Inside Micro
Office Professional

Paul Cassel
Jodi Davenport
Critch Greaves
Michael Groh
Bruce Hallberg
Michael Harding
Forrest Houlette
Kimberly Maxwell
Chris St. Valentine
Rob Tidrow

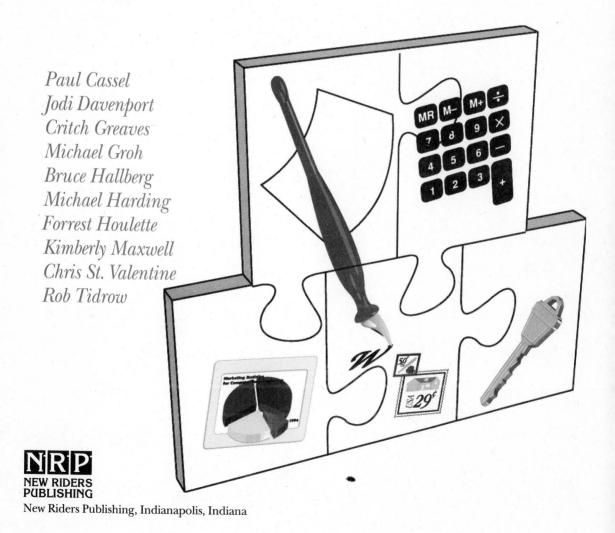

NRP
NEW RIDERS
PUBLISHING

New Riders Publishing, Indianapolis, Indiana

Inside Microsoft Office Professional

By Paul Cassel, Jodi Davenport, Critch Greaves, Michael Groh, Bruce Hallberg, Michael Harding, Kimberly Maxwell, Chris St. Valentine, and Rob Tidrow. Original Access chapters by Michael Groh and Michael Harding.

Published by:
New Riders Publishing
201 West 103rd Street
Indianapolis, IN 46290 USA

Printed in the United States of America 2 3 4 5 6 7 8 9 0

            Inside Microsoft office professional / Jodi Davenport . . . [et al.].
                p.   cm.
            Includes index.
            ISBN 1-56205-228-4 : $39.95
            1. Business—Computer programs. 2. Microsoft Word. 3. Microsoft
        Excel. 4. Microsoft PowerPoint (Computer file). 5. Microsoft
        Access. 6. Microsoft Mail. I. Davenport, Jodi, 1967-   .
        HF5548.2.I427   1994   94-4621
        650'.0285'5369—dc20   CIP

Warning and Disclaimer

This book is designed to provide information about the Microsoft Office computer program. Every effort has been made to make this book as complete and as accurate as possible, but no warranty or fitness is implied.

The information is provided on an "as is" basis. The authors and New Riders Publishing shall have neither liability nor responsibility to any person or entity with respect to any loss or damages arising from the information contained in this book or from the use of the disks or programs that may accompany it.

Publisher	Lloyd J. Short
Associate Publisher	Tim Huddleston
Product Development Manager	Rob Tidrow
Marketing Manager	Ray Robinson
Director of Special Projects	Cheri Robinson
Managing Editor	Matthew Morrill

About the Authors

Paul Cassel has used and programmed mainframe computers, minicomputers, and microcomputers since 1967. Since 1982 he has specialized in PC database consulting for large, medium, and small businesses.

He currently resides in New Mexico with his family.

Jodi Davenport works in marketing for a consumer product company north of Indianapolis, Indiana. Ms. Davenport also trains personnel on Windows applications and serves as a software troubleshooter. She has an extensive background in desktop publishing and presentation software.

Having completed her undergraduate work in public and corporate communications at Butler University, Ms. Davenport lives in Indianapolis with her husband. She enjoys traveling, theater, and home improvement projects.

Critch Greaves is an Indianapolis, Indiana resident and vice president of marketing for Imaging Office Systems, Inc. He has a background in digital document imaging systems and optical disk storage and retrieval systems.

Critch has experience with IBM and compatible PCs, Novell networks, UNIX, Xenix, and a variety of application software packages. He has been involved in the design, setup, installation, training, and documentation of numerous microfilm and optical disk systems in Indiana and the Midwest.

He attended Depauw University in Greencastle, Indiana, and graduated with a B.A. in psychology.

During the last 15 years, **Michael Groh** has worked in a wide variety of situations such as programming in C and Pascal, selling expert systems, and designing user interfaces for Windows applications. His first personal computer was an Osborn I (circa 1982) with 64K of memory and two 180K floppy drives. Mr. Groh is the author of *DOS for Non-Nerds* and a contributing author to *Inside Windows 3.1, Windows 3.1 End-User Programming, Inside Microsoft Access,* and several other books, all by New Riders Publishing. He welcomes your questions and comments at (317) 581-3724 or through CompuServe at 70031,2231.

Bruce Hallberg is the director of information systems for a biotechnology company located in Redwood City, California. He has been heavily involved with PCs since 1980 and has specialized in accounting and business control systems for the past seven years. He has consulted with a large number of local and national companies in a variety of areas and has expertise in networking, programming, and system implementations. He works with a wide variety of PC computer platforms, including DOS, Windows, OS/2, UNIX, and Macintosh. Mr. Hallberg is the author or contributing author of numerous books from New Riders Publishing, including *OS/2 for Non-Nerds, WordPerfect for Wimps,* and *Inside OS/2.*

Michael Harding attended North Carolina State University and has worked for the Department of Defense as a programmer for fighter aircraft systems. Michael formed his own consulting firm, DataSoft, to develop custom networkable software solutions for small businesses. In 1990, DataSoft merged with another company to form UNICORP, of which he was president and chief consultant. He presently is president of Visual Access Corporation and is responsible for product development.

Forrest Houlette began programming in 1979 when he took a course in FORTRAN as part of his M.A. Since then, he has developed software in BASIC, C, CH, and Visual Basic. He has authored two books for New Riders Publishing and worked on seven jointly authored books. Mr. Houlette holds a Ph.D. in linguistics and rhetoric, does research on artificial intelligence and the writing process, and teaches English at Ball State University.

Kimberly Maxwell has authored computer trade publication articles and computer books on computer networking and communications products and technologies since the late 1980s. She holds a B.A. in journalism and an M.S. in management of information systems. Her experience includes writing hundreds of articles as contributing writer or editor for such publications as *PC Magazine, PC Laptop Computers Magazine, LAN Times, Windows Magazine, Network Computing, Computer Reseller News, LAN Magazine,* and *Computer Shopper.* Her books include *Windows 3.1 Networking, The Modem Coach,* and *Guide to Field Computing.*

Chris St. Valentine is an experienced Windows developer with a 12-year background in database design on the IBM PC. He is a former member of the Microsoft Access User Education Team and is an award-winning author of computer books, specializing in Microsoft Access. You can reach Chris through CompuServe at 72702,724.

Rob Tidrow is the product development manager for New Riders Publishing and specializes in operating systems, Windows-based applications, and online communications. During his tenure at New Riders, Rob has edited and developed several popular NRP titles, including *Inside Novell NetWare, Inside Windows 3.1, Inside MS-DOS 6.2, Inside Excel 5 for Windows, Inside WordPerfect 6 for Windows,* and *Riding the Internet Highway.* He also is coauthor of the best-selling *Windows for Non-Nerds,* published by New Riders, and is a contributing author to the *AutoCAD Student Workbook* and *Inside WordPerfect 6 for Windows,* which are published by New Riders Publishing. Mr. Tidrow has created technical documentation and instructional programs for use in a variety of industrial settings and has a degree in English literature from Indiana University. He resides in Indianapolis with his wife, Tammy, and his two boys, Adam and Wesley. He can be reached on CompuServe at 75250,1443.

Trademark Acknowledgments

All terms mentioned in this book that are known to be trademarks or service marks have been appropriately capitalized. New Riders Publishing cannot attest to the accuracy of this information. Use of a term in this book should not be regarded as affecting the validity of any trademark or service mark. Network World, Inc., is the copyright owner for all NetDraw images used in this book.

Product Director
Michael Groh

Production Editor
John Kane

Editors
Nancy Albright
Amy Bezek
Laura Frey
Patrice Hartmann
Paul Mangin
Howard Peirce
Cliff Shubs
John Sleeva
Steve Weiss
Lisa Wilson
Phil Worthington

Acquisitions Editor
Alicia Krakovitz

Technical Editor
Robert L. Bogue

Acquisitions Coordinator
Stacey Beheler

Editorial Assistant
Karen Opal

Publisher's Assistant
Melissa Lynch

Cover Designer
Jay Corpus

Book Designer
Roger S. Morgan

Production Imprint Manager
Juli Cook

Production Imprint Team Leader
Katy Bodenmiller

Graphics Image Specialists
Teresa Forrester
Clint Lahnen
Tim Montgomery
Dennis Sheehan
Susan VandeWalle

Production Analysts
Dennis Clay Hager
Mary Beth Wakefield

Production Team
Troy Barnes
Mona Brown
Elaine Brush
Cheryl Cameron
Steph Davis
Rob Falco
Kimberly K. Hannel
Mike Huff
Greg Kemp
Jamie Milazzo
Michelle Mitchell
Casey Price
Ryan Rader
Kim Scott
Marc Shecter
Susan Shepard
SA Springer
Scott Tullis
Suzanne Tully

Indexers
Charlotte Clapp
Jennifer Eberhardt
John Sleeva

Contents at a Glance

Table of Contents

INTRODUCTION

Welcome to *Inside Microsoft Office Professional*! This book is designed specifically to meet the needs of users who have invested in the Microsoft Office suite of applications, including Microsoft Word 6 for Windows, Microsoft Excel 5 for Windows, Microsoft PowerPoint 4, Microsoft Access, and Microsoft Mail. Even if you don't have the Professional version of Office, you still can use this book.

How *Inside Microsoft Office Professional* Is Designed

Four of the six parts in this book are dedicated to the separate applications in the suite. The other parts show you how to get more out of your Office suite of products by using more advanced features such as integration and networking. This approach enables you to use Office as most users use it—as separate applications—as well as understanding how to use these applications in harmony.

Inside Microsoft Office Professional is written for those users who might be comfortable or even expert with one or two of the Office suite applications, but who must or want to learn the other applications in the Office line. Many users find that they spend so much time in one application, such as Word, that when they have to use another application, such as PowerPoint, they really are not that comfortable with it.

How many times have you had to complete a presentation, but you didn't know how to use PowerPoint, so you just created it in Word? Or, perhaps, your boss wants that report with charts, graphs, and pretty pictures done in "FIVE MINUTES" or else. But when you get back to your workstation, you can't get that sales history out of Excel so that it imports into Word just right. Eventually, you get frustrated with this approach, so you close Excel in a huff and rekey the data into a Word table and hand in a report blander than ice cubes boiled in water. The information is there, but it is not as presentable as you would like.

What's Different About This Book

The power of a suite like Microsoft Office is the integration, or as Microsoft labels it, *component reuse,* you get when all your major applications work together seamlessly. This integration enables you to create sparkling presentations, "smart" spreadsheets, highly automated word processing documents, and powerful databases.

What Is Integration?

Although Windows 3.1 has made it easier to integrate your applications, not many users are comfortable designing elaborate OLE and DDE links to make their various applications work together. Office is designed around the theory that users want to use two or three applications at once without having to reengineer or reformat data once time has been spent creating it. Users don't want to create worksheets in Excel that are filled with thousands of numbers, only to have that data available only to Excel. Why not use that data in another applications, such as Word or PowerPoint—or even Access? This is the magic of Microsoft Office, and *Inside Microsoft Office Professional* shows you how to do this.

Integration enables you to create a Word document, such as a sales letter, using an Excel worksheet or Access database to plug in sales figures in the letter. Or, you might have an Access database that keeps your inventory. For accounting purposes, you can have Access send specific inventory data to Word to create a monthly report that you can turn in to your accountant or manager. Microsoft Office enables you to do all this and more.

Part One: Word for Windows

Part One is devoted to Microsoft Word for Windows 6. Many users devote most of their working time using a word processor for correspondence, business proposals, memos, or other reports. For these users, the word processor is the key application on their desktop, with all other applications supporting its documents.

Using Word for Windows 6 to complete your work is easy. The goal of Part One is to introduce you to the basics of Word 6, including creating a document, changing text formats, and printing documents. Part One also gets you up and running on the more advanced uses and features of Word 6. You learn, for example, how to create tables and to customize dictionaries, macros, and graphics.

Word is a powerhouse application and is simple enough that you can work with it as soon as it is installed. Word's more advanced features enable you to build complex documents such as an office newsletter. Whether you want to type a quick to-do list or create a one-page trifold brochure containing pictures and drop caps, you can do it in Word with equal ease. Word's advanced capabilities are as easy to use as its simple features.

Part Two: Excel

The second part of *Inside Microsoft Office Professional* is devoted to Microsoft Excel 5 for Windows. Excel is one of the most popular spreadsheets available for Windows and is probably the second most popular application in the Office suite. With Excel, you can quickly and easily create powerful worksheets, colorful charts, and focused reports and presentations.

In Part Two you are introduced to Excel 5's new interface, including folder-like tabs; how to create and format worksheets; and how to build charts from the data you have in your worksheets. In later chapters, more advanced features are covered to help you get the most out of your Office investment. If you are interested in setting up loan calculations, mortgage analysis, or other powerful spreadsheet applications, *Inside Microsoft Office Professional* shows you how to use functions, macros, and the new Visual Basic for Application features.

Part Three: PowerPoint

When you need to put together a presentation replete with slides, handouts, and reports, use Microsoft PowerPoint. Part Three gives you an introduction into this easy-to-use Office application. Although you might not do all of your work in PowerPoint, you might need to use it from time to time to put together that "perfect" presentation for the board of directors. For that reason, Part Three shows you the best information and instructions to get the job done.

After you have put together your presentations on the computer, you can transfer them onto plain paper, color or black-and-white overheads, or 35mm slides, or you can show them on a video screen or computer monitor. To complete your presentation package, PowerPoint's printing options include formats ranging from audience handouts to speaker's notes.

Part Three discusses using the PowerPoint AutoContent Wizard, entering presentation text in the outline, and viewing slides. You also learn ways to apply PowerPoint templates to a presentation, add to presentation shapes with text inside, and insert a new slide and clip art into a presentation.

What you will learn with PowerPoint and other Office applications is that many design and formatting tools are identical to those in Word and Excel. If you know how to use these applications, you already know how to use many functions in PowerPoint. This feature helps transfer your skill in one application to another, making the learning curve for that application much smaller.

Part Four: Microsoft Access

Everyone working in a typical business environment needs to manage data. In Part Four, you learn how to use Microsoft Access to help you manage, manipulate, and use various forms of data by creating databases. Do you have a stack of business cards you've received from business contacts, hairdressers, and friends sitting in your desk drawer with a rubber band around them? Would you like a better way to manage them? Do you produce products that are identified by obscure parts numbers and have varying prices? Would you like to have a better way to inventory and record the manufacturing and selling of these product?

If you answer yes to these or any other questions that deal with data, whether it is text or numbers, you should consider creating an Access database. The principal author of Part Four calls Microsoft Access "a personal database system designed to help you manage the flood of data and information."

In Part Four, you learn how to create tables, queries, forms, and reports. If you are not familiar with these terms, don't worry; Part Four also provides an introduction to database basics and the terms and phrases that are unique to database applications such as Access. For those interested in more advanced database features, there is an introduction to Access Basic, the programming environment in Microsoft Access.

The nicest thing about Microsoft Access is that it has been designed for normal people like you. Part Four is designed to give you more than just a basic understanding of what you can do with Access; it shows you how to create an actual database using Access.

Part Five: Data Sharing and Integration

Have you ever created a Word document and decided to include a summary of data that you have stored in an Excel spreadsheet? Do you wish you could just place the data in there and not worry about updating that same data in the Word document every time you change or manipulate it in the Excel worksheet? With the integration features of Word and Excel (and the other Office applications), you can do just that. Link the data you want from Excel into the Word document using dynamic data exchange (DDE) and rest assured that your data will always be updated. No need to enter the same updates in two different documents.

DDE is an internal communications protocol Windows uses to enable one application to "talk to" or exchange data with another application. Normally used to transfer information between applications, DDE also can be used within an application. Part Five shows you ways to create and use DDE links, use macros to control DDE, and share information between applications.

Part Six: Extending the Office Suite

Although Microsoft Office Professional is a complete suite of Windows applications for your business and personal needs, you might find that you need to enhance it or your basic Windows environment with other applications. Part Six introduces you to some of the latest Windows applications that complement and help you get the most from your Office investment.

Appendix

One of the most helpful ways to learn anything is through hands-on learning. *Inside Microsoft Office Professional* includes several tutorial-like steps and procedures that you can do right along with the discussions. The appendix discusses what is on and how to use the *Inside Microsoft Office Professional* companion disk of worksheets, documents, databases, and integration macros that accompany this book.

Special Conventions and Sidebars

Inside Microsoft Office Professional includes special conventions that help you follow along with various discussions and procedures. Most New Riders Publishing books use similar conventions to help you distinguish between various elements of the software, Windows, and sample data. This means that once you purchase one New Riders book, you will find it easier to use all the others.

Before you look ahead, you should spend a moment examining these conventions.

Typeface Conventions

When you see the following typeface, you know that the same information literally appears on-screen:

```
This appears on-screen
```

When you see this same typeface with bold lettering, you know that you are supposed to type the information, as in the following example:

```
Type this information.
```

Anytime you see a word, letter, or number highlighted with boldface, you know to type it in. You might, for example, be instructed to type **WIN** at the DOS prompt. When you see this, you should type WIN as instructed.

New terms, when defined, appear in *italic*.

Key Combinations

Inside Microsoft Office Professional uses a special convention to help you know which keys to press and in what order:

✔ Key1+Key2: When you see a plus sign (+) between key names, hold down the first key while pressing the second key. Then release both keys.

✔ Key1,Key2: When a comma (,) appears between key names, press and release the first key, and then press and release the second key.

Hot Key Characters

The Microsoft Office applications adhere to Windows functionality and specifications, including menu placement, dialog box functionality, and command syntax. One of these specifications includes the use of hot key characters in menu names, commands, and dialog box items. *Hot keys* enable you to use Alt+hot key to activate that menu, command, or dialog box item. The hot key character for the File menu, for example, is F. To activate this menu, press Alt+F.

Inside Office shows hot keys for these application elements by boldfacing and underscoring the hot key character. The hot key character for the File menu, for example, is shown as **F**ile.

Notes, Tips, Warnings, and Disk Elements

One way to fully understand and exploit the power of the Office applications is to find shortcuts, enhancements, tips, and other insider information. *Inside Microsoft Office Professional* is packed with Notes and Tips to give you those shortcuts and enhancements just when you need them!

Another way to take advantage of the power of Office and to increase your efficiency with its applications is to know when you might get in trouble with a feature or procedure. *Inside Microsoft Office Professional* provides warnings to help you get around these problem spots.

The following gives you more information about the special icons in this book:

This icon marks a shortcut or neat idea that will help you get your work done faster.

A Note includes extra, useful information that complements the discussion at hand, instead of being a direct part of it. A Note, for example, might describe special situations that can arise when you use Word 6 under certain circumstances, and tells you what to do.

This icon flags documents, worksheets, or other resources that are found on the *Inside Microsoft Office Professional* companion disk you can use to test the concepts you are learning.

This icon tells you when a procedure might be dangerous—that is, when you run the risk of losing data, locking your system, or damaging your software. These warnings generally tell you how to avoid such losses or describe the steps you can take to remedy them.

New Riders Publishing

The staff of New Riders Publishing is committed to bringing you the very best in computer reference material. Each New Riders book is the result of months of work by authors and staff, who research and refine the information contained within its covers.

As part of this commitment to you, New Riders invites your input. Please let us know if you enjoy this book, if you have trouble with the information or examples, or if you have a suggestion for the next edition.

Please note, though: New Riders staff cannot serve as a technical resource for Microsoft Office or for related questions about hardware- or software-related problems. Please refer to the documentation that accompanies Microsoft Office or to the applications' Help systems.

If you have a question or comment about any New Riders book, there are several ways to contact New Riders Publishing. We will respond to as many readers as we can. Your name, address, or phone number will never become part of a mailing list or be used for any purpose other than to help us continue to bring you the best books possible. You can write us at the following address:

New Riders Publishing
Attn: Associate Publisher
201 W. 103rd Street
Indianapolis, IN 46290

If you prefer, you can fax New Riders Publishing at (317) 581-4670.

As well, you can leave a voice mail message to New Riders at (317) 581-3871.

You can send electronic mail to New Riders from a variety of sources. NRP maintains several mailboxes organized by topic area. Mail in these mailboxes will be forwarded to the staff member who is best able to address your concerns. Substitute the appropriate mailbox name from the list below when addressing your e-mail. The mailboxes are as follows:

ADMIN	Comments and complaints for NRP's Publisher
APPS	Word, Excel, WordPerfect, other office applications
ACQ	Book proposals inquiries by potential authors
CAD	AutoCAD, 3D Studio, AutoSketch and CAD products
DATABASE	Access, dBASE, Paradox and other database products
GRAPHICS	CorelDRAW!, Photoshop, and other graphics products
INTERNET	Internet
NETWORK	NetWare, LANtastic, and other network-related topics
OS	MS-DOS, OS/2, all OS except UNIX and Windows
UNIX	UNIX
WINDOWS	Microsoft Windows (all versions)
OTHER	Anything that doesn't fit the above categories

If you use an MHS e-mail system that routes through CompuServe, send your messages to:

mailbox @ NEWRIDER

To send NRP mail from CompuServe, use the following to address:

MHS: *mailbox* @ NEWRIDER

To send mail from the Internet, use the following address format:

mailbox@newrider.mhs.compuserve.com

NRP is an imprint of Macmillan Computer Publishing. To obtain a catalog or information, or to purchase any Macmillan Computer Publishing book, call (800) 428-5331.

Thank you for selecting *Inside Microsoft Office Professional*!

Part One

Word for Windows

Chapter Snapshot

Using Microsoft Word for Windows 6.0 to accomplish your work is easy. The goal of this chapter is to introduce you to using Word 6 rapidly and efficiently. You will be given a guided tour of getting started with Word, with an emphasis on showing you the following steps:

By the time you have finished this chapter, you will have created, formatted, and printed your first Word document. You will have learned the features of Word that you use most often, and you will be ready to create and work on the documents that get your job done.

CHAPTER

Word for Windows Quick Start

by Forrest Houlette

Word for Windows, the word processor in Microsoft Office Professional, probably is the application you will use most as you work with Office. Word is a powerhouse application. It is simple enough that you can work with it as soon as it is installed, yet it contains all the features that you need to build complex documents such as an office newsletter. Whether you want to type a quick to-do list or create a one-page trifold brochure containing pictures and drop caps, you can do it in Word with equal ease. Word's advanced capabilities are as easy to use as its simple features.

Word also possesses the capability of teaching you how to use it as you work. The most obvious feature that helps you learn appears on the screen as soon as you start Word—the Tip of the Day (see fig. 1.1). Each time you start Word, this dialog box presents one new feature of the word processor that you might not be using effectively. Over time, these daily reminders add up to a stronger knowledge of the less frequently used features of your software than if you rely on recalling information from the manual.

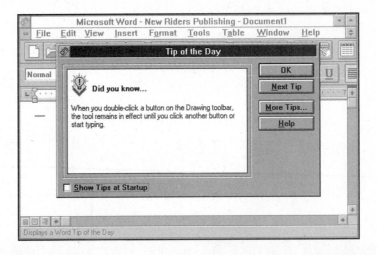

Figure 1.1
Word's Tip of the
Day dialog box.

In addition to the Tip of the Day, Word for Windows 6.0 contains *Wizards* and *Helpers*, special programs that step you through complex tasks. Even when you are working on a familiar task, a Wizard or Helper can be useful. These programs structure your thinking around making your decisions in the right order and with the correct options. For example, you never need to worry about whether you did everything you needed to do to set up a mail merge correctly. The Mail Merge Helper, shown in figure 1.2, makes sure that you did. You activate the Helper by selecting Mail Merge from the Tools menu.

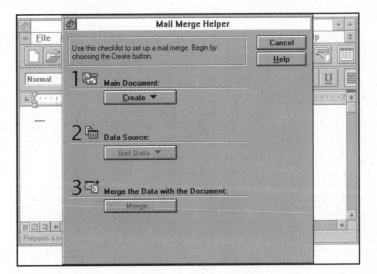

Figure 1.2
The Mail Merge
Helper included in
Word.

Tip Have you ever puzzled over what the picture on a toolbar button means? Word for Windows 6.0 ends such puzzling. Place the mouse pointer over any toolbar button and wait. In about two seconds, a ToolTip window appears, giving the name of the command or feature represented by the button. Also, the status bar at the bottom of the screen shows an explanation of what the command or feature does.

Creating a Document

The first step in learning to accomplish a task with Word for Windows 6.0 is learning how to create a new document or open an existing document. A *document* in Word is the data you type onto the screen and the file that contains the saved data. Word provides powerful document-management features that enable you to handle both these tasks.

Creating a New Document

Word enables you to create both simple and complex spaces into which you can type information. At the simple end of the scale, you can create a blank screen into which you can insert characters. At the complex end, you instantly can create an invoice form into which you can enter the sales information necessary to enable the purchasing party to complete payment. You create both simple and complex documents in just a few easy steps. In the examples included in this chapter, you create three different documents.

Using the Toolbar or Menu

The easiest way to create a new document is to use the Standard toolbar. Table 1.1 shows and describes the buttons found on the standard toolbar.

Table 1.1
Standard Toobar Buttons

Button	Name	Description
	New	Creates a new file based on the Normal template
	Open	Displays the Open dialog box so that you can select an existing file to open
	Save	Saves the current document

continues

Table 1.1, Continued
Standard Toobar Buttons

Button	Name	Description
	Print	Prints the current document
	Print Preview	Activates Word's print preview features
	Spelling	Initiates a spelling check
	Cut	Cuts selected material to the Windows Clipboard
	Copy	Copies selected material to the Clipboard
	Paste	Pastes material from the Clipboard into your document
	Format Painter	Copies the formatting of a selection to the text you specify
	Undo	Undoes the commands you select from the list presented
	Redo	Redoes the commands you select from the list presented
	AutoFormat	Formats your document automatically
	Insert AutoText	Inserts an AutoText entry
	Insert Table	Inserts a table into your document
	Insert Excel Worksheet	Inserts an Excel worksheet into your document
	Columns	Formats your document using columns
	Drawing	Opens the drawing application and enables you to draw a picture in your document
	Insert Chart	Inserts a chart into your document

Button	Name	Description
¶	Show/Hide Paragraph	Shows or hides the paragraph, tab, and space symbols
±	Zoom Control	Scales your view of the document by the percentage you select
?	Help	Activates context-sensitive help

To create a new document by using the Standard toolbar, follow these steps:

1. Point with the mouse to the left button on the Standard toolbar, the one representing a page with the upper-left corner folded down (see fig. 1.3).

2. Click with the left mouse button.

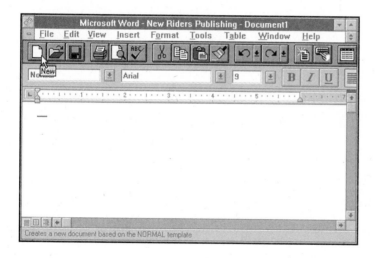

Figure 1.3
Using the New Document button on the Standard toolbar.

In response to your click on the New Document button, Word creates a new document and displays it in a *document window,* the workspace that displays the information you type. If you have a document on your screen already, the new document window appears in front of the existing document window. Both documents, however, are active in the word processor. The section "Navigating the Document" later in this chapter shows the way to move among and within your documents.

Word for Windows 2.0 limited you to nine open documents. Version 6.0 has removed this limit, but you must have enough memory available to open new documents. If a dialog box appears announcing an out-of-memory error message, you have received a cue to close one or more of your documents. You also might choose to close another program that you have running simultaneously with Word. (See "Closing a Document" later in this chapter for instructions.)

The New Document button creates the simplest kind of document Word for Windows uses, a blank workspace with a default font and margins into which you can insert text. Word uses a *document template,* a file that contains instructions for creating a document, to create this simple document. The name of the document template associated with this basic document is Normal, and it is stored in a file called NORMAL.DOT. NORMAL.DOT contains instructions about the margin width, the default font, the page size, and so on that define the appearance of a Normal document.

You also can create a document using Word's menu by performing the following procedure:

1. Open the File menu.

2. Select the New menu item (see fig. 1.4).

3. In the New dialog box, select the template on which the document should be based in the Template combination box. (Normal is selected by default for you, even though the scroll list starts at the top.)

4. Click on the OK button.

You also will see items named *Wizards* in the Template combination box. Ignore them for now. The next section explains how to use them.

If you used Word's default template selection, you just created a new document based on the Normal template, exactly as you did when you clicked on the New Document button. However, for purposes of illustration, use the menu procedure to open a new document based on the Invoice template (see figure 1.5 for the resulting document). The Invoice template illustrates how useful (and complex) document templates can be. The document you create using the Invoice template appears with all the standard text necessary for the invoice already on-screen. You need only to fill in the appropriate amounts and customer information and print the invoice.

There are two reasons to use the menu instead of the Standard toolbar to create a new document. First, you can access the menu from the keyboard by pressing Alt and the under-lined hot keys in the menu name and menu items. (For instance, Alt+F, N selects the New menu item on the File menu.) If you prefer to keep your hands on the keyboard instead of reaching for the mouse while you are working, the menu provides you with a more convenient option for creating a new document. Second, the menu gives you access to the New dialog box and its associated list of templates and Wizards. If you want to create a document based on an alternate template or a Wizard, the menu is your only choice.

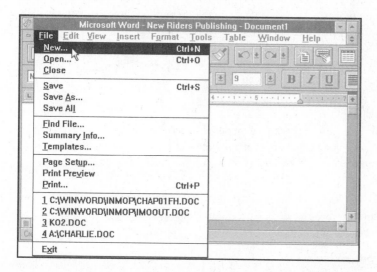

Figure 1.4
Using the File menu to create a new document.

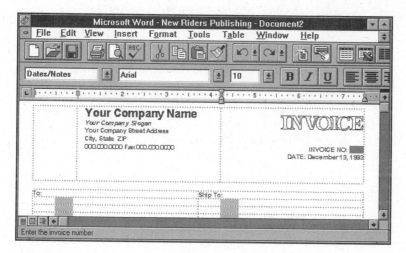

Figure 1.5
A document based on the Invoice template.

Word for Windows

Note It might not seem like it now, but soon you will come to know the hot keys. By knowing these hot keys, you will be able to improve your speed with Word.

Using a Wizard

Wizards are Microsoft's answer to the problem of improving the usability of software. Software manufacturers have known for some time that many features always lie just outside a user's knowledge of the program. In Word, for instance, there are many features that you might not use because you do not use them frequently enough to remember how to use them. Calendar-making is an example of such a feature for the average user of a word processor. Small offices might create calendars only a couple of times each year, often enough to want to use the feature but not often enough to remember how to use it. Wizards step you through such procedures, serving as your memory in such instances.

Although Wizards are nice features, they do take up memory. When you try to run one, you might receive an out-of-memory error message if you have lots of documents or other applications open. Close unnecessary documents and applications to free memory if you receive such a message.

Microsoft provides 10 Wizards in Word for Windows 6.0 to help you create complex documents from document templates. Each Wizard is listed in table 1.2 with a brief explanation of what it helps you create.

Table 1.2
Word for Windows New Document Wizards

Wizard	Function
Agenda	Creates an agenda for a meeting in one of three styles
Award	Creates an award to honor an achievement in one of four styles
Calendar	Creates calendars
Fax	Creates forms for faxed documents in several styles
Letter	Creates a standard letter and enables you to select text from prewritten letters
Memo	Creates a standard memorandum
Newsletter	Creates a newsletter document in one of two styles
Pleading	Creates a standard pleading document for use by lawyers
Resumé	Creates a standard resumé in one of four types
Table	Creates tables of text in several different formats

To use a Wizard, follow this procedure:

1. Open the <u>F</u>ile menu.

2. Select the <u>N</u>ew menu item.

3. In the Template combination box in the New dialog box, select the Wizard you want to use.

4. Click on the OK button.

5. Follow the directions provided by the Wizard dialog box and use the <u>N</u>ext and <u>B</u>ack buttons provided by the Wizard to move among the steps.

Each Wizard offers different choices specific to its tasks. To get a sense of how a Wizard works, start the Agenda Wizard. The initial screen for the Agenda Wizard appears, as shown in figure 1.6.

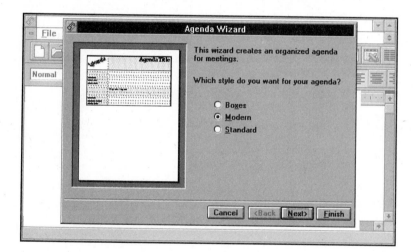

Figure 1.6
The first screen offered by the Agenda Wizard.

I

Word for Windows

Next, perform the following procedure:

1. Select the Bo<u>x</u>es style for the agenda and click on the <u>N</u>ext button.

2. Enter the correct date and time and click on the <u>N</u>ext button.

3. Enter the title and location for the meeting, then click on the <u>N</u>ext button.

4. Select the headings you want to use on the agenda by clicking on the check boxes. Click on the <u>N</u>ext button to move to the next screen.

5. Select the names you want to use on the agenda by clicking on the check boxes. Click on the <u>N</u>ext button to move to the next screen.

6. Enter the topics of discussion, people responsible, and time allocated in the text boxes provided. Click on the <u>N</u>ext button when you are finished.

7. Arrange the topics by selecting one and clicking on the Move Up or Move Down button. Click on the Next button when you are finished.

8. Indicate whether you want a form for recording minutes, using the option buttons provided. Click on Next to move to the final screen.

9. You have reached the end of the information you need to provide to the Wizard. Indicate whether you want Help displayed as the Wizard creates the agenda using the option buttons provided. (Display Help if you want to learn the exact steps the Wizard follows in creating the agenda.) Then click on the Finish button. The Wizard next creates your agenda and displays it in a document window.

10. Fill in the agenda with the appropriate information and print the number of copies you need. A sample of such an agenda is shown in figure 1.7.

Figure 1.7
An agenda completed using the Agenda Wizard.

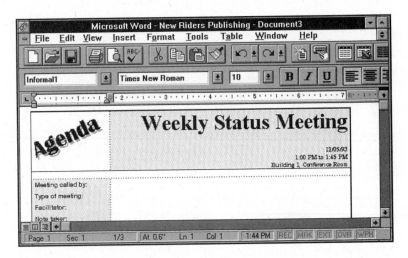

As you can see, you can use Wizards to create complex documents quickly and easily. Wizards save you time and energy, and they give your work a professional look. They enable you to use the advanced features of Word right from the start, even though you might not understand what all those features are when you use them. With the Wizards on your side, knowing how to use the basic New command on the File menu gives you an extraordinary amount of power over the Word application.

Entering Text

To enter text into a document, type at the keyboard. The text you type enters at the *insertion point*, the flashing vertical bar that appears in the document window. If you already have some text in your document—as you do if you created the agenda or the invoice—you can position your insertion point anywhere in the existing text by clicking at that point with the mouse.

The insertion point is different from the mouse pointer, which appears as the I-beam selection cursor and does not flash when it is over a document window.

Closing a Document

If you have been working along with the examples, you have created three to five documents using Microsoft Word. You might find it useful at this point to know how to close a document. Word provides several methods.

The fastest method for closing a document is to press Ctrl+F4 while the document is active. If there are no changes to save, the document closes immediately. If there are changes to save, a Microsoft Word dialog box appears asking if you wish to save changes. Click on Yes to save, No to close the document without saving changes, or Cancel to cancel the document closing operation. If you click on Yes and the document is not yet named, the Save As dialog box appears, which enables you to enter a name for the document (see fig. 1.8). Enter a name in the File Name text box and click on OK to complete the document closing operation. Clicking on Cancel cancels the close operation entirely.

You also can close a document from one of two menus. From the Word menu, open the File menu and select the Close item (see fig. 1.9). Alternatively, from the document window's control menu, select the Close command. Both these menu actions initiate the same sequence of dialog boxes and actions as pressing Ctrl+F4.

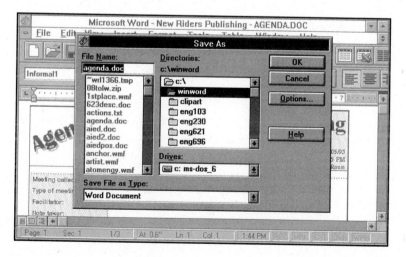

Figure 1.8
The Save As dialog box appearing as part of a document closing operation.

Figure 1.9
Using the Close
command from
Word's File menu.

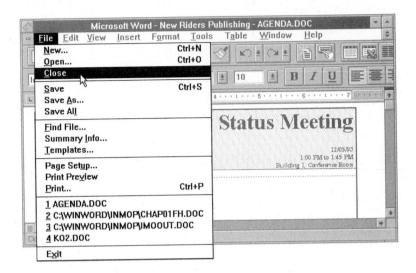

Tip

A document window's control menu always appears in the upper-left corner of the document window as the control menu box. The control menu box might be difficult for you to locate if the document window is maximized. Look to the immediate left of the File menu on Word's menu bar. The control menu box for a maximized window always appears in this position. Click on this box or press Alt+hyphen to open the menu.

To follow through with the exercises you have done so far, close your active documents and save at least one of them. The agenda is a good one to save because it is reused later in this chapter. In the next section you learn how to open a document that you have created, saved, and closed.

Opening an Existing Document

Word provides two methods for opening a document you have created, saved, and closed. To use the Standard toolbar, perform the following procedure:

1. Click on the Open Folder button (the second button from the left) to bring up the Open dialog box (see fig. 1.10).

2. In the Open dialog box, select the file you want to open from the File Name combination box.

3. Click on OK.

At this point, Word opens the file and displays it in a document window.

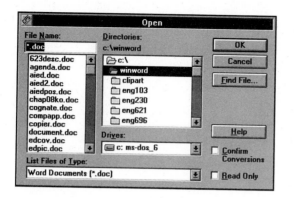

I

Word for Windows

Figure 1.10
The Open dialog box, used to select a file to open.

Alternatively, you can open a file from the Word menu. Click on the File menu and select the Open menu item. Word displays the Open dialog box; from here, the procedure is the same as using the Standard toolbar.

The Open dialog box enables you to select any file from any directory to be opened. To change the directory whose contents is displayed in the File Name combination box, double-click on the name of a directory in the Directories list box. Double-clicking switches a directory open or closed; if the directory currently is open, it closes, and vice versa. To see subdirectories that branch off a parent directory higher in the directory tree, double-click on the parent directory. This action closes lower-level subdirectories and displays the subdirectories that branch from the parent directory. You can navigate to other drives by using the Drives drop-down list box. Simply open the box and select the new drive from the list.

The Open dialog box also controls which files are displayed in a directory. When it opens, it shows only Word documents that end in a DOC file extension, the default extension for Word documents. If you want to see files that end in other extensions, open the List Files of Type drop-down list box near the bottom edge of the dialog box. Select the type of file you want to see by clicking on it, and the display in the File Name combination box is updated accordingly.

Navigating the Document

Word for Windows provides you with several methods for *navigating* within a document—that is, changing which portion of the document is displayed and where the insertion point is. There are many key assignments available in Word; table 1.3 lists the basic ones.

Table 1.3
Basic Key Assignments for Navigating a Document

Key	Action
Up arrow	Moves the insertion point up one line
Down arrow	Moves the insertion point down one line
Right arrow	Moves the insertion point right one character
Left arrow	Moves the insertion point left one character
Ctrl+up arrow	Moves the insertion point to the beginning of the previous paragraph
Ctrl+down arrow	Moves the insertion point to the beginning of the next paragraph
Ctrl+right arrow	Moves the insertion point right one word
Ctrl+left arrow	Moves the insertion point left one word
Home	Moves the insertion point to the beginning of the line
End	Moves the insertion point to the end of the line
PgUp	Moves the insertion point up one screen
PgDn	Moves the insertion point down one screen
Ctrl+PgUp	Moves the insertion point to the top left of the current screen (Word overrides Windows' default action of scrolling the screen to the right)
Ctr+PgDn	Moves the insertion point to the bottom right of the current screen (Word overrides Windows' default action of scrolling the screen left)
Alt+Ctrl+PgUp	Moves the insertion point to the beginning of the previous page
Alt+Ctrl+PgDn	Moves the insertion point to the beginning of the next page
Ctrl+Home	Moves the insertion point to the beginning of the document
Ctrl+End	Moves the insertion point to the end of the document
Tab	Moves the insertion point to the next cell in a table

Key	Action
Shift+Tab	Moves the insertion point to the previous cell in a table
Alt+Home	Moves the insertion point to the first cell in a row in a table
Alt+End	Moves the insertion point to the last cell in a row in a table
Alt+PgUp	Moves the insertion point to the first cell in a column in a table
Alt+PgDn	Moves the insertion point to the last cell in a column in a table

In addition to these key assignments, you can navigate by clicking the mouse where you want the insertion point to appear on your screen.

You also can use the scroll bars that border the right and bottom edges of a document window to navigate in a document. Clicking on the arrow at either end of a scroll bar moves you one line or one column in that direction. Clicking on the scroll bar itself to the right or left (or above or below) of the scroll box moves you one screen in the direction of the arrow at that end of the scroll bar. Dragging the scroll box moves you several screens at a time in the direction you drag.

If you have multiple documents open, you also need to know how to move from one document window to another. When you open a document, its name is appended to the end of the <u>W</u>indow menu (see fig. 1.11). Opening the <u>W</u>indow menu and clicking on the name of the document you want to view moves its document window to the top of the stack.

Figure 1.11
Using the Window menu to navigate among open document windows.

In addition to using the <u>W</u>indow menu, you can press Ctrl+F6 to move to the next document window and Ctrl+Shift+F6 to move to the previous document window.

Word for Windows provides many more keyboard shortcuts for navigating documents and windows. For the complete listing divided by category, select <u>S</u>earch for Help from the <u>H</u>elp menu and go to the topic "Using Keyboard Shortcuts in Word."

Word for Windows

Changing the Format of the Text

The second step in learning to accomplish a task with Word for Windows 6.0 is learning how to define the appearance of your document. Word provides you with several options for defining the basic look of your document. You can select different fonts, change the size of the text, select a style, and work with a variety of special features.

 Tip Before you begin this section, open a document so that you can practice each procedure. A good choice would be your agenda. You can fill in some of the blanks and adjust its look to suit your needs.

Choosing a Font

The most noticeable element in the appearance of your document is the font you use to create it. A *font* in Word refers to the physical and artistic design of the letters as they appear on the page. In different fonts, the same character is designed in a different way. Table 1.4 shows the same words presented in several fonts.

Table 1.4
A Comparison of Fonts in Word for Windows 6.0

Font Name	Sample
Arial	The lazy red dog jumped over the wall.
Century Schoolbook	The lazy red dog jumped over the wall.
Lucida Blackletter	The lazy red dog jumped over the wall.
Monotype Corsiva	The lazy red dog jumped over the wall.

A font in Word also refers to the particular collection of characters that can be displayed in a typeface. A particular font in Word may not have exactly the same characters in it as any other font you use in Word. A good example is the Wingdings font that ships with Windows. The example sentence in table 1.4 appears as follows when typed using the Wingdings font:

✿≈♏ ●☺✼☒ ▢♍♐ ♐▢Ᏸ ☞◆○▢♍♐ ▢◆♍▢ ◆≈♏ •☺●●☜

Obviously, Wingdings does not contain the same collection of characters as any of the four fonts shown in table 1.4. In fact, it contains no alphabetic characters at all. Remember, when working with fonts, the concept really refers to two things: the design of the characters and the selection of characters available. On occasion, as in choosing to use Wingdings or a special foreign language font, your choice will be based on the selection of characters the font makes available rather than the look of the characters.

If you feel you need more fonts than you have, you can purchase several different font packs from both Microsoft and other vendors. Fonts are available as downloadable shareware or freeware programs from sources such as the Desktop Publishing Forum on CompuServe. Some software vendors include fonts with their programs; CorelDRAW!, for instance, includes 750 fonts!

Word provides you with two methods for selecting a font for use in your document. First, there is a drop-down list box on the Formatting toolbar from which you can select the font for use. The Formatting toolbar displays three drop-down list boxes. The one that displays the current font is the middle one. To select a font, perform the following procedure:

1. Click on the arrow button to the right of the drop-down list box to open it (see fig. 1.12). (Pressing Ctrl+Shift+F activates the drop-down list box. After it is activated, pressing the down arrow opens the drop-down list.)

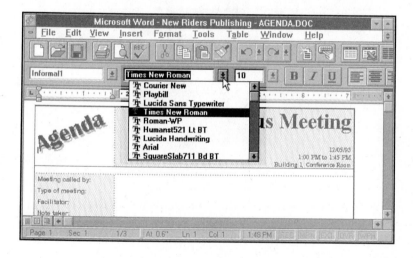

Figure 1.12
Opening the font drop-down list box in the Formatting toolbar.

2. Scroll through the list box by clicking on the scroll bar, and select a font by clicking on it. (You also can use the standard navigation keys to move up and down the list. Once the font you desire is highlighted, press Enter to select it.)

3. Begin typing. Your text will appear in the font you just selected.

If the Formatting toolbar is not visible, open the **V**iew menu and select the **T**oolbars item. In the Toolbars dialog box, check the box next to Formatting in the **T**oolbars list box. The Formatting toolbar then will appear on-screen. If it appears as a floating toolbox and you would rather it appear as a toolbar beneath the menu, double-click on it. Double-clicking switches any toolbar's appearance between toolbar and floating toolbox.

The second way to choose a font is to use the Font dialog box by performing the following steps:

1. Open the F__o__rmat menu and select the F__o__nt item.

2. If the Fonts tab is not on top, click on it.

3. Select the font you want by clicking on it in the F__o__nt list box (see fig. 1.13).

4. Click on the OK button.

5. Begin typing. Your text appears in the font you selected.

Figure 1.13
Selecting Times
New Roman from
the Font list box.

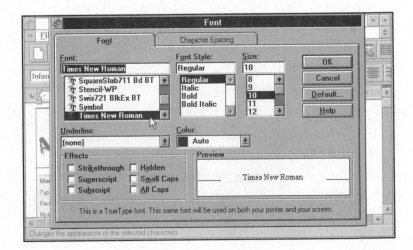

What happens when you select a new font depends on whether you have a selection active. If you select text by dragging over it with the mouse and then select a font, the text in the selection changes to the font you selected. The font used for typing depends on which font is active for the area of the screen in which you type next.

If you have a document for which the Arial font is the active font, for example, but you want your section headings to appear in Monotype Corsiva, you can set the font for the headings only by using the following steps:

1. Select a heading by dragging over it with the mouse.

2. Select Monotype Corsiva as the font.

The selected heading changes to Monotype Corsiva. However, if you move your insertion point to the end of the document and start typing, your text appears in Arial. Changing the font for a selection affects the selection only, not the entire document.

If you have no selection active and choose a new font, the new font appears when you start typing—as long as you do not move the insertion point before you start typing. Moving the insertion point before typing causes the font selection to revert to the font active for that region in the document.

Tip

To change the font for an entire document, open the **E**dit menu and choose the Select **A**ll item. Then select a new font. The new font affects the entire selection. If the selection is large, you have to click on the selection before the new font displays on the screen.

I

Word for Windows

Choosing a Size

You can adjust the size of the font displayed on your screen by using either the Formatting toolbar or the Font dialog box. On the Formatting toolbar, the font size is adjusted using the right drop-down list box. To use the Formatting toolbar, perform the following procedure:

1. Click on the arrow button to the right of the drop-down list box to open it (see fig. 1.14). (Pressing Ctrl+Shift+P activates the drop-down list box. After it is activated, pressing the down arrow opens the drop-down list.)

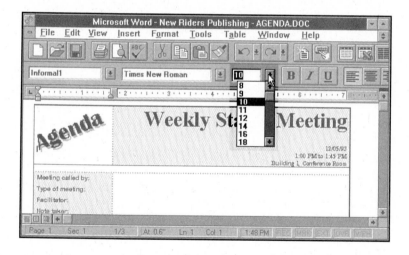

Figure 1.14
Opening the font size drop-down list box in the Formatting toolbar.

2. Scroll through the list box by clicking on the scroll bar, and select a size by clicking on it. (You also can use the standard navigation keys to move up and down the list. Once the size you desire is highlighted, press Enter to select it.)

3. Begin typing. Your text will appear in the font size you just selected.

To adjust the size of a font using the Font dialog box, follow this procedure:

1. Open the F**o**rmat menu and select the **F**ont item.

2. If the Fo**n**ts tab is not on top, click on it.

3. Select the size you want by clicking on it in the **S**ize list box (see fig. 1.15).

Figure 1.15
Selecting 8 points
in the Size list box
of the Font tab.

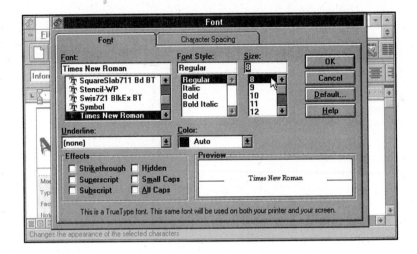

4. Click on the OK button.

5. Begin typing. Your text appears in the font size you selected.

What happens when you select a font size depends on whether you have a selection active, just as when choosing a font. If a selection is active, the change in font size affects the selection only. If a selection is not active, the change in size affects the next character you type—as long as you do not move the insertion point first. If you move the insertion point before you begin typing, the font size reverts to the size already set for that region in your document.

The font sizes available depend on the design of the font. Typically, for the TrueType fonts shipped with Windows, you can select from a range of sizes between 8 and 72 points. A *point* is a unit of measurement used by printers that is equal to 1/72 of an inch. The size of a font refers to its height rather than its width. A common font size for composing letters is 10 or 12 points.

Choosing a Style

A font's *style* describes whether the font has any special attributes, such as bold or italic. In Word for Windows 6.0, fonts can have one of the following four styles:

✔ Regular

✔ Bold

✔ Italic

✔ Bold italic

You adjust a font's style using either the Formatting toolbar or the Font dialog box. On the Formatting toolbar, you adjust style with the two push buttons to the left of the Size drop-down list box labeled B and I (see fig. 1.16).

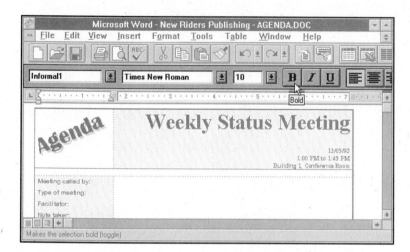

Figure 1.16

Using the Formatting toolbar to set the font style.

Perform any of the following procedures to change a font's style:

✔ Click on the button labeled B to set the bold feature on. (You also can press Ctrl+B from the keyboard.)

✔ Click on the button labeled I to set the italic feature. (You also can press Ctrl+I at the keyboard.)

✔ Click on both buttons to set both bold and italic features. (You also can press Ctrl+I followed by Ctrl+B at the keyboard, or vice versa.)

✔ To clear either feature, click its button again (or press its keyboard equivalent again).

To use the Font dialog box to set the font style, perform the following procedure:

1. Open the Format menu and select the Font item.

2. If the Fonts tab is not on top, click on it.

3. Select the style you want by clicking on it in the Font Style list box (see fig. 1.17).

4. Click on OK.

5. Begin typing. Your text appears in the font style you selected.

What happens when you select a font style depends on whether you have a selection active, just as when choosing a font or choosing a font size. If a selection is active, the change in font style affects the selection only. If a selection is not active, the change in style affects the next character you type—as long as you do not move the insertion point first. If you move the insertion point before you begin typing, the font style reverts to the style already set for that region in your document.

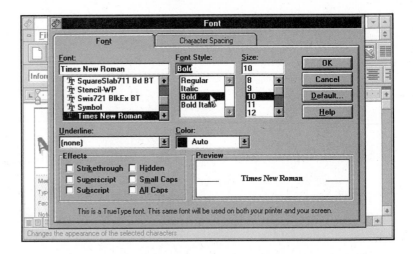

Figure 1.17
Selecting Bold in
the Font Style list
box.

In Word for Windows 6.0, *style* is a word that can refer to two things: font style or document style. For an explanation of document styles, see the section "Understanding Styles" in Chapter 2, "Understanding Word for Windows Concepts."

Selecting Special Features

You can set several special features that affect the appearance of your document. Using the Font dialog box, you can set these features of your text:

✔ Underlining

✔ Color

✔ Special effects

Using the Paragraph dialog box, you can set these features of your paragraphs:

✔ Indentation

✔ Spacing

✔ Alignment

Some of these features can be set from the Formatting toolbar, but many of them must be set using the dialog boxes.

Setting the Underline

You can set underlining for text from both the Formatting toolbar and the Font dialog box. To set underlining from the Formatting toolbar, use the following procedures (see fig. 1.18):

✔ Click on the button labeled U to set the underline feature on. (You also can press Ctrl+U from the keyboard.)

✔ To clear the underline feature, click on its button again (or press Ctrl+U again).

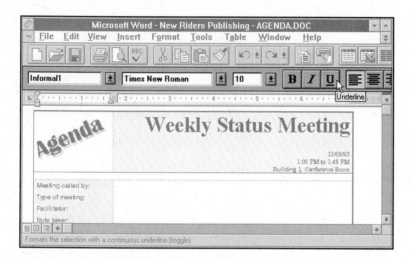

Figure 1.18
Setting the underline feature using the Formatting toolbar.

When you set underlining using the Formatting toolbar, the underline is a single, solid underline that appears under both words and spaces, as in the following example:

<u>Here is an example of underlining set from the Formatting toolbar.</u>

To set underlining using the Font dialog box, use the following procedure:

1. Open the Format menu and select the Font item.

2. If the Fonts tab is not on top, click on it.

3. Select the type of underline you want by opening the Underline drop-down list box and selecting it from the list.

4. Click on OK.

5. Begin typing. Your text appears with the type of underline you selected.

The Font dialog box gives you much greater control over the type of underline you can use in your text than does the Underline button. The possible types are listed in table 1.5.

Table 1.5
Underlining Available in Word for Windows 6.0

Underline	Example
Single	Here is an example of single underlining.
Words Only	Here is an example of words only underlining.
Double	Here is an example of double underlining.
Dotted	Here is an example of dotted underlining.

What happens when you select a type of underlining depends on whether you have a selection active, just as when choosing a font or choosing a font style. If a selection is active, the change in underlining affects the selection only. If a selection is not active, the change in underlining affects the next character you type—as long as you do not move the insertion point first. If you move the insertion point before you begin typing, the type of underlining reverts to the type already set for that region in your document.

Setting the Color

Word for Windows 6.0 enables you to use up to 16 different colors for text. You can use colored text for display purposes only, or you can print colored text if you have a color printer. You can set the color of text by performing the following procedure:

1. Open the F_o_rmat menu and select the _F_ont item.

2. If the Fo_n_ts tab is not on top, click on it.

3. Select the color you want by opening the _C_olor drop-down list box and selecting it from the list (see fig. 1.19).

Figure 1.19
Selecting Black in the Color drop-down list box.

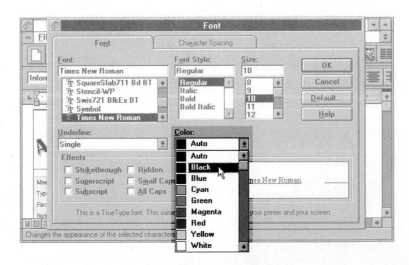

4. Click on OK.

5. Begin typing. Your text appears in the color you selected.

One item in the list of colors is not a color: Auto. When you select this color, Word uses the text color set by the Color dialog box in Control Panel. This color is determined by the overall Windows color scheme or the custom color scheme that you use. Choosing one of the color names from the list overrides the default text color and causes text to appear in the color you have selected.

Tip

Colored text is useful for identifying section headers of different types in a long document. You might see this technique used in New Riders books. Section headings are often set in a different text color from the body text.

What happens when you select a color depends on whether you have a selection active, just as when choosing a font or choosing a font style. If a selection is active, the change in color affects the selection only. If a selection is not active, the change in color affects the next character you type—as long as you do not move the insertion point first. If you move the insertion point before you begin typing, the color reverts to the type already set for that region in your document.

Setting Special Effects

In Word, you can use a variety of special text effects:

✔ Strikethrough

✔ Superscript

✔ Subscript

✔ Hidden

✔ Small caps

✔ All caps

To set any of these features, use the following procedure:

1. Open the Format menu and select the Font item.

2. If the Fonts tab is not on top, click on it.

3. In the Effects group box, select the check box that represents the special effect you want to turn on.

4. Click on OK.

5. Begin typing. Your text appears with the special effects you selected.

You can combine up to four of the special effects if you want. The strikethrough and hidden features combine with either the small caps or all caps features and with either the superscript or subscript features. You can combine only four effects because superscript and subscript are mutually exclusive effects, as are small caps and all caps. Text cannot be both superscript and subscript, or small caps and all caps, at the same time.

What happens when you select special effects depends on whether you have a selection active, just as when choosing a font or choosing a font style. If a selection is active, the special effect affects the selection only. If a selection is not active, the special effect affects the next character you type—as long as you do not move the insertion point first. If you move the insertion point before you begin typing, the special effects revert to the type already set for that region in your document.

Setting the Indentation

If you are used to a typewriter or to one of the early word processors, you probably are familiar with handling indentation with tabs. In Word for Windows 6.0, the word processor handles indentation for you. Using the Paragraph dialog box, you can tell Word how to set up paragraph indentation. Each paragraph you create then fits that template.

To set up paragraph indentation, use the following procedure:

1. Open the F̲ormat menu and select the P̲aragraph item.

2. If the I̲ndents and Spacing tab is not on top, click on it (see fig. 1.20).

3. In the Indentation group box, use the L̲eft and R̲ight spin boxes to set the indentation from the left and right margins. Click on the arrow buttons until the measurement is correct, or select the text in the box by highlighting it with the mouse and then type the exact measurement you want.

4. To set first-line or hanging indentation, open the S̲pecial drop-down list box by clicking on its arrow, and select the appropriate item. Then use the B̲y spin box to set the measurement for the first-line indentation or the hanging indentation.

5. Click on OK. Your current paragraph takes on the indentation you just set. Each subsequent paragraph you create takes on this pattern, unless you reset the indentation using the dialog box.

Typical indentation patterns are easy to apply. Typical paragraph settings include those shown in table 1.6.

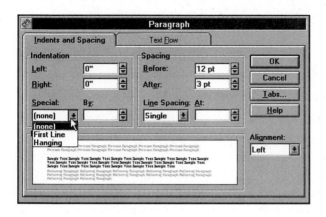

Figure 1.20
Setting indentation using the Indents and Spacing tab of the Paragraph dialog box.

Table 1.6
Indentation Settings for Common Paragraphs

Paragraph Type	Left	Right	Special	By
Standard	0	0	First line	.5
Blocked quote	.5	.5	(none)	blank
Hanging (bibliographic entry)	0	0	Hanging	.5

Because the Paragraph dialog box shows you an example of what the paragraph looks like in the Preview box, you easily can experiment with the indentation settings until you have the paragraph format that meets your needs.

Tip

You can use two buttons on the Formatting toolbar to increase or decrease the left indentation setting by .5 inches (or the equivalent metric setting) with each click. These buttons are the second and third from the right on the toolbar.

When you change indentation settings, they affect your current paragraph and each subsequent paragraph you create. You do not have to select your current paragraph for the effect to take place. However, if you want to affect a group a paragraphs—putting them all into the same format—select them and then open the Paragraph dialog box. The changes then occur in all the selected paragraphs.

Tip

You also can adjust indentation settings by dragging the pointers on the ruler. The right pointer adjusts the right margin. The left pointer has upper and lower halves. Drag the lower half to adjust the left margin. Drag the upper half to adjust the first line or hanging measurement. Drag the box at the bottom of the lower half to adjust both halves of the pointer at the same time.

Setting Line Spacing

You also can use the Paragraph dialog box to set the line spacing within each paragraph:

1. Open the Format menu and select the Paragraph item.

2. If the Indents and Spacing tab is not on top, click on it.

3. In the Spacing group box, use the Before and After spin boxes to set the distance in points from the previous paragraph and from the following paragraph. Click on the arrow buttons until the measurement is correct, or select the text in the box by highlighting it with the mouse and then type the exact measurement you want.

4. To set line spacing within the paragraph, open the Line Spacing drop-down list box by clicking on its arrow, and select the appropriate item. Then use the At spin box to set the measurement for number of lines or distance between lines, whichever is active.

5. Click on OK. Your current paragraph takes on the line spacing you just set. Each subsequent paragraph you create takes on this pattern, unless you reset the line spacing using the dialog box.

The Line Spacing drop-down list box offers the settings shown in table 1.7.

Table 1.7
Line Spacing Settings in the Paragraph Dialog Box

Setting	Explanation
Single	Single spacing, with the line set to a height just a bit greater than that of the font
1.5 Lines	One and one-half line spacing, with the height calculated as 1.5 times the height of a single-spaced line
Double	Double spacing, with the height of the line calculated as twice that of the single-spaced line
At Least	A minimal height for each line, in points, that Word can adjust to accommodate larger fonts or inserted objects
Exactly	A fixed height for each line, in points, that Word cannot change
Multiple	A line height, expressed as a multiple of the single-spaced line height, that you can adjust to any value you want (the default is three, triple-spaced, but you can enter any factor to serve as a multiplier—1.4, for example)

As with indentation, because the Paragraph dialog box shows you an example of what the paragraph spacing looks like in the Preview box, you can experiment with the spacing settings until you have the paragraph format that meets your needs.

When you change line spacing settings, they affect your current paragraph and each subsequent paragraph you create. You do not have to select your current paragraph for the effect to take place. However, if you want to affect a group of paragraphs—setting them all to the same line spacing—select them and then open the Paragraph dialog box. The changes then occur in all the selected paragraphs.

Setting Alignment on the Page

Word offers you two means of setting the alignment of paragraphs on the page. You have four choices for paragraph alignment:

- ✔ **Left-justified.** A straight left margin and a ragged right margin.
- ✔ **Right-justified.** A straight right margin and a ragged left margin.
- ✔ **Centered.** Each line centered and both right and left margins ragged.
- ✔ **Fully justified.** Straight right and left margins.

You can set the paragraph alignment using the four buttons on the Formatting toolbar to the right of the underline button (see fig. 1.21). Click on the button that represents the alignment you want. The pictures on the buttons graphically illustrate the type of alignment that the button provides. These buttons are mutually exclusive. Only one can be pressed at a time, and one must always be pressed.

Left-justified
Centered
Right-justified
Fully justified

Figure 1.21

The paragraph alignment buttons on the Formatting toolbar.

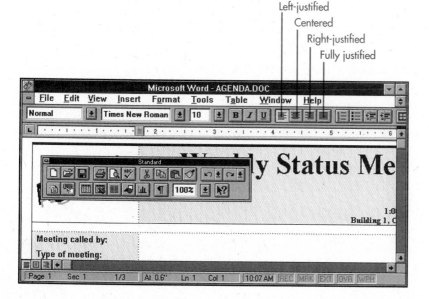

I

Word for Windows

You also can set paragraph alignment from the Paragraph dialog box by performing the following steps:

1. Open the Format menu and select the Paragraph item.

2. If the Indents and Spacing tab is not on top, click on it.

3. Open the Alignment drop-down list box by clicking on its arrow, and select the type of alignment you want from the list.

4. Click on OK. Your current paragraph takes on the alignment you just set. Each subsequent paragraph you create takes on this pattern unless you reset the alignment using the dialog box.

 Many desktop publishers feel that a ragged right margin is easier to read than fully justified text.

Changing the Text

The third step in learning to accomplish tasks with Word for Windows 6.0 is learning how to edit the text of your document. The feature that captivated most users of the original word processors was the capability to edit the text of a document. As word processors have developed, the editing features have become more flexible and useful.

 Open a document to practice with before you start reading these sections. Again, try working on the agenda. You can fill it out for your next meeting while you practice.

Inserting Text

By now you have discovered how to insert text. When you press text keys, characters are inserted at the insertion point, and the insertion point moves to the right of the last character inserted. You can move the insertion point with the navigation keys or by clicking with the mouse. (See the section "Navigating the Document" earlier in this chapter.) Inserting text probably is the most intuitive action you take with Word.

Overstriking Text

There are times, however, when you want to type over existing text. To switch to this editing mode, press the Insert key. When you type, the characters you type replace any characters to the left of the insertion point. To turn off the overstrike mode, press the Insert key again. Use this mode when you need to replace a section of text completely with one of about the same length. Using overstrike saves you the time of removing the outdated text by some other means.

Tip   You can switch the overstrike mode on or off by double-clicking on the OVR box on the status bar at the bottom of the Word window.

Cutting and Pasting

As you work with your document, there are, of course, times when you want to delete a block of text or move a block of text. In Word, you perform these tasks with the cutting and pasting features.

Before you can cut and paste text, however, you first must select the block of text on which you want to take action. You select text using one of two methods:

✔ Drag the mouse pointer over the text to be selected.

✔ Hold down the Shift key and press any of the navigation keys. (Table 1.3 provides a list of the navigation keys.)

Selected text is highlighted in inverse screen colors, usually a black background with white text. (The actual colors depend on the color scheme you have selected using the Control Panel.)

Note   You can lock Word in the text selection mode by pressing F8 or double-clicking on the EXT box in the status bar at the bottom of the Word window. As long as EXT remains highlighted, you can extend your selection using any of the navigation keys or by dragging with the mouse. You will not stop extending your selection until you double-click again on the EXT box.

Once you select a block of text, you can perform on it the operations listed in table 1.8.

Table 1.8
Cutting and Pasting Operations in Word for Windows 6.0

Operation	Result
Cut	Removes text from your document and places it on the Clipboard
Copy	Copies the selected text to the Clipboard, but does not remove it from your document
Paste	Inserts text from the Clipboard, placing the text at the current insertion point (if you have a block of selected text active, it replaces the selected block with the text on the Clipboard)

Tip The Clipboard is an area of memory in which Windows stores material that is cut or copied.

These operations are the same as in any other Windows program that enables editing in this manner. Word provides a standard Edit menu with the usual Cut, Copy, and Paste items for performing these operations. (Accelerator key combinations for these three menu items are Ctrl+X, Ctrl+C, and Ctrl+V, respectively.) However, the Standard toolbar provides buttons for these three common operations (see fig. 1.22).

Figure 1.22
The Cut, Copy, and Paste buttons on the Standard toolbar.

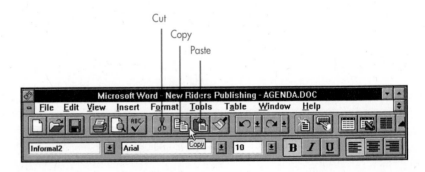

Note The Windows standard keys Ctrl+Ins, Shift+Ins, and Ctrl+Del also are available to do Cut, Copy, and Paste.

Undoing and Redoing

When you are editing, you can, of course, make mistakes. Nothing is more disappointing than deleting an entire section of a document and then realizing it was the wrong section! Word for Windows 6.0 helps you recover from such mistakes by offering undo and redo features.

If you do make a mistake, you can undo it by selecting the Undo option from the Edit menu. This procedure undoes the last change you made to the file. (The accelerator key combination for this undo operation is Ctrl+Z.) Word always will add the name of the operation you are about to undo as the second word of the Undo menu item. If you cannot undo anything, this option changes to Can't Undo and is dimmed.

However, what if you have made lots of changes and discovered you made them in the wrong place? Word helps you compensate for such problems by offering the Undo button on the Standard toolbar. The Undo button is the one with an arrow curved to the left on it. Click on the arrow to the right of the button to display a list of the things you can undo (see fig. 1.23). Select the items on the list you want to undo by dragging with the mouse or extending the selection with the down-arrow key. Then release the mouse button (or press Enter if you are working from the keyboard). Word undoes the last set of actions you indicated. You must always undo actions in the sequence they were taken.

Figure 1.23
Using the Undo button on the Standard toolbar.

You also can redo actions. To redo a single action from the Edit menu, select the Repeat option from the Edit menu. Word always will add the name of the operation you are about to redo as the second word of the Repeat menu item.

You can redo multiple actions using the Redo button on the Standard toolbar. The Redo button is the one with the picture of an arrow curved to the right. It works the same way as the Undo button (see fig. 1.24). Click the arrow to the right of the button, select the sequential items you want to redo, and release the mouse button (or press Enter if you are working from the keyboard). Word redoes the set of actions you have indicated.

Tip   Multilevel Undo and Redo are new features in Word for Windows 6.0. In version 2.0, you could undo or redo only your last action.

Figure 1.24
Using the Redo
button on the
Standard toolbar.

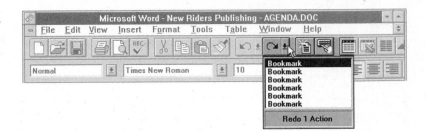

Using Advanced Formatting Features

The fourth step in learning to accomplish work with Word for Windows 6.0 is learning how to apply advanced formatting features. Word gives you almost all the capabilities associated with desktop publishing programs. Taking advantage of these advanced features enables you to give your documents a professional look.

> **Tip**   If you don't have a document open, it is a good idea to open one now so that you can practice with these advanced features. The Normal document you created earlier is a good choice. This document gives you a chance to experiment without spoiling the formatting of your agenda or your invoice.

Adding a Border

In Word, you can add borders around paragraphs to create lines and boxes of different styles on the page. Such borders can be useful for highlighting information, dividing sections of documents, or giving some artistic flair to a document. You also can shade sections of a document using Word's bordering tools. These features enable you to underscore the relative emphasis each section of the document should have.

Word provides two methods for creating borders and shading sections of your document. The most accessible is the Borders toolbar, which you can show by clicking on the last button on the Formatting toolbar. (Clicking on this button again hides the Borders toolbar.) As shown in figure 1.25, the Borders toolbar provides seven buttons and two drop-down list boxes, which enable you to specify the nature of the border and the amount of shading for a block of text.

> **Tip**   An *inside border* is a border that appears between paragraphs in a multiparagraph section surrounded by a border or between the cells of a table.

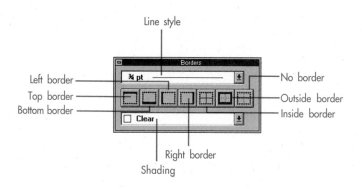

Figure 1.25
The Borders toolbar.

Word for Windows

To use the Borders toolbar, follow this procedure:

1. Place the insertion point inside the paragraph, or select the group of paragraphs you want to surround with a border.

2. Click on the button that provides the kind of border you want.

3. Open the upper drop-down list box and select the line style for the border.

4. Open the lower drop-down list box and select the shading for the bordered area. (Keep in mind that you can shade an area that does not have a border around it.)

The second method for creating borders and shading sections of text is by using the Paragraph Borders and Shading dialog box. This dialog box, shown in figure 1.26, gives you more control over the nature of the borders and shading. You can set colors for each line or shading, for instance, which you cannot do from the Borders toolbar. You also can define shadow borders and set the distance of the border from the text.

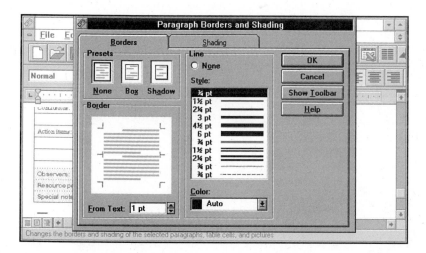

Figure 1.26
The Paragraph Borders and Shading dialog box showing the Borders tab.

To set a border using the dialog box, perform the following procedure:

1. Place the insertion point inside a paragraph or select the group of paragraphs you want to surround with a border.

2. Open the Format menu.

3. Select the Borders and Shading item.

4. Click on the Borders tab if it is not on top.

5. Use the Preset controls to select the type of border, or click on the junction point (defined by the angle markers) in the Border control to define where the border should be.

6. Use the From Text spin box to set the distance in points of the border line from the text.

7. Select the line style from the Style list box.

8. Select the color from the Color drop-down list box.

9. Click on OK to implement your border.

To set shading using the dialog box, perform the following procedure:

1. Place the insertion point inside a paragraph or select the group of paragraphs you want to surround with a border.

2. Open the Format menu.

3. Select the Borders and Shading item.

4. Click on the Shading tab if it is not on top (see fig. 1.27).

Figure 1.27
The Shading tab in the Paragraph Borders and Shading dialog box.

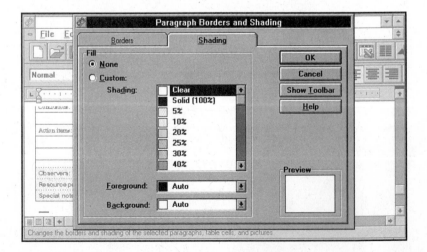

5. Select the type of shading from the Shading list box.

6. Select the foreground color for the shaded area, using the Foreground drop-down list box.

7. Select the background color for the shaded area, using the Background drop-down list box.

8. Click on OK to implement the shading you have designed.

Tip

You can set both borders and shading in one session with the Paragraph Borders and Shading dialog box.

Building Tables

Word for Windows 6.0 includes an advanced table editor that enables you to create tables that include the following features:

✔ Split cells

✔ Formulas that define the contents of cells

✔ Complex formatting

✔ Predefined table formats

Word provides three methods for creating tables; the method you choose depends on how you want to use the table. If you need a quick table with just a few cells, or a table with lots of cells that are of equal sizes, use the Insert Table button on the Standard toolbar by performing the following steps:

1. Place the insertion point where you want the table to appear in your document.

2. Click on the button to open the grid.

3. Drag across the grid until the appropriate number of cells is highlighted (see fig. 1.28).

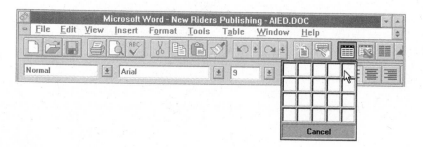

Figure 1.28

Using the Insert Table button on the Standard toolbar to define the table's size.

4. Release the mouse button to insert the table.

5. Insert your data into the table's cells.

Tip   Table 1.3 explains how to use key combinations to navigate a table.

If you need to have more control over column widths or you want more control over the format of your table, use the Insert Table dialog box to create your table. To use this dialog box, perform the following steps:

1. Place the insertion point where you want the table to appear in your document.

2. Open the Table menu.

3. Select the Insert Table item. This brings up the Insert Table dialog box (see fig. 1.29).

Figure 1.29
The Insert Table
dialog box.

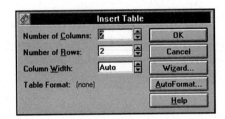

4. In the dialog box, use the three spin boxes to set the Number of Columns, Number of Rows, and Column Width.

5. To select a special format, click on the AutoFormat button to bring up the Table AutoFormat dialog box (see fig. 1.30).

6. In the Table AutoFormat dialog box, select one of the predefined formats in the Formats list box. (The Preview box shows you what each table format looks like.)

7. Use the check boxes in the Formats to Apply group to select whether to use Borders, Shading, Fonts, Colors, AutoFit, or any combination of these features. (You can experiment with different combinations of these features and view the results in the Preview box.)

8. Use the check boxes in the Apply Special Formats To group to select whether the formats you chose in step 7 are applied to Heading Rows, First Column, Last Row, Last Column, or any combination of these. (You can experiment with different combinations of these features and view the results in the Preview box.)

9. Click on OK to accept the AutoFormat you have chosen.

10. Click on OK in the Insert Table dialog box to insert your table.

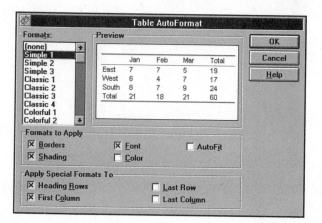

Figure 1.30
The Table AutoFormat dialog box.

If you have an active selection in your document when you choose the Insert Table item from the Table menu, Word converts the text in the selection to a table and does not display the Insert Table dialog box. If you did not intend such a conversion, use the Undo feature to remove the table and return your text to its former state.

The final method for inserting a table is to use the Table Wizard, shown in figure 1.31. Use this method when you want to build a complex table with row and column headings preinserted. The Table Wizard is best at building tables for storing time-oriented data, such as monthly reports.

To use the Table Wizard, follow these steps:

1. Place the insertion point where you want the table to appear in your document.

2. Open the Table menu.

3. Select the Insert Table item.

4. Click on the Wizard button to bring up the initial Table Wizard screen.

5. Select the table format from the six presented, using the option buttons. Click on the Next button to move to the next screen.

6. Use the drop-down list box to set the number of columns. Click on the Next button to move to the next screen.

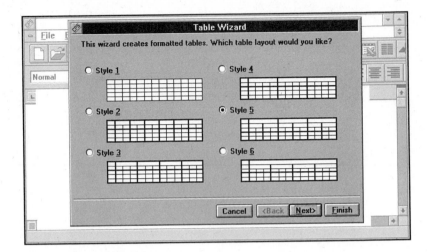

Figure 1.31
The initial screen
of the Table
Wizard.

7. Use the option buttons to set the type of column headings you want. Click on the Next button to move to the next screen.

8. Use the option buttons to set the type of row headings you want. Click on the Next button to move to the next screen.

9. Use the option buttons to indicate the contents of the cells. Click on the Next button to move to the next screen.

10. Use the option buttons to select the printing orientation for the table. Click on the Next button to move to the next screen.

11. Use the option buttons to determine whether you want to see each step in the table's creation on your screen. Click on the Finish button.

12. When the Table AutoFormat dialog box appears (refer to figure 1.30), select one of the predefined formats in the Formats list box. (The Preview box shows you what each table format looks like.)

13. Use the check boxes in the Formats to Apply group to select whether to use Borders, Shading, Fonts, Colors, AutoFit, or any combination of these. (You can experiment with different combinations of these features and view the results in the Preview box.)

14. Use the check boxes in the Apply Special Formats To group to select whether the formats you chose in step 13 are applied to Heading Rows, First Column, Last Row, Last Column, or any combination of these. (You can experiment with different combinations of these features and view the results in the Preview box.)

15. Click on OK to accept the AutoFormat you have chosen. The Wizard then inserts your table in the document.

Word's Table menu provides robust table editing features. If you create a simple table and decide later you want to apply AutoFormat to it, for instance, select the table and then select the Table AutoFormat item from the Table menu. If you want to split a cell into two subcells, select the cell (or cells) and then choose Split Cells from the Table menu. You can split a table into two sections using the Split Table menu option. You also can convert text to a table using the Convert Text to Table option, which divides the text into cells based on the appearance of a special character in the text. If you have a list in which the items are separated by commas, for instance, the chunks of text between the commas are inserted into separate cells.

Perhaps the most exciting table feature in Word for Windows 6.0, however, is the capability to assign formulas to cells in a table. The contents of the cell are the results of the calculation. You can, as a result, build miniature spreadsheets into your Word tables. If you are familiar with entering formulas into Microsoft Excel spreadsheet cells, you already know how to enter formulas into Word table cells. The process is very much the same.

To insert a formula in a cell, follow these steps:

1. Place the insertion point in the cell.

2. Open the Table menu.

3. Select the Formula option. The Formula dialog box appears, as shown in figure 1.32.

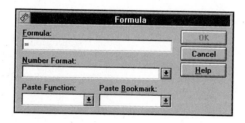

Figure 1.32
The Formula dialog box.

4. In the Formula dialog box, type the formula in the Formula text box after the equal sign. Use standard mathematical operators (+, -, *, /) and parentheses to build your formula.

5. If you want a number format associated with the cell, select one from the Number Format drop-down list box. The *number format* determines the way the number is displayed in the cell, governing such things as number of decimal places and whether a dollar sign is present.

6. If you want to use one of Word's mathematical functions, select it from the Paste Function drop-down list box.

7. If you want to use a cross-reference to a bookmark, paste it in using the Paste Bookmark drop-down list box.

8. Click on OK. The result of your formula now appears as the cell's contents.

Tip   If you have a formula stored at a bookmark, you can reference it in the formula you are building by pasting in the bookmark name. You can create cross-references to formulas outside the table in this manner.

Inserting Pictures

In addition to providing robust table creation and editing, Word also makes it easy to insert pictures into your document. Word can import graphics in most graphics file formats. If your drawing program's file format is not supported directly, chances are that your drawing program can convert the graphic to one of Word's supported file formats.

To insert a picture into your Word document, perform the following steps:

1. Place the insertion point where you want the picture to go.

2. Open the Insert menu.

3. Select the Picture menu item.

4. In the Insert Picture dialog box, select the graphics file from the File Name list box. You can navigate to other drives and directories using the Directories and Drives controls just as you can in the Open dialog box. You can limit the type of file displayed in the File Name list box by selecting a new file type descriptor from the List Files of Type drop-down list box (see fig. 1.33).

Figure 1.33
The Insert dialog box showing a picture previewed.

5. If you want to preview the picture before inserting it, check the Preview Picture check box.

6. If you want to create a link to the graphics file, check the Link to File check box. (See Part Five of this book, "Data Sharing and Integration," for more information about links. If you choose to link, you can uncheck the Save Picture in Document check box if you want.)

7. Click on the OK button. Word then inserts the picture into your document.

Tip

If you cannot find the file you want, use the Find File button in the Insert Picture dialog box to invoke Word's file finder. This feature searches your drive for files that match the specifications you provide.

If you want to edit the picture after you have inserted it, double-click on the picture. This action starts Microsoft Picture, which enables you to edit the picture while it is in place in your Word document. (See Chapter 4, "Sharing Data with Word," for more information about picture editing.)

Printing the Document

The fifth and final step in learning how to accomplish tasks with Word for Windows 6.0 is learning how to print your document. Word provides access to all its document formatting features from the printing menu commands. Although you can access these same features at any time as you work, you probably don't think much about them until you are ready to print. The remaining sections in this chapter explain how to get ready to print by saving and formatting your document, and finally how to print your document.

Tip

Be sure to have a document open so that you can practice with Word's printing features. Your agenda is a good choice. If you filled it out in the earlier exercises, you can print enough copies to distribute for your next meeting.

Saving Your Work

Although not required before printing, it is a good idea to save your work at this time. If your computer locks up because of a printer problem, your document is protected as a file on disk. Word offers several save options, the easiest of which is the Save button on the Standard toolbar. This button is third from the left and has a picture of a 3.5-inch floppy disk on it (see fig. 1.34).

Figure 1.34
The Save button on the Standard toolbar.

To save using this button, click on it with the mouse. The following actions take place:

- ✔ If the file already has a name, Word saves the file.

- ✔ If the file has not been named, Word displays the Save As dialog box, prompting you to name the file (refer to fig. 1.8). After you provide a name for the file and click on OK, Word saves the file.

- ✔ After Word starts to save the file, it might display a dialog box asking for information. If the file is not in Word 6.0 format, for instance, the dialog box asks if you want to convert to Word 6.0 format, save in the existing format, or cancel the save operation.

The Word File menu offers three save options (see fig. 1.35). The first, Save, initiates the same actions as clicking on the Save button on the Standard toolbar. The second option, Save As, brings up the Save As dialog box. Use this option when you wish to save a file under a new file name or in a new location. The third option, Save All, initiates the save action for all files that currently are open in Word.

Figure 1.35
The save options on Word's File menu.

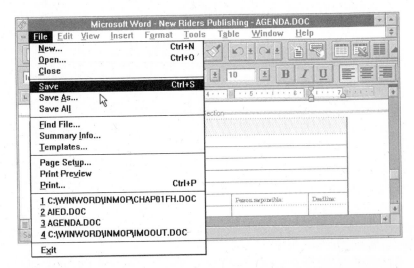

Tip

The AutoSave option is a useful option to set. Click on the **O**ptions button in the Save As dialog box and check the Automatic **S**ave Every check box. Enter the number of minutes to wait between saves in the spin box just to the right of the check box. The default is 10 minutes, but if you work quickly you might want to reduce that setting to 3 minutes. Click on OK, and then cancel the Save As dialog box. Word now will save your document at the regular interval you specified.

The only disadvantage to this is that if you have AutoSave turned on and you are working on large files it might take Word a few seconds to respond to your command when it is saving—which can become a nuisance.

Setting Up the Page

You always can print a document without checking the page setup, but when you do, you accept default values that might not be what you want for your document. By checking the page setup, you can make sure that all the settings for your document are correct. You get access to all the page features through one dialog box, so the process does not take much time.

Tip

The one feature that Word does not let you check from the print dialog boxes is page numbering. Before you print, be sure you have the pages numbered if you so desire. To add page numbers, select Page Numbers from the Insert menu.

To check page setup, perform the following steps:

1. Open the File menu.

2. Select the Page Setup option.

3. Click on the Margins tab (see fig. 1.36).

4. Use the Top, Bottom, Left and Right spin boxes to adjust the width of these margins.

5. Use the Header and Footer spin boxes to adjust the distance between the header and footer and the edge of the page.

6. Use the Gutter spin box to create a gutter if you plan to bind the document. The *gutter* is an additional margin added to allow room for binding. An extra margin is added to the left side of odd-numbered pages and to the right side of even-numbered pages.

7. Check the Mirror Margins check box if your document needs to be printed with right and left pages. This can be used in a similar manner to the gutter.

8. Use the Apply To drop-down list box to determine if these settings apply to the whole document or to the document from the insertion point forward.

9. Click on the Paper Size tab (see fig. 1.37).

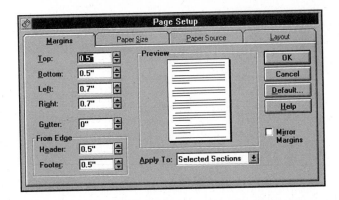

Figure 1.36
The Margins tab in the Page Setup dialog box.

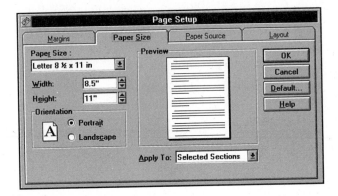

Figure 1.37
The Paper Size tab in the Page Setup dialog box.

10. Use the Paper Size drop-down list box to select predefined paper dimensions, or the Width and Height spin boxes to set custom dimensions.

11. Use the option buttons in the Orientation group to set Portrait or Landscape as the printing direction.

12. Use the Apply To drop-down list box to determine if these settings apply to the whole document, to the document from the insertion point forward, or to the current section of a multiple-section document.

13. Click on the Paper Source tab (see fig. 1.38).

14. Use the First Page and Other Pages list boxes to determine from which tray the paper for those pages feeds.

Tip

Being able to set a different paper source for the first page can enable the first page to be printed on letterhead and the remaining pages to be printed on standard stock.

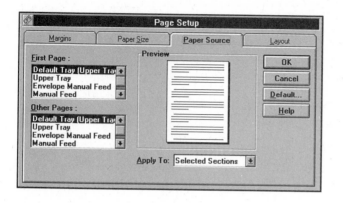

Figure 1.38
The Paper Source tab in the Page Setup dialog box.

15. Use the <u>A</u>pply To drop-down list box to determine if these settings apply to the whole document, to the document from the insertion point forward, or to the current section of a multiple-section document.

16. Click on the <u>L</u>ayout tab (see fig. 1.39).

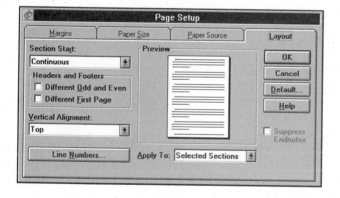

Figure 1.39
The Layout tab in the Page Setup dialog box.

17. Use the Section Sta<u>r</u>t drop-down list box to determine whether the document is one continuous section or new sections starting at New Columns, New Pages, Odd Pages, or Even Pages. (See Chapter 3, "Using Advanced Formatting Features," for an explanation of sections.)

18. Use the check boxes in the Headers and Footers group to set whether headers and footers will be different on odd and even pages and whether the first page will have a different header and footer than the rest.

19. Use the <u>V</u>ertical Alignment drop-down list box to set the alignment of text on the page relative to the top of the page, relative to the center of the page, or justified between the top and bottom edges of the page.

20. Check the <u>S</u>uppress Endnotes check box to prevent endnotes from printing.

21. Click on the Line <u>N</u>umbers button to open a dialog box with controls that enable you to add line numbers to your document.

22. Use the <u>A</u>pply To drop-down list box to determine if these settings apply to the whole document or to the document from the insertion point forward.

23. Click on OK to close the dialog box and make your settings effective.

After you are satisfied with the page settings, you should preview the document to make certain that it looks the way you want.

Previewing the Document

The print preview feature of Word for Windows 6.0 enables you to see the way your document will appear on the page before you print it. This option gives you a chance to verify that the formatting is correct and to make any final changes before the document goes to paper. In fact, you can edit your document in the print preview mode if you notice any details that need to be adjusted.

You can work with your document in the page layout view mode at all times if you want, which is like being in the print preview mode except that the Print Preview toolbar is not available. Open the <u>V</u>iew menu and select the <u>P</u>age Layout menu option, or click on the center button to the left of the horizontal scroll bar at the bottom left edge of the document window.

To enter the print preview mode, open the <u>F</u>ile menu and select the Print Pre<u>v</u>iew option. Your screen adjusts to show a 19 percent reduced picture of your documents page, and the Print Preview toolbar appears (see fig. 1.40). The percentage of reduction depends on your screen resolution.

While in the print preview mode, you can use the Print Preview toolbar to perform the following actions:

✔ You can print the document by clicking on the Print button.

✔ You can switch the magnifier on and off by clicking on the Magnifier button.

✔ You can switch to a one-page view by clicking on the One Page button.

✔ You can switch to view multiple pages by clicking on the Multiple Pages button and dragging across the grid that appears, releasing the mouse button when you have the multiple-page view you want to use.

✔ You can zoom in or out on your document by adjusting the zoom percentage in the Zoom Control drop-down list box.

✔ You can switch the view of the ruler on and off by clicking on the View Ruler button.

✔ You can squeeze a small amount of text on the final page into the other pages by clicking on the Shrink to Fit button.

✔ You can expand the preview screen to show only the page, the toolbar, and the status bar by clicking on the Full Screen button.

✔ You can get context-sensitive help by clicking on the Help button and then clicking on other buttons or screen elements.

✔ You can exit the preview mode by clicking on the Close button.

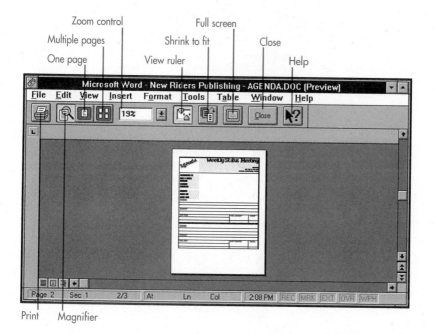

Zoom control
Multiple pages
One page
Full screen
Shrink to fit
View ruler
Close
Help
Print
Magnifier

Figure 1.40
The Print Preview toolbar.

When the magnifier is on, your mouse pointer becomes a magnifying glass. You can switch between a 100 percent view of a document page and the reduced view of a document page by clicking on that page. You have to shut off the magnifier, however, to do any editing while in the preview mode.

When you are satisfied with the document in the preview mode, the next logical step is to print the document.

Printing

Word provides three methods of initiating printing. You can click on the Print button on either the Standard toolbar or the Print Preview toolbar. When you do so, Word prints one copy of the document, using the settings in place at the time you clicked on the Print button.

For more control over the printing process, you can select the Print option from the File menu. (The accelerator key combination for this menu action is Ctrl+P.) This action causes the Print dialog box to appear (see fig. 1.41).

Figure 1.41
The Print dialog
box.

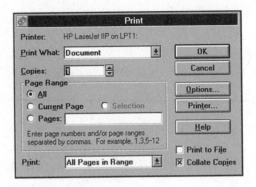

To exert maximal control over your print job, perform the following steps from the Print dialog box:

1. Select the object to be printed using the Print What drop-down list box. Word enables you to print the document or several items ancillary to the document, such as Summary Info, Annotations, Style, AutoText Entries, and Key Assignments.

2. Use the Copies spin box to set the number of copies to print.

3. Use the option buttons in the Page Range group to determine how much of the document to print. You can print All the document, the Current Page, or selected Pages. (If you select Pages, you must enter the page range to print in the text box. Separate discontinuous pages with commas, and express page ranges using a hyphen; for example: 2,4,6-8,12.) If a selection is currently active, you can opt to print the Selection.

4. Use the Print drop-down list box to specify whether to print All Pages in Range, just the Odd Pages, or just the Even Pages.

5. Check the Collate Copies check box to cause Word to finish printing the first copy before printing the second copy. Otherwise, Word prints all the copies of one page, then all the copies of the next, and so on.

By not selecting Collate Copies, some printers might print the document faster because Word will attempt to tell the printer to print copies of the page itself. If the printer supports this it will reduce the size of the file being sent to the printer, and should improve printing time.

6. Check the Print to File check box to cause Word to print the document to a disk file. When you print to a file, you then can print the document on a computer that does not have Word installed with the operating system print command.

7. If the Printer line at the top of the dialog box does not list the printer you want, click on the Printer button to open the Print Setup dialog box (see fig. 1.42). This enables you to choose from a list of available printers. Select the printer you need from the list box and click on the Set As Default Printer button. Click on Close or Cancel, whichever caption appears on this button, to close the Print Setup dialog box. If you need to adjust the setup of the printer, click on the Options button to open the dialog box provided by the printer driver that enables adjustment of printer settings.

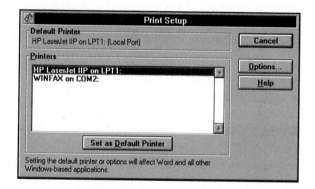

Figure 1.42
The Print Setup dialog box.

8. To adjust Word's printing options from the Print dialog box, click on the Options button. This action opens the Print tab in the Options dialog box, shown in figure 1.43. You can use the Include With Document check boxes to determine which of the ancillary materials to print along with the document. You can use the Printing Options check boxes to set output quality, the print order, whether fields and links are updated before printing, and whether printing can occur in the background. You can use the Default Tray drop-down list box to set the default paper tray for your printer. And you can set the Options for Current Document Only controls to set up settings that refer only to the current document.

9. When all is set correctly, close all the dialog boxes you have opened from the Print dialog box, and click on the Print dialog box's OK button. Word then prints your document.

Figure 1.43
The Print tab in the
Options dialog
box.

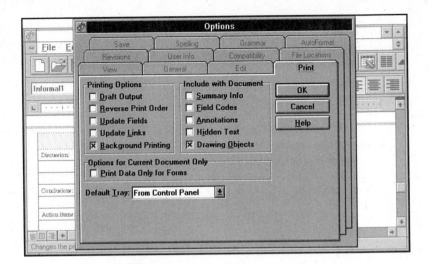

Chapter Snapshot

Every piece of software has a set of concepts—a mindset—behind it. To exploit Word to your best advantage, you have to get used to a few metaphors and concepts that drive the design of the software. In this chapter, you will learn the following items:

This chapter also will acquaint you with toolbars, headers and footers, and multiple document handling. After you are familiar with all these concepts, your work with Word will become more intuitive.

CHAPTER

2

Understanding Word for Windows Concepts

by Forrest Houlette

To get the most out of Word for Windows 6.0, you need to go beyond a knowledge of how to perform basic tasks. You need to understand how Word is organized. To plan solutions for the sophisticated word processing problems you face, you need to think a bit like the designers of Word thought when they put the software together. Any software product is built around metaphors that guide you in using the product.

Windows is based on a desktop metaphor. The screen is like the top of a desk on which you arrange the tools with which you do your work. The Media Player included with Windows is based on a metaphor of a VCR or a compact disc player. The controls have the same symbols on them and the same shapes. These familiar metaphors help you to plan how to use the Media Player. If you want to play a WAV file with Media Player, you already know something about how to do it because you already know how to use the same kinds of controls to run your VCR.

Almost all word processors share some characteristics with their predecessor the typewriter. You have a page onto which to type characters. You have a ruler that tells you where you are as you type across the page. You have tab stops and margin settings. The insertion point moving across the page even acts like the print head moving across the page.

However, word processors offer much more than do typewriters. You cannot shade the background of a paragraph using a typewriter. Typewriters can do borders, but you work very hard at building those borders. You can do footnotes at the bottom of the page using a typewriter, but you need a numbered backing sheet and good skills at guessing exactly how many lines are left at the bottom of the page.

The way you worked with a typewriter illustrates the difference in the way metaphors (or symbols) are used to build word processors. Your method for changing font styles on a typewriter was changing the typing element. You had to stop typing, disassemble the machine, reassemble the machine, type in the new font style, and then repeat the process to get back to the original font style. Using italic was a rather cumbersome process. Word offers a different method. Changing font styles is done by clicking a button. It's just that easy.

Word for Windows 6.0 still shares the typewriter similarities with earlier word processors, but it adds several new features to its design, like changing font styles by clicking a button. These additional features, once you understand them, enable you to exploit the power built into Word.

Once you can think in terms of these features, you can see ways to use Word effectively to provide solutions for your document needs. This chapter helps you to learn how to use them to your advantage.

Understanding the tools that organize Word for Windows 6.0 helps you to plan how to use Word effectively in conjunction with the other Office applications as well.

Defining Document

Word uses the metaphor of a *document* to describe the data you can enter and maintain with the word processor. A Word document has a lot in common with the typical document you could produce with a typewriter; for instance, both types of documents consist of printed pages containing text. However, a Word document can be much more.

Word documents can exist in your computer's memory and can be stored on a disk. Word documents can be viewed on your computer's screen or can be printed on your printer. Because they are electronic in form, Word documents can be sent by electronic mail as well as postal mail. In addition, Word documents can contain several different kinds of data. They are not just text documents, as typewritten documents are.

The Document Window

Probably the best way to begin understanding how Word for Windows 6.0 extends the document metaphor is to look at the way a document appears on the screen.

Each document appears in a *document window,* a child window that Word creates in its workspace when you create a document (see fig. 2.1). Essentially, a document window is an on-screen container for your document. This window not only controls the appearance of your document, but also provides you with means of interacting with your document.

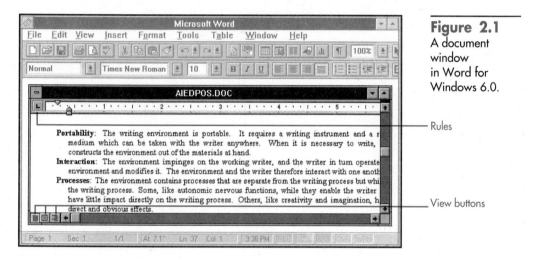

Figure 2.1

A document window in Word for Windows 6.0.

Rules

View buttons

A Word document window is like the standard document window that you see in any other Windows application. It has the familiar title bar, control menu box, minimize button, maximize button, and scroll bars. These items are standard for any document window. They enable you to view the contents of a document and to scroll that view.

Word adds two elements to this familiar scheme that give you much greater control over your document. At the top of the document underneath the title bar is a horizontal ruler. At the right edge of the horizontal scroll bar are three view buttons.

Using the Ruler

The ruler enables you to control the margins, the paragraph indentation, and the tab settings for your document. (Figure 2.2 shows the ruler and its parts in detail.) The margin settings are controlled by the upward facing pointers at the bottom edge of the ruler. Dragging these pointers adjusts the position of the right or left margin. When you drag these pointers, Word displays a vertical dashed line down your screen showing the position of the margin in the document. You can align margins easily in different portions of your document by matching this line to the position of the relevant characters on the screen.

Figure 2.2
The details of
Word's horizontal
ruler.

Indentation pointer

Click here to
choose tab type

Left margin pointer

Drag here to adjust
both left margin and
indentation

Left-aligned tab

Center-aligned tab

Right-aligned tab

Bar tab

Decimal tab

Default tab

Right margin pointer

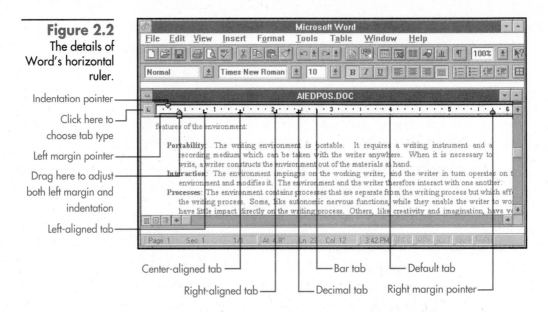

The paragraph indentation setting is controlled by the downward-facing pointer at the top edge of the ruler. Dragging this pointer adjusts the indentation of the first line of a paragraph. When you drag the pointer, Word displays a vertical dashed line down your screen so that you can see the exact position of the new indentation setting.

You can align indentations easily in different portions of your document by matching this line to the position of the relevant characters. You can use the ruler to create both hanging and standard indentations.

You also can adjust the paragraph settings using the Paragraph dialog box as explained in Chapter 1, "Word for Windows Quick Start." To do this, select the **P**aragraph option from the F**o**rmat menu.

After setting the indentation for a paragraph, you often will want to move both the left margin setting and the indentation setting at one time. In this way, you preserve your indentation pattern while adjusting the margin. You can accomplish this sort of adjustment by dragging the box under the left margin pointer.

As in the other margin and indentation adjustments, Word displays a vertical dashed line down your screen to indicate the position of the left margin. In this mode, Word does not display a line to indicate the position of the indentation pointer.

You can adjust tab settings by clicking or double-clicking on the ruler. Clicking on the box at the left edge of the ruler enables you to select which type of tab you will place on the ruler. Clicking on the box cycles you through the following four kinds of tab types:

✔ **Left-aligned.** Characters extend to the right of the tab as you type; indicated by an L-shaped angle in the box.

✔ **Center-aligned.** Characters are centered about the tab position; indicated by an angle with the vertical member centered over the base line.

✔ **Right-aligned.** Characters extend to the left of the tab as you type; indicated by a reverse L-shaped angle.

✔ **Decimal.** The decimal point aligns with the tab position; indicated by the symbol for a center-aligned tab with a decimal point to the right of the vertical member.

After you have selected the type of tab you want, follow these procedures to set the tabs:

✔ Click once on a marked position on the ruler to place a tab at that position.

✔ Double-click on the ruler to place a tab at an unmarked position.

As you are clicking or double-clicking to set a tab, Word displays a vertical dashed line down your screen to show you the position of the tab relative to the text on the screen.

The action of double-clicking not only places the tab but opens the Tabs dialog box, shown in figure 2.3. In this dialog box you can specify the exact position of the tab on the ruler as well as the tab's type and the positions of default tabs on the ruler.

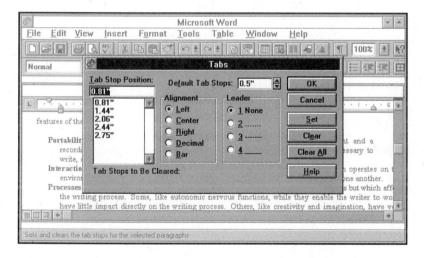

Figure 2.3
The Tabs dialog box.

Tip You also can access the Tabs dialog box by selecting the **T**abs option from the F**o**rmat menu.

The exact position of the tab you are setting appears in the Tab Stop Position combination box in the Tabs dialog box; the positions of other tabs you have set appear in the list box portion of the combination box. To adjust the position and character of the tab, perform the following steps:

1. To specify a more exact position for the tab, enter a number representing the exact position you want in the text box portion of the Tab Stop Position combination box.

2. Select the type of the tab using the option buttons in the Alignment group. You can select from the four options already discussed plus the Bar tab option. A *bar tab* places a vertical line through a paragraph at the tab position.

3. Use the option buttons in the Leader group to select characters that fill in the space between the last text on the line (or the margin, if there is no text) and the tab position.

4. Click on the Set button, then click on OK to complete the action of setting a tab at an unmarked position on the ruler.

A tabs leader enables you to place all the periods, or *leader dots,* between a chapter title and a page number in a table of contents or similar document. You do not have to type all those periods by hand!

The Tabs dialog box also enables the three following actions:

✔ You can clear the tab indicated in the Tab Stop Position combination box by clicking on the Clear button and then clicking on OK.

✔ You can clear all the tabs you have set by clicking on the Clear All button and then clicking on OK.

✔ You can adjust the width between the default tab stops using the Default Tab Stops spin box.

Default tabs are present in the document even when you have set no other tabs. They are indicated on the ruler by faint dots along the bottom edge.

As you can see, a Word document adds all the settings provided on the ruler to the design of a document. Embedded in each document is the equivalent of the tabulator bar and margin setting controls on a typewriter. Word merges these concepts related to document control into the concept of a Word for Windows 6.0 document.

Changing the View

Word merges concepts of three different types of documents into its formula for the document. Writers often talk of outlines, drafts, and final copy. Word enables you to view any document in any of these three ways; you do not need to create separate documents for your outlines, drafts, and final copies. In Word for Windows 6.0, you shift among these points of view on a document by clicking on the view buttons at the left edge of a document's horizontal scroll bar (see fig. 2.4).

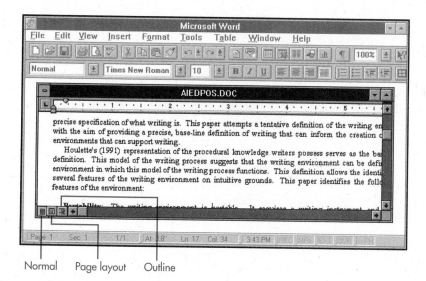

Normal   Page layout   Outline

Figure 2.4
The view buttons on the horizontal scroll bar.

To see a document as an outline, click on the outline button. The Outlining toolbar appears, as shown in figure 2.5. Now when you type, each block of text is either a heading for the outline or body text. The single arrow buttons on the Outlining toolbar reformat a block of text as a heading. The left and right arrows also promote and demote headings to different levels within the outline's structure, whereas the up and down arrows move a heading up and down the list within its level in the outline.

You do not have to display every level of the outline at once. The number buttons indicate how many levels are displayed. Headings that contain undisplayed, or collapsed, levels appear underlined. The plus and minus buttons expand and collapse the topic containing the insertion point. You also can limit the display to the first line of any heading with the Show First Line button.

You can switch between using special font and paragraph formats for each level of heading and not using these formats by using the Show Formatting button.

Figure 2.5
A document in
outline view.

Outline toolbar

Promotion/demotion
buttons

Movement buttons

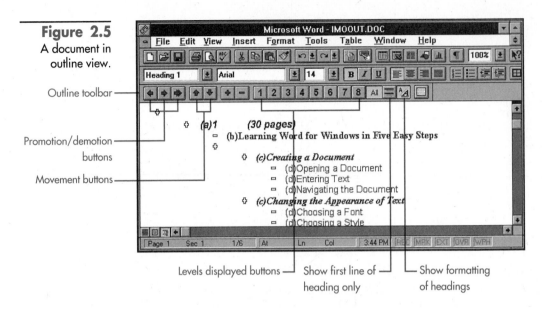

Levels displayed buttons ⎯ Show first line of ⎯ ⎯ Show formatting
heading only of headings

Tip You also can adjust the view of your document by selecting the appropriate options from the **V**iew menu.

To see a document as a draft, click on the Normal button. You see a simplified version of your document, without special formatting applied, as shown in figure 2.6. In this view, you can enter text the fastest, scroll the fastest, and apply proofreading tools the fastest. It is the best view for rapidly developing your document.

Figure 2.6
A document in
normal view.

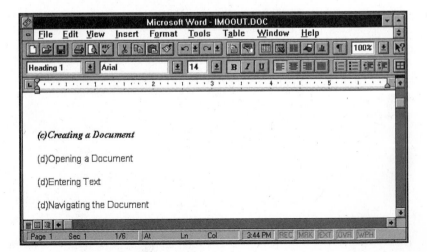

To see a document as final copy, click on the Page Layout button (see fig. 2.7). The view you have now shows you exactly how the document looks when printed. All formatting is applied and all the document's contents are shown in their correct position on the page. You can edit the document to adjust its final appearance in preparation for printing, and Word provides some additional tools to help you.

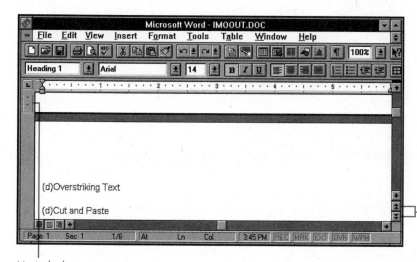

Figure 2.7
A document in page layout view.

Page scrolling buttons

Vertical ruler

Down the left side of the active page is a vertical ruler that displays the vertical margin settings. If you need to adjust these settings, double-click on the vertical ruler to display the Margins tab of the Page Setup dialog box. On the vertical scroll bar are two additional buttons displaying double arrows. These buttons advance you through the document, up or down, a page at a time.

Using Word's tools, you can rapidly shift among outline, draft, and final views of your document. A single document can represent what you ordinarily might see as three different documents.

Zooming and Splitting

Word adds the capability to view more and less of a document. You can zoom in or zoom out on portions of a document, exploding and reducing the size of your view, and you can split a document into two window panes so that you can see different portions of the document simultaneously.

To zoom in or out on your document, follow this procedure:

1. Open the Zoom drop-down list box on the Standard toolbar, the next-to-last control on the right (see fig. 2.8).

2. Select the reduction or enlargement factor you wish to use.

Your document immediately shifts to that size on the screen.

Figure 2.8
Using the Zoom
drop-down list
box on the
Standard toolbar.

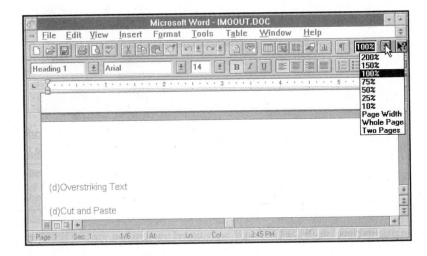

Zooming out beyond 50% makes a document difficult to read and edit, but does give you a sense of its overall look and structure. Zooming above 100% can ease eyestrain and help you to examine details like fine print at the bottom of a contract. To gain the maximum amount of screen space for viewing your document, open the **V**iew menu and select the F**u**ll Screen option.

To split your document into two panes, double-click on the split bar, the black region at the top of the vertical scroll bar, as shown in figure 2.9. You can drag the split bar to adjust the relative dimensions of the two panes. Click on either pane to make it active for editing, just as you would on any other window. To return to a single-pane view of your document, double-click on the split bar again.

By merging the concepts of enlargement, reduction, and multiple views with its concept of the document, Word provides you with greater flexibility and control over your documents. Documents become objects that you manipulate electronically within your computer's memory the same way you might by spreading them out on a table and using a magnifying reader to study details. Documents provide you with all the tools you need to create and use them as a part of their functionality. You do not need lots of external tools to be able to use your documents.

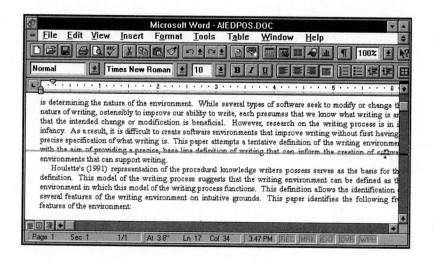

Figure 2.9
Using the split bar.

The Document's Contents

Another way to see how Word revises your concept of a document is to look at the contents of a document. Normally a document contains words and, at a higher end of publishing, pictures, graphs, and tables. In Word for Windows 6.0, documents can contain any type of data. You can create documents whose contents cannot be presented on paper.

To illustrate this concept, you need to examine only one of the applets that comes with Windows, the Sound Recorder. If you have a microphone attached to the sound system in your computer, try the following exercise:

1. Open any Word document.

2. Position the cursor to a location where you would like to add a voice annotation to the document.

3. Open the Insert menu and select the Object option.

4. If the Create New tab is not on top, click on it.

5. In the Object Type list box, select Sound, and then click on OK.

6. Click on the microphone button.

7. Record your message by speaking into the microphone.

8. Click on the Sound Recorder's stop button.

9. Open the Sound Recorder's File menu and choose Update. A sound icon appears in your Word document, as shown in figure 2.10.

10. Close the Sound Recorder by selecting Exit from the File menu.

11. To play back your voice annotation, double-click on the sound icon.

Figure 2.10
A Word document
that contains a
voice annotation.

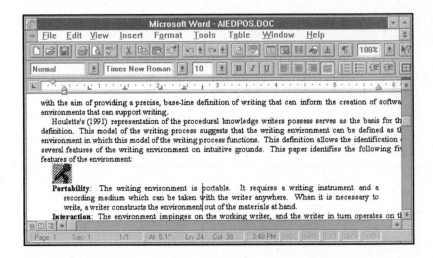

As you can imagine, you can add all sorts of nontext data into a Word for Windows 6.0 document. If you own Video for Windows, you can embed full-motion video clips to illustrate your text. You can include sound files of all types to illustrate your points. Using the Object Packager included with Windows, you can include data of any type prepared by any other application that can run under Windows.

Of course, you also can include pictures, tables, spreadsheets, and other typical illustrations that can be printed on paper. If you are using electronic mail to route documents for review and revision, you easily can include voice comments as well as written comments in the documents. If you are creating the text of a presentation slide show, you can embed the kind of data you need to make your points and present the slides electronically.

The application of Word's document metaphor radically redefines the nature of a document. Think of a Word document as a stack of paper with a home theater system hooked up to one of the futuristic interactive cable systems attached to it, along with an information service like CompuServe. These are the capabilities that Word can provide for you if your computer has the hardware to use them.

Master Documents

In Word for Windows 6.0, documents can serve to contain other documents. A document that serves this function is called a *master document*—a collection of separate documents, each contained in its own file, managed by another document file. As a result, the master document features of Word facilitate working with long documents like the text of a 1,000-page book. Scrolling from the beginning to the end of such a work would take forever.

Using the master document features, you can work with smaller chunks of the full document so that scrolling and spell-checking time no longer become horrendous problems. You also can work with the whole document.

Master documents are really special types of outlines. If you look back at figure 2.5, you will note that there is an extra button on the Outlining toolbar. It is the last one on the right—the Master Document button. When you click on that button you enter master document mode, in which you can convert an existing set of documents into a master document.

Note

You can view a master document in master document view, in which case you see the list of subdocuments. You also can view it in normal view, in which case you see the entire document as a single document. In normal view, sub-documents are indicated by section boundaries in the continuous text that you see. (Click on the Paragraph button on the Standard toolbar to make the section boundaries visible.)

To create a master document from scratch, follow these steps:

1. Click on the New button on the Standard toolbar to create a new file.

2. Open the <u>V</u>iew menu and select the <u>M</u>aster Document item.

The new document you created is now a master document. You can outline your overall document using Word's outlining features, and you can group headings on your outline and define them as subdocuments.

After writing your outline, perform the following procedure to create subdocuments:

1. Select the headings on the outline that should represent the subdocument.

2. Click on the Create Subdocument button on the Master Document toolbar (see fig. 2.11).

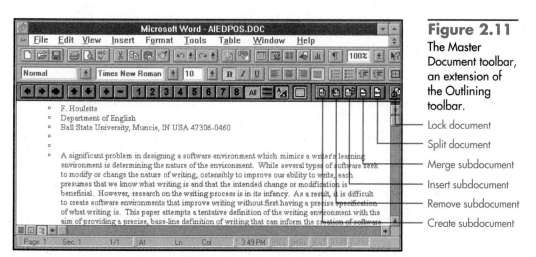

Figure 2.11
The Master Document toolbar, an extension of the Outlining toolbar.

Lock document

Split document

Merge subdocument

Insert subdocument

Remove subdocument

Create subdocument

Word for Windows

Word encloses each subdocument that you create on the outline in a box and identifies that the box's contents are a subdocument by displaying the subdocument icon in the upper left corner of the box.

To open a subdocument for editing, double-click on its subdocument icon. Word creates a new file, displays it in a document window, and displays the contents of the subdocument's segment of your outline for your additions and editing. To save the changes you have made to a subdocument, open the File menu and select the Save option, and accept the file name that Word has assigned. Close a subdocument just as you would close any other document.

To save your work on the entire project, return to the master document and select one of the save options from the File menu. Word automatically provides file names for the sub-documents based on the first header in the outline for the subdocument. As long as you keep the file name Word assigns to a subdocument file, you can edit it either outside of the master document as a separate file or from within the master document.

Never change the name of a subdocument file when you edit it outside the master document. Doing so destroys the link between the subdocument and the master document.

If you need to rename a subdocument, first open it from within the master document. You then can use the File, Save As menu option to rename the file. After renaming the subdocument, you should save the master document as well so that the new file name is recorded as a part of the master document.

You can remove subdocuments just as easily as you can create them by following these steps:

1. In master document view, place the insertion point inside the subdocument you want to remove.

2. Click on the Remove Subdocument button.

When you remove a subdocument, you do not lose any of its contents. Word makes the contents of the subdocument into a new segment of the master document. Instead of appearing as a subdocument that you open from the master document, the information appears as a part of the master document. If you want to delete the information, you should delete it from the master document.

If you need to add information stored in a separate file as a part of a master document, perform the following steps:

1. Open the master document.

2. Click on the Insert Subdocument button to display the Insert Subdocument dialog box (see fig. 2.12).

3. Select the name of the file to insert in the File Name list box.

4. Click on OK.

The file becomes a part of the master document, and its original file name is reserved.

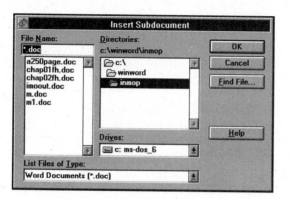

Figure 2.12
The Insert
Subdocument
dialog box.

Master documents and subdocuments can be based on different templates. When you open subdocuments from the master document, however, Word applies the formatting used by the master document's template first and then picks up the nonconflicting features of the subdocument's template.

When you open the subdocument outside the master document, Word applies the formatting used by the subdocument's template. You should eliminate as many conflicts as possible between the master document's template and subdocument templates to avoid surprise changes in a document's format.

When managing a long project using a master document, you eventually will find the need to merge two subdocuments into a single subdocument. This situation might occur when you discover that two chunks of text covering the same issue in separate places need to be combined into one. To merge two subdocuments, you need to make sure they are next to each other in your master document's outline. If they are not, follow these steps:

1. Click on the subdocument icon for the subdocument you want to move up or down in the outline.

2. Drag the subdocument into its new position and drop it into place.

After the two subdocuments are next to each other, perform the following actions to merge them:

1. Select the subdocuments to merge. Holding the mouse button down but not pointing to the subdocument icon, drag the mouse over the text of the documents.

2. Click on the Merge Subdocument button.

Word merges the selected subdocuments into a single subdocument.

You might want to split a long subdocument into shorter ones to improve the speed of working with the text. To split a subdocument, open the master document and perform the following steps:

1. Select the text that should be in the first new subdocument.

2. Click on the Split Subdocument button.

3. Select the text that should be in the second new subdocument.

4. Click on the split subdocument button.

Word breaks the old single subdocument into the chunks you have defined.

 Note   For information about printing master documents, see Chapter 5, "Understanding Printing and Printers."

When you are working as a part of a workgroup, you will want to lock subdocuments to prevent confusion about who is working on what section of the master document. Word keeps track of who created which subdocuments. When workgroup members open the master document, they have read-write editing privileges on the subdocuments they created, but those created by others are locked, providing only read-only access.

You can open a document created by another user to make changes, but you must first unlock it. After you are done, you should lock it again.

To unlock a document, follow these steps:

1. In master document view, place the insertion point in the subdocument to be unlocked.

2. Click on the Lock Document button.

To lock a document, follow the same procedure. The Lock Document button switches the state of the document lock. When a document is locked, Word displays a padlock icon underneath the subdocument icon.

 Tip   If you want to avoid making accidental changes to a subdocument, always lock your subdocuments. You can read and review them, but you will not be able to make changes unless you first unlock the document.

By bundling the document window, the ruler, the capability to split and zoom, and master documents into the concept of a document, Word for Windows 6.0 extends the document metaphor considerably. Working with a Word document now can mean editing a graphic, changing the volume of a sound, or adjusting the playback characteristics of a movie. These extensions can make your Word document a multimedia experience without requiring you to be a multimedia expert.

Defining Template

Word uses a *template* to describe a set of directions for creating a document. Whenever Word creates a new document, it follows the directions stored in one of its templates. Templates all carry the file extension DOT. If you open a file with this extension, it looks just like an ordinary Word document—in fact, it is. When Word constructs a new document, it copies all the characteristics of the template to the new document. When you save the new document, you save it as a file with its own name.

The characteristics of the document template are not modified when you save the document based on the template unless you have taken an action that explicitly modifies the template, such as recording a macro or creating a new style.

Tip Chapter 3, "Using Advanced Formatting Features," explains styles, and Chapter 6, "An Introduction to Word Macros," explains how to record macros.

Templates in Word are files from which characteristics are inherited. As a result, to build a template, you simply create a Word document that has the characteristics you want, and save it as a template. When you create a new document based on the template, the new document inherits all the features you gave to the template. It appears on your screen with all those features in place, ready for you to make additions.

The best way to see how to create a template is to make and save one. Suppose that you want a memo format that clearly shows that a document is confidential. You would like to have your company name and information on the document and a clear indication that the information in the document is to be treated with confidentiality. You could create a template for such documents by following these steps:

1. Open the File menu and select the New option.

2. In the New dialog box, select the Template option button in the New group and click on OK.

3. Enter the information you want for your company into the workspace; figure 2.13 shows an example.

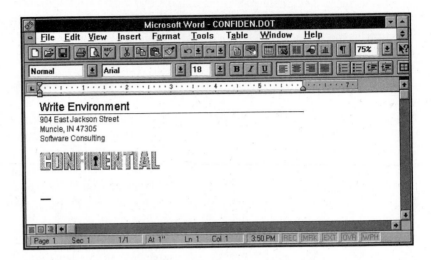

Figure 2.13
Creating a
confidential memo
template.

4. Place the insertion point where you would like a confidential label to appear.

5. Open the Insert menu and choose the Picture option.

6. In the Insert Picture dialog box, select the file CONFIDEN.WMF in the File Name list box and click on OK.

7. Place the insertion point where you would like to begin typing once the new confidential memo document is created.

You now have created the image of the documents you want based on this template. To save the template, follow these steps:

1. Open the File menu and select the Save option, or click on the Save button on the Standard toolbar.

2. Enter a name for the document template and click on OK. Word has already limited the Save As dialog box to saving a template because you already defined the file as a template.

Word automatically saves the template file to your template directory, where it is ready for use the next time you create a new document.

Tip

You actually can save any file as a template. After you have entered a file name in the Save As dialog box, open the Save File as Type drop-down list box and select Document Template, then click on OK.

Templates can contain anything a document can contain. They can be simple, like this confidential letterhead, or they can be complex. Imagine setting up a standard contract as a document template. All the text that never changes could become a part of the template. You could use bookmarks, a feature of Word explained later in this chapter, to indicate where you need to add the text related to each client who signs the contract. Writing a contract is then as simple as creating the document, moving to each bookmark, and entering the text necessary there.

You also can change a document's template if you find it necessary to do so. You might have formatted a document using the Normal template, and discovered afterward that the person sitting two desks over has created a template for just that kind of memo. To substitute the new template for the old one, you attach the new template to the document, following this procedure:

1. Select the Templates option from the File menu to display the Templates and Add-ins dialog box (see fig. 2.14).

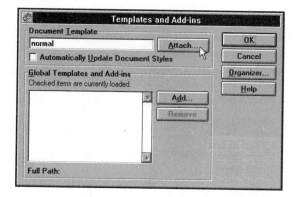

Figure 2.14
Using the Template and Add-ins dialog box to attach a template to a document.

2. Click on the Attach button to display the Attach Template dialog box. Select the template to attach from the File Name list box.

3. Click on OK in the Attach Template dialog box and then click on OK in the Templates and Add-ins dialog box.

Templates also are the repository for things like styles and macros, both explained briefly later in this chapter and in more detail in Chapters 3 and 6. The template can contain toolbars, custom menus, and default settings for dialog boxes. Using templates, you can set up each type of document you work with so that your work is focused on exactly the options of Word necessary to the task at hand.

If you want styles, toolbars, or other such items stored in a special template available to any document you open, load the template globally. Open the File menu, select the Templates option, click on Add, select the name of the template in the File Name list box, and click on OK.

Templates define a plan of action for creating a document. When you create the template, you decide how the document will be created and how you will interact with the document after it is created. As a result, you should plan templates with your work flow in mind. Let the template perform repetitive tasks for you so that you save time and focus on the items in the document that demand your attention.

Understanding Styles

Word for Windows 6.0 uses style to mean a way of doing things with a format. Word extends this meaning into a concept that helps you to accelerate much of the typical work you do in formatting a document.

A *style* is a collection of formats that you save as a unit. After you have saved this collection of formats, you can apply them to any block of text by placing the insertion point within the paragraph to be formatted and selecting the style from the Style drop-down list box on the Formatting toolbar. The Style drop-down list box is always the one farthest left on the toolbar. It contains the styles currently in use in the document.

Word provides two kinds of styles: paragraph styles and character styles. *Paragraph styles* contain formatting information that applies to paragraphs, including font formats. *Character styles* contain formatting information that applies only to characters. Paragraph style names appear in bold characters, while character style names do not.

Word provides a number of built-in styles that you can use to format your own documents. The Style drop-down list box on the Formatting toolbar shows you only the styles currently in use. If you want to see all the styles available to you, perform the following steps:

1. Open the Format menu and select the Style option.

2. In the Style dialog box, use the List drop-down list box to select All Styles. The Styles list box then displays all the styles available in the current template and in templates available globally (see fig. 2.15).

3. To apply any style built into Word, select its name in the Styles list box and click on Apply. The paragraph containing the insertion point takes on the formats saved as that style.

To see how to create a style, turn to "Creating Custom Styles" in Chapter 3, "Using Advanced Formatting Features." To learn how to make a template available globally, see the preceding section.

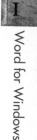

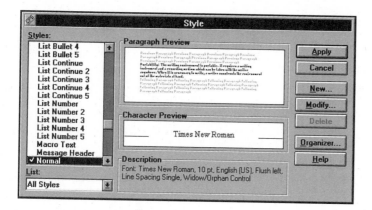

Figure 2.15
Displaying available styles in the Style dialog box.

Styles are saved as a part of a document or a document template. Because of this fact, document templates can serve as collections of styles that you can apply to format the document based on the template. If you are wondering whether Word includes a template with appropriate styles for the document you need to create, investigate the Style Gallery. Open the Format menu and select the Style Gallery option. The Style Gallery dialog box appears, as shown in figure 2.16.

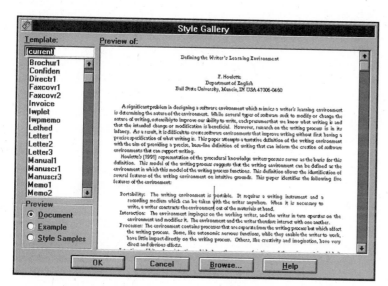

Figure 2.16
The Style Gallery dialog box.

The Template list box displays the list of document templates in Word's \TEMPLATE directory. (If you need to see templates stored in another directory, use the Browse button to change directories.) By selecting a template from the list, the document shown in the Preview of box takes on the style of that template.

By default, Word shows you a preview of the document you currently are working on. Unfortunately, the current document is probably the worst example of the template and its styles, because none of the contents of the template are added to the document and only the default paragraph text style is applied. As a result, you see very little of the automatic formatting available to you in the template. Better examples are provided by the alternate option buttons in the Preview group. You can choose to see an example document or a list of the styles available in the template, with each item in the list formatted in the style it names.

If you find styles available in a template that you would like to use in your current document, you have four choices:

✔ **Copy the styles from their home template into your current document.** The styles are available in that document only, unless you copy them again to another document. To exercise this choice, click on OK in the Style Gallery dialog box.

Use this option if you are interested only in formatting your current document but not in creating similar documents on a regular basis.

✔ **Attach the template to the document.** Do this by canceling the Style Gallery dialog box and selecting the Templates option from the File menu. Click on the Attach button and select the template to attach from the File Name list box in the Attach Template dialog box. Click on OK in the Attach Template dialog box and then click on OK in the Templates dialog box. Keep in mind that the template you attach replaces the template that previously was attached.

Use this option when you want to take advantage of other items that might also be stored in the template, such as macros and toolbars, and when you are certain that the template is not missing features you might need.

✔ **Copy the styles into the NORMAL.DOT template.** See Chapter 3, "Using Advanced Formatting Features," for more information about how to perform this operation.

Use this option when you expect to use the styles stored in the template in the documents you create by clicking on the New button on the Standard toolbar. Keep in mind that the styles will not be available in templates from which you have deleted some of the items stored in NORMAL.DOT.

✔ **Make the template available globally.** In this case the styles in the template become available to every document in the Style dialog box. For the procedure, see the preceding section of this chapter.

Use this option when you want the styles to be available to every document.

Tip   You can remove a character style from a selection by pressing Ctrl+space bar.

Understanding Toolbars

Word provides toolbars to assist you with various editing tasks. Each toolbar consists of a bar-shaped window that appears beneath Word's menu and contains buttons and other controls that enable you to perform with a single mouse click tasks that otherwise might take several keystrokes or mouse clicks.

Toolbars display visual images that Word uses to represent to you how to perform these tasks. A toolbar therefore serves as a visual reminder of the nature and organization of the task represented by the toolbar. To facilitate your work, Word presents 15 different toolbars, described in table 2.1.

Table 2.1
Word for Windows 6.0 Toolbars

Toolbar	Function
Borders	Helps in placing borders around paragraphs and selecting shading
Database	Assists in inserting, building, and maintaining databases in Word documents
Drawing	Enables the drawing of pictures in Word documents
Equation Editor	Enables you to insert mathematical and scientific equations into a document
Formatting	Helps you to format a document
Forms	Enables you to insert custom fields on templates so that you can create on-line forms
Header and Footer	Enables you to edit headers and footers for your documents
Macro	Assists in editing, testing, and debugging macros
Mail Merge	Helps in conducting a mail merge operation
Master Document	Enables you to manage a master document
Microsoft	Enables you to launch other Microsoft applications from within Word
Outlining	Helps you to create and manage outlines
Standard	Contains typical tools that you want to access frequently
WordArt	Helps in constructing artful text

continues

I

Word for Windows

Table 2.1, Continued
Word for Windows 6.0 Toolbars

Toolbar	Function
Word for Windows 2.0	Provides the Word for Windows 2.0 toolbar for those who need to use it

To use a toolbar, you manipulate the controls on the bar just as you would if they appeared in a dialog box. You can adjust your view of the toolbars in two ways. First, you can determine which of several toolbars are displayed. The easiest way to adjust which toolbars appear on your screen is to click on any toolbar with the right mouse button. A floating menu that gives you access to all toolbar functions appears, as shown in figure 2.17.

Figure 2.17
The toolbar
floating menu.

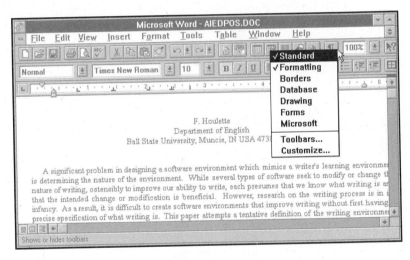

On the toolbar floating menu you can choose to have up to 7 of the 15 toolbars on-screen just by clicking on the menu item that bears the toolbar's name. A check appears next to the names of toolbars already showing on-screen. To hide a toolbar from this menu, click on its checked menu item, and the toolbar will disappear.

In addition to being able to control your view of toolbars, you can select the Toolbar and Customize dialog boxes from this menu. For more about customizing toolbars, see Chapter 7, "Customizing Word for Windows."

Also, you need to know how to float toolbars so that you can avoid limiting a document's workspace. The toolbars shown in figure 2.17 are *anchored;* that is, they are stationary and fixed underneath the Word menu. To make them *float* over your work as separate, movable, and sizable windows, double-click on the toolbar somewhere outside the controls. The toolbar floats away from its anchored position and into the body of the document (see fig. 2.18).

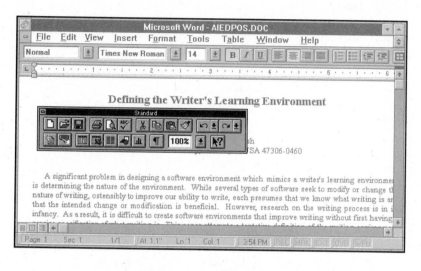

Figure 2.18
A floating toolbar.

You can adjust the size of the toolbar just as you would any window. To anchor the toolbar again, double-click on it.

To manage toolbars effectively, you must know how to access the Toolbar dialog box from the View menu. If you have hidden all your toolbars, you have no other means of getting access to them again. To change your view of the toolbars, follow this procedure:

1. Open the View menu.

2. Select the Toolbars option.

3. Check the toolbars you want to appear in the Toolbars list box. Uncheck those you do not want to appear.

4. Click on OK.

Using the Toolbars dialog box, you can also create new toolbars, customize existing toolbars, and reset toolbars to default tools. For more information about these processes, see Chapter 7, "Customizing Word for Windows."

Defining Headers and Footers

Word enables you to place headers and footers in your documents. These are special regions of the page in which you can insert information you want repeated on each page. The header appears at the top of the page and the footer appears at the bottom. Common uses for these regions are displaying running titles, printing page numbers, and printing information about the document itself, such as file name, print date, last edit date, or version number. Headers and footers remind us of the process printers use to place running titles, tool lines, and other graphics on each page.

Tip   The footer of a document is a good place to store any version tracking information you want to keep as you revise a collaborative document.

Word reserves space for a header and footer in each document. If you insert nothing into these regions, then your text takes them over. On the other hand, if you do insert information, the header or footer is displayed.

One of the most common uses for either the header or footer is to display page numbers. To add page numbers, perform the following procedure:

1. Open the Insert menu and select the Page Numbers option to display the Page Number dialog box (see fig. 2.19).

Figure 2.19
The Page Numbers dialog box.

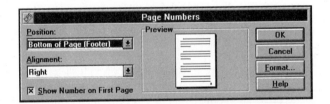

2. Open the Position drop-down list box and select whether you want the page number in the header or the footer.

3. Open the Alignment drop-down list box and select whether you want right, left, center, inside, or outside alignment for the page number. Right, left, and center place the page number at the corresponding position within the header or footer. Inside and outside place the page number at the inside of the binding edge or the outside of the binding edge if you are using mirror margins. The Preview box displays the exact position you have selected.

4. Check the Show Number on First Page check box if you want to display a page number on the first page of your document.

5. Click on the Format button to open the Page Number Format dialog box, shown in figure 2.20.

6. Use the Number Format drop-down list box to select the number format you want to use.

7. Use the option buttons in the Page Numbering group to determine whether the number sequence should Continue from Previous Section or Start At a particular number. If you choose Start At, enter the starting number in the spin box.

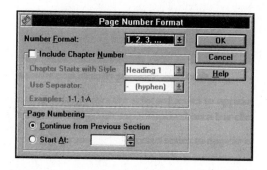

Figure 2.20
The Page Number
Format dialog
box.

8. Check the Include Chapter **N**umber check box to include the chapter number as a part of the page number. If you select this option, you must select a style using the Cha**p**ter Starts with Style drop-down list box. This tells Word how to recognize chapter beginnings. You also must open the Use S**e**parator drop-down list box to indicate what character separates the chapter number from the page number in the page number string.

9. Click on OK in the Page Number Format dialog box and in the Page Number dialog box.

You also can directly edit the header and footer for each page. To prepare to do so, open the **V**iew menu and select the **H**eader and Footer option. Your screen will switch to page layout view and the Header and Footer toolbar appears, as seen in figure 2.21.

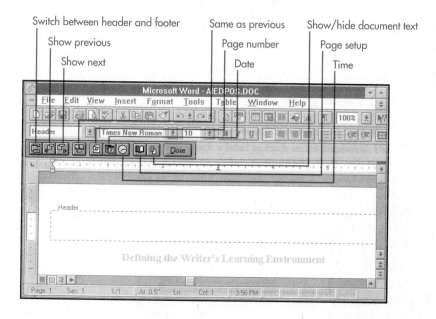

Figure 2.21
Editing the header
and footer using
the Header and
Footer toolbar.

Tip   You can float the Header and Footer toolbar by double-clicking on it.

While the Header and Footer toolbar is visible, you can take the following actions to define your headers and footers:

✔ You can enter and edit text in the header or footer section of the document. You can use any text, field, or control that you can use anywhere else in a Word document.

✔ You can switch between editing the header and footer by clicking on the Switch Between Header and Footer button.

✔ You can move between headers and footers for each section of your document by clicking on the Show Previous or Show Next buttons.

✔ If you want to continue a header or footer from the previous section of the document, click on the Same as Previous button. The button stays depressed to indicate that all sections have the same header and footer. If you want to use different headers and footers in a section, place the insertion button in that section and click on the Same as Previous button again. It pops up to indicate that each section has different headers and footers.

Note   Word enables you to define sections in your document, each of which can have different formatting characteristics.

✔ You can insert page number, date, and time fields by clicking on the buttons with those names.

✔ You can hide the document text if it distracts you, or re-show it, by clicking on the Show/Hide Document Text button.

✔ You can access the Page Setup dialog box by clicking on the Page Setup button. See the section "Setting Up the Page" in Chapter 1 for more information about how to use the controls in this dialog box. The most important controls for headers and footers appear in the Headers and Footers group on the Layout tab and the From Edge group on the Margins tab. These controls enable you to select Different Odd and Even and Different First Page for headers and footers, as well as to set the distance from the edge of the page to the header and footer.

✔ You can exit the header and footer editing mode by clicking on the Close button or by selecting the Header and Footer option from the View menu.

Explaining Document Tools

Word uses the metaphor of a tool to represent an electronic automation of a proofing process that you ordinarily would perform by hand in preparing a document. Word provides you with several tools that help you to improve your documents in one way or another. These tasks range from proofreading to maintaining lists of common phrases to automatically changing a date to match the current day. Using these tools simplifies and speeds up your work.

Spelling Checker

Probably the most familiar document tool is the *spelling checker,* which compares each word in your document to the correct spellings stored in its dictionary and asks you to verify the spelling of any words not in the dictionary. You can add words not in the standard dictionary to a custom dictionary, and you can maintain several custom dictionaries specific to specialized types of documents. The spelling checker, therefore, is a flexible tool that automates the process of proofreading for spelling errors.

Spelling checkers are wonderful, but they do not eliminate typographical errors. In fact, they can serve to hide certain kinds of typos. After the spelling check is over, you can be certain that all the words in the document have correct spellings; however, you cannot be certain that you have used the correct form of the word in the right place. The spelling checker, for instance, will not point out that "to" should have been spelled "too" when you meant "also." Such incorrect forms can be difficult to find once they all are correctly spelled.

To access Word's spelling checker, perform the following steps:

1. Click on the Spelling button on the Standard toolbar, open the <u>T</u>ools menu and select the <u>S</u>pelling option, or press F7. The Spelling dialog box appears, as shown in figure 2.22.

Figure 2.22
The Spelling dialog box.

2. Verify the spelling of the word in the Not in Dictionary text box. If it is correct, take one of the following steps:

   ✔ Click on the Ignore button.

   ✔ If you expect that the word will occur later in your document, click on the Ignore All button. Word then will ignore the word for all spelling checks during the current Word session.

   ✔ If you frequently use the word, select a dictionary in the Add Words To drop-down list box and click on the Add button. Word then will accept the word as being correctly spelled during all Word sessions.

3. If the word in the Not in Dictionary text box is incorrect, select one of the suggestions from the Suggestions list box so that the word in the Change To text box is the word you want. Or type the correct word in the Change To text box, then perform one of the following steps:

   ✔ Click on the Change button to change to the correct form displayed in the Change To text box.

   ✔ Click on the Change All button if you expect to encounter the same misspelling throughout the document. Word then will change all encountered forms of the word to the form you specified as correct.

Be careful when selecting the Change All button, especially if the incorrect form is close to the correct spelling of two different words. You might encounter the word *all* incorrectly spelled as *al* in a document containing the male first name Al. You could accidentally misspell Al's name throughout the document by clicking on the Change All button.

4. If you recognize the misspelling in the Not in Dictionary text box as a common typing error that you make, click on the AutoCorrect button. Word adds this wrongly typed word and its correction to the AutoCorrect list, and will perform the correction on the fly as you type. (For more information about AutoCorrect, see the section "AutoCorrect" later in this chapter.)

5. If the Not in Dictionary box is empty, the Change and Change All buttons take on the labels Delete and Delete All. Usually this change occurs when the spelling checker encounters a repeated word or some similar occurrence. Use Delete and Delete All just as you would Change and Change All in dealing with these circumstances.

6. Click on the Undo Last button to undo the last spelling correction. Using this button, you can reverse the course of the spelling checker through the file to

correct any errors you might have made when clicking on buttons. <u>U</u>ndo Last remains active as long as you can back up to an earlier correction and undo the action.

7. Click on the <u>O</u>ptions button to set the options for the spelling checker. The Options dialog box appears with the Spelling tab active, as shown in figure 2.23.

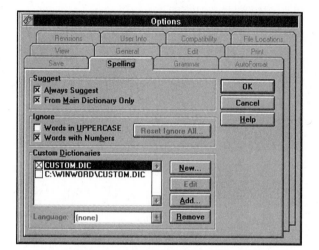

Figure 2.23
The Options dialog box with the Spelling tab active.

In the Options dialog box, perform the following steps:

✔ Use the option buttons in the Suggest group to control how the spelling checker suggests possible correct forms. Select A<u>l</u>ways Suggest if you want Word always to suggest alternate forms. (If you uncheck this box, you can always get suggestions by clicking on the <u>S</u>uggest button in the Spelling dialog box.) Check From <u>M</u>ain Dictionary Only if you want suggestions only from the main dictionary. Uncheck this box if you want suggestions from custom dictionaries as well.

Tip

The fewer suggestions the spelling checker has to make, the faster it runs.

✔ Use the controls in the Ignore group to control the way in which the spelling checker ignores certain words. Check the Words in <u>U</u>PPERCASE box to ignore words in all capitals. Check the Words with Num<u>b</u>ers box to ignore such words. Click on the Reset <u>I</u>gnore All button to clear the Ignore All list for the current session.

✔ Use the controls in the Custom Dictionaries group to set up and maintain your custom dictionaries. Use the Custom **D**ictionaries list box to select which dictionaries are active by checking or unchecking the box next to the dictionary's name. Use the Lan**g**uage drop-down list box to select the language formatting that applies to the dictionary. Use the **N**ew button to create a new custom dictionary. This button opens a dialog box that enables you to create a file in dictionary format. Use the **E**dit button to open a dictionary as a Word document so that you can add words to it. Use the **A**dd button to open a dialog box that permits you to add a third-party dictionary to the list of custom dictionaries. Use the **R**emove button to remove a custom dictionary from the list.

Word's spelling checker enables you to define words that should not be included in the spelling check. The list of words to exclude from the spelling check is called the *exclude dictionary.* It must have the same name as the main dictionary it should work with, end in an EXC extension, and be stored along with its main dictionary in the \MSAPPS\PROOF directory. For example, the American English dictionary shipped with Word is named MSSP2_EN.LEX. The corresponding exclude dictionary must be named MSSP2_EN.EXC.

This capability permits you to use variant spellings not accepted by the main dictionary. For example, if you prefer *judgement* to *judgment,* a commonly accepted spelling variant in American English, you should add *judgment* to the exclude dictionary. This action causes Word's spelling checker to question the spelling *judgment,* so that you can change it to your preferred spelling of *judgement.*

To create an exclude dictionary, perform the following procedure:

1. Create a new file by clicking the New button on the Standard toolbar or by opening the **F**ile menu and selecting the **N**ew option.

2. Type the list of words to exclude. Press Enter after each word.

3. Open the **F**ile menu and select the Save **A**s option.

4. Open the Save As File **T**ype drop-down list box and select Text Only.

5. Enter the appropriate name for the exclude dictionary in the File **N**ame text box.

6. Click on OK.

7. Start the spelling checker to complete the installation of the exclude dictionary.

Grammar Checker

Word for Windows 6.0 provides a grammar checking tool that can help you to catch common errors in writing. The grammar checker examines your document sentence by sentence, searching for patterns that might indicate errors. This tool also can suggest improvements to each sentence that it flags as containing a possible error. You can accept the suggested change, seek an explanation of the possible error, edit the sentence, or ignore the possible error.

Although grammar checkers get better and better all the time, they do not catch all errors and they flag some sentences as containing errors that are in fact correctly formed. For example, Word's grammar checker responds to the sentence *This here be a boo boo* by suggesting that you consider deleting the repeated word. You should proofread your document after checking the grammar to catch any errors the grammar checker missed.

To use the grammar checker, open the <u>T</u>ools menu and select the <u>G</u>rammar option to display the Grammar dialog box, as shown in figure 2.24.

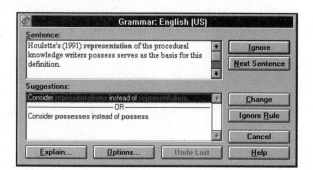

Figure 2.24
The Grammar dialog box.

In the Grammar dialog box, examine the sentence containing the possible problem in the <u>S</u>entence text box and read the suggested course of action in the Suggestions text box. Then take one of the following courses of action:

✔ Click on the <u>I</u>gnore button to ignore the suggested change.

✔ Click on the <u>N</u>ext Sentence button to move to the next sentence without either correcting the error or ignoring the error. You can bypass an error this way so that you can return later with the grammar checker after considering how you want to express the sentence.

✔ Edit the sentence in the <u>S</u>entence text box, making the changes you desire.

✔ Click on the <u>C</u>hange button to make the suggested change or to substitute your edited version of the sentence for the original. Your edited version takes precedence over the suggested change.

✔ Click on the Ignore <u>R</u>ule button to prevent the grammar checker from applying the rule indicated during the remainder of the grammar check.

✔ Click on the <u>E</u>xplain button to open a dialog box, seen in figure 2.25, that offers a more detailed explanation of the possible problem.

✔ Click on the Cancel or Close button, whichever appears, to end the grammar checking session.

Figure 2.25
Getting an
explanation of a
grammar
checker rule.

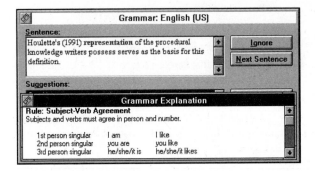

✔ Click on the Undo **L**ast button to reverse the last action you took with the grammar checker. You can repeat this undo action to move backwards through the actions you have taken with the grammar checker.

You can adjust which rules the grammar checker applies to your text by clicking on the **O**ptions button or opening the **T**ools menu and select the **O**ptions item. When the Options dialog box appears, click on the Grammar tab if it is not active (see fig. 2.26).

Figure 2.26
The Grammar tab
in the Options
dialog box.

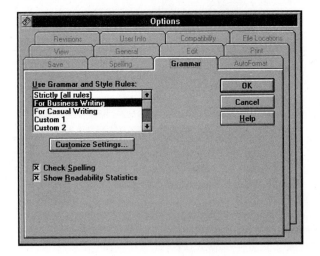

Now, perform the following steps:

1. Use the Check **S**pelling check box to control whether the grammar checker runs a spelling check on each sentence before checking its grammar. Turning off the spelling check speeds the grammar checker, but you need to perform a spelling check before you check your document's grammar.

2. Check or uncheck the Show **R**eadability Statistics check box to control whether the grammar checker shows readability statistics after the grammar check is completed.

3. Select the type of writing whose grammar you are checking in the Use Grammar and Style Rules list box.

4. If you wish to create a custom set of grammar and style rules or to change the rules applied in a predefined type of writing, click on the Customize Settings button and take one or more of the following actions:

   ✔ In the Customize Grammar Settings dialog box (see fig. 2.27), open the Use Grammar and Style Rules list box to select the type of writing for which you want to modify the rules applied.

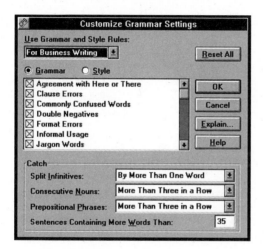

Figure 2.27
The Customize Grammar Settings dialog box.

   ✔ Use the Grammar and Style option buttons to select which set of rules to modify.

   ✔ Click on the sets of rules displayed in the list box to switch whether they will be used in the grammar check.

   ✔ Open the Split Infinitives, Consecutive Nouns, and Prepositional Phrases drop-down list boxes to determine how the grammar checker handles these constructions.

   ✔ Enter a number in the Sentences Containing More Words Than text box to determine the largest sentence (in number of words) that the grammar checker considers acceptable.

   ✔ Click on the Explain button to open a dialog box that explains more about each rule set.

   ✔ Click on the Reset All button to change a rule group back to its default settings if you feel you have made an error in making changes.

   ✔ Click on OK to accept the changes you have made in the rule settings.

At the end of each grammar checking session, Word displays a set of readability statistics unless you have turned this feature off using the Grammar tab in the Options dialog box. These statistics can help you to determine whether you have matched your writing appropriately to your intended readers.

Each of the means of calculating readability applies a slightly different method of calculating reading ease. In general, the lower the value the easier the reading. You can use these statistics as guidelines for determining how well you meet the reading ability of your intended audience.

Note   Under certain circumstances, you might want to have your document meet rigid reading ease guidelines, such as when preparing technical repair manuals for an aircraft maintenance crew. In this setting, the need to understand the steps to follow on first reading is mission critical, since errors in procedure can lead to airplane crashes. In other settings, however, you might not need to adhere tightly to such guidelines. Many of the classics often recommended to adolescents for enjoyment score well off the top of the Flesch and Flesch-Kincaid scales.

Thesaurus

Word for Windows 6.0 includes a thesaurus to help you vary your vocabulary and find more useful words by association with the less useful word you might be able to think of. To use the thesaurus, place the insertion point on the word you want to look up. Then, open the Tools menu and select the Thesaurus option, or press Shift+F7, to display the Thesaurus dialog box (see fig. 2.28).

Figure 2.28
The Thesaurus
dialog box.

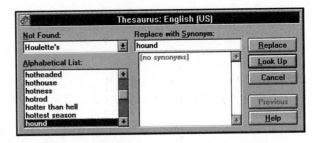

In the Thesaurus dialog box, perform one of the following actions:

✔ Verify that the word you want to look up appears in the Looked Up drop-down list box. (If the word was not found, Looked Up becomes the Not found drop-down list box.) If it does not, enter the word in the text box portion of the Replace with Synonym combination box and click on the Look Up button.

If the insertion point is not on a word when you invoke the thesaurus, the dialog box will be empty and the Replace with $\underline{S}$ynonym combination box will be labeled $\underline{I}$nsert. Type the word to look up in the $\underline{I}$nsert control and click on $\underline{L}$ook Up.

✔ Select the meaning you want to work with in the $\underline{M}$eanings list box. (If the word was not found, $\underline{M}$eanings becomes the $\underline{A}$lphabetical List list box.) You can select antonyms and related words if you want to explore opposites or related word families.

✔ Select a synonym you want to work with in the list box portion of the Replace with $\underline{S}$ynonym combination box.

✔ Click on the $\underline{L}$ook Up button to look up synonyms for the word that currently appears in the text box portion of the Replace with $\underline{S}$ynonym combination box.

✔ Click on the $\underline{P}$revious button or open the Look$\underline{e}$d Up drop-down list box to select words previously looked up during the thesaurus session.

✔ Click on the $\underline{R}$eplace button to replace the word containing the insertion point with the word that appears in the text box portion of the Replace with $\underline{S}$ynonym combination box.

Hyphenation

Word provides a hyphenation facility that enables you to give your documents a professional look by reducing excessive raggedness along a margin or unusually long spaces between words in a fully justified document.

Word enables you to insert two types of hyphens into words. *Optional hyphens* break a word only when the word appears at the end of a line and using the hyphen would improve the appearance of the ragged margin. *Nonbreaking hyphens* always appear in the word but never break at the edge of a line. They are useful in compound words such as *Somerset-Upon-Thyme* or hyphenated personal names in which you do not wish parts of the compound to wrap around a line. To insert an optional hyphen, press Ctrl+- (hyphen). For a nonbreaking hyphen, press Ctrl+Shift+-.

Tip   Word treats a hyphen typed using the hyphen key only as an ordinary punctuation mark.

You can read your text on-screen and guess where hyphens ought to appear if you want. Word, however, provides two alternative methods of inserting hyphens in a text: automatic and manual. Ordinarily, it is best to apply hyphenation toward the end of the writing process. Changes in the text alter the locations at which you need to apply hyphenation.

To apply hyphenation automatically, perform the following procedure:

1. Open the <u>T</u>ools menu and select the <u>H</u>yphenation option. The Hyphenation dialog box appears, as shown in figure 2.29.

Figure 2.29
The Hyphenation
dialog box.

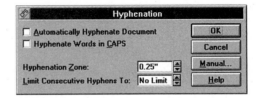

2. Check the <u>A</u>utomatically Hyphenate Document check box.

3. Check the Hyphenate Words in <u>C</u>APS check box if you want to hyphenate words in caps; otherwise, Word will not hyphenate these words.

4. Use the Hyphenation <u>Z</u>one spin box to adjust the width of the zone between the word and the margin where the hyphen break can occur. A wider zone produces a more ragged margin.

5. Use the <u>L</u>imit Consecutive Hyphens To spin box to set the maximum number of consecutive lines that can be hyphenated. (A text in which many consecutive lines are hyphenated can be difficult to read.)

6. Click on OK, and Word hyphenates the text.

To insert hyphens manually, follow this procedure:

1. Open the <u>T</u>ools menu and select the <u>H</u>yphenation option to display the Hyphenation dialog box (refer to figure 2.29).

2. Click on the <u>M</u>anual button to display the Manual Hyphenation dialog box (see fig. 2.30).

Figure 2.30
The Manual
Hyphenation
dialog box.

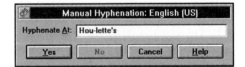

3. Word searches through your document, displaying each word to be hyphenated in the Hyphenate <u>A</u>t text box. For each word, perform one of the following actions:

✔ Click on the <u>Y</u>es button to accept the suggested hyphenation.

✔ If you disagree with the location of the suggested hyphen, click on the word in the Hyphenate <u>A</u>t text box to indicate where the hyphen should go.

✔ Click on the <u>N</u>o button to prevent Word from hyphenating the word shown.

Automatic hyphenation is faster and more convenient, but you should proof your document to make certain you agree with the hyphens inserted. Manual hyphenation is slower, but gives you control over the process at the screen. If hyphenation is the last step in producing your document, you can switch from manual hyphenation to print preview (see the section "Setting Up a Document" in Chapter 5) to verify the final look of the document. You then are ready for printing.

> You can turn off hyphenation for individual paragraphs by opening the F**o**rmat menu, selecting the **P**aragraph option, selecting the Text **F**low tab, and checking the **D**on't Hyphenate check box.

AutoCorrect

AutoCorrect, a new feature in Word for Windows 6.0, is a Wizard that runs in the background as you type, watching for preprogrammed patterns in the stream of characters that you type. When AutoCorrect encounters one of these patterns, it substitutes a corresponding preprogrammed pattern.

AutoCorrect can therefore watch for your most frequent typing errors of common words and automatically correct them for you. As a result, *teh* automatically becomes *the* as soon as you press the space bar after typing the word. You can extend this capability, however, to cover more than spelling errors. Common phrases can be AutoCorrect entries. You can set up the string *slogan* to expand into your company's slogan. You can set up quick key combinations that expand into frequently used addresses, chemical formulas, specialized vocabulary, and so on.

> Keep in mind that AutoCorrect entries can take effect at unwanted times. If you store lots of specialized AutoCorrect entries, you will want their invoking strings to be unique and infrequently used words.

To build an AutoCorrect entry, perform the following steps:

1. Open the **T**ools menu and select the **A**utoCorrect option to display the AutoCorrect dialog box (see fig. 2.31).

2. In the AutoCorrect dialog box, type the text to replace in the R**e**place text box.

3. Type the text to substitute in the **W**ith text box.

4. Click on the **A**dd button.

5. Make sure the Replace **T**ext as You Type check box is checked; otherwise, AutoCorrect is turned off and will not substitute text as you type.

6. Click on OK.

Figure 2.31
The AutoCorrect
dialog box.

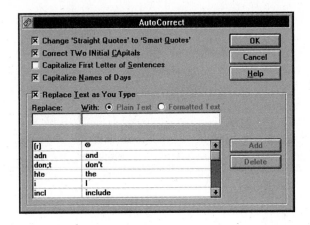

The next time you type the sequence of characters you designated to be replaced, AutoCorrect substitutes the characters you typed in the With text box.

AutoCorrect also can substitute graphics and formatted text for a string of characters. Suppose you need your company logo and slogan to appear in the first heading for each section of your document. You have the logo and slogan already entered in your letterhead template. The logo has been scanned as a clip art graphic, and the slogan is a block of 14 point text sitting to its right. To make the logo and slogan an AutoCorrect entry, perform the following procedure:

1. Select the graphic and the text as a unit.

2. Open the Tools menu and select AutoCorrect.

3. Type a name for the entry in the Replace text box.

4. Select either the Plain Text or Formatted Text option button. Formatted Text preserves the formatting of the text and the graphic image. Plain Text converts both formatted text and graphics to characters in the system font. The With box previews your entry for you.

5. Click on the Add button.

6. Make sure the Replace Text as You Type check box is checked.

7. Click on OK.

The following check boxes in the AutoCorrect dialog box enable you to correct additional text problems:

✔ Replace Text as You Type switches the AutoCorrect Wizard on and off.

✔ Change Straight Quotes to Smart Quotes switches the substitution of curly quotation marks for straight quotation marks on and off.

✔ Correct TWo INitial CApitals switches the correction of this common Shift key error on and off.

✔ Capitalize First Letter of Sentences switches this self-explanatory correction feature on and off.

✔ Capitalize Names of Days switches the capitalization of these names on and off.

Tip   If AutoCorrect corrects something you did not want corrected, just click on the Undo button on the Standard toolbar.

AutoCorrect enables you to change your entries any time you want by simply editing the Replace or With text boxes. You can insert any entry into these boxes by clicking on it in the list box. (If your entry is formatted text or graphics, make the change in your document, select the changed material, and then open the AutoCorrect dialog box.) To complete the change, click on the Add or Replace button, whichever appears.

If you are editing the Replace box, the Add button appears. When you click on it, the entry you changed is not deleted in its original form. Instead, a new entry is added as a new Replace segment paired with the same With segment. If you edit the With text box, the Replace button appears, and the new entry is substituted for the old.

You will need on occasion to delete an AutoCorrect entry. To do so, select the entry in the list box and click on the Delete button.

Document Statistics

Often you need to make a document fit into guidelines of various lengths. Word has a document statistics facility that provides you with various length statistics. To use this facility, open the Tools menu and select the Word Count option. The Word Count dialog box appears, as shown in figure 2.32, and Word updates the counts for you. If you wish to include footnotes and endnotes, check the Include Footnotes and Endnotes check box.

The counts reported are based on the counting rules shown in table 2.2.

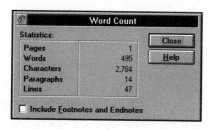

Figure 2.32
The Word Count
dialog box.

Table 2.2
Counting Rules for Document Statistics

Count	Rule
Word	Words in the document, exclusive of footnotes and endnotes unless the check box is checked, and exclusive of headers and footers
Pages	Number of pages as defined by page breaks in document and section breaks where relevant
Characters	Alphabetic characters, numeric characters, and punctuation marks
Paragraphs	Number of paragraphs defined by paragraph marks
Lines	Number of lines, including blank lines following paragraphs even if they are defined by paragraph marks

Every time you use the word count feature, Word repaginates your document and counts the relevant items. In a long document, this can take quite some time. You might want to use this feature sparingly as a result.

Multiple Language Support

Word enables you to work in multiple languages, even within the same document. You will not even know that Word is changing from one language format to another as you are working. You need only to designate which sections of your text are written in which language, and Word handles the rest automatically.

If you have to work with people in Quebec with whom you must use French Canadian words, for instance, you can designate such words as French Canadian using the Language option on the Tools menu. When Word encounters such a word in a spelling check, for example, it automatically switches to the French Canadian dictionary to look up the words designated as French Canadian. If such a dictionary is not installed, Word switches to the nearest equivalent if possible—in this case, a French dictionary.

If you work with multiple languages frequently, make sure you have the appropriate dictionaries installed. If Word does not ship with the dictionary you need, you might be able to purchase one from a third party or find one available as shareware. You install such dictionaries as custom dictionaries. See the section "Spelling Checker" earlier in this chapter for the procedure.

To change the language support for a portion of your document, perform the following procedure:

1. Select the text to be treated as a different language.

2. Open the Tools menu and select the Language option to display the Language dialog box (see fig. 2.33).

Figure 2.33
The Language dialog box.

3. Select the language you want to use from the Mark Selected Text As list box.

4. If your text is primarily in a language other than the one you normally work with, you might want to set this language as the default language for Word. To do so, click on the Default button, then click on the Yes button in the dialog box that appears.

5. Click on OK.

After you have adjusted the language format, use the proofing tools just as you normally would. Word will treat appropriately the blocks of text you marked as being in particular languages.

Tip

If you often work in multiple languages, consider creating a style for each language. Such styles can contain all the appropriate language formatting, and you can set them from the Formatting toolbar quite easily.

AutoText

Word provides the AutoText facility to enable you to create *boilerplate text,* common chunks of text that you use frequently. AutoText is the perfect place to store addresses, standard contract paragraphs, openings and closings for letters, distribution lists you use frequently, fax headers for clients, and other such items. Using AutoText, you can create boilerplate items, save them, and insert them into documents easily.

AutoText items are stored in a document template. Each item has a name that by default is the first few characters in the entry. You can, however, supply a name for each AutoText item when you create it. Because these items appear as entries in the AutoText dialog box, they frequently are called AutoText entries.

To create an AutoText entry, perform the following steps:

1. Enter the text, including graphics if you want, exactly as you want it to appear in any document.

2. Select the text (and graphics, if they are included). If you want the text to retain its formatting, be sure to select the paragraph mark as well. (Click on the Show/ Hide Paragraph button on the Standard toolbar to reveal the paragraph mark, if necessary.)

3. Click on the Edit AutoText button on the Standard toolbar, or open the Edit menu and select the AutoText option. This displays the AutoText dialog box, as shown in figure 2.34.

Figure 2.34
The AutoText
dialog box.

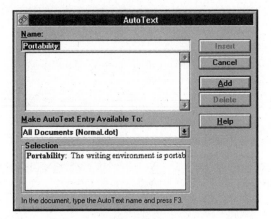

4. In the AutoText dialog box, enter a name in the Name text box if you do not like the default. Names can contain up to 32 characters, spaces included.

5. Open the Make AutoText Entry Available To drop-down list box and select the document template in which you want the entry stored.

6. Click on the Add button.

Tip

Because AutoText entries are stored in document templates, you easily can customize templates with boilerplate text that meets typical goals for documents based on that template. A client letter template, for instance, might contain the addresses of your 10 most frequent clients, three typical opening paragraphs, three typical closing paragraphs, and frequently used enclosure and copy lists.

To insert an AutoText entry, follow these steps:

1. Place the insertion point at the beginning of a line or in an area surrounded by spaces.

2. Open the Edit menu and select the AutoText option. The AutoText dialog box presents the insert options, as shown in figure 2.35.

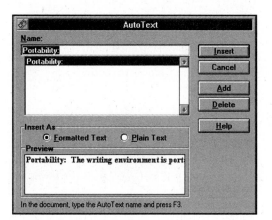

Figure 2.35
The AutoText dialog box showing insert options.

3. Select the name of the entry in the Name combination box.

4. Select either the Formatted Text or Plain Text option button in the Insert As group.

5. Click on the Insert button.

Alternatively, you can type the name of the entry in your document and click on the Insert AutoText button on the Standard toolbar. (The button ToolTip changes name according to the function available at the time.) Pressing F3 or Alt+Ctrl+V invokes AutoText as well. AutoText inserts the entry you have named, or the closest match to the characters you have typed, at the insertion point.

Note   The Insert AutoText button on the Standard toolbar must operate on a selection. Select the paragraph mark where you want to insert AutoText, then click on the button.

If you ever need to change the content of an AutoText entry, insert it into a document, make the changes you want, and then repeat the entry creation process described previously using the same name for the entry as it had before editing. To delete an AutoText entry, open the AutoText dialog box, highlight the name of the item to delete, and click on the Delete button.

The Spike

The Spike is a special AutoText entry that functions as a multiple cut and paste tool. (Microsoft uses the visual image of a desktop spindle holding several slips of paper to represent the Spike in the Word manual.) You can use the Spike to cut several items from a document and insert them elsewhere in the same document or in another document. When you insert the items, they are inserted in the order you cut them.

To cut multiple items using the Spike, follow these steps:

1. Select the text or graphics you want to cut from the document.

2. Press Ctrl+F3. Word cuts the selection and places it on the Spike.

3. Repeat steps 1 and 2 for each item you want to cut.

To paste items from the Spike, locate the insertion point at which the items should appear, but make certain that it is at the beginning of a line or surrounded by spaces. Then, perform one of the following steps:

✔ If you want to paste the material and clear the Spike, press Ctrl+Shift+F3.

✔ If you want to paste the material without clearing the Spike, type **spike** and click on the Insert AutoText button on the Standard toolbar. You can also open the Edit menu, select the AutoText option, select the Spike in the Name combination box, and click on the Insert button.

Find and Replace

Word provides a powerful search and replace routine to help you locate information in your documents. Using this utility, you can locate just about anything and substitute something else for it if you want. To access the find utility, perform the following steps:

1. Open the Edit menu and select the Find option, or press Ctrl+F, to display the Find dialog box (see fig. 2.36).

Figure 2.36
The Find dialog box.

2. Enter the text to find in the Fi**n**d What drop-down list box. The find strings from previous searches are stored in the list box portion of the control to facilitate repeated searches.

3. Select a search direction using the **S**earch drop-down list box. The choices are Up, Down, and All.

Use the check boxes to set the following search specifications:

✔ Checking Match **C**ase requires the matching item to be an exact upper- and lowercase match for the Fi**n**d What string. **Intern** would not match **intern**, for example. Leaving the box unchecked allows a match with a string containing the same letters, but not necessarily the exact cases. **Intern** would match **intern**, **Intern**, and **INTERN**, for example.

✔ Checking the Find **W**hole Words Only box allows matches only with whole words. **Intern** would not match **internment**, for example. Leaving the box unchecked allows the Fi**n**d What string to be matched with parts of words; therefore, **Intern** would match **internment**.

Be careful of using Replace without checking Find **W**hole Words Only. You can replace the string in fragments of words, an action you probably do not intend.

✔ Checking the Use Pattern **M**atching check box enables the use of the advanced wild cards shown in table 2.3 in your Fi**n**d What string.

Table 2.3
Advanced Search Wild Cards

Wild Card	Use	Example
?	Single character	w?t finds **wit** and **wet**
*	String of characters	w*t finds **wit**, **wet**, **wheat**, and so on
[]	One of the characters	w[ie]t finds **wit** and **wet**
[-]	Any character in range	[p-t]at finds pat, rat, sat, and tat
[!]	Any single character except these	p[!a]t finds **pit**, **pet**, **pot**, and **put**, but not **pat**
[!*m-n*]	Any single character	p[!a-e]t finds **pit**, **pot**,

continues

Table 2.3, Continued
Advanced Search Wild Cards

Wild Card	Use	Example
	except in this range	and **put**, but not **pat** and **pet**
{n}	n occurrences of the character or expression to the left	ble{2}d finds **bleed** but not **bled**
{n,}	n or more occurrences of the character or expression to the left	ble{1,}d finds **bleed** and **bled**
{n,m}	From m to n occurrences of the character or expression to the left	20{1,4} finds **20**, **200**, **2000**, and **20000**
@	One or more occurrences of the character or expression to the left	ble@d finds **bled** and **bleed**
<	Character or characters to the right at the beginning of a word	<(intern) finds **internment** and **internally**
>	Character or characters to the right at the end of a word	(intern)> finds **commintern**

✔ Checking the Sounds Like check box enables Word to find words that sound like the one in your Find What string, but are spelled differently. Common variants like **Katherine** and **Catherine** or **sum** and **some** can be found this way.

✔ Click on the Format button to select Font, Paragraph, Language, and Style formats to search for. The items that appear on this button's menu open the same dialog boxes that you can open from Word's Format menu, in which you specify the format you wish to look for. Using these options, you could look for italic text in paragraphs with hanging indents, if you wished. You do not need to enter text in the Find What drop-down list box to search for a format—you can search for the format alone. Click on the No Formatting button to clear formatting information from a search.

✔ Click on the Special button to search for one of the special characters that Word uses, like paragraph characters or section breaks.

✔ Click on the Find Next button to execute the search.

✔ Click on the Replace button to switch to the Replace dialog box in the midst of a find operation.

To replace text with some other text, perform the following steps:

1. Open the <u>E</u>dit menu and select the R<u>e</u>place option, or press Ctrl+H. The Replace dialog box appears, as shown in figure 2.37.

2. Set the controls in the dialog box exactly as you would for a find operation.

3. Enter the text or format to replace with in the Re<u>p</u>lace With drop-down list box.

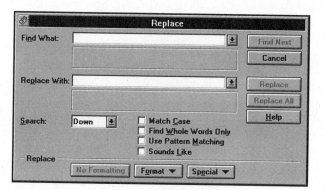

Figure 2.37
The Replace dialog box.

You can use the F<u>o</u>rmat and Sp<u>e</u>cial buttons to enter formats or special characters.

4. Perform one of the following actions:

✔ Click on the <u>F</u>ind Next button to find the next occurrence of the Find What string without replacing the currently found selection.

✔ Click on the <u>R</u>eplace button to replace the currently found selection and find the next selection.

✔ Click on the Replace <u>A</u>ll button to replace all matching strings without having to confirm each replacement.

Tip

You can change the order of the words in the Fi<u>n</u>d What drop-down list box and insert them into the Re<u>p</u>lace With drop-down list box by entering the number of each word in the Re<u>p</u>lace With drop-down list box preceded by a backslash. If the Find What string is **Darrow Clarence**, you can enter **\2\1** in the Re<u>p</u>lace With control to make the Replace With string **Clarence Darrow**.

Bookmarks

Word provides a bookmark facility so that you can easily find specific locations in a document. A *bookmark* is a named location in a document. It functions like a Post-it note inserted as a reminder tab in a book, except that each electronic reminder tab has its own name so that you can find it easily. After you have named a location in your document, however, you not only can move to that location quickly, but you also can insert information at that location.

To create a bookmark, perform the following steps:

1. Select the item you want to mark with a bookmark. This item can be text, graphics, or an insertion point location.

2. Open the Edit menu and select the Bookmark option, or press Ctrl+Shift+F5, to display the Bookmark dialog box (see fig. 2.38).

Figure 2.38
The Bookmark dialog box.

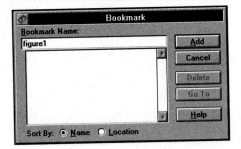

3. Enter a name for the bookmark in the text box portion of the Bookmark Name combination box. The name must begin with a letter and can contain only letters, numbers, and underscore characters. The name must be 40 or fewer characters in length.

4. Click on the Add button.

Tip
You can choose to view or hide your bookmarks. You make this selection using the View tab in the Options dialog box. Open the Tools menu and select the Options item to gain access to these settings.

The most common use for a bookmark is to provide a speedy means of locating a particular spot in a document. To move to a location marked by a bookmark, follow these steps:

1. Open the Edit menu and select the Bookmark option, or press Ctrl+Shift+F5.

2. Select the name of the bookmark in the Bookmark Name combination box.

3. Click on the Go To button.

Tip
You also can move to a bookmark using the Go To dialog box. Double-click on the Status Bar or open the Edit menu and select the Go To option. Select Bookmark in the Go To What list box and select the bookmark name using the Enter Bookmark Name drop-down list box. Then click on the Go To button.

When you edit items marked with bookmarks, you can use the following procedures to get the corresponding actions:

✔ Copy a marked item, or part of it, to another place in the same document. The bookmark stays in place. It is not moved or copied. The copy is not marked by a bookmark.

✔ Cut a marked item and paste it somewhere else in the same document. The bookmark moves with the item cut and marks the item at its new location.

✔ Copy or cut a marked item and paste it to a location in another document. The bookmark both stays in place and moves to the other document. Both documents contain an identical bookmark. If the other document already has a bookmark of the same name, the bookmark does not move and the pasted text is not marked with a bookmark.

Bookmarks enable you to perform calculations on marked numbers. Suppose you mention three sales figures in a memo and want to add them to present a grand total at the end of the memo. If each figure is marked with the bookmarks figure1, figure2, and figure3, you can use this procedure to perform the calculation:

1. Open the Insert menu and select the Field option.

2. In the Field dialog box, select = (Formula) in the Field Names list box. It is the first item in the list when (All) is selected in the Categories list.

3. Enter = **figure1+figure2+figure3** in the Field Codes text box (see fig. 2.39).

4. Click on OK.

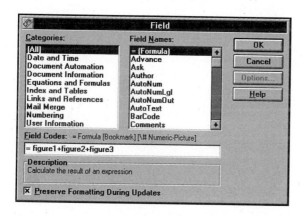

Figure 2.39
Entering a formula based on bookmarks in the Field dialog box.

You will, of course, want to delete a bookmark occasionally. Word offers the following three methods for doing so:

✔ Open the Edit menu, select Bookmark, select the name of the bookmark in the dialog box, and click on the Delete button. The bookmark is deleted, and none of the text or other items marked are affected.

✔ Select the item marked by the bookmark, then press Del or Backspace. Both the item marked and the bookmark are deleted.

✔ Create a bookmark in a new location with the same name. The bookmark is moved to the new location, and the item previously marked is no longer marked by a bookmark. The item previously marked is not otherwise affected.

Note For more information about the advanced uses of bookmarks, see *Inside Word for Windows 6*, also published by New Riders Publishing.

Fields

Word uses fields to enable the entry and updating of information automatically. A *field* is a set of codes that instruct Word to perform an action of this sort. Although you can enter a field by hand, you have to know the appropriate codes for doing so. Word does not require you to learn these codes. The Field dialog box assists you in creating any type of field you want to use, and Word provides many types of fields to choose from.

As an example of how to use fields, consider how often you need to create a letter to a client, typing the date each time you do. You could place a date field in the template for the document that would automatically insert today's date when the document is created. To insert such a field, perform the following procedure:

1. Open the document template and place the insertion point where you want the date to go.

2. Open the Insert menu and select the Field option to display the Field dialog box (refer to figure 2.39).

3. Select the category of field you want to insert from the Categories list box. In this case, select Date and Time. Select the type of date and time field you want in the Field Names list box—in this case, Date.

4. Click on the Options button to display the Field Options dialog box. Select the General Switches tab and select the date format you want, as shown in figure 2.40.

5. Click on the Add to Field button and click on OK. Click on OK in the Field dialog box to insert the field.

6. Close and save the template.

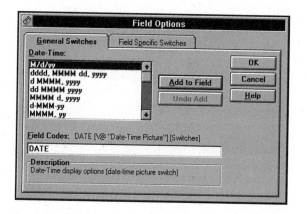

Figure 2.40
The Field Options dialog box, enabling the choice of date formats.

Now each time you create a letter based on the template, the date is automatically inserted in the format you have chosen. When you reopen the document you have created, the date is not updated unless you specifically request it by selecting the field and pressing F9.

If you want to see the codes Word uses in a field, select the field and press Shift+F9; this keystroke switches the display of the actual codes. To switch all fields in this way at the same time, press Alt+F9. You can lock a field, preventing any updates, by pressing Ctrl+F11 or Ctrl+3. You can unlock the field by pressing Ctrl+Shift+F11 or Ctrl+4. If you need to *unlink* a field, that is, convert it to text that displays the last result of the field, select it and press Ctrl+Shift+F9.

If your service bureau uses a desktop publisher that does not recognize Word fields, you can unlink your fields to convert them to plain text that can be imported into the desktop publisher.

For more information about fields, see *Inside Word for Windows 6*, published by New Riders Publishing.

Symbols

Word has a special utility that enables you to insert symbols into a document from any font, as well as from a list of commonly used special symbols like em dashes and trademark symbols. Using this utility, you can give your documents a professional look without having to look up and remember all the special character codes that enable you to enter such symbols using the ASCII character set.

To insert a symbol, perform the following procedure:

1. Open the **I**nsert menu and select the **S**ymbol option to display the Symbol dialog box.

2. In the Symbol dialog box, select either the **S**ymbols or S**p**ecial Characters tab (see figs. 2.41 and 2.42), depending on whether you want to select the symbol from a font or from the list of special characters.

Figure 2.41

The Symbol dialog box showing the Symbols tab.

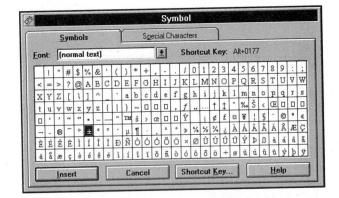

Figure 2.42

The Symbol dialog box showing the Special Characters tab.

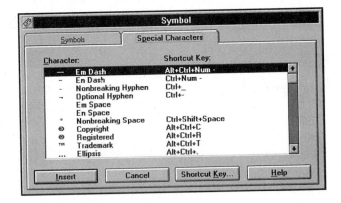

3. Using the **S**ymbols tab, shown in figure 2.41, perform one of the following actions:

   ✔ Select a font using the **F**ont drop-down list box.

   ✔ Select a character from the grid displayed and click on the **I**nsert button. The character is inserted at the insertion point.

   ✔ Select a character from the grid displayed and click on the Shortcut **K**ey button. When the Customize dialog box appears, press the keystroke you want to use to insert the character in the future, click on the **A**ssign button, and click on the Close button. You can insert the character now using the keystroke you just assigned.

4. Using the Special Characters tab, shown in figure 2.42, perform one of the following actions:

✔ Select a character from the list displayed and click on the Insert button. The character is inserted at the insertion point.

✔ Select a character from the list displayed and click on the Shortcut Key button. When the Customize dialog box appears, press the keystroke you want to use to insert the character in the future, click on the Assign button, and click on the Close button. You can insert the character now using the keystroke you just assigned.

Defining Macros

You might think that macros are mysterious things that you will never use. *Macros,* after all, are user-created commands, and you must use some sort of programming language to create them. Word for Windows 6.0, however, has you using them all the time. Macros are a part of the document metaphor, so much so that you could not have a document without macros. Each Word command that you invoke from the menu is, in fact, a macro created by the Word programmers for your use.

To demonstrate this point, follow these directions:

1. Open the Tools menu and select the Macro option to display the Macro dialog box.

2. In the Macro dialog box, use the Macros Available In drop-down list box to select Word Commands (see fig. 2.43).

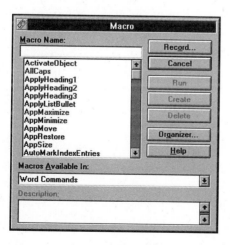

Figure 2.43
The Macro dialog box with Word Commands selected in the Macros Available In list box.

3. Scroll through the <u>M</u>acro Name combination box and select the InsertSymbol macro.

4. Click on the <u>R</u>un button.

The Symbol dialog box should now be on your screen, and you can work with it just as you can if you had invoked it from the menu. The macro and the menu command are equivalent. (The menu, however, makes the Symbol dialog box much easier to find and use.)

All the Word commands are stored in the document template NORMAL.DOT. Any macro is stored as a part of a document template. As a result, you can keep macros that relate to special document types in the templates for those documents. In this way, Word integrates commands and documents entirely. Commands are parts of documents.

You might wonder why Word is structured this way. Building a word processor as a set of macros that you run as you work on your document has the following advantages:

✔ You can choose to use any command in any way at any time, whether it is on the menu, attached to a button, hidden away, or dimmed on the menu. You always can get access to a command through the macro dialog box.

✔ You can decide which commands are attached to the menu and to the toolbars.

✔ You can build your own Word commands that perform custom functions by combining the already familiar commands you use from the menu. You can use your own commands or Word's commands interchangeably.

✔ User-created commands are composed of already existing, already tested Word commands.

✔ With this structure, most users never need to learn the command names in order to create new commands. They can use the macro facility to record the command sequences generated by using the menu and to play these back to Word at will.

In Word, macros are not mysterious—you use them all the time. They are the core of the word processor, a part of every document, and a key concept behind the software. Chapters 6 and 7 show the way to create your own Word macros and how to assign them to the menu or to toolbar buttons. For now, just be aware of how important these macros are to you.

Working with Multiple Documents

The reason that Word couples a document and a window together as a part of the document metaphor is that Word enables you to open multiple documents without having to open a separate copy of the word processor. Each open document runs in its own window and has all the capabilities associated with that window.

You can have open as many documents as can fit in the available computer memory. As a result, you need to know how to manage multiple documents.

Each document window has the familiar maximize and minimize buttons. When a document is maximized, it occupies the entire Word workspace. Its ruler tucks up under the toolbars, its maximize button appears at the right end of the menu bar, and its control menu button appears at the left end of the menu bar. These features define the default appearance of any new document you open when you start Word.

When a document is not maximized, its window has a title bar and looks like any other document window used by any other Windows program, with the addition of the ruler and the view buttons already noted earlier in this chapter. When a document is minimized, it appears as an icon at the bottom of Word's workspace.

You can manage multiple document windows using Word's Window menu, shown in figure 2.44.

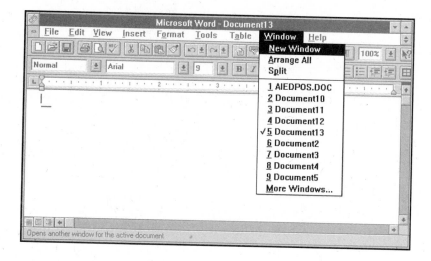

Figure 2.44
Word's Window menu.

The commands on the menu control the following actions:

✔ The New Window command opens a copy of the active document window. When you close the document, all copies of its window close as well.

✔ The Arrange All command arranges all the open document windows so that they are visible on-screen. If you have only a few documents open, their windows appear as horizontal bands in your workspace. If you have more windows open, Word automatically arranges them in a tiled fashion in the workspace. To change the active window, simply click on the window you want to be active.

✔ The Split command activates the split bar. Click in the active window where you want the split to occur.

✔ The list of document names enables you to switch to any document at any time. Simply select the name from the list. If your **M**ore Windows option is available, selecting it opens the Activate dialog box (see fig. 2.45), which gives you access to the list of windows by means of a list box. Scroll through the list, select the document you need, and click on OK.

Figure 2.45
The Activate
dialog box.

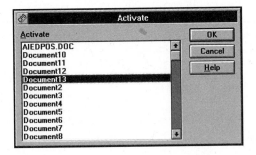

Through the facilities provided by the Window menu, you can keep track of all the documents on your screen. Word makes it easy to have multiple documents open and to avoid getting lost in the maze of multiple documents.

Chapter Snapshot

Now that you know the basic concepts on which Word is built, it is time to teach Word how to support the way you work. In this chapter, you will learn the following advanced features and techniques for customizing Word:

Using these features, you can create professional-looking documents with a minimum of effort.

CHAPTER

Using Advanced Formatting Features

by Forrest Houlette

Having mastered the basics, you can apply your knowledge of Word to create sophisticated documents. Most users accommodate themselves to their software—that is, they learn how to perform tasks the way the software was designed to perform them. Word, however, accommodates itself to your working style. You don't need to build your documents a certain way because Word does it that way; you can teach Word to build documents your way.

You need only two tools to set up Word to work the way you do: document templates and styles. The templates you create provide your documents with the formatting you want, and the styles you create and store in your templates define how you work with your documents. This combination provides you with a tool that facilitates your work by automating it as much as possible.

To illustrate how to use templates and styles to teach Word the way you work, this chapter presents a scenario to help you imagine building your own solutions to working problems. This scenario involves a consulting firm, Write Solutions, Inc., that specializes in helping companies find ways to simplify and automate writing tasks by taking advantage of the features built into their word processing software. The firm has clients in the United States, the United Kingdom, Belgium, and France. Members of the firm have French language skills, and often both correspondence and contracts must contain some passages in French. Of course, Write Solutions practices what it preaches: all its documents are based on Word templates, including its letterhead.

The template and documents described in this chapter are provided on the *Inside Microsoft Office Professional* companion disk.

As an employee of this firm, your job is to set up Word for Windows to handle the letters its representatives must write. You do not write in French, but you need to incorporate passages written in French by others in your correspondence. You also want to match your writing as closely as possible to the conventions used in the United Kingdom when you write to clients in that country.

Creating a Custom Template

The first step in setting up Word to meet your goals is to create a new document template. Follow these steps to perform this task:

1. Open the File menu and select the New option.

2. In the New dialog box, select the Template option button in the New group (see fig 3.1).

Figure 3.1
Creating the new template using the New dialog box.

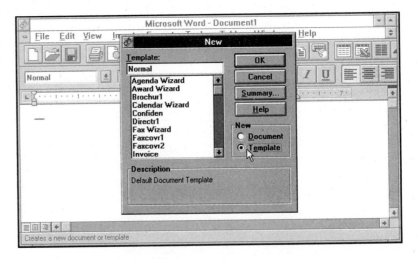

3. In the Template combination box, select the existing template—in this case, the normal template—on which you want to base this new template.

4. Click on OK to create the file.

After you create the new template, click on the Save button in the standard toolbar to save it under its own name. When the Save As dialog box appears, give the template the name **WRITESOL** and click on OK. After you name and save the template, add to it the information you need each document to have whenever you create correspondence.

Because documents based on this template will bear the Write Solutions letterhead, use the document header to contain the letterhead information. Open the <u>V</u>iew menu and select the <u>H</u>eader and Footer option. Add the following information, as shown in figure 3.2, to serve as the letterhead:

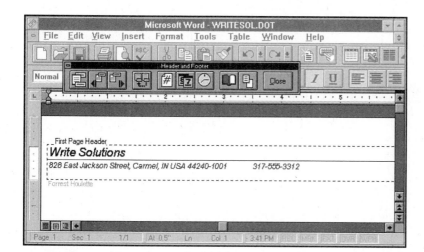

Figure 3.2
The letterhead information for Write Solutions entered on the template.

The Write Solutions letterhead information is in the Arial font that ships with Windows. The upper line is in 14-point Arial, and the lower line is in 9-point Arial. The phone number is placed at the first default tab after the address text. The rule between the two lines of text is the upper border for the second paragraph of the letterhead information. To create the rule, place the insertion point on the second line, open the F<u>o</u>rmat menu, and select the <u>B</u>orders and Shading option. In the <u>B</u>orders tab of the Paragraph Borders and Shading dialog box, click on the upper border line in the Bo<u>r</u>der box and click on OK.

In addition to entering this information, you should perform some other adjustments while working on the header. These adjustments make your document more useful to the people who receive it.

Follow these steps:

1. Click on the Page Setup button in the Header and Footer toolbar and select the <u>L</u>ayout tab in the Page Setup dialog box. In the Headers and Footers group, check the Different <u>F</u>irst Page check box to prevent the letterhead information from appearing on each page of a multipage letter. Then click on the OK button. Click on the <u>C</u>lose button in the Header and Footer toolbar.

2. Enter a page break to create a second page. Open the <u>V</u>iew menu and select <u>H</u>eader and Footer again. Click on the Switch Between Header and Footer button on the Header and Footer toolbar to move to the footer for the second page.

3. Click on the Align Right button in the standard toolbar.

4. Click on the Page Number button in the Header and Footer toolbar. Press Enter.

5. Click on the Date button in the Header and Footer toolbar. Press Enter.

6. Type **Write Solutions**. Select the material you have just entered and use the Font drop-down list box in the formatting toolbar to set the font to Arial.

7. Click on the <u>C</u>lose button on the Header and Footer toolbar, and delete the page break that you entered into your template file. (You no longer need it there.)

The people to whom you send correspondence now know the name of your firm from the letterhead you have created. They also can tell from the second and following pages which company the correspondence is from and on what date it was sent. This information helps if the pages of a long letter ever become separated. The final step in preparing this template is to add your name on the first line of the first page. Your clients can then tell who to contact in response to the correspondence.

After performing all these steps, save the template to protect your work against loss. At this point, you are ready to consider what styles you might want to add to the document template you have just created.

Creating Custom Styles

To simplify working with documents based on your new template, create a selection of styles that automate the formatting of the document. The easiest way to create a style is by example. Format a paragraph of text the way you want it, then perform the following steps:

1. Open the Style drop-down list box on the formatting toolbar.

2. Clear the current style name by pressing Del.

3. Type a new name for the style.

4. Press Enter.

Return to the WRITESOL.DOT template. Format your name the way you would like it to appear beneath the letterhead on the document. To keep the font consistent, select your name and set the font to Arial using the Font drop-down list on the formatting toolbar. Set the size to 8 points using the Font Size drop-down list. Next, open the F<u>o</u>rmat menu and select the <u>P</u>aragraph option. In the Paragraph dialog box, select the <u>I</u>ndents and Spacing tab. Use the

After spin box to set the space after your name to 12 points. Then open the Style drop-down list, clear the current style, type **Name**, and press Enter. You've just created a style for the name block on your letter.

Press Enter and type a date. Select the date text and change the font size to 9 points. Name this style **Date**. You will use it to format the date block on all documents.

Next type a sample inside address and apply formats from the appropriate dialog boxes until it looks the way you want it to. For example, set the font to Arial and the size to 9 points. Set the space after the paragraph to 0 points. Name this style **Address**. You now have a style for the inside address of letters you might write.

Figure 3.5 later in this section shows an example of each of these formats, if you need a visual target for creating these styles.

Create a similar style for the greeting. Set the space before the paragraph and after the paragraph to 12 points so that the greeting automatically spaces itself between the inside address and the body of the letter. Name this style **Greeting**.

Creating Language Styles

The body of your planned document places considerable demand on Word. You might be working with text in U.S. English, U.K. English, or French. As a result, you need to create three body paragraph styles, one for each language. In this way, you signal to Word's document tools to apply the appropriate language information as they operate on the document. As a result, during a spelling check the French dictionary applies to the French paragraphs, the U.K. English dictionary to the U.K. English paragraphs, and the U.S. English dictionary to the U.S. English paragraphs automatically. Word also automatically applies the appropriate exception dictionaries that you might have created.

To create styles for the body of your document, type some sample text. Keep the 9-point Arial font and set the paragraph spacing to 0 points before and 12 points after. Select the text, open the Tools menu, and select the Language option. Select English (US) from the Mark Selected Text As list box and click on the OK button. Then open the Style drop-down list box and create a style named **BodyUS**. Repeat the process of selecting the language, this time choosing English (UK). Create a style called **BodyUK**. Repeat the process one last time, selecting French and creating a style called **BodyFR**. You now can create paragraphs in all three languages, and Word will automatically handle them appropriately.

Create a style in U.S. English that has no lines before or after the paragraph. It should remain in the 9-point Arial font. Name this style **Close**. You will use it to format the closing of letters.

I

Word for Windows

Creating Character Styles

The styles you have created so far are *paragraph styles*, so named because they involve paragraph formats. When you apply these styles to text, the paragraph containing the text is modified to fit the style. You also can create *character styles*—styles that apply only a font format to text. To create character styles, you must use the Style command on the Format menu.

You also can create paragraph styles using the **S**tyle command. The process is the same as for creating character styles, except that you set Style **T**ype to Paragraph. The one advantage of creating paragraph styles in this way is that you can set the style of the text following the paragraph using the **S**tyle for Following Paragraph drop-down list box. The F**o**rmat button in the New Style dialog box provides access to all the Format dialog boxes applicable to paragraphs.

To create a character style, perform the following steps:

1. Open the F**o**rmat menu and select the **S**tyle option to bring up the Style dialog box (see fig. 3.3).

Figure 3.3
The Style
dialog box.

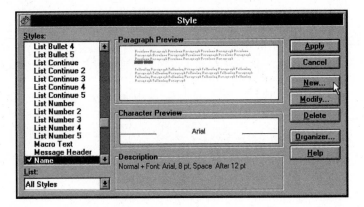

2. In the Style dialog box, click on the **N**ew button to bring up the New Style dialog box (see fig. 3.4).

3. In the New Style dialog box, open the Style **T**ype drop-down list box and select Character.

4. Enter a name for the style in the **N**ame text box.

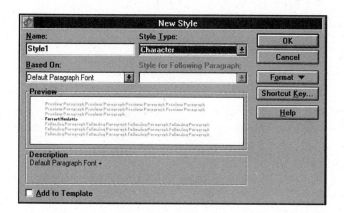

Figure 3.4
The New Style
dialog box.

5. Select the style to base the new style on from the **B**ased On drop-down list box. Word must always use information about an existing style as the basis for creating the new one.

6. Click on the F**o**rmat button and select either **F**ont or **L**anguage from the list that appears. Use the Font and/or Language dialog boxes to set the characteristics for your style.

7. Check on the **A**dd to Template check box if you want to store the style to the current document template; otherwise, it is stored in the document only.

8. Click on OK. Word creates your new style.

9. Click on the Close button in the Style dialog box.

For the WRITESOL.DOT template, you might need a number of character styles: bold italics for foreign words and phrases embedded in your document, for example, and superscript and subscript styles for use in describing some elements of the programs your firm writes. Create these styles according to the procedure outlined. Name them **ForeignPhrase**, **Subscript**, and **Superscript**.

 Style names can contain up to 253 characters, but cannot contain backslashes, braces, or semicolons.

Putting the Styles Together

To get a sense of the usefulness of your custom styles, create a brief document based on WRITESOL.DOT. Follow these steps:

1. Create a new document based on the WRITESOL template.

2. Press the End key to move to the end of the name block, press Enter, select the Date style, and type the date.

3. Press Enter, select the Address style, and type the address.

4. Press Enter, select the Greeting style, and type the greeting.

5. Press Enter, select the Body style appropriate to the country of your client, and type a body paragraph. Repeat this process until the body of the letter is complete.

6. Press Enter, select the Close style, and type the closing.

A portion of the completed letter is shown in figure 3.5 with the styles applied to each paragraph showing in the style area. As you can see, the appropriate formatting is automatically applied to each section of the letter. You do not need to make repeated adjustments using the menu to change the format for each section of the letter. Each section is also set up for the appropriate spelling check procedures.

Figure 3.5
A sample letter based on WRITESOL.DOT, showing the use of custom styles.

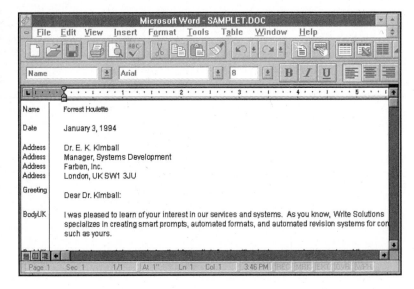

Tip You can open the style area on your screen by adjusting the **S**tyle Area Width in the View tab of the Options dialog box.

Figure 3.6 shows the same letter in page layout view, showing the advantage of using the document template to contain the boilerplate text of the letterhead. Entering the text and the styles in the template once saves you a considerable amount of work as you create subsequent documents.

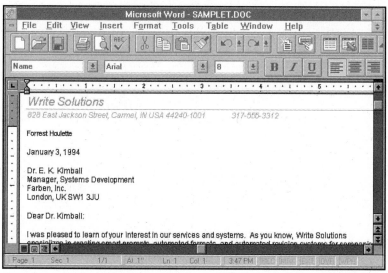

Figure 3.6
The sample letter based on WRITESOL.DOT in page layout view.

Modifying and Deleting Styles

Occasionally you might need to modify a style that you use for creating documents with the WRITESOL.DOT template. You might decide that because you write most of your documents in U.S. English, for example, you would like to limit your use of U.K. English and French to single paragraphs only. You might like to automatically reset the following paragraph to the U.S. English style. Making this change requires you to modify the style.

To modify a style, perform the following steps:

1. Open the <u>F</u>ormat menu and select the <u>S</u>tyle option to bring up the Style dialog box (refer to figure 3.3).

2. Open the <u>L</u>ist drop-down list box and select the view that causes the style you want to modify to appear in the <u>S</u>tyles list box.

3. Select the style in the <u>S</u>tyles list box and click on the <u>M</u>odify button. The Modify Style dialog box appears (see fig. 3.7).

4. To change the name, enter a new name in the <u>N</u>ame text box.

5. Open the <u>B</u>ased On and <u>S</u>tyle for Following Paragraph drop-down list boxes to change these aspects of the style. (If you are working on a character style, the <u>S</u>tyle for Following Paragraph control will not be active.)

6. Click on the F<u>o</u>rmat button and select the appropriate formatting dialog boxes. Make the changes you want to the style.

7. When you are finished, click on the OK button, then click on the Close button in the Style dialog box.

Figure 3.7
The Modify Style
dialog box.

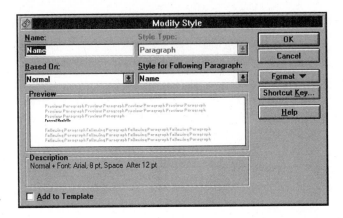

To change the BodyUK and BodyFR styles, select each in the Style dialog box, click on the Modify button, and set the Style for Following Paragraph for each to BodyUS. When you press Enter after you write a paragraph in either of these formats, the style for the new paragraph reverts to BodyUS.

When styles logically follow one another in a document, you might want to modify them so that each style selects the style for the next paragraph as the next style in the sequence. Address, for example, could format the next paragraph as Greeting. After you complete the inside address for the letter, press Enter to type the greeting using the appropriate style.

Occasionally you will need to delete a style from a document template. To delete a style, open the Style dialog box and select the style in the Styles list box. If you can delete the style, the Delete button becomes active. Click on the Delete button to delete the style.

Merging Existing Styles

As noted in Chapter 2, "Understanding Word for Windows Concepts," Word provides a large number of built-in styles you can use in documents. You might want to use some of these styles in your own custom templates, or you might want to move some of your custom styles from a custom template into NORMAL.DOT to make them available globally. Word provides a facility for doing this type of copying and moving—the style organizer dialog box.

To access the style organizer dialog box, follow these steps:

1. Open the Format menu and select the Style option.

2. In the Style dialog box, click on the Organizer button to display the Organizer dialog box. Then select the Styles tab (see fig. 3.8).

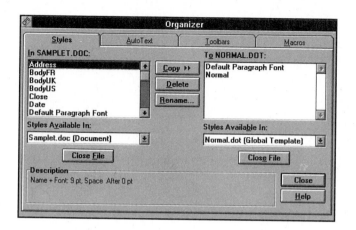

Figure 3.8
The Organizer dialog box displaying the Styles tab.

3. In the left half of the Style Organizer, set up one of the documents or templates that you want to work with. By default, Word places your current document in the left portion of the Organizer and NORMAL.DOT in the right portion. If this arrangement suits you, proceed to step 8. If not, follow steps 4–7.

4. Click on the Close File button on the left.

5. Click on the Open File button that replaces the Close File button.

6. In the Open dialog box that appears, select the file you want to work with and click on OK.

7. Repeat steps 4–6 with the Close File button under the list box and drop-down list box in the right portion of the Style organizer.

8. Select a style in either list box, then choose from the following options

   ✔ Click on the Copy button to copy the style to the other document or template. (The arrow on the Copy button reverses direction depending on which list box contains the selected style.)

   ✔ Click on the Delete button to delete a style. Confirm the deletion by clicking on the Yes button in the confirmation dialog box. The list boxes in the Style Organizer allow multiple selections. You can select contiguous style names using Shift+left mouse button. You can select discontiguous style names using Ctrl+left mouse button.

   ✔ Click on the Rename button to rename a style. Type the new name in the Rename dialog box and click on the OK button.

9. When you have finished with the Style Organizer, click on the Close button.

Using the Style Organizer, you can copy styles among documents and templates, rename styles within documents and templates, and delete styles from documents and templates. After you have defined a set of styles, those styles need not stay isolated in your template or on your machine. You can easily make them available to colleagues, just as colleagues can share styles with you. You can mix and match styles to your advantage.

Changing Case

Word also provides the capability to alter the capitalization of your text on the fly. This capability goes beyond changing the case of selected letters from upper to lower. Word provides several options.

The easiest way to become familiar with Word's case-changing capabilities is to type a sentence, select it, and then press Shift+F3. When you first press this key combination, the sentence changes to all uppercase letters. On the next press, the sentence changes to all lowercase. On the third press, the sentence changes to normal sentence capitalization: an uppercase first letter for the first word and the remainder in lowercase. For any group of selected characters, press Shift+F3 repeatedly to cycle the text through these three options. Just press this key combination until you have the results you want.

Tip

Shift+F3 works on blocks of text longer than a single sentence. This key combination can be useful if you are not a skilled typist. Keep in mind, however, that Word will not preserve the capitalization of proper names in the sentences for which you adjust capitalization using this technique.

In addition to the Shift+F3 key combination, Word provides the Change Case command on the Format menu. This command offers you even more flexibility. When you choose this command, if no text is selected, Word automatically selects the nearest word for you. If text is selected, Word operates on the selection you have made.

When you select the Change Case menu option, the Change Case dialog box appears, as shown in figure 3.9. Choose from the following options:

  ✔ Select Sentence Case to place an initial capital letter on the selection and make the rest of the characters lowercase.

  ✔ Select lowercase to make the selection all lowercase characters.

  ✔ Select UPPERCASE to make the selection all uppercase characters.

  ✔ Select Title Case to make the selection have initial uppercase characters each word.

  ✔ Select tOGGLE cASE to reverse the capitalization of the characters in the selection.

After you have made your selection in the dialog box, click on OK. Word applies the formatting you have chosen to the selection on the screen.

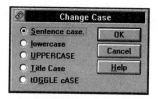

Figure 3.9
The Change Case
dialog box.

Using Drop Caps

Word also provides you with a simple way to create *drop caps,* large capital letters that mark the beginning of the first word in a section. Drop caps can make your documents visually exciting. They also serve a practical purpose—you can use them like bullets on a list. Drop caps help the person reading the document to find the relevant sections. While you might not use them in formatting a letter that you prepare using WRITESOL.DOT, you might use them in preparing a report using that template. Figure 3.10 shows an example of a drop cap in use in a report prepared with the Write Solutions template.

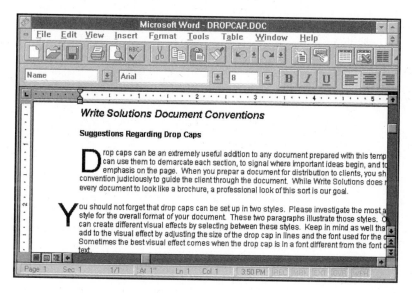

Figure 3.10
A drop cap in a
report prepared with
WRITESOL.DOT.

To create a drop cap, follow this procedure:

1. Place the insertion point in the paragraph that will receive the drop cap.

2. Open the F**o**rmat menu and select the **D**rop Cap option. The Drop Cap dialog · box appears, as shown in figure 3.11.

3. In the Drop Cap dialog box, select the position of the drop cap, either **D**ropped or In **M**argin.

Figure 3.11
The Drop Cap
dialog box.

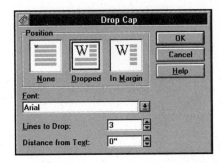

4. Using the Font drop-down list box, select the font for the drop cap. The default is the font of the text in the paragraph.

5. Using the Lines to Drop spin box, adjust the size of the drop cap in lines.

6. Using the Distance from Text spin box, adjust the distance of the drop cap letter from the rest of the text on the right.

7. Click on OK. If you are not in page layout view, Word will ask if you want to switch to that view before you insert the drop cap. You need to be in page layout view to adjust the position and size of the drop cap by dragging with the mouse.

You often will want to use a different font from the rest of your text for the drop cap. To create visual unity, however, it helps to use no more than two fonts. If you use Universal for titles and subheads and Palatino for body text, for example, use Universal for the drop cap at the head of a section to tie the elements together visually.

If, after creating your drop cap, you do not like it, you have the following options:

✔ Open the Edit menu and select Undo Drop Cap. You can select this option from the Undo button on the standard toolbar if the option no longer shows on the menu.

✔ Select the drop cap and press Del. You will need to retype the character you deleted from your text.

✔ Select the drop cap, open the Format menu, and select the Drop Cap option. You can adjust the controls in the Drop Cap dialog box to change the font, distance, and position of the drop cap until you are satisfied with it.

✔ Select the drop cap, select Drop Cap from the Format menu, and then select None in the Position group.

Creating Document Sections

Word enables you to control the formatting you apply to any part of a document completely. In Word, a *section* is a part of a document that can be formatted separately from other sections. You define a section by inserting a section break into a document. Whatever comes before the section break can be formatted differently from whatever comes after the section break. You can create as many sections as you want in a document, and sections can be as short or long as you want them to be.

When you create a new Word document, it has a single section by default. To break a document into more than one section, you must perform the following steps:

1. Position the insertion point where you want to insert the section break.

2. Open the Insert menu and select the Break option.

3. In the Break dialog box, shown in figure 3.12, use the option buttons in the Section group to select one of the following kinds of section breaks:

   ✔ Next Page: The new section begins on a new page.

   ✔ Continuous: The new section begins on the same page, unless the two sections have different settings for page size or page orientation, in which case the section starts on a new page.

   ✔ Even Page: The new section begins on the next even-numbered page.

   ✔ Odd Page: The new section begins on the next odd-numbered page.

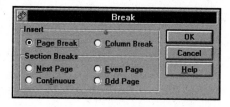

Figure 3.12
The Break
dialog box.

Word inserts a visible break line labeled End of Section into your document, which you can see in Normal view. If you ever need to delete a section break, select it and press the Backspace or Del key. If you delete a section, the formatting of the section above the break in the document becomes the same as the following section.

Defining sections enables you to mix all sorts of formatting styles in the same document. Suppose you are creating a report on recent research and development efforts undertaken by Write Solutions. You want to have an abstract that occupies the full page width, the research report in two-column format, and the bibliography in full-page format. You can accomplish this formatting using sections.

To set this document up, enter the text, applying the styles you have created. To format this document, create a TitleWS style that formats a centered title, a HeadingWS style that formats a left-aligned bold title, and a BiblioWS style that formats each bibliography entry. After you format your text, break it into three sections so that you can separately format the column section.

You can see these additional formats in figure 3.13, and the template including them is on the *Inside Microsoft Office Professional* companion disk.

To create the sections, position the insertion point at the title of the research report, open the Insert menu, select the Break command, select a Continuous section break, and click on OK. Repeat these steps with the insertion point at the title for the bibliography. Figure 3.13 shows this report with the section break inserted after the abstract.

Figure 3.13
A report for Write Solutions that uses sections.

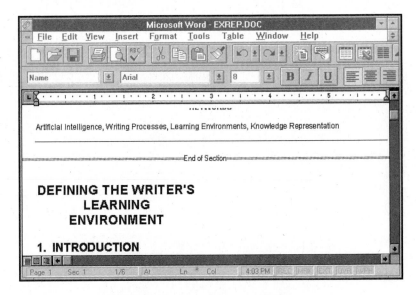

To give each section a different header and footer, make sure that the Same As Previous button is not active on the Header and Footer toolbar. If the button is active, your new section has the same headers and footers as the previous section. To break this link, click on the button.

Using Columns

To create columns in a section of a document, you have two courses of action: you can use the Columns button on the standard toolbar, or you can use the Columns command on the Format menu. Each action achieves the same result. But as usual in Word, the menu command gives you more control over the column creation process.

To use the Columns button, place the insertion point in the section that is to have columns. Point to the Columns button, depress the left mouse button, and drag over the grid until the correct number of columns is highlighted (see fig. 3.14). Release the mouse button, and Word formats your section with the number of columns you indicated.

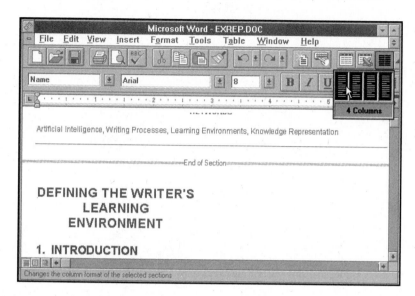

Figure 3.14
Creating columns using the Columns button on the standard toolbar.

To use the menu command to create columns, perform the following steps:

1. Open the Format menu and select the Columns command.

2. In the Columns dialog box, shown in figure 3.15, you can set the following options:

   ✔ To set up columns quickly in one of five preset formats, click on one of the controls in the Presets group to select One, Two, Three, Left (two columns, the narrower on the left), or Right (two columns, the narrower on the right).

   ✔ To set a custom number of columns, enter the number using the Number of Columns spin box.

   ✔ To place a vertical line between the columns, check the Line Between check box.

   ✔ To set up custom column widths and spaces between columns, use the Width and Spacing spin boxes in the Width and Spacing group. Select which column you are working on using the Col. # control. To set equal column widths easily and quickly, check the Equal Column Width check box.

   ✔ To start a new column at the insertion point, check the Start New Column check box, located beneath the Preview box.

✔ Use the Apply To drop-down list box to control whether the column formatting applies to the entire document or simply from the insertion point forward. Word inserts a section break to protect the previous formatting if you elect to apply the column format from the insertion point forward.

3. When you have the column format set up properly, click on the OK button.

Figure 3.15
The Columns
dialog box.

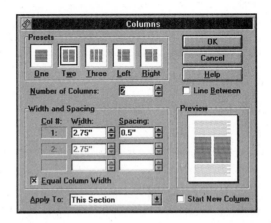

To create the columns in the second section of your Write Solutions report, place the insertion point in the second section. Use the Columns button on the standard toolbar to select two columns. Word adjusts the format of the section as shown in figure 3.16.

Figure 3.16
The Write Solutions
report with two-
column format in the
second section.

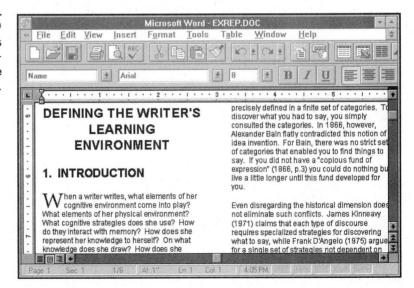

To fine-tune your columns, you need to master a few tricks:

✔ If you have unbalanced columns on the final page of your document, insert a continuous section break at the end of your document. Word automatically balances the columns for you when a continuous section break follows them.

✔ If headings or other text is orphaned at the bottom of a column, insert a column break ahead of the problem text to force it into the next column. Open the Insert menu, select the Break command, select Column Break in the dialog box, and click on the OK button.

✔ If you need two paragraphs or some text and a graphic to stay within the same column, select the items that need to stay together, open the Format menu, select the Paragraph command, select the Text Flow tab, check the Keep With Next check box, and click on the OK button.

✔ If you have a document with a different header on the first page and you want to start your section on a new page, the first page header will appear on the first page of the new section. If you want to maintain the same header and footer for the remaining pages throughout your document, do not want the first page header to appear in the new section, and need the new section to start on a new page, insert a continuous section break followed by a page break. The bibliography section of the example Write Solutions report begins this way.

Using Bullets and Numbering

Word automates the process of using bulleted and numbered lists for you. Word offers two buttons on the right side of the formatting toolbar: the Numbering and Bullets buttons. These buttons switch numbered and bulleted lists on and off. When you are numbering or bulleting, these buttons appear pressed. When you are not using these features, these buttons appear normally. Click on the button to turn this feature on and off.

To enter a bulleted or numbered list, follow these steps:

1. Set up the paragraph's left indent the way you want it to be. If you want your list indented further than the rest of your text, you need to set that up in advance.

2. Click on the Bullets or Numbering button. The first bullet or number will automatically appear.

3. Type the items in your list. Each time you press Enter, a new bullet or the next number appears. Figure 3.17 shows this process in action.

4. When you finish your list, click on the button to exit bullet or numbering mode.

If you've already entered a list of items and decide later that it should be bulleted or numbered, select the list and click on the appropriate button. Word converts your list by adding the appropriate bulleting or numbering.

Figure 3.17

Entering a numbered list.

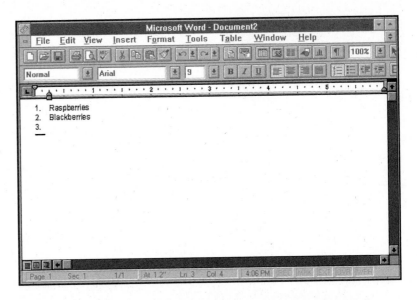

Word supplies styles for formatting lists, bulleted lists, and numbered lists, which you can apply using the **S**tyle command on the F**o**rmat menu. There are five forms of each list style. Each form is increasingly indented. The number ending the style name indicates the level of indentation. List5, for instance, is the furthest indented of the standard list styles.

The buttons on the standard toolbar offer default bullets and numbering. Your list items are formatted with hanging indentation. The numbers are Arabic numbers followed by periods. The bullets are a standard round dot in a default size based on the font size associated with the paragraph marker.

If you want to modify these defaults or to use a different style of bullets and numbering, you need to apply the format using the Bullets and **N**umbering command from the F**o**rmat menu. Using this command, you can create lists that are bulleted, numbered, or multilevel with the levels indicated by alternating numbers and bullets. To use this command, perform the following procedure:

1. Place the insertion point where you want to begin your list, or select the text that will be formatted as a list.

2. Open the F**o**rmat menu and select the Bullets and **N**umbering option. The Bullets and Numbering dialog box, shown in figure 3.18, appears.

3. The three tabs in the dialog box, **B**ulleted, **N**umbered, and M**u**ltilevel, offer different default styles. Select the style you want by clicking on its preview box; then click on the OK button.

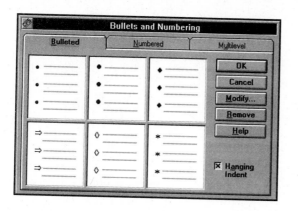

Figure 3.18
The Bullets and
Numbering
dialog box.

Word applies the bullet, numbering, or multilevel style that you select. If you apply the style to a selection, the list is formatted. If you enter the list after applying the style, Word applies the style as you type.

When you are working with a list, point the mouse to the list and click the right button. Word displays the shortcut menu for lists. You can use this menu to stop numbering, skip numbering an item, or access the Bullets and Numbering dialog box.

You can create custom bullet and numbering styles using the Bullets and Numbering dialog box. On any of the tabs, click on the Modify button. A Modify dialog box for the tab appears, offering controls that enable you to adjust the settings for the type of list you want to have. The Modify dialog box for the Bulleted tab is shown in figure 3.19.

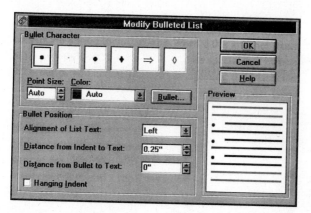

Figure 3.19
The Modify Bulleted
List dialog box.

To modify the bulleted list options, you can choose from the following options:

✔ Select the bullet character from the Bullet Character control by clicking on the preview that suits your needs. If you want a different bullet character, click on the

Bullet button and select one from the Symbol dialog box that appears. Click on OK after you make your selection.

✔ Set the point size and color of the bullet character using the Point Size spin box and the Color drop-down list.

✔ Use the drop-down list box in the Bullet Position group to set the Alignment of List Text.

✔ Use the spin boxes in the Bullet Position group to set the Distance from Indent to Text and Distance from Bullet to Text.

✔ Check the Hanging Indent text box if you want your list to have hanging indentations.

Click on the OK button to apply your custom format.

 Stop   When you create a new style, you replace one of the existing styles displayed by the tab.

The remaining two Modify dialog boxes have basically identical controls in the Position group; however, they offer different controls in the top portion of the dialog box specific to the format being modified. The Modify Numbered List dialog box is shown in figure 3.20.

Figure 3.20
The Modify
Numbered List
dialog box.

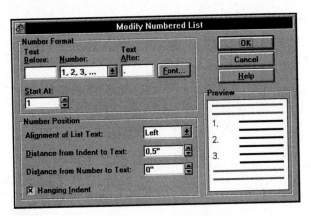

To adjust the numbered list format, you can choose from the following options:

✔ Enter any text that should appear before the number in the Text Before text box.

✔ Use the Number drop-down list box to select a number format.

✔ Enter any text that should follow the number in the Text After text box.

✔ Click on the Font button to select the font and character styles from the Font tab in the Font dialog box. Click on OK after you have made your selection.

✔ Set the starting number in the <u>S</u>tart At spin box.

✔ Use the drop-down list box in the Number Position group to set the Alignment of List Text.

✔ Use the spin boxes in the Number Position group to set the <u>D</u>istance from Indent to Text and Dis<u>t</u>ance from Number to Text.

✔ Check the Hanging <u>I</u>ndent text box if you want your list to have hanging indents.

Click on the OK button to apply your custom format.

The Modify Multilevel list box is very similar to the Modify Numbered List dialog box, except that it adds a control for specifying the level of the list you are modifying (see fig. 3.21).

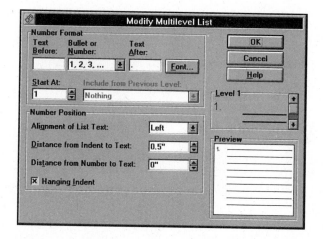

Figure 3.21
The Modify
Multilevel List
dialog box.

Choose from the following options to modify a multilevel list:

✔ Select the list level to modify using the <u>L</u>evel list box. Your list can have up to nine levels.

✔ Enter any text that should appear before the number in the Text <u>B</u>efore text box.

✔ Use the Bullet or <u>N</u>umber drop-down list box to select a number format.

✔ Enter any text that should follow the number in the Text <u>A</u>fter text box.

✔ Click on the <u>F</u>ont button to select the font and character styles from the Fo<u>n</u>t tab in the Font dialog box. Click on OK after you have made your selection.

✔ Set the starting number in the <u>S</u>tart At spin box.

✔ Select what to include from the previous level using the Include from <u>P</u>revious Level drop-down list box. The Preview box shows the results of your selection.

✔ Use the drop-down list box in the Number Position group to set the Alignment of List Text.

✔ Use the spin boxes in the Number Position group to set the Distance from Indent to Text and Distance from Number to Text.

✔ Check the Hanging Indent text box if you want your list to have hanging indentations.

Click on the OK button to apply your custom format.

Using Word, you can create lists of any type you want—bulleted, numbered, multilevel, or plain. You can convert list types easily. After you have formatted a list as one style, select it and open the Bullets and Numbering dialog box. The tab representing the format of the list is automatically selected, and the Remove button is active. To remove the list format, click on the Remove button. You then can apply a new list format (or not) as you like.

Tip You can sort a list using Word. Select the list, open the Table menu, and select the Sort Text option. Word sorts numbered lists alphabetically and automatically renumbers numbered lists after sorting.

Bibliographies often appear in different formats for different audiences. Some publishers prefer the items numbered, for example, whereas some do not. Write Solutions is a company that has to work for both kinds of clients. Converting the bibliography from numbered to unnumbered format is a simple proposition once the basic list is typed into a document. Select the list, apply the appropriate list format, and the job is done. Figure 3.22 shows the converted bibliography in the Write Solutions report you have been preparing in this chapter.

Figure 3.22
A portion of the finished bibliography for the Write Solutions report.

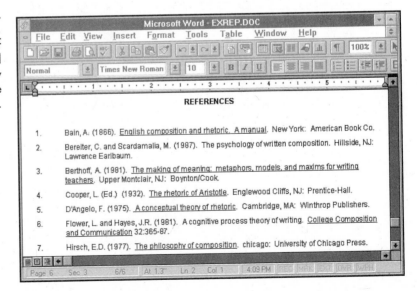

Using Numbered Headings

Word provides you the same flexibility with numbered headings as it does with numbered and bulleted lists. As long as you use the built-in heading styles, you can choose among several formats for these styles using the Heading Numbering dialog box. You apply the built-in heading formats using the Style command on the Format menu, and you adjust the formatting of these styles using the Heading Numbering command on the Format menu.

Tip

If you are creating a custom document template, you might want to copy the heading styles from NORMAL.DOT to your custom template using the Style Organizer. See the section "Merging Existing Styles" in this chapter for more information.

To adjust the formatting of heading styles, perform the following steps:

1. Open the Format menu and select the Heading Numbering command to bring up the Heading Numbering dialog box (see fig. 3.23).

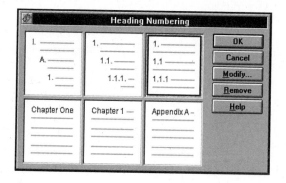

Figure 3.23
The Heading Numbering dialog box.

2. In the Heading Numbering dialog box, select the style you want by clicking on its preview box.

3. Click on OK to apply the format.

You could, for example, number the headings in your Write Solutions report by applying the built-in Heading 1 style to all headings except the elements of the learning environment. These should be formatted in Heading 2. Open the Heading Numbering dialog box and choose either the Roman or Arabic numbering style. Click on OK, and the headings are numbered.

In the example document, only the second section is reformatted using this technique. The remaining sections retain the custom styles created as a part of this chapter. If you want, you can redefine the built-in styles to meet your needs. You probably want to copy them to your custom template beforehand to preserve the default formats in NORMAL.DOT. If NORMAL.DOT becomes hopelessly changed in unwanted ways from the default, you can always reinstall it.

If you outline your document before you apply heading numbering, Word automatically applies the default heading styles as you create the outline. You easily can apply heading numbers to documents created using this procedure. If you use numbered headings often, you might want to develop the habit of using Word's outline capabilities as you develop the structure of your document.

Using AutoFormat

Word can automatically format a document for you after you have typed it. Word applies the built-in styles associated with the template on which the document is based, according to rules Word contains which allow the analysis of a document's parts. Word can recognize titles, headings, lists, and so on. When it recognizes such a structure in your document, Word applies the appropriate style to it.

Word comes with several document templates that it can use with the AutoFormat feature, each representing different types of documents. To take advantage of these templates, you can either base your document on the template when you create it (see Chapter 1) or copy the styles associated with the template using the Style Gallery (see Chapter 2). To see a list of the document types available to you, open the Format menu and select the Style Gallery option. The Style Gallery dialog box offers previews of Word's companion document templates.

You can automatically format a document in two ways. To automatically format without reviewing Word's changes, click on the AutoFormat button on the standard toolbar (see fig. 3.24). Word formats the document and presents the finished version to you. If you do not like the changes, you can use the Undo feature to reverse them.

You can use AutoFormat to review the changes Word makes, accepting some and rejecting others. Open the Format menu and select the AutoFormat option. Word then displays the AutoFormat dialog box, as shown in figure 3.25. Use the controls in the AutoFormat dialog box to control the formatting process.

At this point, you can click on OK to proceed with the AutoFormat process or Cancel to cancel it, or you can choose Options to set options for the process. If you click on Options, Word displays the AutoFormat tab in the Options dialog box, shown in figure 3.26.

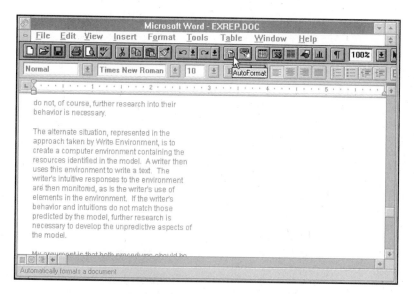

Figure 3.24
The AutoFormat
button on the
standard toolbar.

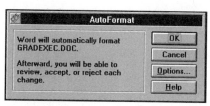

Figure 3.25
The AutoFormat
dialog box.

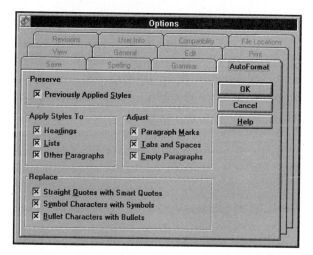

Figure 3.26
The AutoFormat tab
in the Options
dialog box.

The AutoFormat tab controls what Word does as a part of the AutoFormat process. Word can perform the following types of actions:

✔ Word can preserve existing formats. Check the Previously Applied <u>S</u>tyles check box in the Preserve group to enable this.

✔ Word can apply styles to various document structures. Check any or all of the Hea<u>d</u>ings, <u>L</u>ists, and Other <u>P</u>aragraphs check boxes in the Apply Styles To group to enable these actions.

✔ Word can delete extra symbols and characters in a document to improve the formatting. In the Adjust group, check the Paragraph <u>M</u>arks check box to delete extra paragraph marks (such as hard returns inserted instead of using word wrap), check <u>T</u>abs and Spaces to delete empty or extra tabs and spaces, and check <u>E</u>mpty Paragraphs to delete empty paragraphs.

✔ Word can replace certain characters with other characters. In the Replace group, check Straight <u>Q</u>uotes with Smart Quotes to replace regular quotation marks with the curly kind; check S<u>y</u>mbol Characters with Other Characters to replace, for example, (C) with a true copyright symbol; and check <u>B</u>ullet Characters with Bullets to replace characters often used to represent bullets with true Word bullets.

Tip If you work with a typist who formats text the way you would on a typewriter, AutoFormat can convert such formatting to standard Word styles.

If you click on OK in the AutoFormat dialog box, the AutoFormat dialog box changes to show different options (see fig. 3.27). Use the buttons in this dialog box to control which changes you accept for the document.

Figure 3.27
The AutoFormat dialog box after clicking on OK to start the AutoFormat process.

Review the new format Word has given the document. You can choose from among the following options:

✔ Click on the <u>A</u>ccept button to accept all changes. (You can always undo the changes using Word's Undo feature.)

✔ Click on the <u>R</u>eject All button to reject all changes.

✔ Click on the <u>S</u>tyle Gallery button to open the Style Gallery dialog box. Here you can review the types of document formats available by selecting each in the list box, preview them in the Preview box, and choose the one you like by clicking on OK after having selected it in the list box. Word then repeats the AutoFormat process.

✔ Click on the Review <u>C</u>hanges button to review each change, accepting or rejecting each change on an individual basis.

If you click on the Review <u>C</u>hanges button, the Review AutoFormat Changes dialog box appears (see fig. 3.28). Use the controls in this dialog box to determine which changes to accept and which to reject.

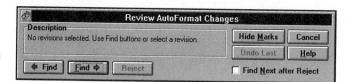

Figure 3.28
The Review AutoFormat Changes dialog box.

You can perform the following actions:

✔ Click on the <u>F</u>ind button or the <u>F</u>ind button to scroll to the previous change or the next change, respectively.

✔ Click on the <u>R</u>eject button to reject a change.

✔ Click on the Hide <u>M</u>arks/Show <u>M</u>arks button to turn the display of paragraph marks off and on.

✔ Click on the <u>U</u>ndo Last button to undo previous actions. Each click undoes one action.

✔ Check Find <u>N</u>ext after Reject to automatically move to the next change after you click on the <u>R</u>eject button.

✔ Click on the Close or Cancel button (whichever appears) to accept all remaining changes.

 Tip   You can also scroll through your document using the scroll bars while reviewing AutoFormat changes.

While you are reviewing changes, Word represents its AutoFormat changes to you visually using the cues shown in table 3.1.

Table 3.1
Visual Cues to AutoFormat Changes

Cue	Change Made
Blue Paragraph Mark	New style applied to paragraph
Red Paragraph Mark	Deleted this existing paragraph mark
Strikethrough Character Style	Deleted these characters or spaces
Underline Character Style	Added these characters
Bar in Left Margin	Changed the formatting of this text

AutoFormat thus helps you to identify its changes quickly and efficiently. You can easily recognize which parts or elements of the document have changed.

AutoFormat is a useful new feature in Word for Windows 6.0. It enables you to type as you might be comfortable typing and to convert what you do to a correctly formatted document using styles. It also enables the quick conversion of a document from one style to another. If AutoFormat makes a mistake, you can easily correct it. AutoFormat can be a very useful first step, if nothing else, in the final formatting of a complex document.

Chapter Snapshot

When you use a suite of applications, you find occasions to want to use the data stored by one application in the other suite applications. Word makes it easy for you to include data from other applications in documents, and to include documents in other applications. In this chapter, you will learn ways to perform the following tasks:

After you know how to share data, you easily will find opportunities to take advantage of your new skills in your work with Word.

Sharing Data with Word

by Forrest Houlette

P art of the power of Word for Windows 6 is its capability to accept data from other applications as if the data had been generated by Word itself. A block of such data is called an *object*. Word can both contain and display objects without the other applications being installed on your machine.

Word can also maintain links to files created by other applications. A *link* is simply a channel of communication with a file of data. Using links, portions of the data in another application's file can be brought into a Word document as an object. These links can be *automatic,* so that every time the other application changes the data the changes are reflected in your Word document. They also can be *manual,* so that after data is brought in it is not updated unless you request the update. They also can be *locked,* so that no updates are possible unless the link is first unlocked.

Using objects and links, you can use Word documents to present pictures, sounds, spreadsheet data, presentation graphics, and other types of data. You can plan to display these documents on-screen, or you can plan to print the documents for display. Some types of data, such as sound, might be useful only in on-screen presentation, whereas others might make sense only in paper presentations. The capability for including objects in your documents removes the limits from your word processor. You now can create documents that include any kind of data that your Microsoft Office applications can create.

Understanding OLE and DDE

For our purposes, OLE is not something you shout at a bull fight and DDE is not a mistaken stutter. These are the technical specifications that enable Windows programs to accept data as objects and maintain links with other applications. DDE, or dynamic data exchange, is the earliest of these specifications. OLE, or object linking and embedding, is the later specification. OLE, especially in version 2.0, is absorbing DDE into itself. In the future, you will hear mostly about OLE, especially OLE 2.0. DDE will drop out of your active vocabulary.

Microsoft implemented DDE in version 2 of Windows and OLE as a part of version 3 of Windows. The OLE capabilities of Windows have been updated several times since the release of Windows 3.1, and the updates have been included as files with your new application software.

Both OLE and DDE give applications names that indicate the application's role in the exchange of data. Sometimes you hear the names *client* and *server* applications. At other times you hear the name *container* and *source* applications.

At present, discussions of these two technical specifications confuse the two names, but they are really very easy to keep straight. Equivalent names begin with the same letter. *Client* applications are *container* applications; they receive the data from another application and hold it within their data file. *Server* applications are *source* applications; they possess data that they share with other applications. *Container* and *source* are the later, more explanatory, terms. As a result, they will be used in this chapter.

Applications can be container applications, source applications, or both. They can play each role at the same time in relationship to any of the applications running on your computer or your network. Sometimes understanding which application is playing which role can be confusing. To you it is mostly unimportant, except that you need to understand container and source applications well enough to manage a data exchange. Which is container and which is source is dependent on your point of view at the moment you initiate a data exchange. If your application is accepting data, it is the container. If it is providing data, it is the source.

It is easiest to understand these technologies if you look at the metaphors that drive them. The metaphor behind DDE is that of a conversation. Imagine that each application on your computer that supports DDE has a phone.

If a container application needs some data, it goes to its phone booth, checks the directory of which applications are available, and dials each one, asking if it can borrow a cup of data. Each source application can do one of two things in response to the phone call. It can ignore the ring because it is too busy to be bothered. In this case, the container and source never have a conversation.

If the source application answers the phone, the container asks if it can borrow the cup of data. If the source application does not have the data, it tells the client application that it has no data, and both applications hang up the phone.

If the source application has the data, it sends the data down the phone line. The container application receives the data and thanks the source application after the data has arrived. When the source application hears the thank you message, it sends an acknowledgment to the container application and both applications hang up the phone. However, if the link is an automatic link, the phone line stays open between the applications permanently, and the applications call each other back if the line is broken. If the link is locked, the container application has padlocked its phone booth, and you must unlock the phone to call the source application back.

OLE also depends on the conversation metaphor, only not as completely. In an OLE exchange, especially in Word 6.0, the container application calls the source application to ask if the source can share data with the container or custom design some data for the container. If the source is available, it answers the phone, but the conversation is very different. The source application does not send just the data down the phone line. Instead, it sends part of itself down the phone line to become a temporary part of the container application.

The source application sends either its menu or a toolbar to the container application. The container application displays the menu or toolbar along with any data that is sent. The user manipulates the data using the menu or toolbar. When the user is finished, the container accepts the data, removes the menu or toolbar from the screen, and hangs up the phone. If the container application ever needs the source application to manipulate the data again, the container calls the source and the conversation is repeated.

Under the earliest version of OLE, the container is the only application that possesses the data. Under OLE 2.0, containers and sources can maintain DDE-style links with one another.

You need to remember that not all application programs are DDE- or OLE-enabled. Some of them simply have no phone. In such cases, you cannot link to or embed from the application.

Linking to Data in Other Applications

Translating these example telephone conversation metaphors into your work with Word 6.0 is straightforward. In the example of a link, you establish the link using the Windows Clipboard as your telephone booth. Both the container application and the source application use the Clipboard as a shared phone booth, and both applications place and answer calls using the Copy and Paste commands on the Edit menu.

This section shows you the way to create links between Word and other applications. The first example demonstrates using Word as a source application, and the second example shows using Word as a container application.

Creating Links with Word as the Source Application

To create a link between a Word document (as source) and another application (as container), perform the following procedure:

1. Save and name your Word document.

2. Select the material to be linked.

3. Place your call by opening Word's Edit menu and selecting the Copy option to place the selected material on the clipboard (see fig. 4.1).

Figure 4.1
Creating a link by copying material from a Word document to the clipboard.

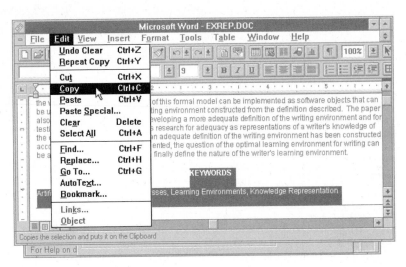

4. Switch to the intended container application—in this case Excel.

5. Receive the call by opening the Edit menu and selecting Paste Special.

6. In the Paste Special dialog box, examine the options available in the As list box, shown in figure 4.2. The options in the As list box describe the format the data can take in the container application. The Result box contains an explanation of the currently selected data format.

7. Select a data format in the As list box and select the Paste Link option button.

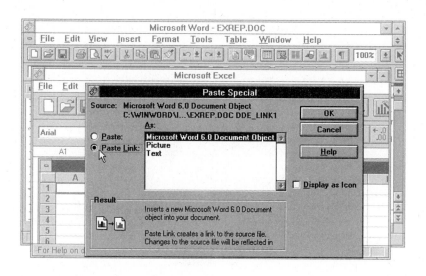

I

Word for Windows

Figure 4.2
The Paste Special
dialog box in
the container
application, Excel.

8. If you want the data to be hidden by an icon, check the Display as Icon check box. When the data is hidden by an icon, you must double-click on the icon to see the data. When you double-click, Word starts, if it is not already running, and displays the data.

> Only some data formats can use all the options offered in the Paste Special dialog box. When you select a data format, the options it can use are active and the options it cannot use are not active. If you cannot link a certain data format, you might be able to paste it as an embedded object. The container application determines which data formats it can accept and whether it can link to the source application or only accept objects from the source application.

9. Click on the OK button to complete the conversation and create the link. Figure 4.3 shows two links from Word to Excel involving the same data. In the first case, the data is not hidden by an icon. In the second case, the data is hidden by an icon.

Links always are maintained by the container application. To see how Word maintains links, open Excel's Edit menu and select the Links option. The Links dialog box, shown in figure 4.4, appears.

Link maintenance really involves only the following three actions:

✔ You can specify a link as automatic (the default) or manual by selecting the Automatic or Manual option buttons. If you make a link manual, you can update it only by opening this dialog box, selecting the link in the Source File list box, and clicking on the Update Now button.

✔ You can open the source application (if it is not running) and load the linked data file by clicking on the Open button.

✔ You can change the name of the source file associated with the link if the file has been renamed. Click on the Change Source button and edit the file name in the Change Links dialog box (see fig. 4.5). The file name appears between the vertical bar (|) and the double exclamation points (!!).

Figure 4.3
An Excel file showing two links.

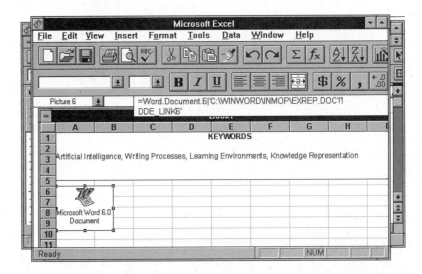

Figure 4.4
Excel's Links dialog box.

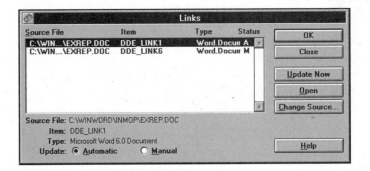

You should always name a file before creating links from it and you should never change the name of a file that has links. The file name is a critical part of the link. If a file name changes after a link is created, the container application can no longer find the source application data for the link and the link is broken. You must repair it by supplying the correct file name.

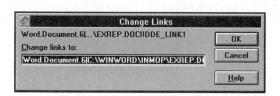

Figure 4.5
The Change Links
dialog box in
Excel.

Creating Links with Word as the Container Application

To create a link between another application (as source) and Word (as container), reverse the process you used to link Word as source to another application and perform the following procedure:

1. Save and name your file in the other application—in this case, Excel.

2. Select the material to be linked.

3. Place your call by opening Excel's Edit menu and selecting the Copy option to place the selected material on the Clipboard (see fig. 4.6).

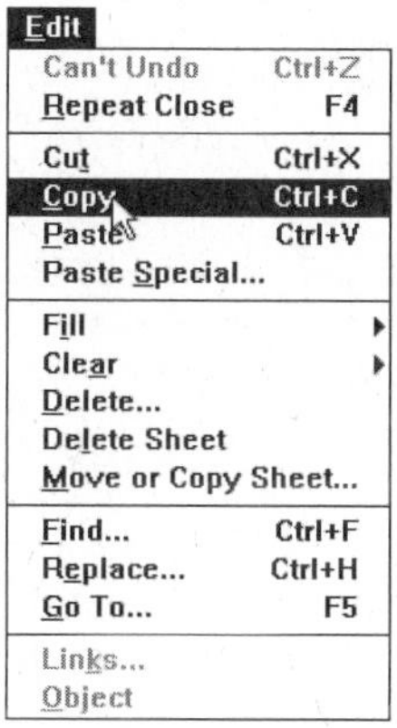

```
Edit
Can't Undo        Ctrl+Z
Repeat Close      F4
Cut               Ctrl+X
Copy              Ctrl+C
Paste             Ctrl+V
Paste Special...

Fill              ▶
Clear             ▶
Delete...
Delete Sheet
Move or Copy Sheet...

Find...           Ctrl+F
Replace...        Ctrl+H
Go To...          F5

Links...
Object
```

Figure 4.6
Initiating a link
with Word from
Excel.

4. Switch to the intended container application—in this case, Word.

5. Receive the call by opening the Edit menu and selecting Paste Special.

6. In the Paste Special dialog box, examine the options available in the As list box, shown in figure 4.7. The options in the As list box describe the format the data can take in the container application. The Result box contains an explanation of the currently selected data format.

Figure 4.7
Word's Paste Special dialog box.

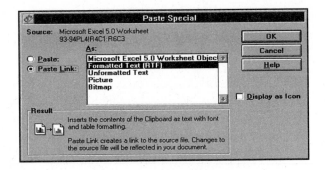

7. Select a data format in the <u>A</u>s list box and select the Paste <u>L</u>ink option button.

8. If you want the data to be hidden by an icon, check the <u>D</u>isplay as Icon check box. When the data is hidden by an icon, you must double-click on the icon to see the data. When you double-click, Excel starts, if it is not already running, and displays the data.

9. Click on OK to complete the conversation and create the link. Figure 4.8 shows two links from Excel to Word involving the same data. In the first case, the data is not hidden by an icon. In the second case, the data is hidden by an icon.

Figure 4.8
A Word document showing two links.

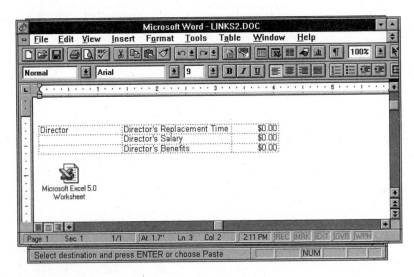

To see how Word maintains links, open Word's <u>E</u>dit menu and select the Lin<u>k</u>s option. The Links dialog box, shown in figure 4.9, appears.

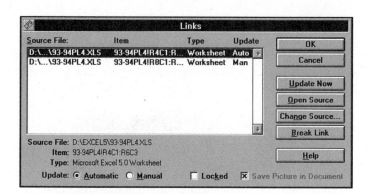

Figure 4.9
Word's Links
dialog box.

Link maintenance in Word involves the following four actions after you have selected a link in the list box:

✔ You can specify a link as automatic (the default), manual, or locked by selecting the Automatic, Manual, or Locked option buttons. If you make a link manual, you can update it only by opening this dialog box, selecting the link in the Source File list box, and clicking on the Update Now button.

> **Tip**
>
> If you are linking your Word document to several graphics files, you can choose where the actual graphic image is stored. If you do not mind having a large file size for your Word document, store the graphic in the document itself by checking the Save Picture in Document check box (the default). If you need to reduce the file size for the Word document, clear this check box so that Word saves only the link to the graphics file in the document.

✔ You can open the source application (if it is not running) and load the linked data file by clicking on the Open Source button.

✔ You can change the name of the source file associated with the link if the file has been renamed. Click on the Change Source button and change the link information using the familiar controls in the Change Source dialog box (see fig. 4.10). This dialog box works in the same way as the Open dialog box, except it provides an Item text box for editing the name of the data item involved in the link.

✔ You can break a link, leaving the data as it is intact in your document, by clicking on the Break Link button.

> **Note**
>
> A link name consists of four items. The first is the source file name. The second is the *link item*, which specifies the location of the data. This might be a specification like a spreadsheet range and column, or it might simply be a name like DDE_LINK10. The third is the type of link; an indication of the nature of the data linked to. The most common type is a document link. The final item

is the *update item*, which indicates whether the link is automatic, manual, or locked. These items are concatenated for use by Windows using the vertical bar and exclamation point concatenators you saw in the Excel Change Links dialog box. In most cases, the only part of the link name that should concern you is the source file name.

Figure 4.10
Word's Change
Source dialog
box.

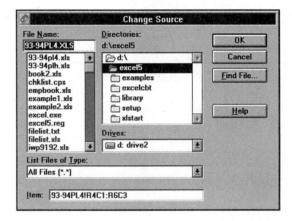

You should use links to data objects whenever the data object meets the following criteria:

✔ The data is likely to change on a frequent basis.

✔ You plan to use copies of the data in several different documents or files.

✔ You want to have the latest copy of the data available in each place the data appears.

Links are especially useful, for example, for spreadsheet data that needs to appear as charts in documents that you have to produce on a weekly or monthly basis, such as sales summaries. They also are useful for database queries that you need to use in mailmerge documents, in which you know that the data is updated on a continuing basis and you want the latest addresses for your labels and form letters. Links like these, coupled with boilerplate text inserted from a template, can save you hours of time. When you open the document to create the report, standard text is inserted and the latest data appears. The data is updated automatically as long as you use automatic links. You need only to do a quick edit of the document to make it say what it needs to say this time.

Inserting Objects from Other Applications

In the example of embedding an object, you embed the object using the Windows Clipboard as your telephone booth, just as you do with a link. As with links, both the container application and the source application use the Clipboard as a shared phone booth. Both applications place and answer calls using the **C**opy and **P**aste commands on the **E**dit menu, just as with links.

This section shows you the ways to embed objects in Word documents and Word objects in other applications. The first example demonstrates the use of Word as a container application. The second example shows the use of Word as a source application.

Embedding with Word as the Container

To embed an object in a Word document (as container) and another application (as source), perform the following procedure:

1. Select the material to be embedded in the source application—Excel in this example.

2. Place your call by opening Excel's **E**dit menu and selecting the **C**opy option to place the selected material on the Clipboard (refer to figure 4.6).

3. Switch to Word and position the insertion point where you want the object to appear.

4. Receive the call by opening the **E**dit menu and selecting Paste **S**pecial.

5. In the Paste Special dialog box, examine the options available in the **A**s list box, shown in figure 4.11. The options in the **A**s list box describe the format the data can take in the container application. The Result box contains an explanation of the currently selected data format.

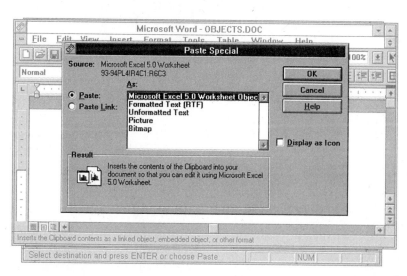

Figure 4.11
The Paste Special dialog box in the container application Word.

6. Select a data format in the <u>A</u>s list box and select the <u>P</u>aste option button.

7. If you want the data to be hidden by an icon, check the <u>D</u>isplay as Icon check box. When the data is hidden by an icon, you must double-click on the icon to see the data. When you double-click, Excel starts, if it is not already running, and displays the data.

8. Click on OK to complete the conversation and embed the object. Figure 4.12 shows an object embedded in a Word document. When you want to edit the data in the object, you must double-click on the object. Excel starts, if it was not already running, and enables the capability of editing the object.

Figure 4.12
An Excel object embedded in a Word document.

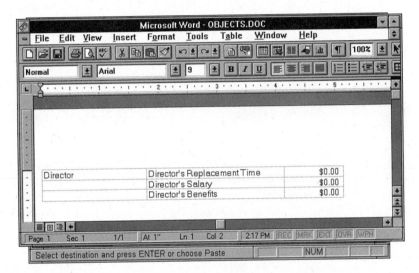

The difference between a link and an object is that objects are always contained in the container application and not in a file maintained by the source application. While you can have several copies of the same object in several different documents, they are independent of one another. They can be changed at different times independently of one another. The changes are made in one copy of the object and are not reflected in other copies of the object.

Tip If you want changes in one copy to be reflected in all copies of the object, link them.

Maintenance for embedded objects is different from maintenance for links. If you need to change an object, simply double-click on it to open its source application and make the changes. In most cases, when you double-click, the source application replaces Word's menu with its own and provides a toolbar for your use. (This is the case with Excel.)

You also can access an object for maintenance from the Edit menu. As figure 4.13 shows, the last item on this menu is the object option. It changes name according to the type of object selected. This option opens a cascading menu that offers different options depending on the type of object.

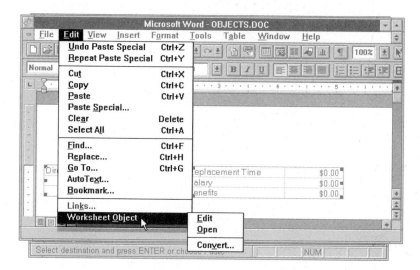

Figure 4.13
Word's Edit object option.

In the case of an Excel worksheet object, you have the following options:

✔ Edit causes Excel's menu toolbar to replace Word's so that you can edit the worksheet object while it is in place in the document. This form of editing is called *in-place editing*.

✔ Open causes the Excel window to open and load the object. This is the form of object editing that you might be used to from version 2.0 of Word for Windows. When you close the Excel window, the worksheet object is updated in the Word document.

✔ Convert opens the Convert dialog box, shown in figure 4.14, which enables you to convert the object from one form to another or to make active the object for editing in one of its possible forms. Select the form of the object you prefer in the list box, select the conversion or activation action that you want, and click on OK to carry out the action.

Figure 4.14
Word's object
conversion
dialog box.

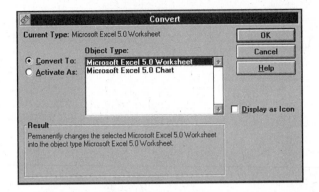

Tip

Embedded objects can take several possible forms, as determined by the source application. Just because you embedded the object in one form does not mean that it must remain embedded in that form. The object conversion option enables you to change the form of the object. Be aware, however, that some non-Microsoft applications might include one-way conversions as an option.

Embedding Data Using Word as the Source

To embed Word data (using Word as the source) in another application (as container), reverse the process for embedding an object in Word and perform the following procedure:

1. Select the material to be embedded from your Word document.

2. Place your call by opening Word's Edit menu and selecting the Copy option to place the selected material on the Clipboard (see figure 4.15).

Figure 4.15
Preparing to
embed Word data
in another
application using
the Copy option.

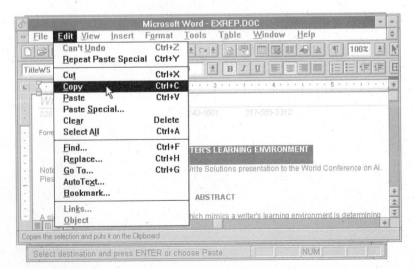

3. Switch to the intended container application—in this case Excel.

4. Receive the call by opening Excel's **E**dit menu and selecting Paste **S**pecial.

5. In the Paste Special dialog box, examine the options available in the **A**s list box, shown in figure 4.16. The options in the **A**s list box describe the format the data can take in the container application. The Result box contains an explanation of the currently selected data format.

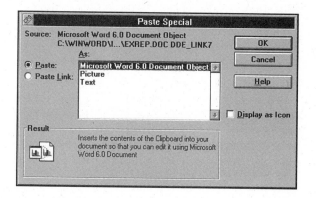

Figure 4.16
Excel's Paste Special dialog box.

6. Select a data format in the **A**s list box and select the **P**aste option button.

7. If you want the data to be hidden by an icon, check the **D**isplay as Icon check box. When the data are hidden by an icon, you must double-click on the icon to see the data. When you double-click, Word starts, if it is not already running, and displays the data.

8. Click on OK to complete the conversation and create the link. Figure 4.17 shows a Word object embedded in an Excel worksheet.

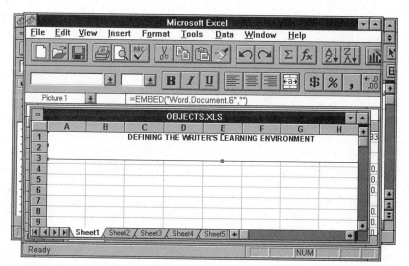

Figure 4.17
Word text embedded in an Excel worksheet.

Objects in Excel are maintained in exactly the same way as they are in Word. Double-click on the object to edit it in place, or use the Object option on the Edit menu to Edit, Open, or Convert the object.

In general, you should embed data objects whenever they meet the following criteria:

✔ The data is not likely to change on a frequent basis.

✔ You do not plan to use copies of the data in several different documents or files.

✔ You are not concerned whether this copy of the data remains the latest copy of the data.

Embedded objects are useful any time that data from external applications needs to appear in a document. You might need to include a spreadsheet table, for example, in a Word document. Rather than build the spreadsheet in Excel and have to maintain the file with Excel, you can keep the spreadsheet in the document that uses it. As a result, the spreadsheet is never divorced from the document. You can never accidentally delete the file from your Excel directory and need to re-create the worksheet from the data in your Word document. Embedded objects keep related data in the same container, making your work with that data much more efficient. Very often, Word documents make the best containers for your data.

Using Word's Drawing Capabilities

A good example of the usefulness of embedded objects in Word documents is the insertion of pictures that you can create using Word's Drawing application. You can access this application by clicking on the Drawing button on the Standard toolbar. When you click on this button, the button stays depressed and Word displays the Drawing toolbar (see fig. 4.18). You then can use the tools on the Drawing toolbar to embed graphics in your Word document. Clicking on the Drawing button again removes the toolbar and returns you to editing your document.

Drawing in Word

To draw in your Word document, you must be in page layout view. When you click on the drawing button, you enter page layout view. You can switch to any view you want while working on your drawing, but use of any of the drawing tools on the toolbar will return you to page layout view.

You can draw in one of two ways in your document. First, you can use any drawing tool to draw directly on your document. You can create the line shown in figure 4.19, for instance, by selecting the Line button and dragging in your document. In this way, you can add graphics to emphasize text, draw arrows that demonstrate the relationship between text elements, or add callouts to tables to make special points. No matter which way you choose to draw, the graphics are embedded as objects in your Word document.

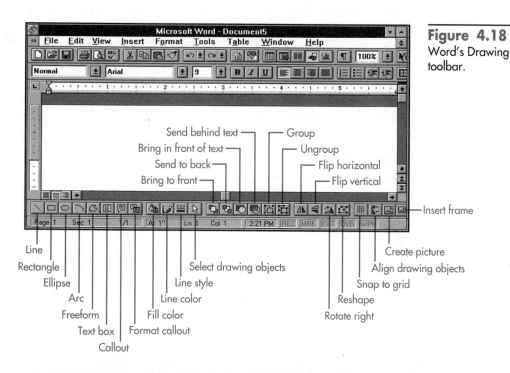

I

Word for Windows

Figure 4.18
Word's Drawing toolbar.

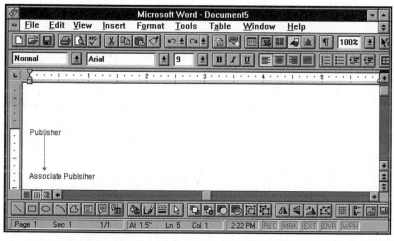

Figure 4.19
A line drawn directly in a Word document.

You also can create a picture by clicking on the Create Picture button. When you click on the button, the draw picture screen appears, as does the Picture toolbar (see fig. 4.20).

The drawing screen shows you the current picture boundary. You can draw on this screen using the drawing tools. After selecting a drawing tool, drag to draw the shape you have selected. Adjust its dimensions using the sizing handles that are visible when you select the shape by clicking on it. You are not limited to the picture boundary shown on the screen—you can draw beyond it.

Figure 4.20
Word displaying
the draw picture
screen and
toolbar.

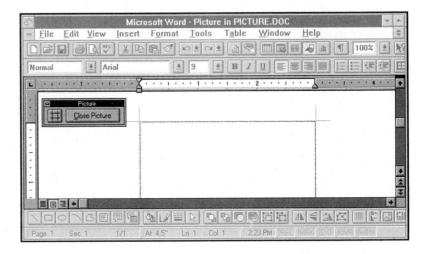

When you are finished with your drawing, click on the Reset Picture Boundary button on the Picture toolbar. Word then makes the picture boundary fit what you have drawn. To exit the drawing screen and see the picture in place in the document, click on the Close Picture button. Word inserts the picture at the current location of the insertion point.

Tip You can remove the Picture toolbar from the screen before you have closed your picture by clicking on its control menu box. Without the toolbar on the screen, however, you cannot close the picture. To get the toolbar back, open the **V**iew menu and select the **T**oolbars option. In the Toolbars dialog box, check the box next to the Picture item in the list box and click on the OK button.

Fine-Tuning Your Word Drawing

After you have inserted a picture, it appears wherever the insertion point was when you clicked on the Create Picture button. Text does not flow around it, and it might create large white spaces in your document that you do not want.

To control the way the picture fits into your document more effectively, you should place it in a frame. To do so, select the picture and click on the Insert Frame button. Word places a frame around your picture. Text will now flow around your drawing, you can place your drawing more effectively by dragging it on the screen, and you can resize your drawing by selecting the frame and dragging the sizing handles.

Word's drawing application provides you with additional drawing tools that you might need. You can select the fill color by clicking on the Fill Color button and selecting a color from the palette that appears (see fig. 4.21). You can select the line color in similar fashion using the Line Color button. The Line Style button enables you to select the type of line you want to draw from a palette as well.

Figure 4.21
The fill color palette.

You can insert text boxes with the Text Box button and callouts with the Callout button. As with the shape tools, drag on the screen to create the item. You can format your callouts by selecting each in turn and clicking on the Format Callout button. This action brings up the Callout Defaults dialog box (see fig. 4.22), which enables you to choose from several default patterns and to adjust the characteristics of your callouts using the controls provided.

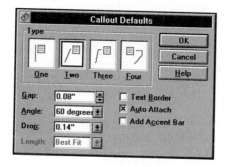

Figure 4.22
The Callout Defaults dialog box.

You also can place any object in front of or behind others by selecting the object and clicking on the Bring to Front or Send to Back buttons. You can place a text box over or behind a shape by performing the same procedure with the Bring in Front of Text and Send Behind Text buttons. You can create groups of objects by clicking on the Select Drawing Objects button (arrow button), selecting the objects to be in the group by dragging, and clicking on the Group button. You then can manipulate the grouped objects as a single object, and you can ungroup them by selecting the group and clicking on the Ungroup button.

The flip and rotate buttons do just as their names indicate—flipping or rotating the selected object. The Reshape button enables you to change the dimensions of any freeform object you have drawn. The Snap to Grid button aligns the objects in your drawing on a grid with the dimensions you specify in the dialog box that appears when you click the button (see fig. 4.23). Select the dimensions for the grid using the controls and then click on OK.

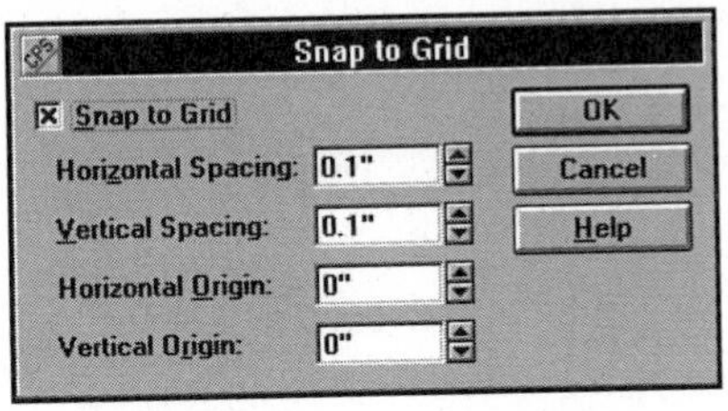

Figure 4.23
The Snap to Grid
dialog box.

Clicking on the Align Drawing Objects button brings up a dialog box, shown in figure 4.24, that enables you to place objects in particular places on the page. First select the object or objects you want to align. You then select their location using the option buttons. Clicking on OK aligns the objects.

Figure 4.24
The Align Drawing
Objects dialog
box.

Setting the location relative to the page means relative to the Word page, not relative to the current picture boundary. Bottom right relative to the page means the lower right corner of the page as it prints, as shown in figure 4.25.

Figure 4.25
An object aligned
to bottom right
with respect to the
page.

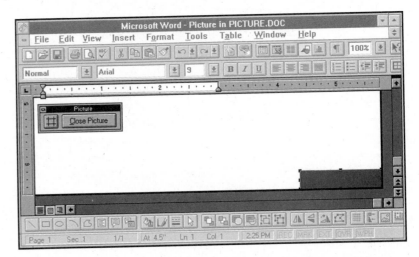

Setting the locations relative to each other superimposes the objects over one another with the positioning you specify. Figure 4.26 shows several objects aligned relative to each other.

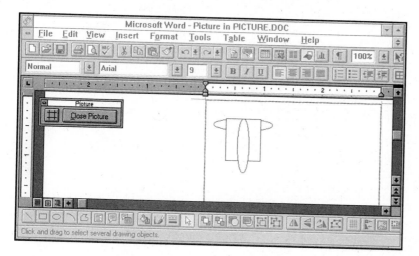

Figure 4.26
Three objects with top center alignment relative to one another.

Tip

Word 6.0's new drawing capabilities enable you to create pictures of any type for use in your Word document. However, if you miss the capability to import a picture as you could in the Microsoft Drawing applet included with Word for Windows 2.0, you can still import pictures. You do so using the **P**icture option on the **I**nsert menu.

Using WordArt

The WordArt 2.0 applet included with Word 6.0 is another example of how to embed objects in documents. WordArt enables you to create special text effects and embed them into your Word documents. You access WordArt by opening the **I**nsert menu and selecting the **O**bject option. This action causes the Object dialog box to appear (see fig. 4.27). In the **O**bject Type list box on the **C**reate New tab, select Microsoft WordArt 2.0, then click on the OK button.

When WordArt opens it provides you with both a menu and a toolbar. Although all the effects you can create with WordArt can be accessed from the menu, the toolbar is easier and more convenient to use. WordArt also presents you with a dialog box into which you enter the text for your special effect and a representation of the text object embedded in your document, as shown in figure 4.28.

Figure 4.27
The Object dialog box showing the selection of WordArt 2.0.

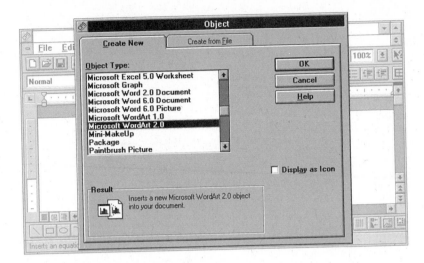

Figure 4.28
The WordArt menu, toolbar, and dialog box.

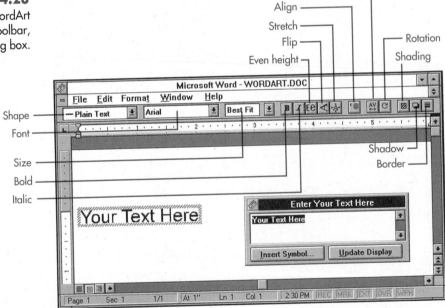

To create a special text effect, enter your text in the Enter Your Text Here dialog box. If you need to insert a symbol not readily available from your keyboard, click on the Insert Symbol button to open the Insert Symbol dialog box (see fig. 4.29). You can select any symbol available in your current font for insertion into your text. Just click on the symbol and then click on OK. If you need a symbol not in your current font, select a new font from the font drop-down list box described later in this section.

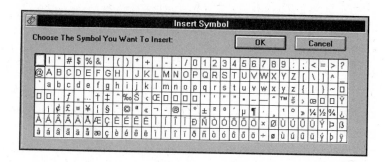

Figure 4.29
WordArt's Insert Symbol dialog box.

You can design your special effect by working with the controls on the WordArt toolbar. First, select a shape by opening the Shape drop-down list box. This action displays a grid of the preset shapes you can give to your text, as shown in figure 4.30. Just click on the shape you want.

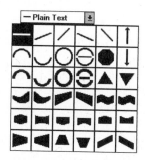

Figure 4.30
WordArt's Shape drop-down list box.

Next, select the font and size you want to use from the Font and Size drop-down list boxes. These controls work exactly the same as those offered by Word on the Formatting toolbar. You also can apply the character styles **bold** and *italic* using the Bold and Italic buttons, exactly as you might from Word's Formatting toolbar.

Tip

Most of the time your text is updated immediately in your Word document. If you feel you need to update the text, click on the **U**pdate Display button in the Enter Your Text Here dialog box.

The next few buttons apply special effects to your text. You have the following options:

✔ The Even Height button causes all the characters in your text to be the same height, regardless of whether they are upper- or lowercase.

✔ The Flip button causes each character of your text to lay over on its left side, so that the text reads vertically from bottom to top.

✔ The Stretch button causes your characters to expand to fill the space allotted for your WordArt effect. To cancel the effect, click on the button again.

✔ The Align button opens a drop-down list of alignment options, most of which should be familiar from working with Word (see fig. 4.31). The less familiar options are letter justify, stretch justify, and word justify. *Letter justify* increases the spaces between letters to justify a line. *Stretch justify* stretches the width of the characters to justify a line. *Word justify* increases the space between words to justify a line.

Figure 4.31
The Align
drop-down list.

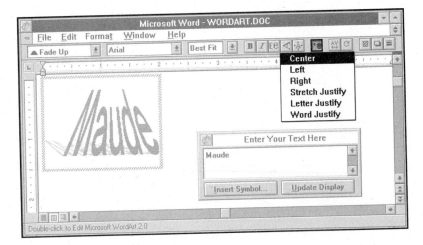

✔ The Spacing Between Characters button enables you to adjust the spacing between characters to achieve a more readable effect. Experiment with the options described by the option button captions, which represent the range from very close together to very far apart, until you find the option that works for you (see fig. 4.32). You also can experiment with clearing the Automatically Kern Character Pairs check box to see whether your effect benefits from turning this feature off. (Pairs of characters that present odd spacing problems are automatically *kerned*, or adjusted closer, by WordArt unless you clear this check box.)

✔ The Rotation button opens the Special Effects dialog box, as shown in figure 4.33. This contains two spin boxes that control the angle of rotation and the slider, or slant from vertical, of the rotated text. Adjust the controls so that your text effect appears the way you want it.

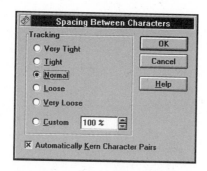

Figure 4.32
The Spacing Between Characters dialog box.

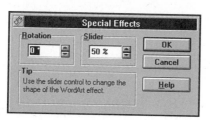

Figure 4.33
The Special Effects dialog box in WordArt.

✔ The Shading button gives you access to the Shading dialog box (see fig. 4.34). This enables you to select among various shading patterns and colors for your characters. Experiment with the controls to achieve the effect you want.

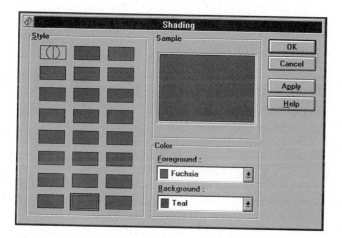

Figure 4.34
WordArt's Shading dialog box.

✔ The Shadow button opens a list box that offers you several choices of shadows for your characters, as shown in figure 4.35. The MORE option gives you access to the Shadow dialog box, which enables the additional option of selecting the color of the shadow. (The default color is silver, which is a good complement for most text colors.)

Figure 4.35
The Shadow drop-
down list box.

✔ The Border button opens the Border dialog box, as shown in figure 4.36, which enables you to select the border width for the characters you use and the border color. The border referred to is the one that snakes along the edge of each character itself. Widening the border of the character reduces the area of the shading pattern you might have applied to your text effect.

Figure 4.36
The Border dialog
box.

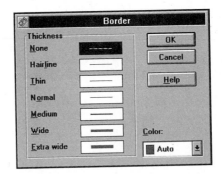

When you are finished creating your WordArt effect, click anywhere on the Word workspace to return to working on your document. This action closes WordArt and embeds the text effect in your document as an object. To return to working on your text effect, double-click on it.

Tip

WordArt effects are not automatically enclosed in frames; that is, your text cannot flow around them. If you want to use a frame, select your WordArt object and select the **F**rame option from the **I**nsert menu.

Using Microsoft Graph

Microsoft Graph is yet another example of the OLE tools provided with Word 6.0, giving you the opportunity to place charts in your documents as illustrations. You can either import an Excel chart for use with your document, or you can create one using the built-in spreadsheet capabilities of Microsoft Graph. In either case, Word treats the chart in the same way.

To start Microsoft Graph, click on the Graph button on the Standard toolbar. The Graph window opens, as shown in figure 4.37. This window is an application window. It remains open until you close it, and the Word window can hide it. The Graph window does not appear on the Window menu because Graph is an independent application from Word. To locate the Graph window if the Word window obscures it, you should use the Task List.

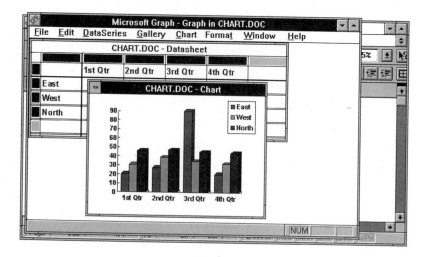

Figure 4.37
The Microsoft Graph window.

The Graph window provides two document windows in which you build your chart. One represents the datasheet from which the chart is built, and the other represents the chart itself.

Word opens the Graph window with a default datasheet and chart in place. You can edit the datasheet to prepare the chart for your Word document by changing the names of the rows and columns, adding rows and columns, deleting rows or columns, or changing the character of the chart.

The sample datasheet is intended to show you the most common situation for creating a chart and to suggest possibilities for your data by example. Editing the datasheet and pressing Enter after each edit causes an automatic update of the chart.

In addition to editing the example datasheet, you can import a datasheet from a spreadsheet. In the case of the Office suite of applications, this would be from Excel. To do this, select the datasheet, open the File menu in the Graph window, and select the Import Data option.

Graph displays the Import Data dialog box, shown in figure 4.38. Select the file containing the data. If you want to select only a row:cell range of data or a named range of data, select the Range option button and enter the row:cell specification or the name of the range in the text box, then click on OK.

Figure 4.38
The Import Data
dialog box.

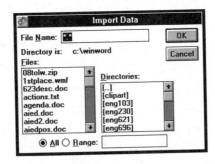

You also can import an Excel chart that you have already created using Excel. In this case, open the File menu and select the Open Microsoft Excel Chart option. Graph displays the Open Microsoft Excel Chart dialog box (see fig. 4.39). Use the controls to navigate the directories until you find the chart you want. When you do, click on OK. Graph imports the chart and the data on which it is built.

Figure 4.39
The Open Microsoft
Excel Chart
dialog box.

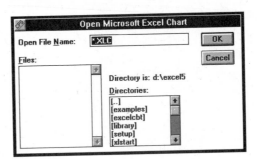

The Edit menu in Graph provides you with all the familiar options; however, there are some options that need further explanation (see fig. 4.40). The Copy option copies the chart to the Clipboard. The Clear option deletes the selected item on the chart or the datasheet. Delete Row/Col and Insert Row/Col perform the named options, exactly as they do in Excel or Word's table editor.

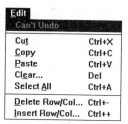

Figure 4.40
Graph's Edit menu and options.

The Gallery menu enables you to select the type of chart you want to present. Each of its menu items names a type of chart. Selecting a menu item opens a dialog box that enables you to choose from several preset formats for that type of chart. You simply select the format you want by clicking on it, and then click on the OK button. Selecting the 3-D Column menu option, for example, displays the Chart Gallery dialog box shown in figure 4.41. To select the type of 3-D column chart you want, click on its picture, then click on OK. Graph automatically converts the format of the chart it displays in the Chart document window to the format you have selected.

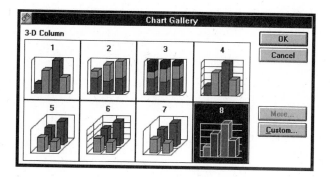

Figure 4.41
Choosing the type of 3-D column chart from the Chart Gallery dialog box.

If the More button is active in the Chart Gallery dialog box, clicking on it reveals more predefined chart formats that could not be presented in the dialog box because of limited space.

Each of the Chart Gallery dialog boxes displays the available formats for the type of chart named by the menu item that displays the dialog box. If none of these formats is appropriate for your task, click on the Custom button. This action displays the Format Chart dialog box (see fig. 4.42), from which you can build a customized format.

Figure 4.42
The Format Chart
dialog box.

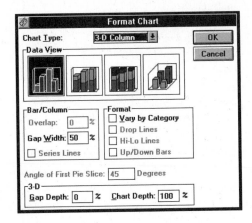

To build a custom chart using the Format Chart dialog box, perform the following steps:

1. Select the type of chart using the Chart Type drop-down list box.

2. Select the data view by clicking on one of the boxes in the Data View group.

3. Use the activated controls in the Bar/Column, Format, and 3-D groups to set the characteristics of the chart.

4. Click on OK.

Tip

The best way to create a custom chart is to experiment with the controls in the Format Chart dialog box and view the results in the Graph document window.

The DataSeries menu enables you to describe the data series you want to use in your chart. A *series* is a set of rows or columns that provide the basis for drawing the data markers such as lines and pie slices on the chart. A series contains the data that defines the heights of the columns or the width of the pie slices. The various options on the DataSeries menu enable you to take the following actions:

✔ Plot on X-Axis enables you to select the series that defines the tick-mark labels for the x-axis in a scatter chart. Place the focus in the row or column to serve as the series and select this menu item.

✔ Include Row/Col enables you to indicate which rows and columns to include in the chart. Select the rows or columns and select this menu item.

✔ Exclude Row/Col enables you to indicate which rows and columns to exclude from the chart. Select the rows or columns and select this menu item.

✔ Series in **R**ows causes each row to be included as a series on the chart. Simply select this menu item to produce this result.

✔ Series in **C**olumns causes each column to be included as a series on the chart. Simply select this menu item to produce this result.

✔ Move to **O**verlay causes the selected series to appear as an overlay on the chart—for example, as a line graph superimposed on a bar chart—if the chart allows overlays.

✔ Move to **C**hart causes the selected series to appear on the chart rather than as an overlay.

Tip Only the items relevant to the chart type you selected from the Gallery menu are activated on the DataSeries and Chart menus.

The **C**hart menu enables you to specify the characteristics for the type of chart you have chosen to build. Each menu option changes one of the characteristics of the chart's display. You have the following options:

✔ **T**itles opens a dialog box, shown in figure 4.43, that enables you to attach a title to one of the five items that can carry a title. Use the option buttons to select the item that will bear the title.

Figure 4.43
The Chart Title
dialog box.

✔ Selecting the **D**ata Labels option brings up the Data Labels dialog box (see fig. 4.44), which enables you to attach a label to each series displayed. Use the option buttons to select the type of label appropriate for your chart.

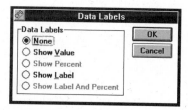

Figure 4.44
The Data Labels
dialog box.

✔ Arrow enables you to add or remove an arrow pointing to some portion of your chart. This menu option appears as Add Arrow or Delete Arrow, depending on whether the arrow is present. You can drag each end of the arrow to the position you want.

✔ Legend enables you to add or remove a legend for your chart. This menu option appears as Add Legend or Delete Legend, depending on whether the legend is present.

✔ Axes presents a dialog box (see fig. 4.45) that enables you to add and remove the axis lines from your chart if your chart type allows them. Use the check boxes to add or remove the lines you want.

Figure 4.45

The 3D Axes dialog box.

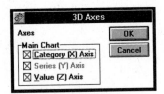

✔ Gridlines presents a dialog box, shown in figure 4.46, that enables you to add and remove grid lines from your chart, if your chart type permits them. Use the check boxes to add or remove the lines you want.

Figure 4.46

The Gridlines dialog box.

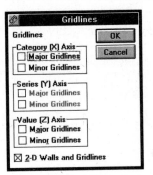

Graph's Format menu gives you access to all the formatting dialog boxes that are appropriate for each element of your chart. To change the format for any element of the chart, select that element and then open the Format menu. The results of your action depend, of course, on the element you have selected, so experimentation is the key to achieving the look you want for your chart. The Format menu gives you the following options:

✔ Patterns opens the Area Patterns dialog box, shown in figure 4.47, which enables you to determine the nature of the border and area shading associated with the selected element. Use the option buttons and drop-down list boxes to select the options you want. The Sample box previews the results of your choices.

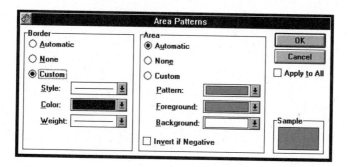

Figure 4.47
The Area Patterns
dialog box.

✔ Font opens the Chart Fonts dialog box (see fig. 4.48). This dialog box enables you to select a font for use with the element you have selected. The controls should be familiar from your work with Word's Format Font menu option; however, the Chart Fonts dialog box enables you to select the background for characters using the option buttons in the Background group. Automatic selects the best background for readability. Transparent lets the pattern and color of the chart background show through. Opaque surrounds each character with an opaque background in the color you select, in effect boxing the characters for readability.

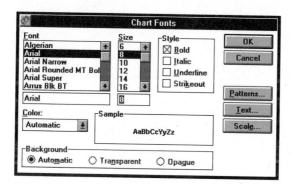

Figure 4.48
The Chart Fonts
dialog box.

✔ Text opens the Axis Text dialog box, which offers option controls that enable you to select the orientation of text along a chart axis. The controls are self-explanatory (see fig. 4.49), with Automatic providing the best fit possible.

Figure 4.49
The Axis Text
dialog box.

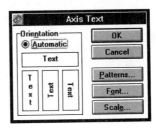

✔ Scale opens the Format Axis Scale dialog box. This provides check boxes and text boxes that enable you to define the scale lying along the selected axis of the chart. As figure 4.50 shows, placing a check in the first five check boxes sets the value automatically according to the values entered on the data sheet. If you enter a value into a text box, you override the automatic setting, and the check box clears. The controls vary according to the type of chart you have created, so experimentation is the key to achieving the look you want.

Figure 4.50
The Format Axis
Scale dialog box.

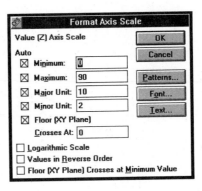

✔ Legend opens the Legend dialog box, which provides option buttons for placing the legend on your chart (see fig. 4.51).

Figure 4.51
The Legend dialog
box.

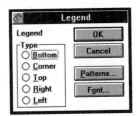

✔ <u>N</u>umber applies to the datasheet and determines the way numbers are displayed in the cells and on the chart you build. <u>N</u>umber opens the Number dialog box shown in figure 4.52. This dialog box provides formats similar to Excel's number formats. Select the format that applies and click on OK.

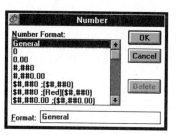

Figure 4.52
The Number dialog box.

✔ Column <u>W</u>idth opens the Column Width dialog box (see fig. 4.53). You can choose the <u>S</u>tandard Width check box, which provides an automatic setting, or you can enter a number in the text box. This menu option applies to the datasheet only.

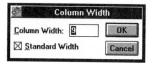

Figure 4.53
The Column Width dialog box.

✔ <u>C</u>hart opens the Format Chart dialog box discussed earlier in this section and shown in figure 4.42.

✔ <u>O</u>verlay opens the Format Overlay dialog box (see fig. 4.54). This dialog box activates the controls appropriate to your chart type to place an overlay series on the chart, along with various lines that show its relationship to the other series. Experiment with the controls to achieve the look you want.

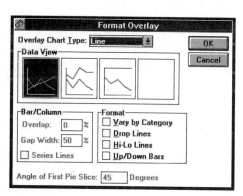

Figure 4.54
The Format Overlay dialog box.

✔ 3-D View opens the Format 3-D View dialog box, which presents controls to adjust the elevation and rotation angles for your 3-D chart (see fig. 4.55). Experiment with the controls to get the look you want for your chart.

Figure 4.55
The Format 3-D
View dialog box.

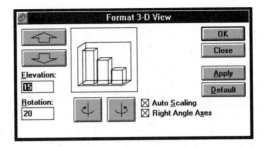

✔ Color Palette opens the Color Palette dialog box, from which you can select the color for your element, as shown in figure 4.56. If you wish to create a custom color, click on the Edit button to open a color editor much the same as that offered by the Control Panel for creating Windows colors.

Figure 4.56
The Color Palette
dialog box.

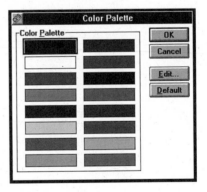

Because of its many features, Microsoft Graph enables you to build custom charts for your documents quickly and easily. You do not have to load your full spreadsheet unless you want to.

When you finish creating your chart, select the Exit and Return to option on the File menu. Graph asks if you want to update the object you have embedded in your Word document. If you answer Yes in response to the dialog box, Graph embeds the chart you created as an object in your Word document. If you answer No, Graph exits without embedding, or without updating the existing object.

As with any OLE-enabled application, objects you create with Graph are stored as a part of your Word document. To edit your charts, just double-click on them.

Chapter Snapshot

The last sections of Chapter 1 introduced you to printing with Word. In this chapter, you will learn the finer points of printing by working through realistic scenarios. The topics discussed in this chapter include the following:

After you finish reading this chapter, you will know why to follow particular printing procedures, and you will see ways in which you can extend Word's printing capabilities.

5 CHAPTER

Understanding Printing and Printers

by Forrest Houlette

C hapter 1 covered the basic printing features of Word 6.0. Now it is time to explore these features in greater detail and see the ways in which you can fully exploit them. Printing does involve a few tricks, and thinking through what you want can save you time and paper. The guided tour of the printing controls in Chapter 1 is only an introduction to printing with Word. Working through some practical examples will help you see how you can use the printing controls effectively.

Setting Up a Document

Before you prepare a document for printing, you need to review why you are printing the document. Is the document something you need fast and that no one else really needs to see? Is it the final draft of a major presentation, something that needs to look magnificent to impress someone? Answers to questions like these help determine the way you want to set up the document for printing.

Setting Up a Template

You can set the default page setup for a document template so that it is appropriate for documents based on the template. The page setup information is stored in the document template. As a result, when you are ready to print, you don't have to modify the controls in the Page Setup dialog box to suit your document.

Creating a default page setup for a document template is easy. Follow these steps:

1. Open the document template or create a new document based on the template.

2. Open the File menu and select the Page Setup menu option.

3. Adjust the controls on the tabs in the Page Setup dialog box to suit your needs.

4. Click on the Default button in each tab, as shown in figure 5.1.

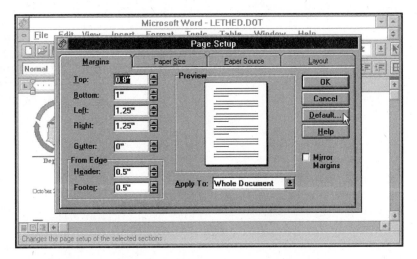

Figure 5.1
Setting the default page setup for a template by clicking on the Default button.

5. When the Confirmation dialog box appears, click on the Yes button.

Clicking on the **D**efault button to save the default information also closes the Page Setup dialog box. If you want to adjust the defaults in another tab, you need to reopen the dialog box.

Your document template now contains the page setup information that you want to use for your documents.

A practical example clarifies why you might want to make these adjustments. Suppose that each month you have to write a 10-page sales report that you present to the sales management team. Each month, the sales managers for each product line meet with the marketing vice president to review progress toward sales goals. Each division produces such a sales report, and these documents are distributed, photocopied on both sides and three-hole punched, to the sales management team. Each member of the team stores these reports in a three-ring binder for future reference.

When you set up the pages for such a document, you need to leave room for the holes that are punched along the left margin of the odd pages. You need to print using odd and even pages, opposing headers and footers, and opposing page numbers so that the document looks good in the binder. But remembering to make all these adjustments each time you print might be a hassle. You might have to make several test prints before you get a usable print.

The best solution is to create a template for these reports and store the page setup in the template. You would go through steps like these:

1. Open a document based on the template.

2. Open the **F**ile menu and select the Page Set**u**p option.

3. On the **M**argins tab, use the G**u**tter spin box to create a 0.5-inch gutter to accommodate the punched holes (see fig. 5.2).

4. Check the M**i**rror Margins check box because the completed document will be printed on both sides of the page.

5. Make sure the **A**pply To drop-down list box shows Whole Document as the selection.

If you have a selection active in your document, the Apply To drop-down list box automatically shows Selection as the current option. Always verify that this control shows the correct selection before you set the default.

6. Click on the **D**efault button and accept your changes in the confirmation dialog box.

7. Open the Page Setup dialog box again.

Figure 5.2
Adjusting the Gutter
and Mirror Margins
controls on the
Margins tab.

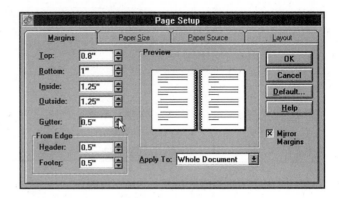

8. Click on the Layout tab and check the Different Odd and Even Pages box in the Headers and Footers group, as shown in figure 5.3. Check the Different First Page check box to keep the first page clear of the headers and footers for the rest of the document.

Figure 5.3
Setting up opposing
headers in the
Layout tab.

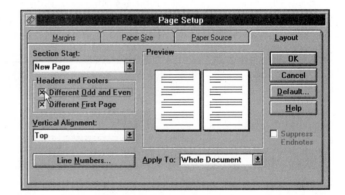

9. Make sure the Apply To drop-down list shows Whole Document.

10. Click on the Default button and accept your modifications.

You now should print a test document to make sure you have set up the page correctly. If you see other changes that are necessary, make them as well and save them as the template defaults. After you are satisfied with the test prints, your document template is ready. Now you do not have to adjust the page setup controls every time you print.

Setting Other Printing Options

There are other printing options of which you will want to take advantage, even though you cannot store them in each template. These are the options that you set on the Print tab of the Options dialog box. You should set these controls to reflect the majority of your printing needs and adjust them only as you need to for your less frequently printed documents.

You can get to these controls in two ways. You can open the File menu, select the Print option, and click on the Options button, or you can open the Tools menu, select the Options item, and click on the Print tab. In either case, you reach the Print tab of the Options dialog box, shown in figure 5.4.

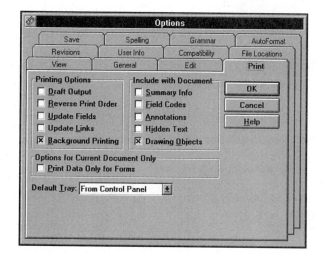

Figure 5.4
The Print tab in the Options dialog box.

The Printing Options group provides check boxes that you can use to specify the default behavior of your printer driver. You might choose to use these options for reasons such as the following:

✔ Check **D**raft Output for the fastest printout possible. The document will not look its best, but it will print quickly. This option is especially useful if you have a dot-matrix printer that slows down considerably when it does letter-quality printing and you are in a hurry.

✔ Use **R**everse Print Order if you are using a laser printer or similar printer that sorts the printed sheets in the reverse of page order to avoid curling the sheets around the printing rollers. By reversing the print order, your sheets stack in page order.

✔ Check **U**pdate Fields if you insert fields into your document that can go out of date. Suppose you use sequence numbers to number the figures in a document, then insert two new figures after the most recent print. You can easily forget to manually update the sequence fields. Checking this check box causes the sequence fields to be updated for you before each printing operation.

✔ Use Update Links if your documents have automatic links to data that is updated frequently. Checking this box assures that each document has the latest data.

✔ Background Printing is checked by default because this option enables you to continue working while Word prints your document. This is the preference of most users. If you are in a hurry for your printed copy, however, uncheck this box. This forces you to wait, of course, until Word finishes printing before you can work again.

The Include with Document group provides check boxes that enable you to specify the additional information that prints with the document. You might want to use these options for reasons such as the following:

✔ Check Summary Info to print the information displayed by the Summary Info dialog box. To see the Summary Info dialog box or to update its contents, open the File menu and select the Summary Info option.

✔ Use the Field Codes option to print the text that makes up each field code in your document. If you are searching for a problem with the way a field is behaving, a printout of the field codes can be extremely useful.

✔ Check the Annotations box if you need to see the annotations that various reviewers leave on a document. This option is most useful if you want to work on a printed copy as you revise a document.

✔ Select Hidden Text when you want to print characters formatted as hidden text in your document. If you have formatted notes to yourself embedded in the document as hidden text, you might want to print them if you are going to work with a printed copy as you revise.

✔ Drawing Objects is checked by default to enable the embedded pictures in your document to print. If you are printing a draft on a slow printer, however, you might want to uncheck this box to speed printing.

After you store your desired page setups in your document templates and set your print options to cover the majority of jobs, printing is easier. Usually you simply click on the Print button on the Standard toolbar, and Word does the rest. The only time you need to review your print options and page setup is when you encounter special circumstances.

Exploiting the Preview Feature

The print preview feature in Word 6.0 can be extremely useful. After you reach the final stages before printing, you should use the previewer to examine your document. Make sure all the details are correct on-screen. To access this feature, open the File menu and select the Print Preview option.

Print preview has gained several features in Word 6.0, including providing you with the capability to edit in preview mode. By editing in preview mode, you easily can see formatting problems in your document and make the necessary changes. Just click on the Magnifier button on the toolbar to take the magnifier out of its default activated status. You then see the insertion point flashing in your document. You can edit the document just as if you were in normal or page layout view, as shown in figure 5.5. You can even edit in a multiple page view. As a result, you do not have to jump into and out of preview mode to make changes to your document's format.

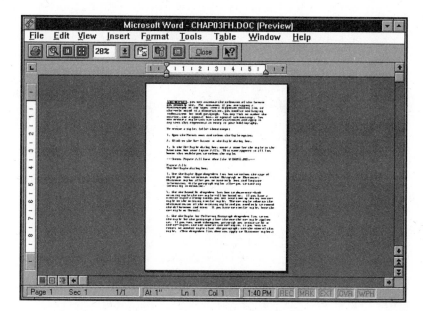

Figure 5.5
Editing a document in preview mode.

In addition to editing, you can access any of Word's menu options while you are in preview mode. If you need to set font formatting or insert a field, you can do so. (Figure 5.6 shows an example.) You must remember that some menu options are incompatible with preview mode. If you change to page layout view, you exit preview mode. In general, you can make any insertion you need to make or change any formatting while remaining in preview mode.

Tip

The major exception to editing while staying in preview mode is changing the contents of the headers and footers.

Using print preview, you can carefully review your documents and get them into proper shape without doing a test print, thus saving the paper and time used on test prints.

Word for Windows

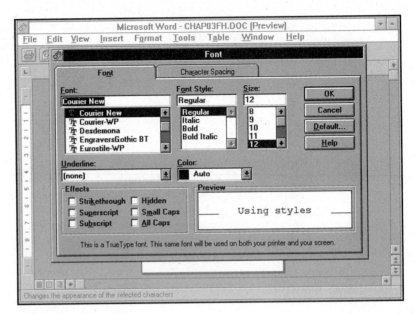

Figure 5.6
Changing a font
format while in
preview mode.

Printing Documents

Word 6.0 provides several options for printing a document. Of course, you will want to print an entire document. You might also want to print segments of a document. And you certainly need to know the way to handle printing from the new master document format.

Printing an Entire Document

As Chapter 1 explained, you print an entire document by clicking on the Print button on the Standard toolbar or opening the File menu, selecting Print, and clicking on OK. There are some tricks to printing an entire document, however, that you might be glad to know about.

If you proofread a document that has different odd and even pages, you might want to print it differently than when you print the final copy. You can open the Print drop-down list box in the Print dialog box and select Odd Pages or Even Pages (see fig. 5.7). Printing odd or even pages separately enables you to compare headers and footers, margins, gutters, and similar features to more easily make certain that they are correct. If you look only at pages that have the same layout in a single stack, you can detect errors in the layout faster because a deviation from the norm is more obvious.

If you print multiple copies, you can collate them by checking the Collate Copies check box in the Print dialog box, also shown in figure 5.7. The box is checked as the default because most people want their copies collated. If you plan to distribute a document page by page in a meeting, however, it is more convenient not to collate the copies as they print. You might readily prepare a set of one-page handouts as a single Word document, each page representing one of the handouts. Unchecking the Collate Copies check box prints them as you need to distribute them. Also, if a printer has the capability to make multiple copies of the same page, you will have to unselect Collate Copies so that the printer internal copies command will be used.

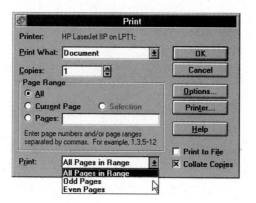

Figure 5.7
Using the Print drop-down list in the Print dialog box.

You might also find the Print to File check box useful on occasion. When you check this check box, also shown in figure 5.7, Word does not print your document to a printer. Instead, Word formats the document for the printer selected but prints the document to a disk file. You then can submit that file to the printer you have specified at a later time by using the DOS PRINT command or by dragging and dropping the file icon from File Manager to Print Manager.

The capability to print to a file is most useful for preparing a document to print at a service bureau. You can install the driver for the printer type used by the service bureau, print to a file, and take the file to the service bureau. The service bureau need not use the same word processor as you; it needs only the correctly formatted file and a means of submitting the file to the printer.

This capability also is useful if you need to print a document on a printer that is not attached to your computer or LAN. You can put the document on a disk, take the disk to the appropriate computer, and print the document. You can use this technique to avoid carrying bulky loads of paper to meetings at remote locations. It is especially useful to avoid carrying lots of paper on an airline trip to one of your company's clients or one of your company's sites.

Printing Portions of a Document

As noted in Chapter 1, Word also enables you to print portions of a chapter. In fact, Word offers three methods for printing parts of a document. The method you should choose depends on your goals.

If you discover an error in a single page and you can correct the error without changing the pagination, for example, you can select the Current Page option button in the Print dialog box (see fig. 5.8) to print that single page. Scroll through your document until you reach that page. Next, make your correction. Make sure the insertion point is on the page you need to print. Then open the File menu, select Print, click on the Current Page option button, and click on OK. The problem in the printed version is corrected with a minimum of effort.

Figure 5.8
Selecting the
Current Page
option.

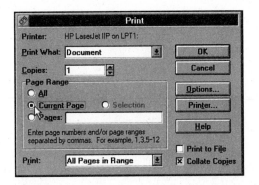

You might also use the Current Page option if you need to provide a copy of a single page in a document to someone else, possibly to proofread or to provide important data for an oral presentation. At times, however, you might need to print more than a single page for such purposes. You could, of course, perform the current page procedure repeatedly, but there is an easier way.

Word permits you to print multiple pages and page ranges. To use this option, select the Pages option button in the Print dialog box, as shown in figure 5.9. Then, in the text box next to the option button, type the pages and/or page ranges you want to use. You can enter single page numbers (like 3), or page numbers indicating a range by using a hyphen (like 12-15). You can enter several pages and page ranges, as shown in figure 5.9, as long as you separate them with commas. When you click on OK, Word prints only the pages and page ranges indicated.

Figure 5.9
Using the Pages
option in the Print
dialog box.

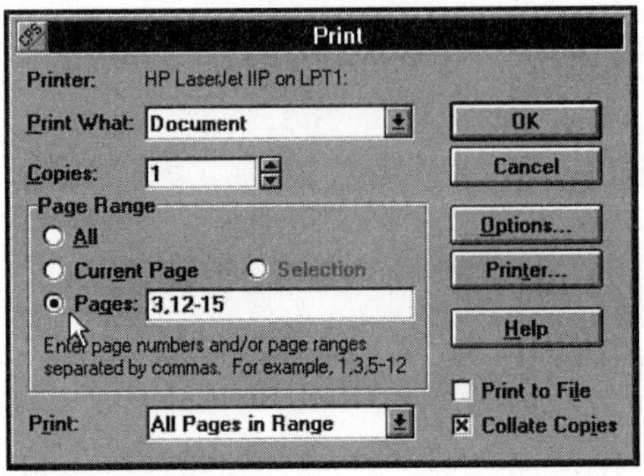

Sometimes you need a part of a document that begins at the middle of one page and ends at the middle of another to present as a separate document. You'd like for this to start at the top of a page and to look like a stand-alone document. You can, of course, copy that part of the document to a blank document and then print the new document, but there is a simpler way. Select the section you need to print, just as if you were going to copy it. Then open the File menu, select Print, and choose the Selection option button in the Print dialog box (see fig. 5.10). When you click on OK, Word adjusts for the new page numbers and prints the section as a regular document. You save a few steps and get the same results.

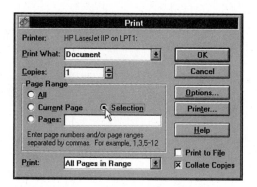

Figure 5.10
Using the Selection option in the Print dialog box.

Word 6.0 offers printing scenarios that meet your needs. When you decide how to print just part of a document, just think about what you need the part for and how you need it to look on the page. You can achieve the results you want straight from the Print dialog box.

Printing Master Documents

When you organize a document as a master document, you have flexible control over printing. Master documents add one more level of control. If you display a document in master document view, as described in Chapter 2, "Understanding Word for Windows Concepts," you can select which portions of the document to print by expanding and collapsing different headings. The expanded headings print the text included under them, the collapsed ones do not. Figure 5.11 shows an example of a master document being prepared for partial printing.

Tip

You also can use the techniques described earlier in this chapter in the section "Printing Portions of a Document" when you print a master document.

To print an entire master document, display it in normal view. Print the document using the techniques described earlier in this chapter in the section "Printing an Entire Document." Your entire master document prints with the formatting you have applied.

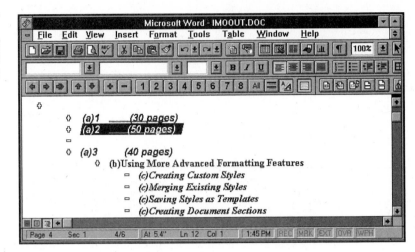

Figure 5.11
A master document
set up for partial
printing

Changing the Printer

You might work with several different printers, especially if your computer is attached to a network. Using Microsoft Office, you probably have at least two printer drivers installed, even if you have only one printer. One of the drivers is for your printer. The other is for a Genigraphics graphics printer so that you can prepare PowerPoint slides to be printed in special image formats, such as 35mm slides, by a service bureau. Using the Genigraphics printer driver is one of the more likely occasions you might have for printing to a file. You can take the correctly formatted files directly to your service bureau for production as slides.

A *printer driver* is a control program that translates a Word document into instructions for your printer. You install printer drivers using the Printer icon in the Control Panel. Installing a printer driver and installing a printer are one and the same operation in the Control Panel.

Obviously, if you have more than one printer, even a phantom one, you need to know how to change printers. The process is straightforward, as shown by the following steps:

1. Open the File menu and select the Print option.

2. In the Print dialog box, click on the Printer button.

3. In the Print Setup dialog box (see fig. 5.12), select the printer you want to use in the Printers list box.

4. Click on the Options button to verify that the printer is set up correctly for your print job. A dialog box like the one shown in figure 5.13 appears, specific to your printer. Adjust the controls as necessary and click on OK. This returns you to the Print Setup dialog box.

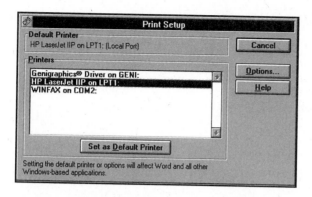

Figure 5.12
The Print Setup dialog box.

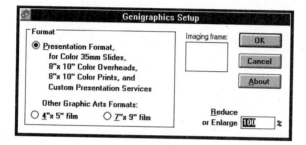

Figure 5.13
The options dialog box for the Genigraphics printer.

5. Click on the Set as <u>D</u>efault Printer button to select the printer as the one for Word to use next (and until you change the default).

6. Click on the Close button in the Print Setup dialog box and continue the print operation as normal.

One common reason you might need to change printers is to print envelopes or labels. You might have a printer that is set up with an envelope feeder, or a specialized label printer. Or you might have a dot-matrix printer dedicated to printing checks for your company or similar special-purpose forms. You might also have a color printer on the network, as well as a black-and-white local or network printer to select from.

Changing the Printer Setup

After you select the printer to use, you might want to adjust its setup to reflect the printing job you have to do. If you are used to other applications offering a printer setup menu option, you might be surprised not to find such an option on the Word 6.0 menu. Word spreads out the controls typically found in a print setup dialog box among several other dialog boxes that are more logically named.

As described in the preceding section, Word's Print Setup dialog box enables you to choose a printer and to set a few options relating to the printer. In fact, these are the limited set of printer options not handled by other dialog boxes. They relate most directly to the printer hardware and hardly at all to the page setup and formatting of your document.

The controls most often offered by print setup dialog boxes in other applications are offered in the Paper Size and Paper Source tabs of the Page Setup dialog box, shown in figure 5.14. The use of these controls is described in detail in the section "Setting Up the Page" in Chapter 1.

Figure 5.14
The Paper Size tab in the Page Setup dialog box.

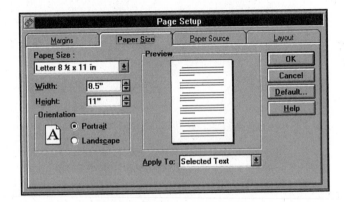

In Word 6.0, customary printer setup is handled as part of formatting your document. Word communicates the appropriate settings to your printer. You do not need to be concerned with the details of printer setup, because Word effectively hides them from you. How your printer handles margins, character spacing, fonts, and such matters is between Word and your printer. You design the document; Word handles the printing details.

Working with Special-Purpose Printers

You already have seen the example of the Genigraphics printer driver included with PowerPoint. It is a special-purpose printer driver intended to facilitate the work of creating presentations. You might encounter other special-purpose printer drivers. These drivers usually cause some other kind of device to masquerade as a printer. Delrina's WinFax LITE driver is a good example, because it is bundled with so many fax modems.

The WinFax LITE driver causes your modem to masquerade as a printer. Word sees your fax modem as a printer, and sends documents to it. The WinFax LITE driver receives the documents and treats them as faxes, transmitting them to their destinations over your modem. This ingenious deception enables you to create a fax in any application that can print.

Such drivers often require more extensive setup than do printers for Word because they are, in fact, not printers. Word cannot treat their special needs during page setup because the drivers demand much more in terms of setup than Word knows how to provide. As a result, when you select one of these "printers," you need to pay special attention to the Options dialog box that appears when you click on the Options button in the Print Setup dialog box.

WinFax LITE's options dialog box is shown in figure 5.15. As you can see, it contains controls that go beyond Word's page setup capabilities.

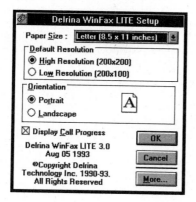

Figure 5.15
The WinFax LITE options dialog box.

This dialog box asks you to set the fax resolution, the page orientation for the fax, and whether a dialog box appears to display the progress of the fax call. None of these options can be under Word's control because Word, as an application, has no knowledge of faxing.

Figure 5.16 shows the additional settings displayed when you click on the More button. Again you see controls that Word has no means of managing. You can set the type of modem and the modem command string to use. You can select the speaker setup, transmission rate, speaker volume, and dialing procedure. You also can enter information for the fax cover sheet and fax station information. All these are settings that Word cannot adjust as it prepares your document for you.

Figure 5.16
Additional settings
for the WinFax
LITE driver.

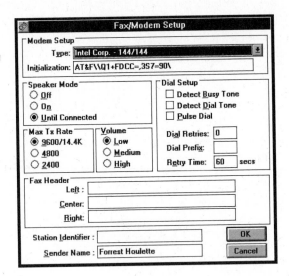

If you are using special-purpose printer drivers, the most important point is that you must handle more of the setup yourself. Be sure to click on the <u>O</u>ptions button when you select the printer and make certain the options are set correctly. Word cannot always control these drivers as you might expect. You have to exercise more control over such devices yourself.

Chapter Snapshot

This chapter explains how to create Word macros. You will learn the way in which to record macros and assign them to the keyboard, menu, and toolbars. You also will learn the basics of Word Basic macro programming. More specifically, you will learn the following:

By the time you have completed this chapter, you will be able to build simple macros—just by recording your actions with the menu, keyboard, toolbars, and mouse—and more complex and useful macros.

CHAPTER

An Introduction to Word Macros

by Forrest Houlette

As explained in Chapter 2, "Understanding Word for Windows Concepts," Word 6.0 is a word processor that is based on the concept of macros. Each command that you can execute from the menu constitutes a named block of code created by the Word programmers. When you execute a command from the menu, your menu action selects the block of code by name and has it executed. As a result, the action you wanted Word to take occurs exactly as you asked when you selected the menu option.

This chapter extends the concept of Word macros by showing you how to create your own commands, which you can attach to the menu or to toolbar buttons. You need not think that this business of creating custom commands is beyond you. Word makes the process easy—as easy as clicking a few buttons and taking the action you wanted to make with a single command. You need to know little about programming to build your own macros.

Explaining Macros

In Word, a macro is a special type of document, for two reasons. First, a macro is a document that is stored as a part of a template. In that sense, a macro bears the same relationship to a template that a subdocument bears to a master document. Second, a macro consists of only certain kinds of "sentences": the names of Word commands, the same names you saw listed in the Macro dialog box in Chapter 2.

The names of the Word commands make up Word's macro programming language, officially named Word Basic. Word Basic contains a few additional commands that do not appear on the Word menu. These commands enable you to open special-purpose files and to create dialog boxes. As a result, by using Word Basic you can make Word do anything you want it to do. You have complete control over all Word's commands, all its file-handling capabilities, and even its capability to create and display dialog boxes.

Tip Use macros to automate your most frequently repeated actions. If you perform a multistep action repeatedly as you work, you can use a macro to do it for you.

You have two ways at your disposal to create macros. You can sit down and figure out exactly what you want Word to do. You can read through the list of Word commands and decide which ones would accomplish the task, then you can type each of the commands into a macro file in the proper order, hoping you did not make any typing mistakes. And you would have a macro that has taken you a lot of time and effort to build, even assuming that you had gotten all the commands right and the macro works correctly.

On the other hand, you can have Word record the macro for you. First, you open the Macro dialog box, click on the Record button, and fill in some information in a dialog box. You then take the action you want to have automated as a macro, performing all the menu and mouse steps exactly as if you were not recording them. When you are finished, click on the Stop button. You would have a macro correctly built that does exactly what you did as you were recording. Word builds a macro file for you containing all the commands necessary, and it works exactly as you did with the mouse and keyboard. Unless you made a mistake, your macro will not take the wrong action.

Recording Macros

To show you why and how to record a macro, let's examine the case of a computer-book author. When a chapter is finished and ready to send to the publisher, several tasks have to be performed. The line of text needs to be set to 6.5 inches throughout the document. The fields used to number figures and tables need to be updated. Since the publisher needs a text-only document, the links in the fields need to be broken. The document needs to be checked for spelling. The spacing between a period and the next sentence needs to be cut from two spaces to one. Finally, the document needs to be saved in Word for Windows 2.0 document format, the version that the publisher uses.

 While this example relates to only one type of document, every document has finishing steps that need to be taken once the text and layout are complete. **Tip** Record these steps as a macro saved in the template for the document and you will never forget to do any of them again.

Odds are that on any given day the author of a chapter is going to forget to do one or more of those things, especially as deadlines approach and the writer tires out struggling to produce the chapters due. The writer could use a checklist, but checklists have a way of getting lost or forgotten. The best solution for the author is to record a macro that performs all these steps and save it in the template used to create the chapter. Word then is responsible for maintaining the checklist of things to be done. The writer only needs to remember to run the end-of-chapter macro, and Word takes care of all the details.

The code for the following project, as with all the macros included in this chapter, can be found on the book's companion disk in the NEWRIDE.DOT template.

To record such a macro, follow these steps:

1. Open the Tools menu and select the Macro option, or double-click on the REC box on the status bar. (If you double-click on the REC box, continue to step 3. Word skips the Macro dialog box when you use this method.)

2. When the Macro dialog box appears, as shown in figure 6.1, click on the Record button; this brings up the Record Macro dialog box (see fig. 6.2).

3. Enter a name for the macro in the Record Macro Name text box in the Record Macro dialog box. You cannot use punctuation or spaces for the macro name. Keep it short but descriptive. You may wish to use capital letters at word beginnings to make it more readable. For this example, type **EndNRPChapter**.

4. Open the Make Macro Available To drop-down list box and select the template in which the macro will be stored. If you want the macro available to all documents, store it in NORMAL.DOT. If not, store it in the template for the documents that will use it. In this example, we will store the macro in NEWRIDE.DOT.

Figure 6.1
Starting the
macro-recording
process from the
Macro dialog box.

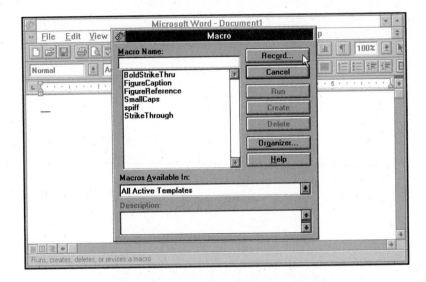

Figure 6.2
The Record Macro
dialog box.

5. Enter a description of what the macro does, up to 255 characters, in the Description text box. A description is good protection against forgetting what the macro
   does. While the description is optional, it appears in the Description text box in
   the Macro dialog box and appears on the status bar when the macro is selected as
   a menu command or as a toolbar button. For this example, enter **Ends New**
   Riders chapter.

6. If you want to assign the macro to a toolbar, the menu, or the keyboard, click on
   the appropriate button in the Assign Macro To group. Each button opens the
   Customize dialog box (discussed in detail in Chapter 7, "Customizing Word for
   Windows") to the appropriate tab. In this example you will assign the macro to the
   keyboard, so click on the Keyboard button.

7. In the Customize dialog box (see fig. 6.3), press the key combination that you want to use to run the macro. In this example, press Ctrl+Shift+E. Word displays the keys you pressed in the Press New Shortcut Key text box. Word also warns you if the key combination is already assigned to another command or macro. (If it is and you do not want to disturb the assignment, press Backspace to clear the text box and try again.)

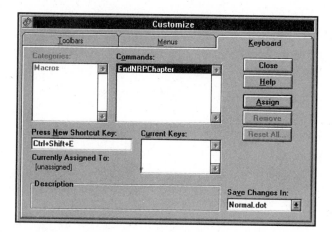

Figure 6.3
The Customize dialog box.

8. Click on the Assign button, then click on the Close button. At this point, the Macro Recording toolbar will float above your Word screen and the pointer will display a cassette tape below the arrow (see fig. 6.4). You are recording your macro.

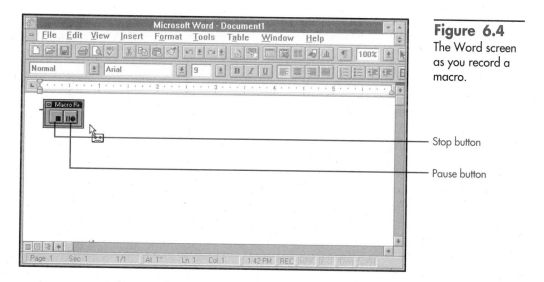

Figure 6.4
The Word screen as you record a macro.

9. To record your macro, perform the following actions in sequence:

    ✔ Open the Edit menu and choose the Select All option. (You select the entire text because your next actions must affect the entire text.)

    ✔ Drag the right margin pointer to the 6.5-inch indicator. If it is already there, click on it to set that right margin for all paragraphs.

    ✔ Press F9 to update the figure-number fields. (Number fields are explained later in this chapter.)

    ✔ Press Ctrl+Shift+F9 to unlink the fields. (This action converts all number fields to plain text that represents the last update of the field.)

    ✔ Press Ctrl+Home to clear the selection and move to the beginning of the document.

    ✔ Click on the Spelling button on the Standard toolbar and check the spelling in the document.

    ✔ Open the Edit menu and select the Replace option. Enter two spaces in the Find What box and one space in the Replace With box. Click on the Replace All button.

    ✔ Open the File menu and select the Save As option. In the Save As dialog box, open the Save As File Type drop-down list box and select the Word for Windows 2 option. Click on the OK button.

10. Click on the Stop button on the Macro Recording toolbar. Your macro has been recorded and saved.

Tip

If you are unsure as to the next action to perform during your recording of the macro, you can use the Pause button on the Macro Recording toolbar to pause the recording. You then can try out the next step until you are sure how it should go. Click on the Pause button again to record your well-practiced action.

You can run your new macro in any document you create with the NEWRIDE.DOT template. However, there are two cautions to using this macro. First, do not use it in a document that does not have active fields. The unlink-fields action that you recorded has nothing to do under such circumstances and causes an error. Word presents a dialog box informing you that a command failed, and then exits the macro procedure, doing none of the rest of the work.

Second, if you run your new macro on a document, it will name the document using the same name as the file with which you recorded the macro. You could accidentally overwrite a file.

Obviously your macro needs to be modified slightly before it is ready for use. The next section tells you how.

Modifying Macros

You have seen how you can record some rather complex actions as a macro very easily. However, you also have seen how some recorded macros can have unfortunate side effects. Typically, unfortunate side effects include the following:

✔ Commands that cause errors when they cannot perform the intended action. Virtually every Word command and every macro you create can have this unfortunate consequence.

✔ Commands that record specific file names or other document-specific information.

You can easily modify your macros to resolve these side effects. To make the modifications, you need to know how to edit a macro, how to test a macro, and how to debug a macro. Fortunately, these are not complex tasks. Word makes it easy to solve both of the problems associated with recording macros.

Word Basic is designed to report an error every time a command cannot carry out its action, for whatever reason. The reason Word reports the error and stops the action is that it has no other instructions. However, you can add a command to each macro you record that tells Word what to do when it encounters an error.

Word also identifies document-specific information in easy-to-spot ways. Typically, if you delete the document-specific information from the command, Word carries out the command using the defaults for the document at hand. In the case of the Save As command, if the command has no file name to use, it uses the file name for the document on which the macro is operating. You easily can scan your macro commands and remove such information.

Tip

Before you read through the next few sections, you might want to make sure that the Word Basic Help file is available on your computer. When you select the typical installation using Setup, this file is not installed. Double-click on either the Word or Office Setup icon and add the Word Basic Help file to your installation.

Editing

The procedure for editing a macro is much like the procedure for editing a document, because a macro is just a special type of document. To open a macro for editing, follow these steps:

1. Open the Tools menu and select the Macro option.

2. In the Macro dialog box, select the name of the macro to edit from the Macro Name combination box (see fig. 6.5). You might need to open the Macros Available In drop-down list box to select the appropriate template so that your macro shows in the list box.

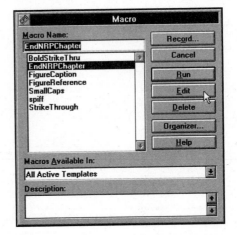

Figure 6.5

Preparing to edit a macro using the Macro dialog box.

3. Click on the Edit button.

At this point, Word opens the macro and displays it as a document. Word also displays the Macro toolbar, which assists you in working with the macro. Figure 6.6 shows the EndNRPChapter macro you just recorded opened for editing.

You edit a macro exactly as you edit a document; all the same editing actions apply. There are a couple of cautions, however. Keep each macro command in its own paragraph. Turn on paragraph marks by clicking the Show/Hide ¶ button to see how Word defines the end of each macro command with a paragraph mark. If a paragraph mark does not separate two commands, Word will display an error message indicating that it could not interpret the command.

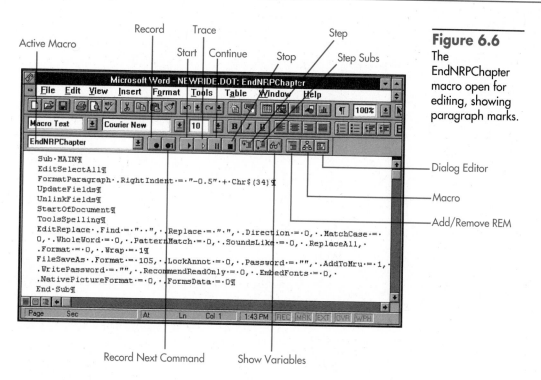

Figure 6.6
The EndNRPChapter macro open for editing, showing paragraph marks.

In addition, do not add extraneous characters to a macro command, place extra characters before the command, or misspell a command keyword. Word Basic does not know how to deal with such issues except to display an error message that explains it could not understand the command. When you make changes, you want to make them with the precision of a surgical air strike. Go into the file, add or delete or change what you need to, and exit the file leaving the rest intact.

As you are editing, the macro toolbar provides a button that can be of great assistance—the Record Next Command button. If you want to add a command to your macro, you need not type the command. You can switch to a document, click on this button, and perform the action representing the command. Word adds the command to the active macro file at the current insertion point position, then stops the recording process. You do not need to type commands, and you can record and modify commands as necessary. (There are a few exceptions to this rule, as you will see, but not many.) In general, if you have the choice of recording or typing, select record. Word does not make typing errors while it records.

Tip

The active macro is the one that runs when you click on the Start button on the Macro toolbar. The Active Macro drop-down list box (see fig. 6.6) always indicates which macro is active. If you have more than one macro open for editing and testing, you can change which one is active by selecting its name from this list.

To make the specific changes necessary in the EndNRPDocument macro, you need to add one statement and delete a portion of another. To solve the problem of an error being generated, you need to add a statement telling Word what to do if a statement cannot carry out its action. Word Basic provides a family of three such commands, each of which gives Word different directions. In the case of this macro, you want simply for the command that cannot complete its action to give control to the next command so that the rest of the macro can run. In other words, if a command cannot be carried out, you want to ignore that command and get on with the rest of the macro.

To add this functionality to your macro, perform the following procedure:

1. Position the insertion point at the end of the SubMAIN line.

2. Press Enter to create a new line.

3. Type **On Error Resume Next**.

The line you have just added tells Word that when it encounters an error to resume running the macro with the next command. No dialog box appears, and the macro keeps running until it ends. You have to type this command; it is one of the few that you cannot record.

To solve the problem of Word using the default document name inappropriately, you need to remove document-specific information. In this macro, only one element needs to be removed. If you look at the line that begins FileSaveAs, you see that it contains a specification of the file name to use. If you remove that specification, Word will use the name of the file on which the macro is running instead. To solve this problem, follow these steps:

1. Select .Name = "CHAP06FH.DOC", (include the space at the end).

2. Press Del.

Save the changes you have made in your macro by pressing the Save button on the Standard toolbar—just as you would in any other file. You can close a macro-editing window by opening the File menu and choosing the Close option.

Testing

Testing your revised macro is largely a process of running the macro and verifying that it works. If it does not work, then you need to proceed to the stage of debugging. When you test your macro, you should have its editing window open to take advantage of the Macro toolbar's testing aids; however, you cannot test a macro while its editing window is the active document window. You must make a document window active and run the test from the Macro toolbar, which remains available as long as you have a macro-editing window open.

The macro toolbar offers the following buttons that can help with testing, as shown in figure 6.7:

✔ **Start** runs the active macro, the name of which is always shown in the Active Macro drop-down list box on the left side of the toolbar. You can change the active macro if you want by selecting a new macro name from this list. Your first step in testing should be to run the macro to see what happens.

✔ **Trace** runs the active macro with a slight variation. Each command in the macro-editing window is highlighted as it runs. If you arrange your document windows so that the active document and the macro-editing windows are both visible, you can watch the actions performed and also see which lines are responsible for them. This is a variation of the testing procedure that provides more information to you about which line caused the problem, if a problem should occur. (If a problem does occur, Word highlights the command that caused it.)

✔ **Continue** restarts the running of a macro if it has stopped for some reason. You might have stopped it using the Stop or Step buttons, for instance.

✔ **Stop** halts the execution of a macro. This button is extremely useful if your macro runs away from you and continues executing after it should have stopped.

✔ **Step** causes one command in a macro to execute and then stops the macro. You can click on Step repeatedly to work through a macro line by line, or you can click on Continue to allow the remainder of the macro to run without interruption.

✔ **Step Subs** functions exactly like Step, except it does not pause after each action taken when you run a macro from within a macro. Step Subs pauses only after the commands in the active macro's editing window are completed. If the active macro were to have another macro you wrote as one of its commands, which is perfectly allowable, Step Subs does not pause after the execution of each command in the embedded macro. It pauses again when it encounters the next command after the embedded macro, whereas Step would pause after each command in the embedded macro. Step Subs is useful when you know that all the commands in the embedded macro are running properly.

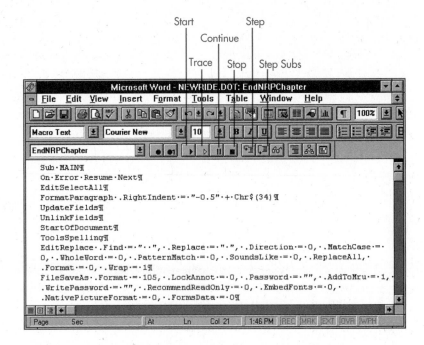

Figure 6.7
The testing buttons
on the Macro
toolbar.

Testing is a no-brainer process. You run the macro if necessary, looking for an error message or a failure of the macro to perform its action. If the macro runs correctly, you are finished with it. If it fails to run correctly, you need to proceed to the step of debugging.

Debugging

Debugging is not a no-brainer process. It can be tedious and time-consuming. That is why your first step in debugging should be to re-record the macro. If this course of action solves the problem, you do not have to proceed further. If recording again does not solve the problem, use the Step button to move through your macro line by line. You need to have both your active document and your misbehaving macro visible on your screen, and you need to follow some straightforward, commonsense rules.

The first rule to follow is that Word is doing exactly what you told it to do, which is not necessarily what you want it to do. You need to look first at what you told Word to do to see if you can find the problem. If a paragraph format is not set correctly, did you set it correctly in the dialog box when you recorded the macro? If fields are not updating, did you press F9 (or was it F8) when you recorded the macro? If the file name is not correct on the save, what file name did you tell it to use? Chances are the source of the problem is something you told the macro to do that was not what you intended to say.

The second rule to follow is that Word Basic commands consist of a name and some parameters that the command might require. The name of the command invokes the action named.

Most Word Basic commands are named after the menu items that you use when you take the same action by hand, as in `FileSaveAs`. Some commands take no parameters, others do. Parameters can appear as an item or list of items separated by commas in parentheses after the command name, as in `AppMaximize ("Microsoft Excel")`. Parameters also can appear as an item or list of comma-separated items following the command name, as in `Font "Arial", 8`. Parameters also can appear in similar lists, but in a form wherein some begin with a period and have an equal sign followed by a value, as in `EditReplace .Find = " ", .Replace = " ", .Direction = 0, .MatchCase = 0, .WholeWord = 0, .PatternMatch = 0, .SoundsLike = 0, .ReplaceAll, .Format = 0, .Wrap = 1`. In this form of a Word Basic command, each item beginning with a period serves to represent the state of a dialog box control bearing a similar name. The value after the equal sign, if it is present, represents the state of that dialog box control. Violating these conventions always leads to problems.

The third rule to follow is that there are just a few things, really, that can go wrong in writing a macro. The following list describes these possibilities, along with common symptoms:

✔ **Infinite Loops.** The macro just keeps on running and will not stop unless you click on the Stop button on the Macro toolbar. The most likely cause is a command that causes the macro to execute a second command, which in turn causes the first command to be reexecuted, causing the second to reexecute, and so on. The most likely cause in a recorded macro is an incorrect On Error statement. Examine the macro carefully using the Step button on the Macro toolbar. When you have found the two statements that are calling each other, break the chain of calls in the most convenient way.

✔ **Misspelled Statements.** You receive a Syntax Error or a Label Not Found Error. Word cannot compensate for your mistakes in typing. Prevention is to record commands whenever possible. Correction is to compare what you typed, character by character, to the examples given in the Word Basic Help file, accessible from the Word Help contents by clicking on Programming with Microsoft Word.

✔ **Extra Characters.** You receive any of a variety of errors, but they will all have "incorrect" or "missing" or a similar word in their description of the problem. Word is interpreting the extra characters as a part of a command and cannot make sense of the command. The solution is to compare what is in the macro-editing window, character by character, to the example in the Word Basic Help file.

✔ **Incorrect Information.** Your macro does not do what you want it to do, but everything else seems correct. Check the values you have assigned to the parameters of your commands; one of these probably is wrong. The easiest way to correct the problem is to select the problem command, switch to an available document, and re-record the command using the Record Next Command button while paying close attention to the settings in the dialog boxes you use. If you have typed the command because you cannot record it, select the command and retype it.

A Note from the Author

The instruction to retype a problem command sounds totally stupid, but sometimes, under the most mysterious of circumstances, it works. In typing the command you did something wrong that you did not see. You might never see it. But the focused activity of retyping the command might cause you to do it correctly the second time.

Debugging a macro can be frustrating. It can be so frustrating that continuous, long efforts at it usually are unproductive. You easily can get trapped in a rut and not see the problem from a fresh perspective. Debugging is best done in short bursts with breaks in between. Stay with the procedures suggested above for the best results. Change only one thing at a time in your macro between each test run. If you change more than one command, you might fix the problem you had but introduce another one.

Tip

You can prevent a command from executing by placing the characters REM, for REMark, in front of them. To do so, place the insertion point in the line you want to remark out, or select the lines, and click on the Add/Remove REM button. This button switches the presence of the remark characters.

If all else fails, both the Word Help file and the Word manual explain how to get technical assistance from Microsoft. The good news about Word Basic, however, is that if you record when you can and type only when you have to, and if you follow these suggested procedures, you should rarely run into a problem with a macro that you cannot solve yourself very quickly.

Using Word Basic

As stressed in Chapter 2, if you use Word, you use the Word Basic macro language. Word is simply a set of Word Basic commands organized into a menu, a set of toolbars, and a set of keystrokes with which you can create documents. Once you go beyond using what Word provides to you, you have entered a new level of using Word Basic. Your involvement with Word Basic can take you to any of three levels of using the language.

The Beginning User

If you are working at the beginning level, you are recording your own macros and adding an `On Error Resume Next` command after the `Sub MAIN` line that begins your macro. You probably are assigning your macros to keystrokes so that you can conveniently use them just by pressing mnemonic keys. Your macros work well. You rarely run into errors or debugging problems. You are automating frequently repeated tasks very effectively, but you are not trying to program in Word Basic. This chapter has shown an example of the kind of macro you are likely to create.

The Intermediate User

When you break into the intermediate level, you start using more commands that cannot be recorded, and you start using commands that look as though they have to be programmed. Your macros involve some flow control and more planning. They also involve some interdependence.

As an example of a macro that an intermediate user might create, consider the problem of inserting figures into a document. Each figure has to be numbered, and you might not insert the figures into the emerging document in the correct order. As you revise, you might insert a new figure in between two existing ones, and you would very much like for the figure numbers to automatically sequence themselves. Furthermore, the information necessary in each figure caption is the same for all figures, with the exception of figure numbers and possibly chapter numbers.

Along with the figure captions, you must insert a figure reference in the text you create to indicate to readers which figure to look at as they read. If you could automate the sequencing of these numbers and coordinate their numbering with the figure captions, you certainly could save yourself lots of work.

As an intermediate user of Word Basic, you can accomplish this task. You have to learn a bit about how Word Basic describes number fields, and you have to program that description to get the kind of number field you need to use. You also have to create two macros, one to insert captions and one to insert references, and make them cooperate with one another. In fact, this process is rather easy. You just have to master the language Word Basic uses to describe sequential number fields.

The first macro you create builds the figure reference in the text. The reason this is the first macro is that it contains the key figure number. The figure caption has to stay in sequence with its reference, which occurs earlier in the text than the caption. To create this macro, perform the following procedure:

1. Double-click on the REC box on the status bar. This action initiates the process of creating a macro.

2. Enter the name **FigureReference** in the Record Macro Name text box (see fig. 6.8).

3. Enter the following description in the Description text box: **Inserts a figure reference**.

4. Select NEWRIDE.DOT, your template for creating chapters containing figures, in the Make Macro Available To drop-down list box.

5. Click on the Toolbar button to assign the macro to a toolbar. This opens the Customize dialog box.

Figure 6.8
Beginning the
recording of the
FigureReference
macro.

6. In the Toolbars tab of the Customize dialog box, drag the name of the macro from the right-hand Categories list box and drop it on an existing toolbar (see fig. 6.9). Use the Standard toolbar for the purposes of this example.

Figure 6.9
Adding the
FigureReference
macro to the
Standard toolbar.

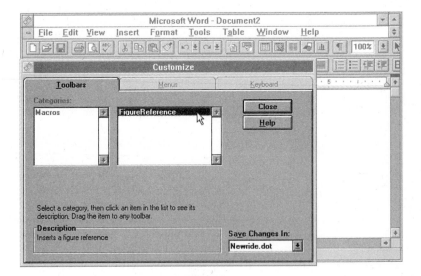

7. In the Custom Button dialog box, which appears automatically, select a button that you want to use, then click on the Assign button. In this example, use a Text button. Abbreviate the name of the macro to FigRef to save space using the Text Button Name text box.

8. Click on the Close button in the Customize dialog box. The recorder starts.

9. Type **figure 1.** at the keyboard.

10. Open the Insert menu and select the Field option.

11. Select Numbering in the Categories list box and Seq in the Field Names list box (see fig. 6.10).

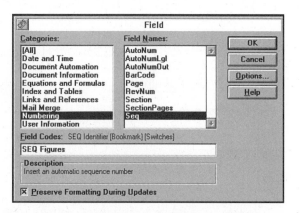

Figure 6.10
Inserting
the number
sequence field.

12. Now practice a bit of Word Basic programming. Enter the name **Figures** in the Field Codes text box. The field code is the Word Basic descriptor of the field. It consists of a field type and several parameters. The name parameter identifies the sequence for Word. You can use several automatic sequences of numbers in the same document as long as they have different names. You could, for instance, have one for figures and one for tables.

13. Click on the Options button.

14. In the Field Options dialog box, shown in figure 6.11, select the type of numbers you wish to use (for this example use 1 2 3) from the Formatting list box on the General Switches tab. Click on the Add to Field button. This action adds the switch \Arabic to the field code, which tells Word Basic to use Arabic numbers to create the figure reference.

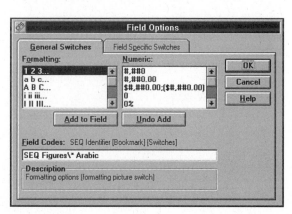

Figure 6.11
The Field
Options dialog
box showing
the General
Switches tab.

15. On the Field Specific Switches tab, as shown in figure 6.12, select the \n switch from the Switches list box. Click on the Add to Field button. This action adds the switch to the field code, which instructs Word to use the next number in the sequence.

Figure 6.12
The Field Options
dialog box
showing the
Field Specific
Switches tab.

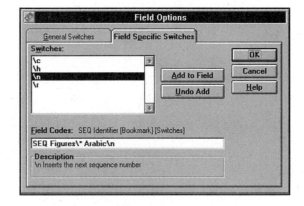

16. Click on the OK button in the Field Options dialog box, and again in the Field dialog box.

17. Click on the Stop button to stop the recorder.

The macro you have created inserts a figure reference of the following form inside the text of your document: **figure 1.1**. Each time you insert another figure reference, the number after the period increments. If you insert a figure reference between two existing figure references, you can update the figure numbers to be in correct sequence by selecting the entire document and pressing F9. (The EndNRPChapter macro you created earlier, in fact, includes this action as one of the things it does!) You do have to edit the macro manually to change the chapter number each time you create a new chapter. Figure 6.13 shows the code recorded for this macro.

After you insert a figure in your text, you need to write a caption for it that matches the figure reference in the figure number. Create such a macro by following this procedure:

1. Double-click on the REC box on the status bar.

2. Enter the name **FigureCaption** in the Record Macro Name text box (see fig. 6.14).

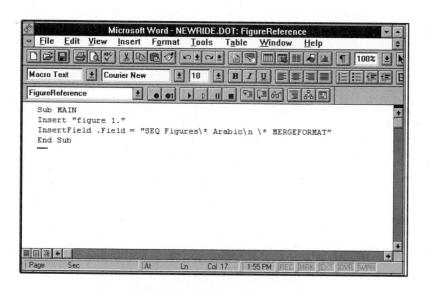

Figure 6.13
The code for the FigureReference macro.

Figure 6.14
Beginning the recording of the FigureCaption macro.

3. Enter the following description in the **D**escription text box: **Inserts a figure caption**.

4. Select NEWRIDE.DOT, your template for creating chapters containing figures, in the Make Macro **A**vailable To drop-down list box.

5. Click on the Toolbar button to assign the macro to a toolbar.

6. In the **T**oolbars tab of the Customize dialog box, drag the name of the macro from the right-hand Categories list box and drop it on an existing toolbar (see fig. 6.15). Use the Standard toolbar for the purposes of this example.

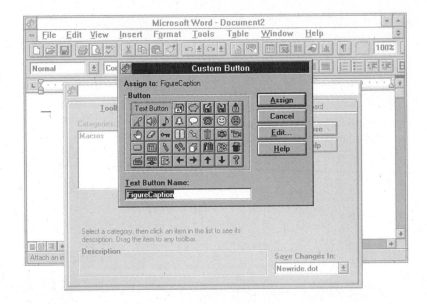

Figure 6.15
Adding the
FigureCaption
macro to the
Standard toolbar
using the Custom
Button dialog box.

7. In the Custom Button dialog box, which appears automatically, select a button that you want to use. In this example, use a Text Button. Abbreviate the name of the macro to FigCap to save space using the **T**ext Button Name text box. Then click on the **A**ssign button to return to the Customize dialog box.

8. Click on the Close button in the Customize dialog box. The recorder starts.

9. Type **Figure 1.** at the keyboard.

10. Open the **I**nsert menu and select the Fi**e**ld option.

11. Select Numbering in the **C**ategories list box and Seq in the Field **N**ames list box (see fig. 6.16).

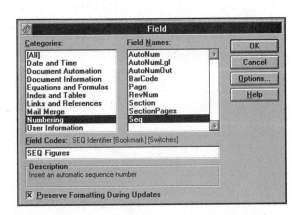

Figure 6.16
Inserting the
number sequence
field for the
figure caption.

12. Now practice a bit of Word Basic programming. Enter the name **Figures** in the Field Codes text box. This number will be in the same sequence as the figure reference.

13. Click on the Options button.

14. In the Field Options dialog box, shown in figure 6.17, select the type of numbers you want to use (for this example use 1 2 3) from the Formatting list box on the General Switches tab. Click on the Add to Field button.

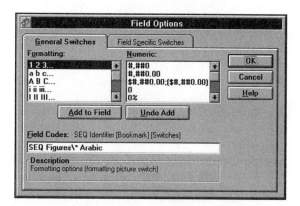

Figure 6.17
The Field Options dialog box showing the General Switches tab for the figure caption.

15. On the Field Specific Switches tab, as shown in figure 6.18, select the \c switch from the Switches list box. Click on the Add to Field button. This action adds the switch to the field code, which instructs Word to use the nearest preceding number in the sequence.

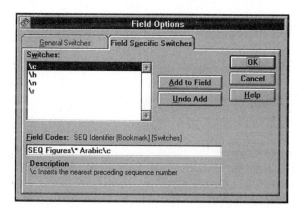

Figure 6.18
The Field Options dialog box showing the Field Specific Switches tab for the figure caption.

16. Click on the OK button in the Field Options dialog box, and again in the Field dialog box.

17. Type a colon and then press Enter.

18. Click on the Stop button to stop the recorder.

This macro inserts a figure caption of the following form:

Figure 1.1:

(blank line here)

The insertion point appears on the blank line following the figure number, ready for you to type the actual caption. The number matches that of the preceding figure reference. Insert your figure reference, then insert your figure. Finally, insert your figure caption. If you insert your figures, references, and captions out of sequence, select your entire document and press F9. The figure numbers will automatically update to the correct sequence. (You do have to edit the macro, however, to set the right chapter number.) Figure 6.19 shows the code recorded for this macro.

Figure 6.19
The code for the
FigureCaption
macro.

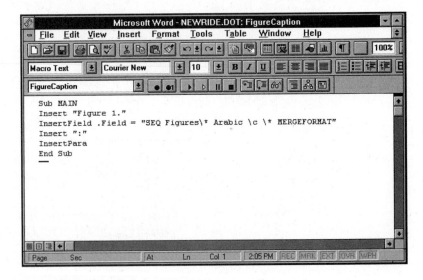

```
Sub MAIN
Insert "Figure 1."
InsertField .Field = "SEQ Figures\* Arabic \c \* MERGEFORMAT"
Insert ":"
InsertPara
End Sub
```

In this intermediate macro, you have mastered some minor aspects of Word Basic programming, mainly with the help of the Field Options dialog box. At this level, more can go wrong with a macro. When debugging, you have to pay special attention to whether all the correct switches appear in all the correct places. Your macros, however, can be very useful, much more so than at the beginning level.

The Advanced Level

At the advanced level, you actually program your macros. You are still recording as much as possible, but you are also entering nonrecordable statements. If you want to get involved with this level of macro building, you need to get the *Microsoft Word Developer's Kit* described in the Word Basic Help file. You also should look for third-party books on the subject of Word Basic. What you can do with macros at this level is absolutely astounding! The next section gives you a peek at what you can do at this level.

Creating Complex Macros

Macros can become very complex and exciting. When you reach the advanced level, you will be creating custom dialog boxes and entering nonrecordable commands. You will be working at the level of a macro programmer. But the benefits of using Word Basic at this level are definitely worth the effort. This section describes the way to create a custom dialog box to manage the macros that you have created in this chapter. It illustrates the way to create a dialog box and how to work with flow control. Your dialog box will present a list of the three macros created in this chapter from which to choose. After you select a macro from the list, clicking on OK starts that macro. The list will be displayed in a combination box.

Recording commands is not the first step in creating a macro at this level and using these features. Few of the commands used by this macro are recordable. You must type the commands instead. Start your macro by performing the following procedure:

1. Open the Tools menu and select the Macro option.

2. Enter the name DialogBox in the Macro Name text box (see fig. 6.20).

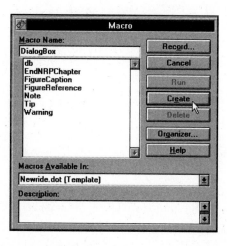

Figure 6.20
Creating the Dialog Box macro using the Macro dialog box.

3. Click on the Create button.

Word opens a macro-editing window that contains only the Sub MAIN and End Sub lines, with a blank line in between. You now are responsible for inserting the macro commands yourself. However, the Macro toolbar gives you some help.

To create the dialog box that you need, click on the Dialog Editor button, the last one on the right. Word's dialog-box editor starts and displays its window on your screen. You use this editor like a drawing program to create your dialog-box code. To create the dialog box for this example, follow these steps:

1. Click on the Dialog Editor button on the Macro toolbar.

2. Drag the border of the dialog box shown in the editor so that it is a convenient size.

3. Double-click on the dialog box to reveal the Dialog Information dialog box, as shown in figure 6.21. Enter the name **My Macros** in the Text$ text box and click on OK. The caption on the dialog box changes to "My Macros".

Figure 6.21
The Dialog
Information
dialog box.

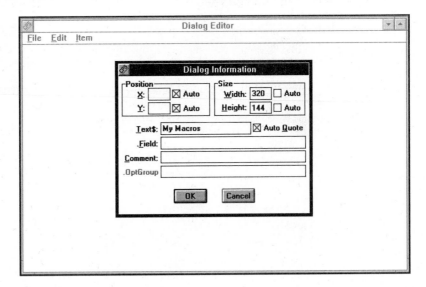

4. Open the Item menu on the Dialog Editor menu bar and select the List Box option. In the New List Box dialog box, select the Combo Box option button and click on OK (see fig. 6.22). Drag the border of the combination box inserted to make it a convenient size.

5. Open the Item menu on the Dialog Editor menu bar and select the Text option. Drag the text control until it is positioned over the combination box and aligned

with the left edge of the combination box. Double-click on the text control. In the Text Information dialog box, type **Select a macro:** in the T̲ext$ text box (see fig. 6.23), then click on the OK button. You now have the directions for using the combination box included in your dialog box.

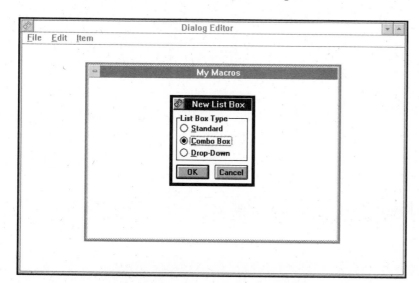

Figure 6.22
The New List Box dialog box.

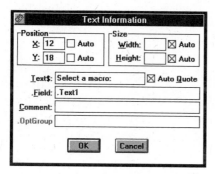

Figure 6.23
The Text Information dialog box.

6. Open the I̲tem menu and select the B̲utton option. In the New Button dialog box, select the O̲K option button and click on the OK button. Drag the button to the position you want it to have.

7. Repeat step 5, except choose the C̲ancel option. This button is automatically aligned under the OK button you just created. Your dialog box is finished. The finished dialog box is shown in figure 6.24.

Figure 6.24
The finished
dialog box.

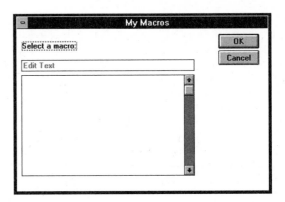

8. Open the File menu and select the Exit option. Answer Yes when the dialog box appears asking if you want to save the dialog box to the clipboard.

9. Place the insertion point between the two commands in the DialogBox macro-editing window and paste the dialog box statements in by clicking on the Paste button on the Standard toolbar.

Examine the dialog-box code that the dialog-box editor has created for you. (The code is shown in figure 6.25. Your code might vary slightly from the code presented here.) It begins with a Begin Dialog command, which announces to Word that you are going to explain the details of how the dialog box will look on the screen. Word reads from the Begin Dialog command to the End Dialog command and learns how to present the dialog box on the screen.

Figure 6.25
The dialog-box
code inserted by
the dialog-box
editor.

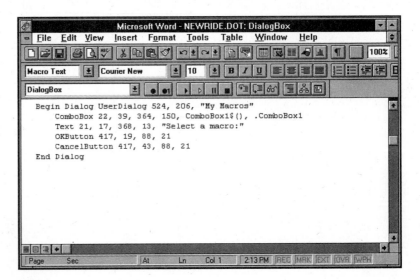

```
Begin Dialog UserDialog 524, 206, "My Macros"
    ComboBox 22, 39, 364, 150, ComboBox1$(), .ComboBox1
    Text 21, 17, 368, 13, "Select a macro:"
    OKButton 417, 19, 88, 21
    CancelButton 417, 43, 88, 21
End Dialog
```

The Begin Dialog command tells Word that this is a UserDialog box (as opposed to other types Word allows), gives its width and height, and provides the caption to display in the title bar.

Each subsequent statement announces a type of control, gives its dimensions, and provides other details about it. The Text control, for example, indicates what text should be displayed within its boundaries. The ComboBox provides the name of the array containing the list of items to be displayed in the combination box, and the name of the variable that will contain the item the user selected. (Variables and arrays are explained in the next three paragraphs.)

You must now add the commands to the macro that fill the list box with options and cause the dialog box to take action when you click on the OK button. To accomplish these feats, you must learn to use both variables and arrays.

A *variable* in Word Basic is a name that refers to a block of memory in your computer. Whenever you use the name, you refer to the contents of that block of memory. You can store information in a variable and use the information you have stored there simply by referring to it by the name of the variable. In this macro, for example, you will use a variable called Dlg.ComboBox1. This variable refers to the place in memory where the characters in the item you select in the combination box are stored after the dialog box is gone from the screen. You can use the characters simply by using the name of the variable, as you will see.

An *array* is a set of variables that share a common name because they are related in the way they are used. Each variable in the array has a subscript number attached to it so that each variable sharing the common name can be differentiated. In this macro, you will use an array called ComboBox1 to store the characters in the items that are displayed in the combination box in the dialog box. This array has three items, because you have three macros that you want to display for selection in the combination box. You reference each variable in the array using the name plus subscript: ComboBox(0), ComboBox(1), ComboBox(2), and so on.

Tip Array subscripts always begin at 0 in Word Basic.

The first code you need to add to your macro must appear before the dialog box code inserted from the dialog box editor. You need to define the array of items to be displayed in the combination box. To do so, add the following lines of code:

```
Dim ComboBox1$(3)
ComboBox1$(0) = "Figure Reference"
ComboBox1$(1) = "Figure Caption"
ComboBox1$(2) = "End NRP Chapter"
```

The first line informs Word to create an array (or dimension it) so that the highest subscript can be 3. This dimensioning statement guarantees you room for four items in the array, because array subscripts start at 0, but it is easier for you to read as a programmer. You look at the statement and you know you have room for your three items because you know you can have at least the three subscripts indicated in the Dimension statement. The next three lines assign the characters between quotation marks to each indicated element in the array.

Now, when Word reads the dialog box code and sees that it is to use an array called `ComboBox$()` to fill the combination box, it takes the array you have just defined and fills the combination box with the items in the array.

After the code inserted from the Dialog Editor, you need to add the following lines:

```
Dim Dlg As UserDialog
Trap = Dialog(Dlg)
If Dlg.ComboBox1 = "Figure Reference" Then
     FigureReference
ElseIf Dlg.ComboBox1 = "Figure Caption" Then
     FigureCaption
ElseIf Dlg.ComboBox1 = "End NRP Chapter" Then
     EndNRPChapter
End If
```

The first line tells Word to take the dialog box that has been described to it and create it in memory. The second line displays the dialog box. You use a variable named Trap to capture the value that the Dialog command passes back to Word when it is finished, because Word will report an error every time the user clicks on the Cancel button. This error simply is normal behavior for Word. If you give Word the variable Trap to store the value that the Dialog command passes back, however, Word does not generate the error.

The remaining three lines create a test to see which item the user selected from the combination box. The variable *Dlg.ComboBox1* is used in this test. This is the variable in which Word stores the item the user selected. The tests are all of the form If Dlg.ComboBox1 contains this value, then take this action. The first test uses the keyword If to create the test. If the characters stored in *Dlg.ComboBox1* are "Figure Reference," then Word executes your macro FigureReference, which is named as the action to take after the Then keyword.

The remaining lines use the ElseIf keyword to initiate the test. These lines execute only if the test immediately preceding them failed. They check to see if the other possible items in the list box were selected, and run the appropriate macro if they were. The End If line simply informs Word that no more tests are following.

Save your macro exactly as you would save any other Word file. Close the file by selecting <u>C</u>lose from the <u>F</u>ile menu.

Obviously, using Word Basic at this level requires some programming skill and some programming knowledge. You have to master variables, arrays, logical tests, and similar concepts. But after you do, you can create custom dialog boxes and get Word to perform even more complex actions in an automated way. For example, you now have a dialog box that, with a little modification, can serve to manage any set of macros you would like to make available through it. You can add this dialog box to the menu, giving yourself and other users a convenient way to access macros. Figure 6.26 shows the finished dialog box running.

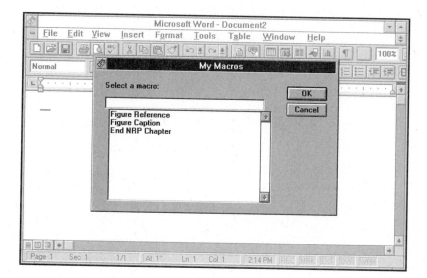

Figure 6.26
The finished My Macro dialog box.

The finished code appears on the *Inside Microsoft Office Professional* companion disk.

Note The next chapter explains how to add the My Macro dialog box to the menu. The process is the same as if you were to assign it to the menu from the Record Macro dialog box.

Chapter Snapshot

Customizing Word enables you to make the word processor do more of the work for you. You make Word tell you what you need to know about a document in the ways you need to know it. In this chapter, you will learn ways to perform the following customization techniques:

By the time you complete this chapter, you will be able to perform tasks that make Word for Windows 6.0 do your bidding.

CHAPTER 7

Customizing Word for Windows

by Forrest Houlette

Microsoft advertises Word as "the world's most popular word processor." One of the reasons for that popularity is that you can customize Word to suit your needs. Migrating from Word 2.0? You can get your familiar toolbar back if you want it. Don't like the way the menu is organized? You can rearrange it if you like. You can make Word work your way.

Making Word Work for You

Customizing Word is a matter of working with two items found on the Tools menu, Customize and Options. Each of these options opens a tabbed dialog box. From the Customize dialog box, you can change the items that appear on toolbars, change key assignments, and add, rearrange, and subtract items from the menu. From the Options dialog box you can adjust many other features of Word, changing the behavior of the word processor by doing so. One other menu option, the Toolbars item on the View menu, also is involved in customization. Using the Toolbars dialog box that this item activates, you can create new toolbars, reset default toolbars, and select which toolbars are displayed. The following sections explain each of the customizations that you can perform to tune Word to your preferences.

Note Four of the tabs displayed in the Options dialog box are covered in the sections of this book that deal with using the features the folders govern. The Print tab is explained in "Printing the Document" in Chapter 1 and "Setting Up a Document" in Chapter 5. The Spelling tab is explained in "Spelling Checker" in Chapter 2. The Grammar tab is covered in "Grammar Checker" in Chapter 2. And the AutoFormat tab is covered in "Using AutoFormat" in Chapter 3. Chapter 7 covers the Customization tabs and the other Options tabs.

Customizing Toolbars

You can use as many toolbars at the same time as you want with Word 6.0. You also can create your own custom toolbars or change existing toolbars, both through the Toolbars dialog box (see fig. 7.1). You access this dialog box by opening the View menu and selecting the Toolbars item.

Using Multiple Toolbars

As noted before, Word enables you to use multiple toolbars. To show a toolbar on the screen, check the box next to its name in the Toolbars list box. To hide a toolbar from view, uncheck the check box. Using multiple toolbars gives you immediate access to most of Word's features, but displaying multiple toolbars does reduce the size of the workspace, as shown in figure 7.2.

Tip The number of toolbars displayed in the Toolbars list box changes depending on what you are using Word to do. If you are in outline view, for example, the Outlining toolbar appears on the list, although it does not normally.

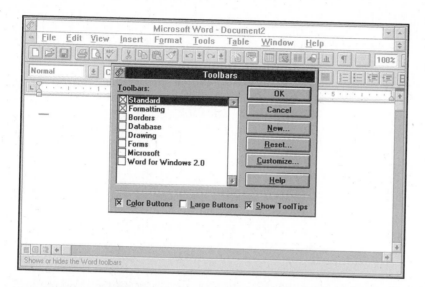

Figure 7.1
The Toolbars
dialog box.

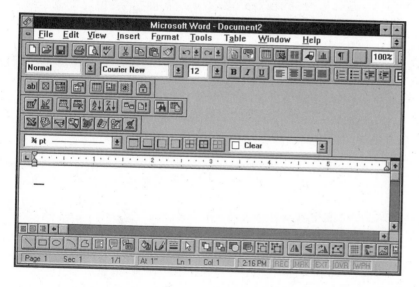

Figure 7.2
Plenty of toolbars,
but little space to
work in!

Changing the Appearance of Toolbars

You can use the check boxes along the bottom edge of the Toolbar dialog box to control the appearance of toolbars. These check boxes control the following characteristics of a toolbar:

✔ Color Buttons switches the display of color buttons. Unchecking this box causes the buttons to appear in shades of gray.

✔ Large Buttons switches the size of the buttons between large and small. The large buttons are easier to see, especially if you work with one of the higher screen resolutions, like 1024×768.

✔ Show ToolTips governs whether ToolTips are displayed when you point the mouse pointer at a button. ToolTips can be useful, but they might become distracting or annoying once you are familiar with the toolbars you display. You can turn ToolTips off by unchecking this box.

Creating New Toolbars

To create a new toolbar, click on the New button in the Toolbars dialog box. Word displays the New Toolbar dialog box, shown in figure 7.3.

Figure 7.3
The New Toolbar
dialog box.

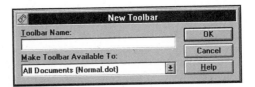

Enter a name for the toolbar, which will be displayed in its title bar when it floats, in the Toolbar Name text box. Open the Make Toolbar Available To drop-down list box to select the template that will contain the toolbar. Then click on the OK button.

Word creates your new toolbar as a floating toolbar and opens the Customize dialog box to the Toolbars tab (see fig. 7.4). You use the Toolbars tab to add buttons to your new toolbar.

Figure 7.4
The floating
toolbar and the
Customize dialog
box opened to the
Toolbars tab.

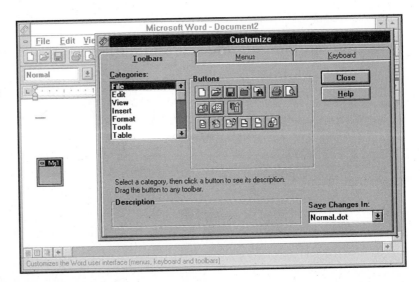

To add a button to your toolbar, follow this procedure:

1. Select a category of Word commands in the Categories list box. Word shows the buttons for that category in the Buttons box.

2. Click on a button to see which function is associated with it. The function appears in the Description box.

3. Drag the appropriate button and drop it in the location you want it on the toolbar.

If you select one of the last four categories on the list, Macros, Fonts, AutoText, or Styles, Word opens the Custom Button dialog box, shown in figure 7.5. This dialog box offers you a variety of graphical buttons and the option of creating a text button.

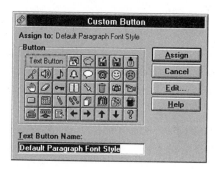

Figure 7.5
The Custom Button dialog box.

You can perform the following actions in this dialog box:

✔ If you like one of the graphical buttons provided, click on it and then click on the Assign button.

✔ If you prefer to use a text button (the default), type the text that you want to appear on the face of the button in the Text Button Name text box and click on the Assign button.

✔ If you would like to create a custom graphical button, click on the Edit button. Word opens the Button Editor, shown in figure 7.6. Select a color from the Colors palette and click on any square in the grid to change the pixels represented by that box to the color you have selected. You can see your work in the Preview box. And you can move your entire painting one square on the grid in any direction by clicking on the appropriate arrow button. Using the arrows, you align your picture on the button.

Tip Even if you click on the Cancel button in the Custom Button dialog box, Word places a button on your toolbar. To remove an unwanted button, open the Customize dialog box by selecting the Customize option on the Tools menu. Select the Toolbars tab, then drag the unwanted button from the toolbar and drop it on the Toolbars tab.

I

Word for Windows

Figure 7.6
The Button Editor.

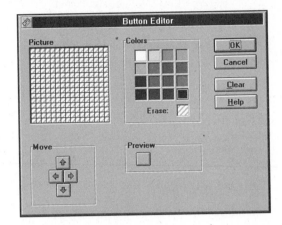

Changing Existing Toolbars

You can change toolbars in several ways. To change the buttons on the toolbar, follow these steps:

1. Open the Toolbars dialog box by selecting Toolbars from the View menu.

2. Select the toolbar to change in the Toolbars list box.

3. Click on the Customize button.

You can also open the Customize dialog box to work on a toolbar by opening the Tools menu and selecting the Customize option.

4. Drag buttons from the Customize dialog box to the toolbar to add buttons, or drag buttons from the toolbar to the dialog box to delete buttons. To create custom buttons, follow the procedure described in the preceding section.

5. Click on the Close button when you are finished.

If you have changed one of Word's default toolbars, you can change it back to its original state easily. Follow these steps:

1. Open the Toolbars dialog box by selecting Toolbars from the View menu.

2. Select the toolbar to reset in the Toolbars list box.

3. Click on the Reset button.

4. Select the template to which the change applies using the drop-down list box titled Reset changes made to '*toolbar name*' for:. Then click on the OK button.

If you have created a custom toolbar and no longer want it, you can delete it by following these steps:

1. Open the Toolbars dialog box by selecting T̲oolbars from the V̲iew menu.

2. Select the toolbar to delete in the T̲oolbars list box.

3. Click on the D̲elete button. (This button replaces the Reset button after you select the toolbar.)

4. Click on the Y̲es button in the confirmation dialog box that appears.

Obviously you can create toolbars that fit your working style and manage them easily in Word. You can also do the same sorts of things with menus.

Customizing Menus

You can customize Word's menus in much the same way as you can customize toolbars. You can add an entire menu to the menu bar or remove a menu from the menu bar. You can also add items to or delete items from any of the menus. You perform these actions using the M̲enus tab in the Customize dialog box, which you access by opening the T̲ools menu and selecting C̲ustomize. Figure 7.7 shows the Menus tab.

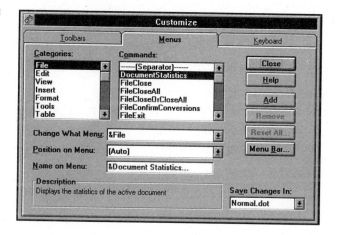

Figure 7.7

The Menus tab in the Customize dialog box.

Tip Before you do any work on the menu, make sure you have selected the correct template in the Sa̲ve Changes In drop-down list box.

Adding and Deleting Menu Items

To add an item to a menu, follow this procedure:

1. Open the Tools menu, select the Customize option, and select the Menus tab.

2. Select the category of the item you want to add in the Categories list box.

3. Select the command you want to add in the Commands list box.

4. Select the menu to which you want the command added in the Change What Menu drop-down list box.

5. Select the position on the menu where you want the item added using the Position on Menu drop-down list box. Selecting a current item changes the Add button to Add Below, and the new item is placed below the current item.

6. Edit the text that will appear on the menu in the Name on Menu text box. The ampersand (&) indicates that the following letter will be the hot key for the menu item. Make sure the hot key does not conflict with any other item on the menu.

7. Click on the Add or Add Below button.

8. When you have finished making changes, click on the Close button.

To delete a menu item, follow these steps:

1. Open the Tools menu, select the Customize option, and select the Menus tab.

2. Select the item you want to remove in the Position on Menu drop-down list box.

3. Click on the Remove button.

4. When you have finished making changes, click on the Close button.

Adding and Deleting Menu Bar Items

To add a menu to the menu bar, follow these steps:

1. Open the Tools menu, select the Customize option, and select the Menus tab.

2. Click on the Menu Bar button. This action opens the Menu Bar dialog box (see fig. 7.8).

3. Type the name of the menu you want to add in the Name on Menu Bar text box. Place an ampersand (&) before the hot key, and make sure the hot key does not conflict with any other item on the menu bar.

4. Select the position where you want to add the menu using the Position on Menu Bar list box. Selecting an existing menu causes the Add button to become Add After, and the new menu is added to the right of the existing menu.

5. Click on the Add or Add After button.

Figure 7.8
The Menu Bar
dialog box.

6. When you have finished making changes, click on the Close button to return to the Customize dialog box, then click on the Close button to end the procedure.

To rename an existing menu, follow these steps:

1. Open the <u>T</u>ools menu, select the <u>C</u>ustomize option, and select the <u>M</u>enus tab.

2. Click on the Menu <u>B</u>ar button to open the Menu Bar dialog box.

3. Type the new name for the menu in the <u>N</u>ame on Menu Bar text box. Place an ampersand (&) before the hot key, and make sure the hot key does not conflict with any other item on the menu bar.

4. Select the menu you want to rename using the <u>P</u>osition on Menu Bar list box.

5. Click on the R<u>e</u>name button.

6. When you have finished making changes, click on the Close button to return to the Customize dialog box.

Once you rename a menu, you can change it back to its original name only by retyping the original name or resetting the menu. If you have to reset the menu, you might lose other changes you have made. Keep a record of the exact name as it was before you changed it to save wasted effort fixing a mistake. The procedure for resetting the menu is the next section in this chapter.

To remove a menu from the menu bar, follow these steps:

1. Open the <u>T</u>ools menu, select the <u>C</u>ustomize option, and select the <u>M</u>enus tab.

2. Click on the Menu <u>B</u>ar button to open the Menu Bar dialog box.

3. Select the menu you want to remove using the <u>P</u>osition on Menu Bar list box.

4. Click on the <u>R</u>emove button. Click on the <u>Y</u>es button in the confirmation dialog box that appears.

5. When you have finished making changes, click on the Close button to return to the Customize dialog box.

Resetting the Menu

If you have made mistakes or want to get back to the menu that shipped with Word, follow this procedure to reset the menu.

1. Open the Tools menu, select the Customize option, and select the Menus tab.

2. Click on the Reset All button.

3. Click on the Close button to return to the Customize dialog box. Click on the Close button in this dialog box to end this procedure.

Customizing the Keyboard

The Word 6.0 keyboard also is completely customizable. You can assign any command, macro, style, AutoText entry, or font to a key so that when you press that key the assigned action is performed. Word is shipped with many keys preassigned, and you can reassign these if you want. If you want to return to the default Word key layout, you can reset the keyboard to its original state.

 If you are wondering which keys are assigned which functions, you can always print a list of the key assignments. Open the File menu, select the Print option, select Key Assignments in the Print What drop-down list box, and click on the OK button.

To make a keystroke assignment, follow these steps:

1. Open the Tools menu and select the Customize option.

2. In the Customize dialog box, select the Keyboard tab (see fig. 7.9).

Figure 7.9
The Customize
dialog box showing
the Keyboard tab.

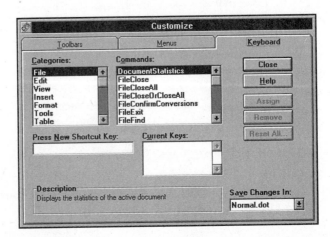

3. Select the template you want to alter in the Save Changes In drop-down list box.

4. Select a category of commands from the Categories list box, and select the exact command from the Commands list box.

5. Make sure that the Press New Shortcut Key text box has the focus. Press the key combination that you want to use to invoke the selected command. The current key assignment for the selected command appears in the Current Keys list box and the Description box shows what the selected command does. If the keystroke you have chosen to assign is already assigned to another command, a Currently Assigned To message appears above the Description box to let you know which command your intended new keystroke already invokes.

6. Click on the Assign button.

7. When you have finished making changes, click on the Close button.

To remove a keystroke assignment from a command, follow these steps:

1. Open the Tools menu, select the Customize option, and select the Keyboard tab.

2. Select the template you want to alter in the Save Changes In drop-down list box.

3. Select a category of commands from the Categories list box, and select the exact command from the Commands list box.

4. Select the key assignment to remove in the Current Keys list box.

5. Click on the Remove button.

6. When you have finished making changes, click on the Close button.

As noted, you can remove key assignments and make new assignments as often as you like. If, however, you want to return to the original key assignments, perform the following steps:

1. Open the Tools menu, select the Customize option, and select the Keyboard tab.

2. Select the template you want to alter in the Save Changes In drop-down list box.

3. Click on the Reset All button.

4. Click on the Yes button in the confirmation dialog box that appears.

You might find that you want to reassign keys so that the commands and macros you most desire to use from the keyboard are assigned to mnemonic keys. Word now is shipped with so many preassigned keys that you might find it impossible to find free keys that you can remember as representing a command. For example, you might find it convenient to assign the FigureCaption macro to the Ctrl+F keystroke, and the figure reference to the Ctrl+Shift+F keystroke, *F* being a good mnemonic key for *Figure*. However, Word already has assigned these keys, along with Alt+Shift+F and Ctrl+Alt+F, to other commands. Do not feel locked in by these assignments. Design your keyboard to meet your needs. You can always reset or change the key assignments later.

Adjusting Other Options

You can customize Word in many other ways. The Customize dialog box offers the ways to change the features most commonly involved in customization. However, the Options dialog box (see fig. 7.10) provides the capability to alter Word's behavior in many other ways. The 12 tabs in this dialog box control the way Word appears on the screen, the way Word interacts with files, and numerous other features. You should be sure to review each of the tabs to make sure that Word is taking the actions you want as it runs.

Figure 7.10

The Options dialog box.

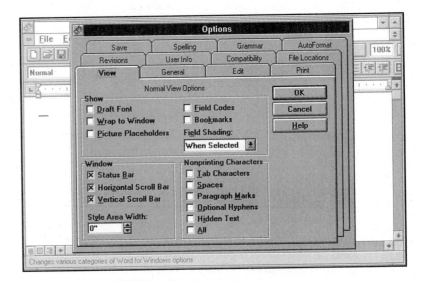

Remember, 4 of the 12 tabs are explained in relation to the processes they govern. The Print tab is explained in "Printing the Document" in Chapter 1 and "Setting Up a Document" in Chapter 5. The Spelling tab is explained in "Spelling Checker" in Chapter 2. The Grammar tab is covered in "Grammar Checker" in Chapter 2. And the AutoFormat tab is covered in "Using AutoFormat" in Chapter 3. The following sections explain the tabs that cover more general features of Word.

General

The General tab (see fig. 7.11) covers some miscellaneous features of Word, including screen appearance, help features, and measurement units.

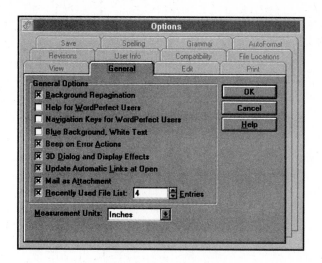

Figure 7.11
The General tab in
the Options
dialog box.

The controls within the General tab are described in the following list:

✔ The Background Repagination check box governs whether Word repaginates documents as you are working. You probably want background repagination most of the time. But if you are working on a long document, the long breaks for repagination at certain working junctures might become annoying.

✔ The Help for WordPerfect Users check box switches on and off special help for those migrating from WordPerfect for DOS. When you press a WordPerfect for DOS keystroke, Word displays help explaining the Word command that performs the same function.

✔ The Navigation Keys for WordPerfect Users enables and disables the Word emulation of WordPerfect keystrokes involving the PgUp, PgDn, Home, End, and Esc keys. If you prefer the WordPerfect key assignments for these keys, check this box.

✔ The Blue Background, White Text check box, when checked, converts Word's workspace to the named color scheme.

✔ Beep on Error Actions governs whether Word beeps when you make a mistake. Check it if you need the audible reminder, uncheck it if you prefer silence from your word processor.

✔ 3D Dialog and Display Effects governs whether the Word window and dialog boxes have a three-dimensional look. Check or uncheck this box to give Word the appearance you prefer.

✔ Update Automatic Links at Open, when checked, causes automatic links to be updated when you open a file. If you would prefer to know when and which links are updating, however, uncheck this box and use the Links option on the Edit menu to update automatic links.

✔ The Mail as Attachment check box allows you to attach documents to mail messages if you have an e-mail system available to you. Check it if you have e-mail, uncheck it if you do not.

Word has special e-mail features that you can use directly from the menus. You can attach to a document routing slips that automatically send a document to the individuals, either sequentially or at the same time, who need to see it. Reviewers also can annotate a document or add revisions to a document using the Annotation option on the Insert menu and the Revisions option on the Tools menu.

✔ The Recently Used File List check box governs whether the list of the last opened files appears on the File menu. If you check it, set the number of files to include in the list using the spin box.

✔ The Measurement Units drop-down list box enables you to choose the unit of measurement that Word displays on its rulers and uses to calculate dimensions in most of its dialog boxes.

Even though the Options dialog box does not offer hot keys for the tabs, you can move from one tab to another using the Ctrl+Tab key combination and the Ctrl+Shift+Tab key combination. The former cycles through the tabs to the right, the latter to the left. If a control on the tab has the focus, however, these keystrokes will cycle through all the controls on the tab before cycling through the tabs.

View

The View tab (see fig. 7.12) governs which elements of a document you see on the screen. It offers three groups of controls that control what to show in the workspace, which elements of a document window to display, and which special characters to display on-screen. The View options vary slightly depending on the view option selected from the View menu.

The Show group offers the following controls in Normal, Outline, and Master Document views.

You can select among Normal, Outline, and Master Document views using the View menu.

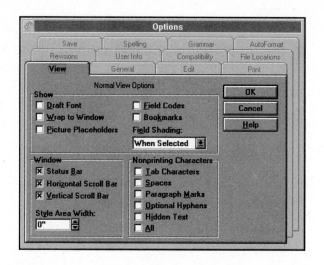

Figure 7.12
The View tab in the Options dialog box.

✔ The <u>D</u>raft Font check box controls whether formats and graphics are displayed as a part of a document. When the box is checked, character formatting appears only as bold and underlined, and graphics appear as empty boxes. Using <u>D</u>raft Font can speed your work with a draft and printing of drafts but does not give you an accurate view of your document's layout.

✔ The <u>W</u>rap to Window option, when checked, causes the text to be wrapped at the current document window border. You can use this option to avoid the annoying horizontal scroll when you are typing on a line wider than the current window can display; however, using this option does not give you an accurate view of your document's layout.

✔ The <u>P</u>icture Placeholders option, when checked, displays a box instead of a picture. Using this option speeds scrolling through a document and gives you a complete sense of the text format; however, you do not see the pictures on screen.

✔ The <u>F</u>ield Codes option, when checked, causes fields to display as the text codes that create the field rather than as the result of those codes. In a date field, for example, you see the instructions for creating the date rather than the date itself. This option is useful if you know how to work with field codes and need to see the codes to make adjustments.

✔ The Boo<u>k</u>marks option, when checked, causes bookmarks and links to be displayed in grayed brackets. This option is useful when you want to see where bookmarks and linked information appear.

✔ The Fi<u>e</u>ld Shading drop-down list box enables you to select whether—and if so, when—Word displays nonprinting shading around fields. You can select from Never, When Selected, and Always. When Selected is the default.

When working in page layout view, the following two controls replace the Wrap to Window check box:

✔ The Object Anchors check box, when checked, causes an anchor icon to appear that shows where an object is anchored to a paragraph. Using this option enables you to tell when moving a paragraph might affect an object.

✔ The Text Boundaries check box switches whether dotted lines appear to show the boundaries of paragraphs, columns, objects, and frames. Using this option enables you to see the exact placement of these items on the page.

The remaining two groups in this tab are fairly self-explanatory. The Window group offers check boxes that control whether the Status Bar, Horizontal Scroll Bar, and Vertical Scroll Bar are displayed. It also provides a spin box that enables you to set the Style Area Width, which displays the style of each paragraph at the left of the workspace. The Nonprinting Characters group provides check boxes that control whether the named nonprinting characters are displayed on the screen. Use these controls to set up your display so that your workspace is comfortable and familiar.

Edit

The Edit tab controls how Word behaves when you use editing features, including when you edit pictures. These controls determine which keys perform certain editing functions and how drag-and-drop features work.

Figure 7.13
The Edit tab
in the Options
dialog box.

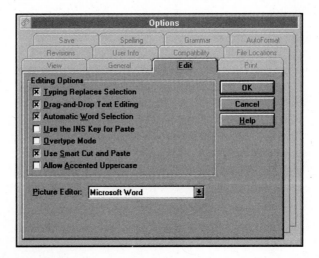

The Edit tab provides the following controls:

✔ The Typing Replaces Selection check box, when checked, causes a selection to be deleted when you start typing, before the characters you type appear on the screen.

The net effect is that the selection appears to be replaced by what you type. When unchecked, this control causes what you type to appear, scrolling the selection to the left.

✔ When checked, the <u>D</u>rag-and-Drop Text Editing option enables you to copy and move a selection by dragging with the mouse. When this box is unchecked you must perform these operations using the <u>E</u>dit menu.

✔ When you check the Automatic <u>W</u>ord Selection check box you can select an entire word just by selecting a part of it. When this box is unchecked you select only the characters you have dragged over with the mouse.

✔ The <u>U</u>se the INS Key for Paste option enables you to paste data from the Clipboard by pressing Ins rather than Shift+Ins.

✔ <u>O</u>vertype Mode, when checked, has the same effect as pressing Ins. Each character you type replaces the character at the insertion point. Unchecking the box returns you to inserting new characters to the right of the character at the insertion point.

✔ Use <u>S</u>mart Cut and Paste deletes unnecessary spaces when you cut information from a document or paste information into a document. If you included extra spaces at the end of a sentence in the cut operation, Word removes the extra spaces (or adds more spaces, if necessary) to fit the context into which you paste.

✔ <u>A</u>llow Accented Uppercase enables Change Case and the proofing tools to suggest and insert accented uppercase letters when you are working in text formatted for the French language.

✔ The <u>P</u>icture Editor drop-down list box enables you to select the graphics editor you want to use to create pictures for your Word documents. The list offers the options of Microsoft Draw, Microsoft Word, PowerPoint Presentation, and PowerPoint Slide.

Save

The Save tab (see fig. 7.14) provides controls that govern Word's behavior in saving documents. These options enable you to set up automatic saving, to embed fonts in a document, and to set passwords on documents.

The Save tab gives you the following controls:

✔ Always Create <u>B</u>ackup Copy, when checked, causes Word to copy the current version of the document to a file with a BAK extension before saving any changes. You then have two versions of the document at all times: the version you opened before making changes and the version you saved with the changes.

✔ Allow <u>F</u>ast Saves causes Word to save only the changes to a document, not the entire file. As a result, the saving process is faster.

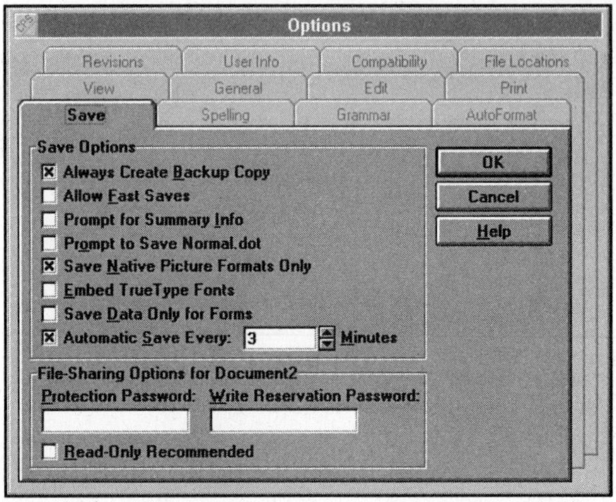

Figure 7.14
The Save tab in the Options dialog box.

Tip You cannot keep a backup copy if you enable fast saves. These two options are mutually exclusive. Word enables you to check only one or the other.

- ✔ Checking Prompt for Summary Info causes Word to display the Summary Info dialog box as you save each new document.
- ✔ Prompt to Save Normal.dot, when checked, causes Word to display a dialog box that asks if you want to save changes to the NORMAL.DOT template each time you close Word.
- ✔ Save Native Picture Formats Only, when checked, causes Word to store only the Windows version of an imported graphic with the document file. This choice saves file space. If you import documents back and forth between the Macintosh and Windows platforms, however, you should uncheck this box. Unchecking this box causes Word to store both versions of the graphic, making transport back and forth across the platform barrier easier.
- ✔ Embed TrueType Fonts, when checked, causes the TrueType fonts used in your document to be stored in its file. When others open and read the document, they can see the fonts you used even if those fonts are not installed on their computer.
- ✔ The Save Data Only for Forms check box enables you to create special templates called forms and use them to create database records. When this box is checked, the data on your form is stored in a single record, enabling you to import the record into a database.

A *form* is a template that you have protected using the **P**rotect Document command on the **T**ools menu. It contains tables and some special fields that you can insert using the For**m** Field command on the **I**nsert menu. When you use a form as the template for a document, you can enter information only in the table grid and controls provided. Because the form is protected you cannot change the rest of the document. You can save the entire form document, or only the data entered into the fields. The purchase order template included with Word is a sample of a form.

✔ The Automatic **S**ave Every check box causes Word to save your document on the schedule of minutes that you set using the spin box. You should select this option to guard against losing parts of your document if your computer loses power or is accidentally reset. These events happen more often than you think. If you work rapidly, three minutes might be a good choice.

The File-Sharing Options group enables you to set passwords on a document. You have the following options:

✔ Enter a **P**rotection Password in the text box to keep other users from opening a document. Unless other users enter the correct password, they cannot open the document.

✔ Enter a **W**rite Reservation Password to prevent users from saving changes to a document. Other users can open the document, but they cannot save it without entering the correct password.

✔ For a moderate level of protection, check the **R**ead-Only Recommended check box. When other users attempt to open the document, they see a message that recommends opening the document for reading only. However, they can open the document for both reading and writing if they want.

Revisions

The Revisions tab (see fig. 7.15) gives you control over the way revisions are marked in your document. You can select the color and style for each type of revision mark. You can make these choices for text inserted into a document, text deleted from a document, and text marked as revised in the margin.

You can mark revisions to a document by opening the **T**ools menu, selecting the Re**v**isions option, checking **M**ark Revisions While Editing in the Revisions dialog box, and clicking on the OK button. All further changes you make to the document are formatted as you specify in this tab. You can use the other controls in the Revisions dialog box to accept revisions made to a document, to compare two documents, and to merge revisions from the revised version of a document into the original document.

Figure 7.15
The Revisions tab
in the Options
dialog box.

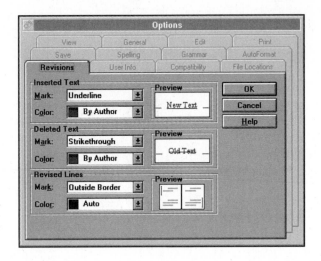

In each of the Inserted Text, Deleted Text, and Revised Lines groups, you can select the Mark used to identify the item and the Color used to code the item using the drop-down list boxes. In the Color drop-down list boxes, you can select to code each different author as a different color or to select a single color for all revisions. In the Mark drop-down list boxes, you can select from the various character styles and formats offered. The preview boxes show you the effects of the changes you have made.

User Info

The User Info tab enables you to set the information for the user of the system, as shown in figure 7.16. The controls are straightforward. Enter your **N**ame, **I**nitials, and **M**ailing Address in the text boxes provided, then click on the OK button.

On systems used by several people, you can build an AutoExec macro that collects the user information from the current user and sets the user information before work starts.

Compatibility

The Compatibility tab (see fig. 7.17) gives you the chance to change the way Word imports files from other word processors. As a rule, you should modify the options presented here only when file conversion has not been successful. However, experimentation is relatively risk free. You can always exit the document without saving and reconvert it by opening the original file again.

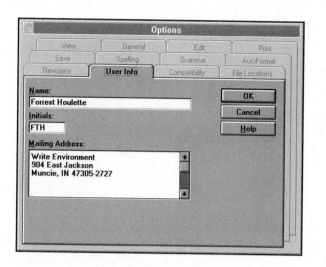

Figure 7.16
The User Info tab in the Options dialog box.

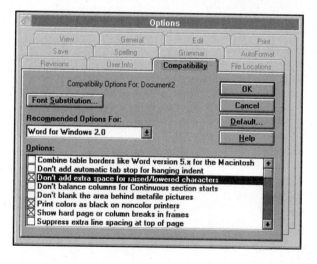

Figure 7.17
The Compatibility tab in the Options dialog box.

If your converted document is not formatted as you wish, perform the following action:

1. Open the **T**ools menu, select the **O**ptions item, and click on the Compatibility tab.

2. Review the available conversion options and make the adjustments you think necessary. When you click on OK, your document's formatting adjusts to reflect the changes you have made.

3. After you have the look you want for documents converted from the word processor in question, click on the **D**efault button to make the conversion options you have selected the default options applied when converting from that word processor.

The specific controls offered by the Compatibility tab are as follows:

✔ The Recommended Options For drop-down list box shows the word processor Word recognizes as having created the converted document. You can make a new selection if Word did not recognize the correct word processor.

✔ The Options list box offers 12 conversion options that Word applies in converting files. The options applied to your document are checked. To indicate that additional options should apply, check the box next to the description of the option. To prevent an option from applying, uncheck its box.

If you have a question about whether an option will help, try it and click on OK. If you do not like the changes, remove it. You can easily experiment using the Compatibility tab.

✔ The Font Substitution button opens a dialog box that enables you to select fonts that substitute for fonts used in the document but not installed on your machine. If any substitution has taken place, clicking on this button reveals the Font Substitution dialog box, shown in figure 7.18.

Figure 7.18
The Font
Substitution
dialog box.

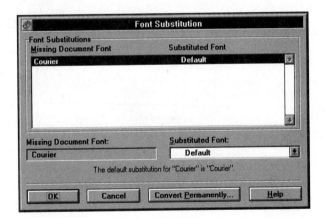

To use this dialog box, click on one of the fonts listed in the Missing Document Font list box. Open the Substituted Font drop-down list box and select the font you want to substitute for the missing font. Click on the OK button to apply your changes. Click on the Convert Permanently button to make the changes permanent for the document. (In other words, Word no longer sees the font as having been substituted.)

File Locations

The File Locations tab displays a list of the directories where Word stores nine types of files (see fig. 7.19). This tab enables you to review these locations and make changes in the directories specified. You should make such changes if you have moved the files from a previous directory to a new directory, as when consolidating all the clip art images installed by various programs on your system into a single directory that all the programs access.

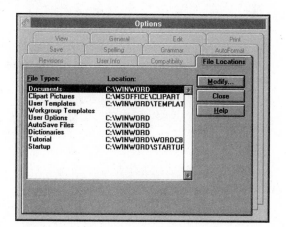

Figure 7.19
The File Locations tab in the Options dialog box.

If you have not installed a network, you will not see a directory for workgroup templates.

To change the directory specifications, follow this procedure:

1. Select the directory to change in the File Types list box.

2. Click on the Modify button or double-click on the directory in the list box.

3. In the Modify Locations dialog box, either type the new location into the Location of Documents list box or use the Directories and Drives controls, which work like those in the Open dialog box, to specify the new directory. If you need to create a directory, click on the New button, type the name in the resulting Create Directory dialog box, and click on OK. Then click on OK in the Modify Locations dialog box.

4. Repeat steps 1–3 for each change you need to make.

5. Click on the Close button in the File Locations tab.

Be careful with the changes you make. Word will look for the exact directory you specify. If you make a mistake, you might experience errors which report that Word could not locate certain files, or dialog boxes that should show a list of files might be blank. If such problems occur, double-check the file locations for accuracy.

Using Macros To Customize Word

As you saw in Chapter 6, "An Introduction to Word Macros," you can customize Word using macros. When you create a macro, you create a custom command. You can attach these commands to a button, a menu, or the keyboard by using the techniques described earlier in this chapter. Besides creating custom commands, you can use special macros to customize the behavior of Word on certain actions. There are five such macros; table 7.1 identifies them and explains when they run.

Table 7.1
The Auto Macros in Word

Macro	Action
AutoExec	Runs when Word starts
AutoOpen	Runs when a file opens
AutoNew	Runs when a new file is created
AutoClose	Runs when a file is closed
AutoExit	Runs when Word exits

Using these macros, you can customize Word's behavior at each of these events. For example, with AutoExec, you could use Word to organize your start of work each day. Word could use the Shell command to launch the contact list you have stored in an Access database, launch Notepad and load your to-do list, and open Excel and load the worksheets you need to use during the day. Such a macro would look like this:

```
Sub MAIN
Shell "msaccess.exe contact.mdb"
Shell "notepad.exe todo.txt"
Shell "excel.exe workday.xls"
End Sub
```

Tip The string included in the `Shell` command must have the name of the application's executable file and any command-line arguments, such as the name of the file to open, that you want to include.

With AutoOpen, you can build appropriate start-up routines into each document template you create. For example, for documents that are lists that have to be updated, such as notes on conversations that you have during the day, you could insert an `EndOfDocument` command in the AutoOpen macro. Then you would not have the need to scroll manually to the end of the file each time you opened it; the AutoOpen macro would do the scrolling for you. In fact, you insert the date automatically as well using an `InsertDateTime` command. Such a macro would look like the following:

```
Sub MAIN
EndOfDocument
InsertDateTime
End Sub
```

With AutoNew, you can automatically save each new file by prompting yourself for a file name and to save the file. This macro would need an `InputBox$()` command to collect the file name and a `FileSaveAs` command to save the new file. Such a macro would have the following lines:

```
Sub MAIN
FName$ = InputBox$("What name do you want to use for this file?",
"New File")
FileSaveAs .Name = FName$, .Format = 0
End Sub
```

With AutoClose you can automatically apply formatting to a document by using the AutoFormat feature. As a result, you would not have to be concerned about how you typed the document or whether you applied the right styles. You type, and when you close the file the right styles are applied by a `FormatAutoFormat` command. Such a macro would look like the following:

```
Sub MAIN
FormatAutoFormat
End Sub
```

AutoExit can easily perform the clean-up operations you would like to perform as Word exits. You could make the macro perform the reverse action of your AutoExec macro. To follow through with these examples, this macro would use the `SendKeys` command to send the equivalent of Alt+F+X (the equivalent of Alt+Eile+Exit) to each running application. You must follow this command with an `AppActivate` command to make sure each application receives the keystrokes. Such a macro would look like the following:

```
Sub MAIN
SendKeys "%fx"
AppActivate "Microsoft Access "
SendKeys "%fx"
AppActivate "Notepad - TODO.TXT"
SendKeys "%fx"
AppActivate "Microsoft Excel - WORKDAY.XLS"
End Sub
```

Tip

The % sign indicates that a keystroke is an Alt+character keystroke in the SendKeys command. You must include the exact title bar title for each running application in the AppActivate command.

How would you create such macros? Follow this procedure:

1. Open the Tools menu and select the Macros option.

2. Enter the name of the macro you want to create in the Macro Name text box. Make sure you are storing the macro in the appropriate template by using the Macros Available In drop-down list box.

3. Click on the Create button.

4. After the macro editing window is open, enter the lines that make up your macro.

5. Close and save the macro file as you would any file.

Using the Auto macros, you can make Word perform some dazzling tasks when any of the Auto events occurs. You can make your work easier by using these macros to automate tasks you would otherwise perform each time one of the events occurred.

Organizing Macros

After you create macros in one template, you might want to move them to another template, delete them, or rename them. Word 6.0 provides a utility for performing such operations: the macro organizer. To use this facility, perform the following steps:

1. Open the Tools menu and select the Macro option to display the Macro dialog box, shown in figure 7.20.

2. Click on the Organizer button to display the Organizer dialog box, then click on the Macros tab (see fig. 7.21).

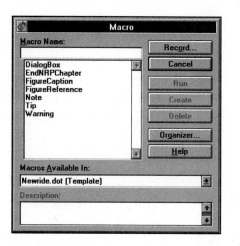

Figure 7.20
The Macro
dialog box.

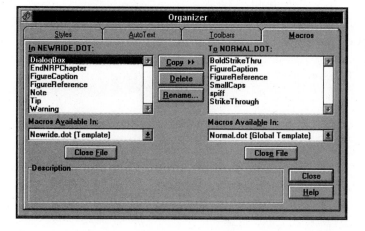

Figure 7.21
The Macros tab in
the Organizer
dialog box.

3. Use the Macros Available In drop-down list boxes to select the files that you want to work with. If you want to work with only one file, click on the Close File button below one of the list boxes. If a file you want is not listed on the drop-down list, use the Close File button, which then converts to an Open File button. Click on the Open File button to reveal a standard Open dialog box, and select the template for use.

4. To copy macros, select the macro or macros in the In list box and click on the Copy button. Use the Ctrl and Shift keys with mouse clicks to select multiple macros—such as Ctrl+click for discontinuous selection and Shift+click for continuous selection—as you would in File Manager.

The In list box is always the one that has the focus, so clicking on either list box switches their names between In and To. The arrow on the Copy button changes direction depending on which list box has the focus.

5. To delete a macro, select it and click on the Delete key. Click on Yes or Yes to All in the confirmation dialog box that appears. You can make multiple selections using the Ctrl and Shift keys.

6. To rename a macro, select it in one of the list boxes and click on the Rename button. In the Rename dialog box, type the new macro name in the New Name text box and click on OK.

7. When you are finished with the macro organizer, click on the Close button.

Part Two

Excel

Chapter Snapshot

Excel 5 is one of the most popular Windows-based spreadsheets in the computer industry. This chapter jump-starts you to using Excel. Specifically, you are introduced to the following Excel 5 basics:

This chapter does not go into much detail about these procedures. The remaining chapters in Part Two will cover Excel 5 much more thoroughly.

CHAPTER 8

Excel Quick Start

by Rob Tidrow

P robably the second most popular application (next to Word 6) in the Microsoft Office suite is Microsoft Excel 5. Excel 5 is a powerful spreadsheet program that helps you collect, chart, manage, and analyze data.

This chapter provides a quick tour of Excel 5, while offering you opportunities to use functions and to create a worksheet, a chart, and formulas. This chapter will not answer all your questions about Excel. Use it as the first of many lessons toward learning and understanding Excel 5.

This chapter provides a hands-on tutorial for creating a simple example worksheet and a chart. Within this tutorial, you are presented with concepts, terms, and procedures that will help you get up and running on Excel quickly.

Looking At Excel's Features

Although Excel 5 has made it easier than ever to build spreadsheets, create charts, and integrate data from various sources, you will need to learn a great deal in order to understand all the components and functions of Excel. Before you start entering numbers and text, acquaint yourself with Excel 5's interface and its vast array of features.

What Excel 5 Offers

With the release of Excel 5, Microsoft has greatly expanded its best-selling spreadsheet to offer many features that have been available in other spreadsheet programs. These features enable novice as well as experienced users to increase their spreadsheet power. Some of the new features include the following:

✔ **More Wizards.** Among the key features in Excel 5 are Wizards, which help you create sophisticated worksheets and charts. The Function Wizard is designed to assist you in creating functions to include in your worksheets. Another Wizard is the TextImport Wizard, which helps you import text files into Excel. The Tip Wizard offers timely suggestions and hints as you are working. You become more familiar with the Function Wizard in Chapters 10, "Mastering Excel Functions," and 11, "Advanced Worksheet Capabilities."

✔ **Tabs in Workbooks.** A workbook now contains several sheets, which can be worksheets, chart sheets, or macro sheets. A *workbook* is a single file on your system. To switch between sheets in a workbook, click on its tab at the bottom of the workbook, much like you use the tabs on manila folders to flip through your filing cabinet to select individual file folders.

✔ **Customizable Toolbars.** Excel 5 provides great flexibility in placing and customizing toolbars. Not only are you offered more toolbars, you also can create buttons on them, reposition buttons, add new ones, and delete buttons and toolbars. You also can create your own toolbars. See Chapter 14, "Customizing Excel 5," for more information on customizing and adding toolbars.

✔ **Pivot Tables.** Sometimes you want to summarize or view your data in different ways. With previous versions of Excel, setting up these situations was like creating brand-new worksheets or charts. With Pivot Tables and the PivotWizard, you can create summary tables and view them as quickly and easily as dragging fields on your tables.

✔ **OLE 2.0.** OLE (object linking and embedding) 2.0 creates an environment in which you can edit embedded data in place. When you embed in Excel data created in an OLE-compliant application, just double-click on the embedded object, and Excel's toolbars and menus take on the "personality" of the native application. This makes editing and updating data quicker and easier.

✔ **Microsoft Query.** Query replaces Q+E from Excel 4 to help you work with external databases so that you can access database files from various sources.

✔ **Visual Basic for Applications.** Sometimes referred to as the "common macro language," Visual Basic for Applications (VBA), Excel version, enables you to extend the programming environment to create full-featured applications in Excel. The Excel macro language still is supported in Excel 5, but VBA is the wave of the future for building your applications in Excel. It also offers debugging tools and dialog box sheets. See Chapters 14, "Customizing Excel 5," and 15, "Mastering Visual Basic for Applications," for more information on using VBA.

This book is limited in the depth that it can go into with each application in the Office suite, and some of these features might not be examined in detail. For a thorough view of these and other Excel 5 features, pick up a copy of *Inside Excel 5 for Windows,* published by New Riders Publishing.

Excel 5's Interface

The elements of the Excel screen include both basic Windows features, such as scroll bars and windows, and Excel-specific items, such as toolbars and menus. The primary document in Excel is called a *workbook*. Think of a workbook as a ledger book or binder that stores all your critical information about a project, sales report, or any other data you need to keep. Like a normal book binder, each workbook is made up of *sheets*. These sheets can be worksheets or chart sheets. As a new feature to Excel 5, you can switch between sheets by clicking on tabs at the bottom of the workbook. Figure 8.1 shows you worksheets, tabs, and a workbook.

Excel 5 provides a number of different toolbars. In Chapter 14, "Customizing Excel 5," you learn how to customize and change the look of these toolbars, but the following sections introduce you to some of the more common elements you will need to know as you work on your worksheets and charts.

You can find the name and function of a toolbar button by moving the mouse over the button and waiting a second or two. Excel shows you the name of the button in a banner next to your pointer and displays its function in the status bar at the bottom of the screen. This feature comes in handy when you have several toolbars and various buttons on your screen.

The standard toolbar at the top the screen helps you select choices that might be buried several menus or dialog boxes deep in the Excel menu structure. From this toolbar, you can open workbooks, print and save worksheets or chart sheets, and ask for help. Table 8.1 shows the individual buttons and tells you their functions.

Figure 8.1
The parts of the
Excel screen.

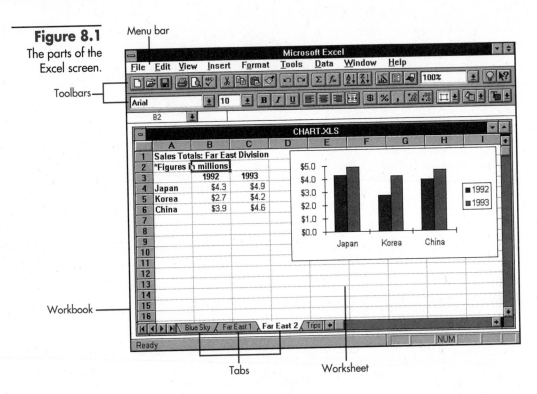

Menu bar

Toolbars

Workbook

Tabs

Worksheet

Table 8.1
Excel's Standard Toolbar

Button	Name	Function
	New Workbook	Creates a new workbook
	Open	Opens a document
	Save	Saves the active workbook
	Print	Prints the active workbook
	Print Preview	Shows the active document in print preview mode

Button	Name	Function
	Speller	Checks the spelling of the document
	Cut	Cuts the selection to the Clipboard
	Copy	Copies the selection to the Clipboard
	Paste	Places the Clipboard contents at the insertion point
	Format Painter	Copies and pastes formats for cells and objects
	Undo	Undoes the last action or command
	Repeat	Repeats the last action or command; this is the same as the redo feature in Word 6
	AutoSum	Inserts the SUM function and shows sum range
	Function Wizard	Starts the Function Wizard
	Sort Ascending	Sorts selected rows in ascending order
	Sort Descending	Sorts selected rows in descending order
	ChartWizard	Activates the ChartWizard
	Text Box	Inserts text or text box
	Drawing	Turns the drawing toolbar on or off

continues

II

Excel

Table 8.1, Continued
Excel's Standard Toolbar

Button	Name	Function
100% ⬇	Zoom Control	Sets the view of the document
💡	Tip Wizard	Turns the TipWizard toolbar on or off
▶?	Help	Displays Help

Immediately below the standard toolbar is the formatting toolbar. This toolbar enables you to select fonts, change point sizes, add character enhancements, and customize other sheet attributes. Table 8.2 shows you each of the buttons on this toolbar.

Table 8.2
Excel's Formatting Toolbar

Button	Name	Function
Arial ⬇	Font	Sets the font for the selection
10 ⬇	Font Size	Sets the font size for the selection
B	Bold	Boldfaces the selection
I	Italic	Italicizes the selection
U	Underline	Underlines the selection
▤	Align Left	Left-aligns the selection
▤	Center	Centers the selection

Button	Name	Function
	Align Right	Right-aligns the selection
	Center Across Columns	Centers the selection across columns
	Currency Style	Changes the selected cells to default currency style
	Percent Style	Changes the selected cells to default percent style
	Comma Style	Changes the selected cells to default comma style
	Increase Decimal	Adds one decimal place to the number format
	Decrease Decimal	Removes one decimal place from the number format
	Borders	Enables you to select a border for the selection
	Color	Sets the color for the selection
	Font Color	Sets the color for the selected font

Creating a New Worksheet

Now that you are familiar with some of Excel's tools and naming conventions, you can start creating your own workbook and adding worksheets to it. The rest of this chapter leads you through some simple examples for getting up to speed quickly with Excel 5 and using some of its basic charting and formatting features.

For details about worksheets, charts, functions, and other Excel components, the remaining chapters in Part Two provide more insight into these areas. Turn to those chapters when you are comfortable with the basics presented in this chapter.

Worksheet Basics: Columns, Rows, and Cells

When you start Excel, it opens up a brand-new workbook that has 16 blank worksheets. You can start working in any of these worksheets, close them, or open up an existing workbook that you have saved previously. For this example, you can just start working on the topmost worksheet, labeled Sheet1.

On the worksheet is a grid of columns and rows (see fig. 8.2). *Columns* run vertically and are labeled alphabetically, starting with *A. Rows* run horizontally and are labeled numerically (1, 2, 3, and so on).

Figure 8.2
Worksheets are divided into rows and columns.

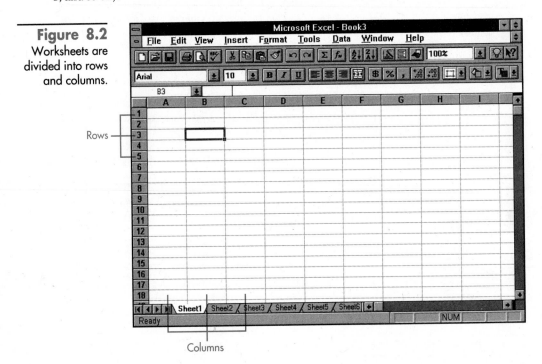

You can tell which column you are in by looking at the top of the worksheet for the corresponding letter, such as A, B, and so on. Likewise, by looking at the left side of the worksheet, you can find the row number you are in. The intersection of a column and row is called a *cell.* Cells are where you do most of your work in Excel and are named by the column and row that make them up. This is called the *cell address* or *reference.* In figure 8.3, for example, the word Team is located at cell reference C5.

Cell reference   Formula bar   Cell

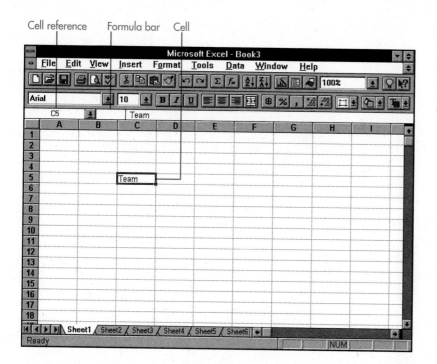

Figure 8.3
Cells and cell references are the basic components of Excel worksheets.

To enter data in a cell, first select it by moving the mouse pointer over the desired cell and clicking. This places the insertion point in the active cell, which is highlighted on-screen with a bold border around it. After you select a cell, you can start entering data from your keyboard or numeric keypad. Above the worksheet, in the formula bar (see fig. 8.3), the cell reference and the text you type appear.

An Example Worksheet: Monthly Team Scores

To help you get acquainted with Excel's basic worksheet components, make sure you have Excel started and a blank worksheet on-screen. Next, follow these steps to create a worksheet of monthly points scored by a hypothetical sports league.

The worksheet for this example is included on the *Inside Microsoft Office Professional* companion disk. It is named SCORES.XLS and can be found in the Chapter 8 files.

1. Move the mouse pointer over cell reference C5 and click. This places the insertion point at C5. Notice that the border around the selected cell is highlighted and that the cell reference is displayed in the formula bar.

2. Type **Team** and press Enter. The insertion point moves to cell C6, and you can continue to enter data. In cell C6 enter **Lions** and press Enter. Continue adding team names using the names **Panthers**, **Eagles**, and **Tigers** until the worksheet looks like the one in figure 8.4.

Figure 8.4
Entering team names in the SCORES.XLS example worksheet.

Although using a mouse in Windows greatly increases efficiency, you might find that keyboard shortcuts help you during data entry in Excel. To move from cell to cell, use the left- and right-arrow keys to move left or right. Use Tab to move to the next cell to the right. You also can use the up- and down-arrow keys to move to the cell above or below your current cell.

3. Enter the months in which the points are scored. In this example, the season runs from January through May. Move to cell reference D5 and type **January.** Press Enter.

Before you continue, you should save the work you've already done on this worksheet. Click on the Save button in the standard toolbar to open the Save As dialog box. In the File **N**ame list box, type the name **SCORES.XLS** and click on OK or press Enter. This saves the workbook with the name SCORES.XLS. The actual worksheet is still named Sheet1 (as shown at the bottom of the worksheet), but you learn in Chapter 9, "Understanding Excel

Worksheet Concepts," how to rename worksheets to fit your needs. As you continue with this exercise, be sure to save your work periodically by clicking on the Save button.

4. Enter the next four months (through May) in cells E5, F5, G5, and H5. The worksheet should now look like figure 8.5.

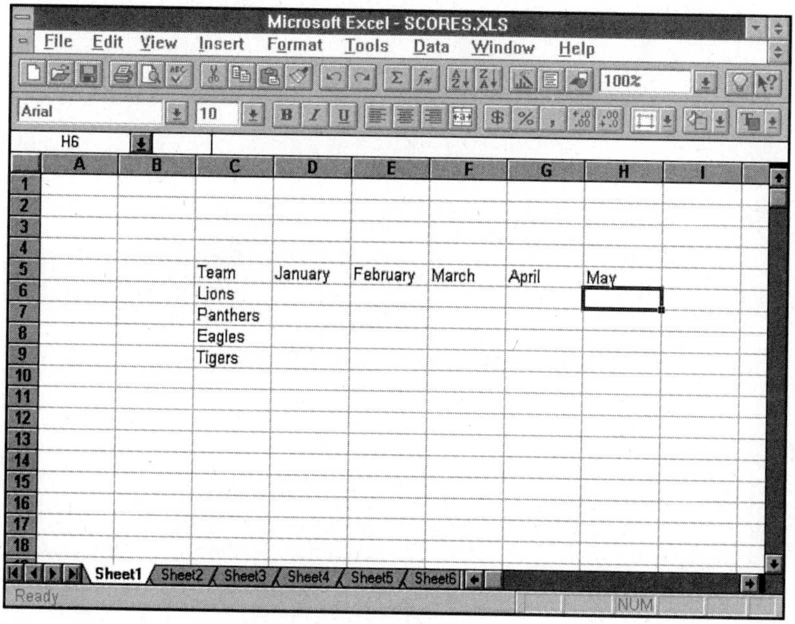

Figure 8.5
Entering the months of the season in the SCORES.XLS worksheet.

(screenshot of Microsoft Excel - SCORES.XLS showing a worksheet with the following data in row 5: Team, January, February, March, April, May. Column C contains: Team, Lions, Panthers, Eagles, Tigers in rows 5-9. The cell reference box shows H6, and Sheet tabs Sheet1 through Sheet6 appear at the bottom.)

Tip

As a new feature to Excel 5, you can automatically fill in certain types of data that you previously had to fill in manually. One example is the months of the year. In the preceding step, to fill in the months after January, just click on the cell containing January and move your mouse pointer to the bottom right corner of the highlighted cell. This is called the *fill handle.* Grab the fill handle with the mouse and drag it to the right until the mouse pointer is in cell H5 and release the mouse button. The months from February through May automatically fill the cells. This is called AutoFill, and you will learn more about this in Chapter 9, "Understanding Excel Worksheet Concepts."

5. Now that you have your teams and months in place, you can fill in monthly score totals for each team. This is sometimes referred to as *raw data.* Use table 8.3 as a guide.

Table 8.3
Monthly Team Scores

Team	January	February	March	April	May
Lions	25	85	49	18	127
Panthers	46	81	107	57	159
Eagles	17	42	23	74	28
Tigers	45	85	43	51	57

The worksheet should look like the one shown figure 8.6.

Figure 8.6
The SCORES.XLS
worksheet with
monthly team
scores entered.

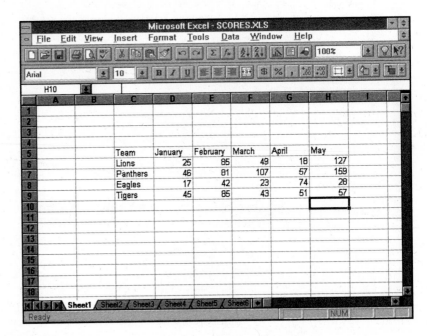

6. To help you remember which type of information you are looking at in this worksheet, place a report title in the upper left corner of the sheet. Move the insertion point to cell A1, type **American Conference**, and press Enter. Notice how the title flows into cell B1 so that you can see the entire title.

7. In cell A2, enter **Monthly Team Scores 1994** and press Enter. The worksheet should look like the one shown in figure 8.7.

You've now set up a worksheet with team names, months, and monthly scores. At this point, you can enhance the worksheet by providing a more friendly looking worksheet, moving

things around, creating a chart, or manipulating the data in a variety of ways to suit your needs. In the next section, you total the monthly team scores to see which team has scored the most points per month.

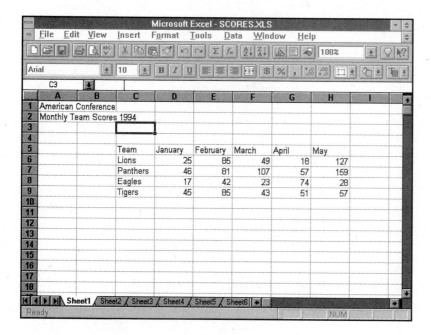

Figure 8.7
Entering the report title in SCORES.XLS.

Data Manipulation: Summing Monthly Scores

One of the main functions of a spreadsheet program like Excel is to calculate data for you automatically. These calculations can be as a simple as basic arithmetic or as complex as a probability statement. In Excel, you use *formulas* to get the results you are looking for. Because many mathematical calculations, such as adding up columns of data, never change, Excel provides you with a number of *functions;* these are predefined formulas that you can use or add to other formulas. The SUM function, for instance, is used so often that it is placed on the default standard toolbar as the AutoSum button (refer to table 8.1).

Later in this chapter, you will see some examples of functions and how to use them in your workbooks. See Chapter 10, "Mastering Excel Functions," however, for more in-depth coverage of functions. You also might want to pick up a copy of *Inside Excel 5 for Windows*, published by New Riders Publishing, to fully exploit these functions.

To become familiar with formulas, and particularly the SUM function, return to the SCORES.XLS worksheet and total the monthly scores for each team. Perform the following steps:

1. In cell I5, enter **Total** and press Enter. This is the column in which the total scores will be placed.

2. Make sure cell I6 is selected and click on the AutoSum button on the standard toolbar. Excel examines the data around cell I6 and assumes that you want to add up (that is, *sum*) the data in the range D6 through H6.

When you select a number of cells in a worksheet, this is called a *range*. When you refer to a range, use the form *ColumnRow:ColumnRow*, such as D3:H6. This is the same as saying "D6 through H6."

3. Press Enter or click on the AutoSum button again to have Excel add up the values in cells D6:H6. The total in this example is 304. If you click on cell I6, the cell shows the sum but the formula bar shows the actual formula, =SUM(D6:H6).

4. You can use the same method to calculate the other teams' scores, or you can copy the AutoSum formula into the cells. To copy the AutoSum formula, first click and hold down the mouse button in cell I7. Next, drag the mouse to cell I9. All three cells are selected now. Click on the AutoSum button, and Excel automatically sums the total scores for the Panthers, Eagles, and Tigers.

Figure 8.8 shows the completed worksheet.

Although many of your Excel spreadsheets might be numerically based (such as sales reports, sports scores, or number of videos sold in a region), you also might have employee lists, address lists, and the like. Excel provides a variety of ways to manage and view lists.

As you look at the totals for each of the teams in this example, you might want to list them in descending order of points scored. This way you can quickly see which team has scored the most runs in the season. This is one way that you can manage lists in Excel.

To sort the scores in descending order (highest to lowest), make sure the SCORES.XLS spreadsheet is still open and perform the following steps:

1. Select cells C6:I9.

2. Choose **D**ata, **S**ort. The Sort dialog box appears (see fig. 8.9).

3. In the **S**ort By pull-down list box, choose Total. Click on **D**escending to sort the team totals from highest to lowest.

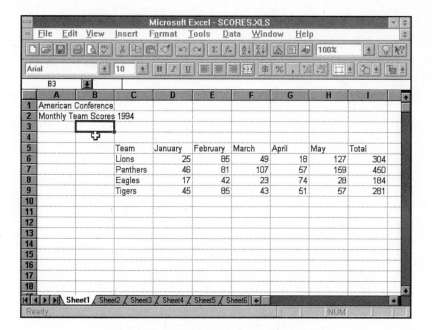

Figure 8.8
Using the
AutoSum button to
automatically
calculate the total
monthly scores.

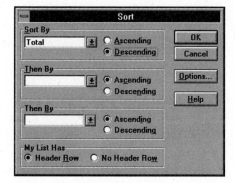

Figure 8.9
The Sort dialog
box asks you how
you want to sort
your selection.

4. Press Enter or click on OK. Excel sorts your data and displays the teams in
   descending order, based on the total points scored during the season (see fig.
   8.10).

Now you need to format the worksheet a little to make it more presentable and readable.

Figure 8.10
Sorting points scored during the season from highest to lowest using Data, Sort.

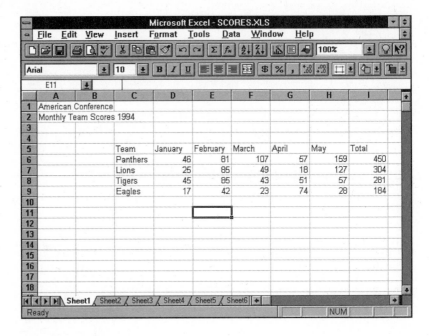

Formatting Data

When you enter data into worksheets, Excel uses the default template to format the data. Usually, this is the Normal template, which is activated when you open a new workbook. Although this format is functional, it is not always that attractive to look at.

You might, for instance, want to make the Total column bold to make it stand out, or make it a different color than the rest of the data. You might want to center the report title to make it clear what data the reader is looking at. Excel also enables you to use TrueType fonts, so you can take advantage of the TrueType font investment you might have made for your other Windows-based applications, such as CorelDRAW!, PowerPoint, or Word for Windows.

To apply different formatting features to your worksheets, you have a couple of choices. You can, for instance, use Excel's AutoFormat feature, which automatically sets up your document in a pleasing and professional-looking way. You also can manually format the worksheet. In the following examples, you will learn how to format using both methods.

The following examples show you how to autoformat the table of team scores in the SCORES.XLS worksheet.

1. In the SCORES.XLS worksheet, select the entire table—the range C5:I9.

2. Select For mat, Autoformat. The AutoFormat dialog box appears, in which you can select the type of formatting you want for your table. In the Table Format list,

Excel provides several different choices, including Simple, Classic 1, Colorful 2, and so on.

See Chapter 9 for more information about each of the **T**able Format options, including examples of what each looks like.

3. Choose the format you want to apply to your table. The Sample area in the AutoFormat dialog box shows you an example of what your table will look like. For this example, scroll down the list of formats, choose 3D Effects 1, and click on OK or press Enter. Figure 8.11 shows the formatted table.

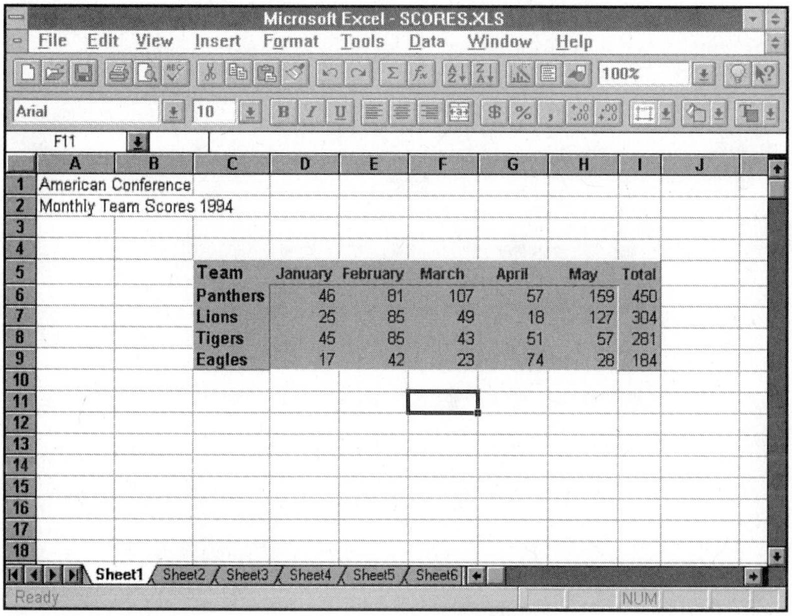

Figure 8.11
The 3D Effects 1 table format displays your data in a professional-looking format.

Now that you have formatted the table, you can set up your title across the top of the worksheet. First, widen the columns the titles are in so that all the text fits in one column.

Move the mouse pointer between the A and B column headings at the top of the worksheet until the pointer changes to a double arrow (see fig. 8.12), then double-click. This changes the column width so that your titles fit in one column (the A column). The worksheet should look like the one shown in figure 8.13.

Figure 8.12
Changing the column width to fit the worksheet title in one column.

Double-click to change column width

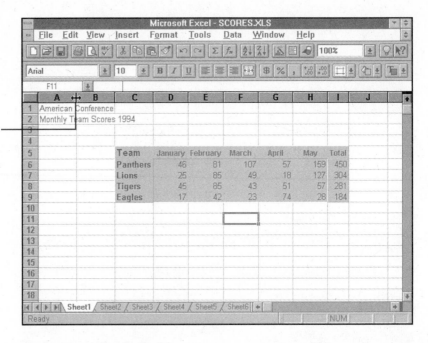

Figure 8.13
The worksheet title fitting into column A.

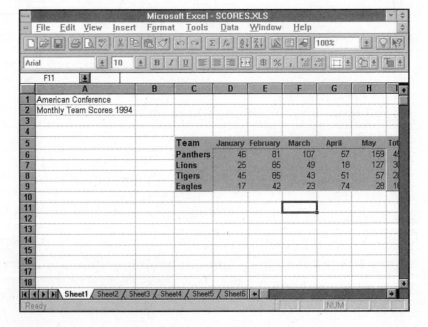

To help readers see the worksheet titles, you might want to add special character formatting to them, such as bold, italic, or underline. Excel makes it easy to add these effects to your data. In most cases, you can select the cell in which the character, number, word, or set of words appear and click on the appropriate formatting buttons on the formatting toolbar.

The following example uses the SCORES.XLS worksheet and formats the titles to make them easier to view and read.

1. Make sure the SCORES.XLS worksheet is open and click in cell A1. This selects the title American Conference and displays it in the formula bar.

2. Because this is to be the top title of the worksheet, you should make the typeface larger than the other characters on the page. One way to do this is to change the font and then change the font size.

   For this example, choose the font named Times New Roman (you should have this font if you installed Windows 3.1 and all its standard fonts) from the Font list on the Format toolbar.

> Remember, you can find the name and function of a toolbar button by moving the mouse over the button and waiting a second or two. Excel displays the name of the button in a banner next to your pointer and displays its function in the status bar at the bottom of the screen. This feature comes in handy when you have several toolbars and various buttons on your screen.

3. Next, click on the Font Size tool on the Format toolbar and choose 20. This changes the font size to 20 points, making it larger than the other characters on the worksheet.

4. Click once each on the Bold and Underline buttons on the format toolbar. This makes the title bold and underlined.

5. Now, select cell B1 and change the font size to 14 points (keep the font the same, which should be Arial in this example). Add bold italic to this title. The worksheet should look similar to the one shown in figure 8.14.

You now can center the title over the table, making the worksheet easy to read and more professional-looking.

1. Select the range A1:L2.

2. Click the Center Across Columns button on the Formatting toolbar (refer to table 8.2).

   You also can choose Format, Cells and click on the Alignment tab. Choose the Center across option and press Enter or click on OK. This centers the title across the range of cells so that it is centered over the table (see fig. 8.15).

Figure 8.14
Adding character formatting to your titles to help them stand out.

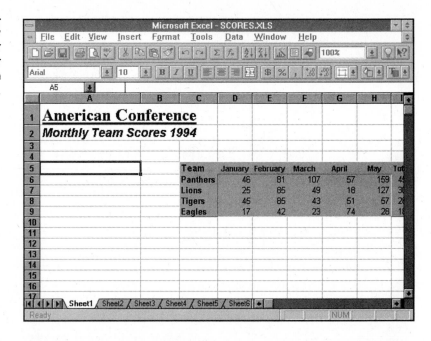

Figure 8.15
Centering the title over the table of team scores.

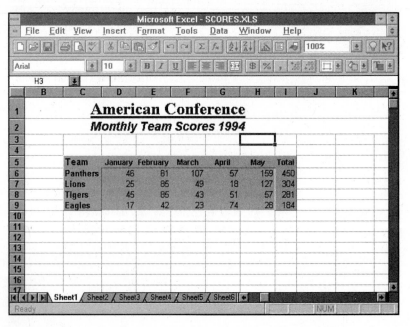

Now the worksheet is set up with its data and is formatted to make it more readable. The following sections show you how to expand the worksheet's functionality and purpose by introducing formulas, functions, and charts.

Using Excel Formulas and Functions

Formulas are the cornerstone of any spreadsheet, including Excel worksheets. You create formulas to perform the calculations that you don't want to, whether because of speed, redundancy, or accuracy. With a calculator or a pencil and pad of paper, a math or accounting whiz could perform all the same functions of an electronic spreadsheet, but why should she? Excel lets you worry about the most important part of the spreadsheet: acquiring and disseminating the data. You don't have to worry about calculating every mathematical formula just to get the results you need.

How To Use Formulas

To enter a formula in a worksheet, you first must decide what calculation you want and where you want to perform it. Earlier, you calculated the sum of the scores for each team using the AutoSum feature. In another worksheet, you might calculate the gross sales of a product during the last fiscal year. Or, you might need to find the interest gained on an invested stock.

When you enter a formula in a cell, you need to preface it with an operator, such as the equal sign (=), plus sign (+), minus sign (-), or at sign (@). (When you use any of the last three operators, Excel changes it to an equals sign.) You must also tell Excel where to find the data, whether it is in an individual cell or a range of cells. You can name these cells or point to them. When you point to cells, these cells are surrounded by a dotted line, called a *moving border*. This border helps you see which cells are selected when you create the formula.

See Chapter 9, "Understanding Excel Worksheet Concepts," for more detail about other ways to enter and use formulas in your worksheets, including how to point to a range of cells.

To create formulas in your worksheets, perform the following steps:

1. Double-click on the cell that you want to include the formula.

2. Enter an equal sign (=) or other operator. Remember that Excel changes these other operators to equal signs.

3. Enter a value, cell reference, range, or function name. You can enter a cell reference or range by typing them or by selecting them with your mouse. The cell reference or range displays in the formula.

4. If the formula is complete, press Enter.

5. If the formula is not complete, enter an operator, such as +, -, or **@**.

6. Repeat steps 3–5 to continue building the formula until it is complete.

One of the easiest ways to understand how to enter formulas is to enter one yourself. The following example, using the SCORES.XLS worksheet from the *Inside Microsoft Office Professional* companion disk, calculates the average monthly points scored for each team.

1. Make sure the SCORES.XLS worksheet is active.

2. In cell J5, type **Average** and press Enter.

3. In cell J6, enter the formula to average the points scored for the Panthers. This formula adds up the total points scored in cells D6 through H6 and divides that number by the number of months for the season (5).

   Because you already have a Total column that adds up D6:H6, you can use this cell as the first part of your formula, as in the formula =I6/5

   See figure 8.16 to see how this looks in the worksheet.

Figure 8.16
Entering a formula to determine the average monthly points scored.

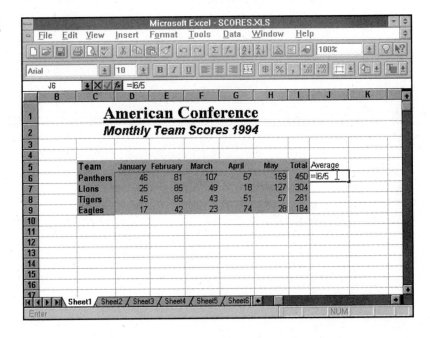

4. Press Enter. This calculates the average monthly points that the Panthers scored this season.

5. You now can calculate the average for each of the other teams by repeating the formulas in cells J7–J9, remembering to use the appropriate Total cell as the first cell reference (for instance, use =I7/5 for the Lions).

Tip

To quickly create the formulas for the other three teams, you can copy the formula by double-clicking on cell J6, moving the mouse pointer to the lower right corner of the cell, and dragging the mouse down to cell J9. Release the mouse button, and the formula is copied to each of the cells; Excel automatically calculates the average points scored for each team.

The completed worksheet should look like the one shown in figure 8.17.

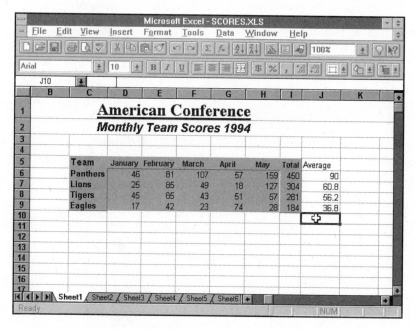

Figure 8.17
The average monthly points for all four teams.

How To Use Functions

As you saw earlier in the chapter, you can use built-in functions to help you calculate the results of your data. These functions help you add up columns of data, calculate averages of a range of cells, or return the interest rate for a fully invested security.

Simple calculations on a number or series of numbers are performed by using formulas. Such formulas, such as adding a column of numbers, are the foundation of many functions. Other functions use a combination of several formulas. Functions can be applied in a variety of different ways.

Note

For in-depth coverage of functions, see Chapter 10, "Mastering Excel Functions."

Functions are used only in formulas, even if they are the only element of a formula. When you create a formula, you must start the expression with an equal sign (=). Functions have parentheses after them; some are empty and some must include values (such as a range of cells). You must also include the function name, information about a cell or range of cells to be analyzed, and arguments about what to do with the selected range of cells (some functions need additional information). The Address function, for example, returns a value about a cell address in a worksheet. The following is the syntax for this function:

ADDRESS (**row_number,column_number**,absolute_number,a1,sheet_text).

The arguments in bold are required arguments; the remainder of the arguments are optional. Chapter 10, "Mastering Excel Functions," goes into more detail about each of these arguments.

You can incorporate up to 1,024 arguments in a function, as long as no single string of characters in the function statement exceeds 255 characters. Functions can be entered into worksheets manually, by a macro, or by using the FunctionWizard.

To help you get acquainted with using functions, use the SCORES.XLS worksheet on the *Inside Microsoft Office Professional* companion disk to find the highest point total for each month.

1. Make sure SCORES.XLS is the active worksheet.

2. Select cell D10.

3. Select Insert, Function. The Function Wizard - Step 1 of 2 dialog box appears (see fig. 8.18).

Figure 8.18

Selecting a function using the Function Wizard - Step 1 of 2 dialog box.

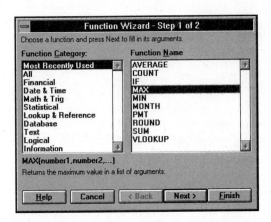

4. In this dialog box, you can choose any function that Excel provides. For this example, click on Most Recently Used in the Function Category list box. This displays the functions that Excel has determined to be the most used functions in worksheets.

5. In the Function Name list box, click on MAX. This tells Excel that you want to use the MAX function, which returns the maximum value in any of the cells you select (in this example, the most points scored in a month).

6. Click on the Next button to display the Function Wizard - Step 2 of 2 dialog box.

7. You now must tell Excel which arguments you want to use to determine the maximum value. To do this, you can enter the cells in the number 1 field. You also can click on cell D6 to highlight it and drag the mouse to select cells D7 through D9 (see fig. 8.19). (You might have to move the dialog box to see the worksheet better.)

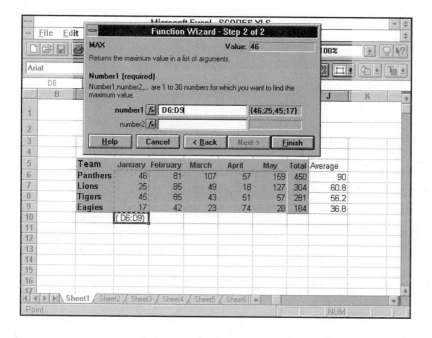

Figure 8.19
Selecting the cells to find the maximum points scored.

8. Notice in the number 1 field that Excel automatically places the cell references to calculate.

9. Click on the Finish button to return to the worksheet and to see the most points scored in January (see fig. 8.20).

10. Copy and paste this same function to find the most points scored for the rest of the months of the season. Figure 8.21 shows the final worksheet.

Figure 8.20
The highest team
score in January
was 46.

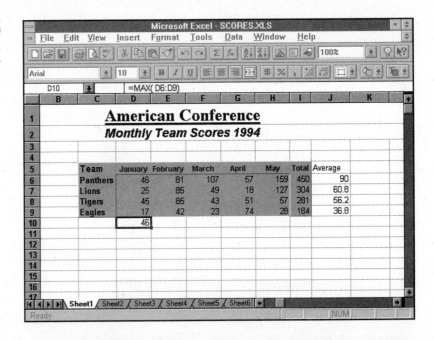

Figure 8.20
The highest team
score in January
was 46.

Figure 8.21
Calculating the
highest points for
each month of the
season.

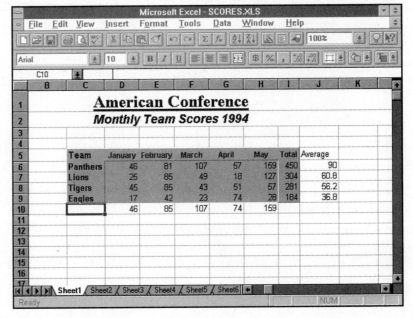

Creating Excel Charts

At some point, you might have to present your data to other people. You can, of course, use your worksheets as-is in your presentation, whether you present them electronically or in printed format. On the other hand, you can present your data in charts. A *chart* is a visual representation of your worksheet data. You can use Excel to create several different types of charts, including pie charts, line charts, and 3-D charts.

 See Chapter 12, "Excel Charts and Graphics," for more information about using and creating Excel 5 charts.

Charts help you and your audience grasp concepts and details about your data quickly and easily. Colorful charts and graphs are seen every day (as in *USA Today,* which uses charts and graphs to display interesting—and sometimes trivial—data).

Excel 5 makes creating, editing, and printing your charts a breeze. You can place the chart either in the current worksheet or on its own chart sheet. When you change the data in the worksheet, Excel automatically updates the chart associated with that data.

The following steps show you the way to create a simple chart using the data in the SCORES.XLS worksheet. For this example, you create a column chart that shows the points scored each month by the Panthers in the 1994 season. This data can be used by coaches, scouts, or the media to assess the team's performance throughout the season. (Of course, other data is important for a thorough analysis of the team's performance, such as schedule, injuries, and playing conditions.)

To chart the Panthers monthly points scored, perform the following steps:

1. Make sure that the SCORES.XLS worksheet is open.

2. Select the range D5:H5. This range represents the labels for the months during the season.

3. Select the data that you want to chart. Hold down Ctrl and select the range D6:H6.

4. Click on the ChartWizard button on the standard toolbar. Notice that the mouse pointer changes to a cross hair with a chart graphic.

    You use this pointer to tell Excel where you want to place the completed chart. For this example, you will place the chart on its own chart sheet.

5. Click on the Sheet2 tab at the bottom of the screen. This displays a blank sheet on which you can place the chart (see fig. 8.22).

6. Drag the pointer from cell B4 to H14. The ChartWizard - Step 1 of 5 dialog box appears (see fig. 8.23).

Figure 8.22
Switching to a new
blank sheet.

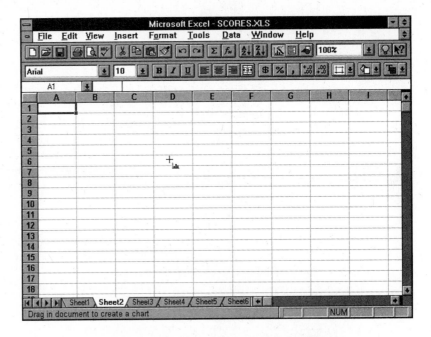

Figure 8.23
The ChartWizard -
Step 1 of 5 dialog
box.

7. The ChartWizard - Step 1 of 5 dialog box asks you to select the range you want to chart. You already have done this in Step 5, so click on the Next button.

8. The ChartWizard - Step 2 of 5 dialog box appears. In this dialog box, you select the type of chart you want to use. To keep it simple, use the default selection, Column, by clicking on the Next button.

Chapter 12, "Excel Charts and Graphics," describes each of the chart options and the formats available, as well as how to use them.

9. The ChartWizard - Step 3 of 5 dialog box appears. Choose the format of your chart. Again, select the default choice, which is number 6, by clicking on the Next button.

10. The ChartWizard - Step 4 of 5 dialog box appears. In this box, you see a sample of your chart using the data that you selected, as shown in figure 8.24. Click on the Next button.

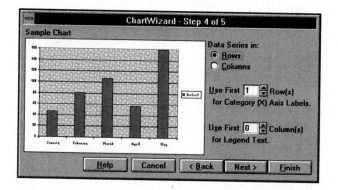

Figure 8.24
Excel shows you a sample of what your finished chart looks like.

11. The ChartWizard - Step 5 of 5 dialog box appears. This dialog box gives you the option of having a legend, adding a title to your chart, and filling in the axis titles (see fig. 8.25). For this example, select the No option under Add a Legend? and type **Panthers 1994 Points Scored** in the Chart Title box.

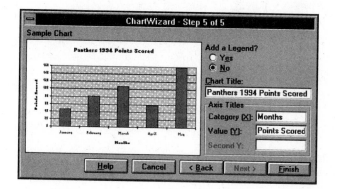

Figure 8.25
The ChartWizard - Step 5 of 5 dialog box.

12. In the Category (X) box, type **Months**. In the Value (Y) box, type **Points Scored**. Click on the Finish button.

The chart appears on Sheet2 in the area you selected in Step 6. The chart should look like the one in figure 8.26.

Figure 8.26
The finished chart,
showing the
monthly scores for
the Panthers.

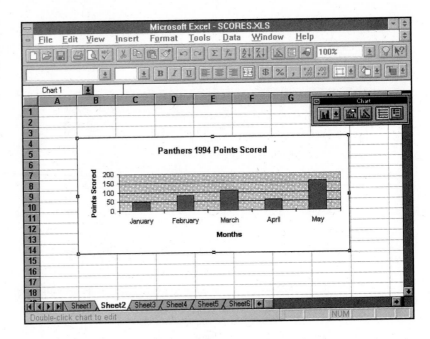

Saving and Printing Your Work

At some point, you will need to save and print your workbooks. By saving your workbooks, you can use them over and over again, without having to enter the data again or create a chart over and over. When you print your work, you can use the hard copy printouts for reports or handouts for presentations. This section shows you the way to save and print your workbooks.

Saving Your Workbook

As you work through your worksheets and chart sheets, you will want to save them periodically. When you use the File, Save option in Excel 5, you save the active workbook, which contains the sheets you are working in. If it is the first time that you save your workbook, Excel displays the Save As dialog box. The name you enter in the File Name text box appears at the top of the workbook. Try to use file names that help you remember the contents of the workbook.

Another way to quickly save your work is to click on the Save button on the standard toolbar. You also can press Ctrl+S.

Save your work often. Too many hours and data have been lost due to system crashes, power glitches, or children experimenting with Reset buttons on computers. Make it a habit to save your work after you make a substantial change to your workbook, enter data into several cells, create a chart, write a macro, or when you think you will be away from your desk for awhile.

If you want to rename a workbook that already has been saved with another name, select File, Save As. This displays the Save As dialog box, enabling you to enter a new name and optionally save the file in a different subdirectory. The original file remains saved under the old name.

The following steps show you how to save the SCORES.XLS worksheet by another name— SEASON.XLS:

1. Make sure the SCORES.XLS worksheet is active.

2. Select File, Save As to display the Save As dialog box.

3. In the File Name text box, type **SEASON**. The extension .XLS is automatically filled in.

4. To change the path to a different drive or subdirectory, use the Directories and Drives lists (this is optional).

5. Press Enter or click on OK. If the Summary Info option is selected, Excel displays the Summary Info dialog box; you can enter the summary information for the workbook if you want.

See Chapter 14, "Customizing Excel 5," for information about customizing Excel and selecting different options, such as Summary Info.

6. Press Enter or click on OK.

Printing Your Worksheet and Chart Sheet

Now that your worksheets and charts are saved for posterity and future work, you can print a copy of one to see how it looks on paper. Excel provides several choices when you are ready to print your workbooks. You can, for instance, add a header and footer to your pages, add page numbers, or insert the name of the workbook on the printout.

Previewing Your Work

One of the handiest tools that Excel provides is the Print Preview command. Print Preview enables you to see exactly how your worksheets or chart sheets will appear when printed. This saves time, paper, and printer toner by showing you what you need to change or modify before you send your print job to the printer. Sometimes, for instance, a chart or worksheet may look fine when you are entering and editing data, but when you print it, the chart or worksheet is too large or too small, or you lose rows and columns from the worksheet. Print Preview can help you prevent some of these problems.

To preview your print job in Excel, select File, Print Preview. Your screen displays a facsimile of the final, printed worksheet or chart. As you can see in figure 8.27, you might not be able to read or see all (or any!) of the details in your sheets. This is because Excel is trying to fit an electronic piece of paper (usually 8 ½ by 11 inches) on your screen. Still, you can get an idea of the information that will printed. (As you see in the following example, you can magnify this view to get a closer, more readable view.)

Figure 8.27
Using Print Preview to view the worksheet before it is printed.

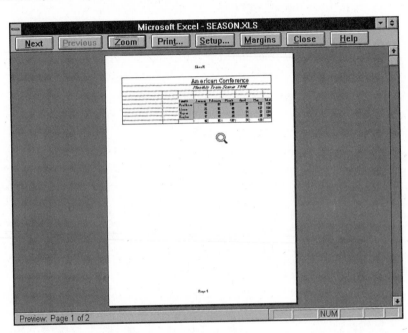

The preview window has the following controls and buttons:

✔ Next. When highlighted, this button enables you to view the next sheet in your workbook.

✔ Previous. When highlighted, this button enables you to view the previous sheet in your workbook.

✔ Zoom. The Zoom button enables you to change the magnification of the print preview. Click on this button to view the sheet in full size.

✔ Print. When you press the Print button, Excel returns you to the normal editing window and displays the Print dialog box.

✔ Setup. This button displays the Setup dialog box, in which you can change page setup options. This dialog box is discussed later in this chapter and again in Chapter 9, "Understanding Excel Worksheet Concepts."

✔ Margins. Use this button to activate or deactivate the margin option, which enables you to view and change the margins of the worksheet. The Margin option is discussed in Chapter 9, "Understanding Excel Worksheet Concepts."

✔ Close. Use this button to close Print Preview mode and return to the worksheet.

✔ Help. If you have a question about any of these options or any other Excel feature, click on the Help button.

See Chapter 9 for information on adjusting the size of the columns and rows in your worksheets.

Use the following steps to view the SEASON.XLS worksheet in Print Preview mode.

1. Make sure that SEASON.XLS is active.

2. Select File, Print Preview, or click on the Print Preview button on the standard toolbar. The worksheet appears on-screen in the preview window (refer to figure 8.27).

3. As you move the pointer over the worksheet, notice how it changes to a magnifying glass. This enables you to click on the worksheet to zoom in on any part of the worksheet you want to see in more detail. You might have to zoom in on different cells to see if everything fits as you want it to. If a cell displays number signs (#####) instead of actual values or figures, for example, you need to widen the columns before you print the worksheet.

4. Everything should look okay in the SEASON.XLS print preview, so click again to zoom out and click on the Close button. This returns you to the normal worksheet screen.

Printing the Worksheet

Now that you have previewed the worksheet, you are ready to print it. Perform the following steps to learn how to use some of the print options that Excel offers.

1. Make sure you have the SEASON.XLS worksheet active.

2. Select File, Page Setup to display the Page Setup dialog box.

3. Click on the Page tab and make sure the Landscape button is clicked. Next, click on the Margins tab to switch to the margins options.

4. In the Center on Page area, click on Horizontally to center the worksheet on the page (see fig. 8.28). Notice how the Preview area in the middle of the dialog box reflects how the worksheet will be set up on the page.

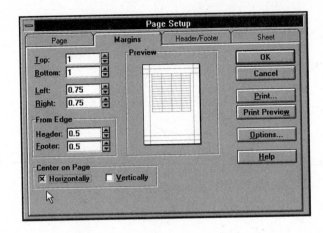

Figure 8.28
Selecting the
Horizontal option
in the Center on
Page area.

5. Click on the Sheet tab. In the Print area, clear the Gridlines check box to turn of the gridlines.

> As you will learn in Chapter 9, *gridlines* are the horizontal and vertical lines that help you locate and set up cells on your worksheets. Usually, you keep gridlines on while you enter and edit your data; you usually turn off gridlines when you want to present your worksheets in a clean, professional way.

6. Click on OK.

Now you are ready to print the worksheet. If you want to take another quick look at your sheet before you print, use the Print Preview feature, as you did in the preceding section.

7. Select File, Print, to display the Print dialog box (see fig. 8.29). In the Print What area, make sure the Selected Sheet(s) option is checked. This tells Excel to print only the selected worksheet(s) or chart sheet(s).

8. Click on OK. The worksheet should start printing.

If you want, click on the Sheet2 tab and preview and print the Lion Season 1994 chart. You can use many or all of the same options you used for the preceding example.

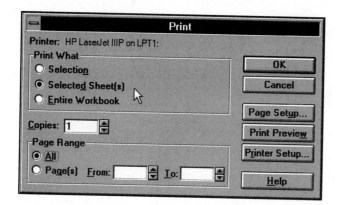

Figure 8.29
The Print dialog box.

Excel

Chapter Snapshot

Worksheets are the primary elements that you work on when you use Microsoft Excel. Worksheets can be simple or complex, depending on your needs. To fully develop your worksheets, you need to understand all their rules, nuances, and features. This chapter gives you this understanding by presenting the following topics:

When you finish this chapter, you will be well on your way to building more spectacular and dynamic worksheets.

CHAPTER 9

Understanding Excel Worksheet Concepts

by Rob Tidrow

Look around your desk. How many piles of papers or notebooks do you have? Do you have key data placed in these piles, such as budgets, sales reports, or invoice statements? Are some of the piles vital to the success of your business, job, or home budget planning? Would you like a better way to manage some of this mess? If you answer "Yes" to these questions, you are a prime candidate for a spreadsheet program such as Excel 5.

Examining Worksheets

As you saw in Chapter 8, "Excel Quick Start," Excel workbooks contain worksheets, which are like the ledger sheets you might have used in high school accounting class. Along the left side of the sheets are rows numbered 1, 2, 3, and so on, and along the top of the sheets are columns lettered A, B, C, and so on. The intersection of these rows and columns are *cells*. Worksheets contain 256 columns and 16,384 rows.

The data that you place in worksheets can be text, formulas, or numbers. Usually, *text* entries are labels, such as American Conference or December Sales Results. You also might use text entries when you have numbers and text combined, such as account codes. *Number* entries might be points scored, dollars earned, taxes paid, interest rates, or any other number that you need to store. *Formula* entries are calculations based on values that you specify, such as cells or ranges.

Selecting and Viewing Sheets

Not surprisingly, each type of data that you can enter in Excel has its own rules and features. The basic means of getting the data into the worksheets, however, is the same: You select the sheet and cell in which you want the data placed, and you type the information.

Before you enter the data, make sure that you are working in the correct workbook and worksheet. When Excel starts, a blank workbook with 16 blank sheets opens. Along the bottom of the workbook are tabs that enable you to select the sheet on which you want to work. These tabs are numbered Sheet1, Sheet2, and so on. If you do not want to start a new worksheet, you also can enter data in a workbook that you have saved previously by selecting File, Open and opening the desired file. You then click on the tab to change to the sheet in which you want to enter the data and select the cell to contain the data.

If you have more than one workbook open, you can move between workbooks by selecting Window and choosing the workbook that you want to make active. This is handy if you are cutting and pasting data from one workbook to another. You also can arrange the workbooks on your screen to make them easier to switch between by using the Window, Arrange option. When you select this option, the Arrange Windows dialog box appears (see fig. 9.1).

This dialog box enables you to arrange your workbooks so that they are placed vertically or horizontally (by using the Vertical and Horizontal options), tiled (by using the Tiled option), or cascaded (by using the Cascade option). You also can arrange only the windows of the active workbook by clicking in the Windows of Active Workbook check box. This puts the active workbook in the foreground and the inactive ones in the background.

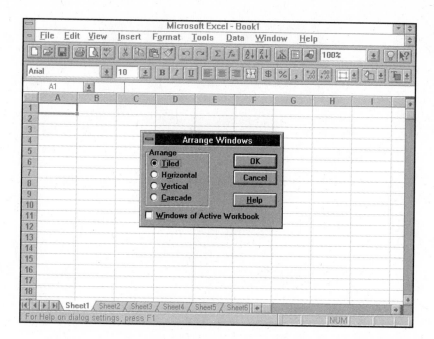

Figure 9.1
Use the Arrange
Windows dialog
box to help keep
your workbooks
organized on-
screen.

As with any other Windows application, you can move individual Excel
workbook windows around by using the mouse and grabbing the title bar. The
Arrange Windows dialog box is useful in some cases when you just cannot
seem to set up the interface to suit your needs and you want a more automatic
way of doing so.

Hiding Workbooks

As your worksheets get more complex, or if you have several workbooks open at once, you
might find it irritating to have your workplace so cluttered. You can keep it clean by hiding
workbooks or worksheets.

As you will see throughout Part Two, you might need to have workbooks open
even though you are not working in them. You might, for instance, have a
workbook linked to another workbook, but not be using the former one for
data-intensive work.

To hide a workbook, select the workbook that you want to hide and choose <u>W</u>indow, <u>H</u>ide.
The workbook disappears immediately from your screen. To unhide any windows that are
hidden, perform the following steps:

1. Select <u>W</u>indow, <u>U</u>nhide. This displays the Unhide dialog box with a list of the
   hidden windows (see fig. 9.2).

Figure 9.2
The Unhide dialog
box keeps a list of
any hidden
windows.

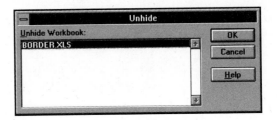

2. In the Unhide Workbook list box, click on the window you want to unhide.

3. Choose OK or press Enter. The window you want to unhide reappears on-screen in its previous size and position.

Hiding Worksheets

What if you want to hide all those other worksheets in a workbook that you are not using? To do this, you cannot use the Windows, Hide command. You have to use the Format, Sheet command, as follows:

1. Switch to the sheet you want to hide.

2. Select Format, Sheet. A submenu pops out to the side of the pull-down menu.

3. Choose Hide. The sheet instantly disappears.

To unhide the worksheet, select Format, Sheet, Unhide to display the Unhide dialog box. Click on the sheet you want to unhide and choose OK or press Enter. The sheet reappears on-screen.

You might want to keep all the windows in place, or you might want to keep other people from moving windows around if they are using your workbooks. To lock a window after you have it in place, select Tools, Protection, Protect Workbook to display the Protect Workbook dialog box (see fig. 9.3). In this dialog box, you can enter a password in the Password (optional) text box so that users will need a password to move the windows or modify the structure of the workbook (such as hide, unhide, delete, or move it). Click in the Windows check box so that the position of the windows cannot be changed. Click in the Structure check box to protect the structure of the workbook.

Remember your password. If you forget it, you cannot unprotect your workbook.

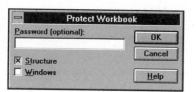

Figure 9.3
Use the Protect
Workbook dialog
box to lock your
workbooks.

Moving Around in Workbooks and Worksheets

From Chapter 8, "Excel Quick Start," you already know that you can click on the sheet tab of your choice to switch to that sheet. Excel offers a few other navigational tools to help you move around in your workbooks. You can, for instance, use scroll bars to move around. You also can type a cell reference to switch to that cell.

Tab scrolling buttons appear at the bottom of workbooks to enable you to move through the worksheet names in a workbook. You cannot switch to a different sheet by using the tab scrolling buttons, but you can view the names of the sheets and then click on the sheet tab that you want to activate. Each workbook has four tab scrolling buttons. The far left and far right buttons move to the first and last sheets in the workbook, respectively. The middle two buttons move one sheet to the left or right in the workbook. See figure 9.4 for the placement of these scrolling buttons.

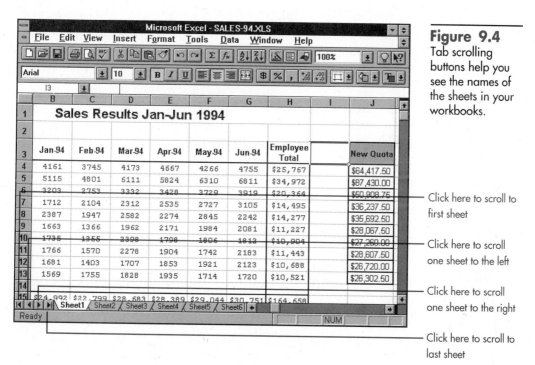

Figure 9.4
Tab scrolling
buttons help you
see the names of
the sheets in your
workbooks.

Click here to scroll to
first sheet

Click here to scroll
one sheet to the left

Click here to scroll
one sheet to the right

Click here to scroll to
last sheet

Selecting More than One Worksheet

You might have to select several worksheets (say, if you have a reference to multiple, noncontiguous workbooks) in a workbook that are not side by side—Sheet2, Sheet4, Sheet 11, and Sheet13, for example. To do this, perform the following steps:

1. Click on the tab scrolling buttons to show the first sheet that you want to select, such as Sheet2.

2. Click on that tab (in this example, Sheet2).

3. Click on the tab scrolling buttons to show the next sheet in the group that you want to select, such as Sheet4.

4. Click on that tab while pressing Ctrl (in this example, Sheet4).

5. Continue scrolling to the next sheet tab, using Ctrl+click, until all the sheets are selected.

As you select the sheets, the tabs change colors to signify that you have selected them.

In other situations, you might need to select several sheets that are in order, such as Sheet3 through Sheet 8. Follow these steps:

1. Click on the tab scrolling buttons to show the first sheet you want to select, such as Sheet3.

2. Click on that tab (in this example, Sheet3).

3. Click on the tab scrolling buttons to show the last sheet in the group that you want to select, such as Sheet8.

4. Click on the last sheet name while pressing Shift. This selects all the sheets between the first and last sheets on which you clicked. Again, the tabs change colors to show that they have been selected.

Using the Go To Command

If you want to move to a specific sheet in an open workbook, but you don't want to scroll through all the sheets and you know exactly the sheet and cell reference, perform the following steps:

1. Select Edit, Go To (or press F5). The Go To dialog box appears.

2. In the Reference text box, enter the name and cell of the sheet to which you want to switch. You have to separate the name and cell with an exclamation point, such as in the following example:

    SCORES!H6

In this example, you are telling Excel to jump to cell H6 in the SCORES worksheet.

3. Choose OK or press Enter.

Understanding Excel's Three Types of Data

You might have stacks of papers on your desk and loose invoices jammed in your filing cabinet. These numbers, dates, products, inventory lists, dollars spent and received, phone numbers, addresses, and other miscellaneous words and numbers are forms of data. You need to find a way to administer all this data so that you can use it quickly and efficiently. Now that you know how to move among workbooks and worksheets, you can start entering all this wealth of information that you have been putting off for months (or years!).

Probably one of the reasons that you purchased Microsoft Office Professional was to take full advantage of multiple applications. You can build a spreadsheet in Excel 5 and then use it in a presentation that you create in PowerPoint. Or, you can use an Access database to manage all your data and then use Excel 5 to manipulate and present that data. (If you are interested in using Excel 5 with Access, see Parts Four and Five of this book. Part Five also provides information to help you achieve integrated solutions with Office.)

When you finally break down all the data and see what you have, you can begin to formulate how you want it to look in your worksheets. Phone numbers and addresses, for instance, can comprise a Black Book worksheet. Sales data for the entire midwestern sales force can be put into a Midwest Sales worksheet. You even can start thinking about creating sophisticated workbooks that rely on macro or Visual Basic for Applications front ends.

One way to get ideas on the types of workbooks and worksheets that you can build in Excel is to view the sample files that come with Excel 5. These files are usually stored in the \EXAMPLE and \EXCELCBT subdirectories in which you have Excel stored. Open these files and see how Excel enables you to present data in several different ways.

Using Text as Data

You can include text entries that are alphabetical characters, numbers, symbols, and spaces. Usually, text entries, which can be up to 255 characters long in a cell, are used to label worksheets and to help readers understand the contents of the workbooks. You also can enter numbers and have them treated as text, such as in the case of addresses, numbers used as labels, and numbers that begin with 0. When you enter a number that has a leading zero, Excel deletes the 0. You can, however, retain the 0 by leading the entry with an apostrophe ('), which tells Excel that the entry is to be accepted as text. (The apostrophe does not appear in the cell.)

Tip

Another way to enter a number as text is to select F**o**rmat, **C**ells. This displays the Format Cell dialog box. Click on the Number tab, select the Text option in the **C**ategory list, and highlight the @ format code in the **F**ormat Codes box. Click on OK or press Enter. This returns you to the active worksheet where you can enter the number, and it is accepted as text.

Excel places text in a cell by aligning it on the left side of the cell. Numbers, on the other hand, are right-aligned. If your text entry is too large to be viewed in the default cell size, you need to resize the cell by using the formatting features explained later in this chapter.

To enter text in a worksheet, select a cell and type the text. In the following example, you enter some text and some numbers as text. Notice how text aligns on the left side of the cell.

The following exercise uses a new worksheet that you can open by choosing **F**ile, **N**ew (the completed worksheet for this example is included on the bonus disk):

1. Make sure Excel is started, and select **F**ile, **N**ew to create a new workbook. A new workbook with blank worksheets appears.

2. Click in the cell in which you enter the text—for example, cell B4.

3. Type the text you want—for example, **Sales**. Notice how the text aligns on the left side of the cell.

4. Enter some numbers that you want to appear as text, such as the current year. To do this, add an apostrophe (') before the number: **'1994**. Excel interprets this data as text and does not think it is a number entry. (You learn about number entries in the next section.)

Another way to enter text (or any other data) is to use the formula bar on the formatting toolbar. To make this your default choice, turn off the in-cell editing feature. This method is nice if you don't want to see your entries made directly in the cell until you are finished entering them.

To turn off in-cell editing, use these steps:

1. Select **T**ools, **O**ptions. The Options dialog box appears.

2. Click on the Edit tab to display the Edit dialog box (see fig. 9.5).

3. Click on the Edit Directly in Cell check box to turn it off.

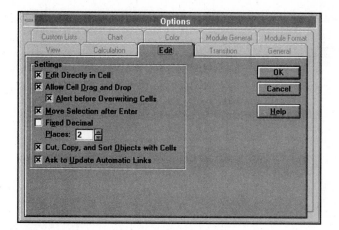

Figure 9.5
Use the Edit dialog box to turn off (or on) the in-cell editing feature.

4. Click on OK or press Enter.

Your default setup now enables you to enter data using only the Excel formula bar. As shown in figure 9.6, when you select a cell to edit, the cell highlights and the formula bar displays four buttons. These buttons—Names list, Cancel, Enter, and Function Wizard—help you enter different types of data, undo an entry, or accept an entry.

The Names box on the formula bar shows you the cell reference for the selected cell. The Cancel button enables you to undo what you have typed before entering the data. You also can press Esc to do the same thing. The Enter button is used to place the entry into the selected cell. The Function Wizard button activates the Function Wizard to help you build formulas that contain functions. (You learn more about the Function Wizard in Chapter 10, "Mastering Excel Functions.")

Tip

Text entries may become lengthy and run too long for the cell in which they are contained. To avoid having text flow into other cells, you can use text wrapping to display the entry in multiple lines in one cell.

To see how the feature works, enter a lengthy string of some data in a cell. Next, select Format, Cells and click on the Alignment tab. Choose the Wrap Text check box and press Enter or click on OK. The cell gets larger to accommodate all the data.

Figure 9.6
Use the formula
bar and its buttons
to enter data into
your worksheets.

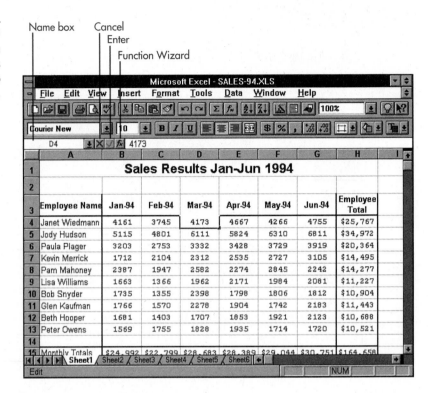

Figure 9.6
Use the formula
bar and its buttons
to enter data into
your worksheets.

Employee Name	Jan-94	Feb-94	Mar-94	Apr-94	May-94	Jun-94	Employee Total
Janet Wiedmann	4161	3745	4173	4667	4266	4755	$25,767
Jody Hudson	5115	4801	6111	5824	6310	6811	$34,972
Paula Plager	3203	2753	3332	3428	3729	3919	$20,364
Kevin Merrick	1712	2104	2312	2535	2727	3105	$14,495
Pam Mahoney	2387	1947	2582	2274	2845	2242	$14,277
Lisa Williams	1663	1366	1962	2171	1984	2081	$11,227
Bob Snyder	1735	1355	2398	1798	1806	1812	$10,904
Glen Kaufman	1766	1570	2278	1904	1742	2183	$11,443
Beth Hooper	1681	1403	1707	1853	1921	2123	$10,688
Peter Owens	1569	1755	1828	1935	1714	1720	$10,521
Monthly Totals	$24,992	$22,799	$28,683	$28,389	$29,044	$30,751	$164,658

Using Numbers as Data

For the most part, your worksheets will contain numbers. The primary function of a spreadsheet is to help you calculate, store, manipulate, and present numbers. These numbers might be dollar amounts, percentages, dates, or other values. Excel lets you enter these characters as number data: 1 2 3 4 5 6 7 8 9 0 E e . % - + / . (Later in this chapter, you are shown how to change the formatting of numbers.)

Numbers are entered the same way text is: select the cell, type the number, and then press Enter or click on the Enter box on the formula bar. Excel right-aligns the numbers in the cells. If you want to enter fractions, type an integer (such as 1 or 0), a space, the numerator, a slash (/), and the denominator: **3 1/2** or **0 5/16**. The first fraction in these examples reads as *three and one-half*, and the second fraction reads as *five-sixteenths*. If you do not use an integer before the fraction, Excel thinks you are entering a date. The second example without the zero (5/16) would read *May 16*.

Some other forms of numbers that you might need to enter are negative numbers, dollar amounts, decimals, and very large or small numbers. Negative numbers are placed inside of parentheses—**(45)** for negative 45, for example. Dollar amounts are entered with the dollar

sign then the number: **$34.90**. Decimal values are entered with the decimal point: **432.89**. If you deal with large numbers, such as scientific notations, you use the form **84.3992 E+3**. (*E* is the symbol that represents scientific notation.)

Tip

To enter a number that has thousands and uses one or more commas in it, you have to place the comma in the correct place or Excel will think it is a text entry. The number 34,45 is not the same as 3,445 to Excel. The first is interpreted as text and the second is interpreted as a number.

The easiest way to see whether an entry is interpreted as a number or text is to see whether Excel aligns it on the left side or the right side when you enter it. If it is aligned on the right side, it's a number. On the left, it's text.

When you enter a number that does not fit in a cell, Excel displays a series of ####s to indicate that the column is not wide enough (see fig. 9.7). To change the ####s to the actual numbers, you can widen the columns or change the numeric format (such as changing the font or point size of the number). To change the numeric format, you might need to change a long number to scientific notation. (Later in this chapter, you are shown how to widen columns.)

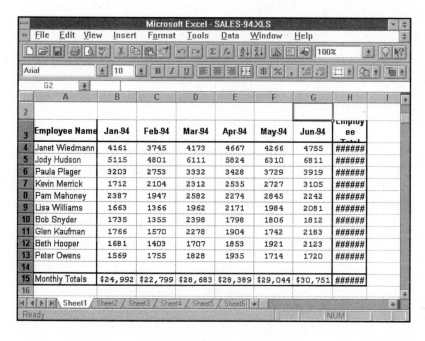

Figure 9.7
When a cell is not wide enough and the number is too long, you see a series of ####s.

Employee Name	Jan-94	Feb-94	Mar-94	Apr-94	May-94	Jun-94	Employee Total
Janet Wiedmann	4161	3745	4173	4667	4266	4755	######
Jody Hudson	5115	4801	6111	5824	6310	6811	######
Paula Plager	3203	2753	3332	3428	3729	3919	######
Kevin Merrick	1712	2104	2312	2535	2727	3105	######
Pam Mahoney	2387	1947	2582	2274	2845	2242	######
Lisa Williams	1663	1366	1962	2171	1984	2081	######
Bob Snyder	1735	1355	2398	1798	1806	1812	######
Glen Kaufman	1766	1570	2278	1904	1742	2183	######
Beth Hooper	1681	1403	1707	1853	1921	2123	######
Peter Owens	1569	1755	1828	1935	1714	1720	######
Monthly Totals	$24,992	$22,799	$28,683	$28,389	$29,044	$30,751	######

Entering Dates and Times

You might need to place actual dates and times into your worksheets, such as February 1, 1994, or 5:13 p.m. When you enter dates and times, Excel stores this data as a serial number. *Serial numbers* represent starting points that are programmed into Excel. A date serial number is computed from the starting point of December 31, 1899. A time serial number is computed using fractions of the 24-hour clock.

If you enter the date December 31, 1993, for example, the serial number is 34,334. This means that 34,334 days have passed between December 31, 1899, and December 31, 1993. If you enter a time of 12:00 noon, Excel saves it as the serial number 0.50; 5:00 p.m. is 0.70833. This means that when it is noon, half the day has passed; when it is 5:00 p.m., you have only about three-tenths of the day left.

Why are serial numbers used by Excel? Serial numbers make it easy to calculate dates and times you might need in your results, such as delivery times and dates or account payable data. All you need to think about, however, is entering dates and times the way Excel accepts them, which is in a number of different formats. You do not need to enter serial numbers, even though you can if you want; Excel handles the conversion itself.

The secret to entering and displaying dates and times correctly is to use Excel's date and time formats (see table 9.1). These formats are found by selecting For̲mat, C̲ell and clicking on the Number tab (see fig. 9.8). In the C̲ategory list box, you can choose the type of number, including Date and Time, that you want to format. The format appears in the F̲ormat Codes box.

Figure 9.8
Use the Number tab to format dates and times.

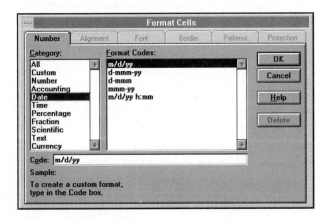

Table 9.1
Date and Time Formats

Date or Time	Format
1/12/94	m/d/yy
12-Jan-94	d-mmm-yy
12-Jan	d-mmm
Jan-94	mmm-yy
1/12/94 11:15	m/d/yy h:mm
11:15 a.m.	h:mm AM/PM
11:15:34 a.m.	h:mm:ss AM/PM
11:15	h:mm
11:15:34	h:mm:ss
1/12/94 11:15	m/d/yy/h:mm

Another key to making your dates and times appear correctly is to make sure your worksheet is formatted correctly. Occasionally, the way you customize Excel affects the way data is interpreted by Excel. (Later in this chapter you are shown some formatting changes that alter the way dates and times are displayed. See Chapter 14, "Customizing Excel 5," for more information about customization in Excel.)

When you enter data that you want to appear as a date or time in the current format (the format you choose), enter the date or time as specified in table 9.1. To format a date in the default format (Setup in Excel), select the cell that contains the date and press Ctrl+#. For numbers, use Ctrl+@. The following steps show you some examples of entering dates and times in your worksheets:

1. In the EXAMPLE.XLS worksheet, select cell G6 and type **15-Jan-94** as the date. Press Enter.

2. Now change this date to the current date format by selecting G6 again and pressing Ctrl+#. This changes the date to the format you specified in the Format Codes box (refer to figure 9.8). In figure 9.9, the date changes to the current format, *m/d/yy*.

Figure 9.9
Changing an
example date to
the default date
format.

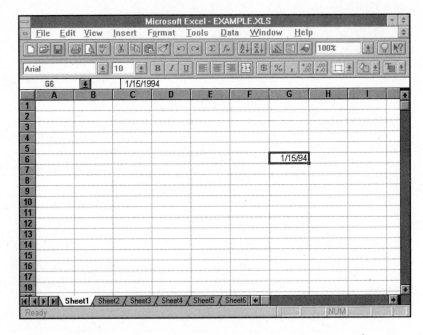

If your format is set as *d-mmm-yy*, your date stays the same as you type it (in this case, 15-Jan-94). If this is the case, type the date as **1/15/94** and press Ctrl+# to see the date change to 15-Jan-94, the default format.

One of the most useful shortcuts when you are entering data is to enter the current date and time automatically in a cell. Press Ctrl+; to enter the current date, and press Ctrl+: to enter the current time.

You also can use the following keyboard shortcuts to apply common date and time formats to your entries:

Ctrl+Shift+@   h.mm
Ctrl+Shift+#   d-mmm-yy

Using Formulas as Data

The third type of data that you can enter in Excel is formulas. Formulas are simple to understand. They calculate results based on values. In Chapter 8, for example, you entered a few formulas to help you calculate totals, averages, and highest points scored in each month. You can use numbers, cell references, text, or functions in formulas.

To enter formulas in your worksheets, perform the following general steps:

1. Double-click on the cell in which you want to include the formula.

2. Enter an equal sign (=) or other operator. Remember that Excel changes these other operators to equal signs.

3. Enter a value, cell reference, range, or function name by typing it or selecting it with your mouse. The cell reference or range appears in the formula.

4. If the formula is complete, press Enter.

5. If the formula is not complete, enter an operator, such as +, -, or @.

6. Go back to Step 3 and continue building the formula until it is complete.

Most of the time, you use Excel formulas to calculate results of numbers. These types of formulas are called *arithmetic formulas*. Generally, arithmetic formulas calculate results by using numbers, function results, and cell addresses with one or more of the following mathematical operators:

=

-

*

/

%

^

The caret (^) operator denotes an *exponentiation operator*. An example of exponentiation is raising a number to a certain power. The formula =5^2 means *5 raised to the second power*, or 25.

Calculating by Order of Precedence

When you enter a formula that contains operators, you need to keep in mind the order by which Excel calculates the formula. This is called *order of precedence*, and is used by Excel to determine which part of the formula to calculate first, second, and so on.

If you have the formula =5*3^2, for example, it is not clear which part of the formula should be calculated first. Excel's order of precedence first calculates the exponentiation part (3^2=9) and then the multiplication part (5*9). The result of this total formula is 45.

If you calculate the parts in the opposite order, the results are quite different (5*3=15; 15^2=225), so it is important to understand Excel's order of precedence when you create your formulas. Table 9.2 shows the order in which Excel calculates formulas and the operators associated with certain operations. (Some of the operations in the table are covered in more detail in Chapter 10, "Mastering Excel Functions," and later in this chapter in the section discussing ranges.)

Table 9.2
Order of Precedence in Formulas

Order	Operation	Operator
1	Range	:
2	Intersection	Space
3	Union	'
4	Negation (such as –9)	-
5	Percent	%
6	Exponentiation	^
7	Division and multiplication	/ and *
8	Addition and subtraction	+ and -
9	Concatenation	&
10	Comparison	= < > <= >= <>

You might want to create formulas that do not follow the natural order of precedence. You might, for instance, want to add two numbers together and *then* multiply the sum by another number. In the order of precedence, however, Excel multiplies first, then adds. To overcome this in your formula, use parentheses to surround the numbers that you want Excel to calculate first.

If, in the preceding example, you want to add 5 and 3 and then multiply the sum by 10, set up the formula as the following:

    =(5+3)*10

When you have more complicated formulas, you might have parentheses inside of parentheses. This is called *nesting*. Keep in mind that Excel calculates what is inside of parentheses first, and the formulas within the inner parentheses are calculated before those within the outer ones.

The following example provides some sample formulas that you can enter in a new worksheet to help you get acquainted with entering formulas. The finished worksheet is saved as FORMULAS.XLS on the bonus disk.

1. In cell B4, enter **=2+2** and press Enter.

2. In cell B6, enter **=2*2** and press Enter.

3. In cell B8, enter **=2/2** and press Enter.

4. In cell B10, enter **=2-2** and press Enter.

5. In cell B12, enter **=2^2** and press Enter.

6. In cell B14, enter **=2*(2^5)** and press Enter.

Figure 9.10 shows the results of these formulas and how your worksheet should look. (A worksheet title, called "Entering Formulas," has been added to cell B2 in this figure.)

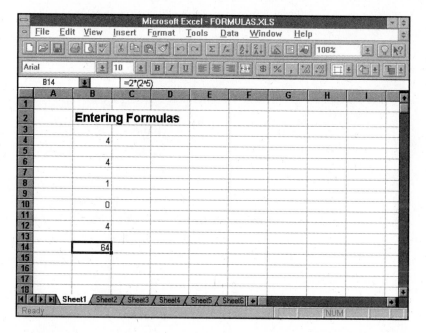

Figure 9.10

Entering example formulas.

Tip

Remember to type the equal sign to start the formula. If you forget to do this and press Enter, Excel interprets your entries as text and does not calculate the formula. To edit the cell after you have entered the formula, double-click in the cell or click in the cell and press F2. This enables you to edit the formula in the cell. You also can click on the cell and then edit the formula in the formula bar. Press Enter to have Excel evaluate the formula.

Copying and Moving Formulas

Recall that you learned in Chapter 8 how to copy formulas from one cell to another. You can click on the cell that contains the formula and select Edit, Copy from the menu bar, then move the insertion point to the new cell and select Edit, Paste. The results of the calculation appear in the cell.

Tip A quicker way to copy a formula to an adjacent cell (one that is above, below, to the right, or to the left) is to use the mouse. Click on the cell that contains the formula and move the mouse pointer to the lower right corner of the cell border. Grab the cell handle that appears and move the selection into the cells where you want to copy the formula. Then release the mouse button.

When you copy a formula, you usually have a number of calculations to perform in a worksheet that use the same formula but have different cell references. The worksheet shown in figure 9.11, for example, has the monthly sales earnings for January through June. Cell H4 shows the total earnings for Janet Wiedmann through June. The formula to calculate this result is the following, as displayed in the formula bar:

=SUM(B4:G4)

Figure 9.11
The formula
=SUM(B4:G4) can
be copied to other
cells.

	A	B	C	D	E	F	G	H
2								
3	Employee Name	Jan-94	Feb-94	Mar-94	Apr-94	May-94	Jun-94	Employee Total
4	Janet Wiedmann	4161	3745	4173	4667	4266	4755	$25,767
5	Jody Hudson	5115	4801	6111	5824	6310	6811	
6	Paula Plager	3203	2753	3332	3428	3729	3919	
7	Kevin Merrick	1712	2104	2312	2535	2727	3105	
8	Pam Mahoney	2387	1947	2582	2274	2845	2242	
9	Lisa Williams	1663	1366	1962	2171	1984	2081	
10	Bob Snyder	1735	1355	2398	1798	1806	1812	
11	Glen Kaufman	1766	1570	2278	1904	1742	2183	
12	Beth Hooper	1681	1403	1707	1853	1921	2123	
13	Peter Owens	1569	1755	1828	1935	1714	1720	
14								
15	Monthly Totals	$24,992	$22,799	$28,683	$28,389	$29,044	$30,751	
16								

Now that you have this formula written, you can use it to add the totals for the other sales-people. When you copy the formula into another cell, Excel assumes that you want to use the same general formula, but the cell references are to be changed. That is, to calculate Jody Hudson's total, you want to use cell references B5:G5, not B4:G4 as in the original formula. The other salespeople also have their own data that needs to be calculated.

How does Excel know which cell references to use? This is known as *relative reference format* in Excel. When you create a formula that asks Excel to "add the contents of cells B4:G4," Excel interprets this as "adding the contents of the cell six rows to the left (cell B4), to the contents of the cell five rows to the left (cell C4), to the contents of the cell four rows to the left (cell D4), to the contents . . ." until all are added and displayed in H4.

When you copy this formula to H5 to add Jody Hudson's sales numbers, Excel automatically adjusts the cell references but interprets the formula the same. In this case, Excel interprets the formula as "add the contents of the cell six rows to the left (cell B5), to the contents of the cell five rows to the left (cell C5), to the contents of the cell four rows to the left (cell D5), to the contents . . ." until all are added and displayed in H5.

Sometimes, however, you cannot just copy a formula from one cell to another and get the correct results. This occurs when you have some references that change in a formula *(relative references)* and some that do not. Those that do not are called *absolute references*. When you use absolute references in a formula, Excel uses the specific cell reference that you enter, regardless of where you copy the formula.

You might, for example, want to add another formula to the worksheet shown in figure 9.11 that determines the total sales quota for the next six months for each salesperson, and the quota is two-and-one-half times the total amount they produced in the first six months. This quota index is placed on the worksheet in cell C18 as 2.5. The formula is =H4*C18 and is created in J4 for Janet Wiedmann.

When you copy the formula to another cell using the techniques you have learned, Excel assumes it is working with a relative reference format and you get $0 in the cells, which obviously is the wrong sales quota (see fig. 9.12). You get this result because Excel interpreted your copied formula to mean "multiply the number that is 2 columns to the left by the number that is 14 rows down and 7 columns to the left." When you copy the formula to Jody Hudson's row (J5), Excel cannot find a value that is "14 rows down and 7 columns to the left," so it multiplies the number 2 columns to the left (in this case, $34,972) by 0.

To get the correct results, use Excel's absolute reference format to anchor the number that you want to use in all the formulas. The anchored value is the cell reference that does not change, regardless of where you copy or move a formula. In the example shown in figure 9.12, you need to anchor the quota index number (2.5) so that each salesperson's total value can be multiplied by this value. To distinguish between absolute and relative references in a formula, use a dollar sign ($) before the row and column of the cell address that you want to anchor—$C$18, for example.

Figure 9.12
Using relative
references does
not always work
when copying
formulas.

	C	D	E	F	G	H	I	J	K
	Feb-94	Mar-94	Apr-94	May-94	Jun-94	Employee Total		New Quota	
4	3745	4173	4667	4266	4755	$25,767		$64,417.50	
5	4801	6111	5824	6310	6811	$34,972		$0.00	
6	2753	3332	3428	3729	3919	$20,364		$0.00	
7	2104	2312	2535	2727	3105	$14,495		$0.00	
8	1947	2582	2274	2845	2242	$14,277		$0.00	
9	1366	1962	2171	1984	2081	$11,227		$0.00	
10	1355	2398	1798	1806	1812	$10,904		$0.00	
11	1570	2278	1904	1742	2183	$11,443		$0.00	
12	1403	1707	1853	1921	2123	$10,688		$0.00	
13	1755	1828	1935	1714	1720	$10,521		$0.00	
14									
15	$22,799	$28,683	$28,389	$29,044	$30,751	$164,658			

The following steps show the way to set up the example worksheet by using absolute references and then copying the formula to other cells:

1. On the bonus disk, open the worksheet file named SALES-94.XLS.

2. In cell J4, type the formula **=H5*$C$18** and press Enter. The result of the calculation is $64,417.50.

Tip

Use Shift+F4 to switch between absolute and relative references.

3. Copy the formula into cells J5:J13 to calculate the new quotas for the rest of the sales force. To do this, click on cell J4 and grab the handle at the bottom right side of the cell border.

4. Drag the selection down to cell J13 and release the mouse button. The new values appear in the selected cells, showing the sales quota for the rest of the staff (see fig. 9.13).

Figure 9.13
Copying the quota
formula using
Excel's absolute
reference format.

	C	D	E	F	G	H	I	J	K
	Microsoft Excel - SALES-94.XLS								
	File Edit View Insert Format Tools Data Window Help								
	Arial		10	B I U		$ % ,		100%	
	B2								
2									
3	Feb-94	Mar-94	Apr-94	May-94	Jun-94	Employee Total		New Quota	
4	3745	4173	4667	4266	4755	$25,767		$64,417.50	
5	4801	6111	5824	6310	6811	$34,972		$87,430.00	
6	2753	3332	3428	3729	3919	$20,364		$50,908.75	
7	2104	2312	2535	2727	3105	$14,495		$36,237.50	
8	1947	2582	2274	2845	2242	$14,277		$35,692.50	
9	1366	1962	2171	1984	2081	$11,227		$28,067.50	
10	1355	2398	1798	1806	1812	$10,904		$27,260.00	
11	1570	2278	1904	1742	2183	$11,443		$28,607.50	
12	1403	1707	1853	1921	2123	$10,688		$26,720.00	
13	1755	1828	1935	1714	1720	$10,521		$26,302.50	
14									
15	$22,799	$28,683	$28,389	$29,044	$30,751	$164,658			
16									

Sheet1 / Sheet2 / Sheet3 / Sheet4 / Sheet5 / Sheet6 /

Ready   NUM

II

Excel

Tip — You can use absolute references to anchor part of a cell reference. You can, for example, anchor just the column part or row part of the reference. To do this, place the dollar sign in front of the column address or the row address, depending on which part you want to anchor. You might want to do this if the column you refer to in a formula stays the same but the row changes with each calculation.

Referencing Another Worksheet in a Formula

If you have a lot of data and you create many worksheets to store this data, you might have occasions when a formula in one worksheet needs to use data from another sheet. These *sheet references* are handy so that you do not have to create redundant data in numerous sheets.

To refer to another cell in another sheet, place an exclamation mark between the sheet name and cell name. You might, for instance, write a formula in cell A9 in Sheet1 that needs to reference cell B5 in Sheet2. This reference looks like SHEET2!B5. (Use the sheet name in place of SHEET2 if you have named the sheet.)

Tip — When the sheet name contains spaces, such as Sales 94, you need to place single quotation marks around it when you are making sheet references.

If you are not sure of the cell reference in another sheet, you can start writing your formula and switch to the sheet that you want to reference when you get to that part of the formula. Then use your mouse and click on the cell or range of cells that you want in your formula. The cell or range reference appears automatically in your formula. You then can finish your formula and press Enter to calculate it.

Using 3D References

What if you have a formula that needs to reference a cell range that has two or more sheets in a workbook? This might happen if you have identical worksheets for different sales teams, regions, or states. You also might have several different worksheets that have totals calculated and entered in identical cell addresses. You then can add all these totals to get a grand total by referencing all the sheets and cell addresses in one formula.

When you have cell ranges such as this, Excel refers to them as *3D references*. A 3D reference is set up by including a *sheet range*, which names the beginning and ending sheets, and a *cell range*, which names the cells to which you are referring. A formula that uses a 3D reference that includes Sheet1 through Sheet10 and the cells A5:A10 might look something like the following:

=SUM(SHEET1:SHEET10!A5:A10)

Another way to include 3D references in your formulas is to use the mouse and click on the worksheets that you want to include in your formula. To do this, start your formula in the cell where you want the results. When you come to the point where you need to use the 3D reference, click on the first worksheet tab that you want to include in your reference, hold down Shift, click on the last worksheet that you want to include, and select the cells you want to reference. When you finish writing your formula, press Enter.

Calculating a Formula

As soon as you enter a formula (that is, type it and press Enter), Excel automatically calculates it. You might not want Excel to do this all the time, however, if you have created a complex, time-consuming calculation that you don't want to do right away. Or, you might want to write a formula before you get all the data in the worksheet.

To tell Excel not to calculate a formula automatically, perform the following steps:

1. Select **T**ool, **O**ptions. This displays the Options dialog box.

2. Click on the Calculation tab to display the Calculations options (see fig. 9.14).

3. Click on the **M**anual option. You also can set up Excel to calculate the worksheet automatically, except items in a table, which you can calculate manually by clicking on the Automatic Except **T**ables option.

The Calc <u>N</u>ow (F9) button can be used to calculate all your open worksheets. Or, you can use the Calc <u>S</u>heet button to calculate only the active worksheet. You can press F9 while you are working in the worksheet to calculate all open worksheets; you do not have to open this dialog box every time you want to calculate your worksheet. Press Shift+F9 to calculate the active worksheet.

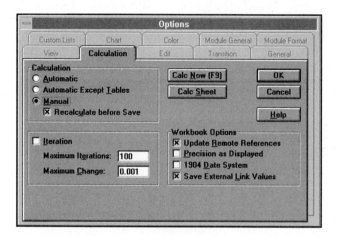

Figure 9.14
The Calculation option tab in the Options dialog box.

4. When you choose the <u>M</u>anual option, you then can decide whether to have Excel calculate before you save the worksheet by clicking the Recalc<u>u</u>late before Save option.

5. Press Enter or click on OK.

Viewing Worksheet Formulas

As you learned in Chapter 8, Excel displays the formula for a selected cell in the formula bar and the results of the calculation in the cell. You might, however, find this inconvenient if you want to view all your formulas at once. To do this, you can press Ctrl+' or perform the following steps:

1. Select <u>T</u>ools, <u>O</u>ptions.

2. Click on the View tab to display the View options (see fig. 9.15).

3. Click on the Fo<u>r</u>mulas check box in the Window Options group. This tells Excel to display formulas instead of values.

4. Press Enter or click on OK.

Figure 9.15
Use the View tab to tell Excel to show all the formulas in their cells.

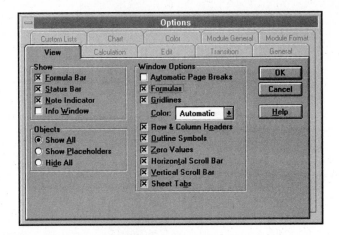

Using Arrays in Formulas

In the SALES-94.XLS worksheet in the preceding examples, notice how there are several areas that use the same formulas but have different cell references. The Employee Total column, for example, uses the same SUM formula to calculate each of the employees sales numbers.

When you have situations such as this, you can save system memory and time by using an *array formula,* a rectangular range of formulas that is treated as one group. Excel denotes array formulas by placing braces ({}) around them. Excel automatically places these braces; you do not have to place them yourself.

To enter an array formula, perform the following steps:

1. Select the range that you want to contain the array formula.

2. Enter the formula and use the range coordinates for the area you want to include in the array formula. You also can use the mouse to select this area.

3. Finish the formula.

4. Press Shift+Ctrl+Enter to tell Excel to make this formula an array formula. Excel places braces around the formula.

Tip

You cannot insert cells or rows within an array, edit a single cell in an array, or delete part of an array. You can edit an array by double-clicking on the array range. Edit the array formula and press Shift+Ctrl+Enter.

Formatting Your Worksheet

Once you enter your data and set up some formulas, your worksheet is functional, but it might not look very appealing. You might, for instance, want to highlight certain columns in your sheet, use color coded-cells, change fonts, or format dates, numbers, and times to improve the appearance of your worksheet.

Alignment

When you enter data into a cell, it aligns automatically to Excel's default. For text, this alignment is left-justified. For numbers, this alignment is right-justified. However, you might want to center the text or align the numbers along the left side of the cell. Excel enables you to align data in a number of different ways by using the Alignment tab in the Format Cells dialog box (see fig. 9.16). To use this option, select Format, Cells and click on the Alignment tab.

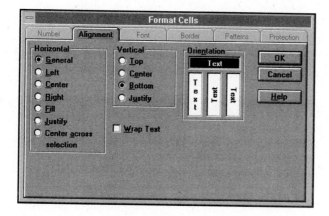

Figure 9.16

Use the Alignment tab to customize the way your data aligns in the cells.

These are the options that you can choose:

✔ **General.** Displays the data in the default alignment.

✔ **Left.** Left-aligns the data in the cell.

✔ **Center.** Centers the data in the cell.

✔ **Right.** Right-aligns the data in the cell.

✔ **Fill.** Repeats the data in the cell until the cell is full.

✔ **Justify.** Aligns the data in the cell with the left and right edges of the cell when you have more than one line of text in the cell.

✔ **Center across selection.** Centers the data in the cell across the range you select.

Tip

The Formatting toolbar contains buttons for aligning text, including the Left, Center, and Right Align buttons. You also can center text across cells by using the Center Text in Selection button.

When you use the Center across selection option, you can set up titles in your worksheets easily. In Chapter 8, for instance, you centered the title "American Conference" over your data.

Later in this chapter you are shown how to modify the height and width of rows and columns. When you do, you can change the way the cell contents are aligned vertically by using the options in the Vertical section of the Alignment tab. You can, for instance, align the data at the top of the cell with the Top option. Use the Center option to align the data in the center of the cell. The Bottom option is used to place the data at the bottom of the cell. Justify is used to justify the data in the cell vertically.

Another problem that you can overcome easily with the alignment options is a long text entry. In figure 9.17, for instance, the text in cell B4 overlaps several neighboring cells. To correct this problem, click in the Wrap Text check box on the Alignment tab to have Excel automatically adjust the height of the cell to accommodate several lines of text. Notice in figure 9.17 how cell D6 is large enough to contain all its text, making it easier to read.

Figure 9.17
The Wrap Text option enables you to place several lines of text in a cell.

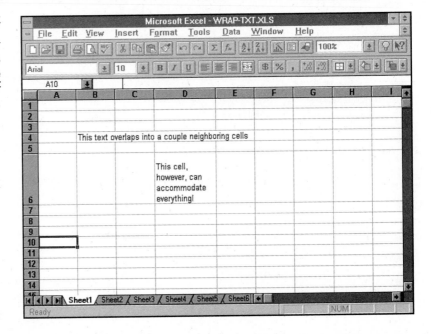

You might want to have text displayed in several different ways. This is handled by the Orientation section of the Alignment tab. The default selection is horizontal. You can choose the vertical option so that the text reads from top to bottom. Or, you might want to read the text sideways, reading top to bottom with the text rotated 90 degrees counterclockwise or 90 degrees clockwise. These latter options are handy when you need vertical titles for reports or charts. (See Chapter 12, "Excel Charts and Graphics," for more information regarding creating and formatting charts.)

Tabs and Carriage Returns

Most computer users are comfortable using a word processor to type text and do elementary tasks such as tabbing and starting new paragraphs. In most word processing applications, you press Tab to tab over or press Enter to start a new paragraph. In Excel, however, these tasks are not as intuitive.

If you press Enter while you are typing text, Excel interprets this as the end of your entry and enters the contents into the cell. Similarly, when you type text and then press Tab, Excel enters what you have typed and moves over to the next cell. To place a carriage return in a cell entry, press Alt+Enter. To place a tab in a cell entry, press Alt+Ctrl+Tab. By using tabs and carriage returns in your cell entries, you have more control over how your final worksheet looks.

You can delete Tab and carriage returns as you do any other character in a cell. First select the cell, press F2 for editing, and press Del to delete the Tab or return.

Fonts

The numbers, letters, and other characters that appear on your screen all belong to a certain font. A *font* is the typeface, type size, and type style of a certain character. With Windows 3.1, you can use TrueType fonts, a specially designed font that you can resize and print with semiprecision. That is, what you see on-screen in your worksheet will be what you should see when it is printed (or a close resemblance to it). (For more information on using and understanding the science of fonts, see *The Fonts Coach,* published by New Riders Publishing.)

The size, type, and variations of fonts you use help make your worksheet stand out among other reports. Keep in mind that when you format your worksheets you ultimately intend to have someone (maybe just you) look over it. For this reason, make your worksheets easy to use, to the point, and functional. A functional worksheet does not have to be drab in appearance or intimidating.

You might, for instance, change the point size from the default 12 points to a larger 14- or 16-point size. You then can make the text bold, italic, or underline. Along with centering titles or justifying text, you can add these subtle formatting changes to make your text pop off the page. Compare the worksheets in figures 9.18 and 9.19. Both contain the same data and same text. Which one are you more likely to read?

Figure 9.18
A worksheet without changing the default font characteristics.

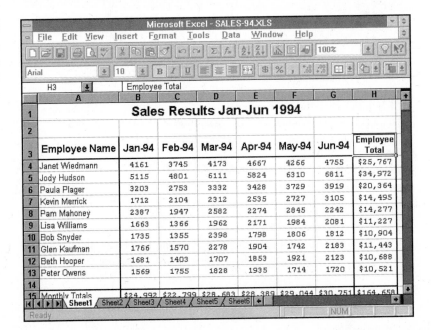

Figure 9.19
The same worksheet with added font enhancements.

Some of the most common character enhancing options are available on the default formatting toolbar. You probably will use this toolbar throughout the time you create your worksheets and enter data. The options available to help you change your font characteristics include the following (see fig. 9.20):

✔ **Font drop-down list.** Use this list to choose the font for the selection.

✔ **Font Size list.** Use this list to change the point size of the selected entry.

✔ **Bold, Italic, Underline buttons.** These buttons enable you to add bold, italic, and underline font styles to your selection.

✔ **Font Color.** Add a little color to your entries by changing the color of the selection from black to a number of different colors. You might, for instance, use red to denote late payments.

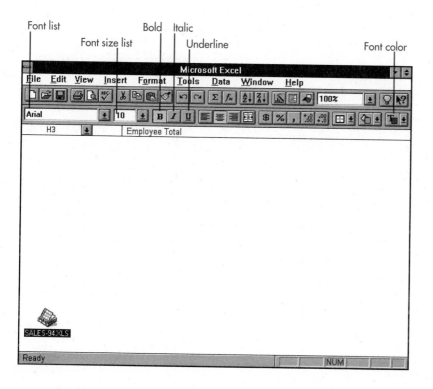

Figure 9.20
Character formatting options on the formatting toolbar.

II
Excel

If you want to use a dialog box interface to change the selected character(s), select Format, Cells and click on the Font tab. This displays the Font tab options (see fig. 9.21):

✔ Font. This option enables you to choose the font for the selection. TrueType fonts appear with a double T logo next to them. Printer fonts appear with a printer icon next to them.

✔ Font Style. Use this list to add character enhancements, such as regular (also know as *roman*), italic, bold, and bold italic.

✔ Size. This option enables you to select a different point size for your selection.

✔ Underline. This drop-down list enables you to select the type of underlining you want for your selection, such as None, Single, Double, and Single or Double Accounting. Accounting underlines only underline the numbers in a cell, not the entire cell.

✔ Color. Use this list to select a color for your selection. You might want to experiment with the way different colors print. Use Automatic for black-and-white printers if you do not want to take any chances.

✔ Normal Font. This check box enables you to select Excel's default font. Chapter 14, "Customizing Excel 5," discusses changing Excel's default settings.

✔ Effects. This area enables you to add Strikethrough, Superscript, and Subscript characteristics to your selection.

Figure 9.21
The Font tab
options.

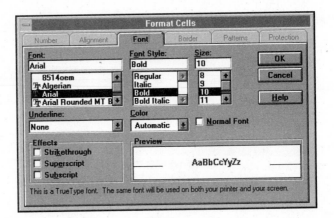

The Preview window in the lower right corner of the tab screen enables you to view what the changes will do to your selection.

A *printer font* is used to print your worksheets and charts from preinstalled fonts in your printer or in cartridges you can plug into the printer. PostScript fonts, for example, are printer fonts. You also can download fonts from your computer to the printer's memory.

When you use a printer font, another font is used to display the characters on your screen. These screen fonts usually are installed when you install your printer in Windows. You might see some differences between what is on-screen

and what actually prints, because the screen fonts might not always have the same font size and styles that the printer font has. You usually will use TrueType fonts when working with worksheets, but you can invest in some professional-quality printer fonts that will add much more to your final presentation.

Numeric Formats

In Chapter 8 you were introduced to the different types of numeric formats that Excel offers. Because spreadsheet applications are designed around conveying numeric data, the format your numbers are in is probably the most crucial part of your worksheet. The way you format your numeric data is up to you, but you should be consistent in the way you handle numbers from worksheet to worksheet in each workbook.

The following are ways that you might want to handle numeric data: make all negative numbers a different color, such as red or blue; use commas for thousands separators; use brackets for special numbers. Excel provides several built-in number formats (see table 9.3), and also enables you to create your own number formats. (For more information on creating your own number formats, pick up a copy of *Inside Excel 5 for Windows*, published by New Riders Publishing.)

Table 9.3
Excel's Built-In Number Formats

Format Category	Format Setting	Examples	
		Positive	Negative
All	General	4500.75	−4500.75
Custom	Lists custom formats (if any)		
Number	0	4501	−4501
	0.00	4500.75	−4500.75
	#,##0	4,501	−4,501
	#,##0.00	4,500.75	−4,500.75
	#,##0_);(#,##0)	4,501	(4,501)
	#,##0_);[Red](##,##0)	4,501	(4501)**
	#,##0.00);(#,##0.00)	4,500.75	(4,500.75)
	#,##0.00_);[Red](#,##0.00)	4,500.75	(4,500.75)*

continues

Table 9.3, Continued
Excel's Built-In Number Formats

Format Category	Format Setting	Examples Positive	Negative
Accounting	_(*#,##0_);_(#,##0);_(*"-"_);_(@_)	4,500	(4,500)
	_(*#,##0.00_);_(*(#,##0.00);_(*"-"??_);_(@_)	4,500.75	(4,500.75)
	_($*#,##0_);_($*(#,##0):_($*"-"_);_(@_)	$4,500	$(4,500)
	_($*#,##0.00_);_($(#,##0.00);_($*"_"??);_(@_)	$4,500.75	$(4,500.75)
Percentage	0%	45%	–45%
	0.00%	45.75%	–45.75%
Fraction	#?/?	45 3/4	–45 3/4
	#??/??	45 31/42	–45 31/42
Scientific	0.00E+00	4.5E+04	–4.5E+04
Text	@ (Text placeholder)		
Currency	$#,##0_);($#,##0)	$4,501	($4,501)
	$#,##0_);[Red]($#,##0)	$4,501	($4,501)
	$#,##0.00_);($#,##0.00)	$4,500.75	($4,500.75)
	$#,##0.00_);[Red]($#,##0.00)	$4,500.75	($4,500.75)

*Denotes red numbers when a negative value appears

To apply a format to an individual cell or range, select that cell or range and perform the following steps:

1. Select Format, Cells to display the Format Cells dialog box.

2. Click on the Number tab to activate it (see fig. 9.22).

3. In the Category list box, click on the type of number that you want to format, such as General, Number, or Percentage. When you select a category, the list in the Format Codes list box changes to show the format of the number (these are the format settings listed in table 9.3).

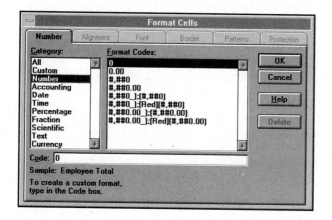

Figure 9.22
Use the Number tab to select the number formatting of your choice.

4. In the Format Codes list box, click on the format that you want to use. Look at the Sample: line at the bottom of the dialog box to help you select the correct format.

5. Press Enter or click on OK

If you want a quicker way to apply common number formats, you can use keyboard shortcuts. The following list shows the key combination and the format code that is applied:

Key Combination	Format Code
Ctrl+Shift+~	General
Ctrl+Shift+!	0.00
Ctrl+Shift+$	$#,##0.00;($#,##0.00)
Ctrl+Shift+%	0%
Ctrl+Shift+^	0.00E+00

When you enter your numeric data, you can specify the type of format you want applied to the number by adding certain characters, such as the dollar sign ($) and percentage sign (%). To enter a dollar amount, begin your entry with a dollar sign, enter the numeric data, and press Enter. Excel interprets your entry as a Currency format. To enter a percent, type the number, then add a percent sign (%) after it. Excel interprets this as the Percentage format and enters it as such.

Tip A quick way to display the Number dialog box is to select the cell that you want to format, click the right mouse button, and select **N**umber from the pop-up menu. This immediately displays the Number dialog box, enabling you to add or change number formats.

Modifying Columns

One of the common problems you run into with any spreadsheet application, including Excel, is the default size of the cells. They usually are too small to hold all the data you want to place in them. Excel 5 makes it easier to resize the rows and columns of your worksheets.

Recall that when you enter a number, or after a calculation is evaluated, you might have cells that contain #### characters. These characters tell you that the cell is not large enough to display the number. You need to widen the column to display the number.

You can change one or several columns by performing the following steps:

1. Select the cells in the column that you want to widen. Select a cell in each column that you want to adjust if you are resizing multiple columns.

2. Select Format, Column to display the pop-out menu shown in figure 9.23.

Figure 9.23
Adjust the size or columns using the Column options.

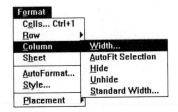

The Column options provide you with the following choices:

✔ Width. This option enables you to modify the selected columns to a width based on the Normal font. When you select this option, the Column Width dialog box appears (see fig. 9.24). You can enter a specific width in the Column Width field box.

Figure 9.24
Use the Column Width dialog box to enter a specific column width.

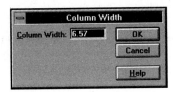

✔ AutoFit Selection. This option probably is the most convenient option to use because it modifies the column widths to accommodate the widest cell contents in your selection. When you choose this option, Excel automatically increases or decreases the size of the selected columns to best fit your entries.

✔ Hide. You can hide specific columns to keep sensitive data secure. You learn more about this option later in this chapter.

✔ Unhide. Use this option to unhide hidden columns. This option is discussed in more detail later.

✔ Standard Width. This option enables you to select the default standard column width for the selected columns. When you select this option, the Standard Width dialog box appears (see fig. 9.25). You can press Enter or click on OK to accept the default width. Or, you can change the default column width by changing the value in the Standard Column Width field box. The standard column width is 8.43 characters, the number of characters that can be displayed in the cell in the normal font.

Figure 9.25
Accept or change the standard column width in the Standard Width dialog box.

3. Press Enter or click on OK to accept your choice.

To change columns quickly, use your mouse. Select the columns you want to modify and move the pointer onto the column separator directly to the right of the column heading (see fig. 9.26). Drag the column left or right until the column is the width that you want. Release the mouse button.

If you want to fit the column to the widest cell entry, move your mouse pointer to the column heading and double-click on the column separator. This automatically modifies the selected column to fit the widest entry.

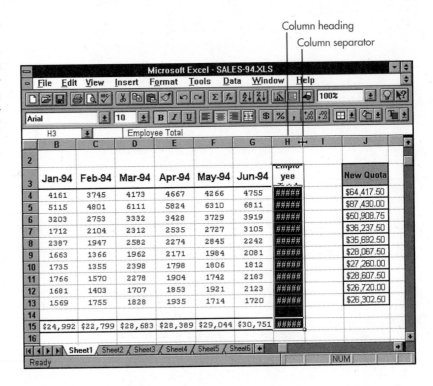

Figure 9.26
Move the mouse pointer to the column separator in the column heading to modify column widths.

Hiding Columns

If you have a budget worksheet, some of the information will be shared with your management and staff, but some, such as management salaries, should not be available to all readers. To get around this problem, you can create two separate worksheets—one with salaries and one without. This, however, separates key data that you need to include in your total budget expectation.

Another way to solve this problem is to hide the columns that contain this information. To hide selected columns of data, choose Format, Column, Hide. Excel automatically hides the selected columns. To reveal a hidden column, select the cells that span the hidden column and choose Format, Column, Unhide. The hidden column appears.

To hide a column using the mouse, move the mouse pointer over the column separator that is to the right of the column heading you want to hide. When the pointer changes to a two-headed pointer, drag the column separator left until it is past the separator on its left.

Reverse the process to unhide the column. Move the pointer until it touches the column separator on the right of a hidden column. The pointer then changes to a two-headed pointer with space between the two heads. Move the pointer so

that its left tip touches the column separator, and drag the separator to the right. Release the mouse button, and the column is revealed.

Modifying Rows

Row size also might be a problem for the type of data you use. The standard row height, for example, usually is not large enough to display readable text or make large enough worksheet titles. You also might want to add more space between different types of numbers, such as monthly and annual totals.

You can adjust the height of rows much the same way you can columns. The standard row height is 12.75 points, enabling it to fit the default Excel font, Arial 10 point.

 Tip

If you change the point size of a font, to 20 points, for example, Excel automatically resizes the row height to fit the new font size. You do not need to adjust the row height manually.

To change the row height of selected rows, perform the following steps:

1. Select the rows you want to resize.

2. Select Format, **R**ow to display the pop-out menu shown in figure 9.27.

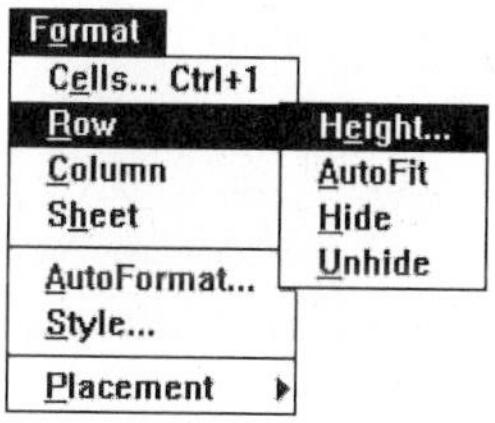

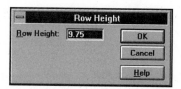

Figure 9.27
Use the Row option to change row height of selected rows.

The Row options provide you with the following choices:

✔ H**e**ight. Use this option to enter a specific height for the selected rows. When you select this option, the Row Height dialog box appears (see fig. 9.28). Fill in the desired height in the **R**ow Height field box.

Figure 9.28
Use the Height option to specify row heights precisely.

✔ AutoFit. Use this option to change the row height quickly to accommodate the best fit for the row. This option is nice if you don't want to mess around with changing row heights manually.

✔ Hide. This option enables you to hide selected rows. You learn more about this later in this chapter.

✔ Unhide. This option enables you to unhide selected rows. You learn more about this later.

3. Press Enter or choose OK when you specify the row height in the Row Height field box.

To change row heights quickly, use your mouse. Select the line under the row header you want to modify and drag the pointer up or down until the row height is what you want. Release the mouse button.

If you want to change the row to fit the tallest entries in a cell, move your mouse pointer to the row heading and double-click on the row separator. This automatically modifies the selected row to fit the tallest entry.

Hiding Rows

If you have data entered in certain rows in your worksheets that you want to hide, select those rows and choose Format, Row, Hide. You then can reveal the rows by selecting the cells that span the hidden rows, as you learned earlier in this chapter.

To hide a row using the mouse, move the mouse pointer over the row separator that is below the row heading you want to hide. When the pointer changes to a two-headed pointer, drag the row separator up until it is past the separator above it.

Reverse the process to unhide the row. Move the pointer over the row number that is under the hidden row until it changes to a two-headed pointer with space between the two heads. Drag the line down to reveal the row.

Mastering Borders, Patterns, and Colors

Pick up your favorite magazine and notice how the layout adds to the readability of the information. Most of the design features that professional designers employ are subtle, yet effective: colors, borders, shading, and patterns. Excel 5 enables you to improve the presentation of your worksheets with these same tools.

Borders

One of the easiest ways to enhance the appearance of your worksheets is to add borders to cells or ranges of data. You can, for instance, add a border around a table of data, use borders to highlight totals, or place a border to call attention to data-entry areas on your worksheets. Excel gives you a number of different borders, as shown in figure 9.29.

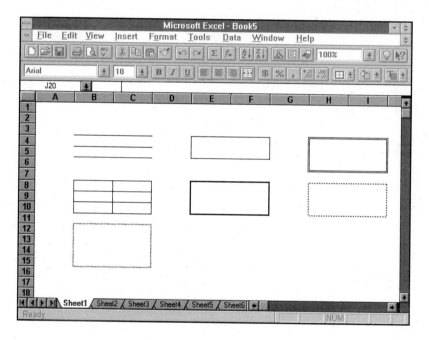

Figure 9.29
Use borders to enhance your worksheets.

The quickest way to add a border to a selected cell or range of cells is to use the Border button on the Formatting toolbar:

1. Select the cell or range of cells that you want to enclose in a border.

2. Click on the down arrow on the Border button to display the borders list box (see fig. 9.30).

3. Pick the border style you want to use and click on it. This places the selected border around your selection.

Figure 9.30
Click on the down
arrow on the
Borders button to
display the
borders list.

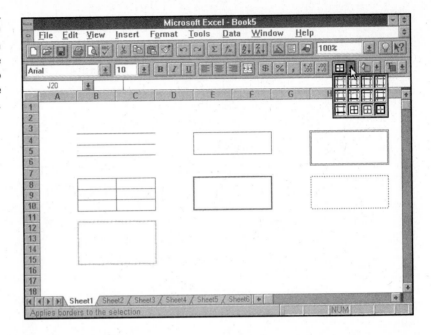

One of the new features of Excel 5 is the use of tear-off menus and tools. If you plan to use the Border button several times in succession, you can "tear" it off the toolbar and let it float on your desktop. To do this, click on the down arrow on the Border button, grab the border list with your mouse, and drag it to someplace convenient on your desktop. When you release the mouse button, the border list floats on your worksheet, waiting for you to use it.

Another way to select borders for your worksheets is to use the Border tab in the Format Cells dialog box. To access this dialog box, select F$\underline{o}$rmat, $\underline{C}$ell, and click on the Border tab (see fig. 9.31).

The Border tab contains the following options:

✔ $\underline{O}$utline. Use this option when you want to add a border to the outside edges of your selection.

✔ $\underline{L}$eft. This option applies a border to the left edge of the selection.

✔ $\underline{R}$ight. This option applies a border to the right edge of the selection.

✔ $\underline{T}$op. This option applies a border to the top edge of the selection.

✔ $\underline{B}$ottom. This option applies a border to the bottom edge of the selection.

✔ Styl$\underline{e}$. This option shows the eight different border styles you can choose, including double lines, dashed lines, thin line, and so on.

✔ **Color.** Use this pull-down list box to apply different colors to your borders. Keep in mind that these colors do not print if you have a black-and-white printer. You can, however, achieve high-quality and easier-to-read worksheets using various color schemes with your borders.

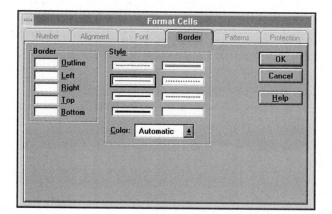

Figure 9.31
Use the Border tab to select borders for your selections.

Patterns

Another effective tool for formatting your worksheets is the use of patterns. Excel enables you to use patterns to add background effects to your lists, tables, and other entries. The patterns can be used for your printouts and for your on-screen or visual presentations. You can, for example, output your worksheet to Microsoft PowerPoint and use it in an overhead presentation. To make your worksheets more powerful, experiment with the patterns until you find ones that do not overpower the information in your sheets, but add to its effectiveness.

To apply patterns to your worksheets, use the Pattern tab in the Format Cells dialog box. Excel 5 gives you 18 different types of patterns to choose from. To add a pattern to your selection, select Format, Cells, and click on the Patterns tab (see fig. 9.32).

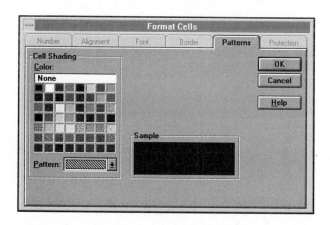

Figure 9.32
Apply patterns and shading to your worksheets using the Patterns tab.

Click on the Pattern pull-down list box and examine the various types of patterns available to you. You can see an example of each one by clicking on it and looking at the Sample area of the dialog box. When you decide on a pattern, press Enter or click on OK. The pattern is applied to the worksheet selections.

You might want to set off a row, column, or specific cells that should not contain any data. To help you and others keep from entering data into these cells, use a pattern, such as a diagonal pattern, that makes it impossible to read the data.

Colors

As you have seen, Excel enables you to apply several different formatting enhancements to your worksheets. Probably the most effective and underused feature is color. You can brighten your on-screen presentations by effectively using color to point out areas of interest, key data points, or data-entry areas.

Although you should use as much color and shading as you can to enhance your worksheets, you should keep in mind your printing limitations. If you have a black-and-white printer, you cannot, of course, print color images.

Many times, these colors are converted to gray-scale images when you try to print them. If you have key data separated by color, such as a light blue and a yellow, these colors usually print as similar gray tones, making it nearly impossible to distinguish them from each other. The best way to determine what works best for your individual situation is to experiment with different shading and colors.

To apply colors to your cells or range of cells, perform the following steps:

1. Select the cell or range to which you want to add color.

2. Select, Format, Cells.

3. If you want to add color to your border, click on the Border tab and, using the Color drop-down list box, choose the color you want.

   If you want to add color to your pattern, click on the Patterns tab and choose the color you want from the Color area. If you want a foreground color, click on the Pattern drop-down list box and select a color.

4. Press Enter or click on OK to apply the color to your selection.

Tip

You also can click on the Color button on the Formatting toolbar to add color to a cell. Click on the down arrow on the button and choose the color of your choice.

If you plan to use the Color button several times, remember to tear it off the toolbar and let it float on your workspace. To do this, click on the down arrow on the Color button to display the color list. Then, grab the color list with the mouse and drag it off the toolbar. When you release the mouse button, the color list floats on your desktop, enabling you to use it over and over.

Examining Advanced Printing Options

You learned in Chapter 8 how to use some of Excel 5's printing options and how to print your worksheets. This section adds to that discussion and shows you how to perform more sophisticated printing operations.

Setting Print Ranges

When you print a worksheet, Excel prints the entire worksheet by default. You can, however, adjust the print range to include only those cells or portions of worksheets that you want to print. To do this, use the File, Page Setup command. You also can click on the Page Setup option when you are in the Print dialog box.

To set up a print area, perform the following steps:

1. Select File, Page Setup and click on the Sheet tab. This displays the Sheet tab in the Page Setup dialog box (see fig. 9.33).

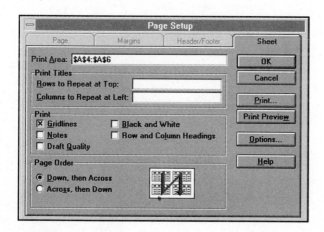

Figure 9.33
Set the print range using the Sheet tab options.

II

Excel

2. Click in the Print Area text box. This is where you tell Excel which area of the worksheet you want to print.

3. Move your mouse pointer back to the area of your worksheet that you want to print and select the cells you want to print. Excel automatically places the cell addresses in the Print Area text field.

To select the cells you want to print, you might have to move the Page Setup dialog box to the lower part of your screen to get it out of the way. This does not affect the selection or the options you have picked in the Sheet tab.

4. Press Enter or choose OK when you finish selecting the print range. Excel marks the print range with dashed lines to remind you what the print range is.

To remove the print range, select File, Page Setup and click on the Sheet tab. In the Print Area text box, delete all the cells to print the entire worksheet. Or, you can delete only those cells you do not want to include in the print range.

Controlling Page Breaks

After you select the print range, you might want to modify a few of the print settings to make sure that what you want to print fits on a page. One such option inserts a page break to reposition an automatic page break that Excel has added to your worksheet.

When you insert manual page breaks, Excel inserts them above and to the left of where you have the insertion point (or the active cell). Another feature of Excel is that the manual page breaks appear as longer and darker dashed lines than automatic page breaks. If you cannot see the page breaks very well, turn off the gridlines. This helps automatic and manual page breaks stand out better.

Perform the following steps to insert manual page breaks:

1. Select the cell below and to the right of the place where you want a manual page break to be inserted.

To select a vertical page break, move the insertion point to row 1 of where you want the vertical break to be. If, for instance, you want a vertical page break to occur between columns D and E, move the insertion point to cell E1.

2. Choose Insert, Page Break. Excel places a manual page break at the point you specify.

To remove the manual page break, select the cell below and to the right of the page break. Choose Insert, Remove Page Break, which appears on the menu only when you select a

manual page break to remove. If the menu item does not appear, you have not selected the correct cell in the worksheet. Try again.

If you want to remove all manual page breaks in your worksheets, select the entire worksheet and choose Insert, Remove Page Break. This clears all the manual page breaks. It does not, however, clear automatic page breaks, which cannot be removed. You can reposition them by inserting manual page breaks, as prescribed in the preceding steps.

Resizing Margins

Sometimes you create worksheets that contain a ton of data, but you do not want to print out pages and pages. You want to print out the fewest number of pages possible to get all your data on hardcopy reports. One way to do this is to reset page margins so that you can squeeze as much onto a page as possible.

Check your individual printer to see what the minimum margin can be on your documents. Some printers must have at least a 1/4-inch margin on the paper's edge. This means, of course, that your worksheet margins must be at least 1/4 inch.

If you cannot fit everything on the page even by modifying the margins, try different fonts and font sizes until you find one that can fit everything you want on a page or a few pages. Keep in mind, too, that you need to be able to read the data, so don't choose a point size that is too small, such as 6 point. You would need to carry around a magnifying glass just to read your worksheets.

To change the margins in your worksheets, change to Print Preview mode first. This way you can see the entire page and resize the margins. To do this, choose File, Print Preview, then perform the following steps:

1. Click on the Margins button in the Print Preview toolbar.

2. Move the mouse pointer to the margin or column you want to change. The pointer changes to a two-sided arrow indicating that you can drag the handle. Look in the status bar to see the margin size or column width of your selection.

3. Hold down the mouse button and drag the handle until it is placed where you want the new margin or column. Continue Steps 2 and 3 until your worksheet is set up as you want it.

Selecting Printers

If you have more than one printer set up under Windows, you might want to use more than one to print your worksheet, depending on the type of paper or other options available for a specific need. You might, for instance, choose to print out all your rough drafts on a dot-matrix printer to conserve laser printer resources. Or, you might have a color printer set up for your finished worksheets.

To select a printer that is not the default printer, select File, Print, Printer Setup to display the Printer Setup dialog box (see fig. 9.34). In the Printer area, click on the printer of your choice. You also can click on the Setup button to modify the printer's options. Click on OK or press Enter.

Figure 9.34
Select a printer or change its setup options using the Printer Setup dialog box.

One way to dress up your printouts is to include titles on your worksheets. To do this, select File, Page Setup and click on the Sheet tab. Click in the Rows to Repeat at Top text box or the Columns to Repeat at Left text box to specify where you want the title to appear. Choose the rows or columns (they must be adjacent rows and columns) that you want to have printed on each page. Press Enter or click on OK.

Chapter Snapshot

This chapter introduces you to Excel 5.0 functions. *Functions* are tools you can use to analyze data and get information in the form of values. These values result from a calculation or group of calculations on information from your worksheets. Put another way, functions help give you answers to questions for evaluation, examination, and projections in your business. In this chapter, you will learn about the following:

Excel version 5.0 has new functions not included in prior releases and some powerful new ways to use them. If you are new to functions, you will find the first part of this chapter most helpful. If you are experienced with functions, you might want to go directly to the section containing the functions that you want to apply to your workbooks.

10 CHAPTER

Mastering Excel Functions

by Critch Greaves

This chapter begins with a discussion of what functions are and the concepts behind them. Throughout this section you will use sample worksheets and workbooks and have an opportunity to practice using several popular functions. Each function has a step-by-step explanation of its use, purpose, and syntax.

For many of the function categories available in Excel 5.0, you will learn about several functions and see examples of how to use them. The following functions are covered in this chapter:

- ✔ **Financial.** FV is the future value. CUMIPMT is the cumulative interest payment. CUMPRINC is the cumulative principal payment. EFFECT is the effective annual interest rate.

- ✔ **Statistical.** AVERAGE averages a group of values. SUM adds a group of values. MAX returns the largest number in a group. MIN returns the smallest number in a group. RANK ranks values from largest to smallest, or vice versa.

✔ **Math and Trigonometry.** MEDIAN returns the median in a group of values. ABS returns an absolute value for a number or range of numbers. COUNTIF sums values, provided certain criteria are met. EVEN and ODD round numbers to the nearest integer as even or odd. MOD returns the remainder of a division calculation. PI returns the value of pi. ROMAN returns the roman numeral counterpart to Arabic numeral values. ROUND rounds numbers to specific levels. POWER raises a number to a specific power. SUMIF adds a group of numbers, provided certain criteria are met. PRODUCT sums a group of numbers.

✔ **Text.** CONCATENATE joins multiple arrays of text. DOLLAR formats numbers as text, with the currency format. FIXED formats numbers with a fixed number of decimal places. LEFT and RIGHT extract a certain number of characters from the left or right of a string of characters. UPPER, LOWER, and PROPER change the case for the display of text. UPPER displays in all uppercase, LOWER displays in all lowercase, and PROPER displays the first character of each word capitalized. TRIM removes spaces from strings of text.

✔ **Lookup and Reference.** ADDRESS returns information about the cell address of a reference. AREAS returns a value about an area in a reference. CHOOSE returns a value based on an index number and a list of values. HLOOKUP and VLOOKUP return values based on the location in a row or column. MATCH returns the location of a string in an array.

✔ **Information.** CELL returns information about a cell and its contents. COUNTBLANK counts blank cells in a range or array. INFO returns information about your system, environment, and setup. ISEVEN and ISODD return values of TRUE or FALSE based on whether a value is even or odd. N converts numbers to other formats for use in other spreadsheet programs. TYPE returns a numeric value based on the type of information contained in a cell.

✔ **Logical.** AND and IF return TRUE or FALSE values about a statement or calculation. AND needs all arguments to be true to return a TRUE value. NOT reverses the logic of an argument; true arguments become false, and vice versa. OR returns a TRUE value if any statement in a set of statements separated by OR is true (otherwise false is returned). TRUE and FALSE return TRUE and FALSE as values.

With Excel 5.0, there are several changes and additions to the list of available functions. Here are the new and changed functions, by category:

✔ **Database and List.** SQLREQUEST enables connection with an outside data source and runs a query from Excel, returning the result as an array done without macros. SUBTOTAL returns subtotals from lists or databases.

✔ **Date and Time.** DAYS360 returns the number of days between two dates in a 360-day year (if your accounting year is based on 12 30-day months). WEEKDAY converts a serial number to a day of the week. YEARFRAC returns a fraction figured on the number of days between two dates.

✔ **DDE and External.** SQLREQUEST (see the Database and List entry).

✔ **Financial.** AMORDEGRC is the depreciation that prorates assets for accounting periods function. AMORLINC is the depreciation that calculates on the life of assets for accounting periods.

✔ **Information.** COUNTBLANK counts the number of blank cells in a specified range of cells.

✔ **Lookup and Reference.** HLOOKUP returns a value for an indicated cell from the top row of an array. VLOOKUP returns a value from the leftmost column of an array.

✔ **Math and Trigonometry.** COUNTIF counts the number of cells in a range, if they are not blank and if certain conditions are satisfied. POWER returns the value of a number raised to a particular power. ROMAN converts Arabic numerals to roman numerals. ROUNDDOWN rounds numbers down. ROUNDUP rounds numbers up. SUMIF adds cells based on given criteria.

✔ **Text.** CONCATENATE merges text from multiple locations into one item.

Using Functions

Simple calculations, such as adding or subtracting, on a number or series of numbers are executed by using simple formulas. The simple formula SUM(A1..A5), for instance, inserts the sum of the numbers contained in the range A1..A5 into the cell containing the formula. These formulas are the foundation of many functions. Other functions use a combination of several formulas or procedures to achieve a desired result.

Functions, like formulas, all follow the same basic format:

✔ They must begin with an equal sign (=).

✔ The function name must be entered.

✔ Information about a cell or range of cells to be analyzed must be included.

✔ Arguments about what to do with the selected range of cells are entered last.

Some functions need additional information, and those examples will be discussed as they arise. For example, the following is the syntax for the ADDRESS function, which returns a value about a cell address in a worksheet:

```
ADDRESS (row_number,column_number,absolute_number,a1,sheet_text)
```

The arguments `row_number` and `column_number` are required arguments, and the remainder of the arguments are optional.

Some functions permit a variable number of arguments; for instance, use as many arguments in the SUM function as necessary. You can incorporate up to 1,024 arguments in a function, as long as no single string of characters in the function statement exceeds 255 characters.

Functions can be entered into worksheets manually, with a macro, or by using the Function Wizard.

Using the Function Wizard

One of the most exciting new tools Excel 5.0 has is the Function Wizard. It makes functions easier to use and understand by organizing them into logical categories by type, and by prompting you to complete the arguments required to make the function return a correct value.

Starting the Function Wizard can be done several ways. Clicking on the Function Wizard button on the Standard toolbar (see fig. 10.1) invokes the Wizard's first screen, which indicates that you are working on the first of two steps. The same button also appears on the formula bar when you double-click on a specific cell in your worksheet. This button works the same way that the Standard toolbar button does.

Figure 10.1
The Standard toolbar, showing the Function Wizard button.

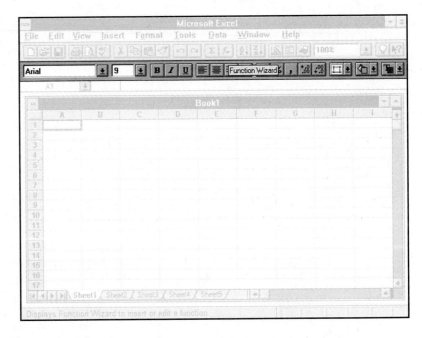

When you add a toolbar from the Toolbars dialog box (opened by selecting the Toolbars option in the View menu), it first appears as a floating toolbar on top of the current worksheet. To move the floating toolbar to the top of the Excel screen as shown in figure 10.1, double-click on the title bar of the floating toolbar. The floating toolbar will be installed in a fixed location at the top of the Excel screen.

To move a toolbar from its fixed location to a floating window, double-click anywhere on the toolbar other than a button.

You also can start the Function Wizard from the menu selections in the title bar, by selecting Function from the Insert menu. A keyboard shortcut for starting the Function Wizard is Shift+F3. Yet another way to start the Wizard is to enter the name of the function in a cell and press Ctrl+A.

Clicking on either of the Function Wizard buttons, using the pull-down menu, and using the keyboard method all produce the same result—the first of two dialog boxes. In the Function Wizard dialog box title, the status of the function insertion process is displayed as Step 1 of 2. You select which function you want to use by function category and function name. The function categories are listed on the left side of the box, and the associated functions are listed on the right.

The most recently used category of functions also appears in the Category window. This is useful especially if you use a particular group of functions regularly (the list changes and maintains the last 10 functions used). When a function is highlighted, its name, a brief description, and its arguments are displayed below the category list.

After the function is chosen, clicking on the Next button advances you to the second step: entering arguments or instructions for calculation.

If you invoke the Wizard by typing an equal sign, the name of the function, and pressing Shift+F3, typing the name in lowercase provides a validation of the function name. If the name is entered correctly, Excel will convert it to uppercase automatically. If your entered name is incorrect or invalid, Excel will insert a plus sign and leave the invalid name in lowercase.

In this second step, the name, description of the function, and arguments appear along with boxes showing the values of each argument. The resultant value of the function is shown in the top right corner of the box.

Using the manual name entry method, the Wizard skips to the Step 2 of 2 dialog box (entering arguments) because you have already selected the function you wish to use.

Arguments that require cell addresses or range information can be entered by keyboard or mouse. Other arguments that are not associated with specific cells on the worksheet must be entered manually. Some arguments are required for a value to be returned, and some are optional. Arguments that are required appear in bold and (required) appears above the edit boxes when the field is selected. Optional arguments appear in regular typeface, with (optional) next to the name (see fig. 10.2).

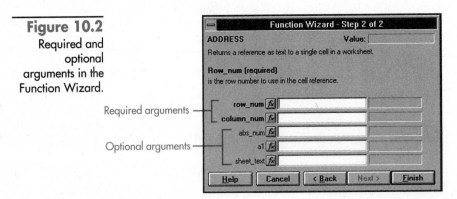

Figure 10.2
Required and optional arguments in the Function Wizard.

Required arguments —
Optional arguments —

Note that to the left of each function edit box is a Function Wizard button. Use this if you need to incorporate additional calculations or functions as arguments, a process known as *nesting functions*. Excel enables nesting of up to seven levels. When you nest functions, another Function Wizard box appears, and the dialog box title indicates that you are editing function 1 of 2. When you click on the Next button, that function is entered into the current function, and editing of the second function is enabled. You will have a chance to practice nesting functions and editing functions later in this section.

Tip

When you want to edit a function using the Function Wizard, click on the cell containing the function to edit and press Shift+F3. This invokes the Function Wizard and takes you directly to the Step 2 of 2 dialog box, with all the arguments in the edit boxes.

The buttons at the bottom of the first screen in the Function Wizard are Help, Cancel, Back, Next, and Finish. If you get stuck on a particular function, click on the Help button. A help session will begin for the topic or formula highlighted. Cancel closes the Function Wizard completely, unless you are nesting a function. If so, it cancels only the function you are nesting. Back is activated when the Step 2 of 2 dialog box is active, and it takes you back to the Step 1 of 2 dialog box so that, if needed, you can select a new function type or name. The Next button takes you from the Step 1 of 2 to the Step 2 of 2 dialog box, and Finish completes the Function Wizard and places the function statement in the cell that was activated when the Function Wizard was invoked.

Using Add-Ins

Some functions require add-ins to work. An *add-in* is a file that can be installed from the Tools menu enabling additional commands and functions. The following are add-ins that come with Excel:

✔ Analysis ToolPak is used for financial and engineering functions and provides additional tools for statistical and engineering applications.

✔ AutoSave performs timed saves to disk while you work.

✔ ODBC (Open Data Base Connectivity) Query is a collection of worksheet and macro functions for retrieving data from external database files using Microsoft Query.

✔ Report Manager prints reports based on views and scenarios.

✔ Slide Show is used for making presentation slides from worksheets and charts.

The PowerPoint program within Microsoft Office Professional has many more presentation features. See Part Three of this book to learn more about PowerPoint.

✔ Solver is installed at setup, enabling you to analyze what-if scenarios based on changing information.

✔ View Manager saves the current window display as a view and enables you to look at worksheets in varying ways.

Add-ins are located in the Excel LIBRARY directory or one of its subdirectories. If an add-in does not appear in the Tools, Add-Ins menu selection, using Microsoft Excel Setup will enable you to install it.

See Chapter 11, "Advanced Worksheet Capabilities," for a more detailed explanation of add-ins.

Financial Functions

Excel has over 50 financial functions prewritten and available for use in worksheets. Many of them require the use of add-ins. If a function does not appear, you may need to check which add-ins are installed in the Tools, Add-Ins menu selection. A good example of financial functions is the Future Value function.

The Future Value Function (FV)

FV, the Future Value function, calculates the future value of an investment. The syntax used for this function is the following:

```
=FV(rate, nper, pmt, pv, type)
```

The required arguments are rate (the current percentage rate fixed for the term of the investment), nper (the number of periods of payment), and pmt (the payment amount per period). In the optional arguments, pv is the present value of a lump sum of future payments and type is 0 or 1 depending on whether payments are due at the beginning or end of a period.

Figure 10.3 shows the process of finding the future value of a monthly $100.00 payment into an annuity that yields 10 percent over a five-year period, with payments at the end of each period.

Figure 10.3

The values in the Function Wizard edit boxes for FV.

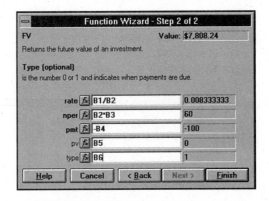

One technique you can use to organize your worksheets in a workbook is to name the sheets with unique identifiers, as you will see in many of the figures throughout this chapter. To name a worksheet, double-click on its tab to display the Rename Sheet dialog box. Type the new name and click on OK. The new name will appear on the tab.

Using the same function with worksheet cell addresses rather than values enables you to change numbers and see the effect of different interest rates, payment amounts, or terms, without having to reenter the entire function or go through all the Wizard's steps.

Enter the following in B8:

```
=FV(B1/B2,B2*B3,-B4,B5,B6)
```

This enables you to enter all the pertinent information into your equation and see immediate results. Try performing the function using the manual typing method (use lowercase letters for function validation), and then do the same thing using the Function Wizard.

Manually typing the functions usually is more time-consuming and cumbersome than using the Function Wizard. Shorter, more frequently used functions can be faster and easier to

enter using the keyboard, though. Experimenting with both methods will allow you to find the most effective way to use your software.

If your value returned is a cell full of ### signs, double-clicking on the column top (where the letter designation is) will make the column big enough to display its largest value entered so far.

Notice in the formula entry, the payment and present values have a negative value. This is important to several financial functions because the functions return negative values, which can be confusing. Adding the negatives to the function cell references enables you to enter positive numbers, which for many people might make more sense. If you are setting up a worksheet for another person to use who is not familiar with functions or financial analysis, this can be very helpful. The negative references can be entered either from the keyboard or prior to cell selection using the Function Wizard.

The rate for a five-year annuity at 10 percent should be entered as **10%/12**, and the number of periods of payment as **12*5**. The payment amount should be entered as a negative value.

Using the Function Wizard, you can enter the values used for the calculation in a similar way. Click on the Function Wizard button on the Standard toolbar to display the Step 1 of 2 dialog box. Select Financial Functions from the Category of functions list on the left side of the box. On the right, select FV, either by clicking once and then clicking below on the Next button, or by double-clicking on FV.

In the Function Wizard Step 1 of 2 dialog box, you can press Alt+C to choose Function **N**ames, and by typing the first letter of the desired function, the highlight bar will advance to the first function that begins with that letter. The same applies to Function **C**ategory.

This takes you to the Step 2 of 2 dialog box, in which arguments are completed. To complete this function, and return the future value, type the values directly into the edit boxes (**10%/12** for 10 percent over a 12-month period). For each value entered, an adjacent value for calculation purposes is displayed at the right side of the edit box (see fig. 10.4).

Upon completion of argument entry, the value of the FV function is displayed in the Value box at the top right of the dialog box. Clicking on the **F**inish button returns you to the cell in your worksheet where the function will go. Press Enter to complete the insertion of the function into the sheet.

You also can use the Function Wizard to enter values as cell references by opening and choosing the type of function and specific function name, and then proceeding to the Step 2 of 2 dialog box. Once there, instead of entering numeric values into the sheet, use the mouse to click on cells in the worksheet where values are located.

II

Excel

Figure 10.4
The completed
Function Wizard
dialog box, with
data, ready to be
inserted into the
worksheet.

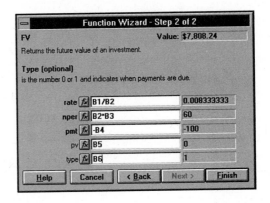

In the sample worksheet, Interest Rate is in cell B1, Number of payments per year is in B2, Number of years in Annuity is in B3, Payment amount is in B4, Present Value is in B5, and Time of Payment (Beg=0 End=1) is in B6.

For entry of the rate, click on cell B1, type /, and click on cell B2. This yields the rate, divided by the number of months in a year. Tab to nper, and click on cell B3. Type * and click on B2 again. This yields the total number of payments, or number of years multiplied by the number of months per year. Tab again. Be sure when you click on the payment and present value arguments to give the cell reference that preceded it a minus value, or your ending value will be negative.

In the process of evaluation, if you enter a number in the present value cell and later remove it, you need to replace it with a 0, or the #value! message will appear in the FV cell B16. When the function is first entered, if there is no value, FV assumes 0. After it is cleared, the formula sees the cell as text-formatted and empty. This produces the error message.

Figure 10.5 shows the finished product, inserted into the worksheet with the function syntax in the formula bar.

The CUMIPMT Function

The CUMIPMT function returns a value that represents the cumulative interest paid between two periods. It is one of the functions that requires the Analysis ToolPak add-in.

If you borrow $1,000.00 from the bank at a 13.5 percent interest rate for a term of two years beginning on March 1, and you want to know how much interest you have paid for a calendar year, this function does the job.

The syntax of CUMIPMT is the following:

```
=CUMIPMT(rate,nper,pv,start_period,end_period,type)
```

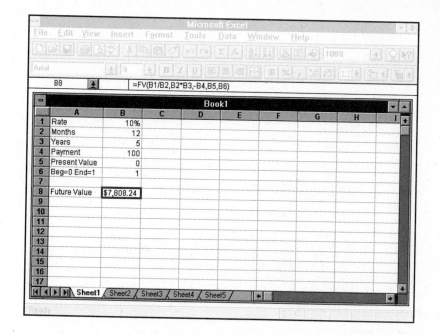

Figure 10.5
The completed
future value
calculation.

All the arguments are required for this function: `rate` is the interest rate, `nper` is the number of payments per period, `pv` is the present value, `start_period` is the number of the first period to calculate from, `end_period` is the number of the period to complete the calculation, and `type` is either 0 or 1 based on whether payment is made at the beginning or the end of each period.

To compose the function, enter the following:

```
=cumipmt(13.5%/12,12*2,1000,1,10,1)
```

The resulting value (shown as a negative number) is the cumulative amount of interest in the 10-month period between March and December that you paid on your $1,000.00 loan: $81.27799685.

As you enter formulas and function statements, pay close attention to spacing in the formula bar. An added space or missed comma can result in errors in the results or in not having the command executed.

You can use the Function Wizard to create your own interest payment evaluation function. Then you can determine what the benefits of borrowing money over certain periods of time at various interest rates might have on your corporate or personal finances.

Using the worksheet shown in figure 10.6, you can enter values for the arguments in the cells and see the results of different loan calculations. Begin by typing the cell labels in column A, row 4. The first value label should be **Interest Rate:**. Press Enter, which drops the active cell to A5, and type **Payments per Year:**. Complete the cell labels as shown in figure 10.6.

Figure 10.6
The worksheet format for the CUMIPMT formula.

	A	B	C	D	E	F	G
1							
2							
3							
4	Interest Rate:	13.50%					
5	Payments Per Year:	12					
6	Years of Loan:	2					
7	Value of Loan:	1000					
8	Starting Period to Evaluate:	1					
9	Ending Period to Evaluate:	10					
10							
11	Cumulative Interest Payment:						
12							
13							
14							
15							
16							
17							

Book1 — FV \ CUMIPMT \ Sheet3 \ Sheet4 \ Sheet5

Now, enter the values for the loan interest calculation so that your screen looks like the following (see fig. 10.7):

```
Interest Rate:               13.5%
Payments Per Year:             12
Years of Loan:                  2
Value of Loan:               1000
Starting Period to Evaluate:    1
Ending Period to Evaluate:     10
```

Double-click on cell B11, and click on the Function Wizard button on the formula bar. In the first dialog box, select Financial in Function Category, select CUMIPMT from the Function Name list, and click on the Next button, or press Enter. The dialog box changes to Step 2 of 2 and the arguments in the form of cell references or values can now be entered.

For the rate, click on the worksheet cell B4, type / and click on cell B5, which shows a value for that argument of 0.01125. Tab to the next argument, nper. Click on B6, type *, and click on B5. The resulting value to the right of the nper edit box shows 24. The value box at the upper right corner of the sheet does not show a value because all the required arguments are not complete yet. Tab to the pv edit box and click on B7. The value shows 1000 to the right of the edit box. Tab to the start_period field, click on B8, tab to end_period, click on B9, tab to type, and click on B10. The B10 cell is blank and returns a value of 0 until it is cleared manually. If you want to evaluate the difference between paying at the beginning or the end of a period, which is an optional argument, add a cell for Beg=1 End=0 in A10, and the value 0 or 1 in B10. The calculations should now equal -81.27799685.

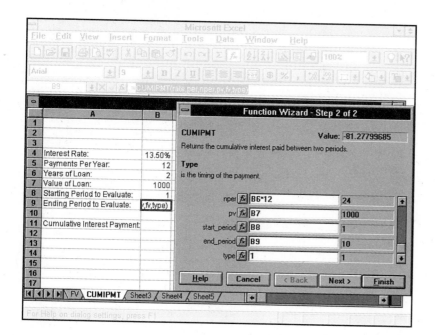

Figure 10.7
The Function Wizard displaying the variables for CUMIPMT.

Click on the Finish button, and the function, complete with arguments, is ready to be entered into the sheet. Pressing Enter or clicking on the check mark in the formula bar inserts the calculation and shows the result. On the workbook where the value is returned, with that cell highlighted, click on the $ button on the Standard toolbar. The result is formatted as currency with two decimal places and is rounded to $81.28.

The CUMPRINC Function

The CUMPRINC function takes the CUMIPMT function one step further. It returns the value of the principal paid on a loan during a period of time. The two functions can be used together on one sheet because they share the same arguments and structure. Use the previous loan example and type the following:

```
=CUMPRINC(13.5%/12,2*12,1000,1,10,0)
```

This returns a value of 391.18 total principal paid in the 10-month period between March and December. Click on the cell, and click on the $ button in the Formatting toolbar to display the value as currency.

The worksheet now looks like figure 10.8, formatted with dollar values in the cells that contain the CUMIPMT and CUMPRINC functions.

Figure 10.8
The resultant values from both the CUMIPMUT and CUMIPRINC functions.

	A	B	C	D	E	F	G
			Book1				
1							
2							
3							
4	Interest Rate:	13.50%					
5	Payments Per Year:	12					
6	Years of Loan:	2					
7	Value of Loan:	1000					
8	Starting Period to Evaluate:	1					
9	Ending Period to Evaluate:	10					
10							
11	Cumulative Interest Payment:	$81.28					
12	Cumulative Principle Payment	$391.18					
13							
14							
15							
16							
17							

FV \ **CUMIPMT** \ Sheet3 \ Sheet4 \ Sheet5 /

The EFFECT Function

The EFFECT function returns the effective annual interest rate, given the nominal interest rate and the number of compounding periods per year. For an annual interest rate of 18.25 percent that is compounded four times per year, the syntax is the following:

```
=EFFECT(18.25%,4)
```

With this function, the effective interest rate is 19.54 percent.

Examining Statistical Functions

Statistical functions frequently return values about arrays of data or groups of numbers. The example here provides you with a foundation of how statistical functions can help you look at data in interesting ways.

The AVERAGE Function

The AVERAGE function returns the arithmetic mean of a group of numbers. This function can have up to 30 arguments, and arguments can be names of cell ranges or individual cells.

Tip

Blank cells in an array to be averaged are counted and figured into the average, unless the cell has been designated as empty. Empty cells are not counted. To check or change the zero values options, select Options, Tools. In the View tab, check or clear the Zero values box.

For this example, you will create a worksheet with information about a group of salespeople. The example in figure 10.9 shows the basic information that you will build on to learn about statistical functions.

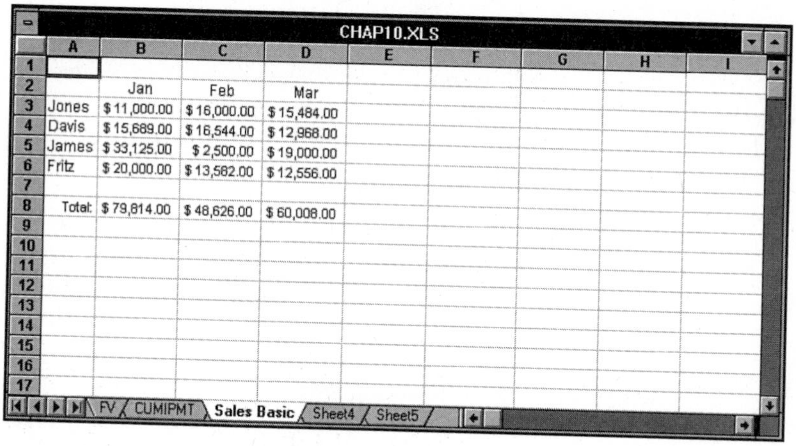

Figure 10.9
The Sales worksheet.

There are four salespeople, with three columns of information adjacent to each name. Each column represents one month's sales. To place headers on the worksheet, type **Jan** in cell B2. Click once with the mouse on that cell, and, using the AutoFill handle, drag it across the other columns from B to D to fill in **Feb** and **Mar**. If the result is ####s across your cell, double-click on the right side of the column header to adjust the width of the columns.

To continue the formatting of this sheet, highlight cells B3 to H13. This is the range of cells you will use for the statistical analysis, where currency format is important. On the Standard toolbar, click on the $ button. See table 10.1 for the data for the sales worksheet.

Table 10.1
Data for Sales Worksheet

Salesperson	Jan	Feb	Mar
Jones	11,000	16,000	15,484
Davis	15,689	16,544	12,968
James	33,125	2,500	19,000
Fritz	20,000	13,582	12,556

The SUM Function

In analyzing sales performance, sales totals are critical. You can add quarterly and monthly totals to your worksheet quickly by using one of Excel's most popular functions, the SUM function. It even has its own button on the Standard toolbar. In your worksheet, below the names in column A, skip one row and type **Total:** in cell A8. Then, in the column to the right of the Averages Column, in cell F2, enter **Quarterly Total** as the heading of the new column. Position the mouse on cell F3, and, holding the left mouse button down, highlight the cells to cell F6. Then move the cursor over to cell B8, hold down the Ctrl key on the keyboard, and highlight the cells from B8 to F8. You now should have two separate ranges of cells highlighted (see fig. 10.10).

Figure 10.10

The cells prior to pressing the SUM button.

	A	B	C	D	E	F	G	H	I
1									
2		Jan	Feb	Mar	Averages	Quarter Total			
3	Jones	$11,000.00	$16,000.00	$15,484.00	$14,161.33				
4	Davis	$15,689.00	$16,544.00	$12,968.00	$15,067.00				
5	James	$33,125.00	$2,500.00	$19,000.00	$18,208.33				
6	Fritz	$20,000.00	$13,582.00	$12,556.00	$15,379.33				
7									
8	Total:								

CHAP10.XLS

FV / CUMIPMT / **Sales Basic** / Sheet4 / Sheet5 /

Once you have your ranges highlighted, on the Standard toolbar, click on Σ, the Greek letter that represents the SUM function. Excel automatically totals the number in the rows and columns you have selected, and returns the values. The SUM button on the toolbar can save a lot of time in arriving at totals for large worksheets and projects.

For this example, you will find out what the average sales amount is for each representative. To do this, click on the cell in the first empty column of data, on the same row as salesperson Jones. This is cell E3. On the Standard toolbar, click on the Function Wizard. Choose function category Statistical and function name AVERAGE, and click on the Next button. For the Step 2 of 2 dialog box, hold the mouse button down on cell B3 and drag to cell D3. The keyboard entry is **=AVERAGE(B3:D3)**. The value returned by the formula is the sum of cells B3 through D3, divided by the number of entries in the range: $14,161.33.

You can complete the averages for the rest of the salespeople by using the AutoFill feature. To do this, click on E3, the cell for the average of the first person, and position the cursor over the fill handle in the lower right corner of the cell. Then, hold the left mouse button down, and drag the pointer down to cells E4, E5, and E6. The averages automatically fill in for the remainder of the sales force (see fig. 10.11).

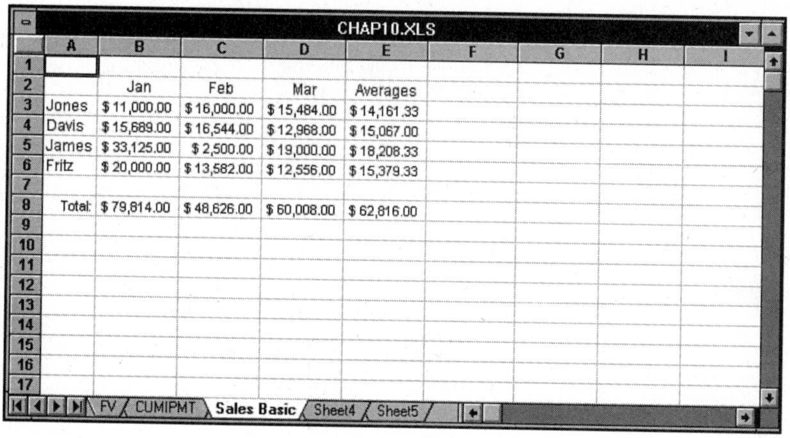

	A	B	C	D	E	F	G	H	I
		CHAP10.XLS							
1									
2		Jan	Feb	Mar	Averages				
3	Jones	$11,000.00	$16,000.00	$15,484.00	$14,161.33				
4	Davis	$15,689.00	$16,544.00	$12,968.00	$15,067.00				
5	James	$33,125.00	$2,500.00	$19,000.00	$18,208.33				
6	Fritz	$20,000.00	$13,582.00	$12,556.00	$15,379.33				
7									
8	Total:	$79,814.00	$48,626.00	$60,008.00	$62,816.00				
9									
10									
11									
12									
13									
14									
15									
16									
17									

FV / CUMIPMT \ **Sales Basic** / Sheet4 / Sheet5 /

Figure 10.11
The Sales worksheet showing averages.

The next step is to determine what the high sales month was for each salesperson.

The MAX Function

Of course, it is easy to look at the sheet and determine what the current high number is for each person, but you might want to monitor these figures over a period of months or years to determine the top month of each one. (There also is a formula to look at the lowest month.) The MAX function is the answer.

In cell G2, type the Heading **High** and press Enter. The active cell is now G3. On the Standard toolbar, click on the Function Wizard button.

Select function category Statistical and function name MAX, and click on the Next button. The Wizard prompts you for the first argument entry, which is Column B3 through D3. Position the pointer on B3, hold the left mouse button down, and drag to cell D3. Now, in the Function Wizard box, click on the Finish button. Pressing Enter inserts the function in the sheet and returns the value $16,000.00. This represents the highest value in the range for salesperson Jones.

You can use the AutoFill feature again to complete the rest of the sales staff's MAX months and provide a new entry for the MAX month for the company's total sales. Position the mouse on cell G3, click once to make G3 the active cell, and position the pointer to the lower right corner of the cell until the pointer changes to a small, black +. While holding down the left mouse button, drag the pointer down to cell G8. This action AutoFills the MAX function in all the highlighted cells, returning the maximum values for each representative and the company. Figure 10.12 shows the result of the MAX function.

You can accomplish the same result with the keyboard. With cell H3 active, type **=max(B3:D3)** and press Enter. The function returns the maximum value found for cells B3, C3, and D3. Using the AutoFill, you then can fill in the rest of the cells by dragging the AutoFill handle to the appropriate cells.

Figure 10.12
The MAX results, showing the high month for each salesperson.

	A	B	C	D	E	F	G	H	I
1									
2		Jan	Feb	Mar	Averages	Quarter Total	High		
3	Jones	$11,000.00	$16,000.00	$15,484.00	$14,161.33	$42,484.00	$16,000.00		
4	Davis	$15,689.00	$16,544.00	$12,968.00	$15,067.00	$45,201.00	$16,544.00		
5	James	$33,125.00	$2,500.00	$19,000.00	$18,208.33	$54,625.00	$33,125.00		
6	Fritz	$20,000.00	$13,582.00	$12,556.00	$15,379.33	$46,138.00	$20,000.00		
7									
8	Total:	$79,814.00	$48,626.00	$60,008.00	$62,816.00	$188,448.00			

CHAP10.XLS

FV / CUMIPMT \ Sales Basic / Sheet4 / Sheet5 /

The MIN Function

The MIN function is the opposite of MAX; it returns the smallest numeric value found in a range of cells. MIN uses the same arguments and syntax.

In cell H2, type **Low** and press Enter. Your active cell is now H3. Type **=min(B3:D3)** and press Enter. The dollar amount for salesperson Jones is returned, and the active cell is now H4. Click again on cell H3, and, from the lower right corner, AutoFill the rest of the salespeople and company information with the MIN function. The MAX and MIN function columns for sales are now complete.

The RANK Function

Now that you have calculated what the highs and lows are for the salespeople and the company, you can use the RANK function to assign a numeric rank to each person, based on their sales. Click on cell A2, making it active. Type the header for that column, **First Quarter Rank**, and press Enter. In cell A3, invoke the Function Wizard from the Standard toolbar. Statistical Functions still should be active, if that was the last function category used. From the function name box, select RANK, and click on the Next button.

The Step 2 of 2 dialog box is now active, and the first argument is the number you want to rank. Because our heading was First Quarter Rank, you should choose the First Quarter Total Cell for Jones, which is in cell F3. Click once on F3, and press Tab to move to the next argument. The next argument is called ref, which indicates the numbers to compare to the first argument, or the total for the quarter.

With the ref edit box active, highlight cell F3, and, holding the left mouse button down, drag the pointer to cell F6. This creates the reference for the first representative's monthly total compared to all other salespeople. Press Tab to move to the last edit box in the Function Wizard, and type **0**. Note that the value in the upper right of the Wizard dialog box is now filled in.

In the order edit box, Excel ranks in ascending order for nonzero characters, descending order for zero characters.

In order to rank the remainder of the salespeople, we can use the AutoFill feature to drag the function to the remaining cells. However, this operation will return incorrect results because the cells referenced will change. In other words, our goal is to move the function to analyze a new number, but compare it to the same original arguments chosen in the Jones ranking. In order to have RANK look to the same cells for each comparison, you need to make the cells referenced in the function absolute cell references. This means that regardless of the location of the function, or where it might later be moved, it still will rank the number we wish to compare to the first quarter totals, located in cells F3:F6.

The following example illustrates the effect of absolute and regular cell references on a simple array of numbers:

| | | | Totals | |
Jan	Feb	Mar	Normal Cell Reference: B8:D8	Absolute Reference: $D$10:$F$10
1	1	1	3	3
2	2	2	6	3
3	3	3	9	3
6	6	6	18	3

The example shows normal referencing in the next-to-the-last column. To input this total, type **=sum(B8:D8)** and press Enter in the D10 cell. Then AutoFill down to E10 and F10. Each time the formula or function is moved, its cell pointers adjust accordingly.

The formula in D14 now reads =SUM(D10:F10), which returns the correct sum for that row. The last column uses absolute cell references, which point only to D10:F10. When the function is moved or copied to another location, it still returns a value associated with that original range of cells.

This example uses absolute cell references to return an incorrect set of values for three of the four entries. With the RANK function, use of absolute cell references is essential to producing accurate results.

Tip

You can make cell references absolute from Excel's Formula bar as formulas and functions are entered, or when editing an existing one. To do this, select the cell with the function or formula you want to make absolute, click on the cell reference, and press the F4 key. The row and column references cycle through the levels of reference type each time you press the F4 key. Using this method, you can choose to make both row and column absolute, or just one or the other.

The MEDIAN Function

The median value returned by the MEDIAN function represents the number in the middle of a set of values. In other words, half the numbers in the set have a value that is higher than the median, and half have values that are lower. This is similar to averages, yet the median is not representative of a calculation on a value or values in a worksheet. It is simply the middle value from a group.

To add the MEDIAN function to our sales analysis spreadsheet, click once on cell I2. Type the heading for this column, **Median Month**. Press Enter, moving the active cell to I3. Try invoking the Function Wizard by pressing the keyboard key combination shortcut, Shift+F3. From the function category, select Statistical, and from the function name window, select MEDIAN. Pressing Enter or clicking on the Next button moves you to the next step.

The first edit box shows the caption Number1. Position the mouse pointer on cell B3, and drag the pointer to D3. The first argument is the only one required for this function, so you can click on the Finish button to return the value to your worksheet. For this function, because you do not need absolute cell references, use the AutoFill feature to complete the MEDIAN function for the remainder of the salespeople. Figure 10.13 shows what the finished sheet should look like.

Figure 10.13
The Sales worksheet showing the MEDIAN function.

	A	B	C	D	E	F	G	H	I
1									
2		Jan	Feb	Mar	Averages	Quarter Total	High	Low	Median
3	Jones	$11,000.00	$16,000.00	$15,484.00	$14,161.33	$42,484.00	$16,000.00	$11,000.00	$15,484.00
4	Davis	$15,689.00	$16,544.00	$12,968.00	$15,067.00	$45,201.00	$16,544.00	$12,968.00	$15,689.00
5	James	$33,125.00	$2,500.00	$19,000.00	$18,208.33	$54,625.00	$33,125.00	$2,500.00	$19,000.00
6	Fritz	$20,000.00	$13,582.00	$12,556.00	$15,379.33	$46,138.00	$20,000.00	$12,556.00	$13,582.00
7									
8	Total:	$79,814.00	$48,626.00	$60,008.00	$62,816.00	$188,448.00			

CHAP10.XLS

FV / CUMIPMT / **Sales Basic** / Sheet4 / Sheet5 /

Math and Trigonometry Functions

Excel 5.0 has nearly 60 different mathematical and trigonometric functions available for use in worksheet analysis. Several of these are discussed in the following sections.

The ABS Function

The ABS function returns the absolute value of a number; that is, the number without its sign. This function can be used in calculations that require positive numbers in order to work properly, such as the CUMIPMT example.

Earlier in this chapter, you were able to display the resulting value from CUMIPMT by placing a negative value in the argument edit box for present value. For this example, you use that CUMIPMT function with the same numbers, and nest the ABS function so that the result is a positive value.

Recall the syntax of the original CUMIPMT function formula:

```
=CUMIPMT(rate,nper,pv,start_period,end_period,type)
```

The result is a negative number. Using cell address arguments in the formula and placing a minus before the cell containing present value enables a positive number as the result. Another way to accomplish this is to nest the ABS function with CUMIPMT.

 Tip You can use ABS by itself to change the contents of a cell from a negative number to a positive number, and if the cell already contains a positive value, no changes are made to the contents.

If you already have put your formula in place and it returns a negative value, and you want to change it to a positive one, you can accomplish this quickly. Click on the cell that contains the negative value and press F2. This displays the value in the cell and displays the formula in the formula bar, located near the center of the screen. Figure 10.14 shows the result of this action.

Click on the formula bar, and you then can edit the formula.

 Tip The cursor will go where the pointer is at the time of the click on the bar. Once there, the End, Home, and left- and right-arrow keys on the keyboard can help you move to the spot at which you need to make additions or corrections.

Press the Home key, which moves you to the first character in the formula, and press the right-arrow key. This action takes you inside the = where you can insert the ABS function to return a positive value always. Type **abs(**, then press the End key and type **)**.

II

Excel

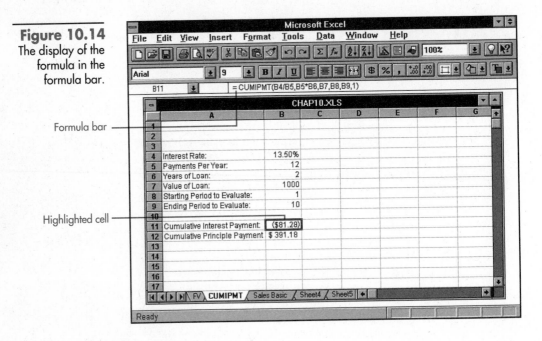

Figure 10.14
The display of the formula in the formula bar.

The original formula was the following:

```
=CUMIPMT(D22/D23,D24*D23,D25,D26,D27,1)
```

and the resultant value was ($81.27). This is the new formula:

```
=ABS(CUMIPMT(D22/D23,D24*D23,D25,D26,D27,1))
```

and its value is $81.27. Using ABS changes the negative value returned by CUMIPMT to a positive one so that it can be used in other calculations with the desired sign.

Nesting the ABS function with the keyboard is fast, and using the Function Wizard to either edit an existing function or nest a function as it is created is fast as well.

To use the Function Wizard to create a new CUMIPMT that returns an absolute number, select the cell where the value is to be returned to the worksheet, and invoke the Function Wizard. First, select Math & Trig Functions from the function category list and ABS from the function name list.

When you click on the Next button, to the right of the edit box there is another Function Wizard button, which facilitates nesting. Click once on that button, and the Function Wizard Step 1 of 2 (Nested) dialog box appears. Select Financial Category CUMIPMT from the function category list, and proceed to the next dialog box, Step 2 of 2 (Nested), by pressing Enter or the Next button.

At this point, enter the arguments that are needed to return the cumulative interest payment value. As the arguments for CUMIPMT are completed, the value displayed in the Function Wizard value box is a negative value. Click on Finish, and the original function Step 2 of 2 dialog box appears, with the CUMIPMT information highlighted and entered in the ABS argument. Note here that the resulting value in the Wizard shows as a positive number. Clicking on the Finish button completes the nesting process and returns the calculation to your worksheet (see fig. 10.15).

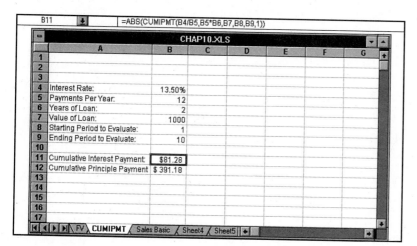

Figure 10.15
The CUMIPMT results entered in the ABS argument.

The ABS function is a good example of a simple function that has immediate results. It is relatively easy to add to an existing formula, either from the keyboard or the Function Wizard.

The COUNTIF Function

The COUNTIF function examines a range of nonblank cells and counts the number of cells that match certain criteria. In the sales worksheet example, if each salesperson had to sell $10,000 every month to reach quota, and you wanted to have a column in your sheet that indicates how many months they reach their goals in a certain time period, COUNTIF is the perfect function to use.

To add this entry to your sheet, make cell J2 active by clicking on it. Then type the heading **# Mths. over Quota** and press Enter. Next, invoke the Function Wizard in J3. Select the Math & Trig category, the COUNTIF function, and click on the Next button. In the first edit box (range), position the mouse pointer on cell B3, hold the left button down, and drag the pointer to cell D3. Tab to the next edit box (criteria), type **>10000**, and press the Finish button.

The result is the number of months that Jones finished above quota, or with sales over $10,000. Using AutoFill, position the mouse pointer on the lower right corner of cell J3 until the cursor becomes a plus sign. Holding down the left mouse button, drag the highlight box down to cells J4, J5, and J6. The resulting calculations appear.

The keyboard entry for this function is **=COUNTIF(B3:D3,">10000")**. A salesperson who sells exactly $10,000.00 for a given month does not get credit for having achieved quota based on this calculation. If the goal is $10,000 or greater, the operand in the formula should be changed from > to >= (greater than or equal to). Figure 10.16 illustrates the results. (For clarity, the High, Low, and Median columns in figure 10.16 have been hidden with the <u>H</u>ide command under the <u>C</u>olumn option in the Fo<u>r</u>mat menu.)

Figure 10.16
The Sales worksheet showing COUNTIF results.

	A	B	C	D	E	F	J	K
1								
2		Jan	Feb	Mar	Averages	Quarter Total	Months Over Quota	
3	Jones	$11,000.00	$16,000.00	$15,484.00	$14,161.33	$42,484.00	3	
4	Davis	$15,689.00	$16,544.00	$12,968.00	$15,067.00	$45,201.00	3	
5	James	$33,125.00	$2,500.00	$19,000.00	$18,208.33	$54,625.00	2	
6	Fritz	$20,000.00	$13,582.00	$12,556.00	$15,379.33	$46,138.00	3	
7								
8	Total:	$79,814.00	$48,626.00	$60,008.00	$62,816.00	$188,448.00		
9								

CHAP10.XLS

FV / CUMIPMT \ Sales Basic / Sheet4 / Sheet5

The EVEN and ODD Functions

The EVEN and ODD functions are simple and useful for certain applications. The keyboard entry is about as fast if not faster than using the Wizard; the syntax is the following:

```
=even(number)
```

or

```
=odd(number)
```

The EVEN function takes a number, or extracts a number from a cell reference, and rounds it up to the nearest whole even number. The ODD function does the same, to the nearest odd whole number.

An application for which this function can be useful is an inventory/ordering worksheet in which particular stock items are shipped in quantities of two only. A customer ordering one could be notified upon order entry that this was the case. You can accomplish this by having the quantity ordered in one column, and the shipping quantity (with the function performed on its contents) drawn from the quantity ordered cell.

The MOD Function

MOD is a function that returns the remainder from division of a number. This calculation can be used in figuring a check digit for an account number for security purposes. An example of this might be a formula that takes a customer's telephone number, divides it by a constant number, and adds the remainder to the end of the phone number as a verification.

The syntax for MOD is the following:

```
=mod(number,divisor).
```

Using the previous example, if a customer's phone number is 555-1212, and you chose 8 as your special divisor, the formula =mod(5551212,8) returns a value of 4. The customer account number would be 55512124. The worksheet uses the MOD function and the CONCATENATE function from the Text function category. The former returns the remainder, and the latter returns the value needed for displaying the account number as one complete number. (The CONCATENATE function is discussed in more detail later in this chapter.)

First, set up a column for phone numbers (in the example, column A, cell 3), a column for the remainder (column B, cell 3), and a column for new account number (column C, cell 3). When the phone number is entered in the first cell, the function automatically figures the remainder and joins, in the third column, the original number with the remainder.

To set up the MOD function using the Function Wizard, click on cell B3 and invoke the Wizard. From the Function Category list, choose Math & Trig, and select MOD from the Function Name list. Press Enter, or click on the Next button, and the arguments section appears. Click on the cell containing the number, or cell A3. Tab to the Divisor field, and type the number **8** (a number chosen at random). Press Enter, or click on the Finish button, and the MOD is placed in the remainder column. Then, move to cell C3, the account number column.

Invoke the Wizard again, and select Text as the type and CONCATENATE as the function to be used. When you click on the Next button, the arguments required are to select the text items you wish to join together. Select A3 for the first item and B3 for the second. When you press Finish, the 55512124 account number, complete with check digit, is returned as the value.

The PI Function

PI is one of the few function selections that does not require any arguments. It can be used in formulas or calculations to return special values. The geometric equation for figuring the circumference of a circle is pi × (radius)^2. The syntax for this calculation is the following:

```
=pi()*(12^2)
```

where the value **12** is the radius of the circle whose circumference you wish to obtain.

The ROMAN Function

The ROMAN function takes numeric values and converts them to Roman numerals, and it can display the numerals in one of five different formats. The ROMAN function can convert numbers only up to a maximum of 3,999, and it can convert only positive values. Negative values, and those exceeding 3,999, return the #value! error message.

The syntax for using the ROMAN function is the following:

```
=roman(number,style)
```

where number is the numeric value you wish to convert, and style is a number from 0 to 4. The help information about ROMAN says that style 0 is the Classic Roman style, and 1 through 4 are More Concise.

To use the Function Wizard to enter the ROMAN function, highlight the cell in which to display the value, and invoke the Wizard. From the Function Category list, choose Math & Trig, and from the Function Names window, select ROMAN. Clicking on the Next button enables argument entry, where you can preview the conversions by entering a number and style, or enter a cell address for the numeric value and 0–4 for the style.

You also can enter TRUE and FALSE for style arguments, where TRUE is Classic format, or 0, and False is More Concise, such as style 4.

The ROUND Function

ROUND is a straightforward function that takes a number and rounds it to a specified number of decimal places. The rounding feature is important for many calculations because the values that come from calculations might be different from the rounded number. Figure 10.17 illustrates how rounding can affect one number used in a simple calculation.

The syntax for the ROUND function is the following:

```
=round(number,num_digits)
```

If num_digits is less than 0, the number is rounded to the left of the decimal. If it is 0, the number is rounded to the nearest integer. If it is greater than 0, it is rounded to that number of decimal places.

Using the Function Wizard in the example in figure 10.18, after selecting the category and function name, the argument selection uses cell addresses. The number to be rounded has an absolute address ($F$7) and the num_digits argument is variable (G8). When the formula is AutoFilled to adjacent cells, the rounding takes place on the same number each time because of the absolute cell address.

	A	B	C	D	E
		CHAP10.XLS			
1					
2		Original Number = 155.258965			
3					
4		Number of decimal places	155.258965 Rounded is:	X 6.5 / 1.5	
5					
6		-1	160	693.3333333	
7		0	155	671.6666667	
8		1	155.3	672.9666667	
9		2	155.26	672.7933333	
10		3	155.259	672.789	
11		4	155.259	672.789	
12		5	155.25897	672.78887	
13		6	155.258968	672.7888613	
14					
15					

FV / CUMIPMT / Sales Basic \ **Rounding** / SH

Figure 10.17
The effects of rounding on calculations.

The POWER Function

The POWER function returns the result of a number raised to a power. If you want to take the number 10 to the second power, for example, the keyboard entry to your selected cell is =power(10,2), and the result is 100. You can accomplish the same result in Excel by typing =10^2.

The SUMIF Function (with PRODUCT)

The SUMIF function adds values from a list of numeric values, provided certain criteria are met. This is an interesting function and has many potential uses. Revisiting the sales worksheet used earlier in this chapter, if your company has a bonus program for salespeople that is calculated as a percentage of total sales over quota, the SUMIF function can help you calculate the bonuses automatically.

If you pay a quarterly bonus of 1/2 percent of total sales for those salespeople who exceed their quota of $10,000.00 for a given month, the SUMIF syntax is the following:

```
=PRODUCT(SUMIF(C3:E3,">=10000"),0.5%)
```

In the example, SUMIF is nested within PRODUCT, which is a function that multiplies its arguments. The result of this function yields a number that includes only those months' sales that are greater than or equal to quota (10000), and multiplies that number by 0.5%, which is the bonus.

To use the Function Wizard with SUMIF, choose the PRODUCT function from the Math & Trig category, and when the first argument edit box is on screen, press the Function Wizard box next to it. This brings up the nested Function Wizard box. Then highlight the cells and the criteria added as an argument to the SUMIF function. Upon completion, enter the multiplier for the PRODUCT function; the returned value is displayed (see fig. 10.18).

Figure 10.18
The worksheet showing PRODUCT, with SUMIF nested, resulting in the Bonus column.

	A	B	C	D	E	F	J	K	L
							Months		
2		Jan	Feb	Mar	Averages	Quarter Total	Over Quota	Bonus	
3	Jones	$ 11,000.00	$ 16,000.00	$ 15,484.00	$ 14,161.33	$ 42,484.00	3	$ 212.42	
4	Davis	$ 15,689.00	$ 16,544.00	$ 12,968.00	$ 15,067.00	$ 45,201.00	3	$ 226.01	
5	James	$ 33,125.00	$ 2,500.00	$ 19,000.00	$ 18,208.33	$ 54,625.00	2	$ 260.63	
6	Fritz	$ 20,000.00	$ 13,582.00	$ 12,556.00	$ 15,379.33	$ 46,138.00	3	$ 230.69	
8	Total:	$ 79,814.00	$ 48,626.00	$ 60,008.00	$ 62,816.00	$ 188,448.00			

CHAP10.XLS

FV / CUMIPMT \ Sales Basic / Rounding \ Sheet5 /

Using Database Functions

There are two types of database functions: those that do calculations on worksheet databases and those that can be used to retrieve external data. The worksheet commands have counterparts as statistical functions. The only difference between them is that the database functions perform their calculations on database worksheets, and statistical functions perform theirs on lists in worksheets. (The external data commands are covered in detail in Chapter 13, "Excel Data Input and Export.")

Working with Text Functions

Text functions, unlike many of the other function types, manipulate numbers and characters for formatting, sorting, display, and computation.

The CONCATENATE Function

The CONCATENATE function can be used in a variety of different ways to extract information from worksheets. Text can be joined to form sentences about values located in your worksheet. For example, the following text:

```
Salesperson Jones averaged 14112 for the first quarter
and exceeded quota 3 times for a bonus amount of
$211.68!
```

was extracted directly from the sales worksheet using the CONCATENATE function with this syntax:

```
=CONCATENATE("Salesperson ",$B$3," averaged ",$F$3," for the first
quarter "," and exceeded quota ",$K$3," times"," for a bonus amount
of",$M$3,"!")
```

The cell references are absolute, so the function formula can be moved anywhere in the workbook and maintain integrity. The example was formulated using the Function Wizard, but can be done from the keyboard as well.

> **Tip**
>
> When joining entered text and cell references, make sure to enter the two items in separate edit boxes in the Function Wizard. This is important because the Wizard places quotation marks around entered text. If you have the text `"Salesperson"` and the cell reference in the same edit box, the result will be `Salesperson $B$3`, not Salesperson Jones.

The DOLLAR Function

The DOLLAR function converts numbers into text and formats the value as currency, with any number of decimal places. The difference between using DOLLAR and formatting numeric values as currency is that Excel converts DOLLAR formatted cells to text. The results still can be used in formulas and calculations, because Excel also converts them to numbers when it calculates.

Figure 10.19 shows the difference in appearance between cells formatted using DOLLAR and those using the $ button from the toolbar.

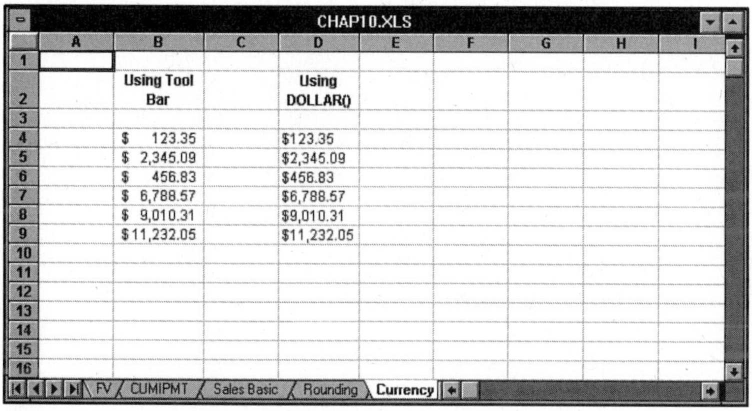

	A	B	C	D	E	F	G	H	I
1									
2		Using Tool Bar		Using DOLLAR()					
3									
4		$ 123.35		$123.35					
5		$ 2,345.09		$2,345.09					
6		$ 456.83		$456.83					
7		$ 6,788.57		$6,788.57					
8		$ 9,010.31		$9,010.31					
9		$11,232.05		$11,232.05					

CHAP10.XLS

FV / CUMIPMT / Sales Basic / Rounding / Currency

Figure 10.19
The formatting differences using the DOLLAR function and the toolbar $ formats.

The FIXED Function

FIXED is a text function that formats numeric values as text with a given number of decimal places. The FIXED function also can insert commas for formatting appearance. The syntax for FIXED is the following:

```
=fixed(number,decimals,no_commas)
```

Excel

and is similar to the DOLLAR function because of its text-to-numeric conversion for calculation purposes.

To use the Function Wizard with FIXED, select text from the Category Function window, and FIXED from the Function <u>N</u>ame window. Click on the Next button, and arguments can be entered.

The LEFT and RIGHT Functions

The LEFT and RIGHT functions extract a certain number of characters from the left or right of a string of text. If the word MICROSOFT is in cell L23, for example, and you enter the function **=left(L23,5)**, the resulting value is MICRO. If you then enter the function **=right(L23,4)**, the value is SOFT. This could be used as an account identifier, in a similar fashion to the prior example in the function MOD.

The UPPER, LOWER, and PROPER Functions

The UPPER, LOWER, and PROPER functions change the case of text strings in a worksheet. UPPER and LOWER modify the entire text string. Entering **=lower(MICROSOFT CORP)** yields microsoft corp as its value, and entering **=upper(microsoft corp)** yields MICROSOFT CORP as its value. Either all upper- or lowercase text using PROPER capitalizes the first letter of each word and converts, if necessary, the remaining characters in the string to lowercase.

The TRIM Function

The TRIM function removes spaces from text. This function is handy if your worksheet has received data from an external source that has added too many spaces between words in a string. Figure 10.20 illustrates how TRIM can be effective.

Figure 10.20
Trimming a cell
with spaces.

	A	B	C	D	E	F	G	H	I
6	Original->		This is an example		of too many	spaces	in	text	
7	Trimmed ->		This is an example of too many spaces in text						

CHAP10.XLS

FV / CUMIPMT / Sales Basic / Rounding \ Spaces

Functions related to TRIM include the following:

- ✔ CLEAN removes all nonprintable characters from a text string

- ✔ MID returns a specific number of characters from a string

- ✔ REPLACE replaces characters within a string

- ✔ SUBSTITUTE replaces certain characters with new ones

Using Lookup and Reference Functions

Lookup and reference functions are functions that return values about locations of rows, cells, columns, and data in worksheets. They also can extract information from a table.

The ADDRESS Function

The ADDRESS function returns the location of a cell, given the row and column numbers, as text. The syntax used for this function is the following:

```
=address(row_num,col_num,abs_num, a1,sheet_text)
```

row_num is the number of the row, col_num is the number of the column, abs_num is a value from 1 to 4 (referring to the type of reference), a1 is a logical value that determines if the returned value is in A1 or R1C1 format, and sheet_text is the name of the worksheet from which to return the value.

The abs_num argument's values are the following:

1=Absolute value, such as $A$1

2=Absolute Row, Relative Column, such as $A1

3=Relative Row, Absolute Column, A$1

4=Relative reference, A1

An example of the Address function is **=address(1,1,1,1)**, which returns the value $A$1. To use the Function Wizard to enter this formula, select the category and name, then type the argument entry.

If you use a mouse to select a cell for the row and column, the cell addresses are inserted rather than only the row and column identifiers. The end result is a #value! error. Additionally, clicking on the row or column names at the top of each respective worksheet inserts the value C:C if you click on the C column. This insertion also returns an error.

The AREAS Function

The AREAS function returns a value for the number of areas in a reference. An *area* is a range of contiguous cells or a single cell or both.

Tip If you want to include several references in a single argument, you need to include an extra set of parentheses so that Excel will not interpret the comma separator as a field separator.

The syntax for AREAS is the following:

```
=areas(reference)
```

A multireference entry example is =areas((B3:G3,A4,C5:H5)). This function as entered returns the value 3.

The MATCH Function

The MATCH function returns the relative location of a value in an array of text. If you enter **=MATCH("davis",C5:C8,1)**, the function searches the text in the range C5 though C8 to find the string davis. The value it returns is 1, and the text davis appears as the first match in the array.

If the data array is resorted alphabetically in descending order, the new position returned by MATCH is 4. Figure 10.21 shows examples of how MATCH can work in the worksheet.

Figure 10.21
The worksheet showing MATCH results.

D3	▼	=MATCH("Davis",A3:A6,0)

CHAP10.XLS

	A	B	C	D	E	F	G	H
1	Rep							
2								
3	Jones	"Davis" is found in row:		4				
4	James							
5	Fritz							
6	Davis							
7								

SalesBasic / Rounding / **Logical & Ref** / Spaces

Ready

Working with Information Functions

Information functions return values based on how a cell is formatted or what it contains.

The CELL Function

CELL returns specific information about all types of numeric formats and date formats, about whether a cell is blank or contains a label or value, or even what or where that value is. If you need to determine what the width is for cell A3, type this formula: **=cell(width,A3)**. It can give this information by individual row and column. CELL is used for compatibility with other spreadsheet programs.

The COUNTBLANK Function

The COUNTBLANK function returns a value based on how many empty or blank cells it locates in a given array. This function is especially handy in the Function Wizard (see fig. 10.22). If you need to find out how many entries in a particular array contain no entry, highlight that entry with the mouse after you have selected the function from Step 1.

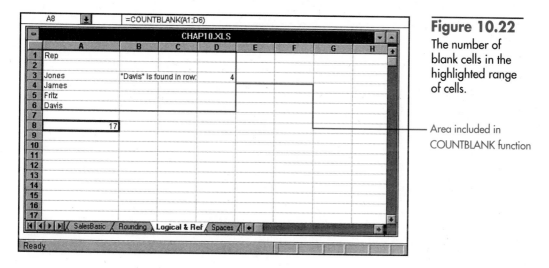

Figure 10.22
The number of blank cells in the highlighted range of cells.

Area included in COUNTBLANK function

Note   The COUNTBLANK function does not count blank text cells that contain quotation marks as true blank cells. Value cells that have 0 are counted, however.

The ISEVEN and ISODD Functions

The ISEVEN and ISODD functions return the values TRUE or FALSE. ISEVEN returns TRUE if a number is even and FALSE if the number is odd. ISODD, naturally, returns FALSE if a number is even and TRUE if odd.

Note ISEVEN and ISODD return a #value! message if run on a cell that contains a non-numeric value. If a number is a decimal, the ISEVEN and ISODD functions test only the integer, not the value to the right of the decimal point.

The N Function

The N function is like the CELL function in that it is included with Excel for compatibility with other spreadsheet programs. The syntax for N is the following:

```
=N(number)
```

where number is the value you want to convert. If N encounters a number, that number is returned. If N sees a date, it converts that to a serial number. If N sees TRUE, it converts it to a 1, and everything else N sees returns the value 0.

The TYPE Function

The TYPE function is like the INFO function, except that TYPE returns values 1, 2, 4, 8, 16, and 64 only. If a selection is a number, the value is 1. If it is text, the value is 2. If it is a formula, the value is 8; if it is an error, the value is 16; and if it is an array, the value is 64. TYPE has a simple syntax:

```
=type(value)
```

The argument value can be a cell or array reference, or a direct value entered.

Logical Functions

Logical functions return values based on whether certain values in a worksheet are met.

The AND and IF Functions

The AND function returns a TRUE or FALSE value, based on worksheet values. This can be useful if you want to display information about a number or numbers in a sheet. AND enables up to thirty arguments. The syntax is the following:

```
=AND(logical1)
```

Figure 10.23 shows two examples of the AND function. The first is the function by itself, and the second is nested with another logical function, IF, and returns a different value based on similar criteria.

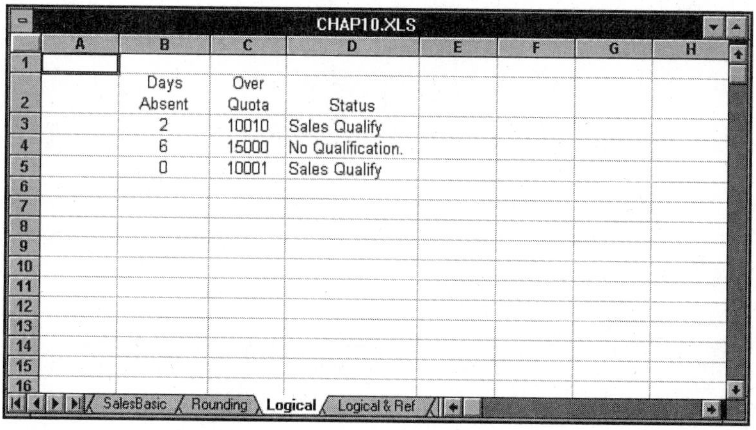

Figure 10.23
IF and AND
nested together.

The problem solved in figure 10.23 is to determine whether salespeople qualify for a contest. The criteria for qualification are: less than five days absent from work and sales greater than $10,000.00. If those two criteria are met, the salesperson qualifies. The functions used are IF, to satisfy the criteria examination, and AND, to return a value based on IF's determination of TRUE or FALSE, based on the criteria. The syntax is the following:

```
=IF(AND(B8>10000,A8<5),"Sales Qualify","No Qualification.")
```

The NOT Function

The NOT function is a simple one: it reverses the logic of an equation or argument. For example, in the formula **=not(10=11)**, the returned value is TRUE. The numbers, of course, are *not* equal. The NOT function reports FALSE for the formula **=not(10=10)**.

The OR Function

The OR function, like AND, returns a TRUE or FALSE value based on its argument. Unlike AND, however, OR returns a TRUE value if *any* argument is true, whereas AND returns a TRUE only if *all* arguments are true. If you change the qualification rules for the example in the AND and IF discussion—either less than five days of absenteeism or greater than $10,000.00 in sales—the OR statement returns Sales Qualify! for all the arguments in figure 10.23.

The TRUE and FALSE Functions

The TRUE and FALSE functions are among the easiest to use of all the Excel functions because they do not require any arguments at all. They simply return the values TRUE or FALSE when entered. You can use these functions through the Function Wizard or they can be typed directly into a worksheet.

Troubleshooting Excel Functions

The process of troubleshooting functions has improved drastically over previous releases of Excel because of the Function Wizard. The Wizard enables immediate feedback and prompting through each step of the function, which can be invaluable.

As you gain more comfort with Excel functions and formulas, you might find that function entry is faster from the keyboard than through the Wizard. It makes little sense to use some simple functions, such as TRUE and FALSE, with the Wizard. However, the Function Wizard and some of Excel's built-in features make most function entries easier and more accurate, and error recognition faster.

When you are troubleshooting functions, the Function Wizard can do all the formatting, typing, and arranging of function statements for you. If you invoke the Wizard and choose the function name you want to use, the entry in the formula bar is made for you before any arguments are entered. After clicking on the Next button, the arguments are displayed, and after all the required functions are completed (and prior to clicking on <u>F</u>inish), the value is displayed in the upper right corner of the Step 2 of 2 dialog box. You can see the results prior to actual entry into your sheet.

If your function returns #value!, #name!, or another error message, you can change values by moving back to your arguments to determine what the cause of the problem is. For newer users of Excel, the Help button also is a good way to work through problems.

As you enter functions and determine which ones you will need to analyze your worksheets and workbooks adequately and completely, the Help button brings up specific syntax notes, tips, and, in many cases, examples of ways in which functions can be used. Often, mistakes in value entry can be spotted by looking at Help's examples and working back through the arguments to determine the root of the problem.

You might wish to use the Bookmark/Define feature in on-line help if you are going back and forth on different kinds of function questions or varying types of examples. The bookmark takes you to the spot you last were and saves time and keystroking or mouse clicking.

As you become more comfortable with functions, entering them from the keyboard can become more effective. If you get in the habit of entering the formula, Excel converts lowercase entries to all uppercase—if it is typed correctly and is a function name Excel recognizes.

Using this method, you can skip the first dialog box with the Wizard as well, by first typing the equal sign, then typing the function name in lowercase with opening parenthesis, then pressing Shift+F3. This action brings up the Step 2 of 2 dialog box, in which you then can enter arguments, using the mouse for cell or array references or the keyboard.

Another way of editing function statements is to position the mouse pointer on the cell that contains the statement and press F2. This brings up the formula and makes it available for editing in the cell in which it is written. It also brings up a copy in the formula bar, but you must click on the formula bar to edit the function there. When the formula is opened for editing, the arrow keys can move you one space at a time through the statement so that you can make any necessary changes. Pressing Enter ends the editing session and returns the value of the function.

While the statement is open for editing, whenever the cursor is on a cell reference, you can press the F4 key to modify the cell reference's type from absolute row or column to relative row or column, or vice versa. This is helpful when moving functions or when copying them with AutoFill or copy/paste and cut/paste features. Figure 10.24 shows a function that is being edited and the mouse pointer clicked on the formula bar for easier editing.

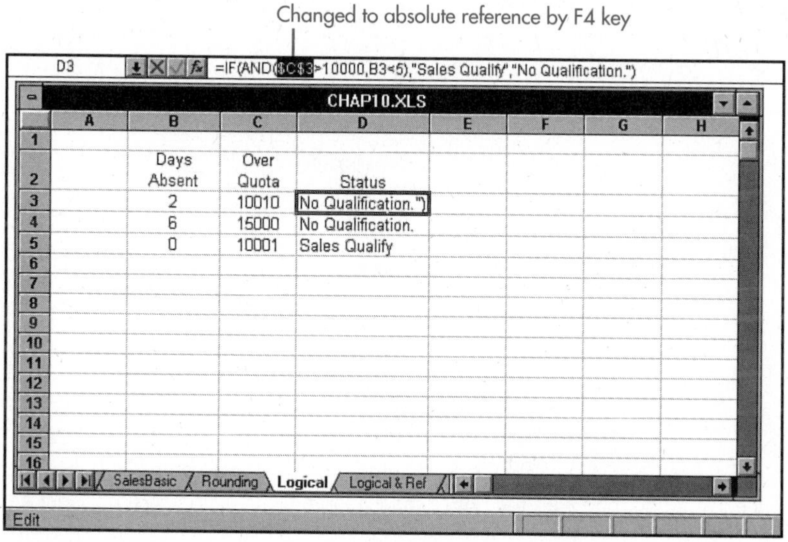

Changed to absolute reference by F4 key

Figure 10.24
Absolute references changed using the F4 key (note the formula bar).

Linking Functions

Data from one sheet in a workbook can be linked to cells located in another worksheet, another workbook, or even an external source such as a database or another spreadsheet program. Sharing information between sheets can be accomplished in a variety of ways, depending on your specific needs and application.

If you have a workbook with information related to a separate workbook, and you want to use information from the first one, the first workbook is called the *source workbook*. The sheet that receives the information from this source is called the *dependent worksheet* (or *workbook*). An *external link* refers to another Excel cell or range of cells or specific named region.

To create a link between workbooks, highlight the cells that you want to link in the source workbook. From the toolbar or the Edit menu, select Copy, which places a flashing dotted line around the cells that you have selected. Click on the Window menu. Select the workbook to which you want to take the selected referenced cells, and make it the active window. (You also can have both books open at one time on a single screen.)

In the dependent sheet, or the one you want to receive the cell references, choose Paste Special from the Edit menu. In the resulting dialog box, you can choose to copy all information about the selected cells—such as formulas, formats, values, and notes—and you can perform operations on the data. If you check All and select Paste Link in the Paste Special dialog box, the entire cell group, along with its entire contents, are copied to the new worksheet. Now, any time items are changed on the original or source workbook, those changes are passed along to the dependent reference. Figure 10.25 displays an example of this procedure.

Figure 10.25
The Paste Special menu.

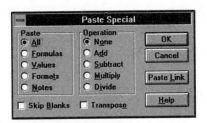

There is a shortcut to this paste process. Highlight the cells to which you want to copy the references and click the right mouse button. This brings up a cell menu that includes Cut, Copy, Paste, Paste Special, Insert, Delete, Clear Contents, and Format Cells. Move to your dependent worksheet, click on a cell to receive the information, and click the right mouse button again. Choose Paste Special to complete the process.

When you link workbooks in this manner, Excel creates absolute references in the formulas that are transferred so that if you move the information in the workbooks, the references to the source remain intact. Movement in either the source or dependent workbooks is protected.

Linked formulas use this syntax:

```
{='[WORKBK.LXS]Worksheet_Name'!abs_cell_ref}
```

For example, the formula `{='[SALES.XLS]Sales Report'!$C$4:$D$8}` in the SAMPLE1.XLS workbook is dependent on `SALES.XLS` workbook, `Sales Report` worksheet, and cells `C4` to `D8`. At the point when those cells are updated on the source link, the dependent links will be updated automatically as well.

Excel also will update dynamically any charts or related information you are using that are linked to your source reference.

Excel includes visual auditing capability. For a detailed discussion, see Chapter 11, "Advanced Worksheet Capabilities."

Example Application

The following example uses many of the formulas and concepts outlined in this chapter.

Creating an application requires some forethought and planning to be effective. Key issues to a successful application include what data to use, where it comes from, what level of sensitivity it carries, what format it is in, and who needs to use it.

Other important issues include what new data will be entered into a worksheet and what will be calculated. How will updates be made, and by whom? What level of experience does the person doing the updates have? What portions of the data are meaningful for some, but not for others?

Often, you will find that changes need to be made and documentation needs to be done. Excel has some great tools and methods for these tasks, as described in the section "Using Excel's Auditing Functions" in Chapter 11, "Advanced Worksheet Capabilities."

Because several different people will need the sales information generated from this example application, three separate workbooks will be created. The first is MASTER.XLS, the second is SLSRES.XLS, and the third is SALACCT.XLS. The MASTER workbook is the source for much of the data that the other two workbooks will receive, so the amount of work needed to maintain current information in all of them is minimized because of the links created.

MASTER.XLS contains raw sales numbers, received from the billing department, about each salesperson. The data can be extracted from a monthly billing analysis report generated by accounts receivable, an external source (see Chapter 13, "Excel Data Input and Export"). For this example, data will be entered manually from customer billing analysis reports by a sales support person.

SLSRES.XLS contains a recap of the sales reports by region and by salesperson. Information in this workbook is distributed to regional sales managers, and can be used to track performance by region, by person, and by product.

SALACCT.XLS is the sales accounting workbook. This data is used in payroll, where bonuses, contests, and commissions are calculated and checks are written.

The MASTER.XLS workbook has four active worksheets, one for each region of the company. Each region has two salespeople, and the MASTER workbook is the source for a portion of all the worksheets. The columns that list sales by product type for each month of the year are totaled, with running year-to-date sums for each category and one grand total.

Most of the SLSRES workbook is extracted from the MASTER. The sales totals by product category and region are calculated and presented on this sheet. In addition, an average sales figure by salesperson, by product category, and by month is listed. The sheet also includes a range of cells that represent the percentage of sales for the company by product type and by representative.

The SALACCT workbook also is linked to the source MASTER workbook. In this workbook, the totals are calculated and profits are figured from cost data. The profit report is broken out into profits by line of business, salesperson, and region. Sales managers are paid a bonus for profit growth and increased revenue.

Salespeople in this organization are paid a percentage of profits of their quarterly sales for hardware. They are paid a straight percentage of revenue for software and service. They also get bonuses for each month that their quota is exceeded, and the bonus is figured on quarterly dollars.

The information from these workbooks is distributed to different locations, and people throughout the company.

In the MASTER.XLS workbook, each worksheet has a new name to assist with organization. To rename a worksheet, double-click on the worksheet tab at the bottom of the screen. This brings up a dialog box in which you can enter the new name. Clicking on OK changes the name in the tab.

When you name a worksheet in a source workbook and change the worksheet name later, the formulas in the dependent workbooks are updated automatically.

Because the base values for this example come from sales data about each representative in the company, the best place to begin is with the salesperson sales data (see fig. 10.26). The basic information about the people, territories, and regions are the headers for the sheet. In the data range, the column headings are product categories, and the row headings are months of the year.

	A	B	C	D	E	F	G	H	I	J	K
1	Sales Person:	Anderson, Kate			YTD TOTAL:	Hardware	Software	Service			
2	Territory:	R1850									
3	Region:		1			98000	12000	24000			
4	Quota:	10000									
5											
6											
7		Hardware	Software	Service	Total						
8	January	10000	1000	2000	13000						
9	February	8000	1000	1	9001						
10	March	8000	1000	2000	11000						
11	April	8000	1000	2000	11000						
12	May	8000	1000	2000	11000						
13	June	8000	1000	2000	11000						
14	July	8000	1000	2000	11000						
15	August	8000	1000	2000	11000						
16	September	8000	1000	2000	11000						
17	October	8000	1000	2000	11000						
18	November	8000	1000	2000	11000						
19	December	8000	1000	2000	11000						

Anderson, KT. / Sheet2 / Sheet3 / Sheet4 / Sheet5 /

Figure 10.26

The base format for the MASTER worksheet.

The three product headings are Hardware, Software, and Service. The fourth column heading is for monthly totals. There is a number at the bottom of each column representing year-to-date (YTD) totals—by product category—and summary information at the top of the sheet using the same totals as cell references. The totals are copied from the bottom of the columns and pasted as links for the YTD totals at the top. This automatically creates absolute references to the totals numbers.

The SLSRES.XLS sheets use the values from MASTER for many of the calculations. To create the SLSRES workbook, select New from the File menu. Rename the first worksheet tab Region 1. From the Window menu, click on Arrange. Select Tile in the dialog box, and click on OK. This displays both the MASTER and SLSRES workbooks on-screen, which makes creating the link between the two easier.

Make the MASTER workbook and the Anderson, K. worksheets active by clicking on them. Highlight the range of cells from A1:H4 and click the right mouse button. Choose Copy from the Cell menu, and move to the SLSRES workbook. In the worksheet Region 1, click on cell A1 and click the right mouse button. Select Paste Special from the menu, and click on the Paste Link button in the dialog box. This action copies the cell references from MASTER to SLSRES and completes the link between the two. Now, each time data is updated for a salesperson, the changes will be updated in the dependent worksheets.

The Paste Special command can copy cells a number of different ways. You can paste all the attributes of a cell, or formats, formulas, values, or nothing. You also can perform operations during the copy. You can copy the cells, or you can add, subtract, multiply, or divide the target values with the cells you have chosen to copy (see fig. 10.27).

Figure 10.27

The result of the Paste Special command.

B2			=[MASTER.XLS]Anderson, KT.'!$A$1:$H$5					
	A	B	C	D	E	F	G	H
1	Sales Person:	Anderson, Kate			YTD TOTALS:	Hardware	Software	Service
2	Territory:	'!$A$1:$H$5						
3	Region:	1				$ 98,000.00	$ 12,000.00	$ 24,000.00
4	Quota:	10000						

Sheets: Region 1 / Region 2 / Sheet3 / Sheet4 / Sheet5 / Sheet6 / Sheet7 / Sheet8

The SLSRES workbook has three active worksheets. The first two are the sales recap sheets for the salespeople in each region. Each salesperson has a group of cells that contains her year-to-date sales in each of the product categories. In addition, the summary shows the last active month entered. This number is calculated by using the HLOOKUP function. The function is written in SLSRES as the following:

```
=hlookup(IF***) CG: fill in the formula to do the lookup if
sales>1.and return the value of the month.**
```

This updates the regional managers with the values for the current month's sales.

The third worksheet in the SLSRES workbook is the company totals and rankings worksheet. It shows the total sales for each salesperson, followed by that person's respective ranks for Hardware, Software, and Service. It also shows the percentage of total sales for each product category, as well as percentage of total sales for the region. The last area of the sheet shows the values that reflect the averages by region for all salespeople in all categories.

The last workbook in the series, SLSACCT, is the sales accounting workbook. This group has three sheets in it as well. The first is the Quota % worksheet. In this sheet, the quota performance is calculated for each salesperson, and for each region. These numbers are all drawn from the MASTER workbook. The salespeople again are ranked, but this time by percentage of quota achievement, and the number of months over quota is listed as well.

The second worksheet in this book is Bonus $, or the place where the bonuses are figured. This sheet figures its values from the individual sales recap sheets in MASTER. The bonuses are paid if the salesperson is over quota for the month, and paid on the dollars sold during the current quarter. Quarterly totals are figured here, and the bonuses are figured on those numbers.

The third sheet in the book is Commission $, which figures the commissions paid to each person, along with the tax information for each check and for the year. The profits for hardware are figured here from the fourth sheet, Costs. Because the salespeople are paid for hardware on percentage of profit, the values are linked together, and the commissions are

calculated from that. In addition, the sales manager's bonus is figured from these calculations. The growth for each region is figured here, too.

The last worksheet in this application is the Performance Recap. The recap shows the total sales, the total commissions, and rank for overall sales for each region and each salesperson. Each person also has a cell for contest bonus points and for performance against quota. The total dollars are graphed for distribution to all offices to post so that salespeople can see how they are doing in relation to the rest of the group.

Chapter Snapshot

Microsoft Excel version 5.0 has some new and powerful capabilities. This chapter will introduce these capabilities to you so that you can learn to use them in your applications. The advanced capabilities covered in this section include an in-depth discussion of several of the Add-ins and advanced features that are part of Excel 5.0. In this chapter, you will learn about the following:

After you finish this chapter, you will know how to install add-ins, use advanced features, and apply them in applications. You also get a chance to use some of Excel's advanced tools, like Auditing and Report Manager. Excel's other powerful advanced tools include Microsoft Query, ODBC Add-in, Pivot tables, and DDE functions. These topics are covered in Chapters 13 and 15.

11 CHAPTER

Advanced Worksheet Capabilities

by Critch Greaves

Add-ins in Excel 5.0 are worksheet tools that bring new and advanced power to your desktop. The Add-ins included with Excel are AutoSave, Analysis ToolPak, Slide Show, Goal Seek, Solver, Scenario Manager, View Manager, and Report Manager. A brief description of each follows:

✔ **AutoSave.** Automatically saves your work at specified intervals.

✔ **Analysis ToolPak.** Provides a number of worksheet functions and macro functions that help with data analysis in the workbook, the Function Wizard, and the Tools menu.

✔ **Slide Show.** Enables you to create customized slide shows of your worksheets, graphs, and reports by using the customizable Slide Show template.

✔ **Goal Seek.** Enables you to find values to complete questions based on a specific outcome.

✔ **Solver.** Enables you to determine answers to complex what-if questions by analyzing cells and determining the optimum value adjustments to arrive at a desired result.

✔ **Scenario Manager.** Enables you to create and analyze results from various groups of changing cells. The scenario manager enables you to define custom assumptions and to answer complex what-if questions.

✔ **View Manager.** Helps you arrange and look at your information in a variety of ways.

✔ **Report Manager.** Enables you to format your information contained within workbooks and worksheets and scenarios in an organized, uniform report output format.

Installing and Removing Add-Ins

The add-in files are located in the \EXCEL\LIBRARY subdirectory. To look at the available add-ins, choose Add-Ins from the Tools menu. A list of the available add-ins appears; add-ins that are installed have their check boxes selected. You install the add-in you want by clicking on the check box to the left of the description of the add-in. Removal is just as simple. To remove an add-in that is already installed, just click on the appropriate check box.

Many add-ins bring with them menu choices. When you install an add-in, the menu options are made available; when you remove an add-in, the options are made inactive. Additionally, with Analysis ToolPak you can choose from 50+ more functions than without it activated.

Selecting Add-Ins from the Tools menu displays the Add-Ins dialog box (see fig. 11.1). Note which add-ins are currently selected. For examination, click in the check boxes currently marked with an X so that all add-ins are deselected. After you do this, close the Add-Ins dialog box by clicking on the OK button. This removes the add-ins from Excel, and changes the functions, selections, and menu selections that you can access throughout the various menu choices on the main toolbar, from the pull-down menus, and through several of the Wizards, such as the Function Wizard.

Figure 11.1
The Add-Ins
dialog box.

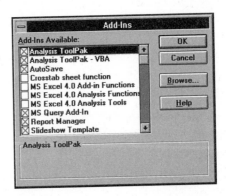

If you have an add-in loaded and resident in a separate window, such as Slide Show, removing it does not deactivate it from the active workbook. You can continue to use Slide Show just as you always do within Excel. The next time the program is terminated, however, the Slide Show add-in is not available until it is reactivated through the use of Tools, Add-Ins.

Even after you remove all the add-ins from Excel, several of them remain available from pull-down menus, such as Solver, Goal Seek, and Scenario Manager. When they are invoked under the Tools pull-down menu, they are resubmitted to the add-ins list that Excel uses to track what is automatically loaded when starting up the software, so that the next time you use the program, the same tools are available.

Using all add-ins with Excel changes the time required to load the program and slows down other operations such as Cut and Paste because of the extra demands on system memory and resources, such as the Virtual Memory swap file.

Using the Add-Ins

The following sections describe the features of the Excel add-ins and get you up to speed in working with them.

AutoSave

AutoSave is one of the easiest add-ins to use, and offers one of the greatest benefits: it saves your work for you in specified intervals.

To activate AutoSave, choose Add-Ins from the Tools menu. When the Add-Ins dialog box appears, click in the AutoSave check box.

Configuring the AutoSave add-in is straightforward. Again click on the Tools menu, and if you have properly installed the add-in, AutoSave appears in the drop-down menu with a check mark next to it. Click on AutoSave, and the AutoSave dialog box appears with several options you can use to modify the add-in (see fig. 11.2). The default values are to autosave every 10 minutes, to save the active workbook only, and to prompt the user before saving. You also can configure AutoSave to save workbooks or workspaces automatically, with or without user intervention.

Figure 11.2
The AutoSave dialog box.

If the <u>P</u>rompt Before Saving check box is selected, you can save the current workbook, skip the save, cancel the operation, or get help.

If you have AutoSave activated under the default settings and you switch to another Windows application while working on an Excel Workbook, the Excel title bar beneath whatever application you are running flashes, indicating that user input is required. When you switch back to Excel, the AutoSave dialog box is in the foreground of the workbook, and the Excel title bar stops flashing.

If you want to change the interval of time between saves, or save all open workbooks instead of just the active workbook, change the options from within the AutoSave dialog box. You can disable AutoSave, change the Automatic <u>S</u>ave Every setting, choose Save Active <u>W</u>orkbook Only or Save <u>A</u>ll Open Workbooks, and decide whether to check Prompt Before Saving. If you are working on a new workbook and have not previously saved your work, AutoSave takes you through the normal steps required to save a workbook, such as assigning a name and location for storing the workbook.

Analysis ToolPak

After you install the Analysis ToolPak, a new option appears on the <u>T</u>ools menu—<u>D</u>ata Analysis, which lists the Analysis tools available in Excel.

Before you use the Analysis ToolPak, you need to organize your worksheet data as an input range, and select an output range in which to place results. The contents of the output vary, depending on which tool you use. Excel assists you by providing labels for cells in an output range if you do not supply them.

The tools available in the ToolPak are shown in table 11.1.

Table 11.1
Tools Available in the Analysis ToolPak

Tool Name	Description
Anova: Single Factor	Performs simple variance analysis based on rows or columns of data
Anova: Two Factor with Replication	An extension of the single factor Anova, which includes more than one sample for each group of data
Anova: Two Factor without Replication	Performs two sample Anova, which does not include more than one sampling per group
Correlation	Finds a correlation coefficient for a group of numbers

Tool Name	Description
Covariance	Averages the deviations of two ranges of data from their respective means
Descriptive Statistics	Reports on the variability and central tendencies of data
Exponential Smoothing	Returns a value based on a prior forecast, using a constant that determines the magnitude of how strongly forecasts respond to numbers in a forecast
F-Test Two-Sample for Variance	Compares two population groups for variance
Fourier Analysis	Solves problems in linear systems analyzing periodic data
Histogram	Calculates individual and cumulative frequencies for ranges of cell data and bins, and generates the number of occurrences of a value in a set
Moving Average	Projects values based on previous periods, such as sales or inventory
Random Number Generation	Fills cells with random numbers for a variety of different statistical uses
Rank and Percentile	Provides the percentage rank of each value in a data set
Regression	Using the "least Squares" method, analyzes a set of observations about an event, to enable forecasting of other events
Sampling	Creates a sample of data from an existing sample or population
t-Test: Paired two Sample means	Compares whether two Sample for Means are distinct
t-Test: Two-Sample, equal variances	Determines whether two sets' means are equal, assuming equal variances
t-Test: Two-Sample, unequal variances	Determines whether two sets' means are equal, assuming unequal variances
z-Test: Two Sample	Tests the difference between two population means

II

Excel

Each of the Analysis ToolPak functions has similar requirements to return values, like regular worksheet functions. All require *input values*, cells or ranges that Excel assigns as absolute values using the ROWCOLUMN reference type. In addition, you are prompted for arguments specific to the type of analysis required so that a meaningful number or report is returned as you use the functions.

The information for most Data Analysis tools can be output to a range of cells, a new worksheet ply, or its own workbook. A *worksheet ply* is simply another worksheet in your existing workbook, which you can name in the dialog box under output options, as shown in figure 11.3.

Figure 11.3

Outputting in the Covariance dialog box to a new worksheet ply, with new name Report.

Covariance	
Input	
Input Range:	$A$9:$B$15
Grouped By:	● Columns
	○ Rows
☐ Labels in First Row	
Output options	
○ Output Range:	
● New Worksheet Ply:	Report
○ New Workbook	
	OK
	Cancel
	Help

Many of the Data Analysis tools are specific for exact specific analysis, and extensive help is available in the user's guides, and through on-line help. When you want more specific information about one of the Data Analysis tools, highlight it with the mouse and press F1 or click on the Help button.

The results generated by many of the Data Analysis tools are extensive, as typified by an Anova: Single Factor, for example. Taking a simple sample of six numbers, in two worksheet cells, selecting the input range as two columns by three rows, and output range as a new worksheet ply called Anova, the resulting report is extensive, showing the count, sum, average, variance, and an analysis of the variance in detail.

The Analysis ToolPak was developed by GreyMatter and KRISTECH companies.

Slide Show

The Slide Show add-in is used to make presentation graphics images from workbook data. You can present the slides on a monitor, save the slides as files on a floppy disk, and share the slides across a network, but you cannot print the slides out to hard copy to use in overheads. You should also save the slide as an additional file besides the SLIDES.XLA, so that you can keep the add-in in its original condition.

You can activate the Slides add-in by opening a new file and specifying Slide as the file type, provided you have selected the add-in from the Tools, Add-Ins menu selection already. Other ways to open a new file are to press Ctrl+N or choose File, New. Both methods activate the New dialog box. Pressing W or S will highlight your selection so that you quickly can select the file type you want.

To make a slide, you need to decide which information from your workbook you want to appear in the display. By highlighting the information with the mouse and copying it to the Clipboard (by using the Copy button on the standard tool bar, or the Edit, Copy command, or the right mouse button), you can bring information from worksheet to slide format. After you highlight and copy your data, choose Window from the main menu and switch to the Slide window. After the Slide window is active, press the Paste slide button on the slide add-in. The data is then brought into the sheet, and the Edit slide dialog box is invoked for additional information on how your presentation should look.

You can choose different transitions from the Transition Gallery in the Edit Slide dialog box, as shown in figure 11.4. This gallery has over 40 transition effects to change the appearance of the screen as you move through your slide presentation. The Edit Slide dialog box can be displayed by clicking on the Edit Slide button in the gallery window.

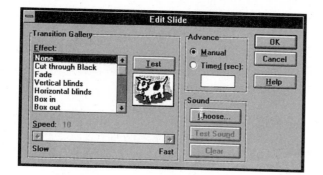

Figure 11.4

Choosing effects in the Edit Slide dialog box.

As you experiment with the Slide Show add-in, be aware that the most effective presentations probably do not use all different types of transitional effects. You should experiment with the transition effects so that your show flows nicely, without being distracting. The data should be the focus of the presentation, not the way your slides move up, down, or around the screen.

You can test the way the transitions work by selecting the particular effect from the Effect list box in the Edit Slide dialog box, then clicking on the Test button. The small dog then gives way to another image of a key, using the effect you choose.

You can affect completion speed of a transition in the Speed slider of the Edit Slide dialog box, where 1 is the slowest and 10 the fastest. The correct setting depends on the transition you choose and the effect you want. After you decide upon your effects, you can choose to advance the slide manually, or within a chosen number of seconds. The Timed advance holds the image on-screen for the time you specify, then advances to the next frame, using the transitions. Note that the time for the slide transition is different from the automatically timed slide advancement.

You can attach .WAV files to your slides by clicking on Choose in the Sound group. As with transitions, you can test the sounds you choose by clicking on Test Sound.

If your PC does not have a sound board, you still can use Windows' sound capability. The driver for using your PC's internal speaker is available from Microsoft, either by writing Microsoft and requesting the driver on disk, or by using the Microsoft Download Service and downloading the PC Speaker driver. The quality of sound is not near what the 16-bit digital boards deliver, but it can be better than silence.

You can rearrange the order in which your slides appear by using the Cut Row, Copy Row, and Paste and Delete Row buttons on the second row of buttons in the Slide Show add-in. To perform a movement, edit, or deletion, highlight the row number on the far left side of the spreadsheet, or press Shift+spacebar when the cursor is on a cell in the row you want to move. When you want to reinsert the slide, click on the Insert Row button.

In addition to worksheet information (cells, graphs, or other Excel information), you can bring other information into Slide Show. You can paste any information from the Clipboard into the Slide Show to use in your presentation.

If you use AutoSave with the Slide Show, be careful to initially save your Slide Show under another name, so that you don't overwrite the original SLIDES.XLS workbook. Also, keep this in mind if you have the Save All Open Workbooks option selected.

Goal Seek

Goal Seek is a handy tool that you can use to achieve a certain value in a cell that has a formula, by adjusting the value of another cell that has a direct effect on that cell. Suppose that the salespeople's totals for the month were 70,000, and that result was obtained by adding the individual's numbers for each month and displaying it in a cell below the column. You can use Goal Seek to see how much your top representative needs to sell to make the monthly total 80,000.

Goal Seek is invoked by choosing Tools, Goal Seek. The dialog box prompts you to select the cell that has the formula whose result you want to alter, then enter the value you want to reach. The final step in Goal Seek is to select the cell whose value you want to modify to reach the goal or target specified in the first step.

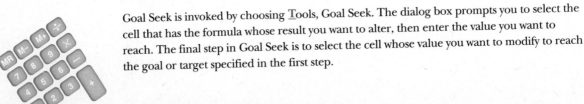

Figure 11.5 shows the Goal Seek dialog box.

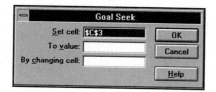

Figure 11.5
The Goal Seek
dialog box.

After you choose the options you want to use with Goal Seek, the Goal Seek Status dialog box appears with several options: stepping through an operation, pausing operations, and seeking additional help. This dialog box also displays the cell information, the target value, and the current value, so that as Goal Seek works, you can see the result and step through, pause, or alter it as you go. Clicking on the Pause button changes the choices to Stop and Continue.

When you click on OK in the Goal Seek Status dialog box, Goal Seek places the value found into the specified cell. If you find that this is not what you want, you can restore the values by choosing Undo Goal Seek from the Edit menu on the main menu bar. If you really can't decide what to do, choose Edit, then Redo Goal Seek, to recalculate the goal seek you just undid.

You can use Goal Seek with data tables to answer what-if questions about multiple variables against a single formula or single variables against multiple formulas. A *data table* is an array or group of cells that shows the effects of different variables on a formula. There are two types of data tables, single-input and two-input tables. A *single-input table* takes a single variable in a formula and displays multiple values in the data table.

If you want to see the results of a varying interest rate on a loan in table format, for example, you would use a single-input data table. Figure 11.6 shows the format for a column-oriented table, and you can do the same thing in a row format. To make a data table, begin by entering a column of the values for which you want to see results. From the first entry in the column, go right one cell and up one cell. At this location, input the formula that contains the target cell where you want your table variables inserted—in this case, interest rates. Now, using the right mouse button, select the area that contains the variables, the formula you entered to the right and up one row, and from the Data menu, select table.

The Table dialog box appears, and you can choose Row Input Cell or Column Input Cell. In a single-input table, you can fill in only one value (in a two-input table, you must input values for both). Your input cell, because this example uses a columnar format, is the second choice, Column Input Cell. The *input cell* is the cell whose value you want to change in the representative table of variables.

To make a two-input table, take the same column of figures and move the formula entered earlier to the cell directly above the first entry in the column. Then, directly to the right of that, enter your second variable—the length of time on a loan. Next, highlight the entire area, including the variables and formulas, as shown in figure 11.7.

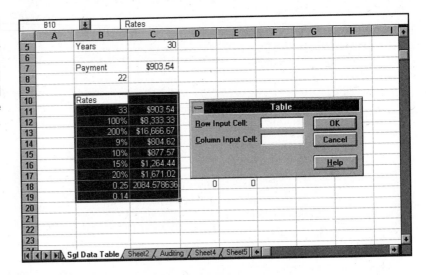

Figure 11.6
The format for a column-oriented table, showing multiple interest rates and payments.

Figure 11.7
The two-input table example, with highlighted variables and formats and the Table dialog box.

Again, choose **D**ata, Table. For the row input cell, choose the time frame from the main portion of the worksheet. Press Tab, or click on the next field—the column input cell. Click on the percentage rate from the main area, and click on the Done button. Goal Seek fills in the values for each corresponding time frame, at each interest rate. At this point, perform the following steps:

1. Choose **D**ata, Table.

2. For the row input, choose the time frame from the main portion of the worksheet.

3. Tab to the column input box and click on the value for percentage rate.

4. Click on OK.

Any changes you make to the interest rate column or the time row are reflected automatically as you enter the numbers, which can be a valuable way to answer what-if questions.

A *two-input table* takes two variables in a formula and returns the values as shown in figure 11.8.

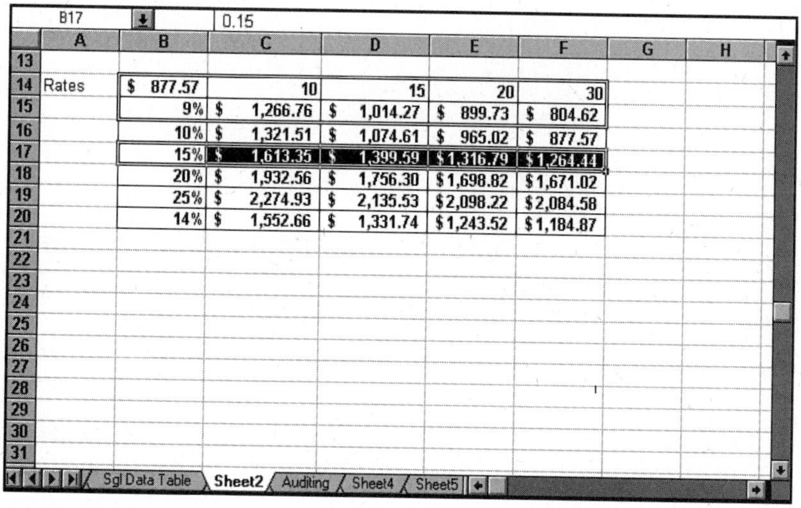

	B17		0.15						
	A	B	C	D	E	F	G	H	
13									
14	Rates	$ 877.57	10	15	20	30			
15		9%	$ 1,266.76	$ 1,014.27	$ 899.73	$ 804.62			
16		10%	$ 1,321.51	$ 1,074.61	$ 965.02	$ 877.57			
17		15%	$ 1,613.35	$ 1,399.59	$1,316.79	$1,264.44			
18		20%	$ 1,932.56	$ 1,756.30	$1,698.82	$1,671.02			
19		25%	$ 2,274.93	$ 2,135.53	$2,098.22	$2,084.58			
20		14%	$ 1,552.66	$ 1,331.74	$1,243.52	$1,184.87			
21									
22									
23									
24									
25									
26									
27									
28									
29									
30									
31									

Sgl Data Table \ **Sheet2** \ Auditing \ Sheet4 \ Sheet5

Figure 11.8
Example of a two-input data table.

Goal Seek can save time in doing tedious what-if type analysis by offering quick solutions to questions that might take a long time using trial and error.

Solver

Solver calculates answers to what-if scenarios by using adjustable cells, and even minimizing or maximizing specific cells in order to attain the desired result.

Solver is useful for three types of problems:

✔ **Integer problems.** Problems that require a yes or no answer (0 or 1), or problems in which no decimal places are required. Integer problems can greatly increase the amount of time Solver needs to reach a solution.

✔ **Linear problems.** Problems that involve functions or operations such as addition and subtraction, or some of the built in functions such as FORECAST.

✔ **Nonlinear problems.** Problems that use any algorithms, pairs of changing cells that are multiplied or divided by one another, or exponents. Growth and SQRT are two functions that might be present in a nonlinear problem.

Solver is similar to Goal Seek; however, it has more options, and can answer questions of greater complexity. In addition, after Solver answers the questions you pose, you can have it generate reports based on the changes you make to your worksheets.

To start Solver, choose **T**ools, Solver. The Solver Parameters dialog box appears (see fig. 11.9), in which you enter the information it needs. The first item Solver needs is a *target cell*, a cell that contains a formula that you want to find a value for by altering other dependent parts of your worksheet or workbook. To select a target cell, click on the cell you want to change. If you highlight the cell you intend to change and then invoke Solver, that cell address is automatically entered in the S**e**t Target Cell edit box.

Figure 11.9
The Solver
Parameters dialog
box.

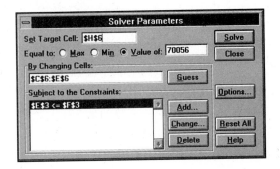

Next, you select an Equal to parameter, **M**ax, Mi**n**, or **V**alue of. There is an entry box to enter the specific value, which is activated if you check the **V**alue of selection. After you complete these two steps, you need to tell Solver which cells to change to arrive at the desired result, and you can use the **G**uess button if you need help for this. Clicking on **G**uess highlights the cells on the worksheet and displays the absolute values of the cells in the box beneath the **B**y Changing Cells text box. **G**uess selects all nonformula cells referred to by the formula in the **B**y Changing Cells text box, which can save you some time.

To further customize your problem setup, you can add constraints to the equations by clicking on the **A**dd box and choosing limits or ranges for the cells to be modified. Suppose you want to see which numbers would need to be modified for each of your salespeople to reach 80,000 sales for a month. The current sales is 55,600, but you want the values for a particular person to remain at or below a certain dollar value. You can, in the Subject to the Constraints box, add the cell reference to the person whose number you want to keep at or below the value, and indicate the Less than or equal to sign and the value.

You can add multiple constraints to the equation to reach the desired goal. If you have multiple constraints and you want to change, edit, or delete them, the boxes to the right of the Constraints window enables these functions. Clicking on the **A**dd button brings up an empty dialog box in which you fill in the appropriate cell, limit, and operator. **C**hange brings up the same box, but with all the values filled in for editing. **D**elete prompts you to confirm the deletion of a particular constraint from the problem.

If you plan on running a similar problem against other worksheets, you can save your model problem and modify those parameters for the new problem. The **O**ptions button in the Solver dialog box presents the following options:

✔ **Max Time.** Limits the amount of time spent in solving the problem by limiting the number of interim calculations. The default value is 100 seconds, and the maximum is 32,767. The default is adequate for most small problems. This value must be a positive integer.

✔ **Iterations.** Limits the amount of time Solver uses to process your problem. Again, the default is 100, which is adequate for most simple problems, and this option has the same maximum value and rules as Max Time.

✔ **Precision.** Determines whether the constraint cell value matches the target value or is within the upper or lower value ranges you specified. The default is 0.000001, and the number you use must be a fraction. The lower the number, the higher the precision, and therefore, the longer Solver takes to reach the solution.

✔ **Tolerance.** Deals with changing cells that are restricted to integers. The *tolerance* is a percentage of error allowed in a calculation in which an integer is used. A higher tolerance level increases solution speed, and this setting has no effect if there are not integer limits placed on the cells to change.

✔ **Assume Linear Process.** Speeds the solution if all the specified relationships are linear.

✔ **Show Iteration Results.** Stops Solver after each iteration and shows the results, which can be useful if you are examining a problem or troubleshooting a scenario.

✔ **Use Automatic Scaling.** Handy when the changing cells and the target have large scale differences. The Estimates box specifies whether you should use T**a**ngent or **Q**uadratic methods to estimate target and changing cells. The Default is Tangent, but Quadratic can improve results in nonlinear problems. Derivative's choices of **F**orward (the default) and **C**entral are useful if the graphical representations are not smooth and continuous. The Central method also might be useful if Solver gives you a message that it could not improve the solution.

✔ **Search.** Defines whether the **N**ewton or C**o**njugate gradient method of searching is used. This tells Solver which algorithm to use, and which direction to search after each iteration. The Newton method requires more memory, but results in less iteration. The Conjugate method is useful with larger problems, if memory is a problem, and can be used to step through a problem.

The Load and Save Model buttons each bring up their own dialog boxes, and can assist you in saving additional models, or bringing them into use in other worksheets. The First Solver model is automatically saved with your work.

Solver calculations can stop for three reasons:

✔ The maximum time limit based on the value in the Options section for Max Time is reached.

✔ The maximum number of iterations or trials is reached.

✔ Solver solves the questions satisfactorily or runs into a problem. If Solver runs into a problem, you receive a message that Solver was unable to adequately solve your problem.

The amount of time Solver needs to operate is affected by two factors:

✔ The number of changing cells

✔ The complexity of the problem

Scenario Manager

Scenario Manager is a tool that enables you to evaluate changes made to worksheets by changing information in a select set of cells. Scenario Manager tracks and maintains the input values you choose, and plugs them into the cells you request. Scenario Manager is a powerful tool for what-if analysis in a worksheet, across multiple sheets in a workbook, or across multiple workbooks.

You can activate Scenario Manager from the Workgroup toolbar or through the Tools menu. Once input, each scenario has a unique name, and its own set of changing cell information.

You can merge scenarios from sheets with other sheets to form consolidation sheets. Suppose you need to borrow money. You have a monthly payment you know you can afford, but you are not sure of how much you should borrow to meet the payment. Furthermore, competing financial programs offer varying interest rates over varying terms. You can set up a model of the loan structure you want to evaluate and use Scenario Manager to evaluate for the best loan structure for your situation. If you use different scenarios to plug in different interest rates available from different banks, the Scenario Manager shows you at a glance what each program offers in terms of the final outcome. Figure 11.10 shows the model, using First from the Scenarios list box.

To create the scenario, choose Scenarios from the Tools menu. The Scenario Manager dialog box appears, and any scenarios associated with the current worksheet are shown in the Scenarios list box. If there are no existing scenarios, click on the Add button to display the Add Scenario dialog box. Scenarios do not require much information, but the results can be very useful.

The scenario needs a name that can offer an indication of its purpose. The example shown earlier is called First. The next box of information Scenario Manager needs is the Changing Cells box. This is the area where the variables appear on your worksheet so that Scenario Manager can provide what-if analysis.

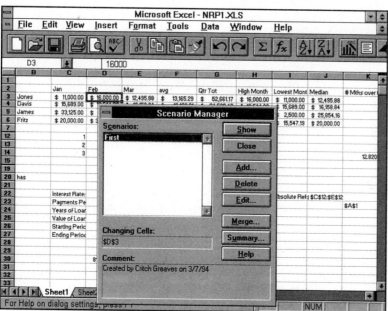

Figure 11.10
The loan model
with Scenario
Manager.

Select the cells you want to change and insert values in them by clicking and dragging with the left mouse button. If there are cells outside the contiguous range you want to include in the changing cells, use Shift+click to include them. Insurance cells can be included by pressing Ctrl+click.

The next information box in this step is the user Comment box, which indicates the registered user's name and the date that the scenario was created or modified. Scenario Manager uses this information to track names and maintain order in the Merge function.

After you create the scenario, you return to the main Scenario Manager dialog box, in which you should see the name of the scenario you just entered. Several buttons are available along the right side of the box:

- ✔ **Show.** Enters the results of your variables.

- ✔ **Close.** Closes the Scenario Manager.

- ✔ **Add.** Displays the Add Scenario dialog box, which you use to create a scenario.

- ✔ **Delete.** Removes scenarios.

- ✔ **Edit.** Enables you to change or modify the elements of a scenario.

- ✔ **Merge.** Displays the Merge dialog box, which enables you to select the workbook, sheet, and scenario you want to merge.

- ✔ **Summary.** Provides a new worksheet with a complete formatted summary of the variable changes

The Summary button does some interesting things. It provides a formatted report on its own worksheet of the values that were changed and the results of the scenario. The Scenario Summary dialog box appears, and you have a choice of two different types of reports. The first is the scenario summary, which is a report on its own worksheet, showing the complete details of the scenario.

You also can put the results into a pivot table. A *pivot table* is an interactive worksheet table that you can use to organize and analyze data in a variety of ways. After you create a pivot table, you can rearrange data by dragging fields and items.

Note For more information on pivot tables, see Chapter 13, "Excel Data Input and Export."

View Manager

View manager can change the way your worksheets and workbooks appear on-screen and eventually on paper without saving a separate workbook. Because Excel has a vast number of formatting options that can change the appearance of a worksheet, you might want to use View Manager to add additional enhancements to the way your work appears.

The view that you save reflects current window size, in addition to many of the settings in the Options dialog box. Because each view is saved across a complete workbook, it can be helpful to use the name of the worksheet as well as a brief description.

To invoke View Manager, choose View, View Manager. The option at the bottom of the menu choices should indicate View Manager; if it does not, you should reinstall this add-in through the Tools menu.

When you choose View Manager from the View menu, the View Manager dialog box appears (see fig. 11.11). From this dialog box, you can select existing views of your worksheet if available. You can Add a new view, Show the effect of the view, Close the View Manager, or Delete a view.

Figure 11.11
The View Manager dialog box.

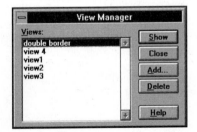

Views save the print settings and displays settings for a worksheet as well as hidden column or row information. You have the option of changing these settings when you create the view in the Add View dialog box. This is done at the same time as you assign a name to the view.

To set up a view, first create the look you want to use by changing the settings, zoom factors, and print settings, and hiding any columns or rows that you want to exclude from the view. After your sheet looks that way you want, choose View from the main menu and invoke the View Manager. Choose Add and name your view. Indicate whether you want to save print settings and hidden columns or rows in the Add Views dialog box, and click on OK to save the view of that sheet.

Note If you do not have any print settings made for a particular sheet, the entire worksheet prints.

Report Manager

The Report Manager provides detailed reports of your workbooks in a variety of ways. You can create customized reports from your information using the Report Manager tools.

Reports can include different views and scenarios, and a report can automatically switch between scenarios and views and print them in a specific order.

To create a report, choose Print Report from the File menu. The main Print Report dialog box appears, in which you can print, close, add, edit, delete, or get help.

The first step is to name the report, followed by creating a section. To do this from the Print Report dialog box, choose Add, then name your report and tab to the section area of the Add Report dialog box. A *section* of the report is defined by simply choosing which worksheet from the workbook you want to use and whether you want to use any predefined views or scenarios from the sheets in your reports.

After you name the report, the default values for Sheet, View, and Scenario are marked in the Section to Add group. The sheet name is the same name as the sheet that was active when you launched Report Manager. The drop-down boxes for View and Scenario are used to select available variables and representations of your workbook.

After you define a particular addition to the Report Manager, click on the Add button, and it will show up on the Print Report dialog box as well as in the Sections of this Report area.

If you want to keep an original report to show a history of a particular sheet, for example, you can choose Add in the Report Manager dialog box, and define a new report that uses your new views or scenarios.

Figure 11.12 shows Report Manager's Add Report dialog box.

Figure 11.12
Report Manager's
Add Report dialog
box.

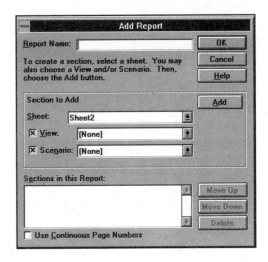

When you add a new report, if you do not want to use views or scenarios in printing, you can keep the default values or uncheck the boxes to the left of the choices. Unchecking the boxes grays the selections available from the drop-down menus for each selection.

With each report you design, you can have multiple sections. In the initial design stages of report design, you can update the sections of this Report section of the dialog box, after you click on the Add button next to the Section to Add group.

You might want to use different sections in a report to illustrate projected changes in business trends. If you incorporate all the selections into one report when you print, all are included together. If, on the other hand, you want to have the flexibility to print all the information but do not want to have all the reports print together, set up separate reports that reflect the same values.

The Add Report dialog box is also where you change the position of sections in your report, such as in what order your sections fall. If you want the report to be one large report, you should select the Use Continuous Page Numbers check box. This option prints the page numbers across multiple sections. Unselecting this box resets the page number at each section.

After you define the information in the section that you want to incorporate in your report, you must click on the Add button in the Sections in this Report area. If you do not, an error message appears, indicating that you cannot have a report that does not have designed sections. It becomes even more important if you add sections, however, because if you define a new section and forget to add it to the report, Report manager discards all your changes.

After adding a section and clicking on OK, the Print Report dialog box is activated. To print a report, select the title of the report you want and click on the Print button. Your screen changes to each sheet, view, and scenario as it generates the report, and a standard dialog box that indicates print status appears after Excel generates the information. Upon completion your original view, scenario, and worksheet are restored so that you can continue work.

Using Report Manager, you can set up one report to print each scenario you create, with the view options you designate for each scenario, in the order you want the reports to appear.

Using Excel's Auditing Features

Excel has auditing tools that you can use to illustrate how values are arrived at and to figure out where problems have occurred.

The Auditing toolbar provides a quick way to use some of Excel's features—using visual tools called tracers. *Tracers* are graphic displays, such as arrows, that show visually where formulas get their values. To display the Auditing toolbar, choose Auditing from the Tools menu. The last selection on the menu is Show Auditing Toolbar, and if it is already active, there is a check mark next to the selection. If you do not want the toolbar to be displayed, simply click in the Show Auditing Toolbar check box.

You also can display the toolbar by choosing Toolbars from the View menu. The dialog box that appears shows all available Excel and add-in toolbars. If the toolbar you want is not on the list, return to the Tools menu and choose Add-Ins to make sure that the add-in you want is loaded. This displays the Add-Ins dialog box so that you can make the selection.

From the Auditing toolbar, you can select and remove tracers of different types: precedents and dependents. You also can add notes, trace errors, and show an information window.

Tracers are graphic representations that display a relationship between cells. Tracers can illustrate two types of relationships: precedent and dependent. *Precedent cells* are cells that are referred to directly by a formula. *Dependent cells,* conversely, are cells that contain formulas that refer to other cells.

Another way to describe the relationships is with the terms direct and indirect. A *direct precedent* is a cell that is referred to by the formula in the active cell. An *indirect precedent* is referred to by a formula in a direct precedent cell or another indirect cell.

A *direct dependent* is a cell that contains a formula that refers to the active cell, and an *indirect dependent* is a cell that contains a direct dependent cell or another indirect dependent cell.

In the worksheet in figure 11.13, for example, the formula for `Total` in cell C6 is directly dependent on cells C2:C4. The average formula in C8 is directly dependent on the formulas in cells C6 and C7, but indirectly dependent on the values in C2:C4. The cells C2:C4 are direct precedents of the formula in cell C6. They are also indirect precedents of the formula in C8.

Using Auditing tools can help understand, visualize, and troubleshoot these concepts and the data associated with them. In the worksheet in figure 11.13, to trace the precedents of cell C6, (the Total), make C6 the active cell by clicking on it. Then, on the Auditing toolbar, click on the Trace Precedents button. A box is drawn around cells C2:C4, and a solid line is drawn from the boxed cells to the formula in C6. Then, by clicking on the Trace Dependents button while C6 is still active, a similar line is drawn from C6 to C8, indicating that C8 is directly dependent on C6. This action shows what the relationships are between the cells.

Figure 11.13
Samples of precedent and dependent cells.

	C6		=SUM(C2:C4)						
	A	B	C	D	E	F	G	H	I
1									
2		Joe	100			Auditing			
3		Bill	1003						
4		Julie	1897						
5									
6		Total	3000						
7		# days	4						
8		Average Day	750						
9									
10			75						
11									
12			#DIV/0!						

Sgl Data Table / Sheet2 \ **Auditing** / Sheet4 / Sheet5

Another way to show this relationship is to make C8 the active cell, and click on the Trace Precedents button. The line is drawn to C6, pointing in the same direction. Click on the Trace Dependents button again to draw the box again on C2:C4, and put the arrow there as well (see fig. 11.14).

Figure 11.14
Tracing precedents from C8, direct and indirect.

	C8		=C6/C7						
	A	B	C	D	E	F	G	H	I
1									
2		Joe	100			Auditing			
3		Bill	1003						
4		Julie	1897						
5									
6		Total	3000						
7		# days	4						
8		Average Day	750						
9									
10			75						
11									
12			#DIV/0!						

Sgl Data Table / Sheet2 \ **Auditing** / Sheet4 / Sheet5

To find out which cells are dependent on which values, select cell C2. Click on the Trace Dependents button, and the arrow points to the cell that contains the formula that is directly dependent on the value in that cell. Click on the Trace Dependents button again to draw the line to the next cell, C8, that is indirectly dependent on C2.

Auditing also can be useful in tracking errors in worksheets. If you have a formula that returns an error message, making the errant cell active and clicking on the Trace Errors button shows where the problem lies in the formula.

 Tip   You can move along a trace line by placing the mouse pointer on the line and double-clicking. This action moves the active cell to the location to which the trace points. Clicking again returns you to the origin point.

Excel shows tracers in three ways. The first is by a solid blue line. The destination point is indicated by an arrowhead on the end of the line. On a monochrome screen, the line appears black. Errors are traced by a solid red line, or by a dotted line on a monochrome monitor. The error tracer also has an arrowhead point. The third type of tracer is a dashed black line that has an icon, and is the same in both color and monochrome. This tracer refers to an external reference in another worksheet. Figure 11.15 illustrates all three types of lines.

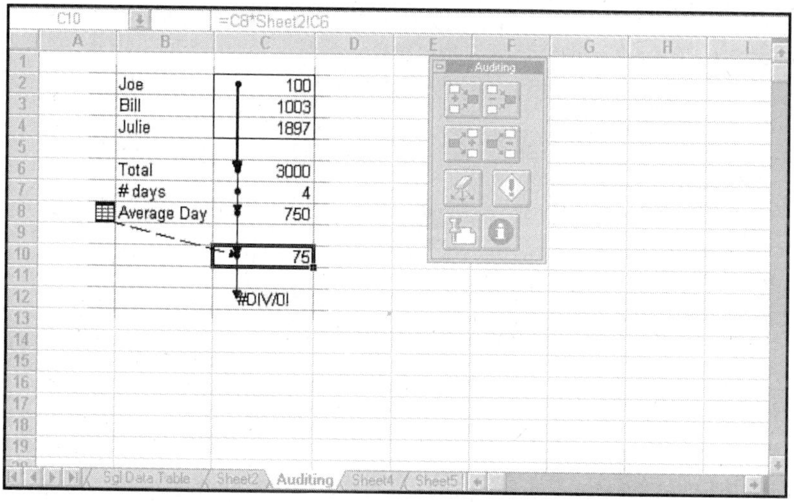

C10		=C8*Sheet2!C6							
	A	B	C	D	E	F	G	H	I
1									
2		Joe	100						
3		Bill	1003						
4		Julie	1897						
5									
6		Total	3000						
7		# days	4						
8		Average Day	750						
9									
10			75						
11									
12			#DIV/0!						

Figure 11.15
Examples of the three types of tracer lines.

You can remove tracer arrows as easily as you can produce them. Press the Remove Precedent Arrows button to undo the most recent trace precedent function; the Remove Dependent Arrows button works exactly the same way.

If when tracing you press the Trace button numerous times to step through a progression of relationships, each set of arrows is removed one at time. You can remove all the arrows on a sheet by clicking on the Remove All Arrows button.

Using the Auditing features, you can add comments to your worksheets. Adding comments is useful if you are going to share your work with others and some explanation is necessary to make certain portions of the worksheet or workbook clear. It also is helpful if you are using complex formulas and references to track your work and trace your footsteps. Users—whether the actual users or just receivers—of larger worksheets can benefit from annotations and explanations of information as well.

Notes

Adding notes or sounds to worksheets is done through the Auditing toolbar. The icon of a pushpin and paper is the Add Notes button. You can type the note, or a note can be a sound that you import. You can even record your own messages if your computer has the appropriate recording hardware and software.

Clicking on the Attach Notes button brings up the Cell Note dialog box, as shown in figure 11.16. The cell that is active when you press the Attach Notes button is where the note indicator is placed, and it is indicated by a small red square in the upper right corner of the cell. If you have multiple cells highlighted when you enter your note, it will be placed in the last cell clicked on.

Figure 11.16
The Cell Note
dialog box.

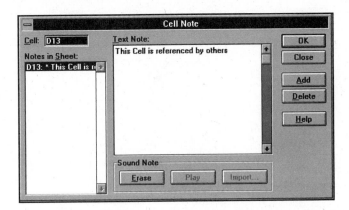

To play or read a note from anywhere on a worksheet, click on the Attach Note button to bring up the Cell Notes dialog box, and the notes in the worksheet are listed in the Notes in Sheet list box. Click once on a note to make it active and display the contents of the written note in Text Note edit box in the center of the dialog box. If there is a sound file attached, the Play button at the bottom is activated. If the note is text only, the Play button is disabled.

You can check the spelling of notes just like worksheets. Just click on the Check Spelling button on the main toolbar, or choose Tools, Spelling. Alternatively, you can press F7.

You also can print text notes. From the File menu, choose Page Setup. On the Sheet tab in the Page Setup dialog box, click on the Notes check box. If you want the row and column references to print as well, click in the Row and Column References check box.

You also can choose not to display notes indicators. Choose Options from the Tools menu. Choose the View tab, and you can select or deselect the Note Indicator check box in the Options dialog box. When the note display indicator is not activated, you can still read, play, and print notes.

To copy the notes from cells to other cells, select the cell that has the note you want to copy. Click the right mouse button, or press Shift+F10, to bring up the Cell menu. Select Copy, and move the mouse to the destination cell. Click the right mouse button again, and choose Paste Special. The Paste Special dialog box containing options appears, and click in the Note check box at the bottom of the box to copy the contents of the note to the new cell. You also can use the pull-down menus to copy notes.

Information Window

The last button on the Auditing toolbar is the Information Window. The Information Window shows detailed information about a cell. You can customize the information you want to display about cells.

To display the Information Window, click on the Show Info Window button on the Auditing toolbar or choose Options from the Tools menu and click in the check box next to Information Window in the View tab.

The Information Window can display the following information:

- ✔ **Cell Address.** Displays the value of the cell location in Row and Column.
- ✔ **Formula.** Displays the contents of the formula in the cell.
- ✔ **Value.** Displays the contents in general format.
- ✔ **Protection.** Displays the protection status.
- ✔ **Names.** Displays the names that refer to the cell.
- ✔ **Precedents.** Brings up the Precedents dialog box with options of either displaying all levels of precedents or just direct ones.
- ✔ **Dependents.** Brings up the Dependents dialog box with options of displaying either All Levels or just Direct.
- ✔ **Note.** Displays the contents of typed notes, and shows whether sound is attached to the file

You can switch between the worksheet and the Information Window by pressing Ctrl+F2. This command works only if the Info Window box is activated.

You can use the Information Window to print information about a range of cells as well. To do this, highlight the cells you want to print information about and switch to the Information Window. From the File menu choose Print, or for a shortcut, click on the Print button on the standard toolbar.

Go To Special

The Go To Special command helps find notes, constants, formulas that meet a particular criteria, blank cells, cells in the current region or array, cells that do not fit a pattern in a row or column, precedents or dependents (direct or all levels), the last active cell in your sheet, visible cells, or objects. The Go To Special dialog box and be accessed by pressing F5 or by selecting Edit, Go and then clicking on the Special button. Figure 11.17 shows the Go To Special dialog box.

Figure 11.17
The Go To Special
dialog box.

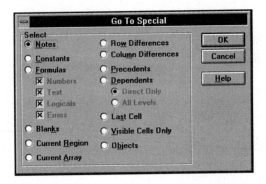

The Notes option selects all cells that contain notes (you also can press Ctrl+Shift+?). *Constants* are cells whose contents are deemed not to be a formula, so those cells whose values do not begin with an equal sign are considered to be constants, whether they are numbers or text.

The Formulas option selects cells that meet the selection criteria of values returned as numbers, text, logical, or errors. Using the Current Region option selects a range of cells as the active cell and all adjacent cells surrounded by any combination of blank rows or columns.

You can select the current array to which a cell belongs by checking the Current Array radio button, or by pressing Ctrl+/. To find cells that do not fit a pattern in a row or column based on the value in the active cell, press Ctrl+\ for rows or Ctrl+Shift+| for columns. This feature finds all the cells in a column or row that differ from the active cell at the time you select the Go To Special command.

You also can use Go To Special to find cells referred to by specific formulas (precedents) or cells with formulas that refer to selected cells (dependents). With the Go To Special dialog box options of selecting just the direct cells or all levels, you can find for precedents:

✔ All cells that are directly or indirectly referred to by a formula and for dependents

✔ All cells that contain formulas that directly or indirectly relate to cells

Figure 11.18 shows the dependents at all levels that relate to a specific cell.

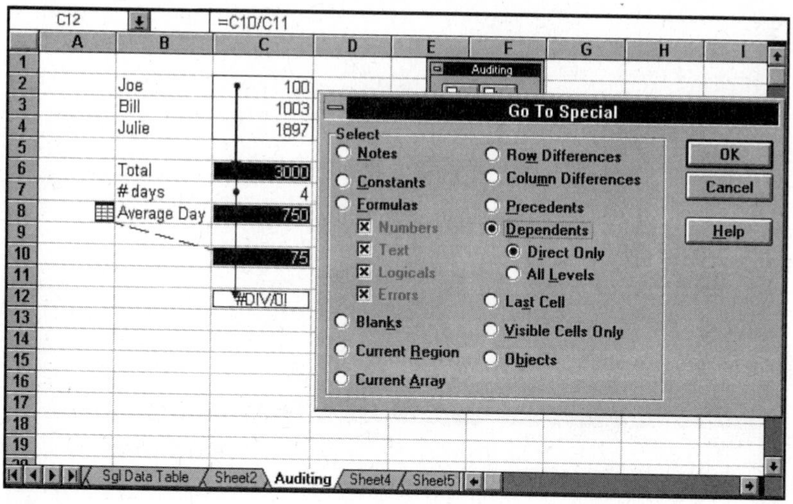

Figure 11.18
Dependent cells with Direct Only selected in the Go To Special dialog box.

Changing the Appearance of Your Worksheet

You can modify the appearance of worksheets in several ways, and you can modify how they can be used in the new ways. You can split worksheets and freeze titles, which is a great way in large worksheets to move to various cells or scroll through the worksheet but still keep the column or row labels visible.

One of the easiest ways to begin to change the way your worksheet looks without changing the original is to choose New from the Window menu. This operation makes a second window of the original worksheet, so you can modify, split, format cells, and vary the appearance in many ways without affecting your original document. Splitting worksheets is a useful tool for viewing different parts of a worksheet, even in drastically different sections on the same screen (see fig. 11.19).

The splitting done to the worksheet in figure 11.19 was performed by positioning the active cell at C1 and choosing Split from the Window menu. The position of the active cell at the time you select split will affect the way Excel performs the command. In figure 11.19, the active cell was in the first row of the sheet, near the middle of the active screen. Excel splits the sheet down the middle, horizontally. Using the mouse, you can move from one side of the split to the next to modify or examine data.

Figure 11.19
Splitting a
worksheet and
viewing different
sections on the
same screen.

	A	B	C	D	E	F	G	H	I
1									
2		Joe	100						
3		Bill	1003						
4		Julie	1897						
5									
6		Total	3000						
7		# days	4						
8		Average Day	750						
9									
10			75						
29									
30		Annual Total	$897,654.00						
31									
32									
33									
34									
35									
36									
37									

Sgl Data Table / Sheet2 \ **Auditing** / Sheet4 / Sheet5

If the active cell had been C15, Excel would have split the worksheet into four separate areas. If you position the active cell in column A, no matter what row, Excel splits the worksheet vertically. In essence, Excel splits the window into panes at the active cell. Excel splits horizontally above the selected cell, and vertically to the right of the selected cell.

Another way you can create a split is to drag the split box to the position you want. One split box is located above the scroll bar, to the far right side of the screen, just above the up arrow. Another is located on the horizontal scroll bar, toward the right end. They appear as small black separations, and when you position the cursor on the box, the pointer changes from the regular arrow to the split pointer, enabling you to drag down to create the split. You can create horizontal or vertical splits using split boxes.

After you finish with either the horizontal or vertical splits, you can drag the bar back to the bottom or side of the worksheet where it originated, and it removes that portion of the split.

After you split sheets, you can position the pointer on any of the split bars to reposition them for ease of viewing.

Regardless of how you split a worksheet, or whether you split it into two or four panes, you can undo the effect of the split by choosing the Remove Split option from the Window menu.

After you split worksheets, you can freeze panes from the same menu. Freezing panes automatically freezes or prevents scrolling of the upper or left pane. This keeps information visible in the upper or left pane, while allowing freedom of movement or change of view in any other section of the worksheet.

The Zoom command on the standard toolbar enables you to reduce or enlarge the size of the cells so that you can see more or less. Excel sets some common useful zoom factors but also enables you to set your own. To use Zoom, click on the drop-down arrow in the edit box on

the standard toolbar or choose <u>V</u>iew, <u>Z</u>oom. This displays the Zoom dialog box. You get a range of choices from 200% to 25% in the drop-down menu, and <u>S</u>election. You can even select an entire worksheet by clicking on the box at the upper left corner of the worksheet, above the column numbers, and to the left of the row numbers, click on Zoom, choose Selection, and see zoom at its smallest possible size. Experimenting with some of the choices provides you with a clear understanding of how you can use zoom.

Perhaps a more practical use of Zoom is to select a range of cells that you want to get a better look at, and <u>Z</u>oom Selection on the selected cells. They can be used in this manner for a Slide Show or to view as well. Zoom can help display slightly larger portions of your sheet for easier data entry or analysis. If 100%, or normal viewing, does not enable you to see all your worksheet by just a few columns or rows, using zoom to shrink your worksheet by a small percentage can save a great deal of time scrolling back and forth.

Another way to change the way a worksheet appears is to hide rows or columns of information. Excel has the capability of hiding and unhiding so that you can view or print just what you want. In a worksheet that has a column for each month of the year and a grand total column at the end, for example, you might want to hide the month columns and display only the labels and grand totals.

Additionally, you might want to hide the rows for individual salespeople, and just display region totals for the summary view or printed report. Hiding rows and columns does not affect formulas or delete information—it only keeps them from the display.

To hide a column or row, choose either <u>C</u>olumn or <u>R</u>ow from the F<u>o</u>rmat menu. The <u>H</u>ide command becomes available in a submenu.

Using Outlining

Outlining is a method of creating summary reports that enables you to hide or display as much information as you want. An outline can have up to eight levels of groups, both on the horizontal axis and the vertical axis. One worksheet can have only one outline.

Excel can outline automatically or manually. To create an outline, first highlight or select the data you want to outline. Then choose Group and Outline from the <u>D</u>ata menu. If your data is in a format that you can easily outline, select Auto Outline. Figure 11.20 shows the effect of automatic outlining on the sales worksheet.

The result is a grouping of related items in row and column orientation that you can then hide, expand, or change based on the way your data is formatted. If, for example, you want to show the sales totals for the quarter and the monthly high only, just click on the minus signs above the lines that indicate which areas to eliminate from view in the worksheet (see fig. 11.21).

Figure 11.20
The Auto Outline
of a worksheet.

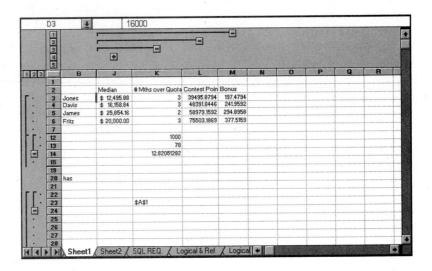

Figure 11.21
Quarterly Sales
totals without the
Monthly detail,
hidden by
reducing the
outlined portions.

As you experiment with hiding and displaying different levels within your outline, Shift-clicking on the outline levels shows what will be hidden if you reduce the outline area.

If your data is not organized in a way that makes sense to automatically outline, you can use the manual method. From the **D**ata menu, choose Group and Outline, then S**e**ttings. The Outline dialog box appears prompting you for information about the location of summary information—whether row summaries are to be located below the detail and if column summaries are located right of the detail. You can choose to have **A**utomatic Styles, **C**reate the outline, or apply **S**tyles.

Chapter Snapshot

After you have entered your data into a worksheet, you can use Excel's powerful charting and graphics capabilities to display your data in different ways. Excel can display data from cells—called *data points*—in a worksheet as bar graphs, pie graphs, line charts, or in relation to other data points from other worksheets. Showing information graphically makes the understanding, comparison, and evaluation of data easier.

In this chapter you will learn about the following:

Excel's charting and graphics capability goes far beyond simply showing values or data points in a graph. Using the Chart Wizard, you can create presentations that can be incorporated into documents, embedded in workbooks, or even placed into a slide show. And because your data was linked to your charts at their creation, the charts are automatically updated when data in the worksheet is changed.

Excel Charts and Graphics

by Critch Greaves

C harts and graphs can be very simple, or they can be created to display complex relationships among data. Through the use of Excel's Chart Wizard, the creation and display of a chart is made simple. Like the other Excel Wizards, the Chart Wizard is a series of dialog boxes that take you step-by-step through the chart-making process, providing various options to make it quick and easy. After you have generated a chart, it can be changed to appear exactly as you want.

Using the Excel Chart Wizard

The Chart Wizard button, located on the Standard toolbar, prompts you to select a location, such as an a new or existing worksheet, for your chart to appear. The instruction "Drag in document to create chart," appears in the status window at the bottom of the screen. Simultaneously, the cursor changes from the regular mouse pointer to a cross with an icon of a chart attached to it.

The area you select can be as small as a single cell or as large as you want your chart to be.

> **Note**
>
> After you have chosen an area for your chart, you can later change its size, depending on the amount of data points selected and the chart's type. Experimenting with area size to find a chart's optimum size is discussed later in this chapter.

For the chart you will create in this exercise, first open the SALES.XLS worksheet on the *Inside Microsoft Office Professional* companion disk.

1. With the first sheet active, click on the Chart Wizard button, and select a range of cells below the data that is five cells wide and five rows deep, starting at A10. This area represents the display area in which Chart Wizard will place the graphic representation you will create.

> **Tip**
>
> To expedite the charting process, highlight the cells you want to represent in the graph before starting the Wizard. The Chart Wizard presumes that the data points you want to use in your graph have been highlighted, as noted in figure 12.1.

Figure 12.1
The Chart Wizard's main dialog box with the cell $A$1 selected as the active range.

> **Note**
>
> When you select a range of data points to include in your graph, be sure to include the column and row headers, as they can be used for descriptors in the graphic.

2. To highlight the actual range you will graph for this example, use the mouse to select cells A1..D6. The range indicated in the Chart Wizard dialog box is automatically updated with the new range information.

3. Now you must choose a chart type. There are 14 different Excel chart types, and each one has a variety of options available to it. Select the Column chart type from the Chart Wizard Step 3 of 5 dialog box and click on the Next button. Note that there are 10 different Column chart types from which to choose (see fig. 12.2).

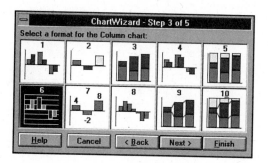

Figure 12.2
The 10 types of column charts available, in the Chart Wizard - Step 3 of 5 dialog box.

4. Click on the Next button to accept the default column chart type (type 6). The Chart Wizard then takes you to a dialog box that gives a preview of the chart selected with the data you have chosen.

At this point, you can change the orientation of your graph by clicking on one of the Data series choices to change from Row orientation to Column orientation, and you can specify (if necessary) from where Chart Wizard will obtain the data labels used in the graph.

A *series* in an Excel chart is a set of data that will be graphed as a single entity on the chart. When charting the performance of a group of salespeople, for instance, each person's monthly sales for the year 1994 will be a series on the chart.

Using the Row orientation, the Wizard picks the axis labels from the first row of data by default. Use this option when the first row of data contains labels or other information you intend to use as the X-axis label. You can change this default to be either the first row by itself, or multiple rows.

For the chart's legend (which is descriptive text across the top of the chart), the same operation can be performed by clicking on the arrow buttons to use the first column or multiple column information for legend labels.

5. Click on the Finish button, and the Chart Wizard places the final graph in the area that was selected. The graph is displayed as shown in figure 12.3.

Figure 12.3
The final sales
graph display.

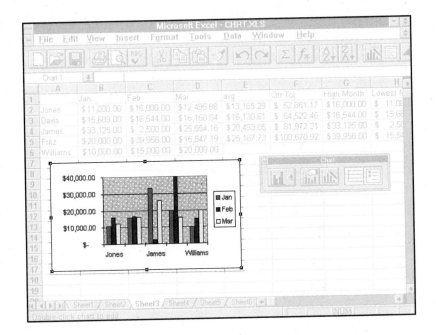

As you noticed as you stepped through the options in Chart Wizard, there are numerous choices that you can pick to make your graph appear the way you want. One of the choices that makes the biggest difference in the appearance of your graph is chart type.

Understanding Chart Types

Excel has 14 chart types to choose from to display your graphics in documents or worksheets. Choosing a particular chart type is an important step in making your presentation effective and clear. The chart types are the following:

- ✔ Area chart
- ✔ Bar chart
- ✔ Column chart
- ✔ Line chart
- ✔ Pie chart
- ✔ Doughnut chart
- ✔ Radar chart

✔ XY (scatter) chart

✔ 3-D area chart

✔ 3-D bar chart

✔ 3-D column chart

✔ 3-D line chart

✔ 3-D pie Chart

✔ 3-D surface Chart

Area Charts

Area charts show the relative change of values over a period of time. Figure 12.4 illustrates an area chart.

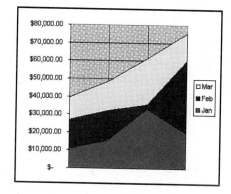

Figure 12.4
An example of an area chart.

Bar Charts

Bar charts illustrate relationships among items. Use stacked bar charts to show the relationship between specific items and the rest of the data set used to build the chart. Bar charts are organized and displayed horizontally to emphasize differences in values, as shown in figure 12.5.

Column Charts

Column charts are similar to bar charts, except their orientation is vertical instead of horizontal (see fig. 12.6). This shifts emphasis from a comparison of difference in values to an emphasis on a change over a certain period of time.

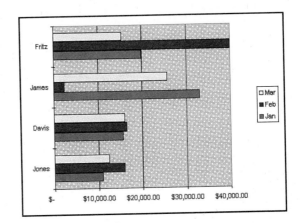

Figure 12.5
A bar chart
example.

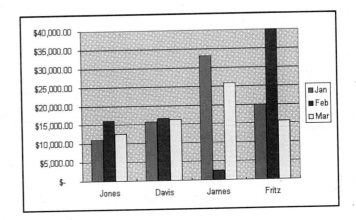

Figure 12.6
A column chart
example.

Line Charts

Line charts are great for showing trends in data over a period of time. This type of graph is similar to an area chart, but emphasizes the change of data over time in a somewhat different manner, as figure 12.7 illustrates.

Pie Charts

Pie charts show how data points relate to a whole set of data. The pie contains only one data series, even if you have selected more than one. Figure 12.8 shows an example of the pie chart. In this pie chart, the relationship of each salesperson to the whole group is displayed in percentage figures.

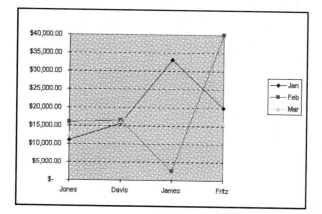

Figure 12.7
A line chart
example.

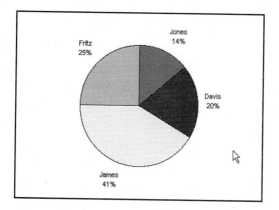

Figure 12.8
A pie chart
example.

Doughnut Charts

A doughnut chart is similar to the pie, but can be used to display more than one data series at a time. Each concentric ring of a doughnut chart contains the data from a different series in the data set (see fig. 12.9).

Radar Charts

The radar chart shows changes in data relative to a central point and individual data points. The value categories are scattered around the center point of the graph with lines connecting the values, as shown in figure 12.10.

Figure 12.9
A doughnut chart showing multiple data series.

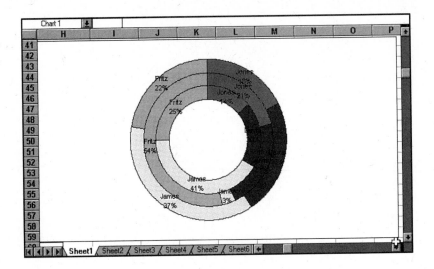

Figure 12.10
A radar chart.

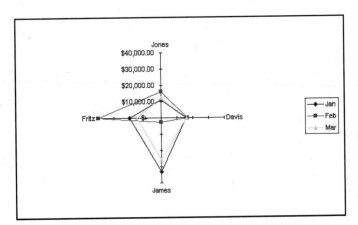

XY or Scatter Charts

XY or scatter charts show the relationships among data points by plotting dots on a graph relative to two or more groups of numbers as a series. The XY chart clearly shows data clusters, and is commonly used in scientific data analysis.

You can use a line to connect the points in an XY chart by selecting the correct autoformat choice when creating the chart. Or, to connect the lines in an existing XY chart, double-click on the data series, which displays the Format Data Series dialog box, and choose a line in the **P**atterns tab.

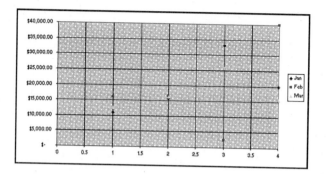

Figure 12.11
The XY or scatter chart.

3-D Area Charts

You can create a number of three-dimensional charts using Excel and the Chart Wizard. The 3-D area chart is good for showing totals and illustrating the differences among the series, as shown in figure 12.12.

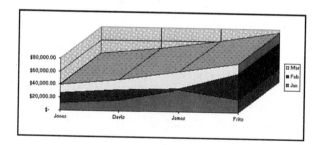

Figure 12.12
A 3-D area chart.

3-D Bar Charts

Another type of 3-D chart is the 3-D bar chart. This type shows data and draws a graphic relationship between items or series of data. You also can use the stacked 3-D bar to show relationships to a whole with a different twist.

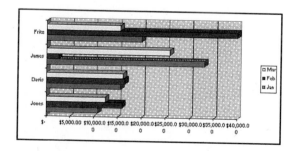

Figure 12.13
The 3-D bar chart.

3-D Column Charts

3-D column charts can be used to display relationships in two different ways. The simple 3-D column chart shows columns along the X axis. The perspective column chart compares the data along the X and Y axes. In both instances, data is plotted along the Z axis. Figures 12.14 and 12.15 illustrate the different views.

Figure 12.14
The simple 3-D column chart.

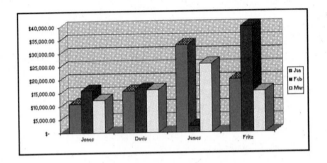

Figure 12.15
The 3-D perspective column chart.

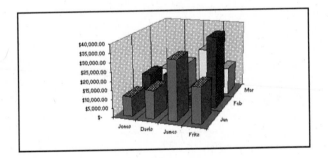

The 3-D perspective column chart often is used to display "three-dimensional" data. An example of three-dimensional data would be the total sales figures for all the salespeople in a company over a number of years. There are three dimensions to this data: an individual salesperson's total sales, the sales totals of all the salespeople for the previous year, and the sales totals of all salespeople for all previous years.

3-D Pie Charts

You also can make pie charts appear three-dimensional. Figure 12.16 shows a single data series, just like the standard pie chart. To show more than one data series, the two-dimensional doughnut chart should be used.

3-D Line Charts

The 3-D line chart shows data trends so that they look like ribbons, as shown in figure 12.17.

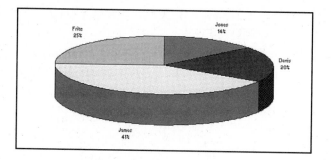

Figure 12.16
A 3-D pie chart.

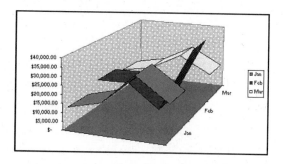

Figure 12.17
A 3-D line chart.

II

Excel

3-D Surface Charts

Finally, the 3-D surface chart shows a "flexible" continuum for data display (see fig. 12.18). This type of chart is useful for showing relationships among large amounts of data.

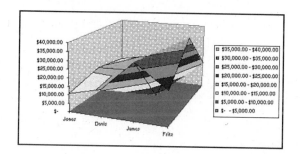

Figure 12.18
A 3-D surface chart.

Understanding Data Organization

Because you have used the same worksheet data across all the different chart types, data points appear in a graph with specific relation to other data points or data series. The horizontal and vertical lines along which data are displayed are called the chart *axes*.

A two-dimensional graph shows data along two separate axes, the X axis and the Y axis. The X axis typically is horizontal and the Y is vertical.

3-D charts can have two or three axes. The third axis, perpendicular to both the X and Y axes, is the Z axis, and it is present only in 3-D charts. While there is no such thing as a three-dimensional screen (or printout), imagine that the Z axis is sticking out towards you.

 Note Pie charts and doughnut charts do not use axes of any kind.

The value axis is usually the Y axis, and the category axis is the X axis. In a two-dimensional graph, you can change the orientation of a chart from X to Y by double-clicking on the chart, and then double-clicking on a portion of the data range. This brings up the Format Data Series dialog box. Selecting the Axis tab, you can plot the data on the primary or secondary axes, changing the appearance of the data completely.

Figure 12.19
Changing a chart's orientation in the Axis tab of the Format Data Series dialog box.

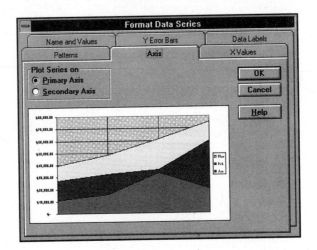

Exploring Chart Options

Using the Chart Wizard, you can add a number of options while you are building your chart. After your chart has been completed, it can be modified using methods discussed later is this chapter.

The first choice you have when building your chart is its location on your Excel worksheet. You can select for a chart's location a single cell, a specific area (highlighted with the mouse), or an individual sheet.

The next step is selecting the range of data you want to display graphically. If you selected a range of data prior to invoking the Chart Wizard, the information appears in the range window of the dialog box. If you did not select a data series to chart, or if you want to modify your selection, highlighting a range of worksheet data by clicking and dragging with the mouse will update the range box.

After these two choices have been made, you will need to choose a chart type. The prompt for this appears in the Step 2 of 5 dialog box. Because there are several types available, you must think about how your data would best be displayed and choose a chart type accordingly. The Step 4 of 5 dialog box in the Wizard displays a sample of the chart based on the chart type, data, and format you have chosen.

At this point, you can choose to have you data series appear in row or column orientation. In figure 12.20, for example, a data series is shown in row orientation. This places the X axis values as Dollars and Y axis values as Months. Changing to Column orientation places the Months as the X axis data, and the Representatives as Y axis. Figure 12.21 shows the change.

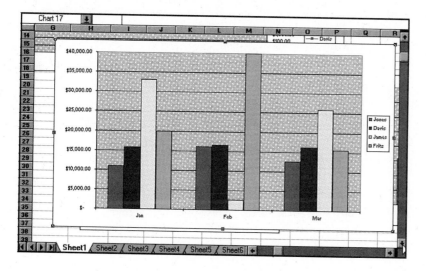

Figure 12.20
The sales graph with row orientation for the data series.

Additionally, select the data labels for your graph. In the Chart Wizard Step 4 of 5 dialog box, you can select the contents of the first 0, 1, 2, 3, or 4 rows to appear as labels for the X axis labels. In addition, you have the same options for the Legend.

The effect that choosing the labels has on the appearance of the chart is interesting. Choosing more labels in this example reduces the number of data points on the graph. Similarly, choosing additional legend columns reduces the number of data series across the X axis.

Specify the title of your graph and the labels of your axes in the last dialog box of the Chart Wizard. This box also enables you to decide whether you want to include a legend. Clicking on the Finish button closes the Chart Wizard and creates the graph on your workbook.

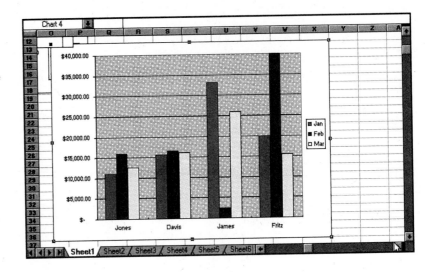

Adding Text to Your Chart

You can add text to your charts in a number of ways. If you decided not to include a legend in your chart, you can add one later. Legends are especially useful on large, complex graphs where they help the reader keep track of what is going on.

The first method to add text to an existing chart is to activate it by double-clicking on the chart. Sizing handles will appear in the corners and along the sides of the chart. Right-click anywhere on the chart to open the shortcut menu. From this menu you can add titles, edit titles, and make changes to existing text in these areas.

You can also add text boxes to your graphs. A *text box* clarifies a graphic representation, emphasizes a particular point, or simply annotates some detail on your graphs.

The standard Excel toolbar contains the Text box button, located to the right of the Chart Wizard button. A text box can be placed next to a graph or directly within the chart.

Note If you add a text box on or next to graph while the graph is not activated, the box will not move with the graph when it is moved. If, however, the graph is activated, the box and graph become one object. Then, if you want, the box still can be moved around within the graph.

Adding a New Series to Your Chart

After you have defined a chart and have it displayed on a worksheet, Excel will automatically update the chart as the data displayed within it changes. If you want to add a data point or an entirely new data series, however, you can modify the structure of your chart by following a few simple steps.

If you add a new person to your staff, you will need to update the chart with that person's sales figures. To include this series of figures in this chapter's example chart, add a new row with the new person's data to the worksheet. For this example, the person's name is Williams, and his sales totals for January, February, and March are 10,000, 15,000 and 20,000, respectively.

After you have entered that information into your worksheet and have formatted the numbers appropriately, select the range (including the name) with the mouse. Then, using the shortcut menu (brought up with the right mouse button), choose Copy.

Next, choose the graph to which you want to add the data series. Click on the graph to highlight it, then bring up the shortcut menu again and choose Paste. The new data series will be added to the graph (see fig. 12.22). If the results are what you expected, your graph is complete. If something did not transfer as you wanted, you can undo the paste by choosing Undo from the Edit menu.

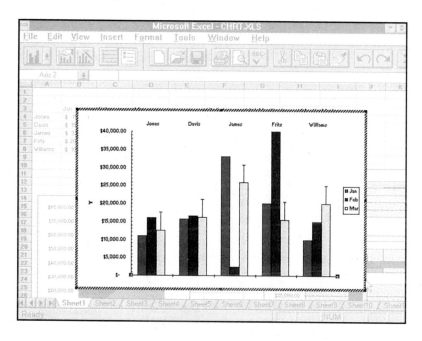

Figure 12.22
The new data series pasted into an existing graph.

You also can copy-and-paste highlighted worksheet data by using toolbars or pull-down menus.

To add new data to a chart using a pull-down menu, double-click on the chart, then select the New Data option from the Insert menu to display the New Data dialog box. This dialog box walks you through the steps necessary to add a new range of data to your chart. The New Data dialog box enables you to specify the location of the new data and how you want it displayed on the chart.

Modifying Charts

After your chart is in place in a given location, there are options available that affect the appearance of the data.

Activating a Chart

Before trying to change its appearance, you first must activate a chart by double-clicking on it. To indicate that it is ready for modification, an activated chart is shown with a wide border.

The first way to modify an area of a graph is to double-click on the area of the chart (legend, labels, text boxes, and so on) to be changed. Separate format options are available for each area. If you want to modify the plot or type area, bring up the formatting shortcut menu by clicking on the background of the chart and then the right mouse button (see fig. 12.23).

Figure 12.23
The shortcut menu after clicking on the plot area.

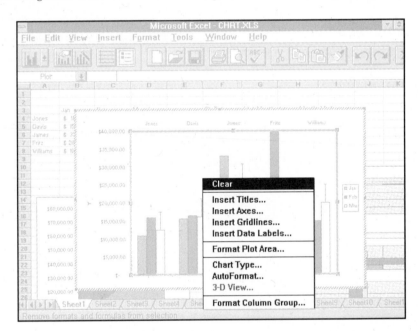

When you activate a chart, the choices in the Excel menu bar become chart- and graph-specific. The F̲ormat choices with an active graph are different from those available when a cell or range of cells is active, for example.

Double-clicking on the plot area of the graph invokes the Format Plot Area dialog box, which is one of the options available on the shortcut menu.

Making Text Changes

The Insert Titles dialog box enables you to insert titles on charts, value axes (y axis), and category axes (X axis). If your graph has secondary value or category titles, these options can be used, too.

The Insert Axes menu enables you to add or remove axes from your graph's display. This can change the way your data appears by either bringing in a new axis to view data or by removing one.

The Insert Gridlines shortcut menu selection adds X or Y lines in major or minor categories. This means that you can show background lines to make your data easier to view across a graph. Figure 12.24 shows all gridlines enabled.

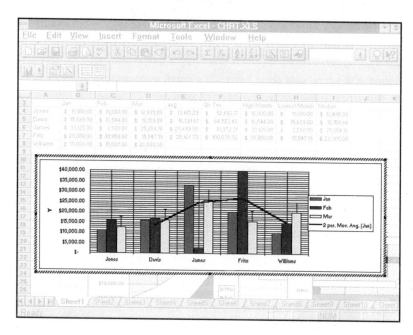

Figure 12.24
The sales graph with all gridlines enabled.

The Insert Data Labels dialog box provides options for viewing data labels. You can decide to show data labels as values, percentages, labels, or labels and percentages. There also are options to show the legend key beside the label or even to not show labels at all.

Changing the Chart Type

The Format Chart Area dialog box (invoked by double-clicking on the chart area itself) is used to change borders, lines, and colors that display on the graph that is active.

The Chart Type dialog box selected from the shortcut menu enables you to actually switch from a column graph to the other types of Excel graphs, such as doughnuts, pie, area, and so on. Here, you can select two or three dimensions. Furthermore, after a graph type is selected, you can choose the subtype of graph from the options dialog box (opened with the options button). From there, you can modify sort orders within your selected data series, vary colors, change the axes, and so on.

Using AutoFormat

The AutoFormat selection (again, from the shortcut menu) combines many of the formatting options available by using galleries of different chart and subchart types. With AutoFormat, you can select from any of the available chart types in Excel, as well as some of the popular subtypes. In addition, you can define and save your own customized chart types and formats, adding uniformity and customization to a worksheet or presentation.

The Format Column Group selection from the shortcut menu contains many of the same options. You can change chart types in the Options tab. Choices also are given to change colors, to modify the overlap of columns or data shapes on your graph, to change the series order that the chart has, and even to change the subtype of the graph.

If you need to modify the appearance of a column or group of columns, double-clicking anywhere on the them will open the Format Data Series dialog box.

To open the shortcut menu for modifying a single series on the chart, click on an individual column or line in a data series area, then right-click on the highlighted column or line. The options on this menu are the following:

- ✔ Clear
- ✔ Insert Data Labels
- ✔ Insert Trendline
- ✔ Insert Error Bars
- ✔ Format Data Series
- ✔ Chart Type
- ✔ AutoFormat
- ✔ 3-D view
- ✔ Format Column (or Line) Group

Some of the options on this menu overlap those on other formatting menus. Others, however, are new additions that can be performed only on the data series and cannot be done from the plot area as previously described. Specifically, you can add trendlines and error bars to your graph.

Adding Trendlines

Trendlines show trends in the data by drawing lines across data points. The line represents and displays the movement of a data point over time.

There are several ways to format trendlines. There are six different types to choose from and numerous ways to format each. Format types include the display of linear trends, logarithmic, polynomial, power, exponential, and moving average. The type of trendline you choose for your information is determined by the type of information your chart contains.

After you have inserted a trendline, you can change its pattern or type of line. Activate the line by clicking on it once, then double-click on any of the blocks on the line or column.

Formatting Axes

You can change the formatting of the X or Y axis. Double-clicking on the axis information opens the Format Axis dialog box. Here, you are presented with tabbed choices for formatting the pattern of the axis, the scale, font selection for number displays, and alignment of text on the axis.

The Format Axis dialog box provides flexibility for formatting the graph's axes. Formatting options includes changing the text font on titles, data labels, and legends. The scale of the graph—the way that the data points are plotted—relative to the Y axis values is automatically calculated based on the values displayed in the range of data. You can modify the value if you want your axis values to be different than the values shown on the default selection.

You can directly modify sheet data by moving information on a chart. To do this, click on the border of a particular data point to place an "active" box around the data point. The values in the worksheet actually change to represent the new graphic label, relative to where a data shape is as you drag it.

Graph axes are delimited by *tick marks,* variable indicators of where data labels are located in relation to the data points graphed. In the Format Axis dialog box (see fig. 12.25), you can change tick mark location and appearance, as well as where axis labels will appear in relation to their tick marks. Tick marks can be *major,* meaning that each axis label value has only one mark, or *minor,* meaning that each label has numerous marks to indicate many small steps in value before the next label is reached.

II

Excel

Figure 12.25
The Format Axis
dialog box.

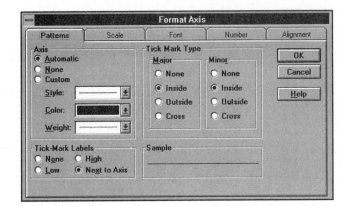

Chapter Snapshot

Excel 5.0 has some extremely powerful data import and export capabilities. Excel's capabilities for importing and exporting data is significant because it enables you to use existing data in a variety of standard popular database formats in Excel worksheets and workbooks. The benefit is that you can use data to update worksheets without having to enter the same data repeatedly.

In this chapter, you learn about the following:

Using MS Query, you can open databases, retrieve and sort information based on the criteria that is meaningful to you, and port that information into Excel, or other applications by clicking a mouse. Not only can you move all or selected data records from one data source into a worksheet, you learned how to create Pivot tables, which summarize information from not one but many potential data sources. Using MS Query and Excel, you can even export your information back to numerous formats, and even operating systems.

CHAPTER

Excel Data Input and Export

by Critch Greaves

Being able to import and export data can lead to more effective use of office staff and increased productivity, as well as increased accuracy. It also means added power in terms of the type of information you can have in a worksheet and the steps for getting it there.

Excel uses Microsoft Query to perform a number of data import and export tasks. In this chapter, you have a chance to learn about MS Query, how it works, and what it can do for you when used with Excel Worksheets and on its own. In addition, you can learn how Excel shares data with other applications—in other words, how you can send information from your workbooks to other applications or coworkers for additional analysis and use.

Because Excel and MS Query are very flexible, you have a chance to evaluate a number of different ways to harness the power of data import and export to and from your applications.

Using Microsoft Query

Microsoft Query is a tool that enables you to retrieve and sort data from a wide range of sources. Some of these sources include the following:

- ✔ Microsoft Excel
- ✔ Microsoft Access
- ✔ Microsoft FoxPro
- ✔ Microsoft SQL Server
- ✔ ASCII Text
- ✔ dBASE
- ✔ Paradox
- ✔ Btrieve

You need to install Query with the drivers to access these different data sources, and drivers for some of these sources come with MS Query. After you use MS Query to access the data source that you need, you can use it to sort, filter, and display information that you need, and then send it to an application that you choose, such as Excel.

Note If you do not have drivers for the source you need, contact Microsoft.

In MS Query, you can perform several functions that manipulate data. The most common operation is called a query. A *query* is a question about a group of data, for example, "For which customers do we have information?" or "How many customers do we have in the 12345 ZIP Code?" MS Query translates your questions into a format that your computer can understand, and returns the answer in the form of a table.

A *table* is a group of information in rows and columns. An example of a table is an Excel worksheet. Tables usually are organized by topic or related item, such as customers, parts numbers, or the like. The rows and columns equate to records and fields from the database perspective. A *field* is one portion of a record. Name, Address, and ZIP Code are examples of fields. A *record* is a row of related fields. A *customer record* might be a collection of 10 fields of data, all relating to one customer.

You can start MS Query from its own program icon as a stand-alone application, or you can invoke it from within Excel, Word, or Access. After you start MS Query, you can use it in a number of ways.

You can access MS Query from within Excel in several ways. One way is to use the MS Query button on the Query and Pivot toolbar (see fig. 13.1).

Figure 13.1
The Query and
Pivot toolbar.

Another way to start MS Query is to choose **D**ata, Get E**x**ternal Data. If the Get External Data option is not available on your **T**ools menu, select Add-ins to see whether the Query Add-in is installed. Odds are, it isn't, in which case, you can use the Excel Setup program to configure it for your system.

You also can use certain other external data retrieval functions to launch MS Query, such as Pivot Tables, which are explored in greater detail in "Using Pivot Tables" later in this chapter.

To begin, from the Microsoft Office Program Group in Windows Program Manager screen, double-click on the MS Query icon. This launches the program, and the CUE Card help along with it.

Figure 13.2 shows the opening screen of Microsoft Query, and MS Query Cue Cards, which launches along with it. If you do not want Cue cards to appear with Query, you can click in the lower check box.

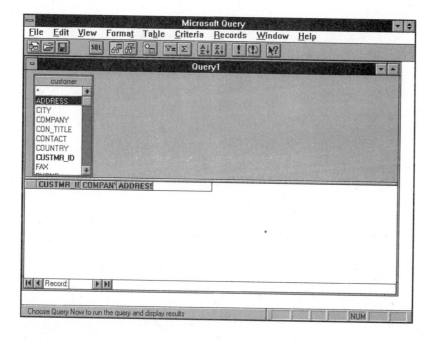

Figure 13.2
MS Query's
opening screen.

The opening screen of Query has two menu commands, <u>F</u>ile and <u>H</u>elp, and the toolbar. The toolbar has the following buttons available:

- ✔ **New Query.** Enables you to define a new question or questions about a group of data.

- ✔ **Open Query.** Starts a query that has already been defined and saved.

- ✔ **Save Query.** Enables you to keep the query you designed in the New Query Steps for future use.

- ✔ **View SQL.** Enables you to look at the Structured Query Language associated with a query of a data source.

- ✔ **Show/Hide Tables.** Enables you to look at or suppress view of tables.

- ✔ **Show/Hide Criteria.** Enables you to look at or suppress certain information.

- ✔ **Add Tables.** Enables you to add tables to a query or data set.

- ✔ **Add Criteria.** Enables you to ask additional "questions" or further filter the information that you request.

- ✔ **Totals.** Provides totals for the selected information.

- ✔ **Sort Ascending.** Sorts the selected tables in ascending order.

- ✔ **Sort Descending.** Sorts tables in descending order.

- ✔ **Automatic Query.** Automatically performs any query..

- ✔ **Help.** Enables you to access Cue Cards or regular MS Query help screens.

Before Query can do anything for you, you need to define a data source for it. Because MS Query's job is to retrieve existing data, the data should be on your hard disk, and you should have an idea about what you want to accomplish ahead of time.

Importing Data from External Data Sources

To identify a query, click on the New Query button on the toolbar. The Select Data Source dialog box appears. Available Data Sources might be empty, so click on the Other button. The ODBC dialog box appears. *ODBC* is an acronym for Open Data Base Connectivity. Any previously defined data source appears in the ODBC box, and you can create your own data source. Click on the name of the data source you want, or type it in the selection box.

Click on dBASE files, click on OK, and the dBASE file's name now appears in the Available Data Sources window. Click on the Use button, and the Query1 window appears in the background and the Add Tables dialog box appears in the foreground.

The Add Tables dialog box lists the files that are compatible with the data source you chose in the previous steps. Because you chose dBASE files, all files in the current directory that have a DBF extension appear as choices. To begin, select the sample data file called CUSTOMER.DBF and click on the Add button. Then close the window. Now the Query1 window is active, and the Customer table or data file is shown in the upper portion of the window.

The Query1 window is divided into two sections called *panes.* The upper pane is referred to as the *table pane* and the lower pane is the *data pane.* The selected tables or data sources you select appear in the table pane, and any fields and records you select appear in the data pane.

Several ways are possible for selecting fields from a table or data source to appear in the data pane. You can select a field by double-clicking on the name, which places the field in the data pane, or you can drag-and-drop a name from the table pane to the data pane.

Figure 13.3 shows the result of double-clicking on the CUSTMR_ID field and COMPANY field, and dragging the ADDRESS field to the data pane.

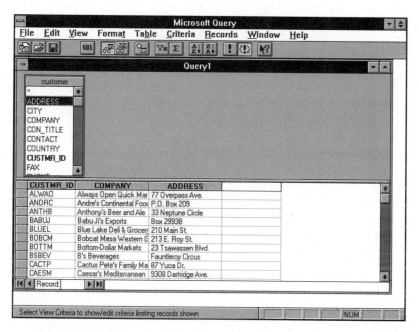

Figure 13.3
The results of adding fields from the table pane to the data pane (note the Auto Query button is off).

The Auto Query button defaults to On, which means that when you add a field from the table pane to the data pane, the corresponding data from the table is displayed. If you click on the Auto Query button, it no longer appears recessed, and the resulting data associated with the fields is no longer displayed. If you want the data to be displayed with each entry of a field, leave the Auto Query button on at all times. You also can activate Auto Query from the **R**ecords menu. Figure 13.4 shows the difference between Auto Query on and Auto Query off.

Figure 13.4

Results of selecting fields with the Auto Query button on.

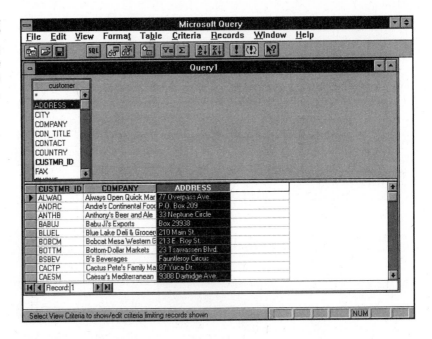

After the fields from the selected table appear in the data pane, you can manipulate your information, add fields, edit fields, or select data that you want to move into other applications.

Thus far, you have learned how to select tables or databases, select fields, and display them. The section that follows concentrates on the MS Query toolbar and the file functions that you can perform. In addition, because you can format and display your information in numerous ways, you get a chance to move and manipulate the windows or panes within MS Query.

If you want to insert a field from the table pane into the data pane, you have a couple different avenues to take. You might want to insert a field from the table pane to the data pane to rearrange existing fields or to insert a field where you had already chosen another. To insert a field, choose the field from the table list, and drag it down to the data pane. Position the field just above the label of the column where you want to insert it. MS Query automatically moves over the existing field, and inserts the new one at the point you choose.

If you need to rearrange the order of your data fields in the data pane, you can select an entire data column and move it. To select an entire column, click on the column label at the top of the column or press Ctrl+spacebar with any field in that column active (see fig. 13.5). After you select the column, you can drag it to a new location and drop it into place, similar to the insert operation described earlier.

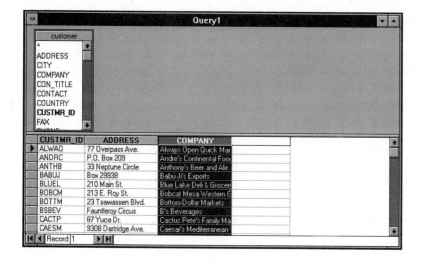

Figure 13.5

Selecting an entire data column.

You also can use the **R**ecords menu to insert a column. Begin by selecting the column directly to the left of the column that you want to insert. After that column appears in reverse video, select Add **C**olumns from the **R**ecords menu. The Add Column dialog box appears. Choose the field name from the active table, and select the field you want. Select the asterisk (*) if you want to select all fields in the table.

You can change column headings and determine whether your totals are displayed at the bottom of each column in the Insert Field dialog box. The total can appear as a sum, average, minimum, or maximum. Figure 13.6 shows the Add Column dialog box.

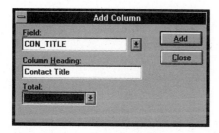

Figure 13.6

The Add Column dialog box.

If you want to edit the columns you drop into the data pane, double-click on the top bar of the column. The Edit Column dialog box appears. You can replace the field with another field, or you can change the column header. You also can add or remove a total to or from the pane.

You can use the Add Column dialog box to insert more than one field at a time. To do so, hold down the Ctrl key as you click on the field, or click on the * (asterisk) to insert all the fields into the data pane. Yet another way is to double-click on the title bar of the table whose fields you want to add, and hold the Ctrl key, click on the fields you want to deselect, and drag them down.

If you want to remove a field from a table, select the field in the data pane section and press the Del key. When you delete the field, the data actually is not removed from the table, only from view on the data pane. To remove a field using the menu system, select **R**emove column from the **R**ecords menu.

If you delete a row, unlike a field, it is deleted from the data table. This is a very important distinction, and you should deal with it carefully.

You cannot remove or delete a blank column from the data pane.

After you select the fields that you want from the data pane, you can save that particular "request" as a query. To do so, click on the Save Query button, or select **S**ave Query from the **F**ile menu. The Save **A**s dialog box appears the first time you save a query. After you name the query, click on OK.

If you modify a query and you want to save it along with the original, select the Save **A**s option from the **F**ile menu. Rename the query, and click on the OK button. Your modified query is saved under the new name, and the original is still the same. You can use the Save button on the toolbar to save your query for the first time, and to save modifications if you do not want to maintain a copy of the original.

You can alter the appearance of selected fields in the data pane when the fields are displayed. You might, for instance, want to change the size of a row or column, move columns, sort the data in a particular order, hide or display columns, or change the font. MS Query enables you to do any of these actions.

If you want to change the width of a column so that you can see more or less of the field, you can do so in any of the following ways:

✔ Place the mouse pointer on the right side of the column heading and drag it. There's a trick to this; wait until the pointer changes to a two-headed arrow, and then click and drag.

✔ Click anywhere on the column, and then select the Column Width option from the Format menu. Enter the value for the width of the column in the Column Width dialog box.

To restore the original size of the column, select Standard Width from the Format menu.

If necessary, you can change the width of several columns at the same time. Drag across the headings of several columns at one time to select those columns. Then position the mouse on the right side of the far right column. When the pointer changes to a double arrow, change the size of the width displayed, which modifies all the selected columns.

To make the width of a column the same as the maximum width of your largest data field, click on the right side of the column header, just as you would in Excel—a very quick and easy way to make an optimum adjustment.

To change the height of the rows of data shown in the data pane, position the mouse pointer above the row number on any row. When the pointer turns into a double arrow, resize the row. If you increase the height of a column, information in the row might word wrap. If you reduce the height of a column so that the display font is too large to fit, the font is reduced to fit. MS Query attempts to make the adjustment for you. Changing the height of one row modifies all rows in a query.

Another way to modify row height is to select Row Height from the Format menu. The value is displayed in points in the Row Height dialog box. One point is equivalent to 1/72 inch. All rows change to the value you specify. Select Standard Height to restore the rows to the default value.

To hide, but not delete, a column of information, click on the column you want to hide, then select Hide from the Format menu. The column disappears from view. To unhide a hidden column, follow the same procedure used to hide a column, only select the Show Columns option from Format menu. Show Columns is the multipurpose display manager for MS Query. The Show Columns dialog box provides a list of columns. You can select column names, and hide or show them, depending on the current status of the column.

MS Query enables you to sort data in the data pane. Select the fields you want to sort, and choose Sort from the Records menu. The Sort dialog box appears, as shown in figure 13.7.

II

Excel

Figure 13.7

The Sort
dialog box.

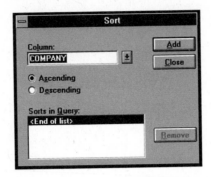

The Sort Ascending and Sort Descending buttons on the toolbar are good for sorting tasks. Select a column that you want to sort, and click on the appropriate button. MS Query returns the results immediately.

The Sort dialog box has the following options:

✔ **Column.** Initially, all of the column titles available in the data pane appear. After you select the column you want to sort and select the order, click on the **A**dd button. Two things happen:

    ✔ The requested sort of the data in the result set is performed

    ✔ The Sort command is added to the list of sorts available in the query

After you select a column for sorting in the query, that column no longer appears in the list of columns. If you want to resort the data in a different order, or at a different time in relation to other sorts, highlight it in the Sorts in **Q**uery list box and click on the **R**emove button. Then resubmit the data using the same steps.

✔ **A**s**cending and D**e**scending radio buttons.** Use these to change the order in which a sort is performed. Before you click on the **A**dd button, highlight the sort in the Sorts in **Q**uery list box just after where you want the new sort to be added. Then, when you add the new sort, it is inserted preceding the one you specify.

✔ **Sorts in Query list box.** This provides a list of the sorts in the query.

After you sort the data, click on the **C**lose button to close the dialog box.

MS Query uses the field name from selected data tables for the title of the column that is displayed. If you want a more meaningful name, double-click on heading bar at the top of the column where the name appears. The Edit Column dialog box appears (see fig. 13.8). This dialog box has three boxes:

    ✔ **F**ield. Use to select a column (it uses the one you click on as the default).

✔ **Column Heading.** Use to change the column header.

✔ **Total.** Use for totals.

If your data table has a column named CON_TITLE, you might want to change the heading to read Contact Title for aesthetic, or even proper identification, purposes.

You can accomplish the same result if you click anywhere in the column and then select **E**dit Column from the **R**ecords menu to display the Edit Column dialog box (see fig. 13.8).

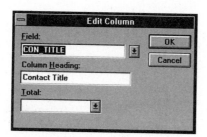

Figure 13.8
The Edit Column dialog box.

Changing Fonts

You can change fonts for your data display or result set. You can use any font on your system, however, you cannot change individual rows, columns, or cells. The font you use applies to all data in the set.

When your data is displayed in the data pane, MS Query enables you to manipulate your data in several ways, including sorting, which you just reviewed. You also can edit, change, copy, and delete information or records.

Before you can change or delete information, you must check **A**llow Editing in the **R**ecords menu.

If you need to make a change to a field within a record, highlight the contents of the cell by clicking on the field cell. Enter information while the cell is highlighted to overwrite the existing contents. If you only need to make a modification, just click on the field. One click selects the entire cell, two clicks selects the text in the active cell, and three clicks gives you the individual edit cursor. At this point, you can scroll through the field to the where you need to do your editing. If a cell is highlighted, you can press F2 to get into Edit mode. The cursor is positioned at the end of the field, and you can use the Home, End, and arrow keys to move through the cell to edit the part that you need to change.

If the entire cell contents are highlighted, the arrow keys move from cell to cell rather than from character to character.

Before you attempt to edit a record, you should be aware of a few other rules. You must enter the correct type of information into the cell. For example, you cannot enter alpha characters in a date field. You also have a limited amount of space. In addition, you must follow any other rules defined by the source data.

Any permitted changes to a record or field are automatically saved when you leave that record. If you make a mistake while editing a field, press Esc to revert the contents of a cell to its original state. While in Edit mode, a pencil appears in the row box to the left (see fig. 13.9), indicating that the changes being made are penciled in and not yet permanently saved to disk.

Figure 13.9
Changes are "penciled in" while in Edit mode.

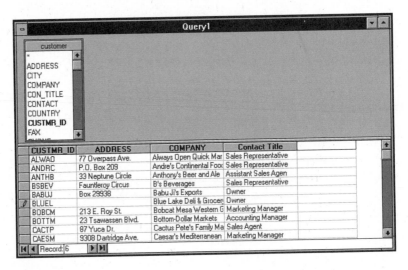

Adding records to your database is easy in MS Query. Navigate to the bottom of the result set where there is a blank record. Position the pointer in the first cell, and make an entry. After you complete the entry for that cell, press Enter to move to the next cell to the right, or use the arrow keys. As you enter data, the row indicator changes from the active row triangle to the pencil, indicating that you are making unsaved changes. After you press Enter on the last cell in the set, the pencil disappears, and your new record is saved.

If you need to delete a cell, highlight the information in the cell, and press the Del key. If you have deleted the contents of a cell, but haven't yet left it, you can still press Esc to abort the deletion. If you leave the cell, but make no other changes, you can still undo your deletion by selecting Undo Current Record from the Edit menu. But as soon as you make any changes after leaving the cell, you cannot undo the deletion.

Before you can manipulate multiple rows or columns of information, you must select the data you want to manipulate. To select an entire column, click on the title bar, or click anywhere in the column, then press Ctrl+spacebar. To highlight an entire row, click on the corresponding row button or press Shift+spacebar.

When you delete a row, you actually are deleting data from your database. And unlike individual cell deletion, which you can undo, you cannot undo row or record deletion.

Times do arise when you cannot delete or add information to a result set. These times depend on the application, the rules associated with specific data fields, and the setup of the query.

For instance, you cannot edit data in queries that use more than one data table. You cannot edit data in fields whose totals are calculated. Some applications can lock records or fields, and these prohibit changes and deletions. Some applications require unique entries in certain fields. If you get the Duplicate Key error, the value you entered is already in the data file, and you cannot have multiple copies of that value.

Sharing Data in MS Query

To share data from one cell in a result set to another, highlight the cell you want to share, and from the Edit menu, choose Cut if you want to move the data permanently, or Copy if you want to copy it to another cell. Then place the mouse pointer where you want the data, and select Paste from the Edit menu. Your data is moved or copied to the destination.

Sharing data with other applications also is possible. You can share two different types of data, and MS Query provides two different ways to copy the information.

The two data types that exist in databases and tables are referred to as static and dynamic. *Static data* are constant, unchanging groups of fields and records. When you make updates with static data, copied information does not reflect changes. The copy is an exact duplicate of the original, unconnected after the copy is made. *Dynamic data*, on the other hand, is linked to the source. With dynamic data, when you make changes to the source data, the changes are passed on dynamically to the copy, and the updates are kept current with the original records. If you dynamically copy information from a dBASE file to an Excel workbook, for instance, whenever changes are made to the dBASE file, the changes are passed along so that the data in the Excel workbook is always current.

To copy data from MS Query to another application, select the data that you want to copy in the result set. Then choose Edit, Copy, or press Ctrl+C. If you want to copy the headings and row numbers as well as the information, choose the Copy Special option. The Copy Special dialog box appears in which you can choose whether to include column headings and row numbers. Make your selection (the default is Column Headings), and click on OK. Then switch to the destination application, or start it if it is not already running. Open the file that you want to receive the data, and place the cursor in the upper left corner.

If you want static copy of data, choose **P**aste from the **E**dit menu in the other application. The information is placed in the area of the application you choose, and the data is an exact, unchanging representation of the original. If you want to make a dynamic copy, choose **E**dit, Paste Link. The information and the update link are pasted to the source application.

After you finish with the file you have pasted information to and saved it to disk, the next time you open the application, you can reestablish the link and update any changes to your data. Figure 13.10 illustrates a static copy of selected information from MS Query to Excel.

Figure 13.10

Copying select data from MS Query.

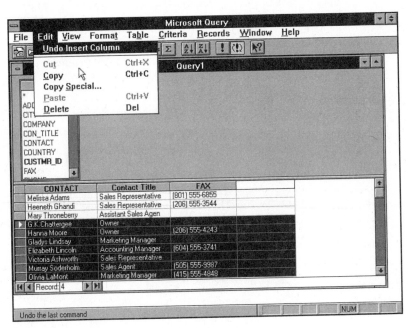

In Excel, data are placed into respective columns as in the original format. You can paste the same information by clicking on the Paste button in the standard toolbar. You can paste data as many times as needed and to multiple applications, until new data is entered into the Clipboard.

The Paste Special dialog box enables you to paste data as text, or to paste a link to the data. If choose Paste Link, you also can paste the link as an icon. If you paste the link as an icon, Excel pastes the icon of the MS Query application into the worksheet rather than the data. The link, however, remains so that when you double-click on the icon from your worksheet, it launches or switches to MS Query and brings up the file to which the links point.

To illustrate the way a dynamic link differs, edit one of the fields in the source application. Go to MS Query, and edit the title of one of the pasted records. For this example, you add the title President to G.K. Chattergee's record. Save the information in MS Query simply by

moving the cursor to another record. Then switch back to Excel. Your data might still be the same as it was prior to the switch. Save the workbook, then close it. From the File menu in Excel, reopen the file and see what happens.

First, a dialog box appears that tells you this sheet contains links to other applications. You can reestablish those links by clicking on the Yes button. As the worksheet opens, the values in the sheet go to #N/A errors for a few seconds, and then the data reappears along with the changes made from MS Query.

Take special note of the format of the cells on the dynamic paste. The static copy of information treated everything as text only, and the dynamic copy treated blank fields in the FAX number column as 0. Also, each cell has the following information in the formula bar and cell.

```
=MSQuery.exe¦FISRST.QRY!'R4:R12'
```

The preceding line includes the name of the application (MSQUERY.EXE), the associated query file from the dynamically linked application (FISRST.QRY), and the positions of the file, in this case from row 4 to row 12.

Keeping the preceding line in mind, return to MS Query, and choose Sort from the Records menu. Select Contact as the column, Ascending, add the sort, and close. The order of the data changes.

Now, switch back to Excel. Click on the Save button, and observe the changes that result after the save. The data in rows 4 through 12 in the source application changes, and so do the values linked to the worksheet.

You can further maximize this powerful tool by using the additional features that MS Query has available for asking specific questions about data, and selecting only data that meets your criteria.

Another pane you can use to filter the records display in MS Query is the *criteria pane.* To display the criteria pane, click on View, and select Criteria. You also can find this command on the toolbar, called View Criteria. The criteria pane appears between the table and data panes.

You can create a typical example of a simple criteria entry by double-clicking on the CITY field in the table pane, which adds the CITY column to the data pane. Then drag the CITY label to the Criteria Field cell in the criteria pane. Press Enter to move the cursor to the value cell directly below the CRITERIA field cell. Type **Auburn** and press Enter. This represents the question "Display all the customers whose CITY is Auburn."

If the field that contains Auburn is displayed, you can click on the cell, which makes it active, then click on the Criteria Equals button. This runs the query in exactly the same way.

Query automatically displays all matching records from the table or database. There is one entry for this query, and it is displayed alone.

Query uses Structured Query Language, or SQL, to "ask" questions. The questions you enter in plain language are automatically converted to the format MS Query needs to execute properly.

You can adjust the size of the criteria pane by using the horizontal bar and dragging, just like the other panes. To take your question further, for example, "Display all customers whose CITY is Auburn or London," press Enter again, then move one box down to the OR field in the criteria pane and type **London**. Press Enter to get the answer to your question. Although simple questions like this are helpful, MS Query can do much more complex tasks with ease.

You can perform the same function with the mouse for all entries. Clear all criteria from the criteria pane. Click the down arrow in the Criteria field box. Select CITY. Move down to the Value box, and double-click on the empty box. The Edit Criteria dialog box appears. Here, you can select different operators, and different values from the table to match the question you need to ask.

The operators that you can use are as follows:

- ✔ Equals
- ✔ Does not equal
- ✔ Is greater than
- ✔ Is greater than or equal to
- ✔ Is less than
- ✔ Is less than or equal to
- ✔ Is one of
- ✔ Is not one of
- ✔ Is between
- ✔ Is not between
- ✔ Begins with
- ✔ Does not begin with
- ✔ Ends with
- ✔ Does not end with
- ✔ Contains
- ✔ Does not contain
- ✔ Like

✔ Is not like

✔ Is null

✔ Is not null

Some operators obviously are more useful for certain data types than others. For instance, it might make sense if you're looking for a letter or character string to look in a text field, but not in a numeric or date field.

After you select a field and an operator, click on the Values button to bring up a list of the values in your table in that field. You can select any of the values from the list of available values, and look for that value, or edit the value once in the edit box. For instance, if you want search for a city that begins Aust, rather than type that, you can select Austin from the values list, and delete the last two letters from the result displayed in the box. Closing the dialog box puts the query in motion (as long as the Auto Query button on the toolbar is pressed), and returns the result set.

To ask a more complex question, click on the Criteria choice on the main menu and select Remove All Criteria. This clears the prior question. Click again on Criteria, and select Add Criteria. The Add Criteria dialog box appears, which enables you to ask new types of questions.

For instance, to identify people in your customer base who are in Sales or Marketing for a mass marketing campaign, select Add Criteria, and click the down arrow in the field box. Then select the CON_TITLE field. Tab down to the Operator's box, press the down arrow, and choose the operator "contains." Enter Sales in the Value box, then click on the Add button. The dialog box stays active, but the query is executed in the background. Click on the OR button at the top of the box, and delete the word Sales and type **Marketing** in the Values box. Click again on the Add button, and close the dialog box. Your list now includes those contacts whose title has either the word Sales or Marketing in them (see fig. 13.11).

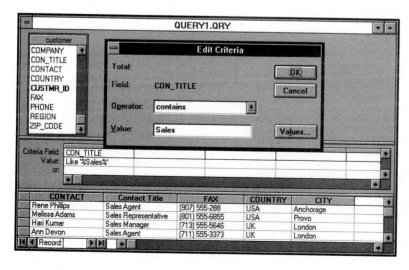

Figure 13.11
The result of the Sales and Marketing query.

The search is case-sensitive. The same search for sales and marketing would return no records.

Another way you can use this criteria is to track records. If you want to test the completeness of your contacts database and find out, for instance, for which customers you lack fax numbers, MS Query can fulfill your needs easily.

Click on the Criteria Field box, and select FAX. Then, from the Value box, double-click on Is Null from the operators list. Close the box, and you have your answer. All those customers need to be contacted so that the records can be completed.

You can clear criteria in much the same way as you delete columns from view. If you click on the top of the column of cells in the criteria pane, the entire group of cells is selected, and pressing the Del key removes them.

The criteria on which you perform your queries can belong to fields that you can't see in the data pane. For instance, if you want to search on REGION equal to IL, but do not include it in the data pane, select REGION in the criteria pane only. If you do want it in the data pane, you can always hide the column later if you want to display it for some users only.

You can use expressions to evaluate criteria in the criteria pane. For instance, to see a list of customers whose orders averaged 500.00 or more, you need to add an expression to your criteria search.

To illustrate this example in MS Query, click on the New Query button on the toolbar. Follow the steps to bring up a new database from dBASE files, called orders.

First, select a data source. dBase files should be highlighted, and click on Use. Then, in the Add Tables dialog box, double-click on ORDERS.DBF. Close the box, and you are returned to your query screen.

Select the fields to appear in the data pane by double-clicking on the labels in the table box. Choose CUST_ID, SHIP_NAME, and ORDER_AMT. Then from the toolbar, choose the Show/Hide Criteria button, which displays the criteria pane. Double-click on the Criteria Field box in the criteria pane, and the Edit Criteria box opens. Choose the down arrow in the Total box. The values Sum, Avg, Count, Min, and Max appear as choices. Select AVG, and tab to the Fields choice. Select ORDER_AMT, and click on OK.

Double-click on the Values field, and select the operator "is greater than," tab to Values, and enter 500. Close this box, and your result set will be a set of the customers who have orders greater than 500.00.

MS Query can perform calculations on your data, too. You can perform calculations on all

records in a table or selected records in a group, and you can use the five most common operators—Sum, Avg, Count, Min, and Max—or create your own.

To create your own operators, use the same orders database and clear the data pane of all fields except ORDER_AMT. Then click on the Cycle Through Totals button. The sum of all orders is displayed first, then the Average, the minimum, the maximum, and the count (see fig. 13.12).

For each type of total, there are some qualifiers that must be met, as follows:

✔ **SUM.** Sums the values in a field; works on numeric fields only.

✔ **AVG.** Calculates the average value of a numeric field.

✔ **Count.** Returns the number of entries in a field, except blank or null records.

✔ **MIN.** Returns the lowest value of the field (for Text fields, A is the lowest); it also works with numbers, dates, times, logical fields (yes or no).

✔ **MAX.** Returns the highest value in the field; (for Text fields, Z is the highest); it also works on numbers, date and time fields, and logical fields.

To create a report of all the totals, select the ORDER_AMT field five times for your data pane. One-by-one, double-click on each column head bringing up the Edit Column edit box. Select each total for each column, and the For Each in the fifth ORDER_AMT column. The totals for each category are displayed, as well as the individual order values in the last column. Figure 13.13 shows the end result.

II

Excel

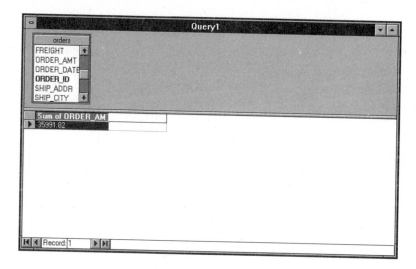

Figure 13.12
The ORDER_AMT field, selected, cycling through totals.

Figure 13.13
The end results of
the order totals
report.

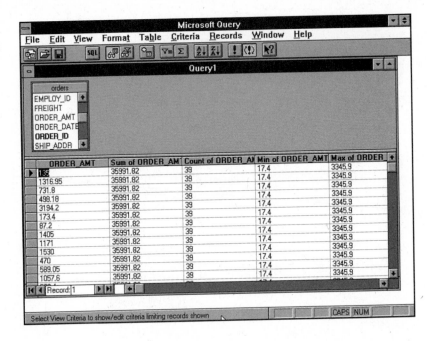

Before you can perform a calculation on a group of records in a table, you must determine what field you want to total, how you want the total to appear, and how to organize the group.

In this example, you find the sum of the ORDER_AMT field for each CITY in the database. First, clear the data pane of all fields, and resubmit the ORDER_AMT and CITY fields. Next, edit the column for ORDER_AMT by double-clicking on the column header, or by selecting the column, and choosing Records, Edit Column from the pull-down menu.

Then, in the Edit Column dialog box for ORDER_AMT, select SUM as the total. Click on OK. The total of the orders for each city are combined and shown in the Sum of ORDER_AMT column.

Note Click on the Cycle Totals button on the toolbar to show each category of total for the group. To see the other values, continue to click through the cycle.

In MS Query you can change the order and the type of records you display by changing the query criteria. For instance, if you want to display the sum of the orders for CITIES that have two or more orders, select the same setup as in the previous example. Using the ORDER_AMT column, set with the Sum for the total and the CITY column in the criteria pane, add the information for the criteria field of Count as the total, ORDER_AMT, and the value as Greater than or equal to 2. This displays the total order values for those cities that generated two or more orders.

Taking that one additional step, if you want to see which of those cities that had two or more orders averaged orders of over 1000, add another criteria column. Choose for field the ORDER_AMT field, the Total of AVG, and for values, choose greater than or equal to 1000. The list now is smaller and more defined than before.

To change the display to show the average order for those cities that had two or more orders and averaged over 1000, select the ORDER_AMT Column in the data pane, and click on the Cycle Totals button until the Average ORDER_AMT heading appears.

You can cycle through all the values and get an idea of the power of this type of lookup. Figure 13.14 shows an example of such a search.

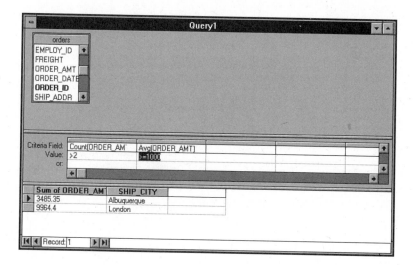

Figure 13.14
Cities that had more than two orders, which averaged more than 1000.00 per order, shown with total sales.

You have a great amount of flexibility in how you can set up your queries to obtain a desired result set. You can select the records you want first, then calculate totals, or you can calculate first, then display records based on the calculations. The best method for a particular application varies, yet having the capability to adjust and modify can produce some powerful and specific results.

There are additional calculations that you can perform on your data other than the five most popular functions offered by MS Query. Adding your own calculations is easy and straightforward.

In the data pane, select the column heading where you want to put your calculation. If you want to project what orders for a time period might be based on current orders, you can take the order amount field and multiply it by a value to result in a new set of data in the result set. If your data displayed is for one month, and you want to multiply that month by 12 to determine year totals, type **(ORDER_AMT)*12** in the column header box and press Enter.

The information that results is the projection, with new numbers. By adding a new label to the column header, your custom calculation is complete. Figure 13.15 shows the annual projections, and the Edit Column dialog box showing how the information was entered.

Figure 13.15
The annual projections, with the Edit Column dialog box present.

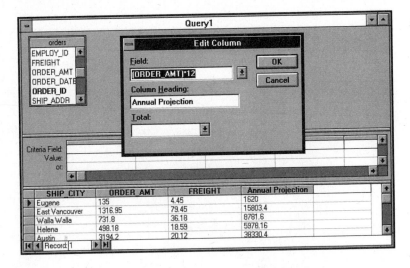

So far, you have experimented only with single table queries. MS Query can use multiple tables to build specific result sets. You get a chance later in this chapter to evaluate multiple table queries and see the difference between that and single table queries, and to link tables by using joins.

The biggest operational difference between single table and multiple table joins is that when you use multiple table queries you cannot edit the data in your result table. Also, field names appear differently, with the table name first, followed by a period, and then the field name.

To make a relationship between tables, MS Query performs a join between one field in each table if possible. Before a meaningful join can occur, the fields must be similar in some way. The most common way to create a join is to use a primary index from one data table to the next.

To illustrate this concept, click on the New Query button. Then choose dBASE Files again as your data source, click once on CUSTOMER.DBF, choose the Add button, and select ORDERS.DBF. Close the dialog box, and look at the table pane. Notice that the two tables have a line drawn between them, going from CUSTMR_ID in the CUSTOMER.DBF to CUSTMR_ID in the ORDERS.DBF (see fig. 13.16). This line represents the join between these tables. Because the data fields in each file share the same name and have the same type of data, Query automatically makes the join and draws the line to illustrate the relationship.

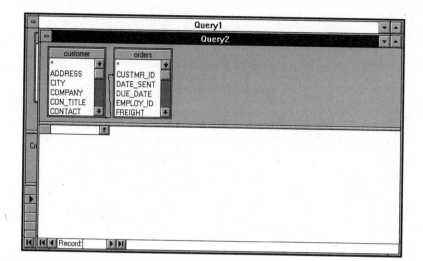

Figure 13.16
The join between
CUSTOMER.DBF
and ORDERS.DBF
on CUSTMR_ID.

Now that your data is joined, you can perform queries based on criteria in either or both tables, and your result set displays the result set of the query. To set up your data pane, choose COMPANY and CONTACT from CUSTOMER.DBF, and choose DATE_SENT, SHIP_CITY, and ORDER_AMT from ORDERS.DBF. The resulting data displays records only for those customers who have placed orders because there has to be a customer ID in both the customer and orders data files.

If you want to produce a result set of customers who have been shipped orders between two dates, select Criteria from the View menu. The criteria pane appears, and in the first selection box, choose the field ORDERS.DATE_SENT. As indicated by the pull-down choices, the fields now are preceded by the table name so that query can track the data source.

Select the field, and in the Values box, choose Is Between as the operator, tab to the Values box, and click on the Values button. From the Values box, choose the two values of 05-17-1989 and 07-15-1989. Click on OK. The orders sent between those two dates for customers whose CUSTMR_ID matches in CUSTOMER.DBF and ORDER.DBF, and who shipped orders within the selected date range, appear.

You can sort your new result set by any of the columns displayed. If you want to see who had the largest order in that time frame, select the ORDER_AMT column, and click on the Sort Descending button. The result set should look like figure 13.17.

Figure 13.17
A joined multitable
query, sorted by
order value.

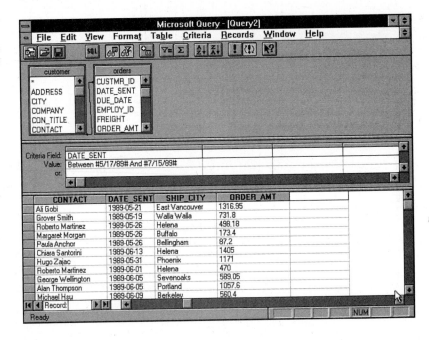

Figure 13.17
A joined multitable
query, sorted by
order value.

This type of join is called an *inner join,* and the default is that the values in the two joined fields (CUSTMR_ID) must contain the same value for data from either table to be displayed. If MS Query does not create the join automatically, you can use the Joins command from the Table menu to modify or create joins.

You also can delete joins. To illustrate how this works, first click on the line that joins the two tables you have selected in the query. Press the Del key, and the line and join disappear. Also, press the Auto Query button on the toolbar so that the result set is not updated for each change. Choose Remove All Criteria from the Criteria menu so that the result set will be complete.

The fastest way to create (or re-create) a join between two tables is to drag the name of the first field to the second. To re-create the join you just removed, click on CUSTMR_ID in CUSTOMER.DBF, and drag it over to CUSTMR_ID in ORDERS.DBF.

To evaluate further the way the inner join works, click on the join line between the tables, and select Joins from the Table menu. Click on the line prior to choosing Joins to ensure that you are editing the existing join and not creating a new one. As you can see, you can harness the power of joining information from multiple tables in a number of ways.

The top of the Joins dialog box shows the field from the first table that is joined, and its relationship to the field from the second table. In this case, an *equi-join,* a join involving two fields whose values equal one another, is used, and the result is a display of only records from the two tables whose values are equal. This is called an inner join.

The Joins Include section of the Joins dialog box enables you to choose an outer join instead of an inner join. An *outer join* is one that selects all records from one table, and only records from the second table that have equal joined values.

In the example, this process shows all customers who have IDs that are equal in both tables, and it displays all the records from the orders table and shows blank cells where the fields cannot be matched. This can show you missing information and help track down errors.

You also can display the opposite of the previous example by choosing the last Join includes option, which takes all values from Orders and only those from customers whose IDs are equal.

 Outer joins cannot be performed with more than two tables in a query.

Another type of join, known as the *self-join*, compares values within a single table by adding two copies of the same table in a query.

Click on the New Query button, select data sources as dBASE Files, and select the EMPLOYEE.DBF twice. Query informs you that the table is already in the query one time, so you need to confirm that you do want another copy. Choose OK to close the dialog box, and return to the query.

Query gives the second copy of the table a new name that has the extension _1 for differentiation. To create a list of employees and their managers, delete the join that exists between the two tables if MS Query joins them automatically. Drag the name REPORTS_TO from the first table to EMPLY_ID in the second table. Add the fields of First Name, Last Name, and EMP_TITLE to the data pane from the first table, and add LAST_NAME from the second table.

The self-join returns a list of employees and their managers. The REPORTS_TO and EMPLY_ID fields are the same data type. When the tables are joined by this link, the information from the first table appears along with the information of each employee's boss. The link displays the name of the manager (REPORTS_TO) for each EMPLY_ID.

You can use MS Query to add new tables to provide new information in addition to just looking at existing data. Select Table Definition from the File menu after you select a data source. The Select Table dialog box appears. Click on New. The New Table Definition dialog box appears.

To define a new table, name it, and tab to the field section of the dialog box. From here, you must give each field a name, data type, and length. After you define each field, click on the Add button, and the field appears in the lower section of the window.

You can specify whether the field is required. After you define the table you want to add, click on Create and the table appears on the list of available data sources. You also can use the Table feature to view the definition of other existing data sources or tables in MS Query.

You cannot change fields after a data table has been created. The best way to add or modify tables is to bring up the existing definition, use the Add and Remove features to get the table in the correct format, and save it under a new name. You then can use MS Query to transfer all the information from the old table to the new corrected one.

The types of fields and lengths available vary with different ODBC Driver types.

You also can use <u>T</u>able Definition from the <u>F</u>ile menu to delete a table you no longer need. Select the file from the Available Sources list and click on <u>R</u>emove.

Another way to create a new table is to use a result set from a query. This is a powerful way to transfer information from one format to another and create meaningful new data files.

To do this, run the query you want, and display the result set in the data pane. Select Save <u>A</u>s from the <u>F</u>ile menu. You then can select the data source you want to use. You can save your query as a query file, or as a new database table. In the window for available data sources, the list might not include all the different types of data files you might want to use. If it doesn't, click on <u>O</u>ther, and a new ODBC Sources box appears.

If you have chosen to define new files or sources, they appear in on the ODBC Sources box. To create a new data source category, click on the New button. The following list shows some of the ODBC Driver data types that are available from MS Query.

- ✔ Microsoft Access Files
- ✔ Btrieve Files
- ✔ dBASE Files
- ✔ Excel Files
- ✔ FoxPro Files
- ✔ Oracle
- ✔ Paradox
- ✔ SQL Server
- ✔ Text Files (*.TXT, *.CSV)

You can transport your result set to a wide variety of popular formats. This is extremely important for several reasons. Because information sometimes needs to be shared between applications, computers or even companies, having the capability to deliver data in a format

that others can use can same time and money. In addition, being capable of accepting data in all these formats and porting it to the format you want to use is very powerful.

For instance, if you have a client that has a dBASE application that he has been using for some time, and you need to use some of his data for a project, but your company uses Access as a database, you can use MS Query to read his dBASE file, filter out what you don't need, and create a new Access file directly from his information. The original data is unchanged, you have the information you need to use (in the right format), and it was accomplished with a minimum of time, hassle, and money spent.

MS Query performs its tasks by using a special language called SQL. Each time MS Query examines, retrieves, updates or does any function with a database, an SQL statement controls the way the process runs.

When MS Query builds a query, the software composes an SQL statement that begins with the SELECT command. Figure 13.18 shows a simple SELECT statement after choosing three fields from CUSTOMER.DBF for display in the data pane.

The view in the preceding figure is displayed by clicking on the SQL button on the toolbar. It also can be displayed by choosing **V**iew, **S**QL from the pull-down menus.

When the SQL box is active, you can edit or customize your statement. Using the toolbar, pull-downs, and tools that you have learned about in this chapter, MS Query translates that into SQL terminology. You can also type it directly. Figure 13.19 shows what the last self-join and query looks like in SQL.

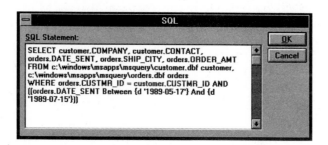

Figure 13.18
The SQL state-
ment syntax.

Some of the SQL statements that you use, either by entering them directly into the SQL box or by using the graphical interface provided by MS Query include the following:

✔ **From.** Specifies tables added to the table pane, where Select gets its fields.

✔ **Outer Join, Left or Right.** Joins tables and changes the way the join is set up.

✔ **AND.** Use for inclusive evaluation of more than one criteria.

Figure 13.19
The self-join and
query in SQL.

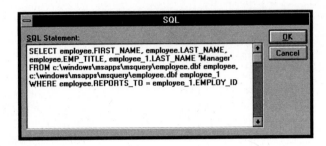

SQL

SQL Statement:

```
SELECT employee.FIRST_NAME, employee.LAST_NAME,
employee.EMP_TITLE, employee_1.LAST_NAME 'Manager'
FROM c:\windows\msapps\msquery\employee.dbf employee,
c:\windows\msapps\msquery\employee.dbf employee_1
WHERE employee.REPORTS_TO = employee_1.EMPLOY_ID
```

OK
Cancel

✔ **OR.** Use for exclusive evaluation of more than one criteria.

✔ **DISTINCT.** Use if the Unique Values Only box in Query Properties is used.

✔ **ORDER BY.** Use on selected fields for sorting.

✔ **GROUP BY.** Use to display records together.

✔ **WHERE.** Use to evaluate or change criteria in a calculated field; joins tables using equi-join

✔ **HAVING.** Use when working with an untotaled field in a set that contains totals.

Some types of queries cannot be created using the Query window, which involves granting of privileges, modifying tables, or creating indexes on data. You can use the Execute SQL dialog box to define and create custom statements.

Retrieving External Data from Excel

You can launch the power of MS Query from within Excel to bring data to your workbooks.

Earlier you learned how to select and copy data either in a static, unchanging mode, or dynamically, from Query to other applications. Now, you will learn how to retrieve external data from Query, and the external sources available to it from within Excel 5.0.

To begin, load Excel, and have a blank workbook on screen. Select Get E̲xternal Data from the D̲ata menu. If the menu option is not available, make sure that the XLQuery and ODBC add-ins are activated in the Add-in dialog box.

Selecting Get External Data launches MS Query, and prompts you to select a data source, choose a table, and complete the basics of retrieving the data you want. You can create a new query, run an existing one, or change queries as you learned earlier in this chapter. After the result set displays what you request, select Return Data to Excel from the F̲ile menu.

An options dialog box appears in Excel asking you to specify whether to keep Query References (default is yes), Include Field Names (default is yes), Include Row Numbers (default is

no), and destination for the data in the workbook. The default destination is the cell that was active when you invoked the Get External Command. You can change it to be specific for the sheet and cell range you need.

Clicking on OK brings the data from Query into Excel, places each column in an Excel column, and adjusts the width of the cells that receive the information.

Your data is now copied and ready use in the worksheet however you want (see fig. 13.20).

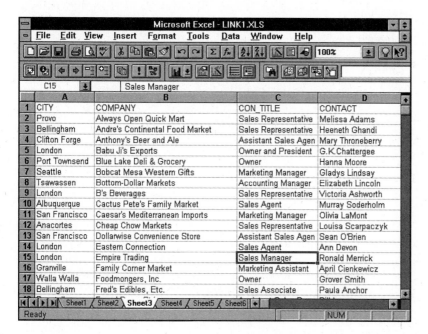

Figure 13.20
The completed worksheet, with data captured from MS Query.

If you need to return to the data source and edit the information, you can double-click on the worksheet data, and the data is brought up from the source. This is a feature that can come in quite handy. Using the Query and Pivot toolbar accomplishes this as well. Click on the Get External Data button to launch or switch to MS Query.

Excel has other tools that you can use to obtain external data as well, such as the Pivot Table.

Using Pivot Tables

Pivot tables are tools used in Excel to summarize large lists, databases, worksheets workbooks, or other collections of data. They are called pivot tables because you can move fields with the mouse to provide different types of summary listings, that is, the tables can change, or pivot.

Pivot tables can get their source information from a number of different sources. For this discussion, you extract data for the pivot table from external sources using MS Query.

Begin with a blank worksheet. The first part of creating a pivot table is to invoke the Pivot Table wizard. This is the first button on the Query and Pivot toolbar. The first screen of the Pivot Table Wizard is the data source selection step. You have the following choices:

✔ Microsoft Excel List or Database

✔ External Data Source

✔ Multiple Consolidation Ranges

✔ Another Pivot Table

Choose External Data Sources and click on Next. The Step 2 of 4 dialog box appears. Click on the Get Data button, which has the notation `no data retrieved`. MS Query is launched.

Follow the steps involved in choosing a data source, choosing a table, and setting up a result set. You can, if you have already done so, retrieve a saved query. After the result set is the information you want to summarize in the Pivot Table, select Return Data to Microsoft Excel from the File menu and click on Next.

The Data is then sent to Excel through the Clipboard. The PivotTable Wizard - Step 3 of 4 dialog box appears. Figure 13.21 shows the Pivot Table setup screen.

The fields that you select in your result set show along the right side of the dialog box. The areas of the pivot table you work with are Row information, Column information, Data, and Page. You can drag the selected fields into these separate areas for table formatting.

In the query, for example, the ORDERS.DBF file was chosen. The fields selected were: Customer Id, Order Id, Ship City, Order Date, and Order Amount. If you want to create a

Figure 13.21
The Pivot Table setup.

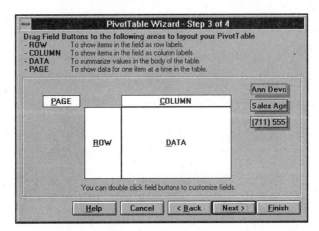

summary table of this information, you might want to see it as a break down by customer and city, with the orders totaled, but listed separately by customer ID and order ID. The Pivot table can easily provide you with this information.

Because a separate breakdown by City is desired, drag the City field over to the PAGE section of the Pivot Table Setup, Step 3 of 4 dialog box. This means that for each city, you can see a separate page of data, or a recap of the sales in that city. Next, take the Order Amount field, and drag it into the data area. That information is summarized and totaled in the table. For row, take the Order Date field. Drag it over and your table provides a row breakdown in date order. The column information is the Customer ID and Order ID fields. Click on Next, then click on Finish. The resulting pivot table is shown in figure 13.22.

C5 — Sum of ORDER_AMT

	C	D	E	F	G	H	I	J
3	SHIP_CIT	(All)						
4								
5	Sum of ORDER_AMT		CUSTMR ID	ORDER ID				
6			ANTHB	ANTHB Total	BLUMG	BLUMG Total	BOBCM	BOBCM Total
7	DATE_SE	ORDER_AMT	10028		10017		10032	
8	5/17/89	135	0	0	0	0	0	0
9	5/17/89 Total		0	0	0	0	0	0
10	5/19/89	731.8	0	0	0	0	0	0
11	5/19/89 Total		0	0	0	0	0	0
12	5/21/89	1316.95	0	0	0	0	0	0
13	5/21/89 Total		0	0	0	0	0	0
14	5/26/89	87.2	0	0	0	0	0	0
15		173.4	0	0	0	0	0	0
16		498.18	0	0	0	0	0	0
17	5/26/89 Total		0	0	0	0	0	0
18	5/31/89	1171	0	0	0	0	0	0
19	5/31/89 Total		0	0	0	0	0	0
20	6/1/89	470	0	0	0	0	0	0

Sheet1 / Sheet2 / Sheet3 / **Sheet4** / Sheet5 / Sheet6

Figure 13.22
The pivot table.

The resulting pivot table looks somewhat ominous at this point because it shows all the information for all facets of the data. In the Ship City box at the top of the table, there is a drop-down arrow. Click on the arrow to bring out a list of each city in the data. Click on the city whose sales numbers you want to see. When you select an individual value for the page criteria, such as London, the table automatically recalculates and displays the recap of sales, complete with grand totals at the bottom and to the right, for total sales by date for that city, and total sales by customer for that city.

The pivot table is a very powerful analysis tool. You can summarize a vast amount of information in a friendly, informative, interactive worksheet table.

You cannot edit information in a pivot table because it maintains a link to the source data, but updating the source file does pass any new or changed information to the table. In this example, for instance, any new orders for customers show up on the pivot table if they are entered into the source database. When the table is retrieved, on the Query and Pivot toolbar, the Exclamation Point button is the Refresh Data tool. Clicking on this button performs the original query and returns any new or changed information to your table.

If you decide you want to change the orientation of the table, you can change it dynamically by dragging the field identifier to the location you want it. As an example, if you want to see the Customer ID information in a row instead of a column, click and drag the field name for Customer ID from the its present column to the Row area. The pivot table automatically reformats itself with the new information.

Another way to modify your table is to click anywhere on the table and then click on the PivotTable Wizard. This process takes you directly to Step 3 of 4, the set up, where you can drag row, page, column or data information around to format the table the way you want.

You also can double-click on a field name to customize it. The customization can change where it is located, row, column or data, and how it is totaled, if at all. You also can choose to hide items if you want. For instance, if you drag the Order ID field from column to row, you get a detail breakdown by Order ID of order total, and by date (the other row identifier) for each customer within each city.

The totals that show on the table are figured for each subcategory in the row and for the column. When you add an additional row field, the pivot table provides a new subtotal field on the row. The same occurs with column information. The information in every row and every column is totaled. There is a grand total field for the table.

After you create your table, you can change the way it displays information in addition to dragging row and column and page fields to new locations. By highlighting a range of cells in the detail section of the table, and selecting Group from the toolbar, the pivot table combines the information into a combined section. Then, using the Hide Detail button, you can just display the totals. Another way to use this is to highlight the information under the Date Sent field, and click on the Hide Detail button. This suppresses the display of the subtotals for each Order ID for each date, but still shows the dates and the grand total.

You can also hide the detail on a row-by-row or column-by-column basis.

Highlighting an entire column of information, such as the row data, which is the Date Sent field, and clicking on the Group button makes an interesting display. You then can view or hide the detail on an entire group of cells by double-clicking on the cell that contains the Group label—Group 1, in this case. Figures 13.23 and 13.24 show the effect of grouping and changing the view of your pivot tables.

To obtain a great amount of detail about a pivot table, you can output each sheet of the table to its own worksheet if necessary. You can do this to allow further individual data manipulation or calculation. Just click on the Show Pages button on the Query and Pivot toolbar to take each page from the table and create a worksheet for each one.

If you combine this with large collections of data, minus proper organization, a great deal of space and time can be required. In this example, Show Pages creates a recap of sales for each city.

	C8			Group1						
	C	**D**	**E**	**F**	**G**	**H**	**I**	**J**		
3	SHIP_CITY	(All)								
4										
5	Sum of ORDER_AMT			CUSTMR_ID	ORDER_ID					
6				ANTHB	ANTHB Total	BLUMG	BLUMG Total	BOBCM		
7	DATE_SE	DATE_SENT	ORDER_AMT	10028		10017		10032		
8	Group1	5/17/89	135	0	0	0	0	0		
9		5/17/89 Total		0	0	0	0	0		
10		5/19/89	731.8	0	0	0	0	0		
11		5/19/89 Total		0	0	0	0	0		
12		5/21/89	1316.95	0	0	0	0	0		
13		5/21/89 Total		0	0	0	0	0		
14		5/26/89	87.2	0	0	0	0	0		
15			173.4	0	0	0	0	0		
16			498.18	0	0	0	0	0		
17		5/26/89 Total		0	0	0	0	0		
18		5/31/89	1171	0	0	0	0	0		
19		5/31/89 Total		0	0	0	0	0		
20		6/1/89	470	0	0	0	0	0		

Sheet1 / Sheet2 / Sheet3 \ **Sheet4** / Sheet5 / Sheet6

Figure 13.23
The group in full display.

	C8			Group1						
	C	**D**	**E**	**F**	**G**	**H**	**I**	**J**		
3	SHIP_CITY	(All)								
4										
5	Sum of ORDER_AMT			CUSTMR_ID	ORDER_ID					
6				ANTHB	ANTHB Total	BLUMG	BLUMG Total	BOBCM		
7	DATE_SE	DATE_SENT	ORDER_AMT	10028		10017		10032		
8	Group1			970	970	1148	1148	94.88		
9	Grand Total			970	970	1148	1148	94.88		
10										
11										
12										
13										
14										
15										
16										
17										
18										
19										
20										

Sheet1 / Sheet2 / Sheet3 \ **Sheet4** / Sheet5 / Sheet6

Figure 13.24
The group after double-clicking.

Now, with each city on its own sheet, in its own pivot table, you can drag and move information around to create the views you want, and if you do not like the way your result looks, you can use the Edit menu to undo your pivot changes and revert back to the original design.

Another way to reformat your pivot table is to click once on the field you want to alter, and from the Query and Pivot toolbar, click on Pivot Table Field. The Edit Field dialog box appears, where you can change the orientation, from page, to row or to column, you can modify the type of subtotal that is applied to the information, such as SUM, COUNT, AVERAGE, MAX, MIN PRODUCT, Standard Deviations, and so on. And, if you want to suppress the display of information, you can hide items on the list of values for the field.

If you want to suppress the display of certain cities in the table, you can selectively click on the values you do not want to show, and they remain hidden until you go back and tell the pivot table edit field criteria to redisplay them.

Double-clicking on any of the field names brings up the Edit Field dialog box.

When you double-click on the Totals fields, the information that is used to calculate that total is copied into an additional worksheet tab within the workbook. For instance, if you select all from the Ship City Page selection, to bring up all the information in the table, and go to the end of the table to the last grand total, double-clicking copies the summary into its own worksheet, which you can then manipulate, edit, and work with separate from the pivot table (see fig. 13.25).

Figure 13.25
The summary sheet, made by double-clicking on the pivot table grand total cell.

	A	B	C	D	E	F	G	H
	SHIP_CITY							
1	SHIP_CITY	EXPR_1	ORDER_AMT	CUSTMR_ID	ORDER_ID	DATE_SENT		
2	Helena	17.4	17.4	MORNS	10026	6/28/89		
3	Bellingham	87.2	87.2	FREDE	10006	5/26/89		
4	Auburn	91.8	91.8	MANZH	10019	7/14/89		
5	Seattle	94.88	94.88	BOBCM	10032	7/11/89		
6	Ithaca	97.3	97.3	SAWYH	10029	7/7/89		
7	Eugene	135	135	FRUGF	10000	5/17/89		
8	Buffalo	173.4	173.4	WALNG	10005	5/26/89		
9	Albuquerque	185.8	185.8	RATTC	10025	6/25/89		
10	Berkeley	192.1	192.1	GRUED	10014	6/14/89		
11	San Francisco	351	351	CAESM	10036			
12	Denver	371	371	TOMMI	10023	6/30/89		
13	Austin	438.43	438.43	VALUF	10037	7/19/89		
14	Seattle	448	448	VINEA	10020	6/28/89		
15	Helena	470	470	SILVS	10010	6/1/89		
16	Helena	498.18	498.18	SILVS	10003	5/26/89		
17	Berkeley	560.4	560.4	RITEB	10013	6/9/89		
18	Sevenoaks	589.05	589.05	WELLT	10011	6/5/89		

Sheet1 / Sheet2 / Sheet3 / **Sheet17** / Sheet4 / Sheet

You can change the way your data appears by moving fields around from different orientations. You also can change how the sheet looks. You change a pivot table by selecting Autoformat from the Format menu, because the changes made to individual cells or ranges are not passed along to the other worksheets.

Autoformat provides a consistent look across the sheet. Using Autoformat, you can choose from many varying styles of background colors, styles, column and row display changes, from simple to complex.

Finally, if you want to sort your data as displayed on your pivot table, Excel provides the appropriate tools. Highlight the range of cells you want to sort. Click on the last column of order totals. Then, from the standard toolbar, click on the sort Ascending or Descending button. Your data will be displayed in rank, in the order that you requested. You can customize your sort, by highlighting the data in the table, or range that you wish to put in order, and from the Data Menu, select Sort. The sort menu prompt you for the order, the key, and provides you with options about how to process your request (see fig. 13.26).

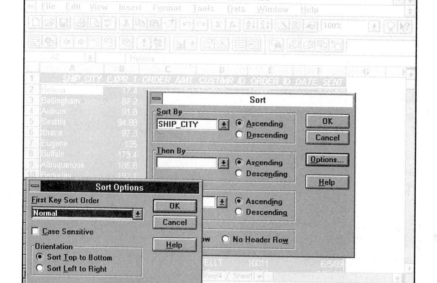

Figure 13.26
The Sort and Sort Options dialog boxes.

The figure shows the dates in the table highlighted, and the Data, Sort, options dialog boxes displayed. Note also the changed format, using the Autoformat feature, from the Format pull-down menu. The selection chosen for the format is the Colorful 2 format.

The following is a list of the data output formats that Excel 5.0 supports.

✔ Microsoft Excel workbook

✔ Template

✔ Formatted Text (Space delimited)

✔ Tab delimited text

✔ Comma delimited text (CSV)

✔ Microsoft Excel 4.0 Worksheet

✔ Microsoft Excel 3.0

✔ Microsoft Excel 2.1

✔ Microsoft Excel 4.0 Workbook

✔ WK3, FM3 (1-2-3)

✔ WK3 (1, 2, 3)

✔ WK1, FMT (1, 2, 3)

- ✔ WK1 All (1, 2, 3)

- ✔ WKS (1, 2, 3)

- ✔ WQ1 (Quattro Pro)

- ✔ dBASE IV

- ✔ dBASE III

- ✔ dBASE II

- ✔ Text for Macintosh

- ✔ Text for OS/2 or MS-DOS

- ✔ Character separated (Macintosh)

- ✔ Character separated (OS/2, MS-DOS)

- ✔ DIF (Data Interchange Format)

- ✔ SYLK (Symbolic Link) Format

To save data to these formats, select Save As from the File menu, then use the pull-down menu selection at the bottom of the Save As dialog box to choose the format you want.

Saving information to many of the supporting file types supports only the active worksheet because the resulting programs might lack the capability to process multilevel worksheets the way Excel does. Experiment with the format to which you need to export, to come up with a workable solution.

Chapter Snapshot

Now that you are a little more comfortable using Excel, you might want to add a little of yourself to the way Excel works and looks. Excel 5 gives you great flexibility in deciding the types of toolbars you want to display, the menu items you want available, and where you want toolbars to be placed. This chapter shows you the way to take advantage of these customization features and provides the following insights into Excel:

Although this chapter contains more advanced features, even beginners can take advantage of Excel 5's customization routines.

CHAPTER

Customizing Excel 5

by Rob Tidrow

Have you ever pulled down a menu or looked at the standard toolbars and thought, "Why do I have to rummage through all these options I never use to choose the Options command?" Although the Excel interface is easy to use, it also is packed with dozens of commands and options you might never use. You can eliminate, add, move around, and create your own menus, dialog boxes, toolbars, and toolbar buttons to make Excel work the way you work.

Exploring Excel's Customizable Menus

One of the unique features of Excel 5 is the Menu Editor. The Menu Editor enables you to customize the menu system, giving you the capability of creating your own menus. You can use this feature when you build macros or Visual Basic applications to create your own worksheet applications.

To use the Menu Editor, you first must activate a Visual Basic module or create a new one. Perform the following steps to start and use the Menu Editor:

1. Activate a Visual Basic module, or select Insert, Macro, Module to start a new one. The Visual Basic toolbar appears on-screen.

2. Select Tools, Menu Editor to display the Menu Editor dialog box (see fig. 14.1).

Figure 14.1

The Menu Editor dialog box enables you to customize your menus.

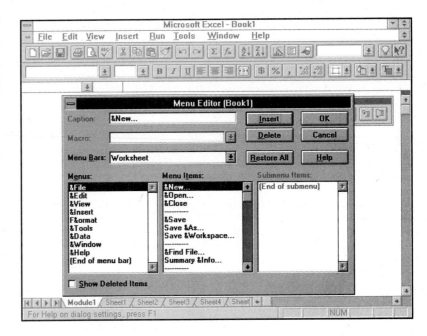

Tip

You also can click on the Menu Editor button on the Visual Basic toolbar to start the Menu Editor. This button is the second button from the left and looks like a pull-down menu.

At this point, you need to use some of your knowledge about Windows applications. Most Windows applications, for instance, have standard menus that are on a menu bar, such as File, Edit, Window, and Help. Standard menus also have standard elements, including menu items (commands), separator bars, submenu items, and the ellipsis (if the menu item activates a dialog box). For the most part, you take these elements for granted when you learn and use a Windows application.

Another feature that usually is taken for granted when you use Windows applications is how menu bars change depending on what you are doing. Notice, for instance, that when you performed the previous Step 1, the menu bar changed, giving you new menus with different menu items. This enabled you to select commands that are specific to the Visual Basic module. The menu bar that is activated when you choose this module is called the Visual Basic Module menu bar.

Excel has seven types of menu bars from which you can choose when you create or modify menus. You can choose these menu bars from the Menu <u>B</u>ars drop-down list box in the Menu Editor dialog box. The following are descriptions of the menu bars:

Excel

- ✔ **Worksheet.** This is the standard menu bar that you see when you work with worksheets.

- ✔ **Chart.** This menu bar is active when you have a chart active.

- ✔ **No Documents Open.** You see this menu bar when there are no open workbooks. This menu bar contains only <u>F</u>ile and <u>H</u>elp.

- ✔ **Visual Basic Module.** This menu bar appears when you have a Visual Basic module active.

- ✔ **Shortcut Menus 1.** This is the menu that appears when you right-click on a toolbar, row or column header, window title bar, tool, cell, desktop, or workbook tab.

- ✔ **Shortcut Menus 2.** You see this menu when you right-click on a drawing object, button, or text box.

- ✔ **Shortcut Menus 3.** This is the menu that appears when you right-click on parts of a chart, including data series, text, arrow, plot area, gridline, floor, and legend. You also see this menu when you click on the whole chart.

In the Menu Editor dialog box, the <u>M</u>enus, Menu I<u>t</u>ems, and S<u>u</u>bmenu Items lists contain the actual menu names and commands (items) for each menu bar. You work from these lists to determine which menus and menu items you want to include in each customized menu bar.

Adding Menus to a Menu Bar

Although creating your own menus requires you to know a different language of sorts, you already are familiar with most of it just by using Windows applications on a regular basis. The menu bar that you use can be one of the seven Excel menu bars or one that you create from scratch. The following steps show you the way to add your own menu to a menu bar:

1. In the Menu <u>B</u>ars drop-down list box in the Menu Editor dialog box, select the menu bar you want to customize. You might, for instance, want to add a menu to the Worksheet menu bar. If so, click on Worksheet.

2. You now need to tell Excel where you want to place the new menu on the selected menu bar. To indicate this, select from the M<u>e</u>nus list box the menu that is immediately left of where you want the new menu to appear.

   Suppose, for example, that you want to add a menu named Fiscal and place it to the left of the Data menu. To do this, click on &Data in the M<u>e</u>nus list box.

Note The ampersand (&) is an instruction that tells Excel to underline the next character. This underlined character denotes the accelerator key, or hot key, in the menu name.

3. Click on the <u>I</u>nsert button, telling Excel that you want to insert a new menu. This activates the <u>C</u>aption field box in the Menu Editor dialog box (refer to figure 14.1).

4. In the <u>C</u>aption field box, type the name of the new menu: **Fi&scal**, for example. You can place the ampersand to the left of any other character to denote a hot key. Just be sure that the hot key does not conflict with other hot keys that already are set up on the menu bar.

5. Return to Step 1 to add more menus. Press Enter or choose OK when you finish adding menus.

This returns you to the Visual Basic module. If you created a new menu on the module, you will see it displayed on the menu bar. If you created a menu on another menu bar—the Worksheet menu bar, for example—click on a sheet tab to switch to a worksheet. You can see your new menu on the menu bar. In figure 14.2, for example, the Fiscal menu appears on the menu bar.

Adding Items to a Menu

If you click on a newly created menu, nothing happens. This is because you have just created the menu and not any menu items under it. The following steps show you the way to create menu items and place them on your new menu:

1. Be sure you switch back to the Visual Basic module, and select <u>T</u>ools, Menu E<u>d</u>itor to display the Menu Editor dialog box.

2. In the Menu <u>B</u>ars drop-down list box, select the menu bar that includes your new menu; Worksheet, for example.

3. In the M<u>e</u>nus list box, click on the menu that you want to add items to; Fi&scal, for example.

4. In the Menu Items list box, select the menu item before which you want your menu item to appear. If this is a new menu (as in the Fiscal example), the only option is (End of menu), as shown in figure 14.3. Click on (End of menu) if this is the only option or if you want the item to be at the bottom of the menu.

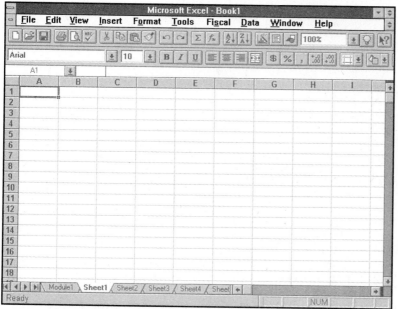

Figure 14.2
Adding the Fiscal menu to the Worksheet menu bar.

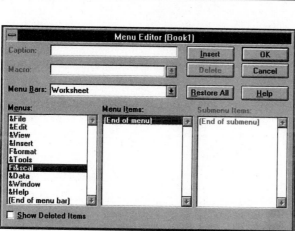

Figure 14.3
The Menu Items list includes all the menu commands for the selected menu.

5. Click on <u>I</u>nsert. This activates the <u>C</u>aption field box.

6. Type the name of the menu item you want to add to the menu; **&Budget**, for example. If you want to include a separator bar, use a hyphen (-) instead of a name.

> Some menus use separator bars to group different types of commands or items. In the <u>F</u>ile menu, for example, the printing commands are grouped and separated from the other commands by two separator bars. Try to use separator bars to group similar items. The separator bar is created by using a hyphen (-) when you include a caption name.

7. To add another menu item, return to the Menu I<u>t</u>ems list box and click on the menu item before which you want your menu item to appear. Do not click on OK or press Enter yet; this would return you to the Visual Basic module.

8. Repeat steps 4–7 until you finish adding all the menu items. Click on OK or press Enter when you finish.

You can see your new menu structure by returning to the menu bar that contains the new menu, such as a worksheet. You now are ready to add some functionality to your menu items so that they do more than just sit on a menu.

> You also can add submenu items to menu items by following the preceding steps, but selecting the item before which you want your submenu item to appear in the Su<u>b</u>menu Items list box.
>
> If, for example, you want to include a submenu item called Equipment to the &Budget menu item, click on &Budget in the Menu I<u>t</u>ems list box and then click on (End of submenu) in the Su<u>b</u>menu Items list box. Click on Insert and fill in the Caption field box with **&Equipment**.

Adding Functionality to Menu Items

When you create new menu items and customize them, you have to assign a command or procedure to them. In other words, you must attach a macro or Visual Basic subroutine to them. If, for example, you create a Visual Basic subroutine that runs a budget analysis worksheet, you can attach this routine to the &Budget menu item in the preceding examples.

> See Chapter 15, "Mastering Visual Basic for Applications," for more information on creating macros and Visual Basic subroutines. Also, pick up a copy of *Inside Excel 5 for Windows*, published by New Riders Publishing, for in-depth coverage of these features.

The following steps show you the way to attach a macro or subroutine to a menu item:

1. Make sure the Menu Editor dialog box is active by returning to a Visual Basic module and selecting Tools, Menu Editor.

2. Select the menu item or submenu item to which you want to attach the macro or subroutine. Select &Budget in the Menu Items list box, for example, to attach a macro or subroutine to it.

3. In the Macro pull-down list box, select the macro or subroutine name you want to attach to the menu item (see fig. 14.4). If you don't have any macros to attach, see Chapter 15, "Mastering Visual Basic for Applications," in which you learn to create macros.

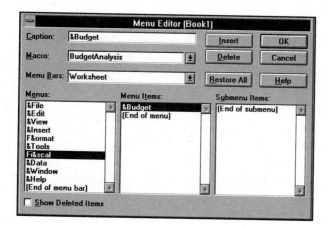

Figure 14.4
Attaching a macro or subroutine to a menu item using the Macro pull-down list box.

4. Return to Step 2 to continue adding macros and subroutines to menu items.

5. Press Enter or click on OK when you finish.

You now can return to the menu bar that you customized and use the new menu and menu item(s).

Tip

When you want to delete a menu, menu item, or submenu item, start the Menu Editor, select the item you want to delete, and click on the Delete button. Use the Restore All button to return the menus to their original, built-in state.

Customizing Toolbars

Excel 5 makes it very easy—too easy in fact—to customize the toolbars that appear on your screen. They are so easy to customize that you might overdo adding new icons and macros to your toolbar. This clutter slows down your system. On the other hand, you can add or delete tools that you use a lot or never at all.

If, for example, you use the double-underline formatting feature often, you might get tired of navigating menus, tabs, and dialog boxes to insert a double-underline to a word or phrase. To speed up this process, you can add the double-underline tool to the Formatting (or any other) toolbar. Excel includes several predefined tools that you can add to your desktop, including the double-underline tool, making it easy to customize the look and functionality of your toolbars. You also can add your own macros and Visual Basic subroutines to toolbar buttons.

Understanding Toolbar Options

When you first install and start Excel 5, you are shown the default toolbars and tool buttons. These include the Standard and Formatting toolbars. Unbeknownst to new users, there are several other toolbars that you can display, including the Query and Pivot toolbar, Chart toolbar, and Forms toolbar. To display these toolbars, use the following steps:

1. Select View, Toolbars to display the Toolbars dialog box, as shown in figure 14.5.

Figure 14.5
The Toolbars dialog box displays the available toolbars.

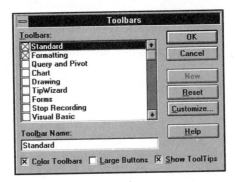

2. Click in the check boxes to display toolbars of your choice. If you want to deactivate one, be sure its check box is empty.

3. Along the bottom of the dialog box, you can tell Excel to show color in the toolbars (the Color Toolbars option), display large buttons (the Large Buttons option), or show the tool button names (the Show ToolTips option).

Tip   Use the Large Buttons option if you use a high resolution video display, such as 1024×768. This makes the buttons a little larger, helping you to see and use them better.

4. If you want to add specific buttons to (or delete them from) a toolbar, click on the Customize button. This displays the Customize dialog box (see fig. 14.6).

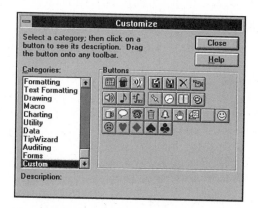

Figure 14.6
Add buttons to a toolbar using the Customize dialog box.

5. In the Categories list box, click on the category that contains the button you want to add. The Buttons area changes to display the buttons included in the selected category.

   You might, for instance, want to add the double-underline button to the Formatting toolbar. To do so, click on Text Formatting in the Categories list box.

6. To see the button's function, click on the button in the Buttons area. A brief description of the button's function appears at the bottom of the dialog box.

7. Grab the button you want to add to the toolbar and drag the button to where you want it. If, for example, you want to place the double-underline button between the italic (I) and the underline (U) buttons on the Formatting toolbar, drag the double-underline button there and release the mouse button.

Cleaning Up a Crowded Toolbar

If you get carried away or your display is not large (you might be using standard VGA display or a laptop display, for instance), your toolbars might get too crowded or disappear off the right side of the screen. If this happens, you need to clean up your toolbar and move around or remove some toolbar buttons. You also can resize the width of a pull-down list box—the Font pull-down list box, for example.

To remove or move a button, perform the following steps:

1. Select View, Toolbars, Customize to display the Customize dialog box.

2. To remove a button, drag the button you want to remove off the toolbar and drop it onto the worksheet area. This automatically removes the button from the interface.

3. To move a button, drag the button that you want to move and drop it in its new place on the toolbar. You should drag it so that its center is placed between the buttons where you want it.

4. Click on Close in the Customize dialog box when you are finished reorganizing your toolbars.

Customizing a Button with a Macro

You might create a macro that you want to assign to a button on a toolbar. You can assign it to a built-in button or create your own button. You might, for instance, create a macro that assigns various formatting features to a selected cell or range of cells. You then can create a toolbar button using the Button Editor and assign the macro to it.

To assign a macro to a built-in or custom button, perform the following steps:

1. Make sure the toolbar that contains the button you want to modify is on your screen.

2. Select View, Toolbars. This displays the Toolbars dialog box. Click on Customize to bring up the Customize dialog box.

3. Select the button you want to assign the macro to and drag it to the toolbar. If you want to use a custom button and place it on the Formatting toolbar, for example, click on Custom in the Categories list, pick one of the buttons, and drag it to the Formatting toolbar.

4. Select Tools, Assign Macro from the menu bar. The Assign Macro dialog box appears, as shown in figure 14.7. If you are assigning a macro to a Custom button, the Assign Macro dialog box displays automatically.

5. Click on the macro name you want to assign in the Macro Name/Reference list.

6. Press Enter or click on OK to return to the Customize dialog box. Click on Close or press Enter. This displays the active worksheet.

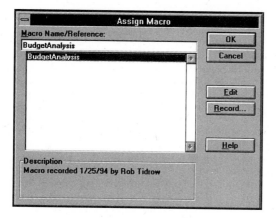

Figure 14.7
Assigning a macro
to a toolbar button
with the Assign
Macro dialog box.

Designing Your Own Toolbar

Suppose, for example, that you don't want to use any of the built-in toolbars that Excel provides. This might be the case if you have several customized buttons that you created (see the following section on creating your own buttons) or you just want to group certain buttons together.

To design your own toolbar, perform the following steps:

1. Select View, Toolbars to bring up the Toolbars dialog box.

2. In the Toolbar Name field box, type the name of the new toolbar you want to create, such as **Quick Tools** (see fig. 14.8). Use as many characters and spaces as you like in the name.

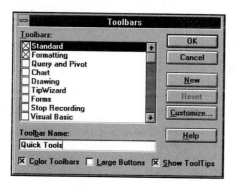

Figure 14.8
Naming the new
toolbar in the
Toolbar Name
field box.

3. Click on the New button, which places the toolbar on the screen.

4. The Customize dialog box appears, with a toolbar large enough to fit one button on it. From the Buttons group, drag any buttons you want onto the new toolbar.

5. After you place all the buttons, click on Close. The new toolbar displays, with the buttons available for use.

Figure 14.9 shows an example of a custom toolbar with several buttons added to it.

Figure 14.9
Adding buttons to
a custom toolbar.

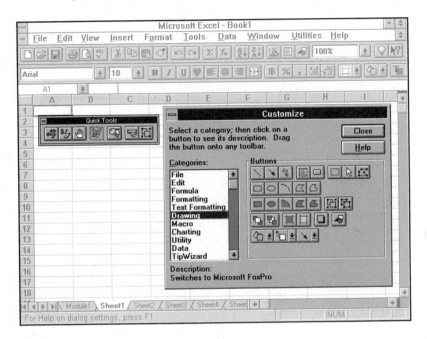

Designing Your Own Buttons

Excel 5 enables you to draw your own toolbar buttons or modify existing ones using the Button Editor. If you have ever used an icon editor or Woody Leonard's WOPR utility, you'll feel at home with the Button Editor.

The following steps show you how to use the Button Editor:

1. If you want to modify a button, make sure its toolbar is displayed.

2. Select View, Toolbars to display the Toolbars dialog box.

3. Right-click on the button you want to edit and choose Edit Button Image from the menu. This displays the Button Editor dialog box (see fig. 14.10).

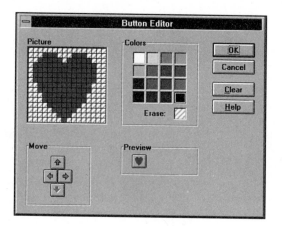

Figure 14.10
Use the Button Editor to create your own button face.

If you want to create a new button, click on the Clear button in the Button Editor dialog box.

4. In the Colors area, click on a color. Next, click on the boxes in the Picture area to create the picture that you want to appear on the button. Use the Preview area to see what the actual button looks like.

5. Continue clicking on the colors you want to finish the drawing. Press Enter or click on OK to place the finished button on the toolbar.

Assigning Toolbars to Workbooks

Let's say you want to assign a toolbar to a specific workbook. Or, you want to trade toolbars with a friend or co-worker. To execute both of these tasks, you must attach the toolbar to a workbook. Perform the following steps:

1. Open the workbook file to which you want to attach the toolbar.

2. Activate the Visual Basic module by switching to a Visual Basic module or selecting Insert, Macro, Module.

3. Select Tools, Attach Toolbar to display the Attach Toolbars dialog box (see fig. 14.11).

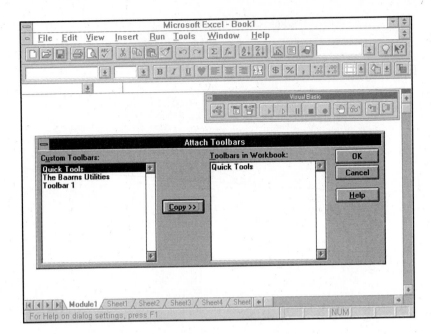

Figure 14.11
Attaching custom
toolbars to
workbooks using
the Attach
Toolbars dialog
box.

4. Click on the toolbars you want to attach in the Custom Toolbars list box.

5. Select Copy. Excel places the name(s) in the Toolbars in Workbook list box.

6. When you finish adding names to the Toolbars in Workbook list, press Enter or click on OK.

7. Save the workbook.

Floating Toolbars

Excel 5 enables you to reposition toolbars to fit your editing needs. You might, for instance, like to have certain toolbars handier than others. One way to keep them close at hand is to tear them off the top of the screen and let them float on your desktop.

To tear off a toolbar, move the mouse pointer to a blank area on the toolbar, grab the toolbar, and drag it onto the worksheet area. Release the mouse. The toolbar becomes a floating "toolbox" that stays visible on your screen as you enter and edit data. You can grab the title bar of the toolbar and move it around as you do any other Windows window. See figure 14.12 for examples of floating toolbars.

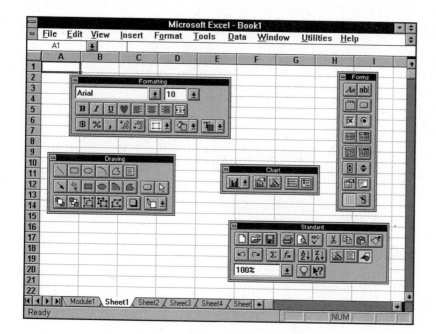

Figure 14.12
Floating toolbars
to the extreme.

To place the floating toolbar back on top of the screen, grab the toolbar, drag it to the top of the screen where you want to place it (it must be above the worksheet area), and drop it. The toolbar elongates into a rectangular object to help you get an idea of where it will be placed when you release the mouse button.

II

Excel

Chapter Snapshot

The Microsoft Office Package incorporates two powerful and exciting common features within each application: automating tasks and customizing applications and functions. Each application in the Microsoft Office—both Standard and Professional versions—includes a new, easy-to-use language for customizing, simplifying, and automating routine tasks. The language is called Visual Basic for Applications (VBA).

This chapter covers the following topics:

VBA itself is not new. In fact, it has been around for some time. Microsoft has taken the best of VBA and written a version of it that is easy to use and learn, flexible, and powerful. In this chapter, you learn about VBA in general, and how to record, edit, and troubleshoot macros. You also will learn about some of the ways to customize Excel using VBA.

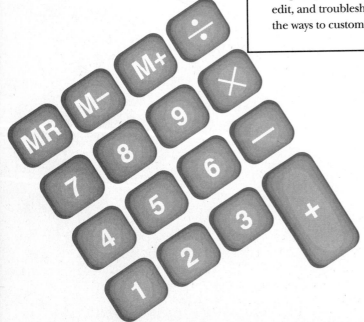

CHAPTER 15

Mastering Visual Basic for Applications

by Critch Greaves

Probably the most widely used feature of Visual Basic for Applications (VBA) is macros. *Macros* are shortcuts—instructions that are recorded and played back to tell Excel what to do. VBA does an excellent job of simplifying the process of recording and playing back these instructions.

Excel has extensive on-line help available for VBA, and if you plan on doing much with this powerful language, this is a good place to begin learning some of its capabilities.

To get help information for VBA, choose Contents from the Help menu. You will see toward the bottom of the screen the topic Programming with VBA. Click on this topic, and you will be led to answers to all your VBA questions—and more. There is information about common tasks and operations using VBA, functions, Excel objects in VBA, properties associated with objects, methods associated with objects, common statements, keywords and the tasks they perform, and much more information.

In the VBA Reference, most of the help information is related to keywords and their functions, operation, use, syntax, and so on. One of the things that makes VBA so powerful is that in the help section on a particular keyword, you can find related topics, examples of code that can be compared or even copied into your own code, descriptions, elements, and remarks.

If you are familiar with macros and the Excel 4 macro language, you will want to evaluate the new language carefully. Excel 5 fully supports Excel 4's language, so all macros written in Excel 4 will work with Excel 5. The language has been updated to support the new features of Excel as well.

You still can create macro sheets and record and write macros in the previous language, and there is full online help. Microsoft will not, however, update the language in future releases of Excel.

If you want old macros to work with newer programs, you might want to consider rewriting the macros in VBA. Another option is to set up a call to the old macro language from VBA modules. There is not a translation from the previous language to VBA.

Understanding Macro Concepts

A macro automates tasks that you perform regularly. As you work, you will find that there are certain tasks that you do repeatedly, such as typing a certain phrase, heading, number, or group of numbers. Anything that you do on a regular basis can be a possible candidate for a macro. In this section, you will record some simple macros, run them, look at them, and figure out ways you can make use of macros in your applications.

Recording a macro is not a difficult task, once you have an idea about what it can do and how you can use it. Think about how the toolbar works, and how using some of its features speeds things along. Macros work the same way—they help automate routine functions.

For your first few macros, you might want to experiment with the processes; but in general, once you get the hang of it, the process becomes very simple and straightforward.

The macro recorder can be turned on prior to opening a workbook. For this example, you will learn to create a macro to open a new worksheet, rename the first four sheets, and set up data-entry fields on them. The first thing you need to do is close any workbooks and save them so that you have everything in Excel closed except the File and Help menus. Closing worksheets is not an essential part of macro creation; you'll do it just for this example.

Select Record New Macro from the File menu to display the Record New Macro dialog box. The system will provide you with a suggested name of Macro#. Then, click on the Options button. Your screen should look something like figure 15.1.

Excel defaults to Macro1 for the name of the macro, where the *1* at the end of the name is the next number available that can make it a unique name. Using the suggestions for macro names might not be very descriptive, but you can organize your macros in other ways within your personal macro sheet.

On the main screen, you have several choices you can make about your macro prior to recording it. You can choose a different name, and you can change the description. These

default to the user name from Excel's setup and a nondescriptive statement that this is a macro. You also can assign the macro to the Tools menu from here with whatever description you want to give it. You can assign a shortcut key to the macro, which defaults to Ctrl+E unless you have already assigned Ctrl+E to something else. You can add additional keys to the keyboard shortcut; for example, holding down the Shift key and typing **E** makes Ctrl+Shift+E become the shortcut keystroke combination.

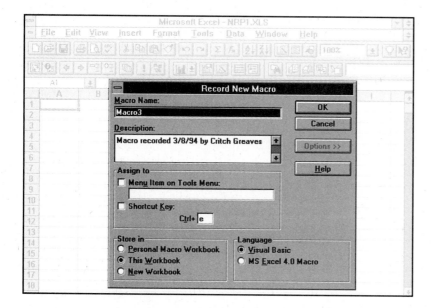

Figure 15.1
Excel's Record New Macro dialog box.

II

Excel

You can store the macro in one of three places:

- ✔ A personal macro book
- ✔ This workbook
- ✔ A new workbook

Most macros probably should be saved in your personal macro book, which keeps them available for wherever you are working. It is, however, a choice you need to make based on the task at hand.

The last item to decide is the language you will use. For obvious reasons, the macros you create in this chapter will use VBA.

Tip

If, in your macro-recording session, the AutoSave add-in displays and asks if you want to save your sheet, it will come up each time you run your macro. If you do not want this to happen, you can edit the code to remove that function from the macro.

To begin the recording process, click on OK. The Stop Recording toolbar, which consists of one button, appears. The status line at the bottom of the screen indicates that you are recording. To use VBA to record your macro, use the mouse and keyboard to do the tasks you want to save as an automated task. When you are finished, click on the Stop Recording button.

If you assign the macro to the Tools menu, it will show up there with the name you gave it. If you give it a keyboard shortcut, the combination of the keystrokes you assign it should run it as well. For this example, call the Tools menu name **New Sales Sheet**, and the keyboard shortcut Ctrl+U, and click on OK. Next, perform the following steps:

1. Open a new workbook by selecting New from the File menu. Choose Workbook, OK, and Excel will open a new book for you.

2. Double-click on the Sheet 1 tab and rename the sheet North. Rename the second sheet South, the third East, and the fourth West. When you are finished, click on the North worksheet again.

3. Make cell B1 active, and type **January** in it. Using the AutoFill feature, drag the handle to M1.

4. Go to cell A3, and enter the words **Hardware**, **Software**, **Service**, **Rental**, and **Other** in column A.

5. Highlight the entire area from A1:M8, position the cursor over the selected area, and click the right mouse button. Select Copy from the cells menu.

6. Click on the South worksheet. Hold down the Ctrl key, and click again on the East and West sheet tabs. Press Enter to select the destinations you just chose.

7. Click on the Stop Recording button, and your macro is finished.

To test it and make sure it recorded properly, run it and verify the results. First, close the sheet you just created and open a new one. Then, from the Tools menu, choose Macro. Choose PERSONAL.XLS!Macro1 from the macro list, and click on Run. Your macro should now do all the functions that you recorded.

You can add a help line to the Tools menu and change the help status line, and even add a help file with a special editor. To add the help line, select Macro from the Tools menu. Choose the macro name PERSONAL.XLS!Macro1 and click on the Options button. In the Options dialog box, you can edit the same options that you did when you set up your macro. When editing after macro creation, however, you also can set up a few other options.

You can specify a help line for your macro that will show in the status line at the bottom of the screen when your item on the Tools menu is highlighted. This appears in the same location in the dialog box as the file location choices on the original options before recording (see fig. 15.2).

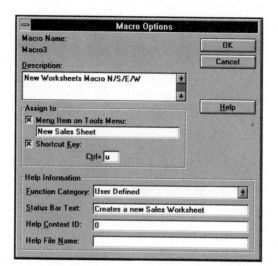

Figure 15.2
The Macro Options dialog box for macros that already have been recorded.

After your macro is recorded, you can run it by selecting Macro from the Tools menu, selecting your macro, and clicking on the Run button. Or, you can run your macro by selecting Name from the Tools menu or by using the keyboard combination. All these methods have been used and set up as part of the recording process or editing process. You also can assign your macro to an existing toolbar that appears on Excel's main screen, or to a graphic button or object somewhere in a worksheet.

Assigning a Macro to a Toolbar

Assigning a macro to a toolbar is a great way to keep your macros close and useful. As you will experience, though, the more the worksheet and software do for you, the more you will find for them to do.

VBA, Excel, and the rest of the Microsoft Office package take full advantage of the toolbars and VBA integration. Through VBA, you can create much more than just macros.

Deciding where you want to place your macro for most effective access is an important step in creating and using automation in Excel. The good news is that you can choose one or all of the locations, so regardless of where you place your macro, you can get to it to use it. If you are not pleased with its location, you always can change it.

You already assigned your first macro to the Tools menu and to a keyboard shortcut. The next step is to assign it to a toolbar button.

From the View menu, select Toolbars, then the Customize option. At this point, you need to decide whether you want your macro to be assigned to a button on an existing toolbar or to a toolbar that you create. For this exercise, you should create your own toolbar. To do this, in the Categories section of the Customize box, scroll down until you see the Custom category.

For the Custom List, a group of buttons appears on the right side of the window; you can use any of them to represent the macro you have recorded. To assign a macro to a button on this custom toolbar, select the button you want, click and drag it to an open spot on the toolbar area, and the Assign Macro dialog box will become active.

At this point, you can click on the macro name you want to select and click on OK, and the macro will be assigned to the button on the custom toolbar, which now is called Toolbar 1.

You also can bring up the Customize dialog box by clicking the right mouse button anywhere on the toolbar area. This brings up the Toolbar menu, and Customize is shown at the bottom. You also can display or suppress the display of any toolbar this way.

If you drag a button into the toolbar area, you can assign the macro to it by the method described previously. When the Customize dialog box is active, clicking the right mouse button on any button on any toolbar also activates the button shortcut menu. From this menu you can assign macros; cut, copy, or reset the button image; or even edit the image of the button to create your own customized buttons for easy recognition.

Tip
When you are in the customize mode, clicking on any button on any toolbar will show the definition or function of that button in the bottom of the window, regardless of the category of toolbar.

Use the Button Editor to edit the button image and customize your macro buttons. While in the customize mode, click the right mouse button on the button you want to customize or edit, and choose the edit image choice from the menu to display the Button Editor dialog box (see fig. 15.3).

In the Button Editor box, you can select colors, change the overall design, move the image on the button, and get a preview of the changes as you work.

After your macro is assigned, clicking on this button in any worksheet invokes the macro.

Editing Your Macro

Now that you have recorded at least one macro, you need to find out how to edit it. Advanced users will want to take the VBA code and write their own applications, add-ins, macros, and functions. Less-experienced users might want to automate a few tasks at some point.

Editing macros is done from the same menu as the options menus, with which you already are familiar. Because you saved your first macro to the PERSONAL.XLS sheet, you need to unhide the worksheet to edit the macros saved on your personal macro sheet.

If you have at least one workbook open, the Unhide option is available in the Window menu;

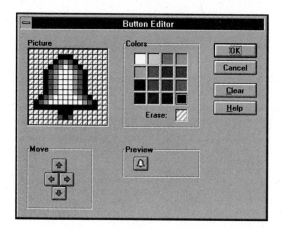

Figure 15.3
The Button Editor
dialog box.

otherwise, it can be found on the File menu. After the sheet is unhidden, if you save the changes to the sheet when you exit Excel, the PERSONAL.XLS workbook will appear automatically the next time you begin the program. To get back to the original format after editing, choose Hide from the Window menu and close Excel.

Macros placed on the personal workbook can be edited easily after the workbook is unhidden. Macros are placed in areas called *modules,* either in workbooks or in their own sections, such as the PERSONAL.XLS workbook. The module is an area that is especially suited for VBA code and nothing else. When Excel has a VBA module displayed, the menu selections change, and some of the functionalities of the commands change to programming instead of workbook tasks.

Getting to the modules to edit your code can be done using the Macro Edit feature (once PERSONAL.XLS is unhidden) or, if a macro is written to a module on the current workbook, by clicking on its tab. The tabs are clearly labeled Module 1, Module 2, and so on, and if you choose to have a macro recorded on the current workbook, the module is placed at the end of the current worksheets by default.

After you have the module to which your macro is written loaded and active, you can make additions and edits to your macro text. At the top of the module is the description of what you have prepared. It can be edited if you want the description to change. The macro name also appears here, in the headings. Changing that information will have no effect on the operation of the macro. The guts of the code lie between the first word in blue type, Sub, and the last words, End Sub.

The green text at the top is informational, and can be edited and changed without too much problem. Visual Basic tracks this section as information because of the apostrophe (') at the beginning of the line. While you edit in this area, the text changes color as you actually begin to edit or add information. Upon completion, provided you have preceded the line with an apostrophe, it returns to green when you leave the line.

If you enter a line that is information, but you forget to put the leading apostrophe, you likely will receive an error message to the effect that what you have entered is not a valid keyword or statement, or there is some other VBA error. This is another special feature of the modules.

The material in the middle, between Sub and End Sub, is a collection of statements and instructions. VBA has numerous instructions and statements it can perform. To find out how they work, you can invoke the VBA Reference. One easy way to do this is to highlight a word in your macro that you want to learn about. You can highlight Sub if you wish. Then press F1. If there is a reference to this word in the VBA Reference, it will be displayed at this time. If there is no reference, the main menu will be displayed.

While you are in the module, you can adjust the screen setup and macro display. As with several screens in other applications, you can split the window into separate areas. This can be done by choosing the Window, Split menu choice, or by double-clicking or dragging the split bar located at the top of the vertical scroll bar.

If it would be helpful, you can add comments to your code as it is entered. This might help you track a procedure down later. To do this, position the cursor at the end of the code line to which you want to add a comment. Press Enter twice. Enter a single apostrophe, and type a comment about the field.

VBA takes the comment and stores it along with your code. You can use standard movement keys to move the cursor in VBA. The Ctrl key in conjunction with the arrows, for example, moves the cursor one word to the right or left.

Sometimes, when you record a macro, you might include a step that you want to get rid of down the road. If that is the case, you use the edit mode.

You can use code that was written in other macros within your own, if needed. You can find existing code in the VBA Reference, which can be copied from online help to your modules.

To do this, invoke the VBA Reference and find the process that you want to do. At the top of each section, you will see, in green letters, See also and Example. Click on Example. There is some sample code written for the function you are working on so that you can get a better feel for the code and the way it is supposed to look and feel in your modules.

Another powerful editing feature of VBA is the capability of recording a macro and inserting it as new code in an existing macro. To do this, perform the following steps:

1. Click on the point at which you want the code to be inserted.

2. Select Record Macro from the Tools menu, and choose Mark Position for Recording.

3. Switch to the sheet on which you want to record your actions.

4. Choose Tools, Record Macro, Record at Mark, and record your actions.

5. When you are finished, click on the Stop Macro button and the code will be updated. The new VBA code will be inserted where you marked the code.

You also can enter a text file of code into a macro by selecting Insert, File and choosing the file you wish to include. Then click on OK.

Switching with a Macro

Macros can act as a toggle for an operation. If you create a simple macro that changes the display of a worksheet, and you want the macro to change it from one status to the next—such as turning the bold font on and off with the use of only one button—use the Not keyword. Using Not works to switch the status of a line where appropriate. To do this for a display of gridlines on a worksheet, for example, type the following:

```
Sub DisplayGridlines()

ActiveWindow.DisplayGridlines = False


End Sub
```

To make this macro work as a toggle to turn gridlines on with one click and off with the next click, change the lines to read like the following:

```
Sub ToggleGridlines ()

ActiveWindow.DisplayGridlines = Not
ActiveWindow.DisplayGridlines

End Sub
```

Interactive Macros

Macros can be made interactive as well. You can have your macro ask you or others for input. Interaction is accomplished through the use of an input box. To see what an example of the code looks like, type the word **inputbox** on your VBA module, select it with the mouse, and press F1. This invokes the VBA Reference.

A selection box will come up, prompting you to select VBA:Input box or Excel:Inputbox. Click on Visual Basic for Applications:Inputbox, and click on OK.

A help screen about Inputbox for VBA appears, with a full explanation of how input boxes work. At the top of the screen, See Also and Example are displayed in green letters; click on Example. This activates an example of how the function can be used. The VBA Reference Example window has three buttons located in the upper right corner of the dialog box: Close, Copy, and Print. Click on the Copy button. This brings up a sample of the code (see fig. 15.4), which you can highlight with the mouse and copy to the Clipboard (using the copy button in the next window). Then you can bring it into your own module so that you can practice and learn from the example.

Figure 15.4
Copying sample code from VBA Reference.

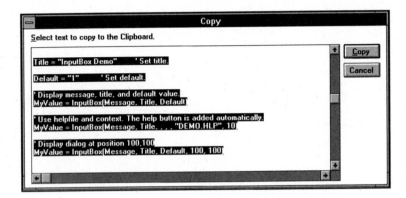

If you want to print your topic, press the Print button or choose File, Print. Referring to a printed copy can be handy in documenting errors, troubleshooting, or working on your code when you are not at your keyboard.

You can perform customization items in your modules as well, such as changing the colors of the elements of your code; changing the way your code looks; and changing the automatic formatting, such as automatic tabbing, that VBA will do for you.

To begin customization, select Options from the Tools menu, then choose Module General or Module Format. In the Module Format section, you can change the font that is used in your modules, the size that the font uses, and the colors that various code elements appear in (Comments, Code, and so on). From the Module General tab you can specify whether VBA will *autotab*, which means that the code on the next line will be at the same indentation as the preceding line. You also can specify the width of the tab (default is 4, max is 40), break options, and syntax checking, and require variable declaration.

The break option has VBA stop on all errors, and the syntax-checking option automatically reviews each line of code as it is entered for the correct syntax. Require Variable Declaration specifies whether or not each variable must be declared explicitly.

There also are international settings you can adjust if needed for multinational use.

Creating User-Defined Functions

VBA also enables you to create and use your own customized functions, as referred to in Chapter 10, "Mastering Excel Functions." User-defined functions are like other Excel functions, except that you can specify exactly what they do. User-defined functions can combine

mathematical expressions, text, dates, logical and other values, Excel functions, and VBA to return the values you need from your data.

This can be an especially handy tool to use if you have formulas that are long and complex, because they can be reduced to a single function, making them easier to use and remember. User-defined functions also are more accurate because you do not need to remember each step when you want to use them; all you need to do is insert the function and Excel does the rest.

As with macros, functions are designed in a VBA module. Unlike macros, however, functions cannot be recorded and do not perform actions—they merely return values. On the module, they begin with `Function` and end with `End Function`, whereas macros begin with `Sub` and complete with `End Sub`.

The syntax for most user-defined functions is `Function argument1, argument2` and so on. You also can create functions that do not require any arguments.

VBA statements, called *assignment statements*, are similar to worksheet function statements, with a few differences. VBA statements begin with a variable name and an equal sign, followed by the function statement:

```
NetSales = (Territory1 + Territory2)
```

In this statement, `NetSales` is the variable, and `Territory1` and `Territory2` are the arguments being used in the calculation. You can include `If`, `For`, and `Do` statements in user-defined functions as well. To figure a bonus of three percent on sales over 100,000, for example, the following function statement would be used:

```
Function BONUS(Territory1, Territory2)

  NetSales = (Territory1 + Territory2)
  If NetSales >= 100000 Then
      BONUS = NetSales * 0.03
  Else
    BONUS = NetSales * 0#
  End If


  End Function
```

Figure 15.5 shows the Function Wizard step for performing this user-defined function.

You can assign your function to one of Excel's categories of functions to make the function more accessible. Move to the module where the function is located and, from the View menu, choose Object Browser. The Object Browser dialog box first asks you to select the macro or function that you want to assign. Then you can choose a category or create a new one, and place your function there.

By default, Excel puts user-defined functions in the User Defined category.

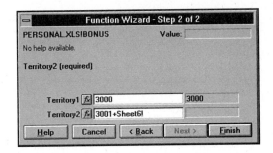

Figure 15.5
The Function Wizard, showing the new user-defined function BONUS.

Working with VBA Procedures

So far you have used VBA modules to input macros and functions. There is another way to refer to instructions entered in VBA: procedures. Procedures can be either macros or functions but are slightly different in scope than either of them.

Procedures are classified as code that performs some type of activity or returns a value as a subroutine of a macro or function. Procedures can be called from a macro or function, and can be located anywhere within Excel in a VBA module.

Generally, when you want to automate a process, the most effective way to do it is to break that process down into subprocesses. This makes sense from the programming perspective, because smaller chunks of a task are easier to conceive, troubleshoot, and manage than their larger counterparts.

In simple format, the grouping of processes in Excel Visual Basic is very easy to do. A sample of such a grouping might look like the following:

```
Sub Territory()
     CalcTotals
     RunCommRpt
     RunInvent
     FigureBonus
     PrntRecaps
End Sub
```

This routine, or group of procedures, can be assigned to a button on a custom toolbar that breaks up the macro into the following tasks:

✔ Calls `CalcTotals` (a macro that gets data from a dBASE data file, using MS Query), puts it into a worksheet, and figures sales totals by person and by month

✔ Calls `RunCommRpt`, another VBA routine that calculates the commissions for each rep, based on the values from the first `CalcTotals` macro

✔ Calls `RunInvent`, the inventory run, which, based on the sales from the totals sheet, prints a list of the items that need to be reordered or inventoried

✔ Calls FigureBonus, which takes the information from RunCommRpt and, for those who qualify based on sales volumes, calculates the bonuses and generates a worksheet for accounting

✔ Calls PrntRecaps, which generates a listing by sales rep for each customer, along with the amount of the sales and the types of products purchased

When Excel calls a subroutine, it can look anywhere to find it. It starts in the module where the original call is, then looks in other modules in the active workbook, in other active sheets, and in other modules on the disk. A module can be called from anywhere. You need to plan carefully what your modules are named and who needs to use them.

You can make a module private if you know that it is not going to be used outside a specific workbook. To make a module private, select the module and type **Option Private Module** prior to any code.

Tip

Your organization of modules should make sense and be documented as you create your procedures so that when you go back to update, fix, or modify, the areas that are affected are easy to find.

Looking At VBA Objects

VBA uses objects to enable you to control what you want to have happen. An *object* is something that has a use, such as a worksheet. Objects have *properties*, and the control of the properties determines partially how your objects will respond. Objects also have *methods*, or actions that objects can do.

Understanding Properties

The reason for using VBA code is to control your objects. The code typically refers to changing some property so that your object looks or does something different. ColumnWidth, for example, is a property because you can control the width of a column automatically by using VBA. The following are some of the more common properties:

✔ **ActiveCell.** The active cell of the active window.

✔ **ActiveSheet.** The active sheet of the active workbook.

✔ **ActiveWorkbook.** The active workbook in Excel.

✔ **Bold or Italic.** The type style displayed by a font.

✔ **Column or Row.** A number that identifies the area of a range.

✔ **ColumnWidth.** The width of all columns in a specified range.

✔ **Height or Width.** The size of an object in points.

✔ **RowHeight.** The height of all rows in a range specified in points.

✔ **Selection.** The object selected in the active window.

✔ **Value.** The value of a cell.

VBA works with ranges, not individual cells. To work with an individual cell, VBA uses a range that contains only one cell.

Understanding Methods

Methods are the actions used on the properties of objects to modify how something looks, or to control the actions that take place on the object.

VBA methods include Calculate, Clear, Copy, and Justify. The syntax used for these arguments in your VBA code is the following:

```
object.method
```

If a method takes arguments, the arguments are listed after the method:

```
object.method (arguments)
```

VBA works with objects and collections of objects to automate the processes you want to simplify within your work environment.

Examining Types of Errors in VBA

As you work with VBA code, errors sometimes creep up. VBA provides a number of debugging tools that can help you trap and fix errors in code. You need to learn about the following three types of errors to understand how to debug VBA code:

✔ Language

✔ Run-time

✔ Logic

A *language error* could be one of punctuation, spacing, or misspelling. VBA detects errors in language before you run the code if that option is turned on in the options tab, discussed earlier in this chapter.

Run-time errors are encountered when VBA tries to carry out a task that is impossible to do. This might occur if your code refers to a range of cells when there is not an active worksheet open and, therefore, no cells available.

Logic errors occur when your code may work, but not as you had intended. Logic errors also can contain run-time errors.

There are four buttons on the VBA toolbar that can be helpful in debugging code:

✔ Instant Watch

✔ Toggle Breakpoint

✔ Step Into

✔ Step Over

Instant Watch shows the current value of an expression while the code is stopped in break mode. Toggle Breakpoint enables you to set a point in your code at which operation is halted. Step Into runs only one line of code, and if the code calls another procedure, the view changes to the called code. Step Over runs the next line of code, and if a call to another procedure occurs, does not shift your view to the other called procedure.

The *break mode* occurs when running code stops and enters the troubleshooting mode of VBA. The break mode is entered when one of the following occurs:

✔ Your code has a breakpoint listed in it

✔ Your code has a Stop command

✔ Your code has an untrapped run-time error

You also can enter the break mode manually by pressing Ctrl+Break or Esc during the running of the code. To insert a breakpoint in your code, select the line at which you want operation of the code to halt. Then from the VBA toolbar, click on the Toggle Breakpoint button. You also can insert a breakpoint from the Run menu. When you set a breakpoint, VBA highlights the line of code and bolds the text that falls at the breakpoint.

Entering a Stop command in your code does the same thing as switching a breakpoint. There is one major difference, however: when you close and reopen a worksheet with your code, all breakpoints are cleared. Stop statements remain a part of the code until you actually remove them (see fig. 15.6).

Figure 15.6
Code with two
breakpoints
entered.

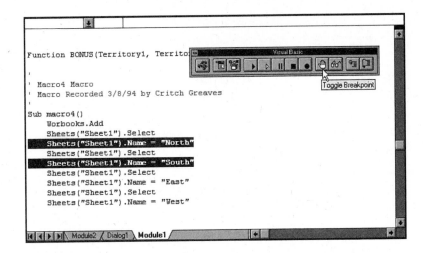

When errors occur in code, a Macro Error dialog box appears (see fig. 15.7). From this box, you can choose to halt execution (End), Continue, Debug, Goto (a specific area of the code), or get Help.

Figure 15.7
A run-time error
dialog box.

Figure 15.7 shows the dialog box for run-time errors. If you choose Debug, the debug window shows the code in the lower portion and one of two panes in the upper half of the window (see fig. 15.8). The top pane can be either the Immediate pane or the Watch pane.

Figure 15.8
The Debug
window, with the
Immediate pane
active.

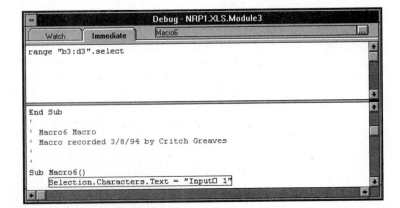

The Debug window's panes can be used for two different functions. The Watch pane, made active by selecting the Watch tab in the top portion of the window, enables you to view an operation or code that returns a result with the expression, the value returned, and the context in which it is used.

The Immediate pane, on the other hand, is used to evaluate sections of code you enter into the window directly for troubleshooting purposes. You can type a statement to see the immediate effect of the code on the operation at hand. There is a wipe bar between the two windows that you can use to enlarge or reduce the size of the windows so that you can get a better view of your code or a better view of the active pane at the top (see fig. 15.9).

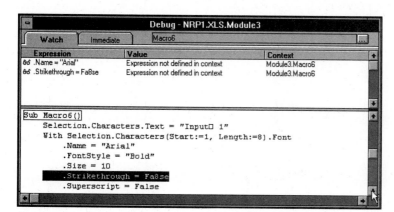

Figure 15.9
The Watch pane of the Debug window.

You can select a portion of your code to run in order to troubleshoot it. Select the module tab of the sheet that contains the code to be run, and highlight the code with the mouse. Then, click on the Step Into button on the VBA toolbar. This immediately invokes the Debug window and enables you to evaluate the execution of the macro one step at a time. By pressing the Resume Macro button on the toolbar, you can complete the procedure.

Additionally, you can highlight the entire macro or procedure and click on the Run Macro button on the toolbar. This begins execution of the code.

There are numerous types of VBA code examples illustrated in the VBA Reference. As you define the procedures you want to run, browsing through the code and examples will help you get a better idea of what is involved in creating macros, functions, and procedures.

Creating and Customizing Menus

You can use VBA in Excel to customize menus for all levels of your applications. Custom menus can be created and edited to suit your own applications and needs. After you become comfortable with Excel, you can remove items that you do not use, or put them on other menus for less frequently accessed functions.

Use the Menu Editor to make the customized changes to a menu system or to create your own unique system. To begin the Menu Editor, first select a VBA module tab of a worksheet or PERSONAL.XLS. From the Tools menu, select Menu Editor to display the Menu Editor dialog box (see fig. 15.10).

Figure 15.10
The Menu Editor
dialog box.

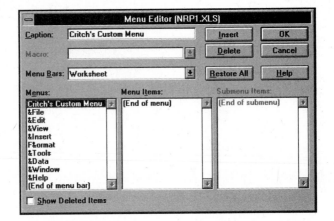

The Menu Editor is a great tool to customize Excel. It can be useful for the advanced and beginning user by taking the items that you use most frequently—or that might not appear on a menu at all—and adding them to the menu. It also can be used to take away the stuff you do not need.

The Caption text box refers to the title of the menu selection you want to modify or add to. The ampersand (&) preceding the selection in the Menus list box designates the keyboard equivalent of the command. For instance, pressing Alt+W invokes the Window menu, which is shown on the list of menus as &Windows. If you changed that to display Window&s, the Alt+S combination would be the keyboard equivalent of the command.

Clicking on the menu you want to edit brings up a list of menu and submenu items for the main menu. The control buttons at the upper right of the Menu Editor dialog box enable you to insert new items, depending on what section of the window you have active. You also can delete items from the menu, restore all the changes, cancel them, and get online help about the process. In addition, you can assign macros that you have created using VBA to the menu system, just as you can by attaching a macro to the Tool menu from the Edit Macro dialog box you learned about earlier in this chapter.

You might have noticed that when you change sections of the program, such as from a worksheet to a module, the menu selections change as well. Using the Menu Editor, you can modify seven menu bars:

✔ Worksheet

✔ Chart

✔ No Documents Open

✔ Visual Basic

✔ Shortcut Menu 1

✔ Shortcut Menu 2

✔ Shortcut Menu 3

You can add an entirely new menu to the main menu by selecting the Caption box and typing a new name, with & for the keyboard shortcut. Then click on Insert. Move to the Menu Items list box and insert the items you want to add to your menu. If you want items to have submenus, insert them in the Submenu Items list box.

The highlighted option in the Menus window when you click on Insert to add a new menu item indicates where the new item will appear on your menu bar. Inserting at the top will make your menu choice be first on the bar, and inserting at the bottom of the list will make your menu selection be last.

To create a separator bar on your menus, type a hyphen (-) after the items you wish to separate.

The Menu Editor modifies only the menu of the workbook that is active when you invoke it.

To make a menu change more permanent or show it on all worksheets and workbooks, choose the PERSONAL.XLS sheet when you do your menu editing. Make sure when your changes are complete that you save your sheet, and if you do not want it to be opened each time you begin Excel, hide it from the Windows menu prior to saving the file.

By using VBA, you also can control the menu and toolbar appearance and functionality of Excel's menu system. There are numerous ways to modify which menus are activated and which ones are dimmed, how they appear, and when they can be used. The scope of the modifications is beyond the scope of this book; however, for even more in-depth discussion on VBA, see *Inside Excel 5 for Windows* and *Understanding Visual Basic 3 for Windows*, both from New Riders Publishing.

Part Three

PowerPoint

Chapter Snapshot

PowerPoint is a presentation software program that helps you quickly and easily create professional-quality presentations. Your presentations can be transferred onto plain paper, color or black-and-white overheads, or 35mm slides, or they can be shown on a video screen or computer monitor. To complete your presentation package, PowerPoint's printing options include formats ranging from audience handouts to speaker's notes.

This chapter discusses the following topics:

This chapter will get you up to speed and comfortable with PowerPoint in a short period of time. The explanation behind many exercises is brief; the remaining chapters in Part Three discuss PowerPoint's features in more detail.

Marketing Statistics
for Computer Book Publishing

1994

16 CHAPTER

PowerPoint Quick Start

by Jodi Davenport

Many PowerPoint design and formatting tools are identical to those in Microsoft Word and Microsoft Excel. If you know how to use these applications, you already know how to use many functions in PowerPoint.

PowerPoint automates many layouts and formatting functions to take the fear out of using a presentation software—even if you are not a professional designer. Preformatted templates and color schemes eliminate the need for time-consuming formatting. PowerPoint Wizards (the AutoContent Wizard and the Pick a Look Wizard) guide first-time presenters through creating first-rate presentations and speed experienced presenters through the building stages. Also, extensive customization enables you to use presentation formats over and over. As you will see, the endless presentation enhancements let you professionalize your work without a lot of hassle.

PowerPoint presentations can be *data-driven*. That is, graphs and charts in PowerPoint presentations can derive, for example, from data in Excel spreadsheets or contain text from Word documents.

Whether you are producing slides, color overheads, black-and-white overheads, plain-paper printouts, or any other format, PowerPoint uses the word *slide* to refer to each individual screen of information in your presentation. Each PowerPoint presentation is a series of slides, each of which contains a graphic or text.

To get started quickly, you will work through creating a 35mm slide presentation about the Shipshape Cruise Lines training program. This training program focuses on handling passenger complaints.

If you haven't already, double-click on the PowerPoint icon to start PowerPoint. PowerPoint opens with the Tip of the Day (see fig. 16.1).

Figure 16.1
PowerPoint's Tip of the Day.

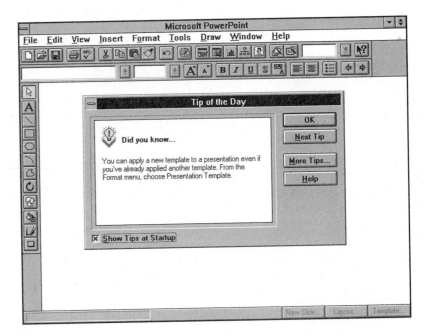

These helpful tips offer suggestions about PowerPoint functions, shortcuts, and slide design. These tips help you quickly learn how to use PowerPoint, and you can access them through the Help menu anytime PowerPoint is open. To see another tip, click on the Next Tip button in the Tip of the Day dialog box. Click on the More Tips button to take you to the Help index. To keep the Tip of the Day dialog box from appearing each time you open PowerPoint, click on the check box in front of Show Tips at Startup at the bottom of the Tip of the Day dialog box to deselect it. When you are done viewing the tips, click on OK.

Choosing a Presentation Format and Entering Presentation Text

The purpose of your presentations can range from discussing strategy to selling a product to delivering bad news. PowerPoint's flexibility enables you to present any kind of information and customize a presentation format. PowerPoint also includes preformatted outlines to help you determine the ideal content of a specific type of presentation. If you are delivering bad news to a group of employees, for example, PowerPoint suggests ways to organize the presentation material to ease the blow.

Using the PowerPoint AutoContent Wizard

After the Tip of the Day, the PowerPoint dialog box appears and presents many paths through which you can begin creating a new PowerPoint presentation (see fig. 16.2).

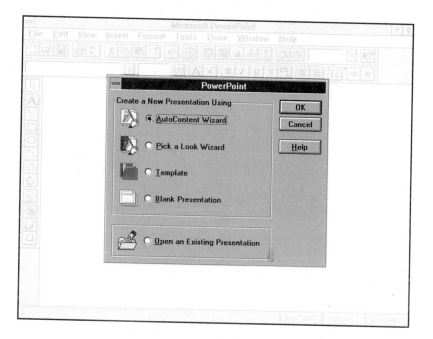

Figure 16.2
PowerPoint offers many paths to help you create a new presentation.

This dialog box appears every time you open PowerPoint, but you can turn it off through the Tools menu. Sometimes when you open PowerPoint, you might want to begin working with a favorite template or go directly to a blank presentation. Or, you can choose to open an existing presentation.

Each of these options will be discussed in later chapters. For this exercise, select AutoContent Wizard and click on OK.

The PowerPoint AutoContent Wizard opens at Step 1 of 4 and explains that the wizard will help you to begin creating a presentation (see fig. 16.3).

The PowerPoint AutoContent Wizard helps you to organize your thoughts and makes suggestions about the content of a presentation based on the type of material you want to cover.

To continue, click on Next to go to Step 2.

The AutoContent Wizard automatically begins by creating the title slide for a presentation. The picture of the title slide shows how the levels of information will appear on the first slide.

First, the AutoContent Wizard asks, "What are you going to talk about?" A flashing cursor waits for you to enter the presentation title. Type **Handling Passenger Complaints**, then press Tab to go to the next text box.

The AutoContent Wizard asks, "What is your name?" This box might already be filled in with your name or a department name because this data comes from the PowerPoint setup information. When you press Tab, any information in the box is highlighted. Type **Shipshape Cruise Lines** to overwrite the highlighted text. Press Tab to proceed to the third text box.

With the current information highlighted, type **Become part of the crew!**. After filling in all three fields, your screen should look like the one in figure 16.4.

Figure 16.3
Step 1 of 4 in the AutoContent Wizard.

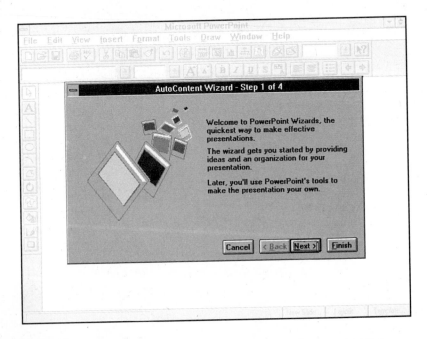

If you want to return to a previous box to change information, press Shift+Tab to highlight the text and type new information. After you have filled in the information, click on Next.

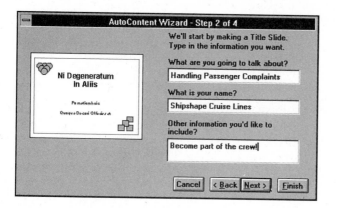

Figure 16.4
Filling in the text boxes.

Tip If you want to go back a step at any time in the AutoContent Wizard, click on **B**ack.

Step 3 of the AutoContent Wizard asks you to choose the type of presentation you are going to give (see fig. 16.5).

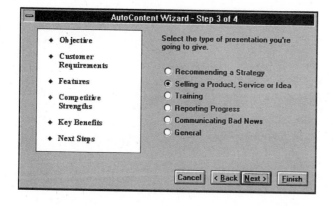

Figure 16.5
Step 3 of the AutoContent Wizard.

The AutoContent Wizard offers six presentation types for you to use:

✔ Recommending a Strategy

✔ Selling a Product, Service or Idea

✔ Training

✔ Reporting Progress

✔ Communicating Bad News

✔ General

The skilled presenter knows that, depending on the presentation type, key information should be delivered to an audience in a certain order. The PowerPoint AutoContent Wizard guides you through building an effective presentation by offering content outlines designed for a particular type of presentation.

For this example, click on the presentation type Communicating Bad News. Notice the bullet points in the white box change when you make the selection, as shown in figure 16.6. Instead of opening a presentation with the bad news, the AutoContent Wizard suggests that you begin by presenting background on the situation to inform the audience.

Figure 16.6
Selecting the presentation type Communicating Bad News changes the suggested content outline.

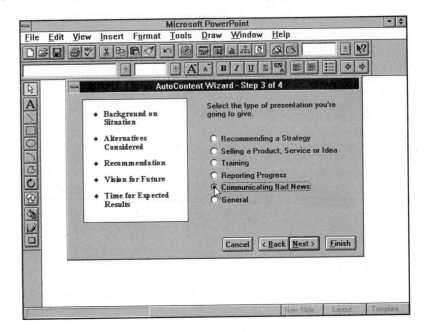

For the Shipshape Cruise Lines training presentation, select the presentation type Training, and note the new content outline (see fig. 16.7).

Click on Next to continue to Step 4.

In Step 4, the AutoContent Wizard explains that you have completed the initial steps to building a presentation (see fig. 16.8).

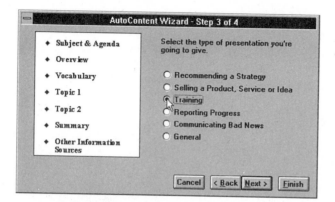

Figure 16.7
Selecting the
Training
presentation type.

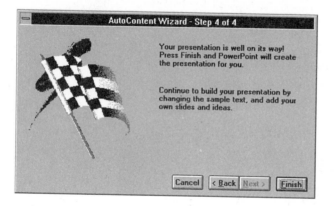

Figure 16.8
Step 4 of the
AutoContent
Wizard.

Now, by changing the sample text in the Outline view and adding new slides, the Shipshape Cruise Lines training presentation will unfold.

To continue, click on **F**inish. PowerPoint takes a moment to prepare the outline, and then opens the Outline view for you to input presentation text.

Entering and Editing Slide Text in the Outline View

PowerPoint's Outline view helps you to organize your thoughts. Think of the PowerPoint Outline view as an outline in Microsoft Word. Many of the word processing functions are identical. Using the word processing functions, you replace the existing content suggestions with information pertaining to the Shipshape Cruise Lines training program.

PowerPoint provides many ways for you to delete text and replace it with new information in the outline. You can highlight the text and overwrite it with new information by simply typing. You also can highlight the text, press Del, and type the new information. Or, you can highlight the text and press the Cut button on the toolbar. In this chapter, you will have a chance to try each method.

By working through the PowerPoint AutoContent Wizard, you already have the Title Slide text completed (see fig. 16.9) and need only to input text for the additional slides.

Figure 16.9
The PowerPoint Outline view with text suggestions from the AutoContent Wizard.

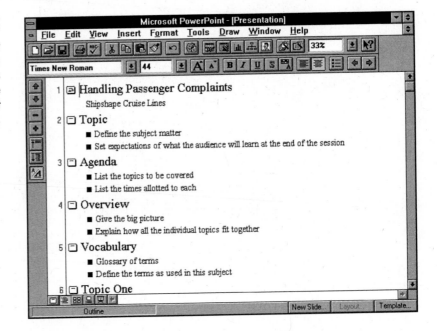

Don't worry that the third level of information ("Become part of the crew!") does not appear in the Outline view. This text will appear on the title slide but not in the Outline view. Editing this text is covered in Chapter 17, "PowerPoint Tools and Concepts."

Each slide in a presentation usually has a slide title. In the Outline view, text on the same line as the slide number and slide icon is the slide title; for example, the current slide title for Slide 2 is Topic.

To replace the title with a more appropriate title, select the word *Topic* using the I-beam cursor and click on the Cut button on the Toolbar. Then, with the cursor flashing, type **How to handle complaints** (see fig. 16.10).

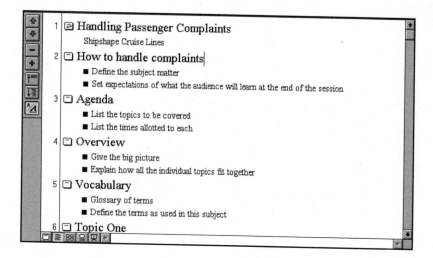

Figure 16.10
Typing a new title
for Slide 2.

The PowerPoint AutoContent Wizard suggests that you should next define the subject matter. Highlight the words *Define the subject matter* using the I-beam cursor and click on the Cut button on the Toolbar. Type **The standard procedures for handling passenger complaints on Shipshape Cruise Lines**. Then, in the second bullet point, type **Become a certified member of the Shipshape crew** (see fig. 16.11).

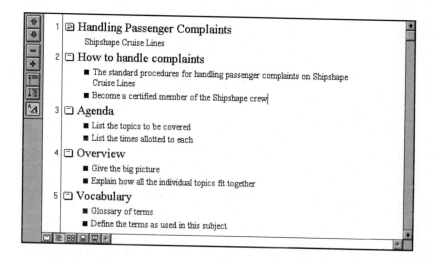

Figure 16.11
Completing the
bullet points on
Slide 2.

The PowerPoint AutoContent Wizard suggests that you discuss the agenda next. Leave the slide title Agenda, but replace *List the topics to be covered* with **Shipshape complaint compliance**.

Suppose you want another blank bullet point on Slide 3 to present an additional topic to be covered in the Shipshape Cruise Lines presentation. To add another bullet point, click at the end of the first bullet point and press Enter (see fig. 16.12).

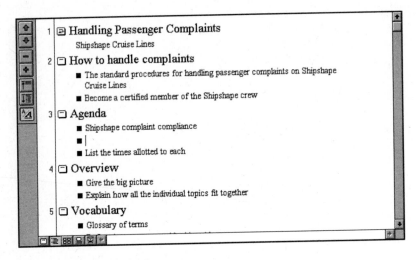

Another blank bullet point appears with the cursor flashing, waiting for you to type. Type **Complimentary Lunch**. Then, replace the text in the third bullet point with **Role playing**. The bullet points in Slide 3 now are completed, as shown in figure 16.13.

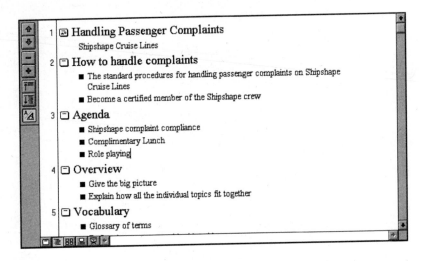

In Slide 4, leave the slide title as Overview but replace the content suggestions with the following text:

- ✔ Replace *Give the big picture* with **Keep the passengers happy.**

- ✔ Replace *Explain how all the individual topics fit together* with **Learn the techniques then practice for perfection.**

The Shipshape Cruise Lines training procedures do not include any special vocabulary, so you can delete Slide 5. To delete an entire slide, move your cursor over the Slide icon to the right of the number 5 until the arrow turns into a four-headed arrow. Click once with the left mouse button. Notice that all the slide text including bullet points is selected (see fig. 16.14).

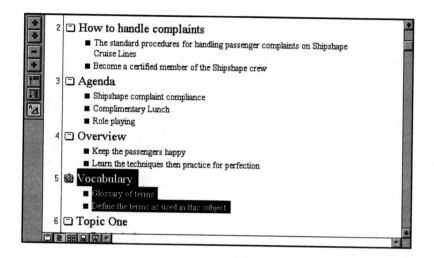

Figure 16.14
Selecting an entire slide.

Click on the Cut button on the Toolbar; the slides are automatically renumbered. The slide titled Topic One becomes Slide 5.

The first topic to discuss in the Shipshape Cruise Lines training program is Shipshape complaint compliance. Replace the content suggestions in Slide 5 with the following text:

✔ Replace *Topic One* with **Shipshape complaint compliance.**

✔ Replace *Explain details* with **Follow the manual.**

✔ Replace *Give an example* with **If a passenger wants a towel, get him a towel.**

✔ Replace *Exercise to re-enforce learning* with **Role playing.**

The text for Slide 5 should be complete except for the last bullet point suggesting that you add more slides if necessary (see fig. 16.15).

Because you do not need to add any more text, delete the last bullet point. To delete this point, move the mouse pointer over the bullet until it changes to a four-headed arrow and click the left mouse button to select the line of text (see fig. 16.16).

PowerPoint

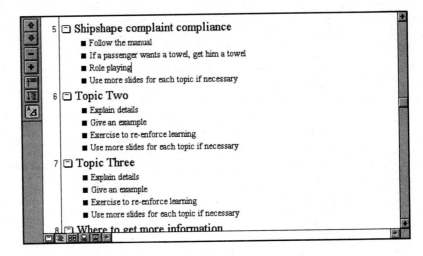

Figure 16.15
The outline with replaced text in Slide 5.

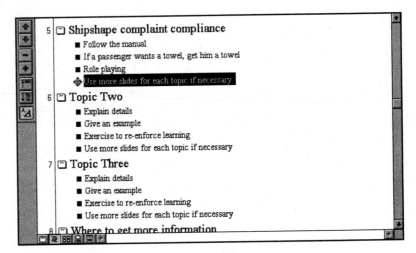

Figure 16.16
Selecting a single line of text.

Click on the Cut button on the Toolbar or press Del to delete this bullet point.

You can continue to replace the content recommendations with presentation text using these same word processing steps. Replace the content suggestions in Slide 6 with the following text:

✔ Replace *Topic Two* with **Role playing.**

✔ Replace *Explain details* with **Talking to a passenger with a complaint.**

✔ Replace *Give an example* with **A passenger does not like his room.**

The last two bullet points are not required for topic two, so you can delete both of them. Rather than deleting one at a time, you can delete both bullet points at one time.

Move the mouse pointer over the third bullet point in Slide 6 until the four-headed arrow appears, and click the left mouse button to select the line of text. Next, move the mouse pointer over the fourth bullet point until the four-headed arrow appears.

Hold down the Shift key and click the left mouse button. Holding the Shift key enables you to select multiple lines of text or multiple slides, as shown in figure 16.17.

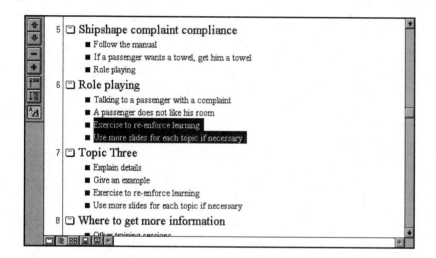

Figure 16.17
Selecting multiple lines of text.

Click on the Cut button on the Toolbar or press Del to delete the text.

To move forward in this section, delete Slides 7 and 8. You can highlight multiple slides using the same technique as for highlighting multiple lines of text.

To delete these slides, move the mouse pointer over Slide 7's slide icon until it turns to a four-headed arrow, and click to highlight the entire slide. Move the mouse pointer over Slide 8's slide icon, hold down the Shift key, and click the left mouse button. Click on the Cut button on the Toolbar or press Del to remove these slides.

Congratulations! You have a slide presentation with six slides. Before moving to the next step, click on the Slide icon before the Title Slide to select it. Use the vertical scroll bar if necessary to move to the top of the outline.

Viewing Slides and Adding a PowerPoint Template

Now that you have organized your thoughts using the AutoContent Wizard and revised the outline using the Outline view, you can view the slides you have created by changing to the Slide view.

III

PowerPoint

Look at the group of five buttons at the bottom left corner of the workspace. The first four buttons are called *View buttons* (see fig. 16.18).

Figure 16.18
The View buttons.

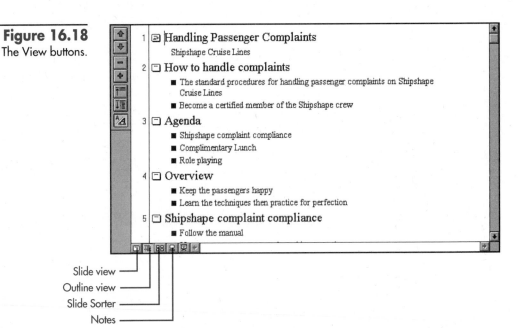

Slide view
Outline view
Slide Sorter
Notes

These buttons manipulate the PowerPoint views and enable you to see a presentation in other formats such as a Slide view, Slide Sorter view, or Notes view. The currently pressed button with the picture of an outline indicates that you are in Outline view. These views will be discussed in depth in Chapters 17, "PowerPoint Tools and Concepts," and 18, "Enhancing PowerPoint Presentations."

To view the Shipshape Cruise Lines presentation in Slide view, click on the Slide view button at the bottom of the workspace. This button has the Slide icon on it.

The title slide appears in the workspace in 8-by-11-inch landscape mode. PowerPoint has applied some formatting and graphics that you will alter later in this chapter.

Using the PowerPoint Slide Changer

The vertical scroll bar at the right moves you through the PowerPoint presentation to look at other slides.

Click on the vertical scroll bar handle and drag it slowly down. PowerPoint shows you which slide will appear when you release the left mouse button (see fig. 16.19).

Figure 16.19
Using the vertical scroll bar to move through the slides.

You also can move from slide to slide by clicking on either the Previous Slide or Next Slide buttons at the bottom of the scroll bar (refer to figure 16.19). The Next Slide button moves you forward one slide; the Previous Slide button moves back one slide.

For presentations with multiple slides, using the handle method enables you to move more quickly to the specific slide you want to view. You also can press PgUp or PgDn on the keyboard to move through presentations, or click in the scroll bar above or below the scroll box to move forward or back.

Keep in mind that you can see the entire slide in the workspace. The vertical scroll bar works differently when you view slides at reduced views. Scaled views will be discussed in depth in Chapter 17, "PowerPoint Tools and Concepts."

Applying a PowerPoint Template

Applying a PowerPoint template transforms the look of every slide in a presentation with graphics, color, and text formatting. Altering these preformatted templates enables you to further customize your work. You can apply a template to a presentation at any time.

To apply a template to a presentation, click on the Template button at the bottom right corner of the workspace. This displays the Presentation Template dialog box, as shown in figure 16.20.

PowerPoint automatically takes you to the directory in which the templates are stored. PowerPoint also opens the subdirectory holding templates for slides. To display all the available subdirectories under the template directory, double-click on the template directory. The three subdirectories include the following:

✔ bwovrhd for black and white overheads

✔ clrovrhd for color overheads

✔ sldshow for video screens and 35mm slides

Figure 16.20
The PowerPoint template directories in the Presentation Template dialog box.

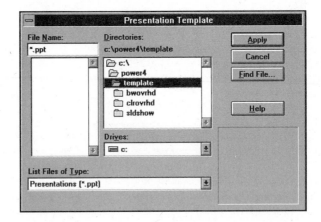

Double-click on the sldshow subdirectory to access these templates because Shipshape Cruise Lines requested 35mm color slides. Click once on the first template, awards.ppt. A thumbnail sketch of the template appears, enabling you to roughly preview the template's colors, graphics, and text formatting (see fig. 16.21). Click once on a few other templates to see some of the other preformatted templates available.

Figure 16.21
Previewing a template.

Tip

This miniature slide preview also appears when you open any presentation you have created. When you are looking for a specific file, it provides a quick way to preview a presentation before opening it.

For the Shipshape Cruise Lines presentation, the tropics.ppt template is most complimentary. Scroll down the file list and highlight tropics.ppt. Notice the preview; then click on **A**pply. All the slides in the presentation assume the tropics.ppt template formatting; an example is shown in figure 16.22.

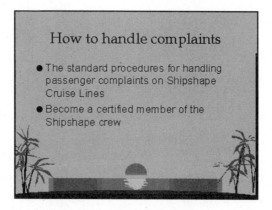

Figure 16.22
The tropics.ppt
template format.

PowerPoint templates specify the font, style, placement, and color of the title on every slide in the presentation. Even the placement of the body text and the bullet style used for each slide subpoint are stored in the tropics.ppt template. Using templates greatly reduces the amount of work you have to do to prepare PowerPoint presentations. Modifying and creating templates is discussed in Chapters 17, "PowerPoint Tools and Concepts," and 18, "Enhancing PowerPoint Presentations."

Adding an Object Containing Text on Every Slide

Shipshape Cruise Lines requests that its name appear on each slide. Carefully adding the word SHIPSHAPE in exactly the same place on each individual slide would be time-consuming.

The PowerPoint Slide Master solves this problem; any object on the Slide Master appears on every slide in a presentation. Rather than place SHIPSHAPE on every slide, you can place it once on the Slide Master.

Opening the Slide Master

To access the Slide Master, open the <u>V</u>iew menu and choose <u>M</u>aster. Masters are available for other PowerPoint formats, including Outline, Handout, and Notes. So, a cascading menu appears for you to select the Master you want—in this case, the Slide Master.

Tip

To open the Slide master, you also can hold down the Shift key and click on the Slide view button at the bottom of the workspace. This shortcut works to open any other master corresponding to a view.

The tropics.ppt template Slide Master contains the following elements (see fig. 16.23):

✔ The Title Area for AutoLayouts box

✔ The Object Area for AutoLayouts box

✔ The graphics associated with the template

Figure 16.23
The Slide Master for the tropics.ppt template.

Notice that the text *Click to edit Master title style* in the Title Area box includes character formatting such as the font, font size, and alignment. This Title Area text shows the formatting of the Slide Titles on every slide except the Title Slide. To change the look of the Slide Titles throughout a presentation, make those changes here in the Slide Master to save time.

The text in the Object Area also is formatted. Everything from the bullet styles to the indentation of the subpoints is retained in the Slide Master.

Drawing an Object and Adding Text

To add a rectangle containing the word SHIPSHAPE to every slide in the presentation, first click on the Rectangle button on the tool palette, as shown in figure 16.24.

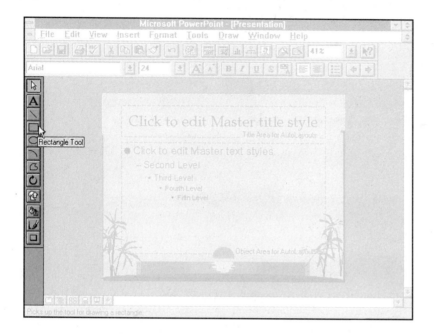

Figure 16.24
Selecting the
Rectangle drawing
tool.

When you move the mouse cursor onto the slide, the pointer changes to a cross hair. In the upper right corner of the slide, click and drag the cursor to the right to draw the box. Don't worry if the rectangle overlaps the Title Area for AutoLayouts box. Release the left mouse button when the box is the size you want; the box displays square resizing handles in each corner and on the top, bottom, and sides (see fig. 16.25). These handles indicate that the shape is selected and that you can resize the object at this time.

Figure 16.25
The box displays
square resizing
handles.

With the handles still showing, type the word **SHIPSHAPE** (see fig. 16.26).

Notice that when you begin typing, the square handles disappear and a crosshatched frame appears. This crosshatched frame indicates that the shape is selected and currently in text-edit mode.

III

PowerPoint

Figure 16.26
Typing text inside
the rectangle.

PowerPoint center-aligns the word and positions it in the middle of the rectangle automatically. Changing this alignment and positioning within shapes is discussed in Chapters 17 and 18.

If the rectangle you have drawn is not large enough to accommodate the entire word, you need to make the rectangle larger. To enlarge the rectangle, you must first get the square resizing handles to reappear. Currently, a text cursor is flashing at the end of the word *SHIPSHAPE* (although it might be difficult to see).

To make the square handles reappear, click on the crosshatched frame of the rectangle. This click takes you back to Object edit mode, and the square handles reappear.

Move the cursor over one of the square handles; notice that the cursor changes to black arrows (see fig. 16.27).

Figure 16.27
Moving the cursor
over a square
handle.

These arrows show you which direction you can resize the object. Grab the bottom left resizing handle in the rectangle's corner by clicking on the handle and holding down the left mouse button. Drag the outline of the rectangle to the left to make the rectangle wider. The cursor changes to a cross hair as you enlarge the rectangle, and a dotted outline of the rectangular shape shows the rectangle's new size.

After you have made the rectangle the size you want, open the <u>V</u>iew menu and choose <u>S</u>lides or click on the Slide view button to return to Slide view (see fig. 16.28).

Figure 16.28
Clicking on the Slide View button to return to the Slide view.

Move through the slides using the vertical scroll bar; notice that the rectangle containing SHIPSHAPE is on every slide in the location where you drew it on the Slide Master (see fig. 16.29).

Figure 16.29
SHIPSHAPE appears on every slide, including the Title slide.

The PowerPoint tropics.ppt template assigns the rectangle's text and fill color automatically. These colors can be changed, so don't worry if they are not to your liking.

Adding a New Slide with Clip Art

You often will want to insert a new slide within a presentation even after you have finished entering text in the Outline view. Also, adding graphics or pictures to individual slides adds interest to presentations and helps to effectively communicate to your audience.

PowerPoint provides a quick and easy way to add a new slide with clip art using preformatted AutoLayouts. The PowerPoint Clip Art library offers a vast selection of images so that you can select just the right picture for a presentation.

Before the Agenda slide, Shipshape Cruise Lines wants a slide that shows what its average cruiser looks like.

Adding a New Slide and Choosing a Layout

PowerPoint inserts a new slide after the current slide you are viewing in Slide view or the highlighted slide in Outline or Slide Sorter view.

You want to insert a Slide before the slide titled Agenda. Using the vertical scroll bar, move to Slide 2. Ensure that the Agenda slide is Slide 3 by scrolling down one slide; then return to Slide 2.

To add a new slide, click on the New Slide button. The New Slide dialog box appears, enabling you to select the AutoLayout for the new slide (see fig. 16.30).

Figure 16.30
Selecting an AutoLayout in the New Slide dialog box.

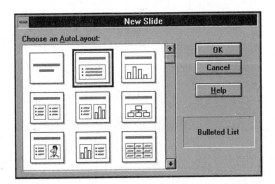

Tip To bypass the AutoLayout dialog box and insert a new slide with the same layout as the slide before it, press Shift while clicking on the New Slide button.

The AutoLayout box includes 21 layouts, ranging from a title slide to a blank slide. Click once on an AutoLayout with the cursor and notice the layout description that appears on the right (see fig. 16.31).

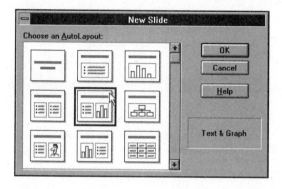

Figure 16.31
The layout description for a selected AutoLayout.

PowerPoint enables you to add one or a combination of the following to a slide:

✔ Bulleted text

✔ A graph

✔ An organizational chart

✔ Clip art

✔ A table

✔ Other objects, such as media clips or Word Art

Use the vertical scroll bar within the dialog box to view the additional AutoLayouts beyond those shown in the box.

For the new slide in the Shipshape Cruise Lines presentation, find the AutoLayout described as Text & Clip Art (see fig. 16.32).

Click on this AutoLayout and click on OK in the New Slide dialog box, or double-click on the AutoLayout. The new slide appears with a slide title box, a bulleted text box, and a clip art box, as shown in figure 16.33.

III

PowerPoint

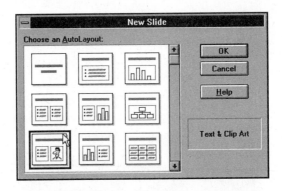

Figure 16.32
Selecting the Text
& Clip Art
AutoLayout.

Figure 16.33
The new slide with
the AutoLayout.

Adding Slide Text and Clip Art

You can add slide text directly to the slide as well as in the Outline view. PowerPoint leads you through placing and aligning text to save you time.

Click inside the box labeled Click to add title. A flashing cursor appears in the crosshatched frame for you to type the title; type **A Shipshape Cruiser**. Next, click inside the bulleted text box labeled Click to add text; a flashing cursor appears after the bullet. Type **Take a vacation on a Shipshape Cruiser!** (see fig. 16.34).

Now you're ready to add clip art. Double-click inside the box labeled Double-click to add clip art. The Microsoft Clip Art Gallery appears, as shown in figure 16.35.

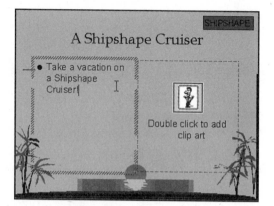

Figure 16.34
Adding a title and text to the slide.

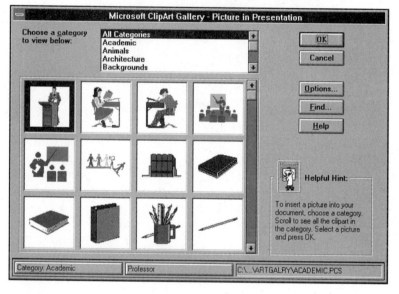

Figure 16.35
The Microsoft Clip Art Gallery.

 The first time you add clip art to a slide, PowerPoint loads all the graphics into the Clip Art Gallery. This might take some time. Do not interrupt this process—all the images might not transfer into the gallery.

PowerPoint arranges the individual pieces of clip art by different categories; clip art featuring modes of transportation are in the Transportation category, for example. The Microsoft Clip Art Gallery opens showing all categories of clip art.

You know that you are looking for a picture of a ship, which is a mode of transportation. To move quickly to the pictures in the Transportation category, use the vertical scroll bar in the box displaying the categories to scroll down. Click on Transportation to select it. A new set of clip art appears, but no picture of a ship is visible. Use the vertical scroll bar in the clip art box to scroll down and find a picture of a ship (see fig. 16.36).

Figure 16.36
Scrolling to find a
picture of a ship.

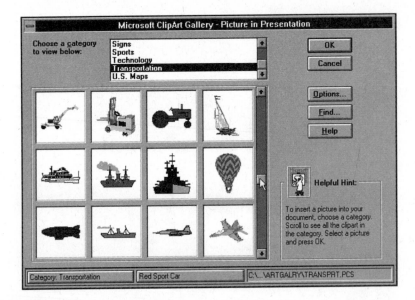

At the bottom of the Microsoft Clip Art Gallery dialog box are two buttons and a text box. The buttons show which category you are viewing and the name of the highlighted clip art. The text box displays the clip art's directory path. These buttons enable you to relocate and rename a piece of clip art to customize the Clip Art Gallery. If there are a few pieces of clip art you often use, for example, you can move them into a new category that you can call "Frequently Used." Further customizing the Microsoft Clip Art Gallery is discussed in Chapter 18, "Enhancing PowerPoint Presentations."

The picture titled Yacht resembles a Shipshape Cruiser. Click on this picture, and then on OK (see fig. 16.37).

Tip   If you forget how to use the Microsoft Clip Art Gallery, a Helpful Hint at the bottom right of the dialog box walks you through inserting clip art into a document.

After clicking on OK, the Microsoft Clip Art Gallery closes, returns you to the presentation, and inserts the picture of the yacht in the designated area (see fig. 16.38).

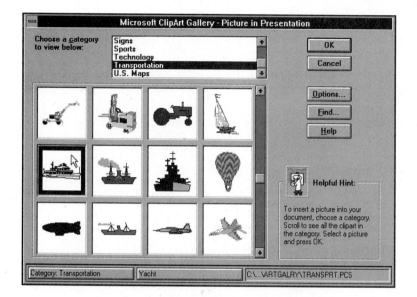

Figure 16.37
Selecting the clip art titled Yacht.

Figure 16.38
PowerPoint inserts the clip art into the designated area.

Moving Clip Art

Unfortunately, the picture is covering up some of the Slide template graphics. This section discusses how to move clip art.

Square resizing handles surround the picture of the yacht showing that the picture is selected. To move the picture, place the cursor over the picture. Click and hold the left mouse button to grab the clip art. Now, drag the picture up and to the left, away from the palm trees (see fig. 16.39).

Figure 16.39

Moving and positioning the clip art.

When the picture is positioned where you would like it, release the left mouse button.

You can insert clip art on a slide without working through the AutoLayout, and you can paste multiple pictures on one slide. Sizing and altering clip art is discussed in Chapter 18.

Previewing, Printing, and Saving the Presentation

This final step helps you to preview the Shipshape Cruise Lines presentation before printing, and shows you the way to print and save your work.

Using PowerPoint Slide Show

PowerPoint Slide Show enables you to view a presentation without the menus, toolbar, tool palette, or scroll bars. This feature lets you see how the presentation would look on slides, overheads, or a video screen without the PowerPoint workspace.

Before beginning the Slide Show, make sure you are viewing the first slide in the presentation. The Slide Show starts on the current slide seen in the workspace, instead of automatically beginning on Slide 1.

To begin the Slide Show, click once on the Slide Show button at the bottom left of the workspace. This button shows a picture of a slide screen (see fig. 16.40).

Figure 16.40
Selecting the Slide
Show feature.

A black screen appears moments before showing the first slide. Don't worry—you haven't lost your work! The first slide eventually comes into view on-screen without showing the Slide workspace, as shown in figure 16.41.

Figure 16.41
Viewing the first
slide of the
presentation using
the PowerPoint
Slide Show.

III

PowerPoint

Notice the icon with the drawing pencil in the bottom right corner of the screen. This icon provides the Freehand drawing tool for you to emphasize slide information during a presentation. For example, suppose you want to emphasize Become part of the crew! on the title slide by drawing a circle around it as you talk about it. Click on the Freehand drawing tool, then move the cursor off the square and notice that it changes to a pencil.

Move the pencil somewhere near the words Become part of the crew!. Click and drag with the left mouse button to draw a circle around the text (see fig. 16.42).

Figure 16.42
Drawing a circle
using the
Freehand drawing
tool.

You can continue to draw on the slide by holding down the left mouse button. To turn off the drawing tool, click on the Pencil icon or press Esc.

Press E on the keyboard at any time to erase the freehand drawing on a slide. Otherwise, the drawing appears until you move to the next slide. When you return to the slide, the drawing is gone.

The left mouse button works like a slide projector button, moving you through the slides with a single click. Clicking the right mouse button takes you back one slide.

Move through the presentation until you see the final slide. Click again to return to the PowerPoint Slide view with the workspace.

Printing a Presentation

Even if you intend to transfer a presentation to slides or overheads, printing the slides on plain paper can save time and money because you can preview your work. Printed presentations can be routed among many people and allow for written comments or corrections. You will not be able to check the colors, but you can preview the overall look, proof spelling, and so on. PowerPoint includes a spelling checker tool that is discussed in Chapter 17, "PowerPoint Tools and Concepts."

To print the PowerPoint presentation, open the File menu and choose Print, or click on the Print button on the toolbar (see fig. 16.43).

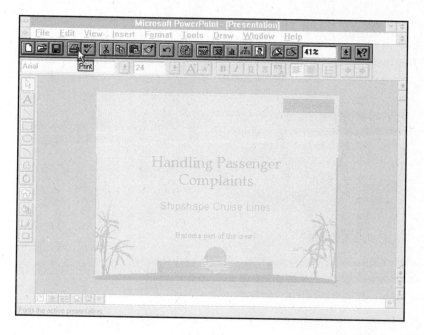

Figure 16.43
Clicking on the Print button.

The Print dialog box appears, showing PowerPoint's default print settings. PowerPoint is set to print one copy of all the slides in the presentation (see fig. 16.44).

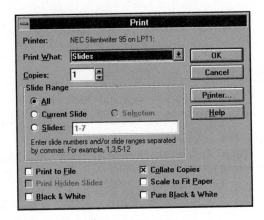

You also can choose to print the current slide on-screen or only a few specific slides. Additional printing options will be discussed later in Chapter 17.

Be aware that printing times can vary depending on how many graphics are on a slide, so be sure to allow adequate time for your printout. It's probably not a good idea to start printing a presentation five minutes before you are scheduled to present it!

To begin printing, click on OK to print all the slides.

Saving Your Work

As shown in the PowerPoint title bar, PowerPoint labels the file "[Presentation]" until you give it a permanent name. You must save the presentation to access it at a later time. All PowerPoint presentations have the file extension .ppt.

To save the presentation, open the File menu and choose Save, or click on the Save button on the toolbar (see fig. 16.45).

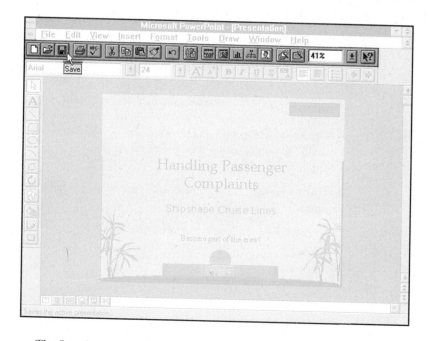

Figure 16.45
Clicking on the
Save button.

The Save As dialog box appears and prompts you to name your presentation file (see fig. 16.46).

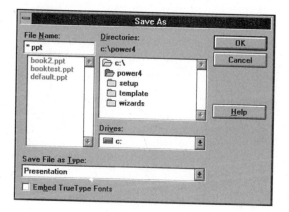

Figure 16.46
The Save As
dialog box.

III

PowerPoint

The file type is preselected for a PowerPoint presentation so that PowerPoint will automatically add the .ppt extension. Type the name **shipshap** in the File Name box. Select the directory and path where you would like to save your file and click on OK. The file name now appears in the PowerPoint title bar.

Chapter Snapshot

Understanding PowerPoint concepts such as the PowerPoint toolbars or the Slide Master means smarter and faster presentation construction. For example, the PowerPoint Slide Master holds for every slide in a presentation formatting details that you can use to reduce design time and eliminate potential frustration.

This chapter explains many PowerPoint design tools in detail by discussing the following topics:

To help illustrate some of the PowerPoint concepts and tools in this chapter, we will return to the Shipshape Cruise Lines training presentation you created in Chapter 16.

Marketing Statistics
for Computer Book Publishing

1994

CHAPTER

PowerPoint Tools and Concepts

by Jodi Davenport

As you saw in Chapter 16, "PowerPoint Quick Start," PowerPoint supplies many tools to help you quickly create a professional presentation. PowerPoint templates provide preformatted slide layouts, but you can implement your own creative presentation designs using the additional tools and Wizards that PowerPoint offers.

Beginning a New Presentation When You Open PowerPoint

Many times you will open PowerPoint to access an existing presentation. Sometimes you will open PowerPoint knowing exactly what kind of file you want to create—a one-page handout or flyer, for example. In both cases, you would not necessarily want to utilize PowerPoint's Wizards or AutoLayouts.

PowerPoint lets you decide how you want to begin every time you open the application by offering options in the PowerPoint dialog box (see fig. 17.1). At this point, you can choose from the existing options and click on OK, or click on Cancel to bypass this dialog box.

Figure 17.1
PowerPoint's initial
dialog box offers
many options.

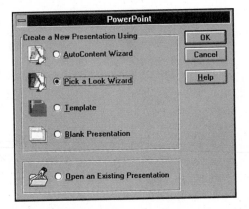

You can choose to not have this dialog box appear when PowerPoint first opens. To keep this dialog box from appearing, open the **T**ools menu and select **O**ptions. The Options dialog box appears and presents many options to customize the way PowerPoint works. The General section appears at the bottom of the box and includes the option Show Startup **D**ialog. To turn this feature off, click on the check box. For now, however, leave the setting on.

When you are in PowerPoint and want to begin a new presentation while an existing presentation is currently on-screen, open the **F**ile menu and select **N**ew. A dialog box appears, providing exactly the same options as the beginning dialog box, except for the option **C**urrent Presentation Format. This option opens a new presentation with the same presentation format as the presentation currently on-screen.

The following sections discuss the options offered in the PowerPoint dialog box and where each one takes you. By understanding these various paths when starting out, you can make the best choice for your particular task.

AutoContent Wizard

The PowerPoint AutoContent Wizard provides suggestions about the kind of information you might include in a presentation, depending on the type of presentation you are creating. To use the AutoContent Wizard, select AutoContent Wizard and click on OK. See Chapter 16, "PowerPoint Quick Start," for more information.

Pick a Look Wizard

The PowerPoint Pick a Look Wizard uses nine steps to help you to create a complete presentation package that can include audience handout pages or speaker's notes. To use this Wizard, select Pick a Look Wizard and click on OK.

In Step 1 (see fig. 17.2), the Pick a Look Wizard tells you that this Wizard presents choices to help you organize a complete presentation. Click on Next to move to Step 2.

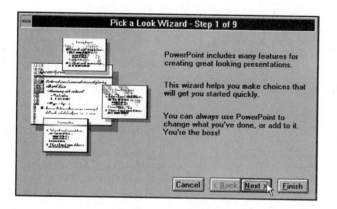

Figure 17.2
Step 1 of the Pick
a Look Wizard.

Step 2 (see fig. 17.3) asks you to choose the output you will use for this presentation. Step 2 reminds you that you can make a different output selection at a later time if you are not sure which one to use right now. This reminder applies to many decisions throughout the Pick a Look Wizard, so don't feel as though your choices cannot be changed. Click on Next when you have made an output decision.

Step 3 (see fig. 17.4) guides you through selecting a template to use for this presentation. Even though you can apply a template at any time, the Pick a Look Wizard helps you to think through initial presentation setup decisions before you begin. Four template choices already appear in Step 3. A preview of the template appears to the left of the choices when you click on the template name.

Figure 17.3
Step 2 of the Pick
a Look Wizard.

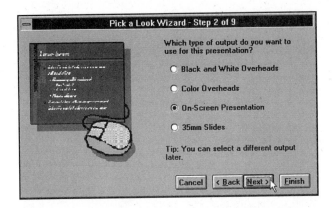

Figure 17.4
Step 3 of the Pick
a Look Wizard.

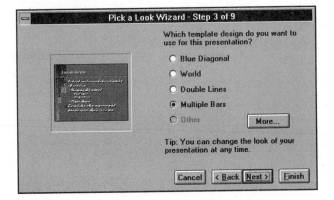

To view more templates, click on More. PowerPoint directs you to the template directory that corresponds with your presentation output format. If you choose black-and-white overheads as the output format, for example, PowerPoint takes you to the \bwovrhd directory. Select a template and press Apply. PowerPoint returns you to Step 3 in the Pick a Look Wizard; click on Next.

Step 4 in the Pick a Look Wizard (see fig. 17.5) explains that PowerPoint offers four ways to print a presentation, including:

✔ **Full-page slides.** Full-page printouts of slides without menus, toolbars, or scroll bars.

✔ **Speaker's notes.** The top half of the printout includes a miniature slide; the bottom half features notes that the speaker can refer to while delivering a presentation.

✔ **Audience handout pages.** Multiple slides printed on one page.

✔ **Outline pages.** The outline of the presentation.

Outline pages

Speaker's notes

Full-page slides

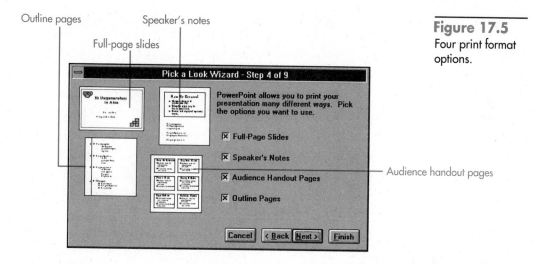

Audience handout pages

Figure 17.5
Four print format options.

Clicking on the check boxes selects and deselects the printout options. Selected options will be included when you print the final presentation. Select the print options you want and click on **N**ext.

In the next series of Pick a Look Wizard screens, the Pick a Look Wizard enables you to easily place text objects automatically on every slide in the presentation. If you want the date to appear on each slide, for example, you could click the check box in front of Date. PowerPoint then positions the date for you. If, however, you want to reposition or edit these options later, you can access the Slide Master. To add a name, company name, or any other text, select the text with the I-beam cursor in the box and retype.

Depending on which printouts you selected in Step 4, the next Pick a Look Wizard steps vary. If you selected only Full-Page Slide and Outline Pages to be printed, for example, the Pick a Look Wizard shows you options for only those two formats.

Step 9 in the Pick a Look Wizard (see fig. 17.6) tells you that you have made the selections for the look of your presentation. Click on **F**inish to implement these selections.

After you click on **F**inish, wait for PowerPoint to set up the slides. The title slide appears first with the template format and text objects you chose (see fig. 17.7). From this point, you can add new slides as you work by clicking on the New Slide button and selecting an AutoLayout.

III

PowerPoint

Figure 17.6
Step 9 in the Pick a
Look Wizard.

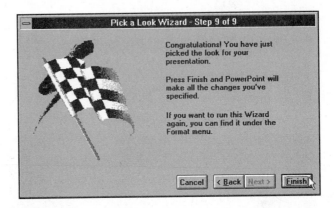

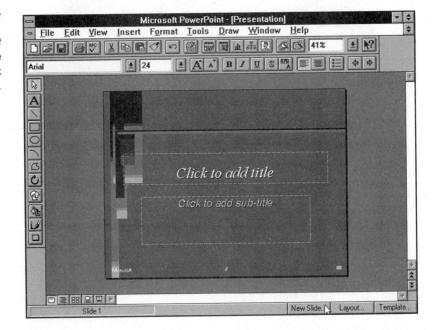

Figure 17.7
PowerPoint
implements the
Pick a Look
Wizard selections.

Template

When beginning a new presentation, you might simply want to select the slide template and
add the slides as you work using the AutoLayouts. If this is the case, choose Template from the
PowerPoint dialog box when it first opens. PowerPoint takes you directly to the template
directory for you to make a template selection. To find out more about previewing templates
and opening directories that utilize your presentation format, see Chapter 16, "PowerPoint
Quick Start."

Blank Presentation

You might want to begin creating a new presentation by selecting an AutoLayout for the first slide and working from there. You can always select a template, add objects, or choose to print outputs during or after you have finished entering slide text. When you select **B**lank Presentation from the initial PowerPoint dialog box, PowerPoint takes you to the AutoLayouts and asks you to make a selection. Continue to click on the New Slide button and choose an AutoLayout to build a presentation.

Open an Existing Presentation

To access an existing presentation, select **O**pen an Existing Presentation from the initial PowerPoint dialog box. The Open dialog box appears for you to choose a file. Click on OK to open the file.

Establishing Slide Setup

At times you might create a presentation on custom-sized paper or need the slides to be in a certain orientation. In PowerPoint, slide setup includes slide size, numbering, and orientation for slides, notes, handouts, and outlines.

Changing the slide size or orientation after you have completed a presentation results in graphics or text on the slides adjusting proportionally in size to accommodate the new slide size. However, these changes may result in distortions of clip art, text, or other graphics, so it is important to make these changes at the beginning if your presentation requires an unusual setup.

Note Remember that whatever presentation type you ultimately choose, a PowerPoint presentation is a series of slides.

When you begin creating a new presentation, the basic PowerPoint slide appears in the landscape position and is sized for letter paper (10 inches wide by 7.5 inches tall). PowerPoint allows some margin space to accommodate slide and overhead holders. To make changes to the slide setup, choose S**l**ide Setup from the **F**ile menu. The Slide Setup dialog box appears (see fig. 17.8), enabling you to change the slide size, numbering, and orientation.

Slide Size

PowerPoint offers five slide-size formats to accommodate various presentation types. Open the **S**lides Sized for list box to show the following sizes (see fig. 17.9):

✔ On-screen Show is used for video-screen or computer-monitor presentations.

✔ Letter Paper is used for presentations on 8.5-by-11-inch paper.

✔ A4 Paper is used for presentations on 210-by-297mm or 10.83-by-7.5-inch paper. This paper is an international size.

✔ 35mm Slides is used for presentations on 35mm slides.

✔ Custom is used for presentations on materials with a special, custom size.

Figure 17.8
The Slide Setup
dialog box.

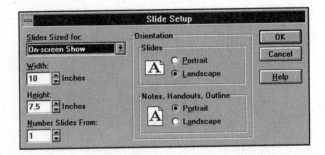

Figure 17.9
The slide-size list
box options.

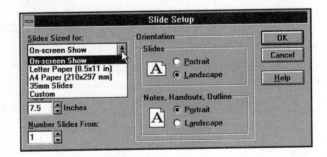

To adjust the slide height or width, click on the up- or down-arrow buttons, or select the numbers using the I-beam cursor and enter the slide size. Notice when you click on the up- or down-arrow buttons or enter numbers that the slide size automatically changes to Custom.

Slide Numbering

PowerPoint numbers slides automatically, beginning with Slide 1. However, a presentation can begin with any number. You might, for example, create a presentation that is the second half of a 100-slide presentation. The slides should begin with Slide 51 to keep the order exact.

To change the beginning slide number, click on the up or down arrows or select the number using the I-beam cursor and enter a number.

Slide Orientation

At times you might want to create and print PowerPoint slides for use in a booklet or binder that already includes portrait-oriented pages. To keep the orientation uniform, you can change the slide setup orientation to portrait. To change the slide orientation, click on the button before Portrait or Landscape in the Slide Setup dialog box.

The small sheet of paper with an *A* will adjust to show which orientation you have chosen. These same orientation changes also can be made to notes, handouts, and outline pages. Click on OK when you are finished making your selections.

Using PowerPoint Views

PowerPoint offers four views in which you can work on one presentation: Slide view, Outline view, Slide Sorter view, and Notes view. These views play a role in organizing an impressive presentation package. You can switch smoothly between these views while working on a presentation by using the four view buttons at the bottom of the workspace or selecting them from the View menu (see fig. 17.10). The Status bar indicates which view you are in.

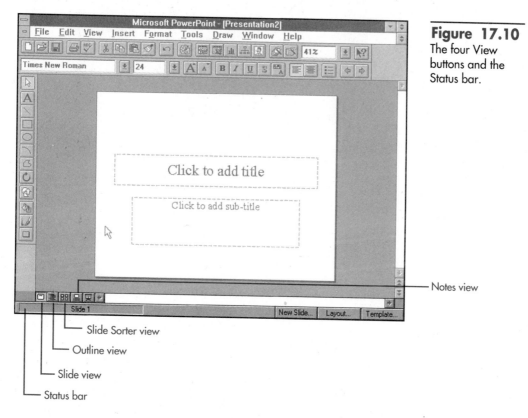

Figure 17.10
The four View buttons and the Status bar.

III

PowerPoint

— Notes view

— Slide Sorter view

— Outline view

— Slide view

— Status bar

Many views share toolbars. However, the Outline and Slide Sorter views each have a toolbar that offers functions particularly useful in that view. For example, the slide transition tools appear on the Slide Sorter view toolbar because you can apply transitions only in this view.

Slide View

To select the Slide view, click on the view button with the slide icon on it or choose <u>S</u>lides from the <u>V</u>iew menu. The Slide view is the basic PowerPoint view (see fig. 17.11). Most of the slide formatting and design work is done in the Slide view. PowerPoint includes many default settings in the Slide view that you can change so they appear automatically when you begin PowerPoint. To see which toolbars are available in the Slide view, open the <u>V</u>iew menu and choose <u>T</u>oolbars. The Toolbars dialog box lists the toolbars available in the Slide view (see fig. 17.12).

Figure 17.11
The PowerPoint
Slide view.

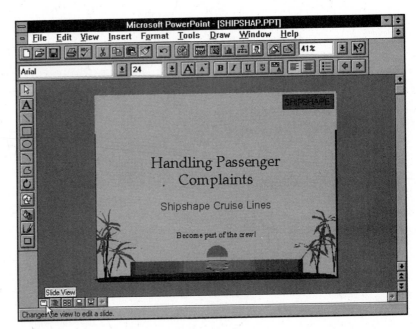

The Standard, Formatting, and Drawing toolbars are checked, indicating that they are currently in use. For a discussion of manipulating and customizing toolbars, see the section "Manipulating PowerPoint Toolbars," later in this chapter. To exit the Toolbars dialog box and return to the Slide view, click on OK.

Outline View

To select the Outline view, click on the Outline view button or choose <u>O</u>utline from the <u>V</u>iew menu. The Outline view shows the Slide titles and text (see fig. 17.13). As shown in Chapter

16, the Outline view enables you to organize your thoughts when creating a presentation. You can insert additional text in the Outline view, create a new slide, and rearrange text or slide order.

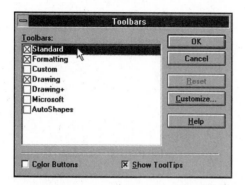

Figure 17.12
The toolbars available in the Slide view.

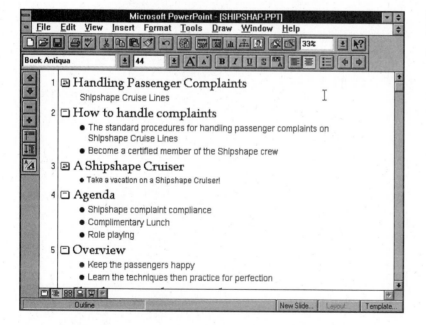

Figure 17.13
The PowerPoint Outline view.

The Slide icon before each Slide title indicates whether the slide contains Clip Art or objects not shown on the Outline. In figure 17.14, Slide 1 and Slide 3 both have shapes inside each Slide icon, but the other slide icons do not. Do you remember from Chapter 16 that the text *Become part of the Shipshape Crew!* did not appear on the Outline? It is an additional object, which accounts for the shapes inside Slide 1's icon. The yacht picture accounts for the shapes inside Slide 3's icon.

Figure 17.14
Shapes inside the
slide icons.

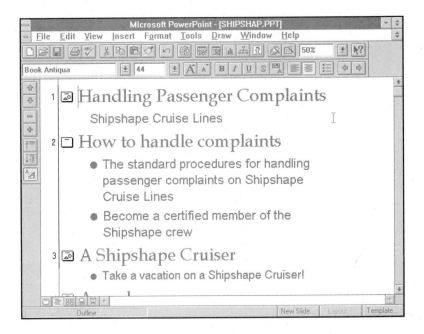

The Outlining toolbar appears on the left when you select the Outline view. The functions of each button will be discussed later in this chapter, and refer to Chapter 16 to review entering text in the Outline view. From the Ⅴiew menu, choose Ⅰoolbars to view the toolbars available in the Outline view (see fig. 17.15). Notice that some of the toolbars available in Slide view do not appear as choices in the Outline view, but there is a toolbar named Outlining. Click on OK to continue.

Figure 17.15
Toolbars available
in the Outline
view.

Slide Sorter View

To select the Slide Sorter view, click on the Slide Sorter view button or choose Slide Sorter from the Ⅴiew menu. The Slide Sorter view shows each slide, numbered (see fig. 17.16). The Slide Sorter view enables you to rearrange a presentation's slide order; delete, copy, or add new slides; and assign slide transitions to each slide. Slide transitions are discussed in Chapter 18, "Enhancing PowerPoint Presentations."

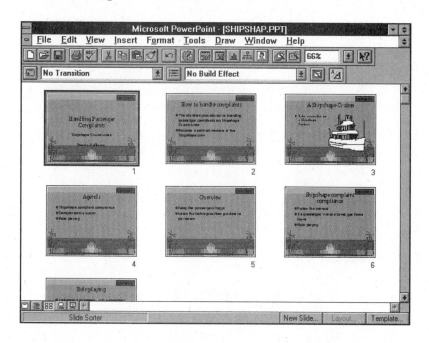

Figure 17.16
The PowerPoint Slide Sorter view.

A dark box surrounds the first slide, meaning that it is selected and can be moved, deleted, copied, or assigned a slide transition. To move a slide, place the mouse pointer on the selected slide. Click and hold the left mouse button, then drag the mouse pointer between Slide 2 and Slide 3 and release the left mouse button (see fig. 17.17). The mouse pointer changes to a slide icon with an arrow pointing down when you move it. Notice that the first slide moved and the slide numbering automatically adjusted.

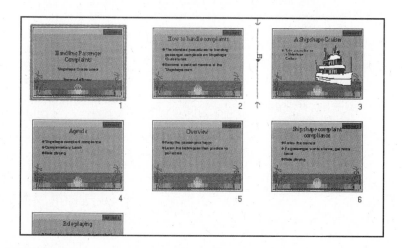

Figure 17.17
Rearranging the slide order.

To select more than one slide in the Slide Sorter view, hold down the Shift key and click on the slides you want to select. To move multiple slides, follow the same steps outlined for moving one slide.

Deleting one or more slides is as easy as selecting the slide or slides and pressing Del. Alternatively, you can select the slide, open the Edit menu and choose Delete Slide. To copy a slide, select the slide and click on the Copy button. Click the mouse where you want the copied slide to appear and click on the Paste button.

To add a new slide, click on the spot at which you want the new slide to appear. If you want a new slide between the second and third slide, for example, click in the space between these slides. A large flashing cursor appears where you clicked the mouse pointer. Click on the New Slide button in the bottom right corner of the workspace. When the cursor is flashing, you also can open the Insert menu and choose New Slide or press Ctrl+M. PowerPoint asks you to choose an AutoLayout for the new slide, then inserts the new slide with the same color scheme and format as the other slides in the presentation.

Open the View menu and choose Toolbars to see which toolbars are available in the Slide Sorter view. Notice that there is a Slide Sorter toolbar (see fig. 17.18). Click on OK. For a discussion of the Slide Sorter toolbar, see Chapter 18, "Enhancing PowerPoint Presentations."

Figure 17.18
The toolbars available in the Slide Sorter view.

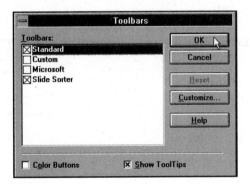

Notes View

To select the Notes view, click on the Notes view button, or open the View menu and choose Notes. The Notes view shows a small picture of a slide with a text box below it (see fig. 17.19).

The Notes format is ideal for speaker's notes or for creating audience handouts with speaker's comments about each slide. The box labeled "Click to add text" works like a word processing box in which you can type comments or additional information. Words wrap just as in word processing software. To add text in that box, click inside the box and begin typing.

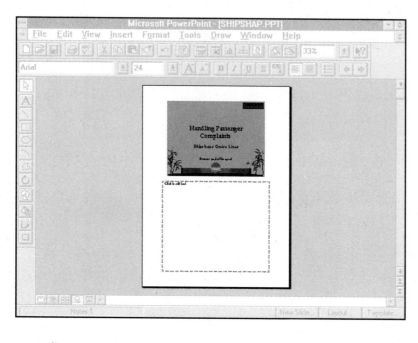

Figure 17.19
The PowerPoint
Notes view.

 Any text inside this box in the Notes view will not appear in the Outline view.

The same toolbars available in the Slide view also are available in the Notes view.

Manipulating PowerPoint Toolbars

Located initially across the top and down the left side of the workspace, PowerPoint toolbars provide easy access to frequently used PowerPoint functions. The toolbar buttons work just like the toolbar buttons in Microsoft Word and Microsoft Excel, requiring one press to execute the function.

PowerPoint includes Tool Tips to let you know the button name and the button function. When you activate a Tool Tip, a button name appears next to the button and a button function description appears in the status bar in the lower left corner of the workspace (see fig. 17.20). To activate the Tool Tips, move the mouse pointer over a button and wait a moment. These tips help you learn and recall the functions of these toolbar buttons.

As you work more and more in PowerPoint, you will begin to recognize functions you are performing regularly. You can customize PowerPoint toolbars just like in Microsoft Word and

Microsoft Excel. Customization can help you work more quickly and efficiently. The way to customize toolbars is discussed in "Customizing Toolbars," later in this section.

As in Microsoft Word and Microsoft Excel, PowerPoint requires that you select the text or numbers you want to change before performing a function. However, depending on the PowerPoint formatting function, you can select text or numbers in many time-saving ways. If you want to boldface a single word in a sentence, for example, you simply can place the flashing cursor within the word and click on the Bold button on the Formatting toolbar.

Figure 17.20
Activating
PowerPoint Tool
Tips.

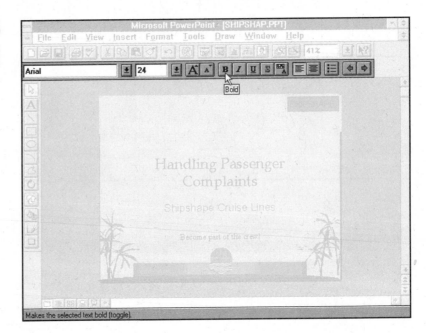

Floating Toolbars

When you first open PowerPoint, some toolbars are docked at the top and down the left side of the workspace. By double-clicking in the gray area in between toolbar buttons, you can float the toolbars in the workspace and move them where you like.

Move the mouse pointer between the Spell Check and Cut buttons on the top toolbar. Double-click, and watch the toolbar pop out into the slide area (see fig. 17.21). Following these steps, you can float any toolbar in the workspace. Notice the toolbar name is at the top of the window and the control menu icon in the upper left corner of the window. You can float as many toolbars at one time as you would like.

Move the mouse pointer in the gray area around the buttons. Click and drag the window anywhere in the slide area. An outline of the window moves to show you where the toolbar will land when you release the left mouse button.

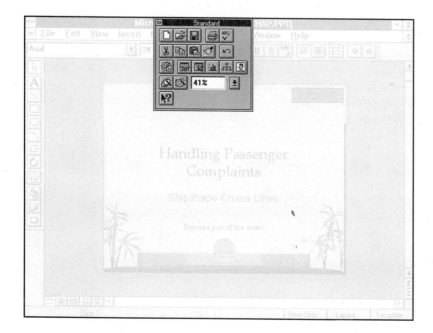

III

PowerPoint

Figure 17.21
The Standard
toolbar is floating.

To remove a toolbar from view, click once on the control menu icon in the upper left corner of the window. To make the toolbar reappear, open the <u>V</u>iew menu and choose <u>T</u>oolbars. Click on the check box in front of Standard and click on OK (see fig. 17.22).

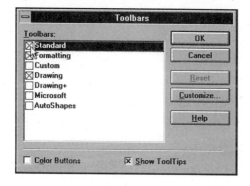

Figure 17.22
Choosing to show
the Standard
toolbar.

The toolbar reappears floating in the workspace because you removed it while it was floating. To dock a toolbar, double-click on the gray space around the buttons and watch the toolbar snap into position.

Moving Toolbars

PowerPoint enables you to manipulate toolbars by dragging them out into the workspace. Move the mouse pointer in a gray space between the Spell Check and Cut buttons. Click and drag the toolbar down into the workspace. The toolbar outline shows you where the toolbar is moving. After the toolbar is well into the workspace, it changes into a square shape. When you move the toolbar down to the bottom of the workspace, it changes back to a long rectangle (see fig. 17.23).

Figure 17.23
The toolbar flattens out to clear the workspace view.

Viewing Additional Toolbars

To view additional PowerPoint toolbars, open the Toolbar dialog box by choosing Toolbars from the View menu. The Toolbar dialog box shows you which toolbars currently are showing and the toolbars that are available to open while in the current view. To remove a toolbar, remove the check in front of the toolbar name by clicking inside the check box. To make a toolbar appear, click in the check box.

In the Toolbar dialog box, you also can choose to have color in the toolbar buttons or hide the Tool Tips. Click to add or remove the checks in the boxes (see fig. 17.24). To implement your changes, click on OK. Toolbars might appear floating at first. You can move them or dock them at the top by double-clicking in the gray area around the toolbar buttons.

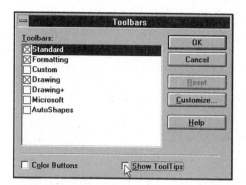

Figure 17.24
Selecting Color Buttons and turning on or off Tool Tips.

PowerPoint offers a shortcut to hiding or showing toolbars. To access this shortcut, move the mouse pointer over any visible toolbar and click the right mouse button. A pop-up menu appears showing the toolbars that are available in the current view; current toolbars have a check mark next to the toolbar name (see fig. 17.25). To make a toolbar appear, click on the toolbar name to make the check appear. You also can access the Toolbars dialog box through this shortcut menu by choosing Toolbars.

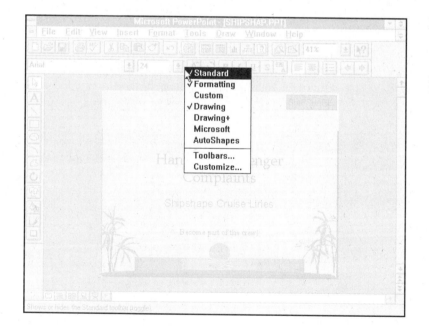

Figure 17.25
Click the right mouse button to access a shortcut menu.

III

PowerPoint

Customizing Toolbars

PowerPoint enables you to customize toolbars to expedite regularly used functions. Notice that PowerPoint provides extra space to the right of horizontal toolbars and at the bottom of the vertical toolbars. This extra space enables you to add toolbar buttons. To customize a toolbar, select <u>C</u>ustomize from the <u>T</u>ools menu to display the Customize Toolbars dialog box, as shown in figure 17.26.

Figure 17.26

The Customize Toolbars dialog box.

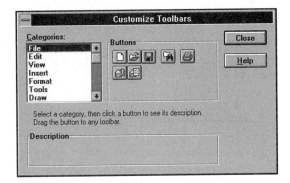

Tip

You can access the Customize Toolbars dialog box through the shortcut menu by placing the mouse pointer over any current toolbar and clicking the right mouse button. Select Customize.

The Customize Toolbars dialog box displays categories of tools from which you can choose. The toolbar buttons available in those categories appear in the Buttons box. To see the buttons available in the Edit category, for example, click on Edit in the <u>C</u>ategories list box (see fig. 17.27).

Figure 17.27

Selecting a category and viewing the available buttons.

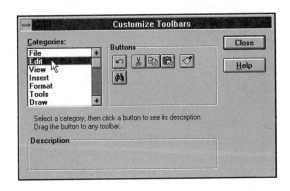

Tool Tips are available on the buttons in the Customize Toolbars dialog box. Move the mouse pointer over a button in the Buttons box and wait a moment. A Tool Tip eventually appears, showing you the name of the button. To see a full description of the button's function, click on the button and view the description in the Description box (see fig. 17.28). To confirm the button description you are viewing, a dotted outline forms around the button to indicate that it is selected. All these steps are outlined in the Customize Toolbars dialog box for your information.

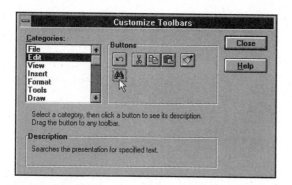

Figure 17.28
Viewing a button's description.

To place buttons on the toolbars already showing in the workspace, click and hold down the left mouse button with the mouse pointer over a button. Notice that when you click and hold the left mouse button, a small plus sign (+) appears on the button.

Drag the button off the Customize Toolbars dialog box and onto the toolbar where you would like it positioned, placing the plus sign on the exact spot. Release the left mouse button and watch the button take its place where you positioned it (see fig. 17.29).

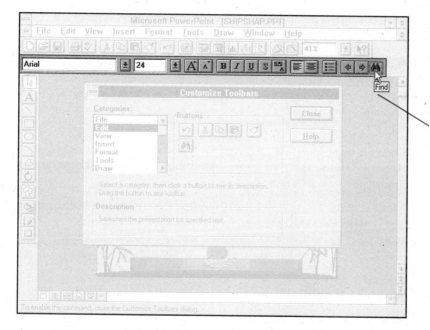

Figure 17.29
Placing the button on a toolbar.

The Find tool being dropped on the Formatting toolbar

III

PowerPoint

The button retains its dotted outline to let you know that you still can move the button to another location. To move the button again, click on the button, drag it to where you want to position it, and release the left mouse button.

You can rearrange other buttons on current toolbars while the Customize Toolbars dialog box is open. Click on any button, then drag the button to another location (see fig. 17.30). The other buttons on the toolbar reposition themselves to accommodate the button.

Figure 17.30
Repositioning a button on a toolbar.

In addition to adding buttons, you can remove buttons from a toolbar with the Customize Toolbars dialog box open. To remove a button, click on the button, then drag it off the toolbar and into the workspace.

If the Customize Toolbars dialog box is not open, you can hold down the Alt key and drag a button off the toolbar to remove it. If you've been following along, drag the Find button off the toolbar using these steps. To copy a button from one toolbar to another, press Ctrl+Alt and drag the button to a new position. When you are done customizing toolbars, click on Close in the Customize Toolbars dialog box.

Using Toolbar Functions

As you can see, PowerPoint toolbars are flexible and designed to help you work in an efficient, comfortable manner. Now that you know how to manipulate the toolbars, you are ready to learn the functions of the buttons on four toolbars. You will recognize many of the functions because they are identical in Word and Excel. Tool Tips can help you to review the button names and functions if you forget.

As in Word and Excel, you must select text or objects before you perform the function. PowerPoint AutoSelect is designed to select entire words rather than individual characters, so selecting text to format is easier than ever.

Button functions that are common across Microsoft Office applications are only briefly explained in the following section. This section will focus on buttons that carry functions unique to PowerPoint. To demonstrate the toolbar functions, return to the Shipshape Cruise Lines training presentation you created in Chapter 16.

The Standard Toolbar

The Standard toolbar (see fig. 17.31) is available in every PowerPoint view. The buttons on the Standard toolbar cover the basic functions such as Save, Cut, Copy, and Paste.

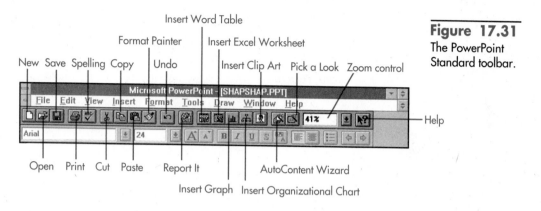

Figure 17.31
The PowerPoint
Standard toolbar.

Common Standard Toolbar Buttons

The first eight buttons on the PowerPoint Standard toolbar are basic tools found also in Word and Excel. If you know how to use these tools in these other applications, you already know how to use them in PowerPoint.

When you are in PowerPoint and want to begin a new presentation while an existing presentation currently is on-screen, press the New button on the Standard toolbar. The New Presentation dialog box appears, presenting the same options as the dialog box that appears when you first open PowerPoint, and one new option: Current Presentation Format, which opens a new presentation with the same presentation format as the presentation currently on-screen.

The Open button brings up the Open dialog box, from which you can select a presentation file to open. The Save button quickly saves a presentation that already is named; if you have not named the presentation, the Save As dialog box appears and enables you to name your file. The Print button brings up the Print dialog box, enabling you to print either a presentation or specific slides in that presentation. The Spelling button begins a spelling check on the current slide or a selected slide if you are in Slide Sorter view. The Spelling dialog box works the same way as in Word and Excel.

The Cut, Copy, and Paste buttons also work just as they do in Word and Excel. In PowerPoint you need to select text or objects by clicking on them before you perform one of these functions.

The Format Painter

The Format Painter button (the button showing a paintbrush) enables you to copy the format of a selected object and apply that same format to another object. This function expedites formatting and saves you time. Suppose you want to make Slide 1's title bold and italic, then decided you wanted the title on Slide 3 in the same format. The Format Painter is ideal for this situation because it copies entire formatting instructions.

III

PowerPoint

This simple exercise is meant as an example to show how the Format Painter works. Changing to Slide 3 and clicking on the Bold and Italic buttons would work, too. However, think of how the Format Painter could save much time when copying an extensively formatted object.

First, select Slide 1's title by clicking on *Handling*, then dragging the I-beam over *Passenger Complaints* (see fig. 17.32). Open the Format menu and choose Font. In the Font dialog box, choose Bold Italic, then click on OK.

Figure 17.32
Selecting the title
slide's title.

With the text still selected, click on the Format Painter button. Move the pointer out to the workspace and notice that it has changed to a paintbrush and I-beam (see fig. 17.33). Use the vertical scroll bar to move to Slide 3. When Slide 3 appears, move the mouse pointer out to the workspace. Notice that the paintbrush and I-beam still appear.

Figure 17.33
The pointer
changes to a
paintbrush and an
I-beam.

Select the title *A Shipshape Cruiser* using the I-beam. Notice that the Format Painter automatically applies the format, including color, of Slide 1's title (see fig. 17.34). By double-clicking on the Format Painter button, you can repeatedly format text. Suppose you want all the text on the title slide formatted the same as the title. Return to Slide 1 and select the title again using the I-beam cursor.

Figure 17.34

Applying a text format using the Format Painter.

Double-click on the Format Painter button and move the paintbrush and I-beam over *Shipshape Cruise Lines* (see fig. 17.35). Next, move the paintbrush and I-beam over the words *Become part of the crew!* and watch the Format Painter apply formatting to this text. Press Esc to remove the paintbrush and I-beam and return to the mouse pointer.

Figure 17.35

Applying formatting to the second level of information.

You also can use the Format Painter to transfer slide color schemes from one slide to another in the Slide Sorter view.

III

PowerPoint

The Undo Button

The Undo button reverses the last edit made to a slide. If you delete an object by mistake, for example, simply click on the Undo button to retrieve the object and place it back where it originally was.

The Report It Tool

The Report It tool quickly transfers the outline text from an open PowerPoint presentation into Word for use in a word processing document. Suppose you want to use the Shipshape training presentation text in an employee manual. Instead of retyping all the text, you can click on the Report It button to transfer the text into Word to get you started quickly.

Clicking on the Report It button automatically begins Word, in which the presentation outline text appears in Rich Text Format (RTF). The text is already formatted and is prepared for you to further manipulate or incorporate into another document.

Adding Objects to a Slide

The following five buttons are used to insert objects on a blank slide. These buttons work in the same way: click on the button and watch the rectangle with square resizing handles appear on the slide to show you where the object will appear after it is created.

The objects you add to a slide using the Insert Microsoft Word Table and Insert Microsoft Excel Spreadsheet buttons are OLE/DDE objects, meaning that when the object is selected, you have access to all the editing and creating tools and menus you would have in the corresponding applications. If, for example, you insert an Excel spreadsheet on a PowerPoint slide and select it by clicking on it, you instantly have access to Excel toolbars and menus. These tools appear where the PowerPoint toolbars are; you do not temporarily exit PowerPoint and work within Excel, then return to PowerPoint.

✔ The Insert Microsoft Word Table button enables you to add a table to a slide conveniently. Click on the button and select the number of columns and rows you want included in the table. When you release the left mouse button, the table appears on the slide.

✔ The Insert Microsoft Excel Spreadsheet button opens a grid, just like the Insert Microsoft Word Table button. Select the columns and rows you want in the spreadsheet and release the left mouse button. The spreadsheet appears for you to add numbers and formulas.

✔ The Insert Graph button enables you to place a graph on a slide. To insert a graph, click on the Insert Graph button on the toolbar and see PowerPoint place a rectangular outline on the slide to show you where the graph will be placed. You can alter the size of the graph after you create it using the square resizing handles. PowerPoint also offers an AutoLayout in which you can insert a graph by double-clicking in a designated area (see fig. 17.36). For more information about using Microsoft Graph, see Chapter 18, "Enhancing PowerPoint Presentations."

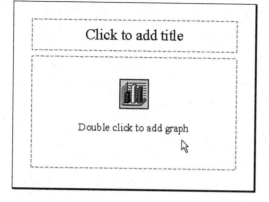

Figure 17.36
An AutoLayout in
which you can
insert a graph.

✔ The Organizational Chart button enables you to insert an organizational chart on a PowerPoint slide. When you click on the Organizational Chart button, PowerPoint shows you where the chart will appear on the slide when you finish creating it by showing a rectangle with square resizing handles just like when you pressed the Insert Graph button. For more information about using the Organizational Chart, see Chapter 18.

✔ The Insert Clip Art button enables you to insert clip art on a PowerPoint slide. Just as a rectangle with black resizing handles appears when you click on the Insert Graph or Insert Organizational Chart button, this same rectangle appears when you click on the Insert Clip Art button. PowerPoint then takes you to the Microsoft Clip Art Gallery. For more information about using the Clip Art Gallery to select an image, see "Adding a New Slide with Clip Art" in Chapter 16, "PowerPoint Quick Start."

Using the PowerPoint Wizard Buttons

The AutoContent Wizard and Pick a Look Wizard buttons take you to Step 1 in each Wizard when you want to begin a new presentation. For more information about the AutoContent Wizard, see Chapter 16. For more information about the Pick a Look Wizard, see the section "Pick a Look Wizard," earlier in this chapter.

Using Zoom Control

PowerPoint Zoom Control adjusts the distance at which you view and work on slides, notes, and outlines. Zoom Control appears on each of the four toolbars and helps you get a closer or more distant look while you work. When altering clip art or drawing graphics in the Slide view, for example, the closer views at 66% and 100% enable you to work with more precision. To assess the overall look of the slides, you might want to step back from the slides to a 33% or 25% view.

To access the preset magnification levels, click on the down arrow to the right of the percentage (see fig. 17.37).

Figure 17.37
Opening the drop-
down list of preset
magnification
levels.

The magnification levels available vary from view to view:

✔ The Slide, Slide Sorter, and Notes views have the following magnification levels: 25%, 33%, 50%, 66%, 75%, 100%, 150%, 200%, 300%, and 400%.

✔ The magnification levels offered in the Outline view include 25%, 33%, 50%, 66%, 75%, and 100%.

You also can select any of these magnification levels by choosing Zoom from the View menu. The Zoom dialog box appears (see fig. 17.38) and presents some preset magnification levels, but it also enables you to select a specific magnification percentage. To increase the magnification level, move the mouse pointer over the up arrow and click to increase the magnification by one-percent increments. To decrease the magnification level, click on the down arrow with the mouse pointer. You also can select the percentage with the I-beam cursor and enter the magnification you would like. Click on OK to activate the view you have chosen.

Figure 17.38
The Zoom
dialog box.

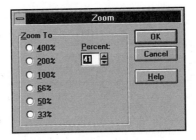

Using Context-Sensitive Help

The Help button enables you to find out more information about a toolbar button function or any menu command. To utilize the Help function, click on the button and move the mouse pointer into the workspace; the mouse pointer appears with a question mark (see fig. 17.39). At this point, you can move the pointer to the area anywhere on the screen where you need more information and click. A Help window appears and provides more information. Open the Help window File menu and choose Exit to return to the presentation.

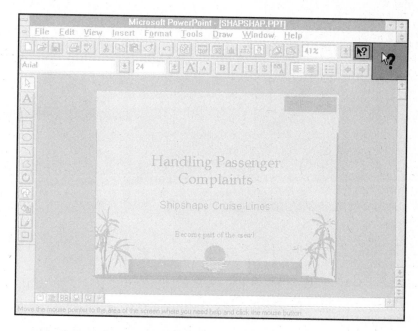

Figure 17.39
The Help cursor.

The Formatting Toolbar

The Formatting toolbar provides functions to help you with formatting operations, such as changing fonts or italicizing text (see fig. 17.40).

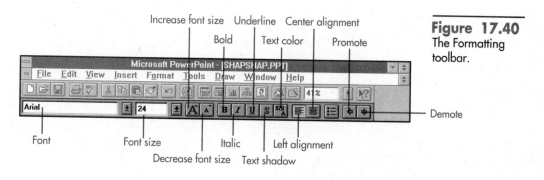

Figure 17.40
The Formatting toolbar.

III

PowerPoint

Choosing and Formatting Fonts

The Font list box works like the list box in Microsoft Word. Simply select the text and click on the down arrow to view the font choices (see fig. 17.41). Notice the three fonts located above the double line. PowerPoint places the three fonts you used last at the top of the font list for easier accessibility as you work. Only three fonts remain at the top of the list at one time.

Figure 17.41
The Font list box.

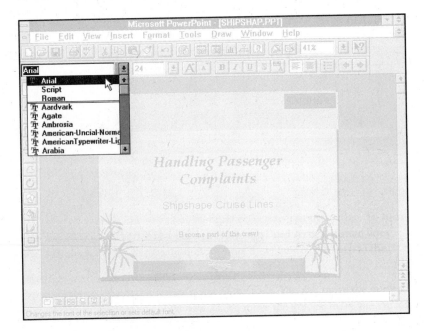

You also can change the font by opening the Format menu and choosing Font. The Font dialog box opens and enables you to choose the font, font style, and size (see fig. 17.42). Click on OK to exit the Font dialog box.

Figure 17.42
The Font dialog box.

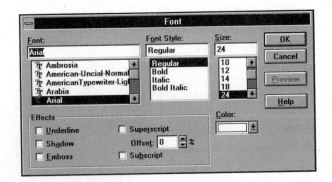

The Size list box drops down so that you can choose the font size you want. These font sizes are preset (for example, 12, 14, 18, 24). You also can select the current font size with the I-beam cursor and type an exact font size.

The Increase Font Size and Decrease Font Size buttons in the Formatting toolbar enable you to quickly change selected text's font size by various increments.

The Bold, Italic, Underline, and Text Shadow buttons on the toolbar perform these character changes on selected text. PowerPoint's Bold, Italic, and Underline buttons work just like in Word. Simply select the text and click on the style you want to apply to the text.

The Text Shadow button enables you to add a shadow to slide text only, not to shapes or other objects. This style is especially effective in slide titles or to emphasize text. To add a shadow to text, select the text and click on the Text Shadow button.

Because you can output your presentation to color slides or overheads, color text is particularly effective. When you click on the Text Color button, a color palette appears with the eight colors you used most recently (see fig. 17.43).

Figure 17.43
The Text Color color palette.

Click on a color block to change the color of the selected text. If you do not see a color you like, click on Other Color for more choices (see fig. 17.44).

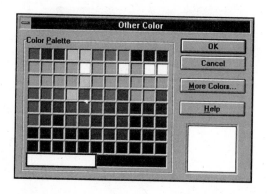

Figure 17.44
Additional text colors in the Other Color dialog box.

You even can create your own color by selecting More Colors from the Other Color dialog box to display the More Colors dialog box (see fig. 17.45). Move the black marker on the color waves to the shade of color you want. Then click on the triangular pointer along the color band and drag it up or down to select the color intensity. When you have chosen a color, click on OK and then OK again to close the Other Color dialog box. This custom color shows on the color palette that appears for you to use later when you click on the Text Color button .

Figure 17.45
Creating your own
color.

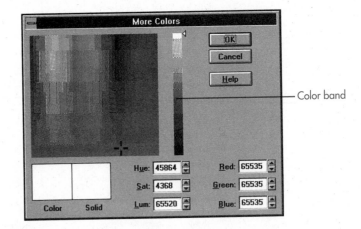

— Color band

Aligning Text

The Align Left and Align Center buttons work exactly as they do in Word. Simply select the text and click on the alignment you would like. You also can access text alignment by opening the Format menu and choosing Alignment (see fig. 17.46). A cascading menu offers you four choices: left, right, center, and justify. Choose the alignment by clicking on it.

Figure 17.46
Aligning text
through the
Format menu.

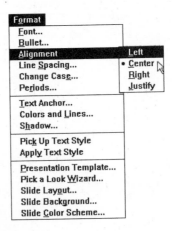

Bullets

PowerPoint can automatically add bullets to lists added in the slide body text box on slides other than the title slide. Notice that if you select this text, the bullet button on the Formatting toolbar is pressed. To bullet text, select the text and click on the bullet button.

You are not limited to a simple dot for your bullets. To access other bullet styles, select the text, open the Format menu and select Bullet. When the Bullet dialog box appears, click on the bullet you would like. You can select the bullet color by opening the list box under Special Color (see fig. 17.47). Notice that if you created a custom color earlier, it also appears on this palette. Click on OK to implement any bullet formatting.

Note As a shortcut to adding a bullet to a line of text, simply place the flashing cursor within the line and click on the bullet button.

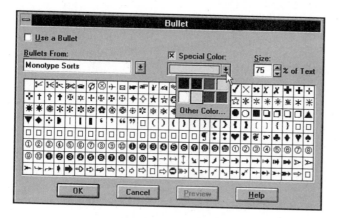

Figure 17.47
Selecting a special bullet color.

Promoting and Demoting Bullet Points

The left- and right-arrow buttons on the Formatting toolbar are the Promote and Demote buttons, respectively. These buttons enable you to create a hierarchy of text using subpoints. Suppose that on Slide 2 you wanted to move the second bullet point under the first bullet point to make it a subpoint. Click the I-beam cursor anywhere in the text, then click on the Demote button on the Formatting toolbar (see fig. 17.48).

Notice how the second bullet indents and assumes another style of bullet. This bullet format is defined in the Slide Master. The Promote and Demote buttons are particularly useful in the Outline view to manipulate text and organize your thoughts.

Figure 17.48
Demoting a bullet
point.

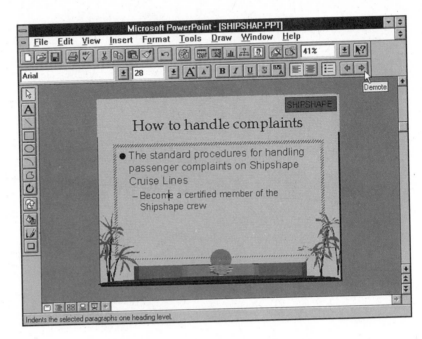

The Outline Toolbar

The Outline toolbar is available only in the Outline view. Change to the Outline view by pressing the Outline view button in the bottom left corner of the workspace. The Outline toolbar automatically appears vertically down the left side of the workspace (see fig. 17.49).

Figure 17.49
The Outline
toolbar.

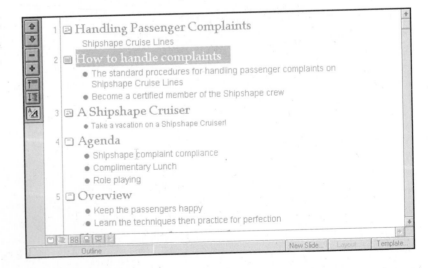

Moving Text or Slides Up and Down

The Move Up and Move Down buttons rearrange text vertically one line to eliminate cutting and pasting. Suppose you want Complimentary Lunch to be the last point on the Agenda slide. To rearrange text, select the bullet point using the four-headed arrow, then click on the Move Down button (see fig. 17.50).

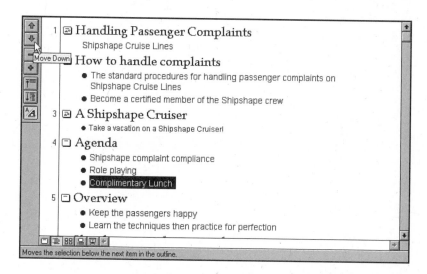

Figure 17.50
Moving text down
the outline.

These buttons also can be used to rearrange entire slides. To move Slide 2 into Slide 3's position, select Slide 2 by placing the mouse pointer over the slide icon until it turns to a four-headed arrow, then click (see fig. 17.51). Click on the Move Down button once and watch the slide begin its descent (see fig. 17.52). Click on the Move Down button again to position all the highlighted text completely into the Slide 3 position. The slides automatically renumber. You also can use these buttons to move multiple slides.

Collapsing and Expanding Selections

The Collapse Selection and Expand Selection buttons work like the Collapse and Expand buttons on Microsoft Word outlines. For example, you currently are viewing all slide titles and subpoints. To view only the title of a slide, select the entire slide and click on the Collapse Selection button. Watch the subpoints hide (see fig. 17.53). Click on the Expand Selection button to expand the slide text.

The Show Titles and Show All buttons enable you to see only the slide titles in the Outline view. No text needs to be selected. Click on the Show Titles button (see fig. 17.54). If you move a title when Show Titles is pressed, all the subpoints under the title also move. This is especially helpful when organizing long presentations. To see all the presentation text, click on the Show All button.

III

PowerPoint

Figure 17.51
Selecting Slide 2.

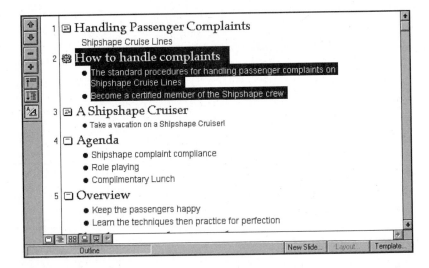

Figure 17.52
Slide 2 moves one
level with one click
of the Move Down
button to assume
the Slide 3
position.

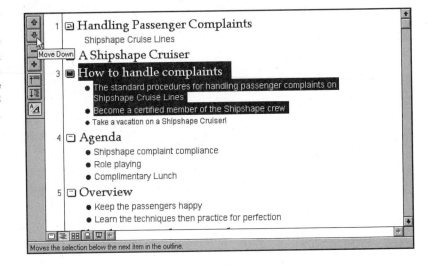

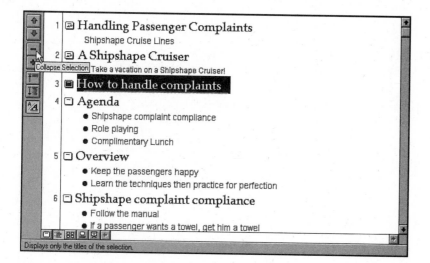

Figure 17.53
Collapsing a section of the outline.

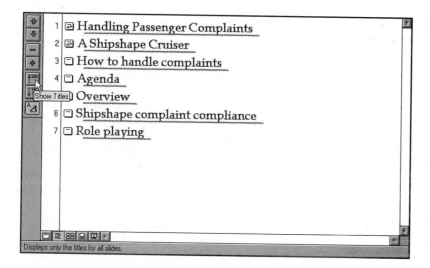

Figure 17.54
Viewing only the slide titles using the Show Titles button.

III

PowerPoint

Showing and Hiding Text Formatting

The Show Formatting button changes the outline text to reflect the font and font size as they appear on the slides. To revert to a default font and font size while working in the Outline view, click once on the Show Formatting button (see fig. 17.55). This default text formatting enables you to see more of the outline text at one time. To change back to viewing the actual fonts and font styles, click on the Show Formatting button once again. Change to the Slide view to continue.

Figure 17.55
Viewing Outline
text in a default
font and font size.

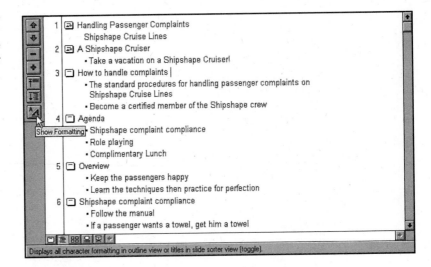

The Microsoft Toolbar

The Microsoft toolbar (see fig. 17.56) is available in all four views and enables you to switch
instantly between other Microsoft applications. You are able to access these applications,
however, only if they currently are available on your computer or through a network.

Figure 17.56
The Microsoft
toolbar.

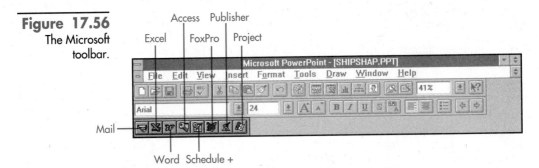

To make the Microsoft toolbar appear, display the Toolbars dialog box by selecting Toolbars
from the View menu, then check the box next to Microsoft. Or, as a shortcut, you can move
the mouse pointer on any current toolbar and press the right mouse button. When the pop-
up menu appears, click on Microsoft. The Microsoft toolbar appears floating in the
workspace. Double-click in the area around the toolbar buttons to dock the toolbar at the top
of the workspace. As you move the mouse pointer over each button, a Tool Tip shows you
which button accesses what application.

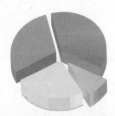

The Custom Toolbar

The Custom toolbar is a blank toolbar that is available for you to customize with buttons that you frequently use. To open the Custom toolbar using the right mouse button shortcut, move the mouse pointer on any current toolbar and press the right mouse button. Select Custom from the pop-up menu.

The Custom toolbar appears floating and initially is very small because there are no buttons on it. The toolbar will enlarge as customized buttons are placed on it by using the Customize Toolbars dialog box. Or, you can hold down the Alt key and move buttons from any current toolbars to the Custom toolbar. You also can use Ctrl+Alt to copy buttons from a current toolbar to the Custom toolbar.

Using Drawing Toolbars

Three of PowerPoint's toolbars pertain to drawing and manipulating shapes: the Drawing toolbar, the Drawing Plus toolbar, and the AutoShapes toolbar. You can manipulate all three drawing toolbars just as you can the others. You can dock them on either side of the workspace or at the top and bottom of the workspace (see fig. 17.57). You also can customize these toolbars using the same customization techniques discussed earlier in this chapter.

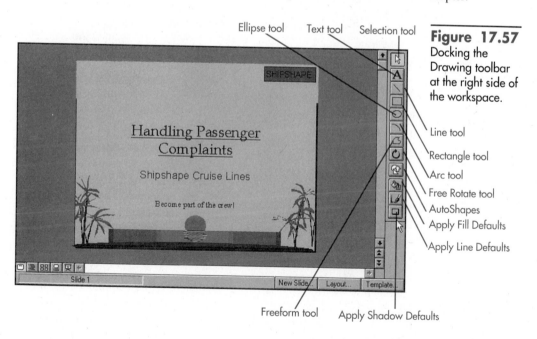

Figure 17.57
Docking the Drawing toolbar at the right side of the workspace.

The Drawing Toolbar

The PowerPoint Drawing toolbar offers many basic drawing and object-formatting tools for you to enhance your presentations.

The Selection Tool

The Selection tool is used to select objects using the mouse pointer. All objects need to be selected to apply formatting. You also use the Selection tool when you want to move objects. PowerPoint reverts to the Selection tool when you finish performing a function, so sometimes it is unnecessary to click on the Selection tool button to activate it. After you draw a rectangle, for example, the mouse pointer automatically changes from a cross hair back to the Selection tool. To select multiple objects, select the first object, hold down the Shift key, and click once on the other objects you want to select.

The Text Tool

Using the Text tool, you can add to a slide text that is separate from the text typed in the Outline. Often single words or phrases showcased on a slide add interest and help communicate a thought or process. Also, a company name included on slides—such as *SHIPSHAPE* on the Shipshape Cruise Lines training presentation—creates recognition and promotes awareness.

The two options for adding text with the Text tool are a text label and a word processing box. Text doesn't automatically wrap in a text label. Text labels are ideal for single words or phrases that you want to place on a slide.

To create a text label, first move to Slide 3 in the Shipshape Cruise Lines presentation. Then click on the Text tool button on the Drawing toolbar and move the mouse pointer on to the slide. Notice that the mouse pointer turns to a text cursor. Click on the slide where you want to place the text label, and a flashing cursor appears inside a crosshatch frame. Type **Service!**. The cursor remains flashing at the end of the text label. Move the mouse pointer off the slide and click.

After typing the text label, you might want to move it somewhere else on the slide. To move the text label after you have typed it, click once on the word or words to select it. A crosshatch frame appears, letting you know you have selected the label and that the text can be edited (see fig. 17.58).

Place the mouse pointer on the crosshatch frame and click again; the edit-object frame appears with square resizing handles (see fig. 17.59). Click directly on the edit object frame but not on the square resizing handles. Then, click and drag the label to another location on the slide. The label's dotted outline shows the size of the label as you move it. Release the left mouse button when the label is where you would like it. From this point, you can make text-formatting changes by selecting the text label and making style selections, such as enlarging the font size or changing the text color.

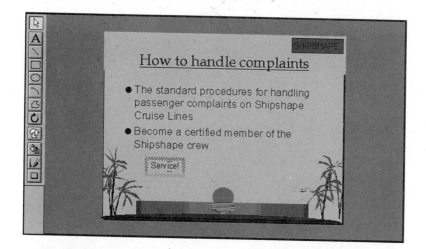

Figure 17.58
Selecting the text
label.

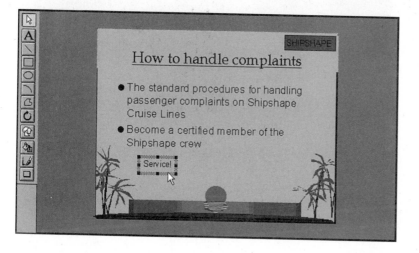

Figure 17.59
The edit-object
frame.

III

PowerPoint

Use these same steps to move other text labels, word processing boxes, or clip art. You can move objects one pixel at a time using the arrow keys on the keyboard while the object is selected.

Text wraps inside the boundaries of a word processing box. If you plan to type a long sentence or more than one sentence, use a word processing box. To create a word processing box, click on the Text Tool button and move the text cursor over the slide. Click and drag the text cursor down to the right to draw a box. Notice that the text cursor turns into a cross hair when you begin to drag the cursor to draw the word processing box.

After you draw the box, a flashing cursor appears inside a crosshatch frame and waits for you to begin typing. Type **Shipshape Cruise Lines wants you to be a well-trained crew member.** Move the mouse pointer off the slide and click. To move the word processing box, follow the same steps outlined for moving a text label.

The Line, Rectangle, Ellipse, and Arc Tools

The Line, Rectangle, Ellipse, and Arc tools all work the same way. To obtain a clean palette to draw objects, move to the end of the presentation and insert a blank slide. Click on the New Slide button and choose Blank from the AutoLayouts. Click once on the rectangle button and move the mouse pointer onto the slide. Notice that the cursor turns into a cross hair (see fig. 17.60). Click and drag the cross-hair cursor down and to the right or left, depending on where you want the object on the slide. Release the left mouse button when the rectangle is the size you want.

Figure 17.60
Preparing to draw a rectangle.

Tip

As noted in the status bar, you can hold down the Shift key to constrain the angle when drawing a line, to draw a square when using the Rectangle tool, to draw a circle when using the Ellipse tool, or to draw a circular arc when using the Arc tool.

The cross hair immediately returns to the mouse pointer. Also, PowerPoint instantly attaches an object frame to the shape and provides square resizing handles for you to alter the shape.

Tip

If you double-click on a drawing-tool button, you can draw shapes one after another. After drawing the first object, the cross hair remains instead of reverting to the mouse pointer, enabling you to draw another object. Press Esc to remove the cross hair.

The following procedure resizes any PowerPoint object. Move the mouse pointer over the bottom right square resizing handle. Notice that the mouse pointer turns to arrows, showing you which way you can resize the rectangle (see fig. 17.61). Grab the square resizing handle, and click and drag the mouse in the direction you want to alter the rectangle. PowerPoint shows you an outline of the object as it is being resized to let you judge how big or small you want the object. Release the left mouse button when the object is the size you would like.

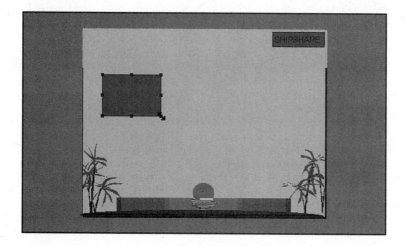

Figure 17.61
Resizing an object.

Sometimes when you resize an object, it becomes difficult to keep the object proportional; a circle can become elliptical, for example, or a square rectangular. To resize an object around the center so it maintains its proportionality, hold down the Ctrl key as you drag the resizing handle. The status box also gives you this information.

If you accidentally alter the object's size too drastically and want to restore the object to its original proportions, press Ctrl and double-click on any square resizing handle.

The Freeform Tool

The Freeform tool enables you to draw objects with freeform lines and straight lines. To use the Freeform tool, click on the Freeform tool button and move the mouse pointer onto the slide. Just as with the other tools, the mouse pointer turns into a cross hair when you move it into the workspace. Now, hold down the left mouse button and watch the cross hair turn into a pencil. Still holding down the left mouse button, move the mouse to draw in freeform (see fig. 17.62). Release the left mouse button, and the pencil returns to a cross hair. Move the mouse down to draw a line. Press and hold the left mouse button to return to the freeform drawing using the pencil. When you are done drawing, double-click the left mouse button. The object immediately acquires the square resizing handles and can be altered using the same steps discussed earlier in this section.

Figure 17.62
Drawing in
freeform.

You can use the Freeform tool to draw polygons, too. Click on the Freeform tool and move
the cursor into the workspace. Using the cross hair, click the left mouse button once but do
not hold it down. Now, move the mouse to draw a line. Click the left mouse button once again
to end that line, and drag the mouse to draw another line. The status bar tells you to continue
clicking for each point of the polygon and to double-click to end your drawing.

The Free Rotate Tool

The Free Rotate tool enables you to rotate any object; even text will rotate within an object.
Suppose you want to rotate the rectangle you drew. Select it by clicking on it, then click on the
Free Rotate tool button and move the cursor onto the slide. The cursor changes to a circular
shape with a plus sign (+) in the middle. The status bar tells you to position the cursor over
any square resizing handle (see fig. 17.63). When you have done this, hold down the left
mouse button and drag the object to rotate it, as shown in figure 17.64.

Figure 17.63
Positioning the
mouse pointer
over a square
resizing handle.

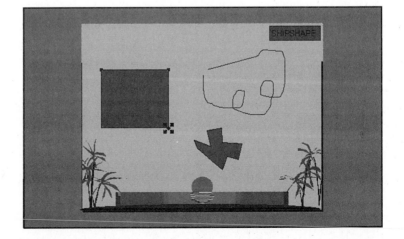

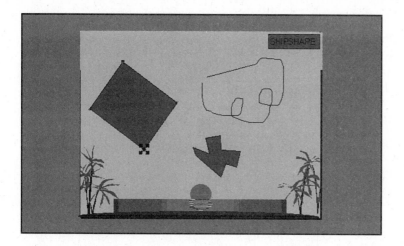

Figure 17.64
Rotating the object.

To rotate an object on restricted angles such as 45 or 90 degrees, hold down the Shift key while you rotate the object. The status bar informs you of this information if you forget. Release the mouse button when you are finished rotating the object, then press Esc to exit the object-rotating mode.

The Apply Fill Defaults Button

The Apply Fill Defaults button shows a paint can filling up a square. This button functions as a toggle. When this button is pressed, PowerPoint automatically fills objects after you draw them. You can remove the fill by selecting the object and clicking on the Apply Fill Defaults button again to turn it off.

To change the rectangle's fill color, select Colors and Lines from the Format menu to display the Colors and Lines dialog box, as shown in figure 17.65. In the Colors and Lines dialog box, you can change an object's fill color, line color, and line style, including dashed lines and arrowheads.

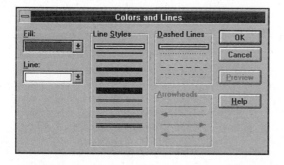

Figure 17.65
The Color and Lines dialog box.

To select another fill color, open the Fill list box by clicking on the down arrow. The menu offers the same eight color blocks and any custom colors you created. To remove the fill, select No Fill. To make the fill the same color as the slide background, choose Background. PowerPoint also enables you to create a shaded fill that adds interest to any shape. To add a shaded fill, select Shaded. The Shaded Fill dialog box opens, displaying the various shading patterns (see fig. 17.66).

Figure 17.66
Choosing a shaded fill.

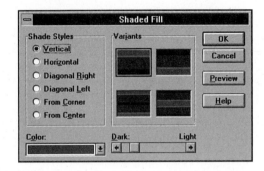

The shading styles direct the shading within the shape. PowerPoint provides a number of patterns with which to spice up a shape's fill. Click through the various Shade Styles and watch the examples appear in miniature in the dialog box. Select the shading style you like and click on OK. Click on OK again in the Color and Lines dialog box to apply the shading.

You also can add a colored pattern inside an object. In the Color and Lines dialog box, open the Fill list box and choose Pattern (see fig. 17.67). This displays the Pattern Fill dialog box, which presents many patterns from which you can choose (see fig. 17.68). You can change the background and foreground colors by opening the color palettes and clicking on a color block (see fig. 17.69). Click on the pattern you would like and click on OK. Click on OK again in the Colors and Lines dialog box to apply the pattern to the selected object.

Figure 17.67
Preparing to insert a pattern into an object.

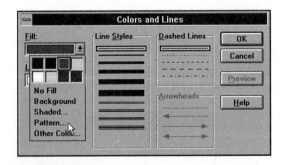

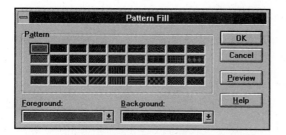

Figure 17.68
The Pattern Fill
dialog box.

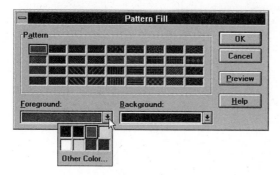

Figure 17.69
Selecting another
foreground color.

The Apply Line Defaults Button

The Apply Line Defaults button switches on or off to show or remove an object's outline. You can change a line's color by opening the Color and Lines dialog box through the Format menu and following the same steps as changing an object's fill color; however, you want to open the color menu under Line (see fig. 17.70). The Color and Lines dialog box also enables you to change the line's thickness in the Line Styles box.

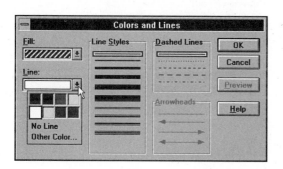

Figure 17.70
Changing a line's
color.

The Apply Shadow Defaults Button

The Apply Shadow Defaults button, showing a rectangle with a black shadow, switches on or off to apply a shadow to an object. You can color or offset shadows in many ways. To shadow an object, select the object and click on the Apply Shadow Default button (see fig. 17.71).

Figure 17.71
Shadowing the rectangle using PowerPoint defaults.

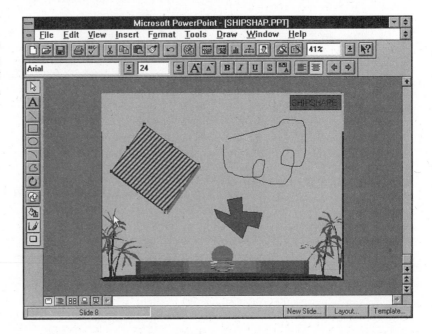

To change the shadow's color, open the F**o**rmat menu, choose S**h**adow, and select the color you would like from the Shadow dialog box. In the Shadow dialog box you can adjust the shadow's offset direction and thickness. To increase the thickness of the shadow going up or down, click on the up or down arrow (see fig. 17.72).

Figure 17.72
Two objects with different shadows.

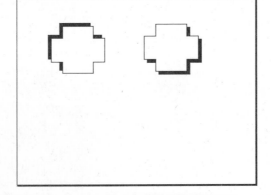

The Drawing Plus Toolbar

The Drawing Plus toolbar (see fig. 17.73) puts many of the object-formatting options discussed in the previous section at your fingertips. For example, the Fill Color button, picturing a color palette with a tipped paint can, enables you to access the fill options without working through the Format menu (see fig. 17.74). The Line Color, Shadow Color, Line Style, and Dashed Line buttons present these formatting options right on the toolbar to save you time (see figs. 17.75–17.78).

 In figure 17.73, the Drawing Plus toolbar appears at the top of the PowerPoint screen, whereas it appears at the left side in figures 17.74–17.78.

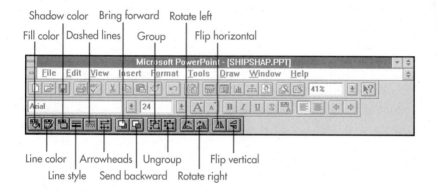

Figure 17.73
The Drawing Plus toolbar.

Figure 17.74
The Fill Color button options.

Figure 17.75
The Line Color
button options.

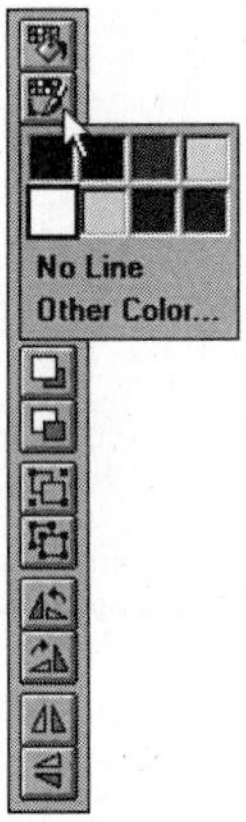

Figure 17.76
The Shadow Color
button options.

Figure 17.77
The Line Style
button options.

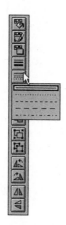

Figure 17.78
The Dashed Line
button options.

The Arrowhead button applies only when you draw a line or an arc and want to place an arrowhead at one end or another, or both. For example, click on the Line button and draw a line on the slide. With the line still selected, click on the Arrowhead button (see fig. 17.79). Click on the arrowhead style you want to apply to the line.

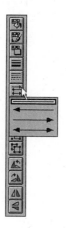

Figure 17.79
The Arrowhead
button options.

The Bring Forward and Send Backward buttons work in tandem and help you arrange multiple objects. The following steps illustrate how these buttons work. First, insert a blank slide by choosing New Slide, then another using AutoLayout. Then draw a line, a rectangle, and an ellipse on the blank slide using the techniques described earlier in this chapter. Move the objects so that they are overlapping each other as shown in figure 17.80.

Select the ellipse by clicking on it. You will know it is selected when the square resizing handles appear. To move the ellipse behind the rectangle, click on the Send Backward button on the Drawing Plus toolbar (see fig. 17.81).

Figure 17.80
Overlapping the
objects.

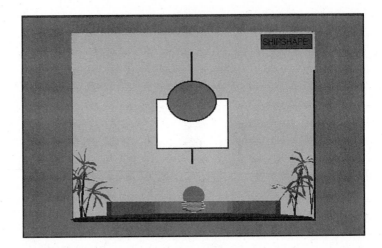

Figure 17.80
Overlapping the
objects.

Figure 17.81
Sending the circle
back one level.

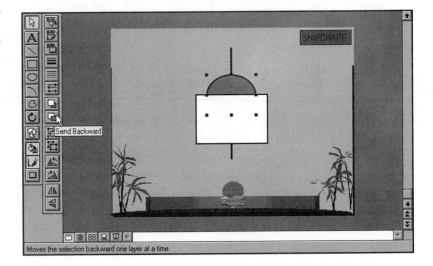

Notice that the circle is behind the rectangle but still on top of the line. Click on the Send Backward button again (see fig. 17.82). Notice now that the line is on top of the circle. To bring the circle forward on top of the line, click on the Bring Forward button (see fig. 17.83).

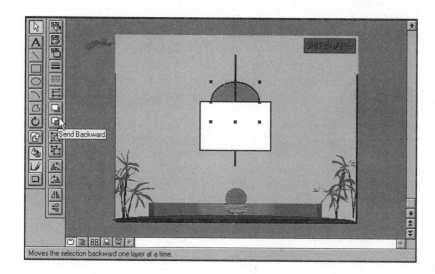

Figure 17.82
Sending the circle
back another level.

You also can access these positioning functions from the **D**raw menu. The **D**raw menu offers four choices for positioning shapes or objects:

✔ Bring to Fron**t** positions the highlighted shape on top of all other shapes or objects on the slide.

✔ Send to Bac**k** positions the highlighted shape behind all other shapes or objects on the slide.

✔ Bring **F**orward positions the highlighted shape one level forward relative to the other shapes or objects on the slide.

✔ Send **B**ackward positions the highlighted shape one level backward relative to the other shapes or objects on the slide.

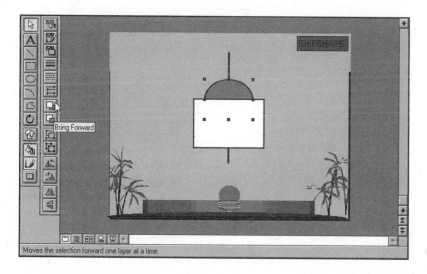

Figure 17.83
Bringing the circle
forward one level.

Grouping Objects

Right now, the three objects are separate. You can select each one individually by clicking on it. To move these objects, you would have to move them one at a time. Sometimes you will want to group objects in order to move them or ungroup objects to edit them separately. Ungrouping objects is especially useful when altering clip art, as shown in Chapter 18, "Enhancing PowerPoint Presentations."

To group the line, rectangle, and ellipse, you must select all of them at one time. Remember, you can select one object, hold down the Shift key, and select the rest; however, PowerPoint provides a shortcut. You can drag a selection box around the objects using the cursor. To drag this selection box, place the cursor in the area to the upper left of the objects. Press and hold the left mouse button until the cursor changes to a cross hair.

Drag the cross hair so that you drag a box around the three objects. A dashed outline of the box shows you whether you have surrounded all the objects. Release the left mouse button. All the objects acquire square resizing handles, which let you know they are selected (see fig. 17.84).

Figure 17.84
All objects are
selected.

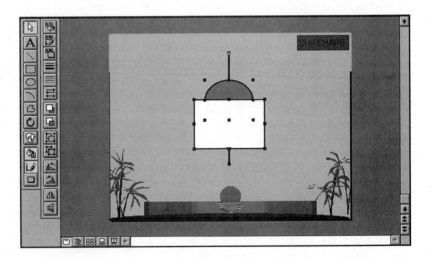

Click on the Group button on the Drawing Plus toolbar and notice that the square resizing handles encompass all the objects (see fig. 17.85). At this point, you can move or resize all the objects at one time. For example, click in the center of the rectangle and drag the mouse pointer over to the left. Notice that all the objects move together. Place the mouse pointer over a square resizing handle, grab the handle by clicking the left mouse button, and hold. Now, drag the handle the way that it will let you move. Notice that all the objects either increase or decrease in size, depending on which way you move the mouse.

Figure 17.85
Grouping the
three objects.

Flipping Objects

The next four buttons rotate and flip objects both horizontally and vertically. To flip or rotate a shape, select the shape using the Select tool and select the rotation or flip direction. Experiment with the objects you have just drawn. You can rotate or flip any object including clip art. When you are finished experimenting with objects, select them and click on the Cut button on the Standard toolbar or press Del to remove them from the slide.

AutoShapes Toolbar

The Drawing toolbar features the AutoShapes button. This button opens the AutoShapes toolbar, which is a palette of shapes for you to use in your presentations. Click on the AutoShapes button on the Drawing toolbar. The AutoShapes toolbar appears floating in the workspace (see fig. 17.86). You can move or dock the AutoShapes toolbar just as you can the other toolbars.

Use the same drawing techniques described earlier in this chapter to draw these shapes. Click on the button with the shape you want to draw and drag the cross hair on the slide until the shape is the size you want. You also can double-click on these buttons to draw the shape repeatedly.

PowerPoint AutoShapes provide an additional, diamond-shaped resizing handle that enables you to alter these shapes even further (see fig. 17.87). This handle works like the square resizing handles, but adjusts the shape's look rather than its size. To use it, place the mouse pointer on the handle until it turns into a white triangle. Click and drag the mouse to make adjustments. This shape flexibility enables you create unique shapes to emphasize and illustrate key points in a presentation.

III

PowerPoint

Figure 17.86
The AutoShapes
toolbar.

AutoShapes button

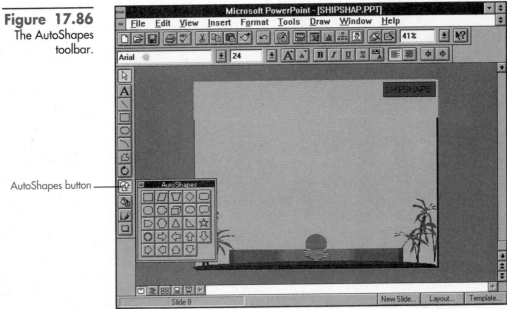

Figure 17.87
A small, diamond-
shaped handle lets
you adjust
AutoShapes.

Diamond-shaped handle

If you draw an AutoShape and decide you would like to change it to another shape, select the shape and open the Draw menu. Choose Change AutoShape and make your selection from the palette of shapes that appears. The original shape changes and can be adjusted at this time.

Working with Text within Shapes

Adding text to shapes enables you to highlight words in an interesting way. Text inside shapes can be edited just like other slide text; however, PowerPoint enables you to anchor and align text within shapes in creative ways.

Adding Text inside Shapes

To add text within a shape, open the AutoShapes toolbar if it is not already open and click on the up arrow. Draw the shape on the blank slide (see fig. 17.88). While the arrow is still selected, type **Arrow**. Notice that the word automatically appears centered in the middle of the arrow in the default font (see fig. 17.89). To add text inside a shape that has already been drawn, select the shape and begin typing.

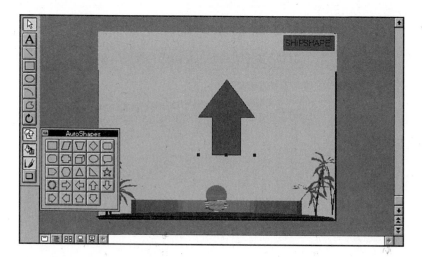

Figure 17.88
Drawing an arrow facing up.

III

PowerPoint

Understanding Text Anchor

Text anchor refers to where text is located within shapes. PowerPoint defaults to the Middle anchor point, but you can change this anchor to better suit your needs. With the arrow shape selected, select **T**ext Anchor from the F**o**rmat menu to display the Text Anchor dialog box (see fig. 17.90). Within the Text Anchor dialog box you can change the **A**nchor Point. Open the list box by clicking on the down arrow; you can choose from Top, Middle, Bottom, Top Centered, Middle Centered, and Bottom Centered. Select Bottom Centered and click on OK. Notice how the word *Arrow* moves to the bottom of the shape.

Figure 17.89
Adding text within
a shape.

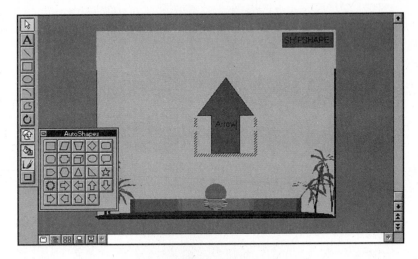

Figure 17.90
The Text Anchor
dialog box.

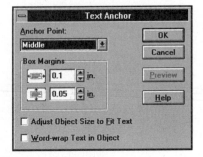

Adjusting Text within Shapes

Text does not wrap automatically within shapes. To illustrate this, click the I-beam cursor at
the end of the word *Arrow* so the cursor is flashing. Then, press the space bar and type **facing
up** (see fig. 17.91).

Notice that the words extend beyond the outline of the shape and do not wrap. However, you
can choose to have text wrap or to have the object adjust automatically to accommodate the
text. With the arrow selected, open the Text Anchor dialog box by selecting Text Anchor from
the Format menu. At the bottom of the Text Anchor dialog box there are two options: Adjust
Object Size to Fit Text and Word-wrap Text in Object. To make the text word-wrap within the
arrow, check the box in front of Word-wrap Text in Object, then click on OK. The words
Arrow facing up now wrap within the shape (see fig. 17.92).

Suppose you want the shape to automatically adjust its size to accommodate the amount of text. In this case, there is more than enough room inside the arrow to accommodate the text, so you can draw another shape. Choose the Ellipse tool and draw a small ellipse on the slide. With the shape still selected, type **Adding text inside a shape** (see fig. 17.93). Open the F̲ormat menu and choose T̲ext Anchor. Click on the Adjust Object size to F̲it Text check box and click on OK. Notice that the ellipse adjusted its size to accommodate the words (see fig. 17.94). If you type more text inside the ellipse, it will continue to adjust in size.

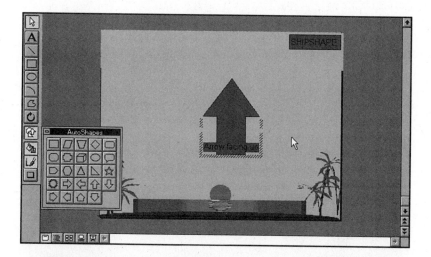

Figure 17.91
Adding more text
inside the shape.

Figure 17.92
The text wraps
inside the shape.

If you have been following along, delete the objects and hide the AutoShapes toolbar to continue.

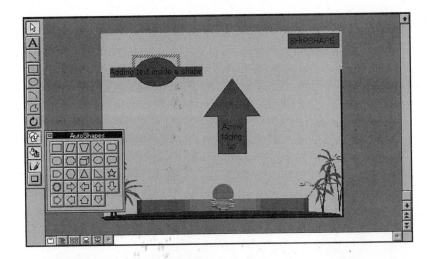

Figure 17.93
Adding text inside
a small ellipse.

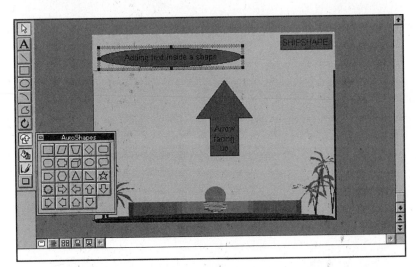

Figure 17.94
The ellipse
adjusted to fit the
text.

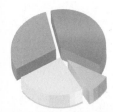

Using Alignment Tools

PowerPoint makes precisely aligning and positioning shapes or objects easy by providing tools to help. When you have many objects on a slide, adjusting each object individually to line up with other objects can be time-consuming. This section discusses the ways in which you easily can make these adjustments.

Ruler

The PowerPoint Ruler is similar to the Microsoft Word ruler. You can add tabs and define text margins within text labels or word processing boxes or shapes. To turn on the PowerPoint Ruler, open the View menu and choose Ruler. The Ruler is available only in the Slide and Notes views and extends only as wide and tall as the slide size in the Slide view and the page size in the Notes view.

The PowerPoint Ruler shows you where the cursor is positioned on the slide or notes page with dotted lines that move as you move the mouse. The ruler is in inches. On each axis, the ruler places the 0-inch mark in the center of the slide or notes page. So, if the dotted marks on each axis are on 0, the mouse pointer is positioned in the middle of the slide or notes page (see fig. 17.95).

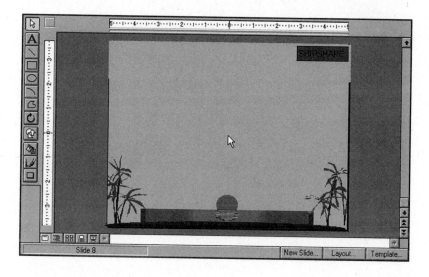

Figure 17.95
The mouse pointer is positioned in the middle of the slide.

The ruler is ideal for helping you draw sizes with specific dimensions. If you want to draw a 2-by-2-inch rectangle, for example, click on the rectangle tool and position the cross hair so that you begin to draw at 0.

Click and drag the cross hair down to the right. Make sure the dotted marks line up on 2 on both axes (see fig. 17.96). Release the mouse button when you have lined up the dotted marks.

To remove the Ruler from view, open the View menu and click on Ruler to remove the check mark.

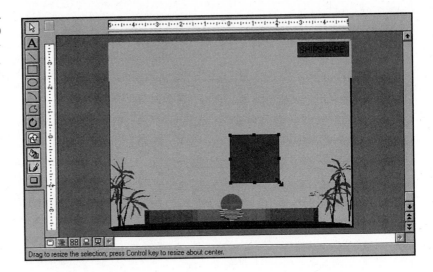

Figure 17.96
Drawing a 2-by-
2-inch rectangle.

Guides

PowerPoint guides help you to align one object or multiple objects to a straight edge. To turn the guides on, open the View menu and select Guides. Horizontal and vertical dotted lines appear on the slide. Any shapes that you draw and move near these guides will snap to the guides.

The Guides first appear intersecting at the center point of the slide. You can move the guides separately and reposition them to help you align objects. To move the guides, move the cursor on the dotted line and hold down the left mouse button. Notice the box that appears when you hold down the mouse button, showing the current location of guide in inches. Move the horizontal guide up or down and the vertical guide left or right; the guide location adjusts as you move the guide. To remove the guides from view, open the View menu and select Guides to remove the check mark.

Snap to Grid

PowerPoint's Snap to Grid option helps you to precisely align objects by providing an invisible grid of lines on the slide. To turn this grid on, open the Draw menu and select Snap to Grid.

To get a feel for working with the grid, draw a rectangle on the slide. Place the cursor inside the rectangle and hold down the left mouse button. Move the rectangle slowly down the slide. Notice how the rectangle seems to jump as it moves; this is the rectangle adhering to the invisible gridlines. You can temporarily override the grid by holding down the Alt key as you move the object. To turn off the Snap to Grid, open the Draw menu and select Snap to Grid to remove the check mark.

Understanding the Masters

PowerPoint Masters are powerful because they enable you to make formatting changes that apply to all the slides, outline pages, audience handout pages, and notes pages included in your presentation package. By making changes or additions in one place, you do not have to take the time to make changes on each individual slide or page.

PowerPoint provides masters for Slides, Outlines, Handouts, and Notes. Handouts are paper printouts that show two or six slides on a page. Sometimes you want to pass a printout of the presentation slides to audience members for their information. Handouts provide an easy, automatic way to prepare these pages.

Often you will want the date or a page number to appear on audience handouts or slides. The Masters are a perfect place to add these objects and automate them for even more time savings. This section discusses each of the four PowerPoint Masters and which objects can be inserted on the Master. A basic understanding of the PowerPoint Masters can help you save formatting time.

The Slide Master

The PowerPoint Slide Master contains formatting information that is applied to every slide in a presentation. The Slide Master enables you to conveniently change slide characteristics, such as the slide title position, the body text position, slide background colors, text formatting, and bullet formatting. By making changes in one place, you do not have to take the time to make changes on each individual slide. For example, in the Shipshape Cruise Lines training presentation, when you placed the word *SHIPSHAPE* on the Slide Master, you placed it on every slide in the presentation.

To view the Slide Master, open the View menu and select Master, then choose Slide Master. Or hold down the Shift key as you click on the Slide View button. The Status bar reads Slide Master. Notice that the toolbars do not change when changing views from the PowerPoint Slide view to the Slide Master. At this point, you can make any text-formatting changes or add objects that you want to appear on every slide. You work in the Slide Master just as you would in the Slide view; the difference is that additions or changes affect every slide in the presentation.

To change text formats, select the text and make changes using the toolbar buttons or the menus. If you want every slide title to be underlined, for example, select *Click to edit Master title style* and click on the Underline button on the Formatting toolbar (see fig. 17.97).

Suppose you wanted to change the bullet color from yellow to pink on every slide. Click on the words *Click to edit Master text style* (see fig. 17.98). Open the Format menu and choose Bullet to display the Bullet dialog box. Open the Special Color list box and click on the pink color block (see fig. 17.99). Click on OK and notice the bullet turns to pink. You can change the bullet colors and styles on any level of text by following these same steps. To view these changes in the presentation, click on the Slide View button.

Figure 17.97
Formatting the
slide titles
throughout a
presentation.

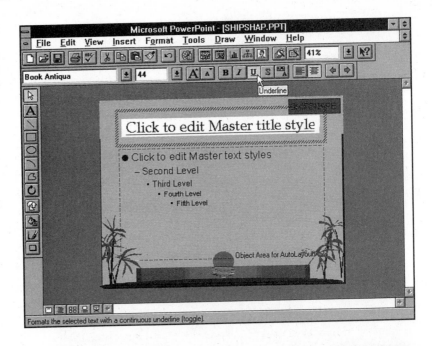

Figure 17.98
Selecting the first
bullet point.

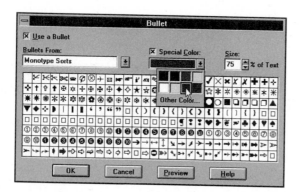

Figure 17.99
Changing the
bullet color.

The Outline Master

To view the Outline Master, open the <u>V</u>iew menu and choose <u>M</u>aster. Then, from the dialog box, select <u>O</u>utline Master. The status bar tells you that you are viewing the Outline Master.

The Outline Master appears as a clean sheet of paper (see fig. 17.100). At times you might want to add a company logo or name to the Outline master for identification. Remember, by adding these objects on the master, they appear on every printed page.

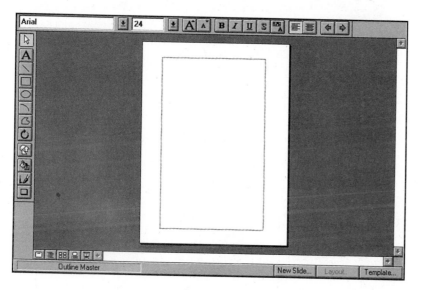

Figure 17.100
The PowerPoint
Outline Master.

The Handout Master

To view the Handout Master, open the <u>V</u>iew menu and choose <u>M</u>aster. Then, from the dialog box, select Han<u>d</u>out Master. The Handout Master appears much like the Outline

Master—a blank page—except the Handout Master outlines where slides appear if you print handouts with two or six slides (see fig. 17.101).

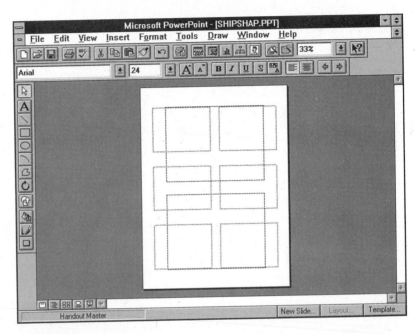

The Notes Master

To view the Notes Master, open the **V**iew menu and choose **M**aster. Then, from the dialog box, select **N**otes Master. The Notes Master shows a small Slide Master and a box labeled Notes Area for AutoLayouts (see fig. 17.102). You are able to type in this box any notes that you want to appear on every note printout. Commonly, however, you will not want to type any text here because the notes will differ from slide to slide. You might want to add a logo or page numbers.

Inserting Items on the Masters

Many times you will want the date, time, or page numbers to appear on every slide, notes page, handout page, or outline page. PowerPoint Masters are the perfect place to add these items. PowerPoint even takes this process a step further by using items similar to field codes in Microsoft Word. These items automatically keep track of dates, times, and page numbers so you don't have to.

To place the date on every handout page, for example, open the **V**iew menu and choose **M**aster. Then choose Han**d**out Master. Open the **I**nsert menu and choose D**a**te. Two slashes appear side by side on the Handout Master in a box with black resizing handles (see fig. 17.103). The actual date will not appear until you print the handout pages.

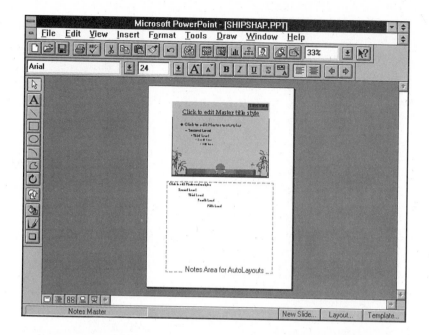

Figure 17.102
The PowerPoint
Notes Master.

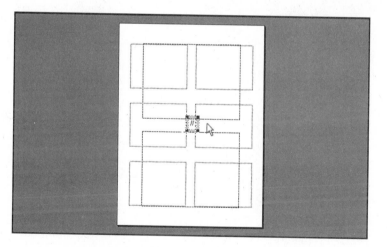

Figure 17.103
How the date first
appears on the
Handout Master.

To move the date to the lower left corner of the handout master, place the cursor on the gray border of the box. Click and drag the box down into the left corner. Release the left mouse button when the box is positioned where you want it (see fig. 17.104).

You can format text by making selections from toolbars. Follow these same steps to insert the time or page numbers on other PowerPoint Masters. Notice the other items you can add on the Masters. All these other items come into the Masters in the same way as the date did. In many cases, however, you have to decrease or increase the size of the objects.

Figure 17.104
Placing the date in
the lower left corner
of the handout
page.

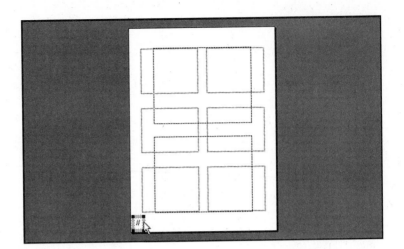

Chapter Snapshot

PowerPoint provides a number of tools to help you enhance your presentations, such as adding color schemes and slide transitions. PowerPoint also provides tools to help you become a more effective and polished presenter, including Drill Down and hidden slides containing information you can retrieve during a presentation to answer difficult audience questions. PowerPoint automates creating graphs and organizational charts to make developing these objects easy and quick, while keeping them professional-looking. Customizing existing clip art helps to further customize your presentations and make them look as though you hired a professional designer.

This chapter will help you further enhance your presentations by providing tools to perfect your delivery. This chapter discusses the following topics:

Most importantly, PowerPoint provides continuous help when executing most common tasks while creating a presentation. PowerPoint Cue Cards present the directions for completing PowerPoint features such as editing clip art or adding sound or video.

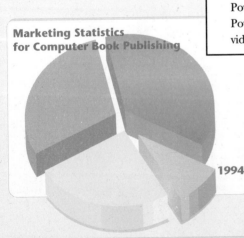

Marketing Statistics
for Computer Book Publishing

1994

CHAPTER

Enhancing PowerPoint Presentations

by Jodi Davenport

To begin this chapter, assume you are beginning a new presentation about learning PowerPoint. Open PowerPoint and select a blank presentation from the PowerPoint dialog box. If you currently are in PowerPoint, click on New on the Standard toolbar and select Blank Presentation. From the selection of AutoLayouts, choose Title Slide. This first slide in the Blank Presentation assumes PowerPoint's default template, which includes a white slide background and black text (see fig. 18.1). Type **Learning PowerPoint 4.0** for the title and **Making presentations easy!** for the subtitle (see fig. 18.2).

Figure 18.1
The first slide
assumes the
default template.

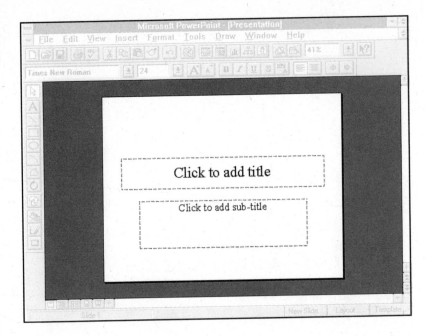

Figure 18.2
Adding title slide
text.

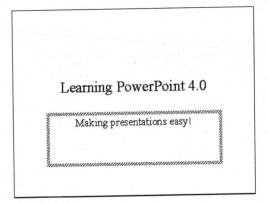

Using Color Schemes

PowerPoint guides you through choosing a presentation color scheme by offering colors based on the slide background color. PowerPoint uses color combinations that work well together so that you don't have to worry about getting into a color nightmare. You can change the color scheme for an individual slide or an entire presentation using the same techniques.

Shading a slide background can be particularly effective if you want to add a professional touch to a presentation. Making the top half of a slide dark can highlight a slide title. Leaving the bottom half light can make slide text pop off the screen.

Selecting a Color Scheme

Before you select a slide background, you need to think about the conditions under which you will deliver the information. If you will be in a dark room that seats many people, for example, slides with a dark background and lightly colored text will be easy to read for audience members in the back of the room.

PowerPoint enables you to select different color schemes for slides and notes. Normally, however, you will want to keep the background for notes white so that you do not detract from the slide image or text (not to mention use a lot of printer toner).

To begin constructing a color scheme, open the Format menu and choose Slide Color Scheme.

Because you currently are in the Slide view, the Format menu offers only options that affect slides. If you were in the Notes view, the Format menu option would read Notes Color Scheme.

The Slide Color Scheme dialog box appears and shows you the current presentation color scheme (see fig. 18.3). This color scheme is defined in the default template. The color scheme includes the slide background color, text and lines color, object shadow color, title text color, object fill color, and three accent colors. A slide preview shows you where each color is used. As seen in the slide preview, the accent colors appear in objects such as graphs.

If you want to change a single color in this scheme, click on the color block you want to change and then click on Change Color. A color palette appears; make a color selection and click on OK. To create a new color, click on More Colors in the color palette box and follow the steps outlined in the section "Choosing and Formatting Fonts" in Chapter 17, "PowerPoint Tools and Concepts."

To use PowerPoint's preset color schemes to change the scheme of a single slide or an entire presentation, click on Choose Scheme in the Slide Color Scheme dialog box to display the Choose Scheme dialog box (see fig. 18.4). The far left box in the dialog box presents multiple slide background colors. PowerPoint asks you to select the slide background color. Use the vertical scroll bar next to the Background Color selection box to view other colors. For this presentation, choose a light background color by clicking on the color.

III

PowerPoint

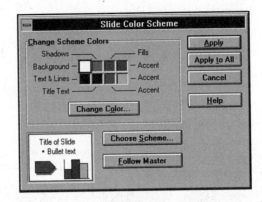

Figure 18.3
The Slide Color
Scheme dialog
box.

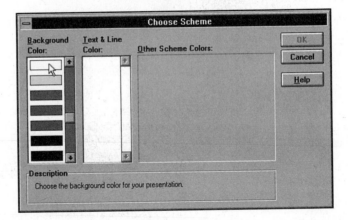

Figure 18.4
The Choose
Scheme dialog
box.

When you click on a color, PowerPoint presents color options for text and lines in the Text & Line Color box (see fig. 18.5). Scroll through these colors to see which colors PowerPoint suggests based on the slide background color you chose. Choose a dark color for the text and lines. PowerPoint then offers options, pictorially, for a title color, an object fill color, and three accent colors. PowerPoint suggests these colors because they blend well with the text and line color you chose (see fig. 18.6).

PowerPoint tells you that if you want to see other color options, select a different background or text and line color. Mixing and matching to get just the right combination is easy with PowerPoint's suggestions. Click on OK to feed these colors into the color palette in the Slide Color Scheme dialog box. To apply these colors to a single slide, click on Apply. You want to apply this scheme to all the slides in the presentation, so click on Apply to All. The color scheme you designed is implemented in the title slide.

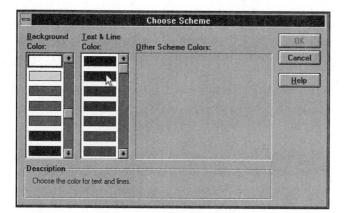

Figure 18.5
Colors for text and lines appear in the Text & Line Color box.

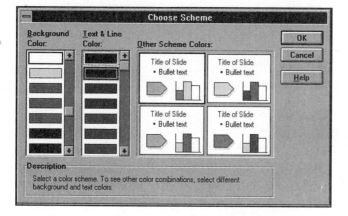

Figure 18.6
PowerPoint shows you color options in the Other Scheme Colors box.

Shading

Shading can add interest to an ordinary slide background. PowerPoint lets you choose from various shading directions to highlight certain areas of the slides depending on the slide background color you chose. To access the shading options, choose Slide Background from the Format menu to display the Slide Background dialog box. Currently there is no shade style on the slide background. Click on the Vertical shade style and observe the variants that appear in the Variants box (see fig. 18.7). Below the Variants box is a dark to light scale that enables you to change the shading color. Move the handle closer to Light and notice the changes in the Variants box.

Through the Slide Background dialog box, PowerPoint enables you to select a different background color. Select Change Color and work through the Background Color dialog box if you decide to alter the color. Remember, however, that this background color will not be in sync with the color scheme you developed earlier in this section. If you really want to change the slide background color, work through the Color Scheme dialog box to keep the colors compatible. To revert to the shading defined in the current Slide Master, click on the Follow Master button. Clicking on this button also reverts to no shading style, because the default master defines no shading.

Figure 18.7
The Variants box shows the different combinations of shading.

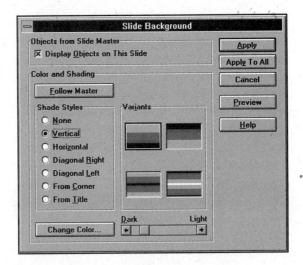

Click on Apply to change the shading style on an individual slide. To implement the shading on every slide in a presentation, choose Apply to All. To see how the shading looks on your slide, choose a shading style and variant and click on Apply (because you currently have a single title slide).

If you want to add shading to the background of Notes pages, change to the Notes view by clicking on the Notes View button. Then, open the Format menu and select Notes Background. Experiment with a few shading styles and variants to change the background on the Notes page. You probably will want to keep the Notes background white to keep the focus on the slide and notes.

Using Microsoft Graph

On the second slide in this presentation, you want to present a graph showing how many new PowerPoint users there will be in the next three months. PowerPoint makes creating a graph easy with Microsoft Graph. Insert Slide 2 by clicking on the New Slide button. From the AutoLayouts, select Graph (see fig. 18.8). Type **New PowerPoint Users** for the title. Double-click where it says to add a graph to access Microsoft Graph.

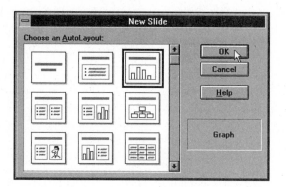

Figure 18.8
Selecting Graph from the AutoLayouts.

Microsoft Graph Datasheet

Microsoft Graph opens over the PowerPoint presentation and uses a datasheet to capture data to drive the chart. The datasheet appears on top of the chart with data already in some of the datasheet cells (see fig. 18.9). The menu bar now includes drop-down menus with commands pertaining to Microsoft Graph. Microsoft Graph uses its own Standard toolbar, which appears docked at the top of the workspace. Under the datasheet is the current slide and how the graph appears on the slide. You can edit this chart directly when the datasheet is not showing using Microsoft Graph functions discussed in this section. Clicking on the slide will take you back to PowerPoint.

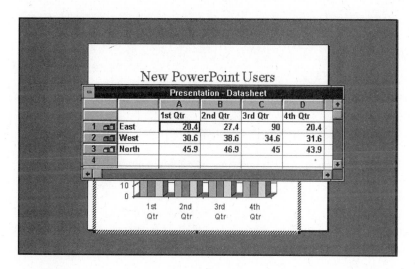

Figure 18.9
A Microsoft Graph datasheet.

III

PowerPoint

Tip

If at any time you accidentally click on the slide and return to your presentation, double-click on the chart to take you back to Microsoft Graph.

The Microsoft Graph datasheet looks like a Microsoft Excel spreadsheet with rows, columns, and cells; however, the datasheet does not use formulas. You can import Microsoft Excel spreadsheet information into a datasheet or cut and paste it into the datasheet to save time. Also, you can export datasheet information.

To change data in the cells, double-click on a cell. A flashing cursor appears, waiting for you to enter data. The mouse pointer also changes to an I-beam, enabling you to select, delete, and reenter information. Just as you can select multiple cells in Excel spreadsheets, you also can select multiple cells in the datasheet. You can edit information using the Cut, Copy, and Paste buttons on the Standard toolbar, just as you edit data in Excel spreadsheets. Click on the Cut button on the standard toolbar to remove the data.

To clear the current information in the datasheet, select all the cells by clicking on the button where the column and row headings intersect (see fig. 18.10) and press Del. The datasheet now is clear for you to input new PowerPoint users information. Click on the cell under column A and type **January** (see fig. 18.11).

Figure 18.10
Selecting all the cells in the datasheet.

	A	B	C	D	
	1st Qtr	2nd Qtr	3rd Qtr	4th Qtr	
1 East	20.4	27.4	90	20.4	
2 West	30.6	38.6	34.6	31.6	
3 North	45.9	46.9	45	43.9	
4					

Presentation - Datasheet

Figure 18.11
Entering text in the datasheet.

	A	B	C	D	
	January				
1					
2					
3					
4					

Presentation - Datasheet

Press the right-arrow key once and enter **February** under column B. Under column C, enter **March**. Click in row 1 and type **# of Users**. If the text does not fit in the column, open the Format menu and choose Column Width. Enter a larger number to widen the column. In the datasheet, in row 1, column A, type **50**. In row 1, column B, type **75**. In row 1, column C, type **100** (see fig. 18.12).

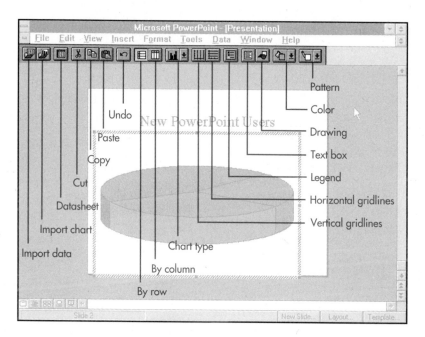

Figure 18.12
Entering data in
the datasheet.

Figure 18.13
The Microsoft
Graph Standard
Toolbar.

To become quickly proficient with Microsoft Graph, a discussion of the Microsoft Graph Standard toolbar functions will be helpful.

The Standard Toolbar in Microsoft Graph

The Standard toolbar in Microsoft Graph enables you to quickly perform many Microsoft Graph functions (see fig. 18.13). The Standard toolbar in Microsoft Graph cannot be customized like the toolbars in PowerPoint. It can, however, be moved and floated in the workspace.

The Import Data Button

The Import Data button enables you to bring in data from an entire spreadsheet or a range of cells. When you click on the Import Data button, the Import Data dialog box opens and enables you to select the file from which you want to obtain the data (see fig. 18.14). To change the type of file you want to find, open the List Files of <u>T</u>ype list box. To select only a range of data, enter the range in the space provided. When you have typed the file name or range, click on OK. Another dialog box might open and ask if you want to overwrite the current data in the datasheet. Click on OK or Cancel depending on your situation.

Figure 18.14
The Import Data
dialog box.

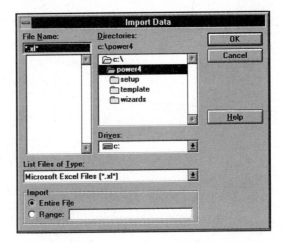

The Import Chart Button

Microsoft Graph enables you to import a chart using the Import Chart button. This button works the same way as the Import Data button. Clicking on the Import Chart button takes you to an Open Chart dialog box from which you can select a chart.

The Datasheet Button

The Datasheet button currently is pressed because the datasheet is showing. To remove the datasheet from view, click on the Datasheet button or choose <u>D</u>atasheet from the <u>V</u>iew menu. Removing the check mark removes the Datasheet from view. For now, however, click on the Datasheet button again to show the Datasheet.

The Editing Buttons

The Cut, Copy, Paste, and Undo buttons work just as they do on the Standard toolbar in PowerPoint. Select the text or object, then perform the function.

Viewing Data by Row or Column

Currently the new data is shown in rows. This is why the By Row button on the Standard toolbar is pressed. Click on the By Column button and see what happens (see fig. 18.15). Microsoft Graph assumes that you want the data to be read by columns and have the different months represent individual series of data. Click on the By Row button to change # of Users back to the data series. You also can make this change through the <u>D</u>ata menu by selecting either Series in <u>R</u>ows or Series in <u>C</u>olumns. To remove the datasheet from view to see the chart, click on the Datasheet button on the Standard toolbar.

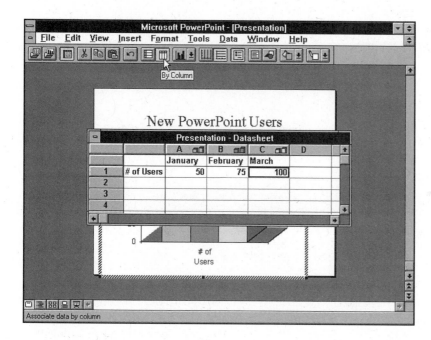

Figure 18.15
Clicking on the By Column button.

Choosing a Chart Type

Currently the information is shown in a column chart. The Chart Type button on the Standard toolbar enables you to revert quickly to a default column chart or change the type of chart through which the data is shown. Click on the down arrow next to the Chart Type button to access the types of charts Microsoft Graph offers (see fig. 18.16).

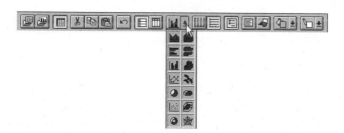

Figure 18.16
Viewing the other type of charts Microsoft Graph offers.

The first column of chart types are two-dimensional. The second column shows three-dimensional charts. The types of charts available include the following:

✔ Area charts

✔ Bar charts

✔ Column charts

✔ Line charts

✔ Pie charts

✔ Donut charts (two dimensional only)

✔ Radar charts (two dimensional only)

✔ XY Scatter charts (two dimensional only)

✔ Surface charts (three dimensional only)

You also can access the chart types by opening the Format menu and choosing Chart Type. The Chart Type dialog box opens and ask you to choose either a two-dimensional or three-dimensional chart. The chart options will change depending on the dimension you select. Choose 3-D bar chart as an example. Click on the chart type with the mouse pointer and click on OK. Now you are viewing the new information in a 3-D bar chart.

Formatting a Chart

The Horizontal Gridline button is pressed in the Standard toolbar because these gridlines appear on the chart (although they appear vertically on the bar chart). The Legend button is pressed because a legend is currently showing. You can move the legend anywhere within the chart. The chart size might adjust to accommodate the legend. Move the cursor over the legend. Click and hold the mouse button and move the legend off the bar on the chart.

The legend has black, square resizing handles. Move the cursor over the bottom middle handle; notice the black arrows show you in which direction you can adjust the size. Grab the handle and make the legend larger by dragging the mouse down (see fig. 18.17). To remove the legend, click on the Legend button.

To insert a text box in the graph, click on the Text Box button and move the cursor over the chart. You cannot draw a text box anywhere outside the parameters of the chart. The mouse pointer changes to a cross hair. Drag a rectangle just as you would in PowerPoint, by holding down the left mouse button and dragging the mouse. Type the sentence **Many people will want to learn PowerPoint in the future** (see fig. 18.18).

The text size is very small. With the Text Box selected, open the Format menu and choose Font. The Format Object dialog box opens. Enlarge the text size to 12 point and click on OK (see fig. 18.19).

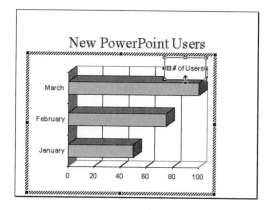

Figure 18.17
Enlarging the legend.

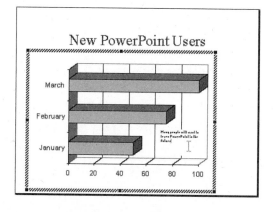

Figure 18.18
Adding a text box to the chart.

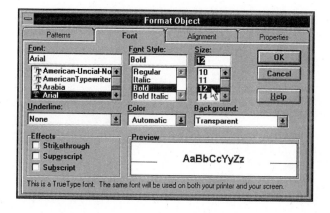

Figure 18.19
Enlarging the text size in the Format Object dialog box.

III

PowerPoint

The Graph Drawing Toolbar

Microsoft Graph features a Drawing toolbar that is similar to the Drawing and Drawing Plus toolbars in PowerPoint. Click on the Drawing button to show the Drawing toolbar, as shown in figure 18.20. You can manipulate and move the Drawing toolbar just like other toolbars. Move the toolbar off the chart by dragging the title bar with the cursor (see fig. 18.21).

Figure 18.20
The Drawing toolbar in Microsoft Graph.

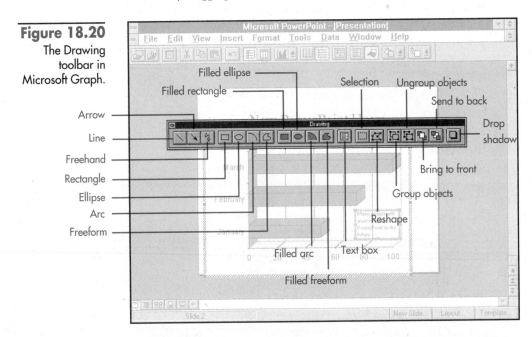

Figure 18.21
Moving the Drawing toolbar off the chart.

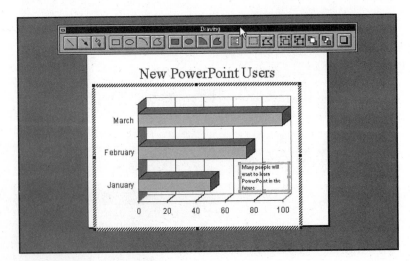

The toolbar buttons show which objects you can draw, using the same techniques as for the PowerPoint Drawing toolbar. Many buttons even look the same. To find out which buttons draw which objects, move the cursor over the button to activate the Tool Tip. To draw an object, click on the button, then move the cross hair within the chart area. Click and hold down the left mouse button, then move the mouse to draw the object.

Unlike the Freeform tool in PowerPoint, the Freehand tool remains in freehand mode and never reverts to drawing straight lines like the Freeform tool. The Selection tool enables you to drag a selection box around a number of objects or to select them at one time. This feature also is available in PowerPoint on the Drawing toolbar, but pictures a white arrow rather than a dashed outline of a rectangle.

Use the Reshape button to alter the vertices of a polygon. When the polygon is selected, click on the Reshape button to apply square resizing handles to each vertex of the polygon. You can grab these handles to reshape the polygon. Click on the Reshape button again to remove the square handles from the vertices and return to having the entire object selected.

The Group Objects, Ungroup Objects, Send to Back, Bring to Front, and Shadow buttons on the Microsoft Graph Drawing toolbar work just as they do in PowerPoint. Leave the Drawing toolbar open for the next exercise.

The Color and Pattern buttons on Microsoft Graph's Standard toolbar function to fill objects that you have drawn on the chart. To show how these buttons work, draw a filled ellipse on the chart (see fig. 18.22) using the Ellipse button on the Drawing toolbar.

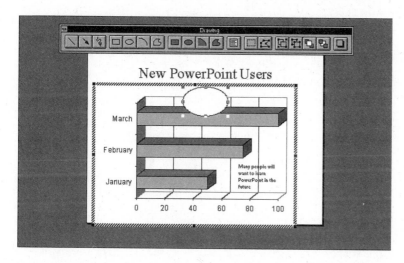

Figure 18.22
Drawing a filled
ellipse on the chart.

III

PowerPoint

The Color button shows a tipped paint can and a block of color. If you want the ellipse to be filled with this color, click on the button. If you want to select another fill color, click on the down arrow next to the Color button to display a palette of colors (see fig. 18.23). Click on the fill color you want and watch the ellipse fill with that color. If you want the ellipse to have no fill, click on None in the color palette.

Figure 18.23
Opening the fill color options.

The Pattern button pictures a pencil drawing and a block with no pattern inside. If you want the object to have no pattern, click on the Pattern button. If you want to select a pattern, click on the down arrow and select a pattern from the choices presented on the pattern palette.

To continue following along with the examples, remove the filled ellipse and the text box by selecting each and clicking on Cut on the Standard toolbar or pressing Del.

Editing the Chart

Microsoft Graph makes editing a chart's formatting easy with AutoFormat. To use AutoFormat, make sure the chart is selected and select A̲utoFormat from the Fo̲rmat menu. The AutoFormat dialog box opens and presents many possible formats for the current chart (see fig. 18.24).

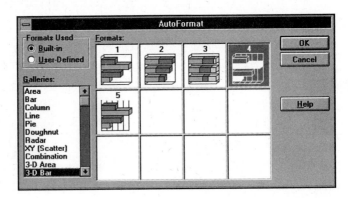

Figure 18.24
The AutoFormat dialog box, showing different formats for a 3-D bar chart.

The 3-D bar chart appears with gridlines or without gridlines, or with bars side by side or stacked. You don't have to worry about finding the gridlines buttons; you can make these stylistic changes in the AutoFormat dialog box. You can also change the chart type in this dialog box by making a selection in the G̲alleries box that lists two-dimensional and three-dimensional chart types. Click on 3-D Column and choose Format 4, then click on OK.

Microsoft Graph enables you to change the 3-D view of a chart. Open the Fo̲rmat menu and select 3̲-D View. The Format 3-D View dialog box opens and shows a wireframe of the current chart (see fig. 18.25). To change the elevation at which you view the chart, click on the up- or

down-arrow buttons; the wireframe of the chart reflects these changes (see fig. 18.26). To change the chart's rotation, click on the rotate right or left buttons; the outlined chart also reflects these changes. When the view is where you want it, click on OK. If you want to return to the original view, click on **D**efault.

Microsoft Graph enables you to quickly make many changes to the chart in one dialog box. Suppose you want to change the font and font size for January, February, and March. Click on January on the chart and notice that the axis on which these labels fall acquires black handles. You now can make changes to the text that falls on this axis and changes to the axis itself.

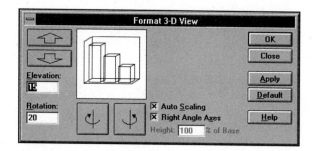

Figure 18.25

The Format 3-D View dialog box.

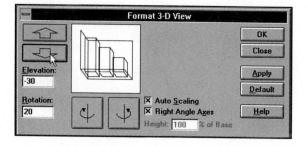

Figure 18.26

Changing the chart's elevation.

III

PowerPoint

Open the F**o**rmat menu and choose **F**ont. The Format Axis dialog box opens with the Font tab in front (see fig. 18.27). Notice the tabs running along the top of the dialog box labeled Patterns, Scale, Font, Number, and Alignment. Think of these as tabbed cards that you can pull forward depending on the formatting changes you want to make. You can make changes to all these chart aspects in one dialog box.

Tip

The Format Object dialog box in PowerPoint uses these same tabs, enabling you to make multiple formatting changes to a selected object in one dialog box.

Figure 18.27
The Format Axis
dialog box with
the Font tab in
front.

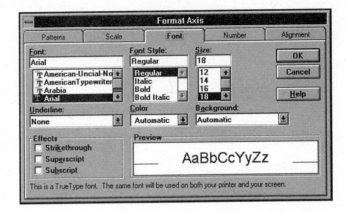

Figure 18.27
The Format Axis
dialog box with
the Font tab in
front.

Make the text bold, then click on the tab labeled Alignment to move the Alignment tab to the front. Select the vertical text facing down (see fig. 18.28). Click on OK to see how the text changes orientation. With the axis still selected, click the right mouse button to access a shortcut menu (see fig. 18.29). You can select Format Axis to open the dialog box again and make changes.

Figure 18.28
Changing the
direction of the
text.

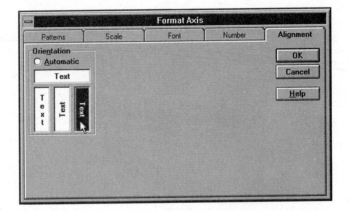

Tip

Microsoft Graph provides many shortcut menus that open and present options that relate to the selected chart objects. Experiment by selecting chart objects and pressing the right mouse button to see the options on the shortcut menu that appears.

Remove the Drawing toolbar by clicking on the Drawing button on the Standard toolbar. Click on the Datasheet button to show the datasheet.

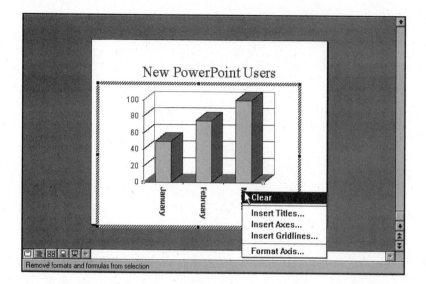

Figure 18.29
Accessing the right-mouse-button shortcut menu.

Changing Graph Colors

PowerPoint shows pictorially on the datasheet which color represents which row or column of information; for example, any information in row 1 is shown by a blue bar on the column chart. To better illustrate this, change the chart type to a 3-D pie by opening the Format menu and selecting AutoFormat. Select 3-D Pie in the Galleries listing and select Format 5 (see fig. 18.30). Notice on the datasheet that a different color pie slice is next to A, B, and C.

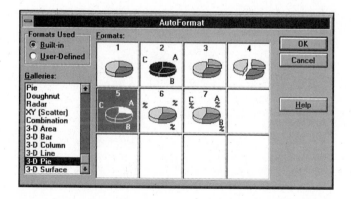

Figure 18.30
Selecting Format 5 for the 3-D Pie chart.

Remove the datasheet so that you can view the chart. To change the color of an individual pie slice, click directly on the pie slice labeled February to select it (see fig. 18.31). Square handles indicate that the slice is selected. With the cursor on the slice, click the right mouse button to open a shortcut menu.

Figure 18.31
Clicking directly on the pie slice to select it.

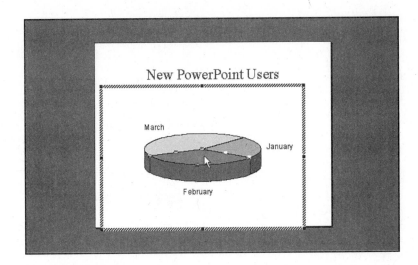

 You also can access the Format Point dialog box by double-clicking on the pie slice.

From the shortcut menu, select Format Point. The Format Data Point dialog box opens and shows the Patterns tab in front (see fig. 18.32). Select a color from the Area color palette. Next, click on the Data Labels tab to bring it forward. On the Data Labels tab, you can choose to show values or percentages on the chart. Leave the current selections and click on OK. The pie slice changes to the new fill color.

Figure 18.32
The Patterns tab in the Format Data Point dialog box.

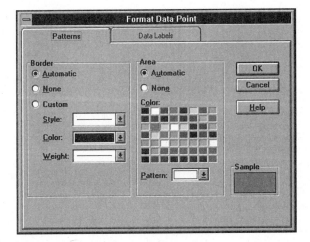

PowerPoint lets you draw attention to a pie slice by pulling the slice out from the pie. With the pie slice still selected, place the cursor in the center of the slice. Hold down the left mouse button, drag the slice down and out from the pie, and release the left mouse button (see fig. 18.33). You can move the pie slice back in by clicking and dragging it back in place.

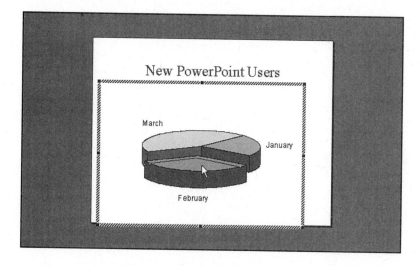

Figure18.33

Separating a pie slice to draw attention to it.

When you are done making any formatting or data changes to the chart, click on the slide outside the chart to return to the PowerPoint presentation. The chart positions itself on the slide. If you want to access Microsoft Graph again to make changes, double-click on the graph. To enlarge the chart once it is on the slide, grab a black resizing handle and adjust the size just as you would for an object.

Using Microsoft Organizational Chart

The next slide in the presentation will include an organizational chart. Making an organizational chart is easy with Microsoft Organizational Chart. Instead of tediously drawing rectangles and lines and adding text, the chart appears before you, waiting for you to fill in names, titles, or comments.

Click on New Slide. From the AutoLayouts select Org Chart (see fig. 18.34). Click to add a title and type **Potential PowerPoint Users**. Double-click where it says *Double click to add org chart* and wait for the application to open over your PowerPoint presentation. It might take some time, so don't be alarmed. When Microsoft Organization Chart opens, the beginnings of a chart already appear in the workspace just as data appears in the Microsoft Graph datasheet. This chart helps to get you started. To work through making a chart, you will select text and retype the information for your presentation.

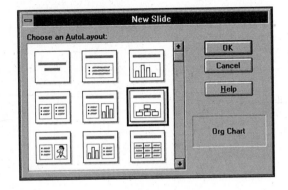

Figure 18.34
Selecting the AutoLayout featuring an organizational chart.

Changing Information

To change the organizational chart title, select the words *Chart Title* with the I-beam cursor and type **Our department structure** (see fig. 18.35). You replace the text in the organizational chart boxes in the same way. Select the top box by clicking on it, then select *Type name here* with the mouse I-beam and replace it with the name **Kelly** (see fig. 18.36).

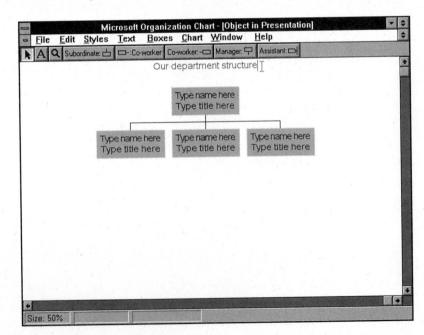

Figure 18.35
Replacing the existing text with your own.

Our department structure

Figure 18.36
Replacing the text
in the top box.

Notice that when you select the text, two lines of text labeled Comment 1 and Comment 2 appear. You can replace these comments with job functions or any comments pertaining to the position. Press the down-arrow key to select the next line of text. Replace *Type title here* with **Department Manager**. Replace *Comment 1* with **Oversees department activity**.

When you are done filling in information in the top box, click anywhere outside the box. The box resizes itself and the label *Comment 2* disappears. Fill in the information in the other boxes the same way, using the following text for examples:

✔ In the right box at the second level type **Craig**; then type **Section Manager**.

✔ In the left box at the second level type **Carol**; then type **Section Manager**.

To edit text in a box, select the box and click the mouse I-beam inside the box. Make any edits and click outside the box to implement the changes.

Suppose there were only two people directly reporting to the department manager, so you need to remove one of the three boxes. Click the mouse pointer inside the middle box and press Del. This removes the box while the remaining boxes reposition themselves.

Adding a Box

The buttons at the top of the workspace show which level each box represents. You can tell Kelly is in a Manager position, for example, because his box is identical to the picture on the Manager button.

Kelly has an assistant who needs to be placed on the organizational chart. To add this box, click on the Assistant button and move the mouse pointer into the workspace. Notice the mouse pointer assumes a miniature of the new box to be added on the chart. Because the Assistant reports to Kelly, click the mouse inside Kelly's box. Another box appears as an Assistant (see fig. 18.37). Initially there is no text in the new box. However, click the mouse pointer inside the box to make text appear. Select *Name* and type **Jeri**. Replace *Title* with **Assistant**. Then click outside the box. You can add other boxes to the organization chart in Subordinate, Co-worker, or Manager capacities in the same way you added the Assistant box.

III

PowerPoint

Figure 18.37
The Assistant box
appears on the
chart under Kelly.

Editing the Chart Style

Fonts or text colors often are used to identify levels of employees on an organizational chart. To change the characteristics of multiple boxes, you must first select them. To select more than one box, click on one box, then hold down the Shift key and click on the other boxes you want to select.

Often, however, there are many boxes with many levels of employees on an organizational chart. Selecting each box individually would be time-consuming. Microsoft Organizational Chart provides a speedy way to select multiple boxes at different levels. Suppose you wanted to select all the boxes except for the Department Manager's. Open the Edit menu and choose Select; a number of choices appear (see fig. 18.38). Because you want to select everyone except for the department manager (who is in a Manager box), choose All Non-Managers (see fig. 18.39). At this point, you can make any formatting changes you would like to the selected boxes. Then, click outside the boxes to deselect them.

Figure 18.38
The choices under
Select.

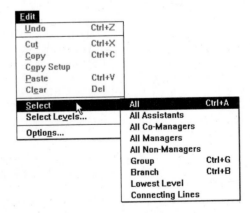

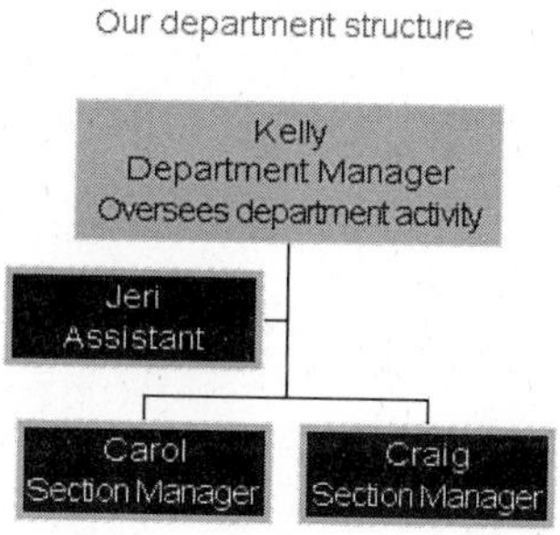

Our department structure

Figure 18.39
Selecting all the people under the Department Manager.

Microsoft Organizational Chart enables you to change the format of the boxes at each level. Currently, the bottom two boxes are side by side with lines coming out of the tops of the boxes. To change this format, select the two boxes by holding down the Shift key; then open the Styles menu to display a palette of chart styles (see fig. 18.40). Under Group styles, a button is pressed showing the current style. Click on the button under Group styles showing the boxes lined up vertically to change the group style.

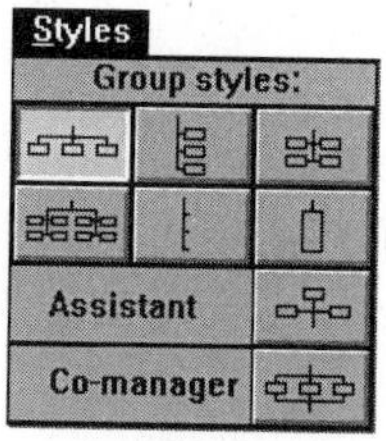

Figure 18.40
The chart styles available.

Now, suppose you want to change the text color and font size for these boxes. With the two boxes selected, open the Text menu and select Color. Choose a color, then click outside the boxes to deselect them and see the text assume that color. To change the font size, select the boxes and select Font from the Text menu. The Font dialog box appears for you to make changes to the text. To change the alignment of the text inside boxes, select the box. Open the Text menu and select the alignment: Left, Right, or Center.

You can stylize any box even further with various borders, colors, or shadows. To make these changes, select a box or boxes and open the Boxes menu; a number of choices appear. The first three options pertain to boxes. To change a box border, select Box Border and make a selection from the palette of borders. The remaining options work the same way.

To change the chart's background color, open the Chart menu and select Background Color. A palette of colors appears from which you can choose. Remember that this color appears on the slide and might clash with your color scheme.

Changing the Zoom Level

Microsoft Organizational Chart enables you to view the chart at four magnification levels and provides shortcuts to access these levels:

Magnification Level	Shortcut Key
Size to Window	F9
50% of Actual	F10
Actual Size	F11
200% of Actual	F12

You also can access these views through the Chart menu. Use the button picturing a magnifying glass on the toolbar to quickly zoom in to the 200% of Actual view. Click on the Zoom button and place the magnifying glass anywhere on the chart. Click the left mouse button to zoom in. When you zoom in, the Zoom button on the toolbar changes to a button picturing an organizational chart (see fig. 18.41). Click on on this button and click anywhere on the chart to see the entire chart in the window.

Figure 18.41
The zoomed-in chart. Note that the Zoom button changes to a button with an organizational chart.

Zoom button, changed to organizational chart

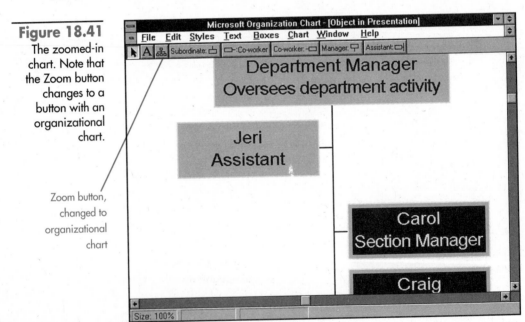

Drawing Tools

Microsoft Organizational Chart provides drawing tools to help you highlight certain areas of the chart. To show the drawing tools on the toolbar, open the <u>C</u>hart menu and select Show <u>D</u>raw Tools. The tools appear as buttons on the toolbar, as shown in figure 18.42.

Figure 18.42

The Microsoft Organizational Chart drawing tools.

The first drawing tool shows a crosshair and enables you to draw only vertical or horizontal lines. To draw a vertical or horizontal line, click on the button and move the cursor into the workspace; the cursor changes to a crosshair. Hold down the left mouse button and drag the mouse vertically to draw a vertical line, or horizontally to draw a horizontal line. The second drawing tool is used to draw lines, and works just as it does in PowerPoint. Simply click on the button, move the cursor into the workspace to change the cursor to a crosshair, and click and drag the mouse. To change the thickness, style, or color of any line drawn on the organizational chart, select it and then open the <u>B</u>oxes menu. The line formatting choices appear at the bottom of the drop-down menu.

Sometimes on an organizational chart, some boxes need to connect to other boxes to show additional relationships. Suppose one of the section managers occasionally reports directly to the department manager; you would want to draw a dotted line to show this unconventional channel of reporting. Microsoft Organizational Chart provides a drawing tool to help you draw these lines without having to draw multiple straight lines. To demonstrate this, click on the dotted line drawing button on the toolbar.

Move the crosshair inside the department manager's box. Click and hold the left mouse button and move the cross hair into one of the section managers' boxes. Notice that the faint outline of a line appears. Release the left mouse button to show the new dotted line (see fig. 18.43). This line shows the additional reporting path.

You can add a rectangle to the chart by clicking on the Rectangle button and using drawing techniques outlined in Chapter 17, "PowerPoint Tools and Concepts."

The Text Tool button just to the right of the Selection Tool button enables you to add a text label to the chart outside of a chart box. This tool works just like the Text tool in PowerPoint. Simply click on the button and move the mouse I-beam near the chart. Click the left mouse button to anchor a flashing cursor and begin typing.

After you have created and formatted the organizational chart, open the <u>F</u>ile menu and choose E<u>x</u>it and Return to Presentation to close Microsoft Organizational Chart and return to PowerPoint. The organizational chart appears on the slide, and you can resize it using the square resizing handles.

Figure 18.43
Automatically
drawing a new
dotted line.

Adding Clip Art

The images from the Microsoft Clip Art Gallery enable you to enhance a presentation or emphasize a key point. You can rotate or flip clip art like any other object and cut, copy, and paste it. Most of the time, clip art comes into the presentation either too large or in colors that do not compliment a color scheme. PowerPoint enables you to modify clip art extensively to make it work for your presentation. This section discusses resizing clip art and manipulating it to fit your needs.

Recategorizing Clip Art

To begin, add a new slide to your presentation by clicking on New Slide. From the AutoLayouts, select Text & Clip Art. For the title, type **PowerPoint Presentations**. Double-click on the box to access the Microsoft Clip Art Gallery.

The Microsoft Clip Art Gallery opens and presents images in All Categories. Suppose you wanted to use the first image, Professor, from the Academic category in your PowerPoint presentation. You also think this image would work well in future presentations about sales techniques. In fact, moving through all the clip art, you notice that there are a number of images in different categories that would work well in those presentations. Microsoft Clip Art Gallery enables you to recategorize clip art into categories that you specify.

Select the image of the professor by clicking on it; a blue box shows that the image is selected. Move the cursor down to the bottom of the workspace and click on the Category: Academic button (see fig. 18.44).

Clicking on this button takes you to the Edit Picture Information dialog box. In this dialog box you can create a new category and reassign the selected clip art into this category. The dialog box asks you to type a new category or description for the image. With the category Academic selected, type **Sales Presentation**. Click on the Tab button to select the image

description Professor. Type **Man Presenting** (see fig. 18.45). Click on OK to make these changes and return to the Clip Art Gallery. Notice that the descriptions of the image have changed but the image remains in its original location.

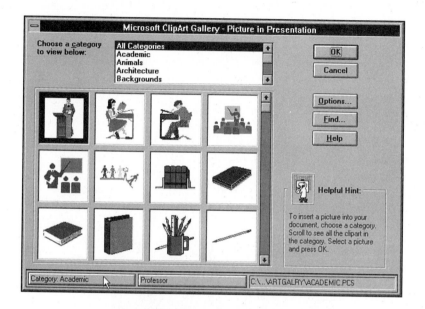

Figure 18.44
Clicking on the Category button.

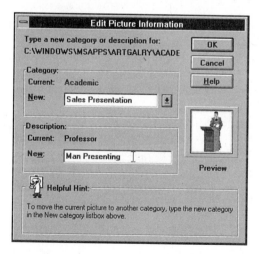

Figure 18.45
Retyping a new category and description.

III
PowerPoint

In the categories box, scroll down and find the category Sales Presentation. Select that category and notice that the Man Presenting is the only image in this category. Return to the Academic category and notice that the Professor image is now gone because it has been moved to the Sales Presentation category. Microsoft Clip Art Gallery rearranges the images after you have reassigned their categories.

Return now to the Sales Presentation category and double-click on the Man Presenting image to bring it into the presentation. Notice how the image comes into the presentation distorted. The next section discusses the way to remedy this problem.

Resizing Clip Art

The Man Presenting image needs to be elongated vertically. Move the cursor over the top middle square resizing handle until it turns to black arrows (see fig. 18.46). Grab the handle and pull the image up over the title box. Release the left mouse button and notice that the image looks much more proportional (see fig. 18.47).

Figure 18.46
Preparing to elongate the disproportional image.

Figure 18.47
The image is proportional, but too large.

Now the image is too large for the slide and must be reduced; however, you do not want to disturb the proportions. If you used the square resizing handles to adjust the size of the image, the image would no longer be proportional. You need to scale the image down. With the clip art selected, indicated by the square resizing handles, open the Draw menu and choose Scale. The Scale dialog box opens and shows you that the image is currently showing at 100 percent. Reduce the image to 80 percent by clicking on the down arrow, or select 100 with the I-beam cursor and retype **80**. Click on OK. The clip art is a much better size for the slide and maintains its proportions. To move the clip art down a little bit, move the cursor on the image and hold down the left mouse button to drag the image down.

Using these same steps, you can alter the size of any clip art but keep the proportions the same. Use the square resizing handles when proportions are not a concern or when you purposely want to adjust the image.

Recoloring Clip Art

PowerPoint enables you to change the colors incorporated in clip art. Suppose you wanted to change the man's tie from blue to pink. Select the image by clicking on it, then open the Tools menu and select Recolor. The Recolor Picture dialog box opens and presents the original colors and the new colors (see fig. 18.48).

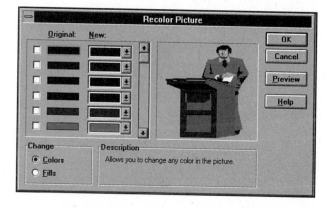

Figure 18.48
The Recolor Picture dialog box.

You can choose to change the colors in the picture or change only the fill colors and not the line colors. The Description box tells you this information when you choose either choice in the Change box. Leave the option at Colors for this exercise.

From the miniature of the image in the dialog box, you can see that the man's tie is blue. Find the matching blue color in the Original column of colors, using the vertical scroll bar if you have to. The second color from the top appears to be the blue color of the tie. Open the color palette of the blue in the New column by clicking once on the down arrow (see fig. 18.49). Select the pink color block. To see a preview of the pink tie, click on Preview. If you don't like how the new color looks, remove the check mark in the box before the original color. If you do like the new color, leave the check box and click on OK. The clip art on the slide reflects this color change.

Figure 18.49
Opening the new color options for this color.

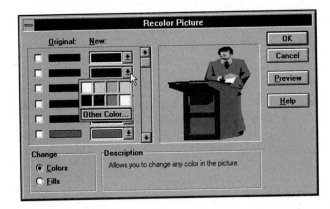

Cropping Clip Art

At times you will want to crop an image for a presentation. You could, for example, crop the image of the man at the podium from the waist up if you wanted to make more room on the slide. To crop clip art, select the image, then open the Tools menu and choose Crop Picture. Move the cursor over the slide and notice that the cursor changes to a cropping pointer. The status bar tells you to move the cropping pointer over a square resizing handle. Move the cropping pointer over the bottom right square resizing handle.

Now, click and drag the pointer up to the man's waist to crop the bottom of the picture (see fig. 18.50). Release the left mouse button to see the cropping. To remove the cropping and return the picture to its full size, drag the bottom right handle back down using the cropping pointer. The cropping pointer will not move any further down when the picture is at its full size. To turn the cropping pointer off, press Esc.

Figure 18.50
Cropping the bottom of the picture.

Editing Clip Art

PowerPoint clip art is composed of multiple shapes with different fill colors and shading grouped together. The clip art you bring in from the Clip Art Gallery, however, needs to be converted to PowerPoint clip art to be edited. To illustrate, select the Man Presenting image by clicking on it with the cursor. The image acquires square resizing handles to indicate that it is selected.

From the Draw menu, select Ungroup. An information box appears, explaining that the image is not a group of objects and will be converted to a PowerPoint object (see fig. 18.51). Doing this, however, will eradicate any linking or embedding information associated with the image. If you did not want to change these associations, you could press Cancel. Click on OK, however, to ungroup the image for editing purposes.

Figure 18.51
The imported object information box.

After you ungroup an image, you cannot use the Recolor or Crop Picture commands through the Tools menu. Do any recoloring or cropping before you begin ungrouping the image.

Notice now that the image has two sets of square resizing handles, one around the man and one around the podium (see fig. 18.52). Click off the slide to remove the resizing handles. Then, click once directly on the podium to select that piece. Move the podium off the man by clicking and dragging it to the left. Notice that the man's legs are behind the podium (see fig. 18.53). You can separate all clip art in this way and use it as separate pieces. You could delete the image of the man if you wanted only a picture of a podium, or vice versa. Just think—you now have even more pieces of the clip art than you originally saw in the Clip Art Gallery. Delete the podium by selecting it and clicking on Cut on the Standard toolbar or pressing Del.

Suppose you wanted to remove the piece of paper from the man's hand. The images ungroup in levels, meaning that the man's hand and paper could be one group that needs to be further ungrouped. Click the cursor directly on the piece of paper; square resizing handles appear around the man (see fig. 18.54). Select Ungroup again from the Draw menu. A smaller square appears around the man's hand and piece of paper. With this small square selected, open the Draw menu and choose Ungroup again. Continue to select Ungroup until you can click on the piece of paper and square resizing handles appear around it. Click off the slide again to remove the selections, then click directly on the piece of paper. With it selected, click on Cut on the Standard toolbar. The piece of paper is removed.

If you make a mistake and delete part of the man that you didn't want to, you can select <u>U</u>ndo from the <u>E</u>dit menu or click on the Undo button on the Standard toolbar.

Figure 18.52
Square resizing handles appear around the man and around the podium.

Figure 18.53
Viewing the man behind the podium.

Figure 18.54
Clicking directly on the piece of paper produces resizing handles around the man.

You want to regroup the entire image so that you don't mistakenly move a piece out of place. Grouping the image makes moving it easier. To make sure you select all the images associated with the man, use the Selection tool to drag a selection box around the man. To drag this box, move the cursor somewhere above the man but not in the title window. If you click in the title window, you will select the title box (which is not associated with the man). Click and drag the mouse to draw an invisible box around the entire image of the man. Release the left mouse button to select all the pieces of the image (see fig. 18.55). Now, open the Draw menu and choose Group. The square resizing handles show that the image is now just one piece.

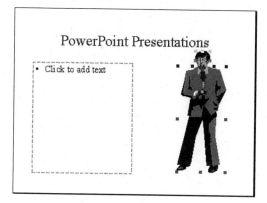

Figure 18.55
Selecting all the pieces associated with the image of the man.

Remain on the slide titled "PowerPoint Presentations" showing the image of the man to work through the next sections.

Exploring Further Text Editing

PowerPoint provides many text editing tools that make formatting presentation text quick and easy. Many times you can select multiple lines of text and apply formatting at one time to save time.

For the following exercise, click in the box that reads Click to add text and type the following in a bulleted list:

- **Designer templates**
- **Decorator color schemes**
- **Professional clip art**

This section will show you ways to further manipulate text in presentations.

Moving Text

PowerPoint supports drag and drop. You can use drag and drop to reposition text just as you do in Microsoft Word. In PowerPoint, text can be moved using drag and drop on slides, in the Outline, or on a Notes page. Select the text, then hold down the left mouse button until the drag and drop cursor appears. Drag the text to the new location and release the left mouse button.

You can use the four-headed arrows to move entire lines of text directly on a slide. Suppose you want *Professional clip art* to be the first bullet point. Move the cursor over the bullet in front of *Professional clip art* until it changes to a four-headed arrow. Hold down the left mouse button and slowly move the four-headed arrow up. Do not release the left mouse button.

Notice that the four-headed arrow turns to a two-headed arrow and a horizontal line moves in between the bullet points. This horizontal line shows to where the selected text will reposition when you release the left mouse button. Release the left mouse button when the vertical line is at the top of the bulleted list and watch this bullet point assume the top position. You can demote text using the same techniques, except that you move the four-headed arrow to the right. Select the second bullet point and move the four-headed arrow to the right (see fig. 18.56).

Figure 18.56
Demoting a bullet
point.

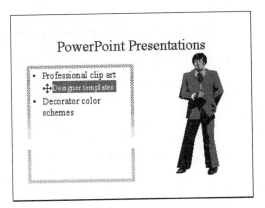

The subpoint assumes the formatting that is defined in the slide master. You also can use the Promote and Demote buttons on the Formatting toolbar to indent text. With the subpoint still selected, promote the subpoint by clicking on the Promote button on the Formatting toolbar (see fig. 18.57).

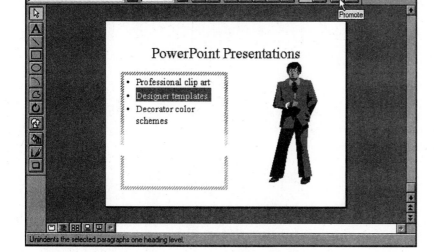

Figure 18.57
Promoting a bullet point.

Spacing Lines

PowerPoint automatically uses single line spacing for text. You can override this spacing using the Line Spacing command from the Format menu. Select all the bullet points in the text box by moving the cursor over the first bullet until it changes to a four-headed arrow. Click the left mouse button to select the line of text. Move the cursor over the third bullet until it turns to a four-headed arrow, then hold down the Shift key and click the left mouse button to select all three bullet points. With these bullet points selected, select Line Spacing from the Format menu to display the Line Spacing dialog box (see fig. 18.58).

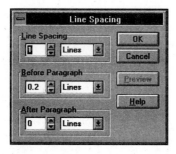

Figure 18.58
The Line Spacing dialog box.

You can choose to change the line spacing or the spacing before or after paragraphs. To change the line spacing to 1.5 lines between paragraphs, click the up arrow in the line spacing box until 1.5 shows or simply type **1.5**. To see a preview of the spacing, click on Preview. You might need to move the Line Spacing dialog box off the text box to view the preview. Click on OK to implement the new line spacing. Adjusting interparagraph spacing is particularly effective when you want very little text to fill a lot of slide space.

Changing Case

PowerPoint enables you to switch through different cases to save formatting time. This function works the same way as in Microsoft Word. With the three bullet points still selected, open the Format menu and choose Change Case. The Change Case dialog box appears and provides five options (see fig. 18.59).

Figure 18.59
The Change Case dialog box offers five choices.

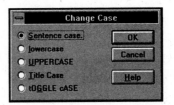

These options are shown in the dialog box just as they will appear on the slide. Select lowercase, for example, and click on OK; the slide text adjusts to reflect this choice. PowerPoint enables you to toggle through Sentence case, lowercase, and UPPERCASE using Shift+F3, just as in Microsoft Word. With the text currently selected, press Shift+F3 until the text turns to UPPERCASE. Using the Change Case function is especially helpful when you have a lot of text that needs to be changed.

Adding and Removing Periods

PowerPoint helps you to add or remove periods on multiple lines of text with one click. With the three bullet points selected, open the Format menu and choose Periods. The Periods dialog box opens and asks whether you would like to Add Periods or Remove Periods (see fig. 18.60). Click on Add Periods and click on OK. Periods appear at the end of every bullet point. Click anywhere off the slide to deselect the text. To continue, use the vertical scroll bar to move back to the title slide.

Using the Slide Sorter Toolbar

After you have created slides for a presentation, PowerPoint supplies tools to help you add even more features to the delivery. Also, PowerPoint enables you to hide slides that supply information to answer audience questions or provide backup information to clarify a key point.

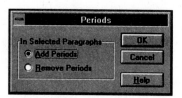

Figure 18.60
The Periods dialog box.

The Slide Sorter view conveniently helps you to view all the slides in a presentation with slide numbers and to insert, delete, or rearrange slides. You also can copy and paste slides. The Slide Sorter toolbar supplies the additional tools you need to apply slide transitions, create build slides, and hide slides. You can customize and move this toolbar like the other PowerPoint toolbars.

Change to Slide Sorter view by clicking on the Slide Sorter View button in the bottom left corner of the workspace to continue.

Slide Transitions

PowerPoint slide transitions add excitement during a slide show and interest to a presentation. Instead of simply clicking through the slides, you can make a slide enter the screen from the left side or fade out when moving to the next slide. To add a slide transition to a slide, select the slide by clicking on it. A black box indicates that the slide is selected. Click on the Transition button on the Slide Sorter toolbar (see fig. 18.61).

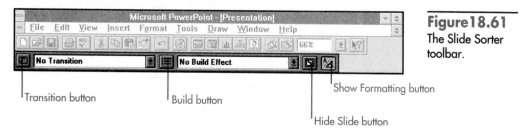

Figure18.61
The Slide Sorter toolbar.

The Transition dialog box appears and shows that there currently is no transition selected for this slide. To view the effects available for the selected slide, open the Effect list box by clicking the cursor on the down arrow (see fig. 18.62). Use the vertical scroll bar to view additional effects. When you get ready to make a selection, watch the picture of the dog in the bottom right corner of the dialog box. This picture illustrates the transition so that you can get a preview. Select Checkerboard Across and watch the picture. You can regulate the speed of the transition in the Transition box: choose Slow, Medium, or Fast. The picture will preview the speed combined with the selected transition.

Figure 18.62
The list of available effects for slide transitions.

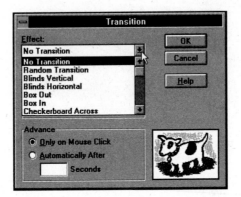

The Transition dialog box also enables you to decide if you want to move through a slide show using the mouse buttons or if you want the slides to change after a certain number of seconds. You can type directly into the box. When you have made your selections, click on OK.

A transition icon appears under the slide to show you that there is a transition assigned to the slide. The Transition Effects box on the Slide Sorter toolbar shows you that Checkerboard Across is the current transition. If you want to change the transition, you can access the Transition Effects list box on the toolbar and make another selection (see fig. 18.63). The selected slide will show you what the transition looks like when you make a selection.

Figure 18.63
Opening the Transition Effects toolbar to make another selection.

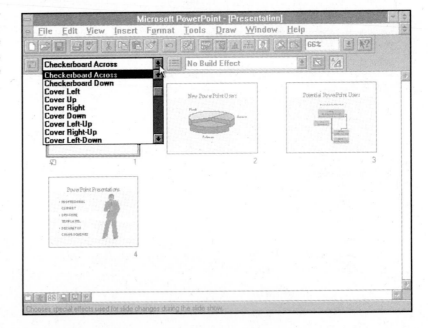

Build Slides

Build slides help the audience to focus on one slide point at a time. Bullet points appear on the slide one by one, and only the most current point is shown in the default text color. The other bullet points are dimmed to focus the audience's attention. You can change any slide with bulleted text to a build slide.

Select Slide 4 and click on the Build button on the Slide Sorter toolbar to display the Build dialog box (see fig. 18.64). First, decide what color you want to dim the previous bullet points. You do not have to dim these bullet points, but the effect can help a audience focus its attention on single points. Open the color choices by clicking on the down arrow, and select a color. To access other colors, click on Other colors. When you select a color, the check box acquires a check mark to indicate that you want to dim previous points.

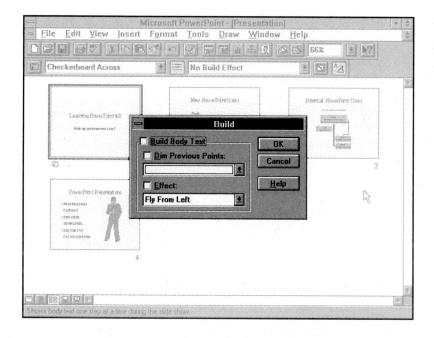

Figure 18.64
The Build dialog box.

PowerPoint enables you to choose the way in which the bullet points enter on the build slide; however, you do not have to use these effects. Simply leave the check box empty if you do not want an effect. To access the different effects, open the Effect list box by clicking on the down arrow (see fig. 18.65).

Make a selection and click on OK. You can change the build effects by opening the Build Effects box on the Slide Sorter toolbar. Notice that the Build Slide icon appears next to the Slide Transition icon to indicate that the slide is a build slide.

PowerPoint

Figure 18.65
The effects
options.

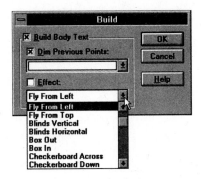

Figure 18.65
The effects
options.

To see how the build slide looks, select it and click on the Slide Show button at the bottom left corner of the workspace. Remember that the screen momentarily goes black, but the first selected slide will eventually appear with the slide transition, if it has one (see fig. 18.66).

Figure 18.66
Showing the
selected slide with
no bullet points.

PowerPoint Presentations

Click to make the first bullet point appear. Notice that it appears as defined by the Build Effects selection. Click again to evoke the second bullet point and watch the first point dim. Continue to click through all the bullet points until you return to the Slide Sorter view.

To remove the Build Slide settings on a slide, select the slide and click on the Build button on the Slide Sorter toolbar. In the Build dialog box, remove the check mark in front of Build Body Text and click on OK.

Note Slide transitions and build slides can be used only for an on-screen show on a computer monitor or video screen.

Hide Slide

At times you might want to hide a slide during a slide show. For example, you might decide you don't want to share the information, but want to hold on to the slide for now. Instead of quickly clicking through the slide, which looks unprofessional and risks the audience reading the information, PowerPoint enables you to hide slides.

To hide a slide, select the slide and click on the Hide Slide button on the Slide Sorter toolbar. Notice that a slash mark appears over the slide number to indicate that this slide is hidden. To remove the Hide Slide instructions, select the hidden slide and click on the Hide Slide button again.

Show Formatting

Sometimes in the Slide Sorter view, you simply want to add transitions or create build slides. You cannot edit the information on the slides in this view. If a presentation includes many slides with a lot of clip art, working in the Slide Sorter view can become tedious and slow. PowerPoint enables you to remove the slide formatting so that you do not slow down. Click on the Show Formatting button on the Slide Sorter toolbar to remove the formatting.

Notice that the slide titles remain in the default font, so that you can identify the slides. You now can perform any Slide Sorter toolbar function more rapidly. To return to a formatted view, click on the Show Formatting button again; this feature switches on and off.

Using PowerPoint Presentation Help

PowerPoint provides many tools to help you perfect your delivery and to supply backup information if you get stuck. PowerPoint can track the length of a slide discussion, for example, or access files containing supportive data during a presentation.

Rehearse New Timings

Often you do not know how long it will take to show an individual slide until you are actually making the presentation. This inaccuracy can lead to rushing through the last few slides in a presentation or completely skipping over information. As you rehearse a presentation, PowerPoint can keep track of how much time you take to cover the information on a slide.

To use Rehearse New Timings, select Slide Show from the View menu to display the Slide Show dialog box (see fig. 18.67). In this dialog box, you can choose to show all the slides or only specific slides. You also can select how to advance through slides; choose Manual Advance if you want to use the mouse buttons or keyboard. After you have rehearsed the timing on each slide, you can choose to use those times to control the slide advancement if you do not want to use the mouse or keyboard.

Figure 18.67
The Slide Show
dialog box.

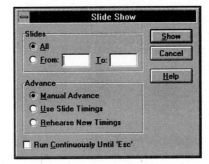

To rehearse new timings, select Rehearse New Timings and click on OK; the Slide Show begins immediately. A timer appears in the bottom left corner of the first slide and begins timing as soon as the slide appears (see fig. 18.68).

Figure 18.68
The timer begins
as soon as the first
slide appears.

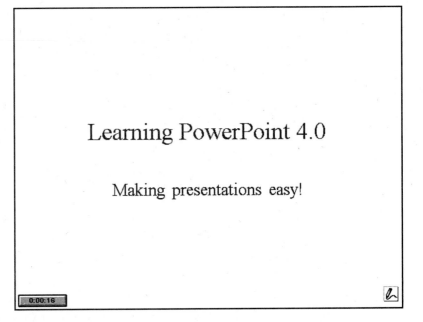

Talk through the slide just as you would during a presentation. When you are done covering a slide, click on the timer button. The next slide appears and the timer begins timing. When you have worked through all the slides, a dialog box tells you the total time for the presentation (see fig. 18.69). The dialog box also asks if you want to go to the Slide Sorter view and see the timing for each slide. Click on Yes. In the Slide Sorter view, the times appear below the slides for your reference.

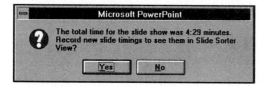

Figure 18.69
A dialog box appears to tell you the length of your presentation.

Drill Down

PowerPoint utilizes a *multiple document interface,* meaning that it enables you to access other files while it is currently running. Often, as a presenter you would like to have critical information at your disposal when an audience member asks a question or a concept is not understood. Drill Down enables you to access information directly from a slide in a presentation without closing PowerPoint and opening another application.

If someone asks what formula was used to calculate a number that is graphed on Slide 2, for example, you can open the spreadsheet from which you pulled the information. To add a Drill Down file, select Slide 2 and change to the Slide view. Select Object from the Insert menu to display the Insert Object dialog box. Select Create from File (see fig. 18.70).

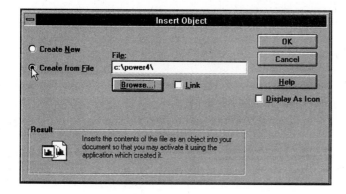

Figure 18.70
Selecting Create from File from the Insert Object dialog box.

In the File box, enter the path and file name of the file you want to be able to access from the slide. Click on Browse if you want to find the file using the Browse dialog box (see fig. 18.71).

Figure 18.71

Using the Browse dialog box to select a file.

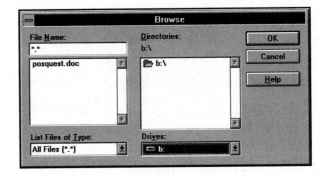

Select Display as Icon in the Insert Object dialog box because you want only an icon displayed on the slide, not the entire file. The default icon appears in the bottom right corner of the Insert Object dialog box. If you do not care for this icon, select Change Icon in the Insert Object dialog box to view other choices. Click on OK in the Insert Object dialog box. The icon appears on the slide (see fig. 18.72).

Figure 18.72

The icon appears on the slide.

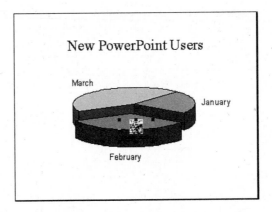

To move the icon to a more inconspicuous place, move the cursor over the icon. Click and drag the icon to the bottom left corner of the slide (see fig. 18.73). To access the drill down file during a presentation, double-click on the icon. You can have multiple drill down files on one slide.

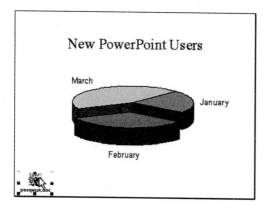

Figure18.73
Moving the icon to a more inconspicuous place on the slide.

Branching Presentations

PowerPoint enables you to branch to another presentation during a Slide Show to access other slides. You can choose to branch to a presentation when you click on an object or to go immediately to the other presentation.

To branch presentations during a slide show, move to the slide from which you want to branch. Open the additional presentation by clicking on the Open button on the Standard toolbar. When the other presentation opens, select the slides you want to show and click on the Copy button on the Standard toolbar. Open the File menu and select Close to leave the presentation. When you return to the first presentation, open the Edit menu and select Paste Special. From the Paste Special dialog box, select PowerPoint Presentation Object, then click on OK. On the current slide, a miniature of the first slide from the branched presentation appears (see fig. 18.74).

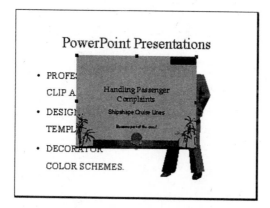

Figure 18.74
A miniature first slide from the branched presentation appears.

You can resize the miniature slide using the square resizing handles, or move it anywhere on the current slide. This picture appears on the slide during a slide show. To branch to the other presentation, click on the picture. After all the slides from the branched presentation are shown, you return to the original presentation and can continue.

Using Additional PowerPoint Help

PowerPoint makes remembering how to use PowerPoint easy with Tool Tips and the status bar. PowerPoint goes even further with additional instructions on Cue Cards to lead you through performing commonly used procedures. Also, taking presentations out of the office is easy with PowerPoint Viewer.

Cue Cards

PowerPoint Cue Cards present step-by-step instruction on procedures commonly asked on the Microsoft Help Lines. To access the Cue Cards, open the Help menu and choose Cue Cards. Cue Cards can remain open while you work on a presentation in PowerPoint. The main menu asks "What do you want to do?" To make a selection, click on the arrow buttons preceding the topics.

Suppose you want to change presentation defaults so that when PowerPoint opens, it already is formatted for your needs. Click on the arrow before Change presentation defaults (see fig. 18.75). PowerPoint Cue Cards explains that you can change the text object defaults and graphic object defaults. Choose to find out more about changing the default for text objects by clicking on the arrow button before that choice (see fig. 18.76). The next window in PowerPoint Cue Cards leads you through six steps to change the text object default settings. You can execute these steps while the Cue Cards window remains open.

Figure 18.75
Selecting to find out how to change presentation defaults.

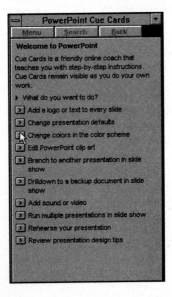

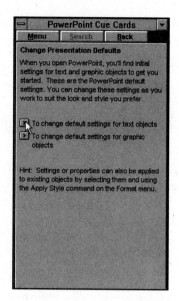

Figure 18.76
Choosing to find
out more about
changing the text
object defaults.

Read through the steps or make the changes if you like. You can always click on the **B**ack button to revert to a previous Cue Cards window. To see the Cue Cards menu again, click on the **M**enu button. PowerPoint Cue Cards even offer design tips to helps you create professional, effective presentations. To close Cue Cards, double-click on the control menu icon in the upper left corner of the window.

PowerPoint Viewer

PowerPoint Viewer is an application that enables you to show a PowerPoint presentation without loading all the PowerPoint application files on a computer. Suppose you want to take a presentation on a sales call to show on a computer monitor. You don't have room to take a computer but know there is a computer and color monitor where the sales call is taking place. You also know that the location does not have the PowerPoint software.

PowerPoint Viewer software files fit on a single disk. You can take the software and your presentation file and load both on the on-site computer. Don't worry if the fonts you use in a presentation are not on the computer you intend to use. PowerPoint temporarily installs the fonts used in a presentation on the computer then removes them after you are finished presenting.

To use PowerPoint Viewer, install the software by inserting the supplied disk into an external disk drive. If the computer includes Windows, open the **F**ile menu in the Program manager. Select **R**un and enter the external disk drive letter and then type **VSETUP.EXE** (see fig. 18.77). Click on OK. The PowerPoint View icon appears, letting you know it has been installed. Double-click on the icon and the Microsoft PowerPoint Viewer dialog box opens. Select the presentation file you want to run and click on Show. When the presentation opens, move through the slides using the mouse buttons or the keyboard. After you work through all the slides, PowerPoint Viewer returns you to the Microsoft PowerPoint Viewer dialog box again. Click on Quit to exit.

Figure 18.77
Preparing to install
PowerPoint Viewer
through the
Program
Manager.

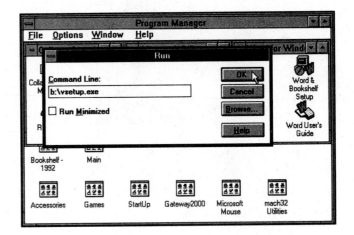

Part Four

Microsoft Access

Chapter Snapshot

Generally speaking, database systems such as Microsoft Access require a significant amount of time and effort to learn well enough to build successful, useful databases. This chapter is intended to lead you through the basic steps required to build a small Access database without spending a great deal of time on the mechanics of learning Access. In later chapters you will come to understand the details of building Access applications and why certain things were done here the way they were. In this chapter, however, you learn about the following:

By the time you reach the end of this chapter, you will have a working database that you have built with Microsoft Access. Please just work your way through each of the steps in this chapter without spending too much time trying to figure out why things work the way they do. Your database ought to look a lot like what you see in this chapter's figures.

CHAPTER

Access Quick Start

by Chris St. Valentine

The title of this chapter is somewhat misleading. It just is not possible to learn Access quickly (or any other database system, for that matter). What you can do, however, is break the process of building a database into a few logical steps and learn how to perform each of those steps using Access.

If any of the terminology in this chapter is unfamiliar to you, don't panic. The next chapter explains each of the terms and concepts you will be using here.

Here are the steps in building any Access database:

1. Create the database tables

2. Build queries to extract data

3. Design and build forms

4. Create the macros and code needed for the forms

5. Design and build any reports to be included in the database

A Note from the Author

For the most part, there aren't any "right" or "wrong" ways to do things in Access. Although it is easy to use an inefficient technique to build a table or form, it is just as easy to use the most efficient methods as well. This part of *Inside Microsoft Office Professional* is intended to keep you on the right track as you begin work with Microsoft Access.

Understanding Access Databases

All too often, books on Microsoft Access assume the reader already understands what an Access database is and what the major components of an Access database are. For most people new to Access, however, a minimal amount of orientation to the tasks ahead is in order.

What Is an Access Database?

An Access *database* is a method to store and retrieve a variety of data. The data can be anything from collections of names and addresses that would otherwise be stored in a desktop card file, on up to corporate-wide systems that store millions of bits of information on employees, customers, inventory, and other disciplines.

An Access database is composed of a number of different *objects* that are called tables, queries, forms, macros, reports, and modules. Each of these components is described a little later in this chapter. You can think of the objects as parts of an Access database, much like a car is a carefully assembled collection of parts. You build an Access database by carefully constructing and assembling the various parts to perform the overall job expected of your database. Just as a car is intended to provide transportation, Access databases are intended to provide management for your data.

A *database application* is a database complete with a user interface and data retrieval and printing options. An application is meant to be used by people who are not personally familiar with Access, yet who need to use the data stored in an Access database. The Northwind Traders, Order Entry, and other samples that come with Microsoft Access are examples of simple database applications.

Access is ideally suited for small- to medium-sized databases. The Access environment is easy to learn and understand, and Microsoft has built many features into Access designed to help database beginners build successful applications with Access.

Each Microsoft Access database application is stored as one large file on your computer's hard disk or network server. All the Access database objects described in this chapter are contained within a single file with an MDB extension. (Most other database systems store each component in its own file.)

Access Views

Most of the objects in an Access database can be displayed in multiple views. Generally speaking, Access database objects can be displayed in either Design view or in a working view. The exact name for the working view depends on the type of object. The working view for tables and queries is called the Datasheet view, for example, whereas the working format of forms is Form (as well as Datasheet) view.

Any time you see the expression *Design view* applied to an object, it means that the object is being edited by the Access developer.

Tables

A *table* is the primary storage component of an Access database. Access tables look a lot like spreadsheets. They are made of rows and columns of data that is managed by Access. As you soon will see, defining the rows and columns in a table can be a daunting task. Fortunately, there are only a few simple rules that must be followed to ensure success as you build tables in your Access database.

Figure 19.1 shows a typical Access database table.

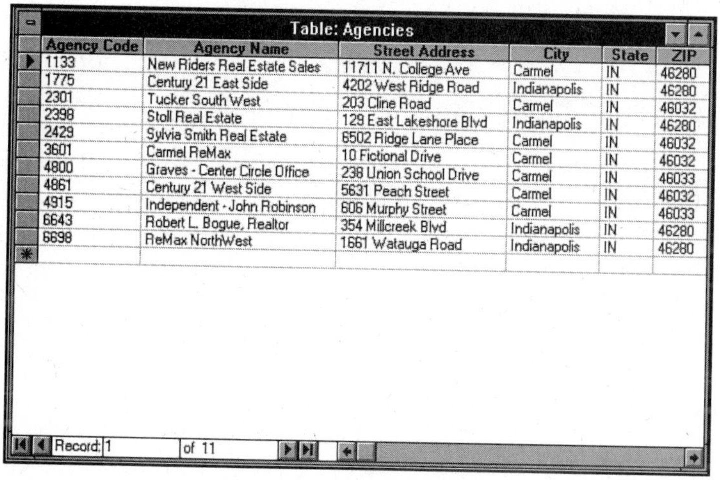

Table: Agencies					
Agency Code	**Agency Name**	**Street Address**	**City**	**State**	**ZIP**
1133	New Riders Real Estate Sales	11711 N. College Ave	Carmel	IN	46280
1775	Century 21 East Side	4202 West Ridge Road	Indianapolis	IN	46280
2301	Tucker South West	203 Cline Road	Carmel	IN	46032
2398	Stoll Real Estate	129 East Lakeshore Blvd	Indianapolis	IN	46280
2429	Sylvia Smith Real Estate	6502 Ridge Lane Place	Carmel	IN	46032
3601	Carmel ReMax	10 Fictional Drive	Carmel	IN	46032
4800	Graves - Center Circle Office	238 Union School Drive	Carmel	IN	46033
4861	Century 21 West Side	5631 Peach Street	Carmel	IN	46032
4915	Independent - John Robinson	606 Murphy Street	Carmel	IN	46033
6643	Robert L. Bogue, Realtor	354 Millcreek Blvd	Indianapolis	IN	46280
6698	ReMax NorthWest	1661 Watauga Road	Indianapolis	IN	46280

Record: 1 of 11

Figure 19.1

A typical Access table.

A precise and complete lesson on database tables is beyond the scope of *Inside Microsoft Office Professional*. It is important to know, however, that the rows of data in tables are called *records* and contain related information (for example, a person's name, address, and phone numbers). Each column in a table represents the different *fields* that make up the records. A person's name will be one field, the address another, and a phone number will be a third field.

Using the card file analogy, an individual card in the box is a *record* and contains all the contact information for one person. Each line on the card (name, address, phone numbers) is a separate *data field* of the record. You will become very familiar with these terms as you work with Access.

Queries

A *query* is a question you ask of the database. Queries are how you extract selected information from the tables in the database. Constructing Access queries is simplified by the Query By Example (QBE) grid, shown in figure 19.2. To learn more about queries, see Chapter 22, "Understanding Access Queries."

Figure 19.2
The Access
QBE grid.

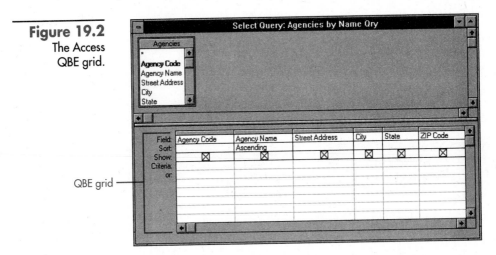

As you will see in Chapter 22, the QBE grid is quite easy and intuitive to use. Without a doubt, the QBE grid is a much simpler approach to constructing queries than using traditional database programming languages.

Forms

Access databases are sometimes described as *forms-oriented* applications. Nearly all the user interaction with an Access database application is through one form or another (although menus can be used as well).

Access forms contain text boxes, command buttons, labels, and other components that enable the user to input or change data, view query results, and, in many other ways, interact with the database. These objects are called *controls* because they control most of the user interaction with the Access database application.

Figure 19.3 shows an Access form from the HomeFinder application. (HomeFinder is included on the *Inside Microsoft Office Professional* companion disk.)

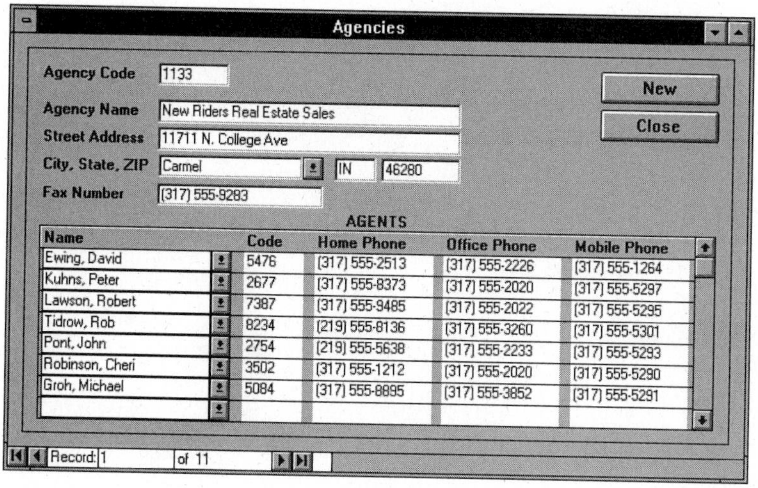

Agencies	

Agency Code 1133

Agency Name New Riders Real Estate Sales

Street Address 11711 N. College Ave

City, State, ZIP Carmel IN 46280

Fax Number (317) 555-9283

New

Close

AGENTS

Name		Code	Home Phone	Office Phone	Mobile Phone	
Ewing, David		5476	(317) 555-2513	(317) 555-2226	(317) 555-1264	
Kuhns, Peter		2677	(317) 555-8373	(317) 555-2020	(317) 555-5297	
Lawson, Robert		7387	(317) 555-9485	(317) 555-2022	(317) 555-5295	
Tidrow, Rob		8234	(219) 555-8136	(317) 555-3260	(317) 555-5301	
Pont, John		2754	(219) 555-5638	(317) 555-2233	(317) 555-5293	
Robinson, Cheri		3502	(317) 555-1212	(317) 555-2020	(317) 555-5290	
Groh, Michael		5084	(317) 555-8895	(317) 555-3852	(317) 555-5291	

Record: 1 of 11

Figure 19.3
The HomeFinder
Agencies form.

Macros

Access macros are a way to automate activities associated with Access applications. You add macros to the components on Access forms to respond to events such as mouse clicks and text changes initiated by the user of the application. Macros are a way for you to tell Access how you want your application to behave. Macros are discussed more fully in Chapter 24, "Using Macros."

Reports

Reports are printouts of the data extracted from the database, or summaries of the information obtained from the database. Not all databases include reports, although most databases feature at least a few different reports. The sample database described in this chapter does not include a report. Understand, however, that many Access databases include dozens of different reports, each designed to present different data extracted from the database.

Access reports are discussed in detail in Chapter 25, "Building Reports."

Access Basic Modules

Microsoft Access contains a complete database programming language called Access Basic. Although many successful Access databases have been built without any programming in Access Basic, you will find it well worth the effort to learn enough Access Basic to become reasonably proficient with its syntax and structure. The actual "words" making up the computer program in figure 19.4 are usually referred to as *code*.

IV

Microsoft Access

Figure 19.4

Access Basic code in the Edit window.

```
━  Module: Miscellaneous                                ▼  ▲
Function csvMinValue (ByVal X As Variant, ByVal Y As Variant) As Vari▲

   ' Revision History
   ' ------------------------------------------------------
   ' 1.00  15-Mar-93 Chris St. Valentine
   '                     Initial version.
   ' ------------------------------------------------------

   If IsNumeric(X) * IsNumeric(Y) Then
        csvMinValue = X + (X - Y) * (X > Y)
   Else
        MsgBox "Invalid numeric argument.", MB_ICONEXCLAMATION, "MinV
        csvMinValue = Null
   End If

End Function
```

Access Basic code is stored within your databases in *modules*. Your databases can contain as many modules as necessary. Most Access database developers create separate modules for each type of task: navigating through forms, checking system resources such as available disk space, and so on.

Access Basic is, admittedly, a complex subject. *Inside Microsoft Office Professional* presents only the essentials of programming in Access Basic. The reader is encouraged to acquire a book such as the *Access Developer's Guide* by Roger Jennings (Sams Publishing, ISBN 0-672-30178-4) if you determine that Access Basic is important to your databases. Users of Excel 5 and Word 6 will be happy to know that the syntax and structure of Access Basic is very similar to the macro languages found in each of those applications. If you have worked with Excel or Word macros, you will benefit from this head start as you begin working with Access Basic.

Creating the New Database

As an example of an Access database, this chapter describes how to build "Hyperdex," a replacement for the ubiquitous card file found on most business desktops. Hyperdex will help you keep track of names, addresses, and phone numbers and can be easily expanded to include much more information such as birthdates, Social Security numbers, and other data.

The first step of any Access database project is to create a new, empty database with no tables, queries, forms, or other database objects in it. As described earlier, you build Access databases by adding tables, queries, and other objects to the empty database container.

To create a new, empty database, perform these steps:

1. Start Access. The empty Access screen will appear (see fig. 19.5).

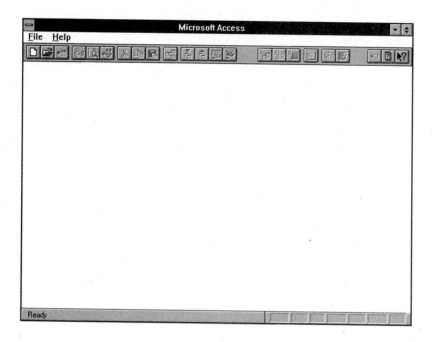

Figure 19.5
The initial Access screen.

2. Choose the <u>N</u>ew Database command from the <u>F</u>ile menu. The New Database dialog box will appear, as shown in figure 19.6.

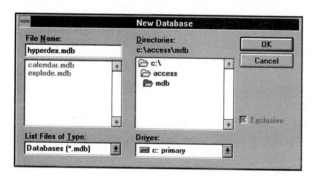

Figure 19.6
The New Database dialog box.

3. Type **HYPERDEX.MDB** (or **hyperdex.mdb**—Access doesn't care) into the File <u>N</u>ame box of the New Database dialog box and click on the OK button.

4. After a short delay, Access will display the soon-to-be-familiar Database window, as shown in figure 19.7. You will learn more about the Database window later in this chapter.

IV

Microsoft Access

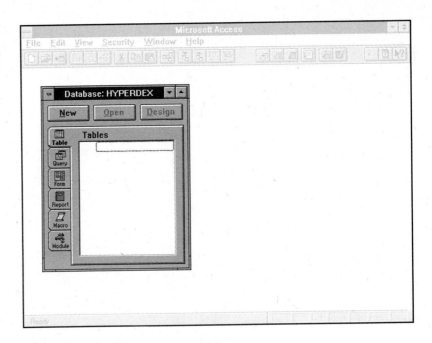

Figure 19.7
The Database
window and
toolbar.

You now have a clean, empty database named HYPERDEX.MDB on your computer's hard disk. If, for some reason, the toolbar at the top of the Database window does not appear, choose <u>V</u>iew, Tool<u>b</u>ars and make sure Database is checked in the list of available toolbars.

Creating the Database Tables

Because tables are the primary data storage mechanism in Access databases, considerable time is spent designing and building efficient tables.

There are two ways you can build a new table. First, you can use the built-in Table Wizard. The Table Wizard is a tool included with Access that helps you create a table by presenting a series of dialog boxes in which you can select a specific table type and certain fields. The Table Wizard is ideal if you want to create a table that closely resembles one of the more than 40 tables included with the wizard.

The second way to build a new table is to create the table yourself from scratch. When you click on the <u>N</u>ew button near the top of the Database window, Access displays the New Table dialog box (see fig. 19.8), in which you can choose to either create the table using the Table Wizard or manually.

The following sections describe each of these techniques. For this sample database, you will create a small table with 10 different fields in it, without paying too much attention to table-building rules, and the manual approach is more appropriate. For now, though, a brief discussion of the Table Wizard would be useful for future reference.

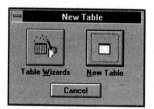

Figure 19.8
The New Table
dialog box.

Using the Table Wizard

When you choose Table Wizards in the New Table dialog box, Access displays the first of
several Table Wizard dialog boxes (see fig. 19.9).

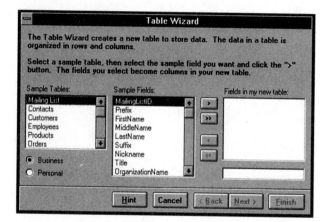

Figure 19.9
The first Table
Wizard dialog
box.

In the first Table Wizard dialog box, you choose the table that most closely
matches the kind of table you want to create. If you want to create a table that
tracks contact information, for example, you might select the Contacts sample
table.

The Sample Fields column contains typical fields for the kind of table. The
Contacts table contains fields for name, address, name of organization, and so
on. Select the fields you want to include in the new table by highlighting them
and then pressing the right-arrow button (see fig. 19.10).

IV

Microsoft Access

Figure 19.10
Selecting a field
for the new table.

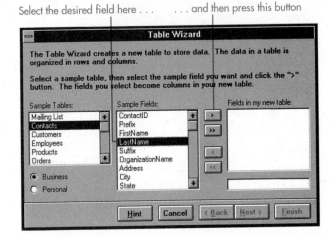

When you are finished selecting fields, click on the Next button; Access displays a dialog box in which you can name the table. For this example, type **Contacts** (see fig. 19.11).

Figure 19.11
Naming the
new table.

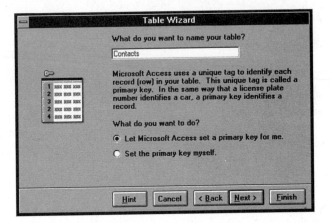

Also in this dialog box, you specify whether Access will assign the primary key or you will assign the key yourself. Keys are described in Chapter 21, "Creating and Using Access Tables," but for now you should allow Access to assign the primary key.

When you click on the Next button, Access displays the last Table Wizard dialog box (see fig. 19.12). You have three options:

✔ Open the table in Design view and make any necessary design changes

✔ Open the table in Datasheet view and begin entering data

✔ Enable Access to create a form, and then use that form to enter data into the new table

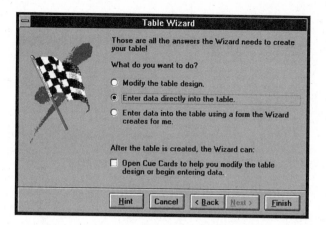

Figure 19.12
The final Table
Wizard dialog
box.

How you proceed now depends on what you want to do. If you are like most users, you will want to add a bit of sample data to give meaning to the other database objects such as queries and reports.

Creating a Table from Scratch

When you choose to create a table manually by clicking on the <u>N</u>ew Table button in the New Table dialog box, Access displays a new table in Design view (see fig. 19.13).

Design view   Datasheet view   Click here to close the property sheet

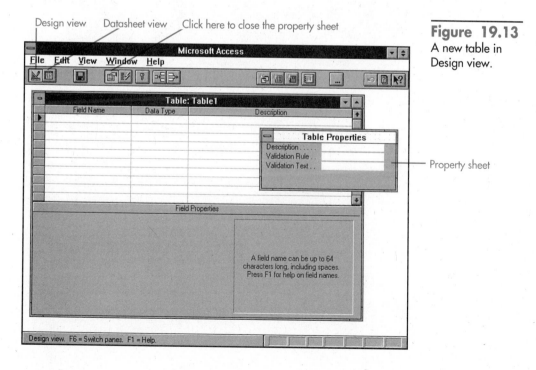

Figure 19.13
A new table in
Design view.

Property sheet

IV

Microsoft Access

The following procedure outlines the steps to build a new table:

1. If the Table Properties property sheet appears, as shown in figure 19.13, close the sheet by pressing the Properties button on the toolbar or by choosing the Close command from the property sheet's control menu. You will not be setting the table properties in this small example.

2. Notice that the table in Design view looks something like an Excel or Lotus 1-2-3 spreadsheet. The column heads (Field Name, Data Type, and Description) indicate the kind of information expected in each column. Click in the top row right under Field Name and enter **ID** in the box. The table now should look like figure 19.14.

Figure 19.14
Adding the first
field to the table.

Enter the name
of the field here

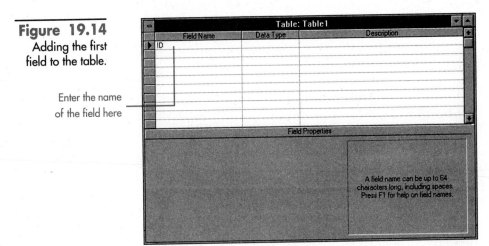

3. Use the Tab key to move to the Data Type column (or click in the Data Type column) in the same row as the name of the field (ID). A downward-pointing arrow, indicating a drop-down list, will appear. Click on the downward-pointing arrow and select Counter from the list (see fig. 19.15).

The ID field will serve as an arbitrary identifier for each record in the database. As you will see a bit later in this chapter, Access takes care of entering data into this field for you.

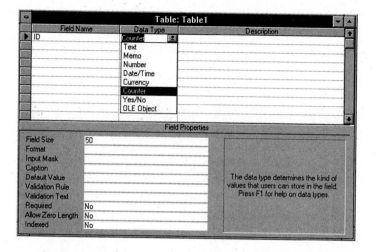

Figure 19.15
Selecting the data
type for the ID
field.

Figure 19.15
Selecting the data
type for the ID
field.

4. The Description column can be used to enter a short description for the field. For now, however, you can ignore the Description column.

5. The next field will contain the first name of each person stored in the database. Therefore, enter **FirstName** in the Field Name column. This time, instead of selecting Counter from the Data Type drop-down list, select Text. The data you store in text fields are simple words and numbers (in this case, first names).

6. Continue adding fields to the table by tabbing to the Field Name rows under the ID field and filling in the names and data types shown in figure 19.16.

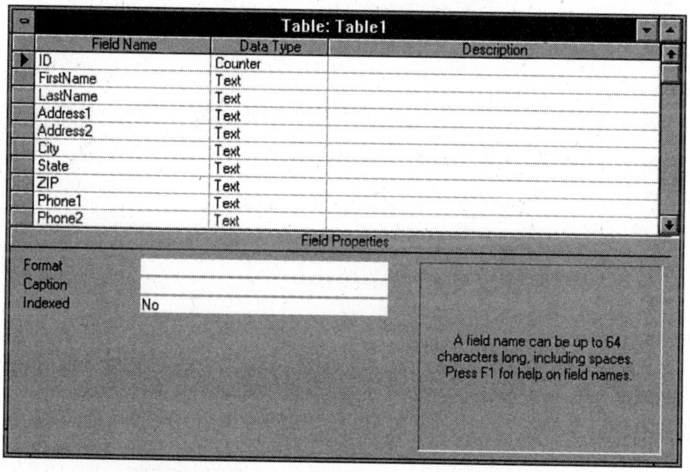

Figure 19.16
The completed
table in Design
view.

IV

Microsoft Access

7. Switch the table to Datasheet view by clicking on the Datasheet View button or by choosing View, Datasheet. Access displays the dialog box illustrated in figure 19.17. Access cannot display the table in Datasheet view until you save the design changes.

Figure 19.17

Access makes sure you save the new table.

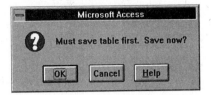

When you click on OK, Access displays yet another dialog box in which you can enter the name for the new table. Type **People** in this dialog box and click on OK.

8. Access will not let you go quite yet. The next dialog box Access displays is shown in figure 19.18. As you will read in later chapters, a *key* is one way that the different tables in your database are connected together. For this small database, click on the Yes button and let Access create the primary key for you.

Figure 19.18

Access can create the primary key for you.

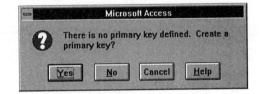

9. Finally, Access displays the new, empty table in Datasheet view (see fig. 19.19).

Figure 19.19

The completed table in Datasheet view.

Control menu button
First record

Fields
Minimize button
Maximize button
Horizontal scroll bar

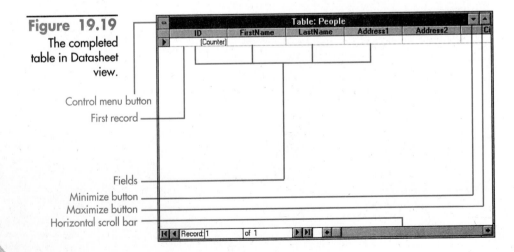

Don't be disappointed, even though there's not much to look at. The table, after all, is empty. It will be more interesting after some data has been added.

Breaking Some Rules

You have not followed every accepted table-building rule as you created this table. You did not, for example, include a description for each of the fields, and you did not change the default field size (you might have noticed the Field Size in the bottom half of the window in figure 19.15). Descriptions in a simple table like this are not really necessary because the purpose of each field is rather obvious. The field sizes have been left at the default (50 characters) to keep this exercise simple.

> The field size setting defines the maximum number of characters allowed in a field. Unlike other database systems that allocate as much space as you define, Access stores only the number of characters actually entered into the field. There is no penalty for leaving the field size at 50.

You should be aware, however, that you usually will want to adjust the field size, include descriptions, and modify the other properties associated with each field in your tables. Descriptions help you remember the purpose of the fields in a table. Adjusting the field size and other field properties helps keep your database running quickly and efficiently.

Adding Data to the Table

The next step is to add some data to the table. Notice that the fields you entered while the table was in Design view are now arranged horizontally across the table window. There are too many fields in the table to display all of them without moving from side to side with the scroll bar at the bottom of the window.

Adding data to the table is easy. Simply type a person's name (first and last names are kept separate), address, and phone numbers into the fields of each record. (Remember, each row of a data table is a *record*.) Use the Tab key to move from field to field; Shift+Tab will move you back one field. When you reach the end of a record (the table will scroll to provide access to the fields that are off the screen), Access automatically drops you down to the next record.

Enter data horizontally in the table. Unlike most spreadsheets, in which the data can be entered in rows across the sheet or as columns down the sheet, you enter data in Access datasheets only horizontally across the table.

Add the names and addresses of 10 or more people you know. You can even use the phone book or make up names and addresses if you do not have 10 names and addresses handy. Be sure to enter one record with the following information:

FirstName: Steve

LastName: Miller

Address1:	11326 Rolling Rock Drive
Address2:	(none)
City:	Orlando
State:	FL
ZIP:	33936
Phone1:	(813) 555-4104
Phone2:	(none)

The "Steve Miller" record will be used to test the select query you build in the next step. After you have added 10 or more records, your table should look something like figure 19.20.

Figure 19.20
The People table, complete with data.

ID	FirstName	LastName	Address1	Address2	City	State	ZIP
1	Steve	Miller	11326 Rolling Rock Drive		Orlando	FL	33936
2	Paul	Helms	7840 Southbay Drive		Carmel	IN	46032
3	Richard	Lyons	9039 Fall Creek Rd		Carmel	IN	46032
4	Lee	Perkins	9551 Vest Mill Road		Winston-Salem	NC	27103
5	Brad	Pease	8854 Sunblest Lane		Hingham	MA	02186
6	Harry	Slabosky	11918 College Drive		Indianapolis	IN	46110
7	David	Allen	1350 Pennsylvania Ave		Indianapolis	IN	46130
8	Tim	Murray	1473 Stormy Ridge		Galesburg	FL	33936
9	Linda	Matthews	8713 Woodstock Ct.		Hingham	MA	02187
10	Tom	Reid	6244 Dover Court		Marlboro	MA	02173
11	Darryl	Ryan	680 West Piper		Erie	PA	16506
12	Steve	Taylor	615 Dayton Ct.	Apt J-7	Hialeah	FL	32897
13	Cliff	Flanagan	861 Gulfview Terrace	#136	Ft. Meyers	FL	33935
14	Sarah	Miller	7127 Plaza Lane	#23	Carmel	IN	46032
15	David	Lovett	8415 Deer Ridge Rd	#I-2	Speedway	IN	46910
16	Jim	Wagner	9201 Keystone Way		Indianapolis	IN	47101
(Counter)							

Table: People

Record: 17   of 17

Again, notice that you do not enter values for Counter fields—Access enters the values for you.

When you have completed entering data into your table, click on the Minimize button to set the table aside, or double-click on the control menu button to close the table. Both of these buttons can be seen in figure 19.19.

Building Queries

Now you will build a query to extract records from the table (you named it People) you built in the last step.

Access supports several different kinds of queries. By far the most commonly used is the select query. As its name implies, a *select query* selects certain information from the database. You then display the selected data in a form or datasheet.

Select queries are what most people think of when they think about databases. For example, the phone company performs a select query on its databases to determine your monthly phone bill. When you call to make airline reservations, the agent uses a select query to find the most convenient and cost-effective flight (theoretically, at least) that still has seats available.

Building simple Access select queries is quick and easy. First, go to the Database window, click on the Query button, and then click on the <u>N</u>ew button at the top of the window (see fig. 19.21).

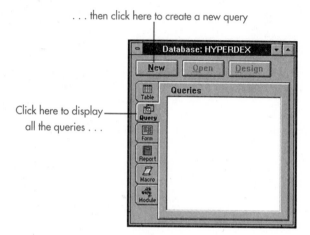

. . . then click here to create a new query

Click here to display
all the queries . . .

There are two ways you can build a new query. First, you can use the built-in Query Wizards. The Query Wizards are tools included with Access that help you create a query by presenting a series of dialog boxes in which you can select certain query properties and attributes. The Query Wizards are ideal if you want to create a query that closely resembles one of the styles produced by the Wizards.

The second way to build a new query is to create the query from scratch. When you click on the <u>N</u>ew button near the top of the Database window, Access displays the New Query dialog box (see fig. 19.22) in which you can choose to create the query either manually or by using the Query Wizards.

IV

Microsoft Access

The following sections describe each of these techniques. For this sample database, you will create a simple select query manually. For more complicated queries, using the Query Wizards approach may be more appropriate.

Using the Query Wizards

When you choose to use a Query Wizard, Access displays the first of several dialog boxes in which you can choose to build one of four kinds of queries:

- ✔ **Crosstab.** Summarizes information in a row-and-column format.
- ✔ **Find duplicates.** Identifies duplicate records.
- ✔ **Find unmatched.** Identifies records that exist in one table but have no matching or corresponding record in a second table.
- ✔ **Archive.** Purges a table of old or obsolete data.

As each dialog box appears, enter or select the information required by the Wizard. Using the Query Wizards to build a new query is covered more fully in Chapter 22, "Understanding Access Queries."

Creating a Query from Scratch

When you choose to create a query manually by clicking on the New Query button in the New Query dialog box, Access displays an empty QBE grid and the Add Table dialog box in which you can enter the name of the table or query on which to base the new query.

The following procedure outlines the steps to build a new query:

1. The Add Table dialog box (see fig. 19.23) is somewhat misnamed because you can display the names of tables, queries, or both. For this example, you have only one table from which to choose: People. Either double-click on the name of the table or highlight the table name and choose Add.

2. Access adds the People table to the top portion of the Query window (see fig. 19.24). Close the Add Table dialog box by choosing Close.

   Access is now ready for you to specify how you want select data from the People table.

3. Look closely at the People table in the top portion of the Query window. This is called a *field list:* Access displays the names of all the fields in the table and it waits for you to select the fields you want to add to the QBE grid.

   Double-click on LastName in the field list and watch what happens. Access adds LastName to the first column of the QBE grid in the lower portion of the Query window, as shown in figure 19.25.

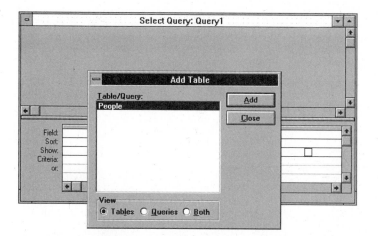

Figure 19.23
The Query window with Add Table dialog box.

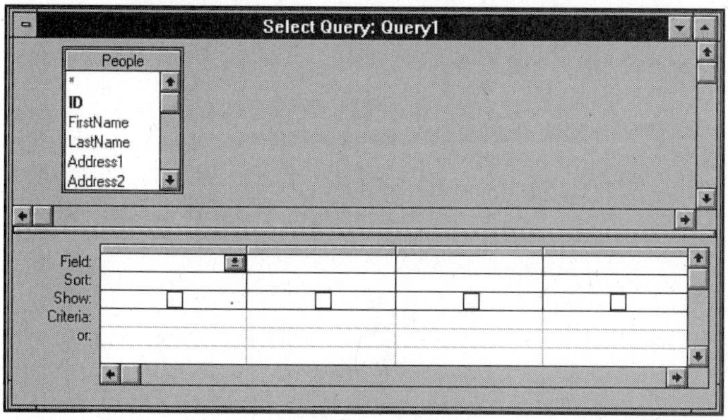

Figure 19.24
The Query window with the People table added.

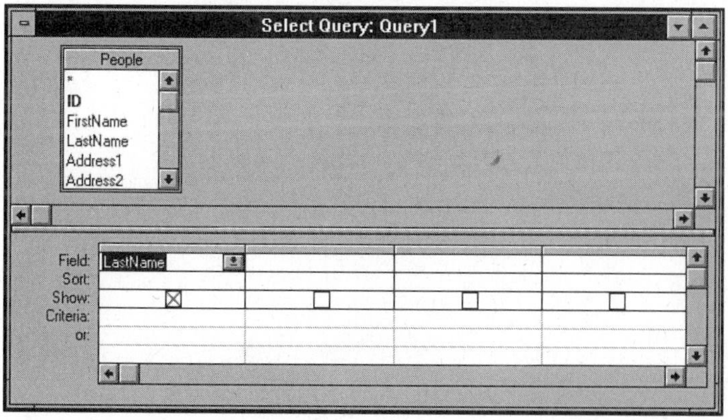

Figure 19.25
Adding the LastName field to the QBE grid.

You will specify the field, sort options, and search criteria in the QBE grid later. In the meantime, however, continue to add fields to the QBE grid by double-clicking on the field names in the People field list (be sure to add FirstName as well). You might need to use the field list scroll bar to view all the fields in the list. The only field you do not need to add is the ID field.

As you add fields to the QBE grid, the new fields appear to the right of fields already in the grid. When you are done adding fields, the QBE grid should look something like figure 19.26.

Figure 19.26
The query in the QBE grid, with all fields added.

Field list scroll bar

Sort box

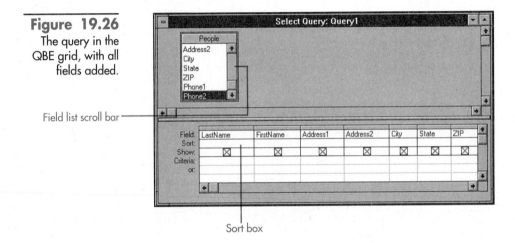

4. When you have added all the fields in the field list, click in the Sort box beneath the LastName field in the QBE grid. A drop-down arrow will appear, permitting access to the list of sort options (see fig. 19.27). Select Ascending from this list.

Figure 19.27
Selecting the Ascending sort option.

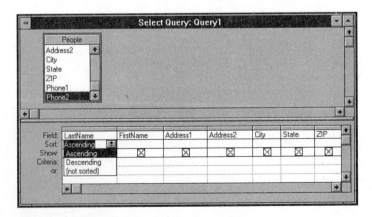

5. To display the results of the query, click on the Datasheet View button on the toolbar or choose <u>V</u>iew, Datasheet. Your results should look something like those illustrated in figure 19.28.

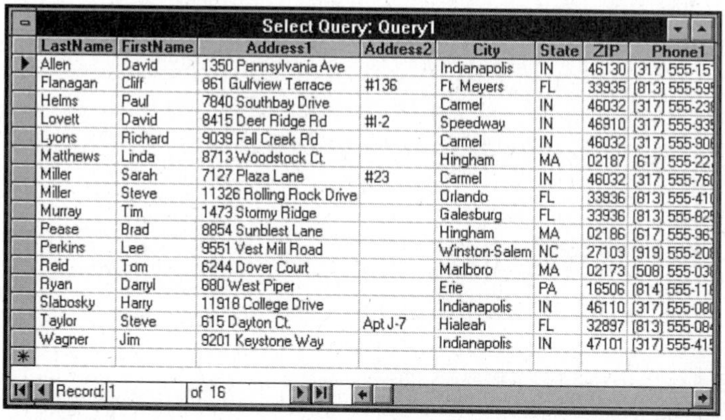

	LastName	FirstName	Address1	Address2	City	State	ZIP	Phone1
▶	Allen	David	1350 Pennsylvania Ave		Indianapolis	IN	46130	(317) 555-15
	Flanagan	Cliff	861 Gulfview Terrace	#136	Ft. Meyers	FL	33935	(813) 555-59
	Helms	Paul	7840 Southbay Drive		Carmel	IN	46032	(317) 555-23
	Lovett	David	8415 Deer Ridge Rd	#I-2	Speedway	IN	46910	(317) 555-93
	Lyons	Richard	9039 Fall Creek Rd		Carmel	IN	46032	(317) 555-90
	Matthews	Linda	8713 Woodstock Ct.		Hingham	MA	02187	(617) 555-22
	Miller	Sarah	7127 Plaza Lane	#23	Carmel	IN	46032	(317) 555-76
	Miller	Steve	11326 Rolling Rock Drive		Orlando	FL	33936	(813) 555-41
	Murray	Tim	1473 Stormy Ridge		Galesburg	FL	33936	(813) 555-82
	Pease	Brad	8854 Sunblest Lane		Hingham	MA	02186	(617) 555-96
	Perkins	Lee	9551 Vest Mill Road		Winston-Salem	NC	27103	(919) 555-20
	Reid	Tom	6244 Dover Court		Marlboro	MA	02173	(508) 555-03
	Ryan	Darryl	680 West Piper		Erie	PA	16506	(814) 555-11
	Slabosky	Harry	11918 College Drive		Indianapolis	IN	46110	(317) 555-08
	Taylor	Steve	615 Dayton Ct.	Apt J-7	Hialeah	FL	32897	(813) 555-08
	Wagner	Jim	9201 Keystone Way		Indianapolis	IN	47101	(317) 555-41

Record: 1 of 16

Figure 19.28
The query in Datasheet view.

When you switch to Datasheet view, Access executes the query and then displays the results of the query. Query Datasheet views look just like tables. In fact, tables and Datasheet views usually are indistinguishable, and Access treats them as if they were the same kind of database object. Adding, changing, or deleting data in Datasheet view is the same as changing the data in the table underlying the query.

6. Save your new query by choosing <u>F</u>ile, Save Query <u>A</u>s; Access displays the Save As dialog box (see fig. 19.29). Enter **People by Name Qry** as the name of your query. This identifies the source of the data (the People table) and something about the query output (it is sorted by name).

Save As

Query <u>N</u>ame:
People by Name Qry

OK

Cancel

Figure 19.29
Saving a new query.

7. Close the query by either double-clicking on the control menu button in the upper left corner of the Query window or choosing <u>F</u>ile, <u>C</u>lose.

At this point, you have not specified any criteria for the query to use when selecting records. By default, Access shows all the records in the People table, sorted in alphabetical order. Later in this chapter you will return to the People by Name Qry query to make a few changes that enable you to specify exactly which records you want to retrieve from your database.

IV

Microsoft Access

Designing and Building Forms

Work styles differ, but the next step in building Access databases usually involves creating a few forms to handle the data stored in the tables and extracted with queries.

Access forms substitute for the paper forms that sometimes dominate our lives. Forms almost always have tables and queries "under" them. The text boxes, scrolling lists, and other objects on the form are connected to fields in the query or table underlying the form. Access forms provide a clean, easy-to-understand interface to the queries and tables that provide the underlying structure of the forms.

Using the Form Wizards

The easiest and most direct method of building a form is with the Form Wizards. As you soon will see, the Access Form Wizards are a series of dialog boxes that perform most of the repetitive tasks involved in creating new forms. Each dialog box asks you a question or two about the form you want to build. Then, based on your responses to these questions, the wizard builds a form corresponding to your responses.

To demonstrate the way Form Wizards work, you will quickly build a simple form. You will not be using this form in your final project; it's for demonstration purposes only.

To create a new form using the Form Wizards, follow these steps:

1. In the Database window, click on the Form button, then choose <u>N</u>ew (see fig. 19.30).

Figure 19.30
Creating a new form.

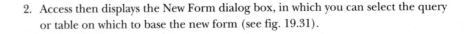

2. Access then displays the New Form dialog box, in which you can select the query or table on which to base the new form (see fig. 19.31).

Figure 19.31
Specifying the underlying query or table.

In this exercise, the form will be based on the query you just created, People by Name Qry. You can either enter the name in the text box, or open the drop-down list and select the name of the query.

3. There are two ways you can build a new form. First, you can choose Form Wizards to use the built-in Form Wizards. The Form Wizards are ideal if you want to create a form that closely resembles one of the styles produced by the wizards. The second way to build a new form is to create the form yourself from scratch, by choosing Blank Form. For this exercise, choose Form Wizards.

It should now be rather obvious why you added the letters *Qry* to the name of the query. If you had not added this suffix, there would be no way to distinguish the query from another database object with another, similar name. Of course, you could have named the table and the query almost anything you like (Access supports object names up to 64 characters in length), but giving queries names that are similar to the tables on which they are based provides you with a quick way to check which queries are associated with which tables.

4. When you choose Form Wizards, Access displays the first Form Wizards dialog box (see fig. 19.32).

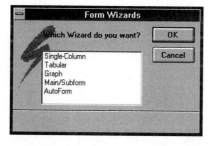

Figure 19.32
Creating a new form with a Form Wizard.

There are five different Form Wizards in Access: Single-Column, Tabular, Graph, Main/Subform, and AutoForm. Each of these wizards creates a distinctive look. You should feel free to come back to the Form Wizards later on and try out the various looks you can achieve.

For this exercise, however, highlight the Single-Column Wizard in the list and then click on OK. Access displays the next wizard dialog box, in which you can specify the fields you want to include on the new form (see fig. 19.33).

Figure 19.33
Selecting fields for
the new form.

Select the desired fields here . . .

...then click on this button

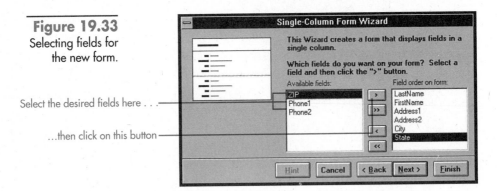

5. The Available fields list contains the names of all the fields included in the People by Name Qry query. Select the fields you want to include by highlighting each field and then clicking on the right arrow button. Repeat this for each field you want on the form. For this form, select all the fields.

6. After you have selected all the fields (see fig. 19.34), choose Next to continue to the next Wizard dialog box.

Figure 19.34
Selecting all the
fields to include on
the form.

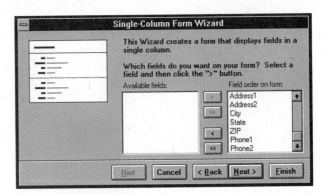

7. This dialog box (see fig. 19.35) enables you to select the overall appearance of the new form. As you click on the various options (Standard, Chiseled, Shadowed, and so on) the sample under the magnifying glass changes to give you a preview of the way the form will look when complete. Most people pick Standard, Embossed, or Chiseled. For this exercise, select the Embossed look and choose Next.

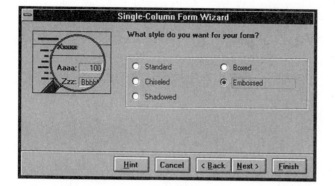

Figure 19.35
Selecting the look
of the new form.

8. Access displays the final Form Wizard dialog box (see fig. 19.36). In this dialog box, you type the name you want to appear as the caption in the title bar of the form (along the top of the window). By default, Access assumes you want to use the name of the underlying table or query—in this case, People by Name Qry.

The name of the underlying query rarely makes a good form caption, so you usually will change the default setting. For this exercise, type **Hyperdex Lookup** as the title of the form.

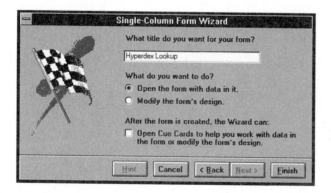

Figure 19.36
Specifying the
caption for the
new form.

9. If you know you will need to make changes to the form design, you can open the form in Design view. Otherwise, open the form with data in it. When you choose Finish, Access opens the form in Form view (see fig. 19.37).

Figure 19.37
The new form
created with the
Form Wizard.

Record navigation buttons

Notice that the default width for text fields is much too wide for state abbreviations and ZIP codes. In the next section, you will build a new version of this form from scratch. Although the Form Wizard makes a good guess at how a form should be constructed, the default design is rarely perfect.

> **Note** If you are not happy with the exact appearance of the form, Chapter 23, "Creating and Using Forms," describes the process of modifying forms.

10. Experiment a bit with the form. Notice that you can change the contents of any of the text boxes on the form. As you change the data displayed on the form, you are changing the contents of the underlying People table.

    Notice also the navigation buttons in the lower left corner of the form. The navigation buttons enable you to sequentially step through the records or jump to the beginning or end of the records.

11. Save your work by choosing File, Save Form As. Name the form **Hyperdex Lookup**, and then close the form by double-clicking on the form's control menu or by choosing File, Close.

When you close the new Hyperdex Lookup form, notice that the form name appears in the list of forms in your database (see fig. 19.38).

Your experiment with the Access Form Wizards is now complete.

Figure 19.38
The Database window with the new form in the list.

Building a Form from Scratch

The first steps of building a form from scratch are the same as using the Form Wizards:

1. In the Database window, click on the Form button, then choose <u>N</u>ew.

2. Wait for Access to display the New Form dialog box (refer to figure 19.31), and then select the name of the table or query on which you want to base the form. For this exercise, select the People by Name Qry query.

Beginning with the next step, however, the process is quite different:

3. Choose <u>B</u>lank Form to open a new, empty form in Design view (see fig. 19.39). If you do not see the toolbox right away, either click on the Toolbox button on the toolbar or choose <u>V</u>iew, <u>T</u>oolbox.

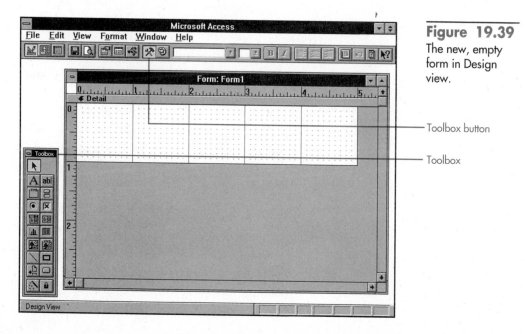

Toolbox button

Toolbox

Figure 19.39
The new, empty form in Design view.

IV

Microsoft Access

4. At this point, the design area, or detail section, is a little small. Enlarge the detail section by moving the mouse pointer to the bottom edge of the section and dragging the edge until the section is about 2 1/2 inches high. Notice that the mouse cursor changes to a two-headed arrow as you drag the edge of the detail section.

Figure 19.40
Dragging the detail section to a larger size.

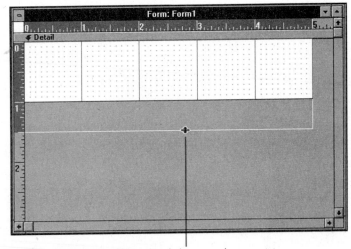

A two-headed arrow indicates resizing

If you later discover that the detail section is either too large or still too small, you can resize it again.

5. You usually build forms by clicking on tools in the toolbox and then dragging the tools onto the form's detail section. The toolbox can be seen somewhat more clearly in figure 19.41.

The most commonly used tools in the toolbox are the Label, Text Box, Command Button, List Box, and Combo Box (which creates drop-down lists). The form in figure 19.37 has only labels and text boxes on it.

6. Add a label for the form by clicking on the Label tool in the toolbox. Notice how the mouse cursor changes as you move it anywhere on the form. Click near the location where the label should appear (don't worry about exact placement just yet); Access displays a small rectangle in which you can enter the text of the label (see fig. 19.42).

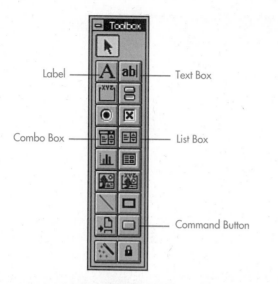

Figure 19.41
The form toolbox.

Label — Text Box

Combo Box — List Box

Command Button

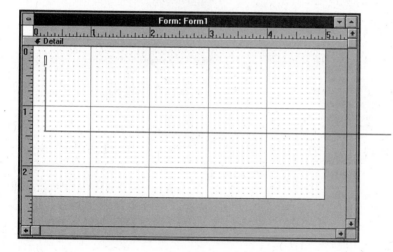

Figure 19.42
Adding a label
control to the form.

Click wherever you want the
label to appear

7. Type **Hyperdex Lookup 2** into the label control, and then press Enter. As you type the text for the label, notice how the label control automatically widens.

8. The label contains the correct text, but it is too small and needs to be emphasized somehow. Before you can change a control, you must first select it. The easiest way to select a control is to drag a rectangle through the control (see fig. 19.43).

IV

Microsoft Access

Figure 19.43
Select a control by dragging a rectangle through it.

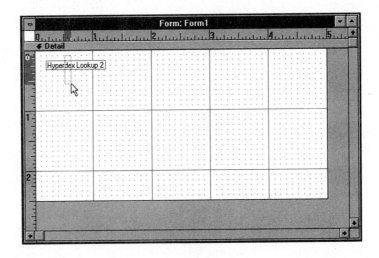

9. Make the text larger by setting its font size to 14 points in the Font Size list box, and make it boldfaced by clicking on the Bold button on the toolbar (see fig. 19.44).

Figure 19.44
Adjusting the font attributes for a label control.

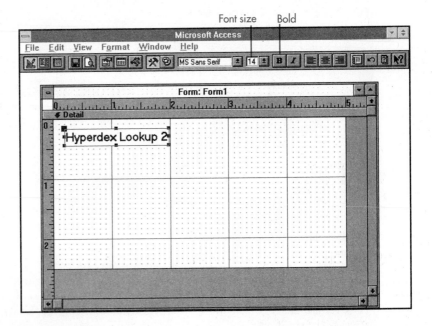

10. The text is now larger and bolder, but the control itself has not changed size (it is much too small). Resize the control by opening the Format menu, choosing the Size command, and then choosing the to Fit subcommand (see fig. 19.45).

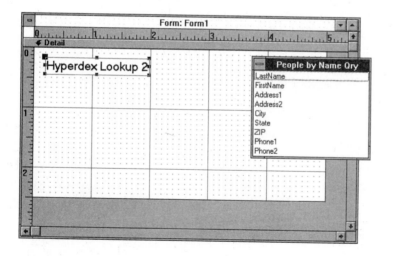

Figure 19.45
Resizing a control.

11. The label is the only control you will add to the form directly from the toolbox. See Chapter 23, "Creating and Using Forms," for more detailed information about the other form controls. For now, hide the toolbox by choosing View, Toolbox.

12. Open the field list by choosing View, Field List; Access displays the field list (see fig. 19.46). In this example, the field list has been enlarged by dragging on its borders with the mouse; this makes it easier to read the contents of the list.

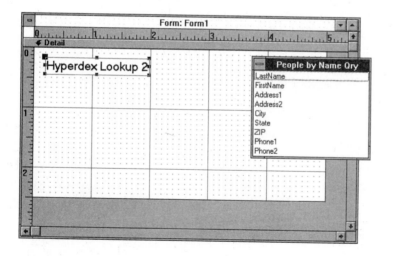

Figure 19.46
The new form with the field list revealed.

The field list contains all the fields in the People by Name Qry query. You will add the rest of the controls to the form by dragging fields from the field list and dropping them on the form.

13. Click on LastName in the field list and drag it onto the form about midway under the form label. Access adds a new text box where you release the mouse button (see fig. 19.47).

IV

Microsoft Access

Figure 19.47
Adding a text box
by dragging a field
onto the form.

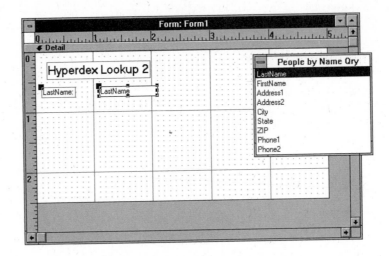

Figure 19.47
Adding a text box
by dragging a field
onto the form.

14. Continue adding controls to the form by dragging the field names from the field list. Although you can place the controls anywhere you like on the form, you should try to pattern your form after other applications that place address information under the person's name, and the city, state, and ZIP code information under the address. Figure 19.48 shows what the form might look like when you have added all the fields.

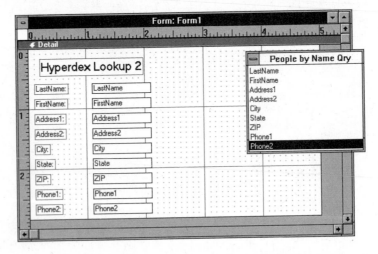

Figure 19.48
The form with all
the controls
added.

Close the field list by choosing View, Field List.

15. Notice that the control widths are the same as they were in the form created by the Form Wizard: the state and ZIP code controls are too wide. Also, the name and address fields might be a bit too narrow for the data you expect to enter.

Resize a control by first selecting it (draw a rectangle through the control), and then dragging the sizing handle to a more appropriate width (see fig.19.49).

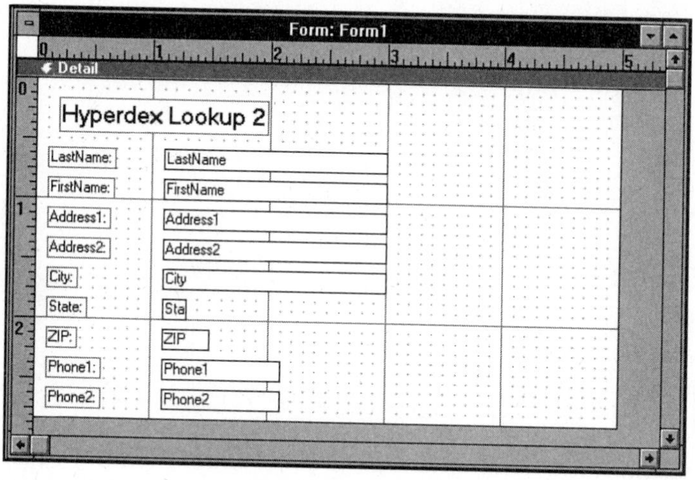

Figure 19.49
Resized controls on the form.

You can change the widths for more than one control at a time. First, widen the LastName control. Then, select the desired controls by dragging a rectangle through them. Make sure you don't drag the mouse through controls you don't want to resize. Next, choose F**o**rmat, **S**ize. Finally, choose one of the subcommands to make the controls the same as the widest or narrowest of the selected controls. You also can use this technique to adjust the height of the controls by choosing the to **T**allest or to **S**hortest subcommands.

16. Switch to Form view by clicking the Form view button or by choosing **V**iew, **F**orm. The result (see fig. 19.50) is much like that produced by the form created with the Form Wizard. The navigation buttons in the lower left corner of the form work as they do with the Wizard-created form, and any changes to the data displayed on the form will be reflected in the underlying table.

    Admittedly, this is not the best-looking Access form possible. Still, the form is functional and provides an easy-to-use interface to the underlying data. In Chapter 23, "Creating and using Forms," you learn many of the techniques required to produce more aesthetically pleasing forms.

17. Save your work by choosing **F**ile, Save Form **A**s. Name the form **Hyperdex Lookup 2**, and then close the form by choosing **F**ile, **C**lose.

You've now completed your second Access form. Although both techniques discussed so far required quite a few steps to describe, no more than a few minutes of work is required to build simple forms like these.

Figure 19.50
The completed
form in Form view.

> **Form: Form1**
>
> ### Hyperdex Lookup 2
>
> LastName: Allen
>
> FirstName: David
>
> Address1:   1350 Pennsylvania Ave
>
> Address2:
>
> City: Indianapolis
>
> State: IN
>
> ZIP: 46130
>
> Phone1:   (317) 555-1514
>
> Phone2:
>
> Record: 1   of 16

Automating the Database Search

Recall that the People by Name Qry query returns all the records in the People table. In the absence of specific query criteria, Access will return all the records from the tables included in the query.

You now will create a small form that will supply the query with just enough information to select specific records from the People table. This new form will serve as a query criteria input form and will contain three controls:

- ✔ A text box you can use to enter the last name of the person you want to find

- ✔ A command button, Search, that will trigger the query to extract the person's name from the table

- ✔ Another command button, Cancel, that you can click on to cancel the search

You also will need a small Access Basic procedure that will respond when you click on the Search button. Finally, a minor modification of People by Name Qry is necessary so that the query criteria can be read from the new query criteria form.

The following steps are required to automate your database:

1. Create the new criteria form by following the general procedures outlined earlier for constructing a new form from scratch. When you get to the New Form dialog box, however, don't enter the name of a table or query; this will be an unbound form. An *unbound form* is a form that has no underlying query or table.

   The new form should look something like that shown in figure 19.51.

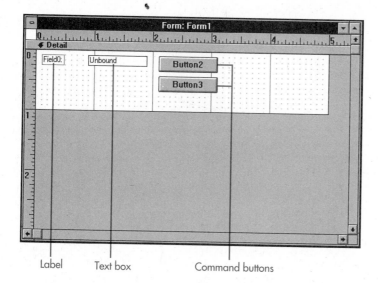

Figure 19.51
The new criteria form in Design view.

Label   Text box   Command buttons

2. Each control on an Access form has a number of properties that define the appearance and behavior of the control. To view the properties, display the property sheet by choosing <u>V</u>iew, Proper<u>t</u>ies (see fig. 19.52), or by pressing the Property Sheet on the Toolbar.

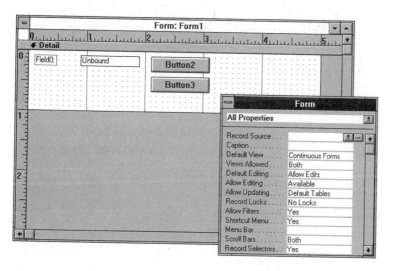

Figure 19.52
The form property sheet.

3. Labels, text boxes, and command buttons have different properties. Some are the same, and some are unique to each kind of control. All controls have a Name property, for example, but only the label and command buttons have a Caption property.

By default, Access assigns names such as Text0, Button4, and so on. Not only are these names meaningless, they can be confusing if you later need to refer to a control by its name.

Select each control in turn and change its Name property to something more meaningful. Name the label **LastNameLbl**, the text box **LastName**, the first command button **Search**, and the other command button **Cancel**.

4. Again select the label control and set its Caption property to **Last Name**. Change the Search command button's Caption property to **Search** and the Cancel button's Caption property to **Cancel**.

Your form should look something like that illustrated in figure 19.53.

Figure 19.53
The criteria form with the control captions set.

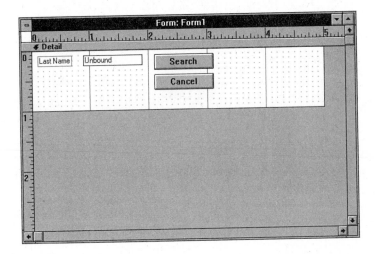

5. Select the Search command button and then locate the On Click property in the property sheet. Open the drop-down list and select [Event Procedure] (see fig. 19.54).

6. Click on the small button (the one with the ellipsis—...) to the right of the drop-down list button; Access displays the form's code module in which you can add the code that will be triggered whenever you click on the Search button. Enter the code illustrated in figure 19.55, and then close the code window.

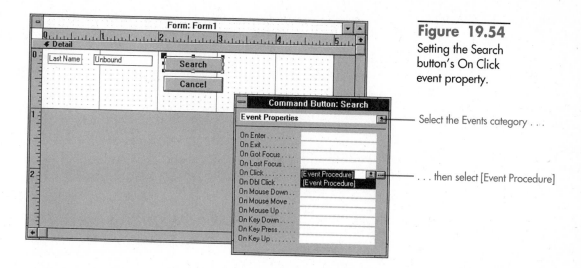

Figure 19.54

Setting the Search button's On Click event property.

Select the Events category . . .

. . . then select [Event Procedure]

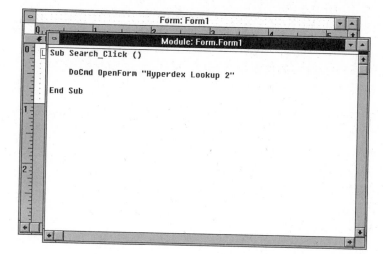

Figure 19.55

Entering code for the Search button.

Don't worry about trying to understand how the code works or what the exact syntax, or wording, is. All that matters right now is that you understand that whenever you click on the Search button, Access will run this code and open the form named Hyperdex Lookup 2.

7. Repeat step 5 for the Cancel button's On Click event. Then, open the code module (by pressing the button with the ellipsis) and set its code as illustrated in figure 19.56.

IV

Microsoft Access

Figure 19.56
Entering code for
the Cancel button.

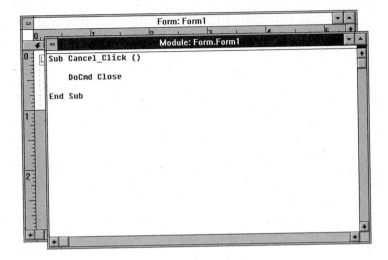

All this button needs to do is close the current form.

8. Save the new form by selecting File, Save Form As. Name the form **Search Criteria**. Then, switch to Form view by choosing View, Form, but don't try clicking on the command buttons yet (you need to modify the People by Name Qry query first). Your new form should look something like figure 19.57.

Figure 19.57
The completed
criteria form.

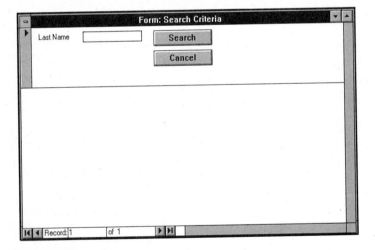

Minimize the form and continue with the next section, in which you will see how you can modify the query to accept a last name from the new form.

Modifying the Query

The following procedure outlines the steps you can follow to modify the People by Name Qry query.

1. In the Database window, click on the Query button, and then click on the People by Name Qry query.

2. Click on the Design button; Access opens the query in Design view.

3. Click on the Criteria box in LastName column. This is where Access looks to obtain the specific query criteria you want to apply to the database search.

4. Enter the following text into the criteria box exactly as it appears here:

   `Like [Forms]![Search Criteria]![LastName] & "*"`

   Include everything from the word Like to the closing quotation mark (").

   Your completed query should look like figure 19.58. The LastName column has been widened a bit to display all of the text for the criteria.

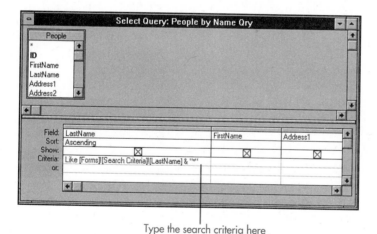

Type the search criteria here

Figure 19.58
The query in Design view.

5. Save the query by choosing <u>F</u>ile, <u>S</u>ave, then close the query.

Your database is now complete.

Using Your New Database

Using the database is quite simple:

1. If you minimized the criteria form while you followed along in the last section, reopen the form by double-clicking on the form's icon.

2. If you closed the criteria form, return to the Database window, click on the Form button, and highlight the Search Criteria form. Next, open the Search Criteria form by either double-clicking on the name or by clicking on the Open button.

3. Type **Miller** in the text box (see fig. 19.59).

Figure 19.59
Using the criteria
form.

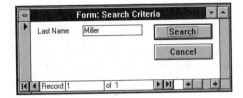

4. Click on the Search button; Access opens the form named Hyperdex Lookup 2 and shows the first of two records for people whose last names begin with Miller (see fig. 19.60).

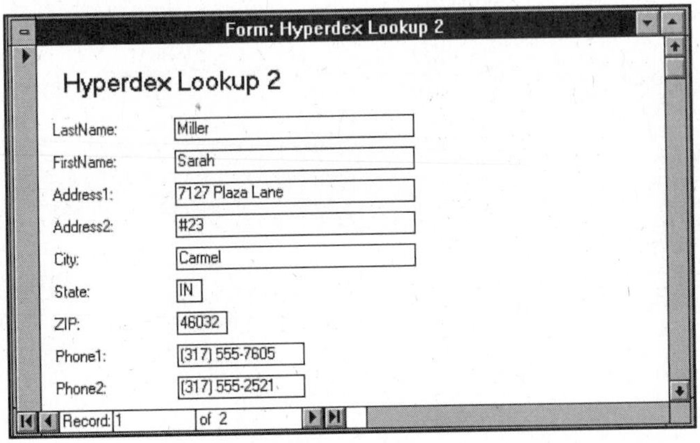

Figure 19.60
It works! Only
Miller records
appear in the
Hyperdex Lookup
2 form.

Did it work for you? If so, congratulations! You should be proud that you were able to manipulate Access to the point at which the database yielded precisely the information you expected.

If this exercise did not work as described, don't despair—you have plenty of company. Building databases is complex, detailed work that not many people fully master. There are many things that can go wrong. Be sure to read the next section to get an idea of what to look for to fix your database. Then read the following section to get an understanding of how this simple database is supposed to work behind the scenes. Maybe that will help you make whatever changes are necessary to complete the project.

What Could Go Wrong

There are many things that could go wrong with the database described in this chapter. If you saw a blank Hyperdex Lookup 2 form with no data in it, check the following:

✔ Make sure there is at least one record in the People table for which the last name starts with Miller. If there isn't, try the name of someone that you did enter into the table.

If the form opened up with the wrong name in it:

✔ Make sure you specified People by Name Qry and not some other query or table name in the Record Source property of the Hyperdex Lookup 2 form. To check this, open the form in Design view, open the property sheet, and check the form's Record Source property.

✔ Make sure you put the query criteria in the LastName column in the query QBE grid. Your query really has to look exactly like figure 19.58. If you need to stretch the LastName column wider to see the entire criteria text, move the mouse pointer to the right edge of the gray bar just above LastName in the QBE grid until the pointer changes to a double-headed arrow, then drag the right margin of the column wider. (This action is exactly like adjusting the width of columns in Excel.) Or, click in the Criteria box, and then press Shift+F2 to open the Zoom box.

If Access pops up a dialog box like in figure 19.61, you didn't name the text box in the criteria form correctly. Remember: the name of the box is LastName, exactly as indicated in the search criteria entered into the QBE grid in People by Name Qry.

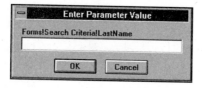

Figure 19.61
This dialog box means you misnamed something.

How It Works

It is important to understand the flow of the data through this database example. The primary storage mechanism is the People table. It goes without saying that Access cannot find data that is not in the People table or that is incorrectly entered into this table.

The People by Name Qry query extracts data from the People table. Initially, you applied no query criteria to the query, so the query returned all the records in the underlying table. Later, you had the query look for something named [Forms]![Search Criteria]![LastName] to determine what records to look for.

[Forms]![Search Criteria]![LastName] refers to a control named LastName on a form named Search Criteria. LastName, of course, is the text box on the Search Criteria form in which you enter the last name of the person you want to retrieve from the database.

The Search button on the Criteria form opens the Hyperdex Lookup 2 form by calling code in its event procedure. This code is known as *code behind form* because it is stored "behind" the form in an event procedure. When you click on the Search button, Access triggers the On Click event and automatically runs the code, which in turn opens the form.

The data source for the Hyperdex Lookup 2 form is the People by Name Qry query. When the lookup form opens in response to the OpenForm macro action in the Search button's event procedure, Access automatically runs the query to ensure that the lookup form displays the most recent—and properly selected—data.

It should be clear that all the parts of an Access database are intricately linked to each other. The names you assign to the various database components are important. Always check your work to ensure that you have used the correct syntax and carry your naming conventions throughout your database projects.

When something goes wrong, stop a moment and think about the flow of the data through the database. Make sure you fully understand what is supposed to happen when you click on a button or enter text into a text box. Nothing happens in an Access database by accident. Careful planning is necessary to make sure that whatever does happen is anticipated and desirable. A little thought ahead of time can save you many hours of frustration later on.

Chapter Snapshot

Everyone working in a typical business environment needs to manage data. Without even thinking about it, we all manipulate huge amounts of data during the workday. The names and addresses of customers and clients, holiday and vacation schedules, and the periodic reports you prepare all are examples of data. Microsoft Access is a personal database system designed to help you manage the flood of data and information that threatens to overwhelm you every day in your job. This chapter discusses the following topics:

The nicest thing about Microsoft Access is that it has been designed for normal people like yourself.

Learning Access Concepts

by Paul Cassel

I f some kind of control is not applied, the names, numbers, and words flowing through an office might overwhelm the unprepared office worker. The office professional of the '90s needs to keep an enormous amount of information easily accessible. The most efficient people are those who best manage information, whether that information takes the form of schedules, client lists, inventory, or financial data.

Imagine how difficult it would be for a law office to conduct business if efficient filing systems weren't in place to handle client records. How could a video rental store continue to do business if no attention were paid to its video inventory?

On a more personal basis, can you imagine how difficult it would be if you had to rebuild your Christmas card list from scratch every year? Or if you had to use the phone book or directory assistance every time you made a phone call?

Over time, a number of data management systems have been established to help people control the data that dominates our lives. These systems include everything from those compact name-and-address books you can buy at the drugstore to massive computer programs running on million-dollar computers. The more sophisticated computerized database systems require highly skilled professionals to maintain, while managing a pocket address book can be handled by almost anyone.

Understanding Databases

A *database* is anything that helps you organize information into a structure that makes the information easier to manage. Most people, when confronted with the word *database*, immediately think of some kind of complicated, mysterious computer program. However, as you soon will see, there are many kinds of databases all around you that you have already mastered.

A key concept with Microsoft Access—or any database—is that data by itself is practically worthless. No one cares for raw numbers, name lists, or card files full of disorganized data. Not until some organization and structure has been applied to the data does it become *informative*, and therefore, *information*.

Your copy of Microsoft Office Professional includes Microsoft Access, a Windows database application designed to enable the non-database professional to manage a wide variety of data-management tasks. Access has been applied to all manner of data management tasks, from the simple HYPERDEX desktop card file systems like you built in Chapter 19, "Access Quick Start," to sophisticated time-and-expense billing systems.

Traditional Databases

We all are familiar with simple, traditional database systems. Although you may not have thought about it in these terms, the desktop card file you use every day is a database of names and addresses. Similarly, the address book in your briefcase or purse is another form of a name-and-address database.

Figure 20.1
A desktop card
file.

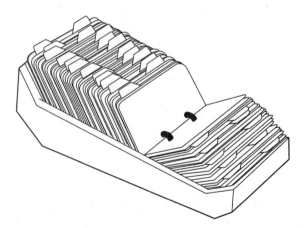

A nicely organized filing cabinet is a database of documents. A dictionary is a database of words and their definitions. A cookbook is a database of recipes, and *Chilton's* automobile manual is a database of car repair instructions. Surely you have been using one or more of these types of databases for a long time.

See? You have been a database user and expert for a long time and didn't even know it!

Computerized Databases

For many years, huge computerized databases have been churning away inside giant computers, tended by highly trained, highly specialized computer professionals. Everyone's life is touched by these computers and the data they manage. When you submit your income tax return each year, it, along with the returns of millions of other people, is fed into one of these gigantic computer systems for analysis. The SAT, GRE, GMAT, and other standardized tests that millions of high school and college students agonize over each year are graded and scored by another of these giant computers and their programs.

Fortunately, a simpler solution is available to the layperson—one with smaller data management requirements. In the past dozen or so years, a wide variety of computerized databases have become available for desktop computers. Although the very first successful personal computer application (VisiCalc) was a spreadsheet strictly designed for numerical analysis, it soon was followed by a number of database applications. Foremost among the early database systems was dBASE from Ashton-Tate.

Traditional Database Systems

Until fairly recently, PC databases required you to learn a complicated database language before you could master your data. The language, which often was different for each type of database, was used to write *database programs* that controlled the way the database engine stored, retrieved, and manipulated data. These programs determined how the screen looked and how data was to be input into the database, and, generally speaking, controlled the way in which the user interacted with the database and its data.

The early versions of dBASE were typical of PC database systems. When started on a computer, the only indication that dBASE was ready to work was a dot (actually, a period) that appeared on the screen as soon as dBASE was running. dBASE required the user to type certain commands after the dot, instructing dBASE what to do. A large number of dBASE commands had to be memorized to get dBASE to do any kind of work at all.

Obviously, the dBASE dot prompt required a certain level of competence before you could build databases with it. (It's not really fair to single out dBASE in this regard; most other PC databases were not much easier to use.) Although the dBASE interface improved over time, there are still dozens of different commands to learn before useful work can be performed with dBASE.

Most often, the expert dBASE user would use the programming language built into dBASE to write a database application to make it easier for laypeople to use the data stored in the database. The database application would include some kind of user interface with words, lines, and boxes on the screen. The interface would control how the data was entered or used. A well-designed and carefully written dBASE application shielded the nonexpert from having to learn the dBASE commands before using the database.

IV

Microsoft Access

Because database languages were most often used by database professionals, the structure and terminology of the database languages were almost always difficult to learn. It was a rare individual who would produce a complete database application without first undergoing extensive training in database techniques and programming. Even the most experienced database programmer needed weeks to produce a useful database application.

Finally, because older database systems like dBASE worked only on simple DOS computers, they did not use many of the graphical elements you take for granted in Windows applications: scroll bars, menus, tool bars, and so on. The only "graphics" that could be displayed by many DOS-based database applications were simple lines and boxes.

Using a database application written in dBASE or another DOS-based system is just like learning any DOS application. Under DOS each application has its own appearance and style, and interacts with the user in completely unique ways. There are none of the menus, mouse actions, or other Windows interface elements you have become so familiar with.

Microsoft Access: A Truly Modern Database

Microsoft has completely changed the way people use PC databases. Because it is a Windows-based database system, you will feel right at home with the menus, dialog boxes, buttons, and other Access interface elements. Most of your interaction with Access will involve the keyboard and mouse. Help is always available by pressing the F1 key or by using the Help command on the Access menu bar. Access is truly WYSIWG (What You See Is What You Get). When you design a report that will be printed on a laser printer, you can see on the screen exactly what the report will look like when it comes out of the printer.

Although Access contains a complete programming language (called *Access Basic*), powerful and useful Access databases can be built without any programming at all. When necessary, the Access programming language can be used to customize certain aspects of your Access database applications.

You are not required to learn Access Basic before building sophisticated, useful database applications. As you will see, the Access development tools were designed with the non-database professional in mind. Furthermore, the Access environment (see fig. 20.2) is easy to learn and use; any experienced Windows user will feel right at home in the Access environment. All the familiar Windows features—scroll bars, buttons, menus, and so on—are included in Microsoft Access and can be used in database applications built with Access.

In spite of its deceptively empty appearance, you soon will find that Microsoft Access quickly provides you with a wealth of design and construction aids to help you build powerful databases. In the meantime, it probably is enough to recognize that the Access environment (sometimes called the *desktop*) looks like any other Windows application.

You will, however, have to learn the rules and techniques required to build queries, forms, reports, and other components of an Access database application. Most first-time (and many experienced) Access users become confused or frustrated as they begin database projects because they haven't spent a little time learning the basics.

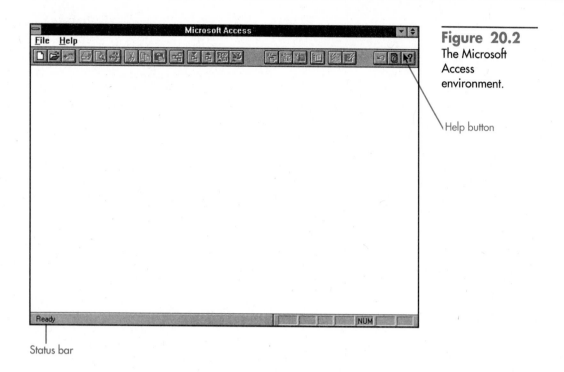

Figure 20.2
The Microsoft
Access
environment.

Help button

Status bar

Using Microsoft Access

Access is an application for building databases, much like Windows Paintbrush is an application for drawing pictures or Word for Windows is an application for creating documents. Databases almost always contain a number of different components, such as tables, forms, and queries (in Access, these things are called *objects*). Access contains a number of different tools that you will use to build the database objects.

There are three main ways to use Microsoft Access:

✔ You can use Access to design and build databases.

✔ You can use Access to work with databases built by other database systems.

✔ You can use Access to work with the databases built with Access.

It's almost as if you could read a Word document only while the document is open in Word or view a Paintbrush picture only while the picture is in Paintbrush. Figure 20.3 illustrates how Access is used.

IV

Microsoft Access

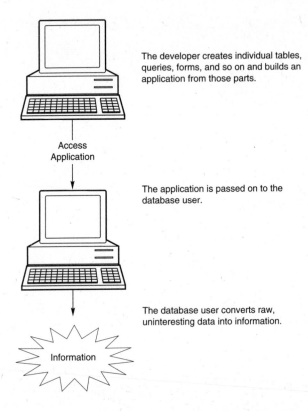

Figure 20.3
The way Access
is used.

The developer creates individual tables,
queries, forms, and so on and builds an
application from those parts.

Access
Application

The application is passed on to the
database user.

The database user converts raw,
uninteresting data into information.

Information

Actually, Access is most like Excel in that, for the most part, Excel is used to create worksheets of information and charts that display that information. Even though the worksheets and charts can be printed, Excel often is used for viewing the worksheets and charts.

Defining Access Database Terminology

Back when you were learning to drive a car, you probably were taught the various components of automobiles before you sat down in the driver's seat. Similarly, there are a number of terms that you will use frequently as you build Access databases:

- ✔ **Data.** As used in this book, *data* is a very general term for all the facts, figures, and other items people need to manage in their jobs and businesses. Access can handle many different types of data—names, addresses, other text, numbers, pictures, dates, even sound and video clips.

- ✔ **Information.** After data has been captured and managed in some way or other, it qualifies as *information*. To put it another way, information is organized data.

- ✔ **Table.** Data usually is stored in a database as a *table*. Database tables look a lot like spreadsheets; data is arranged in rows and columns (see fig. 20.4).

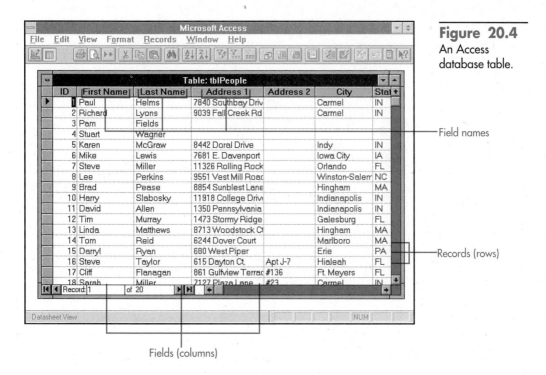

Figure 20.4
An Access
database table.

Field names

Records (rows)

Fields (columns)

✔ **Record.** A *record* is one row of a database table. All the data in a database record is somehow related. If you think of a desktop card file as a database, a database record is one card from the desktop card file. All the data (name, address, and so on) on the card relates to one person. New data is added to the database by adding new records to a database table.

✔ **Field.** Database records are made up of fields. A *field* is one piece of data (like a phone number) within the record and corresponds to the columns of a database table. Generally speaking, a database is designed by deciding which fields to include in the database tables, and the number of fields do not change as data is added to the database. As you will see, certain rules or guidelines should be followed when deciding which fields should be added to a database table at design time.

✔ **Query.** A database wouldn't be much good if there was no way to extract data from it. Although you can "browse" a database table, the most common way to retrieve data from database tables is with a *query,* which is a set of rules for finding data. For instance, "Give me all the records for people with last names beginning with *S*" is a valid database query.

✔ **Form.** Everyone has encountered forms at some time or other. Sometimes it seems as though our lives are ruled by forms: income tax forms, time cards, insurance benefit forms, driver's license applications, and so on. Windows-based database applications

IV

Microsoft Access

like Access enable you to include on-screen forms (see fig. 20.5), database applications that make it easier for users to enter, change, or retrieve data. Often the on-screen forms mimic the appearance of their paper equivalents.

Figure 20.5
A typical form in an Access database application.

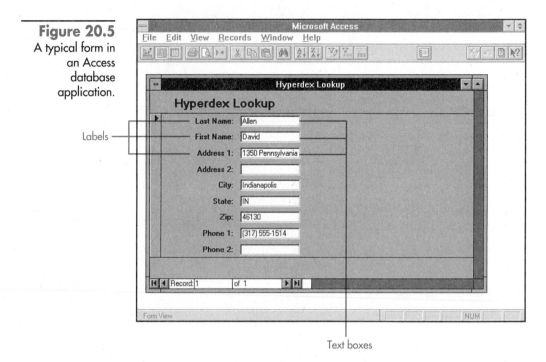

The form in figure 20.5 displays a person's first and last names, as well as the person's address and phone number. Generally speaking, an Access form displays one record of data. The buttons in the lower right corner of the form move through a "stack" of forms, each form displaying the data from a different record: the person's name, address, and phone number.

✔ **Module.** Access Basic code is not added directly to forms or the controls on forms. Instead, Access Basic functions and procedures (explained in Chapter 26, "Understanding Access Basic") are kept in modules within the database. The functions stored within the modules can be called by macros and other database objects at runtime. An Access database can contain as many modules as necessary. Access Basic often is used for validating data, deleting obsolete information, and performing complex calculations on data stored in the database.

✔ **Database.** The term *database* has been applied to many different data-management methods. A Microsoft Access database consists of all the tables, forms, queries, and other components used to manage data within a project. As you soon will see, the

people who use an Access database do not need to know anything at all about how the data is stored within the database. The creator of the database, however, has to learn quite a bit about how to build Access databases.

In this book, the term *user* applies to the person who actually sits at the computer and has to get data out of the database. The person who builds the Access database is the *developer*.

✔ **Object.** Access databases are made up of database objects such as tables, forms, and queries. Each Access object type has its own design tool (which you use to build the object) and rules for making the object perform as expected.

✔ **Event.** An *event* is any action for which you can define a response. An event occurs whenever the user presses a key on the keyboard, moves the mouse, or clicks a mouse button. Events are actions, normally initiated by the user. One of the biggest advantages of Access (and other Windows databases as well) is that the user is not restricted to interacting with the database in any particular sequence. Data can be entered into any field at any time (unless a restriction has been placed on the fields by the developer). Similarly, buttons and menu items can be accessed as needed by the user (the same restrictions apply). A well-designed Access database will respond to essentially any meaningful event initiated by the user and ignore events that are meaningless or possibly dangerous to the data.

✔ **Event-driven.** This is a broad term applied to any application or system that is able to respond to arbitrary events like mouse clicks or key presses. *Event-driven* applications are contrasted to *procedural* applications, which require input and actions to occur in a predetermined sequence. Most Windows applications are event-driven.

Understanding the Access Environment

Although the initial Access environment is quite barren (refer to figure 20.2), after you start creating new database objects and opening existing ones, the environment gets much more interesting.

Creating a New Database

Creating a new, empty Microsoft Access database is no more complicated than selecting New Database from the File menu. The New Database dialog box opens, asking for the name of the new database and enabling you to select the directory that will serve as the database's home (see fig. 20.6).

Figure 20.6
The New
Database dialog
box.

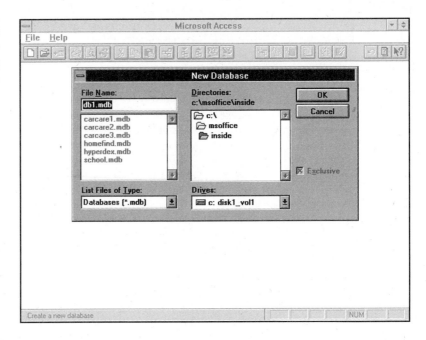

Access database names must conform to the DOS *filename.ext* naming convention. That is, the name must be eight characters or less, cannot include any punctuation, and must be followed by the three-character MDB extension. (MDB stands for Microsoft DataBase, by the way.)

If a database is already open, there is no **N**ew Database option in the **F**ile menu. The **N**ew option in the **F**ile menu opens a cascading menu enabling you to select Table, Query, Form, and the other database objects. If a database is already open, Access assumes that you want to add new objects to the database, not create an entirely new database. If you want to create a new database, be sure to close any open databases before selecting **N**ew Database from the **F**ile menu.

You might notice the List Files of **T**ype drop-down list box in the lower left corner of the New Database dialog box in figure 20.6. Although the 2.0 and 1.0 file formats are very similar, they are not exactly the same. A 2.0 database file cannot be opened by Access 1.0, although Access 2.0 can open the older (1.0) database files. Microsoft has provided limited backward compatibility in Access 2.0 to accommodate developers working in environments that contain a mix of Access 2.0 and 1.0 users. One of the limitations of this backward compatibility is that Access 2.0 cannot change the structure of 1.1 or 1.0 databases. To do this you must convert the 1.0 or 1.1 database to 2.0 format using the **F**ile, Convert menu selection.

Even a brand-new, empty database requires about 64K of disk space. The empty MDB file contains certain information and reserved space for database object names to occupy 64K of disk space.

Exploring the Database Window

After you enter a name for the database and click on the OK button in the New Database dialog box, the Access environment changes quite dramatically (see fig. 20.7). A fairly large window opens in the upper left corner of the Access environment, several items are added to the menu bar, and several additional icons appear on the toolbar.

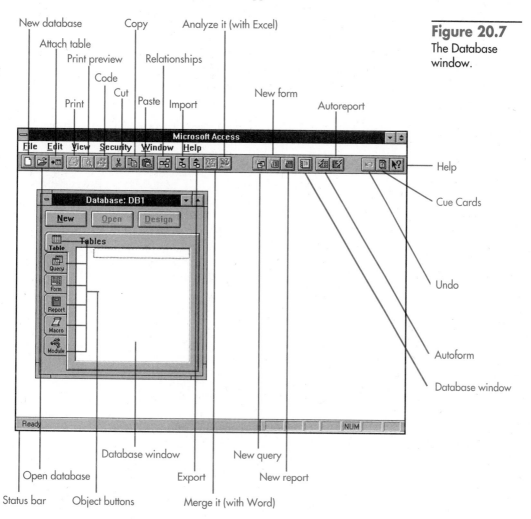

Figure 20.7
The Database window.

The menu bar has several new options and the toolbar under the menu bar has more buttons active than in figure 20.2. By far the most important change has been the addition of the database window (which is sometimes called the database container). This window serves as the switchboard to access all the components of the database.

IV

Microsoft Access

Down the left side of the database window are a number of object buttons. These buttons enable access to each of the six types of major database objects: tables, queries, forms, reports, macros, and Access Basic modules. When you click on an object button, the display area to the right of the object buttons shows all the items of that type currently in the database.

When an object button is pressed, such as the Tables button in figure 20.7, you can use the New button at the top of the database window to create a new object of the type indicated by the active object button. In figure 20.7, the New button will start the process of building a new database table. After you have built a table, its name appears in the (now empty) list to the right of the object buttons, and the Open and Design buttons will become active. The Open and Design buttons enable you to quickly open an existing object for work or open an existing object in design view (see the section "Understanding Design Windows" later in this chapter).

At the far right of the toolbar near the top of the Access screen are the New Query, New Form, and New Report icons. As their names imply, these icons enable you to quickly create new queries, forms, and reports. Using the toolbar icons bypasses the need to press the appropriate object button on the database window and then the New button at the top of the database window.

It might take a while, but soon you will instantly recognize the icons used to represent each type of major database object (tables, queries, forms, and so on) in Access. Notice that the icons at the right end of the toolbar contain the same graphics as the object buttons on the database window. You will see other instances in Access for which these same icons are used for other purposes.

Understanding Design Windows

Initially the database window is empty. Right after you create the database, even though the empty database occupies a significant amount of disk space, there are no tables, queries, forms, or other accessible objects in the database. (This statement is not exactly true, but is sufficient for our purposes. If you are really interested in Access system objects, please consult a more advanced Access book such as *Inside Access 2.0, Special Edition,* also from New Riders Publishing.)

The first step in creating a Microsoft Access database is to build a table to hold data. Although this process is covered in more detail in Chapter 21, "Creating and Using Tables," it might be interesting to look at the table design window.

Most of the major objects in an Access database (tables, forms, queries, and so on) can be viewed from more than one perspective. Given an Access table, you can look at it from the datasheet view or in design view. Figure 20.8 shows the same table shown in figure 20.4 in design view.

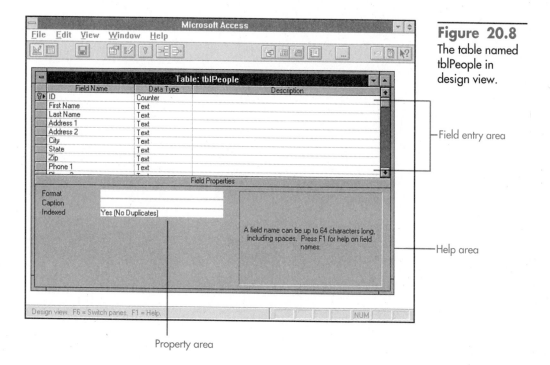

Figure 20.8
The table named
tblPeople in
design view.

In design view, changes to the structure of the table can be made, including naming the fields, specifying the data types handled by the fields in the table, and other parameters such as designating the key field. Notice that while in design view, the area in the lower right corner of the table provides help as you build the table.

Similarly, each type of database object has its own design view. In later chapters, you will become familiar with designing and creating each type of Access database object.

Menus

Like all Windows applications, Microsoft Access features a menu bar across the top of the main window. Unlike many applications, however, the menu items change to reflect the activity occurring on the Access desktop. Notice the menu bar in figure 20.8. There are only five menu items: File, Edit, View, Window, and Help. Figure 20.9 shows the menu bar while the Hyperdex Lookup form is open. The same five menu items are present, but a sixth (Records) has been added.

IV

Microsoft Access

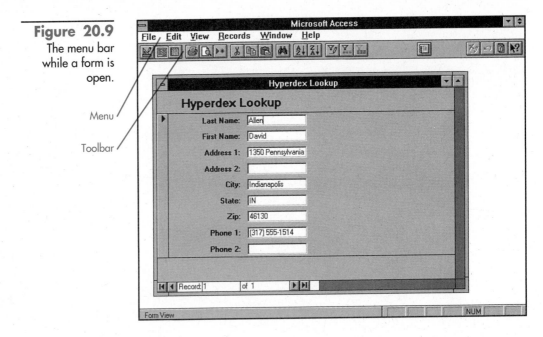

Figure 20.9
The menu bar
while a form is
open.

Menu

Toolbar

The Records menu contains all the functions necessary to manage the records displayed in the Hyperdex Lookup form.

The buttons that appear on the toolbar change, depending on the activity taking place on the Access desktop. For more information, see the "Toolbars" section later in this chapter.

To make the situation more confusing, the Access application itself can take over the menu bar, adding new menu items or suppressing items that normally would appear on the bar. There are good reasons for applications to control the menu bar. New functions can be added that would otherwise have to be implemented with command buttons, and certain functions that might prove dangerous to the data can be removed from the menu bar.

Toolbars

You probably have noticed the Access toolbar, which appears just below the menu bar in figures 20.8 and 20.9. Although Access seems to be suffering from the icon mania that affects most Windows applications, you will find the toolbar to be a great time-saver. Each button on the toolbar represents a shortcut method to perform some Access function. The binoculars

icon, for instance, enables you to quickly find a particular record, instead of having to manually search through each record displayed by the form.

As with the menu bar, the toolbar changes to reflect the activity on the Access desktop. The icons on the toolbar in figure 20.9 are quite different from those in figure 20.8. As you read through each chapter in Part Four, you will become quite familiar with the most frequently used buttons on each Access toolbar. You can learn what each button in the Toolbar does by placing your mouse cursor over it. Access pops down a short tool tip—like a cartoon balloon— telling you the button's function. In addition, you will see a longer explanation of the button's function on the far left of the status bar.

Access Help and Cue Cards

Because databases can be quite complicated to design and build, Microsoft pays particular attention to helping you learn Access. Cue Cards, a new help feature, appears in the Access Help menu (see fig. 20.10). Cue Cards provide a unique interactive approach to learning common Access tasks and procedures. Access Cue Cards are implemented as a series of help screens that provide specific help and instructions for the most common Access tasks.

Figure 20.10

The Cue Cards command appears in the Access Help menu.

When you select Cue Cards from the Help menu, the main Cue Card menu opens (see fig. 20.11). Just to the left of each item in the main Cue Card menu is a button that triggers the next Cue Card in the series.

Assume that you have some questions about building Access tables, so you select the option titled Build a Database with Tables by clicking on the button just to the left of this option. After a moment, you are returned to the Access desktop and the Build a Database with Tables Cue Card is positioned on the right side of the screen, as shown in figure 20.12.

IV

Microsoft Access

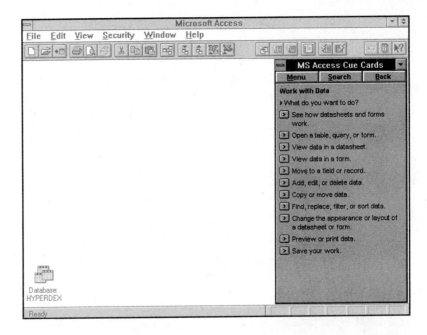

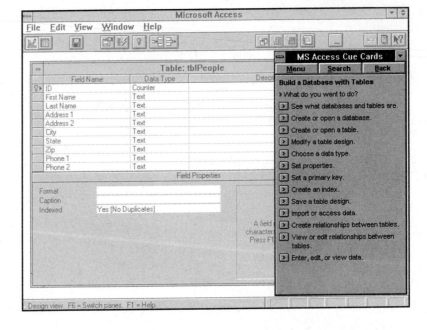

Cue Cards are designed to help you as you build Access databases. For instance, they always appear on top of the Access desktop. Although you can move the Cue Card around on the screen (by dragging the Cue Card title bar) so you can see what you are doing, you cannot use the Alt+Tab key combination to move Access on top of the Cue Card.

Cue Cards provide step-by-step instructions and explanations of important Access tasks. Figure 20.13 shows the Cue Card that explains how to create a database. The help on this Cue Card is quite specific, telling you which buttons to push and what happens in response to your action.

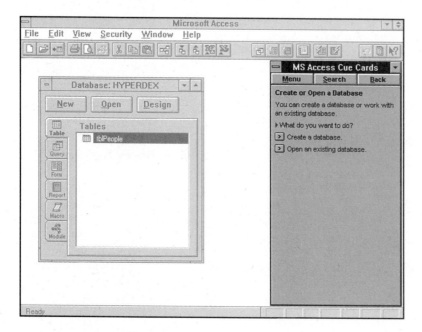

Figure 20.13
The Create or Open a Database Cue Card.

It is likely that soon after you start working with Access, you will no longer need to use Cue Cards. Although the instructions and explanations they present are valuable learning tools, you will soon master most of the tasks described by Cue Cards. It is nice to know, however, that they are always there if you need them.

Cue Cards are an installation option and might not have been installed on your computer. They do require a significant amount of disk space (somewhat less than 2M), but are well worth the time and effort to install.

If, for some reason Cue Cards refuse to start when you select the Cue Card command in the **H**elp menu, check whether the file named MSACCESS.CUE appears in the ACCESS directory, which probably is under the OFFICE or MSOFFICE directory on drive C on your computer. It is possible that Microsoft

IV

Microsoft Access

Office has been installed on the network in your office as well, which means that MSACCESS.CUE might not appear anywhere on your computer.

If MSACCESS.CUE does not appear in the ACCESS directory, you will have to find the Access installation disks to install them. Fortunately, you can install the Cue Cards without installing all of Microsoft Access.

Looking At Tables

Modern databases like Access are extremely flexible in the types of data they can hold. You can store numbers, text, pictures, sound, video, and many other types of data in an Access database. You can keep all these in a single table, if you need to.

When you build a database table, Access needs to know what kind of data you plan to store in the table. Because you have to specify the types of data stored in the database tables, a little advanced planning helps during this phase of the project. Chapter 21, "Creating and Using Tables," discusses the information that is required for successful database table design.

Building Tables

The best analogy for a database table is a folder within a filing cabinet. Figure 20.14 illustrates how a computer database can be compared to a traditional office filing cabinet. The filing cabinet itself is a paper database that holds, for example, all the business records for a small company. Within the filing cabinet are a bunch of different folders, each holding all the paperwork for a single customer. There might even be separate folders for each customer. One folder holds orders from a customer, another folder contains all of the payment receipts from the same customer.

In a filing cabinet, folders normally are arranged alphabetically to make them easy to find. Separate drawers in the cabinet might be used to hold similar folders (orders in one drawer, payment receipts in another). Alternatively, each folder might contain all orders received for a certain month, or all payments received over some period of time. The exact arrangement depends on the filing method set up by the business.

In an Access database, you might create an Orders table to hold all the orders submitted by customers and another table to store payments from the customer. Each time a new order or payment is received from a customer, a new record is added to the appropriate table.

So far, so good. But what happens if you want to see *all* the orders or payments from a particular customer? Using a filing cabinet is easy; all you do is pull out the customer's order or receipt folder and you have all the information you need on that customer (a different filing system, of course, might make this search more difficult). How do you do the same thing using an Access database?

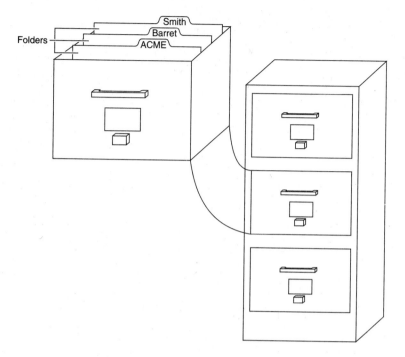

Figure 20.14
Database tables
can be like folders
in a filing cabinet.

Understanding Table Relationships

You might have seen Access described as a *relational* database system. This technical-sounding expression simply means that the data in tables within the database are *related* to each other in some way. Instead of putting all the data in one massive table, Access lets you break up the data into smaller, more manageable sets of closely related data in separate tables.

Many people use spreadsheets (like Excel) to store information like names and addresses. This approach works fine as long as the information does not get too complicated. As soon as you want to add another layer of complexity (like vacation schedules) to this information, the spreadsheet approach can get pretty unmanageable.

In the filing cabinet analogy, the papers in the customer orders and payment receipts folders are related to each other by the customer name. Most businesses use a customer number to track orders and payments. The files in the orders and payments folder can be related by the customer number, customer name, or invoice number. Figure 20.15 illustrates this concept.

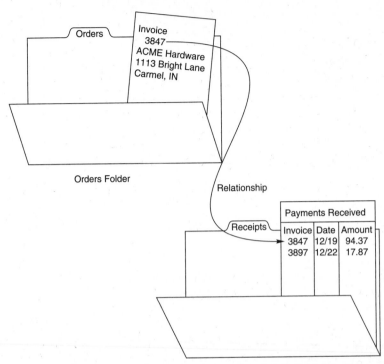

Figure 20.15
Relationships between folders in a filing cabinet.

In the same way, records in the Orders and Payments tables in an Access database can be related by a customer number, customer name, or invoice number. Almost always, some kind of number (such as the customer number) or other data will be used to tie tables together. The bit of data tying tables together is called a *key field*.

When you build tables in Access, you always will want to add a key field (remember, fields in a record correspond to columns in a table) to the table that ties the table to the other tables in the database. The account number on your electric bill is the key field used by the electric company to track your outstanding balance and payments, for example. As you build Access databases, you will add similar fields to track the data you store in its tables.

Understanding Access Queries

The whole reason you build a database is to get data back out of it again. A *query* is how you ask the database for information. Think of queries as highly structured questions you give Access to get the information you need out of the database. Without a doubt, queries are the most important database object you will design in Access.

Figure 20.16 shows the results of a simple query. Looks a lot like the table in figure 20.4, doesn't it? In fact, queries build a kind of temporary table called a *dynaset* that you can then use pretty much as you use tables. You can add, delete, or change records in the dynaset.

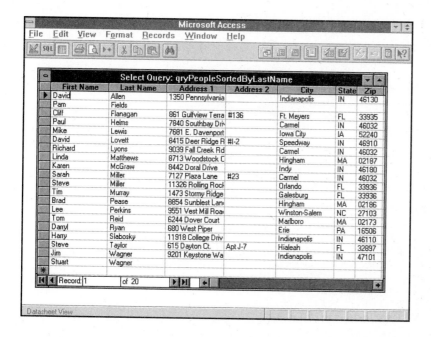

Figure 20.16
The results of a query look like a table.

In figure 20.16, notice that the dynaset's title bar tells you where the data came from. In this case, the title bar contains the name of a select query (which will be explained in detail in Chapter 22, "Understanding Access Queries"), one of several types of queries available in Access.

The biggest difference between tables and dynasets is that a table is permanent, whereas a dynaset goes away when you close it. Dynasets are connected to the tables involved in the queries that create them. Changing data in a dynaset changes the data in the underlying tables. These changes to the underlying table are permanent, and persist after the dynaset is closed.

Simple Queries

Most Access queries are pretty simple. In the case of an electronic card file, you will need queries for retrieving a person's address or birthday when you know the last name of the person. If you call the electric company to find out why the payment you sent in the previous month wasn't credited, a fairly simple query on the electric company's database will show all the payments they have received from you.

These are simple queries because only a single table needs to be searched. Looking up a person's address in the Hyperdex card file database is quick and easy because only the Address table needs to be searched. The electric company only needs to look in their giant Payments table to find all the records keyed on your account number.

More Complex Queries

A small business managing customer accounts with Access might want to match up invoices with payments. Or the company might want a list of its best-selling products and the customers who are buying those products.

Queries like these will access multiple tables. It is unlikely you will store invoices and payments in the same Access table. Similarly, you couldn't really keep a list of all the customers who have bought a particular item in the same table storing the item's sales history.

 In Chapter 22, "Understanding Access Queries," you will look at a number of simple and complex queries and learn how, with a little work, Microsoft Access can make even fairly sophisticated data management easy.

The dynaset built by a complex query can contain data from more than one table.

Mastering Forms Concepts

Although you can enter data directly into Access tables, there are a lot of problems associated with working with tables. You usually won't want untrained people changing data in your database tables. It is too easy to make a mistake, particularly if the table is very large. Many Access database tables contain dozens of columns and thousands of rows; making sure you are on the right row and column when entering or changing data can be difficult.

Much of the data contained in business databases is pretty sensitive. You wouldn't want just anyone reading salaries or medical histories stored in your database tables. Using forms restricts users of the database to only that data that you decide should appear on the form.

The following is a simple example of an Access database that will illustrate forms concepts. This database will handle videotape rentals for a neighborhood video store. Although incomplete, the MOVIES database effectively demonstrates some important concepts.

Understanding How Forms Work

Each form in a Microsoft Access database application is connected to a database table or query. The fields and other data areas on a form represent the values in the underlying table or query. Figure 20.17 shows a table and its corresponding form from the MOVIES database.

In this example, the form named Movies for Rent is connected to the table named Movies. Each field on the form (Video ID, Name of Movie, Category, and Year) is linked to the corresponding field in the Movies table. The Movies for Rent form displays one record of data. In this case, the record contains information on the movie *Starstruck*.

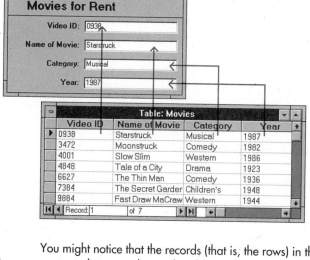

Figure 20.17
A form and its
underlying table.

You might notice that the records (that is, the rows) in the table in figure 20.17 are sorted in ascending order of the Video ID column. As long you have defined a key field, Access automatically sorts a table on the key field. The Video ID field in the Movies table has been defined as the key field, so Access keeps the table sorted on the Video ID field.

It is important to note that not all fields in the table underlying the form need to be represented on the form. Often only a portion of the fields in a table are shown on the form. This practice makes it easy to restrict the data available to the user. Because only those fields chosen by the Access developer are shown on the form, all other fields are kept secure.

Access forms often are linked to queries. Figure 20.18 shows a query underlying a form similar to the one shown in figure 20.17. The main difference in these forms is that the data in figure 20.17 has been sorted on the name of the movie by the query named MoviesSortedByName.

The qryMoviesSortedByName query overrides the default sort imposed by the table's key field. As you will see in Chapter 22, "Understanding Access Queries," there are many different ways to sort data using queries.

Look closely at the forms in figures 20.17 and 20.18. In figure 20.17, the movie in the form is *Starstruck* and its Video ID is 0938. *Starstruck* is the topmost movie in the table underlying the form in figure 20.17 because the table is sorted by the Video ID field. By default, Access tables are sorted on the table's key field, which in this case is Video ID. In figure 20.18, the movie in the form is *Fast Draw MaCraw*, which is the topmost movie in the dynaset underlying the form. The records in the dynaset are sorted by the Name of Movie field by the Select Query that created the dynaset. Queries, sorting, and other issues involving dynasets are discussed in Chapter 22.

IV

Microsoft Access

Figure 20.18
A query
underlying a form.

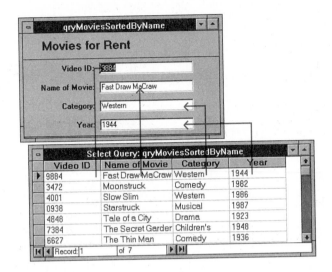

Normally when a form is using data from a table, there is only one table underlying the form. The exception to this general rule is when a subform (see Chapter 23, "Creating and Using Forms") is used on a form.

If showing data from more than one table is necessary, an easier way is to use a query to join the data from the tables; then display the query results on the form.

Creating Access Forms

Access provides a powerful forms design utility you will use to build forms like the one shown in figure 20.19. This form displays data contained in an Access database designed to manage membership for clubs and churches. The data you see displayed on the form in figure 20.19 has been extracted from a number of different tables by a complex Access query.

Don't worry if you do not recognize the names of the parts of the form labeled in figure 20.19. You will learn all these names and more in Chapter 23, "Creating and Using Forms." In the meantime, it is enough to know the following about the parts of Access forms:

✔ **Control.** *Control* is a general term applied to all the objects placed on Access database forms. The expression indicates that the objects on the form control the data being displayed and the way in which the user interacts with the data. Essentially, all objects on Access forms are controls—even those objects that are inanimate.

✔ **Text boxes.** *Text boxes* on Access forms are normally connected to fields in the tables or queries underlying the form. If a text box is enabled, changing the text in the text box changes the data in the underlying table.

✔ **Labels.** A *label* is simple text placed on the form. In figure 20.19, the word Members at the top of the form is a label. Labels cannot be changed by the user, and they are not connected to the underlying database tables.

✔ **Option buttons.** Option buttons are familiar to all Windows users. *Option buttons* enable the user to select between mutually exclusive options; this means that only one of the buttons in an option group can be selected at a time. Option buttons usually are connected to fields in the underlying database tables.

✔ **Combo boxes.** A *combo box* is a special type of list. When the user clicks on the down arrow, a list of values is revealed. Only one of the values can be selected.

✔ **Command buttons.** The form in figure 20.19 has a large number of command buttons. Certain actions occur when the user clicks on a *command button*. When the user clicks on the <u>C</u>lubs command button in figure 20.19, for instance, the area above the row of command buttons displays all the clubs that the person shown in the form belongs to.

Notice also that Access command buttons can be instantly triggered with accelerator keys. Like most Windows applications, anything that is underlined is an accelerator (sometimes called a *hot key*) that can be triggered by holding down the Alt key and pressing the letter indicated by the underline. Pressing Alt+C instantly displays the list of clubs.

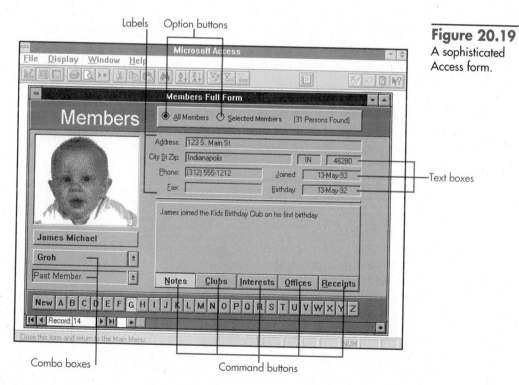

Figure 20.19
A sophisticated Access form.

IV

Microsoft Access

The data on the form in figure 20.19 comes from a number of different tables. As the user clicks on each of the buttons (**N**otes, **C**lubs, **I**nterests, **O**ffices, **R**eceipts) at the bottom of the box in the lower right quadrant of the form, information drawn from different tables in the database is displayed in the box. Each time the user clicks on one of these command buttons, a query is triggered that returns the requested information.

The boxes holding the person's name, address, and other information can be changed by simply entering new data into the boxes. When data in these boxes is changed, the data stored in the tables underlying this form changes as well.

The important concept behind the form shown in figure 20.19 is that the person using the form does not have to be concerned about how the database tables or queries were constructed. The user does not have to learn a database language or know anything at all about Microsoft Access. A well-designed form like the one in figure 20.19 effectively shields the user from all technical details of the database containing the data.

The form in figure 20.19 is exceedingly complex and was designed by an Access developer with several years of experience. Fortunately, forms this complex are very rare and the typical Access user will never create a form this complicated. All the examples described in this book are much simpler and easier to understand.

Working with Control Properties

Every control on a form has a number of properties associated with it; for instance, text on the form can be displayed in any of a number of fonts, in many different sizes and colors, and in any of several different typefaces (bold, italic, and so on). All these characteristics of text appearing on Access forms are called *control properties*.

Figure 20.20 shows the Hyperdex Lookup form from figure 20.5 in design mode. The properties list for the first name field is open to show you some of the many properties there are for text boxes.

There are 53 different properties for text boxes. Fortunately, only a few of these control properties are ever changed by the typical Access developer. For the most part, the default values are adequate and not often changed (several control properties have no default values, whereas other properties are required). As you will see in Chapter 23, "Creating and Using Forms," most properties are easy to change if you need to, and you even can specify the default values for most of the properties.

Each property has a name and a value. Many of the names make intuitive sense. Obviously, the values of properties such as Left, Top, Width, and Height specify the position and dimensions of the text box. Other properties and their values are not so obvious. The Can Grow property, for instance, means that the dimensions of the control will change to accommodate the data displayed in the control (which can happen for some text boxes and areas displaying graphics). Chapter 23 discusses control properties and their values in detail.

The properties that appear in an object's properties list depend on the nature of the object. A command button (see figure 20.21) has a very different list of properties than a text box

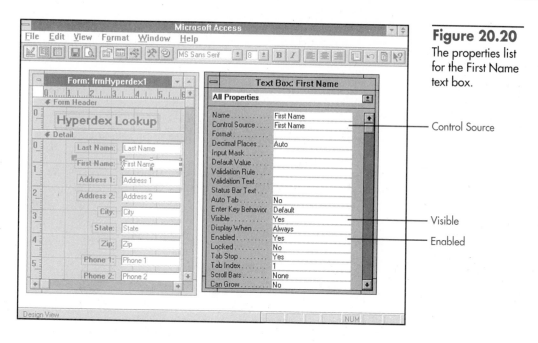

Figure 20.20
The properties list for the First Name text box.

— Control Source

— Visible

— Enabled

because the function of a command button is very different from a text box. Access command buttons have no Border Width or Special Effect properties, for instance, although both objects have Font Name and Font Size properties. Even so, there are 36 different properties for command buttons.

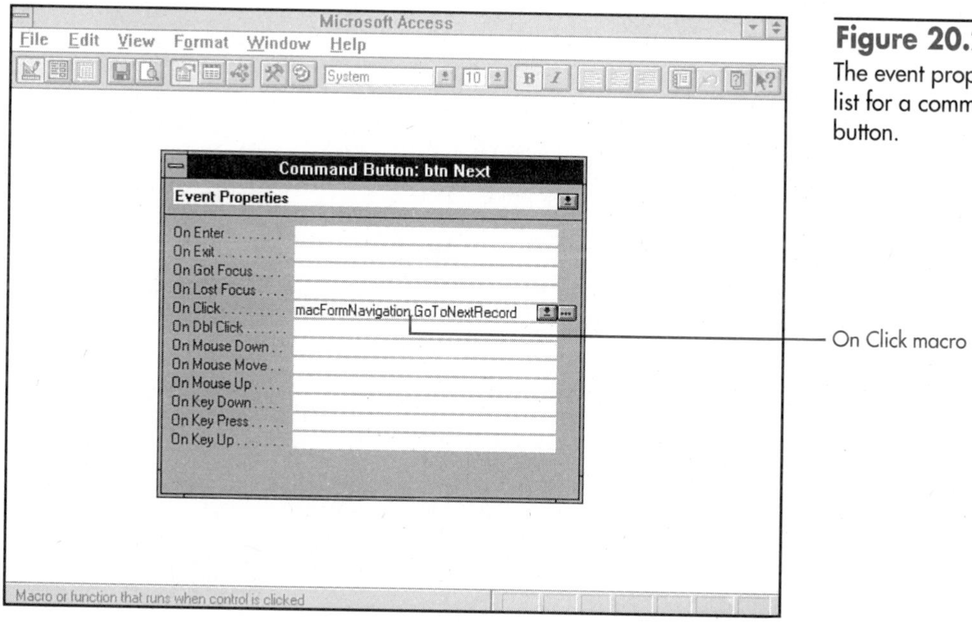

Figure 20.21
The event property list for a command button.

— On Click macro

The successful Access developer soon learns which object properties are important and which values work best for the application being built. Most of the differences in the appearance of different Access applications shown in this chapter are due to the different property settings used by the developers of those applications. It is likely you will quickly adopt a particular style, learn the properties that produce that style, and apply those properties to all the forms in your Access applications.

Working with Macros

As you might expect, a form like that shown in figure 20.21 doesn't just happen. Even though it is easy to add things like text boxes and buttons to a form, you have to tell Access what to do when the user clicks on the buttons with the mouse or enters text into the fields.

In figure 20.22, when the user clicks on the <u>N</u>ext button (or presses Alt+N) the next record in the query underlying this form is displayed. Similarly, the <u>P</u>rev button displays the previous record and the C<u>l</u>ose button closes this form.

Figure 20.22
The Hyperdex Lookup form, with Next, Previous, and Close buttons.

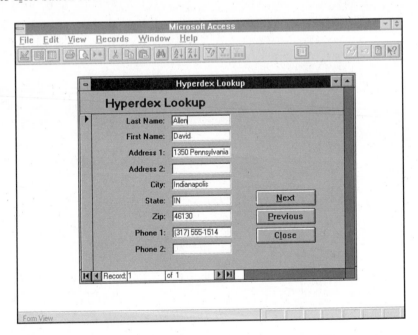

Each of these command buttons triggers a macro that performs the action specified on the button. Look again at figure 20.21, which shows the properties list for the Next command button. Notice the property named On Push in the properties list has a value of `macFormNavigation.GoToNextRecord` (part of the `Record` part has been cut off by the edge of the properties list). The On Click, On Enter, On Exit, and On Dbl Click properties all are events that can occur at essentially any time. Whenever the user is ready to move on to the next record, all that is required is a click on the <u>N</u>ext button, and Access will dutifully comply.

Macros are discussed in detail in Chapter 24, "Building Macros." Meanwhile, it is sufficient to take a look at the macros controlling the Next, Prev, and Close buttons in enough detail to understand they way in which macros fit into the larger picture. Figure 20.23 shows the macFormNavigation macro.

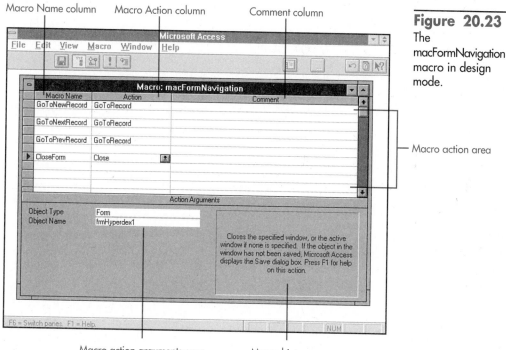

Figure 20.23
The macFormNavigation macro in design mode.

A macro is made up of one or more macro actions that define the behavior Access will exhibit when the macro is triggered. In the case of the Next button on the Hyperdex Lookup form, the user expects the next record to be displayed when the Next button is pressed.

The actions making up a macro are listed in the macro action column of the macro design window. In figure 20.23, one of the macro actions is GoToRecord. Access has a total of 47 different built-in macro actions. Not all the actions are used frequently. In fact, there are several actions that are rarely if ever used by any but the most advanced Access developers.

The macFormNavigation is a *compound macro* that contains four small single-action macros. When the Next button's On Click event is triggered, the submacro named GoToNextRecord runs, executing the GoToRecord action. But how does Access know that the user wants to go to the next record? From figure 20.23 it looks as though each one of the first three submacros all execute the same macro action, yet each button exhibits unique behavior.

It turns out that most Access macro actions require one or more arguments to complete the macro action. In the case of the Next button, the arguments for the GoToRecord action include the Next argument in the arguments section of the macro design screen. Although it sounds complicated when described in this manner, building macro actions is fairly straightforward and is described in Chapter 24, "Building Macros."

Creating Useful Reports

Finally, most people like to have a printout of their work. When working with an Access database, you might want a hard copy of the data extracted from the database, including summaries (totals or sums of data from one or more tables), graphics such as a company logo or image stored in the database, and other information such as the date and the database user's name.

Because reports are based on tables and queries, anything that can be displayed on a form can be shown on a report. Because a sheet of paper is much larger than a computer screen, the data can be arranged in a more useful manner than when displayed in an on-screen form. The data that would otherwise occupy several different on-screen forms, for instance, can easily fit on a single piece of paper.

Figure 20.24 shows an Access form from the HOMEFINDERS database, displayed in report design preview mode. Although this figure might be a little hard to interpret, notice that each column shows a different type of data. The columns in the report in figure 20.24 display data from the fields and records stored in the HOMEFINDERS database.

Figure 20.24
An Access report in design preview mode.

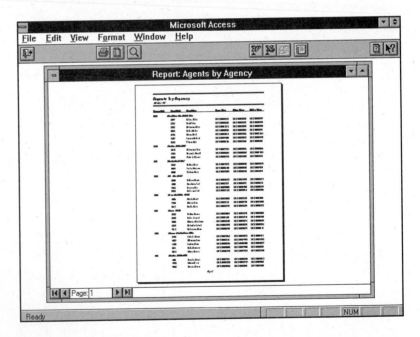

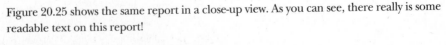

Figure 20.25 shows the same report in a close-up view. As you can see, there really is some readable text on this report!

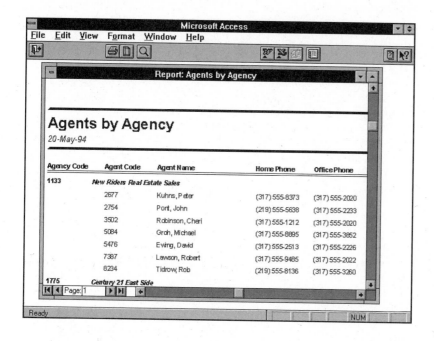

Figure 20.25
The report in a close-up view.

One of the easiest ways to build a report in Access is to let Access do it for you by using either a Report Wizard or the Autoreport button on the toolbar. Figure 20.26 shows a simple report created using the Autoreport feature of Access.

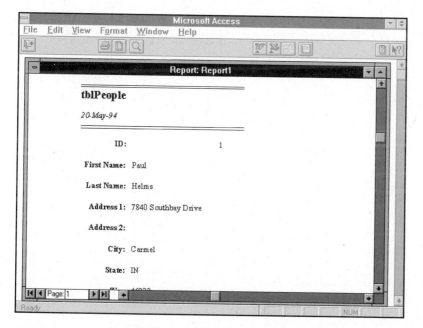

Figure 20.26
A report created by the Autoreport button.

IV

Microsoft Access

As you can see, you will have to clean up the design a little bit. The Autoreport creates usable reports, but doesn't have much of an imagination or aesthetic sense. Reports will be covered in much greater detail in Chapter 25, "Building Reports."

Access Basic: The Ultimate Control

Even if you make copious use of the Access Wizards, macros, and other design aids provided to make your job as a database developer easier, you eventually will end up using Access Basic. Most people avoid Access Basic because it entails "programming."

Most Access users would like to leave programming to the type of database developer described earlier in this chapter: hard-core, technologically oriented, out of touch, nerdy. However, that's not necessarily true when it comes to Microsoft Access. The computer language built into Access is much more approachable than traditional database languages. Even its name, Access Basic, sounds friendly. How could something named Basic be hard to learn or use?

We will not look at Access Basic here because you won't need it until your applications become fairly complicated, and even then Access often will program itself, saving you the effort of doing any real programming. In the meantime, it's probably enough to know that you can create your own custom behavior and capabilities into your Access applications. Think of Access Basic as a method of extending the basic capabilities of Microsoft Access. If you don't like the way something is built into Access, write your own!

Access Wizards: Your Humble Servants

The software geniuses at Microsoft sure put in some overtime when they made Access. Access forms and reports can be visually stunning and impressive. There is almost no limit on the types of data that can be displayed or how that data is presented. All this flexibility, however, comes at a price.

Most first-time Access users are bewildered by the wide variety of options and decisions that must be made when building forms and reports. When it comes to building forms, for instance, there are dozens of decisions to make: colors, fonts, font sizes, position on the screen of each control, appearance of text boxes, and so on. Also, because Access is a *visual* application (that is, most of its user interaction takes place on the screen with the mouse and keyboard), you will be making a lot of forms and reports. You will almost certainly build a form for each of the tasks the users of your database will have to perform. Users are almost never satisfied with the reports you produce, as well. There's always something else, something more they want or need.

Without some kind of help, designing and building forms and reports can be daunting tasks. As you soon will discover, however, you will have hard-working, dedicated helpers available any time you need to make a new form or report.

When you tell Access you want to create a new form, the New Form dialog box (see fig. 20.27) appears. Notice the button on the left side of the dialog box that offers Form_Wizards as an option. A similar button on the right side of this dialog box enables you to "do it yourself"; that is, to build a form from scratch without the aid of the Form Wizards.

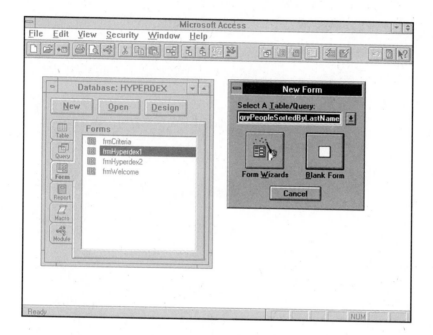

Figure 20.27
The New Form dialog box.

Recall that most forms have a table or query "under" it. The text box at the top of the New Form dialog box enables you to specify the table or query that will be under or bound to the new form. This text box contains a drop-down list to help you find the table or query you want to use so that you won't have to memorize the names of each of your tables and forms.

After you have specified the table or query to use for your form and have clicked on the Form_Wizards button, the first window of the Form Wizard appears (see fig. 20.28).

The Form Wizard selection dialog box in figure 20.28 enables you to select from among five different Form Wizards. The sequence of dialog boxes that follows depends on which wizard is selected.

Going through the entire process of creating a form with the Form Wizard has been left to Chapter 23, "Creating and Using Forms." Meanwhile, however, notice how the Wizard works. Access Wizards are implemented as a number of windows like the one in figure 20.28. This window shows you a list of options from which you make a selection. The design and appearance of the new form will be based on your responses to these options.

Think of the Wizard as someone asking you a number of questions about the form you are building. The Wizard's questions and your responses constitute a dialog that determines the appearance of your forms.

The nice thing about Wizards is that you do not have to use them if you do not want to. Some people don't like the default appearances created by the Wizards. Others find that the Wizard "dialog" gets in the way of getting work done. On the other hand, some long-term Access users have never made a form or report without using the Wizards.

Figure 20.28
The first Form
Wizard window.

The five different Form Wizards

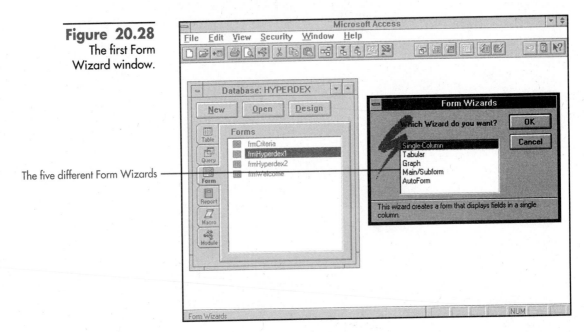

Chapters 23, "Creating and Using Forms," and 25, "Building Reports," show you how to build forms and reports without using the Access Wizards.

Chapter Snapshot

Previous chapters explored how you can create a new database and how each of the six database objects (tables, queries, forms, reports, macros, and modules) store, organize, display, and print your data. Of these database objects, tables are by far the most central to the content of your database. This chapter covers the following information about tables:

Well-designed tables make it much easier to build the forms and reports needed by your users when they work with your database application. Furthermore, the structure of the tables in your Access database determine what kinds of data can be managed by your database.

CHAPTER

Creating and Using Tables

by Paul Cassel

Back in Chapter 19, you built a simple card file database to manage names and addresses. This chapter and those that follow in this section of *Inside Microsoft Office Professional* take the basic Hyperdex application and enhance it to form the basis of a small business's customer management system. In this case, the business is an independent automobile repair shop called Carmel Car Care.

The manger of Carmel Car Care wants to automate some of the procedures associated with handling repair jobs done in his shop; for instance, the database eventually will handle billing, service interval notification, and service history.

A complete description and implementation of such a database is quite beyond the scope of this book. The chapters in *Inside Microsoft Office Professional* that discuss Access focus on an in-depth examination of several of the tables, forms, queries, and other database components.

The Carmel Car Care database as described in these chapters can be found on the *Inside Microsoft Office Professional* companion disk as CARCARE1.MDB. In addition, HYPERDEX.MDB is available on the companion disk as well. Please feel free to open these databases and examine the tables described in this chapter.

Building the Carmel Car Care Database

The main table in the Carmel Car Care database (tblCustomers) is nearly identical to tblPeople in the Access Hyperdex application discussed in Chapter 19, "Access Quick Start." The same basic information is required: the person's name, address, phone numbers, and so on. Because the main table is similar to tblPeople, you are better off using this table than re-creating the same table from scratch.

To begin building the Carmel Car Care database, locate the Access database file CARCARE1.MDB (from the *Inside Microsoft Office Professional* companion disk). If the companion disk is not available, consult Chapter 19 to see how tblPeople was built and create your own copy of this table. Or, use the Windows File Manager to copy the file named HYPERDEX.MDB to a new file named CARCARE1.MDB. If you choose to copy HYPERDEX.MDB to CARCARE1.MDB, please note that you will have to either ignore or delete the database objects in the Hyperdex application that are not relevant to the Carmel Car Care application.

Next, open the CARCARE1.MDB database in Access (see fig. 21.1).

Figure 21.1
The beginning of the Carmel Car Care database (CARCARE1.MDB).

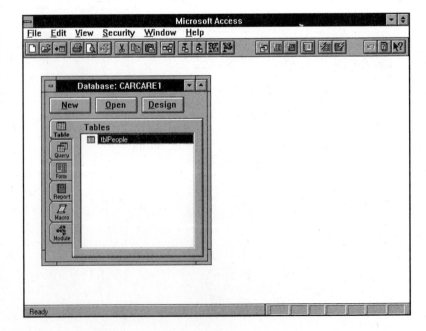

Notice that the tblPeople table from HYPERDEX.MDB is present in the new database. A more descriptive name for this table in the Carmel Car Care database might be tblCustomers. Renaming a database table in Access is easy. With the table highlighted in the database window, choose Rena<u>m</u>e from the Access <u>F</u>ile menu, and the dialog box shown in figure 21.2 appears.

Figure 21.2
Renaming tblPeople to tblCustomers.

When you click on the OK button after entering the new name for the table, the table name in the database window changes as well (see fig. 21.3).

Figure 21.3
The new table name appears in the database window.

The same process can be applied to queries, forms, macros, reports, and modules. Be forewarned, however: After you begin implementing an Access database, the objects within the database become highly dependent on each other. Recall from Chapter 20, "Learning Access Concepts," that tables or queries can lie under an Access form. If you change the name of a table or query underlying a form, the connection between the form and the table or query is broken. You will have to manually "reconnect" each of the form's controls to the appropriate component of the underlying table or query.

Certain data in the copy of tblPeople contained in CARCARE1.MDB on the *Inside Microsoft Office Professional* companion disk is different than described in Chapter 19. Some of the addresses and phone numbers have been changed so that most of the people contained in the table live in Indiana, for instance. Otherwise, the tblCustomers table is essentially identical to tblPeople.

IV

Microsoft Access

Understanding Naming Conventions

As your databases grow in size and complexity, the need to establish a naming convention for the objects in your database increases. Access imposes few restrictions on the names assigned to database objects. Therefore, it is entirely possible to have two distinctly different objects (a form and a report, for instance) with the same name. You cannot, however, have a table and a query with the same name.

Although it is adequate to name the single table in the Hyperdex database "People", as the database grew larger and more forms and reports were added, you would find it difficult to distinguish between a form named People and a report named People. This is especially true when using expressions in queries or Access Basic routines (expressions are discussed in later chapters).

The very simple naming convention used in this chapter and the ones that follow can save you a lot of trouble later on. In the Carmel Car Care database, the names of all tables begin with the three-character *tbl* prefix, while queries have a *qry* prefix. Forms, reports, and macros use *frm, rep,* and *mcr,* respectively.

Furthermore, compound table names will be displayed in mixed case (tblCustomerInformation, not TBLCUSTOMERINFORMATION or tblcustomerinformation). Most people find mixed case names easier to read than all upper- or lowercase.

In these chapters, even though the name of a table is tblCustomers, it might be referred to as the *customers* table. Generally speaking, the users of your Access applications will never see the names that you have assigned to tables, forms, and other database objects. As you will see in this chapter and the ones that follow, you can control what appears in the title bar at the top of a form that accesses data stored in a table or extracted by a query.

Whenever possible, take advantage of the long names that Access accommodates for your database objects. There is no need to abbreviate the name of a table to CUSTINFO (as some database systems require) when tblCustomerInformation is more descriptive and easier to remember.

Finally, although Access allows spaces in the names of database objects, this book avoids using spaces in object names. This book is set in a proportionally spaced font, and it can be easy to miss a space between characters. Leaving spaces out of names entirely will avoid this problem.

Understanding the Importance of Database Tables

Tables are the most basic of the database objects. You might think of tables as containers for your data that supply information to all the other database objects. After you create a new database, you can either create new tables or attach to existing tables in another database.

You can work with tables in two views: Datasheet view and Design view (see figs. 21.4 and 21.5). Switching between Datasheet view and Design view requires only pressing the correct button on the Access toolbar.

Datasheet View button

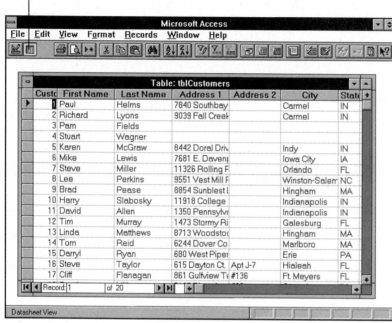

Figure 21.4
The Carmel Car Care customers table in Datasheet view.

Whether you open a table in Design view or Datasheet view depends on what you want to do:

✔ **Datasheet view.** Use this view when you want to view or edit the data in a spreadsheet-like row-and-column format. Each row (down the table) represents a record and each column (across the table, from left to right) represents a field in the table. Datasheet view is what comes to mind most often when thinking of database tables.

✔ **Design view.** Use this view if you want to alter the table structure by adding or deleting fields or changing the properties of fields (like Field Size) in the table. In figure 21.5, for example, notice that the name ID field has been changed to Customer ID. Each row represents a field in the table.

Do not be confused by the different views in figures 21.4 and 21.5. In datasheet view, fields are arranged horizontally from left to right across the table. In design view, the field definitions are arranged vertically down the screen.

IV

Microsoft Access

Figure 21.5
The Carmel Car
Care customers in
Design view.

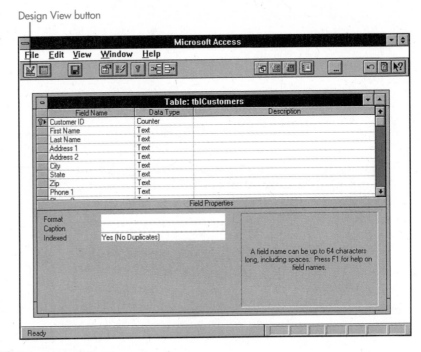

You will find many reasons for changing a table's structure after the database table is finished and contains data. Often, users will want some new feature to be added to the database. Sometimes adding a feature requires additional information in the database and the best way to add the information is by adding new fields to an existing table. Or, you might find that the field size specified at design time is just too small to handle all instances of that data. It's easy, for instance, to underestimate how big a field holding people's last names should be.

There are three ways you can add tables to your database. You can create a new table yourself, or you can import or attach a table from another database program, such as FoxPro, dBASE, or Paradox (or another Access database). Importing and attaching are discussed later in this chapter.

Creating a New Table

The Carmel Car Care database needs a table to hold data about the different cars the customers own. Although at first glance it would appear that a number of fields could be added to the customer table (tblCustomers) to hold data about customer's cars, this is not a practical approach for a number of reasons.

For instance, not every customer owns just one car. Some people have two or even three cars that they bring to Carmel Car Care. It would be difficult to know how many fields had to be added to the customers table to accommodate all the cars owned by the people in that table. Furthermore, when a customer buys a new car, sells an old one, or otherwise changes ownership, the data in the customers table would have to be changed, raising the possibility of making errors in the address, phone number, or other data that is unrelated to the car's data.

The data within a table should be closely related, like a person's name and address or Social Security number. A separate table should be used for data that is not directly related to the primary purpose of the main table. A car's vehicle identification number (or VIN, a unique serial number applied to every car sold in the United States), for instance, is not related to your name or address, yet it is closely related to your car. Therefore, create a separate table for "car information."

What this means is that all the data stored within a table should be related in some way or other. The customers table contains all the contact information (name, address, phone numbers) related to customers. A separate table would contain all the data relating to the cars that the customers own. These two tables would then be related through one or more of their fields so that it would be easy to find all the cars owned by a particular customer. Figure 21.6 illustrates the way in which the customers and cars tables are connected (we soon will discuss building the cars table).

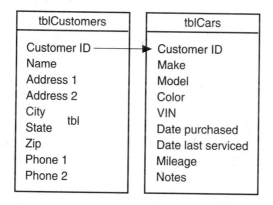

Figure 21.6
How customers and cars tables are connected.

Both the customers and the cars tables contain a key field named Customer ID. As you soon will see, Access makes it easy to relate two tables through their primary key fields. Figure 21.7 shows a schematic of how tblCustomers and tblCars interact. The ID field in tblCars contains the same data as the ID field in tblCustomers and is used to connect these two tables together.

Figure 21.7
Customers might own more than one car.

tblCustomers	
ID	Cust Name
1	Paul Helms
2	Richard Lyons
3	Pam Fields
4	Stuart Wagner

tblCars	
ID	Car Info
1	1993 Grand Am
2	1989 Ford Taurus
1	1987 BMW 325is
3	1992 Toyota Corolla
3	1990 Jeep Cherokee
4	1988 Honda Civic

Each customer might own more than one car. For instance, Paul Helms (ID = 1) owns two cars (1993 Grand Am and 1987 BMW 325is) whereas Stuart Wagner (ID = 4) owns one car (1988 Honda Civic).

Notice that the car information in tblCars does not fall in any particular order. As long as the ID assigned to each car matches a record in tblCustomers, Access will always be able to find all the cars belonging to a particular owner. Similarly, given some piece of unique information about a car (such as its VIN number), Access will always be able to find the owner of the car.

As you soon will learn (or maybe have already learned from Chapters 19 and 20), you will use some unique bit of information to tie Access database tables together. In the Carmel Car Care application, avoid using data such as the car's license plate number as the unique identifier—it's possible the license number will change as new plates are issued or if the owner acquires vanity plates for the car. Always look for some unique, unchanging bit of information, such as a Social Security number or vehicle identification number, to link tables together.

As you build an Access database, you will more than likely construct many drawings similar to figure 21.7 to test the basic design of your application. Always make sure you thoroughly understand the data management requirement of your database before you begin work, and, as you build the database, make sure the implementation suits the initial data management specification.

Examining Table Relationships

Since tblCars does not exist yet, it's too early to connect tblCars to tblCustomers. However, give some thought to connecting these tables because the relationship to be established between them determines, in some respects, the way to construct tblCars.

One-to-Many Relationships

The connection between tblCustomers and tblCars is described as a *one-to-many relationship*. This means that each customer (the *one* side) might own several cars (the *many* side). As you will see later in this chapter, Access makes it easy to establish one-to-many relationships between tables.

Without a doubt, one-to-many relationships are the most common type encountered in relational databases like Microsoft Access. There are many examples of one-to-many relationships to consider: A family might have several children attending the local school system. A person may make several contributions to charity organizations during the year. A person or business might own several cars or trucks.

A one-to-many relationship is illustrated in figure 21.8. The table on the left shows families that have children attending a local elementary school. The table on the right shows pupils attending the school, sorted by the Family ID field. Notice that for each family in the table on the left, there may be one or more pupils attending the school.

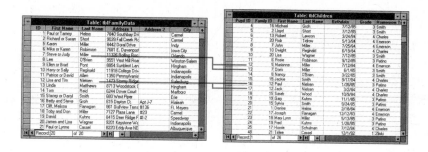

Figure 21.8
One-to-many relationships.

One-to-One Relationships

Pure *one-to-one relationships*—each record in one table has one and only one matching record in another table (as in figure 21.9)—are less common in relational databases. Most often the data in the second table would be included as part of the primary table, at least in relational databases. Generally speaking, if there is a one-to-one relationship between data, the data should all be part of the same table.

IV

Microsoft Access

Figure 21.9
One-to-one
relationships.

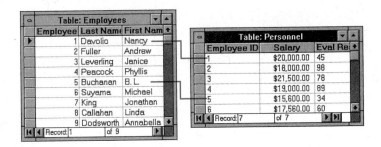

There are times, however, when one-to-one data should not be contained within the same table; figure 21.9 illustrates such an example. Normally a company would not keep confidential information such as salaries and performance evaluations in the same table as the employee names. It is much easier to control access to the confidential information by using a one-to-one relationship between these tables than it would be including all the data in one big table.

Many-to-Many Relationships

From time to time you will encounter many-to-many relationships. In these situations, each record in each of two tables can be related to one or more records in the other table. Figure 21.10 illustrates an example of a many-to-many relationship between two tables. The table at the top (Employees) contains the names and employee IDs of a number of different people working for a company. The table at the bottom contains a list of departments that employees may work for. As you can see, Greg Wallen (Employee ID = 1) is listed under both Administration and Sales & Marketing departments. This could mean that Greg works as an administrator of some kind within the Sales & Marketing group.

This explanation might seem a bit misleading. Because the relationship is from an Employee to the Departments table, it might seem like a simple one-to-many relationship. If you look in the Employee ID column in the Departments table, however, you will see the same IDs appearing multiple times.

To join these two tables, you need a common field, of course. But adding the Dept ID field to the Employees table results in multiple records containing the same data. For instance, the record containing the name Greg Wallen appears twice—once for each department he works for.

The arrangement shown in figure 21.10 is very inefficient of disk space. The words "Sales & Marketing," "Administration," and "Customer Support" appear multiple times in the Departments table. Also, any time data is updated, more than one record might have to be changed; for instance, changing a name or the number assigned to a department might require changes to multiple records. A more efficient design is shown in figure 21.11.

Table: Departments

Dept ID	Dept Name	Location	Employee ID
100	Administration	Indianapolis	1
102	Sales & Marketing	Gresham	2
101	Customer Support	Indianapolis	3
103	Customer Support	Carmel	4
105	Sales & Marketing	Carmel	1
102	Sales & Marketing	Gresham	5
100	Administration	Indianapolis	2
100	Administration	Indianapolis	5
102	Sales & Marketing	Gresham	4
104	Customer Support	Gresham	10
106	Administration	Carmel	7
106	Administration	Carmel	6

Record: 13   of 13

Figure 21.10
A many-to-many relationship.

Table: Employees

Employee ID	Last Name	First Name	Department
1	Wallen	Greg	100
1	Wallen	Greg	105
2	Sampras	Timothy	102
2	Sampras	Timothy	100
3	Boyd	Fred	101
6	St. Valentine	Chris	106
7	Younger	Edna	100
8	Andrews	Stephen	106
9	Caren	Renee	104
10	Dalt	Sam	104

Record: 1   of 10

Figure 21.11
A many-to-many relationship using a join table.

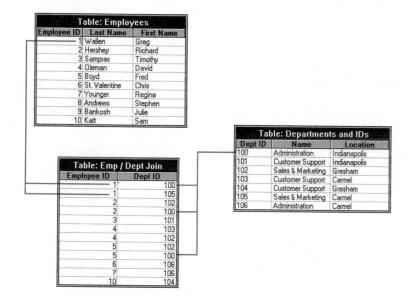

Table: Employees

Employee ID	Last Name	First Name
1	Wallen	Greg
2	Hershey	Richard
3	Sampras	Timothy
4	Oleman	David
5	Boyd	Fred
6	St. Valentine	Chris
7	Younger	Regina
8	Andrews	Stephen
9	Bankosh	Julie
10	Katt	Sam

Table: Emp / Dept Join

Employee ID	Dept ID
1	100
1	105
2	102
2	100
3	101
4	103
4	102
5	102
5	100
6	106
7	106
10	104

Table: Departments and IDs

Dept ID	Name	Location
100	Administration	Indianapolis
101	Customer Support	Indianapolis
102	Sales & Marketing	Gresham
103	Customer Support	Carmel
104	Customer Support	Gresham
105	Sales & Marketing	Carmel
106	Administration	Carmel

In figure 21.11 a new table named Emp / Dept Join is used to hold the instances in which employee data and department data meet. Using this technique, an employee name or department number has to appear only once in the database, making maintenance easier and requiring less disk space.

Given how complicated many-to-many joins can be to construct, it is fortunate that many-to-many relationships are quite a bit less common than straightforward one-to-many situations.

Building the Cars Table

To create the Carmel Car Care table (named tblCars) to hold car data, make sure the Table object button is pressed in the Database window. The New button will create an empty table in design view (see fig. 21.12). If the Table Properties list is not displayed, click on the Table Properties button.

Figure 21.12
A new table
(Design view).

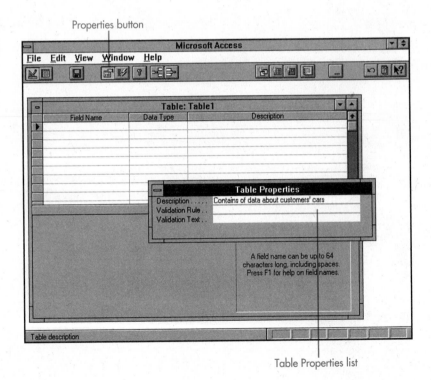

The Table Properties sheet contains information about the table as a whole. The Description is an optional, brief entry you can use to provide internal documentation for the table. The table description entry does not appear in the table's title bar or anywhere else in the application.

When you attach a table, Access enters the Description for you. Access automatically enters the path and file specification for the attached table. If you would rather use a different description for an attached table, simply enter the new description in place of the default value. For regular, nonattached tables, you can enter whatever comment you like.

Primary Key

The Primary Key identifies the table's primary key (when one is assigned to the table). The primary key and indexes both are optional.

Primary keys are used in most Access tables. As described in earlier chapters, a table's *key* is used to create relationships between the table and other tables in the database. A table without a key cannot be connected to other tables in the database. As described later in this chapter, keys are so important that if you choose not to specify a key for your table, Access will ask you to assign a key when you try to leave design view.

Indexes

Indexes are used somewhat less frequently and are used by Access to quickly locate or order information in the table. If you expect your tables to grow quite large as data is added, you should specify indexes for the fields that will most frequently be searched.

Primary keys and indexes are described in more detail later in this chapter.

Defining Fields in the Cars Table

After you create a new table, you must define the table structure, create the fields that will store data, and set the appropriate field data types. In Design view, each row represents one field in the table. The first column (see fig. 21.13) stores the name of the field.

In this example, the field name is Customer ID and will be used to connect tblCars to tblCustomers. Field names must be unique; that is, you cannot have two fields in the same table with the same name. Field names can contain blanks and punctuation. Be careful not to use extremely long names when naming fields, however. As you will see in subsequent chapters, very long object names can be a nuisance.

When you use the Tab or right-arrow keys to move to the Data Type column, Access displays a button you can press to open a drop-down list of data types, as shown in figure 21.14.

Figure 21.13
Defining the name
of the field.

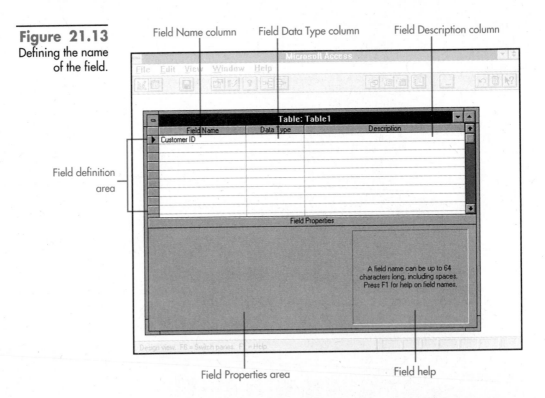

Field Name column · Field Data Type column · Field Description column

Field definition area

Field Properties area · Field help

Figure 21.14
The Data Type
drop-down list
box.

The default field data type is Text. The Customer ID field in the customers table, as you might recall, is a Counter field. Because fields used to form relationships between tables must have the same data type, you must change the field data type for the Customer ID field in tblCars. Select Number from the drop-down list and the list box will close. The Field Properties section of the window changes to reflect the selected data type; for example, the field properties for the Number data type includes entries for Field Size, Format, Decimal Places, Caption, and other properties.

The Customer ID field in the customers table is a Counter data type. This data type was selected for the customers table because (as explained later) it makes an ideal primary key. By changing the Field Size property of the Customer ID field in tblCars to Long Integer (see fig. 21.15), we can (later in this chapter) form a relationship between this field and the Customer ID field in tblCustomers.

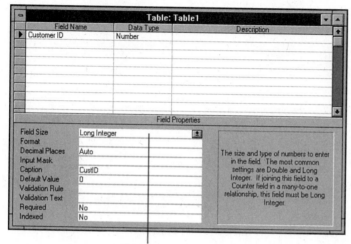

Field Size property

Figure 21.15
Setting the Customer ID Field Size property to Long Integer.

A quick way to switch between the field definition area of the table design window and the field property area is to use the F6 key. Pressing F6 will instantly move the mouse cursor from one area to the other.

What's so special about the Counter field type? Counters are nothing more than integer numbers that can range from 1 to 2,147,483,648. As you soon will see, the value of a Counter field is automatically filled in by Access, and the value cannot be changed by the user. Also, the value of a Counter cannot be duplicated within a table. These unique properties of Counter fields make them ideal to use as primary key fields to connect tables.

Finally, enter a short comment in the Description column (see fig. 21.16).

Figure 21.16
Entering a field description.

Description for the Customer ID field

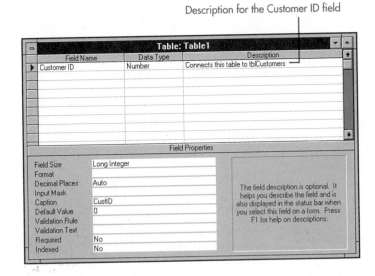

The process is repeated for each of the remaining fields (see figure 21.17). You define the field name, select a data type, enter or change field properties as necessary, and enter a short description that describes the field, unless the name of the field makes its use completely obvious.

Figure 21.17
The new tblCars table with all fields defined.

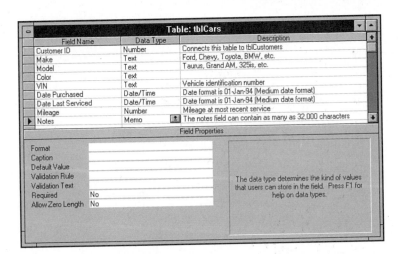

The next section of this chapter discusses the different properties to apply to each of the fields of the cars table.

Setting Field Properties

When you create a field and choose its data type, Access automatically assigns certain default field properties. For example, the default Field Size for the Number data type is Double (as can be seen in figure 21.14).

Frequently, however, you will want to change some of the default values. The new field properties can be assigned at any time. Many Access users assign property values for every field as the fields are defined, whereas others wait until all fields are designated.

As an example of changing field properties, the default field size of Text fields is 50—the field can contain 50 characters. This field size is excessive for data like the make of the car, so the Field Size property of this field was changed to 15 (see fig. 21.18), a more reasonable size to hold data like "Chevy" and "Ford".

		Table: tblCars
Field Name	**Data Type**	**Description**
Customer ID	Number	Connects this table to tblCustomers
Make	Text	Ford, Chevy, Toyota, BMW, etc.
Model	Text	Taurus, Grand AM, 325is, etc.
Color	Text	
VIN	Text	Vehicle identification number
Date Purchased	Date/Time	Date format is 01-Jan-94 (Medium date format)
Date Last Serviced	Date/Time	Date format is 01-Jan-94 (Medium date format)
Mileage	Number	Mileage at most recent service
Notes	Memo	The notes field can contain as many as 32,000 characters

Field Properties

Field Size	15
Format	
Input Mask	
Caption	
Default Value	
Validation Rule	
Validation Text	
Required	No
Allow Zero Length	No
Indexed	No

A field name can be up to 64 characters long, including spaces. Press F1 for help on field names.

Current field   Field Size for Make field

Figure 21.18
The modified Field Size property for Make field.

Notice in figure 21.18 that a right-pointing triangle indicates that Make is the current field. Therefore, the properties that appear in the field properties area pertain to the Make field. The downward-pointing arrow in the Data Type column of the Make field appears only when the mouse pointer is in the Data Type column.

For more information about using custom formats and Access Basic to change the appearance of date fields, search the Access Help system for "formatting dates". For more information about formatting in general, see Chapter 23, "Creating and Using Forms," and Chapter 26, "Understanding Access Basic."

IV

Microsoft Access

You also can set a field's format when you create forms and reports. Form and report controls have a Format property you can set that overrides whatever format you specify in Table design. For example, you might want dates to appear in one format in datasheets (using the format set in Table design) and in another format when they appear in reports (using the Format property of the control that contains the date).

As you move from row to row in the cars table, the number of properties in the Field Properties list changes according to the particular data type. Fields defined as the Counter data type have only three properties (Format, Caption, and Indexed), Number fields have eight properties, and so on.

In many cases, you will not need to change the default values. You probably can leave the Caption property blank, for example, because Access uses the field name when you do not supply a caption. When you create a form or report and drag a field from the field list, Access uses the Caption property to assign a value to the field's label (this process is described in Chapter 23). If there is no caption, Access uses the field name. Most field names are short enough to serve as captions, but others are too long to be used on forms and reports and in datasheets.

The Customer ID field is an example of a field whose field name is too long to be used in Datasheet view, particularly because the data itself is only a few characters wide. This effect can be seen in the table when it is switched to Datasheet view (see fig. 21.19). The field name is much wider than the width of the data in the field. When the width of the column is made narrower (by selecting Column Width under the Format menu) to make the width more appropriate for the data in the column, the column heading (which is the field name) is hard to read.

When the Caption property of the Customer ID field is changed to CustID, the corresponding column heading is easier to read (see fig. 21.20). The name of the field is still Customer ID, as indicated by the Field box on the toolbar. The only thing that has changed is the heading Access uses on the column in the table. Similar captions have been established for the Date Purchased and Date Last Serviced fields in this figure.

"Customer ID" does not fit in the field

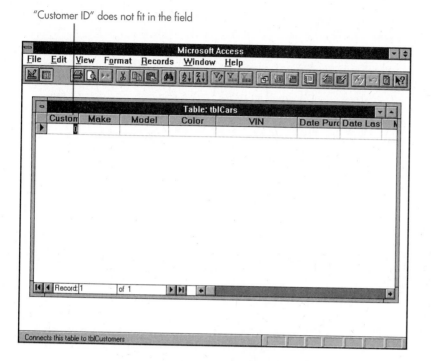

Figure 21.19
An example of a too-long field name.

New column headings

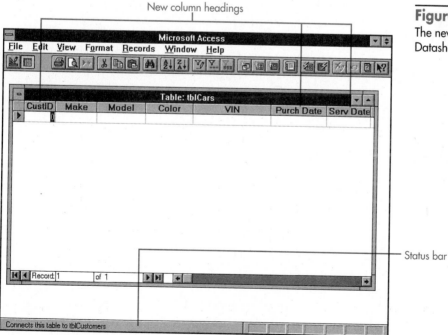

Figure 21.20
The new table in Datasheet view.

Status bar

In figure 21.20, notice that the Access status bar contains the text of the description entered for the Customer ID field. Access is trying to help you or your users understand the purpose of each of the fields in the table. If you have special instructions to your users, you can put them into a field's description while in Design view. As the mouse pointer moves from field to field, the status bar will display the description of each field in turn.

Table 21.1 describes the various Access field properties. For more information about any of these properties, search the Access Help system for the particular property name.

Table 21.1
Field Properties

Property	Description
Field Size	For Text fields, defines the maximum number of characters that can be entered in the field. For Number fields, Field Size property defines the type of number (Byte, Integer, Long Integer, Single, Double) that can be stored in the field.
Format	The Format property specifies how data will be displayed. You can use the predefined formats or create a custom format using an expression or Access Basic.
Input Mask	A pattern to control the appearance of a field.
Decimal Places	For Number fields, the Decimal Places property determines how many numbers will appear to the right of the decimal point.
Caption	When present, the Caption property defines the default field label on forms and reports, and as columns in datasheets.
Default Value	Value entered in a field when you add a new record to the table.
Validation Rule	A Validation Rule is an expression that defines data entry rules and validates the data.
Validation Text	Text that appears in a message box when the entered data fails the validation rule.
Required	Whether a field requires an entry.
Indexed	Indicates whether the field is indexed (Yes - no duplicates, Yes - duplicates allowed, or No - not indexed).

Note Not all properties apply to all data types. For example, the DecimalPlaces property does not apply to Text fields and does not appear in the Field Properties list.

There are several things you should notice about tblCars, including the following:

✔ The Date Purchased and Date Last Serviced fields both are defined as Date data types. Many different formats can be used for data: Long Date (January 1, 1994), Medium Date (01-Jan-94), Short Date (1/1/94), and so on. The Medium Date format was selected for these fields. The Date field type can also display time values (2:04 PM or 14:04).

✔ The Mileage field is a number data type. Access provides five different field sizes for number fields: Byte, Integer, Long Integer, Double, and Single. The Long Integer field size was selected because it can display very large numbers (for high-mileage cars).

✔ The default field type for all Access fields is Text. Whereas Text fields can contain up to 255 characters, however, Memo fields can store as many as 32,000 characters. Because the Notes field will likely need to hold more than 255 characters, change its field data type to Memo.

Each number field size has a different numeric range that it can accommodate:

Byte: 0 to 255

Integer: –32,768 to 32,767

Long Integer: –2,147,483,648 to 2,147,483,647

Single: –3.402823E38 to 3.402823E38

Double: –1.79769313486232E308 to 1.79769313486232E308

Setting a Primary Key

A *primary key* consists of one or more fields that uniquely identify each record in a table. Typically, a table's primary key is a single, unique field such as an employee's Social Security number or a product identification number.

When you create a primary key, Access automatically creates an index on the field specified as the primary key. Access uses indexes to quickly locate records, so tables with primary keys are generally more efficient than tables without primary keys.

Tip

When you display tables in Datasheet view, Access displays the records in primary key order. When you use tables to fill combo boxes and list boxes, however, Access displays the records in order entry—that is, the order in which the records were added to the table. To fill a combo box or list box in a particular order, create a query and use the query for the box's Row Source. For more information on sort orders, see Chapter 22, "Understanding Access Queries."

If your table already has a field with unique values, you can set that field to be the primary key. Because the Customer ID field in tblCustomers was defined as a Counter field, Access guarantees that each value in this field is unique and this field can be used as a primary key for tblCustomers. As designed, however, tblCars has no truly unique fields (except, perhaps, for the VIN number).

Realizing the Importance of Primary Key Fields

Primary keys are important in relational database design. Because the value assigned to a primary key field cannot be duplicated within the table, each and every record in the data is guaranteed to be unique and different from all other records in the database. Just as the Dewey decimal system used in a well-run library ensures that any book on any shelf can be quickly and easily located, a primary key in each of your database tables makes the data contained in the tables quick and easy to find.

Access uses a table's primary key to determine the default relationship between that table and other tables in the database. Data access is much faster on a table with a primary key because the index to the primary key is updated every time data is added or changed in the table. Whenever practical, you should establish primary keys for each of your tables and use the key to build relationships between the tables in your databases.

Adding a Primary Key to tblCars

So far, the tblCars table does not contain a primary key. Rather than use the VIN number (which, although a unique value for each car, is a 15- or 20-character text field), use a Counter field instead. Access is much quicker accessing data through key fields that are Number or Counter data types than text key fields. Also, in practical terms, a car's VIN number might not always be available (for instance, if the customer drives away before the VIN number is recorded). As you will see, after a primary key field is defined, Access *requires* a unique value to be entered into the primary key field for every record—you cannot leave a primary key field empty. Because Access automatically assigns Counter values for you, no problem arises if the VIN number or other data is not available.

Adding a Field to a Table

You will have to add a new field to tblCars just to hold the primary key for this table. A suitable name for this field is Car ID, because it will serve to uniquely identify each car contained in the database.

Adding a field to an existing table presents no problem to Access. Open tblCars in Design view and position the cursor in the Customer ID field. By default, the cursor will already be in this field when you open the table in Design view. From the Edit menu, select Insert Row to insert a new, empty row above the Customer ID row.

After the new row has been added, tblCars looks as it does in figure 21.21. Notice that Customer ID and the other fields have all shifted down one row and a new, empty row is inserted above Customer ID.

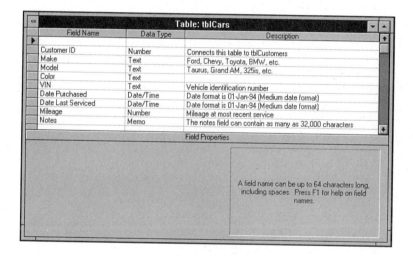

Figure 21.21
The new row has been added to tblCars.

Adding the new Car ID field involves nothing more than specifying the name (Car ID, of course) and data type (Counter). To set the Car ID field as the primary key for the tblCars table, click on the Primary Key button, as shown in figure 21.22. The Indexed property in figure 21.22 is set to No because the Customer ID field has not yet been designated as the primary key.

Figure 21.22
Indexing the Car
ID field in tblCars.

Primary Key button

Row pointer

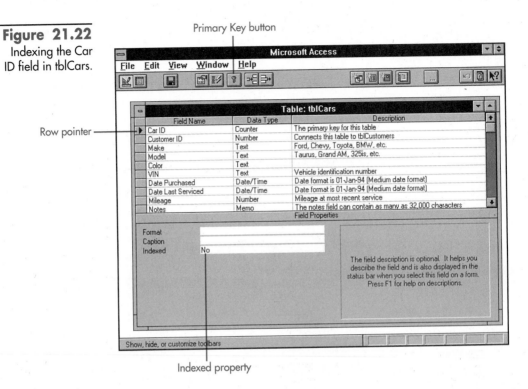

Indexed property

The primary key for tblCars, however, will be a simple Number field, without the special attributes of a Counter field. Access enables us to ensure, however, that whatever field is designated as the primary key will contain unique values.

After you click on the Primary Key button, Access displays the primary key field indicator, which looks like a little key, next to the Car ID field (see fig. 21.23). Notice also that the Indexed property box in the field properties now reports that the Car ID field is indexed with No Duplicates. A field designated as the primary key for a table must be indexed with No Duplicates; if duplicate values were allowed, the field would not qualify as a primary key.

The Car ID field is indexed to permit fast lookups of records in this table when using the Car ID to find records. The No Duplicates parameter means that Access will not allow duplicate values in the Car ID field. No Duplicates is not a problem because the Car ID field was defined as a Counter field. As mentioned earlier in this chapter, Access will guarantee that each value in a Counter field is unique.

Key field indicator

Figure 21.23
The Car ID field
defined as the
primary key.

```
┌─────────────────────────── Microsoft Access ───────────────────────┐
│ File   Edit   View   Window   Help                                  │
├─────────────────────────────────────────────────────────────────────┤
│                        Table: tblCars                               │
│        Field Name          Data Type              Description        │
│  Car ID                   Counter    The primary key for this table │
│  Customer ID              Number     Connects this table to tblCustomers │
│  Make                     Text       Ford, Chevy, Toyota, BMW, etc. │
│  Model                    Text       Taurus, Grand AM, 325is, etc.  │
│  Color                    Text                                       │
│  VIN                      Text       Vehicle identification number  │
│  Date Purchased           Date/Time  Date format is 01-Jan-94 (Medium date format) │
│  Date Last Serviced       Date/Time  Date format is 01-Jan-94 (Medium date format) │
│  Mileage                  Number     Mileage at most recent service │
│  Notes                    Memo       The notes field can contain as many as 32,000 characters │
│                            Field Properties                         │
│  Format                                                             │
│  Caption                                                            │
│  Indexed      Yes (No Duplicates)                                   │
│                           The field description is optional.  It helps you │
│                           describe the field and is also displayed in the │
│                           status bar when you select this field on a form. │
│                           Press F1 for help on descriptions.        │
│                                                                     │
│ Change window position                                              │
└─────────────────────────────────────────────────────────────────────┘
```

Indexed property for Car ID field

Selecting a Field To Use as the Primary Key

After you set the primary key and save the table (using the <u>S</u>ave command in the <u>F</u>ile menu), Access checks to see if the primary key field contains any duplicate values. This can happen if the field you designate as the primary key contains more than one record with the same value in the field. A customer's last name, for instance, is a poor choice for a primary key field. It is very likely that there eventually will be two customers with the same last name (Smith, Jones, Brown, and so on). You are much better off using fields with truly unique values (Social Security Number, Invoice Number, or a field of the Counter data type) as the primary key to a table.

If you try to make a field with duplicate values a primary key, Access displays the following two error messages:

> Can't have duplicate key; Index changes were unsuccessful.

> Error were encountered during save. Indexes were not added.

If this happens, acknowledge the messages by clicking on the OK buttons. Next, select a different field to be the primary key. Because we used a Counter field as the primary key for tblCars, there is no chance of duplicate value.

IV

Microsoft Access

Even if the table contains a field with unique values, many Access developers elect to add a Counter field to the table to use as the primary key. Access maintains the uniqueness of the Counter field. In fact, once a Counter value has been used, it cannot be reused, even if the record containing the value is deleted.

If you do not create a primary key, Access will prompt you to create one when you save the table (see fig. 21.24).

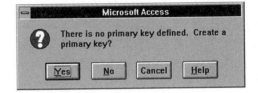

If you let Access create the primary key, it creates a new Counter field named ID. If you already have a field named ID, the new field name will be ID1. If you have an existing field named ID1, Access creates ID2, and so on.

Creating a Multiple-Field Primary Key

Sometimes there is no one field that is unique in a table, but two fields, when joined, create a unique combination. In a table of product orders, for example, the combination of product number, date, and time of order would be unique to each record and could be used as a primary key.

To create a primary key based on two or more fields, highlight the fields by pressing Ctrl while clicking with the mouse before you press the Primary Key button.

Null values are not allowed in the fields used as primary keys (either single field or multiple field). You might, for example, create in an employees table a multiple-field primary key based on first names, middle initials, and last names. If you do this, all the fields must be filled in. If you do not want to require the middle initials, a better choice of primary key would be the Social Security number or employee number, rather than a multifield primary key in which one or more of the fields might contain a null value.

Creating Secondary Indexes

By default, the primary key is indexed automatically. You can create an index on other fields, however, by setting the Indexed property of the fields. In the tblCars table you can create an index on the VIN field that would enable you to quickly retrieve information on a car based on its vehicle identification number (see fig. 21.25).

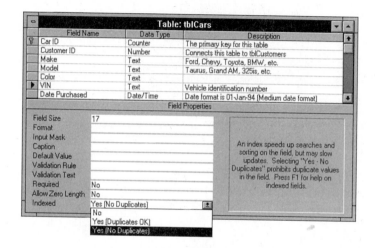

Figure 21.25
Creating an index on the VIN field.

You have the following three options when you set the Indexed property:

✔ **No.** The field is not indexed (default).

✔ **Yes (Duplicates OK).** The field is indexed; you can enter duplicate values in the field (for example, ZIP codes).

✔ **Yes (No Duplicates).** The field is indexed; you cannot enter duplicate values in the field.

Selecting Yes (No Duplicates) is much like setting the primary key. One difference is that records appear in primary key sequence when you open the table in Datasheet view. If you merely create an index (and do not set the primary key), the records appear in the order they were added to the table, even if you create an index.

Tip

Depending on the number of records in a table, the extra overhead of maintaining an index might not justify creating an index beyond the table's primary key. Though data retrieval is somewhat faster with an index than without an index, Access must write index information whenever you enter or change records in the table. In contrast, changes to nonindexed fields do not require extra file activity. You can retrieve data from nonindexed fields.

continues

It is best to add secondary indexes when tables are quite large and indexing on fields other than the primary key speeds up searches. Even with large tables, however, indexing can slow performance if the records in tables are often changed or new records are added frequently. Each time a record is changed or added, Access must update all indexes in the table.

Establishing Multiple-Field Indexes

You can establish multiple-field indexes in a table. To create a multiple-field index, choose View, Indexes . To add an index to a field, enter first a name for the index, the field to index, and a sort order for this field (see fig. 21.26).

Figure 21.26
The Indexes dialog
box.

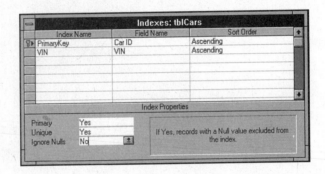

In this example, Access will create an index on the Car ID and VIN fields. To create additional multiple-field indexes, add to this dialog box accordingly.

For more information about multiple-field indexes, search the Access Help system under "Indexes".

Saving the New Table

Save the new table by choosing the $\underline{S}$ave command from the $\underline{F}$ile menu. The first time a new table is saved, Access displays the Save As dialog box and prompts you for the name of the table (see fig. 21.27).

Figure 21.27
The Save As
dialog box.

The name assigned to a table must be unique within the database; you cannot have two tables with the same name. Also, table names can be quite long. Counting spaces and punctuation, the names of tables and other database objects can be up to 64 characters in length.

Entering Data in the Table

At this point, you have created a new table named tblCars for the Carmel Car Care database, defined all the fields, and set all the field properties. Now you are ready to start entering data in the table.

For most applications, you will likely want to create a form that will then be used to enter data. For now, however, it is useful for you to know how to use the table in Datasheet view. Click on the Datasheet button on the toolbar to switch the table to Datasheet view (see fig. 21.28).

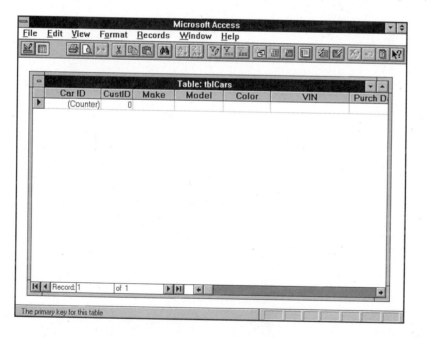

Figure 21.28
The tblCars table
in Datasheet view.

IV

Microsoft Access

Notice just to the right of Car ID is a column headed CustID. Recall that the heading for the Customer ID column was changed to CustID by setting the Caption property of this field.

Adjusting Column Widths

At this point, of course, the table is completely empty; you saw a similar view of tblCars back in figures 21.18 and 21.19. Notice that some of the columns in tblCars are wider or narrower than you would like. The Make column, for instance, is quite a bit larger than necessary to hold values like "Ford" or "Toyota". Columns that are too wide limit the number of columns that can be displayed on the screen at one time.

To quickly resize the column widths, position the mouse on the right boundary of the column head you want to resize, click the left mouse button, and then drag the boundary to the left to make the column narrower (see fig 21.29), or to the right to make the column wider. Notice that the mouse cursor changes to a double-headed arrow as you drag the boundary.

Figure 21.29

Dragging the right boundary to change the column width.

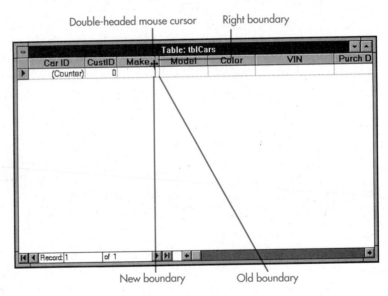

An alternate method of setting column widths was discussed earlier in this chapter. With the mouse cursor positioned in a column, choosing Format, Column Width displays the Column Width dialog box (see fig. 21.30), in which you can precisely specify the width of the column or choose Best Fit to ask Access to automatically size the column widths depending upon already-entered information.

Figure 21.30

The Column Width dialog box.

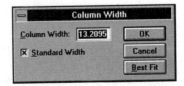

The number in the Column Width text box in figure 21.30 is the number of characters you can show in the column. If the column width is too narrow to display a value, Access will display as many characters as possible, but will not automatically resize the column width to accommodate wide data. By the way, the Column Width text box will accept fractional values such as 10.5 as shown in figure 21.30.

After you have the column widths adjusted to your liking, save the column widths by choosing File, Save. Thereafter, the table will be opened with the previously saved column widths.

Adding Records to the Table

Adding data to the table is simple. Although the Car ID column is highlighted (see fig. 21.31), you cannot enter data into that column. Recall that the Car ID field is a Counter data type field, which means that Access will assign values to this field and will prevent you from changing those values. You must use the Tab key, right-arrow key, or Enter key to move to the Make field before you can enter data. This behavior can be a bit confusing at times!

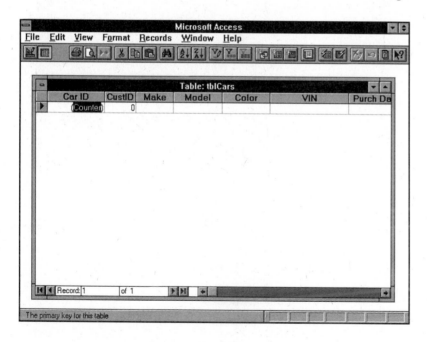

Figure 21.31
Data cannot be entered into the Customer ID field.

Notice in figure 21.31 that Access is trying to help you understand that data cannot be entered into the Car ID field by putting "(Counter)" into the Car ID field. Although useful, it might be more helpful if the cursor would automatically move to the Customer ID field.

As you begin entering data into the Customer ID column, two things happen. The row selector column indicator of the active row changes to a pencil, and a new row appears below the current row with an asterisk in the row selector column. These changes are shown in figure 21.32.

Figure 21.32
The table changes as data is entered.

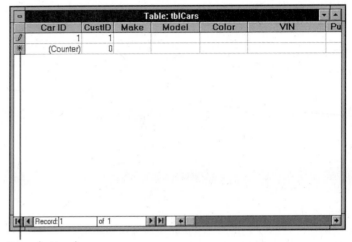

Row selector column

As data is entered into each field, the Tab key, right-arrow key, or Enter key can be used to move the mouse pointer to the next column. Unlike spreadsheets such as Excel or Lotus 1-2-3, the Enter key moves the cursor to the right, not down the table. When the last column in the row is reached, the mouse cursor will automatically drop down to the next row in the table.

After data entry into the row is complete, the asterisk changes to the familiar wedge-shaped record indicator when you move to the next row.

You also can move to a new record by choosing New from the Go To command from the Records menu (see figure 21.33).

Figure 21.33
Choose New to move to a new record.

If the table contains a Counter field, Access fills in the value automatically. When you add a new record, Access increments the most recently used counter value and enters the new value for you. Remember, you cannot enter or change Counter fields yourself. Also, you can have only one Counter field in a table.

Remember the following characteristics of Counter fields:

Counter field values are guaranteed to be unique.

Access automatically fills in the value for you.

Once established by Access, the value cannot be changed.

A Counter value cannot be reused in a table, even if the record containing the value is deleted.

Only one Counter field is allowed in a table.

For a number of reasons, Counter fields are often the ideal primary index field for tables.

For all the other fields in the table, tab to each field in turn and enter data of the appropriate type. During data input, the field data can be changed, deleted, or replaced like text data in a text box in any Windows.

In order for the Carmel Car Care database to work as expected, of course, the value in Customer ID field must match one of the Customer IDs in tblCustomers. In tblCustomers, Customer ID 1 belongs to Paul Helms.

Applying Validation Rules

One of the properties for most field data types is the validation rule to apply to data in the field. A *validation rule* ensures that the data entered into the field meets the criteria determined for the field. In tblCars, for instance, you might want to apply a validation rule to the Mileage field to prevent negative numbers from being entered into this field.

Looking once more at tblCars in Design view (see fig. 21.34), notice the Validation Rule property box for the Mileage field contains > 0 as the validation rule value. This rule will prevent 0 (zero) from being entered into the field as well as negative numbers.

IV

Microsoft Access

Figure 21.34
Setting the Validation Rule property for the Mileage field.

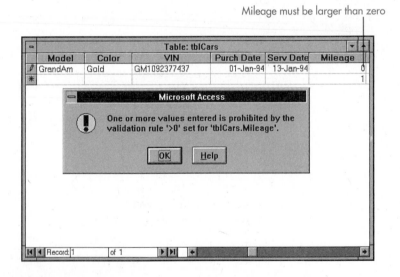

New validation rule

After the validation rule shown in figure 21.34 has been established, Access will warn you when you try to enter invalid data into this field (see fig. 21.35).

Figure 21.35
The default validation rule warning.

Mileage must be larger than zero

The problem with the warning shown in figure 21.35 is that it can be confusing to users. The Validation Text property (located just under the Validation Rule property in figure 21.34) can be used to give a more explanatory warning. The custom validation rule warning is shown in figure 21.36.

Figure 21.36
A custom validation message.

Even without a validation rule, you still must enter the appropriate kind of information. You cannot enter nonnumeric data into a number field, for example, or text into a date/time field. Access checks the type of data without any action on your part. Invalid data entry results in the message shown in figure 21.37.

Data does not match field data type

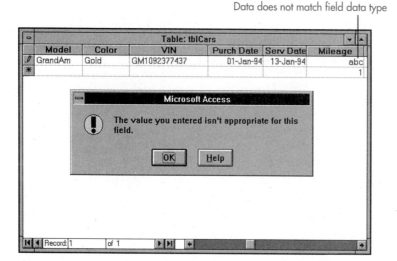

Figure 21.37
The Access error message when input data does not match the field data type.

Using OLE Object Fields

Although the OLE field data type has not yet been examined, you might want to include an example of this field in tblCars. A typical use for the OLE Object field type is to store graphics such as photographs of customers or their cars, Paintbrush bit maps, and product illustrations. Table 21.2 shows some of the many other types of OLE objects you can embed in Access tables.

Table 21.2
Typical OLE Object Types

Object type	Source program
Equation	MS Equation
MakeUp objects	Bitstream MakeUp
Microsoft drawing	MS Draw
Microsoft Excel chart	MS Excel
Microsoft Excel macrosheet	MS Excel
Microsoft Excel worksheet	MS Excel
Microsoft Graph	MS Graph
Microsoft WordArt	MS WordArt
Package	Windows 3.1 Object Packager
Paintbrush picture	Windows 3.1 Paintbrush
Sound	Windows 3.1 Sound
WinPost note	WinPost
Word document	Word for Windows

The actual objects you can add to Access tables, forms, and reports depend on the applications and source programs installed on your computer. Your list of available objects might vary from that shown here.

Embedding an OLE Object

Assume that Carmel Car Care wants to include a picture of the customer's car in the database along with the other data on the car. Returning tblCars to Design view once more, a new field named Picture is added to the field list, and OLE Object is selected from the drop-down list of data types (see fig. 21.38).

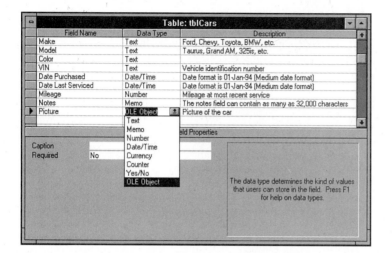

Figure 21.38
Creating an OLE Object field.

Data contained in OLE Object fields is embedded in the table. Embedding an OLE object is much like copying and pasting text: you make a copy of an existing object and insert it into a field. To embed an OLE object, tab to the appropriate field in the datasheet (Picture) and then select the Insert Object command from the Edit menu to display the Insert Object dialog box (see fig. 21.39). Depending on the Windows applications installed on your computer, the list in the Insert Object dialog box can be quite long.

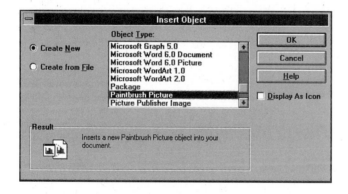

Figure 21.39
Use the Insert Object dialog box to specify the OLE object type.

Next, select the appropriate object type from the selection list. To embed a Picture Publisher bit map, for example, select Picture Publisher.

If the object you want to embed already exists on your computer's disk, click on the Create from File option button. If you want to create a brand-new object, click on OK.

Embedding an Existing OLE Object

When you click on the Create from File option button in the Insert Object dialog box, Access displays a dialog box in which you can specify the name of the file that contains the OLE object (see fig. 21.40).

Figure 21.40
Specifying the name of an existing OLE object file.

To embed the file, locate it by browsing or by specifying the path and file name. Click on OK. Access grinds along for a while and then puts the word *Package* in the OLE field to let you know an object is embedded in the field (see fig. 21.41).

Figure 21.41
Package describes the OLE object.

Double-click on any Picture field to view the bit map

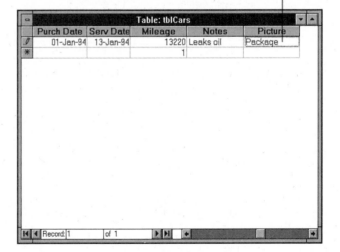

You cannot display the OLE object in Datasheet view. For example, even though you embed a bit map into a table, you cannot see the bit map. To view the OLE object, double-click on the description.

Later, a double-click on the field in the table will open Picture Publisher, or whatever application you have associated with a bitmap image in your Windows registration database, load the picture into the work area, and enable you to either view or edit the picture.

Creating a New OLE Object

To create a new OLE Object, click on OK instead of the Create from File option button in the Insert Object dialog box (refer to figure 21.39). Access opens the source program—in this example, Picture Publisher—and waits for you to create and save the object (see fig. 21.42). Notice in figure 21.42 that the Picture Publisher title bar indicates the image being edited is a "pkg," which is another way of saying it is an OLE object. Windows understands that you intend to embed a Picture Publisher picture in an Access database and is trying to help you understand that this is not an ordinary Picture Publisher session.

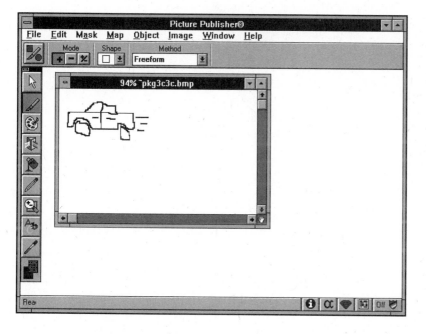

Figure 21.42
The OLE object being created or edited in Picture Publisher.

IV

Microsoft Access

When you are finished creating the new object, choose the E**x**it command from the **F**ile menu (see fig. 21.43).

Figure 21.43
The Exit command
in Picture
Publisher.

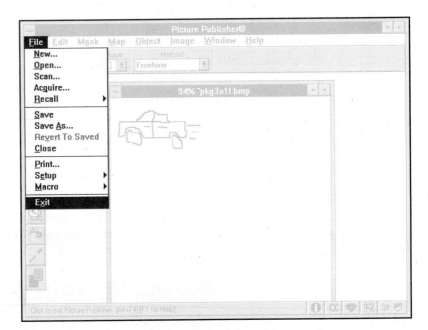

 The exact wording for the Exit command differs in other source programs. In Word for Windows, for example, the Exit command is simply "Exit," while in Paintbrush it is "Exit & Return to Microsoft Access."

In certain applications a dialog box will appear asking if you want to update the embedded objects.

When you have been returned to Access, the picture in the tblCars table is updated with whatever changes you made while in Picture Publisher.

Creating Table Relationships

Earlier in this book, you learned the value of establishing relationships between tables. When you create a relationship, you tell Access the way in which records in one table relate to the records in another table.

For example, the tblCustomers and tblCars tables are related because they both have a common field (Customer ID) that enables one table to refer to the other. If you were to view the tblCustomers table, you would see that each record has a Customer ID that matches one or more records in the tblCars table.

To create a relationship between two tables, close all open tables and go to the Access Database window. Then choose the Relationships command from the Edit menu to display the Relationships grid and the Add Table dialog box (see fig. 21.44).

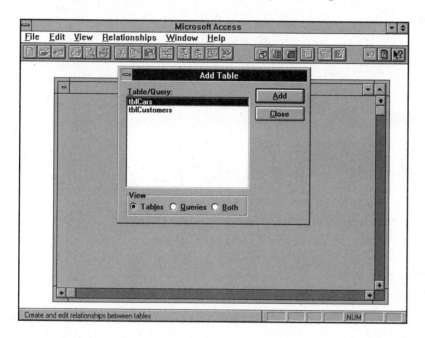

Figure 21.44
The Relationships design grid with the Add Table dialog box.

Note You can define only one relationship between any two tables. If you define a second relationship, Access deletes the first one automatically.

In the Add Table dialog box, select the primary table in the relationship; in this example, the primary table is tblCustomers. Click on the Add button to add this table to the grid. Next, choose tblCars and click on Add to add that to the grid also. These tables will be joined on the Customer ID field. To create this join, click on the Customer ID field in the tblCustomers list and drag it to the Customer ID field in the tblCars list box. Access will respond with a confirming dialog box as shown in figure 21.45. Click on the Enforce Referential Integrity check box to let Access know you want a one-to-many relationship and do not want to permit entries to the many table without a corresponding record previously entered in the one table.

Figure 21.45
Selecting
Customer ID in the
matching fields
drop-down list
box.

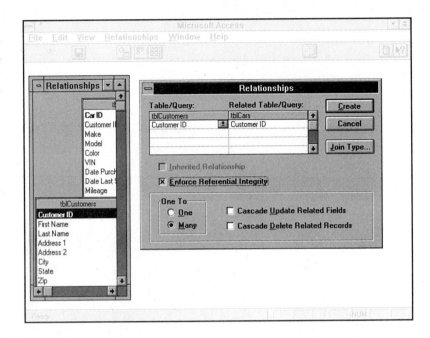

There are two common types of relationships used in Access:

✔ **One-to-One.** Choose this option when one record in the primary table relates to one and only one record in the related table. For example, a customer record could be related to exactly one credit report record.

✔ **One-to-Many.** Choose this option when one record in the primary table relates to one or more records in the related table. For example, a customer might own several different cars.

As described earlier in this chapter, Access is not able to directly form many-to-many relationships between tables. To create many-to-many relationships in Access, you must use a "join" table as described earlier in this chapter. This is why there is no many-to-many choice in the Relationships dialog box.

Referential integrity refers to Access's capability to make sure there are no orphan records. An *orphan record* is a record in the related table that has no matching record in the primary table. You would create an orphan record if you added a car to tblCars and specified a nonexistent Customer ID to the car (that is, there was no matching record in the tblCustomers table).

You also can create orphan records by deleting a record in the primary table while there still are matching records in the related table. Deleting a customer in tblCustomers, for example, would create orphan records in the tblCars table. If you want, you can check the Cascade **U**pdate Related Fields or Cacade **D**elete Related Fields check boxes. This will cause Access to delete or update records in the many tables when you modify or delete records in the one table. For more information on this subject, search Help on "Referential Integrity".

When you enforce referential integrity, Access checks to make sure you do not create orphan records.

When you are done selecting and linking the tables, telling Access which type of relationship to establish, and whether to enforce referential integrity between the tables, click on the **C**reate button near the top of the Relationships dialog box. Access creates the links between the tables and will maintain the relationship until you change it. Figure 21.46 shows the Relationship grid after the join between the tblCustomers and tblCars. Access gives you a good visual clue as to which table is on which side of the one-to-many relationship.

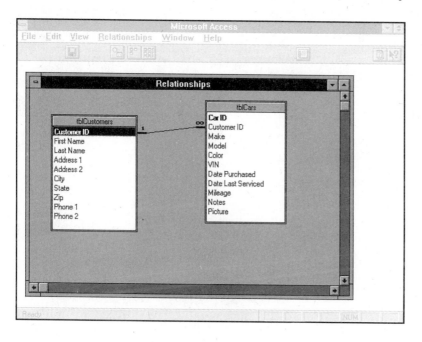

Figure 21.46
The finished relationship link.

IV

Microsoft Access

Modifying an Existing Table

When you first create a table, you might not think of every field that needs to be tracked. Or, you might find that certain fields are not necessary after all and you want to delete them from the table. In addition, you might want to change some of the field properties; some fields might not be long enough, a field might need to be a Long Integer instead of a Double, and so on.

It is easy to make these kinds of changes to an Access table.

 Note
You cannot change the design of an attached table. To change an attached table, you must close the current database and then open the database that contains the attached table. When you are finished making the changes, reopen the first database.

First, open the table in Design view (see fig. 21.47).

Figure 21.47
The tblCars table in Design view.

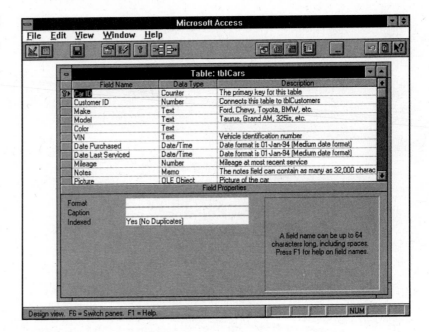

Adding a New Field

To add a new field to a table (for example, tblCars really ought to have a field for the car's year of manufacture), highlight the row where you want the new row to appear by pressing the row selector at the left end of the row (see fig. 21.48).

New row will appear above this row

Figure 21.48
Highlighting a
row.

Table: tblCars

	Field Name	Data Type	Description
🔑	Car ID	Counter	The primary key for this table
	Customer ID	Number	Connects this table to tblCustomers
▶	Make	Text	Ford, Chevy, Toyota, BMW, etc.
	Model	Text	Taurus, Grand AM, 325is, etc.
	Color	Text	
	VIN	Text	Vehicle identification number
	Date Purchased	Date/Time	Date format is 01-Jan-94 (Medium date format)
	Date Last Serviced	Date/Time	Date format is 01-Jan-94 (Medium date format)
	Mileage	Number	Mileage at most recent service
	Notes	Memo	The notes field can contain as many as 32,000 characters
	Picture	OLE Object	Picture of the car

Field Properties

Field Size	15
Format	
Input Mask	
Caption	
Default Value	
Validation Rule	
Validation Text	
Required	No
Allow Zero Length	No
Indexed	No

A field name can be up to 64 characters long, including spaces. Press F1 for help on field names.

Then, press Ins or choose **I**nsert Row from the **E**dit menu. Access inserts above the highlighted row a new, blank row that you can fill in with the new field information. Figure 21.49 shows the Model Year field with all properties (including a Caption, Validation Rule, and Validation Text) defined.

Figure 21.49
The Model Year
field has been
added to tblCars.

Table: tblCars

	Field Name	Data Type	Description
🔑	Car ID	Counter	The primary key for this table
	Customer ID	Number	Connects this table to tblCustomers
▶	Model Year	Number	Year car was built. We only service cars built after 1980
	Make	Text	Ford, Chevy, Toyota, BMW, etc.
	Model	Text	Taurus, Grand AM, 325is, etc.
	Color	Text	
	VIN	Text	Vehicle identification number
	Date Purchased	Date/Time	Date format is 01-Jan-94 (Medium date format)
	Date Last Serviced	Date/Time	Date format is 01-Jan-94 (Medium date format)
	Mileage	Number	Mileage at most recent service
	Notes	Memo	The notes field can contain as many as 32,000 characters

Field Properties

Field Size	Integer
Format	
Decimal Places	0
Input Mask	
Caption	Year
Default Value	9999
Validation Rule	>1990
Validation Text	Model Year must be after 1980
Required	No
Indexed	No

The field description is optional. It helps you describe the field and is also displayed in the status bar when you select this field on a form. Press F1 for help on descriptions.

IV

Microsoft Access

Notice that 9999 has been entered as the Default Value for the this field. Because the Validation Rule has been set to > 1980 (the Carmel Car Care repair shop only works on cars built after 1980), the default value must be larger than 1980, or an error would occur every time a record was added to tblCars and the year of the car was not entered. A default value of 9999 avoids generating a validation rule error.

Deleting a Field

To delete a field from a table, first highlight the row containing the field (see fig. 21.50). Perhaps the manager of Carmel Car Care decides it doesn't matter when the customer bought his car and wants to delete the Date Purchased field from tblCars.

Figure 21.50
Highlighting a row
to be deleted.

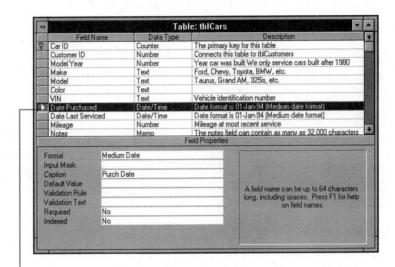

Row to be deleted

Then, press Del or select <u>D</u>elete Row from the <u>E</u>dit menu. Access displays a dialog box asking you to confirm that you want to delete the field (see figure 21.51). Click on OK to delete the field or Cancel to leave the field in the table.

Figure 21.51
Access asks you to
confirm the field's
deletion.

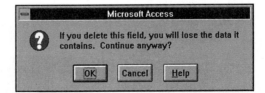

Changing a Field

You can change a field's properties just as you did when you first created the field (see the section "Defining Fields in the Cars Table" earlier in this chapter). To change a field's caption or description, for example, click on the existing text and enter the new text.

If you change the field's data type, be certain you do not lose data by choosing a smaller, more restrictive, or less precise data type.

For example, you can freely change an Integer field to a Long Integer field because all integer values can also be represented by Long Integers. When you change a Long Integer to an Integer, however, some values might be lost if they do not fit within the range of a "regular" integer. If you have an integer field that contains values higher than 32,767, those values will be lost when you convert the field to an Integer field.

You can lose data when you change the Field Size of a text field, as well. If you accept the default length of 50, enter data, and then decide to shorten some of the fields, you must be certain that you have not entered any data longer than the new field length. Access warns you that some data may be lost (see fig. 21.52), but it is up to you to determine it for sure.

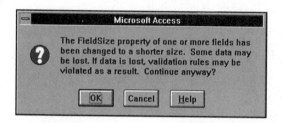

Figure 21.52
Access warns you that data might be lost when you change the field size.

After you have made all the necessary design changes, save the table by choosing the Save command from the File menu. If you want to save the table under a different name, use the Save As command instead.

IV

Microsoft Access

Chapter Snapshot

A *query* is an Access database object you use to ask questions about the data stored in your database. You use queries to select specific data to display in forms and print in reports. In this chapter, you will learn to work with Access queries; specifically, it covers the following topics:

After you finish this chapter, you will know how to use queries to select data to view and use in forms and reports; categorize and summarize data for financial reports and graphs; select records to use in graphs; create new tables; and add records to, delete records from, and update records in existing tables.

CHAPTER

Understanding Access Queries

By Paul Cassel

When working with a database, you might want to select data based on certain criteria, or present the data sorted into a certain order. Queries enable you to retrieve only the information necessary to complete the task at hand. Access queries also can be used to change existing information in the underlying tables of the database.

Queries can extract data from more than one table. In fact, a common use of queries is to combine data from a number of tables for display in a form. In Access, a simple form can display data from just one table. Queries are the only way to display data from multiple tables in Access, unless you use subforms (you will learn all about forms in Chapter 23, "Creating and Using Forms").

There are two broad categories of queries that give you different ways of examining and modifying your data: select queries and action queries. *Select queries* retrieve records, but do not change the underlying tables. *Action queries*, as their name suggests, perform an action; that is, they change the underlying tables.

Select queries include *crosstab queries*, a special form of select query (described in detail later in this chapter) typically used to extract data to be used in charts and graphs.

The action query category includes the following kinds of queries:

- ✔ **Update.** Changes data in one or more tables.

- ✔ **Delete.** Deletes records.

- ✔ **Make-table.** Creates a new table from existing records.

- ✔ **Append.** Adds records to an existing table.

After you create a query, you can open or run it directly from the Database window, or you can use it as the basis for a form or report. Queries are created in the Query window in a manner similar to creating tables.

Exploring the Query Window

The Query window presents a number of features and tools you can use to build powerful queries quickly and easily (see fig. 22.1). All of the various Query window features shown in figure 22.1 are described in this chapter. You also will learn how the query displayed in this figure was created.

The data returned by this query is shown in figure 22.2. Because the data returned by a query comes from database tables, it is not surprising that Access presents the results of a query in a view that looks a lot like a table. The object shown in figure 22.2 is not permanent, however. After it is closed, it disappears until the next time the query is run. The data in figure 22.2 changes any time data is changed in the tables underlying the query. For these reasons, the object in figure 22.2 is called a *dynaset* rather than a table.

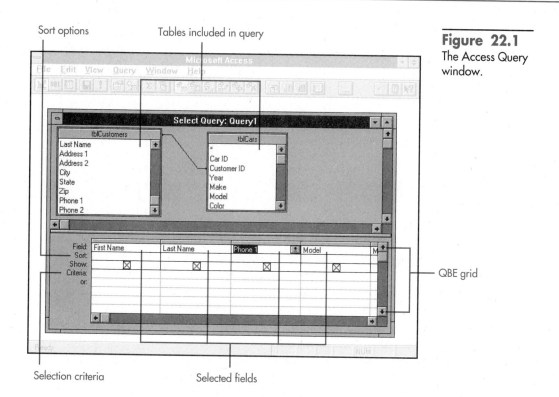

Figure 22.1
The Access Query window.

Sort options

Tables included in query

QBE grid

Selection criteria

Selected fields

Figure 22.2
The dynaset produced by the query.

First Name	Last Name	Phone 1	Model	Make
Pam	Fields	(317) 844-7261	Taurus	Ford
Mike	Lewis	(319) 555-9110	320i	BMW
Lee	Perkins	(919) 555-2085	Civic	Honda
Paul	Helms	(317) 555-2387	Tempo	Ford
Harry	Slabosky	(317) 555-0805	Town Car	Lincoln
Lee	Perkins	(919) 555-2085	Trans Am	Pontiac
Brad	Pease	(617) 555-9639	Probe GL	Ford
Sarah	Miller	(317) 555-7605	Maxima	Nissan
Jim	Wagner	(317) 555-4157	Grand Am	Pontiac
Darryl	Ryan	(814) 555-1162	Sedan DeVille	Cadillac
Tim	Murray	(813) 555-8252	Caprice Classic	Chevrolet
Tom	Reid	(508) 555-0381	Cougar LS	Mercury
David	Allen	(317) 555-1514	Cutlass Supreme	Oldsmobile
Linda	Matthews	(617) 555-2279	Tempo GL	Ford
Steve	Taylor	(813) 555-0844	Stanza	Nissa
Steve	Taylor	(813) 555-0844	325 Convertible	BMW
Cliff	Flanagan	(813) 555-5952	Cavalier	Chevy

Record: 1 of 30

Data from tblCustomers

Data from tblCars

IV

Microsoft Access

As you will see in Chapter 23, "Creating and Using Forms," a dynaset can be the basis of a form that displays the data one record at a time. It also is important to notice that the data in the dynaset in figure 22.2 comes from two different tables. The customer data in the first three columns is from tblCustomers, whereas the vehicle information in the rightmost three columns comes from tblCars. Although data from each table appears in contiguous columns in figure 22.2, the columns can be in any order at all.

To create a query in Access, you use the graphical Query-by-Example (QBE) grid. Unlike other database systems that require you to enter complex expressions on a command line or in a programming language, you can define queries by dragging and dropping table fields from the list at the top of the Query window to the QBE grid. Next you build the query that extracts data from the tables by providing the text, numbers, and expressions to match when selecting records. In other words, you provide an *example* of the data you are looking for (hence the expression *Query by Example*).

Many of the options you might choose for the query (sorting, totaling, and so on) are available in drop-down lists. In most other database programs, these functions are accessible only by entering sometimes confusing command-line expressions or by writing a program in a database programming language.

Figure 22.3 illustrates the ease with which the data returned by a query can be sorted.

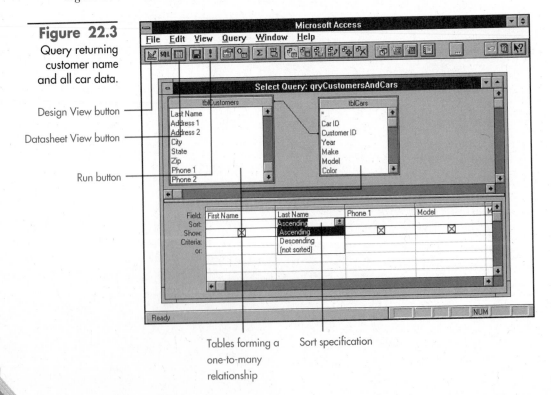

Figure 22.3
Query returning customer name and all car data.

Design View button

Datasheet View button

Run button

Tables forming a one-to-many relationship

Sort specification

In this example, the query sorts the data alphabetically in ascending order by the customer's last name. The sort just as easily could have been specified in descending order by first name. The underlying tables form a one-to-many relationship (each owner might own several cars, but a car cannot be owned by more than one person). This example shows how you need only drag three fields into the QBE grid to display all of the car's data as well as the owner's name (see fig. 22.4).

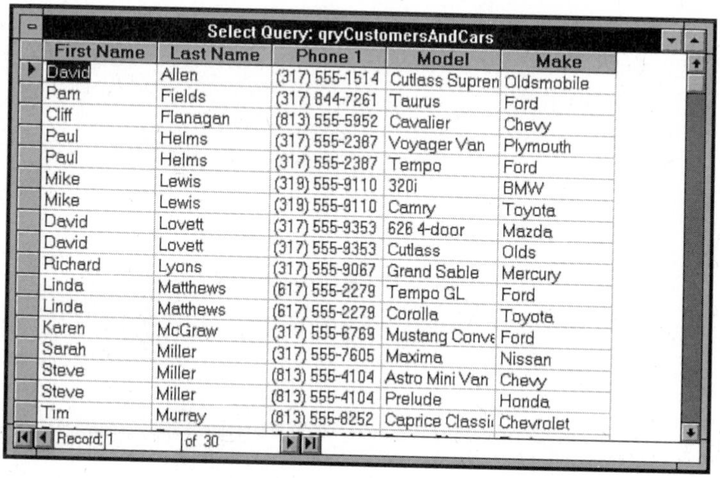

First Name	Last Name	Phone 1	Model	Make
David	Allen	(317) 555-1514	Cutlass Supren	Oldsmobile
Pam	Fields	(317) 844-7261	Taurus	Ford
Cliff	Flanagan	(813) 555-5952	Cavalier	Chevy
Paul	Helms	(317) 555-2387	Voyager Van	Plymouth
Paul	Helms	(317) 555-2387	Tempo	Ford
Mike	Lewis	(319) 555-9110	320i	BMW
Mike	Lewis	(319) 555-9110	Camry	Toyota
David	Lovett	(317) 555-9353	626 4-door	Mazda
David	Lovett	(317) 555-9353	Cutlass	Olds
Richard	Lyons	(317) 555-9067	Grand Sable	Mercury
Linda	Matthews	(617) 555-2279	Tempo GL	Ford
Linda	Matthews	(617) 555-2279	Corolla	Toyota
Karen	McGraw	(317) 555-6769	Mustang Conve	Ford
Sarah	Miller	(317) 555-7605	Maxima	Nissan
Steve	Miller	(813) 555-4104	Astro Mini Van	Chevy
Steve	Miller	(813) 555-4104	Prelude	Honda
Tim	Murray	(813) 555-8252	Caprice Classii	Chevrolet

Select Query: qryCustomersAndCars — Record: 1 of 30

Figure 22.4
The results of the sorted query.

In figure 22.4, notice that customers like Paul Helms and Mike Lewis have more than one car. Therefore, their names appear more than once in this dynaset.

The results of a select query are viewed in Datasheet view by clicking on the Datasheet View button; you also can choose the Datasheet command from the View menu, click on the Run button, or choose the Run command from the Query menu. These buttons can be seen in figure 22.3.

In contrast, you cannot view the results of an action query—you can only run an action query. If you want to see which records will be affected by an action query, first change the query to a select query and then open the query in Datasheet view. This process is described in the "Exploring Action Queries" section later in this chapter.

The Toolbar Buttons in Design View

The toolbar in the Query window changes depending on which view (Design or Datasheet) is active. In Design view, the toolbar has several buttons you can use when you create or run queries (see fig. 22.5). You won't find all of these buttons when the Query window is in Datasheet view.

IV

Microsoft Access

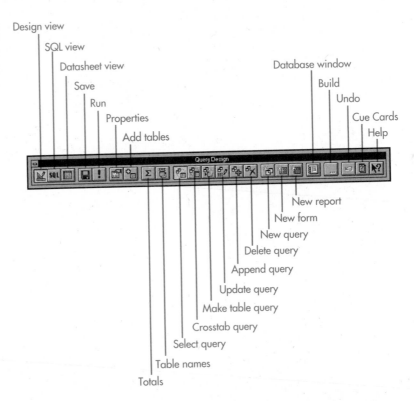

Figure 22.5
The Query window toolbar in Design view.

The following list describes the actions performed by the most-often-used buttons found on the Query window toolbar in Design view:

✔ **Design view, Datasheet view.** For select queries only, use these buttons to quickly switch between Design view, in which you can fine-tune the query's selection and sorting criteria, and Datasheet view, in which you can view the results of the query. Notice that the Design view button is depressed while in Design view.

✔ **Totals.** Clicking on this button turns totals on or off and groups specified fields. Totals are discussed later in this chapter.

✔ **Properties.** This button displays the Query Properties list box (see fig. 22.6), in which you can set the query's properties. The query dialog box closes automatically when you click on the OK or Cancel buttons.

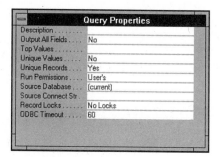

Figure 22.6
The Query
Properties list box.

For more information about the Query Properties list box, see the section "Setting the Query Properties," later in this chapter.

✔ **Run.** For select and crosstab queries only, this button displays the results of the query.

For action queries, clicking on the Run button executes the query and makes the changes specified by the query. When the query is finished, you return to the query's Design view.

✔ **Undo.** Click on this button to undo the very last change you made to the query design. The undo button cannot revert multiple changes, and does not undo changes the query might have made to the underlying data.

✔ **Help.** When you click on this button, Access opens the Help file.

In addition, there are three "new" buttons (New Query, New Form, New Report) on the right side of the toolbar. Press one of these buttons to quickly create a new query, form, or report based on the current query. The same buttons appear on most of the Access toolbars.

The Toolbar Buttons in Datasheet View

In Datasheet view, the toolbar has the same Design view, Datasheet view, Undo, and Help buttons as the toolbar in Design view. It also has the buttons to create new queries, forms, and reports. Other controls available only in Datasheet view enable you to locate particular records or print preview the results of the query (see fig. 22.7).

IV

Microsoft Access

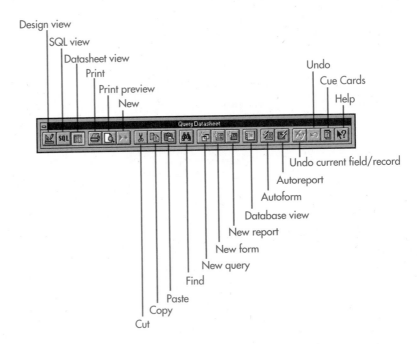

Figure 22.7
The Query window toolbar in Datasheet view.

The following list describes the actions performed by the most-often-used buttons found on the Query window toolbar in Datasheet view:

✔ **Design view.** This button will return the query to Design view.

✔ **Datasheet view.** Notice that the Datasheet view button is depressed while in Datasheet view.

✔ **Print preview.** Click on this button to see how the results of the query will look if you decide to print it.

✔ **Find.** The query's result set often contains so many records that locating any one particular record is difficult. Click on the Find button to open the Find dialog box (see fig. 22.8) and quickly locate a specific record.

Figure 22.8
The Find dialog box.

✔ **Autoform.** Click on this button to have Access create an instant form based on the current query.

✔ **Autoreport.** Click on this button to have Access create an instant report based on the current query.

The Query Commands

Most buttons on the toolbar have a corresponding menu command, but not all menu commands have an equivalent toolbar button. As with the buttons, the commands that are available at any given time depend on whether you are in Design or Datasheet view.

In Design view, useful query commands that do not have buttons include the following:

✔ **Insert Row, Delete Row.** (Edit menu) Use these commands to delete or insert criteria rows. These commands affect all columns in the QBE grid.

✔ **Insert Column, Delete Column.** (Edit menu) These commands insert or delete entire columns in the QBE grid. Another way to insert a new column is by double-clicking on the name of a field in the table's field list in the top half of the Query window. You can delete a column by highlighting it by clicking on the bar at the top of the column, then pressing Del.

✔ **SQL.** (View menu) If you are an experienced SQL programmer, you might want to create queries by entering SQL statements in SQL view. Issuing the SQL command (see fig. 22.9) displays the query in SQL view, as shown in figure 22.10.

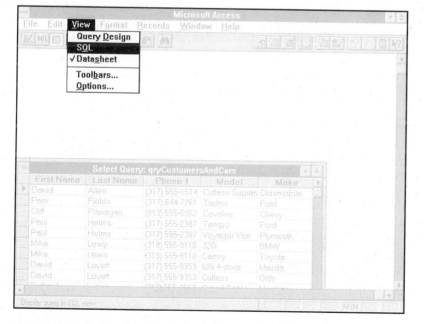

Figure 22.9

Choosing the SQL view from the View menu.

Figure 22.10
The query shown
in native SQL
code.

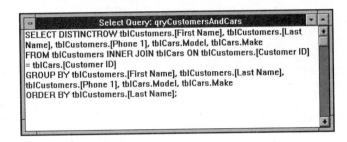

```
Select Query: qryCustomersAndCars
SELECT DISTINCTROW tblCustomers.[First Name], tblCustomers.[Last
Name], tblCustomers.[Phone 1], tblCars.Model, tblCars.Make
FROM tblCustomers INNER JOIN tblCars ON tblCustomers.[Customer ID]
= tblCars.[Customer ID]
GROUP BY tblCustomers.[First Name], tblCustomers.[Last Name],
tblCustomers.[Phone 1], tblCars.Model, tblCars.Make
ORDER BY tblCustomers.[Last Name];
```

When you create a query using the QBE grid, Access automatically constructs an equivalent SQL statement. Figure 22.10 shows the SQL statement required to execute the query shown in figures 22.3 and 22.4. When you enter or modify an SQL statement in the SQL window, Access updates the QBE grid automatically as soon as you close the SQL window.

Generally speaking, unless you know and understand SQL, you should not change the SQL statement in the SQL dialog box. You might make changes in the statement that changes the way your query works. After you have a working Access query that returns the information you want, don't mess with the query or its equivalent SQL statement!

✔ **Remove Table.** (Query menu) Use the Add Table command or toolbar button to open the Add Table dialog box. You can use this dialog box to specify up to 16 tables to include in the query. As its name implies, the Remove Table command removes the highlighted table from the query.

Actually, the Add Table dialog box (see fig. 22.11) is somewhat misnamed because you can add not only tables, but queries as well by choosing the appropriate option button at the bottom of the dialog box.

Figure 22.11
The Add Table
dialog box.

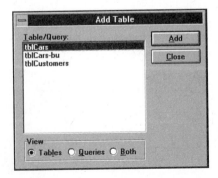

In Datasheet view, you may find the following commands particularly useful:

- ✔ **Print.** (File menu) Use the Print command to print the results of the query.
- ✔ **Refresh.** (Records menu) In a multiuser environment, some of the underlying data might have been changed by another user. Access automatically refreshes, or updates, the records at the interval set by the Options command, but you can make sure you are looking at current data at any time by choosing the Refresh command.
- ✔ **Font.** (Format menu) Depending on the screen resolution, or perhaps your own preferences, you might want to enlarge the screen font used to display the datasheet. If the default font is too thin, you also can change the font to a different style or make it bold. In figure 22.12 the dynaset's font has been changed to 10-point Courier New, which can make numeric data easier to read. Access automatically adjusts the row height to accommodate the new font. Column widths, however, are not changed as the font size changes. The columns in figure 22.12 were manually adjusted to account for the larger font size.

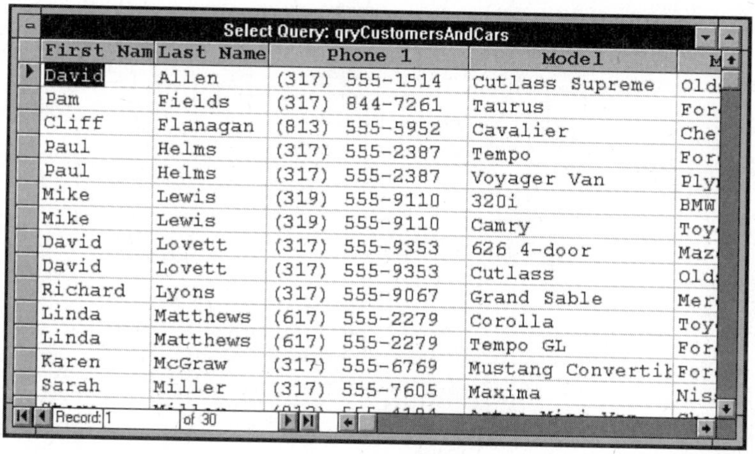
Select Query: qryCustomersAndCars

First Nam	Last Name	Phone 1	Model	M
David	Allen	(317) 555-1514	Cutlass Supreme	Old
Pam	Fields	(317) 844-7261	Taurus	For
Cliff	Flanagan	(813) 555-5952	Cavalier	Che
Paul	Helms	(317) 555-2387	Tempo	For
Paul	Helms	(317) 555-2387	Voyager Van	Ply
Mike	Lewis	(319) 555-9110	320i	BMW
Mike	Lewis	(319) 555-9110	Camry	Toy
David	Lovett	(317) 555-9353	626 4-door	Maz
David	Lovett	(317) 555-9353	Cutlass	Old
Richard	Lyons	(317) 555-9067	Grand Sable	Mer
Linda	Matthews	(617) 555-2279	Corolla	Toy
Linda	Matthews	(617) 555-2279	Tempo GL	For
Karen	McGraw	(317) 555-6769	Mustang Convertik	For
Sarah	Miller	(317) 555-7605	Maxima	Nis

Record: 1 of 30

Figure 22.12
The dynaset displayed in 10-point Courier New.

Creating a Query Using the QBE Grid

Select queries are the most fundamental type of query and the foundation for each of the other types. As mentioned earlier in this chapter, you will use a select query whenever you want to extract data from your database tables. Select queries do not change the data in the underlying tables. This section describes the general procedure for creating a select query, but you can apply these steps to the other kinds of queries as well.

First, go to the Database window, click on the Query object button at the left side of the Database window, and then click on the New button (see fig. 22.13).

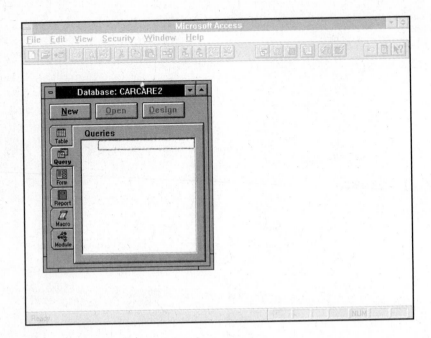

Figure 22.13

Creating a new query.

Adding and Deleting Tables

When you first create a brand-new query, Access will ask if you want to create a new query or use a Query Wizard. If you tell Access you want to bypass the Query Wizard by clicking on the New Query button, Access then displays an empty query window and overlays it with the Add Table dialog box (see fig. 22.14).

Select the tables to include in the query (in our case, tblCustomers and tblCars) and then click on OK, or double-click on the desired table names in the list of tables and queries.

You can base a query on not only tables, but other queries as well. Even though the dialog box says you are adding tables, the list of objects can include queries, too.

Access adds one field list box to the Query window for each table you select in the dialog box (see fig 22.15). If you select a table twice, it will be added to the Query window twice.

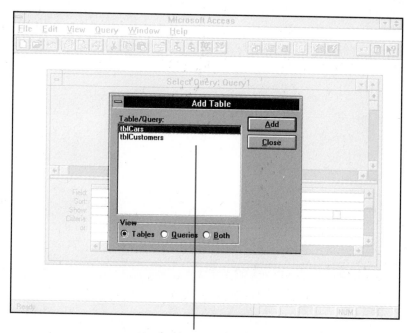

Figure 22.14
The Add Table
dialog box.

List of tables, queries, or both

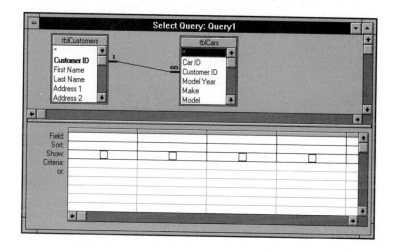

Figure 22.15
The Query window
with two tables
selected.

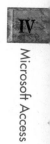

IV

Microsoft Access

Repeat this process until you have selected all the necessary tables or queries, and then click on the Close button.

Tip

Another way to quickly select tables for the query is to drag the table names from the Database window to the upper portion of the Query window.

In figure 22.15 notice that, by default, the boxes in which the tables appear are rather close together and narrow. Long field names, such as Date Purchased, would be hard to read because the box isn't wide enough to display the entire name.

To move a table, click on the table name at the top of the box and drag the box to a new position in the upper portion of the query window. Drag the right or left margin of the box (see fig. 22.16) to change the width of the box.

Border being dragged with the mouse

Figure 22.16
Rearranging the tables in the top half of the Query window.

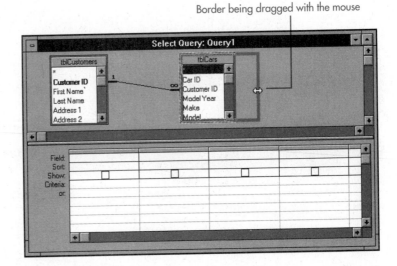

Later, if you need to add another table to the query, you can reopen the Add Table dialog box by choosing the Add Table command from the Query menu or clicking on the Add table button in the toolbar.

If you include a table you no longer need in the query, you can remove it by first selecting the table (click anywhere in the table's field list box) and then pressing Del. You also can select the Remove Table command in the Query menu.

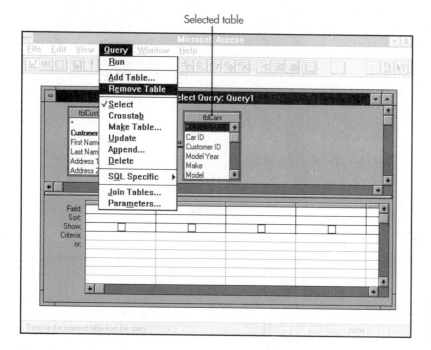

Selected table

Figure 22.17
The Remove Table command in the Query menu.

Joining Tables in Queries

When you add tables to the Query window, Access sometimes displays join lines. A *join line* indicates that a relationship exists between two tables. The join line in figure 22.18 leads from the Customer ID field in tblCustomers to the Customer ID field in tblCars and visually indicates there is a one-to-many relationship between these tables.

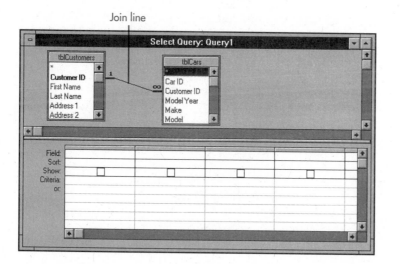

Join line

Figure 22.14
The join line between tblCustomers and tblCars.

IV

Microsoft Access

In this example, Access automatically displays a join line between the tblCustomers and tblCars tables. This happens because the tables were defined as being related using the Relationships command (found in the Edit menu when working with tables). One benefit, then, to defining relationships when building tables is that Access can automatically join tables in the Query window.

 For more information about editing table relationships, see Chapter 21, "Creating and Using Tables."

Not all pairs of tables will have a predefined relationship. In fact, you do not have to define any relationships at all. If you choose not to, however, you will have to define any necessary relationships as you build each query.

 The relationships you establish in the Query window have the same effect as relationships you create using the Relationships command, but they remain in effect only as long as the query is running. This means that when you close the query, the relationship no longer exists.

To join two tables in the Query window, drag a field from one of the tables to the matching field in the other table. Access joins the tables on the selected fields and displays a join line like that between tables in a "real" relationship.

By default, the join you create when you drag a field from one table to another is called an *inner join*, but you can choose a different type:

✔ **Inner join.** Sometimes called an equi-join, this type of join returns only those records for which the matching field value exists in both tables. If a record exists in either table but does not have a matching record in the other, it is not included in the query's result set.

Most multitable queries use inner joins. You might, for example, join an Orders table with a table containing order details. When you run the query, you want to return only orders that have detail records. Orders that have no detail are not returned by the query. Similarly, if there was a customer in tblCustomers who did not own a car, he would not appear in the query's results.

✔ **Left outer join.** With this type of join, the query returns records from the first table (the table on the left side in the Query window), even if there are no matching records in the second (right side) table.

You might, for example, create a query that uses a left outer join to identify order records that do not have any detail records. Orders without detail usually result from canceling an order after the main order record has been committed but before the detail is entered.

✔ **Right outer join.** This has the same effect as a left outer join except that it works in the opposite direction: the query returns records from the second (right side) table, even if there are no matching records in the first table. Depending on which table you add to the query first, you might need to create either a left or right outer join.

Although it is not entirely necessary to learn and understand the exact terminology used with table joins, it is important to know that Access can build a number of different relationships between tables. A little thought will provide the understanding necessary to correctly join your tables to return the data you want.

You can change the type of join by double-clicking on the join line between the two tables. Access then displays the Join Properties dialog box (see fig. 22.19).

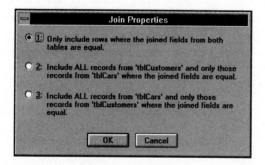

Figure 22.19
The Join Properties dialog box.

Select 1 if you want an inner join (the default), 2 for a left outer join, or 3 for a right outer join. When you select an outer join, the join line in the Query window changes from a solid line to a line with an arrowhead that points to the table whose records will be returned even if there are no matching records in the other table. The join line between the Orders and Order Details tables would point toward the Orders table, for example.

IV

Microsoft Access

Placing and Manipulating Fields in the QBE Grid

After you add the required tables to the upper portion of the Query window, there are several ways you can select the various fields you want to appear in the query:

✔ Drag the field from the field list to one of the columns in the QBE grid.

✔ In the table's field list box, double-click on the name of the field you want to add.

✔ Click on the Field cell in an empty column in the QBE grid and then select the field you want from its drop-down list.

✔ In the Field cell of an empty column, type the name of the desired field.

You can quickly add all the fields from a table to the grid at one time in any of several ways:

✔ Double-click on the asterisk that appears at the top of the table's field list box—the asterisk means "all fields." You also can drag the asterisk to a column in the QBE grid. Access displays a field name that is the name of the table followed by an asterisk (see fig. 22.20).

Figure 22.20
Adding all fields to the QBE grid by dragging the asterisk.

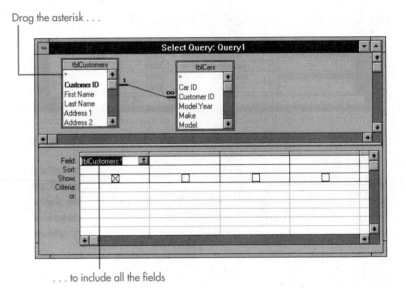

Drag the asterisk . . .

. . . to include all the fields

✔ Double-click on the table's title bar to highlight all the fields, and then drag the fields to the QBE grid. When you use this technique, Access lists each field individually in the grid (see fig. 22.21).

The advantage of using the asterisk method (described first) is that if you later change the table structure (add new fields, rename fields, and so on), the query will reflect the new table structure automatically. The asterisk will make Access use all fields in the table, even if their names have changed.

The second technique, in which you add all the fields individually, is preferable if you want to add most—but not all—of the fields. Add all the fields and then selectively remove the ones you do not need. Each field occupies a slot in the QBE grid. Therefore, if you later change the name of a field or add a field to the table, you will have to update the field names in the QBE grid.

Double-click on the title bar . . .

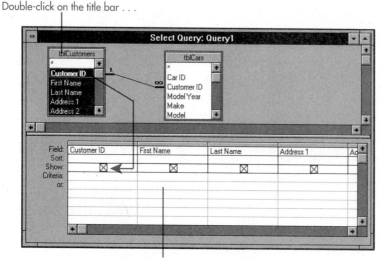

Figure 22.21
Dragging all fields to the QBE grid at once.

. . . and drag the fields to the QBE grid

Removing a Field from the QBE Grid

To remove a column from the QBE grid, click on the field selector (the thin, gray row above the field name in each column). The column in the QBE grid containing the field will be highlighted. Next, press Del or choose the De<u>l</u>ete command from the <u>E</u>dit menu. In figure 22.22, the Customer ID field is being removed because the data it contains is irrelevant to the query.

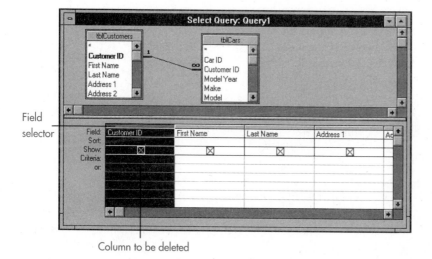

Figure 22.22
Deleting a field in the QBE grid.

Field selector

Column to be deleted

IV

Microsoft Access

Tip

To delete a block of fields from the QBE grid, highlight the first column to be deleted, scroll to the last column, and click on its field selector while holding down the Shift key. This will select the first, last, and all columns in between. You then can delete these columns by pressing Del.

After the column is removed, the other columns in the QBE grid move to the left to occupy the space left by the deleted column (see fig. 22.23).

Figure 22.23
Other columns move to the left.

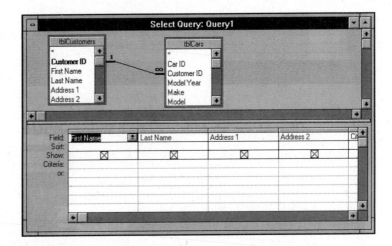

Moving a Field in the QBE Grid

The columns in the dynaset (see figs. 22.6, 22.8, and 22.9) appear in the order in which they occur in the QBE grid. Columns are sequentially added to the QBE grid from left to right, which might not be the order in which you want them to appear in the dynaset. To move a column in the QBE grid, select and highlight the column by clicking on the field selector. Then drag the field selector to its new location (see fig. 22.24).

As you drag the column, a vertical bar will appear where the column will be moved when the mouse button is released. In this example, the Last Name column is being moved to the first column. The vertical bar appears to the left of the First Name column.

When you move a column to the left of an existing column, all the columns to the right are moved over to make room for the new column.

After the move, the column will remain highlighted (see fig. 22.25). Make sure you do not accidentally press Del while the column is highlighted, or you will delete it from the QBE grid.

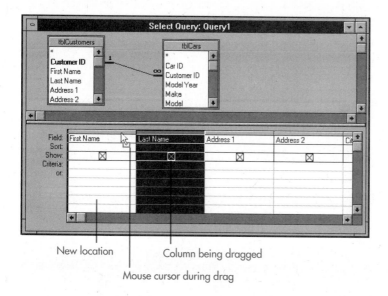

Figure 22.24
Moving a column in the QBE grid.

New location

Column being dragged

Mouse cursor during drag

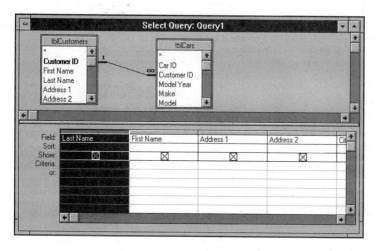

Figure 22.25
The column remains highlighted after the move.

Another way to move columns to the right is to insert a new column. Highlight the column where you want to add a new column (click on its field selector) and then press Ins or choose the Insert Column command from the Edit menu. The inserted column will appear to the left of the highlighted column.

IV

Microsoft Access

Using Aliases

Sometimes the table field names are too short, too long, or too cryptic to be useful. You might have a table with field names such as BusName or Addr1 that you would rather call Company Name and Street Address, for example.

To change the name of a field in a table, you can assign an alias to the field. An *alias* is a name you use in place of the real name of an object (a table field, in this case). Aliases are particularly useful because they enable you to create query results that reflect plain-English column headings instead of the names from the tables.

When you use an alias, you rename fields in the query to make them more meaningful without actually changing the names in the underlying tables. Not changing the real name means that forms, reports, macros, Access Basic code, and other queries that use the existing name will continue to work.

To create an alias, go to the field name in the QBE grid and enter the name of the alias to the left of the existing field name, followed by a colon. In figure 22.26 the alias "Serviced" is being applied to the column Date Last Serviced.

Figure 22.26

Creating an alias for the Date Last Serviced field.

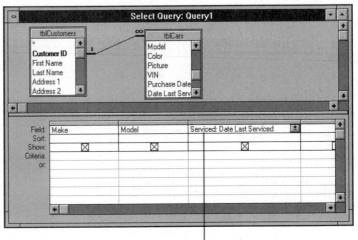

Alias for Date Last Serviced

When the query is returned to Datasheet view (see fig 22.27), the alias appears as the heading for the column holding the Date Last Serviced data.

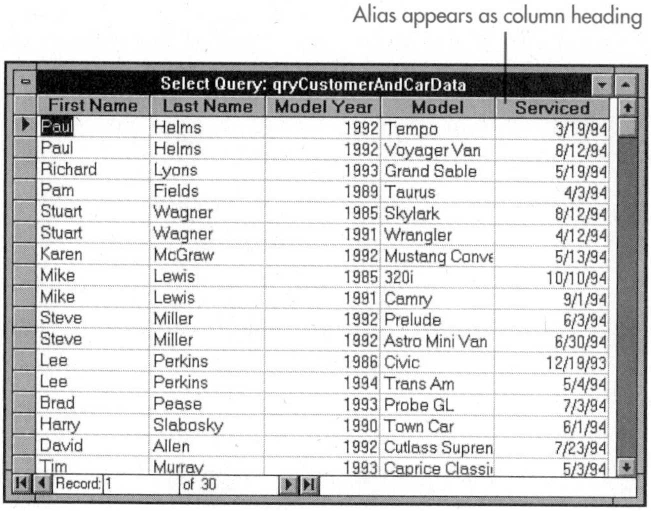

Alias appears as column heading

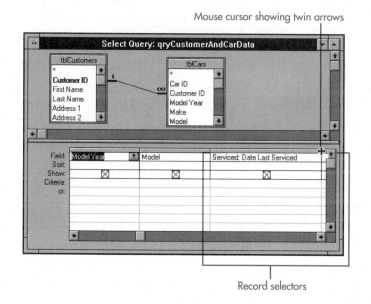

Figure 22.27
The Serviced alias appears as the column heading.

Sometimes the entries in the QBE grid will be too wide to appear in the column without truncating the text. You can make a column wider (or narrower) by dragging on the record selector at the border between two adjacent columns. When the mouse pointer changes to a double-headed arrow, drag the border to resize the column width (see fig. 22.28).

Mouse cursor showing twin arrows

Figure 22.28
Adjusting the width of a column in the QBE grid.

Record selectors

IV

Microsoft Access

In this example, the alias (Serviced) and the field name (Date Last Serviced) are too wide to fit the column width. Resizing the column to make it wider will enable the entire alias and field name to be read.

Sorting Queries

Sorting the data in your query in alphabetic or numeric order often makes the data easier to interpret and analyze. You can sort the results of the query on one or more fields so that you can customize the order in which the data appears. You might sort a list of customers in alphabetical order according to their names, for example, or a list of last-serviced dates in ascending order to put the cars most need in service at the top of the list.

To sort a query by the contents of a single field, click on the Sort cell for the field you want to sort, and then open the drop-down list box to reveal three sort-type options (see fig. 22.29).

Figure 22.29
Selecting a sort order.

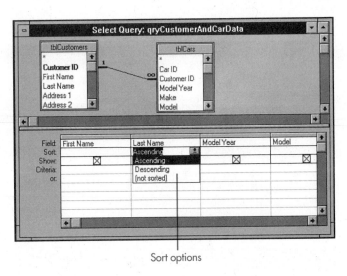

Sort options

The default is to present the data in an unsorted order—not sorted. What this actually means is that Access will not apply any special sorting rules; if the underlying data is unsorted, the query results also will be unsorted. If the underlying data is sorted (as happens when you select a field that is a primary key), then the data will appear in sorted order. As a rule, however, if you want the data sorted in a particular order, you should choose one of the following sort orders, instead of relying on Access to sort it automatically:

✔ **Ascending.** Choose ascending when you want the data to appear with the lower values first (A–Z, 0–9). If you sort customer names in ascending order, for example, names that begin with A appear before names that begin with B, and so on.

✔ **Descending.** Choose descending when you want the values to appear with the higher values first (Z–A, 9–0). If you want to prepare a list of service records with the most recent at the top and older records at the bottom, select a descending sort.

You can sort on more than one field, each with its own sort order. To sort on multiple fields, move the fields to the left side of the QBE grid so that the most significant field (Last Name, in this example) appears first, followed by the other fields (see fig. 22.30).

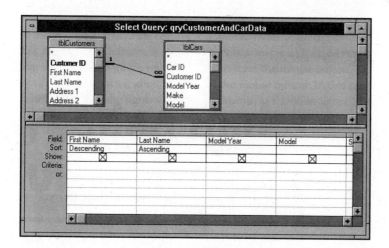

Figure 22.30
Sorting on more than one field.

Access sorts the fields from left to right. In this example, Access sorts the listings by Last Name (ascending) first, then sorts by Date Last Serviced in descending order.

In this particular example, there is not much difference between query results sorted on both the customer last name and service date and results sorted on last name alone. Normally, there must be enough records with the same value in the leftmost column (for instance, a name like Smith or Jones) to make it worth sorting on a second column. If there were 20 or 30 Smiths in the list, the effect of sorting on the second column would be significant. With only one or two Smiths in the list, the difference is negligible.

Entering Criteria for Selecting Records

One of Access's greatest strengths is its capability to present information in a usable format. Instead of listing all the data in the underlying tables in an ordered fashion, you can restrict the records to just those that meet certain criteria.

As you add new listings to the tblCars table, for example, it will quickly grow well beyond the 30 or so records it has today. Over time, the complete listing will become unmanageable—it simply will be too much information to be useful, even when sorted. You might, for instance, want to concentrate a search for cars serviced before a particular date without having to scan listings for all other cars (see fig. 22.31). These cars might be overdue for service, and the Carmel Car Care shop should call them to arrange for a periodic maintenance service.

Figure 22.31 Setting criteria for selecting records.

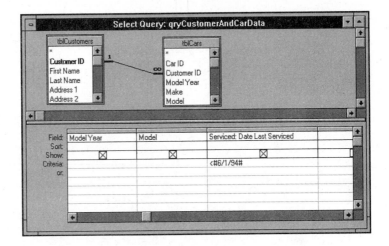

In this example, only those cars serviced before June 1, 1994, will be returned by the query (see fig. 22.32).

Select Query: qryCustomerAndCarData

First Name	Last Name	Model Year	Model	Serviced
Tom	Reid	1992	Villager Van	5/1/94
Tim	Murray	1993	Caprice Classi	5/3/94
Stuart	Wagner	1991	Wrangler	4/12/94
Sarah	Miller	1993	Maxima	5/5/94
Richard	Lyons	1993	Grand Sable	5/19/94
Paul	Helms	1992	Tempo	3/19/94
Pam	Fields	1989	Taurus	4/3/94
Linda	Matthews	1988	Corolla	5/4/94
Lee	Perkins	1994	Trans Am	5/4/94
Lee	Perkins	1986	Civic	12/19/93
Karen	McGraw	1992	Mustang Conve	5/13/94
Jim	Wagner	1989	Spectrum	5/17/94
Jim	Wagner	1993	Grand Am	7/1/93
David	Lovett	1989	626 4-door	4/3/94
David	Lovett	1992	Cutlass	5/30/94

Record: 1 of 15

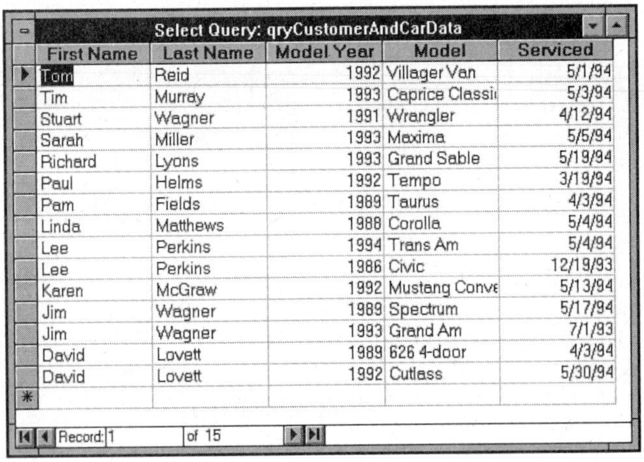

Figure 22.32 The restricted query returns a subset of the underlying table.

In this example, only 15 of the 30 service records appear in the query's results. To restrict the records, you enter an expression (<#6/1/94#) in the Criteria line of the QBE grid for the column you want to restrict (Date Last Serviced). This simple expression means "select all records where the Date Last Serviced field is less (that is, earlier) than June 1, 1994."

Note

Some criteria expressions are relatively simple (a single word or number), whereas others are more complex (specifying functions and logical operators). More complex expressions are discussed in the next section.

The preceding example illustrates how you can enter a simple expression: simply type the text of the criteria. Access even inserts the pound signs (#) it requires around the date. If the text consists of a single word, Access automatically supplies the quotation marks needed to indicate a text string. If the text consists of two or more words, however, you must enter the quotation marks yourself; if you do not, Access displays an error message when you move off the Criteria line.

You can enter dates in any standard date format, such as 6/1/94 or 1-Jun-94. Access automatically recognizes such entries as dates and converts them to the date format specified in the International section of the Windows control panel.

If an expression contains numbers other than dates or parts of text, type the numbers without any special characters (that is, do not enter quotation marks or number signs).

To specify criteria for a Yes/No field, enter Yes, True, On, or –1 to find a Yes value; or No, False, Off, or 0 to find a No value.

To view the results of the query, click on the Datasheet View or Run button on the toolbar, or choose the Datasheet command from the <u>V</u>iew menu or the <u>R</u>un command from the <u>Q</u>uery menu.

Excluding Fields from the Query Results

You might want to sort on a field or apply selection criteria to a field that you do not want to appear in the results of the query. When you select only those service records before June 1, 1994, for example, you might not even need the actual date the car was last serviced to appear in the results of the query. It might be enough to know that the car is overdue for service; therefore, the exact date is irrelevant.

To keep a field from appearing in the results of the query, clear the Show check box in the QBE grid (see fig. 22.33) by clicking on it.

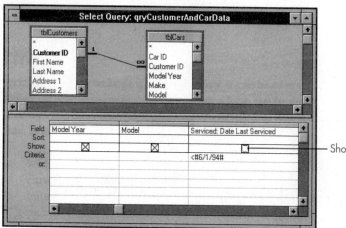

Figure 22.33
The Serviced field will be excluded from the dynaset.

Show check box

IV

Microsoft Access

When you run this query, the selection criteria is still applied to the field; it just does not appear in the results (see fig. 22.34). In fact, any sort directive specified in the QBE grid will be applied as well, even though the column does not appear in the results set. The data in figure 22.34 is sorted in the same order (descending by the Date Last Serviced field) as in figure 22.32, even though the Serviced column does not appear.

Figure 22.34
The results set of
the query with the
Serviced column
excluded.

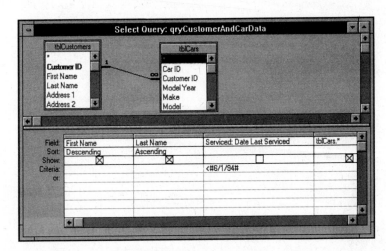

Excluding fields by clearing the Show box is an especially useful technique when you include all fields in a table by dragging the asterisk to the QBE grid but want to apply criteria or sort on one or more fields. You could create a query equivalent to the preceding example by dragging not only the asterisk to the grid, but the other necessary "criteria" fields as well (see fig. 22.35).

Figure 22.35
Excluding fields
when you use the
asterisk.

In figure 22.35, all the fields from the tblCars table will be included in the results set, but the data will be sorted first by the Service field, then by the customer's last name (the customer names, of course, are from tblCustomers). Since the Serviced field appears to the left of the Last Name field, the sort on Serviced will have precedence over the sort on the Last Name field, yet the Serviced field will not appear as the leftmost column in the results set.

To create a query like you see in figure 22.35, first add all the fields by dragging the asterisk to the grid. Then, drag to the grid the fields that need criteria or sorting, and clear the Show check boxes for those fields. If you do not clear the Show check boxes, the fields will appear twice in the query results.

Exploring Select Queries

Select queries are the most common kind of query you will create in Access. Select queries choose records from one or more tables in the database (or attached tables from other database files such as FoxPro, dBASE, or Paradox) according to various criteria you specify. All queries start out as select queries until you change them to one of the other types of queries.

You can view the selected data directly in a datasheet, or you can use the results as the source of information for forms or reports. When you view the results in a datasheet, you are actually looking at a dynaset. A *dynaset* is a real-time representation of the underlying tables. In a multiuser environment, whenever another user changes the tables, Access updates your view of that same data (hence the name dynaset which comes from *dyna*mic *set*). Likewise, whenever you edit data in the query datasheet, other users see your changes.

The following example shows the steps to create a query that returns customers in a specified city, and cars with certain charateristics.

1. Go to the Database window, click on the Query button or tab, and then click on the <u>N</u>ew button. Bypass the Query Wizard by clicking on the <u>N</u>ew Query button in the message box shown in fig 22.36.

2. In the Add Table dialog box, add both the tblCustomers and tblCars to the query design grid, then click on the <u>C</u>lose button (see fig. 22.37).

IV

Microsoft Access

Figure 22.36
Choosing between a Query Wizard or manual design.

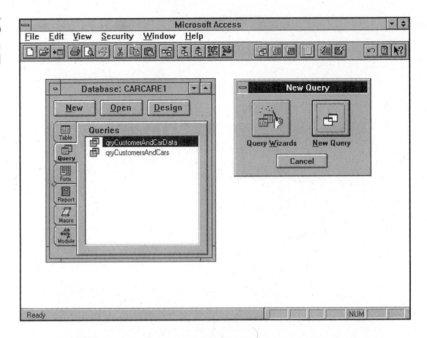

Figure 22.37
The query design grid with tables added.

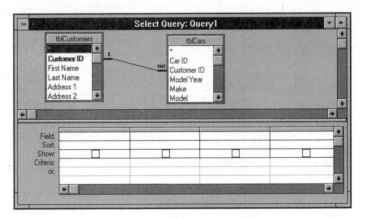

3. Adjust the size and location of the table list boxes to suit you. (see fig. 22.38).

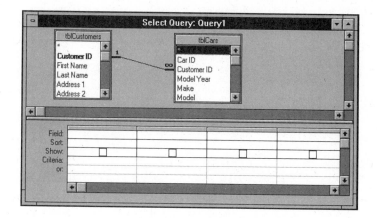

Figure 22.38
Adjusting the table list boxes.

4. Add the First Name, Last Name and City fields from the tblCustomers. The query should return records for only those customers who live in Carmel. In the City column, enter "**Carmel**" as the selection criterion (see fig. 22.39).

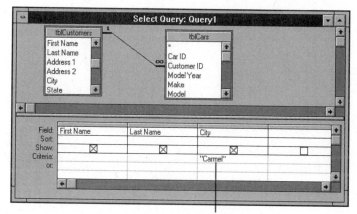

Figure 22.39
Entering the selection criterion in the City column.

Records limited to "Carmel"

5. Because all the records returned will be for customers who live in one city, there is no need to include the City field in the query results. Clear the Show box in the City column (see fig. 22.40).

Figure 22.40
Eliminating the
City field from the
query results.

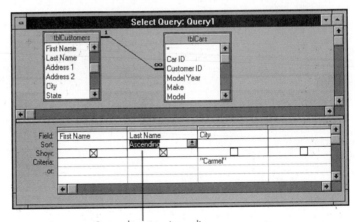

Clear Show check box

6. The customer records should appear in alphabetical order. In the Last Name
    column, set the sort order to Ascending, as shown in figure 22.41.

Figure 22.41
Setting the sort
order for
ascending
alphabetical
order.

Sort order set to Ascending

7. If necessary, enter additional selection criteria for other fields.

8. Review the results of the query by clicking on the Datasheet View button on the
    toolbar. The results are shown in figure 22.42.

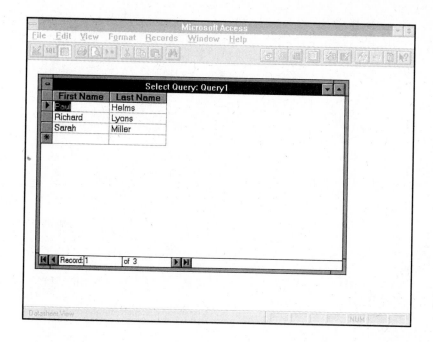

Figure 22.42
The completed query.

In this example, only three records meet the criteria entered in the QBE grid.

9. If necessary, refine the query by changing the criteria or entering additional criteria in other fields.

10. When you are satisfied with the results of the query, choose the Save Query As command from the File menu (if you are in Design view when you save the query, the command is called Save As). Access displays the Save As dialog box (see fig. 22.43), in which you can specify the name of the new query.

Figure 22.43
Entering qryCarmelCustomers in the Save As dialog box.

11. Add the Make and Model fields from the tblCars to the query design grid.

After the query is named, the text shown in the result set title bar changes accordingly (see fig. 22.44).

Microsoft Access

Figure 22.44
The new name
appears in the
title bar.

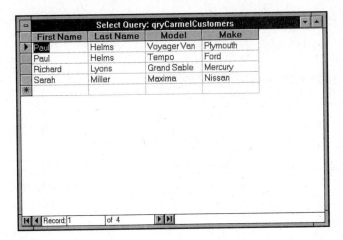

When run, the query now returns four records because one customer has two cars. The select query you just created now appears in the Database window along with the other queries. Any time this query is opened, you will see the records of all customers who live in Carmel. As the data in the underlying tables (tblCustomers and tblCars) changes, the data displayed by this query will change.

You can reopen the query to make changes, or you can open it directly from the Database window by clicking on the Open button. Once a query is named, it becomes a permanent part of the database, even though the data returned by the query might change.

If you use the query as the record source for a form or a report, the form or report will include only the records selected by the query.

Using Operators in Query Expressions

Access is not limited to simple queries such as those presented earlier in this chapter. Indeed, you can create more powerful queries with expressions containing *operators* (words identifying certain operations that should be performed) and *operands* (the words or numbers referred to by the operators).

For example, you can use the Between...And, Like, and Not operators to qualify and select text fields. You can use the mathematical operators (for example, =, <, >, >=, and <=) to work with numbers and dates. In some contexts, you also can use the mathematical operators with text fields.

The Or Operator

In the Criteria row of the QBE grid, you can use the Or operator to choose a record if the value in the field is either of two (or more) values. To return records for customers who live in either Carmel or Indianapolis, for example, enter the following criteria expression:

`"Carmel" Or "Indianapolis"`

In this example, the strings "Carmel" and "Indianapolis" are the operands to the Or operator. Any customer who does not live in either of the specified values will be omitted from the query results.

The Between...And Operator

The Between...And operator enables you to specify a range of values (see fig. 22.45).

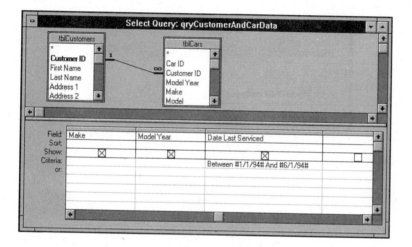

Figure 22.45

Using Between...And to specify a range of criteria values.

In this example, the criteria will select only service records with dates between January 1, 1994 and June 1, 1994. 1/1/94 and 6/1/94 are operands; Between and And are the operators. Remember that Access will automatically add the pound signs around dates, as long as you enter them in a format that Access understands (6/1/94, 1-June-94, and so on).

The results set from the query in figure 22.45 is shown in figure 22.46.

IV

Microsoft Access

Figure 22.46
Only records with service dates between January 1 and June 1 appear.

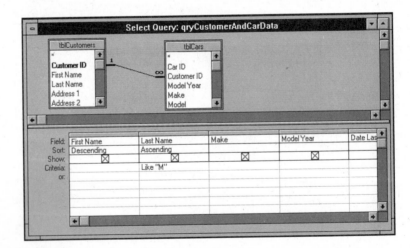

First Name	Last Name	Make	Model Year	Date Last Se
Tom	Reid	Mercury	1992	5/1/94
Tim	Murray	Chevrolet	1993	5/3/94
Stuart	Wagner	Jeep	1991	4/12/94
Sarah	Miller	Nissan	1993	5/5/94
Richard	Lyons	Mercury	1993	5/19/94
Paul	Helms	Ford	1992	3/19/94
Pam	Fields	Ford	1989	4/3/94
Linda	Matthews	Toyota	1988	5/4/94
Lee	Perkins	Pontiac	1994	5/4/94
Karen	McGraw	Ford	1992	5/13/94
Jim	Wagner	Chevrolet	1989	5/17/94
Harry	Slabosky	Lincoln	1990	6/1/94
David	Lovett	Mazda	1989	4/3/94
David	Lovett	Olds	1992	5/30/94

The Like Operator

If you do not need an exact match, you can substitute wild cards for certain characters in a Like expression. In Access, the asterisk (*) wild card stands for any number of characters (including no characters); the question mark (?) wild card stands for any single character.

For example, you can select all customers whose last names start with *M*, as shown in the Last Name field in figure 22.47. The results of the query include all customers whose last names begin with *M* and end with any number of other characters (see fig. 22.48).

Figure 22.47
Using the Like operator to specify a selection pattern.

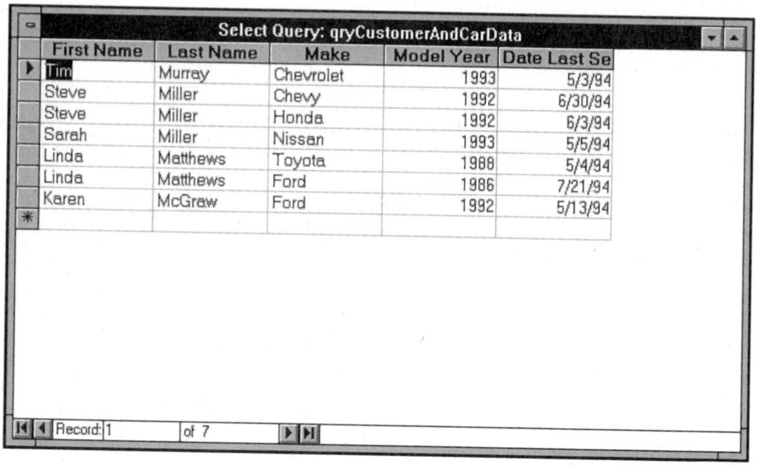

First Name	Last Name	Make	Model Year	Date Last Se
Tim	Murray	Chevrolet	1993	5/3/94
Steve	Miller	Chevy	1992	6/30/94
Steve	Miller	Honda	1992	6/3/94
Sarah	Miller	Nissan	1993	5/5/94
Linda	Matthews	Toyota	1988	5/4/94
Linda	Matthews	Ford	1986	7/21/94
Karen	McGraw	Ford	1992	5/13/94

Record: 1 of 7

Figure 22.48
Results of a query that selects certain customers.

The In Operator

Use the In operator to select records that match one of a list of specific values. This operator has the same effect as using multiple Or operators, but can be more convenient to use when you have a long list of values against which to validate the records. You can use In, for example, to select records for which a state field has values in a particular set of valid states:

> In ("CT", "MA", "NH", "NJ", "NY", "VT")

To achieve the same effect with the Or operator, you would have to enter this longer, somewhat more cumbersome expression:

> "CT" Or "MA" Or "NH" Or "NJ" Or "NY" Or "VT"

The Not Operator

If you want to exclude records based on the selection criteria, add the Not operator. If you want to include all records except those for which the state is in a specified list, for example, use the following expression:

> Not In ("CT", "MA", "NH", "NJ", "NY", "VT")

Tip

To count the number of records found by a query, create a new query and add to it the query whose records you want to count. Then, enter **Count (*)** in the field row of the query. When you switch to Datasheet view, you see the number of records in the dynaset.

IV

Microsoft Access

The Is Null Operator

You can use the Is Null operator to determine whether a field contains a value. You might want to prepare a phone listing of customers, for example, but include only those customers whose records contain phone numbers (see fig. 22.49).

Figure 22.49
Using the Is Null operator.

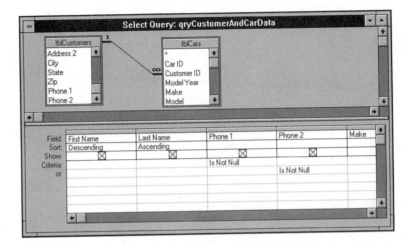

In the example shown in figure 22.49, the criteria are placed on separate lines. If you place them on the same line, Access interprets the criteria as "there is an entry in the Phone 1 field *and* an entry in the Phone 2 field," which is not the goal.

Calculated Fields

Within a column in the QBE grid, you can refer to another field by enclosing its name in brackets ([ ]). This technique is useful when you create calculated fields, such as by multiplying two fields. For instance, you can create an entirely new field named Total in the result set by entering the following in the Field row of the QBE grid:

```
Total: [Unit Price] * [Quantity]
```

where Unit Price and Quantity are the names of fields in one of the tables underlying the query. In this example, the calculated field, Total, is the product of the Unit Price and Quantity fields from the underlying table.

Combining Fields

Another good use of calculated fields is to concatenate (combine) text fields. In tblCustomers, the first and last names are stored in separate fields. It is easy to concatenate the first and last names so that they will appear together in the results set (see figure 22.50).

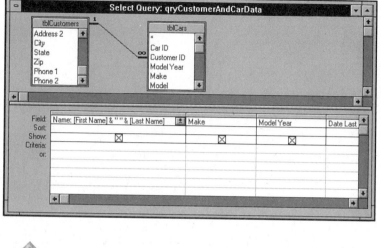

Figure 22.50
Combining text
fields with the &
operator.

Generally speaking, it is a good idea to keep data such as first and last names in separate fields. It is much easier to construct queries to look for people's records when their first and last names appear in separate fields. Also, it is much easier to sort by first or last names when they appear in separate fields.

The expression `Name: [First Name] & " " & [Last Name]` in figure 22.50 does two things. First, it creates a new field in the results set named Name. Second, it combines data from the First Name and Last Name fields and puts it into the Name field.

Notice the search and sorting criteria applied in figure 22.50. The Name field will be sorted in ascending order, and only cars newer than 1991 models will be included in the results set. The Name field concatenates both names into one field, inserting a space between them for readability (the space is added with the `& " " &`).

Unlike other development environments that use the plus sign (+) to concatenate text, Access uses the ampersand operator (&).

The query results in a single field that occupies less horizontal space than do two separate fields (see fig. 22.51).

Figure 22.51
The result of concatenating two text fields.

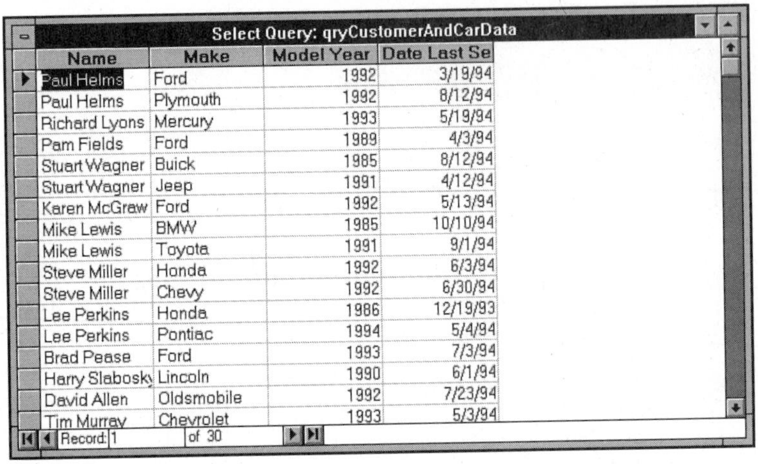

Name	Make	Model Year	Date Last Se
Paul Helms	Ford	1992	3/19/94
Paul Helms	Plymouth	1992	8/12/94
Richard Lyons	Mercury	1993	5/19/94
Pam Fields	Ford	1989	4/3/94
Stuart Wagner	Buick	1985	8/12/94
Stuart Wagner	Jeep	1991	4/12/94
Karen McGraw	Ford	1992	5/13/94
Mike Lewis	BMW	1985	10/10/94
Mike Lewis	Toyota	1991	9/1/94
Steve Miller	Honda	1992	6/3/94
Steve Miller	Chevy	1992	6/30/94
Lee Perkins	Honda	1986	12/19/93
Lee Perkins	Pontiac	1994	5/4/94
Brad Pease	Ford	1993	7/3/94
Harry Slabosky	Lincoln	1990	6/1/94
David Allen	Oldsmobile	1992	7/23/94
Tim Murray	Chevrolet	1993	5/3/94

Select Query: qryCustomerAndCarData
Record: 1 of 30

Tip

When you create more complex expressions that extend beyond the width of the QBE grid column, you can either widen the column or open the Zoom box to view or edit the entry. To open the Zoom box, press Shift+F2. Close the Zoom box by clicking on the OK button or pressing Esc or Enter. (Pressing Esc cancels any editing done in the Zoom box.)

Totaling Fields in Queries

Calculating totals for records in a table is easy—simply drag the field you want to total to the QBE grid, and then click on the Totals button on the toolbar. Access displays a Total row in the QBE grid, as shown in figure 22.52.

Figure 22.52
Adding totals to a query.

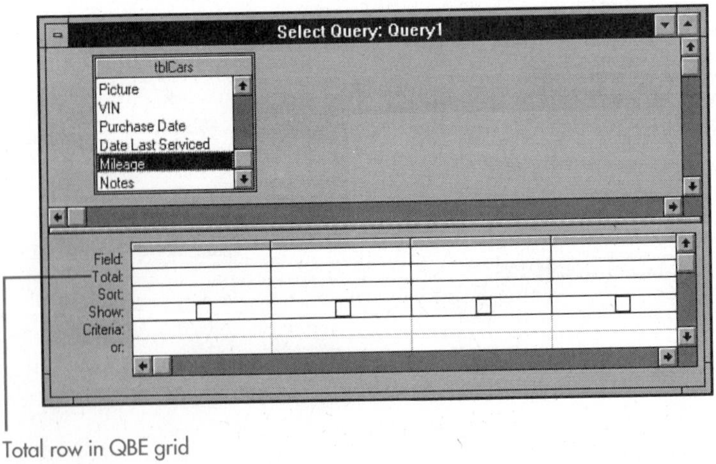

Select Query: Query1

tblCars
Picture
VIN
Purchase Date
Date Last Serviced
Mileage
Notes

Field:
Total:
Sort:
Show:
Criteria:
or:

Total row in QBE grid

You can select from a number of different kinds of totals (see fig. 22.53).

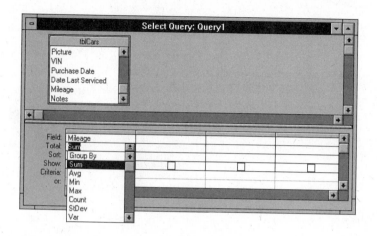

Figure 22.53
Select the desired
kind of total from
the drop-down list.

For instance, although it might not make a lot of sense to compute this kind of total, selecting the Sum total on the Mileage field in the tblCars table returns the results set shown in figure 22.54.

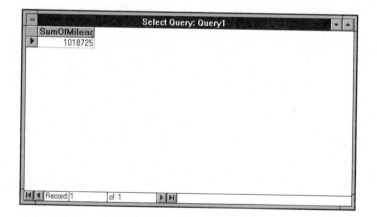

Figure 22.54
The results set for
a sum total on the
Mileage field.

The results in figure 22.54 mean that the cars in the tblCars table have a total of 1,018,725 miles on them. The Sum total adds a field to the results set and calculates the sum on all the records in the field.

More complex totals are possible. Figure 22.55 illustrates the effect of adding a Group By total to the Make field along with the Average total on the Mileage column. The result is that the mileage for all cars of the same make is averaged and displayed in each row in figure 22.55. Similar results could be obtained for the other fields in tblCars (Model Year, Model, and so on). You could even determine if blue cars have more miles on them than red cars!

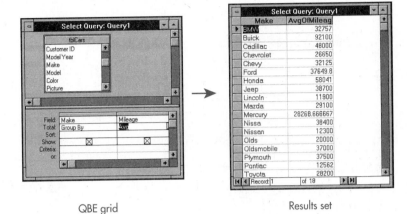

Figure 22.55
The Mileage field
is averaged for
each car make.

QBE grid   Results set

Finally, because queries can combine data from multiple tables, you can determine totals based on relationships between tables. For instance, you quite easily could determine the total number of miles on all cars owned by Paul Helms.

The total options are described in the following list:

✔ **Group By.** Groups records according to the values in the field. This has the same effect as creating a report that has group headers. An example is shown in figure 22.55.

✔ **Sum.** (Total) Returns the sum of the values in the field. This option is particularly useful when you combine this with a field totaled with the Group By option. Figures 22.54 and 22.55 illustrate the Sum total.

✔ **Avg.** (Average) Returns an average of the values in the field. In figure 22.56, the average mileage for each make of car in tblCars has been calculated. The Make column in the QBE grid was set to Group By in the Total row and the Mileage column was set to Ave.

✔ **Min.** (Minimum) Returns the lowest value. For instance, the lowest mileage of any car or any car of a particular year could be determined.

✔ **Max.** (Maximum) Returns the highest value.

✔ **Count.** Returns a count of the number of records. It would be easy to find out how many Fords, Buicks, and other makes of cars were in tblCars using the Count total (refer to figure 22.56).

✔ **StDev.** (Standard Deviation) Returns the standard deviation (a measure of the dispersion of the frequency variation, equal to the square root of the variance).

✔ **Var.** (Variance) Returns the variance of the values in the field; equal to the square of the standard deviation.

✔ **First.** Returns the field value from the first record.

✔ **Last.** Returns the field value from the last record.

✔ **Expression.** Select this option to create a calculated field in the query. Use this when you want to create an expression involving multiple functions.

✔ **Where.** Select this option to specify criteria for a field on which you are not grouping. When you use the Where option, you must clear the Show box.

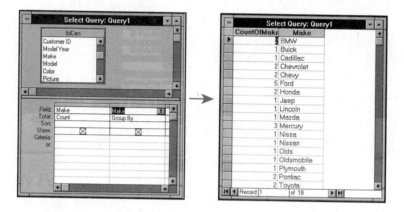

QBE grid

Results set

Figure 22.56
Counting the number of cars of each make in tblCars.

For more information about using the Expression and Where options, search Access Help for Calculating Totals in a Query.

Exploring Action Queries

Unlike select queries that simply retrieve data from the underlying tables, action queries actually change the data in tables. You can use action queries to add, delete, and change data, and even to create new tables from existing records. You can run an action query to delete obsolete records from a table, for example.

Action queries appear in the Database window with an exclamation point next to their names (see fig. 22.57).

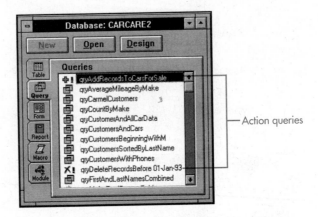

Figure 22.57
Action queries appear in the Database window with a special icon.

The exclamation point is your visual cue that when you click on the **O**pen button, *the query will make changes to data* (unlike select queries, which simply display data when you open them).

To create an action query, create a select query following the steps outlined earlier in this chapter. Then, open the **Q**uery menu and choose the appropriate command for the desired type of query (see fig. 22.58), or choose the appropriate action query button from the toolbar.

Figure 22.58
Selecting the type of query in the Query menu.

You can choose from two kinds of select queries (select and crosstab), plus the following four kinds of action queries:

✔ **Make-table.** Creates a new table based on existing data in other tables.

✔ **Update.** Changes existing records.

✔ **Append.** Adds records to an existing table.

✔ **Delete.** Deletes records from an existing table.

Tip

You can convert one kind of query into any of the other kinds. This is particularly useful when you want to review the records an action query will act upon before you actually run the query. To do this, construct a select query that uses the same selection criteria. Then, open the query in Datasheet view to confirm the correct records have indeed been selected. After you are satisfied with the criteria, convert the query to the appropriate action query.

Make-Table Queries

Use a make-table query when you want to create a new table based on records from other, existing tables. Make-table queries are particularly useful when you want to combine information from two tables and create a single table to be used in other database programs (you can export only tables, not the results of a query).

You might want to create a table that combines various information and export that table to the dBASE database format, for example. If you have a program that can import dBASE databases, a make-table query is a handy way to create a table in Access that the other program can use.

The following example illustrates the steps to create a make-table query that combines information from two tables (tblCustomers and tblCars) and exports the table to a dBASE-compatible file.

1. Create a select query that includes the tables and fields that return all the information you want to export (see fig. 22.59).

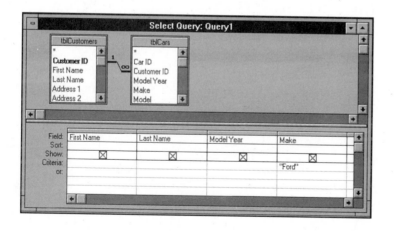

Figure 22.59
Building a select query.

2. Display the query in Datasheet view to make sure the results of the query reflect the records you want to export. In this example, the table includes all customers who own Fords and the year and model of their cars. Return to Design view and, if necessary, revise the query to get exactly the data you expect.

3. Choose the Make Table command from the Query menu or click on the Make Table button in the toolbar. Access displays the Query Properties dialog box (see fig. 22.60), in which you can enter the name of the new table.

Figure 22.60
The Query Properties dialog box.

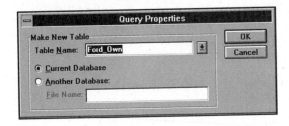

Because the new table eventually will be exported, you can leave the Current Database option button selected; you can build the new table in a different database, however.

As you enter the name of the new table, keep in mind where the table will be used. If you intend to export the table to dBASE, Access will use only the first eight characters (Ford_Own, which will be converted to FORD_OWN during export). If the table will remain in Access, consider longer, more descriptive names (tblAllFordOwners).

4. When you click on OK, Access closes the dialog box. To create the new table, click on the Run button on the toolbar. If you try to run a make table query in a database that already has a table with the same name as entered in the Query Properties dialog box, Access displays a message box with an appropriate warning (see fig. 22.61).

Figure 22.61
Access warns you that you will delete an existing table.

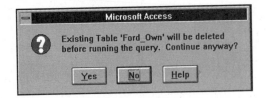

If you click on OK, Access creates the new table.

5. Save the query (if desired) and then go to the Database window (see fig. 22.62), in which the new table now appears.

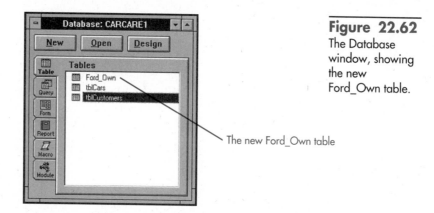

Figure 22.62
The Database
window, showing
the new
Ford_Own table.

The new Ford_Own table

6. Choose the <u>E</u>xport command from the <u>F</u>ile menu. Access opens the Export dialog box, shown in figure 22.63, in which you can select the desired file format for the file.

Figure 22.63
The Export dialog
box.

In this example, the table will be exported to the dBASE IV format.

7. When you click on OK, Access displays a list of all the tables, queries, or both in the database in the Select Microsoft Access Object dialog box, as shown in figure 22.64.

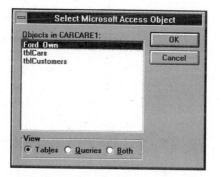

Figure 22.64
The Select Microsoft
Access Object dialog
box.

8. Select the table you want to export and then click on OK. Access displays the Export to File dialog box.

9. In the dialog box, go to the directory to which you want to export the table and then type the name of the new file. When you click on OK, Access exports the table to the specified file.

Update Queries

Use update queries to change information in existing tables. You create an update query much like the other kinds of queries, except that you specify a new value for a specified field.

You might want to update a products table by increasing the product prices by 5 percent, for example, or by setting a field to the same date when you send a mass mailing to selected customers. Update queries save you the time you otherwise would spend if you had to change each record individually.

In the following examples, assume Carmel Car Care has a number of used cars for sale. In order to reduce the unsold inventory, the asking price on all cars that are three or more years old (that is, built in 1991 or earlier) is to be reduced by 15 percent. The update query needs to update the selling price of all the cars in Carmel Car Care's inventory.

The initial data is shown in figure 22.65. Notice the values in the Price column.

Figure 22.65
The tblCarsForSale table.

Car ID	Model Year	Price	Make	VIN
1	1989	$9,000.00	Ford	IFABP7435K1378828
2	1985	$12,300.00	BMW	WBAAA9031H03462
3	1986	$500.00	Honda	
4	1992	$4,500.00	Ford	JFABP754K71344XY
5	1990	$32,000.00	Lincoln	
6	1994	$15,000.00	Pontiac	AJILO23456UXUS11
7	1993	$24,000.00	Ford	JDIU8907XU1287A2
10	1991	$18,000.00	Cadillac	
11	1993	$20,000.00	Chevrolet	
12	1992	$5,600.00	Mercury	MUABZ754K993721
13	1992	$21,000.00	Oldsmobile	
14	1986	$45,000.00	Ford	JFABP754K17388
15	1990	$200.00	Nissa	
16	1993	$4,500.00	BMW	WBABAH234624423
17	1991	$7,000.00	Chevy	
19	1992	$1,000.00	Honda	HKS1U234X7892789
20	1992	$3,800.00	Ford	

Table: tblCarsForSale
Record: 1 of 25

First, start with a select query that returns the desired records. Then choose the Update command from the Query menu. Access displays a new Update To row in the QBE grid (see fig. 22.66).

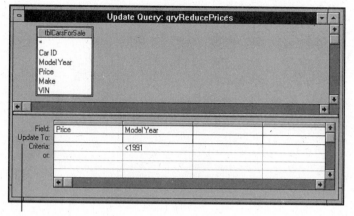

Figure 22.66
Creating an update query.

The Update To row

Next, enter a new value or an expression in the Update To row for the column (field) you want to update (see fig. 22.67). For this example, this is the Price field.

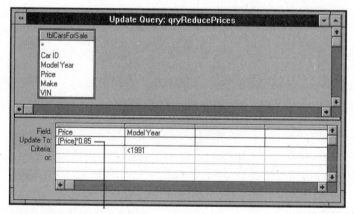

Figure 22.67
Setting a new value for the Price field.

Setting a new value

In this example, the new value will be the existing unit price less 15 percent.

Note If a column has no value or expression in the Update To row, Access treats the column as a selection criterion. Only fields that have an update value are changed by the query. There is no Sort row in the QBE grid because update queries do not return rows and there is no need to sort the data.

IV

Microsoft Access

The result of the update query is shown in figure 22.68. Notice that the asking price of each car built in 1991 or earlier has been reduced by 15 percent.

Figure 22.68
The tblCarsForSale table after updating.

Table: tblCarsForSale				
Car ID	Model Year	Price	Make	VIN
1	1989	$7,650.00	Ford	IFABP7435K1378828
2	1985	$10,455.00	BMW	WBAAA9031H03462
3	1986	$425.00	Honda	
4	1992	$4,500.00	Ford	JFABP754K71344X\
5	1990	$27,200.00	Lincoln	
6	1994	$15,000.00	Pontiac	AJILO23456UXUS11
7	1993	$24,000.00	Ford	JDIU8907XU1287A2
10	1991	$18,000.00	Cadillac	
11	1993	$20,000.00	Chevrolet	
12	1992	$5,600.00	Mercury	MUABZ754K993721
13	1992	$21,000.00	Oldsmobile	
14	1986	$38,250.00	Ford	JFABP754K17388
15	1990	$170.00	Nissa	
16	1993	$4,500.00	BMW	WBABAH234624423
17	1991	$7,000.00	Chevy	
19	1992	$1,000.00	Honda	HKS1U234X7892789
20	1992	$3,800.00	Ford	

Record: 1 of 25

Append Queries

Use an append query to add new records to a table using data from existing tables or the results of other queries. When you append data, the tables involved in the query do not need to have the same structure, although the data types of the appended fields must match. When you append records to a table, the records in the original table remain intact; Access does not delete the original records.

Append queries are particularly useful when you want to merge information from another database. The following example illustrates the steps you would take to create an append query that adds records from a dBASE file.

1. Using the Attach Table command in the File menu, attach the table that contains the information you want to append. Figure 22.69 shows how an attached table appears in the Database window.

    In this example, the query will be based on an attached dBASE file, NEWCARS.

2. Create a select query based on the NEWCARS table that includes all of the fields you want to append (see fig. 22.70).

Figure 22.69
NEWCARS is an attached dBASE table.

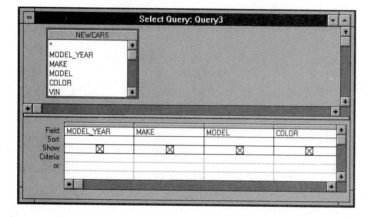

Figure 22.70
The select query here returns all fields.

3. Convert the query to an append query by choosing the Append command from the Query menu or by clicking on the Append Query button in the toolbar. Access displays the Query Properties dialog box, shown in figure 22.71, in which you can enter the name of the table to which the new listings will be appended.

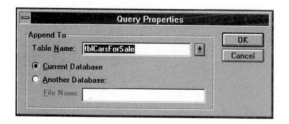

Figure 22.71
The Query Properties box for append queries.

IV

Microsoft Access

If the field names in both tables match, Access displays field names in the Append To row of the QBE grid (see figure 22.72).

Figure 22.72
The Append To
row shows which
fields match.

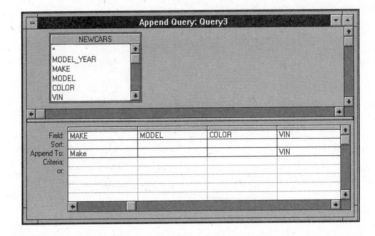

4. In this example, several of the field names do not match (such as MODEL_YEAR). For these fields, the name of the fields to which the new data will be appended must be selected from the drop-down list box shown in figure 22.73.

Figure 22.73
Selecting a field in
tblCarsForSale
to match
MODEL_YEAR.

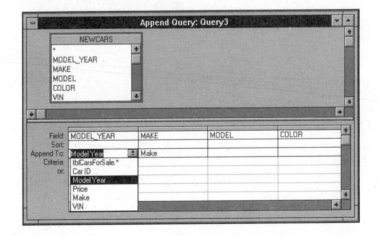

5. After selecting which fields to append to, add the new records by clicking on the Run button on the toolbar or choosing Query, Run. Access runs the query and then displays a message box letting you know how many records will be added. If you click on the OK button, Access briefly displays a progress indicator in the status bar, and then ends without any additional notification.

The modified tblCarsForSale (with new records attached) is shown in figure 22.74.

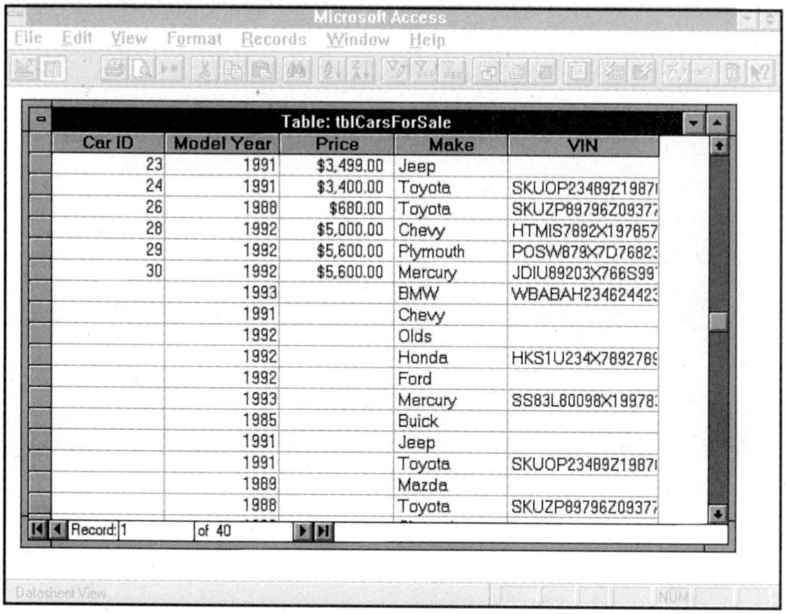

Car ID	Model Year	Price	Make	VIN
23	1991	$3,499.00	Jeep	
24	1991	$3,400.00	Toyota	SKUOP23489Z1987I
26	1988	$680.00	Toyota	SKUZP89796Z09377
28	1992	$5,000.00	Chevy	HTMIS7892X197857
29	1992	$5,600.00	Plymouth	POSW879X7D76823
30	1992	$5,600.00	Mercury	JDIU89203X766S991
	1993		BMW	WBABAH234624423
	1991		Chevy	
	1992		Olds	
	1992		Honda	HKS1U234X7892789
	1992		Ford	
	1993		Mercury	SS83L80098X19978.
	1985		Buick	
	1991		Jeep	
	1991		Toyota	SKUOP23489Z1987I
	1989		Mazda	
	1988		Toyota	SKUZP89796Z09377

Record: 1 of 40

Figure 22.74
The modified tblCarsForSale table.

Delete Queries

Use a delete query to remove selected records from one or more tables—identifying certain groups of records for deletion can save you considerable time.

You can create a delete query, for example, that removes all the house listings that have expired. Checking the listing expiration date, Access can determine whether a listing is still active (and keep it) or if it has expired (and delete the record). Real estate listings are valid or in effect only for a specific period of time, usually six months.

If a delete query specifies two tables in a one-to-many relationship, you can delete records from the "many" table, but not from the "one" table unless you have the Cascade Delete Related Fields check box selected in the Relationships dialog box. If the query is based on tables joined in one-to-one relationships, however, you can delete records from any of the tables.

The following example illustrates the steps to create a delete query that removes records from tblCars if the car has not been serviced since before January 1, 1993.

1. Create a select query (see fig. 22.75) that includes the tables and fields that return all the records you want to delete.

Figure 22.75
The select query
for the Delete
action query.

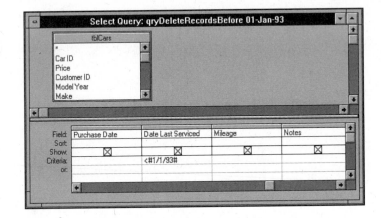

2. Display the query in Datasheet view to make sure the results of the query reflect the records you want to delete. Return to Design view and, if necessary, revise the query.

3. Choose the <u>D</u>elete command from the <u>Q</u>uery menu or click on the Delete query button from the toolbar. Access displays a new Delete row in the QBE grid (figure 22.76).

Figure 22.76
The Delete row
has been added to
the QBE grid.

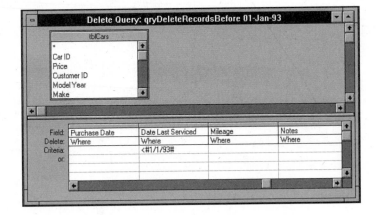

In this example, the query checks to see if the Date Last Serviced was before January 1, 1993. If so, the query will delete the entire record.

4. To remove the selected records, click on the Run button on the toolbar or choose the <u>R</u>un command from the <u>Q</u>uery menu. Access starts to run the query and then displays a message box letting you know how many records will be deleted. If you click on the OK button, Access briefly displays a progress indicator in the status bar and then ends without any additional notification.

Use a delete query when you want to physically remove records from a table. If you only want to hide certain records in forms or reports, use a select query that excludes the undesirable records.

Chapter Snapshot

Data quickly becomes unmanageable unless it is presented in a manner that means something to you and others. Microsoft Access uses forms as the interface between you and your data. Forms can be designed to resemble their paper counterparts or have any other appearance that has meaning to you, and they offer a way to enter data into a table or tables in a logical manner. In this chapter, you will learn about the following:

With a little planning you can view information in many different layouts. Using and designing forms is as much an art as it is data processing. Experimentation will enable you to discover new methods of using and viewing your data.

Creating and Customizing Forms

By Paul Cassel

Entering a sales order or invoice in two different places, one for the order information and one for the line items on the order, quickly becomes tedious. The opportunity to make errors increases because you have to remember information from the order, such as the order number and customer, to properly enter the line items.

With an entry into a single form through the use of a multitable query, you simultaneously can enter information into multiple tables. How often have you entered a name and address into two different systems even though the data is related? That is where the term *relational* in relational database management system comes from. Relational systems can share information from one table to another.

Using the order example, you enter the customer name and address in a master table. When you enter the order and are asked for the customer, all you have to provide is the customer identifier, such as a name or ID number, and Access looks up the address information in the related table and places it in the order automatically. This concept of relational data management has limitless possibilities when applied correctly.

A good example of the effective use of forms is the ever-so-popular invoice, as shown in figure 23.1.

Figure 23.1
An order/invoice form from the Northwind Traders Database.

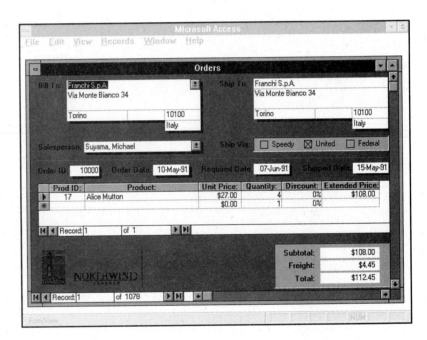

Controlling the flow of a database application is another common use of forms. Look at the Northwind Traders example and notice how a form is used as a switchboard (see fig. 23.2). The form contains buttons that, when pushed, cause other events to occur, such as opening other forms and reports.

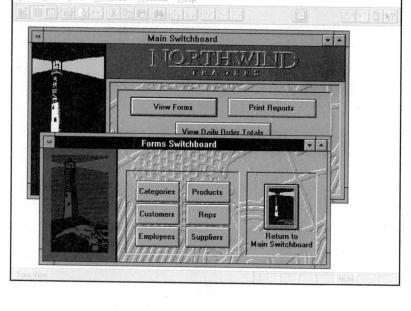

Figure 23.2
The Northwind
Traders
switchboard.

Viewing Data

The presentation of data is one of the most important aspects of data management. If data is not presented in a meaningful manner, understanding what the data is trying to tell you becomes difficult, thus defeating its purpose.

Datasheet View

Access enables you to view data in two ways. The first is called *Datasheet view* (see fig. 23.3), with which you should be familiar from Chapter 21, "Creating and Using Tables."

Form View

The second and more versatile view is Form view. It can be customized to appear differently, depending on your requirements. Even though a form can be displayed in Datasheet or Form view, Form view is more flexible than Datasheet view. Form view is used to view a single record at a time, as shown in figure 23.4.

Figure 23.3
A customer listing
in Datasheet view.

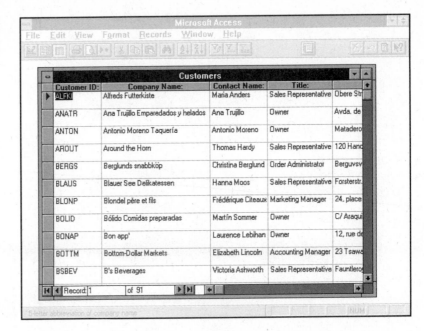

Figure 23.4
The customer
information form
showing a single
record.

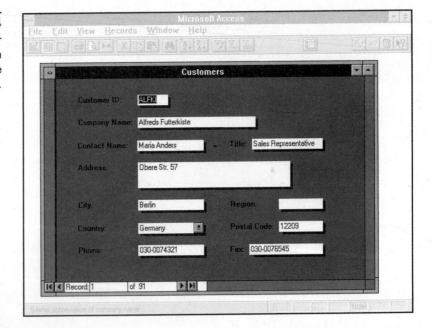

The Form view can show multiple records simultaneously, called *continuous form view*. This view is designed so that the window displaying the record is large enough to show several small forms. The records scroll through the form window from top to bottom, as shown in figure 23.5.

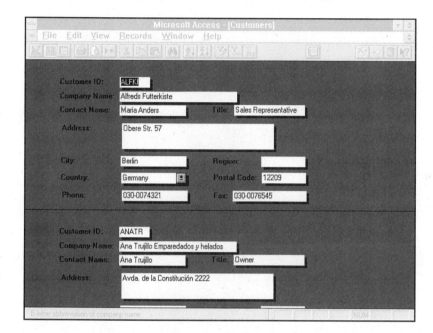

Figure 23.5
The customer information form showing multiple records using the continuous form view.

Using Form Wizards

You may be familiar with the concept of Wizards if you have ever used Microsoft Excel, Microsoft Money, or Microsoft Works. Wizards are automated processes that assist you in creating objects such as forms, reports, and graphs, among others.

The Access Form Wizard does just what it says: it assists you in the quick creation of simple forms. In the following example database, Car Care, you will use the Form Wizard to create a form for the entry of car information.

1. Click on the Table button in the database container and select tblCars (see fig. 23.6).

Figure 23.6
A database container with the Table button pressed and tblCars selected.

2. Click on the New Form button on the toolbar. When the New Form dialog box appears, select Form<u>W</u>izards (see fig. 23.7).

Figure 23.7
The New Form dialog box with the selected table.

3. Access displays the Form Wizards dialog box (see fig. 23.8) and asks which type of form you want to create. For the example, choose Single-Column and click on OK.

Figure 23.8
Access asks which type of form you want.

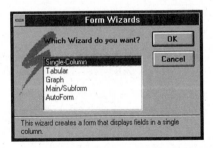

4. Next, the Form Wizard asks you to choose the fields to be on your new form and the order in which they should appear (see fig. 23.9). Select a field and click on the single arrow (>) to move it to the right list box, or click on the double arrow (>>) to move all fields to the right list box. For this example, click the double arrow and move all the fields to the right list box, then click on <u>N</u>ext.

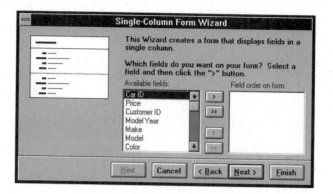

Figure 23.9
The dialog box for choosing fields and field order.

Be careful when choosing your fields. The order in which you choose them will be the order in which they will appear on the right side. This also is the order in which they will appear on your newly created form, and the order in which the cursor will move through the fields on the form.

Tip

When you feel comfortable using the Form Wizard, experiment with reordering the field using the various arrow buttons. Mastery of this technique will save a great deal of time later on. By arranging the field now into the order you want, you will not have to do this manually at a later time.

5. From the dialog box shown in figure 23.10, select the look you want to give your form. The picture under the magnifying glass on the left side of the dialog box changes to reflect the look you have chosen. When you are satisfied with the form's look, click on <u>N</u>ext.

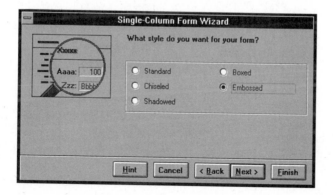

Figure 23.10
The look selection dialog box.

6. In the dialog box shown in figure 23.11, change the title of your new form from tblCars to Car Information and click on <u>F</u>inish.

Figure 23.11
The title dialog
box is the final
step in the Form
Wizard.

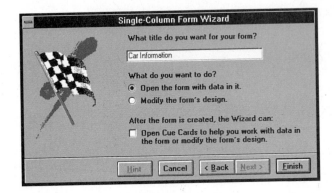

Choosing the Modify the form's design option button in figure 23.11 enables you to begin making manual modifications right now. To get a sense of what the form will look like, however, you usually should choose Finish, get a look at your form, and then decide if any modifications are required.

The form in figure 23.12 should be similar to yours. If you chose a different look or have modified the default colors, the screens still should look similar. Notice that the picture field in not currently visible.

Figure 23.12
The completed
Car Information
form.

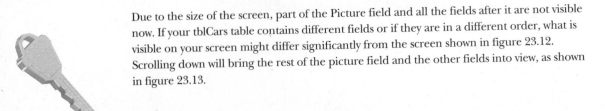

Due to the size of the screen, part of the Picture field and all the fields after it are not visible now. If your tblCars table contains different fields or if they are in a different order, what is visible on your screen might differ significantly from the screen shown in figure 23.12. Scrolling down will bring the rest of the picture field and the other fields into view, as shown in figure 23.13.

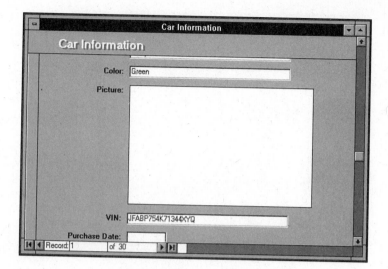

Figure 23.13
The form with the picture field showing.

When you have finished with your form, be sure to save your work. In case you forget, Access will remind you to save a form that has been changed but not yet saved. Perform the following steps to save the form:

1. From the File menu, select Save Form As to display the Save As dialog box (see fig. 23.14).

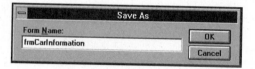

Figure 23.14
The Save As dialog box.

2. Type **frmCarInformation** in the Save As dialog box and click on OK.

3. From the File menu, choose Close to return to the database container.

Tip

For a quick close, double-click on the control box in the upper left corner of the form (see fig. 23.15).

Figure 23.15
The cursor at the window control box.

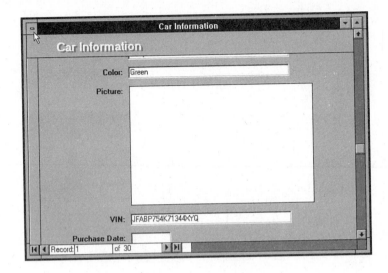

Form Wizards can be quite a time-saver when creating a database from scratch or when converting a database from another system. With a little practice and experimentation, the Form Wizards can be a great productivity enhancement.

Using Forms

Forms enable you to view, add, change, and delete records in your database. To effectively use the data in your records, you need to understand the basics of using these functions and the fundamentals of navigating around a form.

The Form View Toolbar

As with all toolbars, simple design and button layout help speed you through your most common activities with the single click of the mouse. Table 23.1 shows the Form View toolbar buttons and describes the use of each button. The field box will be discussed later in the chapter.

Table 23.1
Form View Toolbar Icons

Icon	Name	Description
	Design View	Switches to Design view to enable you to manually edit the layout of the form.
	Form View	Switches to Form view.

Icon	Name	Description
	Datasheet View	Switches to Datasheet view.
	Print	Prints the current form.
	Print Preview	Sends the current on-screen form to the Print Preview window. This window enables you to see exactly the way your form will look on hard copy, and it even provides a button to begin printing, should you decide to do so.
	New	Jumps to a new record.
	Cut	Cuts to the clipboard.
	Copy	Copies to the clipboard.
	Paste	Pastes from the clipboard.
	Find	Activates the standard Access Find dialog box.
	Sort Ascending	Sorts records in alphabetic order.
	Sort Descending	Sorts records in reverse alphabetic order.
	Filter buttons	These button are used to filter data. *Filters* are used when you want a subset of data based on a specific criteria, such as all the customers in specific state or region. These buttons also are used to sort the data, regardless of whether you are using a filtered subset or the entire database.
	Database window	Jumps to database view.
	Undo current	Reverts to the previous value in a form or field.

IV

Microsoft Access

continues

Table 23.1, Continued
Form View Toolbar Icons

Icon	Name	Description
	Undo	Enables you to reverse your last step or activity. In the event you mistakenly enter data into the wrong field, overwriting the original data, pressing the Undo button will restore the field to its original data.
	Cue Cards	Gets Cue Card-style help.
	Help	Displays context-sensitive help.

Most of the functions performed by the toolbar buttons are available in the pull-down menus. However, the use of the toolbar makes all the functions quicker and more accessible by utilizing single clicks of the mouse. The toolbar eliminates the need to take several steps to work through the menus.

Navigating the Records

After you have taken the time to enter several records into your database, the next concern is viewing them. To move through the different records, use the record navigation box and buttons in the lower left corner of the form (see fig. 23.16).

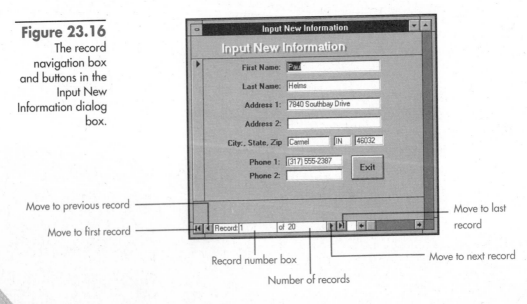

Figure 23.16
The record navigation box and buttons in the Input New Information dialog box.

Move to previous record

Move to first record

Move to last record

Record number box

Move to next record

Number of records

Tip

To remove the navigation tool from your form, turn off the vertical scroll bar property.

The navigation tools look and work much like the buttons on a tape recorder or VCR. The single arrow buttons rewind and advance you one record at a time, and the first and last arrow buttons rewind to the first record in the file or fast-forward to the last one.

Record navigation also can be accomplished using the pull-down menus. By selecting the Records menu and then choosing Go To, you are presented with a submenu, enabling you to move through the records or add new ones.

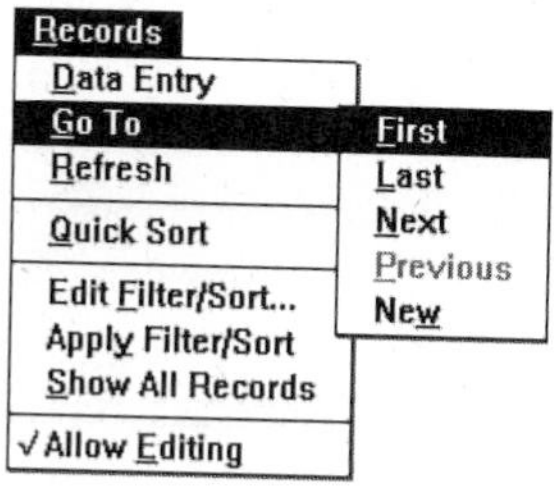

```
Records
 Data Entry
 Go To        First
 Refresh      Last
              Next
 Quick Sort   Previous
              New
 Edit Filter/Sort...
 Apply Filter/Sort
 Show All Records
√Allow Editing
```

Figure 23.17
The Records menu.

Note

Notice the grayed out Previous menu item. This denotes that you are currently at the beginning of the file and have no previous records. If you are at the end of the file, the Next menu item would be grayed out.

Perhaps one of the quickest ways to get to the record you want is to enter the record's ID number in the record number box. To do this, highlight the old record number in the record number box (see fig. 23.18), type the new one (which deletes the old), and press Enter. This method is feasible only when you are dealing with a small number of records. If you could remember the ID number of every record in a database, you probably would not need the database in the first place.

One of the most common method of moving through the data is the *Datasheet/Form toggle technique.* Since most people find it easier and more convenient to spot record that want from a list rather than viewing them one at a time, try switching to the Datasheet view by pushing the Datasheet button on the toolbar. This allow you to view the record in a list rather than individually.

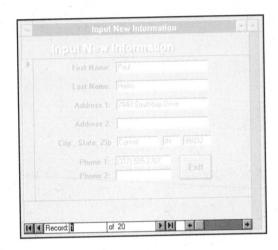

Figure 23.18
Highlighting the record number in the record number box.

One of the most common methods of moving through data is to switch from Form to Datasheet view. Because most people find it easier to spot a record in a list than to look at every record one at a time, try switching to Datasheet view by clicking on the Datasheet button on the toolbar (see fig. 23.19). This enables you to view the records in a list rather than individually.

Figure 23.19
Pressing the Datasheet View button displays the records in Datasheet view.

When you spot the record you want, place the cursor on any field in the record and click on the Form View button on the toolbar to return to the form view (see fig. 23.20).

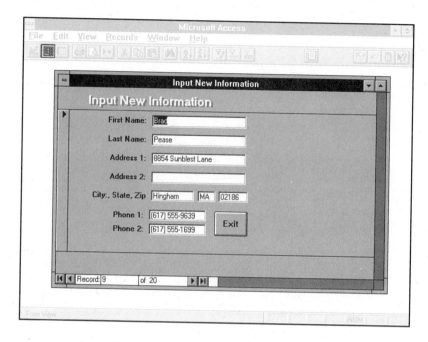

Figure 23.20
Clicking on the
Form View button
returns you to
Form view.

Perhaps the simplest way of all to page through the records is to use the paging keys on the keyboard. Press PgDn to move toward the end of the file and PgUp to move toward the beginning.

Adding New Records

Now that you have created your new form and are comfortable moving through the sample data, it is time to start adding data of your own. Start by selecting frmCarInformation in the Forms section of the database container, as shown in figure 23.21. To open it, either double-click on the name of the form or click on the Open button.

Figure 23.21
The database
container showing
the available
forms.

IV

Microsoft Access

When the form opens, notice that the cursor goes to the first field on the form, Car ID. Click on the New Record button in the toolbar to move to a fresh record. Because the Car ID field has been defined in the table, it shows the word Counter. This means this is a new record with an unassigned counter number. When you finish entering required or validated information in this form, Access will assign a counter number to it. Pressing Tab moves you to the next field, CustID.

In most cases, the cursor will move to the next field when either Tab or Enter is pressed. If, however, you want the Enter key to move to the next record (or not to move at all), you can alter its function by selecting **O**ptions from the **V**iew menu. When the Options dialog box appears, click on the Keyboard category. In the lower-half of the dialog box, you can change the Move After Enter setting as desired.

A little later you will use the CustID field to assign an owner to the car, but skip it for now. Tab to the year field. The default value of 9999 is highlighted, so you can simply begin typing. Enter **1994** and press Tab to move to the next field.

To manually highlight the entire contents of a field, drag the mouse cursor across the text while holding down the left mouse button. A simpler way is to click on the field label.

Enter **Dodge** in the Make field and press Tab. Using the information shown in figure 23.22, complete the form down to the bottom of the screen, but wait before you press Tab to move to the next field.

Figure 23.22
A nearly complete
Car Information
form.

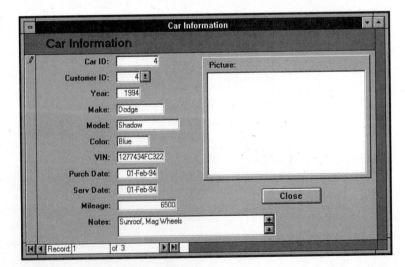

Now Tab to the next field, which is Picture. Notice that the look of the Picture field changes to show it has the focus. At this point you can insert a Picture of the Dodge Shadow—if you have one on your computer—or choose to make one using a drawing package.

Access forms can be 22 inches by 22 inches, so it is possible to design forms much larger than what can be seen on the screen without scrolling. The use of high-resolution monitors set at 1,024 × 768 lpi or 1,280 × 1,024 lpi can show much more than a standard 640 × 480 lpi VGA display. An Access user's resolution must be a consideration as you design your forms. You do not want the user to have to scroll around unless it is absolutely necessary. Also, in multiuser situations, every user might not be set at the same resolution, so what you see on your screen as fitting just fine might not fit on another user's screen.

For now, skip the Picture field and press Tab to move to the next record. When Tab is pressed on the last field of a form, the record is automatically saved, and the next record is displayed. If you experience something other than this, check your Keyboard Option settings for Cursor Stop actions. Table 23.2 shows the values for the second and third records.

Table 23.2
Values for Second and Third Records

Field	Record 2	Record 3
Year	1990	1992
Make	Ferrari	Plymouth
Model	Testarossa	Voyager
Color	Red	Blue
VIN	12345	67890
Purch Date	5/3/90	6/1/92
Serv Date	11/14/93	1/7/94
Mileage	76550	52750
Notes	Gas guzzler	Economical

After you enter the data for the second and third record, you'll naturally move to the fourth record to begin entry. Before you move to the fourth record, you can press Ctrl+PgUp to review the previous records. Pressing Ctrl+PgDn moves you forward through the records to last one.

When large numbers of records exist in your database, it is impractical to page through them individually until you reach the end, just to add a new one. An easier way to reach the end is to use the record navigation buttons in the lower left corner of your form. Press the fast-forward button to place you at the last record in the file and then press the next record arrow button to move you to the next record; Access always places a new record at the end of your file, but does not use it until it has data. In other words, the next record past the last one is a new one.

Access provide two possible menu paths to add new records. The first is to select Data Entry from the Record menu, as shown in figure 23.23.

Figure 23.23
The Data Entry
menu selection.

Using the Data Entry method, Access filters out all the previous data and starts your data-entry session with record 1. This is not actually the first record in the file—other records already exist—but the first record in this session. When you complete your data-entry session, choose Show All Records from the Records menu to view all your data, including the records you just entered.

The second method of adding new records is similar to the first. From the Records menu, select Go To, then choose New from the submenu that appears.

This method also moves you one record past the last one. All records are still available you start your entry session at the end of the file.

Editing Existing Records

Editing existing records is as simple as moving to the record you want to edit and making your changes. There is no special menu to select or button to push to begin editing. Access senses changes in data fields and saves those changes when you leave the field.

You can manually save any changes you make by pressing the record selector bar on the left of the form. The selector bar displays a right arrow when the record is saved but is in a nonedit mode. A small pencil is displayed while the record is being edited (see fig. 23.24).

To use the menus to save a record, choose Save Record from the File menu, as shown in figure 23.25.

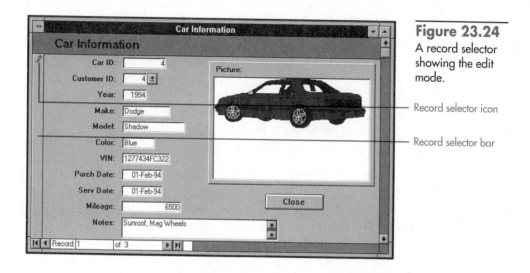

Figure 23.24
A record selector showing the edit mode.

Record selector icon

Record selector bar

Figure 23.25
The Save Record menu selection.

As mentioned earlier, a record also is saved automatically when you move to a different record.

Deleting Records

Deleting records is nearly as simple as editing them. However, Access issues a warning when you are about to delete a record to give you a chance to change your mind.

To delete a record, choose Select Record from the Edit menu. Notice that the record selector bar to the left of the record is now depressed. To delete the record, choose Delete from the Edit menu, or just press Del.

Tip   A shortcut for record selection is to press the record selector bar with the mouse. The bar is actually a large button.

Filtering and Sorting Records

A large amount of data has almost no value in and of itself. What matters is the way the data is used to make decisions. When many records are present in your database, filtering out the unneeded records becomes a priority.

Sorting the data in some logical order is as important as filtering out the undesired records. Because filtering and sorting are so interrelated within Access, both are accomplished using the same technique.

The Records pull down menu contains three selections for filtering/sorting records. Conveniently, these selections correspond to the three toolbar icons labeled Filter/Sort.

Editing the Filter and Sort Order

Editing the Filter and Sort Order uses the same grid as queries (see fig. 23.26). In fact, a filter can be saved as a query and used by other objects in your database.

Figure 23.26
The filter and sorting grid is the same as the query grid.

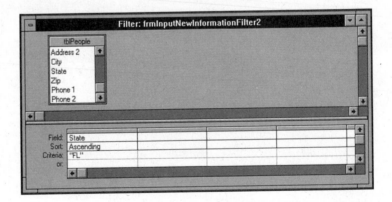

Note   For more information on queries, see Chapter 22, "Understanding Access Queries."

The grid is used in the same way a query is used. Fields are chosen from the available tables and sort orders are chosen if desired. If filtering is needed, criteria is entered. After the grid is filled out, the data is ready to be filtered and sorted.

Apply the Filter and Sort Order

Pressing the second Filter/Sort button on the toolbar applies the filter, sorts the data according to your instructions, then returns you to the original calling form. The form now displays only the data that matches the criteria entered, and also is sorted in the order you chose.

Show All Records

The third Filter/Sort button on the toolbar is used to clear the filter and display all the available records. This also clears the Sort Order and displays the records in the order they were entered originally.

Exploring the Advanced Form Design Tools

The real power and flexibility of Microsoft Access is its use of forms. Forms are used for a myriad of purposes from menus to data entry screens and can be designed to look like just about anything the creative designer wants.

Form Wizards create simple forms in a hurry. Most experienced Access users create the basic forms using Form Wizards and then modify them manually to get a specific look and function. Forms are also created from blank windows as well. This section of the chapter discusses modifying a form and further introduces you to the Form Wizard.

Controls

Forms are much like an artist's canvas. The artist can place almost anything his heart desires on the canvas; forms are the same way. More than just data-entry fields and their labels can be placed on a form. Fields, buttons, bitmap graphics, list boxes, check boxes, radio buttons, and plain text are just a few of the items that can reside on a form.

To simplify the process, anything placed on a form is referred to as a *control*. Any of the preceding items can cause several events to take place. Instead of just being singular in purpose, they can manipulate what happens when certain conditions occur, such as opening a form, moving from one field to another, or pushing a button. Hence the name *control*.

Control Properties

Every control is associated with a corresponding property sheet, as seen in figure 23.27.

Figure 23.27
The property sheet for a label.

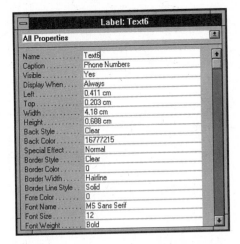

A *property sheet* contains the list of attributes that determine the characteristics and behavior of a control, such as color, size, what happens when it is changed, and whether it is visible. Some controls have only a few properties, whereas others have many. Because there are so many properties associated with most controls, Access has a pull-down selector toward the top of the properties list box that will enable you to specify whether you want the list to display Data, Layout, Event, Other, or All properties at any given time.

Many controls have similar properties, such as size and color, so learning them is not as difficult as it sounds. Besides, help is always a press of the F1 key away. As you use properties more later, you will gain a greater understanding of them.

Modifying Appearances

Controlling the appearance of a form or a control on a form means having to modify the property sheet value related to the effect you desire. However, modifying the property sheet for color becomes a little difficult because Access does not actually store the name of the color in the property. Instead, Access uses a number to represent color.

To modify color, access the Palette toolbox, shown in figure 23.28, by choosing Palette from the View menu or by pressing the Palette button (shaped like a painter's palette) on the toolbar.

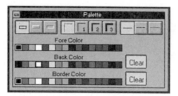

Figure 23.28
The Palette
toolbox

The Palette toolbox enables you to control the colors of the text, fill, and border. You also control the border thickness and the overall appearance. With a little experimentation, the Normal, Raised, and Sunken attributes can yield some very interesting visual effects, as shown in figure 23.29.

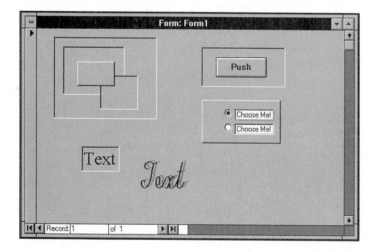

Figure 23.29
A sampling of
visual effects using
the Palette
toolbox.

Text Boxes

Text boxes are placeholders for data or other values. They normally are bound to a field in the underlying table or query, but do have to be. Text boxes enable you to enter data into Access and can hold text, numbers, dates, times, and currency values. Also, a text box sometimes is used to hold temporarily a value for use elsewhere. An example appears in the Order Date Dialog box of the Northwind Trader database container (see fig. 23.30).

The order date is not linked (*bound* as it is known in Access) to an underlying table or query; however, the date is called from another query to filter the data for the report. When the Order Date dialog box is closed, the date it held is lost forever and you must enter a new date the next time it is used.

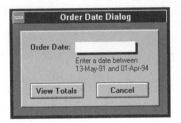

Figure 23.30
The Order Date
Dialog box from
Northwind
Traders.

Labels

Labels are the names given on forms to let you know what is expected in a particular control. The word *Name* besides the text box in which the name is entered is the label. Labels do not necessarily have a one-to-one relationship with controls; a label can be used to reference a group of controls as well (see fig. 23.31).

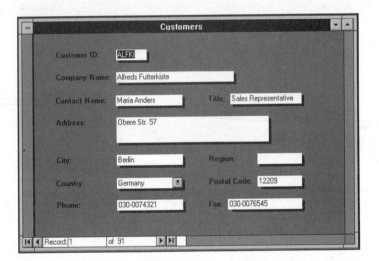

Figure 23.31
The Customers
form uses labels to
identify text fields.

Combo Boxes

Microsoft Windows has made this single control famous. The combo box normally will be your first choice for selecting a single value from a list of other values.

A combo box can be based on tables, queries, or values that you enter into the Row Source property. All combo boxes are used the same way: click on the small down arrow to the right of the text box, and the available values will appear in the drop-down list. There are three combo boxes in figure 23.32.

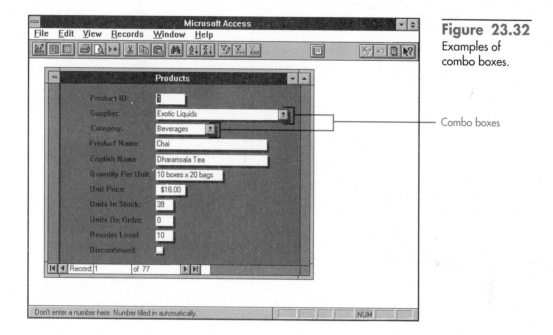

Figure 23.32
Examples of
combo boxes.

Combo boxes

List Boxes

List boxes are similar to combo boxes except they do not require you to push a button to see
the value choices. With the exception of on-screen appearance, list boxes and combo boxes
are almost identical (see fig. 23.33).

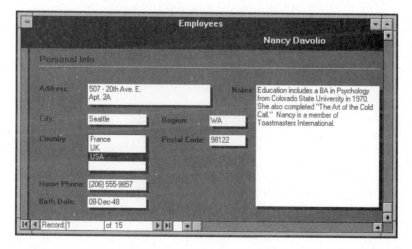

Figure 23.33
The Northwind
Employees form
showing a list box
used for the
Country field.

IV

Microsoft Access

List boxes are normally used only where a small number of records is available. It becomes impractical to scroll through hundred of choices to find the one you want.

Using list boxes for large numbers of records also is impractical due to performance. List boxes are designed to handle only a small number of records.

When using a list box, you will want to be able to see the highlighted value without having to scroll the list to find it. If your list box contains more choices than the list can display on the screen, there is a chance some fields will use choices near the bottom of the list. At first glance, it would appear as if no choice has been made. You will have to scroll down to see which value is used, wasting valuable time.

Option Groups

Option groups contain one or more radio buttons, check boxes, text boxes, or toggle buttons. A separate number is assigned to each control in the group. Because only one control in the group can be selected, option groups are useful in applications where only one answer is correct. Male or Female, Yes or No, FedEx or Airborne, and Mr. or Mrs. are examples of buttons you might find in an option group. Option groups can contain more than two choices, but there never are very many, and the group will hold only one choice at a time. Care should be taken to determine whether your needs are best served by an option group or a list box. In figure 23.34, one of the option group choices, Sales by Category, also has a list box of product choices associated to it.

Figure 23.34
The Report to Print option group, above a list box related to the second option in the group.

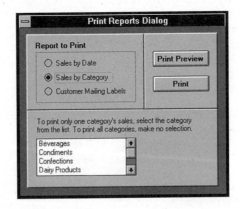

Option Button

These buttons, sometimes called *radio buttons*, are almost always used with option groups. This control generates a Yes/No, On/Off or True/False action. When the button is pushed, it generates a –1 to represent a Yes/On/True condition. When the button is pushed again, it switches to the opposite No/Off/False, and generates a 0. This is how the option group knows which button is pushed. It looks for the button generating a true condition (–1), because only one button in the group can be true. When a specific option button is pushed, all others are reset to false or 0.

Toggle Buttons

Toggle buttons are identical in function to option buttons. Use these buttons when you want to place text on the button to show its function (see fig. 23.35).

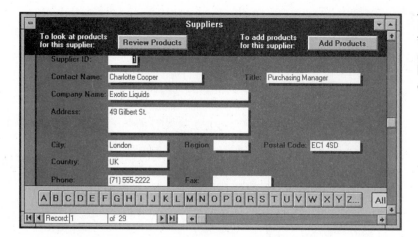

Figure 23.35
The Suppliers form uses toggle buttons to filter data.

Check Boxes

Check boxes are similar to option buttons because they generate the same True/False conditions. The major distinction between option buttons and check boxes is that option buttons normally are used within option groups and check boxes are not. Also, option buttons are used for "pick only one" situations, and check boxes are used for "check all that apply" situations. See the examples in figure 23.36.

Figure 23.36
The Permissions
section of this
dialog box uses
check boxes, and
the List section
uses option
buttons.

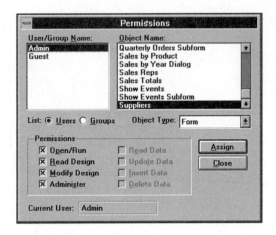

Object Frames

Object frames can contain pictures, sounds, graphs, charts, or documents such as Excel spreadsheets or Microsoft Word documents. These objects can either be applied to a frame using cut and paste or through the use of OLE (object linking and embedding).

Object frames consist of bound and unbound frame types. *Bound frames* are linked to the underlying data source, whether it is a table or a query, whereas *unbound frames* are not tied to your data. They are commonly used to accent the form design, such as a logo or background bitmap, as shown in figure 23.37.

Figure 23.37
The Northwind
Traders Main
Switchboard
contains a logo
bitmap, a title
bitmap, and a
textured
background
bitmap, all
contained in
unbound object
frames.

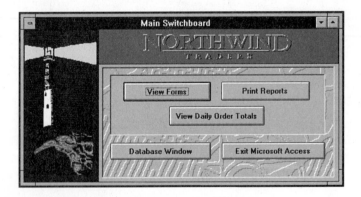

Objects in a bound frame change as the data changes, as exemplified in figure 23.38.

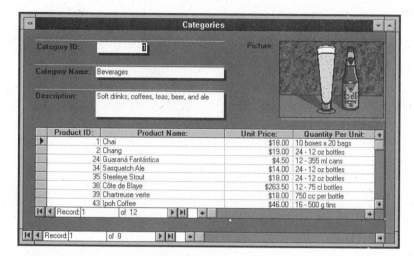

Command Buttons

Command button are the most commonly used control other than the text box. Command buttons give you the ability to automate functions and activities by simply pressing a button. They are most commonly used to activate macros.

Page Breaks

When your forms become too long to display within a single window, you can break them into different pages. The Page Break marks the point treated as both the bottom of one window and the top of the next.

Subforms

Subforms are small forms embedded into a main form. They display records from a data source different from the main form, but they are related to the main form's data by at least one common field.

Line items on an invoice are related by the common invoice number field to the order header. It is confusing, however, to view at the same time two different screens of data regarding an invoice. In figure 23.38, a subform is placed in the middle of the form directly below the invoice header it relates to. The subform and main form are linked through the Order ID field (which contains the number 10217).

Figure 23.39

A product subform embedded on the Orders main form.

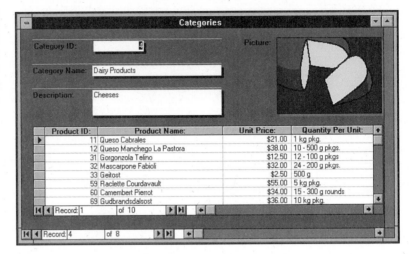

Building Forms

As discussed earlier, forms are the main interface between you and your data. You have learned the definitions and uses of the various components of form design; now you will put that knowledge to use in a practical application.

Design View

All modifications to a form are done in Design view. Microsoft Access provides a special toolbar to assist and expedite your work. The toolbar consists of several buttons that correspond to a particular design function. The first seven are always visible in Design view. The others are visible depending on the type of control you are modifying.

Open the frmCarInformation form in Design view by selecting it in the database container and clicking on Design (see fig. 23.40).

Tip   Clicking the right mouse button pops up an appropriate shortcut menu in many places in Access.

The toolbar is visible at the top of the screen and has the Design View button selected. The second and third buttons are used to switch between Form view and Datasheet view, respectively.

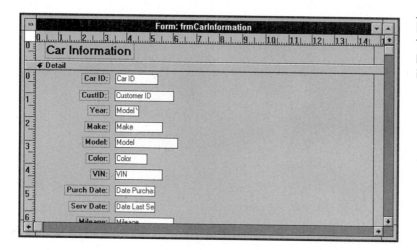

Figure 23.40
The Car
Information form
in Design view.

The fifth button, Print Preview, enables you to see and prepare the current form for printing before issuing the print command.

The sixth button switches the properties list box between opened and closed. The contents of the properties list box vary according to the type of control being modified.

The field list is switched on and off by the seventh button. Designing a form from a blank window requires access to the fields in the underlying table or query. The field list displays those fields and enables you to drag a field from the list to the form.

The tenth button is the Palette button, which switches the formatting palette on and off.

Colors and Appearance

With the car information form in Design view, switch the color palette on by clicking on the Palette button on the toolbar. Click in the area to the right of Car Information in the form header. Using the color palette, click on the dark gray color in the fill row, as shown in figure 23.41, to convert the form header color to dark gray.

Click on the text box for Car ID. The control will be highlighted with handles. These handles can be used to move or resize the control. With the field highlighted, choose the Sunken option in the color palette to give the control a sunken appearance.

A quick way to give all the text boxes a sunken appearance is to place the arrow of the mouse cursor just left of and slightly above the first field you wish to highlight. Press and hold the left mouse button and drag the lasso type box to the right of and just below the last field you wish to highlight. The lasso box does not have to completely engulf the controls in question—it just needs to touch them all. With the controls highlighted, click on the Sunken option in the palette toolbox. All the text box controls now appear with the sunken appearance, as shown in figure 23.42.

IV

Microsoft Access

Figure 23.41
The form header is
changed to dark
gray using the
palette.

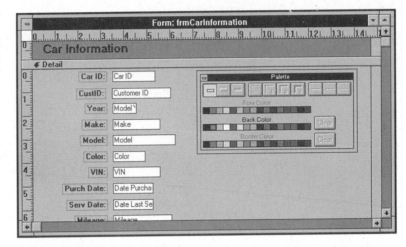

Figure 23.42
The text boxes
with a sunken
appearance.

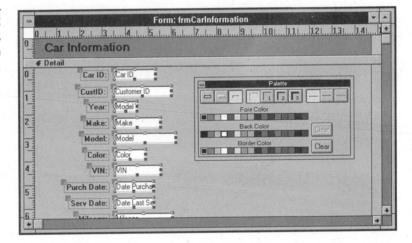

Switch the color palette off by clicking on the Palette toolbar button, then click on the Form View button to see the modified form. When you have finished viewing the form, switch back into Design view.

Saving Your Work

To ensure that your work does not get lost, save your Design view changes frequently by choosing Save from the File menu. If you are designing a new form from scratch, you will be prompted for a name. Give the dialog box a unique name and save your work.

Note If you try to close a form design window but have not saved you changes, Access will automatically sense the changes and prompt you to save them.

Moving a Control

To move a control, find the control you want to move. With the mouse pointer on the control, click and hold the left mouse button; the cursor arrow is changed into a hand. With this hand, drag the control to where you want it and release the mouse button. The control and its label are dropped into place when you release the mouse button. In this case, move the picture control up and to the right of the other controls, as shown in figure 23.43.

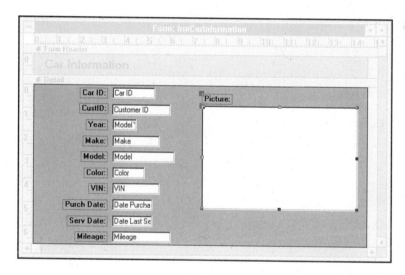

Figure 23.43
The relocated picture control.

If the control needs any slight adjustments, make them by moving the pointer over the edge of a highlighted control. When the pointer converts to a hand, click and hold the left mouse button to move the control again.

Resizing a Control

To resize a control that is too big for the available area or would better be suited by a different shape, adjust the control by using the handles around the edges of highlighted frame.

Click on the picture frame control to highlight it and expose its handles. All controls have eight handles, one in each corner and one on each straight side. When a control is small, as with text boxes, the left and right side handles do not show. Only when a control is large enough to accommodate the side handles will they show.

IV

Microsoft Access

Slowly move your mouse cursor over the different handles and watch the pointer change the arrow shapes to reflect the movement capability of a particular handle. These handles act exactly like the handles on a Windows screen. The diagonal arrows for the corners enable you to control the height and width of a frame, and the horizontal and vertical arrows control movements in their respective directions.

Grab the handle in the upper right corner and drag it in toward the lower left corner about half an inch. Release the mouse button, and the picture control should be resized as shown in figure 23.44.

Figure 23.44

The resized picture control.

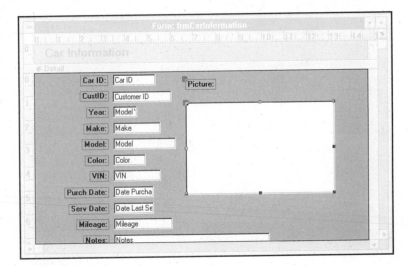

Moving a Label and Independent Control Movement

Notice that when you move a control, the associated label moves along with it. Some situations require the label or some other control to be moved independently of its associated partner.

By now you probably have noticed the special large handle in the upper left corner of a highlighted control. Moving a control using this handle does not resize the control, but moves it independently of any linked controls such as labels.

To move the label independently, highlight the field label for the picture control. Grab the large upper left corner handle, click the left mouse button, drag the label over the picture control, and release the mouse button (see fig. 23.45).

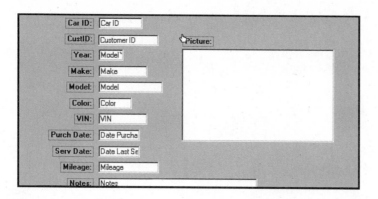

Figure 23.45
A relocated picture
control label.

This technique of moving independent controls works with all controls, not just labels.

Creating Boxes

The use of boxes to create a visual effect is a common technique in the presentation of data. To create a picture box, perform the following steps:

1. Select Toolbox from the <u>V</u>iew menu. A floating toolbox appears with the tools for the controls described earlier.

2. Click on the Rectangle button to choose the Rectangle control tool (see fig. 23.46).

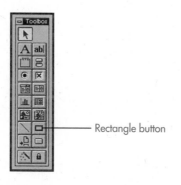

Rectangle button

Figure 23.46
The Rectangle
button in the
toolbox.

3. With the Rectangle tool selected, the cursor changes to a crosshair. Place the cursor to the top and slightly to the left of the picture label. Click the mouse button and drag the rectangle outline just past the lower right corner of the picture control, then release the mouse button (see fig. 23.47).

The new box appears as a solid white box, hiding your picture field.

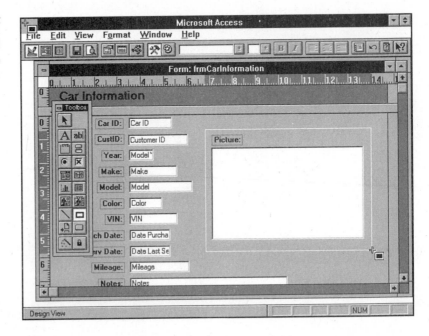

Figure 23.47
The Rectangle tool as it draws an outline.

4. Click on the Palette button on the toolbar to display the Palette toolbox.

5. With your new box still highlighted, click on the Clear check box on the Fill line of the Palette toolbox, then click on the Raised option button. Your new box now takes on the appearance of a raised frame with the actual picture area sunken.

Save your work by choosing Save from the File menu. To view your progress, click on the Form View button on the toolbar. When you are finished viewing your work, return to Design view by clicking on the Design View button.

Adding a Combo Box

Adding combo boxes to your database helps give the database a professional look while ensuring accurate user selections. In this example, the CustID field is a likely candidate to change from a list box to a combo box. Because every car will be assigned a customer, and because customer names easily can be misspelled, selecting from a combo box will eliminate errors users make when typing names in a list box.

To make a professional-looking combo box, perform the following steps:

1. Remove the text box field you don't want so that you can replace it with the combo box field. With your frmCarInformation form in Design view, highlight the CustID control and delete it. Its associated label will vanish as well, but that is to be

expected. When you replace the control with your combo box, a new label will accompany it.

2. Select Toolbox from the **V**iew menu to bring up the Design toolbox. Click on the Combo Box button, then click and drag to draw a new combo box about half an inch long in the location of the old text box.

   When you release the mouse button, the new combo box appears. A new associated label also appear with the word Field*XX*, where *XX* represents the number of the field on the form. If your form already has 31 controls on it, for example, the next one placed on it will be Field32. You can, of course, change theses names.

   Select Toolbox from the **V**iew menu to switch off the toolbox so that your workspace doesn't get cluttered.

3. Highlight the new control label with the mouse. Click on the label again to change to edit mode. You now can change it to something more meaningful, such as Customer ID. Notice that the label expands to fit the increase in size automatically.

   Click on an unpopulated area of the window to stop editing the label; the label change is immediately reflected.

4. Because all the other field labels are right-justified, after you have manually right-justified the label, you must right-justify the text within the label. Highlight the label again with a single mouse click and then move the control to the right using the special large handle in the upper left corner. With the label still highlighted, press the Right-Justify button on the Design View toolbar. Notice that the label did not move, but that the text within the label did.

 Note   By default, all text is left-justified and all numeric values are right-justified.

5. All the colons for the label need to be aligned. To align several control at once, lasso the controls you want to align and select Align from the **F**ormat menu. Choose the direction of alignment from the submenu that appears.

6. Next, highlight the combo box and click on the Palette button on the toolbar to display the Palette. Choose Sunken to create a sunken combo box that looks similar to the other controls on the form, then close the palette toolbox.

7. With the combo box still highlighted, select Properties from the **V**iew menu, or click on the Properties button on the toolbar. Make sure the combo box at the top of the list box has All Properties showing. The property sheet appears, displaying

the list of customizable attributes available. Notice that the Name is still the same name as the temporary field you changed just a moment ago.

8. The Control Source can be referred to as the field in the underlying table or query that holds the data you enter into this control. Select the control source with the mouse. You will notice a button appear to the right to the text area, indicating that this property has a list to choose from. Click on the button and select Customer ID from the list.

9. Notice that the Row Source is, by default, set at Table/Query, which is right for the example because the source of the list for this combo box is a table. Next, you need to select the source for the list of data to be displayed—in this case, the list of customers—when you press the arrow button on the combo box. Click on the Row Source text area, click on the list button that appears, and choose tblCustomers from the list.

10. The next section, Column Count, deals with the number of columns of data you want to display when you click on the list button. To display the first three columns—CustID, First Name and Last Name—enter **3** in the text box.

Tip If you cannot remember which columns you want to display, press F11 to select the database container and review any object you want.

11. To help create a polished look, set the columns to the proper width. The CustID column can be rather narrow, whereas the First and Last Name columns need to be wider. Enter the width for each column, and separate each value with semi-colons: **.25;.5;1** would be a good entry for these columns. You do not have to enter the units of measure; Access follows each entry with the abbreviation for inches.

Tip If your row source table or query has columns you need to include but don't want to display, enter **0** for the width of that column.

12. The *bound column* is the column from the list box you want link to the combo box itself. For this example, link the CustID to the combo box, which itself is bound to the Customer ID field in the tblCustomers table. If you choose column 1 for your bound column, you will be storing the data in column 1 of the combo box in the Customer ID field in tblCustomers. If you chose column 2, First Name, it would be stored in the Customer ID table field. That would not make much sense, because several customer could have the same first name. Good design dictates that you

should try to bind your combo box and control source by a unique value on the Row Source side of the transaction. For our example chose column 1, CustID.

Tip

You can use a 0-inch column as a bound column to bind to a column you do not want to display in the combo box.

13. Although there are many other customization properties you can experiment with, the last required property to be set is List Width. The *list width* determines the width of the drop-down list when the button is pushed. If you have three one-inch columns displayed in your column count and column width properties, and your combo box is only one inch wide, you will have to scroll from side to side to view the data. You can avoid having to scroll by specifying a proper list width.

The best method for choosing the proper list width is to add the column widths together and enter that size into the list width. Because the three columns total 1.75 inches, enter **1.75** in the List Width text area.

Now that you have completed your properties sheet, it should appear similar to figure 23.48.

Combo Box: Field32:	
All Properties	
Name	Field32:
Control Source	Customer ID
Row Source Type	Table/Query
Row Source	tblCustomers
Column Count	3
Column Heads	No
Column Widths	0.25 in;0.5 in;1 in
Bound Column	1
List Rows	8
List Width	1.75 in
Status Bar Text	
Limit To List	No
Auto Expand	Yes
Default Value	
Validation Rule	
Validation Text	
Visible	Yes
Display When	Always
Enabled	Yes

Figure 23.48
A complete properties sheet for a combo box.

IV

Microsoft Access

Now would be a good time to review your work. Select Form view to get a look at your new combo box (see fig. 23.49). When it appears, move to the Customer ID control and click on the arrow button. A list of your customers appears. Make your selection with the mouse or scroll down using the keyboard and press Enter. The bound column 1, CustID, is returned and stored in the Customer ID control in the underlying table.

Figure 23.49
A combo box in
action.

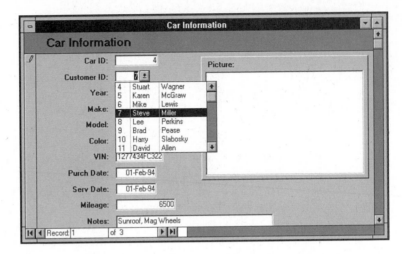

If you are satisfied with what you see, return to Design view and save your work.

OLE Objects in Data

One of the real power features in Microsoft Access is its capability to store pictures, sound, video, and even whole documents with the text data that makes up a record in a database. Access utilizes a Microsoft technology called object linking and embedding (OLE) to accomplish this feat.

OLE objects in Access are used in two different, but similar, ways: unbound and bound. Unbound OLE objects are used mainly for decorative window dressing. An example of this is the logo and textured background of the Northwind Traders database (see fig. 23.50).

Bound OLE objects are linked to the record being viewed. As you page through the car information form or an employee database, all the different photos displayed are bound OLE objects.

In Chapter 21, "Creating and Using Tables," you created an OLE object field in the tblCars table. In this example, you will place a picture with the cars for photo identification.

The first step to adding an image to an OLE object is the same as with any other control: highlight the control so that it has your cursor's focus. Next, select Insert Object from the Edit menu to display the Insert Object dialog box (see fig. 23.51). Choosing the correct object type here creates a link between the object and the software used to create it. Because most images can be used by Microsoft Paintbrush, choose Paintbrush from the list.

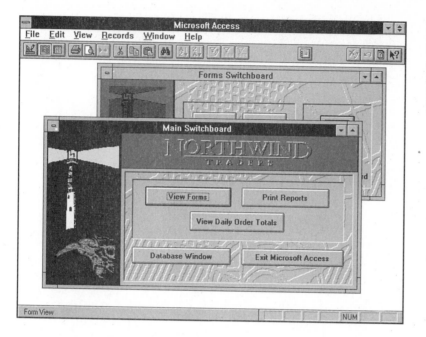

Figure 23.50
Unbound OLE
objects are used to
hold the logo and
background
bitmap images.

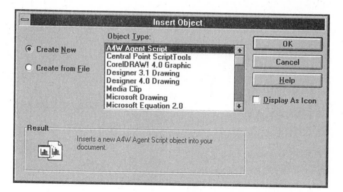

Figure 23.51
The Insert Object
dialog box helps
you locate the type
of object to which
you want to link.

If you want to create a new object from scratch and have it linked to the record, you would click on OK. Next, you are presented with a standard Windows file browse dialog box. Use it to find any BMP, PCX, or other file that can be used by Paintbrush, then click on OK. The image is now pulled in to the OLE object control (see fig. 23.52).

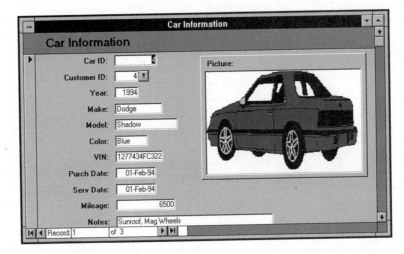

Figure 23.52
The car picture is
linked to its text
record.

Depending on your particular requirement, there are some adjustments you can make to the OLE control. Switch to Design view and highlight the OLE control. Click on the toolbar button to display the properties list if it is not already visible. Use the combo box at the top of the list box to select only Layout properties. You will notice a property call Size Mode. Experiment with this property to create the effect that best suits your needs:

✔ The first setting, Clip, displays the image in its original size without regard to the size of the OLE control. If the image is much larger than the control, you will be able to view only a portion of it.

✔ The Stretch setting stretches the image to fit the size of the OLE control. The image might have to distort in order to accomplish the scaling. Depending on the type of image, this might be undesirable.

✔ Zoom is similar to Stretch except that Zoom maintains the aspect ratio of the image and will only enlarge or reduce to a size that will fit into the OLE control without distortion. This setting sometimes causes a image to appear off-center within the OLE control.

Bound OLE controls have one major benefit that other competing technologies do not possess: because it is linked to its creator, an object can be returned to its creator for use by a simple double-click of the mouse. In the case of images, the image is loaded into the drawing package. For sound or video, the object starts playing.

For a quick example of this benefit, in Form view double-click on the car picture in the OLE control. Paintbrush—or whatever program you have associated with the .BMP extension in your registration database—opens and loads the image of your car, and it is ready for a new paint job (see fig. 23.53). Make any modifications you want to the car using the Paintbrush

tools. When you are finished, close Paintbrush. You will be asked if you would like to update the OLE control. If you answer Yes, the changes you made will be carried back into the OLE control in Access.

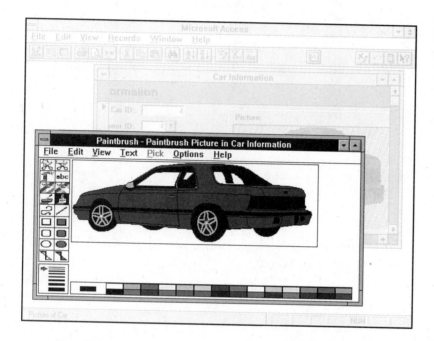

Figure 23.53
Modifying the car object in Paintbrush.

When you decide to delete an OLE object, simply highlight it with a mouse click and press Del.

Tab Order

When you begin to enter data into your new car information form, you will quickly notice that as you move down through the control the cursor does not move in a logical sequence. It jumps around the window, prompting you to enter data in an illogical order.

Windows has gotten us in the habit of pressing Tab to move between field and control rather than pressing Enter, as with older DOS applications. Hence, the tab order. By setting the tab order, you have complete control over the cursor movement as you tab through the controls on your forms.

While you have the car information window open, select Design view and choose Tab Order from the Edit pull down menu. The Tab Order dialog box appears, as shown in figure 21.54.

Figure 23.54
The Tab Order
dialog box
enables you to
control the cursor
movement through
your forms.

The Auto Order button rearranges the order for movement from left to right and top to bottom. Auto Order is a good start, but due to the complexity of most forms, it cannot be used alone. The car information form is such an example. Because the picture control is to the right of the Customer ID control, Auto Order would send the cursor there next. Logically, the picture field should be first or last, but certainly not third.

The small buttons to the left of the field names are the same as record selectors in your forms. By pressing the button, then clicking and dragging the field, you can move it to any location in the tab order you want.

Click the mouse and hold the button down while you highlight several controls. This makes it possible to move several controls at once.

Sizing the Form

After you have finished you basic form design, the last step is to size the form. All forms have two boundaries: one for the right side and one for the bottom (see fig. 23.55).

When you have pulled in the boundaries to just beyond the edges of the outermost controls, choose File, Save Form. When you open your form the next time it will maintain its neat appearance (see fig. 23.56).

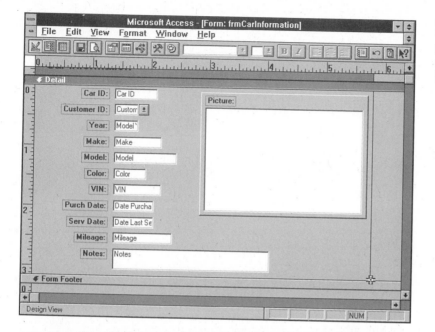

Figure 23.55
Moving both sides
of the form
boundaries.

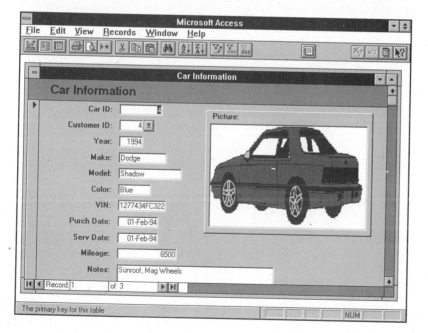

Figure 23.56
A clean finished
form.

Embedding a Subform

Creating a main form or subform can be done quickly using the Main/Subform Form Wizard. For you to understand subforms thoroughly, however, it is best if you create one from scratch.

A *subform* simply is another form embedded to a main form. In the case of an invoice, the main form would contain the header information about the customer, shipping instructions, and so on, whereas the subform would be the scrolling area below the header that contains the items you want to order.

You must, of course, create a subform before you can embed it onto the main form. There is no difference between a main form and a subform in terms of its creation. Forms are only referred to as subforms when they are embedded within other forms.

In this example a new customer main form, called frmCustomer, has been created (see fig. 23.57).

Figure 23.57
The new customer form.

After you have decided which form you will use as the main form, select the table you want as the source of the subform. The subform for this example will be based on the table tblCars.

Highlight the tblCars table in the database container and then click on the New Form Button on the toolbar. You are once again presented with the Form Wizard. Choose to run a Form Wizard instead of a blank form.

Next, you are asked which Form Wizard you want to run. Choose Tabular and click on OK. Access next asks which field you want on the new form. Select Model Year, Make, Model, and Color, then click on Next.

Access now wants to know what look you want for your form. Choose Standard, then click on Next. The next step asks you to give the form a name that will appear at the top of the form;

enter **Car Information**. The final step in creating the form is to choose a mode to view it in. Since you have a few more modifications to make choose Design view.

When designing forms for use as main forms, you will place a large emphasis on appearance. Subforms, however, normally are used as simple lists of associated data, so displaying subforms in Datasheet view makes an excellent alternative to the time spent making a tabular form look like a datasheet.

In the properties sheet for your new form, choose Layout properties and set the default view to Datasheet. Save your new form as frmCarInformationSub (see fig. 23.58).

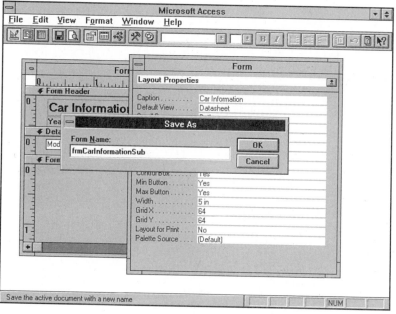

Figure 23.58
The new form with the default view set to Datasheet and about to be saved.

Open the new customer form in Design view and move it to the side to allow a view of the database container. Click and drag your new subform object from the database container and drop it in the blank area at the bottom of the customer form (see fig. 23.59).

Your subform now is embedded in the main form and has become a control on the main form. It can be referred to just like any other control on the main form; however, the controls on the subform are not objects on the main form. They remain objects of the subform. This is why a subform appears as a big white box, instead of displaying its controls.

Tip

To edit the subform, double-click on it while the main form is in design mode.

Figure 23.59
The customer form
in Design view
with a clear view
of the database
container.

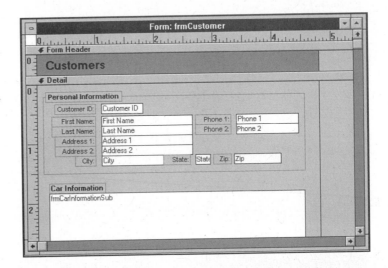

Figure 23.59
The customer form
in Design view
with a clear view
of the database
container.

The subform will only display records that are associated to the record in the main form through the use of a common field. This is call a *parent-child relationship*. The parent (master) is the record in the main form and the child records are those in the subform. In the process of a drag-and-drop, the subform looks for a common field. In this example, it found the Customer ID field to be in both the tblCars and tblCustomers tables. Open the property sheet for the subform and notice the Link Master Field and Link Child Field settings in the Data Properties section have been set to the same field. A simpler way of stating this is, "Display only the record in the tblCars where the Customer ID field matches the Customer ID field in the tblCustomer table."

Now display the main form in Form view. Page through the customers until you find Stuart Wagner. You will notice his car is displayed in the subform. Open the Car Information form and assign the Red Ferrari and the Blue Plymouth Voyager to Paul Helms. Now, back in the Customer form, you will notice that when you get to Paul Helms's record he has two cars assigned to him.

Chapter Snapshot

Technically speaking, *macros* are a sequence of actions that correspond to desired activities that perform when called upon. This chapter explains the composition of macros, covers the structure of the macro window, and describes the different predefined actions. Specifically, by reading this chapter you will learn about the following:

By the time you finish this chapter, you will have created several macros, and will have a firm grasp on the concept of macros and what they can do for your database.

CHAPTER

Using Macros

By Paul Cassel

Macros enable you to automate repetitive tasks. You can automate just about anything with a macro, and macros reduce repetitive tasks to just a mouse click or two. The macro can either be a single action or a series of actions. Macros are similar to small programs within your Microsoft Access application, even though it is not technically a "program."

Suppose, for example, that you want to have one button that closes your customer form, such as the one in figure 24.1. The process of closing a form is simply completed via a command button (the Close button) that has a macro attached to it. Every time you want to close the customer form, you simply click on that button and the macro closes the form for you.

Figure 24.1

Clicking on the Close button generates a close macro.

Input New Information

Phone Numbers

First Name:	Jim
Last Name:	Wagner
Address 1:	9201 Keystone Way
Address 2:	
City, State, Zip:	Indianapolis IN 47101
Phone 1:	(317) 555-4157
Phone 2:	

Close

Record: 20   of 20

You can create macros using many different methods. Keep in mind that no real programming knowledge is necessary, but such knowledge can be helpful—especially if you have a strong sense of logical sequence.

When To Use Macros

When is a good time to use a macro in your Access application? Anytime that you want to automate a routine task. Knowing that macros do the exact same thing every time you launch them, you can utilize macros to make your applications more efficient. You should use macros to:

✔ Make your forms and reports work together more efficiently. You can open your customer form and have a macro that will run a mailing label report.

✔ Set values in controls. An example would be with invoices. If you want your Totals to equal Quantities × Price, you need to state that expression in a macro. The macro executes itself after you enter the price.

✔ Automate data transfers. If, at the end of every month, you need to export the sales numbers out to an Excel spreadsheet, you can create a macro to automate that process.

✔ Customize your applications. By enhancing your macro skills, you make it easier for you and others with minimal computer skills to perform complex tasks.

Exploring the Macro Window

Macros are created and defined in one window called the Macro window, as shown in figure 24.2.

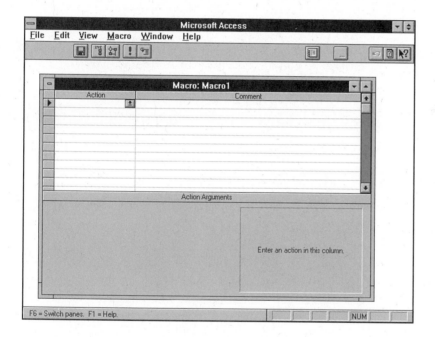

Figure 24.2
The Default Macro window.

The window consists of the Toolbar and the body. The body of the macro window has two sections. The top section is where you add your actions.

The lower section of the window is the action argument section. Most actions have an argument. An *argument* gives Access additional information on how to perform an individual action. If you use the action Open Form, for instance, you need to tell Access which form to open. You do that in the argument section of the macro window.

Toolbar

The toolbar is the section across the top of the Macro window, such as any Access window, which contains buttons for various activities (see table 24.1).

IV

Microsoft Access

Table 24.1
Standard Toolbar Icons

Icon	Name	Description
	Macro Name	Provides the Macro Names column in the Macro window
	Condition	Provides the *Conditions* column in the Macro window
	Run	This button, a shortcut for Run Macro in the <u>F</u>ile menu, executes the macro.
	Single Step	Enables you to execute the macro one step at a time
	Database	Jumps to Database view
	Build	Invokes a builder or wizard
	Undo	Undoes your most recent change
	Cue Cards	Starts Cue Card–style help
	Help	Brings up Access Help

Some of the buttons in table 24.1 provide shortcuts to menu commands used when writing a macro. The first button on the toolbar provides the *Macro Names* column in the Macro window. It is a shortcut from selecting Macro Name from the <u>V</u>iew pull-down menu.

The second button on the Toolbar provides the *Conditions* column in the Macro window. This button is the equivalent to selecting Conditions from the View pull-down menu.

The exclamation mark button is the *RUN* button. This button, a shortcut for Run Macro in the <u>F</u>ile menu, executes the macro.

Note Before you can run any macro, you must save it first. If you forget to save the macro, Access will prompt you to do so before the program executes your macro.

The fourth button from the left—the Single Step method—is helpful when you are debugging a macro. It enables you to execute the macro one step at a time. By executing it one step at a time, you can check to make sure that your actions take place in the correct order. You can also can easily spot a line that causes an error.

The *Undo* button does exactly that. It undoes your most recent change. Remember that the Undo button only undoes your most recent change, unlike other Microsoft products that can store your changes and allow you to undo several changes.

The *Question Mark* (or *Help*) button brings up Access Help. The Help button is context sensitive, meaning that Access knows where you are and offers you help for the area that you are working with. Pressing the Question Mark button is the same as pressing the F1 key.

Tip Another way to bring up the Help feature is to hold down the Shift key and press F1. Your pointer will then have a large, black question mark attached to it, as shown in Fig. 24.3. By pointing and clicking on the subject in question, Access will display the Help menu specific to that subject.

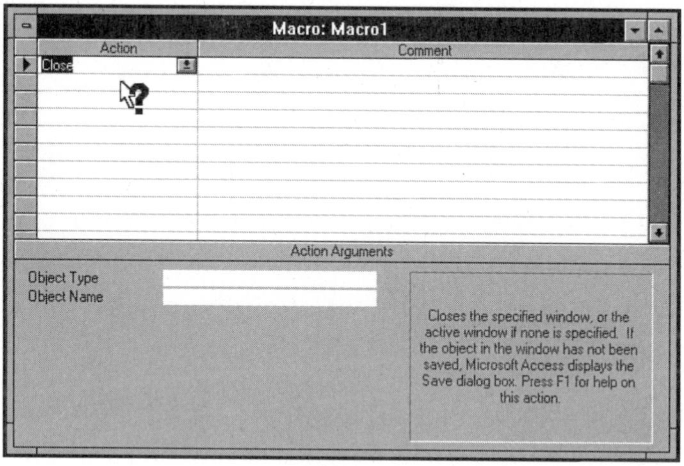

Figure 24.3
The pointer changes when you press Shift+F1.

Actions

In the default Macro window view, the action section appears in columns and rows. Currently, there are two columns. The first is the action and the second is the comment.

Columns

The *comment column* is an area where you can make remarks about the macro or the action. This column is optional, but is highly recommended. When you utilize this column, you can easily find out what each macro does, instead of trying to read every macro in your application. The column also makes for easier debugging. Debugging is covered later in this chapter.

The other column is the *action column*. There are numerous different actions that Access makes available to you through a drop-down *combo box*. By clicking on the arrow, the combo box lists all the different, predefined actions from which you can choose. Highlight the action you desire and press Enter, or use the mouse to click on the desired action.

Rows

Rows show the individual macros that will perform when activated. When a macro executes, each line of the macro is addressed by Access, and it moves from top to bottom.

 The Row Selector is the gray box to the left of the actions column. By clicking on that box, you can highlight the entire row. This can be used for modification purposes.

Comments

Comment is an optional column that is used to remind you about two things:

✔ The result that you are trying to accomplish with the action

✔ To which button on a certain table, form, or report an action is linked.

Arguments

Arguments don't just happen between a married couple or best friends. *Action* arguments define how Access performs an individual action. For example, if you use the action OPENFORM, an argument states which form is to be opened.

For the different actions, the number of arguments differs from action to action. Some arguments are optional. If you are not sure what information the macro needs for an argument, Access provides you with hints in the lower right corner of the macro window, as seen in figure 24.4.

 You can switch between the two sections of the window by pressing the F6 key.

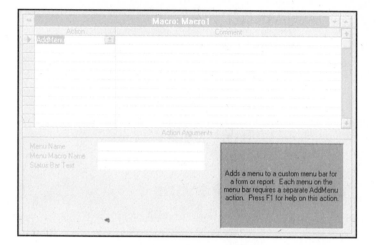

Figure 24.4
Argument hints are in the lower right corner of the macro window.

Defining Macro Actions

As mentioned earlier, there are numerous different, predefined macro actions. Some actions perform tasks that can be accomplished through pull-down menus. Other actions perform tasks that cannot be achieved through pull-down menus: BEEP and MSGBOX, for example. The following discussions explain the different groups of actions and provide a brief description of each action's result.

Tip

You can activate the drop-down box in the action column by holding down the Alt key and pressing the down arrow, or by pressing F4.

Navigating Actions

Navigating actions enables you to move the focus to another window or to a control on a form. To bring *focus* to a screen means to activate that table, query, form, report, macro or module.

If you have two or more windows open at one time, look at the title bar. The window that has focus is the window with the highlighted title bar.

GoToControl

GoToControl enables you to give focus to the control that you named in the Control Name argument. Anything on a form is considered a control: a button, a field, a subform, a list box, and so on. GoToControl gives you the ability to decide which button, field, subform, or list box gets the focus.

GoToPage

If you have a multipage form, *GoToPage* places the focus on the first field on the page that you elect in the GoToPage arguments.

GoToRecord

This action moves the focus to a specific record in a form, table or query. With this action, you specify where you want the focus. GoToRecord is the equivalent to choosing the Go To command from the Records pull-down menu item.

Searching and Sorting Actions

The following actions enable you to search and sort specified records.

ApplyFilter

ApplyFilter runs a query or a filter saved as a query. In your form or report, there are three filtering buttons, as shown in figure 24.5.

Figure 24.5
An example of
filter buttons.

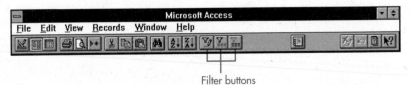

Filter buttons

When you click on the first filter button, Access displays the query that was used to create that form. After you have set your criteria for the information that you would like to sort, you can save that query as a filter. This filter sorts and refines records from the specified query. Of the two arguments listed, only one needs to be filled in.

Tip

To use ApplyFilter on a report, you must assign it to the OnOpen property.

FindRecord

FindRecord locates the first record that meets the criteria that is specified by the arguments in the active table, query, or form. FindRecord should not be confused with find *all* records that match the criteria. FindRecord only finds the *first* record that matches the criteria. If you are sitting on the last record, Access asks you if you want to continue the search from the beginning of the dynaset.

A dynaset is a live subset of your data, usually created by a query.

FindNext

FindNext locates the next record that meets the criteria specified by the previous FindRecord. In essence, FindNext enables you to scroll, one-at-a-time, through the records that meet the criteria that you specified in FindRecord.

Requery

Requery repeats the query that originally filled a control with data. It has the same effect as pressing Shift+F9.

RunSQL

RunSQL runs an SQL statement. Structured Query Language (SQL) is a language used to give you an English-like method of querying data. Some people prefer to work with SQL for its performance abilities. For more information, see Appendix B, "Microsoft Access SQL," in your *Access Language Reference* manual.

ShowAllRecords

ShowAllRecords removes any filter and returns all the records to their original state.

Object-Manipulation Actions

An Access database is made up of different objects, tables, queries, forms, reports, macros, and modules. Objects can be created and edited within each table, query, form, report, macro, and module. You can control those objects through the following actions.

CopyObject

CopyObject enables you to copy a currently selected database object from one location to another. It has the same function as selecting the Export command from the File menu. In the same step, you can copy this object to another database and give it a new name, depending on the arguments you provide.

DeleteObject

DeleteObject removes an object from the database. It has the same function as highlighting the object in database view and pressing Del.

IV

Microsoft Access

Print

Print prints the currently selected database object, which can be the active datasheet, report, or form. Print has the same effect as selecting <u>P</u>rint from the <u>F</u>ile menu. You specify the print settings by providing arguments.

Rename

Rename does just that: renaming the selected object. The object you are trying to rename cannot be open when you rename it. Remember that Rename does not make a copy of the object; it simply renames the original one. Rename has the same effect as selecting the object and then selecting Rename from the <u>F</u>ile menu.

RepaintObject

RepaintObject completes any pending screen updates for the specified database object. If Access is not updating fields quickly, and a number of the fields are updated through SetValue actions, repainting causes the object to recalculate those fields. RepaintObject has the same effect as pressing F9.

If you select an object for repainting from the database window and drag the object to the action arguments section of the Macro window, Access fills in the Object Type and the Object Name arguments as necessary.

SelectObject

SelectObject is designed to give focus to the object specified in the argument.

If you select an object from the database window and drag it to the action arguments section of the Macro window, Access automatically fills in the Object Type and the Object Name arguments.

SetValue

SetValue sets the value of a field, control, or property. An example would be a total field on an invoice. If you enter a quantity and price, the total field requires the calculation of the quantity times the price. The first argument for the SetValue action is the total field. The second argument is the expression required of quantity times price.

Another use of SetValue is to modify a controls property. A common use of this would be to change the visible property to control whether or not you can see a particular field based upon a specific condition.

You cannot use the SetValue action on a calculated control used on a form or report. Also, you cannot use SetValue in Access Basic.

Form and Window Manipulation Actions

In Access, form and window manipulation actions give you greater control over forms and windows. With these macros, you control the forms, queries, tables, and reports as they appear on the screen.

AddMenu

AddMenu is used when you create a custom menu bar for your forms. AddMenu adds a drop-down menu to a custom menu bar. The custom menu bar replaces the standard Access menu bar. If you want to keep some of the standard Access commands on your custom menu bar, utilize the DoMenuItem action for each command you want.

Close

Close has the same effect as choosing Close from the <u>F</u>ile pull-down menu. It closes the specified object or the active window.

If you select an object from the database window and drag it to the action arguments section of the Macro window, Access automatically fills in the Object Type and the Object Name arguments necessary to close that object.

Maximize

Maximize resizes the active window so that it fills the entire workspace. It has the same effect as clicking on the maximize arrow button in the upper right-hand corner of the document.

Minimize

Minimize shrinks the active window down to an icon. Minimize has the same effect as clicking on the minimize arrow button in the upper right-hand corner of the document.

Restore

Restore returns the minimized or maximized window to its original size and position before it was minimized or maximized.

MoveSize

MoveSize offers you the ability to change both the size and/or the location of the active window—depending on the arguments.

OpenForm

OpenForm does just that. It opens the form that you specify in the argument. With this feature, you can launch a form from another form.

An easier way to open a form is to drag the form from the database window to the action column of the macro window. Access automatically fills in your arguments.

OpenModule

OpenModule opens the specified Access Basic module. This can be a sub, a function, or an event procedure. See Chapter 26, "Understanding Access Basic," for more information on subs, functions, and event procedures.

OpenQuery

OpenQuery runs an action query or opens a select or crosstab query. It opens the query specified in the argument.

To utilize OpenQuery more efficiently, drag the query from the database window to the action column of the macro window, and Access will automatically fill in the arguments.

OpenReport

OpenReport opens the report stated in the arguments. When you send a report to the printer with OpenReport, Access prints the report without displaying the Print dialog box. Access uses the most recent printer settings.

OpenTable

OpenTable is the action you want to use when you need to view, modify, or print all the records in a table.

An easier way is to drag the table from the database window to the action column of the macro window. Access automatically fills in your arguments for you.

Macro and Code Actions

You also can use macros that control other macros or other Access Basic modules. The following sections describe those types of macros.

CancelEvent

CancelEvent is an action that has no arguments. It cancels the event that causes a macro to run. Certain event properties can be canceled. When working with a form, the events that can be cancelled include: BeforeUpdate, OnClose, OnDelete, OnInsert, and OnOpen. When working with controls on forms, you can cancel BeforeUpdate, OnDblClick, and OnExit. Reports only have one event that can be cancelled: OnOpen. Report sections, however, have two cancelable events: OnFormat and OnPrint.

It is possible to have a CancelEvent action in a macro that is attached to a form's OnClose property. Keep in mind that the form will not close because the CancelEvent cancels the Close.

To close the form, remove the CancelEvent action from the macro, or fix the circumstances that caused the cancel event in the first place.

DoMenuItem

An Access menu command is carried out by the DoMenuItem action. Use the *DoMenuItem* action when you create a custom menu bar and want some of the Access menu commands to appear on your menu bar. Some of the common menu commands used are Open, Close, and Save.

RunApp

With *RunApp*, you have the ability to launch other Microsoft or MS-DOS applications from within your Access application. Some of the applications that you can launch from your Access application are Word and Excel.

RunCode

RunCode activates an Access Basic Function procedure.

RunCode only runs Functions. If you need to run a Sub Procedure, have a Function that calls that Sub Procedure and then use RunCode to execute that Function.

RunMacro

RunMacro executes a macro, even if that macro is a part of a macro group. This command is similar to the Run Macro command in the File menu. The exception is that the Run Macro command only executes the macro one time. With the RunMacro action, you can specify the number of times that the macro repeats by entering a number in the Repeat Count and/or Repeat Expression found in the argument.

 When you utilize the Repeat Count or Repeat Expression (found in the argument of the RunMacro action), you can run it as many times as you want.

StopAllMacros

StopAllMacros terminates any macro that is currently running. Use this action when an error condition returns true. By using a conditional expression in the macro's action row, you can execute StopAllMacros.

StopMacro

StopMacro terminates the macro that is currently running. StopMacro is different from StopAllMacros in that this stops only one macro: the one that is being called.

Importing and Exporting Data Actions

The following actions enable you to import and export data to and from your database in different formats.

OutputTo

OutputTo exports the data from an Access datasheet, form, report or module to the other Microsoft Office applications in XLS-, RTF-, or TXT-based form.

SendObject

SendObject includes the specified Access object in a MAPI-compliant e-mail message. The object can be a report, form, module, or datasheet in RTF, XLS, or TXT format.

TransferDatabase

Using *TransferDatabase* enables you to exchange information to and from other databases into your Access database. This command is the same as choosing Import, Export, or Attach Table from the File pull-down menu. If you choose Attach Table, then both databases can see any changes you make to either table without having to enter the data in twice.

TransferSpreadsheet

TransferSpreadsheet enables you to exchange information to and from other spreadsheets and your Access database. This command is the same as choosing Import or Export from the File menu.

TransferText

TransferText permits you to transfer text between your Access application and a text file. This action has the same effect as choosing Import or Export from the File menu.

Miscellaneous Actions

Miscellaneous actions are those actions that do not seem to fit in the previous categories, but are nonetheless important. The following sections discuss several miscellaneous actions.

Beep

Beep causes your computer to discharge a beep sound. Beeps are important when you want to signal the user that there has been a change in the screen. When the data that has been entered is not correct, or when a macro has reached a certain point in its steps, a Beep might sound.

Echo

Echo enables you to see what the computer is doing to the screen. The activity that you see when a macro is running is non-essential. If the activity bothers you, you can turn off the Echo by setting Echo to NO. With Echo off, the macro runs behind the scenes. When the macro is finished, Echo is automatically turned back on, and Access repaints the screen.

Hourglass

The *Hourglass* macro changes your arrow cursor to an hourglass. This provides a visual sign that a macro is running, or that the computer is busy with another task. With Hourglass argument set to off, the pointer remains a pointer.

MsgBox

MsgBox displays a message to you. You can type up to 255 characters in the message box. MsgBox offers you other options, such as a beep, a title, or an icon. A combination of these options lets you know whether an error is critical, a warning, or informative. Use the MsgBox action with validation macros. MsgBox can provide information about what kind of data should be entered.

Quit

Quit not only exits the database you are working with, but it also exits Access itself. Any macros that come after Quit will not execute. If, on Quit, you have not saved your data, Access prompts you to do so.

SendKeys

SendKeys action relays keystrokes directly to Access or the active Windows application. Access processes the keystrokes it receives exactly as if you had typed them directly into the active window. You have up to 255 characters per SendKeys action. If the result that you are trying to achieve requires more than 255 characters, you may have a succession of SendKeys actions.

SetWarnings

SetWarnings enables you to turn your system messages on or off. Use this action when you want to prevent modal messages and warnings from stopping a macro.

A *modal* message or warning is a box that appears on your screen that you must respond to before you can continue. Modal forms have focus and will not release it until you answer the modal form questions. An example is the Save Changes dialog box that appears when you make changes on your Form in Design view. No matter what you do, you cannot close that Form until you have decided whether to save the changes.

ShowToolbar

ShowToolbar shows or hides built-in or custom toolbars.

If you need additional information on any of the actions discussed earlier, press the F1 key in Access. After the help menu activates, search for the name of the desired action and press Enter.

Applying Macros

One of the best features of Access, as well as all Microsoft products, is the fact that when you know how to create one new object, you know how to create all new objects. Whether it is a new table, query, form, report, macro, or module, you click on the object button, then the New button. You also can create a new macro by selecting <u>V</u>iew and clicking on Macro. Then click on New or press Alt+N.

Macros are triggered by events. When dealing with forms and reports, events, such as OnOpen, OnClose, On Enter, and On Exit, occur, and most macros run based on the occurrence of an event. The only macro that runs by itself is the Autoexec macro.

Add Action

Bring up a new macro screen. Press the ALT Down Arrow key, or click on the down arrow box in the action column of the new macro. Access displays a combo box of all of the pre-defined actions (see fig. 24.6). Click on the action that you want and Access brings up the arguments, if any, that are associated with that action.

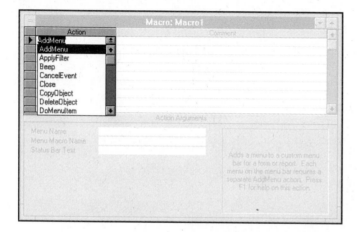

Figure 24.6
The Action combo box.

Fill out the arguments associated with that action. To get to the argument section of the macro, either click in the lower half of the window or press the F6 key. Make sure that you fill out the required arguments associated with that action (see fig. 24.7).

In the lower right side of the window, a hint box appears. This hint lets you know that this action, OpenTable, has a required argument. Access also displays a combo box from which to choose a table.

Figure 24.7
The argument
provides a combo
box.

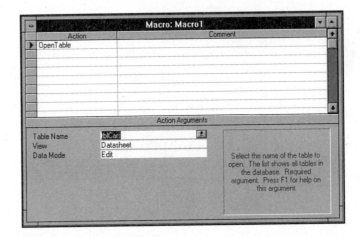

Figure 24.7
The argument
provides a combo
box.

Drag & Drop

When Access opens a table or a form, you can create a macro. With the Drag & Drop feature, creating a macro is as simple as opening a new macro window and dragging the table or form object to the actions column of the macro (see fig. 24.8).

Figure 24.8
Dragging a table
object to the
action column.

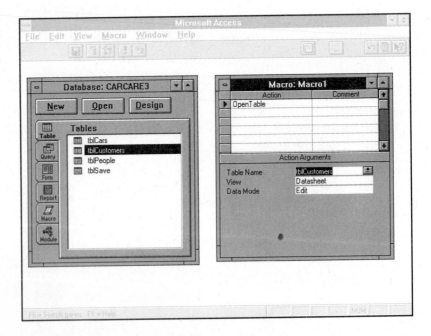

As you can see in the figure 24.8, you need to view the object *and* macro window so that you can utilize the drag and drop feature. After you have dragged and dropped the object, Access automatically fills out the arguments needed to open it.

Running Macros

After you have selected the action and filled in its arguments, you can run your macro. Before any macro will run, you must first save it. Choose **S**ave from the **F**ile menu item or double click on the control box for that macro. Clicking on the control box will would normally close the macro, but because the macro has yet to be saved, Access places a message box on the screen. Would you like to save the macro? Your choices are Yes, No, Cancel, and Help. Yes is the same as pressing File, then Save As. No will return you to the database window. Cancel will return you to the macro. Help is the same as pressing the F1 key.

You can run a macro in many ways, including the following:

✔ Select Run Macro from the **F**ile menu.

✔ Place the macro in an event of a form or report, and then trigger that event.

✔ The third and fourth ways are through buttons found on the macro toolbar. The first icon looks like an exclamation point and the second looks like a stack of papers with a curved arrow.

The Run icon is the one that looks like an exclamation point. By pressing this button, Access executes your macro immediately.

The Step icon is the one that looks like a stack of papers with a curved arrow. This also runs your macro immediately, but it executes only one line at a time. This feature enables you to view your macro as it is being executed.

Editing Macros

Editing or modifying a macro is as simple as editing or modifying any other database object. Simply go to the database window and click on the macro button. All of your macros appear in a database container. Click on the macro that you want to modify and press the Design button, shown in figure 24.9.

Figure 24.9
You edit a macro in the Design mode.

IV

Microsoft Access

Tip

Right-clicking in the macro design grid pops up a handy shortcut menu just as in other Access areas.

After you are in the design mode, you can edit the macro. You can edit the actions, modify the arguments, add, move, or delete rows.

To add new rows to the upper half of the window, simply click on the row where you want the new rows to be inserted. Next, click on the Edit pull-down menu and select Insert Row.

Tip

You can quickly insert rows by clicking on the Row Selector and pressing Ins. The Row Selector is the gray box that appears to the left of the action row (see fig. 24.10).

Figure 24.10
Your pointer will change colors when you are over the Row Selector box.

To move rows around within your macro, use the row selector to highlight the rows that you want to move. With the rows selected, click on one of the darkened rows' row selector box and hold down the mouse button. Drag the mouse to the point that you would like to move the macro to. Release the mouse button and Access will move the action and arguments to the new location for you. This is particularly helpful when dealing with macro groups, which will be discussed on the next few pages.

Deleting Macros

To remove an action, use the row selectors to highlight that row. With that row highlighted, you can either select Delete from the Edit menu or press the Del key.

Tip You can remove a macro by highlighting that macro in the database window and pressing the Del key.

Macro Groups

So far, when discussing macros, each macro had only one action in each macro window. As your applications become more complex, you will probably have more macros. To manage your macros, you can consolidate them under one macro. A *macro group* is a series of one or more macros that appear in the same window. A good example of this would be several buttons on one form. For each button on that form, there is a macro. You can put all of these macro groups in macro objects.

To create a macro group, locate the macro and click on the Design button. The macro appears in Design view. From the View menu, click on Macro Names. Another column called Macro Names now appears on your macro window.

Tip You can activate the Macro Names column by clicking on the Macro Names button—the one with XYZ on it (found on your macro toolbar).

Macro Names

Type in a macro name for each set of actions that make up a macro group. When naming a macro group, use the name of the button or event that will trigger the macro to run. Save the entire macro as the name of the table, form, or report that these macro groups are associated with.

Conditions

Macro groups are addressed by Access beginning with the first action and then continuing down the list, reading the first row, then the next, and so on.

There might be a time when you want to run a macro only when a particular condition is true. This is where the Condition column in the action section of the macro comes in.

Note A *Condition* is a logical expression. The only answers to a logical expression are True or False.

As you enter conditions for your macro, if the condition for that macro row is true, Access performs that action. Within one macro, you can cause a series of actions to perform when the condition is true. By placing an ellipse in the condition column, Access will proceed to the next action. If that condition proves to be true, then Access will execute that action.

 You can change the default macro window to reflect the macro names and condition columns automatically. Simply alter the Macro Category in the **O**ptions pull-down menu.

If the expression in the condition proves to be false, Access skips that row and moves to the next row.

Debugging Macros

After you understand how easy macros are, they can become addictive. Macros make your applications more powerful and flexible. But as surely as a toddler will stumble when it is trying to walk, you will experience problems with your macros.

The following sections discuss a few methods for finding a faulty macro line.

Normal Mode

The first one is the Normal Mode. You can test the macro in Normal Mode by clicking on the Run button on the toolbar. This runs the macro without leaving the macro window.

Single Step Mode

The second method to finding a faulty macro line is the Single Step Mode. Single Step Mode enables you to execute the entire macro one action at a time. By clicking on the Single Step button—the fifth button from the left on the toolbar—Access changes a switch that makes the Run button execute only one action at a time. After clicking on the Single Step, click on the Run button. This begins the single-stepping process.

Before each action is executed, Access displays a dialog box like the one in figure 24.11.

From the Single Step dialog box, you have three choices:

✔ Click on the Step button. This moves you to the next action. If the response is not what you expected, this is where your bug is located.

✔ Click on the Halt button. The Halt button stops the Run process and returns you to the macro window.

✔ Click on the Continue button. This causes the macro to finish out in the normal Run Mode.

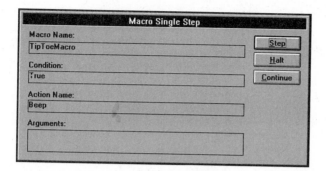

Figure 24.11
The Single Step dialog box.

The Single Step process is like an on/off switch for that macro. If you depress the button to fix a bug, the button will remain depressed until you press it again. (Yes, even if you close the window and re-open it, the button will remain depressed until you press it again.)

Special-Access Macros

As mentioned before, almost all Access macros are triggered by events in your application. Access recognizes that things that you do in your databases cause events to happen. Pushing a button on your form or opening and closing a form are examples of events. Macros are triggered by events that are activated.

There are two macros that do not need to be linked to an event in your database to activate. They are the AutoExec macro and the AutoKeys macro.

AutoExec Macro

The AutoExec macro can perform just about any macro action. The AutoExec macro is activated when the database is opened. Hence, you can have the AutoExec macro do everything from removing the Access toolbar to importing or exporting data to opening a commonly used form. The AutoExec macro can do anything that you want your database to do automatically upon start-up.

To create an AutoExec macro, simply create a macro that performs all the actions that you want executed when the database is first opened. Save the macro as AutoExec. The next time you open that database, the AutoExec macro will kick into action.

If you want to start your database and do not want the AutoExec macro to execute, press and hold the Shift key when you open the database.

IV

Microsoft Access

AutoKeys Macro

The AutoKeys Macro is the other macro that falls under the Special Macros classification. AutoKeys enables you to assign a macro to key combinations. You can either overwrite current key combinations or create new ones. For example, if you press Ctrl+C, Windows copies the highlighted text to the Clipboard. If you reassigned a new action to the Ctrl+C combination, Access performs that action for as long as you are in Access.

Note Because the AutoExec macro runs before the AutoKeys macro, you cannot use the AutoKeys macro in the AutoExec macro.

Building Macros

In the chapter on forms, you created two new main forms and another to be used as a subform. In this section, you will automate those forms as well as use macros.

Command Button Macro

Assuming that your car care database is already open, go to form and highlight frmCarInformation. Open the form in the Design mode, as shown in figure 24.12.

Figure 24.12
The Car Information form in design mode.

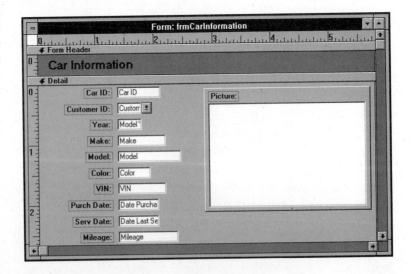

After the form is open, press F11 or click on the Database button in the toolbar to bring the database container in focus. Click on Macros and choose New to begin a new macro.

To better organize your macros, you will put several macro actions within this new macro. To accommodate this organization, you should use the concept of macro groups. Knowing that, you will need to click on the Macro Names button and the Conditions button, or select them from the View menu to display those columns.

Tip

Begin on the second row. It is easier to insert new rows if you have a blank row at the top.

In the Macro Name column, type **CloseButton**. Press the Tab key twice to move the cursor into the Action column. Type **Close** or select Close from the combo box. Note that as soon as you type **Cl**, Access guesses you mean the Close action and fills in the rest of the word for you.

Press the F11 key to bring the database container into focus again. Click on Form and highlight frmCarInformation. Because this is the form that you want to close when the Close button is pushed, click and drag the highlighted object down to the arguments section of the macro window. Access automatically fills in the arguments that are needed to close the frmCarInformation form.

Press the title bar of your macro to bring it back into focus. Save the macro by selecting Save or Save As from the File pull-down menu. In either case, Access prompts you for a Save As dialog box. Save the macro as mcrCarInformation. Using this name, you will know that any macros for the frmCarInformation form can be found in the mcrCarInformation. After saving the macro, close it.

The only two windows visible in your database should be the database container and the frmCarInformation form. Press the F11 key to bring the database container into focus. Click on Macro and highlight the macro you just created, mcrCarInformation. While still pressing the mouse button, drag mcrCarInformation onto the frmCarInformation form and drop it under the OLE Object frame for the car's picture (see fig. 24.13).

Access has automatically created the macro that will close this form when pressed. It has also given this macro's name to the button. To change this, click on the button. This brings the frmCarInformation window into focus and highlights the button. With the button highlighted, press the Properties button on the toolbar or select Properties from the View pull-down menu.

To get the word *Close* to appear on the new button, move your cursor to the Caption line in the properties box. Delete the entire line and type **Close**. Pull down the combo box at the top of the Properties list box and choose Event Properties. Locate the On Click property from the list box and click in the space next to the On Click property—the space that now has mcrCarInformation in it. The macro name is correct, but you have to indicate which macro within that macro group is to occur when the On Click property is activated. Pull down the combo box in the space containing the name mcrCarInformation and locate the CloseForm macro. Click on this macro. Your screen should resemble figure 24.14.

Figure 24.13
Drag and drop
the macro to
create a close
button.

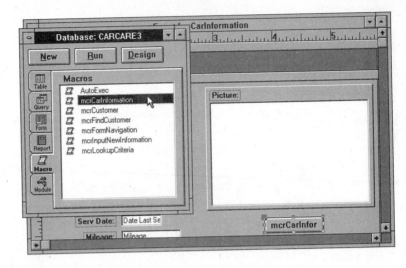

Figure 24.14
A macro within a
macro group.

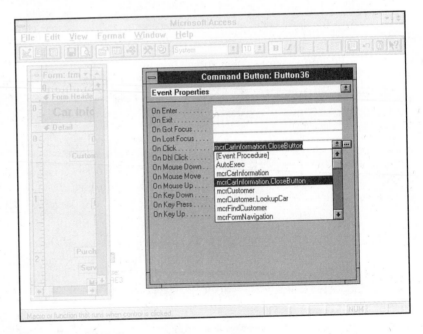

Choose OK and Access returns to the frmCarInformation form. Save the form by selecting
Save from the File menu. Click on the Form View button or select Form from the View menu.
Test the button by clicking on it. Your form should close and the only thing visible is your
database container.

Drill Down Macro

The *Drill Down* macro enables you to gain access to a more detailed view of the same data. In the car care system, you have a table of customers and a table of cars. Each customer has a record. Within that record is stored information about their various cars. However, this list only provides limited information such as color, make, and model. A way is needed to gain instant access to the complete information about a specific car. That's exactly what a Drill Down macro does. It takes you down to a more detailed view of information that is already visible.

Assuming that your car care database is open, click on Macro and choose New to create a macro. Display your Macro Names and Condition columns. The name of this macro group is LookupCar. In the action column, we want to open the car information form. Select OpenForm in the action column. Press the F11 key to bring your database container into focus. Click on Form and drag the frmCarInformation form to the argument section of the LookupCar OpenForm macro. Access automatically fills in the required arguments needed to open that form. Save the macro as mcrCustomer because all macro groups relating to the customer form should be stored within this macro. When you are finished, your macro should look like figure 24.15.

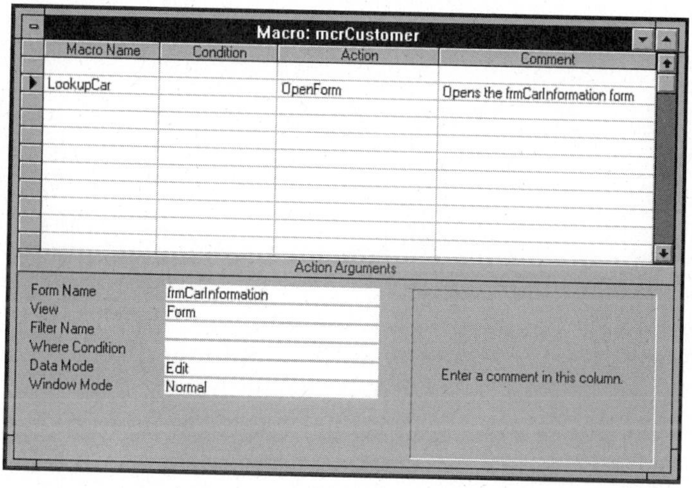

Figure 24.15
The LookupCar macro.

Next, attach your new macro to the frmCarInformationSub found on the frmCustomer form. From your database container window, open the frmCustomer form in design view. Double click on the frmCarInformationSub form found at the bottom of the window. The frmCarInformationSub now comes into focus in design view. Click on the model text box to highlight it. After the model text box is highlighted, open your properties sheet.

On the On Dbl Click property, select mcrCustomer.LookupCar from the combo box. You need to identify which macro in mcrCustomer is supposed to run when the model text box is double-clicked. Click on OK. Save your changes by choosing <u>S</u>ave from the <u>F</u>ile pull-down menu.

There are two ways to reach a subform. First, locate the form you want to open in the database container, then select the design button. This is the normal way to open any object in design view.

In large databases with numerous forms, a specific form may be difficult to locate. In design view, the quickest way to both locate and open a subform is to open the main form in design view and then double click on the subform object.

If you try to run the macro by bringing up frmCustomers and double clicking on the model year, you will notice that it does bring up car information—it might not be the information for that particular car! The macro is half finished. The reason it does not locate the correct car is that the macro has only been told to open the form. The macro does not tell the form which record to display when the form opens.

There are a couple of steps needed to finish this macro and make it work correctly. First, you have to set a unique identifier on the subform. Second, create your Where Condition. Third, attach the macro to a control so that it will drill down to the information you are looking for.

A Where Condition can hold either an SQL Statement or an expression.

Go to the frmCustomer form and double click on the frmCarInformationSub section. Access will display the frmCarInformationSub form in design view. Now, add the unique identifier to this form. Press the Field List button or select Field List from the Yiew pull-down menu. Click on Car Id from the tblCars field list and drag it down to the right side of the Color text box. If necessary, click on the Car Id text box to select it and bring up the Properties list box. Because you do not want to see Car Id on the subform, locate and set the Visible property located under Layout Properties to No. Now you have your unique identifier needed to thread your Where Condition through the subform. Save and Close the frmCarInformationSub and the frmCustomers form.

The WHERE statement must tell Access which field to look at and what value to use. Click on Macro and open the mcrCustomer macro in design view. Place your cursor on the action row and press F6 to move down to the argument section of the macro. You are now going to type in your Where Condition. Type the following expression in the Where Condition argument text area:

```
[car id]=Forms![frmCustomer]![Car Information].Form![Car Id]
```

The preceding expression can be broken down into two sections that are separated by an = mark. The left half of the expression is telling Access which control to look at. "Car Id" is

looking for the Car ID field in the underlying record source (in this case, tblCars). Access is equating "Car Id" to the right half of the expression.

The right half of the expression is known as "referring to controls on a form or subform." The word "Forms" must precede all references to controls on forms. If you need to refer to a control on a report, the word "Report" must precede the reference.

The correct syntax for referring to a control on a form or subform is as follows:

```
Forms![Name of Main Form]![Control Name of Subform].Form![Name of
Control on Subform]
```

The exclamation mark, "!", lets Access know that you have named the form—as opposed to Access naming the form. "[FrmCustomer]" is the name of the form that you are referring to. Remember, the unique identifier is on the subform. You have to tell Access to look on the subform, "![Car Information].form". The last section is the unique identifying itself, "[Car Id]".

Now that you have entered the Where Condition in the macro, you are ready to tie that macro to the subform. You will attach the macro to the double click property of model year control. You are only going to attach it to this control until you see that the macro works. After the macro is working correctly, you should attach it to all controls on the form to enable you to double click anywhere on a specific car and have it drill down to the proper data.

Open frmCustomer form in design view and double click on the frmCarInformationSub form to open it in design view. In the Detail section of the frmCarInformationSub form, highlight the Model Year text box and select Property Sheet from the View pull-down menu. Attach the mcrCustomer macro to the Double Click property. Move your cursor down to the Double Click property and click on the combo box arrow that appears to the right of the line. Select mcrCustomer. Within the mcrCustomer macro is the macro group LookupCar. Because this is the macro group you want to execute, you must also place it on the Double Click property line. Place "LookupCar" after "mcrCustomer" and separate the two with a period so that your line looks like this:

```
mcrCustomer.LookupCar
```

If you cannot see the entire line, press Shift+F2 to activate the Zoom box. Save and Close both the frmCustomer and frmCarInformationSub forms.

To test your new Drill Down macro, open frmCustomer and bring up Paul Helm's record. Move your pointer down to the Model Year box and double click on 1990. Your macro should execute and load the Car Information form with the correct car (see fig. 24.16). Now that the macro is working properly, you can attach it to the other fields in the frmCarInformationSub form.

Figure 24.16
The Drill Down
macro in action.

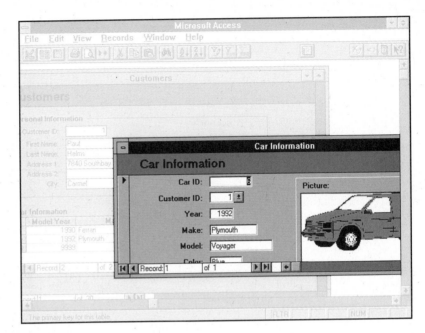

Figure 24.16
The Drill Down
macro in action.

Find Macro

If your databases contain more than a handful of records, paging through each one until you find the one you want is not practical. A method is needed to search for specific information within a specific record. This macro provides a simple means of using the Access Find dialog box. Instead of using the menus, you will create a button to launch the Find dialog box.

From your database container, click on Macro to create a new macro. Place your cursor in the action column and select DoMenuItem from the action combo box. The arguments for this box are listed in order of the keystrokes used to do any particular menu item. The Menu Bar line refers to which menu bar would you like to use. There are several menu bars to choose from. Because you are going to launch the Find macro from your frmCustomer form, choose Form.

Menu Name refers to which item from the menu bar you need to accomplish your task. The combo box associated with the Form menu bar shows you a list of all of the available menu names. Choose Edit. *Find* is the Command needed for this macro. If you choose Records as your menu name and Go To as your command, you would need to fill out the Subcommand line. Because there are no submenus for the Find command, you are finished with this macro. Save the macro as mcrFindCustomer and close the window.

Note Notice in this macro that the Macro Name and Condition columns were not used. If you had more than one action in this macro, the entire macro would run.

Open the frmCustomer form in design view. Press the F11 key to give focus to the database container. Click on Macro and highlight the mcrFindCustomer macro. While keeping your finger depressed on the mouse, drag the macro to the frmCustomer form; drop it over the right corner above the frmCarInformationSub form as shown in figure 24.17.

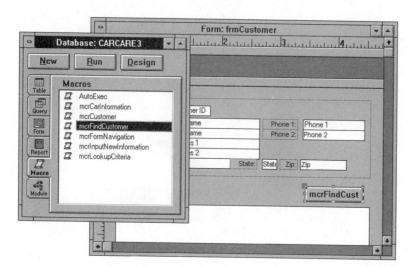

Figure 24.17
Creating the Find Macro button.

Change the name on the button to "Find". To do so, click on the button itself to give the frmCustomer focus and to highlight the button. In the property sheet for the new button, change the caption line to read "Find." Save and close the form.

Test the form by opening frmCustomer and clicking on the Find button. The Find dialog box appears, as shown in figure 24.18.

Figure 24.18
The Find dialog box.

AutoExec Macro

The AutoExec macro gives your database a professional touch. To create an AutoExec macro, open a new macro from the database container. When the database is opened, you want the database container to minimize, so select Minimize from the actions' combo box. There are no arguments for this action, so move down to the next row.

Select MsgBox from the action combo box. Press F6 to move to the argument section of the window. There are four arguments. The first is the message that you would like to display. Type **Welcome to the Car Care System.** The second argument is Beep. Select Yes because you want to alert your users to this message box.

The next argument is Type. There are four icons from which to choose, or you can choose no icon at all. Because this is an information message box, select Information. The last argument is Title. It refers to the bar across the top of the message box. Type in **"Welcome..."**.

Save the macro as AutoExec and close the window. Now, test your macro by highlighting it and pressing Run from the database container. You should get a message box like the one shown in figure 24.19.

Figure 24.19
The AutoExec
Macro in action.

Notice that this message box action produces a modal form. *Modal forms,* such as this message box, hold the focus until explicitly closed. The only way to get past this message box is to click on OK. It appears as if everything is all right. Now for the real test, close the database and reopen it. The AutoExec macro will execute.

Chapter Snapshot

Access reports are similar to forms except that reports normally are meant to be printed, and not displayed on the screen as forms are. Reports almost always are used to produce printed documents containing summarized information from a database. They can be used to document customers with overdue accounts, the names and addresses of customers within a particular ZIP Code area, the most popular items sold by a department store, and so on. In this chapter, you learn about the following:

Although many Access developers spend a great deal of time designing aesthetically pleasing forms and clever queries, most end users of databases are interested in the printed reports the database produces. You will be pleased to know that most of the skills required to create attractive, effective reports are mastered when you learn to build forms.

CHAPTER

Building Reports

By Chris St. Valentine

Constructing a report requires just about the same steps as building a form. The major difference is that because a report is intended to be printed instead of displayed on-screen, laying out controls on a report is a somewhat simpler process. Fewer types of controls are used on reports than on forms. A form might contain elements such as combo boxes, scroll bars, and other components that are inappropriate for printed documents. Constructing reports, therefore, mostly involves moving text boxes around the printable area of a page.

Reports nearly always are based on data returned by queries, although in some cases a table might serve as the source of data used in a report. Usually, you will construct the query used for the report source, debug and test the query by viewing the returned data in an Access form, and then build the report based on the completed query. Alternatively, the same query used for a form can serve as the source for the data in a report.

Access provides two distinct methods for creating reports. The first is to save an existing form as a report, and the second is to build a report from scratch.

Saving a Form as a Report

The easiest way to produce a report is to save an existing form as a report. This technique bypasses the Report toolbox and property lists you use when building a report from scratch.

If you have a form whose design, style, and underlying data can also serve as a report, Access can make a copy of the form that you can use as a report. This saves you time, even if you have to fine-tune the new report to remove those form elements (such as command buttons) that do not belong on the report.

Using the Carmel Car Care database as an example, assume that the form shown in figure 25.1 displays certain information about customers and their cars.

Figure 25.1
The Customers and Their Cars form.

Customers and Their Cars
First Name: Tom Reid
Year and Make: 1992 Mercury Villager Van
Color: White
VIN: JDIU89203X766S997
Phone 1: (508) 555-0381
Phone 2:
Double-click on picture to switch to Paintbrush
Prev Next Close

The Customers and Their Cars form (which is named frmCustomersAndCars) displays the owner's name, a description of the vehicle, and the owner's phone numbers. Carmel Car Care wants a printout of all its customers for the service manager to use. This paper list can be carried into the repair shop, out to the parking lot to help find a particular vehicle, and so on.

To prepare a report based on frmCustomersAndCars, first open the form in Design view and then choose File, Save As Report (see fig. 25.2). (The Save As Report command is not available in Form view.)

Access displays the Save Form As Report dialog box, in which you can enter the name of the new report (see fig. 25.3).

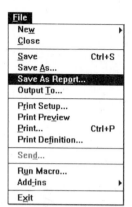

Figure 25.2
The Save As
Report command
in the File menu.

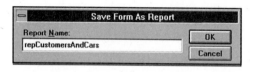

Figure 25.3
The Save Form As
Report dialog box.

The default name is the same as the form you used to create the report, but you can enter any other name if you like. It is a good idea to change the name of the report to avoid confusing it with the form of the same name. In figure 25.3, the name of the report has been changed from frmCustomersAndCars to repCustomersAndCars. The change in the prefix from "frm" to "rep" indicates that the new report is based on the form with the same name.

When you click on OK in the Save Form As Report dialog box, Access silently creates a new report based on the design of the form. To view the new report, click on the Report button in the Database window, highlight the name of the report, and click on either the Preview or Design button in the Database window.

The Preview button runs the query behind the report or data stored in the table behind the report. Figure 25.4 shows the repCustomersAndCars report in Print Preview view. The report screen in Print Preview mode looks somewhat like a piece of paper lying on a gray background.

IV

Microsoft Access

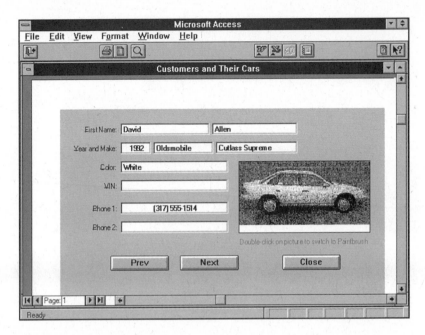

Figure 25.4
The new report in
Print Preview view
mode.

The report in figure 25.4 is an example of a *WYSIWYG* (what-you-see-is-what-you-get, pronounced wizzy-wig) document; what you see on the screen is what you see on the paper after the report is printed. Access helps you determine the report's printed appearance by showing the edge of the paper, margins, and other layout characteristics in Print Preview mode.

You probably will need to make a few changes to the report. If you do not have a color printer, for example, you might want to change some of the colors to black-and-white or shades of gray. You also might want to remove any nonfunctional controls such as command buttons.

The details of making changes to reports appear later in this chapter. For the meantime, take note that you probably will want to change the background, remove the command buttons, and change some of the other minor details of the new report.

Creating a Report from Scratch

The most common way to create a new report is to build it from scratch. The default report created by saving a form as a report usually is inappropriate for printing. As you saw in the last section, these reports contain command buttons, 3D elements, and other components that do not look good when printed on paper. Also, because on-screen forms generally are designed to be viewed one at a time, they can require quite a bit of room when printed. The report shown in figure 25.4 contains only 3 full records and part of another on a piece of paper. Efficient reports often contain data from 30 or 40 records in the database on each page.

To create a report from scratch, first create the query (or table) on which you will base the report. It is likely you will want to use a query that already serves as the basis of an existing form.

Next, go to the Database window and click on the Report button (see fig. 25.5).

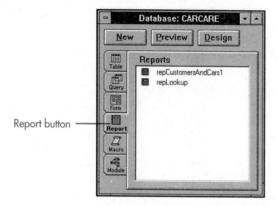

Report button

Figure 25.5
The Report button in the Database window.

Access displays the New Report dialog box and prompts you to enter the name of the query or table on which the new report will be based (see fig. 25.6). Reports can be based only on queries and tables. Select the query or table from the Select a Table/Query drop-down list box in the New Report dialog box.

Figure 25.6
The New Report dialog box.

In this example, the new report will be based on the query named qryCustomersAndCars.

Tip

Another quick way to specify the underlying query or table is to select the table or query in the Database window and then click on the Report button on the toolbar. This opens the New Report dialog box with the selected query or table already entered.

Next, decide whether you want to use one of the Report Wizards and have Access walk you through the steps to create a report, or if you want to create the report manually. To use a

IV

Microsoft Access

Report Wizard, click on the Report Wizards button in the New Report dialog box. To create the report yourself, click on the Blank Report button.

Creating a Report with a Report Wizard

The Report Wizards are similar to the Form Wizards. They sequentially walk you through the process of deciding which fields in the underlying query or table will be used in the new report and how that report will look. Report Wizards have a unique feature, however: you can select a field on which to sort the report (see fig. 25.7).

Figure 25.7
Specifying the sort order for the report.

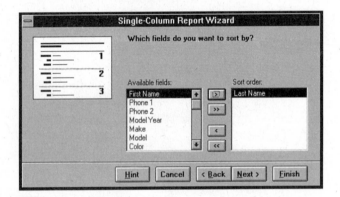

In this example, the report will be sorted according to the customer's last name.

There are three looks you can apply to your report. Each of these looks is handled by its own Report Wizard:

- ✔ **Executive.** This look features the Times Roman font with bold labels to the left of the fields. It has lines that set off a header section.

- ✔ **Presentation.** This look uses the Arial font; labels are bold and underlined. Otherwise, the same as the Executive look.

- ✔ **Ledger.** Like Presentation, this look uses the Arial font to produce a spreadsheet-like format. This look uses report space most economically, is best suited to lengthy (or wide) reports, and often is used when displaying financial data.

Use the Report Wizards to practice with the different report looks. You almost certainly will find a look that suits your requirements. Figure 25.8 shows the default appearance of the report generated by the Single Column Report Wizard, based on the query named qryCustomersAndCars.

Notice that the data in figure 25.8 is nicely arranged in rows and columns. Each column is a different field in the dynaset returned by the query named qryCustomersAndCars, whereas each row is a record of the dynaset. This arrangement of data is extremely efficient and compact. Each page of this printout contains data from about 50 different records.

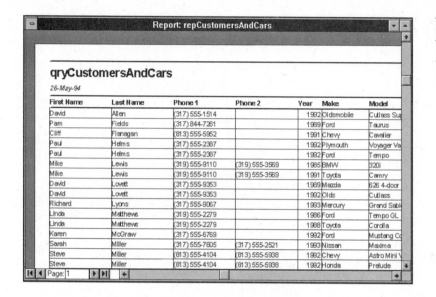

Figure 25.8
The new report created by the Report Wizard.

Creating Reports Manually

You create a report manually much like you create a form. Select <u>B</u>lank Report from the initial New Report dialog box (refer to figure 25.6), and then add controls to the blank report, just as you can on a form.

The blank, empty report appears on the screen after you click on the <u>B</u>lank Report button in the New Report dialog box (see fig. 25.9). You create the report by adding components to the Page Header, Detail, and Page Footer sections of the blank report.

Figure 25.9
The blank, empty report.

Understanding Report Bands

The Design view of an Access report is sometimes described as a banded report. Each band (Page Header, Detail, Page Footer, and so on) represents a different part of the printed report. Typical Access reports can contain a total of five different bands:

- ✔ **Page header.** Appears on every page of the report. Useful for column headings, report date and description, and other information you want on every page.

- ✔ **Detail.** The data itself appears in the detail portion of the report. The data can be laid out in rows and columns, groups, or any of several other designs.

- ✔ **Page footer.** The page footer appears at the bottom of every page in the report. The page footer is useful for holding the page number, report date, or other information you want to appear at the bottom of every page.

- ✔ **Report header.** The report header appears only on the first page of the report. The report header often is used for special information such as the name of the report, name of the person or group of people receiving the report, date of the report, and so on. The report header often is centered on its page and printed in large type. By default, the page footer appears on the same page as the report header; you can change this behavior by setting the Page Header property of the report.

- ✔ **Report footer.** The report footer appears only on the last page of the report. The report footer often is used for information summarizing the data in the report. By default, the page header appears on the same page as the report footer; you can change this behavior by setting the Page Footer property of the report.

If the report header or footer is not visible, choose Format, Report Header/Footer. After data or information has been added to these areas, removing the report header or footer deletes the data. Access stops and warns you if you attempt to remove the check mark on the Report Header/Footer command in the Format menu under these conditions.

To change the dimension of a band's area (that is, to make a band wider or narrower), move the cursor near the lower margin of the band until it changes to a double-headed arrow (much as when changing column widths in Datasheet view), then click and drag the band's lower margin to its new location. You cannot move the upper edge of a band with the mouse.

It is possible to shrink a band's height to zero, if desired. Because you always get page or report footers when page or report headers are activated, you might want to make the footer "disappear" if you will not be using it. Simply drag the lower margin of the unwanted footer area to coincide with the upper margin of the footer. You will find that the unused footer area has disappeared when you view the report in Preview mode.

The print margins (which are set with the P̲rint Setup command in the F̲ile menu) do not affect the area allocated to page and report headers and footers. The area allocated for these report elements is measured from inside the print margins. If you are having trouble getting everything to fit on the printed page, examine the print margins in the Print Setup dialog box to see if they are set unusually wide. Normally, Access establishes a one-inch margin all around the report.

Using the Report Toolbox

As mentioned earlier, reports are built by dragging controls from the toolbox and placing them on the report. The report controls, of course, are used to display data retrieved by the query or contained in the table underlying the report. Each area containing data in figure 25.8 is a report control.

If the Report toolbox is not visible, choose V̲iew, T̲oolbox. The Report toolbox is identical to the Form toolbox you worked with in earlier chapters of Part Four. As you design your report, remember the following:

- ✔ Neither command buttons nor option groups are appropriate for reports, even though these controls appear in the Report toolbox.

- ✔ Report and page headers and footers are useful. The page header and footer appear on every page of the report and are included by default on every new report. The report header and footer appear only on the first and last page of a report, respectively.

- ✔ For reports sorted on several fields, you can use page breaks to ensure that every sort group starts on a new page.

Figure 25.10 illustrates the process of hand-building the Customers and Their Cars report (named repCustomersAndCars). This report features a report header and space for a page header and page footer. This report does not include a report footer because there is no need for it. To remove only the footer and leave the header, resize the footer by setting its height to zero.

The easiest way to add text boxes for each field in the qryCustomersAndCars query is to display the field list (selected from the V̲iew menu) and drag each field from the list to the detail section of the report. The field list, of course, displays each field contained in qryCustomersAndCars.

For the final layout of the Customers and Their Cars report, the fields are arranged side-by-side (rather than vertically as indicated in figure 25.10), with column headings in the page header area. The completed form in Print Preview view can be seen in figure 25.11.

IV

Microsoft Access

Figure 25.10
The Customers
and Their Cars
report (Design
view).

Fields added to
detail area

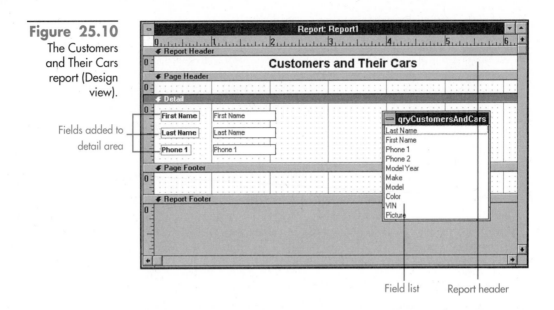

Field list   Report header

Figure 25.11
The Customers
and Their Cars
report in Print
Preview view.

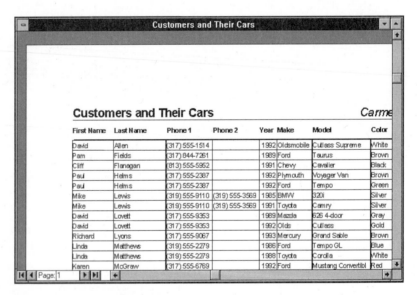

Figure 25.11 looks quite a bit like figure 25.8. The major difference between these reports is
that the hand-built version in figure 25.11 took about five times longer to create than the
Wizard-built report in figure 25.8. The hand-built report in Design view can be seen in figure
25.12.

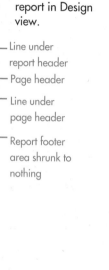

Report header

Figure 25.12
The Customers and Their Cars report in Design view.

Line under report header
Page header

Line under page header

Report footer area shrunk to nothing

Notice the following things about the design of the Customers and Their Cars report:

✔ The space allocated for the detail area permits only one record to be displayed horizontally.

✔ A line is drawn under the report header (Customers and Their Cars) to provide a horizontal rule dividing the report header from the page header.

✔ The page header (which shows the column heading for each column: First Name, Last Name, and so on) has a line drawn under it as well. The line is adjacent to the bottom of the space allocated for the page header area, however.

✔ The report footer space has been reduced to zero by moving the bottom of the page upward to connect with the lower edge of the page footer area.

The page footer contains a calculated control (=`"Page " & [Page] & " of " & [Pages]`) that prints the current page number and the total number of pages. To get the page numbers to appear in the center of the page, the control was made as wide as the report itself. Then, the text alignment was set to Center.

IV

Microsoft Access

Using the Report Toolbar

The left side of the Report toolbar in Design view is different from the Form toolbar in several respects. First, the group of three buttons for Design, Form, and Datasheet views is missing. Instead, reports have Design View, Print Preview, and Sample Preview buttons.

The next group of buttons contains a button not present on the Form toolbar, the Sorting and Grouping button. When you click on the Sorting and Grouping button, Access displays the Sorting and Grouping dialog box (see fig. 25.13).

Figure 25.13
The Sorting and Grouping dialog box.

Sorting and Grouping	
Field/Expression	Sort Order
Last Name	Ascending

Group Properties

Group Header	Yes
Group Footer	No
Group On	Each Value
Group Interval	1
Keep Together	No

Select a field or type an expression to sort or group on

Use this dialog box to select sort fields for the report and to specify whether you want a header or footer for each sort group. In figure 25.14, the Last Name field has been selected for grouping because owners might own more than one car. Grouping all the cars owned by a single owner makes the "group" of records pertaining to the owner easier to see on the report.

If you specify sort fields when you create a report with one of the Report Wizards, they appear in this dialog box. The text-formatting buttons that appear when you select a text control are the same as on the Form toolbar.

The effect on the Design view of the options set in figure 25.13 can be seen in figure 25.14. A new band labeled Last Name Header has been added to the report.

When the report is switched to Print Preview mode, the finished report looks like figure 25.15. A distinct space separates each group of cars associated with each owner. This style of report makes it easy to see which cars are owned by each owner.

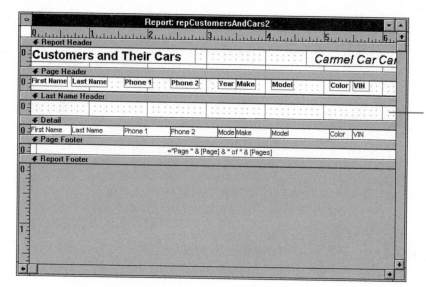

Figure 25.14
A new band has been added to Design view.

Last Name Header band

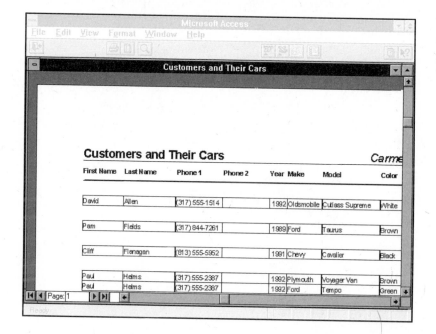

Figure 25.15
The finished Customers and Their Cars report.

Chapter Snapshot

As with macros, you use Access Basic to extend the functionality of Access. Access Basic is a powerful programming language that adds power and flexibility to your applications. In most cases, you do not need more functionality than macros provide; with few exceptions, everything you can do with a macro also can be done easily with Access Basic. However, Access Basic is far more flexible than macros because it features command structures and error handling. This chapter shows you the way to create and manipulate Access Basic code within a module, as well as the following:

Access Basic is a full-function language complete with control structures found in other structured languages such as C. This chapter covers the basics of programming in Access Basic and gives many examples to get you started.

CHAPTER 26

Understanding Access Basic

by Chris St. Valentine

All Access Basic code resides in modules. Because the Module window processes free-form text instead of presenting limited choices, it has more room for error than macros and the other objects in Access. However, macros limit you only to select, predefined groups of actions; Access Basic does not impose this limitation.

From the Database window, you can delete, rename, or print a module. First select the desired module in the Database window, then choose the appropriate command from the File menu:

- ✔ **Delete.** Access prompts you to confirm that you do indeed want to delete the module. You also can press Del instead of choosing the Delete command.

- ✔ **Rename.** Access displays a dialog box in which you specify the new module name. As with the other database objects, you must enter a module name that does not already exist.

- ✔ **Print.** Access displays a dialog box in which you can specify the range of pages you want to print.

The following section discusses the way in which you can create a new module or open an existing module for viewing and editing.

Creating and Opening Modules

To create a new module, click on the Module button in the Database window and then choose the <u>N</u>ew button (see fig. 26.1).

Figure 26.1
Creating a new module in the Database window.

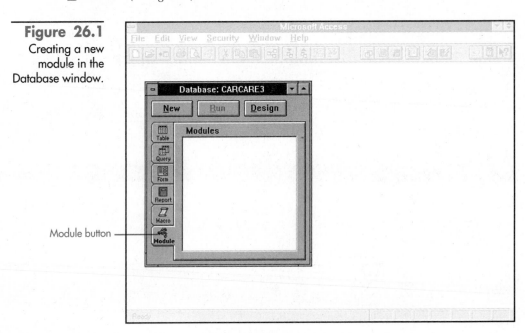

To open an existing module, click on the Module button in the Database window, click on the desired module in the list box, and then choose <u>D</u>esign (see fig. 26.2).

Figure 26.2
Choose Design to open an existing module.

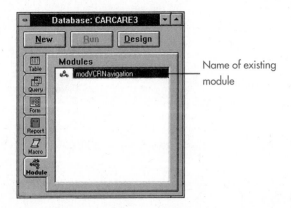

Name of existing module

Understanding the Layout of a Module

A module has two parts: a declarations section and a procedures section (see fig. 26.3).

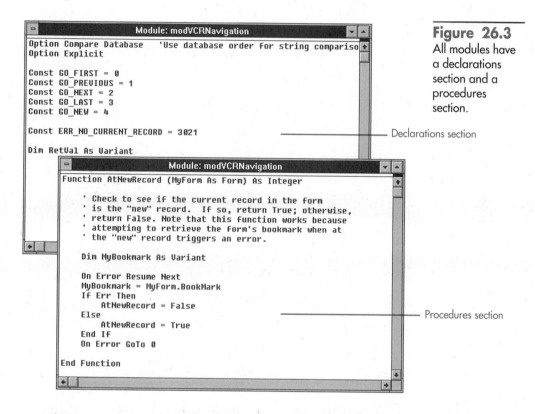

Figure 26.3
All modules have a declarations section and a procedures section.

— Declarations section

— Procedures section

Tip

Although the preceding illustration shows both sections of the system module, you can view a module in only one window at a time. You can, however, split the window to show both sections at the same time. For more information, see the section "Using the Menus" later in this chapter.

As its name implies, the declarations section contains declarations for global and module-wide variables, constants, and arrays. This section also includes statements that define module options and procedure declarations (prototypes) for external functions residing in dynamic link library (DLL) files.

As you might expect, the procedures section contains *procedures,* which are the functions and subroutines that Access executes.

Note Sub (subroutine) procedures are different from Function procedures, however, in that they do not return values as do Function procedures.

Exploring the Module Window

The Module window is where you enter all your Access Basic code (see fig. 26.4).

Figure 26.4
The Module window.

Split bar

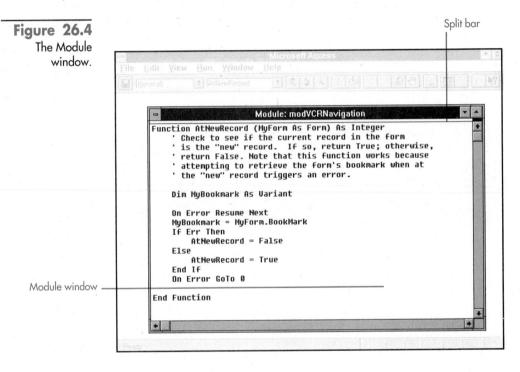

Module window

The Module window is similar to the Code window in Visual Basic. As in Visual Basic, you have a toolbar with buttons for common commands and a movable, sizable window in which you type your code.

Normally, the Module window shows either the Declarations section or a procedure (one Function procedure or one Sub procedure) at a time. To view different sections of a module simultaneously, split the window into two panes, as shown in figure 26.5.

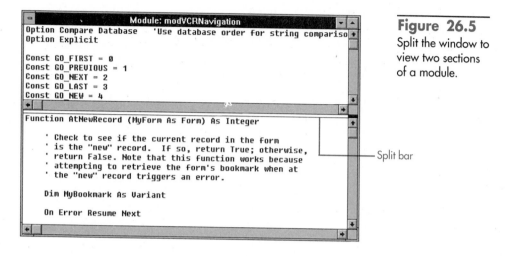

Figure 26.5
Split the window to view two sections of a module.

To split the window, click on the black split bar (located above the vertical scroll bar) and drag it up or down, as appropriate. (You also can choose the Split Window command from the View menu.) Splitting the window is useful when it is necessary to view variable declarations while editing code in a function or subroutine.

Exploring the Toolbar

The Access 2.0 toolbar changes in context according to the window that has the focus. If you are in a Module window, for example, the toolbar contains buttons that apply to modules. If you are in Table design view, the toolbar contains table-related buttons, and so on.

The Procedure box and buttons on the toolbar apply to the Module window that currently has the focus. Table 26.1 shows the toolbar icons and their descriptions.

Table 26.1
Access Toolbar Icons

Icon	Name	Description
💾	Save	While you work, press this button periodically to save the current module.
[general]	Object box	This drop-down list contains a list of all the objects for which you can write code. When you are entering code for a form (code behind

continues

Table 26.1, Continued
Access Toolbar Icons

Icon	Name	Description
		forms), the object box lists all the controls on the form. When you are entering code in a new module, the object box displays only the "gen eral" object.
AtNewRecord	Procedure box	This box contains a drop-down list of all the procedures in the current module. (For more information, see the section following this table.)
	Previous Procedure Next Procedure	These buttons display the module's previous or next Access Basic procedure. Procedures appear in alphabetical order. After you cycle through all the procedures in a module, the Declarations section reappears.From time to time, you might construct a module with many procedures. Use the Previous Procedure and Next Procedure buttons as simple navigation devices to move around the module.
	New Procedure	Press this button to create a new Function or Sub procedure. Access displays the New Procedure dialog box in which you can enter the new name.
	Run	When you are debugging your application and stop the code (or if the code stops as the result of a run-time error), click on the Run button to resume execution of the code from the point at which it had stopped.

Icon	Name	Description
		Later in this chapter you explore a number of powerful debugging tools, including breakpoints, that enable you to stop execution of your code at any point. The Run button resumes code execution from the breakpoint.
	Compile Loaded Modules	Click on this button to compile all the loaded Access Basic modules. Access checks the syntax of your code and reports any errors.
	Step Into	During the debugging process, click on the Step Into button to execute the next line (only) of Access Basic code. If the line of code calls another procedure, clicking on this button single-steps into the second procedure.
	Step Over	This button is similar to the Step Into button. In fact, they are identical in function if the line of code to be executed is not a call to another procedure. If the next line is a call to another procedure, pressing the Step Over button runs the second procedure and then returns to the first procedure and stops.
	Reset	This button terminates execution of all Access Basic procedures and clears all variables.
	Breakpoint	Use this button to either set or clear a breakpoint on the current line of code (the line at which the insertion point is positioned). When Access encounters a breakpoint, execution stops but the values of variables are not cleared.

IV

Microsoft Access

continues

Table 26.1, Continued
Access Toolbar Icons

Icon	Name	Description
		Lines in a procedure or function with a breakpoint appear in bold (see fig. 26.6).M Press F5 or press the Step Into or Step Over buttons to continue execution of your code. Press the Breakpoint button (or F9) to clear a breakpoint.
	Build	Click on this button for help with building expressions in Access Basic; Access displays the Expression Builder.
	Immediate Window	Click on this button to display or hide the Immediate window (for more information, see the section "Using the Immediate Window" later in this chapter).
	Calls	Click on this button to display the Calls dialog box, in which you can trace all the currently active procedures that your code has called.
	Undo and Help	The Undo and Help buttons behave the same as those on other Access toolbars: Undo cancels the effect of the most recent operation, and Help starts Access Basic help.

Procedure Box

Because an Access database can contain multiple modules and each module can contain multiple procedures, Access provides a drop-down list of procedures as a way to quickly move to the procedure or declarations section of the currently active module. When you click on the desired procedure, Access opens the Module window and displays the selected procedure (or declarations section).

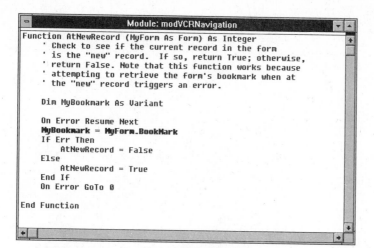

Figure 26.6
Set breakpoints to temporarily stop your code.

```
Function AtNewRecord (MyForm As Form) As Integer
    ' Check to see if the current record in the form
    ' is the "new" record.  If so, return True; otherwise,
    ' return False. Note that this function works because
    ' attempting to retrieve the form's bookmark when at
    ' the "new" record triggers an error.

    Dim MyBookmark As Variant

    On Error Resume Next
    MyBookmark = MyForm.BookMark
    If Err Then
        AtNewRecord = False
    Else
        AtNewRecord = True
    End If
    On Error GoTo 0

End Function
```

If the drop-down list of procedures has more than eight procedures in it, move through the list with the scroll bar attached to the list. The declarations section of the module appears as the special entry (declarations) in the list box; you can select it like any other procedure. To add a new procedure to the list, create a new Function or Sub procedure (for more information, see the next section, "Using the Menus").

You can write as many Access Basic modules as you need for your Access application, and each module can contain as many procedures as necessary.

It is good programming practice to group similar procedures in the same module; for example, string functions go in one module, file-related functions go in another, and so on. This strategy results in more modules, but with fewer procedures in any one module. Smaller modules with few procedures are easier to maintain and share between Access databases.

Using the Menus

The various menus in Access change to show operations specific to the window that has the focus. If the Query window has the focus, for example, commands specific to queries appear in the menus. When a Module window has the focus, the menu commands you see are specific to modules. The following sections describe some of the more commonly used menu commands. For more information about these and the other commands, search Help for the name of the command.

IV

Microsoft Access

Selected File Menu Commands

Several commands in the File menu are used frequently while working with Access modules.

Load Text

Use the Load Text command to perform the following operations:

✔ Replace the current module with the specified text file

✔ Merge the specified text file, inserting its entire contents at the insertion point

✔ Create a new module from the specified text file

When you choose the Load Text command, Access displays the Load Text dialog box (see fig. 26.7).

Figure 26.7
The Load Text dialog box.

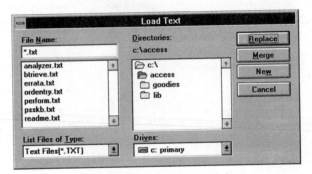

When you choose Replace, Access replaces the existing module and all its procedures with no additional warning. Before you click on this button, be absolutely sure you want to replace the entire module with the text file. If you accidentally choose Replace, immediately close the module without saving the changes when prompted to do so, and then reopen the module and start over.

To import an existing module from another Access database, go to the Database window and choose File, Import.

Save Text

You can create an ASCII file containing all the Access Basic code in the current module. When you choose the Save Text command, Access displays a dialog box in which you can specify the name and location for the new text file.

No page breaks exist between the various procedures in the text file.

To export an existing module to another Access database, go to the Database window and choose File, Export.

Print

When you choose the <u>P</u>rint command, Access displays a dialog box in which you can specify whether to print all the code in the current module, only the currently highlighted text, or a range of pages (see fig. 26.8).

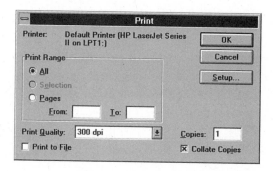

Figure 26.8
Printing the procedures in a module.

Access does not store print setup information with modules as it does with forms and reports. You must reset the print setup information (if necessary) each time you print a module.

Hard-copy printouts of modules are particularly useful for debugging purposes. Because the printout can show more lines than you can see on-screen at one time, it sometimes is easier to see the relationships between sections of code on the hard copy than to see the same information on-screen.

Selected Edit Menu Commands

The Edit menu contains several module-specific commands as well.

Find

In modules, you can use the Find command to search for specified text in the current procedure, the entire module, or all modules in the database. Choosing the <u>F</u>ind command displays the Find dialog box, as shown in figure 26.9.

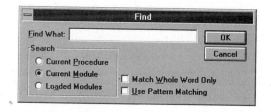

Figure 26.9
The Find dialog box.

IV

Microsoft Access

Type the text you are looking for in the <u>F</u>ind What text box. Next, choose one of the option buttons to tell Access where to look. If you choose the Lo<u>a</u>ded Modules option button, Access automatically opens a Module window for each module in which Access finds the specified text.

Choose the Match <u>W</u>hole Word Only check box if you want Access to look for only whole words that match the search text; otherwise, Access finds any text that matches, even if the search text is found in only part of a word in the module.

Consider a search for the text string *Exp*. When you choose Match <u>W</u>hole Word Only, Access finds only the Access Basic Exp function; when you do not check the Match <u>W</u>hole Word Only box (that is, the box is cleared), Access also finds the variables *Expansion, Expense,* and *HexPoint*. Notice that the search is not case-sensitive; Access finds *Expansion* and *expansion* as acceptable matches to the search text *Exp*.

At times you might want to search for some text but do not know exactly what the text looks like, or you might want to search for several pieces of text that are similar. To do this, select the <u>U</u>se Pattern Matching check box. This enables you to enter a search string containing wild cards. Table 26.2 lists the wild cards you can include in the <u>F</u>ind What text box.

Table 26.2
Wild-Card Matches

Wild Card	Matches	Example
*	Any number of characters	jo* matches jo, john, job, and jolly
?	Any single character	jo?n matches john, jonn, and join
#	Any single digit	12#4 matches 1214, 1234, and 1294
[ ]	Any single character inside the brackets	[hlt]ex matches hex, lex, and tex
!	Any character not in the list	[!lt]ex matches mex and hex, but not lex or tex
-	Any one of a range of characters	[a–f]at matches bat, cat, and fat, but not mat or pat

Replace

Much like the search and replace function available in most word processing programs, you can choose the Replace command to find one character string and replace it with another. When you choose the Replace command, Access displays the Replace dialog box (see fig. 26.10).

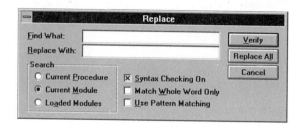

Figure 26.10
The Replace dialog box.

When you check Syntax Checking On, Access automatically checks the syntax of any line affected by the replace operation and displays a message box if the replace operation produces any syntax errors.

Choose Verify if you want to selectively change lines. If so, Access displays the lines that will be changed, one at a time, and asks whether each line should be changed.

New Procedure

Choose the New Procedure command to create a new Function or Sub procedure. Access displays the New Procedure dialog box, as shown in figure 26.11, in which you type the name of the new procedure and then click on OK.

Figure 26.11
Creating a new Function or Sub procedure.

Selected View Menu Commands

All the commands in the View menu are module-specific when you work with Access Basic. You use these commands frequently as you build modules and procedures.

Split Window

Splitting the Module window enables you to view and edit two different sections of your module code at the same time (see fig. 26.12). As described earlier in this chapter, this command has the same effect as dragging the split box to reveal a second window pane.

Figure 26.12
Split the Module window to view two sections at the same time.

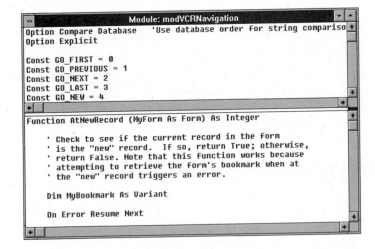

Each of the panes has its own scroll bars, although only one pane can have the focus at any one time. Both panes refer to the same Access Basic module; you cannot view two modules in the same window. To simultaneously view or edit more than one module at a time, open a second Module window.

Procedures

Use the Procedures command to view a list of all the modules and procedures in your database (see fig. 26.13). If you prefer to use the keyboard, press F2.

Figure 26.13
Viewing a list of modules and procedures in the View Procedures dialog box.

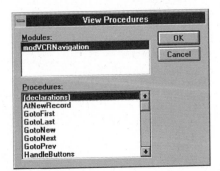

The Procedures command and the toolbar's Procedure box provide similar functionality, but the command enables you to move to any procedure in the database rather than just those in the current module. In figure 26.13, only one module (modVCRNavigation) is available. Many Access applications contain multiple modules.

Immediate Window

For more information about the Immediate Window command, see the section "Using the Immediate Window" later in this chapter. The Immediate window is useful for testing and debugging your Access Basic code.

Options—Module Design

When you choose the Options command from the View menu, Access displays the Options dialog box (see fig. 26.14).

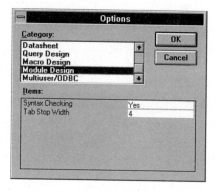

Figure 26.14

Setting options for the Module window in the Options dialog box.

To change Module window settings, select the Module Design category in the top portion of the dialog box. Access displays two settings—Syntax Checking and Tab Stop Width—that apply to the Module window.

When you set Syntax Checking to Yes, Access checks the syntax of each line as you type it and then move to another line. When Syntax Checking is No, Access checks the syntax only when you compile the module or run your code.

Much like tab stops on a typewriter, the Tab Stop Width setting determines the number of spaces between tab stops. When you press the Tab key in the Module window, Access inserts as many spaces as necessary to move to the next tab stop. The default is four spaces.

Run Menu Commands

You use the commands in the Run menu most often as you test and debug your Access Basic code.

Reset

The Reset command has the same effect as the Reset button (see the section "Exploring the Toolbar" earlier in this chapter).

Compile Loaded Modules

Choose the Compile Loaded Modules command to compile every loaded module in the database. *Compiling* is the process of converting the English-like module code into a form the computer can execute. When it compiles, Access reports any syntax errors.

Continue

The Continue command has the same effect as the Run button (see the section "Exploring the Toolbar" earlier in this chapter). The keyboard shortcut for this command is F5.

Step Into

The Step Into command has the same effect as the Step Into button (see the section "Exploring the Toolbar" earlier in this chapter). The keyboard shortcut for this command is F8.

Step Over

The Step Over command has the same effect as the Step Over button (see the section "Exploring the Toolbar" earlier in this chapter). The keyboard shortcut for this command is Shift+F8.

Set Next Statement

While you are debugging your code, you can tell Access which line of code to execute next. Click on the line you want to execute and then choose the Set Next Statement command. The insertion point must be on a line in the current procedure (the procedure in which execution is currently stopped).

Show Next Statement

While you are debugging your code, you might move about looking at different procedures and modules. Choose the Show Next Statement command to return to the current procedure and highlight the next statement that will execute.

Toggle Breakpoint

The Toggle Breakpoint command has the same effect as the Breakpoint button (see the section "Exploring the Toolbar" earlier in this chapter). The keyboard shortcut for this command is F9.

Clear All Breakpoints

Choose the Clear All Breakpoints command to quickly remove all breakpoints in all modules. Access automatically removes breakpoints from a module when you close it.

Modify Command$

When you start Access, you can specify optional command-line arguments. The **Command$** function returns any characters following /cmd on the Access command line. Choose the Modify Command$ command to set or change the command-line arguments without having to restart Access.

Using the Immediate Window

You use the Immediate window primarily to debug code. Use this window to call specific functions, examine or change variables, or print debugging output. To display or hide the Immediate window, choose the Immediate Window command from the View menu.

Perhaps the most common use of the Immediate window is to call a function to see if it is returning the proper value. While you are debugging a Function procedure, for example, you can call it directly without affecting the rest of the module (see fig. 26.15).

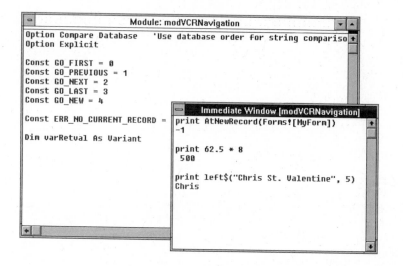

Figure 26.15
Calling a Function procedure directly from the Immediate window.

Figure 26.15 shows how you also can use the Immediate window as a simple calculator or use it to call an intrinsic (built-in) Access Basic function (in this example, Left$).

Tip

Instead of typing the word *print,* you can use the question mark (?). The question mark is shorthand notation for the print statement.

Using Access Basic

Now that you have taken a quick look at the Access Basic environment, including the edit window in which you build and test modules, continue your exploration by studying the Access Basic language itself.

Access Basic is a complete programming language included with Microsoft Access. You can perform nearly everything you can do in a macro, plus much more. In exchange for this increased functionality and power, you pay a price: you have a bit more to learn about the Access development environment.

Access Basic enables you to extend and enhance the capabilities of Access. Through Access Basic, you can add entirely new functions to Access and empower Access with capabilities tailored to your specific work situation.

Because Access Basic is a complete programming language, describing it in its entirety is beyond the scope of this book. However, this chapter does cover the highlights of the parts of the language you are likely to use right away. The examples in this chapter illustrate how you can use Access Basic in a typical application.

Access Basic is similar to Microsoft Visual Basic (VB). In fact, both languages share the same core functions, including those that deal specifically with database manipulation.

Note

VB 3 was the first version of Visual Basic to include the Data Access Object (DAO) that enables the VB programmer to manipulate Access databases.

If you already know Visual Basic, you are well on your way to learning Access Basic. Some features are present in one language but not in the other, however. VB responds to a some-what larger set of events than does Access. On the other hand, Access features the DoCmd statement that enables you to run macro actions, a feature unique to Access Basic.

Exploring Event-Driven Programming

If you have programmed before, but not for the Microsoft Windows environment, you need to develop a new way of thinking about programming. Windows is an *event-oriented* environment, which means the system responds to events instead of the more traditional step-by-step procedural programming.

When you press a command button, for example, Access triggers an event that indicates the button has been pressed. You decide the way to handle the button press by calling a function or running a macro; you define each of these event handlers. No response to an event happens automatically.

Event-driven programs do not follow a predefined sequence of steps. You can move the focus from one control to another, or even from form to form. You cannot predict where the focus moves or what the user does in any control or at any given time.

In contrast, more traditional programming languages such as dBASE are procedural, not event-driven. In these programs, you design a form, ask for input into one or more fields, and then process the input. Such programs are orderly and the underlying code is straightforward: process the first line of code and then go to the next line, and so on until the end of the code.

In Access, you design forms with the built-in forms designer and attach event handlers to the various controls on the form. If you want to perform some action whenever the data in a text box changes, you might attach an event handler to the AfterUpdate property of the text box control. Access and Windows automatically take care of notifying your application when the data changes—you do not have to add any additional code to trap events. All you need to do is make sure that you attach an event handler wherever you want to do something.

Event Handlers

To trigger an action when an event occurs, you attach an event handler to the appropriate event property. Table 26.3 lists the event properties.

Table 26.3
Event Properties

Event	Triggered When
AfterDelConfirm	After you delete a record and the confirmation dialog is closed (forms only)
AfterInsert	After you add a new record (forms only)
AfterUpdate	After you change data (forms only)

continues

Table 26.3, Continued
Event Properties

Event	Triggered When
BeforeDelConfirm	You delete a record, but before the confirmation dialog appears
BeforeInsert	You type the first character in a new record (forms only)
BeforeUpdate	You make changes to data, but before the change is actually made (forms only)
OnActivate	Focus moves to a form or report and becomes the active window.
OnChange	You change the contents of a text box or combo box (forms only)
OnClick	You press a command button or toggle button (forms only)
OnClose	Form or report closes
OnCurrent	Focus moves from one record to another (bound forms only)
OnDblClick	You double-click the mouse (forms only)
OnDeactivate	Focus moves from a form or report
OnDelete	A record is deleted (forms only)
OnEnter	Focus moves to a control (forms only)
OnError	A run-time error occurs.
OnExit	Focus leaves a control (forms only)
OnFormat	Access formats or lays out a report
OnGotFocus	Form or control receives the focus
OnKeyDown	You press a key while a form or control has the focus (forms only)
OnKeyPress	You press and release a key while a form or control has the focus (forms only)

Event	Triggered When
OnKeyUp	You release a key while a form or control has the focus (forms only)
OnLoad	A form is opened; triggered after OnOpen (forms only)
OnLostFocus	Form or control loses the focus
OnMouseDown	You press a mouse button while a form or control has the focus (forms only)
OnMouseMove	You move the mouse while a form or control has the focus (forms only)
OnMouseUp	You release a mouse button while a form or control has the focus (forms only)
OnNotInList	You enter a value in the text box portion of a combo box that is not in the combo box list (forms only)
OnOpen	Form or report opens
OnPrint	Access formats or lays out a report (reports only)
OnResize	You open a form and whenever you resize the form (forms only)
OnRetreat	Access returns to a previous report section during report formatting (reports only)
OnTimer	At regular intervals specified by the TimerInterval property setting (forms only)
OnUnload	A form is closed; triggered before OnClose (forms only)
OnUpdated	You change the data in an OLE object (bound or unbound object frame) (forms only)

An *event handler* is an event procedure, Access Basic function, or a macro you call from one of the event properties. If you want to format a ZIP code, for example, whenever the data in a ZIP code text box changes, you call an event handler that formats the data (see fig. 26.16).

IV

Microsoft Access

Figure 26.16
Calling an event handler from the AfterUpdate event property.

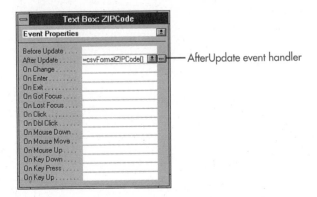

In this example, you want to call the csvFormatZIPCode() function to format the user's entry. Now, whenever the data in the ZIPCode control changes, Access automatically calls the required function. Unlike other development environments, all you have to do is create the function—Access handles calling it for you.

Entering the name of an Access Basic function or the name of a macro is called *attaching an event handler*. Only events that have attached event handlers are active.

Code behind Forms

In addition to calling a function or running a macro, you also can call an event procedure. When an event occurs, Access runs your event procedure. An event procedure is much like any other Sub procedure in Access Basic except that event procedures actually are part of the form in which they are defined (regular Function and Sub procedures reside in modules). These procedures are also called *code behind form* because they are located "behind" the forms.

To create an event procedure, set the event property to [Event Procedure] and then click on the button to the right (see fig. 26.17).

Figure 26.17
Calling a code behind form (CBF) procedure.

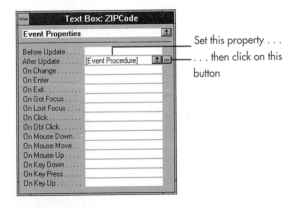

When you click on the button with the ellipsis, Access displays a Module window in which you can define the new procedure.

Looking At a Typical Module

Earlier in this chapter, the section "Creating and Opening Modules" discusses how you can create a module and what the various parts of the module are. All your Access Basic code appears in modules, although you can use the code from many places throughout Access.

To review:

✔ Each database can have as many modules as necessary. It generally is a good idea to organize your modules by function. File-handling functions, for example, would go in one module, string functions go in another, form functions in yet another module, and so on.

✔ Each module has two sections: a declarations section, in which you declare global variables and define function prototypes, and a procedures section, in which you add the actual functions.

✔ You can add comments throughout your code to make it easier to read and maintain.

The following listings show parts of the declarations and procedures sections from some of the modules in the HomeFinder sample database. The HomeFinder application is located on the *Inside Microsoft Office Professional* companion disk and is normally installed in the INSOFFIC directory on your C: drive. To view the modules, first open the HOMEFIND.MDB database and click on the Module button in the Database window. Then, double-click the desired module.

Lines that begin with an apostrophe (') are comments and are ignored by Access (comments are explained later in this chapter).

Unlike some other programming languages, Access Basic does not have a line continuation character to enable one long line of code to continue on the next line. In this book, however, some lines of code are longer than the page width. For these lines and other lines throughout this chapter, a special character (➡) indicates the line appears in the module on a single line and that it appears "wrapped" only in this book.

The Declarations Section

Part of the declarations section from the Declarations module looks like this:

```
Option Compare Database
Declare Function GetModuleHandle Lib "Kernel" (ByVal
```

```
➥ APPNAME As String) As Integer
Declare Function GetPrivateProfileInt Lib "Kernel"
➥ (ByVal Section As String, ByVal Entry As
➥ String, ByVal Default As Integer, ByVal
➥ FileName As String) As Integer
Declare Function GetTickCount Lib "User" () As Long
Declare Function GetWinFlags Lib "Kernel" () As Long
Declare Function OpenSound Lib "SOUND.DRV" () As Integer
```

The declarations section of an Access Basic module informs Access of the various functions and special variables that are used in the module. After a function such as `GetTickCount` has been declared, it can be used in any other module needing the function.

Part of the declarations section from the Global Constants module looks like this:

```
' _ _ _ _ _ _ _ _ _ _ _ _ _ _ _ _ _ _ _ _ _ _ _ _ _ _ _ _
' Global Constants
' _ _ _ _ _ _ _ _ _ _ _ _ _ _ _ _ _ _ _ _ _ _ _ _ _ _ _ _
Global Const ABORT = 3
Global Const APPNAME = "MSACCESS.EXE"
Global Const BLACK = 0
Global Const BLUE = 16711680
Global Const CANCEL = 2
Global Const CASEINSENSITIVE = 1
Global Const GRAY = 12632256
Global Const GREEN = 32768
Global Const HOTPINK = 16711935
Global Const IGNORE = 5
Global Const MB_ICONEXCLAMATION = 48
Global Const MB_ICONINFORMATION = 64
Global Const MB_ICONQUESTIONMARK = 32
Global Const MB_ICONSTOPSIGN = 16
Global Const MB_NO = 7
Global Const MB_RETRYCANCEL = 5
Global Const MB_YES = 6
Global Const MB_YESNO = 4
```

Any variable declared as a global is usable by all modules in the application. Normally, global variables are used for items such as colors, icon names, and other variables that are used throughout the application.

A Function Procedure

The next listing is from the Miscellaneous module. This module contains the declaration of the function `csvMinValue()` and the code defining the function.

```
Function csvMinValue (ByVal X As Variant, ByVal Y As Variant) As
Variant

    If IsNumeric(X) * IsNumeric(Y) Then
        csvMinValue = X + (X - Y) * (X > Y)
    Else
        MsgBox "Invalid numeric argument.", MB_ICONEXCLAMATION,
        ➥ "MinValue"
        csvMinValue = Null
    End If


End Function
```

This function illustrates how you can add new functionality to Access by defining your own functions. In this example, `csvMinValue()` returns the smaller of two specified values.

Adding Comments

As you program in Access Basic, it often is helpful to add comments to your code. *Comments* are remarks or notes you write to yourself to explain what the code does, how it works, or why you chose a certain technique over another.

You begin a comment with an apostrophe (`'`). Comments can appear at the end of a line or at the beginning of a line, but not in the middle: Access ignores not only the apostrophe but also anything that follows. The following example illustrates how you can add a comment to an existing line of code.

```
If MyTable.NoMatch Then ' Couldn't find desired record.
```

In this example, the comment explains what the code means. As useful as comments are, you can find that choosing meaningful names for your variables minimizes the need to add comments to your code. Sometimes, however, even a carefully crafted variable name could use an explanation; in these cases, add a comment above, below, or beside the variable's declaration (`Dim` statement).

Other comments you should add include information in a header at the top of functions. You should consider documenting the purpose of a function, the arguments it accepts, and what it returns. If you do this, you do not have to read through the code later to determine these things. Such commenting is especially helpful to others who inherit your code and do not have the time to study your work.

Because few programmers develop code perfectly the first time around, you are likely to refine a function over time. To keep track of what you have done to a function, add comments that describe the revisions.

IV

Microsoft Access

Indenting Your Code

Most programmers indent their code to show logical program flow and make it easier to see how a function is structured. Access does not require any special formatting, but you benefit from applying a few rules yourself.

The examples in online Help and in some of the sample databases supplied with Access illustrate good programming practices. The coding techniques in the HomeFinder database application generally follow these same guidelines.

When you construct a For...Next loop, for example, indent the inner statements with a single press of the Tab key:

```
For X = 1 To 10
    Debug.Print X
Next X
```

In a long listing, it would be easy to see how and where the For and Next statements delimit the code block. The next example illustrates how you should indent an If...Then...Else block of code:

```
If Not IsNull(PhoneNumber) Then
    On Error Resume Next
    X = Shell("TERMINAL.EXE", 1)
    If Err Then
        MsgBox "Couldn't start Terminal.", 64, "Dial"
        Dial = False
    Else
        SendKeys "%sn", True
        SendKeys PhoneNumber & "{enter}", True
        SendKeys "%pd", True
        Dial = True
        On Error GoTo 0
    End If
End If
```

When you press Tab, Access moves to the next tab stop. Tab stops are initially set every four spaces. You can adjust the size of the tab stops by choosing View, Options to display the Options dialog box, and then choosing the Module Design category (see fig. 26.18).

Typical tab stop widths are four to eight spaces. Widths narrower than four spaces result in code that is slightly harder to read, while widths larger than eight tend to extend lines of code beyond the limits of the Module window. Most programmers use a tab stop width of four spaces.

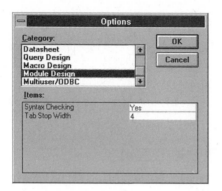

Figure 26.18
Setting the tab
stop width.

Using Constants

Constants represent specific values. You might think of constants as a special kind of variable. Unlike variables, however, the value of a constant does not change during execution of the module. To change the value of a constant, you must alter a line of Access Basic code.

A common example of a constant is PI, defined with the Const statement like this:

```
Const PI = 3.14159265
```

In HomeFinder, the Global Constants module contains a number of constants you can use with the MsgBox statement:

```
Const MB_ICONEXCLAMATION = 48
```

To use the constant, you can enter a line of code like this:

```
MsgBox "Your Message Goes Here", MB_ICONEXCLAMATION
```

In this example, Access substitutes the value of the MB_ICONEXCLAMATION constant, 48, in place of the constant's name. The value of this is that you do not have to remember the various numeric values; you need only remember or look up the name of the constants. This example also illustrates how naming your constants (and variables) can help make your code self-documenting.

Contrast the following example with the preceding version that uses a constant.

```
X = MsgBox("Message", 52)
```

In this example, you would have to remember what 52 means (exclamation point icon, plus two buttons—Yes and No).

Constants make reading and maintaining the code much easier. In the HomeFinder application, for example, the value .0175—representing a real estate agent's typical commission of 1.75 percent—is used in a number of places throughout the code. If the agent's commission changes to 1.85 percent, you must change every instance of .0175 to the new number, .0185, throughout every module in which the number appears. If you miss even one instance, an agent might be underpaid.

IV

Microsoft Access

To prevent this situation and also eliminate having to maintain multiple instances of the actual value, you can use a global constant that defines the value only once:

```
Global Const COMMISSIONRATE = .0175
```

Thereafter, you use the word COMMISSIONRATE wherever you would otherwise use the actual number:

```
AgentCommission = SalesPrice * COMMISSIONRATE
```

When the commission rate changes, you have to change the number in only one place, the Global Constants module.

You can use constants only in Access Basic code. You cannot refer to a constant in an expression on a form, in a query, or elsewhere in your application.

Using Functions and Subroutines

All executable Access Basic code is contained in either Function or Sub procedures (including Sub procedures stored as code behind form). Collectively, these all are known as *procedures*, or simply *functions*.

One reason to create a function is so you can perform a series of actions multiple times without having to repeat the code. You might, for example, want to calculate an agent's commission in a number of places throughout your application. Instead of repeating the same code wherever it is needed, you can call a function that performs the calculation and returns the result.

By using arguments (discussed later in this section) each time you call a function, the function can work with different data each time you call it.

The essential differences between Function procedures and Sub procedures are the following:

✔ Function procedures always return a value, even if you do not assign that value to a variable or to a control. Sub procedures cannot return a value.

✔ More importantly, you can call Function procedures from expressions outside of Access Basic as well as from other procedures. You can call Function procedures from an event procedure on a form, from within a query, from a macro, or from another Access Basic procedure.

✔ In contrast, you cannot call a Sub procedure from anywhere except Access Basic. This means you must call a Function procedure which in turn calls a Sub procedure if you want to run the code in a Sub procedure from a macro, from a form, or from within a query.

Because no compelling reason exists to use Sub procedures, and because Sub procedures are limited with regard to where you can use them, all the procedure examples in this book and in the HomeFinder sample database application are Function procedures.

Most functions begin with the reserved word `Function`, but in some cases you might want to precede this word with `Static` or `Private`.

Static Functions

When you add the word `Static` to the beginning of a function definition, all the variables you declare in the function are made *static:* the variables retain their values between calls to the function. The `Static` reserved word is discussed in greater detail in the section "Using Variables" later in this chapter.

A *reserved word* is text that has special meaning to Access Basic. `If`, `For`, `End`, and `Select` all are reserved words in Access Basic. Other reserved words, such as `Function` and `Sub`, identify parts of your program to Access Basic. The user-defined names you create—the names of variables, constants, functions, and procedures—cannot be named with reserved words.

Private Functions

When you add the reserved word `Private` to the beginning of a function definition, you can call the function only from other procedures in the same module. Access Basic requires that a procedure have a unique name throughout the entire database unless it is marked private. This means you can have multiple modules, each containing functions with the same name.

Drawbacks to using private functions exist, however. Debugging applications that have multiple functions with the same name are harder to debug. Because you can call a private function only from within the same module, the utility of a private function is less than that of a nonprivate function.

Finally, you cannot call private functions from a macro or from form or report event properties. To use a private function, you must call a nonprivate function that in turn calls the private function in the same module.

Note All procedures stored as code behind form are private and can be called only from form, report, or control events.

Function Arguments

When you define a function, you can indicate that the function accepts arguments (arguments are sometimes called *parameters*). An *argument* is a replaceable value (a number, text, or some other value) that you supply to the function when you call it.

The Commission() function, for example, accepts an argument that is the sales price for a house:

```
Function Commission (ByVal SalesPrice As Variant) As Variant
```

Each time you call the Commission() function, the value of the SalesPrice argument is likely to be different. Because the function works with the value of the argument, and not the argument itself, you do not need multiple functions.

Using Variables

Variables are storage places for information in Access Basic. A variable has a user-defined name and a specific data type. Variable names follow the same naming rules as functions: they must begin with a letter and can contain up to 40 characters using letters, numbers, and underscores.

Variable names cannot be the same as a reserved word, although they can contain reserved words. You cannot, for example, create a variable named Print because Print is a reserved word. However, you can name a variable PrintReport.

You can declare a variable in a number of ways:

Explicitly with Dim. The most common (and preferred) way to declare a variable is to use the Dim statement. When you use Dim, you tell Access Basic the name of the variable and its data type (the kind of data you want to store in the variable). The following examples illustrate how you declare variables with the Dim statement.

```
Dim PhoneNumber As String

Dim CustomerID As Variant

Dim X As Integer, Y As Integer
```

For each of these variables, Access can store the specified kind of data. If you try to store an invalid kind of value in a variable, an error occurs. You cannot, for example, store a customer's name in an Integer variable because Integer variables cannot accept text values.

When you declare more than one variable on a single line, you must specify the data type for each variable.

For more information about declaring data types, see the section "Choosing Data Types" later in this chapter.

Explicitly with `Static`. A less common (but not less useful) technique for declaring a variable is to use the `Static` statement. For example:

```
Static Tally As Integer

Static Population As Long
```

When you use the `Static` reserved word, the contents of the variable are preserved between calls to the function. This means that when you call the function, the variable has the same value it had the last time you called the function. This characteristic is useful when you want to call a function and still refer to the last values.

You also can declare an entire function to be static by adding the `Static` reserved word to the beginning of the function definition. When you do this, all the variables throughout the Function procedure are static, even if you do not explicitly declare the variables to be static. In fact, you cannot make some variables static and others nonstatic when you make the entire function static.

Implicitly. If you use a variable that has not been explicitly declared with `Dim`, `ReDim`, or `Static`, Access Basic declares the variable for you. This behavior is generally undesirable, however. For more information about implicit variables, see the following section, "Option Explicit."

Option Explicit

Unlike some other programming languages, such as C, you can use a variable in Access Basic without having to formally declare it. An undeclared variable that has no type declaration character is assumed by Access Basic to be a Variant; such variables are initially empty and contain no value. This feature of Access Basic, although flexible, is nonetheless undesirable for a number of reasons:

✔ It is good programming practice to declare all variables before you use them. This aids in program debugging and helps identify problems in program logic. If you expect a particular calculation to result in relatively small whole numbers, for example, you might store the results in an Integer variable. If your code produces a result too large for an Integer variable (indicating a logical error in your code), Access produces an error message.

✔ A properly declared variable is more memory-efficient than an undeclared variable. An integer variable, for example, occupies two bytes of memory, a double variable occupies eight bytes, and so on. When you declare variables explicitly, the variables occupy only as much memory as necessary. When you use undeclared variables, you waste memory because of the overhead of Variant variables. It is better to declare a variable with the appropriate data type.

✔ Explicitly declaring variables prevents misspellings. The following code contains a misspelling:

IV

Microsoft Access

```
Function GetResources (ByVal Module As String) As Long

    Resources = GetHeapSpaces(GetModuleHandle(Module))
    TotalSpace = High(Resources)
    GetResources = Low(Resources) * 100 \ TotalSpce

End Function
```

The problem with this code is that the fourth line has a typographical error—
TotalSpce should read TotalSpace. If left uncorrected, this function always results in
a division-by-zero error (TotalSpce has a value of zero) because Access automatically
creates a variable named TotalSpce when the fourth line is encountered. This looks
like perfectly good code to Access Basic, and Access does not report any errors when
you compile your code.

When you use Option Explicit, Access forces you to declare all variables. In this
example, compiling the code with Option Explicit present would result in an error
message (see fig. 26.19).

Figure 26.19
With Option
Explicit, Access
tells you about
undeclared
variables.

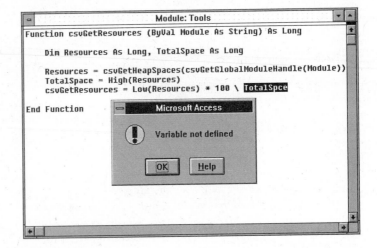

To avoid these and other problems, add the Option Explicit statement to the declarations
section of every module in your database. Option Explicit applies only to the module in
which it appears. If your database has four modules, you need four Option Explicit statements.

The HomeFinder sample database application does not include Option
Explicit in two modules: Declarations and Global Constants. This is by
design because these two modules do not contain any variables. If you follow
the example of HomeFinder and create similar separate modules, you can
safely omit Option Explicit from any module that never contains variables.

Choosing Data Types

When you declare variables or define function arguments, you must choose an appropriate data type. You might, for example, create a variable that needs to store a buyer's name (text), house listing price (currency amount), or a particular room dimension (number). You also might need a variable that contains an unknown kind of data (`Variant`).

Each of these data types are similar to, but distinct from, the data types you use to create a table. Access Basic supports seven built-in data types, and you can define your own types. Table 26.4 lists the built-in data types and the kind of data they can store.

Table 26.4
Allowable Limits of Access Data Types

Data Type	Range of Values
Integer	Integers between –32,768 and 32,767
Long	Integers between approximately –2 billion and +2 billion (–2,147,483,648 and 2,147,483,647)
Single	Numbers between –3.402823 × 10^{38} and 3.402823 × 10^{38}
Double	Numbers between –1.79769313486232 × 10^{308} and 1.79769313486232 × 10^{308}; dates are stored internally as Double values
Currency	Values between approximately –922 trillion and +922 trillion (–922,337,203,685,477.5808 and 922,337,203,685,477.5807), with four decimal places of precision
String	Any characters (letters, numbers, symbols, extended ANSI characters)
Variant	Any of the preceding values

When you declare a variable (or an argument), you follow the name of the variable with the reserved word `As` and the name of the desired data type. If you do not add `As` and the data type, Access Basic automatically assumes you mean to declare a Variant variable.

Because functions return values, you also declare their data types. You do this much like a variable by adding `As` and the data type to the end of the function definition. The following example illustrates how you can declare a function's return data type:

```
Function MyFunction () As Integer
```

In this example, `MyFunction()` returns an Integer value.

Although you do not have to declare a specific data type (Access assumes you want a Variant variable, even if you do not need the flexibility of a Variant), you nonetheless should explicitly declare the appropriate data type. For more information, see the following section.

The Variant Data Type

The Variant data type is very flexible, able to store any kind of data: strings, dates, numbers, and currency values. It also is the only data type that can store the special Null value.

Variants take on the data type of the data stored in it. Access automatically adjusts the data type of a Variant variable or argument to accommodate the data type of the particular value. The following example illustrates one way you can use Variants to store different kinds of data:

```
Function MyVariantTest () As Variant

    Dim MyVariant As Variant      ' Declare Variant variable
    MyVariant = 1                 ' Set to the number 1
    MyVariant = MyVariant + 10    ' Add 10 to it
    MyVariant = "Result = " & MyVariant
    Debug.Print MyVariant


End Function
```

To run this code, add it to a new module, open the Immediate window (choose <u>V</u>iew, <u>I</u>mmediate Window), type **Print MyVariantTest()**, and then press Enter.

Although Variant variables are flexible, a certain amount of overhead is involved with transforming values from one data type to another. Generally, it is better to use a variable with a specific data type (Integer, String, and so on) than it is to use a Variant when you know what kind of data the variable needs to store.

Object Data Types

In addition to the usual data types you use to store string and numeric data, Access supports special types for database objects. Among these objects are the following:

Controls

Databases

Forms

Reports

Tables

Dynasets

Snapshots

Recordsets

Use these object data types when you want to refer to an object with a variable or function argument. You declare object variables just like regular variables using the `Dim` statement. You can declare, for example, a variable that refers to the current database:

```
Dim MyDB As Database
```

A variable that refers to one of the database objects is called an *object variable*. The next example illustrates the way you can refer to the active control (the control that has the focus):

```
Dim MyControl As Control

Set MyControl = Screen.ActiveControl
MsgBox MyControl.ControlName & " is the active control."
```

When you run this code from a command button's Click event, Access displays a message box with the name of the command button control.

Another way to use an object data type is to create a function that requeries a control. You might, for example, want to create a function that updates a combo box or list box, or refreshes a subform. The following function requeries any of these objects:

```
Function csvRequeryControl (MyControl As Control) As Integer

    MyControl.Requery

End Function
```

Creating and Using Arrays

Unlike simple variables that store single values (for example, a customer name or a birthdate), an *array* is a variable that stores a series of related values, such as a list of customer account numbers. Access Basic supports arrays as one way of storing this information. An array is a collection of data with one name. To refer to a particular entry in the list, use an index to point to the desired element in the array.

Note Like all variables, arrays do not store information in the same sense as storing information in tables. You must put information into an array, just as you assign values to regular variables. If you want to save the information that is in an array, you must retrieve the data from the array and in turn store it in a table.

To declare an array variable, use the `ReDim` or `Static` statement followed by the name of the array variable and the number of entries you want in the array:

```
Static MyArray(9) As Integer
```

In this example, Access creates a static array of 10 elements that can store integer values (elements start with number 0; 0–9 results in 10 elements). To refer to the first entry in the array, use `MyArray(0)`. The second element in the array is `MyArray(1)`, and so on, up to `MyArray(9)`. The number within the parentheses is the index into the array.

One common way to use arrays and indexes is to create a loop that works on each array element:

```
For X = 0 To 9
    MyArray(X) = X * 2
    Debug.Print MyArray(X)
Next X
```

In this example, the `For...Next` loop (described later in this chapter) looks at each element of the array and assigns the value of the X variable to the element. When the loop is finished, `MyArray(0)` equals to 0, `MyArray(1)` equals 2, `MyArray(2)` equals 4, and so on.

You also can use `Dim` to create an array with no dimensions, and then later use the `ReDim` statement to change the size:

```
Dim MyArray() As Integer
:
ReDim MyArray(19)
```

You might redimension an array when you do not initially know just how large an array needs to be. When you use the `ReDim` statement, Access erases all the values in the array. If all you want to do is increase (or decrease) the number of elements in an array, yet still keep the remaining values intact, include the `Preserve` reserved word:

```
ReDim Preserve MyArray(29)
```

In this example, the array is increased in size from 20 elements (0–19) to 30 elements (0–29). All the existing elements from 0 to 19 remain intact with whatever values they had before Access processed the `ReDim` statement.

Creating Control Structures

When you run your code, Access Basic follows what is called the *flow of control*. This flow starts at the beginning of a Function procedure and continues through each line of code to the end, unless you change the line-by-line flow of control. To change the flow, you create control structures. This section discusses some of the more common control structures you can use in Access Basic.

In the examples that follow, the exact syntax is somewhat simplified for purposes of illustration. Some optional elements, for example, are not enclosed with brackets, the standard method for indicating optional elements. For more information about the exact syntax, or construction, of the control structures, search Help for the name of the relevant control structure.

If...Then

The most common control structure is the `If...Then` statement. Use `If...Then` when you want to execute a specific section of code, but only when a certain condition is satisfied.

Two forms of the `If...Then` control structure exist:

```
If expression Then statement block

If expression Then
    statement block
End If
```

Access Basic evaluates the expression and, if it evaluates to a true condition, executes the statement block. The following example illustrates how `If...Then` works.

```
If X > 500 Then
    MsgBox "X is greater than 500."
End If
```

In this example, Access displays a message box if (and only if) the value of X is greater than 500; otherwise, the condition is false and Access skips over the statement block.

If the expression evaluates to any value except zero or null, then the statement block is executed.

If...Then...Else

The `If...Then...Else` control structure is similar to `If...Then` except that `If...Then...Else` provides a way to do something if the expression is false.

Only one form exists for the `If...Then...Else` control structure:

```
If expression Then
    statement block 1
Else
    statement block 2
End If
```

If the expression evaluates to true, Access Basic executes whatever code is in the first statement block. When Access gets to the `Else` statement, it skips the rest of the code and goes to the End

`If` statement. If the expression evaluates to false, Access Basic skips the first statement block and goes right to the code following the `Else` statement. The following example illustrates how this works:

```
If X > 500 Then
     MsgBox "X is greater than 500."
Else
     MsgBox "X is not greater than 500."
End If
```

Select Case

The `If...Then` and `If...Then...Else` control structures handle simple testing of two values, but sometimes you need to work with more than two values and do a number of different things. The `Select Case` control structure provides a way of testing a single expression and then performing a variety of operations.

The form for the `Select Case` control structure is:

```
Select Case expression
     Case expression list 1
          statement block 1
     Case expression list 2
          statement block 2
     Case expression list n
          statement block n
     Case Else
          statement block
End Select
```

You can have any number of `Case`-*expression list* pairs. The best way to explain how `Select Case` works is to show an example:

```
Select Case X
     Case 1
          MsgBox "X is the number 1."
     Case "A"
          MsgBox "X is the letter 'A'."
     Case Else
          MsgBox "X is not 1 or 'A'."
End Select
```

In this example, Access Basic evaluates the variable X and determines whether it is equal to 1, "A", or something else. This sample code prints simple message boxes, but you could perform other actions just as easily.

For...Next

You can use a `For...Next` loop to execute a block of code a specific number of times. The form for the `For...Next` loop is:

```
For counter = start value To stop value
    statement block
Next counter
```

The following example illustrates how Access Basic runs the loop for as many times as you specify with the start and stop values.

```
For X = 1 To 10
    MsgBox "Now processing statement number" & Str$(X)
Next X
```

By default, Access Basic begins with the starting value, executes the code inside the loop, and then adds 1 to the counter before it goes through the loop again. It repeats this process until the value of the counter exceeds the value specified by the stop value argument. If you want, you can increment the counter by a number other than 1:

```
For X = 1 To 9 Step 2
    MsgBox "Now processing statement number" & Str$(X)
Next X
```

In this example, Access Basic adds 2 to the counter each time it runs through the loop instead of just 1. The counter equals 1 the first time through (the starting value), 3 the next time, then 5, and so on until the counter equals 11. When it is 11, it exceeds the ending value and Access Basic exits the loop.

In all the previous examples, the starting and ending values were specific numbers. You also can use variables or expressions to set the starting and ending values in a `For...Next` loop.

Do...Loop

At other times, you might want to execute a block of code an undetermined number of times; that is, you want to run some code until a certain condition is true. The `Do...Loop` control structure addresses this need.

Several forms exist for the `Do...Loop` control structure. Three of the more common forms are the following:

```
Do
    statement block
Loop

Do Until condition
    statement block
Loop
```

IV

Microsoft Access

```
Do
        statement block
Loop Until condition
```

In the first form, Access Basic loops through the code in the statement block until it encounters an `Exit Loop` statement. You use this form of the control structure when you need to check a condition inside the loop.

The second form of `Do...Loop` checks to see if the condition is true just before it begins to go through the loop. If the condition is true, Access Basic skips over the loop. This means that the code inside the loop might not be executed at all.

If you want to make sure Access Basic executes the code inside the loop at least once, you want to use the third form. With this form, Access checks the value of the condition after it executes the code. This means the code executes at least one time.

The following example illustrates the third form of the `Do...Loop` structure.

```
Const csvMB_NO = 7
Const csvMB_YESNO = 4

Do
      Response = MsgBox("Show message again?", csvMB_YESNO)
Loop Until Response = csvMB_NO
```

Executing Macro Actions

With few exceptions, you can run any of the macro actions from within Access Basic by using the `DoCmd` statement. The `DoCmd` statement accepts the name of the desired action, along with any arguments required by the action. The following example illustrates how you can open a form directly from Access Basic with `DoCmd` and the `OpenForm` macro action:

```
DoCmd OpenForm "House Information"
```

The next example exports the Agents table to a text file you then can use with an ASCII text editor:

```
DoCmd TransferText A_EXPORTDELIM,, "Agents", AGENTS.TXT
```

In this example, `A_EXPORTDELIM` is one of the intrinsic constants. For more information about constants, see the section "Using Constants" earlier in this chapter or search Help for "constants".

You also can execute an entire macro that in turn calls a number of macro actions. The following example illustrates how you can run a macro from within Access Basic using the `RunMacro` action:

```
DoCmd RunMacro "AutoExec"
```

Calling Functions

You can call a function from within an Access Basic module as easily as you can call it from a form, report, macro, or query. This capability means you do not have to repeat code that you need to execute in various places throughout your modules.

To call a function, simply refer to the function in an expression. The simplest way to call a function is to assign the function's return value to a variable:

```
TotalSpace = HighWord(ResourceSpace)
```

In this example, Access Basic assigns the value returned by the `HighWord()` function to the variable `TotalSpace`.

Filling a Combo Box or List Box

Combo boxes and list boxes contain lists of items from which you can choose. You can fill these boxes with the selectable items in a number of ways, depending on the data you need:

✔ The results of a select query or the contents of a table

✔ A set of fixed values you specify at design time when you create the combo box or list box; this is appropriate when the number of entries is limited and is not likely to change (for example, the names of shipping companies you use).

✔ A list of field names from a table or query

✔ The values returned by an SQL (structured query language) statement

Most of the time, you use one of these techniques to fill a list box or combo box. Sometimes, however, none of these methods supply the exact data you need. In these cases, you can use Access Basic to fill the list.

In Access Basic, you create a fill function. *Fill functions* are unique functions because Access calls the function automatically whenever it needs to—you do not control when the function gets called.

Fill functions also are unique in the way they are constructed. They have a specific structure, and the number and type of arguments they accept cannot be changed. The following example illustrates how you can construct a fill function in Access Basic.

```
Function FillFileNames (MyListBox As Control, ID As Variant,
➥ Row As Integer, Col As Integer, Code As Variant) As Variant

    Const FILEPATH = "c:\windows\*.*"
    Static FileArray(), FileCount As Integer
```

```
Select Case Code
     Case 0 ' Initialize; establish the data set.
          FileCount = 1
          FileArray(1) = Dir(FILEPATH)
          Do Until FileArray(FileCount) = ""
               FileCount = FileCount + 1
               ReDim Preserve FileArray(FileCount)
               FileArray(FileCount) = Dir
          Loop
          FileCount = FileCount - 1
          FillFileNames = True
     Case 1 ' Open; return a unique number.
          FillFileNames = Timer
     Case 3 ' Set the number of rows you want to fill.
          FillFileNames = FileCount
     Case 4 ' Set the number of columns.
          FillFileNames = 1
     Case 5 ' Set the column width; -1 = automatic.
          FillFileNames = -1
     Case 6 ' Get data (and format it, if necessary).
          FillFileNames = FileArray(Row + 1)
     Case 9 ' End; erase any memory used by array.
          Erase FileArray
End Select
```

Whenever Access needs to fill the list (it knows when the list needs to be filled or refreshed), it calls the fill function multiple times with different values for the Code argument (in this example, MyControl) to identify the control you want to fill. Access takes care of the rest of the arguments automatically.

Access calls the function once with Code set to 0, 1, 3, and 4. 0 initializes the list, 1 opens the list, 3 asks for the number of rows of data in the list, and 4 asks for the number of columns.

Access calls the function with the number 5 to determine the width of the list. The first time it asks for the total width of the list; the second time it sets the individual column widths.

Access then calls the function many times with code 6 to fill the list with data. Because you have no way of knowing when Access requires the data, the data must be available at all times. In the preceding example, the function uses a static array to provide the data (recall that a static array or variable retains its values between calls to the function).

Finally, when Access is finished filling the list, it calls the function with Code set to 9.

Manipulating Data

Most of the time, you can process all your data by using tables, queries (including action queries), and forms. At times, however, you might want to do something that requires special handling. For those situations, Access Basic includes functionality to process data. You can use Access Basic, for example, to process in a database other than the current database.

The following example illustrates the way in which you can open a database, open a table, and then list selected contents (in this case, customer names) from the records in the table.

```
Function csvListCustomers () As Integer

    Dim MyDB As Database, MyTable As Recordset

    csvListCustomers = True
    Set MyDB = DBEngine(0)(0)
    Set MyTable = MyDB![tblCustomers].OpenRecordset()

    Do Until MyTable.EOF
        Debug.Print MyTable![Last Name] & ", " & MyTable![First Name]
        MyTable.MoveNext
    Loop

    MyTable.Close
    MyDB.Close

End Function
```

Opening and Closing a Database

To perform data manipulation in Access Basic, you must create a database variable. You declare a database variable like any other variable:

```
Dim MyDB As Database
```

Next, you set it to a value that is a database object. If you want to refer to the current database, you can use the DBEngine object, as shown here:

```
Set MyDB = DBEngine(0)(0)
```

In this example, the trailing (0)(0) identifies the currently active database. The following example illustrates how you can open another database:

```
Set MyDB = DBEngine(0).OpenDatabase("C:\DATA\MYDB.MDB", True, False)
```

In this example, you specify the name of the database, including its full path. In contrast, when you use `DBEngine(0)(0)`, you do not need to know that name of the database.

You must use the longer version that specifies the name of the database:

✔ When you want to manipulate data in another database that is not in an attached table.

✔ When you want to directly manipulate an attached table—you cannot open an attached table. To open the table, you must open the other database first.

`Set` is a reserved word you use to make an object variable "point" to a specific database object. This is much like a pointer in other languages such as C.

When you are finished working with the database, close the database variable with the `Close` method:

```
MyDB.Close
```

A *method* is a special function that operates on the object variable that precedes it. The name of the object variable and the method are separated with a period. In the preceding example, the `Close` method closes the database to which it refers.

Creating and Deleting QueryDefs

Although most of the queries you create in Access are with the Query window and the QBE grid, you can create and manipulate queries in Access Basic, as well.

To open an existing query, you create a `QueryDef` object variable:

```
Dim MyDB As Database
Dim MyQuery As QueryDef

Set MyDB = DBEngine(0)(0)
Set MyQuery = MyDB.QueryDefs("MyQuery")
```

To create a new query, you use an SQL statement:

```
Dim MyQuery As QueryDef

Set MyQuery = MyDB.CreateQueryDef("Agencies by Name Qry")
MyQuery.SQL = "SELECT * FROM Agencies ORDER BY Name;"
MyQuery.Close
```

One easy way to create an SQL statement is to build the desired query using the Query window and the QBE grid. Then, choose View, SQL to display the SQL window (see fig. 26.20), highlight the SQL statement, and copy the statement to the Clipboard.

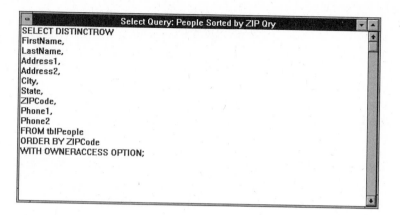

Figure 26.20
The SQL window.

Next, return to your Access Basic function and paste the SQL statement where you need it. You have to fix the bad line breaks to get the statement to fit on one line of Access Basic code, but after you do that you have defined the query without having to write the statement from scratch.

When you use the `CreateQueryDef` method, it actually creates a new query in the database. If you do not want the query to remain when you are finished working with it, delete the query with the `DeleteQueryDef` method:

```
MyDB.DeleteQueryDef("Obsolete Query")
```

When you are finished working with the `QueryDef` variable, close it with the `Close` method:

```
MyQuery.Close
```

Creating and Using Dynasets

You can use three kinds of database objects to manipulate data in your database:

✔ **Tables.** As their name implies, you use Table objects when you want to directly manipulate the actual tables in the database. When you work with indexed tables, this technique can be very efficient. The rules for working with attached tables and native tables are a bit different. For more information, see "Opening and Closing a Database" earlier in this section.

✔ **Dynasets.** The data referred to by a Dynaset object changes dynamically according to the changes in its underlying tables. Dynasets can be based on more than one underlying table, which makes them particularly useful when you deal with tables that are part of relationships. For more information about relationships, see Chapter 21, "Creating and Using Tables."

✔ **Snapshots.** Snapshots are a lot like dynasets: they can be based on one or more tables or on the result of a query. Like dynasets, you can order (sort) or filter the records when you create the snapshot.

IV

Microsoft Access

Unlike dynasets, however, snapshots do not change after they are created. You cannot add records, delete records, nor change any of the data in the underlying tables—they truly are "snapshots" of the underlying data.

To create a Dynaset object, use the `OpenRecordset` method, as shown here:

```
Dim MyDB As Database
Dim MyDynaset As Recordset

Set MyDB = DBEngine(0)(0)
Set MyDynaset = MyDB.OpenRecordset("tblCustomers", DB_OPEN_DYNASET)
```

In this example, `MyDynaset` is a Dynaset object that refers to the tblCustomers table. Another way to create a dynaset is to base the Dynaset object on the name of an existing query:

```
Set MyDynaset = MyDB.OpenRecordset
➥("Agents by Name Qry", DB_OPEN_DYNASET)
```

In this example, the dynaset is based on the results of the `Agents by Name Qry` query. A third way to create the dynaset is to base it on an SQL statement instead of an existing query:

```
Set MyDynaset = MyDB.OpenRecordset("SELECT *
➥FROM tblCustomers ORDER BY [Last Name];", DB_OPEN_DYNASET)
```

This SQL statement retrieves all the records from the tblCustomers table and sorts them by their last names.

After you have created a dynaset, you can examine or change the underlying records. To move from record to record, use the `MoveFirst`, `MoveLast`, `MoveNext`, and `MovePrevious` methods.

You can determine the number of records in a dynaset with the `RecordCount` property. The `RecordCount` property, however, reflects only the number of records you have "visited." To get an accurate count, then, you must go to the last record before you read the record count. The following example shows one way to do this:

```
Function csvRecordCountDemo () As Integer

    Dim MyDB As Database
    Dim MyDynaset As Recordset
    Dim X As Integer
    Dim Bookmark As String

    Set MyDB = DBEngine(0)(0)
    Set MyDynaset = MyDB.OpenRecordset("tblCustomers", DB_OPEN_DYNASET)

    ' First, move beyond the beginning of the records.
    For X = 1 To 5
```

```
        Debug.Print X, MyDynaset![Last Name]
        If X = 5 Then    ' Save the current record location.
            Bookmark = MyDynaset.Bookmark
        End If
        MyDynaset.MoveNext
    Next X


    ' To get an accurate count, go to the last record.
    MyDynaset.MoveLast
    MsgBox "Count: " & MyDynaset.RecordCount & " records."
    ' Return to the previous record location.
    MyDynaset.Bookmark = Bookmark
    ' Print the name to prove it works.
    Debug.Print MyDynaset![Last Name]


    MyDynaset.Close
    MyDB.Close


End Function
```

When you are finished working with the Dynaset object variable, close it with the `Close` method:

```
    MyDynaset.Close
```

Recovering from Errors

Macros might have an edge over Access Basic when it comes to ease of use, but Access Basic is far more flexible and powerful, especially when it comes to handling errors. As you decide between using macros and writing code, you should consider that you cannot trap errors that occur when you run a macro. A macro stops if an error occurs; you probably want your application to handle errors a bit more gracefully, especially if you distribute your application to other users or to clients.

Ideally, Access Basic procedures would not need error-handling code at all. Unfortunately, users sometimes mistakenly delete files, files become corrupted, disk drives run out of space, and network drives disconnect unexpectedly. To handle these and other errors, your applications should include error-handling code.

Building an Error Handler

The best way to detect errors is to construct your code so that your application does not try to perform an operation that could fail. This might mean checking available disk space before you create a report that spools to a disk drive. Some errors, however, cannot be tested ahead of time, or doing so might be impractical. In such cases, you can create your own error-handling routines and trap the run-time errors.

After you have trapped an error, you then decide how your application should proceed. You might retry the operation, ask for additional input from the user, or exit the operation altogether.

Although you can trap many data-entry errors using the ValidationRule event property, other error conditions exist that are not directly related to data entry. These include disk errors, invalid string manipulation, table maintenance, and other activities carried out in code. You can trap these run-time errors with the On Error statement.

The following example illustrates how you can trap an error and change the flow of code.

```
Function csvErrorTest () As Integer

    csvErrorTest = True

    On Error GoTo Err_ErrorTest   ' Enable error trapping.
    Debug.Print 1 / 0             ' Create error condition.
    On Error GoTo 0               ' Disable error trapping.
    Exit Function


Err_ErrorTest:

    MsgBox "Error " & Err & " (" & Error & ") has occurred."
    Resume Next

End Function
```

In this example, csvErrorTest() traps the division-by-zero error and alters the program flow. The error handler, Err_ErrorTest, displays a user-defined error message. Unlike the built-in system error messages Access Basic displays, you can change this message to anything you like.

When you trap an error, Access Basic does not automatically display an error message. If you want the user to see a message, you need to write one yourself. The error code and original message still are accessible, and you can use this information in your own message.

Placing and Naming Error Handlers

You must place error handlers in the procedure in which they are used. You cannot branch to an error handler that is not in the same procedure. If you want to branch to an error handler from within MyFunction(), for example, that error handler must be located in the MyFunction() procedure.

The names of error handlers follow the same naming conventions as other line labels in Access Basic: they must begin with an alphabetic character, must end with a colon (:), must be no longer than 40 characters, and must not be the same as an Access Basic reserved word.

The names of error handlers, like other line labels, must be unique in the module in which they appear. Even though you could have the same label appear in more than one module, you should avoid duplicating line labels because it could lead to confusion as you test and debug your application.

It is convenient to name your error handlers consistently; for example, you might use the format Err_*functionname*, where *functionname* is the name of the function in which the error handler appears. This makes locating the error handlers easy, because they all begin with the same prefix and end with the name of the Function procedure that contains them.

Line labels can begin anywhere on a line as long as they are the first nonblank character on the line. The following example illustrates how you can format your own error handlers. If you choose a different formatting style, use that format consistently throughout your application.

```
Function MyFunction () As Integer

    ' Declarations go here.

    On Error GoTo Err_MyFunction ' Enable error trapping.
    ' Main processing code goes here.
    On Error GoTo 0              ' Disable error trapping.
    Exit Function               ' Avoid falling through.

Err_MyFunction:

    ' Error-handling code goes here.


    End Function
```

The error trap is disabled as soon as it is no longer needed. It is poor programming practice to leave error trapping enabled, even though Access Basic does not require you to explicitly turn it off before you leave a procedure.

If your application requires multiple error handlers in a single procedure, you might name them Err_*functionname*1, Err_*functionname*2, and so on. You also might consider appending a word or two that describe the kind of error—for example, Err_*functionname*BadLength.

Debugging Your Code

Debugging is the process of finding and fixing bugs, or mistakes, in your code. There are three kinds of bugs:

IV

Microsoft Access

✔ **Compile-time errors.** These are the easiest to find and fix. To find them, choose Run, Compile Loaded Modules. If Access detects any errors, it displays an error message indicating the nature of the problem. Access also highlights the line of code that contains the problem.

Another way to catch some compile-time errors is to make sure you leave syntax checking enabled. When you enable syntax checking, Access automatically checks the construction of each line as soon as you press Enter or move to another line.

✔ **Run-time errors.** These errors are slightly more difficult to find than compile-time errors. In Access Basic, this can happen when you try to execute a statement that is inappropriate for the current context. An error occurs, for example, if you try to open a nonexistent query.

Because run-time errors occur only when the code is executed, it might not be apparent for some time that a problem even exists—it can be days, months, or even years before a particular line of code gets executed.

✔ **Logical errors.** These are the hardest errors of all to find and fix. They typically are caused by code that contains the wrong set of statements to solve a particular problem. Because Access Basic relies on you to know which statements to use, and in what order, it is somewhat easy to make mistakes. Even experienced programmers make logical errors.

Access Debugging Tools

You can use the following built-in debugging tools in Design view to help find logical errors in your code:

Breakpoints. A common first step in finding a logical error is to set a breakpoint in your code. A *breakpoint* is a place at which execution stops so that you can see the state of the program. To set a breakpoint on a line of code, place the insertion point anywhere in the line and then press the F9 key. Access displays the line in bold to indicate a breakpoint has been set. To remove the breakpoint, press the F9 key a second time while the insertion point is on the line. You can switch breakpoints on and off by choosing Run, Toggle Breakpoint or by clicking on the Breakpoint button on the toolbar.

Single-stepping. When you encounter a breakpoint, you might want to see which lines of code are coming up next. Access outlines the next line of code with a dotted box, as shown in figure 26.21.

You can single-step through the code by pressing F8, choosing Run, Step Into, or by clicking on the Step Into button on the toolbar. Any of these executes the next line of code. If the code calls another function or a subroutine, step into that function or subroutine and you can see the next line to be executed.

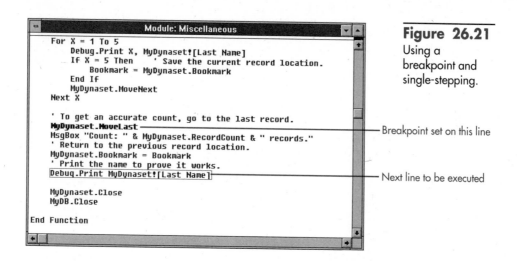

Figure 26.21
Using a breakpoint and single-stepping.

When you are stopped on a line of code that calls another function, you can either single-step into that other function (by pressing F8), or you can press Shift+F8 to execute all the code in the second function and then stop at the next line in the current procedure.

Continuing execution. If you do not need to single-step through the code (perhaps you have fixed the logical error), you can continue code execution at full speed by pressing F5, choosing <u>R</u>un, <u>C</u>ontinue, or clicking on the Run (exclamation point) button on the toolbar.

Execution continues until Access encounters another breakpoint, an error occurs, or until Access reaches the end of the code.

Showing the Next statement. If you have hit a breakpoint and then scrolled around in a module, you might want to get back to where the next statement is executed. Choose <u>R</u>un, S<u>h</u>ow Next Statement to do this.

Setting the Next statement. Sometimes you want to skip over a line of code or go back and reexecute a particular line without having to start over from the beginning. To designate the next line of code that Access Basic executes, place the insertion point anywhere in the line and then choose <u>R</u>un, Set <u>N</u>ext Statement.

Resetting. If you want to resume from scratch, you can use the <u>R</u>eset command from the <u>R</u>un menu or the Reset button on the toolbar. This resets all variables and terminates execution.

Viewing values in the Immediate window. While you have execution stopped in a function, you can view the values in any variables by printing them in the Immediate window. Open the Immediate window by choosing <u>V</u>iew, <u>I</u>mmediate Window.

The Immediate window is so-named because the effect of anything you do in the Immediate window is seen immediately, instead of at run time. In the Immediate window, for example, you can type **?** **MyDynaset.RecordCount** to find out the current record count. In the case of figure 26.22, the value is 20.

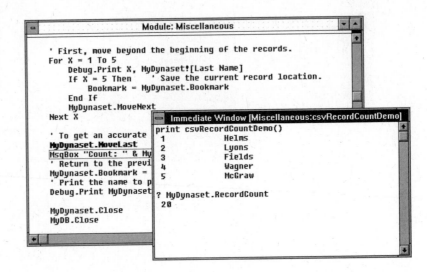

You also can call a function directly from the Immediate window. Simply type **?** plus the name of the function and any arguments.

Another useful thing you can do with the Immediate window is to embed statements throughout your code to print values to the Immediate window. You can enter **Debug.Print**, for example, followed by whatever expression, variable, or function return value you want to see. For example:

```
Debug.Print MyVariable
```

At run-time, the usefulness of the Debug.Print method is rather limited because you cannot see the Immediate window nor any debugging messages.

Chapter Snapshot

From time to time, it might be necessary to use a data file built in another database in an Access database. A file can be imported into Access, where it becomes an integral part of the Access database. Alternatively, an external database file can be attached and maintained as a distinct, independent MS-DOS file, separate from the Access database. In this chapter, you learn about the following:

In the past, transferring data between database systems often was a difficult, time-consuming procedure. Fortunately, importing data into Microsoft Access is quite simple.

CHAPTER 27

Importing and Exporting Data

by Chris St. Valentine

Tables stored in another database format are easily converted to the Access format. You could, for example, import a database built with dBASE III or IV into Access, and thereafter use Access to modify what used to be dBASE data.

Access can import files from a number of database sources:

- ✔ **Microsoft Access.** Databases other than the open database.
- ✔ **Delimited text.** Values separated by commas, tabs, or other specified characters.
- ✔ **Fixed-width text.** Values arranged so that each field has a specified width.
- ✔ **FoxPro.** Versions 2.0 and 2.5 DBF files.
- ✔ **dBASE III and dBASE IV.** DBF files.

✓ **Microsoft Excel.** Versions 2.*x*, 3.0, 4.0, and 5.0.

✓ **Lotus 1-2-3 or 1-2-3/W.** WKS, WK1, and WK3 files.

✓ **Paradox.** Version 3.*x* and 4.*x* DB files.

✓ **Btrieve.** With the data definition files FILE.DDF and FIELD.DDF.

✓ **Microsoft SQL Server.** Using ODBC drivers.

When deciding to import an external table, consider whether you will need to use the table in its native format in the future. Many companies use different database systems within the various groups within the company. In these companies, database tables often are used interchangeably among a number of different databases.

If you are sure that you will not need to use a table in another database system, import the table into Access. Otherwise, you should attach the table to your Access database, which will enable it to be used by its original database system. Once imported, the table will look and behave like any other table you create entirely in Access.

Suppose you have an existing set of business and personal address databases in dBASE format that you now want to use as the foundation of an Access address book application. If you import the files, you can save a considerable amount of time by not having to reenter all of the information.

Importing Files into Access

To import a file into Access, open the Database window and then choose <u>F</u>ile, <u>I</u>mport. Access displays the Import dialog box, providing you with a choice of database formats for importing (see fig. 27.1).

Figure 27.1
Selecting Microsoft
Excel 5.0 in the
Import dialog box.

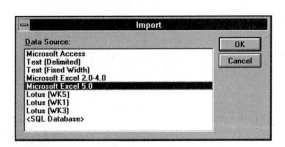

Note   The data sources that appear in the Import dialog box will vary according to the drivers you selected when you installed Access.

Select the appropriate format in the <u>D</u>ata Source list box and then click on OK; Access displays the Select File dialog box (see fig. 27.2). The type of file you selected in the Import dialog box determines which files you will see in the Select File list. If you select Microsoft Excel (any version) as the data source in the Import dialog box, for example, only files with the XLS extension will appear in the File <u>N</u>ame list. Select the file you want to import from this list and click on the Import button.

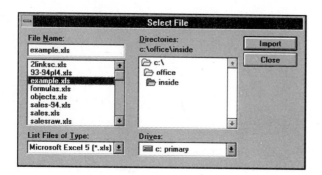

Figure 27.2
Selecting a file in the Select File dialog box.

Depending on the type of file being imported, you might see another dialog box asking for details of the import process. In the preceding example in which an Excel file is being imported, this dialog box asks, among other things, whether you want to use the Excel column heads as field names in the new Access table. If you see a dialog box after the Select File dialog box, simply answer whatever questions that are asked and go on to the next step.

The hourglass mouse pointer appears while the file is being imported, and then Access displays a message letting you know it is finished (see fig. 27.3).

Figure 27.3
Access lets you know when the import is finished.

The imported table now appears in the Access Database window with the same name as the original DOS file (without the DB, DBF, XLS, or other file name extension, of course). If you want, you can change the simple table name to a longer, more descriptive name by choosing <u>F</u>ile, Rena<u>m</u>e.

Attaching Tables

The preceding section describes the way you can import a file from an external database and convert it to the Access table format. Sometimes importing files from an external database is not practical, however.

If, for example, you want to use Access to manage a dBASE table while other users continue to use dBASE with the same table, importing the table will not work. After the table is imported into Access, changes to it within Access will not be seen by the dBASE users—you each will be working with a different copy of the dBASE table.

In cases where the data contained within a table must continue to be used with another database program, it is better to attach the external table, not import it.

When you attach a table, the table stays in its original format; Access can use it almost like a native Access table (the limitations of attached tables are discussed later in this chapter). At the same time, dBASE or Paradox users can continue to add new records and change data in the same table. Attaching the table enables easy access to the data by multiple database management systems.

Although other database users can manipulate attached tables, problems might be encountered when more than one person attempts to use a database file at the same time. Under most circumstances, an error occurs when a user tries to access a file that is already in use. The second user may find that the database (Access, dBASE, Paradox, and so on) the first user is working with has locked the table to prevent simultaneous changes to the table. This mechanism is necessary to prevent data corruption.

Access can attach files from a number of database sources:

- ✔ **Microsoft Access.** Access 1.0, 1.1, and 2.0 databases other than the open database.

- ✔ **Paradox.** Version 3.*x* and 4.*x* DB files.

- ✔ **dBASE III and dBASE IV.** DBF files.

- ✔ **Btrieve.** With the FILE.DDF and FIELD.DDF data definition files.

- ✔ **Microsoft SQL Server.** Using ODBC drivers.

To attach a table, go to the Database window and choose File, Attach Table. Access displays the Attach dialog box, offering you a choice of database formats for attaching (see fig. 27.4). Select the appropriate format in the Data Source list box and click on OK.

Figure 27.4
Selecting dBASE IV
in the Attach
dialog box.

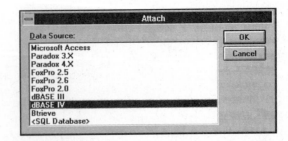

Note The data sources that appear in the Attach dialog box will vary according to the drivers you selected when you installed Access.

Access displays the Select File dialog box; select the table you want to attach and click on the Attach button (see fig. 27.5).

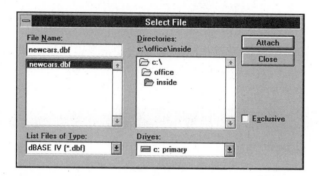

Figure 27.5
Selecting a file in the Select File dialog box.

Tip Checking the Exclusive check box in the Select File dialog box prevents other users from accessing the table while you are using it. Under some situations, even if the Exclusive box is not checked, other users might not be able to use the attached table.

Depending on the kind of external database file you attach, Access might prompt you to specify the names of files related to the table you are attaching. When you attach a dBASE file, for example, Access prompts you to include any index files associated with the dBASE table (see fig. 27.6).

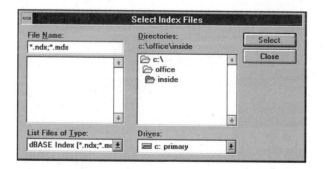

Figure 27.6
Specifying index files for a dBASE table.

IV

Microsoft Access

In this case, the selected file has no associated indexes. When you click on the Close button, the hourglass mouse pointer appears while the table is being attached, and then Access displays a message letting you know it is finished (see fig. 27.7).

Figure 27.7

Access lets you know the file is attached.

The attached table now appears in the Access Database window with the same name as the original file. If you want, you can change the table name to a longer, more descriptive name by choosing File, Rename.

When you change the name of an attached table, the new name appears only in the Access Database window. The file in the external database retains its original name. This enables the table to be used by other users without having to rename the file itself.

If you want to rename imported or attached tables, rename the tables before you create any queries, forms, reports, macros, or Access Basic code that refer to the tables by name. Otherwise, you might have to make time-consuming changes to the queries or other objects to incorporate name changes. Access does not automatically change references to renamed database objects.

In the Database window, attached tables appear with a special icon next to their names, as shown in figure 27.8. In this example, the arrows to the left of the table icons indicate the tables are attached. The icon for the NEWCARS table changes to the letters DB to identify it as an attached dBASE table. Other types of attached tables have other icons. The icon for an attached FoxPro table, for example, is the picture of a fox.

Figure 27.8

Attached table icons in the Database window.

Using Attached Tables

You can use attached tables much like any other Access table. You can use attached tables in queries, forms, and reports, and you can join Access tables and attached tables from other database programs in a single query.

This convenient and powerful feature enables you to set up a query based on data from a variety of data sources. You can create a single query using data stored on a mainframe in SQL format, on PCs in dBASE and Paradox tables, and on data from your own Access tables. After you have constructed the query, you can then design forms and reports based on it. This enables you to easily add, delete, or change data in all the attached tables, and print reports that make use of data from all the sources.

Realizing the Limitations of Attached Tables

Attached tables are still available to other databases. They are subject, however, to whatever limitations the other database program's native format imposes. Accordingly, there are some limitations to the changes you can make to these tables from within Access. You cannot, for example, change the structure of an attached table by adding or deleting fields, and you cannot change a field's data type. You can, however, set certain field properties, such as the text format, the number of decimal places, and the input mask, because these properties are used only within Access.

These limitations are necessary so that users who continue to use the other database programs can use the tables in their programs. If changes to attached tables were possible from within Access, the entry forms, queries, and reports in the other database application would have to be rewritten to accommodate whatever changes you make in Access.

If you need to make a structural change to an attached table (for example, adding a new field), open the table in the other database program and make the change there. When you return to Access, the changes will automatically be reflected in the table.

Exporting Tables and Database Objects

From time to time, it might be necessary to export an Access database object such as a table or form to another database. Once exported, the object then is used by the other database system. Although you can export all Access database objects (tables, forms, queries, macros, and so on) to another Access database, only tables can be exported in a format usable by a foreign database system, such as dBASE, Paradox, or FoxPro.

It is important to note that Access tables and other objects are not removed from the current database. Access creates a copy of the table, form, query, or other object in a format that can be understood by the receiving application.

Exporting tables is, understandably, the opposite of importing files. To export an Access table (or other database object, if exporting to another Access database), choose File, Export. The Export dialog box will open, asking which type of file format you want to export to. By default, the export will be to another Access database. You have a wide range of alternate file types, however, including dBASE, Paradox, FoxPro, Excel, Lotus 1-2-3, and so on.

If you are exporting to another Access database, the Select Microsoft Access Object dialog box appears (see fig. 27.9), enabling you to select virtually any component of your database. You can use the Export command to share tables, forms, queries, macros, and other objects in your database between multiple Access applications.

Figure 27.9
The Select
Microsoft Access
Object dialog box.

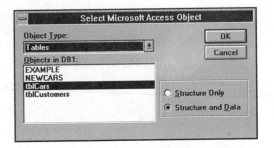

Notice in the lower right corner of the dialog box in figure 27.9 the option to export either the Structure Only or the Structure and Data of the table. When exporting to other Access databases, you have the option to export an empty table (Structure Only) or a table filled with data (Structure and Data). It often is useful to share empty tables between Access applications, instead of building each one from scratch.

Always keep in mind that as you begin new Access applications, some components from other applications you have built might be usable in your new project. Rather than always building from scratch, consider reusing components whenever possible. Often only a few changes are necessary to modify a table, form, or other component for use in another Access application.

On the other hand, if you select a file format other than Microsoft Access, the Select Microsoft Access Object dialog box displays only the names of the tables and queries (or both) in your database (see fig. 27.10).

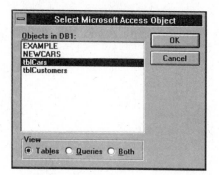

Figure 27.10
The dialog box showing only Access tables.

When you select a file format other than Microsoft Access and export a query, you actually export the results of the query; that is, whatever records are returned by the query.

In either case, select the appropriate object from the list and click on OK. The Export to File dialog box appears, enabling you to specify where on your computer system you want to put the exported object. If you selected Microsoft Access as the destination of the object, the File Name list on the left side of this dialog box will show only Access MDB files.

After you specify the destination for the exported database object, click on OK, and Access will either create a new DOS file containing the Access table or insert a copy of the object in the destination Access database.

Part Five

Data Sharing and Integration

Chapter Snapshot

Dynamic data exchange (DDE) is an internal communications protocol Windows uses to enable one application to "talk to" or exchange data with another application. Normally used to transfer information between applications, DDE can also be used within an application.

This chapter covers the following topics:

DDE enables you not only to share information between applications, but also to send commands from one application to another to control the behavior of the receiving application. Thus, DDE is a tool that implements the Windows standard for both integration and interoperability.

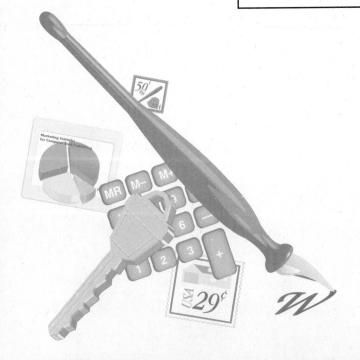

CHAPTER

Examining Dynamic Data Exchange

by Bruce Hallberg

DE creates a *link*—a communication channel, rather like an open telephone line, through which data is sent. When DDE links are live, both the sending (server) and receiving (client) applications are open. While the server data is being edited, you can see the data being transferred in real time: as data in the server document changes, the hourglass flashes briefly as the other application is updated automatically through the link. You can size the application windows so that, with the two documents side by side, you can watch the entire process.

Examining DDE Links and the Way To Use Them

Windows offers two ways to implement dynamic data exchange. The first is through the application's regular interface; you execute directly, from the application's menus, any commands to create and edit links between one application and another. In the second method, you write code in an application's macro language; only through the macro programming construct can you send instructions that control another application's behavior. This chapter teaches you how to create links with each method.

Typically, you use DDE to perform the following kinds of automated data transfers:

✔ Query the data in one application from inside another, and return a result. The query can produce a one-time (static) return of data, or can be set to update the data in the destination document when the query is run again.

✔ Convey a stream of data into an application in real time, such as sending stock market quotes into a spreadsheet.

✔ Link information contained in a compound document to the information's source so that the destination document is updated automatically whenever the source data is changed. Examples of this type of link, sometimes called a *persistent link,* are discussed throughout the chapter.

A Practical Example of Using an Automatic Link

Suppose, for example, that you regularly prepare a summary sales report and send it, at specific intervals, to company managers: once a week to sales managers, twice a month to department heads, and once a month to the chief financial officer. These reports are based on sales figures that you track and total every day in Microsoft Excel. You can create in Microsoft Word a boilerplate report for each manager, including in each report a link to the range (in your Excel worksheet) that shows the running sales total.

As you update the figures in Excel every day, the updated total is sent automatically through the DDE link to the report documents. Whenever you open the Word documents to print and send them to the appropriate managers, the documents reflect the latest data from the Excel worksheet.

Note

A DDE link creates a pointer to the source data. The link is document-to-document (another way of saying file-to-file) rather than document-to-application, as is the case with OLE-embedded data. Chapter 29, "Exploring Object Linking and Embedding," more fully discusses OLE.

After you establish a DDE link, you normally do not need to take any further action to maintain it. But when the source file is moved elsewhere on the system, or its name is changed, you must edit the link manually to tell the destination document the source's new location or name. You learn more about editing links later in this chapter (see the "Managing Links" section).

Different Flavors of DDE

Not all Windows applications support DDE. Some, such as screen savers and font managers, do not need DDE capability. DDE support generally is found in high-end word processors, spreadsheet programs, database applications, fax-generating applications, desktop-publishing programs, and electronic-mail packages.

Windows applications that support DDE can do so as a client, a server, or both. A *client application* requests or receives information from another application. A *server application* supplies information to another application.

Most applications that support DDE do so in a way that is readily accessible to the user, using commands on the application's menus and the familiar Clipboard copy-and-paste metaphor. You can think of this as *end-user DDE*. Other applications require that you access their information through macros written in a programming language. To do this you must understand the inner workings of their DDE implementation. You can think of this method of creating DDE links as *programmed links*. Microsoft Word, Excel, Lotus Ami Pro, and WordPerfect are examples of applications that have their own macro languages and can access other applications through programmed DDE.

How To Discover Whether an Application Supports DDE

To find out whether the Windows application you use (such as Microsoft Word, Lotus Ami Pro, WordPerfect, Excel, or PowerPoint) supports end-user DDE, pull down the menus and look for commands such as Paste Link, Paste Special, or Links. These commands usually are on the File or Edit menus. The presence of these commands indicates that the application supports DDE, using the Clipboard to create the links.

One advantage to using a software suite, such as Microsoft Office, is that they all tend to function very similarly with regard to features such as DDE links. Other applications will generally interface just fine with Office applications, but their implementations might work somewhat differently, depending on the programmers and designers of the other applications.

The way these clues to DDE support are expressed varies from one application to another, as you will see from the first few figures in this chapter.

V

Data Sharing and Integration

Selecting the Paste Special command from Microsoft Word's Edit menu (see fig. 28.1) brings up the Paste Special dialog box (see fig. 28.2.). In this dialog box, you can select a data type and click on the Paste Link button. If the data type you choose cannot be linked, the Paste Link button is grayed out.

Figure 28.1
The Paste Special command in Word.

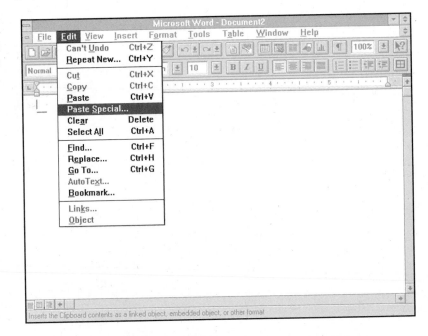

Figure 28.2
Word's Paste Special dialog box.

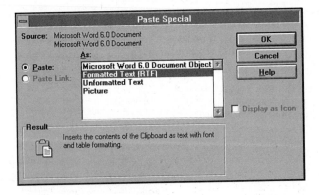

As you can see in figure 28.3, WordPerfect for Windows does things a little differently. The Edit menu command is Paste Link.

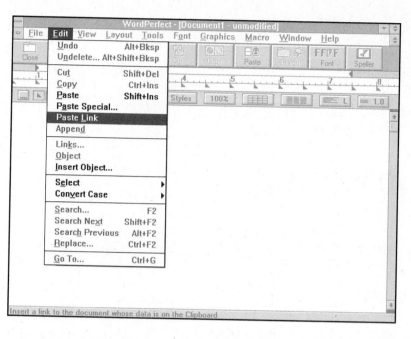

Figure 28.3

WordPerfect's Paste Link Command.

The Paste Special command in Microsoft Excel (see fig. 28.4) works in two different ways, depending on the source of data on the Clipboard. When you copy cells from the Excel worksheet to the Clipboard, the Paste Special command invokes a dialog box (see fig. 28.5) that enables you to paste the data back into the worksheet in several Excel-specific ways.

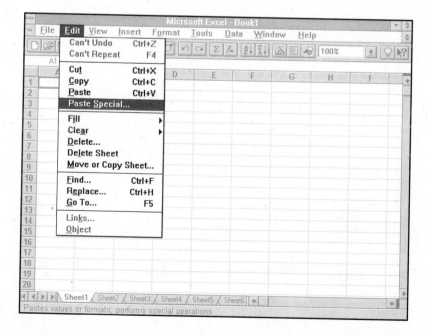

Figure 28.4

Excel's Paste Special command.

Figure 28.5

Excel's internal
Paste Special
dialog box.

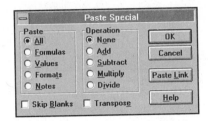

When the data on the Clipboard is from an external source, however, Excel's Paste Special
command works the way it does in Word, offering you various linking options (see fig. 28.6).

Figure 28.6

Excel's external
Paste Special
dialog box.

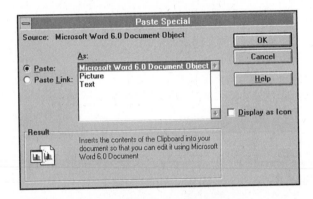

If your application has a macro language, the DDE commands should be
documented in either the language command reference or the on-line help. If
you do not see menu commands that refer to linking, and your program does
not have a macro language, consult the documentation or the vendor to find
out whether and in what form DDE is supported.

These minor inconsistencies between applications can make DDE seem too complicated or
too obscure to use. The obstacle to creating DDE links disappears, however, when you
remember that because end-user DDE is a Clipboard function, a reference to links appears on
one or more menus—usually File and Edit—in applications in which end-user DDE is
available.

Parsing a DDE Link

Whether you create a DDE link through the menu commands or in a macro, the link always
has three parts. To keep track of where the linked information is located and what it refers to,
the system needs to know the following three elements:

✔ Application

✔ Topic (sometimes called *file name*)

✔ Item

Application is Windows' alias for the program (WinWord, for example, when Word for Windows is the server). *Topic* typically is the file name of the source document, and *item* is the information in that document to which the link points. In the case of a spreadsheet, the item is the range, expressed either by a row-and-column address or, if you have named the range, by a name. In the case of a word processor such as Word or Ami Pro, the item is a bookmark name that the application assigns automatically or that you create. In addition to telling the client document where to look for updated source data, these placeholders enable you to "jump" from the destination document to the linked information in the source document, if your application permits.

Using Menu Commands To Create Links

Although you probably would not want to link text from a document created in one word processing application to a document created in another very often, the following example shows you the linking process in action. This example shows you how yet another program implements its DDE-related menu commands.

To copy a block of text from a Word document to the Clipboard, highlight the text and select Copy from the Edit menu (see fig. 28.7).

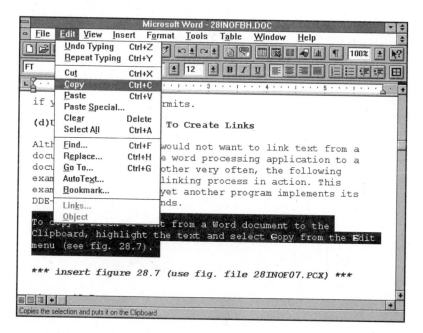

Figure 28.7

Copying data from Word.

Open WordPerfect, pull down its Edit menu, and choose Paste Link. As shown in figure 28.8, WordPerfect's information bar at the bottom of the display shows a brief explanation of the selected command.

Figure 28.8
Pasting a link in WordPerfect.

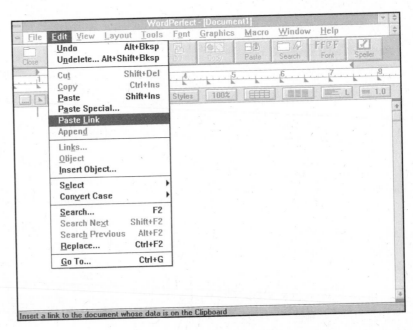

When nothing is on the Clipboard, the Paste commands are grayed out to indicate that they are not available or applicable.

When you choose the Paste Link command, the text is pasted into the WordPerfect document, and a link that points to the original text in Word is established. You can verify the link by selecting the box that contains the linked text (see fig. 28.9). As you can see, the information bar at the bottom of the WordPerfect screen shows the status of the linked data.

Because each open DDE channel requires system memory, the number of links that can be maintained in any document is limited. Factors governing the limit include how much memory is installed on the system and the claims made upon that memory by other resources currently active in the Windows session.

Name and save a server document before you create a link. Otherwise, you have to edit the link later with the source document's name.

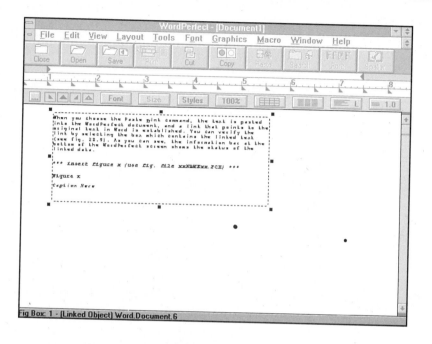

Figure 28.9
WordPerfect's link
status message.

Managing Links

Can you tell, just from looking at a document, whether it contains links and if it does, where they are? Sometimes yes, sometimes no—and sometimes you must do a bit of sleuthing.

Word enables you to explore the links for which it is acting as server. As other applications do, Word creates a bookmark for each server link (these are DDE items). But because Word lists these items as bookmarks in the document, you can use the Go To command in the Edit menu to go to them (see fig. 28.10). Word names the bookmarks DDE_LINKn (n is an automatically incremented number). When you go to a bookmark, Word highlights the block of text to which the bookmark refers. Note that if you delete links, Word does not renumber the remaining bookmarks.

To ensure that Excel's DDE links behave as you want them to, choose **O**ptions in the **T**ools menu and make sure that the **I**gnore Other Applications check box (on the General tab) is cleared. To choose whether to have all links in an individual worksheet updated automatically, select the Calculation tab in the **O**ptions dialog box and then check or clear the Update **R**emote References check box.

Figure 28.10

Finding Links in Word using the Go To dialog box.

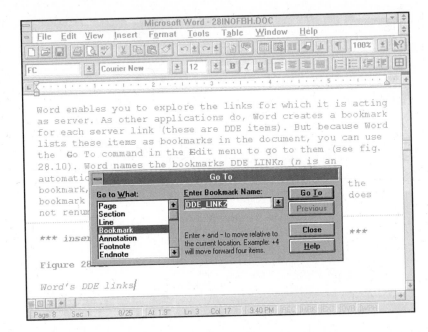

In Excel, the formula that describes the link appears in the formula bar when you select the cell that contains the formula (see fig. 28.11).

Figure 28.11

Excel's link display.

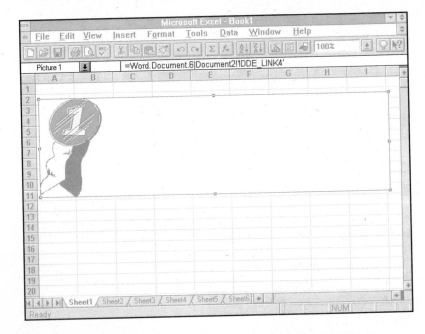

No matter how programs display links, you can always access the links in the document through a menu command. In Word, look for the Links command on the Edit menu. In Excel, the command is on the Edit menu, but is called Links (note the different hot key). And, as you saw in figure 28.8, in WordPerfect you choose Paste Link or Links from the Edit menu. (Some applications gray out the particular menu choice if no links are in the document.)

Each of these commands opens a dialog box that lists the document's links and their attributes. In this dialog box you can update individual links, change their status from automatic (active) to manual (inactive) and back again, cancel or unlink them (leaving the latest result in the document as static text), and edit them. Figure 28.12 displays Word's Links dialog box. The figure clearly shows the three parts of a DDE link: the application, the file name (usually called the topic), and the item.

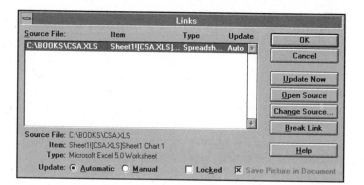

Figure 28.12
Word's Links dialog box.

In this example, you use the Links dialog box to edit the file name (topic) after you name and save the worksheet.

Word not only provides the usual options, but also enables you to jump directly to the source of the link. You can do this by choosing **O**pen Source from the Links dialog box or by selecting the command (named something like Microsoft Excel Worksheet Link) that appears under the **L**inks command on the **E**dit menu when the cursor is placed in a link area.

The best way to edit a link, in general, is to use Change Link dialog boxes. In Word and Excel you can edit the link directly on the face of the document, but the risk of accidentally deleting or mistyping a crucial quotation mark or backslash always exists.

With Excel, you can edit the link directly in the formula bar. Just be sure to press Ctrl+Shift+Enter to save the revised link as an array formula.

Understanding Hot Links

Not only does the terminology and placement of DDE-related menu commands vary from program to program, but discrepancies also exist in the way programs respond to DDE messages. Although DDE links ordinarily are well behaved, you need to be aware of some problems you might encounter.

A *hot* (or automatic) link is one that automatically updates the destination document after the linked information in the source document is changed. A *warm* (or manual) link is one in which the user must manually update the link when the source information is changed. A warm link is sometimes referred to as a *manual link* or an *inactive link*; a hot link is also called an *automatic link* or an *active link*.

Normally, links are hot when you first create them. But because their status can change under certain circumstances—sometimes without the user being aware that what was once a hot link is now a warm one that must be updated manually—you might need to experiment to determine just how your applications operate in this regard.

Not surprisingly, the most reliable DDE integration is between Microsoft Excel as the server and Microsoft Word as the client—the relationship with the longest history. With an Excel worksheet range paste-linked to a Word document, you can expect the following when you open the destination document during a subsequent session:

- ✔ If both Excel and the source document are open, the link updates automatically.

- ✔ If Excel is open but the source document is not, the link updates automatically.

- ✔ If Excel is not open, the link updates automatically.

This is DDE linking at its most efficient.

But what happens when you link Word and Excel in the other direction, with Word as the server? Excel displays a dialog box (see fig. 28.13) asking you if you want Excel to update the links to the unopened document. Clicking on the **Y**es button will update the link to the stored document.

Figure 28.13
Excel's update link
message.

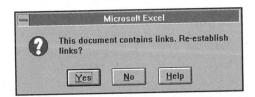

To see how this works in reverse, paste-link some Word text into an Excel worksheet (remember to name and save the source document before you create the link). Close the Excel worksheet. Before you close Word, alter the text so that you can verify the update in Excel. Close Word and then reopen the worksheet. When you answer **Y**es to the message shown in figure 28.13, Excel automatically updates the link. In other words, Excel can find and update the link even though both the application and the Word source document are closed.

Even the most reliable end-user DDE (the one you create when you paste-link ranges from Excel into Word) has one small problem. Start with both applications closed. Open Word first. It correctly reads the changed Excel source data from the disk and automatically updates the link. Then launch Excel and open the linked worksheet. Make changes in the source data.

Word does not update the link automatically. You have to update the link manually, either through the menu and dialog box commands, or by placing the cursor anywhere in the linked data and pressing F9, which is Word's Update Fields key. The link becomes a manual link (even though it still is flagged as automatic in the Links dialog box displayed when you select <u>L</u>inks on Word's <u>E</u>dit menu).

To make sure that the link remains truly automatic, open the linked Excel worksheet *before* you open the Word document.

Despite the peculiarities mentioned in this section, DDE links are a powerful way to share data between Windows applications, and are indispensable to certain kinds of real-time data transfers.

Working with Internal Links

Word and Excel enable you to create internal links. In Word, an internal link is actually a reference to a bookmark.

If you copy Word text to the Clipboard and then use Paste <u>S</u>pecial to place it somewhere else in the same document, Word automatically assigns a bookmark name to the text block, as it does when Word is the server for a regular DDE link. In the case of an internal link, the bookmark name is DDE_LINKn; the number n increments each time you create an internal link.

Internal links are not hot—they are not updated automatically. You can update the links in either of two ways. You can select the field(s) by putting the cursor anywhere in the text (if <u>V</u>iew Field Codes is off) or anywhere in the field (if <u>V</u>iew Field Codes is on) and pressing F9, the Update Fields key. Or you can choose <u>L</u>inks from the <u>E</u>dit menu and then, in the Links dialog box, select the link(s) to be updated and press the <u>U</u>pdate Now push button.

In Excel, you can <u>C</u>opy and Paste <u>L</u>ink a cell or range of cells to different part of the worksheet or to another worksheet. (Note that if you copy a range, the range is pasted as an array.) In this way, you create a reference to the row-and-column or named-range address of the original cell(s). This internal link updates automatically when the source data is changed.

V

Data Sharing and Integration

Using Macros To Control DDE

Now that you have explored the nature of DDE links and how to create and manage them by using menu commands, the next step is to understand how macros can perform many of these tasks for you, truly automating the integration and interoperability of Windows applications.

Looking At DDE Commands— Examples from Excel and Word

Although the exact form of a DDE command can vary from one macro language to another, similarities exist. Table 28.1 lists the most commonly used DDE commands and their meanings in Excel, Word, and Ami Pro.

Table 28.1
Common DDE Commands

Command Name	Application	Action
DDEInitiate	All three	Starts DDE conversation with another application
DDEExecute	All three	Sends a command to another application with which you initiated conversation
DDEPoke	All three	Sends data to another application with which you initiated conversation
DDERequest	All three	Requests data from application with which you initiated conversation
DDETerminate	All three	Terminates conversation with other application
DDETerminateAll	All three	Terminates all conversations with other applications

Using Macros

Frequently, of course, you do not have to create a persistent link because you do not need an ongoing flow of data from one application to another.

The following Word Basic macro queries an Excel worksheet for a particular piece of data. The macro also illustrates how you can control the behavior of one application from inside another. A more sophisticated macro might exercise even more precise control by sending extensive formatting instructions, instructions for the sizing and placement of open windows, and so on.

Using RequestFromExcel

The Word Basic macro RequestFromExcel easily can be created in Word. To see how the macro operates, create a new Word document, pull down the <u>T</u>ools menu, and select <u>M</u>acro. On the Macro dialog box, type **RequestFromExcel** into the <u>M</u>acro Name field, and then click on the Cr<u>e</u>ate button. In the window that appears, type the following program code. Normally, the Word Basic macro's lines are not numbered. Line numbers are included here to help you follow the explanation of the code that follows.

```
 1.  Sub MAIN
 2.  On Error Goto Bye
 3.  DDETerminateAll
 4.  ChanNum = DDEInitiate("Excel", "System")
 5.  TopicsAvail$ = DDERequest$(ChanNum, "Topics")

 6.  If InStr(TopicsAvail$, "GETSTUFF.XLS") = 0 Then
     DDEExecute ChanNum, "[OPEN(" + Chr$(34) +
     "C:\EXCEL\GETSTUFF.XLS" + Chr$(34) + ")]"

 7.  NewChanNum = DDEInitiate("Excel", "GETSTUFF.XLS")
 8.  Name$ = DDERequest$(NewChanNum, "R2C1")
 9.  EditGoTo .Destination = "PutNameHere"
10.  Insert Name$
11.  Bye:
12.  DDETerminateAll
13.  End Sub
```

The macro does the following:

✔ Launches Excel. (A more refined version would check first to see whether Excel were running, and if it were not, would run it automatically.)

✔ Asks which files are open. Open files include the global macro sheet and any other macro sheets and add-ons in the XLSTART subdirectory.

✔ Sees whether the worksheet you want is open; if it is not, instructs Excel to open it.

✔ Requests information from the worksheet.

✔ Inserts the requested information into the Word document.

✔ Ends by closing the DDE channels, which are no longer necessary.

In the following explanation of RequestFromExcel's code, each number refers to the corresponding line of code in the macro:

1. Word Basic's standard opening line.

2. If executing any part of the macro is a problem, the macro branches to the label Bye: (see line 11) so that the command on line 12 (DDETerminateAll) is executed.

3. Closes any stray DDE channels that might be open. For the purpose of this macro, other open channels could cause interference.

4. Launches Excel at its system level, and returns the number of the DDE channel thus opened to the numeric variable ChanNum.

5. Asks which topics (open files) are available and puts the answer in the string variable TopicsAvail$.

6. Looks for the string GETSTUFF.XLS (the file on which subsequent commands are to operate) in the string contained in the variable TopicsAvail$. If the string is not there (that is, if GETSTUFF.XLS is not among the files loaded when Excel is launched by the command in line 4), it sends Excel a command to open that file.

   The syntax, which is complex, must be followed exactly. The command enclosed in square brackets (in this case, the OPEN command) is transmitted to Excel in the style of and with the punctuation required by its own macro commands. Chr$(34) tells Excel that the quotation marks that enclose the text are literal quotes.

7. Now that Excel has opened the required file, a new DDE channel must be opened to communicate with it. In this line, the macro is communicating with the file, not the application.

8. Asks for the item and places it in the string variable Name$. (If you are giving a cell or range address as the item, you must use R1C1 style rather than $A$1 notation. If you have named the cell or range you can use the name as the item. The Excel macro shown later in figure 28.14 uses the name rather than row-and-column address.)

9. Places the cursor at the "PutNameHere" bookmark.

10. Inserts the contents of the variable Name$ at the cursor.

11. The branching label specified in line 2.

12. Closes the DDE channels.

13. Word Basic's standard closing line.

Using ControlWinWord

In this sample macro (shown in figure 28.14), Excel is the server application, but this time Excel itself initiates the DDE conversation, sending commands and data to Word for Windows. Note that this macro is shown using Excel 4 macro code, as opposed to Excel 5 Visual Basic code. While Excel 5 contains the new Visual Basic code, that code would look very similar to the Word Basic code shown previously. Also, some people might wish to continue using Excel 4 macro code while they learn the new Visual Basic module; Excel 5 fully supports Excel 4-style macro code sheets.

ControlWinWord does the following:

✔ Launches Word for Windows and then opens and establishes a DDE channel to the file called RUNWORD.DOC.

✔ Places the cursor after any text in the document.

✔ Inserts a manual link to a named cell in the Excel worksheet GETSTUFF.XLS.

✔ Puts new information in that cell.

✔ Returns to Word and updates the link to reflect the changed data.

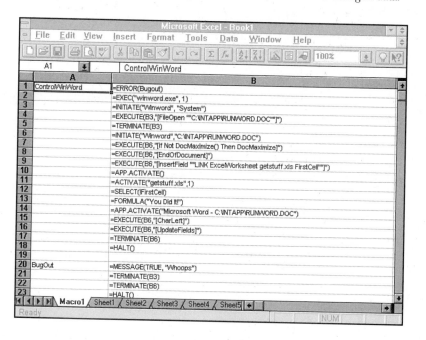

Figure 28.14

The ControlWinWord Excel macro.

The instructions in cells B4 and B6 of the macro (see fig. 28.14) are hardcoded to reflect the location of RUNWORD.DOC in C:\INTAPP. If you are running the macro (as opposed to just reading along), change the directory in the code to indicate where you have stored the RUNWORD.DOC file.

Examining the ControlWinWord Code

The following is a line-by-line explanation of the ControlWinWord code. The numbers (B1, B2, and so on) refer to the cell address of the commands. All commands are in column B; column A contains only labels.

B1.   If the macro encounters an error, branches to a second macro, called Bugout, which begins in cell B19.

B2.   Sends a message to the operating system to launch Word for Windows.

B3.   Opens a DDE channel to the application.

B4.   Tells Word to execute a command—in this case a FileOpen—piped to it through the DDE channel opened in cell B3. Note that the syntax of the command enclosed in square brackets is that of Word Basic. Note also the two sets of quotation marks that enclose the file name. As with the previous macro example, the double set of quotation marks tells the application that the inner quotation marks are literal.

B5.   Closes the DDE channel opened in cell B3. That channel is no longer necessary.

B6.   Opens a new DDE channel to the document.

B7.   Tells Word (through the new DDE channel opened in cell B6) to maximize the document.

B8.   Tells Word to place the cursor at the end of the document.

B9.   Tells Word to insert a link to the Excel topic (the worksheet named GETSTUFF.XLS) and the item FirstCell—a cell whose name is defined in the worksheet. The file RUNWORD.DOC is open on-screen and has the focus.

B10. Returns the focus to Excel. Note that if no argument to the APP.ACTIVATE() function exists, Excel reactivates itself.

B11. Makes GETSTUFF.XLS the active document.

B12. Selects the cell named FirstCell.

B13. Places new data in FirstCell.

B14. Returns the focus to Word. The argument to the APP.ACTIVATE() function must be the name of the Word document, exactly as it appears in the title bar when the document is active. Note that if Excel does not return the focus to Word, it is because it cannot find the exact document name. You can, however, switch the focus to Word manually, either from the Task List or by pressing Alt+Tab. Make sure that the document is maximized (line B7 takes care of this) and that the path is correct. The remainder of the macro executes even if Word does not have the focus.

B15. Moves the cursor one character to the left, placing it inside the LINK field. (CharLeft is a Word Basic command.)

B16. Updates the link (a manual one) to show the changed information in the Excel worksheet.

B17. Because no additional commands are to be sent to Word, closes the DDE channel opened in cell B6.

B18. Ends the macro. Both Excel and Word are open, and Word has the focus.

B20. The error-trapping macro, Bugout, exits from ControlWinWord if ControlWinWord encounters any errors. The command in B2O puts on the status line a message that tells you something has gone awry.

B21. Closes the DDE channel opened in cell B3.

B22. Closes the DDE channel opened in cell B6.

If you want to run the sample macro, type all of the lines exactly as shown in figure 28.14. Then, choose **T**ools **M**acro and then execute from reference B1 in the Macro dialog box.

Chapter Snapshot

In this chapter, you learn what object linking and embedding is and how it is different from dynamic data exchange (DDE). You learn step-by-step the way to create and edit OLE objects and how to use the Object Packager. You will learn about the following topics:

You do not need programming skills to take full advantage of OLE's capabilities. OLE is easy to use yet enormously powerful. In fact, you do not need to know anything at all about its complex underpinnings to enjoy its benefits.

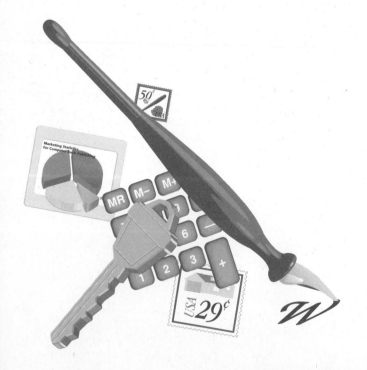

CHAPTER

29

Exploring Object Linking and Embedding

by Bruce Hallberg

With the advent of object linking and embedding (or OLE, pronounced "oh-LAY"), the ideal of giving the user an effortless way to integrate Windows applications is a reality. OLE goes beyond just data sharing; it enables one application to share another application's tools as well.

Excel 5 and Word 6 now support a new version of OLE, called OLE 2.0. This new version of OLE improves the way in which different applications interact in order to create and work with compound documents (the definition of a "compound document" is discussed shortly).

Understanding the Terminology

The following three terms are important to your understanding of the workings of OLE:

- ✔ **Compound Document.** A single document made up of parts created in more than one application.

- ✔ **Container Document.** A document containing either embedded or linked data (such as objects).

- ✔ **Object.** Any piece of data that can be manipulated as a single entity, such as a picture, chart, or section of text.

A compound document is made up of parts created in more than one application. This document is a container for those different parts, which are called objects. Note that the container document is always the client in OLE transactions.

Understanding the Compound Document

As you learned in Chapter 28, "Examining Dynamic Data Exchange," to create a DDE link you first must open the server application and the source document, copy information to the Clipboard, and use the Paste Link command to paste it to the destination document. You also can program the DDE communication with a macro. Although you don't usually have to worry about the link after it is established, you might face difficulties if you want to access, edit, and update the source data. If you move or rename the source document (or, in some cases, move or rename *items*, such as spreadsheet cells or ranges), you must edit the information that Windows needs to maintain the link.

You can perform most of the tasks required to integrate information from one Windows application into another application from within the container document. You might need to leave the container document, however, to edit the linked information at its source. The source information is external to the container document.

Not so with OLE! OLE permits your work to be truly document-centered. You do not need to leave the container document to edit an embedded object. In fact, under most circumstances, you never have to leave it at all. You can initiate an OLE operation directly from within the container document. You just need to know the type of object you want to embed.

If your application can act as an OLE client, you can access a list of available object types from the menu bar. You might need to use a different procedure for each application, though. Look for an Insert menu, and a command on that menu called Object; or you might need to choose the Insert Object command from an application's File or Edit menu, for example. A list of available objects will be displayed, such as in the Word Object dialog box shown in figure 29.1.

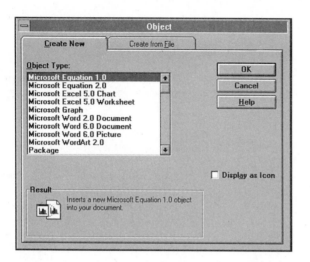

Figure 29.1
Word's Object dialog box and the list of object types you can embed.

Understanding OLE Servers and Clients

To describe the utility of OLE, Microsoft adopted the phrase, "The right tool for the right job." You create text in a word processing program, develop numeric data in a spreadsheet, chart that data in a charting program, and create bit maps in a paint program or illustrations in a drawing program. Each application is optimized for the kind of tasks you ask it to perform. After you create an object in any of these applications, you can embed the object in a container document created in another application.

Modifying a drawing, changing numbers in a spreadsheet, and reformatting text all are forms of editing for which OLE can be used.

In the [embedding] section of WIN.INI, you can see a list of the object types available on your system, along with the application Windows uses to edit those objects (see fig. 29.2).

DDE links point to a source outside the current document. OLE objects reside within the current document.

To use OLE, you do not need to know what Windows is doing behind the scenes. You do not need to know which application will create the object (the server application), nor which application will be used to edit it. To edit an embedded object, just double-click on the object or choose an edit command from the menu. Windows then opens the server application, in which it places a copy of the embedded object and brings it to the foreground on top of the container document. You now can edit this copy of the object. After you finish, Windows asks whether you want to update the original in the container document. After you click on OK, the object is updated and the server application closes.

Figure 29.2

The [embedding] section of WIN.INI.

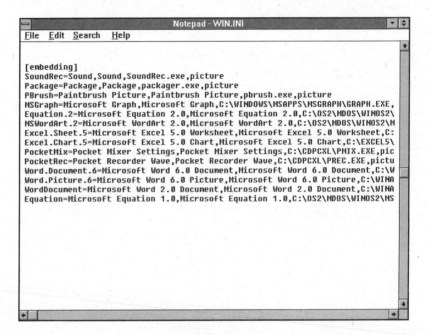

```
                              Notepad - WIN.INI
 File   Edit   Search   Help

[embedding]
SoundRec=Sound,Sound,SoundRec.exe,picture
Package=Package,Package,packager.exe,picture
PBrush=Paintbrush Picture,Paintbrush Picture,pbrush.exe,picture
MSGraph=Microsoft Graph,Microsoft Graph,C:\WINDOWS\MSAPPS\MSGRAPH\GRAPH.EXE,
Equation.2=Microsoft Equation 2.0,Microsoft Equation 2.0,C:\OS2\MDOS\WINOS2\
MSWordArt.2=Microsoft WordArt 2.0,Microsoft WordArt 2.0,C:\OS2\MDOS\WINOS2\M
Excel.Sheet.5=Microsoft Excel 5.0 Worksheet,Microsoft Excel 5.0 Worksheet,C:
Excel.Chart.5=Microsoft Excel 5.0 Chart,Microsoft Excel 5.0 Chart,C:\EXCEL5\
PocketMix=Pocket Mixer Settings,Pocket Mixer Settings,C:\CDPCXL\PMIX.EXE,pic
PocketRec=Pocket Recorder Wave,Pocket Recorder Wave,C:\CDPCXL\PREC.EXE,pictu
Word.Document.6=Microsoft Word 6.0 Document,Microsoft Word 6.0 Document,C:\W
Word.Picture.6=Microsoft Word 6.0 Picture,Microsoft Word 6.0 Picture,C:\WINA
WordDocument=Microsoft Word 2.0 Document,Microsoft Word 2.0 Document,C:\WINA
Equation=Microsoft Equation 1.0,Microsoft Equation 1.0,C:\OS2\MDOS\WINOS2\MS
```

Many new Windows applications and revisions of older applications incorporate OLE technology. Because user demand is high, *OLE-compliant* is a phrase that sells software. CorelDRAW! 4.0, PowerPoint 3.0, Word for Windows 6.0, and Excel 5.0 are examples of high-end applications that can act both as OLE server and client.

In addition to stand-alone applications that have OLE server capabilities, a number of Windows' mini-applications (sometimes called *applets*) are designed to be used exclusively as OLE servers. Note that you can use the applets only from within an OLE client, not as independent programs. Examples of such applets are Microsoft's Note-It, WordArt, MS Graph, and MS Draw. If you try to run an OLE server applet as if it were a stand-alone program (by clicking on the name of the EXE file in File Manager, for example), you receive a message such as "Sorry, Microsoft Draw can only run from within a destination application."

You might want to take data you developed independently in a stand-alone application and embed it in another application. To do so, follow the same copy, paste, and link procedure you use to create DDE links, with one exception: choose Embedded Object from the Paste Link (or Paste Special) dialog box. The data remains an entity in the original file, but has no link to the embedded object in your container document. Editing the original data does not update the embedded object. You can, however, edit the embedded object directly from within the container document.

Figure 29.3 compares the actions you take to create and edit links against the actions you take to create and edit embedded objects. You will find that working with embedded objects is simpler than working with links. Note that you can initiate the embedding procedure in one of two ways. You can create the object in the server application and paste it into the container document. Or, you can choose a command from the container document's menu that gives you direct access to the server application.

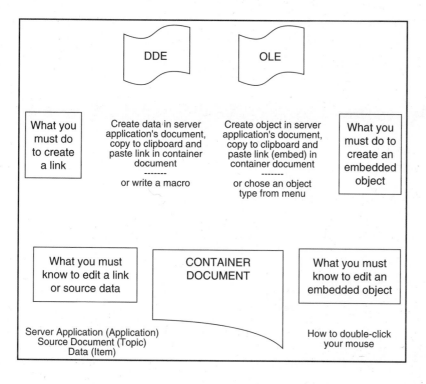

Figure 29.3
Comparing DDE and OLE.

Because an embedded object does not have an independent life—it is not stored in any external file—you must consider when to embed an object and when to link one. In general, you link an object if the server data needs to be shared with more than one client, and you embed an object when the object is to be used only in one container (client) document.

Creating and Editing OLE Objects

This section teaches you step-by-step the way to create and edit OLE objects. The first example uses two of the accessory applications that come with Windows—Paintbrush and Cardfile. The second and third examples use Word and Excel 5.0, and the fourth uses only Word.

Embedding a Paintbrush Object in Cardfile

The first OLE example uses two of the accessory applications that come with Windows—Paintbrush and Cardfile.

To create the embedded Paintbrush object on Card 1 in the file OLE.CRD, perform the following steps:

1. Choose Pictur_e_ from the Cardfile _E_dit menu, and then pull down the menu again to choose I_n_sert Object (see fig. 29.4). If Pictur_e_ is not checked, you cannot select I_n_sert Object.

Figure 29.4
Inserting an object into Cardfile.

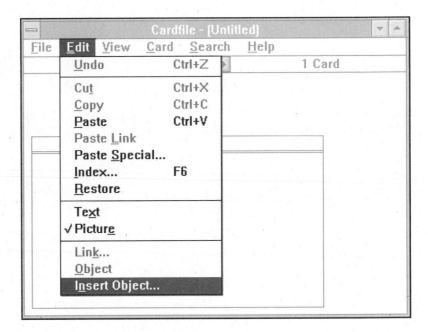

2. Selecting I_n_sert Object displays the Insert New Object dialog box. Choose Paintbrush Picture from the _O_bject Type list (see fig. 29.5).

Figure 29.5
Choosing Paintbrush Picture from the Object Type list box.

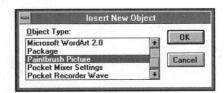

Windows launches Paintbrush. As figure 29.6 shows, you can look at the title bar and see that this is not a separate file, but a "Paintbrush Picture in (Untitled)"—an embedded object.

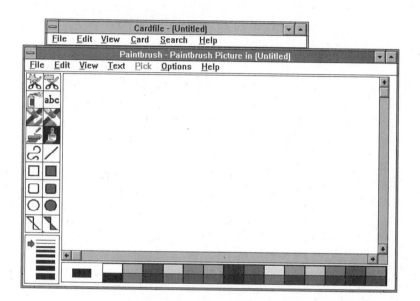

Figure 29.6

Paintbrush is now an OLE server.

3. Create your drawing and then open the File menu. This menu contains two OLE-specific commands: Update and Exit & Return (see fig. 29.7).

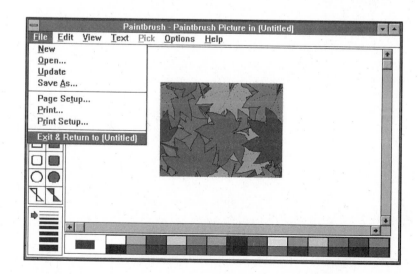

Figure 29.7

The File menu now shows OLE-related commands.

4. If you choose the E̲xit & Return command before you update the container document, Windows issues the warning shown in figure 29.8.

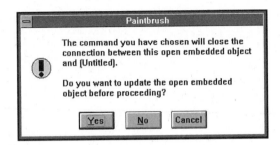

Figure 29.8
Paintbrush's
update alert.

After you create or edit an object, remember to choose U̲pdate before you choose E̲xit & Return.

5. After you update the Paintbrush drawing and exit from Paintbrush, you see the drawing object embedded in Cardfile (see fig. 29.9).

Figure 29.9
The drawing
embedded in
Cardfile.

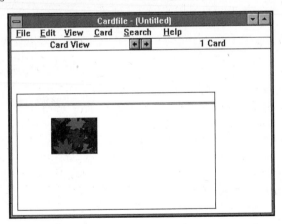

6. To modify the drawing, make sure that a check mark appears next to the Pictur̲e option in the E̲dit menu; then place the mouse pointer anywhere on the object and double-click. You also can click once to select the object, and then choose Edit Paintbrush Picture O̲bject from the E̲dit menu (see fig. 29.10).

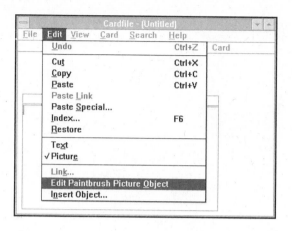

Figure 29.10
You can choose a menu command to edit the object.

As figure 29.11 shows, either action brings Paintbrush to the foreground so that you can use its tools to modify the object.

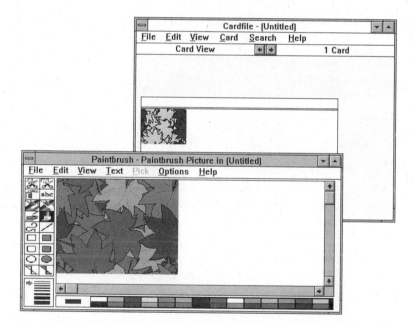

Figure 29.11
Modifying the object in the server application.

7. From the **E**dit menu, select **U**pdate and then E**x**it & Return. You see any modifications reflected in the embedded object (see fig. 29.12).

The procedure is that simple. All applications that support OLE do so in a similar manner. In all cases, the system does for you the work of choosing the editing tools and loading the object. You do not have to leave the container document. Document-centered computing is a reality thanks to OLE.

Figure 29.12
The modified object embedded in Cardfile.

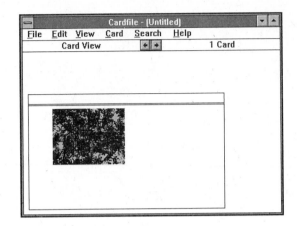

Embedding New Excel Data as an Object in Word

To create an Excel worksheet object directly from within a Word document (the container document), perform the steps in the following example. First, make sure that you have Word running, and then begin a new document by selecting File and choosing the New command.

1. From the new document in Word, select Object from the Insert menu (see fig. 29.13) to display the Object dialog box.

Figure 29.13
Word's Insert menu.

2. Make sure the Create New tab is open. From the Object Type list, choose Microsoft Excel Worksheet (see fig. 29.14).

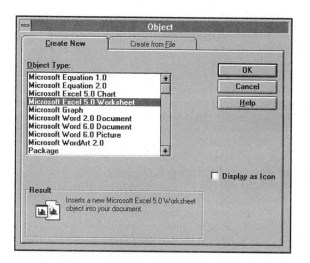

Figure 29.14

Choosing an Excel Worksheet object to embed.

The list of Object Types in the various Insert Object dialog boxes illustrated in this section might not look like the list you see when you follow these examples on your own system. Remember that when you install an application that can act as an OLE server, Windows places the appropriate information about that application in the Registration Database and includes the application in the [embedding] section of your WIN.INI file. When you are working on your computer, the Object Types list will reflect the OLE servers you have installed.

The title bar in figure 29.15 tells you that this is an Excel Worksheet object embedded in a Word document. You can use the worksheet and Excel's tools as you usually do. This capability is evident if you look at the formula bar. The highlighted cell shows the result of summing the two values above it.

An Excel worksheet object gives you access to all the tools and attributes of "native" Excel.

3. From the File menu, choose Update to update the Word document with the embedded information (see fig. 29.16). When you want to return to the Word document, choose Close if you want "native" Excel to remain open, or Exit.

Figure 29.15
The embedded
worksheet gives
you access to
"native" Excel.

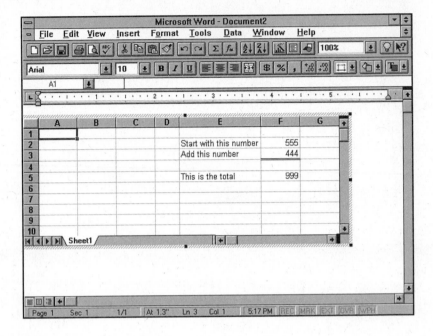

Figure 29.16
Bringing an
embedded object
into the container
document.

In addition to <u>U</u>pdate, another new command appears on the <u>F</u>ile menu when Excel works
with an embedded object. Remember that the embedded object is the original data and is not
permanently stored anywhere external to the Word document. Excel does enable you,
however, to make a copy of the embedded object and save it to a new, ordinary Excel file. To
make a copy of the embedded object and save it to an Excel file, choose Save Copy <u>A</u>s (see fig.
29.16). This brings up the standard Save As dialog box. Excel saves the object as data in the
file you name, but this file does not have an ongoing relationship with the embedded object.
Unlike a DDE-linked object, further changes you make to the embedded object are not
reflected in this file.

Figure 29.17 shows you the Word document with the Excel Worksheet object embedded.

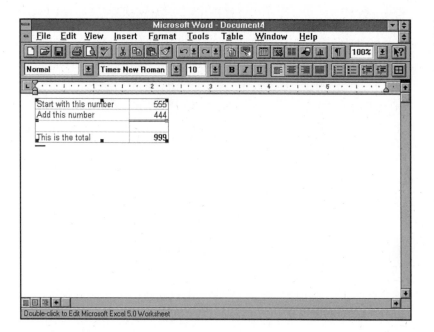

Figure 29.17
The embedded object contained in the Word document.

Embedding Existing Excel Data as an Object in Word

In the preceding example, you created the Excel worksheet object directly from within the Word container document. This example shows you the way to create an Excel object embedded in Word by using existing Excel data.

This example will also showcase the special features unique to OLE version 2. OLE 2 includes an exciting new feature called *in-place editing,* which enables you to edit an embedded document without leaving the compound document. In OLE 1, when you double-click on an object in order to edit it in its source application, the source application starts with the data all ready to be edited. OLE 2, however, leaves you in the compound document, but with the menus and toolbar of the source application appearing instead of the normal document menus and toolbar. This new capability makes working with compound documents much easier, and is a very powerful way to integrate applications.

Word 6 and Excel 5 are the first applications to fully support OLE 2 (although the applets included with Word and Excel also support OLE 2). The other applications in Microsoft Office do not yet support OLE 2, although those capabilities are being added and will soon be available for all the Office applications.

To embed the existing Excel data in word, perform the following steps:

1. Create a file named OLEXMPLE.XLS (use figure 29.18 as a guide). Save the file and then select cells A1 through D5. Copy the highlighted range to the Clipboard as shown in figure 29.19.

Figure 29.18

Creating the OLEXMPLE.XLS file.

	A	B	C	D	E	F	G	H
1		1st Half	2nd Half					
2	These	1500	2000					
3	Those	800	1200					
4	Others	5000	7500					

Microsoft Excel - OLEXMPLE.XLS

2. In your Word document, choose Paste Special from the Edit menu.

Tip

You can bring any running application quickly to the foreground by pressing Alt+Tab until the display shows the name and icon for the program you want. Then, release the Alt key to switch to that program.

3. You have seen the Paste Special dialog box before. This time, choose Microsoft Excel Worksheet Object (see fig. 29.20) and click on OK.

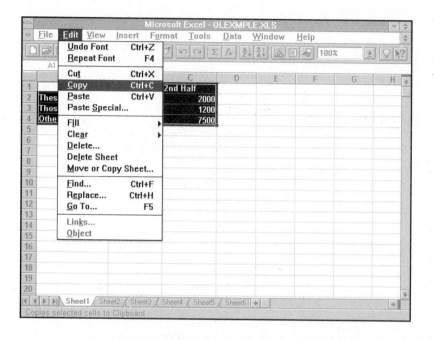

Figure 29.19
Copying data from an existing Excel worksheet.

V

Data Sharing and Integration

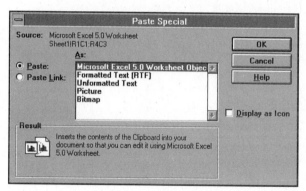

Figure 29.20
Pasting the Excel range as an embedded object.

4. The Excel range now is embedded in your document. Click anywhere in the object to select it. You see a bounding box and sizing handles. *Sizing handles* are the little squares around the perimeter of the object that enable you to change its dimensions. Also, the message Double-click to Edit Excel Worksheet appears in the message bar at the bottom of the document (see fig. 29.21).

Figure 29.21

The Excel range embedded in the container document.

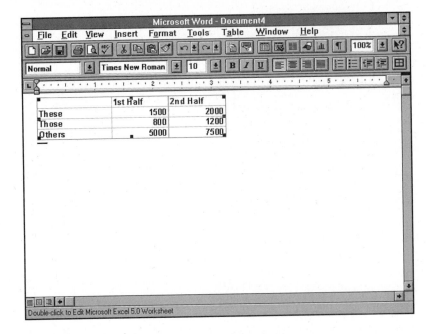

5. To edit the data, double-click on the object, or choose Spreadsheet O**b**ject and then **E**dit from Word's **E**dit menu as shown in figure 29.22.

Figure 29.22

Choosing the Spreadsheet Object option from Word's Edit menu.

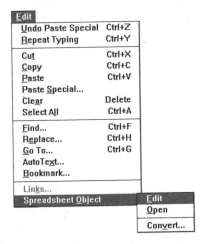

6. Windows starts up Excel "inside" Word and passes to it the embedded worksheet data, which automatically appears highlighted. Notice that you are seeing the Excel menus and toolbar, and that you can even see the Excel window controls bordering the data (see fig. 29.23).

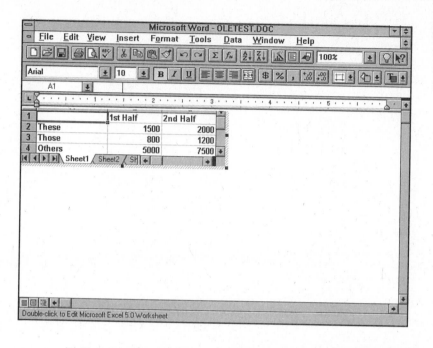

Figure 29.23
Editing the object results in OLE 2 in-place editing.

7. You now can modify the Excel data any way you want by using the tools native to Excel. You can change the numbers or the formatting attributes. After you finish editing the data, click outside the bordered area to return to Word. Notice that the Excel worksheet object embedded in the Word document now reflects the modifications you just made (see fig. 29.24).

The Excel worksheet object embedded in Word can be changed only by its source application, Excel. The font, shading, and borders are Excel's formatting attributes, not Word's.

Exiting from the Excel worksheet object after updating it causes Excel to close silently in the background. You might want to launch Excel normally and examine the file OLEXMPLE.XLS, in which this process started. OLEXMPLE.XLS remains unaffected by the changes you made to the embedded object.

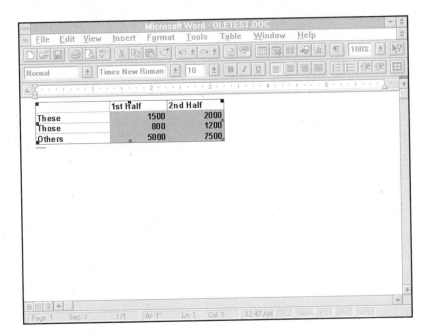

Embedding Word Text in Another Word Document

The final example shows you what happens if you embed Word text in a Word document. Why would you want to do this? Perhaps you want to annotate a document, but find Word's annotations too small and difficult to read (or their placement in the footnote position too limiting) and revision markings too cumbersome.

Annotating with embedded text has the advantage of making highly visible to the reader the place at which the annotations occur, as you can see in figure 29.25. To see this effect, double-click on each of the icons. When you want to return to the main document, choose Close from the Edit menu.

You can create these embedded text objects by using one of two procedures from within the container document. You can copy text from another document and choose Microsoft Word Object from the Paste Special dialog box (you also have to select the Display as Icon checkbox). You also can choose Object from the Insert menu, and from the Object Type list box choose Word Document.

Understanding Object Packager

As is apparent from the preceding discussion, the number of OLE-compliant Windows applications is growing. What do you do if you want to embed in a container document information from an application that does not talk OLE's language? What if you need to access a DOS application while you are working in a Windows document? Windows provides a means to accomplish this task through the use of the Object Packager.

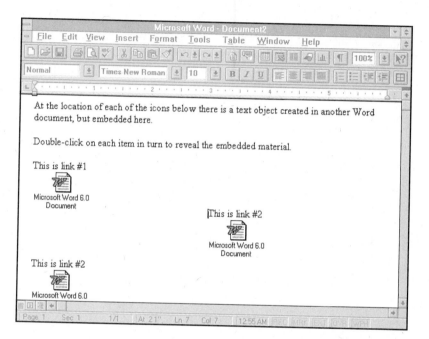

Figure 29.25

Icons represent embedded text from another Word document.

Object Packager, which is OLE-compliant, wraps itself around another application that is not OLE-compliant. Object Packager then contains information about the source that the source itself cannot provide. You then embed this "package" into your container document. Object Packager can wrap itself around Windows applications that are not otherwise OLE servers and even can act as a mechanism for embedding DOS applications, DOS commands, and batch files.

To see how Object Packager works, suppose that you manage a small office in which everybody has a computer that runs Windows, but the computers are not networked. You need to find out which PCs have which OLE servers installed. You write a memo in Word to all the Windows users in the office, and this information is contained in the [embedding] of each user's WIN.INI file. You need a way to capture this text easily and make the process as easy as possible for your users.

So, you decide to put a memo on a floppy disk that is distributed to each user. The memo on the disk asks the users to access their WIN.INI file by double-clicking on the icon in the memo (which represents an object packaged in the memo). When they double-click on the embedded icon, their WIN.INI files are automatically opened for them. They then copy into the Word document the [embedding] section from WIN.INI by simply using copy-and-paste commands (which they all know how to use). After each user adds the information to the document, you will have a complete record of all OLE servers on their system. The users had to do little more than load the Word document to provide you the information you requested.

Using Object Packager

The following example shows you the way to create a Word document into which you embed access to Notepad, which is not an OLE-compliant application. You use Object Packager and have it load your WIN.INI file. Object Packager enables you to represent a Windows or non-Windows object as an icon in your compound document.

Creating a Packaged Object

The first thing you must do to use the Object Packager is to open or create a container document. Then, to create a packaged object from within the container document, perform the following steps:

1. Begin by creating a new document in Word. From the Insert menu, choose Object to display the Object dialog box. From the Object Type list box in the Create New tab, choose Package. Figure 29.26 shows the Object Packager in the Word document.

    The Object Packager is divided into two windows, placed side by side. You specify the content of the package in the right window and the appearance of the package in the left window. The content window of the package usually displays a brief description of the package contents. The appearance window displays the icon to be used to represent the package after it is embedded in a document.

2. You can choose the object to be packaged by using several methods. This example uses the command-line method, where you specify an actual command to be executed when the object is opened . Choose Command from the Edit menu to display the dialog box in figure 29.27.

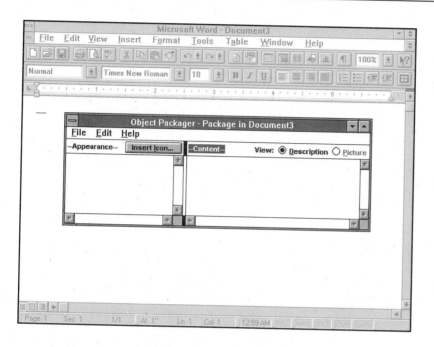

Figure 29.26
The Object Packager's dialog box.

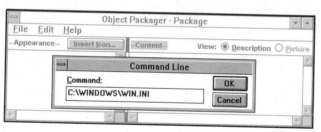

Figure 29.27
Packaging a command line in Object Packager.

Because the extension INI is associated with Notepad, you can run Notepad with WIN.INI loaded by typing the command line shown in the figure. As an alternative, you also can type the following command:

```
C:\WINDOWS\NOTEPAD.EXE WIN.INI
```

If you choose a simple file name to use with the Object Packager, that file name must be associated with an application in order for the object to function correctly. So, if you were to embed, say, CONFIG.SYS, and *.SYS isn't associated with an application on your system, you will get an error when trying to open the final embedded package.

Object Packager does not know which icon to associate with WIN.INI. You can choose any icon on your system, whether it resides in an EXE file, a DLL library, or independently as an icon, which is a file with an ICO extension.

3. To choose an icon, click on the Insert Icon button in the Appearance window of Object Packager. The child window shows you the default for the object you have chosen (or Windows makes its best guess). Click on the Browse button in the Insert Icon dialog box, and you can browse the EXE, DLL, and ICO files on your system to choose the icon you want to represent your packaged object in the container document (see fig. 29.28).

Figure 29.28

You can choose an icon from any application, ICO file, or DLL on your system.

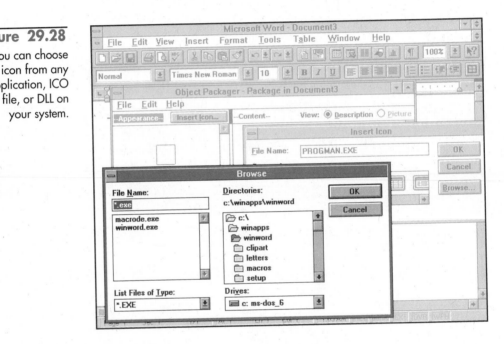

Note

The *appearance* of an OLE package is the icon that you want inserted in the document. The *content* is the command or the file name of the application that is to be packaged.

4. Figure 29.29 shows you how the packaged object appears in your document and the contents of the package.

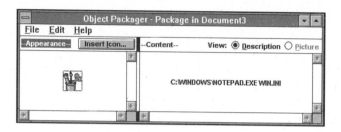

V

Data Sharing and Integration

Figure 29.29
The Appearance and Content windows of the Object Packager.

5. After you have chosen an icon, you can choose E*x*it from the Object Packager's *F*ile menu. Then, click on OK when asked if you want to update the object. Figure 29.30 shows the packaged object embedded in the completed document. It is, in fact, a picture of the icon and the label. You can select it and then format it in any way to set it off.

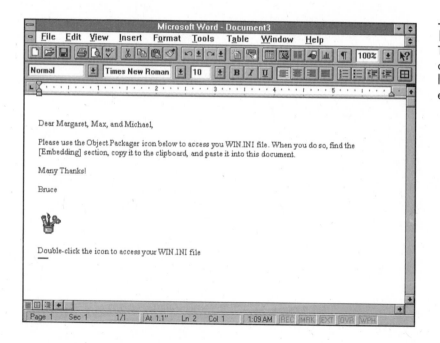

Figure 29.30
The completed document with the labeled object embedded.

Double-clicking on the icon activates the package. (In this example, it runs the WIN.INI file.) If you want to edit the package's content or appearance, you must select the icon with a single mouse click and choose Package O*b*ject from Word's *E*dit menu (see fig. 29.31).

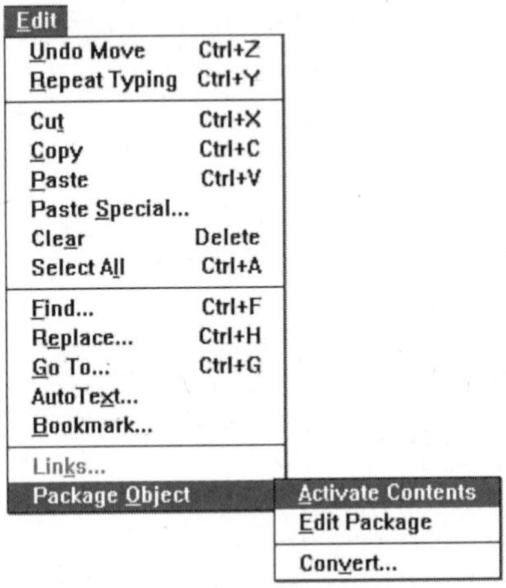

Figure 29.31

Editing the package's content or appearance with Word's Edit menu.

Edit	
<u>U</u>ndo Move	Ctrl+Z
<u>R</u>epeat Typing	Ctrl+Y
Cu<u>t</u>	Ctrl+X
<u>C</u>opy	Ctrl+C
<u>P</u>aste	Ctrl+V
Paste <u>S</u>pecial...	
Cl<u>e</u>ar	Delete
Select A<u>l</u>l	Ctrl+A
<u>F</u>ind...	Ctrl+F
R<u>e</u>place...	Ctrl+H
<u>G</u>o To...	Ctrl+G
AutoTe<u>x</u>t...	
<u>B</u>ookmark...	
Lin<u>k</u>s...	
Package <u>O</u>bject	

<u>A</u>ctivate Contents
<u>E</u>dit Package
Con<u>v</u>ert...

Choosing the Content of a Package

In the previous example, you told Object Packager which object to package by typing a command line. Alternatively, you can choose <u>I</u>mport from Object Packager's <u>F</u>ile menu. This opens a drive and directory window, and from here you can choose a file to embed. This can be an executable file or a document file. If it is a document file, when you choose the icon embedded in your container document, Windows launches the application and loads the file. You also can drag a file from File Manager and drop it into the Content pane of the Object Packager dialog box.

DOS programs, of course, are not OLE-compliant, but thanks to Object Packager you can access a DOS program directly from within your Windows application container document. If you run that DOS program in a window, you can even copy information from it and paste the data directly into the container document.

Just make sure that when you set up the PIF file that controls the DOS program, you choose the radio button labeled Windowed. Then make that PIF file the content of your package. Use the <u>I</u>mport command on Object Packager's <u>F</u>ile menu to find the PIF file in your directory.

When you click on the package that embeds the PIF file, the DOS program runs. Then, by using your mouse and the Mark, Copy, and Paste commands available from the DOS window's control menu, you easily can transfer data between the DOS program and your Windows document.

Examining Multimedia and OLE

A new category of applications that rely heavily on OLE have exciting potential for Windows users—*multimedia.* By using the Windows operating system's multimedia extensions, developers of hardware and software that display sound, video, and animation images on-screen now have the software connections to bring these capabilities to Windows.

You must, however, have additional hardware to use the multimedia technology, such as sound and video boards, CD-ROM players, and so on. Windows comes with an OLE server for sound bites, for example, but you must have a sound board installed in your system (and external speakers that connect to it) to play back the files that Sound Recorder knows how to embed.

You also can plug a microphone into the sound board to record voice or other sounds, and you can create and play back MIDI synthesizer music. With the appropriate hardware, you can embed video clips from a tape or feed real-time, live video directly from a television set.

Even with relatively simple and inexpensive sound hardware you can reap some benefits from linking sound to your documents via OLE. For instance, figure 29.32 shows a letter that has both an embedded graph as well as an embedded recording of a message from the chairman. The reader of this document has only to double-click on the graph icon in order to view the graph using its native application, or to double-click on the microphone icon to hear the recorded comments from the chairman. Using these technologies can enliven documents and make them more powerful. But, of course, these benefits will not be widely available until more PCs have such hardware built in.

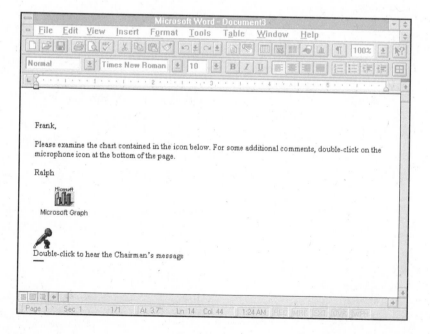

Figure 29.32

Enlivening Windows applications with embedded voice messages.

Chapter Snapshot

Chapters 28 and 29 introduced you to dynamic data exchange and object linking and embedding, two advanced methods by which applications can share data. The purpose of this chapter is to build on your knowledge of these concepts by showing you ways to use them to solve a problem within the context of your work environment. In doing so, this chapter covers the following points:

The goal is to help you to think about these concepts as problem-solving tools that you can use now, not as something you might get to later when you have more time. The trick to using macros, templates, DDE, and OLE to solve problems is to learn to see the problem and the tools in the right way.

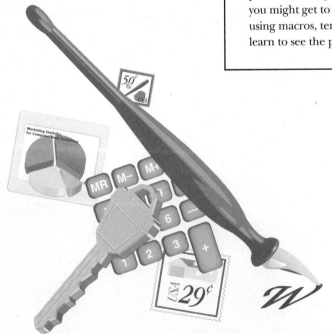

CHAPTER 30

Understanding Automation with Macros and Templates

by Bruce Hallberg

Often computer users look at a tool such as macros and ask, What can I use a macro to do today? Although this question shows that the person is thinking about how to use macros, it probably will not illuminate as many possible uses from which the user might potentially benefit.

A better question for exploring the use of the integration and automation tools provided by the Windows environment is, What tasks or problems do I have that integration tools might simplify or solve? If you begin your exploration of macros, templates, DDE, and OLE from the task and problem end, you are more likely to include possibilities than you are if you begin your exploration from the tool end. To help you explore this task- and problem-oriented focus, this chapter considers a problem faced by anyone who writes correspondence with a word processor: the need to have stationery or letterhead that explains who the correspondence is from and how to return contact. Word for Windows serves as the example word processor, although any full-featured Windows word processor will provide these facilities. (Windows Write even provides most of them.)

In order to meet the need for letterhead, you could propose several solutions. You could have it printed, but then you would have to insert sheets of it strategically in your printer's feed tray if you wanted to print multiple copies of a multipage letter. A more useful solution would be to have your computer print the information on the first page for you. The question, then, is how macros, templates, DDE, and OLE might help you do that.

Learning To Think About Macros

Macros are ways of automating the key strokes and menu commands in your application. As you examine a task or problem, looking for ways to use macros, think in terms of what you would need to do at the keyboard. What would you ordinarily have to type each time you prepare a letter? What menu actions would you have to take before you are ready to write? These are the parts of the task that macros can help you to accomplish.

How To Create Macros

In general, there are two ways to create macros. First, you can turn on a recording feature of your application and record a series of keystrokes; these are later played back to the application at your command as if you were typing the keystrokes at playback time. Alternately, you can write a set of directions and store these directions in a file; these directions are played back at your command and instruct the application to carry out the tasks you have described. The language you use for describing what the application should do is called a *macro language*.

Note Macro languages often look like programming languages. The Word for Windows macro language is in fact derived from the BASIC programming language and is called Word Basic. An explanation of each of the Word Basic statements and commands can be found in the Word for Windows help files, as well as in *Inside Word for Windows 6*, available from New Riders Publishing. If you do not feel comfortable with programming, you should not feel excluded from the capability to use macros. The macro recording facility in Word for Windows enables you to accomplish almost anything you can accomplish by writing a macro in Word Basic.

Word for Windows supports both methods of creating a macro. Recording a macro is by far the easiest. You might, for instance, have noticed that Word does not provide a means of creating bold strikethrough characters on the formatting ribbon. If you want to use the bold strikethrough format as a part of your letterhead logo, you could create a macro to set the bold strikethrough format. The first step, as shown in figure 30.1, is to select the Macro item from Word's Tools menu.

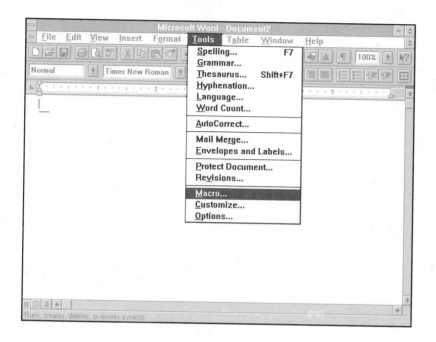

Figure 30.1
Starting the macro
recording process.

When the Macro dialog box appears, type a name for the macro in the text box and then choose the Rec*o*rd button, which then brings up the Record Macro dialog box. Figure 30.2 shows the results of these steps.

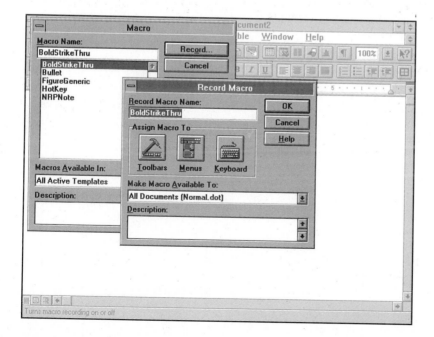

Figure 30.2
Filling in the
Record Macro
dialog box.

You should not assign a macro you have recorded or written to the same key as another macro. You will not erase any of the macros by doing so, but you might lose track of a macro you need if you reassign its keystroke to another macro.

Clicking on the Keyboard button in the Record Macro dialog box displays the Customize dialog box. By selecting the Keyboard tab, you can assign the recorded macro to a keystroke. Place the cursor in the Press New Shortcut Key field, then type the keystroke you want to use to execute the macro after you are done. The example in figure 30.3 shows this with the Alt+Ctrl+K combination.

Figure 30.3

Assigning the shortcut key

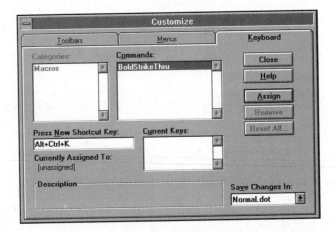

After you type the key combination, Word shows you if that key combination is already assigned to any other function, in the section of the dialog box labeled Currently Assigned To. If you want to override the current assignment and replace it with your new macro, click on the Assign button; the old assignment will be overwritten.

After you have chosen the key assignment and clicked on the Assign button, the macro will start recording, and you will see the small macro toolbar, which contains the Stop and Pause buttons.

Next, type the keystrokes (or perform the mouse clicks) that will turn on the bold strikethrough character format. Hold down the Shift key and press the right-arrow key to select the character to the right of the insertion point. Then select Format, Font to bring up the Font dialog box. Click on Bold in the Font style box and the check box labeled Strikethrough, as shown in figure 30.4. Finally, click on OK.

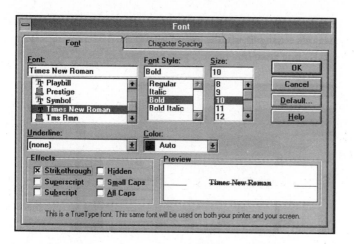

Figure 30.4
Setting the character styles in the Font dialog box.

You now have completed all the keystrokes and mouse clicks necessary for your BoldStrikeThru macro. Click on the Stop button on the Macro toolbar (see fig. 30.5) to end the recording process. Now, whenever you need to create a bold strikethrough character, simply type the text in normal format, place the insertion point to the left of the character that should become bold strikethrough, and press the key combination to which you assigned the macro. If you need to make a string of bold strikethrough characters, type the string in normal format, place the insertion point to the left of the first character, and press the macro key repeatedly until all the characters have been assigned the bold strikethrough format.

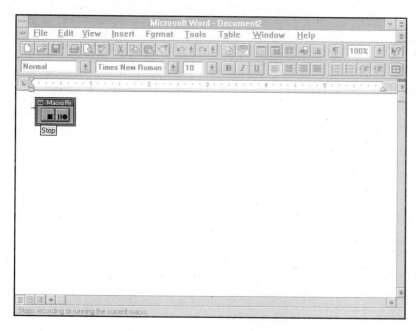

Figure 30.5
End the macro recording process by clicking on the Stop button.

Word for Windows also enables you to create a macro by writing statements in its macro language, Word Basic. To create a macro this way, select the Macro option on the Tools menu. When the Macro dialog box appears, type a name for the macro in the text box, as shown in figure 30.6, and click on the Edit button.

Figure 30.6

Creating a macro using the Macro dialog box.

Word then opens a document window that has a special toolbar, enabling you to test and debug your Word Basic statements. Enter the Word Basic statements that will accomplish the task you have in mind, then close the document window just as you would close any other document window in Word. Your macro will then be ready to use. Figure 30.7 shows the statements for the BoldStrikeThru macro being entered in the special document window.

Tip

You can record a macro and then edit it afterward by selecting the Macro option in the Tools menu. Click on the name of the macro you recorded in the Macro dialog box's list box, then click on the Edit button. Word will open the Word Basic file that it built during the recording process and enable you to edit the Word Basic statements.

What Macros Can Do for You

You can accomplish more with macros than change character formats. If you want to insert a date into your letters automatically, a macro can do that. If you want a dialog box to prompt you for the information in the inside address, a macro can do that. If you want to insert several lines of boilerplate text at several points in a document, a macro can do that also. Any process that you can perform manually from the keyboard, no matter how complex, can be automated as a macro. You need only to identify the tasks and processes you repeat often. They are the candidates for automation as macros.

Figure 30.7
Writing the
BoldStrikeThru
macro in Word
Basic.

Tip

Word for Windows enables you to include dialog boxes in your macros. You can choose from several predefined dialog boxes, or you can create your own using the dialog editor in Word. In order to use dialog boxes effectively to collect information from a user, you must master the rudiments of the Word Basic language. You must write Word Basic statements to display the dialog box, collect the information, and place the information collected into your document. To master these topics, see *Inside Word for Windows 6*, also from New Riders Publishing.

Learning To Think About Document Templates

Because document templates are patterns that you use to create new documents, as you examine a task or problem looking for ways to use document templates, think in terms of how the document should look on the page. How wide will the margins be? Where will graphics appear? Should tables all have the same basic look? These are factors that a document template can automate for you.

Note Document templates, no matter what the software package, look strangely like documents themselves. In fact, they are documents. Word for Windows, for example, stores document templates in files much as it stores a document, except that a document template file has a DOT extension. When Word uses a document template, it inserts all the features of the template into the new Word document. Then Word turns the new document over to you to modify as you wish.

How To Create a Document Template

To create a document template in Word for Windows, select the <u>N</u>ew option on the <u>F</u>ile menu to display the New dialog box (see fig. 30.8). Select the T<u>e</u>mplate option and choose from the list box the template you want to use as your starting point. (The usual choice is NORMAL, the default template, if you have no more specific template from which you want to start.) Then click on OK.

Figure 30.8
Creating a new document template using the New dialog box.

Word displays a new document window with the title Template 1 (or a higher number if this is not the first template you have created during your Word session). You can modify this window any way you want to define the attributes of the document you want to use. You can set the character format, the paragraph format, or the column format, for instance. You can create a special toolbar or menu using the <u>T</u>ools <u>O</u>ptions menu option. Or you can define several styles for different sections of the document.

The example presented in figure 30.9 is a fairly simple one. It does not extensively modify the NORMAL template. It represents an invoice form that a small business might use to invoice one of its regular clients. This document template modifies NORMAL only by adding a date field, boilerplate text, and a table for entering descriptions of services and amounts. While not overly complex, it saves several keystrokes each time the client must be invoiced, as well as the time necessary to locate the information that the template stores ready for use. You can create one template for each regular client, or you could use the same template form and add a glossary in which to store each of the addresses. If you use a glossary, it would be attached to the template, enabling you to choose the client information each time you created a new document using the template.

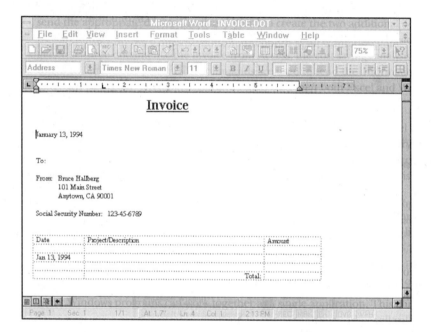

Figure 30.9
Adding boilerplate text to an invoice template.

To save a document template, use the Save **A**s option from Word's **F**ile menu. Enter the name for the template in the text box in the Save As dialog box, and make sure that Save File as **T**ype is set to Document Template. Finally, click on OK to save the template. To use your new template to create a document, select the **F**ile **N**ew menu option, click on the **D**ocument option button in the New dialog box, select your new template in the list box, and click on OK. Word will create the new document on the model defined by your template.

When you save your new template, be careful not to overwrite Word's NORMAL template. NORMAL is the template in which Word stores default options and global macros. If you change NORMAL by overwriting it, you could lose your default settings and global macros.

Document templates can have a special relationship with macros. As noted in the section on macros, macros can be stored in a particular document template so that they will be available only in documents created using that template. In addition, document templates can make use of the following special macros:

- ✔ **AutoNew.** Runs when you create a new document.
- ✔ **AutoOpen.** Runs when you open an existing document.
- ✔ **AutoClose.** Runs when you close a document.

By writing macros with these names and assigning them a template context, you can automate the actions taken when creating a document, opening a document, and closing a document. If there are repeated sets of keystrokes or menu actions that must take place at any of these events, creating these macros will automate them for you for any document based on your template.

Tip Many of the templates included with Word for Windows make use of Wizards to collect common information from the user and insert it into the document. The Letter Wizard template, for instance, is a Wizard that collects the information for the inside address and greeting using dialog boxes.

What Document Templates Can Do for You

Document templates can automate the look and feel of the documents you create using your software. In the Word for Windows example, the document templates manage the visual placement of information on the page, which extensions of Word's capabilities are available as macros to each document, and automatic actions taken at document creation, document opening, and document closing.

You might have imagined a day when, as you create an invoice, your computer offers you a client list from which to select address information, a list of spreadsheets from which to collect the amounts, and a list of services from which to choose. Your computer then inserts the address, collects the amount from the spreadsheet and inserts it into the invoice, and enters the service for which you are invoicing automatically. You can do that today with a document template.

Learning To Think About Compound Documents

In previous chapters, you learned that *compound document* is the name applied to a document that contains information created by several different application programs. The application that creates the document maintains links to the other applications, enabling these applications to update their information when necessary. As you think about integration and automation using compound documents, think in terms of assembling parts. What data is necessary to build the document? Which applications create and manage different data elements? Which application creates the finished document? Are there any processing steps that must take place along the pathways created by the links? These are the issues that compound documents can assist with in integration and automation.

How To Create Compound Documents

As noted in earlier chapters, you create compound documents (documents made up of components from more than one application) using the Edit menu's Paste Special option in the application in which you are assembling the document. In the application from which you wish to link data, you select the data and place it on the Clipboard using the standard Cut or Copy commands, as shown in figure 30.10, which uses Excel as the example source application.

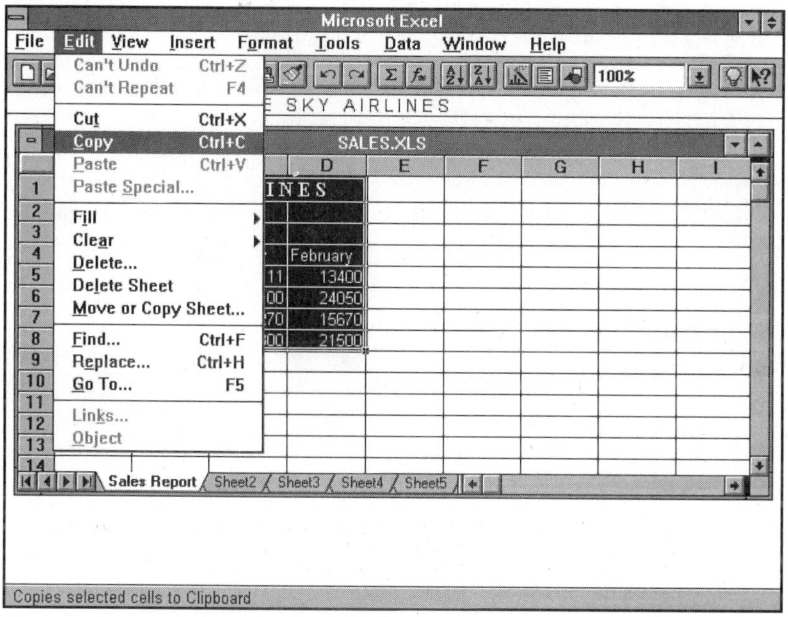

Figure 30.10

Copying data to the clipboard to create a compound document.

When the data to be linked is on the Clipboard, use the Paste Special option from the Edit menu to insert the information at the insertion point and create the link. In the Paste Special dialog box, click on the Paste Link option button and then click on OK to create the link, as shown in figure 30.11, which uses Word as the example destination, or receiving, application.

After the link has been created, the information will be updated in the receiving document whenever it is changed in the originating document. As a result, you can build compound documents that assemble data from a variety of resource applications and stay continuously updated. You do not have to manually move data from one application's files to another's—the applications can now handle that for you.

Figure 30.11
Creating the link
in the Paste
Special dialog
box.

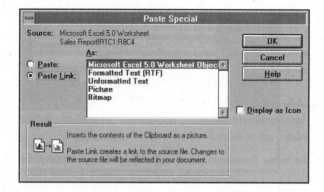

What Compound Documents Can Do for You

Understanding what compound documents can do for you requires you to think in terms of document layers. The lowest layer is the *data origination layer,* at which applications acquire data either through hand data entry or through some form of automated data acquisition. The next layer is the *data manipulation layer,* in which data is transferred from the origination layer applications into a set of documents that manipulate the data by performing calculations or other transformations. The final layer is the *data presentation layer,* the set of documents that you use to communicate with others about the data.

The hierarchy just described is not rigid. Data origination and presentation all might occur within a set of documents managed by one application using Windows' multiple document interface schema. One Word document might be embedded in another, for instance. In addition, the data manipulation layer might merge with the data presentation layer so much that you cannot distinguish between the two of them.

However, the value of this hierarchy is that it aids your thinking as you plan ways to solve problems by integrating applications and automating tasks. If you split your view into these three layers, you are likely to see how you can link data among applications to accomplish very complex tasks automatically. The example of building a letterhead, which begins in the following section, provides a simple demonstration of these concepts. The purpose of the scenarios in the next section of the book is to help you to see ways of using compound documents to solve larger, more complex problems.

Building a Simple Compound Document: A Letterhead

A letterhead need not be a compound document. You can simply build a document template that contains all the requisite items and use that template for all your correspondence. You might, however, want to update parts of a letterhead on occasion. Maintaining those parts as a single file that is linked to all the document templates where the information needs to appear makes the maintenance task easier. You update a single file, and each of the document templates to which the file is linked is automatically updated, including all current correspondence on your hard disk.

Typical items that you would want to be able to update in this way are address and telephone information. All employees could maintain their own letterhead templates on their own machines and customize the address file to suit their needs. On the other hand, if the company were not large, you might want to be able to add an 800 telephone number or a fax number as the company added these services. Linking these items into the document template using DDE makes carrying out such changes as easy as editing a file or two.

Another item that might change occasionally is the company logo. As a result, it would be useful to include the graphics file in the document template. You can do so using either OLE or DDE, but each has a disadvantage to consider. If you use DDE, you will not be able to resize the object, except by resizing it in the application that drew it. (If you use DDE, of course, the advantage is that updating the graphics file automatically updates the image in the document template file.) If you use OLE, you will be able to resize the image at will, but you will have to manually update the image from its source file in each document in which the image is used.

In the example presented here, OLE is the better choice, because the image was originally drawn as an icon for an application. It is a bit map 64 pixels × 64 pixels in size in the original drawing program, and cannot be resized by the original drawing application. Using Paint-brush, which is an OLE client application, you can import the image and resize it. In order to avoid the disadvantage of using OLE, however, the graphics image is embedded into a file that is then linked to the letterhead template. As a result, updating still can be handled from a single file. In planning linkings and embeddings, therefore, it is important to keep in mind that objects can be embedded in files that are then linked.

Creating the Template

The first step in creating the letterhead compound document is creating the document template that you will use to construct letterhead documents. For all practical purposes, this template will serve as the presentation layer. Construct this template as you did earlier in this chapter, using the NORMAL as the template. Access the **F**ile **N**ew command, select the NORMAL template, select the T**e**mplate option button, and then click on OK. Figure 30.12 demonstrates this process.

Figure 30.12
Creating the
letterhead
document
template.

Next, give the new template the name NEWWELET.DOT by saving it using the Save **A**s
option on Word's **F**ile menu. Type **NEWWELET.DOT** in the text box and click on OK
(see fig. 30.13).

Figure 30.13
Naming the
letterhead
document
template.

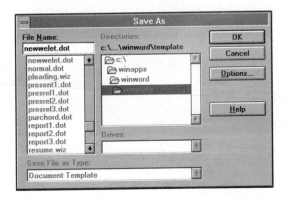

Tip

Saving your documents before creating DDE links among them is a good habit
to get into. If you save first, you cannot accidentally break a link by forgetting
to save a file when you exit an application. This habit is especially important
when you are creating links among several applications and choose to exit
Windows from a crowded desktop. As the save queries appear from various
applications, you could make a costly mistake.

Linking the Name and Address

The first step in linking the address for the letterhead is to create a new file to hold the address information. This file and others like it serve as the data acquisition layer for the template. Click on the New File button on the toolbar to open a new file. (The New File button is the first one on the left end of the toolbar.) Next, create a 1 × 2 table on the first line of the address file. Use the table button on the toolbar to insert the table (see fig. 30.14).

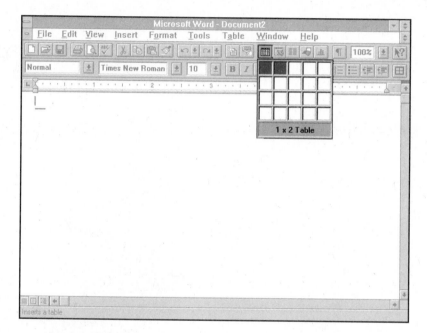

Figure 30.14

Inserting a table in the address file.

Click on the right cell of the table to place the insertion point there. Enter the address information shown in figure 30.15, right-justified, for the company Write Environment. Save the address information using the Save **A**s option on the **F**ile menu, giving the file the name WEADD.DOC. Use the Select **A**ll option on the **E**dit menu to select the table and characters you have entered, and select **C**opy to copy them to the Clipboard.

Use Word's **W**indow menu to switch to the document window that contains NEWWELET.DOT. Use the **E**dit menu's Paste **S**pecial option to paste the address information into the cell. When the Paste Special dialog box appears (see fig. 30.16), select Formatted Text in the list box, then select the Paste **L**ink option button before clicking on OK. The address information appears right-justified in the right cell of the table, and it is linked with DDE to the file WEADD.DOC.

Figure 30.15
Creating the
address file.

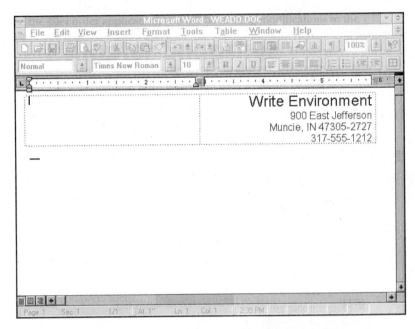

Figure 30.16
Linking the
address file.

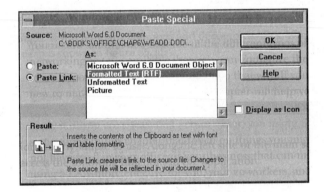

Linking the Footer Information

You might want to display additional information in the footer that appears on the first page
of any correspondence. This information also is a good candidate for DDE linking because it

might change from time to time. The company Write Environment displays its e-mail addresses in this area. You can link them in following steps very like those used to link in the address information.

First, open the footer for the first page of the document created using the template. Make sure you are in the document window that contains NEWWELET.DOT, and use the **H**eader/ Footer option on the **V**iew menu to make the header and footer visible. Select the Switch Between Header and Footer button on the Header and Footer toolbar to jump from the header to the footer. Then, click on the Page Setup button on the Header and Footer toolbar to display the Page Setup dialog box. In the **L**ayout tab of the Page Setup dialog box (see fig. 30.17), select the check box labeled Different **F**irst Page and click on OK.

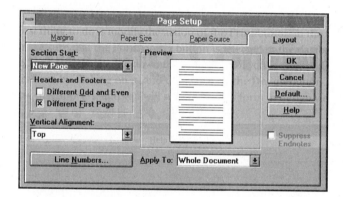

Figure 30.17
Opening the first footer.

Next, create a new file by clicking on the New File button on the toolbar. (This is another file in the data acquisition layer.) Type the information shown in figure 30.18. Save this file using the Save **A**s option on the **F**ile menu, giving it the name WEFOOT.DOC. Use the Select **A**ll option on the **E**dit menu to select the characters you have entered, and copy them to the Clipboard.

Use Word's **W**indow menu to switch to the document window that contains NEWWELET.DOT. Make sure the insertion point is located in the First Page Footer window. Use the **E**dit menu's Paste **S**pecial option to paste the address information into the First Page Footer window. When the Paste Special dialog box appears, select Formatted Text in the list box and select the Paste **L**ink option button before clicking on OK. The address information appears in the First Page Footer window, and it is linked with DDE to the file WEADD.DOC (see fig. 30.19).

Figure 30.18
Entering the information for the footer.

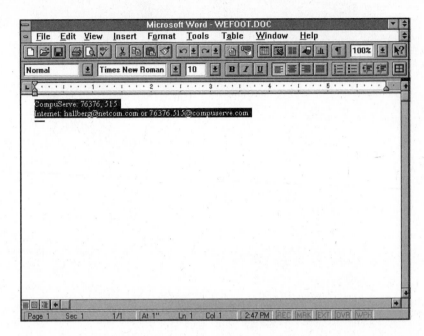

Figure 30.19
The linked information in the First Page Footer window.

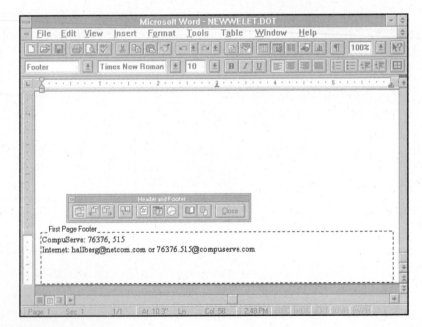

Embedding the Logo

To embed the logo, use the **W**indow menu to switch to the document window that contains WEADD.DOC. Place the insertion point in the left cell of the table you created, and click select **O**bject from the **I**nsert menu. When the Object dialog box appears, select Paintbrush Picture in the list box and then click on OK to open Paintbrush. Next, choose Paste **F**rom on the **E**dit menu. When the Paste From dialog box appears, select the file WE.BMP and click on OK (see fig. 30.20). Next select the **U**pdate option on the **F**ile menu. The graphic will be embedded in the table.

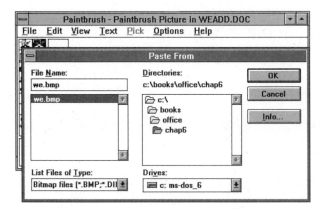

Figure 30.20
Selecting WE.BMP in the Paste From dialog box.

Adding the logo with Paintbrush adds a new layer to the set of documents that make up the letterhead compound document. The graphics file is in the data acquisition layer, and Paintbrush is an application that is in the data manipulation layer. Paintbrush takes the graphic in its native format and prepares it (by changing its format) to be embedded in the WEADD.DOC document. As you plan integration and automation with compound documents, you often will use an application like Paintbrush to take in data in one format from one application and prepare it to be used in another format by another linked application.

After you have embedded the graphic, click on the **U**pdate option in the **F**ile menu, and then click on E**x**it. Then, in Word, click on the logo once to select it. Size it by dragging the boxes on its frame so that it looks appropriate opposite the address text, as in figure 30.21. Save the file using the **S**ave option on the **F**ile menu.

Figure 30.21
The embedded
logo graphic.

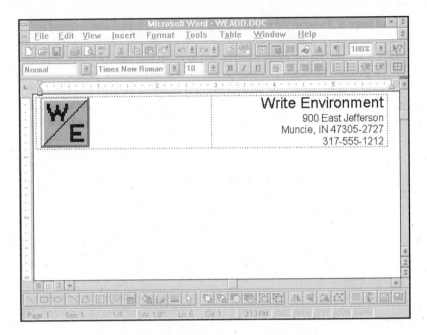

Figure 30.21
The embedded
logo graphic.

Now use the <u>W</u>indow menu to change to the document window that contains
NEWWELET.DOT. Notice that it should already have updated the graphic from the source
file, WEADD.DOC. If the graphic has not been updated, then you will need to do it manually:

Click on the <u>E</u>dit menu and choose the <u>L</u>inks option to display the Links dialog box (see fig.
30.22). In the Links dialog box, click on the link for WEA in the list box and then click on the
<u>U</u>pdate Now button. The table, complete with the embedded graphic, now appears in your
letterhead template.

Figure 30.22
Using the Links
dialog box to
manually update
the link to
NEWWELET.DOT.

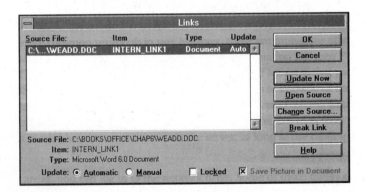

Automating Document Tasks with Macros

The basic look and feel of the letterhead for Write Environment is complete. You might, however, want to add to it using macros so that additional tasks of writing a letter can be automated.

A common task in writing a letter is adding the date and inside address, a task macros can automate considerably. To add the date to a letter automatically, all you need to do is add a date field to the letterhead template. On creation of a letterhead document, Word inserts the current date automatically.

To add the date, first position the insertion point at the location you want the date to appear in the NEWWELET.DOT file. Next, select the Field option from the Insert menu. When the Field dialog box appears, select the Date and Time category in the Categories list box and then CreateDate in the Field Names list box, as shown in Figure 30.23. Click on OK, and Word inserts a macro that automatically displays the current date. (You can see this macro if you select the Field Codes option on the View page of the Tools Options menu.)

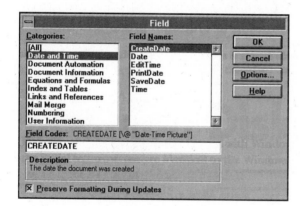

Figure 30.23
Inserting a date field.

Chapter Snapshot

This chapter introduces you to the McGillan-Lewis Corporation. Its sales unit faced the problem of accessing client data located in an Access database from within Word for Windows. Through an in-depth discussion of a DDE application called Turbodex, this chapter covers the following topics:

The word processor is the heart of most office environments, but its capability to access information from database systems is all but nonexistent. Although word processors, such as Ami Pro and Word for Windows, can import remote data for mail merge operations, they still have no real database querying capabilities. The integrating power of dynamic data exchange, however, enables you to bridge this gap between database information and your word processor.

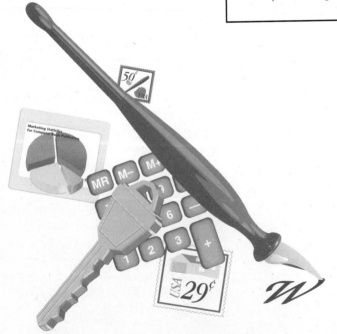

31

CHAPTER

Application Integration: Address Look-Up

by Bruce Hallberg

O ne of the more exciting features of the Microsoft Office package lies in its capability to integrate all the application programs included. Because all the applications are from a single vendor, you also benefit from the fact that they all integrate in similar ways, and you can be sure that integrating all the pieces is possible and has been tested.

When using applications from many different software vendors, you usually can do the same sorts of tricks, but they can be much more difficult to implement. You also run the risk, when the integration isn't working properly, of having each application vendor point its finger at the other vendor as the source of your problem. At least with bundles such as Microsoft Office, you can be sure that the responsibility for a problem lies with only one vendor.

Another notable thing is happening with regard to sharing data between applications—it's getting much easier. Most of this improvement is due to tools such as DDE and OLE that are a part of Windows. Additionally, the Microsoft Office applications work in a similar fashion, at least in the way in which they integrate. And with the advent of the Visual Basic for Applications programming language in each of the Office applications, the code required to link these applications is accessible to nonprogrammers. At least you don't have to learn a different macro language for each application, which used to be common.

Accessing Client Data

The McGillan-Lewis Corporation stores information about its clients in a networked Access database. The sales representatives spend much of their time corresponding with potential and existing clients by mail or fax, and they decided to use Word for Windows to handle these word processing tasks. However, every time they want to do so, they must locate the customer on the current customer listing printout and then type the information about the customer into their document. Obviously, the process is much more tedious, labor-intensive, and error-prone than they would like it to be, especially because they use that information dozens of times a day.

The sales representatives were getting pretty tired of this tedious process. They obviously needed a quick and inexpensive solution that would enable the sales representatives to access client data directly from Word.

Using Available Tools

Because many in the sales unit were already having a hard time adjusting to Windows, the last thing they wanted to do was to learn yet another Windows application (such as Access) just to access the client data. If Word could somehow tap into the power of Access, then their problem would be solved.

One of the sales representatives, who had only limited macro programming experience, decided he would try to develop a solution. He knew a little about Word Basic and had experimented with Access at home. He decided to link the two applications using straightforward DDE commands—and the result was Turbodex. Turbodex extends the built-in capabilities of Word to enable seamless database access through DDE integration with Access. Word acts as the DDE client and Access as the DDE server.

Before looking at Turbodex as both a user and developer, you should first understand the way in which Word and Access operate in their DDE client and server roles. DDE is still relatively young, and a standard implementation of DDE is practically nonexistent—even among products from the same company. Assessing how each acts in its respective roles helps you understand more completely how Turbodex operates.

Word for Windows as a DDE Client

Not only does Word feature a host of word processing attributes, but it also features one of the most powerful macro languages available—Word Basic. Word Basic provides the raw power needed to be a strong DDE client and supports the seven basic DDE commands (Initiate, Poke, Request, Execute, Terminate, and Terminate All), which can be divided up into three main groups: System, Data-Centric, and Task-Oriented.

The System Group

The System group includes DDEInitiate, DDETerminate, and DDETerminateAll. These three commands deal with beginning and ending a DDE conversation. Although these commands are integral to any DDE activity, the real power lies with the remaining two groups of commands.

The Data-Centric Group

The Data-Centric group contains DDEPoke and DDERequest. These two commands are primarily used for exchanging data between the server application and the client application. DDEPoke is used to send data to a specific location within the server application; this location is identified by the item. In the following example, Word begins a DDE conversation with Excel for Windows using a workbook named SALES.XLS as the topic. The DDEPoke command sends the data string "14300" to the A1 cell:

```
ChanNum = DDEInitiate("Excel", "SALES.XLS")
DDEPoke ChanNum, "A1", "14300"
```

DDERequest is used to retrieve data from a specific location (or item) within a server application. The following code begins another DDE conversation with Excel for Windows using the SALES.XLS notebook as the topic. The DDERequest command retrieves the data found at the A1 cell:

```
ChanNum = DDEInitiate("Excel", "SALES.XLS")
SalesTotal$ = DDERequest$(ChanNum, "A1")
```

The Task-Oriented Group

The Task-Oriented group contains a single command, DDEExecute. DDEExecute is used to send a message to the server to execute, making it an ideal way of accessing another application's script or macro language. The message sent to the DDE server must be a macro command in the server's particular dialect. For instance, the Word Basic command for saving a file is "File Save", whereas the command is "Save()" in the Excel 4.0 macro language. (The Excel 5.0 Visual Basic for Applications syntax is similar to the Word Basic equivalent.)

In many respects, DDEExecute is the most powerful aspect of dynamic data exchange. Not only can you access information from another application, but you can actually take full control over the remote application by sending a series of commands remotely. In the following example, Word sends Excel a message to perform the FileOpen command:

```
ChanNum = DDEInitiate("Excel", "SYSTEM")
DDEExecute ChanNum, "[FileOpen]"
```

Remember, DDEExecute generally is not for working with data; in fact, the DDE item is not utilized in a DDEExecute command (remember that the item is a key component of any data requests).

When integrating a Word Basic macro with another application, you probably will find times when you need to send a quotation mark within a DDE command. Because quotation marks are used by Word Basic to signify a character string, you should substitute the embedded quotation mark with Chr$(34). Chr$(34) returns the ANSI character code of the quotation mark to Word which is then passed to the linked application. The following command executes the OpenDatabase function within Access to load the ORDENTRY.MDB database:

```
DDEExecute(AChan, "[OpenDatabase " + Chr$(34) +
"C:\WINAPPS\ACCESS\ORDENTRY.MDB" + Chr$(34) + "]")
```

Although the statement might look confusing within the macro, Word concatenates the literal text and Chr$() codes and passes them as a string to Access. To Access, it will look like the following:

```
[OpenDatabase "C:\WINAPPS\ACCESS\ORDENTRY.MDB"]
```

Access as a DDE Server

Note

DDE Protocol for Access

Application: MSACCESS
Topic: Name of MDB file or System
Item: Name of an Access field

Access is a database program that includes programming tools for data access and management. And although Access often is used interactively, it also can serve as an excellent door through which other Windows applications can access Paradox, Btrieve, SQL, and ASCII-delimited data. You will discover that you do not need to prepare an Access application to act as a DDE server; after it is working interactively, you are ready to link it to a client application.

Note

When you send Access a DDEExecute command, you must surround the function name with square brackets [ ].

Using Turbodex

Turbodex is a small Word Basic program that accomplishes some automatic integration between Word and Access. During the remainder of this chapter, you will learn how to create Turbodex. Near the end of the chapter you can find the complete Word Basic code for Turbodex. You can also save yourself some typing by using the code contained in a file named TURBODEX.TXT from the companion disk that came with this book.

Before you begin building Turbodex, you should review how the program actually works so that you know the purpose of the rest of the chapter. The following text and graphics show you how Turbodex will work when it is complete.

When you install Turbodex, you will define it to be a new item on your Tools menu called Turbodex (see fig. 31.1).

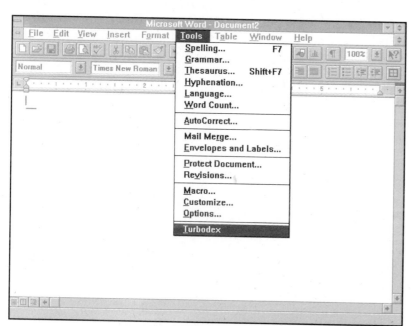

Figure 31.1
Turbodex can be started from the Word Tools menu.

To run, choose the Turbodex menu item. If Access or the ORDENTRY.MDB file is not open, Word will automatically start Access and initiate the DDE conversation. A dialog box will appear, as shown in figure 31.2.

Figure 31.2

The Turbodex dialog box.

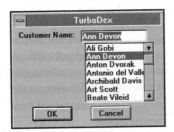

To use Turbodex, simply select the desired name from the dialog box and then click on the OK button. That person's name, company, and address will be automatically inserted into your document.

Turbodex is really a rather simple example of what DDE can accomplish. In fact, you might be wondering why the capability to automatically insert a name and address wouldn't be better accomplished by using Word's mail merge abilities, or by defining the names in the Word AutoText feature. The reason is that by linking Word and Access and using Turbodex to acquire the data from Access, you are always assured of getting current information. If, on the other hand, you crafted a solution using just Word's tools, you would also have the added burden of updating Word's listing on a regular basis from the master listing that is kept in Access, and would run the risk of using information that was not completely up to date.

Although Turbodex simply inserts the name and address into the current document, the possibilities are endless with additional things you could do with the macro. You could, for instance, insert the address into a fax template for quick creation of a facsimile cover sheet or create customized letterhead on-the-fly by inserting the address into a preformatted template.

Developing Turbodex

To end users, Turbodex looks like just another built-in capability of Word. Everything they see and interact with—the menu item, dialog boxes, and so on—is part of Word. Within this fact lies the true power of DDE: it enables the user to access the power of several Windows applications, but to work within a single interface.

As you begin to look at how Turbodex works, you quickly realize that it has two interdependent parts, both of which are joined through that common Windows medium, dynamic data exchange:

✔ **Access, DDE server.** An Access database and application, ORDENTRY.MDB, contains the data that needs to be accessed.

Note ORDENTRY.MDB is included as an example database with Microsoft Access.

✔ **Word for Windows, DDE client.** A Word Basic macro is responsible for communicating with the user, relaying a query request and execution instructions to Access, receiving data back from Access, and placing that data in its appropriate resting place.

Figure 31.3 illustrates the specific, mutually dependent tasks these two modules have. The job of dynamic data exchange is to join these two modules and enable them to work together seamlessly.

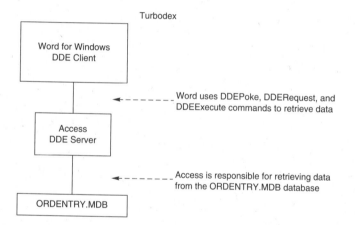

Figure 31.3
Word for
Windows can use
DDE to access
Access data.

Creating the Turbodex Application

You now are ready to integrate the Access application with Word. This is achieved by writing a macro that will be responsible for the following:

✔ Querying the Access database to build a list of all the names in the database

✔ Displaying that list for the user

✔ Retrieving the detailed information on a person after the user has selected the person he or she wants

✔ Inserting the full information into the Word document

To begin, create a new macro named Turbodex and open its edit window.

In the macro window, either key in the Turbodex code, or insert the code from the disk file, TURBODEX.TXT, which is located on the *Inside Microsoft Office Professional* companion disk.

Understanding the Turbodex Application

The Turbodex application, while long, is really fairly straightforward. In pseudocode, the program works like this:

```
Terminate any running DDE conversations
Check to see if Access is running:
        If not running, start Access and load the ORDENTRY.MDB file
Initiate a DDE conversation with Access
Send a SQL query to Access that returns the number of records in the
database
Dimension the CustomerArray to hold all of the customers using the
number returned in the previous step
Submit another SQL statement which will return a single string contain-
ing all the customer names in the database
Parse the names into the array CustomerArray
Sort the array alphabetically
Create a dialog box, which automatically contains CustomerArray in a
combo box
Display the dialog box and wait for input
If the user selects the Cancel button, exit Turbodex
When the user clicks on the OK button, get the selected name
Query the database, using multiple SQL commands, to secure each field
which makes up the customer's company, name, and complete address,
placing this information into variables
Insert the variables into the Word document
End the Turbodex macro
```

If a server application is not running at the time the client attempts to begin a conversation with it, most client applications ask the user if the program should be started. If you are creating a seamless solution, however, you should anticipate this in your macro and load it automatically, if needed, without requiring user interaction. The Turbodex application in this chapter shows how this is done.

Creating the Turbodex Dialog Box

If you examine the Turbodex code, you will see a fairly complex code construction that creates the dialog box:

```
Begin Dialog UserDialog 320, 144, "TurboDex"
      Text 10, 6, 124, 13, "Customer Name:", .Text1
      ComboBox 145, 6, 160, 108, CustomerArray$(), .ComboBox1
      OKButton 38, 117, 88, 21
      CancelButton 166, 117, 88, 21
End Dialog
```

Creating the dialog box would take an enormous amount of time if you had to figure out all the dialog box object positions by hand. Instead, when you are editing your Word Basic code, click on the Dialog Editor button to bring up the dialog box creation tool, shown in figure 31.4.

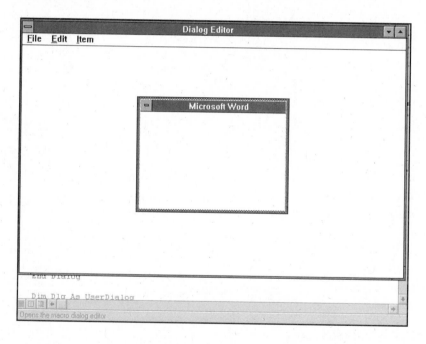

Figure 31.4
Word's Dialog Editor.

You create objects on the dialog box, such as buttons, combo boxes, list boxes, and so forth, with the Item menu. Pull down the Item menu, shown in figure 31.5, and select the object that you want to place in the dialog box.

Figure 31.5

The Dialog Editor's Item menu.

After you select an item from the Item menu, it appears in the sample dialog box. You then can drag it around the dialog box to the location you want and edit the text associated with the object. (For instance, you can name a button OK, or Go Ahead, or whatever.) Figure 31.6 shows the completed dialog box for Turbodex.

Figure 31.6

The completed Turbodex dialog box.

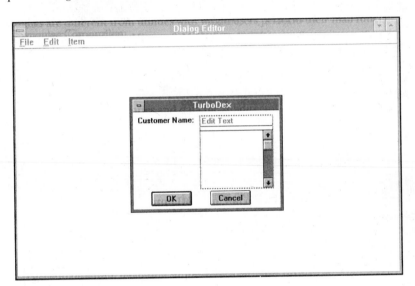

After your dialog box is complete, access the Edit menu in the Dialog Editor and select Select Dialog. Then, choose the Copy command in the Edit menu. Finally, move to your Word Basic macro, and choose Paste in Word's Edit menu. The dialog box "code," such as that which you see in the Turbodex code, is automatically inserted into your macro.

Placing Turbodex on Word's Menu

After you have Turbodex working, you easily can place it on Word's Tools menu. To do this, follow these steps:

1. Pull down the Tools menu and select Customize to display the Customize dialog box.

2. Select the Menus tab in the dialog box, which is shown in figure 31.7.

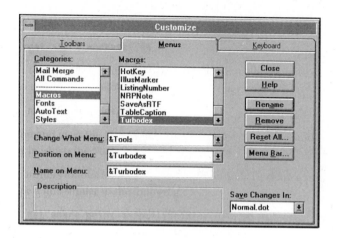

Figure 31.7
The Menus tab in
the Customize
dialog box.

3. In the **C**ategories list box, select Macros.

4. In the Macr**os** list box, select Turbodex.

5. Change the Change What Men**u** option to &Tools.

6. Click on the button to the right of the **P**osition on Menu option and select last item on the list.

7. Finally, change the **N**ame on Menu text box to read **&Turbodex** and click on the Close button.

Turbodex Macro Listing

Here is the complete code listing for Turbodex. Notice that the location of Microsoft Access is "hard wired" to be C:\MSOFFICE\ACCESS\MSACCESS.EXE. If Access is installed in any other directory on your computer system, be sure to modify the line containing the Access Basic "Shell()" command.

```
Sub MAIN

   On Error Resume Next

   'Terminate any running DDE conversations
   DDETerminateAll

   Dim AChan

   'Is Access running? If not, then open Access and the database
   'Be sure to verify the path to Access in the Shell() command
   If Not AppIsRunning("Microsoft Access") Then
```

```
        Shell "C:\MSOFFICE\ACCESS\MSACCESS.EXE"
        AChan = DDEInitiate("MSAccess", "System") \
                DDEExecute(AChan, "[OpenDatabase " + Chr$(34) + \
                "C:\MSOFFICE\ACCESS\ORDENTRY.MDB" + Chr$(34) + "]")
                DDETerminate(AChan)
End If

' Be sure to verify the path to the Access
' sample database named ORDENTRY.MDB
AChan = DDEInitiate("MSAccess", \
    "C:\MSOFFICE\ACCESS\ORDENTRY.MDB;SQL SELECT  DISTINCTROW \
    Count(Customers.ContactName) AS CountOfContactName FROM \
    Customers WITH OWNERACCESS OPTION;")

NumberOfEntries = Val(DDERequest$(AChan, "Data"))

DDETerminate(AChan)

Dim CustomerArray$(NumberOfEntries)

AChan = DDEInitiate("MSAccess", \
    "C:\MSOFFICE\ACCESS\ORDENTRY.MDB;SQL SELECT  DISTINCTROW
    Customers.ContactName FROM Customers WITH \
    OWNERACCESS OPTION; ")

Customer$ = DDERequest$(AChan, "Data")
Print Customer$
b = 0
Index = 1
While 1
    NewIndex = InStr(Index, Customer$, Chr$(13))
    If NewIndex = 0 Then Goto Continue
    CustomerArray$(b) = Mid$(Customer$,Index,(NewIndex-Index))
    Print CustomerArray$(b)
    Index = NewIndex + 1
    b = b + 1
Wend

Continue:
SortArray CustomerArray$()
Begin Dialog UserDialog 320, 144, "TurboDex"
    Text 10, 6, 124, 13, "Customer Name:"
```

```
    ComboBox 145, 6, 160, 108, CustomerArray$(), .ComboBox1
    OKButton 38, 117, 88, 21
    CancelButton 166, 117, 88, 21
 End Dialog

Dim Dlg As UserDialog
Button = Dialog(Dlg)

If Button = 0 Then Goto Exit

 Name$ = Dlg.ComboBox1
 DDETerminate(AChan)

 AChan = DDEInitiate("MSAccess", \
    "C:\MSOFFICE\ACCESS\ORDENTRY.MDB;SQL SELECT \"
    DISTINCTROW Customers.ContactTitle FROM Customers \
    WHERE(Customers.ContactName = " + Chr$(34) + Name$ + \
    Chr$(34) + ")")
 Title$ = DDERequest$(AChan, "Data")
 DDETerminate(AChan)

 AChan = DDEInitiate("MSAccess", \
    "C:\MSOFFICE\ACCESS\ORDENTRY.MDB;SQL SELECT \
    DISTINCTROW Customers.Company FROM Customers \
    WHERE(Customers.ContactName \
    = " + Chr$(34) + Name$ + Chr$(34) + ")")
 Company$ = DDERequest$(AChan, "Data")
 DDETerminate(AChan)

 AChan = DDEInitiate("MSAccess", \
    "C:\MSOFFICE\ACCESS\ORDENTRY.MDB;SQL SELECT \
    DISTINCTROW Customers.Address FROM Customers \
    WHERE(Customers.ContactName \
    = " + Chr$(34) + Name$ + Chr$(34) + ")")
 Address$ = DDERequest$(AChan, "Data")
 DDETerminate(AChan)

 AChan = DDEInitiate("MSAccess", \
    "C:\MSOFFICE\ACCESS\ORDENTRY.MDB;SQL SELECT \
    DISTINCTROW Customers.City FROM Customers \
    WHERE(Customers.ContactName = \
    " + Chr$(34) + Name$ + Chr$(34) + ")")
```

```
City$ = DDERequest$(AChan, "Data")
DDETerminate(AChan)

AChan = DDEInitiate("MSAccess", \
   "C:\MSOFFICE\ACCESS\ORDENTRY.MDB;SQL SELECT \
    DISTINCTROW Customers.Region FROM Customers \
    WHERE(Customers.ContactName \
    = " + Chr$(34) + Name$ + Chr$(34) + ")")
Region$ = DDERequest$(AChan, "Data")
DDETerminate(AChan)

AChan = DDEInitiate("MSAccess", \
   "C:\MSOFFICE\ACCESS\ORDENTRY.MDB;SQL SELECT \
    DISTINCTROW Customers.PostalCode FROM Customers \
    WHERE(Customers.ContactName = " + Chr$(34) + Name$ + \
    Chr$(34) + ")")
PostalCode$ = DDERequest$(AChan, "Data")
DDETerminate(AChan)

AChan = DDEInitiate("MSAccess", \
   "C:\MSOFFICE\ACCESS\ORDENTRY.MDB;SQL SELECT " \
   "DISTINCTROW Customers.Country FROM Customers " \
   "WHERE(Customers.ContactName "\
   "= " + Chr$(34) + Name$ + Chr$(34) + ")")
Country$ = DDERequest$(AChan, "Data")
DDETerminate(AChan)

Insert Company$ + Chr$(13) + Address$ + Chr$(13) \
+ City$ + ", " + Region$ + " " + PostalCode$ \
+ Chr$(13) + Country$ + Chr$(13) + Name$ + ", " + Title$

Exit:

End Sub
```

Turbodex provides a quick and inexpensive solution for the sales unit at McGillan-Lewis Corporation. Instead of the MIS department spending months rewriting C code to meet this need, a sales representative with only limited macro programming experience was able to develop this DDE application.

This scenario illustrates the beauty of dynamic data exchange and applications integration: *you do not need to be an expert C++ programmer to integrate Windows applications.* With limited knowledge of an application's macro language and other "high-level" Windows development tools, you can create DDE applications, such as Turbodex, in a fraction of the time it would take to write a C or C++ program to perform the same task.

Chapter Snapshot

Even simple implementation of dynamic data exchange with shrink-wrapped software can produce powerful results. This chapter introduces you to Addison Fine Furniture and details how this three-man company used applications integration to increase productivity, improve communications with their customers, and reduce their software investment. Demonstrating how easy it is to tap into the power of other Windows applications, this chapter focuses on the following topics:

Getting the most out of your software is important to small businesses. All too often a company buys into an accounting or invoicing system and realizes that it cannot perform everything they wish it could do. Then as software already purchased cannot meet an arising need, the company must buy additional software in an attempt to find a solution. However, the integration technology of Windows combined with Microsoft Office puts a stop to this purchasing cycle.

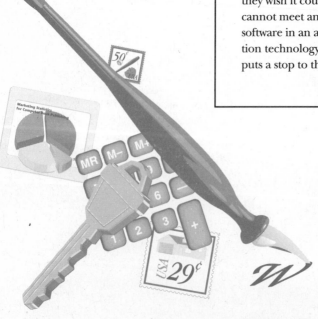

CHAPTER 32

Integrating a Sales Order System with DDE

by Bruce Hallberg

Addison Fine Furniture is a small discount furniture business trying to make a name for itself in the marketplace, and a company in need of maximizing its own software investment. To increase publicity it is selling furniture at a very low profit margin, in an attempt to gain market share from a much larger competitor. In doing so, the owners decided to drive this point home to its customers by sending an "after-sale packet." Sent the day after a purchase, the after-sale packet consists of Addison Fine Furniture's quarterly catalog, a personalized letter, and a cost savings analysis. The cost savings analysis graphically illustrates the amount of money customers save by purchasing their order from Addison Fine Furniture rather than its crosstown rival, Firehouse Jimmy's Furniture Barn.

At the same time, one of the owners created a new sales order invoicing system using Access. This application increased productivity during the order fulfillment process because it enabled rapid data entry and WYSIWYG invoice printing. The owners were discouraged, however, because the new application would not provide the graphing or word processing power they needed for their after-sale packet idea.

The trio discussed the following options: buying a Windows report writer (which would require spending more money on software); using their existing Windows word processor and spreadsheet (which would require considerable time to enter the data for each order); and purchasing an integrated software package (which would require developing their data entry application all over again). The question remained: How could Addison Fine Furniture maximize its time and monetary resources to meet this specific business need?

Using Available Tools

The owners decided that they had to develop a solution with the software they currently owned. Because the company already used Word, Excel, and Access from the Microsoft Office Professional package for other internal purposes, the solution they needed meant they had to be able to tap into the advanced capabilities of these existing applications.

Although they had heard of "dynamic data exchange," the phrase sounded far too complicated for nonprogrammers like themselves. Instead, they began copying data from the Access form to the Windows Clipboard and pasting it into Excel and Word, from which they printed out the Cost Savings Analysis and the form letter. However, this copy/paste solution was too time-consuming for the large number of after-sales packets they planned to send each week.

One of the owners decided to make an effort to learn how to use DDE to link Word, Excel, and Access. To his surprise, he learned how easy it is to set up dynamic links between these three applications and how he could control the output of Excel and Word from within the company's existing Access invoicing system.

This integrated sales order system extended the built-in capabilities of Microsoft Access by linking it to Excel and Word using DDE. Now, the sales data processed in Access is sent to Excel to generate the graphic-based cost savings analysis while the customer's address is sent to Word to generate a personalized form letter. The three pages then are printed out sequentially. And all this is performed with the click of a single button from within Access!

Before looking at how to use and develop the integrated sales order system, it is important to understand how each of these Windows applications operates as a DDE client or server. Because DDE is still a new technology and implemented differently in different applications, it is important to understand the idiosyncrasies that exist with the applications used in this scenario.

Understanding the Sales Order System

For the example presented in this chapter, you build an integrated sales order system using the sample ORDENTRY application that is included with Access. You will modify this application in such a way that, when the user clicks on the button to print the invoice, Access will send the appropriate data to Excel and Word to create the two additional documents that will be sent to the customer. When you are finished, clicking on the button inside of Access will generate three documents: the invoice from Access, the cost savings analysis from Excel, and the form letter from Word. DDE commands are used to send the information from the order entry screen in Access to both Excel and Word, and then both Excel and Word will be instructed (through DDE) to print their respective documents.

Setting up this integrated sales order system is very straightforward in Excel and Word. For both applications, all you need to do is prepare a single file, which has everything except the data from the current sales order. These "template documents" (not to be confused with Templates in either Excel or Word) will be reused each time a sales order is entered and printed.

Creating the system is more complex in Access than in Excel or Word—you will need to restructure the ORDENTRY application somewhat and enter a number of lines of Access Basic code to accomplish the necessary DDE commands.

Understanding the process of integrating Access, Excel, and Word can revolutionize the approach you take to solve problems. When a DDE application is properly developed, three or more Windows programs can work together as a single application. This eliminates the need for a *mega-app:* a word processor, database manager, and spreadsheet all rolled up into one expensive package. DDE enables end users and developers to approach integration in a new and powerful manner—modularizing applications to meet a specific business need.

As was discussed earlier, the integrated sales order system has three parts that work together to produce the three pages of output for each order:

- ✔ **Excel for Windows, DDE server.** Receives the Subtotal field values from Access, uses these as the series for a predefined chart, and prints out the cost savings analysis page.

- ✔ **Word for Windows, DDE server.** Receives the values from address-related Access fields, places them onto a form letter, and prints out the document.

- ✔ **Access, DDE client.** Serves as the data entry application to store data in the Access database and sends specific field values to Excel and Word to generate the after-sale packet.

Figure 32.1 illustrates the interaction between the three applications joined through dynamic data exchange.

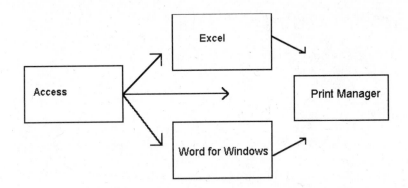

Figure 32.1
Using DDE,
Access pokes data
to both Excel
and Word.

Access as a DDE Client

As you learned earlier in this book, Access is a graphical database system that can be used for a wide variety of data management tasks, such as order entry. Access also can send data to and receive data from other Windows applications. In addition, because Access often is called on to create data entry applications, it might be the sole application many users interact with on a daily basis. As a result, the need for Access to function well as a DDE client is critical.

You can use commands in Access Basic to carry out DDE conversations with other Windows-based applications, such as Word and Excel. To initiate and carry out a DDE conversation with Access, you will use the following Access Basic commands:

✔ **DDEInitiate.** Starts the DDE conversation.

✔ **DDEExecute.** Sends *commands* to the server application.

✔ **DDEPoke.** Sends *data* to the server application.

Excel for Windows as a DDE Server

DDE Protocol for Excel for Windows:

Application: Excel
Topic: Name of XLS file or "SYSTEM"
Item: Cell address or block coordinate

Excel for Windows is a mature, powerful tool in the Windows graphical spreadsheet market and brings with it an extensive macro language and application development capability. These qualities make Excel an excellent candidate for DDE server tasks, such as providing data from a spreadsheet, creating a pie chart on-the-fly, and executing an Excel macro or custom application at the request of another application.

Excel's basic file unit is known as a *workbook*, which consists of 16 or more worksheet pages. Cell addresses are thus identified by the following convention: `page name!cell name`. For example, if you are trying to poke a value to cell G45 on page Stocks, the syntax would be `Stocks!G45`. If no page name is given, Excel assumes the cell is on is the first page of the workbook (but only for DDE requests; Excel otherwise assumes the current page when you just type in a cell reference while using it).

When you use a workbook file as the topic, you can designate a cell address or block coordinate as the item; for example, the following Word Basic macro pokes data to a single cell and requests data from a group of cells:

```
YearlyGains$ = "12,000,000"
ChanNum = DDEInitiate("Excel", "GAINS.XLS")
DDEPoke ChanNum, "1992!S1", YearlyGains$
MonthlyGains$ = DDERequest(ChanNum, "1992!A1..A12")
```

Note that since the `MonthlyGains$` variable contains values from 12 cells, you would need to parse each cell's value to other variables.

To execute an Excel macro or function from a DDE client, use the DDE Execute command of the client application. The following Word Basic macro saves all open notebook files and closes down the application:

```
ChanNum = DDEInitiate("Excel", "SYSTEM")
DDEExecute ChanNum, "[FileSave]"
DDEExecute ChanNum, "[FileClose]"
```

Tip When you send Excel a DDEExecute command, you must surround the macro command or function with square brackets.

Word for Windows

Note DDE Protocol for Word for Windows:

Application: WINWORD
Topic: Name of DOC file, System
Item: Name of a bookmark

Although most of the documentation available on Word deals with it exclusively as a DDE client, Word can also function as a very capable and useful server application. Data can be poked to and requested from a Word document. And, because of Word's comprehensive macro language, you can execute any menu-driven command within Word by sending it the Word Basic equivalent.

If you want to exchange data with Word, you must first define bookmarks within a document. *Bookmarks* are invisible placeholders used by Word to mark a location and are defined by the Bookmark command from the Edit menu. In Word, a bookmark serves as a DDE item.

Because bookmarks usually are invisible, it is easy to lose track of their location. To find a bookmark, use the **E**dit **B**ookmark command and then double-click on a listed bookmark. The cursor will move to the bookmark site.

To delete a bookmark, select the **E**dit **B**ookmark command, select a bookmark from the dialog list box, and click on the Delete button.

You also can enable the display of bookmarks while you work. To do this, access the **O**ptions command in the **T**ools menu. In the Options notebook, click on the View page and then select the Boo**k**marks check box.

If you want to execute a Word Basic command from within your client application, you need to use the DDEExecute statement. For example, if you wanted to create a new Word document, insert text, and then save it all from within Access, you would issue the following statements ("WordLink" is the name of the channel in the following commands):

```
DDEExecute("WordLink","[FileNew]")
        'TYPE THE FOLLOWING TWO LINES IN THE BOOK ON ONE LINE IN WORD
DDEExecute("WordLink","[Insert ""This document was created from another
application!"""]")
DDEExecute("WordLink","[FileSave .Name = ""TEST.DOC""]")
```

When you send Word a DDEExecute command, you must surround the Word Basic statement with square brackets.

Creating the Integrated Sales Order System

To create the sales order system, you will perform the following three steps:

✔ Create the Excel workbook for the cost savings analysis

✔ Create the Word document for the form letter

✔ Modify the ORDENTRY application included with Access

Creating the Excel File

To begin, start Excel and perform the following steps to create the cost savings workbook:

1. In cell A1, enter **Customer Cost Savings Analysis**. Set the font for this line to 16-point Arial and center the text across the visual screen.

2. In cell D3, enter **Addison's Fine Furniture**. Format the text in this cell to be right-aligned.

3. In cell E3, enter **100**. This number is simply a placeholder that you will use to finish the worksheet.

4. In cell D4, enter **Firehouse Jimmy's Furniture Barn**. Format this cell to be right-aligned.

5. In cell E4, enter **125**. Again, this number is simply a placeholder.

6. In cell D5, enter **You Saved:**. Format this cell to be right-aligned.

7. In cell E5, enter the formula **=E5-E3**.

8. Format cells E3:E5 as Currency format with two decimal places.

9. Use the Chart Wizard to create a column chart of the small table contained in cells D3:E4. Create the chart immediately below the information you typed. Format the chart as shown in figure 32.2, adding the appropriate titles.

Figure 32.2 shows the completed worksheet.

Save the file as CSA.XLS and note the directory name in which you store the file. You will need that information later.

Creating the Word File

To create the Word file, start by setting up a fairly standard form letter, but leave the space for the date and addressee blank. When you run the sales order system, Access will provide that information for each letter.

Figure 32.2
The completed
Excel worksheet.

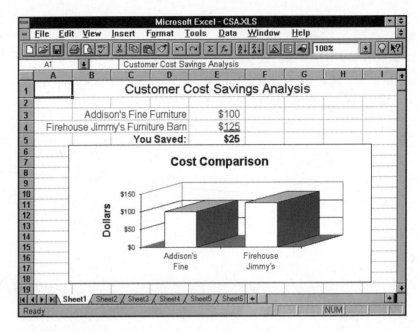

If you want, use the following text for the letter.

Dear Customer,

Thank you for doing business with Addison's Fine Furniture.

We know that one of the primary concerns of our customers is managing expenses in these competitive times. Because of this, we make a commitment to provide you with quality merchandise at a lower price than any of our competitors. In fact, we thought you may be interested in seeing just how our prices stack up to our competition. We have enclosed a complimentary Savings Analysis to show you just how much money you are saving your company by doing business with Addison's as compared to one of our competitors.

If there is anything that we can do to better serve you, please don't hesitate to contact any of us here at Addison's.

Sincerely yours,

Pete Rosewood

General Manager

When you are finished setting up the letter, it should look like the one in figure 32.3.

Figure 32.3
Completed Word form letter.

V

Data Sharing and Integration

In order to receive DDE information in a Word document, you must create bookmarks in the document. The bookmarks let Word know where you want various pieces of DDE information inserted (you will see how this works in the Access Basic code later).

Move to the location at which you would like the date to appear and create a bookmark using the Edit Bookmark command. Call the bookmark **Date**. Similarly, create three more bookmarks, called **Company**, **Address**, and **City_State_Zip**. Create these bookmarks in the location at which you would normally locate them at the top of a business letter.

Note Remember to save your document when you are finished making the changes.

Creating the Access Application

The two supporting parts are now complete, so you are ready to work on the Access application and its links to the other applications. The Access-based sales order invoicing system is a simple order entry system for Addison's Fine Furniture. It is intended to serve three purposes:

✔ Enter sales order data into the Access database

✔ Provide a hard copy printout of the form to serve as the sales invoice

✔ Send data to Excel and Word to generate the after-sale packet

In order to create the sales order application, you will be making modifications to the ORDENTRY application, which is included as a sample application with Access. The sample application is perfect for our purposes, and is almost completely ready. However, you will be modifying the action of the button that prints the invoice to also use DDE commands to update the Excel and Word documents, print them, and then print the Access sales order (which will serve as an invoice).

Start Access and open the ORDENTRY application. Your screen should look like figure 32.4.

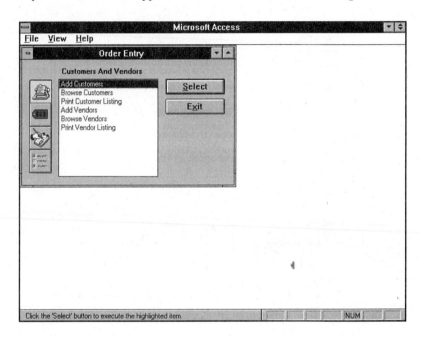

Figure 32.4

The Access ORDENTRY application.

The ORDENTRY application is fairly simple to use. Along the left side of the main screen are four large buttons, which access the following functions in the application:

✔ Customer and vendor maintenance

✔ Product and category maintenance

✔ Order maintenance and reports

✔ Options maintenance

Before changing the application, you must first access the maintenance functions of the database. To do that, click on the bottom button of the application's main screen (options maintenance), select Show Database Window and then click on the Select button. You will then see the Database window, as in figure 32.5.

Figure 32.5
The ORDENTRY
Database window.

The first thing to do is modify the action of the Print button in the Order Entry screen. To do this, make sure that the Form object button is selected in the database window (as it is in figure 32.5) and then scroll down the window until you locate the Orders form. Highlight the Orders form by clicking on it, and then click on the **D**esign button. Maximize the form design window that appears, and you will see the **Orders** form in design view as shown in figure 32.6.

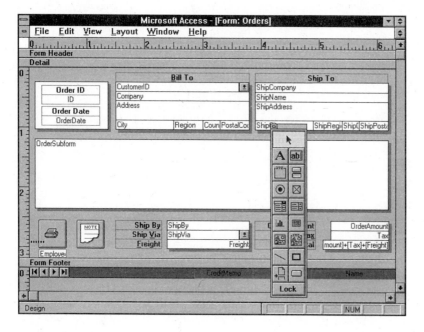

Figure 32.6
The Order form
design screen

The button you need to modify is in the lower left corner of the screen, and has a printer icon on it. Double-click on this button to bring up the printer button's property list, which you can see in figure 32.7.

Figure 32.7
The print button property list in the Command Button dialog box.

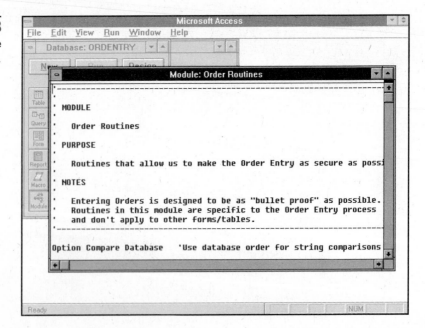

As you can see from the window, the button's On Push event calls a macro named FrmOrders.Print. Modify the On Push event to instead read =PrintInvoice(), which is an Access Basic function that you will create shortly. Close the Orders form design window, saving your changes.

Next, from the Database window, click on the Module button to display the Access Basic modules in the ORDENTRY application. Select the Order Routines module and then click on the Design button. You will then see the screen shown in figure 32.8.

Figure 32.8
The Module window.

Create a new function to hold the new DDE code that you will be adding to the ORDENTRY application. Pull down the Edit menu and choose New Procedure. In the dialog box that appears, click on the Function button and type **PrintInvoice** in the space provided. Click on the OK button to proceed.

You will now see a blank procedure screen. Type the code that follows into the procedure window exactly as it is printed. When you have finished entering the program code (and checking your work carefully!), close the procedure window and save your changes.

```
Function PrintInvoice () As Integer

        'Set error checking so that it continues on errors
    On Error Resume Next

        'Define the variables that we'll use
    Dim ExcelChan, WordChan, Misc, Topics

        'Before doing anything else, print the Access form
    DoCmd RunMacro "FrmOrders.Print"

        'Is Excel running?
    ExcelChan = DDEInitiate("Excel", "System")

        'If not, then start Excel.
    If Err Then
        Err = 0
        'Change the path in the following line to your location for
    Excel
        Misc = Shell("C:\WINAPPS\EXCEL5\Excel.exe", 1)
        If Err Then
            MsgBox "Unable To Start Excel. Aborting DDE Routine."
            Exit Function
        End If
        ExcelChan = DDEInitiate("Excel", "System")
    End If

        'Check to see if the file is loaded
    Topics = DDERequest(ExcelChan, "Topics")
    Misc = InStr(1, Topics, "CSA.XLS")
```

```
        'If not then load it
    If Misc = 0 Then DDEExecute ExcelChan,
➡   "[Open(""C:\BOOKS\CSA.XLS"")]"

        'Terminate the DDE channel for a second
    DDETerminate ExcelChan

        'Reestablish the DDE channel with the file
    ExcelChan = DDEInitiate("Excel", "CSA.XLS")

        'Poke the data into the two cells
    DDEPoke ExcelChan, "R3C5", (Forms![Orders]![OrderAmount])
    DDEPoke ExcelChan, "R4C5", ((Forms![Orders]![OrderAmount]) * 1.25)

        'Print the Excel file
    DDEExecute ExcelChan, "[Print]"

        'Clean up and terminate the DDE connection
    DDETerminate ExcelChan

        'Now for Word. Is it running?
    WordChan = DDEInitiate("WinWord", "System")

        'Not running? Then start it!
    If Err Then
        Err = 0
        Misc = Shell("C:\WINAPPS\WINWORD\WINWORD.EXE", 1)
        If Err Then
            MsgBox "Unable to load Word. Terminating DDE Routine."
            Exit Function
        End If
        WordChan = DDEInitiate("WinWord", "System")
    End If

        'Check to see if the file is loaded
    Topics = DDERequest(WordChan, "Topics")
    Misc = InStr(1, Topics, "CSA.DOC")

        'If not then load it
    If Misc = 0 Then
        DDEExecute WordChan, "[FileOpen ""C:\BOOKS\CSA.DOC""]"
    End If
```

```
     'Terminate the DDE channel for a second
DDETerminate WordChan

     'Reestablish the DDE channel with the file
WordChan = DDEInitiate("WinWord", "C:\BOOKS\CSA.DOC")

     'Poke the data into the bookmarks
DDEPoke WordChan, "Date", (Forms![Orders]![OrderDate])
DDEPoke WordChan, "Company", (Forms![Orders]![Company])
DDEPoke WordChan, "Address", (Forms![Orders]![Address])

      'TYPE THE FOLLOWING THREE LINES ON A SINGLE LINE IN THE ACCESS
SCREEN
DDEPoke WordChan, "City_State_Zip", (Forms![Orders]![City] + ", " +
    Forms![Orders]![Region] + " " + Forms![Orders]![Country] + " " +
    Forms![Orders]![PostalCode])

     'Print the file
DDEExecute WordChan, "[FilePrint]"

     'Tidy up and close the DDE Channel
DDETerminate WordChan

End Function
```

Using the DDE-Enabled Order Entry Application

To test your new DDE-enabled application, close the ORDENTRY database and reopen it. Click on the third button down on the left side of the main window, choose Add Orders, and click on the Select button. You then will see the Add Orders dialog box, which enables you to tell the system which salesperson you are. Click on the arrow to open the left dropbox and select any of the salespeople listed. After you have selected a salesperson, you will see the data entry screen shown in figure 32.9.

First, select a customer. Click on the arrow to open the Bill To drop-down list box and scroll down in the list until you find A Kid's Room. Click on the customer to select it. Click on the Product ID field in the body of the order and press F11 to call up the list of products. Select a product and click on the OK button. Press Tab once to move to Qty field and enter a quantity. Press Tab three more times to complete the line and calculate the order total.

After the order is complete, and most particularly, there are figures in the Order Amount, Tax, and Total fields, click on the print button that you modified earlier. If your printer is on, you should shortly be seeing three documents appearing: the invoice, the cost savings analysis, and finally the form letter.

Figure 32.9
The order entry screen.

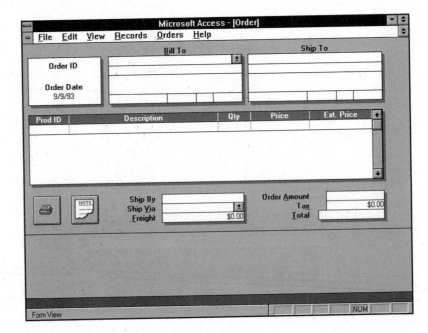

Part Six

Extending the Office Suite

Chapter Snapshot

If you use Microsoft Office, chances are your company is a large corporate environment in which e-mail is needed. Although Microsoft Mail is not necessary to run Office, you can benefit from an e-mail system if you use it as the communications tool between network users. Microsoft Mail caters to corporate environments with multiple satellite offices or staff members who must dial in from remote off-site locations to retrieve their mail. This chapter gets you started with Microsoft Mail by exploring the following topics:

Microsoft Mail offers very straightforward productivity mail tools to provide an effective way to send and receive mail messages. Strong end-user software functionality exists to include hierarchical folders, full-text search of messages, support for object linking and embedding, and the capability to put text from other applications into messages.

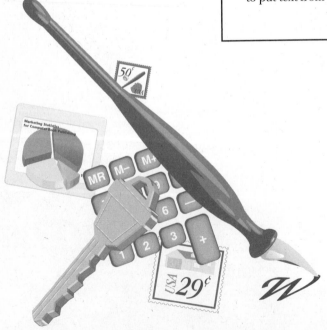

Microsoft Mail

by Kimberly Maxwell

E-mail is something more people are running across in some way, shape, or form. Maybe your company has equipped you with one of the standard network e-mail packages, or maybe you are using an online service such as CompuServe or America OnLine as a vehicle for your e-mail. Maybe you have seen unusual-looking e-mail addresses like john.smith@f47.n282.zl.tdkt.kksys.com. and wonder what they are all about.

When using Microsoft Office, you encounter e-mail because Microsoft Mail is included with the package. Each Office package comes with a site license for one client workstation. If you use Microsoft Mail with your Office suite, a dependable LAN-based system provides you with all the tools necessary to send and receive e-mail—both inside and outside the office network.

Before taking advantage of what e-mail has to offer, however, you should be aware of the different types of e-mail services available, where and how you can access them, and how to use them effectively.

Understanding E-Mail Basics

Defined simply, e-mail is a way for people to communicate electronically. People send and receive text messages using computers through some type of link. The link might be through a modem and telephone line, or the cabling and hardware within your office network.

Regardless of how you access your e-mail, the creation and sending of e-mail messages is basically the same for all types of e-mail packages: A text message is created, addressed to a recipient, and sent. The sender then waits for a return message or a return receipt for the sent message. Figure 33.1 shows the fundamentals of how a message is sent through e-mail.

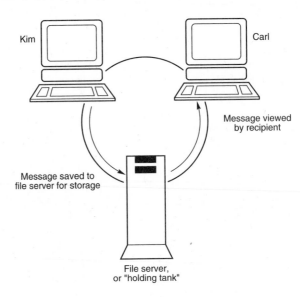

Figure 33.1
A message sent through e-mail.

Kim

Carl

Message viewed by recipient

Message saved to file server for storage

File server, or "holding tank"

Basic e-mail functions include the following:

- ✔ **Create.** Begins a new message.
- ✔ **Read.** Displays the message on-screen.
- ✔ **Send.** Sends the message to the addressed recipient.
- ✔ **Receive.** Accepts the message.
- ✔ **Store and forward.** Places the message in a mailbox and sends it to another user.
- ✔ **Reply to.** Specifies to whom a reply of an e-mail message should be sent.
- ✔ **Carbon copy.** Enables a message to be sent to users besides the addressed recipient.

The E-Mail Process

Most e-mail systems are set up so that messages are stored in a central location. This "holding tank" is the central location from which users send, receive, and retrieve messages. The holding tank often is a specific computer on a computer network that is dedicated to storing messages that are sent and received by network users.

Two types of computers are connected through a LAN: workstations and servers. *Workstations* are the computers through which you do most of your work and you send and receive messages, files, and programs over the network. A *server,* usually located in a separate area of the office, is the computer through which information is stored and transferred from one computer to another. The server contains the software that the workstations use to share information.

If you are using e-mail provided by one of the online services such as CompuServe, MCI Mail, AT&T EasyLink, GEnie, Prodigy, and America Online, you can dial up a central location where all the messages are stored. When users send and receive messages within an online service, the messages are stored in the same central location where they can access other information such as Dow Jones, weather, and group forum messages and logs. Usually, the online services hold messages in the central location for only a certain amount of time, unless otherwise specified by the user.

Users can download messages off the central holding tank onto their local machine's hard drive if they want to store a copy of the message. Users also can create messages on their local computer's hard disk and upload the file as a message onto the system. The user just has to know the necessary information to address the message appropriately.

Examining Microsoft Mail Setup

Microsoft Mail is set up so that the server controls user access to the mail system. The server software maintains data files and temporarily stores messages on the server's hard disk. This storage system is similar to post offices in which all mail is distributed and stored within private mailboxes. Each user on the network receives his own mailbox in which messages are stored. Both the mailbox and messages stored within it are protected by a password that only the individual users know.

The people in charge of distributing or controlling the post offices are the system administrators. These are the same people who install the Microsoft Mail server software, maintain the user lists, define the access to the mailboxes, and manage the server's hard disk.

System Requirements

Before you install Microsoft Mail into a server machine or on your network workstations, you should know the system requirements to run the software. You also need to take note that the server and workstations have different requirements. The following information outlines the system requirements needed for each particular machine.

File server requirements:

- ✔ 4.5 MB of disk space to run the Setup program and install the post office and the other administrative utilities

- ✔ An additional 6 MB is required to install both DOS and Windows clients on the server

Administrator's machine requirements:

- ✔ 640 KB memory

- ✔ One 5.25- or 3.5-inch drive

- ✔ DOS 3.1 or higher

- ✔ Windows 3.1 or higher depending on if you use the Move User utility, which moves users to another post office and deletes users from your post office

External mail functions:

- ✔ An AT-class computer with at least 350 KB of extended or expanded memory

- ✔ DOS 3.3 or higher

- ✔ A 2400–9600 baud modem that is compliant with the Hayes-compatible command set

Windows client machines:

- ✔ 2 MB of memory (4 MB recommended)

- ✔ 286-based or higher

- ✔ Windows 3.0 or higher

- ✔ Windows 3.1 or higher for use with the Move User utility

DOS client machines:

- ✔ 512 KB of memory

- ✔ DOS 3.1 or higher

Macintosh client stations:

- ✔ Macintosh Plus or better

- ✔ System 6.0.3 or higher

Presentation Manager stations:

- ✔ 386-based or above machine

- ✔ 4 MB of memory (8 MB recommended)

- ✔ Microsoft OS/2 version 1.3 or IBM OS/2 version 1.3

A typical setup using all these systems might look like figure 33.2.

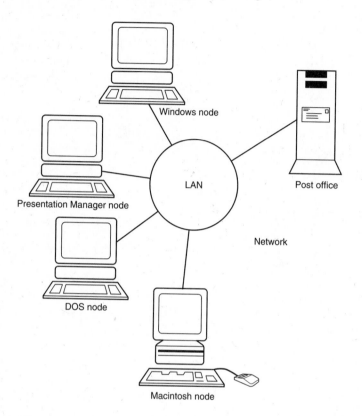

Figure 33.2
A typical single post office setup on a network.

Installation

The Microsoft Mail system is comprised of post office data files and server program files. The Setup program that comes with Microsoft Mail asks you for the name of the directory in which you want to place the data files, and the names of the directories in which you want to install the server and client programs.

The Setup program installs the DOS, Windows, and Presentation Manager client programs. Macintosh clients are installed separately.

When you install the Setup program, you need to connect to a network drive and provide names for the three directories in which you want to install the program's files and data files.

VI

Extending the Office Suite

If you install more than one post office on a single file server, you need to install Windows, Presentation Manager, and Macintosh clients only once. A DOS client, however, must be installed for each post office on a server.

When installing Microsoft Mail, you need to run the Setup program to initiate the process. You are asked where you want the post office, data files, and user information located. Next, provide a post office name and a network name, select the type of network operating system you are using, and choose the components of the Mail system you intend to use. You also are asked to select the client programs you want to install.

Using Mail on the Network

Administrator utilities are different from utilities with which users perform their mail functions. In order for a user to begin using Microsoft Mail, the administrator first must perform certain functions. These functions include connecting users to the mail system, granting access rights, ensuring adequate network resources, and setting up the system to use the network printers.

After the mail server program subdirectories and data file subdirectories are enabled for the users, you can connect the users to the mail system. Microsoft Mail provides two types of security options for its users: advanced and regular security options. If you decide to use the Mail system with advanced security, run the security program on the post office. The security program creates a MAIL.DAT file that automatically connects users to the data files and then hides the contents of the files.

After connecting each user's workstation to the Mail executable files directory, run the SECURITY.EXE program to hide the location of the data files' directory from the users.

Users do not have to enter a shared password to access the post office data files—the MAIL.DAT file is installed by the security program and automatically connects mail users to the post office data files.

Networks unable to use advanced security are those using domain and user-level security rather than share-level passwords on the post office. A network also is unable to use advanced security if it does not support DOS Interrupt 21 function 5F.

Connecting Mail Users

To connect users and grant them access to the mail system, you must run Mail's Net Admin program and create a group for all Mail users. You should assign this newly created group with read and execute permissions to the MAILEXE directory and all permissions to the MAILDATA directory. Then, add all the users who use mail to the group.

To connect a workstation to the mail system, type the following line:

```
net start workstation
```

For users to access the subdirectory that contains the mail system executables, type a line similar to the one that follows (your drive letter might differ):

```
net use d:\\dataserv\mailexe
```

This command gives the location of the drive, the server name, and the location of the directory in which the Mail executables are located.

Sharing printers follows a similar connection method. To share a printer with other network users, type a line similar to the following:

```
net share print 1=lpt1 (printer=device)
```

Table 33.1 lists some of the features that come with the administrator utilities.

Table 33.1
Administrative Capabilities of Microsoft Mail

General Features

Mailboxes can reside on local hard disks

Reads NetWare Bindery for addressing

Runs with NetBIOS networks

E-mail login separate from network login

Notifies user of incoming mail

User can disable notification

Message Configuration

Changes user passwords

Uses a default user profile

Deletes outdated mail

Manages system through dial-in remote

Using Microsoft Mail

Table 33.2 lists the features you can expect as a user of Microsoft Mail.

Table 33.2
Microsoft Mail User Features

Editing Functions

Can move blocks of text

Can import ASCII files

Includes graphics editor

Includes text editor

Includes spelling checker

Attaching Binary Files

Can view directory tree

Includes click-and-drag file attachments

Can save received attachments to disk

Can insert objects in message

Addressing and Organizing Mail

Can create and edit mailing lists

Can select files with cursor

Can assign priorities

Can store and sort received mail

Can create topic folders

Can search mail by date, sender, topic, text, or recipient

Includes optional programming rules

Can route messages sequentially

Message forms are available

When beginning to use Mail, users must type their mailbox name and password (see fig. 33.3). The mailbox name and initial password are provided by the mail administrator, but users can change their password at any time.

After you sign in to the post office, you see an Inbox screen similar to that shown in figure 33.4.

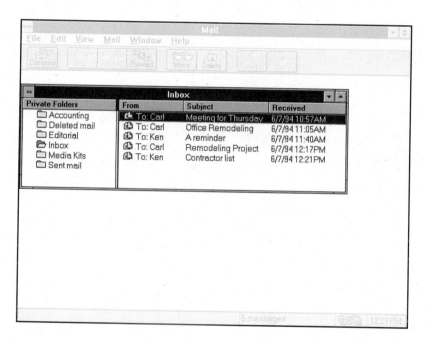

Figure 33.4
The Inbox screen.

The Inbox screen displays messages you have sent and received. It shows the mail message headers, who the mail is from, the subject of each message, the date and time of the mail sent, and whether the message has a priority indicator. You can change the order of the message listing or sort by date, subject, sender, or priority.

You can place the important messages in folders, an efficient way of storing messages according to subject, project, or department. Use the Log Files feature (accessed through the Mail menu) to store messages in folders placed on your workstation's hard disk.

Addressing

Microsoft Mail is set up so that you can form several types of address lists from a global address list provided by your system administrator. This global address list displays all the users in your post office, other post offices, and other mail systems your post office might have access to. You also get a post office address list containing names of users on your local post office and any other users your administrator has included. In addition, you can create a personal address list to include names of users to whom you frequently send messages. You also can create a personal group list when mailing to a group of users such as a department.

Composing a Message

To compose a message, click on the Compose button on the tool bar. This displays the Send Note form (see fig. 33.5), in which you fill out the appropriate information for sending a message.

Figure 33.5
The Send Note form.

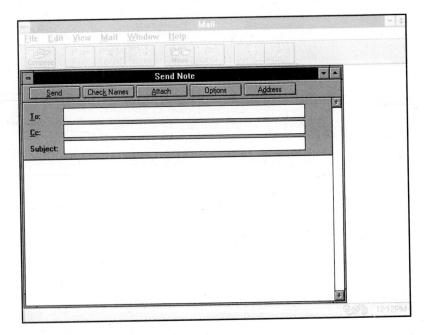

When you address your message, you can select users from address lists. Clicking on the Address button displays the Address dialog box, from which you can get a list of names of other mail users (see fig. 33.6).

For the message body, you can cut and paste text between messages and files. If you want to send formatted files, such as Word or Excel documents, you can send them as attached files. Choosing Attach in the Send Note form displays the Attach dialog box (see fig. 33.7), from

which you can attach an unlimited amount of files. The drives, directories, file types, and file names can be selected from the list boxes, and the file name also can be typed in the File Name edit box.

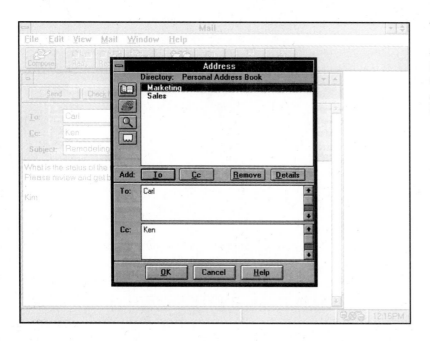

Figure 33.6
Addressing your message using address lists in the Address dialog box.

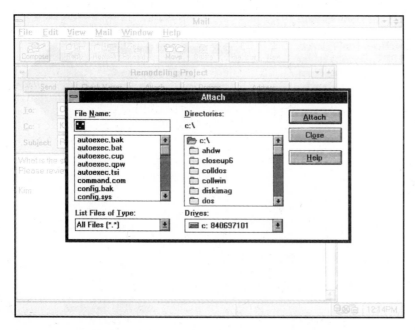

Figure 33.7
Attaching documents is a simple selection process.

Using Mail in Windows

Sending a message is a very simple task. Be aware, however, that the client software for DOS and Windows varies in the way you use Microsoft Mail send and receive functions as well as other standard mail functions. When sending mail using the Windows interface, you get a standard Mail screen with your Inbox overlaid on it. This main screen is where you compose, reply, move, delete, store, and transmit your messages. Most of the work can take place using individual icons representing particular mail actions, or you can use a menu bar to perform your functions.

When you finish composing a message, choose Send in the Send Note form to send the message. After the message is sent, it appears in the recipient's Inbox.

Viewing and Replying to a Message

To view a message, double-click on the new message, or press Tab to move the highlighted bar down the folders list to the message list. The arrow keys enable you to move around to the message you want to view.

When you choose to view a message, you see a screen similar to the one shown in figure 33.8.

Figure 33.8
Viewing the contents of a message.

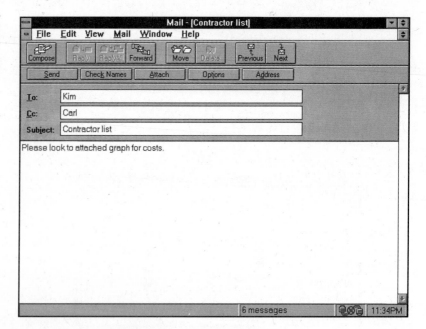

After you read a message, you can send a reply to that message. By choosing the Reply command, you automatically address the message to the person who originally sent it to you, and it automatically includes the original message in the body of your reply. Having the original message within the reply gives you the ability to add comments to different portions of the message.

Deleting Mail

Deleting mail provides you with a way to manage the number of messages in your Mail's Inbox. To delete a message, click on the Delete button or choose File, Delete. This moves the message into the wastebasket area. When you quit Mail, all messages in the wastebasket are deleted. You can change this option by choosing Mail, Options to turn off this feature.

Using Folders To Store Messages

Folders are a good place to store and organize your mail messages. You can create a folder by following these steps:

1. With the Folders list displayed, choose File, New Folder to display the New Folder dialog box (see fig. 33.9).

Figure 33.9
Using the New Folder dialog box to store a message.

2. In the Name box, type a name for the folder. A folder name can consist of any combination of characters and spaces; its length is restricted to eight characters.

3. In the Type group box, choose either Private or Shared, depending on whether you want to enable other users to access this folder.

4. To assign access permissions to a shared folder, choose Options and then select the permissions in the Other Users Can dialog box.

5. Click on OK.

The new folder is included in the Folders list in alphabetic order. If you want to rename a folder, perform the following steps:

1. Select the folder name you want to change.

2. Choose File, Folder Properties.

3. Type the new folder name, then click on OK.

You also can create subfolders within folders. To do this, perform the following steps:

1. Select from the New Folder dialog box, then click on the <u>O</u>ptions button.

2. In the <u>N</u>ame box, type a name for the subfolder.

3. Under Level, click on the Su<u>b</u>folder Of option button, select a folder, and then click on OK.

Note If a folder is selected in the folder list, any new folder you create is a subfolder of the selected folder.

Creating Message Templates

You can create your own message templates to help make messaging to certain people or groups more efficient. To do this, follow these steps:

1. Click on the Compose button in the main Mail window, or choose <u>M</u>ail, Compose <u>N</u>ote.

2. Address the message to the people you send it to regularly.

3. Type the subject and template information.

4. Close the message window by double-clicking on the Send Note window's close box or by pressing Ctrl+F4.

5. Mail asks if you want to save the message; click on the Yes button.

You now can save this message template to any of your mail folders.

To use a message template, perform the following steps:

1. Select the message that was saved as a template, and choose <u>M</u>ail, <u>F</u>orward. Drag the message header to the Outbox icon.

2. Fill in the message. If necessary, change the list of recipients.

3. Click on the <u>S</u>end button.

Tip You might find it convenient to store all your message templates in a single folder.

Working with Embedded Objects

Microsoft Mail enables you to embed an object into a message. To embed an object in a message, follow these steps:

1. Open the document containing the information you want to include in the message and copy the information to the Clipboard.

2. Switch to Mail.

3. Click on the Compose button, or choose <u>M</u>ail, Compose <u>N</u>ote.

4. Choose <u>E</u>dit, Paste <u>S</u>pecial.

5. In the Data <u>T</u>ype list, select the object format.

6. Click on the <u>P</u>aste button.

If you want to create and embed a new object within Microsoft Mail, follow these steps:

1. In the Send Note form, move the insertion point to the location where you want to insert the object.

2. Choose <u>E</u>dit, <u>I</u>nsert Object. This displays the Insert Object dialog box (see fig. 33.10), which lists the Windows-based applications that can create objects.

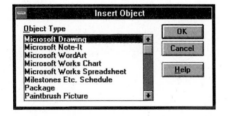

Figure 33.10
The Insert Object dialog box.

3. Select from the <u>O</u>bject Type list the application you want to use, and click on OK.

4. The application's window opens on top of the Mail window. Create the desired object.

5. From the application's <u>F</u>ile menu, choose Update, or close the application.

At this point, the object is inserted in your message.

If you embed an object into your message, you have the ability to modify it. Follow these steps to modify your message:

1. In the message body, double-click or select the object, and choose <u>E</u>dit, O<u>b</u>ject. The application used to create the object opens with the object ready for editing.

2. Edit the object as desired.

3. From the application's File menu, choose the Update command, or close the application. The object in your Mail message is updated to reflect the changes.

Working Offline

You might want to create new messages or work with messages you have received without being connected to the Mail server—when traveling or working at home, for instance. If you have Microsoft Mail workstation software loaded on your local computer, you can compose and work on messages without being connected to the Mail server. This method of mailing is called *offline mailing.*

Before working offline, you must have your message file on the computer or disk you are working with offline. If your message file is stored in your post office, you need to move it to the hard drive in your computer. Your personal address book is copied with the message file.

To move your message file to a computer or disk from your post office, follow these steps:

1. Sign in to Mail.

2. Choose Mail, Options.

3. Click on the Server button.

4. In the Storage box, select the Local option button. In the File box, type the path to the drive or directory in which you want to save your message file.

5. Click on OK.

When you have accomplished moving your message file to the computer you are working with offline, you are ready to begin.

1. Start Mail.

    If the computer is not connected to a Mail post office, a message appears asking if you want to work offline.

2. Click on OK. A dialog box appears, asking for your password.

3. Type your password, then click on OK.

4. If Mail cannot find your message file, you are requested to specify the path to it.

After you finish composing a message, click on the Send button. The message is moved to the Outbox. When you connect to the Mail system after working offline, the messages in your Outbox are automatically sent. When you connect to the Mail system after working offline, you can either leave your message file on your computer or move it back onto the post office.

Using the DOS Client

To begin the composing and mailing process using the DOS client, you must begin by choosing the Compose button in the main mail screen. From here, you can select the users to whom you want to address mail.

After you address the message, you are ready to give the message a subject header, designate the priority of the mail, attach any files you want to send, and type a message in the text box. As with the Windows user interface, you have the capability to edit your message. You can delete, move, and copy blocks. You also can insert text and files.

After you create a message, choose the Transmit command to send it.

Examining Other Features

Some interesting features within Microsoft Mail enable you to organize mail and retrieve mail messages more quickly. Some of these features include moving messages between folders and mailboxes, and a message-finder feature.

Moving messages between folders and subfolders helps you organize your projects efficiently. To move a message, click on the Move button in the main Mail window; the Move Message dialog box appears, as shown in figure 33.11.

Figure 33.11
Using the Move Message dialog box to move messages between folders.

If you are having trouble finding a message, you can use the Message Finder. Choosing File, Message Finder displays the Message Finder template, shown in figure 33.12. You can search by subject, name, recipients, or message text.

Figure 33.12
The Message
Finder template.

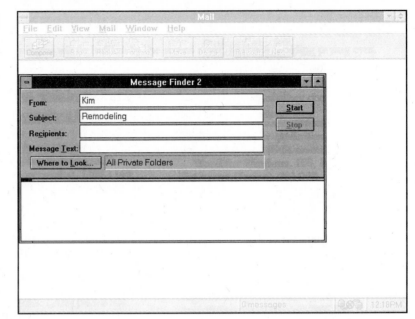

Exploring Add-On Products, Gateways, and Capabilities

Many products are available that work in conjunction with Microsoft Mail. You can use them to expand your network and communicate with remote mail system users and other e-mail systems. These products include the following:

- ✔ **Microsoft Mail Remote.** This enables remote users to connect to their post offices through a modem and regular telephone to access most of Microsoft Mail's features.

- ✔ **Microsoft Mail Gateway to IBM PROFS and OfficeVision.** This gateway provides integration between virtual memory users and Microsoft Mail users.

- ✔ **Microsoft Mail Gateway to MCI Mail.** This gateway connects Microsoft Mail users to MCI Mail, enabling Microsoft Mail users to send mail to MCI Mail and to use the services MCI Mail provides.

- ✔ **Microsoft Mail Gateway to AT&T Mail.** This gateway connects Microsoft Mail users to AT&T Mail, enabling Microsoft Mail users to send mail to AT&T Mail and to use the services AT&T Mail provides.

- ✔ **Microsoft Mail Gateway to X.400.** This gateway enables Mail users to exchange mail with other X.400-compatible systems. This gateway requires an X.25 card and an X.25 line.

✔ **Microsoft Mail SNADS Message Service.** SNADS Message Service enables Microsoft Mail users to interface with SNADS-based mail systems, including IBM's DISOSS. It enables users to send mail and attachments to IBM office hardware such as System 36, System 38, and AS/400.

✔ **Microsoft Mail Gateway to SMTP.** This gateway enables Mail users to exchange mail with SMTP mail systems.

✔ **Microsoft Mail Gateway to Fax and Microsoft Fax and Fax View.** This gateway enables Mail users to send and receive faxes while using the Mail program. Microsoft Fax creates fax image files of documents that you can send to fax users and other Mail users from a Windows application. Users can view, rotate, and scale fax images in Windows and DOS clients.

✔ **Microsoft Mail Gateway to MHS.** This gateway enables Microsoft Mail users to send mail to and receive mail from MHS-compatible systems.

✔ **Microsoft Mail Connection.** This program enables the exchange of mail and files between PC-based networks and Mail for AppleTalk Networks.

✔ **Microsoft Mail File Format API.** This enables you to write custom programs that deliver mail to and retrieve mail from Microsoft Mail post offices. The API interfaces Mail with other mail systems.

The following is a list of gateway and add-on options available for use with Microsoft Mail:

MHS

AT&T Mail

CompuServe

DEC All-in-One

DEC VMS Mail

IBM DISOSS

IBM PROFS

MCI Mail

Wang Mailway

X.400

Remote access module

To connect Microsoft Mail to other types of mail systems by gateways, perform the following steps:

1. Click on the Compose button in the main window, or choose<u>M</u> ail, Compose<u>N</u> ote.

VI

Extending the Office Suite

2. Click on the Address button, or choose Mail, Address Book.

3. Click on the Directory button or press Ctrl+L.

4. From the list of gateways, select the name of the mail system to which you are sending.

5. Click on OK.

6. Address the message.

If the name of the user to whom you are sending the message is in the address list, select it and click on the To or Cc buttons. If the name of the user is not in the list, click on the New Address button or press Ctrl+N to display the New dialog box.

The New dialog box contains the list of mail systems connected to your Microsoft Mail system through gateways. Select the mail system containing the person to whom you want to send mail. A special addressing window for that mail system is displayed. Type the user name and address of the recipient, and click on the To or Cc buttons.

7. Repeat step 6 for each recipient you want in that mail system.

8. Click on OK.

If you often send mail to a gateway recipient, you can add that user's name and gateway address to your personal address book. Then, instead of typing the user's address in the special addressing window, you can select the name from your list.

Chapter Snapshot

Setting up a new network is an important task, and one that needs to be carefully planned, with input from information systems departments, senior management, and most importantly, users. As more organizations move toward rightsizing their information system requirements and migrate more applications from the mainframe environment to LAN/WAN-based environments, the capabilities and performance of network applications will continue to improve.

In this chapter, you learn about the following:

You receive an overview of some of the different types of networking systems available, how you can configure them, and more importantly, why you can use them that way. If you are new to networks, the first part of this chapter will help you better understand some of the terminology, and how you can apply it. If you are a seasoned network user, you might find some topics in this chapter that touch on things you might not have tried in your office or your business that can make using a LAN more effective for you, your co-workers, and your customers.

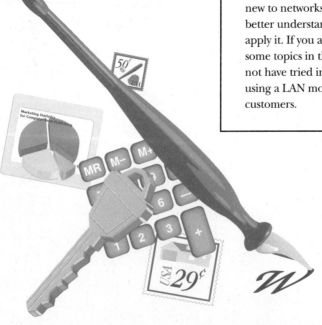

CHAPTER

Exploring Computer Networks

by Critch Greaves

Microsoft Office can turn an ordinary PC into a powerful information processing system. You can beef up that information processing system, however, by taking advantage of the capability of outputting to other computers and data systems. To do that, you use local area networks (LANs), wide area networks(WANs), and other data sharing configurations. The tools of Microsoft Office enable you to share and use information from other systems and applications.

Microsoft Mail is one such tool, and you find it on the Toolbar on each of the integrated packages. A one-user license of Mail is included with both the standard and professional versions of the Office bundle. Mail is a great way to enable communication among computers and users in a group. Part of this chapter discusses how you can use Mail in a network.

Choosing a Network Type

In the past, one of the main reasons for considering a LAN was so that users could share peripherals. With a network, for instance, you wouldn't have to buy a printer for each person in your office, or invest in new hard disk drives for each PC; networks enabled users to share those peripherals and hardware. Today, however, users have even more reasons for moving to a LAN. The LAN arena has boomed in size over the last few years, and every indication suggests that LANs will continue to be popular.

Part of the success of this aspect of the computing industry no doubt stems from the increased power of the PC, the improved applications that are available to solve business problems, and the desire to enhance learning and have fun. The falling prices for increasingly powerful microcomputers have also helped. The size of the machines continues to decrease, the power continues to grow, and even portables (laptops, notebooks, and subnotebooks) are doing things that, three years ago, many in the field thought wouldn't be achieved so soon.

Major companies looked to cut costs by downsizing and changing the way they handled information processing and overall efficiency. The downsizing trend turned to rightsizing. *Rightsizing* often means changing from roomfuls of mainframe computers and DASD to a few well-placed servers and PCs.

PCs are available everywhere. You can buy a PC from any one of thousands of sources—from mail order to retail stores, to large department stores or huge computer super-chains. The power of the applications is incredible, and the power that you can take advantage of when you begin to link computers together is unbelievable.

Not only are personal computers becoming easier to buy, they also are becoming easier to use. Software and operating system options available now offer more power on the worker's desktop than many large corporations had available to them regardless of what they were willing to pay only a few years ago.

Local Area Networks and Token Rings

LANs come in more shapes, sizes, and prices today than ever before. You can still buy the original network design, which has a file server and network cards so that each computer to be added to the network. There are a growing number of reasons for buying this type of design. This type of network is commonly referred to as a *client/server network*.

Applications and resources to be shared on the network are stored on the hard disk of the file server. *Clients* (workstation PCs) connect to the server through some type of cable attached to a network interface card. The file server typically has a faster, more powerful CPU than the client's, with a greater amount of RAM and hard disk space. Generally, file servers have fewer input and output requirements; keyboards, mice, trackballs, and high-resolution video are typically not found on file servers. The file server also has its own *network interface card*, attaching it to all of the PCs on the network. One popular network configuration is called Token Ring.

Token Ring networks earned that name because all of the devices are interconnected in a large circle or ring. The communication passed between stations and the server is handled by the passing of an electronic "token."

Ethernet

Another popular configuration (or topology, as the industry refers to them), is Ethernet. Different types of cables are associated with Ethernet networks, ranging in size from standard telephone wire (twisted pair), to heavy, expensive coaxial cables (thick Ethernet), or to less expensive, thinner coaxial cables—similar to the type cable TV uses (thin Ethernet or thinnet). *Ethernet* networks operate off a "backbone" of cable that has workstation PCs connected to it by a T-connector.

In the client/server networking model, the many different configuration options can help organizations achieve the most efficient use of resources—resources such as computer equipment and, more importantly, the users who have many skill levels. Multi-server networks that distribute workloads on numerous processors are becoming more common, especially for larger, more demanding network applications (such as large, corporate database work, Computer Aided Design, and Document Imaging).

Peer-to-Peer Design

Peer-to-peer design is another network model that is becoming a giant in the computing world. *Peer-to-peer designs* do not use typical servers to accomplish their sharing duties; they share resources from one PC to another—as opposed to using dedicated machines for specific tasks. A few years ago, a typical small office that wanted to attach five computers to a laser printer had to spend a great deal of money and invest time to interconnect the machines. Today, with software packages such as Windows for Workgroups, you can purchase all the hardware and software needed to interconnect and install PCs yourself—saving both money and time.

For the original reasons that networks were a good idea, workgroup computing in the peer-to-peer design model makes a lot of sense. Initial investment costs are low, installation and hook up is much easier. Plus, you still reap the benefits of sharing printers and disk space.

Setting Up a Client/Server Network

Setting up a client server network is much easier to do today than it was a few years ago. If we compare the setup times for the network operating software required for version 2.15 versus version 3.12, the newer version is much faster. The newer version also offers many more powerful options and capabilities. That is why such a large number of support technicians and Certified Novell Engineers (CNEs) are needed; along with the increased power and flexibility comes a whole new set of potentially complicated problems to fix.

After a computer has been chosen to act as server for the client/server network, it must have network operating software installed. A *dedicated file server*, as earlier noted, is a machine that houses the network operating software and many of the software applications that users will be running on the network. Setting up a NetWare server in version 2.15 required running a program called NETGEN—a complex, and time-consuming task. One of the biggest drawbacks to earlier versions of NetWare was that if you wanted to upgrade a portion of your server (such as the network interface card, RAM, or hard disk), you had to "RE-GEN" the whole thing.

With current versions of NetWare, this situation is no longer the case. You can upgrade quickly and easily, and the process involves modular software called *NetWare Loadable Modules* or *NLMs*. NLMs enable users' systems to grow as the users' needs grow, without having to stop and re-create everything.

Current versions of NetWare have new, powerful features that can be complicated to set up—depending on what you need to accomplish—but the software is now more menu-driven and much easier and faster to accommodate.

At the workstation level, configuration issues have not changed much. The first thing you need to do is install and configure a network interface card that can "live in harmony" with other interface cards (such as CD-ROM cards, modems, scanner interfaces, SCSI cards, and so on) that might already be in the PC. Network cards are getting easier to use, too. Not long ago, cards had numerous cryptic jumper settings for hardware interrupts and IO addresses, and after you got the hardware even to boot the PC, the software for the workstation had to be generated before the PC could connect to the network.

IPX and NETX Protocol Setup

Two packages, IPX and NETX, are needed to attach the workstation to the file server. IPX and NETX are two of the more common protocols in use; however, there are numerous others. IPX handles the *internetwork packet exchange*—the basic passing of information between PC and server. The "x" in NETX is a number that corresponds to the version of MS-DOS that your PC uses—version 4 of DOS would use NET4. To find the server, IPX needs to know what the hardware settings of the interface card are; without the proper settings, your PC will not find the server. After the settings are correct and IPX loads without error, you can then load NETX. Loading NETX establishes the connection with the server, as long as the cabling is installed correctly.

After that is all taken care of, you can log in to the network drive. Some of those things are still the same today, except the newer network cards are software controlled—eliminating the jumper settings and generation of workstation shell software programs such as Intel Etherexpress.

The Intel Etherexpress 16 network cards can be installed in an open slot of a PC and configured entirely from the software. A program called SOFTSET will even evaluate your system setup, recommend the appropriate interrupt and IO settings, and then update the card's EPROM Chip for you. This type of network card setup has made configuring all types of networks much easier.

The Peer-to-Peer Design Setup

The peer-to-peer design setup is drastically different. In a typical Windows for Workgroups setup, one of the toughest decisions to make is which package to buy to get the best software licenses. The software is available as an upgrade to Windows 3.1, or to complement Windows 3.1 with Workgroups together, with or without hardware. Similar packaging can make picking up a few boxes a time-consuming process.

In general, however, setting up a Windows for Workgroups network is quite simple. The first step, installing the network card, was described earlier. Microsoft has bundled Windows for Workgroups with the Intel cards because of their easy set-up and high reliability. After the network card is installed in a slot and SOFTSET has been run, you are ready to install the networking software.

The setup procedure for Windows for Workgroups is almost identical to a normal Windows setup. Use the following steps:

1. Put Disk 1 in drive A (or B).

2. Type **SETUP** at the A: or B: prompt.

    Unless your system came preconfigured with Windows or other bundled software, the initial setup screens are identical to the Windows setup screens that most of you are probably familiar with.

3. The screens change from the normal windows setup when the setup software asks you about network setup. The software detects the network card automatically, but it does ask for basic information about how you want to configure your network. Windows makes the necessary changes to your AUTOEXEC.BAT and CONFIG.SYS.

4. Next, you must define a workgroup, give your computer a name so the network will know how to find it, and give yourself a login ID and password. For small networks, there will likely be only one workgroup, and the PC names can be user names or locations such as FRONT_DESK or SERVICE.

5. The rest of the configuration in Windows for Workgroups is all mouse driven, using familiar, control panel functions. Print Sharing is done through the Printers Icon in the control panel. You can enable sharing—and re-sharing at startup for the machine that has the printer should be checked—so that each time that PC loads windows, the other PCs on the network can use the printer.

After the network has been configured, hard disks (as well as floppy drives) can be shared. Disk sharing is all controlled with the File Manager. To share a directory, do the following:

1. Click on the folder that represents the directory to which you want to grant access.

2. From the **D**isk menu, choose Share As.

File Manager assigns to the Shared directory the drive letter of the next available drive after your last hard drive or CD-ROM.

Note You can grant read-only or full-usage rights, with a password or without, to each of the users on the network. You can assign various levels of security.

Figure 34.1 shows what the screen looks like in File Manager.

Figure 34.1
File Manager's
Share As setup
screen.

After the network has been configured, hard disks (as well as floppy drives) can be shared.

Connecting from a Workstation PC

Connecting to a network drive from a workstation PC is just as easy. In the **D**isk menu of the File Manager, select Connect **N**etwork drive. The Connect Network Drive dialog box shows the PCs available on the network, organized by workgroup (see fig. 34.2). If your network has multiple workgroups—such as sales and service—you can connect to the one to which you have been granted rights.

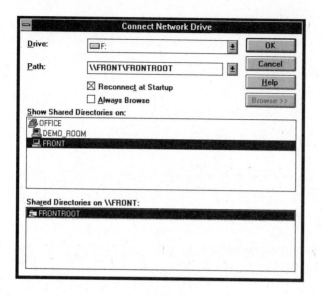

Figure 34.2
The Connect Network Drive dialog box.

Portable Connections

Through the use of parallel port network adapters, you can connect notebooks and laptop computers to client/server and peer-to-peer networks. Network adapters plug into the parallel port and have a place for the standard network cable to attach. The adapters usually have an AC adapter, but some interfaces can run on battery power. Portables that have docking stations can use regular interface cards.

Many types of network operating systems are available now, such as Novell, Windows for Workgroups, LANtastic, Banyan VINES, LAN Manager, OS/2—the list goes on. With any computer decision, trade-offs are inevitable. The client/server system does some things better and faster than peer-to-peer network, but the client/server system also costs more. Peer-to-peer systems also work well, but they are not as fast or powerful as client/server network systems.

Designing and planning a network is a task that should be well planned. Deciding on what type of system you need, the type of cabling you will need, and the applications you need to purchase—along with considerations of the network operating system and client's PCs—is no small undertaking.

Prior to investing in a LAN, you should talk with friends, associates, and vendors who are experienced with networks and who have an idea of the questions you should ask when buying a system.

Originally, network setup was a very time-consuming, technically oriented process that required specialized technicians and installation companies. Today's power networks are configurational works of art that would send the nontechnical computer user to a high frustration level, but the smaller networks are easily configured and implemented by the less experienced user.

Combination Client/Server and Peer-to-Peer Networks

Many organizations are finding that a combination of the two types of networks is the best way to move ahead in the information age. The advantage of a client/server network is that it distributes the processing load across the network so that everyone can work on it. The advantage of a peer-to-peer or workgroup network is that it keeps the network traffic concentrated to the group that will tackle it.

Combined, the two create a powerful, very efficient, network. You can run applications from the server and share them among users in a group, and all the peripherals can still be used by those who need them. This is truly the best of both worlds.

Microsoft Office can help you take advantage of the best of these two networking designs. In any configuration, whether it be client/server, peer-to-peer (or both), Office has tools that can make networking a success above and beyond just peripheral sharing.

In Excel, for example, you can create a worksheet with sales figures for a local office and, by clicking on the Microsoft Mail button on the Toolbar, send the results of your worksheet to someone else on the network (see fig. 34.3). That process is quite simple, as shown in the following steps:

1. Select Send Worksheet from the File menu. This action launches Microsoft Mail and creates a document to be sent.

2. The Excel Icon, with the file name, is embedded in the e-mail message.

3. The recipient, after reading the note, can double-click on the icon (launching Excel), make her own copy of the worksheet into memory, and use the numbers for whatever she needs.

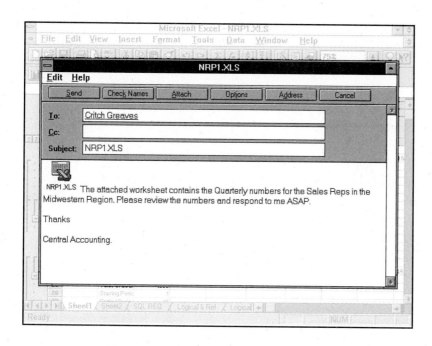

Figure 34.3
The main screen
with the worksheet
icon.

VI

Extending the Office Suite

Excel can also add a routing slip to the worksheet if you need to send it to more than one person. The *routing slip* sends—without printing or mailing—the document to those other people who might need to use the information.

The current version of Windows for Workgroups, version 3.11, also enables users to share fax resources in conjunction with Mail. Users can send their reports via fax to users who are not directly on the network, or who might be out of the office.

Another way Excel can help users take advantage of networks is through the use of MS-Query. *Query* can extract information from a wide variety of network data sources such as SQL Server, a high-end database engine. Using Excel, users can attach to the SQL Server, perform a query, return the data to Excel via DDE or a clipboard copy, and the information can then be used or distributed as needed.

Linking Methods

All the Office packages can take advantage of object linking and embedding (OLE) or Dynamic Data Exchange (DDE). Linking and embedding and dynamic links are both very effective tools to use in the network environment, but deciding which one to use can make a difference to the end user.

Object Linking and Embedding

Suppose that you have a document that you can use on other computers while, at the same time, you do not have access to the source files. Here, object linking and embedding (OLE) would be best. If you do this, all applications used to create the source document must be present on the computer that receives the document.

If you want to transfer from another application to a workbook data extracted from a server that is not always available, you should also use embedding. All the information will be in the embedded object.

If you need to incorporate a large video or sound file, you should create a link to the source file. That way, Excel or the receiving application only stores the link, not the entire source.

If you need to maintain the source data in its original state, linking is better. This way, the source will update the worksheet when it is updated.

Administering Networks

After you have determined the things you want your network to accomplish, it is important to keep the system running, and, more importantly, running smoothly.

Companies and organizations that have large networks installed typically have network administrators on staff to handle the day-to-day training, support, configuration, and problems that arise. Networks might seem easy and trouble-free, but anytime there are multiple users and multiple tasks occurring on a computer system, the unexpected is bound to happen.

The following sections cover helpful guidelines that network users follow.

Backup

The first and probably most important issue regarding networks is backup. It has been said (by the very wise) that you should only not back up that which you can afford to lose—and how many things can you really afford to lose? Because applications and data are often the backbone or core of a business, you should back up everything—often.

Establishing a regular backup routine and sticking to it is always a good idea, and the easier and more automatic the backup becomes, the better. This applies to stand-alone systems, also, but the importance increases exponentially for networks where larger amounts of data affect a wider range of people.

Backup can take place during off-hours, scheduled during times of low/zero activity, and depending on the applications, completely unaffects the users.

Relying on users to back up critical information is typically frowned upon. Users get busy or forget to back up their data, and before you know it, an important chunk of data is missing or

corrupted. The network administrator's full-time task is to make certain that backups are completed, reliable, and complete.

To make the task simpler, several great software packages are available to help you make backups.

Tape has been popular for some time. Because one tape can hold hundreds (or thousands) of megabytes of data, backups can be performed at night, during off hours, unattended. Today's Digital Audio Tapes (DAT) hold multiple gigabytes of data on inexpensive, reliable tapes. Smaller quarter-inch tapes (QIC) hold significantly less data, but—depending on the size of the network—such tapes can represent the best value for your operation.

Application Installation

Another important segment of what is important in network administration is application installation and customization. If a user on a network installs a software package that modifies the configuration files (AUTOEXEC.BAT or CONFIG.SYS), hardware interrupts, or other functions, be careful to avoid the negative repercussions this can have on network applications.

Computer viruses are a problem that can drastically affect entire networks, as well as individual PCs. If a user installs a program on their workstation from a disk infected with a virus, there is the potential to ruin an incredible amount of work. For this reason, the network administrator should always be informed if any application is to be installed on any workstation.

 Avoid unlicensed and unauthorized software. As well as endangering a network with the exposure to viruses, conflicts, and corruption of existing files, the use of unlicensed or unauthorized software poses serious legal problems to a company.

In short, the importance of the information and the number of people relying on that data will proportionally affect the need for network administration and standard policies regarding the use and operation of the system.

Hardware Installation

Because adding a new product, such as a CD-ROM drive, can present interrupt conflicts, the addition of new hardware is critical to the day-to-day operation and schedule of the network administrator. Simple upgrades such as memory or hard disks can present new challenges that should always be carefully planned and implemented.

Communication with the network administrator or network manager is the best way to avoid problems. When in doubt, ask. There truly are no dumb questions. Most administrators would prefer to be asked a simple question rather than being faced with restoring a corporate database.

Windows for Workgroups

In the peer-to-peer world, the addition of Windows for Workgroups has made a big splash. This product is easy to install and expand. As noted earlier, installation is usually straightforward, and there are adjustments that you can make to individual systems that can make a big difference to encourage efficiency within the system.

It is always a good idea when running Windows to add as much memory as you can. Windows for Workgroups is no exception. In fact, Windows for Workgroups slows significantly on a machine with only 4M of RAM. Some applications really need the extra memory, and because of Windows for Workgroups's network background, the extra system memory is a great benefit.

When installing Windows for Workgroups, you should check your swapfile sizes. Adjusting them can improve system performance. Under Windows 3.1, multitasking uses a large amount of system resources. Adding workgroups (plus the sharing of peripheral hardware) adds strain to CPU time. If you notice a slow down in performance, RAM, or swapfile size, WIN.INI/ SYSTEM.INI tweaks can help.

The Windows for Workgroups Resource kit (available from many software houses for about $30) is money well spent. The kit includes an extensive manual that explains many of the settings in the INI files. Also included are some utility applications that you might find invaluable. Resource monitoring becomes easier, and the settings that previously seemed "all Greek" might begin to make more sense.

Cabling and Windows for Workgroups

The cabling that comes with Windows for Workgroups is standard thin Ethernet or thinnet coaxial cable. If you have not set up a network and are getting into Windows for Workgroups for the first time, the hardware kits you can get have most of what you need to get started.

The kits come with the Windows for Workgroups software, the Network interface card, a T-adapter and cable. The only things that are missing for first time setups are terminators for use at the ends of cable runs.

In Ethernet configurations, the backbone of cable that each PC is connected to must be terminated at both ends of the cable run. The terminators tell the signals being sent across the network that there are no more workstations to "poll" for information. One end of the termination should be connected to a ground. Terminators should be available at your local computer vendor. They are very inexpensive and simply plug into the T-connectors at the end of your cable runs.

Chapter Snapshot

With Microsoft Office Professional, you have one of the most powerful collections of application programs available for your Windows-based PC. However, Office doesn't do everything! In this chapter, you learn about various Office add-ons of the following categories:

The products discussed in this chapter are worthy add-ons to your Windows-based PC that will extend its usefulness. Some of the programs discussed here are commercial, while a couple are shareware.

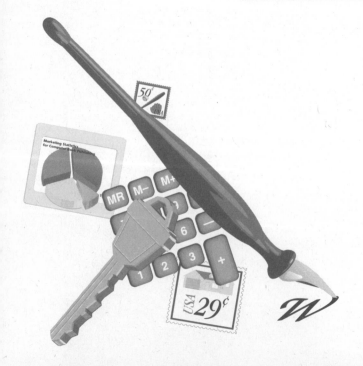

35

CHAPTER

Worthy Office Add-Ons

by Bruce Hallberg and Michael Groh

Y ou have a virtually unlimited number of choices for application software to use with your computer. Because you are reading this book, it is safe to say that you have chosen Microsoft Office to serve your main needs. However, your software needs will not end with word processing, spreadsheets, and database capabilities. To round out your computer, you'll probably also want some other programs.

This chapter discusses some favorite add-ons for Windows and for Microsoft Office. Whether your needs be related to graphics, utilities, home finance, or a desire to enhance the Windows environment, these application programs are worthy add-ons to your Microsoft Office–based computer system.

New Riders Publishing verified most of the ordering information presented. Whenever possible, phone numbers, addresses, and retail prices were verified by calling the vendors mentioned in this chapter. We apologize for any errors or omissions, but we cannot guarantee these products will be available at the suggested retail prices printed here.

Desktop Managers

If there is one thing that most Windows users agree about, it is that the Windows Program Manager and File Manager really do not stack up to more advanced user interfaces, such as those you might see on the Macintosh or with OS/2. Fortunately, there are a couple of third-party desktop managers that present to you a friendlier, more powerful Windows interface than Program Manager.

Norton Desktop for Windows

Current Version: 3.0

Symantec Corporation
10201 Torre Ave.
Cupertino, CA 95014-2132

(800) 441-7234; (408) 253-9600
FAX: (408) 252-4696
Tech support: (415) 892-1424

Suggested Retail: $179
Available through retail software stores

Norton Desktop for Windows (now in version 3) was the first comprehensive desktop manager for the Windows environment. With the Norton Desktop, you can add a host of capabilities that Microsoft does not include with Windows, and also make the desktop a more powerful tool to organize and accomplish your work. The current version includes many useful features.

✔ Enhanced backup program, including support for many tape drives

✔ UnErase, to recover files that you have accidentally deleted

✔ Disk Doctor, which diagnoses and repairs problems on your hard and floppy disks

✔ Integrated file and program management on the desktop

✔ Day Planner, a personal information organizer that helps you manage your schedule and information

✔ An integrated screen saver

✔ FileAssist, which enhances the Open and Save dialog boxes for your other Windows applications

If you want to enhance the function and usability of the Windows user interface, you really can't go wrong with Norton Desktop for Windows.

PCTools for Windows

Current Version: 2.0

Central Point Software
15220 N.W. Greenbrier Pkwy., Ste. 150
Beaverton, OR 97006

(800) 846-5903; (503) 690-8088
Direct sales: (800) 445-4208
FAX: (503) 690-8083
Tech support: (503) 690-8080

Suggested Retail: $179.95
Available through retail software stores or directly from Central Point Software

A worthy competitor to Norton Desktop for Windows is PCTools for Windows, published by Central Point Software. In certain ways, PCTools for Windows is superior to Norton Desktop. It includes features such as the following:

- ✔ An excellent file manager

- ✔ Support for multiple desktops

- ✔ Macro and scripting utilities

- ✔ Enhanced backup program

- ✔ Disk defragmenter

- ✔ Disk repair program

In head-to-head shoot-outs with Norton Desktop for Windows, PCTools for Windows has won more often than it has lost. However, both programs are extremely usable and provide very similar improvements to the Windows environment.

Calendars and Schedulers

Among the most useful Windows applications are planners and scheduling programs. You will find these applications invaluable for keeping track of to-do lists, appointments, birthdays, and other important events. All the calendars and schedulers described in this section include alarms that alert you to impending tasks during the day, as well as perpetual calendars that enable you to schedule events years in advance.

OnTime for Windows

Current Version: 1.5

Campbell Services, Inc.
21700 Northwestern Highway, 10th Floor
Southfield, MI 48075

(800) 345-6747; (810) 559-5955
FAX: (810) 559-1034

OnTime for Windows is a powerful calendar and scheduler that features the following:

- ✔ Lifetime calendar

- ✔ Day planner

- ✔ Scheduler with one-minute resolution throughout the day

- ✔ Week- and month-views of schedules

- ✔ Powerful to-do list manager

OnTime manages your schedule on a daily, weekly, and/or monthly basis. Events are tracked down to the minute (if necessary), and multiple alarms can be set. Schedules can be printed in 8 1/2" × 11", 5 1/2" × 8 1/2", and 3 3/4" × 6 3/4" sizes to fit business organizers like the Franklin Day Planner, Day-Timer, and Day Runner. OnTime also features import/export capabilities that enable you to save your schedule and calendar information as ASCII files and Calendar Creator Plus (a popular calendar program from SoftKey International: (800) 323-8088) format. You even can send your OnTime calendar to popular personal digital assistants such as the Casio Palmtop, Sharp Wizard, and HP 95LX and 100LX.

The Daily Planner and Calendar Publisher (*Far Side* edition)

Current Version: 3.0

Delrina Corporation
895 Don Mills Rd., 500-2 Park Centre
Toronto, ON, CD M3C 1W3

(800) 268-6082; (416) 441-3676
Direct sales: (800) 879-5075
FAX: (416) 441-0333

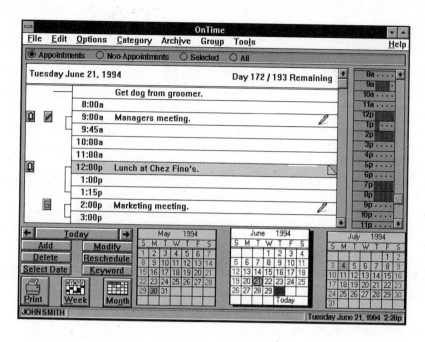

Figure 35.1
OnTime for
Windows works as
a stand-alone
application or on
a network.

VI

Extending the Office Suite

The Delrina Daily Planner gives you five different views of your schedule: day, week, month, year, and as to-do lists. The tabbed notebook design of the Daily Planner enables you to go quickly to the view of the schedule that you want to use. An easy-to-use address card file saves all your important names, addresses, and phone numbers. The Daily Planner is able to import and export ASCII files created with other applications such as FileMaker Pro (a database produced by Claris Corporation: (800) 544-8554) and Lotus Organizer (a personal information manager by Lotus Development Corporation: (800)635-6887). The Daily Planner also prints calendars and schedules in formats that fit the Day-Timer, Day Runner, and the Franklin Planner organizers.

An added feature of Delrina's Daily Planner are the theme packs that can be added to the planner. Figure 35.2 shows the *Far Side* (by Gary Larson) version of the Daily Planner.

SideKick for Windows

Current Version: None assigned

Borland International
100 Borland Way
Scotts Valley, CA 95066-3249

(800) 682-9299; (408) 431-1000
Direct sales: (800) 331-0877
FAX: (408) 439-9262

Retail: $29.95
Sidekick for Windows is available in software stores or directly from Borland

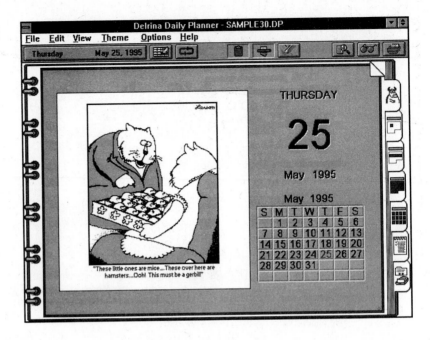

Figure 35.2
The *Far Side* Daily Planner.

Years ago Sidekick was a very popular DOS application. Sidekick for DOS featured a simple calendar, notepad, calculator, and several other functions. It has taken a while for Borland to come up with a Windows version, but the new Sidekick for Windows (see fig. 35.3) is worth the wait. Introduced in the summer of '94, Sidekick boasts a powerful calendar and scheduler, as well as a versatile to-do list, cardfile, and notepad. There are multiple settable alarms, a phone dialer, a calculator, and separate to-do lists for business and personal use. There even is a launch bar that enables you to return instantly to any other Windows application you may have open.

Sidekick directly imports and exports its data in dBASE, Paradox, or Windows cardfile formats without using intermediate ASCII files (you can import or export ASCII files if you want, however). Sidekick tracks the notes you have written and provides a drag-and-drop feature that enables you to drag the data on a person's card to the note for easy addressing. Sidekick even uses drag-and-drop for the phone dialer function.

Graphics Programs

If you are like most people, you probably don't often use graphics programs. However, when you do need them for some task (such as drawing a map to your home for a party, designing how a room will be laid out, or generating an organization chart), you *really* need them! In this section, you will find out about several good programs for Windows that can provide you with all the graphics tools you might ever need. These programs can be used alone or integrated with Microsoft Office through the magic of cut-and-paste and OLE.

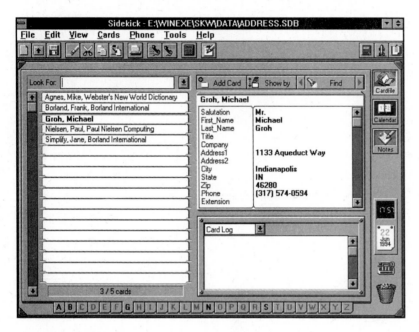

Figure 35.3
Sidekick for Windows from Borland International.

Visio

Current Version: 2.0

Shapeware Corp.
1601 5th Ave., Ste. 800
Seattle, WA 98101-1625

(800) 446-3335; (206) 467-6723
FAX: (206) 467-7227

Suggested Retail: $299
Available through retail software stores or directly from Shapeware

Visio represents a new type of drawing program for Windows. It enables even the artistically challenged to create professional-looking drawings and charts. Visio is based on the idea of drawing with *stencils*, which are predefined shapes that you simply drag onto the drawing area and modify as you like—much like the stencils that you used in kindergarten to learn to print the letters of the alphabet. Visio includes features that make using the stencils a snap. For instance, if you have lines connecting your shapes, and you resize or move a shape, the lines stay intact. You can use Visio to generate, among other things, drawings such as the following:

- ✔ Organization charts
- ✔ Flow charts
- ✔ Room layouts
- ✔ Project timelines
- ✔ Network diagrams

Visio, shown in figure 35.4, is OLE 2.0 compliant, so you can use the OLE 2.0 features in Office to integrate the shapes you draw from Visio. Visio also includes basic drawing tools, aside from the predefined templates, that help you create exactly the drawings that you like.

CorelDRAW! For Windows

Current Version: 5.0

Corel Corp.
1600 Carling Avenue
The Corel Building
Ottawa, ON, CD K1Z 8R7

(800) 77-COREL; (613) 728-8200
Direct sales: (800) 836-3729
FAX: (613) 728-9790

Suggested Retail: $575 (on CD-ROM), $745 (on 3.5" HD floppies)
Available through retail software stores or directly from Corel Corporation

Another graphics add-on for your Windows machine is CorelDRAW! (see fig. 35.5), which is a more traditional drawing program than Visio. CorelDRAW! really shines when you consider all the value it includes in its modest price:

- ✔ CorelDRAW!, a sophisticated drawing program
- ✔ CorelCHART!, used for creating business charts
- ✔ CorelPHOTO-PAINT!, used for modifying photo images
- ✔ CorelSHOW!, used to create on-screen slide shows
- ✔ CorelMOVE!, used to create multimedia presentations
- ✔ 250 additional fonts (on the CD, which is included)
- ✔ 14,000 clip art images (also on the CD)

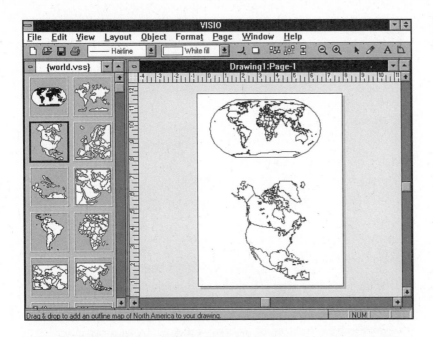

Figure 35.4
Visio.

Figure 35.5
CorelDRAW!

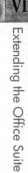

Paint Shop Pro

Current Version: 2.01

JASC, Inc.
10901 Red Circle Dr., Ste. 340
Minnetonka, MN 55343

(612) 930-9171
FAX: (612) 930-9172

Retail: $69
Available directly from JASC or in many retail software stores

Paint Shop Pro is a graphics program that enables you to work with multiple graphics images at a time (see fig. 35.6). With the tools provided in Paint Shop Pro you can display, convert, alter, scan, and print images. You can adjust the brightness or contrast of an image, for instance, or reduce the number of colors in a scanned image. In addition, you can capture screens with Paint Shop Pro and use the screen images in other applications.

Figure 35.6
Paint Shop Pro features a multiple document interface.

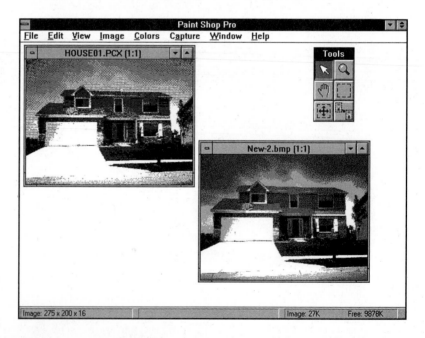

Paint Shop Pro supports all popular image formats: PCX, TIFF, BMP, JPG, WMF, MSP, PCD (Kodak Photo CD), JIF, GIF, IMG, and many others. Paint Shop Pro freely converts images from one format to another, and even functions as an OLE server in integration schemes.

Many of the figures in *Inside Microsoft Office* were processed with Paint Shop Pro.

Image Pro, a software bundle that includes both Paint Shop Pro and Image Commander (discussed next), is available for $99 from JASC.

Image Commander

Current Version: 1.0

JASC, Inc.
10901 Red Circle Dr., Ste. 340
Minnetonka, MN 55343

(612) 930-9171
FAX: (612) 930-9172

Suggested Retail: $39
Image Commander is available as shareware on most bulletin boards or
directly from JASC

Image Commander is a program that enables you to view, convert, and manage different graphics files on your computer. It supports most graphics file formats (such as GIF, JPG, PCX, and so on). You can use it to manage multiple images. See figure 35.7, for example, which shows the thumbnail images for a number of screen pictures. Each image can have attached comments or keywords, and you can search for these comments or keywords in your graphics library, which can contain many different images. If you work with graphics images on your computer frequently, Image Commander is a very useful utility to own.

Home Finance

A nice category of tools to use with your PC is the personal finance tools. These tools help you manage your checkbook, credit cards, investments, and budget. You can automate routine bill-paying and, with checks created for your printer, you even can print out all the checks you create every month. Many of these programs also integrate with tax preparation software, automatically moving your financial data into the tax preparation program to make filing your taxes a breeze.

Using these programs does require a certain amount of discipline because you do have to regularly update your computer files with the activity in your checkbook, and new habits might be required. However, if you can make the effort to fully utilize these programs, they can help you keep better control over your finances and, more importantly, let you know more about your finances.

VI

Extending the Office Suite

Figure 35.7
Image Commander from JASC, Inc.

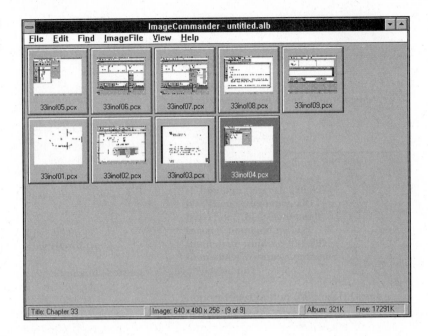

Quicken for Windows

Current Version: 4

Intuit Corporation
66 Willow Place
Menlo Park, CA 94025

(415) 322-0573
Direct sales: (800) 624-8742
FAX: (415) 329-3689
Tech support: (415) 858-6010

Suggested Retail: $69.95
Available through retail software stores or directly from Intuit Corporation

The preeminent home finance program for Windows is Quicken for Windows. It is the most comprehensive home finance software available for Windows, due to features such as the following:

✔ Financial Calendar, which automatically updates your register with regular payments and shows you when money comes in and when it goes out

✔ QuickReports, which reports on a variety of different things about your financial activity—everything from transaction lists, to asset lists, personal balance sheets, and more

✔ Investment management, which tracks your stocks, bonds, and other investments and assets

✔ Graphs that can show you at a glance where you stand financially

✔ Budget management, including multiple budgets

✔ Loan amortization and calculation

✔ Credit card management

Quicken for Windows also can use the Windows Clipboard to move detailed data from Quicken into Excel, where you can use Excel's capabilities to perform tasks that may not be built into Quicken. If you are interested in managing your personal finances on your computer, look no further than Quicken for Windows.

Entertainment

To completely round out any home system (or business system if you don't tell the boss), you probably will want some entertaining software for your Windows-based PC. This section discusses a couple of different choices available to you, although there are hundreds of excellent choices available.

Screen Savers

One of the most popular software categories in recent years (at least in terms of sales) has been software programs called *screen savers*. After your computer has been inactive for a preset period of time, these programs automatically replace the work on your screen with moving images of such things as flashlights, fish, fireworks, and even flying toasters! When you return to your computer, simply move the mouse or press a key to make the images vanish and return to your work.

Screen savers started because earlier PC monitors were subject to a phenomenon known as *screen burn,* wherein images that were left on the screen for a long period of time would eventually become a permanent feature of the screen, and were said to be *burned in.* In fact, if you work in a company with older computers around, you often can see machines that, even when off, show parts of Lotus 1-2-3 or the company's e-mail program on their monitors. Screen savers prevent screen burn by not allowing an image to stay idle on the screen for a long period of time.

Interestingly enough, in the past several years monitors have improved to the point where even relatively inexpensive monitors are proofed against screen burn, even when displaying the same image for hours at a time. At the same time that monitors improved, screen savers took off on the sales charts! In fact, Windows itself has a rudimentary screen saver built into it.

Still, aside from the non-issue (for most people, anyway) of screen burn, screen savers can be useful from two perspectives. First, confidential information left on your screen when you leave for a few minutes will be hidden by the screen saver, passively avoiding prying eyes. Second, many of the screen savers now available have high entertainment value. You can now buy screen savers that generate whatever suits your fancy, from images from Star Trek, to cartoons drawn by *Outland* artist Berke Breathed, to any of a host of other choices. Screen savers generally cost about $50 and are available at any software store.

Microsoft Arcade

Current Version: 1.0

Microsoft Corporation
One Microsoft Way
Redmond, WA 98052-6399

(800) 426-9400; (206) 882-8080
Direct sales: (800) MSPRESS
FAX: (206) 883-8101

Available through retail software stores or directly from Microsoft

Microsoft always has had a healthy presence in the entertainment software category, starting out with their very popular Flight Simulator. For Windows, they have a number of game bundles that sell for around $50. An example of these game bundles is the Microsoft Arcade Pack, shown in figure 35.8.

Figure 35.8
The Classic Battlezone game in the Microsoft Arcade Pack.

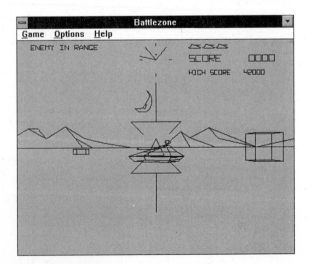

Advanced Tools

Games, personal finance software, graphics software. All these are worthy add-ons to your Office system. But what if your needs run a little hotter than that? If you are an advanced Windows user, you will be interested in two products that really add to the power of Windows and Office.

Visual Basic 3 for Windows Application Development

Current Version: 3.0

Microsoft Corporation
One Microsoft Way
Redmond, WA 98052-6399

(800) 426-9400; (206) 882-8080
Direct sales: (800) MSPRESS
FAX: (206) 883-8101

Suggested Retail: $495
Available through retail software stores or directly from Microsoft

Visual Basic (VB) for Windows is likely the most popular programming environment for Windows (see figure 35.9). It is both easy to learn and powerful. If you need to generate custom Windows programs, but don't want to spend the years necessary to become a competent C programmer, then look to VB to fit your needs. An added advantage to using VB is that it shares the same programming language found in the Microsoft Office products, which will make learning to program with both Visual Basic *and* the Office applications much easier. Furthermore, through DDE and OLE, you can integrate your VB creations with the Office applications to extend the power of your program even further. Using VB, you can create professional-quality applications easily.

OS/2 for Windows Alternative Operating System

Current Version: 2.1

IBM Corporation
Old Orchard Rd.
Armonk, NY 10504

(800) 426-3333; (914) 765-1900
Direct sales: (800) 426-2968 (IBM PC Direct)

Suggested Retail: $59.95 ($49.95 for CD version)
Available through retail software stores

Figure 35.9
Visual Basic for
Windows.

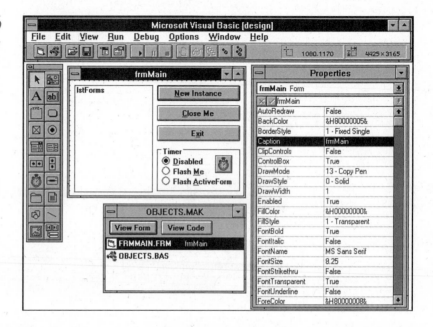

Surprising to some, IBM has come up with a winner with the latest version of its OS/2 operating system. Recently, they have released OS/2 for Windows, which is specially designed to integrate with your existing Windows environment while also allowing the advanced benefits of OS/2:

✔ An advanced, object-oriented user interface called the Workplace Shell.

✔ Better multitasking of your DOS and Windows programs. With OS/2 for Windows, you can carry out processor-intensive tasks in the background, like a large file download, while remaining productive with your foreground application.

✔ Better DOS compatibility than Windows alone offers.

✔ Better performance for some DOS and Windows programs.

✔ Superior memory management as compared to Windows alone. You even can run each Windows application in separate memory spaces, alleviating the memory limitations that Windows sometimes experiences.

OS/2 for Windows is not for everyone. However, if you have sufficient hardware to make good use of it, it can add to the power of your system. To run OS/2 for Windows, you should have a

386 or better processor operating at 25 MHz or faster. You will need 8 MB of RAM (IBM recommends 6 MB, but 8 MB or more is best, particularly for the memory-hungry Office applications) and about 25 MB of free disk space. OS/2 for Windows is shown in figure 35.10.

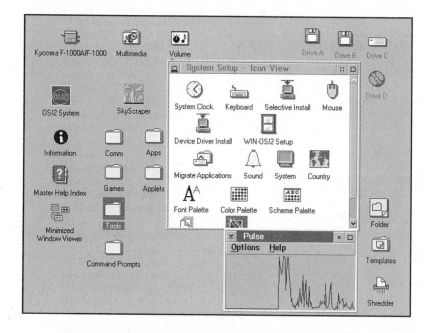

Figure 35.10
OS/2 for
Windows.

A Note from the Author

OS/2 2.1 is the first truly credible 32-bit desktop operating system available for Intel-based PCs, and OS/2 for Windows makes using OS/2 and Windows together easier than OS/2 2.1 by itself. However, all of OS/2's power comes at a price: it really does much better when you have more powerful hardware, and can be sluggish if your hardware isn't up to snuff. In the author's opinion, 8 MB of RAM is a working minimum for OS/2 for Windows, whereas 12 MB or even 16 MB really makes it shine.

Zip File Manager: WinZip

Current Version: 5.5

Nico Mak Computing, Inc.
P.O. Box 919
Bristol, CT 06011-0919

(800) 242-4775; (713) 524-6394
FAX: (713) 524-6398

Suggested Retail: $29
Shareware version available on most bulletin boards or directly from Nico Mak
Computing

File compression programs take files on your computer and compress them using software algorithms. When you *compress* a number of files, you end up with a single file that takes up much less space than the original. In order to use compressed files, they must be decompressed. You use file compression programs for a variety of reasons:

✔ Compress files before transmitting them by modem. Smaller files take less time to send or receive, saving money on telephone or online costs.

✔ If you have files that you want to keep on your computer but do not regularly use, compress them in order to free space on your hard disk.

✔ Most files distributed through bulletin boards are compressed. In order to use these files, you must decompress them.

The most popular programs to accomplish this compression and decompression are PKZIP and PKUNZIP. These two programs are the leader for DOS-based compression programs. WinZip is a Windows-based program that provides a powerful and friendly front end to the PKZIP and PKUNZIP programs. If you regularly compress and decompress files, WinZip will save hours of your time. WinZip is shown in figure 35.11.

Figure 35.11
WinZip.

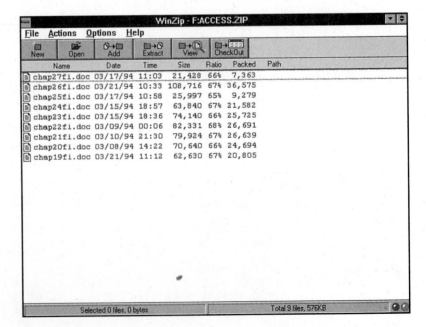

CompuServe Navigator: WinCIM

Current Version: 1.2

CompuServe Information Service
P.O. Box 20212
5000 Arlington Centre Blvd.
Columbus, OH 43220

(800) 848-8199; (614) 457-8600
FAX: (614) 529-1610

Suggested Retail: $10 (includes $10 of usage credit)
Available for download from CompuServe (GO WINCIM) and in retail
software stores. Included with CompuServe sign-up kits.

People are flocking to online services such as CompuServe at a rapid rate. In fact, the best way
to begin to experience the information superhighway is through services such as CompuServe.
Online services contain enormous amounts of data, and, in fact, are the subject of entire
books. (For example, see *Inside CompuServe*, also by New Riders Publishing.)

All the Microsoft Office products are supported by Microsoft through
CompuServe (GO MSOFT). Macmillan Computer Publishing also maintains an
area on CompuServe in which you can interact with publishers such as New
Riders Publishing and Que (GO MACMILLAN).

If you use Windows and CompuServe, you likely will find the most usability from WinCIM,
which is published by CompuServe to help its users more easily access the power of the online
service. WinCIM is shown in figure 35.12.

Modem Communications: Procomm Plus for Windows

Current Version: 1.02

Datastorm Technologies, Inc.
P.O. Box 1471, 3212 Lemone Blvd.
Columbia, MO 65205

(314) 443-3282
FAX: (314) 875-0595

Procomm Plus, a longtime favorite among DOS users, is now available as a Windows application. Procomm Plus for Windows offers superior modem support (containing setups for 437

different modems) and extremely versatile file transfer capabilities (10 different transfer protocols are available). Terminal emulation, commonly used when dialing into other computers, is excellent. Procomm Plus for Windows supports over 30 different emulations. The Procomm documentation could use some improvement, however.

Figure 35.12
WinCIM 1.2.

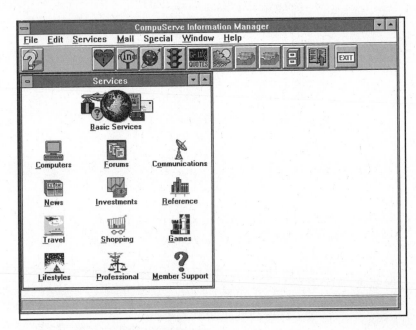

Figure 35.13
Procomm Plus for Windows is a powerful communications package.

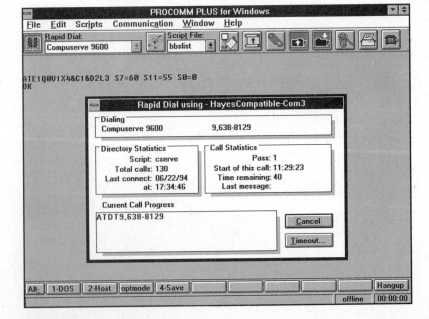

Disk Compression: Stacker

Current Version: 4.0

Stac Electronics
5993 Avenida Encinas
Carlsbad, CA 92008

(800) 522-7822; (619) 431-7474
FAX: (619) 431-9616

Retail: $149

Every serious Windows user eventually runs out of disk space. With applications, document files, clip art, multimedia clips, and other data, even the largest hard disk begins to feel small. Stacker 4.0, the newest version of the successful disk compression utility from Stac Electronics, features a Windows interface that enables you to monitor and manage the "stacked" disk volumes on your computer (see fig. 35.14).

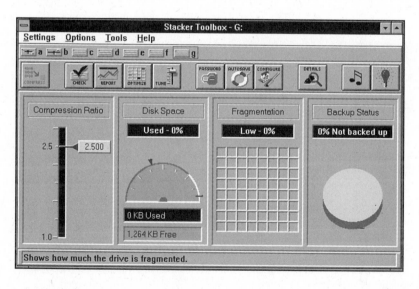

Figure 35.14
Stacker 4.0 features a Windows interface.

Stacker achieves disk compression ratios of 2:1 to 4:1, depending on the type of data being compressed. Image files such as BMPs, text data, databases, and spreadsheets compress much more readily than executable files (EXEs and COMs).

Disk compression utilities always entail a certain amount of risk. A poorly designed compression utility can slow your system, crash unexpectedly, or (catastrophically!) lose all the data stored on the compressed volume. Stacker 4.0 is perhaps the most reliable and best-known of all disk compression applications and has many built-in fail-safe mechanisms to protect your data. Once installed on your system, Stacker 4.0 is completely transparent. The only difference is that you have more than twice as much disk space as you did previously.

Using the *Inside Microsoft Office Professional* Companion Disk

The 1.44MB 3.5-inch disk included with *Inside Microsoft Office Professional* contains all the sample files described in this book. You are free to install these files on your computer and to make any modifications to the documents, databases, and other materials as you wish. It is New Riders Publishing's intention that you continue learning about Microsoft Office Professional by implementing modifications to the materials included on this disk.

Before beginning the installation, please make sure adequate disk space is available. These files require about 2MB of hard disk space to install properly. As you use these files, new files might be made and old files might be expanded. Please ensure that adequate disk space is available for the *Inside Microsoft Windows Professional* companion disk files.

The disk includes a Windows setup program much like other Windows applications you might have installed. To run the installation program, perform the following steps:

✔ Open File Manager or Program Manager and select <u>R</u>un from the <u>F</u>ile menu (open the File menu by pressing the F key while holding down the Alt key).

✔ Enter **A:INSTALL** in the <u>C</u>ommand line input field in the Run dialog box. If your 3.5-inch floppy disk is designated as B, you should enter **B:INSTALL** instead of A:INSTALL.

Alternatively, you could use File Manager to run INSTALL.EXE directly from the floppy disk. If you are unfamiliar with this process, consult your Microsoft Windows documentation to learn how to run applications from File Manager.

✔ The installation program will begin running.

✔ The first screen of the installation program (figure A.1) asks for the path you want to use for the companion files. By default, this path is a directory named INSIDE in the MSOFFICE directory on drive C, although you can put the files anywhere.

Figure A.1
The installation
program
opening screen.

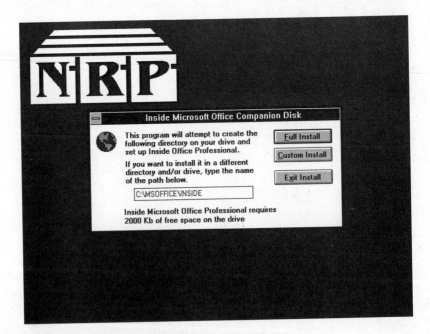

✔ If the specified directory does not exist, the install program will create the target directory.

✔ The install program copies files from the floppy disk to the specified directory on the hard disk.

If you encounter problems with any of the sample applications on this disk, please feel free to contact New Riders Publishing through our fax number, (317) 581-4670, or our reader response line at (317) 581-3871.

Because the sample files included on the companion disk to *Inside Microsoft Office Professional* were created by the authors of this book, we regret that we will not be able to provide technical support for these files.

INDEX

INDEX

INDEX

INDEX

INDEX

INDEX

INDEX

INDEX

INDEX

INDEX

INDEX

INDEX

INDEX

INDEX

INDEX

INDEX

INDEX

INDEX

INDEX

INDEX

INDEX

INDEX

INDEX

INDEX

INDEX

INDEX

INDEX

Inside Microsoft Office Professional
REGISTRATION CARD

Fill out this card to receive information about future Windows books and other New Riders titles!

Name _____ **Title** _____

Company _____

Address _____

City/State/ZIP _____

I bought this book because: _____

_____

I purchased this book from:

☐ A bookstore (Name _____)

☐ A software or electronics store (Name _____)

☐ A mail order (Name of Catalog _____)

I purchase this many computer books each year:

☐ 1–4   ☐ 5 or more

I currently use these applications: _____

_____

_____

_____

I found these chapters to be the most informative: _____

_____

I found these chapters to be the least informative: _____

_____

Additional comments: _____

_____

☐ I would like to see my name in print! You may use my name and quote me in future New Riders products and promotions. My daytime phone number is:_____

New Riders Publishing 201 West 103rd Street • Indianapolis, Indiana 46290 USA

Fold Here

New Riders Publishing
201 West 103rd Street
Indianapolis, Indiana 46290
USA

WANT MORE INFORMATION?

CHECK OUT THESE RELATED TITLES:

	QTY	PRICE	TOTAL

Inside Windows NT. A complete tutorial and reference to organizing and managing multiple tasks and programs in Winows NT! This book focuses on integration capabilities and networking options of Windows NT—an inside look at the operating environment of the future! ISBN: 1-56205-124-5.   ____ $34.95 _____

Integrating Windows Applications. This is the intermediate- to advanced-level Windows user's no-nonsense guide. Readers will learn how to create sophisticated documents through Dynamic Data Exchange and Object Linking and Embedding. This book contains several extras, including a disk loaded with examples, database files, and macros. ISBN: 1-56205-083-4.   ____ $34.95 _____

Inside OS/2 2.1, 3rd Edition. Get the inside story on OS/2, from the industry's best-selling book, on the latest version of this powerful operating system! Completely updated and revised, this book covers installation, memory management, and compatibility—plus detailed coverage of the OS/2 Workplace Shell. With lots of techniques for integrating DOS and Windows applications under OS/2, this book has everything readers need. ISBN: 1-56205-206-3.   ____ $34.95 _____

Ultimate Windows 3.1. If you're looking for the most up-to-date and comprehensive reference on Windows 3.1, your search is over! Loaded with tips, features, bug-fixes—plus coverage of sound boards, CD-ROMs, and video—you'll find only the latest and most relevant information available. A bonus disk includes a hypertext application with "2000 Windows Tips." ISBN: 1-56205-125-3.   ____ $39.95 _____

Name _____

Company _____

Address _____

City _____ State ____ ZIP _____

Phone _____ Fax _____

☐ Check Enclosed   ☐ VISA   ☐ MasterCard

Card #_____Exp. Date _____

Signature _____

Prices are subject to change. Call for availability and pricing information on latest editions.

Subtotal _____

Shipping _____

$4.00 for the first book and $1.75 for each additional book.

Total _____
Indiana residents add 5% sales tax.

New Riders Publishing 201 West 103rd Street • Indianapolis, Indiana 46290 USA

Orders/Customer Service: 1-800-428-5331
Fax: 1-800-448-3804

Fold Here

PLACE
STAMP
HERE

New Riders Publishing
201 West 103rd Street
Indianapolis, Indiana 46290
USA

GO AHEAD. PLUG YOURSELF INTO
MACMILLAN COMPUTER PUBLISHING.

Introducing the Macmillan Computer Publishing Forum on CompuServe®

Yes, it's true. Now, you can have CompuServe access to the same professional, friendly folks who have made computers easier for years. On the Macmillan Computer Publishing Forum, you'll find additional information on the topics covered by every Macmillan Computer Publishing imprint—including Que, Sams Publishing, New Riders Publishing, Alpha Books, Brady Books, Hayden Books, and Adobe Press. In addition, you'll be able to receive technical support and disk updates for the software produced by Que Software and Paramount Interactive, a division of the Paramount Technology Group. It's a great way to supplement the best information in the business.

WHAT CAN YOU DO ON THE MACMILLAN COMPUTER PUBLISHING FORUM?

Play an important role in the publishing process—and make our books better while you make your work easier:

- Leave messages and ask questions about Macmillan Computer Publishing books and software—you're guaranteed a response within 24 hours
- Download helpful tips and software to help you get the most out of your computer
- Contact authors of your favorite Macmillan Computer Publishing books through electronic mail
- Present your own book ideas
- Keep up to date on all the latest books available from each of Macmillan Computer Publishing's exciting imprints

JOIN NOW AND GET A FREE COMPUSERVE STARTER KIT!

To receive your free CompuServe Introductory Membership, call toll-free, **1-800-848-8199** and ask for representative **#597**. The Starter Kit Includes:

- Personal ID number and password
- $15 credit on the system
- Subscription to CompuServe Magazine

HERE'S HOW TO PLUG INTO MACMILLAN COMPUTER PUBLISHING:

Once on the CompuServe System, type any of these phrases to access the Macmillan Computer Publishing Forum:

GO MACMILLAN **GO BRADY**
GO QUEBOOKS **GO HAYDEN**
GO SAMS **GO QUESOFT**
GO NEWRIDERS **GO ALPHA**

Once you're on the CompuServe Information Service, be sure to take advantage of all of CompuServe's resources. CompuServe is home to more than 1,700 products and services—plus it has over 1.5 million members worldwide. You'll find valuable online reference materials, travel and investor services, electronic mail, weather updates, leisure-time games and hassle-free shopping (no jam-packed parking lots or crowded stores).

Seek out the hundreds of other forums that populate CompuServe. Covering diverse topics such as pet care, rock music, cooking, and political issues, you're sure to find others with the same concerns as you—and expand your knowledge at the same time.

What's on the Disk

✔ HomeFinder: A complete real estate management database system written in Microsoft Access

✔ CarCare: A car repair shop application written in Microsoft Access

✔ All the miscellaneous tables, forms, and other database components discussed in *Inside Microsoft Office Professional*

Installing the Disk

The files on the disk are stored in a compressed form and cannot be used directly from the floppy.

The installation program runs from within Windows. Please do not attempt to install the disk from the DOS prompt.

1. From File Manager or Program Manager, choose the **R**un option in the **F**ile menu.

2. Enter **<*drive*>INSTALL** and press the Enter key. *<drive>* is the designation of your 3.5-inch high-density floppy drive and is almost always either A: or B:.

Follow the on-screen instructions in the installation program. By default, the files will be installed in subdirectories under C:\MSOFFICE\INSIDE, unless you change this name during the install process.